T.E. Grade 6

 S0-BDL-183

T.E. Grade 6

T.E. Grade 6

Annotated Teacher's Edition

Prentice Hall

WRITING and GRAMMAR

Communication in Action

Put Students' Words Into Action!

A new approach to language learning designed to produce competent, confident communicators.

- Active learning for today's middle school students.

- Systematic Learning Strategies.

- Easy-to-use handbook style saves time.

- Teacher's Edition provides all the support.

3-Part Organization

Prentice Hall Writing and Grammar: Communication in Action is conveniently divided into the following three sections for ease of use:

- **Writing:** Guides students through each step of the writing process with an emphasis on revision.

- **Grammar:** Provides more grammar practice than any other program, including unique hands-on grammar activities.

- **Academic and Workplace Skills:** Focuses on practical, real-world skills for today's multimedia generation.

Copyright ©2001 by Prentice-Hall, Inc., Upper Saddle River, New Jersey 07458. All rights reserved. Printed in the United States of America. This publication is protected by copyright, and permission should be obtained from the publisher prior to any prohibited reproduction, storage in a retrieval system, or transmission in any form or by any means, electronic, mechanical, photocopying, recording, or likewise. For information regarding permission(s), write to: Rights and Permissions Department.

Prentice Hall

Grade 6-Copper   ISBN: 0-13-043346-2
Grade 7-Bronze   ISBN: 0-13-043347-0
Grade 8-Silver   ISBN: 0-13-043348-9

2 3 4 5 6 7 8 9 10
04 03 02 01 00

Only Prentice Hall Writing and Grammar: Communication in Action...

- Engages today's students with active, hands-on learning.

- Provides extensive practice opportunities and strategies for all stages of the writing process.

- Saves time with its easy-to-use handbook style.

Engage Today's Students

Connections that make instruction relevant for today's students

10.1 Model from Literature

In his Newbery Award-winning book, Holes, Louis Sachar introduces readers to Stanley, a boy who is always in the wrong place at the wrong time. In this excerpt from the book, Stanley is in a boys' camp in the desert. He gets a lecture from the head counselor that sounds like an essay on how to survive in the camp.

How to Survive Camp Greenlake
from Holes

▲ Critical Viewing Why might a person need directions for how to survive in this environment? [Analyze]

GRAMMAR IN LITERATURE

from "The Cat Who Thought She Was a Dog and the Dog Who Thought He Was a Cat"

Isaac Bashevis Singer

In this passage, notice that peasant, a common noun, is often used in place of the proper noun Jan Skiba. The proper noun is also capitalized. Look for other common and proper nouns in this paragraph.

Once there was a poor *peasant*, Jan Skiba by name. He lived with his wife and three daughters in a one-room hut with a straw roof, afar from the village. The house had a bed, a bench bed, and a stove, but no mirror. A mirror was a luxury for a poor *peasant*. And why would a *peasant* need a mirror? Peasants aren't curious about their appear-

Connect to the Language Arts
Connections to literature, writing, and grammar show students the relevance of what they learn.

Grammar in Your Writing
Using Commas to Separate Items in a Series

Use commas to separate items in a series, or list. Separating the items with commas makes your meaning absolutely clear to readers. Look at the following examples.

Examples:

Commas separate individual items in a series:
Add the sugar, baking soda, baking powder, and salt.

Commas separate groups of words in a series:
Begin by gathering your tools, reviewing the recipe, and preheating the oven.

Note: Some writers use a comma before the *and* that connects the last two items in the series. (See the commas following *baking powder* and *recipe* in the examples above.) Others do not use a comma before the final *and*. Follow your teacher's directions about whether to use the comma before the *and*.

Find It in Your Writing Review your essay and circle any lists or series of items. Remember that the series can include either individual words or groups of words. Check that you have correctly used commas to separate the items in each series or list that you find.

Find It in Your Reading Read "How to Survive Camp Greenlake" on pages 12–13. Find an example of commas used to separate items in a series.

Engage Students

Address varied learning styles by actively involving students with Hands-on Grammar activities.

Hands-on Grammar

Subject-Verb Agreement Color Match

Cut three strips of paper of equal length. Draw a blue line across the center of one. Draw a red line across the center of the other. Fold the strip into thirds, as shown in the illustration. Then, write a sentence with a singular subject, a singular verb form, and a phrase across the blue line. Write the subject in the first fold, the verb in the second, and the remaining words in the third fold. Write the same sentence on the strip with the red line, but use a plural subject and plural verb form. Next, cut each strip on the folds. Finally, try to line up the parts of the sentence. You will find that you can't create a color match between a singular subject and a plural verb form.

The Minister	attends	every session

The Ministers	attend	every session

The Ministers	attends	every session

Find It in Your Reading Do this activity with a sentence from the Grammar in Literature passage from "Glory and Hope," on page 578. If the sentence has too many phrases, just use the subject and verb.

Find It in Your Writing Review a recent piece of writing in your portfolio. Use this activity with several sentences from the piece.

Connect to Students' Lives

An authentic student model in every writing chapter tracks the development of one student's writing through a particular writing mode.

What Is a Comparison-and-Contrast Essay?

A **comparison-and-contrast essay** analyzes the similarities and differences between two or more things. It can help you to decide which bicycle to buy. A good comparison-and-contrast essay can even change your perspective—as when a reviewer compares the latest hit song with an old album, letting you hear the startling similarities. A comparison-and-contrast essay includes

- a topic involving two or more things that are neither nearly identical nor extremely different.
- details illustrating both similarities and differences.
- clear organization that highlights the points of comparison.

To learn the criteria on which your essay may be evaluated, see the Rubric for Self-Assessment on page 166.

Types of Comparison-and-Contrast Essays

In addition to an ordinary comparison-and-contrast essay, some specialized essays also use comparison and contrast:

- **Product comparisons** compare two or more products, providing up-to-date information on each and discussing the advantages and disadvantages of purchasing each one.
- **Plan evaluations** compare two or more alternative plans or decisions, discussing the circumstances and comparing the advantages and disadvantages of each plan.

Writers in
ACTION

In his books and articles, Richard Lederer compares English to other languages and different English words to each other. He knows the value of saying more in fewer words:

"... writing is hard work, and writing concisely is even more difficult."

PREVIEW
Student Work
IN PROGRESS

To develop your comparison-and-contrast writing skills, follow the work of Dylan Parker of Carr Lane VPA Middle School in St. Louis, Missouri. In this chapter, Dylan uses featured prewriting, drafting, and revising techniques to develop the comparison-and-contrast essay "Skateboards for Success." At the end of the lesson, you can read Dylan's completed essay.

Persuasion in Everyday Life

Whenever you argue with a friend over which movie to see or debate the merits of one musical group over another, you're using persuasive skills. **Persuasion** is writing or speaking that attempts to convince others to accept a position or take a desired action. Effective persuasion can decide a defendant's fate in a trial, lead to a change in government leadership, or even end a war.

Engage Today's Multimedia Generation

Media and Technology Skills workshops teach students relevant, real-world skills and offer a full array of on-line and multimedia resources.

Prentice Hall
WRITING and GRAMMAR
Communication in Action

Media and Technology Skills

Using Computer Technology

Activity: Getting Help On-line

Computer programs typically come with built-in "how-to's"—on-line help the user can access while using the program. On-line help lets you learn as you work. It is as though the computer were a teacher and a tool rolled into one! By mastering Help, you can turn problems with computers into opportunities to learn.

Learn About It

Balloon Help Turn Balloon Help on or off through a program's menu bar. With Balloon Help on, a balloon appears whenever you roll your mouse pointer over a button, dialogue box, or other feature. Each balloon contains a brief description identifying the function of the feature on which the pointer is resting.

On-line Manuals To consult the on-line manual for a program, select "Help" from the menu bar. "Contents" lists topics by category. "Index" lists topics alphabetically and often provides a Search feature that allows you to search for a particular subject.

Other Kinds of Help Often, the best troubleshooting tips come from the program's "Read Me" file. You may open a "Read Me" file in a text-editor program. Software also comes with a printed manual, which offers detailed information on operating the program.

Apply It Choose an application, such as a word-processing program, to which you have access. Think of a difficulty you have had using the program or a question you might have about the program's use. Use two or more forms of help to solve the problem or answer the question. Take notes in a graphic organizer such as the one to the right. Then, write a mini-manual explaining how to use these different ways of getting help.

Computer Help

Built-in Help
- Balloon Help
- On-line manuals

Other Kinds of Help
- "Read Me" files
- Printed manuals

My Question or Problem _____
Type of Help

How to Use
This Kind of Help
Step 1 _____
Step 2 _____
Step 3 _____

Did I Get an Answer to My Question?
y __ /n __

Easy/Hard to Use
(Explain)

More Practice and Revision Support

Practice, Practice, and More Practice

More grammar exercises than any other program provide the practice your students need to improve their grammar skills and apply them in writing and speaking.

14.2 PRONOUNS

Section 14.2 Section Review

GRAMMAR EXERCISES 18–24

Exercise 18 Identifying Personal Pronouns Identify the personal pronoun in each sentence.

1. My brother and sister want to become pharmacists. They must attend a college of pharmacy.
2. After finishing a five-year program, he will graduate.
3. They must complete a one-year internship before becoming pharmacists.
4. She may choose from many schools.
5. All of them offer similar programs.

5. Who wants to know more?
6. These are copies of fingerprints.
7. Each is unique.
8. Whose is this fingerprint?
9. What can we learn from fingerprints?
10. Few can identify a fingerprint.

Exercise 19 Identifying Antecedents of Personal Pronouns Fill in the blank with the appropriate personal pronoun. Circle the antecedent of the pronoun you supply.

1. Radiologists must attend medical school. ___?___ spend five years studying radiology.
2. If my brother studies radiology, ___?___ will have to complete a residency program.
3. My aunt is a radiologist. ___?___ has her own practice.
4. After completing ___?___ residency, radiologists may decide to specialize.
5. ___?___ may choose to teach instead.

Exercise 20 Recognizing Types of Pronouns Identify ___ of ___ nouns in the sentence ___ demonstrative, interro___

1. My brother is in ___ to study forensic ___
2. That is the study ___
3. It helps police offi___
4. You may have see___ about "crime doct___

Exercise 21 Revision Practice Replace each italicized noun in the sentences below with the type of pronoun indicated in brackets. Some sentences may have to be rewritten as questions. Revise punctuation as needed.

1. *Family practitioners* [personal] provide primary medical care.
2. Family doctors know *famil___* [personal] patients.
3. *Dedication* [demonstrative] ___ son they enter the field.
4. *Family practitioners* [interro___ refer patients to a specialis___
5. *General practitioners* [indef___ had many years of medical___

Exercise 22 Find It in ___ Reading Identify three pers___ nouns in the excerpt from "The ___ Thought She Was a Dog . . ." o___

Exercise 23 Find It in ___ Writing In your own writing ___

Section 14.1 Section Review

GRAMMAR EXERCISES 6–12

Exercise 6 Identifying Nouns Identify the nouns in each sentence.

1. Dogs require attention, including proper feeding and medical care.
2. Dogs need regular exercise.
3. Puppies need a combination of solid foods and milk as they grow.
4. Dogs enjoy rawhide strips ___

Exercise 9 Revision Practice Copy the following paragraph. Replace the italicized words with proper nouns of your choice.

A dog came to *the town.* He walked up *a street* and down *another street. The man,* who lived at the end of *the street,* watched the dog approach.

Exercise 10 Find It in Your Reading Identify two proper nouns, two common nouns, one compound noun, and one collective noun in the following excerpt from "The Cat Who Thought She Was a Dog . . .":

Burek had to be tied outside, and he howled all day and all night. In their anguish, both the dog and the cat stopped eating.
When Jan Skiba saw the disruption the mirror had created in his household, he decided a mirror wasn't what his family needed.

Exercise 11 Find It in Your Writing Look through your writing portfolio. Find five common nouns, two proper nouns, one collective noun, and one compound noun in your own writing.

Exercise 12 Writing Application Write about a dog you've known or read about. Use at least two compound nouns, one collective noun, and two proper nouns.

Chapter 14 Chapter Review

GRAMMAR EXERCISES 25–36

Exercise 25 Identifying Nouns in Sentences Identify the nouns in each sentence below.

1. The pack of wolves chased the rabbit.
2. The rabbit, filled with fear, ran away.
3. Because of their hunger, the wolves continued to hunt.
4. They found no more prey in the forest.
5. The howls of the hungry animals showed their frustration.

Exercise 26 Identifying Nouns in Paragraphs Identify the nouns in the paragraph below.

Wolves are wild animals that look similar to dogs. A wolf has fur that can be white, black, or gray. Wolves travel in packs, using their speed and strength to hunt as a group. They live in most climates, but rarely in deserts or tropical forests.

Exercise 27 Identifying Common and Proper Nouns Identify the nouns in each sentence below. Then, tell whether each noun is *common* or *proper.*

1. My sister Lucy, my mother, and I took our cat to the animal hospital.
2. The hospital is in Philadelphia.
3. We took the cat on the train.
4. The train passed through cities in New York and New Jersey.
5. Our cat Trudy needed special surgery.
6. Dr. Kim, the veterinarian, was very kind.
7. While we waited, my mother and I read a magazine.
8. We saw a dog that looked like a character from the movie *Benji.*
9. A poodle sat on a chair next to us.
10. Before we returned home, we stopped to see the Liberty Bell.

Exercise 28 Identifying Collective Nouns Identify the collective noun in each sentence below.

1. My class went on a trip to the animal hospital last week.
2. The team of veterinarians sees many types of patients.
3. Yesterday, they treated a group of monkeys from the zoo.
4. Sometimes, they go to farms to check a herd of cattle.
5. My family brought our cat to this animal hospital.

Exercise 29 Identifying Compound Nouns Identify the compound noun in each sentence below.

1. My sister-in-law brought a new cat home from the pound.
2. They told her that a police officer had found the cat.
3. It does not get along with the sheepdog in the house.
4. She brought it to the middle school where she teaches.
5. On the way home, they crossed the George Washington Bridge.

Exercise 30 Identifying Personal Pronouns Identify each personal pronoun below as *first person, second person,* or *third person.* Then, tell whether the pronoun is *singular* or *plural.*

1. you
2. she
3. their
4. our
5. them
6. I
7. his
8. yours
9. mine
10. we

Student Work
IN PROGRESS

A Strong Lead

Felix reviewed his prewriting notes and found that his class party gave him the idea for the topic "How to Make Banana Cake." He used an exaggerated image of hungry students to write an attention-grabbing lead.

Our seventh-grade teacher, Mrs. Flood, knows that it takes more than an ordinary cake to feed twenty ravenous seventh-graders. That's why she always asks Mike or me to make our famous Banana Cake. Making Banana Cake takes a little more time than making a cake from a box, but you will find that every bite of the finished product is worth the time it takes. By following the steps outlined here, you can learn how to make this delicious dessert.

Felix introduces his topic with details that make it appealing.

20 • Exposition: How-to Essay

More Strategic Revision

More systematic, hands-on revision strategies help students examine what they write and how to improve it.

10.4 Revising

Looking at Overall Structure

Add an Introduction and Conclusion

After writing your first draft, reread your how-to essay, looking for ways to improve and polish it. You will probably recognize that you don't want to jump right in with step one and end abruptly at the last step. Instead, give a general overview of your topic in an introduction. Then, explain the different steps in the body of the essay and review, summarize, or briefly comment on the procedures in a conclusion.

Revision Strategy
◆ Write a Strong Lead

Begin with an image or idea that "leads" your reader into the essay. Look through your prewriting notes to find details that remind you why you enjoy the activity or why you decided to write about your topic. The detail that grabbed your interest may spark your audience's interest as well. Use one of these details to make that first sentence an attention grabber!

Analyzing Your Paragraphs
Identify Paragraph Purpose

Once you're comfortable with the general structure of your paper, carefully focus on each individual paragraph. The purpose of each paragraph will determine the words or phrases that may need to be added to make your meaning clearer.

Revision Strategy
◆ Use Steps, Stacks, Chains, and Balances

• **Steps** If the paragraph is explaining a step or several related steps for which time order is important, make sure you have indicated the sequence. Use words such as *first*, *next*, and *finally*.

• **Stacks** If the paragraph explains how one part of a process contributes to another, show the connection between ideas with words such as *and*, *furthermore*, and *for instance*.

• **Chains** If the paragraph explains the cause-and-effect relationship between steps, use words such as *so*, *because*, and *consequently*.

• **Balance** If the paragraph shows choice or contrast, use words such as *but*, *however*, *on the other hand*, and *rather*.

▶ Critical Viewing Do you think these boys successfully followed the directions for making a cake? **[Evaluate]**

Student Work
IN PROGRESS

A Strong Lead

Felix reviewed his prewriting notes and found that his class party gave him the idea for the topic "How to Make Banana Cake." He used an exaggerated image of hungry students to write an attention-grabbing lead.

Our seventh-grade teacher, Mrs. Flood, knows that it takes more than an ordinary cake to feed twenty ravenous seventh-graders. That's why she always asks Mike or me to make our famous Banana Cake. Making Banana Cake takes a little more time than making a cake from a box, but you will find that every bite of the finished product is worth the time it takes. By following the steps outlined here, you can learn how to make this delicious dessert.

Felix introduces his topic with details that make it appealing.

Unmatched Assessment Preparation

Assessment resources that you and your students need to succeed

Standardized Test Preparation Workshops

Standardized Test Preparation Workshops after each chapter provide unmatched preparation for PSAT, SAT, ACT, AP, state, and local standardized tests.

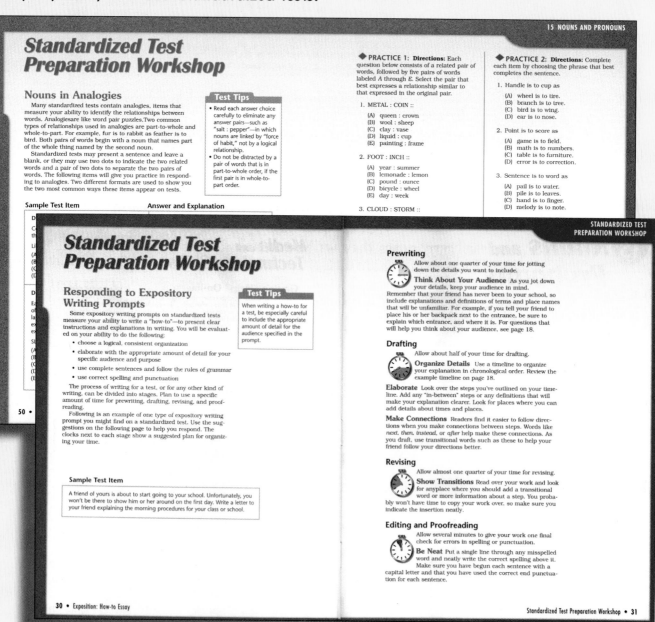

Diagnostic Test

Skill Check A. Identify the nouns in each sentence. Explain why each word is a noun.

1. Dogs can be purchased from a breeder.
2. Good pets can also be found at the shelter.
3. Preparations—such as getting food, dishes, toys, a collar, and a bed—need to be made before the arrival of a new puppy.
4. A veterinarian gives the dog shots for rabies and distemper.
5. All dogs must wear licenses, which ensure identification and immunization.

Skill Check B. Identify the collective or compound noun in each sentence. Tell whether the noun you identify is collective or compound.

1. The whole family should share in taking care of a pet.
2. Dogs need shelter, such as a doghouse, in which to sleep.
3. Supplies can be purchased at a pet shop.
4. Use caution when introducing the new pet to a large group.
5. Avoid packs of stray dogs when walking your pet.

Skill Check C. Identify each italicized noun as common or proper.

The *American Kennel Club* was started in 1884. This *organization* is associated with more than 4,000 *clubs* throughout the *United States*. *Frances* belongs to a group in her *town*. She goes to *shows* in *Austin* with her cousin *Sarah*.

Skill Check D. Identify the pronouns in each sentence. Then, identify each pronoun's antecedent. You may need to refer to previous sentences to find the antecedent.

1. Martin loves dogs. He has three German shepherds.
2. They are very gentle.
3. His sister, Tanya, helps him care for them.
4. She trained them to sit and stay.
5. All the neighbors admire their dogs.

Skill Check E. Identify the italicized pronoun in each sentence as personal, demonstrative, interrogative, or indefinite.

1. *We* went to the pound to see puppies.
2. *My* mother asked, "*Which* do you want?"
3. *That* was a difficult decision.
4. *Those* pups were so cute I wanted them all.
5. *Each* had *its* special qualities.

will be most useful to you in future writing projects?

www.phschool.com
phschool.com

Rubric for Self-Assessment

Use these criteria to evaluate your comparison-and-contrast essay.

	Score 4	Score 3	Score 2	Score 1
Audience and Purpose	Clearly provides a reason for a comparison-contrast analysis	Adequately provides a reason for a comparison-contrast analysis	Provides a reason for a comparison-contrast analysis	Does not provide a reason for a comparison-contrast analysis
Organization	Clearly presents information in a consistent organization best suited to the topic	Presents information using an organization suited to the topic	Chooses an organization not suited to comparison and contrast	Shows a lack of organizational strategy
Elaboration	Elaborates most ideas with facts, details, or examples; links all information to comparison and contrast	Elaborates many ideas with facts, details, or examples; links most information to comparison and contrast	Does not elaborate all ideas; does not link some details to comparison and contrast	Does not provide facts or examples to support a comparison and contrast
Use of Language	Demonstrates excellent sentence and vocabulary variety; includes very few mechanical errors	Demonstrates adequate sentence and vocabulary variety; includes few mechanical errors	Demonstrates repetitive use of sentence structure and vocabulary; includes many mechanical errors	Demonstrates poor use of language; generates confusion; includes many mechanical errors

2 • Comparison-and-Contrast Essay

Success for all Students

Accommodate your students' diverse needs by customizing instruction with assignments that address different ability levels and learning styles.

Diagnostic Tests

Diagnostic Tests before each grammar chapter help you assess students' skill levels and identify areas for improvement.

PRENTICE HALL
Test Bank CD-ROM
Solid Prep for Tests
A COMPONENT OF
WRITING and GRAMMAR
Communication in Action
Bronze Level
Self-Tests • Hints • Tutorials • Test Results • Answer Analysis

PRENTICE HALL
Standardized Test Preparation
CD ROM
Solid Prep for Standardized Tests
A COMPONENT OF
WRITING and GRAMMAR
Communication in Action
Bronze Level
Self-Tests • Hints • Tutorials • Test Results • Answer Analysis

Flexible Assessment Options

Develop confident and successful test-takers with a variety of test-taking opportunities.

Time-Saving Options!

Save time with an easy-to-use handbook style and a variety of integrated ancillary support options.

Easy-to-use

handbook style gives you and your students immediate access to review sections when necessary.

Save time

with point of use support.

Choose from

in-depth, accelerated, or block-scheduling lesson plans to best meet your needs and the needs of your students.

Make planning easier
with a wealth of integrated ancillary support.

Scoring Rubrics on Transparencies
- Scoring rubrics for each writing chapter

Daily Language Practice Transparencies
- Brief daily activities to build skills in grammar, usage, and mechanics

Grammar Exercise Answers on Transparencies
- Answers to all exercises
- Facilitates self- and peer-correction

Test Bank CD-ROM
Solid Prep for Tests
Self-Tests • Hints • Tutorials • Test Results • Answer Analysis

Resource Pro with Literature Database
Teaching resources & classroom management at your fingertips

Writing Support Transparencies
Transparencies to support all writing chapters
- Prewriting, drafting, and revising strategies
- Student Works in Progress
- Responding to Fine Art (Topic Bank)
- Blank graphic organizers for general use

Multimedia Instruction for the Future!

Connect to today's multimedia generation with a variety of fully-integrated technology practice and support options.

Prentice Hall's Internet Homepage

brings the world of writing to your students through support and extension activities and related links.

Resource Pro

helps you manage your lesson planning and resources with a simple click of a mouse.

Formal Assessment CD-Rom

allows you to gauge your students' ability levels and establish your own skills objectives.

TEACHING RESOURCES

Writing

Writing Support Activity Book
Topic Bank for Heterogeneous Classes
Support for Research Writing
Writing in the Content Areas and in the Workplace

Grammar, Usage, and Mechanics

Grammar Exercise Workbook, Teacher's Edition
Daily Language Practice
Hands-on Grammar Activity Book, Teacher's Edition

Academic and Workplace Skills

Academic and Workplace Skills Activity Book, Teacher's Edition
Vocabulary and Spelling Practice Book, Teacher's Edition
Reading Support Practice Book, Teacher's Edition

Assessment

Standardized Test Preparation Workbook, Teacher's Edition
Writing Assessment and Portfolio Management
Formal Assessment/Assessment Resources Software CD-ROM

Professional Resources

How to Manage Instruction in the Block
How to Assess Student Work
Putting Patterns to Work
Kick Off for Success: Organizing for School
Hearing All Sides: Resolving Conflict

Transparency Samples

Transparencies Sampler

ADDITIONAL ANCILLARIES

Workbooks

Hands-on Grammar Activity Book
Writing Support Activity Book
Grammar Exercise Workbook
Reading Support Practice Book
Vocabulary and Spelling Workbook
Academic and Workplace Skills Workbook
Standardized Test Preparation Workbook

Transparencies

Writing Support Transparencies
Daily Language Practice Transparencies
Grammar Exercises Answers on Transparencies
Scoring Rubrics on Transparencies

Technology

Writing Lab CD-ROM
Language Lab CD-ROM
Interactive Writing and Grammar Web site
Resource Pro CD-ROM (including Assessment Resources Software)
Writers at Work Videotape

Spanish Support
Extra Grammar and Writing Exercises
Basic Skills Intervention Kit
Multi-Genre Research Writing

Correlation to the Six Traits Analytical Model

Chapter	Ideas	Organization	Voice	Word Choice	Sentence Fluency	Conventions
1 The Writer in You			p. 3			
2 A Walk Through the Writing Process						
2.1	pp. 16–20					
2.2	p. 22	p. 21				
2.3	pp. 23–24	p. 23				
2.4				p. 25	p. 24	
Spot/Hum.	p. 28					p. 26
3 Paragraphs and Compositions						
3.1	pp. 33–36					
3.2	p. 37	pp. 38–39				
3.3			p. 32	p. 32	p. 32	
Spot/Hum.	p. 44					p. 43
4 Narration: Autobiography						
4.1	pp. 49–53	pp. 49–53				
4.2	pp. 54–57					
4.3	p. 59	p. 58				
4.4	p. 61	p. 60, p. 62		p. 64	p. 63	p. 65
4.5						p. 66
4.7	pp. 68–71	pp. 68–71				
Spot/Hum.	p. 72					
5 Narration: Short Story						
5.1	pp. 74–77	pp. 74–77				
5.2	pp. 78–81					
5.3	p. 83	p. 82		p. 83		
5.4	p. 85	p. 84, p. 86		p. 87		
5.5						p. 89
5.7	pp. 91–92	pp. 91–92		pp. 91–92		
Spot/Hum.	p. 94					
6 Description						
6.1	pp. 100–101	pp. 100–101		pp. 100–101		
6.2	pp. 102–105					
6.3	pp. 106–107	p. 106				
6.4	p. 109	p. 108		p. 111		p. 110
6.5						p. 113
6.7	pp. 115–117	pp. 115–117		pp. 115–119	pp. 118–119	
Spot/Hum.	p. 120					
7 Persuasion						
7.1	pp. 126–127	pp. 126–127				
7.2	pp. 128–131					
7.3	p. 133	p. 132				
7.4	p. 135	p. 134, p. 136		p. 138		p. 137
7.5						p. 139
7.7	pp. 141–145	pp. 141–145				
Spot/Hum.	p. 146					
8 Exposition: Comparison and Contrast						
8.1	pp. 152–153	pp. 152–153				
8.2	pp. 154–157					
8.3	p. 159, p. 161	p. 158, p. 160				
8.4				p. 163		p. 162
8.5						p. 164
8.7	pp. 166–169	pp. 166–169				
Spot/Hum.	p. 170					
9 Exposition: Cause and Effect						
9.1	pp. 176–177	pp. 176–177				
9.2	pp. 178–181					
9.3	pp. 182–183					
9.4	p. 185	p. 184		p. 187		p. 186
9.5						p. 188
9.7	pp. 190–193	pp. 190–193				
Spot/Hum.	p. 194					

Chapter	Ideas	Organization	Voice	Word Choice	Sentence Fluency	Conventions
10 Exposition: How-to Essay 10.1 10.2 10.3 10.4 10.5 10.7 Spot/Hum.	pp. 200–203 pp. 204–205 p. 207 p. 209 pp. 215–217 p. 218	pp. 200–203 p. 206 p. 208 pp. 215–217		pp. 200–203 p. 212 pp. 215–217	p. 210	p. 211 p. 213
11 Research Report 11.1 11.2 11.3 11.4 11.5 11.7 Spot/Hum.	pp. 224–227 pp. 228–229 p. 231 p. 233 pp. 238–241 p. 242	pp. 224–227 p. 229 p. 230 p. 232 pp. 238–241		p. 235	p. 234	p. 234 p. 236
12 Response to Literature 12.1 12.2 12.3 12.4 12.5 12.7 Spot/Hum.	pp. 248–249 pp. 250–255 p. 257 p. 259 pp. 265–267 p. 268	pp. 248–249 p. 256 p. 258 pp. 265–267		p. 255 p. 262	p. 260	p. 261 p. 263
13 Writing for Assessment 13.1 13.2 13.3 13.4 13.6 Spot/Hum.	pp. 274–276 p. 278 p. 279 pp. 283–285 p. 286	p. 277 pp. 279–280 pp. 283–285		p. 280		p. 281
14 Nouns and Pronouns 14.1 14.2						pp. 294–299 pp. 300–309
15 Verbs 15.1 15.2				p. 315		pp. 314–319 pp. 320–325
16 Adjectives and Adverbs 16.1				p. 330		pp. 330–339
17 Prepositions						pp. 352–359
18 Conjunctions and Interjections 18.1 18.2						pp. 364–369 pp. 370–374
19 Basic Sentence Parts 19.1 19.2 19.3 19.4 19.5 19.6						pp. 380–385 pp. 386–389 pp. 390–393 pp. 394–397 pp. 398–403 pp. 404–411
20 Phrases and Clauses 20.1 20.2						pp. 416–423 pp. 424–433

Correlation to the Six Traits Analytical Model

Chapter	Ideas	Organization	Voice	Word Choice	Sentence Fluency	Conventions
21 Effective Sentences 21.1 21.2 21.3 21.4					pp. 441–447 pp. 448–453	pp. 438–440 pp. 454–473
22 Using Verbs 22.1 22.2 22.3						pp. 480–487 pp. 488–493 pp. 494–503
23 Using Pronouns						pp. 508–515
24 Making Words Agree 24.1 24.2						pp. 520–527 pp. 528–533
25 Using Modifiers 25.1 25.2						pp. 538–545 pp. 546–551
26 Punctuation 26.1 26.2 26.3 26.4 26.5						pp. 561–563 pp. 564–573 pp. 574–577 pp. 578–585 pp. 586–597
27 Capitalization						pp. 602–615
Sentence Diagraming Workshop						pp. 620–629
28 Speaking Listening, Viewing and Representing 28.1	pp. 635–636	pp. 635–636				
29 Vocabulary and Spelling 29.1 29.2 29.3 29.4				pp. 656–658 pp. 659–661 pp. 662–665		pp. 666–675
30 Reading Skills 30.1 30.2 30.3	pp. 683–684 pp. 685–688	pp. 683–684 p. 690	p. 693	p. 689 p. 694		p. 693
31 Study, Reference, and Test-Taking Skills						

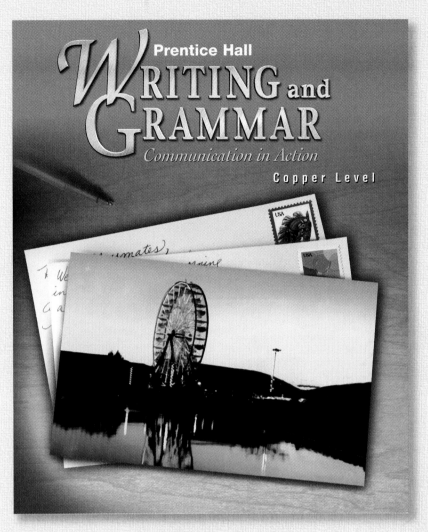

Prentice Hall

WRITING and GRAMMAR

Communication in Action

Copper Level

Copper Level

Prentice
Hall

Upper Saddle River, New Jersey
Needham, Massachusetts
Glenview, Illinois

Copyright © 2001 by Prentice-Hall, Inc., Upper Saddle River, New Jersey 07458. All
rights reserved. Printed in the United States of America. This publication is protected by
copyright, and permission should be obtained from the publisher prior to any prohibited
reproduction, storage in a retrieval system, or transmission in any form or by any means,
electronic, mechanical, photocopying, recording, or likewise. For information regarding
permission(s), write to: Rights and Permissions Department.

ISBN 0-13-436962-9

3 4 5 6 7 8 9 10   04 03 02 01 00

Copper
Bronze
Silver
Gold
Platinum
Ruby
Diamond

Program Authors

The program authors guided the direction and philosophy of *Prentice Hall Writing and Grammar: Communication in Action.* Working with the development team, they contributed to the pedagogical integrity of the program and to its relevance to today's teachers and students.

Joyce Armstrong Carroll

In her forty-year career, Joyce Armstrong Carroll, Ed.D., has taught on every grade level from primary to graduate school. In the past twenty years, she has trained teachers in the teaching of writing. A nationally known consultant, she has served as president of TCTE and on NCTE's Commission on Composition. More than fifty of her articles have appeared in journals such as *Curriculum Review, English Journal, Media & Methods, Southwest Philosophical Studies, Ohio English Journal, English in Texas,* and the *Florida English Journal.* With Edward E. Wilson, Dr. Carroll co-authored *Acts of Teaching: How to Teach Writing* and co-edited *Poetry After Lunch: Poems to Read Aloud.* Beyond her direct involvement with the writing pedagogy presented in this series, Dr. Carroll guided the development of the Hands-on Grammar feature. She co-directs the New Jersey Writing Project in Texas.

Edward E. Wilson

A former editor of *English in Texas,* Edward E. Wilson has served as a high-school English teacher and a writing consultant in school districts nationwide. Wilson has served on the Texas Teacher Professional Practices Commission and on NCTE's Commission on Composition. With Dr. Carroll, he co-wrote *Acts of Teaching: How to Teach Writing* and co-edited the award-winning *Poetry After Lunch: Poems to Read Aloud.* In addition to his direct involvement with the writing pedagogy presented in this series, Wilson provided inspiration for the Spotlight on Humanities feature. Wilson's poetry appears in Paul Janeczko's anthology *The Music of What Happens.* Wilson co-directs the New Jersey Writing Project in Texas.

Gary Forlini

Gary Forlini, a nationally known education consultant, developed the grammar, usage, and mechanics instruction and exercises in this series. After teaching in the Pelham, New York, schools for many years, he established Research in Media, an educational research agency that provides information for product developers, school staff developers, media companies, and arts organizations, as well as private-sector corporations and foundations. Mr. Forlini was co-author of the *S.A.T. Home Study* program and has written numerous industry reports on elementary, secondary, and post-secondary education markets.

National Advisory Panel

The teachers and administrators serving on the National Advisory Panel provided ongoing input into the development of *Prentice Hall Writing and Grammar: Communication in Action*. Their valuable insights ensure that the perspectives of teachers and students throughout the country are represented within the instruction in this series.

Dr. Pauline Bigby-Jenkins
Coordinator for Secondary English
  Language Arts
Ann Arbor Public Schools
Ann Arbor, Michigan

Lee Bromberger
English Department Chairperson
Mukwonago High School
Mukwonago, Wisconsin

Mary Chapman
Teacher of English
Free State High School
Lawrence, Kansas

Jim Deatheridge
Language Arts Department
  Chairperson
Richland High School
Richland, Washington

Luis Dovalina
Teacher of English
La Joya High School
La Joya, Texas

JoAnn Giardino
Teacher of English
Centennial High School
Columbus, Ohio

Susan Goldberg
Teacher of English
Westlake Middle School
Thornwood, New York

Jean Hicks
Director, Louisville Writing Project
University of Louisville
Louisville, Kentucky

Karen Hurley
Teacher of Language Arts
Terry Meridian Middle School
Indianapolis, Indiana

Karen Lopez
Teacher of English
Hart High School
Newhall, California

Marianne Minshall
Teacher of Reading and Language Arts
Westmore Middle School
Columbus, Ohio

Nancy Monroe
English Department Chairperson
Bolton High School
Alexandria, Louisiana

Ken Spurlock
Assistant Principal
Boone County High School
Florence, Kentucky

Dr. Debi Sulzer
Senior Administrator for Instruction
Orange City Public Schools
Orlando, Florida

Cynthia Katz Tyroff
Staff Development Specialist
  and Teacher of English
Northside Independent School District
San Antonio, Texas

Holly Ward
Teacher of Language Arts
Campbell Middle School
Daytona Beach, Florida

Grammar Review Team

The following teachers reviewed the grammar instruction in this series to ensure accuracy, clarity, and pedagogy.

Kathy Hamilton
Paul Hertzog
Daren Hoisington
Beverly Ladd

Karen Lopez
Dianna Louise Lund
Sean O'Brien

CONTENTS IN BRIEF

CONTENTS
PART 1: WRITING

INTEGRATED SKILLS

Chapter 4 Narration

Autobiographical Writing 48

Chapter 5 · Narration
Short Story 72

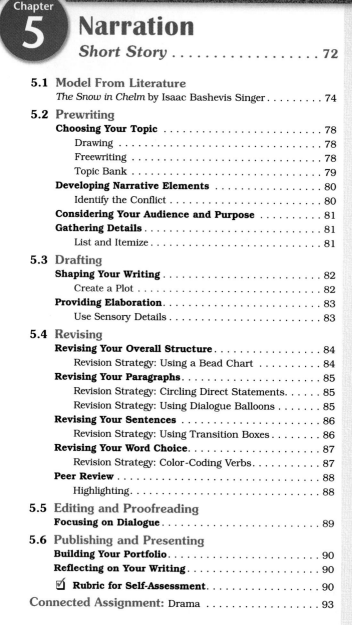

Student Work
IN PROGRESS

Featured Work:
"The Manitoba Monster"
by John Beamer
David Starr Jordan
Middle School
Palo Alto, California

INTEGRATED SKILLS

Chapter 6 Description 98

Student Work
IN PROGRESS

Featured Work:
 "Snow Dance"
 by Leann Goree
 Southside Fundamental
 Middle School
 St. Petersburg, Florida

INTEGRATED SKILLS

Chapter 7 Persuasion

Persuasive Essay 124

INTEGRATED SKILLS

Chapter 8 Exposition

Comparison-and-Contrast Essay 150

INTEGRATED SKILLS

Contents • xiii

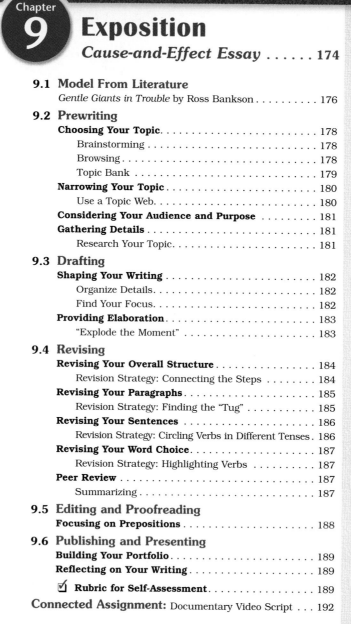

Student Work
IN PROGRESS

Featured Work:
"Saving Our Air"
by Johnny Guo
First Colony Middle School
Sugar Land, Texas

INTEGRATED SKILLS

Chapter 10 Exposition

How-to Essay **198**

Student Work IN PROGRESS

Featured Work:
"Getting to the Pleasant Pedal
Bike Path"
by Jessica S. Lehman
Centre Learning Community
State College, Pennsylvania

INTEGRATED SKILLS

Chapter 11 Research

Research Report 222

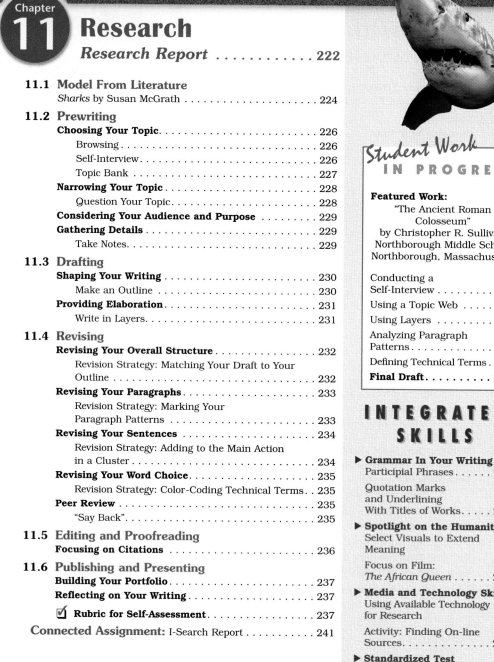

Student Work
IN PROGRESS

Featured Work:
"The Ancient Roman
Colosseum"
by Christopher R. Sullivan
Northborough Middle School
Northborough, Massachusetts

INTEGRATED SKILLS

Chapter 12 Response to Literature 246

INTEGRATED SKILLS

Chapter 13 Writing for Assessment 272

PART 2: GRAMMAR, USAGE, AND MECHANICS

Contents • **xix**

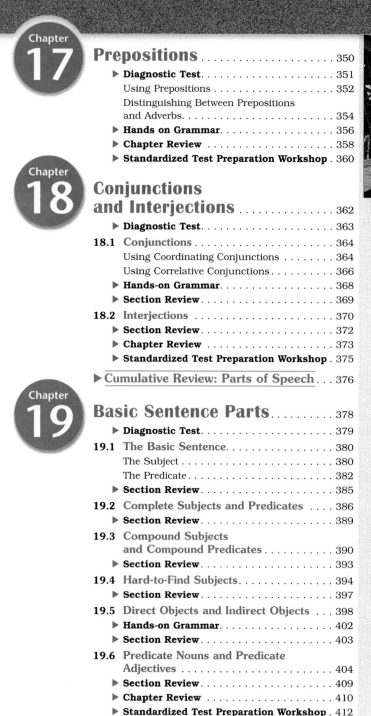

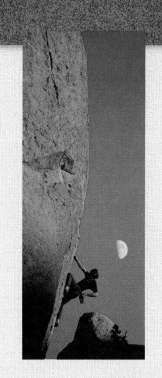

Resources

Lesson Objectives

1. To understand writing as a recursive process and to develop ownership of their own writing processes.

2. To write in a variety of forms, including narrative, descriptive, persuasive, expository, and literary texts, and to develop skills in writing for assessment.

3. To analyze works of literature and student drafts as models and examples of specific writing strategies.

4. To develop voice and adjust their writing to various audiences and purposes.

5. To develop research skills and to use writing as a tool for learning.

6. To apply specific prewriting strategies for generating and narrowing writing topics.

7. To use graphic organizers and other methods for organizing and supporting ideas in drafting.

8. To approach revision in a systematic way in terms of overall structure, paragraphs, sentences, and word choice.

9. To edit and proofread drafts to ensure appropriate usage and accuracy in spelling and the conventions and mechanics of written English.

10. To understand rubrics and to use them to evaluate their own writing and the writing of others.

Writing

Am Kaffeetisch (At the Coffee Table), Carl Schmitz-Pleis, ©Christie's Images, Ltd. 1999

Responding to Fine Art

Am Kaffeetisch (At the Coffee Table)
by Carl Schmitz-Pleis

Use this painting to start a discussion about the process of writing.

1. Have students examine the painting on these pages. You might use the following questions to prompt discussion:

   What does this scene depict? What is the woman doing?

2. Have students describe the seated figure, using details from the painting to support their responses. Ask students what they think the woman is reading.

3. Lead students in a discussion of the role of writing in their daily lives. Aside from school, what other kinds of writing do students encounter? In what ways is writing important to their daily lives?

Time and Resource Manager

In-Depth Lesson Plan

	LESSON FOCUS	PRINT AND MEDIA RESOURCES
DAY 1	**Introduction to Writing** Students discuss the value of writing in everyday life and the qualities of good writing (pp. 2–3).	*Writing Lab* **CD-ROM,** Expression
DAY 2	**Developing Your Writing Life** Students identify strategies for generating and organizing ideas for writing. Coverage of organizing includes notebooks, idea card files, portfolios, and journals (pp. 4–7).	*Writers at Work* **Videotape,** Expression **Teaching Resources** *Writing Support Transparencies,* 1-A; *Writing Support Activity Book* 1-1
DAY 3	**Reflecting on Writing** Students review careers in writing and write a reflective response on their own writing practices (pp. 8–9).	**Teaching Resources** *Formal Assessment,* Ch. 1

Accelerated Lesson Plan

	LESSON FOCUS	PRINT AND MEDIA RESOURCES
DAY 1	**Introduction; Developing Your Writing Life** Students identify qualities of good writing and learn strategies for generating and organizing ideas (pp. 2–7).	*Writers at Work* **Videotape,** Expression *Writing Lab* **CD-ROM,** Expression **Teaching Resources** *Writing Support Transparencies,* 1-A; *Writing Support Activity Book* 1-1
DAY 2	**Reflecting on Writing** Students review careers in writing and write a reflective response on their own writing practices (pp. 8–9).	**Teaching Resources** *Formal Assessment,* Ch. 1

Options for Adapting Lesson Plans

HOMEWORK
Have students complete any stage of the lesson for homework.

FEATURES
Extend coverage with Spotlight on the Humanities (p. 10), Media and Technology Skills (p. 11), and the Standardized Test Preparation Workshop (pp. 12–13).

TECHNOLOGY
Students can complete any stage of the lesson on computer. Have them print out their completed work.

INTEGRATED SKILLS COVERAGE

Integrating Workplace Skills
ATE p. 5

Technology SE pp. 5–11

Viewing and Representing
Critical Viewing SE pp. 2, 4, 6, 7, 10

Integrating Research Skills
ATE p. 9

ASSESSMENT SUPPORT

Standardized Test Preparation Workshop SE p. 12
Standardized Test Preparation Workbook, pp. 1–2
Formal Assessment, Ch. 1

MEETING INDIVIDUAL NEEDS

Less Advanced Students ATE pp. 8, 13; See also Ongoing
Assessments ATE pp. 5, 8
ESL Students ATE pp. 3, 13
Visual/Spatial Learners ATE p. 6
Gifted/Talented Students ATE p. 8

BLOCK SCHEDULING

Resources for Varying Instruction
• *Writing Lab* CD-ROM If your students have access to hardware, a 90-minute block provides an ideal opportunity for students to work on computer.

Professional Development Support
• *How to Manage Instruction in the Block* This Teaching Resource provides management and activity suggestions.

MEDIA AND TECHNOLOGY

For the Teacher
• *Writers at Work* Videotape
• *Resource Pro* CD-ROM

WRITING AND GRAMMAR WEB SITE

The Interactive Writing and Grammar Web site provides a wide array of support for students, teachers and parents. Writing support includes:

• Interactive revision checkers
• Scoring rubrics with complete models

www.phschool.com

LITERATURE CONNECTIONS

Related selections from *Prentice Hall Literature: Timeless Voices, Timeless Themes*, Copper Level:
"Restoring the Circle" and "Loo-Wit, the Fire Keeper," Joseph Bruchac, ATE p. 9
"The Drive-in Movies," Gary Soto, ATE p. 9
"The Wounded Wolf," Jean Craighead George, ATE p. 9
"He Lion, Bruh Bear, and Bruh Rabbit," Virginia Hamilton, ATE p. 9
"Greyling," Jane Yolen, ATE p. 9

The Writer in You

Lesson Objectives

1. To generate and refine ideas and plans for writing.
2. To identify audience and purpose for writing.
3. To use available technology to support aspects of the writing process.
4. To publish for general and specific audiences.

Critical Viewing

Speculate Students may say they would like to ask her what she is writing about and for whom is she writing.

▲ Critical Viewing What two questions would you like to ask this student about her writing? [Speculate]

Writing in Everyday Life

You probably write every day without even thinking about it. You may share e-mail messages with friends or write cards to thank relatives for gifts they've given you. Even something as simple as jotting down a phone message is a form of writing. In addition, you do a variety of forms of writing in school—ranging from taking notes to writing stories to completing research reports. In the chapters that follow, you will learn strategies that will not only help you to become a better writer but will also help you get more enjoyment out of the writing that you do.

⏱ TIME AND RESOURCE MANAGER	
In-Depth Coverage	**Accelerated Pace**
• Cover pp. 2–3 in class. **Option** Divide the class into four groups and assign each group about a quarter of the assigned pages to read and summarize for the rest of the class.	• Have students read, discuss, and summarize pp. 2–3 together.

Why Write?

Like speaking, writing allows you to communicate your thoughts, opinions, and knowledge to others. When you write, however, you can communicate with a wider audience than you can in everyday conversation. Some people might read your work today—and others can read your work next week or next year. By developing strong writing skills, you strengthen your ability to communicate with others.

What Are the Qualities of Good Writing?

Ideas Good writing begins with good ideas. When you come up with ideas to write about, it is important to select those that interest you. The more interested you are in what you write, the better you will write. Consider also whether the ideas will interest the people who read your writing. Be sure to choose ideas that will interest others.

Organization The next characteristic of good writing is a clear and consistent organization. Choose a logical way of arranging your information that suits the topic and the type of writing that you are doing.

Voice When you speak, you sound different from anyone else. The same is true of your writing. A writer's voice is the unique way every writer has of expressing himself or herself on paper. Voice includes everything from the words you use to the types of sentences you choose to the topics you select.

Word Choice Each word should be carefully selected to convey the exact meaning you intend. In addition, consider the associations that certain words call to mind for readers. Two words that have the same meaning can convey different impressions—one positive, one negative. If you wish to convey a positive impression of your subject, choose words that support that impression.

Sentence Fluency Be aware of the sound of your writing as well as its meaning. When you read your work aloud, your sentences should flow smoothly into one another. You can achieve this effect by using transitions to connect your sentences. In addition to using transitions, vary the lengths and types of sentences you use.

Conventions Finally, carefully follow the conventions of English grammar, usage, mechanics, and spelling. A potentially great piece of writing will have a poor impact if it contains errors in these areas. Always proofread your work to eliminate all errors.

Writers in
ACTION

Author Jane Yolen bases many of her fanciful stories on her study of folklore. Even her most fantastic stories, however, contain a grain of realism. She says of her writing: "Anything I've experienced can find its way into one of my stories."

The Writer in You • **3**

PREPARE and ENGAGE

Interest GRABBER Invite a published writer to read from his or her work to the class and talk to students about the rewards and hard work involved in writing for publication. Ask the speaker to describe his or her drafting and revision process in detail. Students will be amazed and impressed to find out that "real" authors may revise their work five, ten, or more times before they are satisfied. (The public librarian should be able to recommend local writers who will visit schools.)

Activate Prior Knowledge

Ask students to describe themselves as writers. Do they write every day? For what purposes? Then discuss school writing assignments: the ones students have enjoyed, the ones they didn't like, and the ones they have found most difficult. Which part of the writing process do students like best: generating ideas, drafting, revising, editing, or presenting their writing to an audience?

More About the Writer

Jane Yolen has written over 150 books for children, young adults, and adults, for which she has received numerous awards. Because of the overwhelming popularity of her fairy tales and fantasy stories, she has been dubbed the Hans Christian Andersen of America and the Aesop of the 20th century.

Customize for
ESL Students

Students learning English may need additional explanation of the five stages of the writing process. Show samples of writing at each stage and explain what it comprises. Label and display the samples for students' reference.

Writer's Notebook and Journal

1. Ask students to describe ways in which the act of writing can help clarify thoughts, desires, and emotions. Challenge students to provide examples from their own experiences.

2. Have students keep a writer's notebook for at least a week. Remind them to bring the notebook with them just about everywhere they go and jot down ideas that intrigue them, quotes from their reading, amusing jokes, bits of conversation, and so on.

3. A customized notebook can inspire a writer to use it, so ask students to choose notebooks that are just right for them. Some students prefer loose-leaf notebooks so they can move pages easily. Others like notebooks small enough to carry in a pocket. Encourage students to personalize their notebooks in some way—perhaps by decorating the covers or inventing hilarious titles.

Critical Viewing

Connect Students may say that the photograph may remind them of a trip they took, which would make a good idea for writing.

Developing Your Writing Life

Part of becoming a good writer is finding an approach to writing that works for you. Your approach includes everything from where you write and when you write to how you go about choosing topics and revising your work.

Keep Track of Your Ideas

One of the first habits that you should get into as a writer is keeping track of your ideas. Having a great idea and then forgetting it is one of the worst things that can happen to any writer. Don't let it happen to you. Try these techniques for keeping track of ideas that come to mind.

Writer's Notebook You can come across a writing idea at any time. That's why many writers carry a small notebook wherever they go. Keep a notebook in which you jot down things you observe, comments people make, and quotations from books, advertisements, and television programs.

Journal A journal is a great way to capture ideas and ensure that you write regularly. Get a notebook or a tablet, and write in it at regular intervals—ideally, every day.

Idea Card File Use note cards to collect ideas about specific topics. For example, if you're writing about the Grand Canyon, you might write a note card about each landform. Use the note cards to experiment with different ways of organizing your information.

▲ **Critical Viewing** How might a photograph like this one help you come up with writing ideas? [Connect]

> **Mesa**
> A flat, raised landform like a mountain or hill, with a flat top

> **Colorado River**
> Runs along the bottom of the Grand Canyon

> **Canyon**
> A valley with steep walls, often created by erosion

⏱ TIME AND RESOURCE MANAGER

In-Depth Coverage	Accelerated Pace
• Cover pp. 4–9 in class. • Share passages from an author's notebook or journal with the class.	• Assign pp. 4–9 for independent student review. • Have students locate, read, and discuss passages from published writers' journals.

Keep Track of Your Writing and Reading

Writing Portfolio Every time you complete a writing project, you will learn and grow as a writer. Creating a writing portfolio helps you to review your progress. Looking back at what you've done can help you to make strong writing choices on your next writing project.

Include a wide range of different types of writing in your portfolio. In addition to final drafts, include notes, graphic organizers, and earlier drafts to capture how the project developed.

Reader's Journal Reading is a good way to provide fuel for your writing. Keeping a reader's journal can also help you to keep track of what you read. Make note of the authors and titles of books and articles you enjoy. Include a couple of quotations that capture each writer's style, too. When you browse through your journal, think of ways you can respond. You might write a review, a sequel, or a letter to the author.

What Works Best for You?

Getting Started There are many different ways to get started on a piece of writing. You may want to plunge in and start typing your ideas on a computer. You may also begin by taking some time to reflect quietly about your topic.

Freewriting Freewriting is another approach to getting started. This involves jotting down any thoughts that come into your mind, with no self-editing. Often, freewriting can provide material for a more formal piece of writing.

Finding Ideas Don't let a blank page intimidate you. Ideas for writing are everywhere! Every day, you can find ideas in newspapers, on television, or in books. If you keep a writer's journal, turn to its pages to find inspiration for your writing.

Improving Your Work One of the great things about writing is that you get a chance to go back and improve what you've done. Take advantage of this opportunity by carefully revising every piece of your writing.

Experiment

As you develop as a writer, experiment with various strategies and techniques. You might try making revisions as you go along. You might also focus on completing a draft in a single sitting. There are many different ways to approach a piece of writing, and one way isn't necessarily better than another. All that really matters is that you find the approach effective.

Technology Tip

If you work on a computer, you can keep an electronic portfolio. Do so by creating a folder for each assignment, and storing those folders within other folders. For example, you may want to create a folder for each type of writing.

Getting Started

1. Even after they have found a suitable place to write, students may still have difficulty getting started. If students are not familiar with freewriting, introduce this technique. They should set a timer for five minutes and write steadily. The idea is to write anything, even nonsense, for that entire time, scarcely lifting pen from paper. Students may find that the act of writing loosens them up and leads to writing they can use in almost the same way stretching loosens up a runner.

2. Engage students in a discussion about improving their work through revision. Do students agree that writers should draft an entire piece before revising? In what way might rewriting be an excuse for not going on? Do students believe that any one procedure works for all writers?

Integrating Workplace Skills

Copy Editors and Proofreaders
Write a short paragraph deliberately including an abundance of errors in spelling, punctuation, grammar, and usage. Give each student a copy. Allow students a few minutes to find and correct as many errors as they can. Then ask students whether they enjoyed this task. Was it easier to find mistakes in someone else's writing than it is to find errors in their own work? Tell students that copy editors' and proofreaders' jobs involve finding and correcting errors in manuscripts.

☑ ONGOING ASSESSMENT: Monitor and Reinforce

For students who are unsure of the steps in the writing process, try the following option.

Have students work together to make a chart that includes a heading for each step of the writing process. With your help, have the group brainstorm ways to accomplish each step of the process and summarize this information on the chart. Post the chart in the classroom so that students can refer to it as necessary.

Organize Your Environment

Teaching Resources:
Writing Support Transparency 1-A;
Writing Support Activity Book, 1-1

1. Reinforce the idea that different writing projects may require different places and environments.

2. Have students suggest possible topics for writing along with places that would be most suitable for that topic; for example, if students were going to write a research report, they would most likely write in a library or other research facility.

Critical Viewing

Apply Some students may say that this environment would be too distracting for them to write effectively. Others may say it would be a good environment because of the reference materials that one might use when writing.

Customize for
Visual/Spatial Learners

Students may enjoy designing their own to-do lists on which they can budget their time for various stages of their writing projects. Students' lists can be as imaginative as they like.

1

Plan to Write

The best way to improve as a writer is to write. Set aside time to write as often as you can. You don't have to wait until you've been given a writing assignment in school. Write on your own. You can write stories, journal entries, letters to your newspaper—any type of writing that interests you. Not only will you improve as a writer, but you'll probably have some fun in the process.

Organize Your Environment

Choose the Right Spot To make yourself more comfortable and efficient when you write, find a special place to do your writing. You might prefer a quiet library or a room with quiet music. Try writing in different places, and decide which environment works best for you. You might even find that you prefer one place for writing poems and another for writing letters.

Be Ready to Write American author Ernest Hemingway once told a friend that he began writing each morning by sharpening twenty pencils! You may not need that many pencils, but it's good to begin with everything you will need. Before you start, make sure that you have pens, paper, and your notes. If you're working on a computer, be sure to use word-processing software with which you feel comfortable and to have access to a printer. Also, have a dictionary and a thesaurus nearby.

Budget Your Time A long writing assignment may take a few days to finish. Make a schedule to help keep you on track. Divide your project into stages, and give yourself a set amount of time for each stage. If one stage takes longer than expected, adjust the amount of time you spend on later stages.

▲ Critical Viewing
Could you write effectively in this environment? Why or why not?
[Apply]

Project To-Do List

Day 1	Begin collecting ideas
Day 2	Continue collecting ideas
Day 3	Decide which ideas to include
Day 4	Write a first draft
Day 5	Revise and proofread piece

6 • The Writer in You

Working With Others

Runners can run by themselves or as part of a team. Writers can also work independently or with others. However, there are many benefits to working with others.

Group Brainstorming It can be challenging to come up with ideas on your own. Group brainstorming helps many writers develop their ideas. Brainstorming means freely suggesting and building on ideas. Don't stop to think about whether the ideas are any good. Just talk about them with the group. Listening to other people's ideas and responses can help you focus your thoughts.

Collaborative and Cooperative Writing Writers can collaborate at all stages of the writing process. A team can draft a letter to the editor by dividing the work. One writer might draft the introduction. Another might draft the conclusion. The same team might take turns proofreading the letter. Using more than one proofreader can really help the team catch any mistakes.

Peer Reviewers As a writer, you are very close to your own writing. Another pair of eyes often sees things that you might have missed. Try to work with a peer reviewer as often as possible. Take turns reading each other's work and offering suggestions for improvement. In each of the chapters that follow, you will find specific strategies and suggestions for working with peer reviewers.

Writers in
ACTION

Every writer has unique writing habits. Robert Frost wrote his poems on a writing board. He said, "I've never had a table in my life. And I use all sorts of things. Write on the sole of my shoe."

◀ **Critical Viewing** Suppose that these students are working together on a school report. How might they share ideas? **[Analyze]**

Step-by-Step Teaching Guide

Work With Others

1. Review the guidelines for successful brainstorming. Mention the following points:
   - One person (or several in turn) is responsible for writing down ideas, preferably on the board or on large sheets of paper so that everyone can see them.
   - No idea is too silly! Group members should feel free to suggest any ideas that come to them. Remind students that judgment does not play a part in brainstorming.

2. Tell students that collaborative and cooperative writing can make the writing process more rewarding because they allow for a greater range of ideas. Remind students that not all writing projects, however, will benefit from collaborative writing. Personal writing, including autobiographical accounts and journal entries, is one such example.

3. Explain to students the importance of peer reviews. These reviews are good opportunities for students to get feedback from their classmates.

Critical Viewing

Analyze Students may say that they might listen to each other carefully, respect each other's ideas, and make a list or outline together before beginning to write.

Publishing

1. Tell students that publishing is usually the last intended stage of the writing process. Where a piece of writing gets published, however, depends on one's purpose for writing and one's intended audience. For example, if students were to write a humorous story for readers their age, they would not want to publish it in a news magazine for adult readers.

2. You may want to design an evaluation sheet, which students can complete and staple to each piece of finished writing. The evaluation sheet might be as simple as the following: What is my favorite part of this paper? What new techniques did I try? What is one part of this paper I could improve?

Customize for
Gifted/Talented Students

Ask students to work together to design a rubric for evaluating writing that includes content and mechanics. When they have developed a draft of the rubric, ask the rest of the class to contribute their ideas. Then have all students use the rubric to evaluate writing products for the rest of the year.

Customize for
Less Advanced Students

Students may have difficulty articulating reasons they like a particular piece of their writing. Suggest that they may be proud of a piece of writing for some of the following reasons:

• They tried a new genre.

• The piece was longer than previous pieces of writing.

• They used interesting words.

• They used a variety of sentence structures.

• Their paragraphs had a main idea and supporting details.

• They enjoyed writing the piece.

1

Publishing

When you finish a writing project, consider sharing it with others. Publishing your work can make you feel proud and may even inspire other writers. There are many magazines, contests, and on-line sites that publish student work. Here are a few resources you might consider:

Periodicals

• *Creative Kids*, P.O. Box 8813, Waco, TX 76714-8813

> Your Name
> Your Street
> Your City, State, and ZIP Code
>
> Place Stamp Here
>
> Creative Kids
> P.O. Box 8813
> Waco, TX 76714-8813

• *Stone Soup*, Children's Art Foundation, P.O. Box 83, 915 Cedar Street, Santa Cruz, CA 95063

On-line Publications

• MidLink Magazine. **http://www.cs.ucf.edu/~MidLink/**

Contests

• National Written & Illustrated By . . . Awards Contest for Students: Landmark Editions, Inc., 1402 Kansas Avenue, Kansas City, MO 64127

Reflecting on Your Writing

Asking yourself questions can help you evaluate your opinions about writing. It can also help you focus on your writing goals. Here are just a few questions you might ask:

• What is my favorite kind of writing?

• Where is my favorite place to write?

• Who is my favorite author?

• At what times do I do my best writing?

• What kinds of writing would I like to complete this year?

Take some time to share your responses with a partner, and then jot down your ideas in a writer's journal.

☑ ONGOING ASSESSMENT: Monitor and Reinforce

For students who are having difficulty evaluating their writing, try the following option.

Have students choose writing buddies to help them evaluate their writing. Buddies can point out confusing passages and suggest revisions.

Integrating Research Skills
Have students find out more about one of the writers listed on this page and read a book or article the person has written.

Writers in Action

Careers in Writing, Writing in Careers

When you think of careers in writing, you probably think of news reporters, novelists, and poets. However, writing plays an important role in many other careers that might not come to mind. Business people write memorandums and proposals. Police officers file crime reports. Nurses report on the condition of patients. In almost any occupation you choose, you will be called on to do some writing.

Meet the Professionals

In the writing chapters of this book, you'll meet nine professionals who use different types of writing on the job. These writers at work include

Jane Yolen, a novelist and short story writer.
In her imaginative tales, Yolen creates memorable characters with whom her readers can identify.

Debbie Behler, a newsletter writer for the Bronx Zoo.
Behler uses writing to provide up-to-date information about events and activities at the zoo.

Virginia Hamilton, a novelist and a reteller of folk tales.
Hamilton writes engaging novels for young readers and retells tales that have been told orally for generations.

Officer Charles Tsang, a police officer.
Writing crime and accident reports requires Officer Tsang to write in a clear and focused manner.

Kevin Powell, a feature writer for popular magazines.
The world of popular culture and entertainment comes to life in Powell's articles.

Doug Raboy, an advertising copywriter.
Raboy uses the power of persuasive writing to spur people to buy the products he represents.

Jean Craighead George, a novelist.
Jean Craighead George tells stories that take place in remote and interesting settings.

Gary Soto, a poet, short-story writer, and essayist.
Soto vividly re-creates humorous stories from his childhood.

Joseph Bruchac, a poet, nonfiction writer, and editor.
In his role as an editor, Bruchac carefully reviews each poem submitted and presents a thoughtful response.

Seeing how these professionals use writing may help you imagine the role that writing will play in your professional life.

Writers at Work Videotape

You can view these Writers at Work demonstrating their writing process in the Writers at Work videos.

Debbie Behler

Virginia Hamilton

Joe Bruchac

The Writer in You • 9

Lesson Objectives

1. To analyze how meaning is communicated through the arts.
2. To study a particular work of art or an artistic performance.
3. To write a poem that captures impressions of a work of art or artistic performance.

Step-by-Step Teaching Guide

Analyzing How Meaning Is Communicated Through the Arts

1. Choose one of the Spotlight elements for class discussion, or have students work in groups or independently on the element of their choice. Give students the initiative to find the necessary books, recordings, or videotapes.

2. Go through the list of different kinds of art with students. Ask for a show of hands of those who create or perform in any of these categories. Have a class discussion of students' reasons for spending time on artistic endeavors. Why do human beings feel the need to create?

3. Remind students that performers are also artists, even though they do not write the plays in which they act or compose the songs they sing. A playwright, composer, or choreographer needs performers to make his or her material come to life. Every performer of a certain piece will interpret it differently and put his or her individual stamp on it.

4. Find a photograph of Michelangelo's great statue *Moses* in an art book. Bring it to class and have students compare it to the statue pictured on this page. Explain that artists of the Italian Renaissance, like Michelangelo, looked back to the statues of ancient Greece and Rome for inspiration. Have students compare and contrast the two statues. Explain how the art of one time and place influences that of another.

Analyzing How Meaning Is Communicated Through the Arts

Introducing the Spotlight on the Humanities

In addition to writing, there are many other ways in which you can express yourself. In the Spotlight on the Humanities features, you will discover how all art is connected and how the inspiration that moved the hearts and minds of creative artists in the past continues to touch artists of today. The following art forms provide some of the best opportunities for self-expression.

▲ **Critical Viewing**
What mood and what ideas does this sculpture convey? **[Analyze]**

- **Fine art** includes paintings, sketches, sculpture, and collages. Through the use of color and form, art expresses feelings and conveys ideas about the world in which we live.
- **Photography** allows us to capture people, scenes, and events. Through the choice of subject, composition, and lighting, photography offers the opportunity for the expression of ideas.
- **Theater** is designed to be performed by actors on a stage. Using props, scenery, sound effects, and lighting, drama brings a story to life. In some cases, music and dance are incorporated into the story line.
- **Film** uses sound and motion to capture events and tell stories. Like dramatic theater, most films tell a story. However, filmmakers can also use the camera angles, sound techniques, and editing to create special effects.
- **Music** uses sound to create meaning. Whether presented as an oboe solo, an operatic aria, or a symphony, music can create moods or present variations on a theme.
- **Dance** creates meaning through organized movement. It can be performed by a single person, a pair, or larger groups.

Writing Activity

Select a work of art from the list above that you consider memorable. Write a poem that captures your impressions about that work of art.

Viewing and Representing Activity

Before students begin the writing activity, have them clear their choices of subject with you. Encourage students to view their works of art again before writing, rather than writing about something that is only a vague memory. Students can view movies again on videotape, find reproductions of paintings and sculptures in art books, and listen to recordings of music.

Critical Viewing

Analyze Students may say that the figure's bowed head and the way he is wrapped in his cloak suggest grief or mourning.

Media and Technology Skills

Making Technology Work for You

Activity: Identify Appropriate Technology

When you do research for a composition or presentation, you choose research tools and sources. Similarly, you have a choice of tools and resources available to share that information with your audience.

Learn About It Choosing the right type of technology for your purpose is the first step in successful communication of your ideas. Learn about the different ways that technology can be used to help you prepare and present information.

- **Writing Tools** Computer *word-processing programs* allow you to store and retrieve text. They also make it very easy to make revisions to your work.

- **Virtual Resources** The *Internet* is an extensive computer network on which individuals get and post information and pictures. Large numbers of individuals and organizations put information on the Internet. Search engines and links between sites allow users to find such information. *E-mail* is a way to send and receive messages nearly instantaneously over the Internet.

- **Audiovisual Tools** Several tools allow you to add sounds and images to your presentations. A *still camera* records still images, which can be displayed on their own or projected in a series with a *slide projector.* A *tape recorder* preserves and plays back sound.

Evaluate It Create a chart with the categories shown below to evaluate which types of technology tools you find most useful and which ones you might want to use in the future.

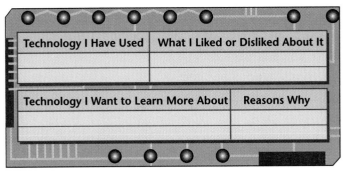

Technology I Have Used	What I Liked or Disliked About It

Technology I Want to Learn More About	Reasons Why

Uses of Technology

Writing Tools
- Writing software—allows easy revisions; helps you organize the writing process by using some feature prompts

Virtual Resources
- Internet—lets you present your work to a wide audience; permits easy research
- E-mail—allows students to share their work and get fast feedback on it

Audiovisual Tools
- Still camera—can show something that is hard to describe
- Slide projector—adds visual interest to oral presentations
- Tape recorder—helps in taking complete notes; reveals the personality of an interview subject

▶ **Lesson Objectives**

1. To identify different forms of communication.
2. To recognize when technology can aid in communication.
3. To use technology to aid communication.

Step-by-Step Teaching Guide

Making Technology Work

Teaching Resources: Writing Support Transparency 1-B; Writing Support Activity Book 1-2

1. Go through the list of "tools" on the page. Ask students how many of them have used each one. Ask them to discuss their experiences with each tool. How did these tools help them accomplish the specific task?

2. Ask students whether they prefer looking something up in a reference book or searching for the same information on the Internet. Ask students who have tried both methods to compare and contrast them. What are the advantages and disadvantages of each? You might tell students that since anyone can post anything on the Internet, not all sites are reliable; published books are held to a much stricter standard of accountability.

3. Use the transparency to take students through the writing exercise. Give them copies of the blank organizer. After students have completed the chart, challenge them to devise a brief activity that will allow them to use a new technology. For example, a student who has never used a camera can take some photographs and use them to illustrate an essay.

Lesson Objectives

1. To read and understand a writing prompt.
2. To use prewriting strategies to generate ideas.
3. To organize ideas to ensure logical progression and support for those ideas.
4. To draft, revise, and edit an answer to a writing prompt.
5. To use correct grammar, spelling, and mechanics.

Step-by-Step Teaching Guide

Responding to Writing Prompts

1. Have a volunteer read aloud the bulleted list of the criteria that test scorers will use to evaluate students' work. Emphasize the first word of the first item: *responded.* This is the most important thing a student must accomplish: the essay must address the question asked. Therefore, the most important first step is to read the question carefully.

2. Remind students not to spend too much time organizing their ideas before they begin writing. A good way to organize details quickly is to sum up the main idea in one sentence, then jot down a few supporting details. Remind students that they need not write in complete sentences at this stage.

3. Have another student read aloud the sample prompt. Then, carefully review the different stages in the writing process on page 13, and have students jot down notes and ideas for each of the stages listed.

Standardized Test Preparation Workshop

Responding to Writing Prompts

Because writing is such an important skill, standardized tests often include writing sections. In these sections, you will be given a writing prompt and asked to write an essay about it. When your essay is evaluated, scorers will look to see that you have

- responded directly to the prompt and performed all of the tasks called for in the prompt.
- presented your ideas in a clear, well-organized manner.
- backed up your main points with facts, examples, and other types of details.
- followed all of the conventions of grammar, usage, mechanics, and spelling.

When you write for a test, you will often be given a time limit. If this is the case, you have to budget your time wisely. Divide up your time among collecting ideas, writing your essay, and revising your essay.

Following is an example of one type of writing prompt you might find on a standardized test. Use the suggestions provided to help you respond. The clocks next to each stage show a suggested plan for organizing your time.

Test Tip

In any test question or writing prompt, look for key words that tell you exactly what is required. Words such as *explain, identify, describe,* and *persuade* indicate specific types of responses.

Sample Writing Situation

> Writer Jane Yolen comments, "Anything I've experienced can find its way into one of my stories."
>
> Write an essay in which you describe an experience you had that you think would make a good story. Provide the details of the experience, and explain why you think it would make a good story. Identify the types of readers who would like to read your story, and tell why.

⚓ TEST-TAKING TIP

Remind students that their essays should fully respond to the prompt. Students should make sure that they answer the entire question, not just a part of it. One way to be sure they have done this is to rewrite the prompt as a series of short questions. Challenge them to try this with the prompt on this page. (Students should write questions similar to the following: What experience in your past would make a good story? Why would it make a good story? Who would want to read the story?)

Prewriting

Allow about one fourth of your time for prewriting.

Choose an Experience Think about the qualities of a good story. Then, search your memory for an experience that could form the basis for a story that would have those qualities.

Make a Timeline Sketch a timeline on which you outline the key events of the experience. Include such details as the people involved and the setting in which the experience took place.

Drafting

Allow about half of your time for prewriting.

Present Your Main Point Begin with an introduction in which you indicate what makes a good story, and sum up with a sentence or two about why the experience you have selected would make a good story.

Describe the Experience Use your timeline to help you describe the experience in detail. Make sure that you describe it in a way that will support your point that it would make a good story.

Support Your Position After you've described the experience, tell why it would make a good story. Back up your opinion by using details from the experience to illustrate how it fits the qualities of a good story.

Identify the Potential Audience Once you've explained why the experience would make a good story, describe the type of audience who would be most interested in your story.

Revising, Editing, and Proofreading

Allow about one fourth of your time to revise, edit, and proofread.

Check for Missing Details Review your essay to see if you have left out any important details from the experience. If you wish to add details, write them neatly in the margin, and draw an arrow and a line showing where they should be inserted.

Eliminate Errors Check your work carefully to eliminate errors in grammar, usage, mechanics, and spelling. Having these types of errors in your work can hurt your score on a standardized test—even if the content of your essay is good.

Customize for
ESL Students

Reassure students that test scorers are not going to expect sophisticated vocabulary and long, complex-compound sentences in writing exercises. Explain that writing prompts are designed to cover the everyday interests and experiences of students so that everyone taking the test should be able to provide an answer.

Customize for
Less Advanced Students

Encourage students who do not write fluently and easily to write more often in their daily lives. Challenge them to write a paragraph every day for two weeks as homework. Devise a series of writing prompts, such as *Describe the way the schoolyard looks in the morning* or *Write about a time when you felt really nervous about an upcoming event.* Make sure the prompts require relatively brief answers so that students can easily finish them as homework assignments, one each night. Give students a time limit within which to write their paragraphs. You may want to go over their assignments with them, or assign classroom tutors from among the best writers in the class. You or the tutor should read the essay, pointing out major flaws in organization and grammar and discussing any concerns the student has. After two weeks, students should show real improvement.

In-Depth Lesson Plan

	LESSON FOCUS	PRINT AND MEDIA RESOURCES
DAY 1	**Introduction to the Writing Process** Students are introduced to the steps of the writing process (pp. 14–15).	*Writing Lab* CD-ROM, Description
DAY 2	**Prewriting** Students walk through the steps of the prewriting process (pp. 16–20).	*Language Lab* CD-ROM, Composing **Teaching Resources** *Writing Support Transparencies 2-A–E; Writing Support Activity Book 2-1–5*
DAY 3	**Drafting** Students walk through the steps of the drafting process (pp. 21–22).	
DAY 4	**Revising** Students walk through the steps of the revising process (pp. 23–25).	**Teaching Resources** *Writing Support Transparency 2-F*
DAY 5	**Editing and Proofreading; Publishing and Presenting** Students walk through the steps of the editing and proofreading and publishing and presenting processes (pp. 26–27).	**Teaching Resources** *Formal Assessment, Ch. 2*

Accelerated Lesson Plan

	LESSON FOCUS	PRINT AND MEDIA RESOURCES
DAY 1	**Drafting** Students explore the introduction, prewriting, and drafting stages of the writing process (pp. 14–22).	*Language Lab* CD-ROM, Composing
DAY 2	**Revising to Presenting** Students explore the revising, editing, and publishing and presenting stages (pp. 23–27).	**Teaching Resources** *Writing Support Transparency 2-F; Formal Assessment, Ch. 2*

Options for Adapting Lesson Plans

HOMEWORK

Have students complete any stage of the lesson for homework.

FEATURES

Extend coverage with the Spotlight on the Humanities (p. 28), Media and Technology Skills (p. 29), and the Standardized Test Preparation Workshop (p. 30).

TECHNOLOGY

Students can complete any stage of the lesson on computer. Have them print out their completed work.

INTEGRATED SKILLS COVERAGE

Speaking and Listening
ATE pp. 16, 18

Vocabulary
ATE p. 19

Technology
SE pp. 25, 29

Real-World Connection
ATE p. 27

Viewing and Representing
Critical Viewing SE pp. 14, 16, 28
Viewing and Representing ATE p. 28

BLOCK SCHEDULING

Pacing Suggestions
For 90-minute Blocks
• Have students complete the Prewriting and Drafting stages in a single period.
• Focus one class period on Revising and Editing and Publishing and Presenting. Allow at least 30 minutes for peer revision.

Resources for Varying Instruction
• *Writing Lab* **CD-ROM** If your students have access to hardware, a 90-minute block provides an ideal opportunity for students to work on computer.

Professional Development Support
• *How to Manage Instruction in the Block* This Teaching Resource provides management and activity suggestions.

ASSESSMENT SUPPORT

Standardized Test Preparation Workshop SE p. 30

Standardized Test Preparation Workbook, pp. 3–4

Formal Assessment, Ch. 2

MEDIA AND TECHNOLOGY

For the Student
• *Language Lab* **CD-ROM,** Composing

For the Teacher
• *Resource Pro* **CD-ROM**

MEETING INDIVIDUAL NEEDS

Less Advanced Students ATE p. 19; See also Ongoing Assessments ATE pp. 17, 22, 24
More Advanced Students ATE p. 31
ESL Students ATE pp. 21, 31
Gifted/Talented Students ATE p. 15

WRITING AND GRAMMAR WEB SITE

The Interactive Writing and Grammar Web site provides a wide array of support for students, teachers and parents. Writing support includes:

• Interactive revision checkers
• Scoring rubrics with complete models

www.phschool.com

LITERATURE CONNECTIONS

Related selections from *Prentice Hall Literature: Timeless Voices, Timeless Themes,* Copper Level:
from *The Pigman & Me,* Paul Zindel, SE p. 21

Lesson Objectives

1. To generate and refine ideas and plans for writing.
2. To identify audience and purpose for writing.
3. To use available technology to support aspects of the writing process.
4. To spell accurately in final drafts.
5. To proofread writing for errors in grammar, spelling and mechanics.
6. To publish for general and specific audiences.
7. To apply criteria to evaluate writing.

Critical Viewing

Analyze Students may say that revising allows you to express your ideas and organize your thoughts more clearly.

Chapter 2 A Walk Through the Writing Process

▲ Critical Viewing
How can revising your writing improve it? [Analyze]

You write every day. The form your writing may take depends on your purpose: You may be working on a school assignment, adding items to a shopping list, writing a postcard while on vacation, or e-mailing a friend. For each different type of writing you do, you may use some or all stages of the writing process, a systematized process for improving your writing.

Types of Writing

To study writing, you can categorize it by **modes,** the forms or shapes that writing can take. The chart at right shows the modes of writing you'll encounter in this book. Writing can also be divided into two broad categories: *reflexive* and *extensive.*

Reflexive writing—such as a postcard to a friend, a note to yourself in your daily planner, or a personal journal essay—is *for* you and *from* you. This kind of writing is tentative and exploratory.

The inspirations for **extensive writing** are *for* others and *from* others. It is usually done for school, and it may be graded and evaluated. The audience for your extensive writing—such as research assignments, persuasive essays, and book reports—is often a general one.

The Modes of Writing

- Narration
- Description
- Persuasion
- Exposition
- Research Writing
- Response to Literature
- Writing for Assessment

⏱ TIME AND RESOURCE MANAGER	
In-Depth Coverage	**Accelerated Pace**
• Cover pp. 14–15 in class.	• Have students read, discuss, and summarize pp. 14–15 independently.

The Process of Writing

These are the stages of the writing process:

- **Prewriting** Freely exploring topics, choosing a topic, and gathering and organizing details before you write
- **Drafting** Getting your ideas down on paper in roughly the format you intend
- **Revising** Correcting any major errors and improving the writing's form and content
- **Editing and Proofreading** Polishing the writing by correcting errors in grammar, spelling, and mechanics
- **Publishing and Presenting** Sharing your writing

These steps may seem to follow a strict order, but writers often jump back to earlier writing stages as they work. For example, when you are drafting, you may discover that you need to do additional research on your topic. When you are revising, you may decide to include more work from your prewriting stage. You might even put aside work in the prewriting or drafting stage, save it in your portfolio, and go back to it sometime later, when you have thought of different strategies for organizing your writing.

A Guided Tour

Use this chapter as an introduction to the stages of the writing process. Consider the steps of the process presented here. Look at some of the strategies used by effective writers, and experiment with them in your own writing. By applying these strategies when you are engaged in the writing process, you will improve the quality of your final draft.

A Walk Through the Writing Process • 15

PREPARE and ENGAGE

Interest GRABBER Show your class notes, drafts, and final copies of your own writing and discuss the process with students: how long it took, the most difficult stages, prewriting strategies, the role of inspiration, and so on. Mention the time and effort you expended. It is always encouraging to be reminded that teachers have to think and work hard too.

Activate Prior Knowledge

Ask students to share some of their writing experiences—perhaps times that they couldn't think of anything to write about and what they did about it, or their favorite writing assignments and why they liked them. Explain that this chapter presents some new prewriting strategies and provides a variety of writing assignments.

Customize for
Gifted/Talented Students

Have students create a bulletin board that shows the steps of the writing process. Ask them to post examples of the steps and challenge them to represent the recursive nature of the process.

Prewriting: Look Through Photographs or Your Scrapbook

1. To model this strategy, show the class a photograph from a trip you took. Have students suggest words and phrases the picture suggests to them. Write the words on the board.

2. Then describe the experiences the photograph brings to your mind. Students will readily appreciate how a photograph can trigger all sorts of memories and associations. That is why this prewriting strategy is so effective for writers.

Integrating Listening and Speaking Skills

Have students bring family photos to class. Divide the class into small groups and ask each student to discuss one of his or her photographs. Listeners should ask questions that help speakers describe the experiences the photographs bring to mind in richer detail.

Critical Viewing

Apply Students may mention birthday parties and relatives.

2.1 # What Is Prewriting?

All writers can feel challenged when faced with a blank sheet of paper. The prewriting stage acts as a preparation for writing by helping to flex and stretch your creative muscles, just as dancers practice and warm up for a recital or performance. Prewriting consists of activities and strategies for getting started—a "mental warm-up" for writing.

Choosing Your Topic

In order to begin writing, you must first have a topic. Often, you produce your best writing when you are addressing a topic you find interesting. Prewriting strategies allow you to explore issues, ideas, and experiences that are meaningful to you. Prewriting techniques, such as the sample strategy presented here, can help you generate your topic.

SAMPLE STRATEGY

Look Through Photographs or Scrapbooks The photographs of significant events and souvenirs from vacations or local celebrations will help you remember amusing or meaningful events. Look through your scrapbooks and family photo albums. Think about the people, places, and activities that were included, and note those things that were meaningful, unusual, funny, or outrageous. Write notes about your most interesting memories. Then, review your notes to find a topic for an entertaining anecdote.

Learn More

For additional prewriting strategies suited to specific writing tasks, see Chapters 4–13.

◄ **Critical Viewing** Name two topics that might be inspired by this photo album. **[Apply]**

16 • A Walk Through the Writing Process

⏱ TIME AND RESOURCE MANAGER	
In-Depth Coverage	**Accelerated Pace**
• Cover pp. 16–20 in class. • Complete the exercises in class.	• Have students read pp. 16–20 independently. • Answer questions as necessary. • Have students complete the exercises independently.

Narrowing Your Topic

After you choose a topic, make sure it is neither too general nor too broad to write about effectively. While you prepare to write, you can use strategies that will help you to narrow your topic and make it manageable.

SAMPLE STRATEGY

Use a Cluster Map Start by writing your broad topic in the center of a sheet of paper. Circle this topic. Then, in the spaces around your topic, jot down and circle related subtopics, connecting ideas to the main topic with linking lines. Then, in the area surrounding each subtopic, repeat the process, circling and linking ideas you have about each subtopic. Review your subtopics and ideas to decide whether any can stand alone as a writing topic. The following model shows a few of the many subtopics of *food*.

CLUSTER MAP

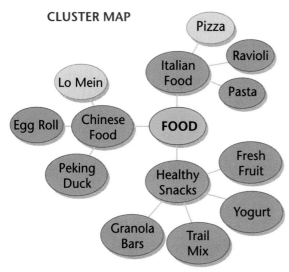

Considering Your Audience and Purpose

Once you have narrowed your topic, think about who will read your work. When you identify your intended audience, you can plan the best way to communicate with it. When you identify your purpose or reason for writing, you can plan what to include or communicate. The suggestions on page 18 will help you to consider your audience and purpose.

Prewriting: Use a Cluster Map

Teaching Resources: Writing Support Transparency 2-A; Writing Support Activity Book 2-1

1. Display the transparency to introduce the strategy of using a cluster map.

2. To help students become comfortable using this strategy, work on a cluster map as a class. Write a broad topic, such as sports, on the board and have volunteers write several subtopics and the ideas that cluster around each subtopic. Then ask students to decide whether the subtopics are suitable for a paper or whether they are still too broad. Would one of the ideas under the subtopic be more suitable?

3. Choose one of the subtopics to use as the center of another cluster map. Write the topic on the board and proceed as in step 1. Students can continue this process until they find a topic whose scope is manageable.

☑ ONGOING ASSESSMENT: Monitor and Reinforce

If some students are having difficulty creating cluster maps, try the following procedure.

Have students work in pairs to develop cluster maps. Consult with the pairs to provide support as necessary.

Prewriting: Considering Your Audience and Purpose

Teaching Resources: Writing Support Transparency 2-B; Writing Support Activity Book 2-2

1. Ask students to identify the purpose and audience for most of the writing they do in school. Most students will say that they write to fulfill assignments and that their audience is the teacher.

2. Urge students to think of broader audiences and purposes: school writing can be shared with classmates and family; an audience might consist of readers of the school newspaper or literary anthology.

Integrating Listening and Speaking Skills

Provide small groups of students a selection of newspapers and magazines for both children and for adults. Have the groups discuss the intended audience and purpose of several of the articles. Urge students to listen carefully to one another and arrive at a consensus. Have volunteers summarize the discussions for the rest of the class.

2.1

Consider Your Audience When you think about the people you want to reach, decide who will read your writing and consider what they already know about your subject. An audience profile can help you plan how to address your audience most effectively. Use your answers to the questions below to prepare an audience profile. Then, use your notes to keep you on target as you write.

CREATING AN AUDIENCE PROFILE

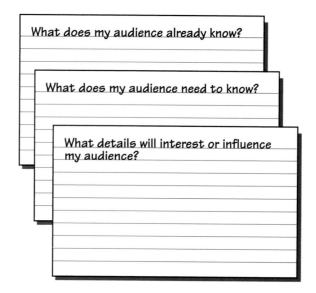

What does my audience already know?

What does my audience need to know?

What details will interest or influence my audience?

Consider Your Purpose Think about your reasons for writing. Your purpose will influence the kinds of language you include. Consider these specific purposes:

TO PERSUADE: Include language and details to sway your readers.

TO ENTERTAIN: Include elements of humor, such as exaggeration and unexpected turns in the events you describe.

TO INFORM: Use objective language that provides information without taking a persuasive stand.

Writing Lab CD-ROM

To prepare an electronic audience profile for a specific writing project, use the Audience Profile activity in the Toolkit.

Gathering Details

To make drafting easier, collect the details and materials that you will need before you write your first draft. This will allow you to concentrate on the form and style of your writing as you draft, instead of trying to locate more information to make your writing clearer. Consider these strategies:

SAMPLE STRATEGY

Make a Sensory Details Chart For many types of writing—both fiction and nonfiction—you'll need to include a variety of details to make your subject clear. If you are describing an object, a place, or an experience, sensory details that tell how your subject looks, smells, tastes, sounds, or feels can improve your draft. Before you start to write, list vivid sensory details that you can use in your description. Create a chart like the one below to help you come up with sensory details.

Topic: New Pizza Restaurant				
Sights	**Sounds**	**Smells**	**Tastes**	**Touch**
checked cloths	chef singing opera	tomato sauce	spicy	gooey
murals from Italy	cheerful hubbub from diners	garlic	fresh	hot
colorful menus		onions	zesty	

🖫 Research Tip

Don't limit detail gathering to your own experiences and knowledge. You may need to conduct library research or interview others to collect the information you need.

SAMPLE STRATEGY

Use Hexagonal Writing When you are writing about literature, a technique called hexagonal writing can help you gather details on six different aspects of a piece of literature. Complete each segment of the hexagon using the directions and questions shown at the right. Then, review your work and add more information to support your ideas. Using this approach, you will be able to write a well-thought-out, thorough analysis.

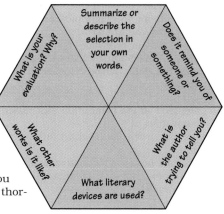

What is your evaluation? Why?

Summarize or describe the selection in your own words.

Does it remind you of someone or something?

What other works is it like?

What is the author trying to tell you?

What literary devices are used?

What Is Prewriting? • 19

Step-by-Step Teaching Guide

Prewriting: Make a Sensory Details Chart

Teaching Resources: Writing Support Transparency 2-C; Writing Support Activity Book 2-3

1. Have students name a story they have read recently in class.
2. Work together to make a sensory details chart for the page. Have volunteers write the topic, set up the chart, and fill in as many of the columns as possible.

Step-by-Step Teaching Guide

Use a Hexagonal

Teaching Resources: Writing Support Transparency 2-D; Writing Support Activity Book 2-4

1. Display the transparency.
2. Have volunteers read each of the questions.

Integrating Vocabulary Skills

Latin and Greek Roots Students will note from the Hexagonal shown on this page that a hexagon has six sides. Have students find out what three-, four-, five-, seven-, eight-, nine-, ten-, and twelve-sided shapes are called.

Customize for
Less Advanced Students

To help students become comfortable using sensory details in their writing, discuss the five senses. Describe a scene, for example the toy department of a department store just before Christmas, and brainstorm sights they might see, sounds they might hear, and textures they might touch. Could the senses of smell and taste be activated too? How?

Prewriting: Create a Character Profile

Teaching Resources: Writing Support Transparency 2-E; Writing Support Activity Book 2-5

1. Students probably will not have enough information to be able to fill in a character profile chart completely for minor characters. When they use character profiles to help write about characters, they should feel free to modify the chart. For instance, they might want to include columns that ask for characters' goals and how they achieve or do not achieve them.

2. Before students begin each item in Applying the Strategies, ask them to turn back to the page in the textbook on which the strategy is discussed and reread the description of the strategy.

2.1

SAMPLE STRATEGY

Prepare a Character Profile To gather details that will bring a fictional character to life for readers, jot down your ideas in a chart like the one below. While you may not need to include all the information you develop, this strategy will help you get to know your characters better, and that will improve the story you ultimately tell.

Categories	Details
Character's appearance	
Character's feelings	
Character's likes and dislikes	
Character's behavior	
Responses of others to character	
Your feelings about character	

▶ APPLYING THE PREWRITING STRATEGIES

1. Look through photo albums or scrapbooks to remember an event, vacation, or moment that was meaningful to you. List several ideas and then identify a topic you might choose to write about.
2. Make a cluster map of actions, places, and people you associate with the word *celebration.* To narrow your topic, suggest a more specific topic based on your cluster map.
3. Imagine that you are writing a speech to welcome an audience to a new or renovated school gymnasium. Prepare audience profiles for the following audiences, and then propose a specific purpose for each.
   (a) students
   (b) parents
   (c) members of the committee that raised funds for renovation
4. Create a sensory details chart for a description of a movie theater.
5. Complete a hexagon for a story you have recently read.
6. Create a new character, using the character profile. When you've completed the chart, share your ideas with a partner.

Collaborative Writing Tip

When you are gathering details to create a fictional character, telling someone else about your ideas may inspire the planning. Just talking about the character may help you identify what you think is most important or decide what needs more thought.

2.2 What Is Drafting?

Shaping Your Writing

Focus on Form Each form of writing has its own set of objectives: narratives tell a story; editorials and reviews present a position in order to persuade; and how-to writing shows the steps for completing a process. Consider the ideas you'd like to communicate, and then match your content to a suitable form. Then, keep the objectives of the particular form in mind as you write.

Pull Readers in With an Enticing Lead Because they invite audiences to read your work, the first few sentences of your writing are especially important. An interest-grabbing lead can command your readers' attention and keep them reading. To create an impressive opener, you might begin with a startling quotation, a strange or unexpected situation, a surprising bit of dialogue, or a vivid visual or sensory description. Then, connect this lead to the rest of your introduction by showing how it relates to your main idea. Look at these examples:

Ⓛ Learn More

Chapters 4–13 provide more information about the specific types of writing and the criteria for writing each one effectively.

WRITING MODELS

Dustin Jones didn't think that he had done anything wrong. So he was curious when his father and mother sat him down for a chat last December 2.

—Susan Fornoff, "Dad Just Got Traded!"

> This lead sparks the reader's curiosity.

When trouble came to me, it didn't involve anybody I thought it would. It involved the nice, normal, smart boy by the name of John Quinn. Life does that to us a lot. Just when we think something awful's going to happen one way, it throws you a curve and the something awful happens another way.

—Paul Zindel, from *The Pigman & Me*

> The writer arouses the reader's interest by beginning with a reference to an unexpected conflict, still to be revealed.

We thought movies would kill live theater. We thought television would kill movies. Now we ask whether video/computer/virtual-reality images streaming into our homes will keep us on the couch Saturday night.

—Ben Stiller, "What Will We Do on Saturday Night?"

> After posing a question in the title of an article, Stiller devotes his lead sentences to the development of a problem. The rest of his article will address a solution.

What Is Drafting? • 21

Step-by-Step Teaching Guide

Drafting: Shaping Your Writing

Have volunteers read aloud the three model paragraphs. Have students discuss why the paragraphs are enticing. All three raise intriguing questions that only further reading will answer.

Customize for
ESL Students

The model paragraphs contain difficult vocabulary and slang. In the first paragraph, a chat is an informal talk. In the second, when life throws you a curve, it presents you with something unexpected.

⏱ TIME AND RESOURCE MANAGER

In-Depth Coverage	Accelerated Pace
• Cover pp. 21–22 in class. • Complete the exercises in class.	• Have students read pp. 21–22 independently. • Answer questions as necessary. • Have students complete the exercises independently.

Drafting: Use the SEE Method

1. To help students understand the SEE method of elaborating paragraphs, work through an example with the class. Write the following sentence on the board: *Moving to a new town is tough.*

2. Explain that the word *extension* in this context means "going beyond." Then have students suggest extension sentences. Help them understand that many sentences would be suitable. For example, *You have to get used to lots of new things all at once.*

3. Then have volunteers think of elaboration sentences: details, examples, facts, and descriptions that support this topic. Finally, explain that the Applying the Strategies exercise on this page asks them to write statement, extension, and elaboration sentences, and direct students to complete the exercise.

2.2

Providing Elaboration

Make your writing as effective as it can be by including enough detail and explanation to let readers completely understand your subject. By using techniques of elaboration, you bring your writing to life. The SEE method is one strategy for developing your ideas and strengthening your writing.

SAMPLE STRATEGY

Use the SEE Method When you follow the steps of the SEE method, you shed more light on your subject. First, write a statement that conveys a main idea. Then, extend the idea by restating or explaining the first sentence. Finally, provide even more detail about the main idea. This elaboration might take many forms, including examples, descriptions, or facts. Look at this example:

STATEMENT: Planting bulbs in the fall produces blooms in the spring.

EXTENSION: With just a little planning and work, you can make a beautiful garden.

ELABORATION: Choose a variety of flowers, plan a pattern, pull on your gardening gloves, plant the bulbs and wait for your spring bouquet.

Statement   Extension   Elaboration

▶ **APPLYING THE DRAFTING STRATEGIES**

1. Write an exciting introduction for an essay about your favorite game. If you're having trouble, consider writing a compelling question to grab your reader's attention.
2. Complete the following sentence, and then use the SEE method to provide elaboration.

   If I could make one change in my town, I would ___?___.

☑ **ONGOING ASSESSMENT: Monitor and Reinforce**

If some students are having difficulty using the SEE method, try the following activity.

Photocopy two paragraphs that contain statements, extensions, and elaboration sentences. Cut the paragraphs apart into sentence strips and have students work	together to sort the sentences into the two paragraphs, put the sentences in an order that makes sense, and identify the statements, extensions, and elaboration sentences.

2.3 *What Is Revising?*

Color-Coding Clues to Revision

When you apply thinking skills to the revision process, you give yourself an opportunity to make educated decisions about improving your writing. For example, the word **ratiocination** (rash´ ē äs ə nā´ shən) describes a method for thinking logically and systematically in order to arrive at a conclusion. When you use ratiocination to revise, you may analyze your draft by coding it in these ways:

- circling verbs
- bracketing sentence beginnings
- highlighting certain language you have used.

Once you've focused on one of these areas, or another specific part of your writing, review the marked areas to evaluate and revise your writing. As you work through the revision sections of Chapters 4–13, you'll find strategies for analyzing and revising structure, paragraphs, sentences, and word choice.

Revising Your Overall Structure

Before you begin to look at the finer points of your draft, review the structure and organization of your ideas. To analyze the soundness of the structure, look at the frame of your writing, For example, look for a main idea and the details you've chosen to support it. Consider this helpful strategy:

SAMPLE STRATEGY

▶ **REVISION STRATEGY**
Color-Coding to Identify Main Ideas

To view the structure of your writing, highlight the main idea of each paragraph. Then review the highlighted sections to decide whether you have presented your ideas in the best order. You may want to insert additional information to make your organization more clear to readers. In the example shown, the writer highlighted main ideas and decided to reorder paragraphs to present ideas more effectively.

Writers in **ACTION**

When she talks about applying a step-by-step approach to revision, researcher Ellen Harkins Wheat acknowledges the value of such a strategy. She encourages writers to devote full attention to the revision process by identifying all the issues they want to address.

"There are lots of checkpoints you have in revising, and you probably need to make a list of all the things you think you need to cover."

IDENTIFYING MAIN IDEAS

Newspaper cartoons add to the joy of childhood. . . .

From a young age, children look forward to reading the comic sections of the paper. . . .

Most of all, Cartoons are something children share with their parents. When children are too young to read. . . .

Sunday comics in color are extra special. . . .

What Is Revising? • **23**

Revising: Color-Code to Identify Main Ideas

1. Suggest that when students apply this strategy, they use markers of three different colors and mark their statements, extensions, and elaboration sentences.

2. Then have them consider whether their sentences flow logically and reorder their sentences as necessary.

3. Finally, they should carefully examine their elaboration sentences. Do all the sentences elaborate on the main idea as stated in the statement, or topic sentence? Students should delete sentences that do not.

⏱ TIME AND RESOURCE MANAGER	
In-Depth Coverage	**Accelerated Pace**
• Cover pp. 23–25 in class. • Complete the exercises in class.	• Have students read pp. 23–25 independently. • Answer questions as necessary. • Have students complete the exercises independently.

Step-by-Step Teaching Guide

Revising: Identify Places to Add Dialogue

Teaching Resources: Writing Support Transparency 2-F

Explain to students that dialogue is a descriptive way of showing how a person or character feels. It is much more interesting to have a character say how he or she is feeling in dialogue than simply to write *She was angry.*

Customize for
Verbal/Linguistic Learners

Some students will be able to distinguish sentence fragments from complete sentences more easily if they read the sentences aloud. Students will find that the rise and fall of their voice sounds incomplete when they read a sentence fragment out loud.

Step-by-Step Teaching Guide

Color-Coding to Evaluate Sentence Length

Let students know that writing, like music, has rhythm. Varying sentence length is one way to create a rhythm that will keep readers interested in what they are reading.

Revising Your Paragraphs

After you have reviewed the overall structure of your draft, study the next level of your writing by looking closely at each paragraph. Whether you are explaining something or narrating a sequence of events, dialogue can draw your readers in to the points you are developing. Consider this strategy:

SAMPLE STRATEGY

▶ **REVISION STRATEGY**
Identifying Places to Add Dialogue

As you read your draft, imagine how dialogue could make your writing more vibrant. Review your writing, placing a check in places where you show a mood, create a character, or build tension through descriptive language or explanation. For each check, draw a dialogue bubble in the margin and jot down notes that reveal a character's thoughts or feelings. Then, consider building some of these quotations into your revision. In this example, the writer deleted some explanation to avoid making a point twice.

ADDING DIALOGUE

We were all waiting on the platform, hoping a train would arrive, but each train that approached roared loudly past the station without stopping. ✓ The wait seemed endless. People shuffled impatiently.

"I've had it," one man said, and sat down with his head in his hands. "How much longer is this going to be?"

Revising Your Sentences

When you examine your writing at the sentence level, review the patterns you have introduced in your writing and introduce variety when you can. Take the time to notice whether you write mostly in short sentences or in long ones. Consider this strategy:

SAMPLE STRATEGY

▶ **REVISION STRATEGY**
Color-Coding to Evaluate Sentence Length

Alternating two different colors, bracket each sentence in your draft. For example, mark the first and third sentences in red and the second and fourth sentences in green. As you do this, pay attention to the length of the sentences in your writing. Then, strive for variety. Introduce a short sentence to break the pattern of long sentences. If you find you have a series of short sentences, combine some of them to improve the flow of ideas.

24 • A Walk Through the Writing Process

✓ **ONGOING ASSESSMENT: Monitor and Reinforce**

If some students are having difficulty identifying sentence fragments, try the following activity.

Have students work together to make a simple chart they can consult to decide whether a group of words is a sentence or a fragment. These three questions should appear on the	chart: Do these words express a complete thought? Do these words tell who or what is doing something? Do these words tell what the person or thing is doing?

Revising Your Word Choice

Review your draft to be sure that the language you have used expresses your ideas most effectively. Look for places in your draft where a specific modifier can help to create a more vivid word picture.

SAMPLE STRATEGY

▶ **REVISION STRATEGY**
Circling Vague or Empty Modifiers

Whenever you write, use modifiers that describe exactly how something looks, sounds, feels, tastes, or smells. Avoid vague modifiers, such as *some* or *many*. In addition, revise empty modifiers—such as *nice, really,* or *great*—that don't add to your draft. Using a red pen, circle any vague or empty modifiers in your draft. In the example below, notice how specific modifiers help to bring the scene to life.

REVISING EMPTY AND VAGUE MODIFIERS

Vague, empty modifiers: Some nice passengers boarded the train for a great trip through the western states.

Specific modifiers: *Four smiling* passengers boarded the train for a week-long *sightseeing* trip through the western states.

Peer Review

As you revise, you'll find it helpful to get someone else's opinion. Each writing chapter offers specific suggestions for inviting peers to review your work.

Get Specific While it may be encouraging to hear your peers say they like your work, challenge your readers to give you specific feedback to help you revise your writing. Avoid questions that can be answered with *yes* or *no.* Consider these focused options:

> **Focusing Peer Review**
> - What did you like best?
> - What would you like to know more about?

▶ **APPLYING THE REVISION STRATEGIES**

Using a draft you have recently written, apply each revision strategy presented here. When you have finished, review the changes you have made. Then, identify the most effective revision you made to your writing.

⊙ Technology Tip

Many word processors have built-in thesauruses to help writers improve their drafts. Highlight a word and use the thesaurus function to preview a list of other words with similar meanings.

Revising: Circling Vague or Empty Modifiers

Modifiers are generally adjectives or adverbs, and they are used to add information and interest. Vague or empty modifiers don't add anything. For example, the word *some* in the example makes the reader wonder how many, and the word *great* makes readers wonder why or in what way the trip is great. When they revise their work, students should be alert for vague modifiers and replace them with specific words that bring images to readers' minds and answer questions they may have.

Revising: Peer Review

1. Remind students that criticism given in peer reviews should be constructive.

2. Before students complete the first activity in Applying the Strategies, you may want to write a student's paragraph on the chalkboard and have the class identify the main ideas and discuss whether more evidence would improve the paragraph.

1. Tell students that good, strong writing does not contain errors in grammar, usage, and mechanics. These types of errors detract from the power of one's writing. Readers will often find a writer's work less credible if it contains too many errors.

2. Review the general areas students should address as they proofread their work.

2.4 What Are Editing and Proofreading?

Once you are satisfied with the ideas your writing expresses, take the time to make sure the form you have used is correct. From correcting errors in grammar, usage, and mechanics to double-checking for neatness, strive to make everything you write error-free.

Focusing on Proofreading

To help you improve your proofreading skills, each writing chapter offers a specific focus and a brief lesson on a related grammar, usage, or mechanics topic. While you can give added attention to each lesson's featured skill, always review your work and correct any errors you see. Here are the general areas you should address as you proofread:

Check Spelling Review the spelling of each word, referring to a dictionary to confirm the spelling of any word about which you are unsure. If no dictionary is available, consider replacing suspect words with synonyms that are easier to spell.

Examine Capitalization and Punctuation At a minimum, check to see that you've begun every sentence with a capital letter and used proper end punctuation. Then, take a close look at the other punctuation you've used.

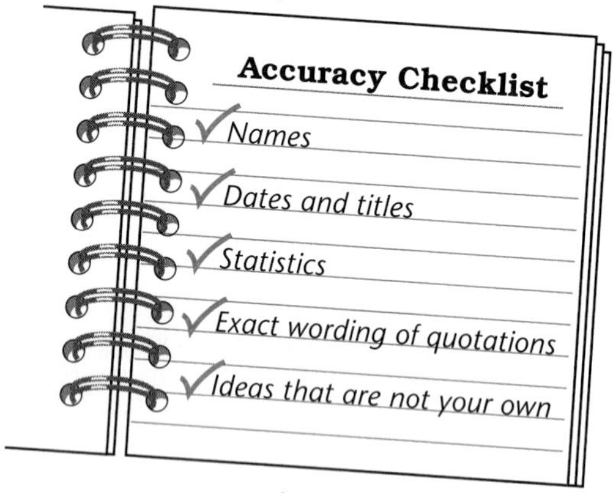

Follow Grammar and Usage Conventions Check your writing to correct errors in grammar and language. To start, be sure you have corrected sentence fragments and revised agreement errors.

Fact-Check Be sure the ideas you include in your writing are true. Use the accuracy checklist shown here to direct your review.

Confirm Legibility If you are handwriting your final draft, make sure that every word is clear enough to be read. Use a single line to cross out deleted information. Then, rewrite any words that may be hard to decipher.

▶ APPLYING THE EDITING AND PROOFREADING STRATEGIES

Using a recent draft you have written, proofread your work according to the categories identified on this page. Identify at least three corrections you have made.

◯ Learn More

Part 2 offers extensive instruction in the conventions of grammar, usage, and mechanics.

Accuracy Checklist
- ✓ Names
- ✓ Dates and titles
- ✓ Statistics
- ✓ Exact wording of quotations
- ✓ Ideas that are not your own

◷ TIME AND RESOURCE MANAGER	
In-Depth Coverage	**Accelerated Pace**
• Cover pp. 26–27 in class. • Complete the exercises in class.	• Have students read pp. 26–27 independently. • Answer questions as necessary. • Have students complete the exercises independently.

2.5 What Are Publishing and Presenting?

Moving Forward

This preview of the writing process gives you just a glimpse of the strategies and techniques that you can use in your writing. Chapters 4–13 will teach you specific strategies to apply to a variety of writing situations.

Build Your Portfolio Because they showcase your best work, your finished writing products are valuable. Organize and save them in a portfolio—a folder, file, box, or other safe container. In addition to illustrating your development as a writer, your portfolio can also serve as a resource for future writing. Reserve a section of your portfolio for writing ideas, peer review notes, and photos that inspire you.

PORTFOLIO

Reflect on Your Writing Every time you complete a piece of writing, you have a chance to learn something about yourself, something about your topic, and something about your writing process. To help you take advantage of this opportunity, review the questions at the end of each writing chapter. Write your responses and save them in your portfolio as evidence of your thoughts and feelings about the writing you have completed this year.

Assess Your Writing At the end of each writing chapter, you will find a rubric, or set of criteria, on which your work may be evaluated. You can refer to the rubric throughout the writing process to be certain that you are addressing the specific conventions for the writing you are creating.

APPLYING THE PUBLISHING AND PRESENTING STRATEGIES

1. Review the prewriting activities you completed in this chapter. Choose one activity to place in your portfolio to be developed at a later time. With a partner, discuss the reasons for your choice.

2. In your notebook or writing journal, reflect on your writing process by answering the following questions:

   - Which strategies in this chapter did you find most worthwhile? Explain.

   - What are your strengths as a writer?

   - What writing goals do you have for the year?

Publishing and Presenting: Portfolio Building

1. To introduce writing portfolios to any students who are not familiar with them, invite an older student to bring his or her portfolio to class, display its contents, and discuss the reasons a few of the pieces were included.

2. Urge students to ask the speaker plenty of questions about the contents of the portfolio and the practical considerations involved in assembling it. Make sure students understand that a portfolio is designed to show a writer's growth and is not necessarily filled with polished, finished pieces.

Real-World Connection

Artists and designers keep portfolios of their work. You might mention that the idea of having students keep portfolios of their writing grew from examining and talking to artists about their portfolios.

Lesson Objectives

1. To examine common themes in the arts.
2. To compare and contrast different versions of the same story.
3. To use a story as a basis for possible topics for a writing project.

Step-by-Step Teaching Guide

Examining Common Themes in the Arts

1. Choose one of the Spotlight elements for class discussion, or have students work independently or in groups on the element of their choice. Give students the initiative to find the necessary books and recordings.

2. Ask the class how many students know the story of *Cinderella*. Challenge students to tell the story. You might go around the room, having each student contribute a sentence or two, until the whole story has been told.

3. Tell students that there are many other musical and dramatic versions of *Cinderella*. Both Gioacchino Rossini and Jules Massenet wrote operas called *Cinderella*, and many students have probably seen the animated Disney movie. Encourage interested students to look up and listen to (or watch videos of) any or all of these musical versions of the fairy tale.

Viewing and Representing

Activity As students consider topics for writing projects, explain that almost any rags-to-riches story can be described as a Cinderella story. Every element of the fairy tale need not appear in a writing project based on the legend.

Critical Viewing

Connect Students may answer that this scene is the turning point of the story—the moment when the prince determines that Cinderella is the woman with whom he danced at the ball and whom he will ask to marry him.

Spotlight on the Humanities

Examining Common Themes in the Arts

Focus on Music: Sergei Prokofiev

Like writers, all artists, dancers, and musicians work to develop inspirations into final performances. Russian composer Sergei Prokofiev (1891–1953) used a well-known fairy tale as the basis for his composition of the music for the ballet *Cinderella*. Whether retelling fairy tales or composing symphonies, Prokofiev was known for taking classical forms and adding satire and playfulness to his compositions.

Theater Connection A theatrical musical adaptation of *Cinderella* was created by American composers Rodgers and Hammerstein in 1964. The musical, which was televised, starred Lesley Ann Warren as Cinderella and Stuart Damon as The Prince. Rodgers and Hammerstein's music and lyrics have made this version of the fairy tale a modern classic.

Literature Connection Over 3,000 versions of the Cinderella story exist, and a version appears in most cultures of the world. The French version, considered one of the earliest, developed among the peasants of seventeenth-century France. Other modern versions of the story include *Just Ella* by Margaret Peterson Haddix and *Ella Enchanted* by Gail Carson Levine, a Newbery Honor Book.

Writing Process Activity: *Cinderella* Inspiration

When underdog teams win championships, announcers often call the unexpected win a "Cinderella story." The expression "if the shoe fits" is a popular cliché. The fairy tale has reached many parts of our culture—and many other cultures. In fact, with over 3,000 versions of the Cinderella story, there must be something universal about this tale. Writing *Cinderella* at the center of a cluster map, work with a group to identify several topics that you could pursue in a writing project. Put your completed map in your portfolio for later development.

▲ **Critical Viewing** Explain the importance of this moment from Walt Disney's version of *Cinderella*. If necessary, conduct research to find the answer. **[Connect]**

Media and Technology Skills

Using Technology to Support Writing

Activity: Building an Electronic Portfolio

Most things get better with practice. The same is true of writing. A good way to track your progress is to save your work in an electronic portfolio that allows you to store your work on a computer's hard drive or on a disk.

Learn About It The first step in organizing your writing on a word processor is to make a single folder for all of your work. You might name it "My Writing." For each project you begin, make a subfolder to hold all your files for that project. Then, in each project folder, make files for each stage of the writing process:

- **Prewriting** Put your freewriting notes, topic ideas, and any research work in a word-processing file called "My Notes" or "Ideas," and save it in your writing folder. You can access this file when you are ready to begin drafting.

- **Drafting** When you are ready to write your first draft, open a new file and name it with a working title. Save your work often as you draft. In fact, try to remember to hit the Save key after every paragraph.

- **Revising** After you have finished a first draft, track any revisions you make by choosing the Save As option and making a file with the title of your work and the ending *.1*. Each time you make a new version, increase the number. To avoid confusion, move your old drafts to a folder called "Old Drafts." Look at this example:

📁 my writing	
Name	Date Modified
▽ 📁 Project 1 – Descriptive Essay	Nov 17
☐ Ideas	Nov 5
▽ 📁 Old Drafts	Nov 14
☐ Grandpa Sam	Nov 9
☐ Grandpa Sam.1	Nov 14
☐ Grandpa Sam. 2	Nov 17
▷ 📁 Project 2 – How To Wrap a Gift	Dec 11

Evaluate It Try the suggested organization for the next writing assignment you complete. Then, get together with a group to discuss the positive and negative aspects of your electronic portfolio.

Media and Technology Skills • 29

Useful Functions

Editing
- Cut—deletes a selected block of text and stores it temporarily so that you can paste it elsewhere
- Copy—duplicates a selected section of text
- Paste—inserts previously cut or copied text

Saving
- Save—stores a file and any changes to it
- Save As—lets you save a new version of a file

Retrieving
- Find—lets you find specific text

▶ *Lesson Objectives*

1. To use a word processor to organize written work.
2. To create and save electronic files.
3. To use word-processing commands and functions to revise and edit writing.

Step-by-Step Teaching Guide

Using Technology for Writing

Teaching Resources: Writing Support Transparency 2-G

1. Ask whether any students regularly do their writing assignments on word processors. You might assign these students as tutors to those who are new to this technology.

2. If you have a computer in the classroom, use it to demonstrate creating new documents and files. If you cannot do this in class, assign tutors to meet with their students at home to demonstrate. If this is not practical, students may have older siblings who can help them. Make sure that all students have someone to show them what to do the first time through.

3. Go through the steps listed on the page. Give students any tips from your own experience of writing on a word processor. Tell students that most word-processing programs can be set up to prompt the writer to save work at the end of a specific time interval, such as every ten minutes. The writer can set this prompt to appear at any interval desired.

4. Stress the importance of saving work every few minutes. A power failure or a computer virus can eliminate hours of hard work in an instant if the writer has not been saving periodically. If work is saved every ten minutes, then only ten minutes' worth of effort can ever be lost.

5. Demonstrate, or have tutors demonstrate, the cut and paste functions of the word processor. Students should be delighted once they learn how easy it is to make major changes to a written text.

Lesson Objectives

1. To read and understand a writing prompt.
2. To use prewriting strategies to generate ideas.
3. To organize ideas to ensure logical progression and support for those ideas.
4. To draft, revise, and edit an answer to a writing prompt.
5. To use correct grammar, spelling, and mechanics.

Step-by-Step Teaching Guide

Using the Writing Process to Respond to Writing Prompts

1. Emphasize that the most important criterion on which a test scorer will judge an essay is if it responds to the question asked. An essay can be literate, entertaining, and well organized, but if it does not respond to the questions in the prompt, it will receive a very low score. Remind students that the most important thing to do when faced with an essay question is to read the question carefully.

2. To make sure that they answer every question in a writing prompt, students may want to paraphrase the prompt as a question or a series of questions. In the example on this page, a student might write the questions *In which extra-curricular activities do you participate? What can you say about them that will encourage other students to join?* Once the essay is written, students can look back at the list of questions and make sure that each one has been answered.

3. Remind students to write for the audience indicated in the prompt—students new to the school. Students should think about questions they would have if they had just moved to a new school, and they should address these questions in their essays.

Standardized Test Preparation Workshop

Using the Writing Process to Respond to Writing Prompts

In order to evaluate the quality of your writing skills, many standardized tests include prompts that offer specific topics for you to address. Use the writing process to generate thoughtful, well-elaborated responses. You will be evaluated on your ability to do the following:

- provide an answer that directly addresses the prompt
- choose an organization suited to your ideas
- elaborate with details appropriate to your specific audience and purpose
- use the conventions of grammar, usage, and mechanics

As this chapter has shown, the writing process can be divided into stages. Even when writing for a test, plan to use a specific amount of time for each stage: prewriting, drafting, revising, and proofreading.

Following is an example of a writing prompt that you might find on a standardized test. Use the suggestions on the following page to help you respond. The clocks next to each stage show a suggested plan for organizing your time.

Sample Writing Situation

> While most people expect to spend time at school in classes required for graduation, many students enjoy participating in extra-curricular activities such as sports and clubs. In a letter to be included in a new student welcome packet, describe your own experiences in order to encourage others to get involved in such activities.

Test Tips

- While you may feel pressure in a test-taking situation, take the time to prewrite and revise. Each of these steps will help you create a better final draft.
- Use any scrap paper available to jot down your ideas. Then, cross off details as you address them in your writing.

TEST-TAKING TIP

Remind students that organizing their ideas in the prewriting stage will help them write their essays more quickly. Suggest the following step-by-step process as a quick way to organize an answer to a writing prompt:

- Decide on the best structure for your answer—comparison–contrast, step-by-step instructions, narrative, pro-and-con, etc.
- Make a simple graphic organizer to match the

structure on which you decide. For instance, a two-column chart is a good way to organize ideas for a comparison-contrast essay.
- Fill in the graphic organizer with all your ideas about your topic.
- Using the completed graphic organizer as the skeleton, flesh out your essay with language and details appropriate to your audience and purpose.

Prewriting

Allow about one fourth of your time for prewriting.

Consider Your Own Ideas Think about your experience with the subject. Review the activities you have enjoyed and think about your friends and their involvement. Jot down the clubs you know best. For each, note the possible benefits of participation.

Consider Audience and Purpose As you begin to gather details for your response, keep in mind the audience indicated in the prompt. Many new students may want to know more about the school and how to make friends. Plan to focus on elements that will appeal to this concern.

Draw Up an Outline Organize your ideas to make them easy to follow. For this assignment, you may choose to focus on one activity and all its rewards. Alternatively, you may want to address several activities and discuss a single benefit of each one. Choose the organizational plan best suited to your experiences.

Drafting

Allow about half your time for drafting.

State Your Position To help your readers understand your ideas, state your main idea in the opening paragraph of your letter. Use the following paragraphs to provide elaboration. Finally, write a conclusion that reminds readers of your key points.

Elaborate With Details An important part of your letter will be the details that you use to prove your points. Include examples or information that encourage students to join school-sponsored activities. Use the SEE method to elaborate ideas in your writing. Review page 22 to see an example of this drafting technique.

Revising, Editing, and Proofreading

Allow about one fourth of your time for revising. Use the few minutes remaining to proofread your work.

Revise to Ensure a Friendly Tone As a student who is thoroughly familiar with your school, take the initiative to make your readers—new students—feel comfortable. Find a level of language somewhere between the formal tone you'd use with adults and the informal slang you'd use with close friends. Revise to achieve this balance.

Make Corrections Review your paper for spelling and punctuation errors. Make all corrections neatly. Cross out text with a single line and use a caret [^] to indicate insertions precisely.

Standardized Test Preparation Workshop • 31

Customize for
ESL Students

Remind students that the audience for the letter in this test question is other students. An audience of their peers means that students can write less formally than they would if the audience were parents or teachers. Students learning English have probably picked up many slang and informal idioms from their classmates. Tell them that when the writing prompt suggests the use of informal English, they should feel free to use these expressions.

Customize for
More Advanced Students

Challenge students to write similar letters for different audiences: perhaps for parents of new students. Give students the same time limit and do not alter the writing prompt except for the intended audience. Afterwards, have students compare and contrast the two letters they have written. This exercise should reinforce the importance of considering audience when answering an essay question.

In-Depth Lesson Plan

	LESSON FOCUS	PRINT AND MEDIA RESOURCES
DAY 1	**Effective Paragraphs** Students learn and apply concepts about writing effective paragraphs (pp. 32–36).	*Language Lab* CD-ROM, Building Paragraphs **Teaching Resources** *Writing Support Transparencies 3-A–B*
DAY 2	**Paragraphs in Essays and Other Compositions** Students learn and apply concepts about unity and coherence of paragraphs and compositions (pp. 37–41).	*Language Lab* CD-ROM, Building Paragraphs **Teaching Resources** *Writing Support Transparency 3-C*
DAY 3	**Writing Style** Students learn and apply concepts about writing style (pp. 42–43).	*Language Lab* CD-ROM, Sentence Style **Teaching Resources** *Formal Assessment*, Ch. 3

Accelerated Lesson Plan

	LESSON FOCUS	PRINT AND MEDIA RESOURCES
DAY 1	**Effective Paragraphs** Students learn and apply concepts about writing effective paragraphs (pp. 32–36).	*Language Lab* CD-ROM, Building Paragraphs **Teaching Resources** *Writing Support Transparencies 3-A–B*
DAY 2	**Paragraphs in Essays and Writing Style** Students learn and apply concepts of unity and coherence of paragraphs. They also learn about the elements of compositions and writing style (pp. 37–41).	*Language Lab* CD-ROM, Building Paragraphs, Sentence Style **Teaching Resources** *Writing Support Transparency 3-C* **Teaching Resources** *Formal Assessment*, Ch. 3

Options for Adapting Lesson Plans

HOMEWORK

Have students complete any stage of the lesson for homework.

FEATURES

Extend coverage with the Spotlight on the Humanities (p. 44), Media and Technology Skills (p. 45), and the Standardized Test Preparation Workshop (p. 46).

TECHNOLOGY

Students can complete any stage of the lesson on computer. Have them print out their completed work.

INTEGRATED SKILLS COVERAGE

Speaking and Listening
ATE p. 36

Vocabulary
ATE p. 43

Technology
SE p. 45

Workplace Skills
ATE p. 43

Viewing and Representing
Critical Viewing SE pp. 32, 35, 43, 44
Viewing and Representing SE p. 44

ASSESSMENT SUPPORT

Standardized Test Preparation Workshop SE p. 46
Standardized Test Preparation Workbook, pp. 5–6
Formal Assessment, Ch. 3

MEETING INDIVIDUAL NEEDS

Less Advanced Students ATE pp. 35, 47; See also Ongoing
Assessments ATE pp. 33, 38, 41, 43
ESL Students ATE pp. 40, 45
More Advanced Students ATE p. 47
Verbal/Linguistic Students ATE p. 34
Gifted/Talented Students ATE p. 40

BLOCK SCHEDULING

Resources for Varying Instruction
• *Language Lab* CD-ROM If your students have access to hardware, a 90-minute block provides an ideal opportunity for students to work on computer.

Professional Development Support
• *How to Manage Instruction in the Block* This teaching resource provides management and activity suggestions.

MEDIA AND TECHNOLOGY

For the Student
• *Language Lab* CD-ROM, Building Paragraphs, Sentence Style

For the Teacher
• *Resource Pro* CD-ROM

WRITING AND GRAMMAR WEB SITE

The Interactive Writing and Grammar Web site provides a wide array of support for students, teachers, and parents. Grammar support includes:

• On-Line Exercise Bank with Auto Check scoring
• Diagnostic and assessment support

www.phschool.com

LITERATURE CONNECTIONS

Related selections from *Prentice Hall Literature: Timeless Voices, Timeless Themes,* Copper Level:
"The Shutout," Patricia C. McKissack and Frederick McKissack, Jr., SE p. 33
"The Sound of Summer Running," from *Dandelion Wine,* Ray Bradbury, SE p. 33
"The Fun They Had," Isaac Asimov, SE p. 40

Lesson Objectives

1. To categorize ideas and organize ideas into paragraphs.
2. To identify types of paragraphs.
3. To identify main ideas and topic sentences in paragraphs.
4. To write topic sentences and supporting sentences.
5. To maintain unity and coherence in paragraphs.
6. To use quotation marks correctly.

Critical Viewing

Connect Most students will understand that the pieces are like the sentences in a paragraph: They must fit together properly in order for the larger unit to make sense.

Paragraphs and Compositions
Structure and Style

Sculpture made from interlocking blocks

What Are Paragraphs and Compositions?

A **paragraph** consists of a group of sentences that work together to support a main idea or to achieve a single effect. Writing in paragraphs helps you to focus information logically in separate sections. Where you break information into paragraphs depends on your subject matter and the type of organization you have chosen.

A **composition** is a group of related paragraphs. They work together to form a composition in the same way that sentences work together to form a paragraph. Among the compositions you will write are responses to literature, research reports, and various kinds of essays. You will also see that well-organized paragraphs are important when presenting ideas in works of fiction. The chapters that follow will cover specific types of compositions.

▲ Critical Viewing
Explain how interlocking blocks could be used in a demonstration of how to construct an effective paragraph. [Connect]

32 • Paragraphs and Compositions

⏱ TIME AND RESOURCE MANAGER	
In-Depth Coverage	**Accelerated Pace**
• Cover pp. 32–38 in class. • Read literature excerpts (p. 33) in class and base a discussion of main idea, topic, and supporting sentences on them. • Complete the exercises with students.	• Assign the Model from Literature for independent reading. • Have students complete the exercises independently.

3.1 *Writing Effective Paragraphs*

Main Idea and Topic Sentence

The main idea of a paragraph is usually stated in the paragraph's **topic sentence.** The remaining sentences support, explain, or illustrate the topic sentence.

A paragraph may also have an **implied main idea.** In this case, the sentences in the paragraph contain related facts and details that together communicate the main idea, which the reader can infer.

WRITING MODELS

from **The Shutout**
Patricia C. McKissack and Frederick McKissack, Jr.

The history of baseball is difficult to trace because it is embroidered with wonderful anecdotes that are fun but not necessarily supported by fact. There are a lot of myths that persist about baseball—the games, the players, the owners, and the fans—in spite of contemporary research that disproves most of them. For example, the story that West Point cadet Abner Doubleday "invented" baseball in 1839 while at Cooperstown, New York, continues to be widely accepted, even though, according to his diaries, Doubleday never visited Cooperstown. A number of records and documents show that people were playing stick-and-ball games long before the 1839 date.

> In this passage, the stated topic sentence is shown in blue italics. This sentence refers to the many myths surrounding baseball. The rest of the paragraph supports and illustrates the opening sentence.

from **The Sound of Summer Running**
Ray Bradbury

Late that night, going home from the show with his mother and father and his brother Tom, Douglas saw the tennis shoes in the bright store window. He glanced quickly away, but his ankles were seized, his feet suspended, then rushed. The earth spun; the shop awnings slammed their canvas wings overhead with the thrust of his body running. His mother and father and brother walked quietly on both sides of him. Douglas walked backward, watching the tennis shoes in the midnight window left behind.

> In this passage, all the sentences work together to support the implied main idea of the paragraph: A pair of sneakers viewed at the beginning of summer exerts a powerful pull on a boy.

Writing Effective Paragraphs • 33

☑ ONGOING ASSESSMENT: Diagnose

Use one of the following options to diagnose students' current level of proficiency in writing effective paragraphs.

Option 1 Ask students to select two examples of strong paragraphs they have written recently. They might choose from reports or essays prepared for a class, or from personal writing. Ask them to think about how their paragraphs are organized and why they are effective. Discuss the paragraphs in conference with each student to determine which students will need extra help learning to write effective paragraphs.

Option 2 Ask students to write a paragraph about a favorite subject, such as an athlete or television program. Have them include a topic sentence and at least three supporting sentences. Plan extra help for those students who have difficulty completing this assignment.

PREPARE and ENGAGE

Interest GRABBER Write the following paragraph on the board.

When the astronauts finally landed on the planet Framis, they were amazed at what they saw. Grass was blue, and water was orange. Animals wore clothes but people didn't. Everyone ate ice cream all day long and never got fat.

Ask students to identify the main idea, the topic sentence. (first sentence)

Activate Prior Knowledge

Have students discuss what they learned about paragraphs from the previous school year. Point out that the paragraph in the Interest Grabber is a good paragraph. That is, it does what a paragraph is supposed to do: It states a main idea; details support the main idea; the paragraph is about only one main idea.

TEACH

Step-by-Step Teaching Guide

Teaching from the Model

1. Have volunteers read aloud the Models from Literature.

2. To aid discussion of the paragraphs, you may want to use webs. Write the topic sentence from the first paragraph on the board in a big circle; then write the detail sentences radiating from it. Write details from the second paragraph around a center circle; then write the implied main idea in the center.

More About the Writer

Ray Bradbury, who writes novels, stories, plays, screenplays, and poems, is best known as a writer of science fiction. His work has received dozens of awards and is represented in more than 700 anthologies. *The Martian Chronicles,* a novel about the colonization of Mars, is generally considered Bradbury's best book. His novel *Fahrenheit 451* was made into a movie and has also been adapted as an opera.

> **Exercise 1**

Have a volunteer explain why the first sentence is the topic sentence. (It tells what the paragraph is mostly about.) Emphasize that the topic sentence may appear at the beginning (as in this case), the end, or the middle of a paragraph.

> **Exercise 2**

The implied main idea can be stated in a phrase (learning to ski) or sentence (The writer finally learns how to ski).

Step-by-Step Teaching Guide

Writing a Topic Sentence

1. Explain to students that writing a topic sentence can be done in different ways.

2. In some cases, students may have a clear idea what the paragraph will be about, so they can immediately unite the main idea in a topic sentence.

3. Other times, it may be more helpful for students to organize the details they will cover in a paragraph and then decide how these details can be summed up in a topic sentence.

Answer Key

> **Exercise 3**

Work through the first item with students by having two or three volunteers write topic sentences and then read them aloud. The sentences will vary slightly, but students should understand that if the sentences express the idea that the writer would like to try or master various winter sports, they are acceptable topic sentences.

Customize for
Verbal/Linguistic Learners

Students may find it helpful to read the paragraphs and topic sentences in the exercises aloud either to themselves or to a partner before attempting to follow the directions.

> **Exercise 1** Identifying a Stated Topic Sentence Identify the stated topic sentence of the following paragraph.

Martin Luther King, Jr., was an important figure in the last century. King spent years working to gain equal rights for all people. He organized many boycotts, demonstrations, and marches. In 1964, he won the Nobel Peace Prize. Four years later, he was assassinated.

> **Exercise 2** Identifying an Implied Main Idea Identify the implied main idea of the following paragraph.

When I first moved to Vermont, I didn't know how to ski. I would stay most weekends during the winter. Finally, I decided to learn to ski. I rented equipment and signed up for a lesson. At first, I moved slowly down the hill, pointing the tips of my skis inward. Then, I learned how to turn. I got better and better, and now, I ski every weekend.

Writing a Topic Sentence

As you plan or outline the subject of your composition, identify the main points you will cover. You can write each main point as a **topic sentence.** A topic sentence states the main idea of a topical paragraph. You can then build your paragraph around the topic sentence.

A strong topic sentence will let readers know what the paragraph is about as well as the point you are making about the subject matter. Here are three pointers for writing a successful topic sentence:

| Review details. |
| Group related details. |
| Write a statement that pulls the details together. |

> **Exercise 3** Writing Topic Sentences Write a topic sentence for a paragraph on each of the following topics.
> 1. Winter sports you'd like to try or master
> 2. A review of the last movie you saw
> 3. A description of your best friend
> 4. How user-friendly or -unfriendly you find your school's computers to be
> 5. Your favorite foods

34 • Paragraphs and Compositions

Writing Supporting Sentences

The topic sentence, whether stated or implied, contains a paragraph's main idea. The sentences in a paragraph that develop, explain, or illustrate the main idea or topic sentence are called *supporting sentences.* You can use one of the following strategies to support or develop the main idea:

Use Facts Facts are statements that are provable. They support your main idea by offering backup, or proof.

TOPIC SENTENCE:	Our playful kitten, Max, will probably grow up to be a very large cat.
SUPPORTING FACT:	Our veterinarian said that, based on his present size and age, Max would grow quite large.

Use Statistics A statistic is a fact often stated numerically.

TOPIC SENTENCE:	Our playful kitten, Max, will probably grow up to be a very large cat.
SUPPORTING STATISTIC:	He weighed just one pound at six weeks, and now, only four months later, he weighs ten.

Use Examples, Illustrations, or Instances
An example, illustration, or instance is a specific person, thing, or event that demonstrates a point.

TOPIC SENTENCE:	Our playful kitten, Max, will probably grow up to be a very large cat.
ILLUSTRATION:	Max is a big eater: He always seems to be waiting for snacks.

Use Details Details are the specifics that make your main idea or key point clear by showing how all the pieces fit together.

TOPIC SENTENCE:	Our playful kitten, Max, will probably grow up to be a very large cat.
DETAIL:	Everyone who sees him now is amazed at how much he's grown in such a short time.

▶ **Exercise 4** **Writing Supporting Sentences** Write two supporting sentences for each of the following topic sentences.
1. It's important to get enough sleep.
2. Programming a VCR can be a frustrating experience.
3. One should never yell "Fire!" in a crowded room.
4. Babies need lots of care.
5. Team sports are fun to play and watch.

▲ **Critical Viewing**
What details could be used to support a topic sentence that says this kitten is adventurous? **[Support]**

Writing Supporting Sentences

1. Discuss the four strategies for writing supporting sentences. Explain to students that when they write, they are like sentence detectives: They need to provide evidence for their readers. Facts and other kinds of details provide that evidence.

2. Write other topic sentences on the board and have students suggest supporting sentences of various kinds: ones that include facts, statistics, examples, or other details.

   Kim is the best player on the soccer team.

   The Call of the Wild *is a really exciting book.*

Critical Viewing

Support Students may mention its ability to climb and its facial expressions.

Answer Key

▶ **Exercise 4**

Have students each write two supporting sentences for the first item. Have volunteers read their sentences aloud so that students can appreciate the range of possible sentences. Urge students to use all four types of supporting sentences as they complete the exercise.

Customize for
Less Advanced Students

Make sure students understand that facts can be proved true or false. Have students explain how they could prove the following statements of fact: The temperature outside is 16 degrees; Mr. Smith's dog is named Lucky; Ben is the tallest kid in sixth grade. Explain that topic sentences can state opinions, but readers should not accept those opinions unless they are supported by facts.

Placing Your Topic Sentence

Teaching Resources: Writing Support Transparencies 3-A–B

1. Go over the example of TRI paragraph construction. The restatement sentence, *The three most annoying kinds of mosquitoes are the Anopheles, the Aedes, and the Culex,* narrows the topic sentence, and the illustration sentence explains why these three kinds of mosquitoes are annoying.

2. Ask students to suggest ways this paragraph might be reorganized to follow the problem/solution or question/answer modes of organization. (One possibility: Which kinds of mosquito, an annoying little insect related to the fly, are most dangerous? The answer is clear: the Anopheles, the Aedes, and the Culex. These mosquitoes spread serious diseases, such as malaria, yellow fever, and encephalitis.)

Answer Key

> **Exercise 5**

Remind students to complete both parts of this exercise: writing a topic sentence and putting the sentences into the proper order and rewriting to follow the PS or QA organization.

Integrating Speaking and Listening Skills

Have small groups read their TRI and PS/QA paragraphs to one another. Listeners should identify the organizational patterns and tell whether any parts were left out.

3.1

Placing Your Topic Sentence

The topic sentence that presents your main idea usually appears at the beginning of a paragraph. Sometimes, a topic sentence can be found in the middle or at the end of a paragraph. Placed at the beginning of the paragraph, the topic sentence focuses the reader's attention before the supporting details are presented. Placed at the end of the paragraph, the topic sentence summarizes the paragraph's details or draws a conclusion.

Paragraph Patterns You can arrange your paragraph in several different patterns, depending on the placement of your topic sentence. Using a TRI pattern, you would put together a paragraph using the following elements:

TOPIC SENTENCE: State your main idea.

RESTATEMENT: Interpret your main idea; put it into other words.

ILLUSTRATION: Support your main idea with an example.

> **T**
> **R**
> **I**
> A mosquito is an annoying little insect related to the fly. The three most annoying kinds of mosquitoes are the *Anopheles*, the *Aedes*, and the *Culex*. These three kinds are especially annoying because they can spread serious diseases, such as malaria, yellow fever, and encephalitis, or inflammation of the brain.

After you have identified the basic parts of your paragraph, try variations of the TRI pattern, such as TIR, TII, or ITR, until you are satisfied with the results.

> **T**
> **I**
> **I**
> Unlike many other insects, ladybugs are charming as well as beneficial. Their nonthreatening small, round shape and their cheerful black-spotted red coloring endear them to children and adults. However, ladybugs are more than just fun to watch. Gardeners love ladybugs because they eat the insects that hurt gardens and crops.

> **Exercise 5** Placing a Topic Sentence Arrange the following sentences in a paragraph. First, identify the topic sentence that expresses the main idea. Then, rearrange the sentences, using the TRI pattern or a variation.

The number of inches refers to the diameter of the wheel. Bicycles come in many sizes: 12, 16, 20, 24, 26, and 27 inches. Many people ride bicycles for recreation, but some people ride them to school or to work. A bicycle is a two-wheeled vehicle powered by turning two pedals with the feet.

Maintaining Unity and Coherence

Establishing Unity

A paragraph has **unity** when all of its sentences relate to the main idea. They support, explain, or develop the topic sentence. To be sure that your paragraphs have unity, think about your topic sentence as you draft. Check that each point relates to your topic. When you revise, strengthen the unity of the paragraph by deleting details or sentences that do not support, develop, or explain the main idea.

In the following paragraph, one sentence is marked for deletion because it interferes with the unity of the paragraph.

WRITING MODEL

> Some dogs are pests. They bark at your guests and jump on your furniture. They chew your shoes and they bother you when you're eating. Maybe these dogs were born that way, but that's unlikely. They probably became pests because their owners never trained them. ~~Puppies are especially cute and loveable.~~ Dogs need to be taught how to behave. They need to learn the family's rules, such as when it's okay to bark. A good obedience class can provide this education. Every pet dog should be required to attend such a class.

▶ **Exercise 6** Revising for Unity On a separate sheet of paper, copy the following paragraph. Mark for deletion any sentences that interfere with the unity of the paragraph.

Obedience schools train the owner as well as the animal. This training is crucial because the owner must know how to control the dog. Otherwise, the dog will forget its training. Dogs love to gnaw on bones. Owners who learn with their pets are rewarded in several ways. Their families and the pets are happier because everyone is following the same rules. Guests feel more relaxed because they don't have to worry about getting dog hair all over their clothes. Regular exercise is also important for dogs.

▼ Critical Viewing
Give three sentences to support the main idea that the dogs in this photograph are well cared for. [**Draw Conclusions**]

Maintaining Unity

1. Have students identify the main idea of the model paragraph. (Dogs need to be trained so that they do not become pests.)

2. Then go through the paragraph sentence by sentence and have students explain why each sentence fits the main idea. They should easily understand why the sentence *Puppies are especially cute and lovable* does not fit the main idea and is crossed out.

Answer Key

▶ **Exercise 6**

Obedience schools train the owner as well as the animal. This training is crucial because the owner must know how to control the dog. Otherwise, the dog will forget its training. ~~Dogs love to gnaw on bones.~~ Owners who learn with their pets are rewarded in several ways. Their families and the pets are happier because everyone is following the same rules. Guests feel more relaxed because they don't have to worry about getting dog hair all over their clothes. ~~Regular exercise is also important for dogs.~~

Critical Viewing

Draw Conclusions Sample answer: These dogs have healthy, shiny coats. They are alert and full of energy. Their weight is just right for their size: They are neither too fat nor too thin.

Achieve Coherence

1. Ask two brave volunteers to tell what they did last Saturday and how to get from school to their home—without using any transitional words. If they manage to do it (which is unlikely), the listeners won't have understood. Whenever the class hears a transitional word sneak into the description, they can make a loud, annoying noise.

2. Examine the words on the chart to help students understand the differences among time-order, spatial, and order-of-importance transitions.

Answer Key

> **Exercise 7**

Make sure students understand that they are to draw information from the facts that follow the paragraph and that these sentences do not have to be incorporated into the paragraph.

3.1

Achieving Coherence

For a paragraph to have coherence, the supporting ideas must be logically connected, and the reader should be able to see how one idea relates to another. When you draft, order the sentences so that one leads logically to the next. Transitional words and phrases, such as those in the chart below, show connections between ideas and help paragraphs to flow.

Time-Order Transitions			
after	during	last week (month, and so on)	previously
ago	earlier	later	simultaneously
already	finally	next	then
at the same time	in the meantime	now	when
before	in the past	once	while
Spatial Transitions			
above	back	east (west, and so on)	middle
across	behind	in	there
around	below	into	under
at	down	left (right)	up
Order-of-Importance Transitions			
as much as best	greatest highest	less main	most (important, unforgettable, and so on)
finally	last	mainly	of all
first	least	more moreover	worst

> **Exercise 7** Revising for Coherence Revise the following paragraph, adding transitions to achieve coherence, and reordering sentences as necessary.

Our vacation in New Mexico was fascinating. We visited the Puye cliff dwellings, which were built into the side of a mesa. We had to climb to reach them. We traveled along desert roads where we saw signs warning "Stock on Highway." We watched for cows but didn't see any on the road. Santa Fe had many Spanish-style buildings. My parents bought jewelry and crafts made by Native Americans. We also visited the charming town of Taos before we went to Santa Fe. I asked my sister if she remembered to bring the camera. Taos is home to Native Americans of the Taos tribe. It was beautiful.

38 • Paragraphs and Compositions

☑ ONGOING ASSESSMENT: Monitor and Reinforce

For students who are still having difficulty revising paragraphs to increase coherence, use the following activity.

Have partners read several paragraphs from nonfiction articles in *Timeless Voices, Timeless Themes,* Copper. Ask them to identify the	transitional words and discuss how these words make the paragraphs more coherent.

3.2 *Paragraphs in Essays and Other Compositions*

Understanding the Parts of a Composition

When you write a composition, you *compose*—that is, you put all the parts together. Your reports, essays, and test answers may not be literary. Nevertheless, they are compositions, and to write them effectively, you must understand each of the parts.

Introduction

The **introduction** presents the subject of your composition. The introduction should capture the readers' interest with a strong **lead,** or first sentence. The main points of your composition should follow next in a **thesis statement.** Several sentences may follow, outlining how you will make each main point.

Body

Forming the **body** of a composition are several paragraphs that develop, explain, illustrate, and support the main ideas in your thesis statement. The body should be **unified** and **coherent** and logically organized. The topic sentence of each paragraph should tie directly to the points in your thesis statement.

Conclusion

The final paragraph of a composition is the **conclusion.** In the conclusion, you restate your thesis statement, usually using different words. You also summarize the support for the thesis and, if appropriate, offer a reflection or an observation on your subject. To make your conclusion memorable, you may want to end it with a forceful statement, a call to action, a quotation, or a question that causes your reader to give your subject more thought.

▶ **Exercise 8** **Planning a Composition** Think of a subject that interests you. Then, on a separate sheet of paper, prepare a brief outline of the parts of a composition that you would write on that topic. Next, write a lead for your introduction— something to engage your readers' interest—and a thesis statement that includes the points you wish to cover in the composition. Now, write a topic sentence for each of your body paragraphs. Finally, choose a quotation or write a forceful statement for your conclusion, or write a question that will keep your readers thinking.

Paragraphs in Essays and Other Compositions • 39

Step-by-Step Teaching Guide

Understanding the Parts of a Composition

1. Explain to students that every composition follows a similar pattern. This pattern helps to organize a piece of writing and give it coherence.

2. Go over each of the three parts of a composition with students. Have students discuss why each part appears where it does. For example, why would it not be a good idea to have the body appear before the introduction?

Answer Key

▶ **Exercise 8**

Have students share their outlines with a partner. Students can review each other's work, suggesting possible ways to reorganize the outlines.

⏱ **TIME AND RESOURCE MANAGER**	
In-Depth Coverage	**Accelerated Pace**
• Cover pp. 39–41 in class. • Complete the exercises in class.	• Have students read pp. 39–41 independently. • Answer questions as necessary. • Have students complete the exercises independently.

Types of Paragraphs

1. Review the two major types of paragraphs. Explain that topical paragraphs are organized around a *topic*, and that functional paragraphs serve a specific *function*.

2. Have a volunteer read aloud the model. Make sure students understand why it is a functional paragraph. Phrases such as *a very old book* and *there was a time when all stories were printed on paper* help to arouse the reader's interest and motivate them to continue reading.

More About the Author

Isaac Asimov (1920–1992) was one of the best-known and most prolific writers of science fiction ever. His interest in science fiction began when, as a very young boy, he became fascinated by science fiction magazines in his family's candy store. Asimov's story "Nightfall" was chosen the best science fiction story of all time in a Science Fiction Writers of America poll. Among his best novels were *The Gods Themselves* and *Foundation's Edge.* He also wrote nonfiction works that explain science topics to ordinary readers.

Customize for
Gifted/Talented Students

Challenge students to imagine what a book in 2155 might look like. Ask them to draw a diagram of the "book," label its parts, and write a short paragraph explaining it.

Customize for
ESL Students

Conventions in the use of quotation marks vary from language to language, so explain to students learning English how quotation marks in English are used. Make sure that students are aware that quotation marks are used in pairs and enclose a speaker's exact words.

3.2

Types of Paragraphs

A strategy is a plan. Just as teams rely on strategies to win games, so do writers employ strategies to write effectively. An effective paragraph strategy involves choosing which types of paragraphs to write and which sorts of details to include.

Topical Paragraphs

A topical paragraph consists of a group of sentences containing one main idea sentence and several sentences that support or illustrate that main idea.

Functional Paragraphs

Functional paragraphs are used for specific purposes. Although they may not contain a topic sentence, they have unity and coherence because the sentences are clearly connected and logically ordered. Functional paragraphs can serve the following purposes:

To Arouse or Sustain Interest A few vivid sentences can work together to capture the reader's attention.

WRITING
MODEL

from **The Fun They Had**
Isaac Asimov

It was a very old book. Margie's grandfather once said that when he was a little boy, *his* grandfather told him that there was a time when all stories were printed on paper.

> This excerpt comes from a story set in the year 2155. It refers to a book that one of the characters has found. The paragraph arouses interest because it describes books on paper as a feature of the past.

To Create Emphasis A short paragraph of one or two sentences breaks the reader's rhythm and adds importance to what is being said.

To Indicate Dialogue One of the conventions of written dialogue is to begin a new paragraph each time the speaker changes.

To Make a Transition A short paragraph can frequently help readers move between the main ideas in two topical paragraphs.

40 • Paragraphs and Compositions

☑ ONGOING ASSESSMENT: Monitor and Reinforce

For students who are having difficulty identifying the three types of paragraphs, use the following activity.

Have students read a page from a nature or science magazine and one from a novel. Then ask them to work in small groups to decide whether the paragraphs are topical or functional. Be sure that group members can explain how they arrived at their decisions.

Exercise 9 Identifying Functional Paragraphs Skim a short story you have read recently. Find one example of a functional paragraph that sustains interest and one example of a functional paragraph that either indicates dialogue or makes a transition. Explain to a partner how these paragraphs work in the context of the short story.

Paragraph Blocks

Sometimes, you can have so much information that you cannot include it all in one manageable paragraph. Then, you may develop a single idea over several paragraphs. This "block" contains several paragraphs that support the same main idea or topic sentence.

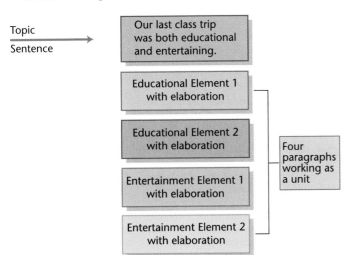

Exercise 10 Writing Paragraph Blocks Write a brief account of a class trip or another interesting experience you have had. When you have finished, mark in the margins the paragraph patterns or blocks you've used. Label each paragraph according to the function it performs. Then, mark your paragraph blocks with braces: { }. Study the patterns you have made, and consider whether you should rearrange or add sentences, or move sentences from one paragraph to another.

Paragraph Blocks

Teaching Resources: Writing Support Transparency 3-C

1. Discuss paragraph length. Ask students why it is difficult to read extremely long paragraphs and whether there is an ideal paragraph length.

2. Talk about the paragraph blocks on the page. Make sure students are aware that the topic sentence indicates how the paragraphs will be organized: first educational aspects will be mentioned, then entertainment.

Answer Key

▶ **Exercise 9**

You may want to choose a short story for all students to use so that you can make sure the story has plenty of dialogue and contains varied paragraph structures. Then divide students into pairs and have them complete the exercise by locating the various types of paragraphs and discussing them.

▶ **Exercise 10**

Students should consider using a topic sentence that sets up the paragraphs to follow in similar fashion to the one in the example.

☑ **ONGOING ASSESSMENT: Monitor and Reinforce**

For students who are having difficulty creating paragraph blocks, try the following activity.

Have students work together to suggest the topics of paragraphs that might appear in the following papers: Parrots Are Great Pets, How to Build a Birdhouse, and Why Kids Should Get the Vote. Then choose one of the paragraphs and diagram how it might be expanded into several paragraphs.

Developing Style

1. Explain to students that they will be learning strategies to help them develop their own personal writing style. The most important thing to remember, however, is that this style be consistent within a single piece of writing.

2. Review the elements of style. You may want to bring in examples of writing to show students how these elements contribute to an overall style.

3. The word *diction* may be unfamiliar to students. Explain that diction means the careful choice of words suitable to an intended audience.

Answer Key

▶ **Exercise 11**

After students have completed the exercise, ask them to choose partners and take turns reading their paragraphs aloud and trying to figure out which Writing Model prompted them.

3.3 Writing Style

Developing Your Style

You express yourself through your personal style. The way you dress, the videos you like, the music you listen to, how you speak—all are expressions of your personal style. Style also refers to the way you express yourself in writing. Almost every feature of a writer's use of language contributes to that writer's style. Several elements contributing to writing style are highlighted here.

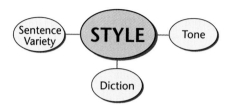

Sentence Variety The different books on your bookshelves indicate some of your literary tastes and styles. You have many options available to contribute to your writing style as well. When you write a paragraph, try to vary your sentence lengths, types, and structures.

Diction The particular words you use add to the style, or overall effect, of a paragraph. Think about your choice of words when planning how to achieve a particular effect. For instance, if you are writing dialogue and want to achieve a realistic conversational tone, you'll probably use informal English. If you intend to convey the seriousness of a certain situation, you will use appropriately formal language. The way words sound can also contribute to a paragraph's style.

Tone Your attitude toward your subject is conveyed in the tone of your writing. You may consider your subject in many ways—for example, with warmth, approval, distance, or admiration. A personal diary entry will probably have a casual tone, while a letter to the editor of your school newspaper will be more serious and formal in tone.

▶ **Exercise 11** Determining a Writing Style Read the two Writing Models on page 33. Study the sentence lengths and structures, the word choice, and the tone of each. Then, write a paragraph of your own, modeled on the style of one of the model paragraphs. Show your paragraph to a classmate, and see whether he or she can determine which style you used as a model.

42 • Paragraphs and Compositions

⏱ TIME AND RESOURCE MANAGER	
In-Depth Coverage	**Accelerated Pace**
• Cover pp. 42–43 in class. • Complete the exercises in class.	• Have students read pp. 42–43 independently. • Respond to questions as necessary. • Have students complete the exercises independently.

Using Formal and Informal English

Standard English can be either formal or informal. Formal English is appropriate for serious purposes. Informal English is appropriate for casual writing, or when you want your writing to have a conversational tone.

Conventions of Formal English

Use formal English for most school assignments and for explanations of processes, reports, essays, speeches, articles, and applications. When writing in formal English, you should follow these conventions:

- Avoid contractions.
- Do not use slang.
- Use standard English and grammar and usage.

Informal English

The English we speak every day is informal English. You can use informal English when you write stories, humorous essays, dialogue, letters to friends, personal notes, and journal entries. When you use informal English, you can

- use contractions.
- use slang and popular expressions.

FORMAL ENGLISH:	This playing field must be rebuilt. It is a hazard to our community. Our children play soccer and baseball on this field, yet it is full of rocks and holes.
INFORMAL ENGLISH:	Hey guys, heads up! This field's a total disaster area. You could break a leg if you're not careful!

Exercise 12 Using Formal and Informal English Rewrite the following sentences, using formal English for those written informally, and informal English for those written formally.
1. I thoroughly enjoyed the soccer season.
2. That last playoff game really rocked!
3. Our new sporting facilities are quite impressive.
4. The stadium cost a bundle and is totally awesome.
5. The best improvement is the Olympic-sized swimming pool.

▲ **Critical Viewing** Describe this scene using formal English, and again using informal English. [Analyze]

Writing Style • 43

Using Formal and Informal English

Discuss formal and informal writing. Ask students to identify the style they would use for the following writing tasks and explain their reasoning:

- an essay for a history class
- a note inviting someone to a party
- a letter thanking a grandparent for a gift
- a cover letter for a résumé

Answer Key

▶ **Exercise 12**

Answers will vary. Samples are given.
1. The soccer season was a blast.
2. That last play was excellent.
3. Our new sporting arena is really neat.
4. The stadium was expensive to construct and is very impressive.
5. The coolest part is the great big swimming pool.

Integrating Vocabulary Skills

Have partners work together to write and perform short, two-person skits. One character should speak in very formal English with an elevated vocabulary, and the other should speak in informal English, including lots of slang.

Integrating Workplace Skills

Using the appropriate written and spoken language is critical to success in the workplace. Ask students to discuss the differences between a formal proposal to the head of a department and an e-mail to a colleague asking for information about a project.

Critical Viewing

Analyze Students' answers will vary. Sentences in formal English should not use contractions or slang and should be grammatically correct. Sentences in informal English should use contractions and "natural-sounding" popular expressions.

☑ **ONGOING ASSESSMENT: Monitor and Reinforce**

For students who are having difficulty distinguishing between formal and informal writing, try the following activity.

Label and display several examples of both types of writing for students to examine. Have students use the examples as models for their own work.

Lesson Objectives

1. To frame questions to direct research
2. To write to inform readers about a musical composition

Step-by-Step Teaching Guide

Examining Musical Compositions

1. Choose one of the Spotlight elements for class discussion, or have students work independently or in small groups on the element of their choice. Give them the initiative to find the necessary books and recordings.

2. Be sure to play one of Mozart's pieces for your students before you discuss the composer and his work.

3. Read aloud a section of a Goethe poem or a paragraph or two from *Faust* or have a volunteer do so. Explain that Faust was a German doctor of legend who was believed to have sold his soul to the devil in exchange for youth, wisdom, and magical powers. Goethe's *Faust* was written in 1808. Several other writers, including Marlowe and Mann, and composers, including Berlioz, Gounod, Liszt, and Schumann, also treated the Faust legend.

4. Ask students who have seen *Amadeus* to discuss the film. What did they think of the depiction of Mozart's character? Could the composer really have been as obnoxious as he was portrayed? Was Salieri really as evil? Ask students to think about how one would check the historical accuracy of these portrayals and whether the film was obligated to "get it right."

5. Before you assign the writing task, play a CD of Mozart's music and model how to find the various themes, and note them in writing.

Spotlight on the Humanities

Examining Musical Compositions

Focus on Music:
Wolfgang Amadeus Mozart

As in a written work, a well-crafted piece of music must have unity, coherence, and other features of good composition. Ranking as one of the great musical geniuses of Western civilization, Wolfgang Amadeus Mozart (1756–1791) was an Austrian composer who could play the clavier (an early keyboard instrument), violin, and organ by the age of six. Also at age six, he composed five short musical pieces, which are still performed today. Mozart came from a musical family and accompanied his father on concert tours throughout Europe. Among Mozart's compositions are sonatas, symphonies, operas, and concertos—music that is technically proficient as well as emotionally stirring. Although Mozart died young, he left us a legacy of astonishing music.

Wolfgang Amadeus Mozart, Barbara Kraft

Literature Connection When German writer Johann Wolfgang von Goethe (1749–1832) was fourteen years old, he saw Wolfgang Amadeus Mozart perform in Frankfurt, Germany. Goethe was to become one of the most prominent and lasting writers in world literature. Not only was he a poet, dramatist, and novelist, but he was also a scientist. Born the son of a government official, Goethe even obtained a law degree. As a philosopher, Goethe believed in the power of the individual. Probably his best-known work is *Faust* (1832).

Film Connection Winner of eight Academy Awards including Best Picture, the 1984 film *Amadeus* chronicles the life of Mozart as seen through the eyes of rival composer Antonio Salieri. Directed by Milos Forman and based on the Broadway play of the same name, *Amadeus* depicts Mozart as a strong, precocious, obnoxious character who was also a genius.

Writing Activity: Response to Music
Listen to a work by Mozart—perhaps *Eine Kleine Nachtmusik* ("A Little Night Music") or the overture to *The Magic Flute.* Notice the musical themes that give the work coherence and the surprises that engage your interest. Jot down notes as you listen; then, use your notes to give a short presentation on how the parts of the composition work together. Use the recording in your presentation.

▲ **Critical Viewing**
How do the elements of this portrait work together to convey a strong image of its subject? **[Evaluate]**

Viewing and Representing

Activity Students may want to enhance their presentations by showing the musical score for the piece they are discussing. If you have any musicians in class, encourage them to play the piece about which they wrote.

Critical Viewing

Evaluate Many students will remark that the simplicity, strength of composition, directness of the subject's gaze, details of clothing and hair, and color palette contribute to a strong image.

Media and Technology Skills

Evaluating Information Media
Activity: Comparing and Contrasting News Sources

Every day, we have an opportunity to get the news from a number of different sources. Together, these sources are called the **media.** Through print, broadcasts, and—more recently—the Internet, we can learn about local, national, and world events. Many media sources don't just report the news; they provide analyses of it, as well.

Think About It The differences between the various types of media include the depth of coverage, the tone, the method of presentation, and the timeliness of the reports.

- **Print media** include newspapers, which are generally published daily or weekly, and magazines, which appear weekly or monthly. The tone in newspapers and magazines is objective, except on the editorial and opinion pages. News coverage in print media is ongoing, and each new issue updates the information. Magazines provide more in-depth coverage; however, they do not update the information as often. Print media draw readers' attention with headlines and key points in bold typefaces. Articles are commonly accompanied by photographs.

- **Broadcast media** come to their audiences through radio, television, and—increasingly—the Internet. These news sources combine sound, images, and live narration. It is possible to watch television broadcasts of the news around the clock, as well as see live coverage of many events. Some broadcasts also feature analyses and discussions of the news. Radio conveniently allows the listener to hear the news while engaging in other activities, and, on numerous sites, the Internet provides users the opportunity to access full coverage of an event at any time of the night or day.

Analyze It Compare the coverage of a current news story in two different sources in print and broadcast media. Which source presented the information most fully? Which, most clearly? In what ways were you affected by each of the different sources? Use a Venn diagram like the one above to help you organize the details for your comparison.

> **Types of Media**
> **Print**
> - Books
> - Magazines
> - Newspapers
> - Photography
> - Print Advertisements
>
> **Broadcast**
> - Television
> - Radio
> - Film
> - Internet Broadcasts

Media Source 1   Media Source 2

Media Sources 1 and 2

Media and Technology Skills • **45**

▶ *Lesson Objectives*

1. To interpret ideas gathered from various media
2. To organize knowledge about a topic in a variety of ways
3. To evaluate the purposes and effects of varying media
4. To write to compare

Step-by-Step Teaching Guide

Evaluating Information Media

Teaching Resources: Writing Support Transparency 3-D; Writing Support Activity Book 3-1

1. Discuss the various sources of news with students. Have students consider what a television broadcast provides that a newspaper can't. What can print media do that broadcast media cannot?

2. Have students choose their news stories and complete a Venn diagram to organize details for a comparison between print and broadcast media. Then have them write the comparison.

Customize for
ESL Students

Students whose first language is not English will find analyzing broadcast media difficult. Their task will be made easier if they or their parents can videotape a news broadcast for them to view several times. You may want to assign all students studying English as a second language the same fairly straightforward news story and choose a newspaper article for them to read and analyze. Introduce difficult vocabulary before students begin reading.

Analyzing Strategy, Organization, and Style

1. Discuss the sample test item with students. Ask them to identify the type of question in the sample (organization question).

2. Have volunteers read the sentences in the paragraph in the order they are shown in items A, B, and C. Decide together why B makes the most sense.

Standardized Test Preparation Workshop

Analyzing Strategy, Organization, and Style

Standardized tests often measure your knowledge about writing an effective paragraph. These types of test items consist of a paragraph in which each sentence is numbered and specific questions are based on the passage. These test questions often ask about the writer's strategy, organization, sequence of sentences, choice of words, and overall style of the paragraph. The following are three types of questions that you will need to answer:

- **Strategy questions** ask whether a given revision is appropriate in the context of the essay.

- **Organization questions** ask you to choose the most logical sequence of ideas or to decide whether a sentence should be added, deleted, or moved.

- **Style questions** focus on conveying the writer's point of view and the use of appropriate and effective language for the intended audience.

The sample test item that follows will give you practice in answering questions on writing strategy, organization, and style.

Test Tip

Read each paragraph, and mark with a check any passages that may be out of sequence or that do not make sense. Refer back to your checks as you answer the questions.

Sample Test Item	Answer and Explanation
Directions: Read the paragraph, and then answer the questions that follow.	
(1) Later on in the afternoon, we helped groom the horses. (2) Right before lunch, we got a tour of the stables. (3) When we arrived at the ranch in the morning, a cowboy greeted us and showed us to our rooms. (4) At night, we sat around a campfire and sang cowboy songs.	
1 Choose the most logical sentence sequence.	The correct answer is *B*. In order to arrange the information in the paragraph in a logical sequence, part 3 should begin the paragraph as a topic sentence. Parts 2, 1, and 4 must appear in this sequence to effectively support the topic sentence and conclude the paragraph.
A 2, 4, 3, 1	
B 3, 2, 1, 4	
C 4, 3, 2, 1	
D Correct as is	

46 • Paragraphs and Compositions

🖎 **TEST-TAKING TIP**

Students should pay particular attention to time order words in organization questions. They might underline these words, which include *first, next, last, finally, before, after,* and so on. When they have to reorder steps in a process, they should consider which steps must happen before other steps can be accomplished.

Practice 1 **Directions:** Read the passage, and then answer the questions that follow. Choose the letter of the best answer.

(1) Yoshi was taken to the emergency medical center at the ski lodge. (2) It was a beautiful January day for skiing. (3) His friend, Maura, drew a cartoon of Yoshi skiing downhill on his cast. (4) Although Yoshi was a pretty good skier, he took a bad spill and broke his leg. (5) Doctors put his whole left leg in a cast. (6) Even Yoshi laughed when he saw the drawing.

1 Which of the following is the most effective topic sentence for the paragraph?
  A Yoshi will never ski again.
  B Maura is a wonderful cartoonist.
  C All skiers have good days and bad days.
  D Yoshi's day on the slopes didn't end as he thought it would.

2 Which of the following is the most logical sentence sequence for this paragraph?
  F 2, 3, 1, 5, 6, 4
  G 2, 4, 1, 5, 3, 6
  H 1, 2, 3, 5, 4, 6
  J 4, 5, 6, 1, 2 ,3

3 If the writer wanted to add more information about this story, which of the following would be most appropriate?
  A Yoshi's favorite hobby was building model airplanes.
  B It didn't snow again that year.
  C Yoshi's leg was going to take a few months to heal.
  D Maura got an "A" in art class.

Practice 2 **Directions:** Read the passage, and then answer the questions that follow. Choose the letter of the best answer.

(1) The doctor told Yoshi that he would have to wear the cast until May. (2) May is in the spring. (3) He had to use crutches in order to move around. (4) It was slow going at first, but then Yoshi got the hang of using them. (5) He even gave the crutches names: Will and Phil. (6) When the cast came off, Yoshi said: "Now, the weather is perfect for skateboarding!"

1 Which of the following sentences is most irrelevant and could be deleted from the paragraph?
  A May is in the spring.
  B He had to use crutches in order to move around.
  C The doctor told Yoshi that he would have to wear the cast until May.
  D It was slow going at first, but then Yoshi got the hang of using them.

2 The tone of this passage can be described as—
  F sad
  G serious
  H humorous
  J mysterious

3 Which of the following sentences would best conclude the paragraph?
  A It's over.
  B With that, he went home and retrieved his skateboard from the garage.
  C Skateboarding is for people who can't ski.
  D Springtime was Yoshi's favorite time of the year.

Answer Key

Practice 1
1. D
2. G
3. C

Practice 2
1. A
2. H
3. B

Customize for
Less Advanced Students
Find an interesting, short, and easy-to-read magazine article. Ask the students to read the article, choose a paragraph, and cut apart the sentences. Students should work together to reassemble the paragraphs in the order that makes the most sense.

Customize for
More Advanced Students
Have students work together to prepare tips for taking standardized tests that ask strategy, organization, and style questions. Remind students that test takers often need shortcuts that help them save time on these timed tests.

Chapter 4

Time and Resource Manager

In-Depth Lesson Plan

	LESSON FOCUS	PRINT AND MEDIA RESOURCES
DAY 1	**Introduction to Autobiographical Writing** Students learn key elements of autobiographical writing and analyze the Model From Literature (pp. 48–51).	*Writers at Work* **Videotape**, Narration *Writing Lab* **CD-ROM**, Narration
DAY 2	**Prewriting** Students choose and narrow a topic, consider their audience and purpose, and gather information (pp. 52–55).	**Teaching Resources** *Writing Support Transparencies* 4-A–C; *Writing Support Activity Book*, 4-1–2
DAY 3	**Drafting** Students organize their ideas and write their first drafts (pp. 56–57).	**Teaching Resources** *Writing Support Transparencies* 4-D–E; *Writing Support Activity Book*, 4-3
DAY 4	**Revising** Students revise their drafts in terms of overall structure, paragraphs, sentences, and word choice (pp. 58–61).	**Teaching Resources** *Writing Support Transparencies* 4-F–H
DAY 5	**Editing and Proofreading; Publishing and Presenting** Students check their work for accuracy and correctness and present their final drafts (pp. 62–63).	**Teaching Resources** *Scoring Rubrics on Transparency*, Ch. 4; *Formal Assessment*, Ch. 4

Accelerated Lesson Plan

	LESSON FOCUS	PRINT AND MEDIA RESOURCES
DAY 1	**Drafting** Students review characteristics of autobiographical writing, select topics, and write drafts (pp. 48–57).	**Teaching Resources** *Writing Support Transparencies* 4-A–E; *Writing Support Activity Book* 4-1–3 *Writing Lab* **CD-ROM**, Narration *Writers at Work* **Videotape**, Narration
DAY 2	**Revising to Presenting** Students work individually or with peers to revise, edit, and proofread their work for presentation (pp. 58–63).	*Teaching Resources* *Writing Support Transparencies* 4-F–H; *Scoring Rubrics on Transparency*, Ch. 4; *Formal Assessment*, Ch. 4

Options for Adapting Lesson Plans

HOMEWORK

Have students complete any stage of the lesson for homework.

FEATURES

Extend coverage with the Connected Assignment (p. 66), Spotlight on the Humanities (p. 68), Media and Technology Skills (p. 69) and the Standardized Test Preparation Workshop (p. 70).

TECHNOLOGY

Students can complete any stage of the lesson on computer. Have them print out their completed work.

INTEGRATED SKILLS COVERAGE

Integrating Grammar
Identifying Nouns SE p. 61
Capitalization of Proper Nouns SE p. 62

Reading/Writing Connection
Reading Strategy SE p. 50
Writing Application SE p. 51

Language Highlight
ATE p. 53

Workplace Skills
ATE p. 60

Technology
SE pp. 56, 63; ATE p. 62

Real-World Connection
ATE p. 54

Viewing and Representing
Critical Viewing SE pp. 48, 50, 51, 55, 64, 65, 66, 68
Viewing and Representing ATE p. 68

ASSESSMENT SUPPORT

Standardized Test Preparation Workshop SE p. 70; ATE p. 51
Standardized Test Preparation Workbook, pp. 7–8
Scoring Rubrics on Transparency, Ch. 4
Formal Assessment, Ch. 4
Writing Assessment and Portfolio Management

MEETING INDIVIDUAL NEEDS

Less Advanced Students ATE p. 71; See also Ongoing
Assessments ATE pp. 55, 57, 63
ESL Students ATE pp. 52, 71
Bodily/Kinesthetic Learners ATE p. 57
Gifted/Talented Students ATE p. 58

BLOCK SCHEDULING

Pacing Suggestions
For 90-minute Blocks
- Have students complete the Prewriting and Drafting stages in a single period.
- Focus one class period on Revising and Editing and Publishing and Presenting. Allow at least 30 minutes for peer revision.

Resources for Varying Instruction
- *Writing Lab* **CD-ROM** If your students have access to hardware, a 90-minute block provides an ideal opportunity for students to work on computer.
- *Writers at Work* **Videotape** Show the Narration segment in class.

Professional Development Support
- *How to Manage Instruction in the Block* This Teaching Resource provides management and activity suggestions.

MEDIA AND TECHNOLOGY

For the Student
- *Writing Lab* **CD-ROM,** Narration

For the Teacher
- *Writers at Work* **Videotape,** Narration
- *Resource Pro* **CD-ROM**

WRITING AND GRAMMAR WEB SITE

The Interactive Writing and Grammar Web site provides a wide array of support for students, teachers and parents. Writing support includes:

- Interactive revision checkers
- Scoring rubrics with complete models

www.phschool.com

LITERATURE CONNECTIONS

Related selections from *Prentice Hall Literature: Timeless Voices, Timeless Themes,* Copper:
from *The Pigman & Me,* Paul Zindel, SE p. 51
"Old Ben," Jesse Stuart, SE p. 53

▶ Lesson Objectives

1. To understand the characteristics of autobiographical writing.

2. To choose and narrow a topic for autobiographical writing.

3. To consider audience and purpose in developing a writing topic.

4. To apply strategies for gathering and organizing details.

5. To draft autobiographical writing that incorporates an effective lead, elements of tension and conflict, and sufficient elaboration.

6. To evaluate and revise the overall structure of autobiographical writing.

7. To analyze the structure of paragraphs and ensure that they are clearly related.

8. To analyze sentences to ensure that they have varied beginnings.

9. To use precise nouns.

10. To benefit from the peer review process in the revision of autobiographical writing.

11. To edit, proofread, and publish autobiographical writing.

Critical Viewing

Analyze Students may mention how they felt at the event and what happened at the event.

Narration
Autobiographical Writing

Autobiography in Everyday Life

Every day, you probably tell other people about events in your life. You might tell a friend about something funny your dog did. You might write a letter to a grandparent about a book you liked. In fact, a big part of life is the stories we tell of it.

When you write autobiographically, you tell a story from your life by writing it down. Developing strong autobiographical writing skills can help you share your life with others and enrich your own experience.

▲ **Critical Viewing**
What details from an event such as this might you include in a piece of autobiographical writing? Why? **[Analyze]**

⏱ TIME AND RESOURCE MANAGER

Resources
Technology: Writers at Work videotape

In-Depth Coverage	Accelerated Pace
• Cover pp. 48–51 in class. • Show Narration section of the Writers at Work videotape. • Read literature excerpt (pp. 50–51) in class and use it to brainstorm narration ideas with students. • Discuss examples of narration you or students know about or bring to class.	• Have students read pp. 48–51 on their own. • Discuss the characteristics of autobiographical writing in class. • Assign the Model from Literature for independent reading.

What Is Autobiographical Writing?

Autobiographical writing tells the story of an event, period, or person in the writer's life. By writing autobiographically, you can share part of your life with others. You can also learn more about yourself. A well-written autobiographical piece includes

- the writer as a character in the story.
- a lead, or opening paragraph, that catches a reader's interest.
- true events presented in clear, logical order.
- a central conflict, or problem, that the writer or another person has to resolve.

To learn how your work may be graded or judged, see the Rubric for Self-Assessment on page 63.

Types of Autobiographical Writing

These are a few of the types of autobiographical writing:

- **Autobiographical incidents,** which are also called **personal narratives,** tell stories of specific events in your life.
- **Autobiographical narratives,** or **sketches,** tell of periods or groups of events in your life. They include your thoughts and insights about the time.
- **Reflective essays** recount an experience and give your thoughts on its meaning.
- **Memoirs** are true stories of your relationship with a particular person, place, animal, or thing.

PREVIEW
Student Work
IN PROGRESS

Coy Walker, a student at Drew Academy in Houston, Texas, wrote an autobiographical essay about a bike accident he once had. In this chapter, you will see how he used the strategies and tips in this lesson to develop his essay. At the end of the chapter, you can read Coy's completed essay.

Writers in
ACTION

Author Paul Zindel's own experiences appear in almost all his books. Zindel remembers when an editor convinced him to write about teenagers.

She "... brought me into an area that I never explored before, my own confused, funny, aching teenage days."

PREPARE and ENGAGE

Interest GRABBER Invite students to retell the last story about themselves that they told to a friend. If they need encouragement, have them recall what they told their friends the last time they talked on the phone or exchanged e-mail. Emphasize that these occasions involve relating short parts of the stories of their lives.

Activate Prior Knowledge

Remind students that every day, they relate some small part of their autobiographies to others. Invite them to look ahead to the evening and discuss what they might tell their families about the happenings that made up their day. After sharing their stories, refer them to the characteristics of autobiographical writing listed in the text.

More About the Writer

Many of Paul Zindel's ideas for stories come from his own troubled teenage years. He says, "Eight hundred and fifty-three horrifying things had happened to me. . . ." In advising would-be writers, he instructs, "Start your story with a bang so you really grab your audience's attention."

☑ ONGOING ASSESSMENT: Diagnose

Use the following option to diagnose students' current level of proficiency in autobiographical writing.

After students read "The Bike," have them write down the main conflict and three details that establish and add to it. Students might need extra support in elaborating and in choosing details that are relevant to the main conflict.

Reading\Writing Connection

Reading: Make Predictions

Explain to students that they are actually making predictions all the time. Each time they think "What will he do if I. . ." or "What might happen if I ask her. . ." they are, in fact, putting into practice the same skill they need when reading. By paying attention to details and getting to "know" the characters, readers are gathering clues to what might happen or how characters will react.

Critical Viewing

Relate Students' responses will vary.

Step-by-Step Teaching Guide

Engage Students Through Literature

Use this model from literature to help students generate a topic for their own autobiographical writing.

1. Read the narrative aloud, or ask students to take turns reading portions.

2. Lead students in discussion by asking questions such as:

   • The writer mentions a near-death experience and a boring vacation in the same paragraph. Do you think this is effective? Why or why not?

   • What conflicting emotions does the story evoke in readers? Which emotion is the strongest?

3. Encourage students to brainstorm for other topics that the passage brings to their minds.

4. Students may add the brainstormed ideas to their own banks of topics for autobiographical writing. Explain that one way to jog their memories about incidents from their lives is to complete a sentence such as: "When I was in the fifth grade, ___ ."

4.1 Model From Literature

In her book My Sister Eileen, *Ruth McKenney (1911–1972) tells a few stories about lifesavers, including one starring her sister.*

Reading Strategy: Predict As you read this narrative, **make predictions**— ask yourself, "What will happen next?" Look for hints left by the author. After you make a prediction, read further to see whether or not it comes true.

▲ Critical Viewing Does this picture remind you of any event in your own life? Explain whether the event would make a good topic for a story. **[Relate]**

My Sister the "Lifesaver"

Ruth McKenney

. . . Long before I ever had any dealings with professional life-savers my sister nearly drowned me, quite by mistake. My father once took us to a northern Michigan fishing camp, where we found the life very dull. He used to go trolling for bass on our little lake all day long, and at night come home to our lodge, deadbeat and minus any bass. In the meantime Eileen and I, who were nine and ten at the time, used to take an old rowboat out to a shallow section of the lake and, sitting in the hot sun, feed worms to an unexciting variety of small, undernourished fish called gillies. We hated the whole business.

Father, however, loved to fish, even if he didn't catch a single fish in three weeks, which on this trip he didn't. One night, however, he carried his enthusiasm beyond a decent pitch. He decided to go bass fishing after dark, and rather than leave us alone in the lodge and up to [who] knows what, he ordered us to take our boat and row along after him.

Eileen and I were very bored rowing around in the dark, and

McKenney opens with an effective lead sentence. By announcing the startling fact that her sister nearly drowned her, she draws the reader in.

McKenney organizes her story logically. First, she gives background information. Then, she starts at the beginning of the story.

50 • Autobiographical Writing

finally, in desperation, we began to stand up and rock the boat, which resulted, at last, in my falling into the lake with a mighty splash.

When I came up, choking and mad as anything, Eileen saw me struggling, and, as she always says with a catch in her voice, she only meant to help me. Good intentions, however, are of little importance in a situation like that. For she grabbed an oar out of the lock, and with an uncertain gesture hit me square on the chin.

I went down with a howl of pain. Eileen, who could not see much in the darkness, was now really frightened. The cold water revived me after the blow and I came to the surface, considerably weakened but still able to swim over to the boat. Whereupon Eileen, in a noble attempt to give me the oar to grab, raised it once again, and socked me square on the top of the head. I went down again, this time without a murmur, and my last thought was a vague wonder that my own sister should want to murder me with a rowboat oar.

As for Eileen, she heard the dull impact of the oar on my head and saw the shadowy figure of her sister disappear. So she jumped in the lake, screeching furiously, and began to flail around in the water, howling for help and looking for me. At this point I came to the surface and swam over to the boat, with the intention of killing Eileen.

Father, rowing hard, arrived just in time to pull us both out of the water and prevent me from attacking Eileen with the rowboat anchor. The worst part about the whole thing, as far as I was concerned, was that Eileen was considered a heroine and Father told everybody in the lake community that she had saved my life. The postmaster put her name in for a medal.

Reading \ Writing Connection

Writing Application:

Leave Clues As you write your own autobiographical narrative, build interest by giving your readers clues about what might happen next.

Here, McKenney develops the central conflict or problem of her story: How will she escape from Eileen's "rescue" attempt?

To enrich her story, McKenney adds details about her thoughts at the time.

⌊ITERATURE

To read another example of autobiographical writing, see *The Pigman & Me* by Paul Zindel. You can find an excerpt from this book in *Prentice Hall Literature: Timeless Voices, Timeless Themes,* Copper.

▼ **Critical Viewing**
Of what experience in your own life does this oar remind you? Briefly compare your experience with McKenney's.
[Compare and Contrast]

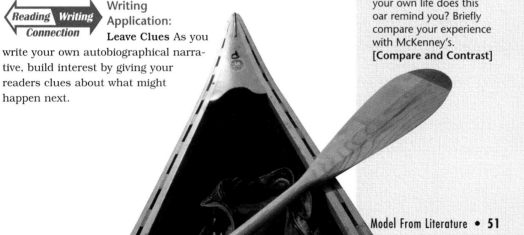

Responding to Literature

Ask students what similarities and differences they notice between McKenney's story and Zindel's. *(Both are about childhood and family, and both involve misunderstandings; however, in "The Pigman," the sister really does help.)* Point out that, since families are such a big part of everyone's life, it is common for family members to appear in autobiographical narratives.

More About the Writer

In the 1930s, Ruth McKenney moved with her sister Eileen from Ohio to New York City's Greenwich Village, an area popular with musicians, writers, and artists. The stories she wrote in a basement apartment were made into a movie, a TV show, and eventually a Broadway musical called *Wonderful Town.*

Critical Viewing

Compare and Contrast Students' responses will vary.

Reading\Writing Connection

Writing Application: Remind students that they will create more reader interest if they leave clues as they draft and revise—hints about what will happen next.

✎ STANDARDIZED TEST PREPARATION WORKSHOP

Mechanics Many standardized tests require students to identify spelling, capitalization, and punctuation errors. Use the following to demonstrate:

(1) The Presidential Medal of Freedom was established in 1945 to honor those who contributed significantly to American life. (2) Among the recipients have been Walt Disney Dr. Martin Luther King, Jr., and Muñoz Marin. (3) Marin was a poet and the first elected president of Puerto rico.

(1) **A** Spelling error   **C** Punctuation error
    B Capitalization error   **D** No error

(2) **A** Spelling error   **C** Punctuation error
    B Capitalization error   **D** No error

(3) **A** Spelling error   **C** Punctuation error
    B Capitalization error   **D** No error

1. **A**; *contributed* is misspelled. 2. **C**; there should be a comma after *Disney*. 3. **B**; *Rico* should be capitalized.

Prewriting: Freewriting

1. Brainstorm with students for possible topics for freewriting. Make sure everyone has topics in mind before the freewriting session begins.

2. The purpose of freewriting is for students to produce a constant stream of thoughts flowing from their minds, through their pens, and onto their papers. You might suggest that they keep their pens constantly in motion, just scribbling circles if necessary until they are ready to continue.

3. Suggest that students use abbreviations if ideas begin to flow faster than they can write.

Prewriting: Quicklist

Teaching Resources: Writing Support Transparencies 4-A; Writing Support Activity Book 4-1

1. Students often feel that they don't "really" know anyone or go anywhere. To help get them started, write on the board *people, places, experiences*. Under *people* write *at school, at home, at club,* and any other places students are likely to go. Under *places* write *daytime, evenings, weekends, vacations*. Under *experiences* write *alone, with friends, with family, with others*.

2. Display the transparency to show how Coy used a Quicklist to help pick a topic.

3. Give students copies of the blank organizer. Demonstrate how to use a Quicklist by listing some people you know from one of the places that will encourage students, such as nearby parks or stores, as well as any interesting vacation spots.

Customize for
ESL Students

Encourage students to use both the freewriting and quicklist exercises as opportunities to remember the countries from which they come. Suggest that they freewrite about the experience of coming to the U.S. or the difficulties of learning English.

4.2 # Prewriting

Choosing Your Topic

A lot of things have happened in your life. To find a good topic for autobiographical writing, think of an event that was special for you. Use these strategies to help:

Strategies for Generating a Topic

1. **Freewriting** Write down whatever thoughts occur to you about a general topic such as *holidays*, *adventures*, or *a problem solved*. Focus more on getting your ideas down than on writing correctly. After five minutes, read over your thoughts, and choose a topic from among them.

2. **Quicklist** Divide a sheet of paper into three columns. In the first, list people and places you know and events you've experienced. In the next, write a description of each. In the last, give an example supporting each general description. Choose a memory on your list as your topic.

Writing Lab CD-ROM

For more help finding a topic, explore the tips and activities in the Choosing Your Topic section of the Narration lesson.

Student Work
IN PROGRESS

Name: Coy Walker
Drew Academy
Houston, TX

Using a Quicklist
Here is how Coy Walker used a Quicklist to generate ideas for a topic. He circled the items connected to his bicycle.

People, Places, and Events	Description	Example
my dad	a smart guy	He warned me about the brakes on my new ten-speed.
Lake Minnetowa	peaceful	We saw deer drinking at the lake last time we were there.
my birthday	a great time!!	I got a bike last time—though I crashed it right afterwards.

My Topic My bike

52 • Autobiographical Writing

⊘ TIME AND RESOURCE MANAGER

Resources
Print: Writing Support Transparencies 4-A–C; Writing Support Activity Book 4-1–2
Technology: Writing Lab CD-ROM, Narration

In-Depth Coverage	Accelerated Pace
• Cover pp. 52–55. • Work with students to choose a topic and gather details for their essays.	• Assign pp. 52–55 for independent student review. • Have students choose a topic and gather details for their essays.

TOPIC BANK

If you're having trouble finding a topic, consider the following possibilities:

1. **Your Clothes** Clothing can be associated with particular events or circumstances. Maybe you have an outfit you wear at holidays or a baseball cap you wore during a championship game. Identify a piece of clothing you associate with a special event in your life. Use this event as the topic of your narrative.

2. **New Kid on the Block** Have you ever felt like the "new kid on the block"? Recall what it was like being with a group of kids who knew each other well but who didn't know you. Write about the experience and your reactions to it.

Responding to Fine Art

3. Think of the events leading up to the action in this painting. Think about the mood the colors create—happy, peaceful, or wild. Then, think of a time you did—or tried to do—something special in a game. Write an autobiographical narrative about this time.

Great Catch, Moses Ros

Responding to Literature

4. Read "Old Ben" by Jesse Stuart, paying attention to all of the details he includes about his pet snake. Then, write the story of a pet you have had, including similar details. You can find "Old Ben" in *Prentice Hall Literature: Timeless Voices, Timeless Themes,* Copper.

✍ Cooperative Writing Opportunity

5. **Illustrated Record** With a group, discuss the best school event you had last year. After you agree on a topic, write a recollection of the event. Some group members should write recollections of highlights from the event. Others should gather photographs and scrapbook mementos from the event, writing a brief explanation of the significance of each. Assemble the work in an album, and make it available to other students in the school library.

Prewriting • 53

Responding to Fine Art

Great Catch, 1991, by Moses Ros

Teaching Resources: Writing Support Transparency 4-B

1. Display the transparency and ask students what story the painting suggests to them.

2. Encourage students to brainstorm for possible topics suggested by this work of art. Was the player surprised that he made the catch? Did it win the game? Was it the only catch he ever made, yet his team still lost?

3. These ideas could lead to writing topics that have to do with sports or an unexpected achievement.

Responding to Literature

If students don't have a pet, they can write about a pet they would like to have. Though the details will not be true, they should be plausible, and any descriptive details about the pet should be accurate and realistic.

Spotlight on the Humanities

For additional topic suggestions, refer students to the Spotlight on the Humanities on page 68.

Language Highlight

Sometimes, words have more than one meaning. Often, by looking at the word's origin, you can discover how this happens. For some words, you can recognize a common idea that relates the various meanings to the root. For example, *direct* comes from the Latin *directum,* led straight, so it is possible to see that the verb meaning "guide" and the adjective "in a straight line" are related. However, many words

continued

continued
with multiple meanings have multiple origins. For example, one meaning of *troll* comes from Old French and another comes from Old Icelandic; one meaning of *compound* comes from Old French and another comes from Malay. These multiple meanings add richness to the language— and make word play possible—but they do mean that it is important to check a dictionary when you are uncertain about a word.

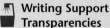 **TIME SAVERS!**

📑 **Writing Support Transparencies**
Use the transparencies for Chapter 4 to facilitate teaching of strategies.

📖 **Writing Support Activities**
Use the graphic organizers for Chapter 4 to facilitate student planning.

Prewriting: Narrowing Your Topic with a Topic Web

Teaching Resources: Writing Support Transparency 4-C; Writing Support Activity Book 4-2

1. Display the transparency. Help students understand the connections between the circled words near the center and the circled words farther out.

2. Demonstrate the topic web strategy on the chalkboard or with the transparency, using the Model From Literature as a starting place. For example, the event might be the entire holiday. Put "holiday" in the center of the web.

3. Ask volunteers to think about parts of the event the writer did not include. *(how they traveled to the camp, where they stayed, what kind of fishing equipment the father used, etc.)*

4. Write these parts around the central "holiday," adding the events that were related. *(father's fishing, near drowning)*

5. Explain how the writer might have continued, if she had used the web, adding details and associations like the girls' boredom, rocking the boat, darkness. Point out that, as the details are added, it would become more obvious which details belonged together and which made the best story.

6. Give students copies of the blank organizer. Have them use the topic web to narrow their topics.

Real-World Connection

Many colleges ask applicants to write an essay. The topics vary, but often the assignment is to tell about a significant event or person in one's life. College is some years away for students, but essays like the one they are writing are good practice.

4.2

Narrowing Your Topic

Once you've chosen a topic to write about, narrow it by focusing on one significant part: a surprise, a problem, or another interesting experience.

For instance, the story of a trip to the zoo might focus on the tigers. When telling the story, you might include your conversations about tigers on the ride, as well as descriptions of the tigers you saw. You might leave out your trip to the snack stand, though. To narrow your topic, you can use a Topic Web.

Use a Topic Web to Narrow a Topic

These are the steps for creating a Topic Web:

1. Write your topic at the center of a piece of paper. Circle it.
2. Write the parts of your topic next to the circle. Circle them.
3. Write down the things each circled topic makes you think of. Circle each new item, and draw an arrow from it to the circled topic that made you think of it.
4. Choose a group of details that belong together to create a narrowed topic.

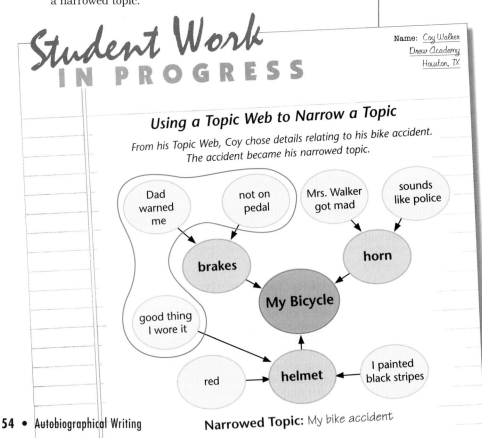

Student Work IN PROGRESS

Name: *Coy Walker*
Drew Academy
Houston, TX

Using a Topic Web to Narrow a Topic

From his Topic Web, Coy chose details relating to his bike accident. The accident became his narrowed topic.

Dad warned me — not on pedal — Mrs. Walker got mad — sounds like police — brakes — horn — My Bicycle — good thing I wore it — red — helmet — I painted black stripes

Narrowed Topic: My bike accident

54 • Autobiographical Writing

Considering Your Audience and Purpose

As you develop your piece of autobiographical writing, think about your **audience**—those who will read the piece. If you are writing for your little brother, you probably will use simple words. If you are writing for a teacher, you will need to explain details your little brother would already know, such as the name of the family cat.

You also need to consider your **purpose** in writing. Autobiographical writing can be used to entertain, to teach a lesson about life, or to capture the personality of a character from your life.

Analyze Your Purpose

To decide on your purpose, think about your topic and ask yourself these questions:

- Is my topic funny or exciting? Is my purpose to **entertain** the reader?
  If so, focus on interesting details and write about them in a funny or exciting way.

- Does my topic involve a lesson I learned? Is my purpose to **instruct** the reader?
  If so, focus on the details that taught you the lesson and draw conclusions from them.

- Am I writing about a particularly interesting person? Can I **capture that character's personality** in words?
  If so, focus on details that bring the character's personality to life.

Gathering Details

Once you have narrowed your topic and considered your purpose, begin gathering the details. Use the strategy of listing and itemizing.

List and Itemize

List words and phrases connected with your topic. Then, circle the most important or most interesting items on your list. Draw arrows between related circled items, and then write a little more about each. Highlight those details that fit together in a story.

Writers in

ACTION

When Paul Zindel decided that he wanted to write for teens, he used the same strategies that you do.

"I thought I knew what kids would want in a book, and so I made a list and followed it."

▼ **Critical Viewing** What do you think made this girl smile? Make up a little story about this picture. **[Speculate]**

Step-by-Step Teaching Guide

Prewriting: Considering Your Audience and Purpose

1. Explain to students that determining your audience involves more than simply identifying age or level of education, but also involves thinking about the audience's background (cultural, ethnic, religious, etc.) and interests.

2. Point out that McKenney might have written her story differently if she were writing for an audience of people who loved to fish. She probably would not emphasize how boring she thought it was, and she probably would have been more enthusiastic about her father's love of fishing.

3. Ask students what kind of reading they prefer—entertaining, instructional, or descriptive.

4. Point out that a story can have more than one purpose. Some writing is both entertaining and instructive, capturing a character's personality can be entertaining, instructive, or both.

Step-by-Step Teaching Guide

Prewriting: Gathering Details

1. Explain to students that details are what create the images, personalities, and emotions of the story, so they are vital to effective writing.

2. Ask students to look around the room and suggest details that make it different from a room that is not a classroom.

3. Give students time to list words and phrases connected to their topics.

4. Explain that, while it is important that details be interesting, it is even more important that they be connected to the topic. If there is a detail that a student loves but that doesn't relate to the story, suggest that it be deleted.

Critical Viewing

Speculate Students may say that she is smiling because she loves her pet.

☑ **ONGOING ASSESSMENT: Monitor and Reinforce**

If students have difficulty determining the audience for their essay, try the following option.

Remind students of other possible audiences: younger siblings or a younger class at school; people who share a specific trait (say, red hair and freckles); an e-mail pen pal; friends and relatives in another country. Students could also write in a different "voice." An autobiography, of course, tells the writer's story. But if the story is about something that happened when the writer was little, it could be written from the point of view of a five-year-old.

Drafting: Present Events in Order; Create Tension

Teaching Resources: Writing Support Transparency 4-D; Writing Support Activity Book 4-3

1. Ask students if they have ever seen a movie that had flashbacks. Point out that, even when a writer moves the story around in time like this, events within the different periods are still presented in order. For example, in Dickens's *A Christmas Carol,* each time Scrooge visits a different time, the events within that time occur in the order in which they occurred.

2. Display the transparency. Review the meaning of *conflict.* Explain that "forces" here refers to impersonal things like nature or time. Wanting to grow up more quickly (or more slowly) is a common conflict. Suggest other nonconfrontational types of conflict *(e.g., being broke and having to earn money for a bike, needing to get in better health to go on a trip, etc.)* Point out that, sometimes the thing the character wants is not a thing, but is simply the resolution of the confict.

3. Have students think about the Model From Literature. If Ruth and Eileen had just gone out in the boat, caught a fish, and gone home, it would have been a boring story. "My Sister the 'Lifesaver'" is interesting because the author includes several conflicts: father likes to fish, but girls don't; Ruth falls in water and Eileen, trying to help her, accidentally hurts rather than helps; everyone makes a fuss over Eileen but not over Ruth, who almost drowned.

4. Have students think about their topics: what is the conflict, who or what is creating the conflict, who is affected by the conflict. Give students copies of the blank organizer so that they can create a conflict map based on their topics.

4.3 Drafting

Shaping Your Writing
Present Events in Order

Most stories have a beginning, a middle, and an end. To help your readers understand your story, it's a good idea to retell events in the order in which they happened.

Think about the items you selected to write about. Which one happened first? What happened next? Make a timeline to show the order of events. As you draft, follow your organizer.

Create Tension

Well-told stories create tension—they keep readers wondering how the story will end. Imagine that you and your sister each want the last piece of pie. When telling this story, it's your job to keep the reader wondering: Who will get it?

Using a Conflict Map Writing about a conflict is one important way to create tension. A **conflict** is a struggle between two or more characters or forces, in which one side stops the other from getting what it wants. In the story of the piece of pie, the conflict is between you and your sister. Before you write, focus your thoughts about the conflict. Make a conflict map similar to the one below.

CONFLICT MAP

Technology Tip

If you use a word processor to write your list, you can cut and paste to move items into groups. Labeling each group will help you organize your information before you begin to write your draft.

⏱ TIME AND RESOURCE MANAGER

Resources
Print: Writing Support Transparency 4-D–E; Writing Support Activity Book 4-3
Technology: Writing Lab CD-ROM, Narration

In-Depth Coverage	Accelerated Pace
• Cover pp. 56–57. • Have students use conflict maps to create tension. • Have students provide elaboration by using the Thoughtshots strategy. **Option** Have students work independently or in small groups with the Writing Lab CD-ROM.	• Have students review pages 56–57 independently, then write their first draft. • Respond to individual drafting issues as necessary.

Providing Elaboration

Picture someone making a sandwich using just bread and nothing else. "That's not really making a *sandwich*," you might say. Similarly, the events you retell in your narrative are just the "bread." To write a finished narrative, you need to add a few other ingredients.

For instance, readers will want to know how the characters in your narrative reacted to events. Use the strategy of Thoughtshots to add such details to your story.

Use Thoughtshots

As you draft, pause for a moment at the end of each paragraph. Then, follow these steps:

1. Scan the paragraph for uses of the word *I*.
2. For each one, ask yourself how you reacted to the events described. For instance, you might have laughed or grown angry or thought, "This is really great!"
3. For each reaction, draw a Thoughtshot in the margin of your draft. (See below for examples.)
4. Inside the Thoughtshot, jot down notes about the reaction.

When it is time to write your final draft, decide which Thoughtshots to include.

Step-by-Step Teaching Guide

Drafting: Providing Elaboration

Teaching Resources: Writing Support Transparency 4-E

1. Use the transparency to show students how Thoughtshots might look in practice. Point out how the writer used Thoughtshots to add more detail about how he felt at various points in the story. Explain that using Thoughtshots can provide the kind of details that enliven writing.

2. Suggest that students consider how characters other than themselves react to circumstances. Remind them that they may not know exactly how these characters felt, but they may be able to figure it out from their actions. For example, characters who throw up their hands and widen their eyes may be startled. Even if the emotions can't be specified with certainty, the reactions can be, whether physical (clenching teeth, smiling, closing eyes, waving arms) or spoken (gasps, shouts, exclaims).

3. Encourage students to add Thoughtshots to their papers. These might be cut-out forms or balloons drawn with markers.

Customize for *Bodily/Kinesthetic Learners*

Partners may find it helpful to act out their conflict maps and/or Thoughtshots.

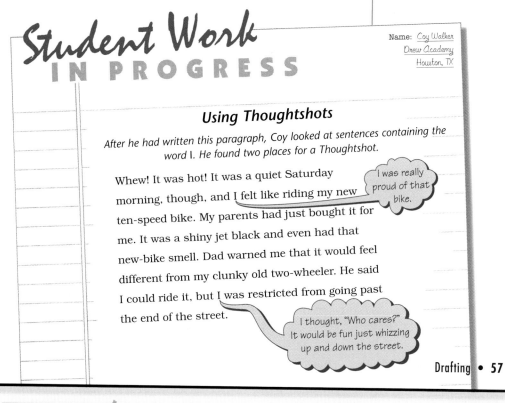

Student Work IN PROGRESS

Name: Coy Walker
Drew Academy
Houston, TX

Using Thoughtshots

After he had written this paragraph, Coy looked at sentences containing the word I. *He found two places for a Thoughtshot.*

Whew! It was hot! It was a quiet Saturday morning, though, and I felt like riding my new ten-speed bike. My parents had just bought it for me. It was a shiny jet black and even had that new-bike smell. Dad warned me that it would feel different from my clunky old two-wheeler. He said I could ride it, but I was restricted from going past the end of the street.

> I was really proud of that bike.

> I thought, "Who cares?" It would be fun just whizzing up and down the street.

Drafting • 57

☑ **ONGOING ASSESSMENT: Monitor and Reinforce**

If students have difficulty providing elaboration, try one of the following options.

Option 1 Have students exchange drafts with a partner. Students should note any places in which further elaboration is necessary.	**Option 2** Remind students that characters' feelings and responses to the events frequently require elaboration to help readers better understand what is going on. Have students carefully scan their drafts for points in which these feelings and responses can be described in greater detail.

Revising: Use Logical Order

Teaching Resources: Writing Support Transparency 4-F

1. Explain to students that, in effective writing, there are connections between its paragraphs that make the piece flow smoothly.

   Point out that the relationships described can be illustrated by the Model From Literature.

   Sequence: Ruth fell in the water in one paragraph, which leads to Eileen trying to help save her in the next.

   Explanation: the paragraph that tells about the father's passion for fishing explains why the two girls are rowing around in the dark in the next paragraph.

   Drama: Ruth sinks beneath the waves in one paragraph; the next paragraph answers the question "will she live," but raises "what will she do to Eileen?"

2. Display the transparency so that students can see how Coy's paragraphs relate to one another.

3. Have students review their writing to identify paragraphs connected with relationships of sequence, explanation, and drama. Encourage them to move, add, or delete paragraphs as needed to create logical order.

Customize for
Gifted/Talented Students

It is common for beginning writers to rely heavily on words like *first, next, then* to show order in a story. Have students come up with four or more examples of ways in which progress can be shown without using any of these words. (Answers will vary; possibilities might include *It started out as. . ., later that day, by 1 o'clock,* etc.)

Revising

After finishing your first draft, look for ways to improve it. Begin revising by reviewing the overall structure of your story.

Revising Your Overall Structure
Use Logical Order

To improve the organization of your draft, use this strategy:

▶ **REVISION STRATEGY**
Identifying Connections

Draw an arrow from each paragraph to the next. Label each arrow with the relationship between the paragraphs it links:

SEQUENCE: The events in one paragraph lead to the events in the next paragraph.

EXPLANATION: One paragraph gives information the reader needs to understand the next paragraph.

DRAMA: One paragraph makes the reader wonder what will happen next. The next paragraph either heightens the curiosity or satisfies it.

If a paragraph is not clearly related to the one before it and the one after it, rewrite it, or consider moving or deleting it.

Student Work
IN PROGRESS

Name: Coy Walker
Drew Academy
Houston, TX

Using Logical Order

When Coy could not determine the connection between two paragraphs, he decided to delete the one that did not add to the action.

...I held the handlebars tight and gained speed. I laughed as I swung wide in order to turn.

explanation

I always loved to do tricks on my bike. I remember watching my cousins popping wheelies. They looked cool.

?

Suddenly, the gate was approaching me fast.... I started to push back on the pedals to lose speed.

drama/sequence

Nothing happened....

58 • Autobiographical Writing

⏱ TIME AND RESOURCE MANAGER

Resources
Print: Writing Support Transparencies 4-F–H
Technology: Writing Lab CD-ROM, Narration

In-Depth Coverage	Accelerated Pace
• Cover pp. 58–61 in class.	• Have students review pages 58–61 independently.
• Have students revise the overall structure of their drafts.	• Have students revise their autobiographical writing independently.
• Do the Grammar in Your Writing on p. 61.	
Options Divide the class into groups for peer review activity. Have students work independently or in small groups with the Writing Lab CD-ROM, focusing on revision activities and tools.	

Revising Your Paragraphs

Open With an Effective Lead

Writing the first sentences of a narrative—the **lead**—is like opening a door. You need to open the door wide and invite the reader in. Use an interest-grabber like one of the following:

- an engaging **description**
  Model car parts lay in oily heaps all over his workbench.
- a **statement** that hints at a story
  Usually, I try to avoid talking to the Moriarty twins.
- **dialogue** or a character's **thoughts**
  "Come in," said the man at the door. "We've been expecting you."
- an exciting **action**
  Running around the corner carrying several cakes, I nearly collided with Mr. Bernstein.

Use the following strategy to make sure your lead is effective.

▶ **REVISION STRATEGY**
Measuring the Effectiveness of Your Lead

Follow these steps to measure the effectiveness of your lead:
1. Create an index card like the one below.
2. Under "Type of Detail," write in the type of detail your first sentence provides. (Refer to the list above.)
3. Under "Reader's Question," write the question that the sentence will make the reader ask.
4. Under "Connects Back/Forward," fill in the words in the next sentences that connect your first sentence to your story.

If you must leave blanks on the card, consider rewriting the lead until you can fill in all the blanks.

MEASURING A LEAD

Our "search party" moved slowly along the path, looking from one side to the next. I was impatient for a sign of Jiffy, my missing turtle, so time seemed to crawl.

1st Sentence		2nd or 3rd Sentence
Type of Detail	**Reader's Question**	**Connects Back/Forward**
Action: search party searching	"What are they searching for?"	"My missing turtle" connects to first sentence; also shows what story is about

Collaborative Writing Tip

Read the lead sentence at the very beginning of your narrative to a group of students. Discuss any questions the sentence raises. What does the audience hope to find out?

Revising: Open With an Effective Lead

Teaching Resources: Writing Support Transparency 4-G

1. Ask students if they have ever started to read a story and quickly lost interest because the beginning just didn't grab them. Explain that many interesting stories probably go unread because they lack an effective lead. Conversely, ask students to recall stories that drew them in right away with an intriguing first sentence.

2. Read aloud these lead sentences from autobiographies:

   My mother started me in newspaper work in 1937 right after my twelfth birthday. (Russell Baker, "Hard as Nails")

   My heart goes out in sympathy to anyone who is making his first appearance before an audience of human beings. (Mark Twain, "Stage Fright")

   When trouble came to me, it didn't involve anybody I thought it would. (Paul Zindel, *The Pigman & Me*)

3. Ask students if these sentences make them want to read more. Why?

4. Display the transparency to show students how to measure the effectiveness of their leads. Give students index cards and encourage them to use the steps of the revision strategy to check the leads in their stories. Explain that it is possible for a lead to leave a blank on the card, but they need to know *why* the omission works for their lead. Otherwise, encourage them to consider a new approach, one that makes it possible to fill in the blanks.

Revising: Vary Sentence Beginnings

Teaching Resources: Writing Support Transparency 4-H

1. Display the transparency to demonstrate how color-coding works. Point out that, as long as colors are different, students don't need to worry too much about the shapes they use.

2. After they have had a chance to color-code their work, ask students to scan their drafts, looking at the beginning of each sentence. Do they notice any pattern, such as too many sentences beginning with *I*?

3. Ask students what could be the effect of several sentences that begin the same way. (Readers could easily lose their place; the writing could sound repetitive or even boring.)

4. Encourage students to revise some sentences if they do not find that too many beginnings are the same.

Integrating Workplace Skills

Explain to students that revising is not a skill limited to short story writing. In business, revising is an important skill, whether it involves rephrasing a memo to make it more diplomatic, revising a proposal to make it more acceptable, or rewriting instructions to make them more logical. The essence of this skill is to be able to look at something and see other possibilities.

4.4

Revising Your Sentences
Vary Sentence Beginnings

Every story has a beat. It can drip along like a leaky faucet, or it can dance about like a butterfly. To give your draft a good rhythm, vary sentence beginnings. Use color-coding to help.

▶ **REVISION STRATEGY**
Color-Coding Sentence Beginnings

Color-code the first word of each sentence, as follows:

Articles include *the*, *a*, and *an*.

Nouns and **pronouns** refer to persons, places, or things. *House*, *Bob*, and *weather* are nouns. *I, you, he, she, it, we,* and *they* are pronouns.

Adjectives tell more about something named by a noun. *Yellow, loud,* and *handsome* are all adjectives.

Adverbs tell more about verbs, adjectives, or other adverbs. *Quickly, brightly,* and *less* are adverbs.

Prepositions show the relationship between things. *In, out, off, on, toward,* and *away* are prepositions.

Find groups of the same colored shape. Rewrite sentences in these groups so that some begin with a different kind of word.

◯ Learn More

To learn more about the different parts of speech, see Chapters 14–18.

Student Work
IN PROGRESS

Name: *Coy Walker*
Drew Academy
Houston, TX

Color-Coding Sentence Beginnings

Coy color-coded his sentence beginnings. When he noticed the number of red rectangles in this paragraph, he rewrote several sentences.

~~I watched the~~ The trees and houses zoomed ~~zoom~~ by in a blur. All I could hear was my own huffing and puffing. The sweat on my back was making my T-shirt cling to me, and it felt sticky and itchy. Then, I was almost home.
Moving to the right side of the street, I squinted my eyes tight, ~~and moved to the right side of the street,~~ preparing to do a daredevil stunt as I turned into my narrow driveway. I held the handlebars tight and gained speed. ~~I laughed as~~ With a laugh, I swung wide in order to turn.

Revising Your Word Choice

Use Precise Nouns

Give your reader a clear picture of events by using precise nouns. For example, if you tell about a family dinner, the sentence "We ate some food" will leave your reader hungry for more details. To feed your reader's imagination, use precise nouns like *lamb chops* instead of general nouns like *food*.

▶ **REVISION STRATEGY**
Highlighting Nouns for Precision

Highlight the nouns in your draft. Then, circle any general nouns. Consider replacing them with precise nouns.

Grammar in Your Writing
Identifying Nouns

A **noun** names a person, place, or thing (including things you can't see). Here are some examples:

Person	Place	Seeable Thing		Unseeable Thing
friend	Texas	raincoat	walking	warmth
Mrs. Oliver	city	dog	flying	brightness
doctor	theater	truck	resting	joy

Find It in Your Reading Identify three nouns in the first paragraph of "My Sister the 'Lifesaver'" by Ruth McKenney on page 50. For each, explain whether it is precise or general.

Find It in Your Writing Find five general nouns in your draft. For each, explain what picture you wanted to give a reader. If the noun does not give enough information to create that picture, replace it with a precise word.

To learn more about nouns, see Chapter 14.

Peer Review

Process Share

Read your draft to a small group. To start off a discussion, your classmates should ask the following questions:

• How did you come up with the idea for your narrative?

• What problems did you have while writing? What did you do to solve them?

• What are you planning to do next to your draft?

Ask group members for suggestions, and consider using their ideas as you create your final draft.

Revising • 61

Step-by-Step Teaching Guide

Grammar in Your Writing: Identifying Nouns

1. Have students skim their drafts and underline or circle the nouns. Then ask them to read the sentences carefully to see if any vague nouns should be more precise.

2. Point out that readers do not need to visualize everything. For instance, Ruth McKenney mentions a lodge at the fishing camp. She doesn't describe the lodge or even use an adjective—because the lodge is not important to the point of her story.

Find It in Your Reading

Nouns identified could include *dealings, lifesavers, sister, mistake, father, Michigan, camp, life, trolling, bass, lake, day, night, home, lodge, Eileen, time, rowboat, section, lake, sun, worms, variety, fish, gillies, business* (precise nouns are underlined). Students may say that they do not need to know more than the general nouns tell them. If they think some nouns are too vague, they should explain why.

Find It in Your Writing

Suggest that students brainstorm for several precise nouns for some of the general nouns before selecting one precise noun as a replacement.

Step-by-Step Teaching Guide

Peer Review: Process Share

1. Keep groups quite small—2–4 students listening to the reader is ideal, if it can be managed.

2. Remind students who are reviewing a classmate's work to offer concrete suggestions for revision. For instance, "You write about a 'building.' A more specific word would help me see the building. Was it a library, a school, a factory, or some other kind of building?"

☑ **ONGOING ASSESSMENT: Prerequisite Skills**

If students have difficulty capitalizing proper nouns, you may find it helpful to review the following to assure coverage or prerequisite knowledge.

In the Textbook	Print Resources	Technology
Nouns, pp. 294–298	Grammar Exercise Workbook, pp. 5–6	On-Line Exercise Bank, Section 14.1

Editing and Proofreading

1. Have students check their writing to make sure they have used logical order and precise nouns.

2. Then have them proofread their writing to catch mistakes in grammar, spelling, and punctuation. Encourage them to use dictionaries when they are uncertain about precise meaning or spelling.

Integrating Technology Skills

If students have access to a computer, suggest that they key in their stories and then use the spelling program to check for errors. However, underscore two important things: spelling programs don't know every word and may challenge them on things that are spelled correctly; these programs don't know if the word chosen is wrong if it is spelled correctly (the/they, to/two/too).

Grammar in Your Writing: Capitalizing Proper Nouns

1. Ask volunteers to suggest some proper nouns. Their suggestions may include nouns that name people, states, cities, countries, rivers, ships, planes, and buildings. Remind them that proper nouns are capitalized.

2. Invite students to brainstorm at least one example of a proper noun in each category listed above.

Find It in Your Reading

Answers will vary but might include: *Michigan* and *Eileen* are capitalized because they are proper nouns. *I* is always capitalized.

Other nouns in the paragraph are capitalized because they begin sentences. All nouns that are not capitalized are general or common nouns, not proper nouns.

Find It in Your Writing

Point out some common errors that students should look for—
Lake Superior versus *the lake*,
Johnny versus *my brother*,
Ms. Valdes versus *our teacher*, etc.

4.5 Editing and Proofreading

Errors in your autobiographical writing can confuse readers or make them impatient. Before you create your final draft, carefully review your essay. Check for errors in spelling, grammar, punctuation, and usage.

Focusing on Capitalization

Check to make sure that you have capitalized

- the first words of sentences.
- people's names.
- place names.
- the first word and all important words in the titles of books, movies, songs, and other works.

Grammar in Your Writing
Capitalization of Proper Nouns

Capitalize words when they are used as the name by which someone or something is called.

> I rode the bus with Aunt Ettie.
> We went to Lake Michigan on vacation.

Do not capitalize words that are not used as names (unless they appear at the beginning of a sentence).

> I rode the bus with my aunt.
> We went to the lake on vacation.

Find It in Your Reading Choose three capitalized words and three uncapitalized words in the first paragraph of "My Sister the 'Lifesaver'" by Ruth McKenney on page 50. For each, explain why it is or is not capitalized.

Find It in Your Writing Review your draft for words you may have capitalized incorrectly. For each, ask yourself: Is this word used as the name of a specific person, place, or thing?

For more on capitalization, see Chapter 27.

⏱ TIME AND RESOURCE MANAGER

Resources
Print: Scoring Rubrics on Transparency, Chapter 4; Writing Assessment: Scoring Rubric and Scoring Models for Autobiographical Essay
Technology: Writing Lab CD-ROM, Autobiographical Incident

In-Depth Coverage	Accelerated Pace
• Cover pp. 62–65 in class, including Grammar in Your Writing. • Distribute and review Proofreading Checklist and Correction Marks. **Option** Have students work on their own with the editing and evaluation sections of the Writing Lab CD-ROM.	• Assign pp. 62–65 for independent student review. • Students edit and proofread their drafts for homework. • Students present their final drafts.

4.6 Publishing and Presenting

Building Your Portfolio

Consider these ideas for publishing and presenting your work:

1. **Skit** With a group, create a skit from your autobiographical piece. Rehearse what each character will say and what he or she will do, and present your skit to the class.

2. **Magazine Submission** Type your work, and mail it to a magazine that publishes student writing. Include a letter introducing yourself and explaining why your story should be published.

Reflecting on Your Writing

Jot down a few notes for your portfolio about the process of writing an autobiographical piece. Begin by answering the following questions:

- What was the hardest part of writing your piece? What was the easiest? Explain why.
- As you wrote, what did you learn about yourself?

 Internet Tip

To review essays scored using this rubric, visit **www.phschool.com**

Rubric for Self-Assessment

Use the following criteria to evaluate your autobiographical writing.

	Score 4	Score 3	Score 2	Score 1
Audience and Purpose	Contains an engaging introduction; successfully entertains or presents a theme	Contains a somewhat engaging introduction; entertains or presents a theme	Contains an introduction; attempts to entertain or to present a theme	Begins abruptly or confusingly; leaves purpose unclear
Organization	Creates an interesting, clear narrative; told from a consistent point of view	Presents a clear sequence of events; told from a specific point of view	Presents a mostly clear sequence of events; contains inconsistent points of view	Presents events without logical order; lacks a consistent point of view
Elaboration	Provides insight into and develops a sequence of events	Contains many details that develop a sequence of events	Contains some details that develop a sequence of events	Contains few or no details to develop a sequence of events
Use of Language	Uses word choice and tone to reveal story's theme; contains no errors in grammar, punctuation, or spelling	Uses interesting and fresh word choices; contains few errors in grammar, punctuation, and spelling	Uses some clichés and trite expressions; contains some errors in grammar, punctuation, and spelling	Uses uninspired word choices; has many errors in grammar, punctuation, and spelling

Publishing and Presenting • 63

Step-by-Step Teaching Guide

Publishing and Presenting

1. Point out to students that parts of the story may need to be rewritten to work as a skit. More dialogue may be needed, and passages of "I thought about it" may need to be reduced. This new "script" version of the story can be created by the original writer or can be accomplished as a group project.

2. Students may want to add photographs, drawings, or other art to their writing for a bulletin-board display.

3. Students can input their autobiographies on a computer and create a class book. They can think of a title and then use a drawing program to design a cover.

ASSESS

Step-by-Step Teaching Guide

Assessment

Teaching Resources: Scoring Rubrics on Transparency, Formal Assessment, Chapter 4

1. Display the Scoring Rubric transparency and review the criteria in class.

2. Before students proceed with self-assessment, you may wish to review the Final Draft of the Student Work in Progress on pages 64–65. Have students score the Final Draft in one or more of the rubric categories. For example, how would students score the essay in terms of audience and purpose?

3. In addition to student self-assessment, you may wish to use the following assessment options.

   - score student essays yourself, using the rubric and scoring models from Writing Assessment.

   - review the Standardized Test Preparation Workshop on pages 70–71 and have students respond to a persuasive writing prompt within a time limit.

   - administer the Chapter 4 Test from Formal Assessment in Teaching Resources to assess students' grasp of concepts presented.

☑ **ONGOING ASSESSMENT: Assess Mastery**

Use one of the following options to assess final drafts of students' autobiographical essays.

Self-Assessment Ask students to score their essay, using the rubric provided. Then have students write a paragraph reflecting on the most valuable strategy they learned in completing this essay.	**Teacher Assessment** Use the rubric and the scoring models provided in Writing Assessment, Autobiographical Essay to score students' work.

Teaching from the Final Draft

1. Help students see that "Those Are the Brakes" includes key elements of autobiographical writing: a lead that catches the reader's interest, real events that happened to the author, a conflict, and Coy's reactions to the events.

2. Ask students what audience and purpose Coy probably had in mind when writing this. *(audience: kids his age; purpose: entertain, possibly inform)*

continued

Critical Viewing

Speculate Students may say that the child loves his bike, because he seems very happy.

4.7 *Student Work*
IN PROGRESS

FINAL DRAFT

Those Are the Brakes

Coy Walker
Drew Academy
Houston, Texas

◀ **Critical Viewing**
How might the child in this picture feel about his bicycle? **[Speculate]**

Whew! It was hot! It was a quiet Saturday morning, though, and I felt like riding my new ten-speed bike. My parents had just bought it for me, and I was so proud of it. It was a shiny jet black and even had that new-bike smell. Dad warned me that it would feel different from my clunky old two-wheeler. He said I could ride it, but I was restricted from going past the end of the street. I thought, "Who cares?" It would be fun just whizzing up and down the street.

As I started my little cruise, Dad called out something. The wind was whipping me in the face, though, and I couldn't really hear. I thought I heard him say something like "Don't break it" and something else about holding the handlebars. But I was having too much fun to stop and ask him to repeat himself. Dad was such a worrywart. Of course, I wouldn't break it. Of course, I would hold the handlebars.

I rode back and forth on the street for about fifteen minutes. The trees and houses zoomed by in a blur. All I could hear was my own huffing and puffing. The sweat on my back was making my T-shirt cling to me, and it felt sticky and itchy. Then, I was almost home. Moving to the right side of the street, I squinted my eyes tight, preparing to do a daredevil stunt as I turned into my narrow driveway. I held the handlebars tight and gained speed. With a laugh, I swung wide in order to turn.

Coy's lead—his first sentences—brings the reader into his story right away.

Coy includes details about his own reactions to events. Each detail helps the reader feel a part of the action.

Coy's story is organized logically. He starts at the beginning (getting the bike). Then, he tells what happened next (his first ride).

Suddenly, the gate was approaching me fast. I needed to slow down, so that I could maneuver into the driveway safely. My old bike had pedal brakes, so naturally I started to push back on the pedals to lose speed.

Nothing happened. I pushed harder with my feet, but the pedals just went around and around in the wrong direction. I could feel them spinning like a wheel of fortune.

Uh-oh. The next thing I knew, I was crashing into our four-foot hurricane fence. Seconds later, I went flying across the top. But that's not the worst part. During my flight, the gate caught my arm, scraping across it. I looked like I'd been in a battle.

Mom and Dad heard the noise and came running outside. I was surprised to see that Dad was almost amused. He said that he could remember his own "Fence Incident." Then he told me that now I was a "soldier" and had received my "war wounds." Mom rubbed peroxide and warm water on me, and it stung like a swarm of bees.

"What happened?" Dad asked.

"The pedal brakes didn't work," I said.

"Oh, no," Dad said and laughed. "I called out to you to remind you. The brakes are on the handlebars, the brakes are on the handlebars."

Coy creates a strong conflict: Will he succeed in controlling his bike, or will the bike go out of control?

Coy's main purpose is to entertain. His conclusion shows the amusing side of the events.

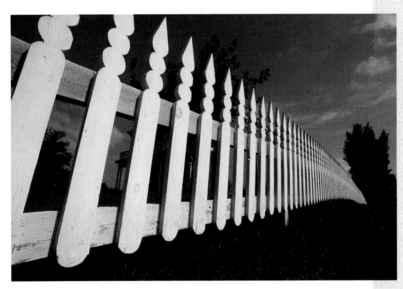

◄ **Critical Viewing** What feelings can you associate with the fence in this picture? Do they match the feelings inspired by the fence in Coy's story? Explain. **[Connect]**

3. If Coy did intend this to inform, what might the "lesson" be? *(don't assume everything works the same; find out where the brakes are; listen to your dad; etc.)*

4. Have students analyze the details that were included. Did Coy succeed in eliminating unneeded details? Is there any additional information that students think should have been included?

5. Ask students if they feel that Coy's story could be refined further.

6. Ask students what elements might help them understand how to approach their own writing.

Critical Viewing

Connect Students may say they associate happy memories of their childhood with this fence.

Lesson Objectives

1. To write a firsthand biography appropriate to audience and purpose.
2. To find a subject for a firsthand biography.
3. To gather details about the subject.
4. To draft, revise, edit, and publish the biography.

Step-by-Step Teaching Guide

Firsthand Biography

Teaching Resources: Writing Support Transparency, 4-I; Writing Support Activity Book, 4-4

1. Go around the room and have each student name a person he or she would like to write about. Have the student explain briefly why this person would be a good subject for a biography. You may want to demonstrate by taking the first turn yourself.

2. If the people students want to write about are alive, available, and willing, students may want to interview them before beginning to write. Make sure students understand that this step is not necessary; they can write about their subjects from memory if they prefer. Simply suggest it as a possibility for those who are interested.

3. Make sure students understand that *firsthand* means they must write about a person they know. Celebrities whom students do not know personally are not acceptable subjects for this assignment.

4. Use the transparency to demonstrate making a timeline for a biography. Point out that a timeline ensures that a writer has not left out any important events. It also ensures that the writer will remember the order in which the events happened. Pass out blank copies of Organizer 6–2 so that students can make timelines for their subjects.

continued

Connected Assignment
Firsthand Biography

A biography tells the story of someone's life. A **firsthand biography** tells the story of someone whom the writer knows or knew personally. Because of the writer's perspective, this kind of biography can give readers unique insights into its subject. A short firsthand biography focuses on one event or period in the subject's life.

A firsthand biography includes

- a subject other than the narrator.
- an organized retelling of events from the life of the subject.
- a first-person point of view—the work is narrated using the pronoun *I*.
- an insight into the subject only the writer could provide.

Prewriting To find a subject for your firsthand biography, list parts of your life, such as "School," "Sports," "Family," and so on. For each heading, jot down your memories of that part of your life. Choose the person you will write about from among these memories. You might choose a topic in one of the following categories:

- **Firsthand Biography of Someone Who Influenced You** Write about a person you know, such as a family member, friend, or teacher, who taught you something important, either in words or by example.

- **Firsthand Biography of a "Character"** Among the people you know, who causes the most trouble? Makes the funniest jokes? Tell the story of such a person.

Once you have selected the person about whom you wish to write, focus on an event involving him or her or on a special characteristic he or she has. To find this focus, list the memories you associate with the person. Choose the most revealing or entertaining memory for your focus.

Then, gather details that reveal your subject's personality and special qualities. Include the following kinds of details:

- things he or she has said
- major accomplishments
- memorable characteristics
- incidents that reveal how he or she has influenced you.

66 • Autobiographical Writing

▲ **Critical Viewing** What kind of firsthand biography might one of these kids write about the other—serious or entertaining? **[Draw Conclusions]**

Critical Viewing

Draw Conclusions Students should say the kids would write an entertaining first-hand biography.

Drafting Once you have focused your topic, organize the events in your story. Retelling events in the order in which they occurred (chronological order) is one of the clearest ways to organize your story. If you select this type of organization, use a timeline like the one below to chart the events of your story.

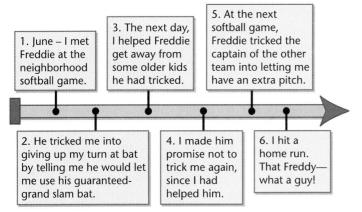

1. June – I met Freddie at the neighborhood softball game.

2. He tricked me into giving up my turn at bat by telling me he would let me use his guaranteed-grand slam bat.

3. The next day, I helped Freddie get away from some older kids he had tricked.

4. I made him promise not to trick me again, since I had helped him.

5. At the next softball game, Freddie tricked the captain of the other team into letting me have an extra pitch.

6. I hit a home run. That Freddy— what a guy!

You might also consider starting with the most important part of your story, and then filling in less important details.

As you draft, make sure that you narrate events in the first person (use the pronoun *I*). Although your focus is on showing your subject as he or she is, elaborate on your story by including your own reactions to events.

Revising and Editing After you have finished your draft, review its overall structure. Make the following kinds of revisions:

- **Check Sequence** Make sure that you have presented events and descriptions in a logical sequence.

- **Add Transitions** Use transitional words, such as *afterward*, *before*, *during*, and *as a result*, to show the order and relation of events clearly.

- **Elaborate** Circle places in your draft where the events are most exciting or where you focus on an important part of your subject's character. Add details at these points to give a complete picture of these events or characteristics.

After you have revised your biography, proofread your paper to make sure that there are no errors in spelling, grammar, or punctuation.

Publishing and Presenting Illustrate your firsthand biography with photographs or drawings. Make copies, and place each in a cover or binder. Present a copy to the subject of the piece. Consider presenting copies to your subject's friends or family or to an organization to which he or she belongs.

Connected Assignment: Firsthand Biography • 67

5. Make sure students understand that they are not required to tell their stories in chronological order; a different text structure may serve some students' purposes better. For example, a student might want to write a biography that explores why her older brother decided to join the Peace Corps. This writer might want to describe events and then analyze possible causes, rather than simply narrating events in chronological order.

6. Emphasize the importance of the biographer's personal reactions to his or her subject. The great value of a firsthand biography is that it offers insight into a subject— insight that a writer who never met the subject cannot provide. The student mentioned in Step 5, for example, may have had long conversations with her brother in which he wrestled with his decision to bypass college and join the Peace Corps. A writer who never met her brother would only be able to speculate about his motives.

7. After all students have written their biographies, have a class discussion about students' views of firsthand biographies versus biographies written by writers and historians who never knew their subjects. What are the advantages and disadvantages of each type? What has this writing assignment taught students about the value of each kind of biography?

Customize for
More Advanced Students

Have each student choose a significant figure from history whom they admire, such as Helen Keller or W.E.B. DuBois. Challenge them to find a firsthand biography of the person (allow them to include autobiographies for this assignment). Have students read an excerpt from the firsthand biography and then compare it to an objective biography (such as an encyclopedia article) on the same person. Finally, have students compare and contrast the two.

Lesson Objectives

1. To interpret visual meaning in works of art.

2. To analyze a painting.

3. To write a journal entry describing the sources of inspiration for a painting.

Critical Viewing

Analyze Students should say that the painting is crowded because there is little open space around the figure; because he is in the corner of the room, and because his head blocks the window, which might have opened up the space.

Step-by-Step Teaching Guide

Interpreting Visual Meaning

1. Tell students that in spite of the critics' failure to appreciate his work, Van Gogh persisted. He spent his final years (1888–1890) in the south of France, where he worked tirelessly, painting hundreds of landscapes and portraits. Explain that Van Gogh's head is bandaged in the self-portrait at the left because he had cut off part of one ear in a fit of despair. He committed himself to a hospital soon after but continued to paint until the day he died.

2. Encourage students to spend some time in the library looking at reproductions of Van Gogh's works. If there are any Van Goghs in a museum in your area, try to arrange a class trip or encourage students to go on their own.

3. Some students may be interested in a screening of the film *Lust for Life,* a biography of Van Gogh starring Kirk Douglas and Anthony Quinn. The film is splendidly photographed and contains closeup views of many of Van Gogh's most famous paintings.

Spotlight on the Humanities

Interpreting Visual Meaning

Focus on the Visual Arts: Van Gogh's *Starry Night*

Writing an autobiographical narrative is one way to show the world something about yourself. Painting a self-portrait is another. The self-portrait on this page is by Dutch painter Vincent van Gogh (1853–1890).

Van Gogh's life was not a happy one. He was troubled by mental illness. Few people appreciated his work during his lifetime. Of the 1,500 paintings and drawings he produced, he sold only one.

Van Gogh's Art Today, though, van Gogh is considered one of the most important modern artists. People value his powerful, dynamic style.

Van Gogh's self-portrait tells you not only what he looked like. It also tells you something about his personality. You can surmise from the many thick brushstrokes and the vivid colors that van Gogh was a passionate painter. He believed in the power of paint to show us new beauty in the world.

When you look at a painting, notice features such as the brushstrokes and the artist's choice of colors. You may discover for yourself some of the beauty van Gogh found in painting.

Music Connections Van Gogh's life and paintings inspired the songwriter Don McLean. In 1971, McLean wrote a tribute to the painter and his artistic originality, called "Vincent (Starry, Starry Night)."

Literary Connections In 1991, the novelist Alice Walker published a poem praising van Gogh's work, entitled "If There Was Any Justice."

Autobiographical Writing Activity: Imaginary Journal Entry
Using library resources, find a reproduction of van Gogh's painting *Starry Night*. Then, as van Gogh, write an entry in your journal about what inspired you to paint the work. Was it a piece of music? An event? Or an actual starlit evening? Explain the feelings and thoughts that led to your painting the scene as you did.

Self-portrait with Bandaged Ear, Vincent van Gogh, Giraudon

▲ **Critical Viewing** Describe van Gogh's use of space in this self-portrait. Is the painting crowded or spacious? **[Analyze]**

▲ **Critical Viewing** What might a poet such as Alice Walker be interested in van Gogh's life and work? **[Hypothesize]**

68 • Autobiographical Writing

Viewing and Representing

Activity You might allow students to write about any Van Gogh painting of their choice, rather than limiting them to *Starry Night*. Require students to study a reproduction of their chosen painting each day for one week. After looking at it, they should write out their reactions to it. At the end of the week, they can begin their journal entries, using these notes as material.

Critical Viewing

Hypothesize Students might say that as an African American and a woman, Walker could empathize with Van Gogh's struggle to succeed in a conservative and unimaginative society.

Media and Technology Skills

► *Lesson Objectives*
1. To create a photo essay.
2. To organize photographs so that they tell a story.

Making Meaning With Visual Images

Activity: Create a Photo Essay

Like van Gogh (see previous page), you can show important things about a person by using images. Learn more about taking photographs, and create a photo essay of someone you know.

Learn About It

Read About It Leaf through an introductory book on taking pictures. Then, read through the owner's manual of your camera to familiarize yourself with its specific features. Get the help of an experienced user of the camera if necessary.

Think About Variables By using different settings on the camera and by taking pictures in different circumstances, you can create different meanings in the photographs you take. For example, a picture taken in a dark room with a flash will look different from a picture of the room with sunlight pouring through the windows.

Experiment Take a few pictures of the same object or scene with different settings or in different conditions. Keep track of the settings and conditions. Look over your developed pictures and take notes on the effects of your choices.

Apply It Take a series of photographs that reveal something about a family member or friend. Choose objects, people, places, and events that tell something about the person, and photograph the person in connection with them. Use a chart like the one below to plan your pictures. Display your results to the class.

Aspect of Person	Type of Photograph	Special Considerations
Mom loves her garden—show her sitting in garden.	Portrait	• Take picture on cheerful, sunny day. • Show some of Mom's favorite roses in the background.

Media and Technology Skills • 69

Types of Images

Action Shot
A shot of a person performing a specific action.

Portrait
A close-up of a person or his or her face.

Still Life
A shot of a group of objects. By selecting the right objects, a photographer can use a still life to show something about their owner.

Making Meaning With Visual Images

Teaching Resources: Writing Support Transparency, 4-J; Writing Support Activity Book, 4-5

1. Not all students may have access to cameras. Students who are exceptionally talented artists may want to draw or paint pictures for their photo essays instead of taking photographs. You might also suggest that students buy small disposable cameras in drugstores; these cameras are quite inexpensive and should suffice for this assignment.

2. Emphasize that students must not use anyone else's camera without the person's permission. Cameras are expensive and people using them need to follow instructions and handle the cameras with care so that they don't damage them.

3. Use the transparency to demonstrate planning a photo essay. Give students copies of the blank organizer to fill out as they work on their own photo essays. You might also bring in magazines like *National Geographic* to show students professional models of photo essays.

Customize for
Visual/Spatial Learners

Van Gogh (see page 68) painted numerous self-portraits. Together, they constitute a sort of "photo essay" of himself in paint. Dutch painter Rembrandt van Rijn is also famous for his many self-portraits. Have each student choose one of these two painters, study his self-portraits, and put together a photo essay on him. Students should accompany their photo essays with written essays describing their interpretation of the painter from his self-portraits.

Lesson Objectives

1. To use narration to respond to writing prompts.
2. To use details to support an opinion.
3. To draft, revise, edit, and proofread an essay.

Using Narration to Respond to Writing Prompts

1. Remind students that the verb *to narrate* means *to tell a story.* Point out the phrase *give your own experiences* in the writing prompt. This phrase suggests that the answer should be given in narrative form. Point out that since *experiences* is in the plural, the answer will probably consist of a series of short stories.

2. Remind students that in a timed essay, they may not be able to discuss every field-trip experience of their lives. In the prewriting stage, students should list the field trips that stand out most prominently in their memories as either worthwhile and fun or dreary and boring, depending on the position they wish to take. For the purpose of this test question, three experiences will probably be enough for a good, detailed answer to the question.

3. When students revise their drafts, they should eliminate irrelevant details. Field trips are great fun for many students because they are able to spend time with their friends in a situation more relaxed than that of the classroom, but details on this aspect of a field trip would not be relevant for the question asked in this essay.

Standardized Test Preparation Workshop

Using Narration to Respond to Writing Prompts

The writing prompts on standardized tests often measure your ability to tell stories for a specific purpose. The following are the criteria upon which such writing will be evaluated:

- Do you organize details in a logical sequence?
- Do you choose words and write in a style that fits the purpose and audience named in the response? (For example, a letter to a company should be more formal than a letter to a friend.)
- Do you use transitions to create a unified, coherent narrative?
- Do you elaborate on events with the effective use of description, characterization, and other details?
- Do you use correct grammar, spelling, and punctuation?

Following is an example of a writing prompt that requires you to use elements of narrative writing. Use the suggestions on the following page to help you respond. The clocks show the suggested percentage of your test-taking time to devote to each stage.

Test Tip

When outlining events for a narrative response to a prompt, place a star next to the most important ones. Focus on these events as you draft.

Sample Writing Situation

> Your school is considering cutting back on field trips. Some think that the money spent on these trips would be better spent on books for the library or on computers that will provide Internet access.
>
> In an essay for the school newspaper, argue for or against eliminating school field trips in favor of buying more library books or computers for Internet access. To support your opinion, give your own experiences on field trips and with the school library and computers for research.

70 • Autobiographical Writing

✎ TEST-TAKING TIP

Warn students that the reasons presented in a written argument must try to persuade a specific audience. In this workshop, the intended audience is made up of school officials who must make a decision about funding. Therefore, students need to provide reasons that these people would find convincing. Have students decide whether the following reasons for enjoying field trips would persuade school officials to continue funding them.

- Students like getting out of the classroom. (not persuasive)

- Discipline is more relaxed on a field trip. (not persuasive)
- In the museum, a student can see the texture of a painting and its actual size and colors—things they cannot see in the small reproductions in library books. (persuasive)

Point out that if the prompt had asked students to persuade other students, their essays might include the first two reasons. Students should always note who the intended audience is, because this will affect the content of their essays.

Prewriting

Allow close to one fourth of your time for prewriting.

Gather Details Begin by gathering information about your experiences on field trips, on the one hand, and with using school library and computer facilities, on the other.

Take a Stand Review your notes on your experiences. Form an opinion on the issue raised in the prompt—whether school money is better spent on field trips or on extra books and computers.

Focus Your Support Next, use the strategy of listing and itemizing to focus on experiences that show something about the value of field trips. (To learn the steps for listing and itemizing, see page 55.)

Drafting

Allow almost half of your time for drafting.

Organization After you have gathered details, make an outline to organize them. Write a sentence for each of your main points. Underneath each main point, list the experiences that illustrate that point. Each story you tell to support your main idea may be organized in chronological order (the order in which events occurred). For instance, one main point might be that field trips motivate students to learn more.

Introduction, Body, and Conclusion After organizing details, begin drafting. Start off with an introductory paragraph that states your opinion and sums up your major reason for it. Then, discuss each of your main ideas in a paragraph or two. In these paragraphs, retell the experiences that support each point. Finally, conclude by restating your opinion in a memorable way.

Revising, Editing, and Proofreading

Allow almost one fourth of your time to revise and edit. Use the last few minutes to proofread your work.

Strengthen Your Case Review your draft. Make sure that each experience you retell clearly supports the point it should support. Eliminate details that distract from your point. Add transitions, such as *next, then,* and *for this reason,* where necessary to make the relation of events and ideas clear.

Make Corrections Check for errors in spelling, grammar, and punctuation. When making changes, place one line through text that you want to eliminate. Use a caret (^) to indicate the places where you want to add words.

Customize for
ESL Students

These students may find field trips especially valuable because they provide a direct experience of history and culture, an experience not obscured by language barriers. All students can get something out of looking at paintings, listening to a concert, or walking through a historic site such as Theodore Roosevelt's birthplace. Suggest this theory to students and see how they respond. They may be able to use material from this discussion in their essays.

Customize for
Less Advanced Students

Encourage students who have trouble with writing assignments to read the writing prompt and write down their immediate reaction to it. A student reading this writing prompt, for example, might respond: *Cut back on field trips? What a rotten idea! Field trips are great because you get to see actual places and works of art instead of just reading about them.* Their immediate reactions are likely to be strong, and a strong opinion is a good beginning for an essay. Having established their opinions, the students can then think back about specific trips they were on that will support their opinion.

Time and Resource Manager

In-Depth Lesson Plan

	LESSON FOCUS	PRINT AND MEDIA RESOURCES
DAY 1	**Introduction to Short Story Writing** Students learn key elements of short story writing and analyze the Model From Literature (pp. 72–77).	*Writers at Work* **Videotape**, Narration *Writing Lab* **CD-ROM**, Narration
DAY 2	**Prewriting** Students choose and narrow a topic, consider their audience and purpose, and gather information (pp. 78–81).	**Teaching Resources** *Writing Support Transparencies* 5-A–C; *Writing Support Activity Book* 5-1
DAY 3	**Drafting** Students organize their ideas and write their first drafts (pp. 82–83).	**Teaching Resources** *Writing Support Transparencies* 5-D–E; *Writing Support Activity Book,* 5-2–3
DAY 4	**Revising** Students revise their drafts in terms of overall structure, paragraphs, sentences, and word choice (pp. 84–88).	*Writing Lab* **CD-ROM**, Narration **Teaching Resources** *Writing Support Transparencies* 5-F–H
DAY 5	**Editing and Proofreading; Publishing and Presenting** Students check their work for accuracy and correctness and present their final drafts (pp. 89–90).	**Teaching Resources** *Scoring Rubrics on Transparency,* Ch. 5; *Formal Assessment,* Ch. 5

Accelerated Lesson Plan

	LESSON FOCUS	PRINT AND MEDIA RESOURCES
DAY 1	**Drafting** Students review characteristics for short story writing, select topics, and write drafts (pp. 72–83).	*Writers at Work* **Videotape**, Narration *Writing Lab* **CD-ROM**, Narration **Teaching Resources** *Writing Support Transparencies* 5-A–E; *Writing Support Activity Book* 5-1–3
DAY 2	**Revising to Presenting** Students work individually or with peers to revise, edit, and proofread their work for presentation (pp. 84–90).	**Teaching Resources** *Writing Support Transparencies* 5-F–H; *Scoring Rubrics on Transparency,* Ch. 5; *Formal Assessment,* Ch. 5

Options for Adapting Lesson Plans

HOMEWORK

Have students complete any stage of the lesson for homework.

FEATURES

Extend coverage with the Connected Assignment (p. 93), Spotlight on the Humanities (p. 94), Media and Technology Skills (p. 95), and the Standardized Test Preparation Workshop (p. 96).

TECHNOLOGY

Students can complete any stage of the lesson on computer. Have them print out their completed work.

INTEGRATED SKILLS COVERAGE

Integrating Grammar
Identifying Verbs SE p. 87
Punctuating Dialogue SE p. 89

Reading/Writing Connection
Reading Strategy SE p. 74
Writing Application SE p. 77

Vocabulary
Integrating Vocabulary Skills ATE p. 81

Language
Language Highlight ATE p. 91

Real-World Connection
ATE p. 80

Viewing and Representing
Critical Viewing SE pp. 72, 74, 75, 76, 77, 82, 85, 91, 92, 93, 94
Viewing and Representing ATE p. 94

BLOCK SCHEDULING

Pacing Suggestions
For 90-minute Blocks
• Have students complete the Prewriting and Drafting stages in a single period.
• Focus one class period on Revising and Editing and Publishing and Presenting. Allow at least 30 minutes for peer revision.

Resources for Varying Instruction
• *Writing Lab* **CD-ROM** If your students have access to hardware, a 90-minute block provides an ideal opportunity for students to work on computer.
• *Writers at Work* **Videotape** Show the Short Story segment in class.

Professional Development Support
• *How to Manage Instruction in the Block* This Teaching Resource provides management and activity suggestions.

ASSESSMENT SUPPORT

Standardized Test Preparation Workshop SE p. 96; ATE p. 91

Standardized Test Preparation Workbook, pp. 9–10

Scoring Rubrics on Transparency, Ch. 5

Formal Assessment, Ch. 5

Writing Assessment and Portfolio Management

MEDIA AND TECHNOLOGY

For the Student
• *Writing Lab* **CD-ROM**, Narration

For the Teacher
• *Writers at Work* **Videotape**, Narration
• *Resource Pro* **CD-ROM**

MEETING INDIVIDUAL NEEDS

Less Advanced Students ATE pp. 81, 97; See also Ongoing Assessments ATE pp. 73, 80, 83, 85, 87, 88, 90

More Advanced Students ATE pp. 92, 97

ESL Students ATE p. 78

Visual/Spatial Learners ATE pp. 76, 92

Interpersonal Learners ATE p. 85

WRITING AND GRAMMAR WEB SITE

The Interactive Writing and Grammar Web site provides a wide array of support for students, teachers and parents. Writing support includes:

• Interactive revision checkers
• Scoring rubrics with complete models

www.phschool.com

LITERATURE CONNECTIONS

Related selections from *Prentice Hall Literature: Timeless Voices, Timeless Themes,* Copper:

"Overdoing It," Anton Chekhov, SE p. 75

"Zlateh the Goat," Isaac Bashevis Singer, SE p. 79

Lesson Objectives

1. To define a short story.
2. To identify three different types of short stories.
3. To read and interpret short story.
4. To utilize strategies for choosing a topic.
5. To use a conflict map to identify story's conflict.
6. To identify audience and purpose.
7. To use Listing and Itemizing to gather details.
8. To use a plot diagram to plan plot.
9. To use sensory details to provide elaboration.
10. To use a Bead Chart to create logical connections.
11. To use strategies to revise paragraphs to show instead of tell.
12. To use strategies to revise transitions and word choice.
13. To participate in peer review.
14. To proofread and correctly format dialogue.
15. To reflect on experience of writing story.
16. To read and review final draft of Student Work in Progress.

Critical Viewing

Interpret Students may mention the story of St. George slaying the dragon.

Chapter 5 *Narration*
Short Story

St. George and the Dragon, Paolo Uccello

Short Stories in Everyday Life

People love to tell stories. You might tell your friends stories when you talk on the phone. You might hear family stories when you get together with relatives—like the one about what you did when you were two or the one about how your grandfather survived a tornado!

True stories like these conjure up other times or places. Once you start writing made-up stories, though, there's no telling where you will stop! A short story can take you right out of your own time and place into a world of imagination.

In this chapter, you'll learn strategies for writing a short story that will hook your readers' interest and even open up a new world to them—the unique world of *your* imagination.

▲ **Critical Viewing**
This painting is an illustration for a famous story—can you guess which one? If you don't know the story, explain what story you might make up about the picture. **[Interpret]**

72 • Narration

⏱ TIME AND RESOURCE MANAGER

Resources
Technology: Writers at Work videotape

In-Depth Coverage	Accelerated Pace
• Cover pp. 72–77 in class. • Show Writing a Short Story section of Writers at Work videotape. • Discuss different types of short stories.	• Assign pp. 72–77 for independent student review. • Discuss definitions and types of short stories.

What Is a Short Story?

A **short story** is a brief, made-up narrative—an account of a sequence of events. The events in a short story can take place in a burning desert, in a mountain fortress, or on a street just like yours. From the ordinary to the extraordinary, a short story can show you the world from a different point of view. Most short stories have

- one or more characters (the people involved in the story).
- a conflict or problem that keeps the reader asking, "What will happen next?"
- a beginning that grabs the reader's interest and introduces the characters, setting, and conflict.
- a middle in which the story reaches a climax—its turning point.
- an ending in which the conflict is resolved and loose ends are tied up.

To learn the criteria on which your short story may be judged or graded, see the Rubric for Self-Assessment on page 90.

Types of Short Stories

The following are some of the different kinds of short stories:

- **Realistic stories** take you on a walk through familiar neighborhoods with people much like those you know.
- **Fantasy and science-fiction stories** might whisk you away to strange, new planets or mysterious ancient kingdoms.
- **Adventure stories** tumble you into a world of brave heroes fighting dangerous enemies.

PREVIEW
Student Work
IN PROGRESS

In this chapter, you'll follow the work of John Beamer, a student at David Starr Jordan Middle School in Palo Alto, California, as he developed his story "The Manitoba Monster." You'll see how he used featured strategies to find a topic, develop a conflict, elaborate, and revise. At the end of the chapter, you'll read his finished short story.

Writers in ACTION

Novelist and short-story writer Isaac Bashevis Singer (1904–1991) received the prestigious Nobel Prize for Literature in 1978. Even when he was a child, he knew which kind of story he liked:

"...from my childhood I have always loved tension in a story. I liked that a story should be a story. That there should be a beginning and an end, and there should be some feeling of what will happen at the end."

Short Story • 73

PREPARE and ENGAGE

Interest GRABBER Read the following passage to students:

Franklin wrapped his arms around the log. He thought—he hoped—he could see the shore. Maybe, just maybe, if he could hold out the wind would bring him in. It was his only chance.

Ask students what questions the passage makes them ask themselves. They might be wondering, Who is Franklin? How did he end up in this situation? What is going to happen to him? Discuss that questions such as these form the basic elements of a short story.

Activate Prior Knowledge

Remind students of some stories they have read: "The Sound of Summer Running" by Ray Bradbury, "Stray" by Cynthia Rylant, "Jeremiah's Song" by Walter Dean Myers, "The King of Mazy May" by Jack London. Ask students which they liked and why (or which they didn't like and why not).

More About the Author

Isaac Bashevis Singer wrote in Yiddish, the vernacular language of European Jews. His stories and novels are filled with a passion for life and simultaneous sadness over the passing of the centuries-old traditions of European Jews. In the tradition of the culture he chronicled, his work also contains strong elements of fantasy. Among his many works are *The Manor, The Estate,* and *Gimpel the Fool.*

☑ **ONGOING ASSESSMENT: Diagnose**

Use one of the following options to diagnose students' current level of proficiency in short story writing.

Option 1 Ask each student to select the strongest example of his or her short story writing from last year. Hold conferences in which you review each student's sample. Use the conferences to determine which students will need extra support in developing a short story.	**Option 2** Ask students to write a sentence that describes a possible character in a short story. Then have them list three qualities that support that description. If students have difficulty completing this exercise, you will need to devote more time on the gathering evidence and elaboration phases of the process.

Reading: Interpret

Interpreting is a key to appreciating and understanding literature. Good writing shows, rather than tells, what happens, making it the reader's job to interpret what the words and actions mean. In the Singer selection, humor and subtlety are achieved through a continued narration without additional commentary on the foolishness of the characters.

Teaching From the Model

You can use this model to help students see tight story structure and the virtues of the "show, don't tell" approach to writing. Point out how even though Singer uses third-person narration, the characters' actions tell the story. The narrator does not intrude beyond initially announcing that the village was populated by fools.

Step-by-Step Teaching Guide

Engage Students Through Literature

1. Have volunteers read the story aloud.

2. After the reading, engage students in a discussion. What do they think of the Elders of Chelm? What possible general comment is the author making about leaders or those in authority?

3. Point out how, in the first paragraph, Singer tells us that the characters are fools and then provides an immediate example with the moon reflected in the barrel.

4. Discuss how the author subtly adds to the fantasy elements with the vagueness about setting. All he tells us is that Chelm is a village. As we read, it quickly becomes apparent that the setting is irrelevant—it could be anywhere—because of the stronger fantasy elements in the story.

 # Model From Literature

Isaac Bashevis Singer (1904–1991) was born in Poland and moved to New York City in 1935. The author of short stories and novels, Singer wrote in Yiddish, the language of Eastern European Jews. He told many tales of life in the small villages of Eastern Europe. Singer received the Nobel Prize for Literature in 1978.

Reading Writing Connection

Reading Strategy: Interpret As you read, **interpret** what you have read by restating its meaning. For example, when you read about an important event, ask yourself: Why did this event happen? When the author mentions a detail that seems to stand out, ask yourself: Why did the writer add this detail?

For example, in "The Snow in Chelm," Singer describes the seven Elders as having "white beards and high foreheads from too much thinking." You might restate the meaning of this detail as follows: "The Elders look the way wise people are supposed to look. Singer says their heads got big from 'too much thinking,' though. He must be poking fun at people who think they are wise."

▲ **Critical Viewing** What features of this man make him look wise? What does the story suggest about judging wisdom on the basis of these features? [Interpret]

 # The Snow in Chelm

Isaac Bashevis Singer

Chelm was a village of fools, fools young and old. One night someone spied the moon reflected in a barrel of water. The people of Chelm imagined it had fallen in. They sealed the barrel so that the moon would not escape. When the barrel was opened in the morning and the moon wasn't there, the villagers decided it had been stolen. They sent for the police, and when the thief couldn't be found, the fools of Chelm cried and moaned.

Of all the fools of Chelm, the most famous were its seven Elders. Because they were the village's oldest and greatest fools, they ruled in Chelm. They had white beards and high foreheads from too much thinking.

Singer begins by introducing his characters with an attention-grabbing statement.

74 • Short Story

Critical Viewing

Interpret Students may note that the man's beard, wrinkles, broad forehead, alert eyes, and hat all suggest wisdom. The story suggests, though, that men with white beards and high foreheads may be very foolish indeed.

Critical Viewing

Relate Students' responses will vary. If students can't think of an example, ask them to tell about a recent movie or TV show that they saw in which the visual effects possibly "tricked" them.

Responding to Literature

Chekhov's story is similar to Singer's in that misunderstandings drive both stories. Singer's village, while vague in setting, comes from the same world and time as Chekhov's story of rural nineteenth-century Russia. Both involve a peasant culture.

◄ **Critical Viewing**
The villagers once thought the moon had fallen into a barrel. Have you ever been tricked by the way something looked? Explain. **[Relate]**

LITERATURE

To read another humorous short story, see "Overdoing It" by Anton Chekhov. You can find this story in *Prentice Hall Literature: Timeless Voices, Timeless Themes,* Copper.

Once, on a Hanukkah night, the snow fell all evening. It covered all of Chelm like a silver tablecloth. The moon shone; the stars twinkled; the snow shimmered like pearls and diamonds.

That evening the seven Elders were sitting and pondering, wrinkling their foreheads. The village was in need of money, and they did not know where to get it. Suddenly the oldest of them all, Gronam the Great Fool, exclaimed, "The snow is silver!"

"I see pearls in the snow!" another shouted.

"And I see diamonds!" a third called out.

It became clear to the Elders of Chelm that a treasure had fallen from the sky.

But soon they began to worry. The people of Chelm liked to go walking, and they would most certainly trample the treasure. What was to be done? Silly Tudras had an idea.

"Let's send a messenger to knock on all the windows and let the people know that they must remain in their houses until all the silver, all the pearls, and all the diamonds are safely gathered up."

For a while the Elders were satisfied. They rubbed their hands in approval of the clever idea. But then Dopey Lekisch called out in consternation, "The messenger himself will trample the treasure."

The Elders realized that Lekisch was right, and again they wrinkled their high foreheads in an effort to solve the problem.

"I've got it!" exclaimed Shmerel the Ox.

"Tell us, tell us," pleaded the Elders.

Here, Singer sets up the main conflict of the story: Will reality force the foolish Elders to realize their mistake?

Singer makes the conflict more interesting by having characters bring up "difficulties" with the plan—all while no one sees the first ridiculous mistake!

Model From Literature • 75

Critical Viewing

Compare and Contrast Students' responses will vary. Make sure they support their answers with details from the painting and the story.

Step-by-Step Teaching Guide

1. Singer reinforces the humor with the names and descriptions of his characters: Dopey, Silly, the potato peeler, Yontel who was in charge of the community goat.

2. Discuss how Singer builds the humor with the Elders' ideas for spending the riches.

Customizing for
Visual/Spatial Learners

Have students choose a passage from the Model From Literature to illustrate. When students are done, you may want to have them present their illustrations to the class. Encourage students to explain why they chose the passage they did and how they decided what to include in their illustrations.

"The messenger must not go on foot. He must be carried on a table so that his feet will not tread on the precious snow."

Everybody was delighted with Schmerel the Ox's solution; and the Elders, clapping their hands, admired their own wisdom.

The Elders immediately sent to the kitchen for Gimpel the errand boy and stood him on a table. Now who was going to carry the table? It was lucky that in the kitchen there were Treitle the cook, Berel the potato peeler, Yukel the salad mixer, and Yontel, who was in charge of the community goat. All four were ordered to lift up the table on which Gimpel stood. Each one took hold of a leg. On top stood Gimpel, grasping a wooden hammer with which to tap on the villager's windows. Off they went.

At each window Gimpel knocked with the hammer and called out, "No one leaves the house tonight. A treasure has fallen from the sky, and it is forbidden to step on it."

The people of Chelm obeyed the Elders and remained in their houses all night. Meanwhile the Elders themselves sat up trying to figure out how to make the best use of the treasure once it had been gathered up.

Silly Tudras proposed that they sell it and buy a goose which lays golden eggs. Thus the community would be provided with a steady income.

One of Singer's purposes is to entertain his audience. Another purpose is to show that all the planning in the world is just foolishness if it loses sight of reality. Both purposes are filled by this funny scene: The men carry Gimpel so he will not tread on the snow—while they walk all over it!

▼ **Critical Viewing**
What is the mood of this painting—serious or silly? Compare this mood to the mood of the story. **[Compare and Contrast]**

Green Violinist, Marc Chagall

Winter Night in Vitebsk, Marc Chagall

Reading\Writing Connection

Writing: Help Readers Interpret

The point here is the value of omission, or what is left out. By describing only the Elders' beards and high foreheads, Singer creates caricatures much like a cartoonist does by emphasizing some features and downplaying, or omitting, others. Remind students of the importance of providing details as they write to help readers interpret.

Critical Viewing

Interpret Students may mention the soft lines as well as the couple on horseback being in midair. The scene of the town itself seems realistic.

◀ **Critical Viewing**
Which details of this painting make it seem like a dream? Which make it seem like a real scene? **[Interpret]**

Dopey Lekisch had another idea. Why not buy eyeglasses that make things look bigger for all the inhabitants of Chelm? Then the houses, the streets, the stores would all look bigger, and of course if Chelm *looked* bigger, then it *would be* bigger. It would no longer be a village, but a big city.

There were other, equally clever ideas. But while the Elders were weighing their various plans, morning came and the sun rose. They looked out of the window, and, alas, they saw the snow had been trampled. The heavy boots of the table carriers had destroyed the treasure.

At the climax of the story, the reader wants to know: Will the Elders see the foolishness of their way of thinking?

The Elders of Chelm clutched at their white beards and admitted to one another that they had made a mistake. Perhaps, they reasoned, four others should have carried the four men who had carried the table that held Gimpel the errand boy?

After long deliberations the Elders decided that if next Hanukkah a treasure would again fall down from the sky, that is exactly what they would do.

Right after the climax comes the resolution of the conflict between reality and foolishness. The Elders will continue in their foolishness!

Although the villagers remained without a treasure, they were full of hope for the next year and praised their Elders, who they knew could always be counted on to find a way, no matter how difficult the problem.

Writing Application: Help Readers Interpret
As you write your short story, emphasize details that will help readers **interpret** a character's personality and actions. You can emphasize a detail by discussing it for one or two sentences. Or, you might make sure it is the only detail of its kind that you include. For instance, Singer mentions little about the looks of the Elders besides their white beards and high foreheads—a sign that these details are meaningful.

Prewriting: Choosing Your Topic

Teaching Resources: Writing Support Transparency 5-A

1. Students may insist that they can't think of an interesting topic, or that all the good story ideas have already been used. Suggest that they think of an interesting place—inside a volcano, the planet Jupiter, the bottom of the ocean—and set their story there.

2. Suggest that students close their eyes and use their imaginations. Have them sketch at first, then add details later.

3. Tell students that the key to freewriting is to suspend judgment or stop thinking. That means they should try not to comment on the quality of the idea, just list ideas as they let their mind roam.

4. Display the transparency to show how John used freewriting to generate a topic. Tell them that they need not write in straight lines or even on the lines. Make sure they have plenty of paper and can write or draw any way they want to do the activity.

Customize for *ESL Students*

Talk with students about people, places, and myths and traditions in their home cultures. These may give them inspiration for a topic. Also suggest that they read "The Yangs' First Thanksgiving" by Lensey Namioka, a story about a Chinese family's difficulties learning American habits. Students probably have a similar experience they could write about. (If they are embarrassed, they can write in the third person.)

5.2 Prewriting

Choosing Your Topic

For some writers, telling a story is easy—the hard part is coming up with a good topic. Here are a few strategies you can use to get your ideas flowing:

Strategies for Generating a Topic

1. **Drawing** Choose a setting in which a story could take place: a house or an apartment where you used to live, a spooky room you wandered into by mistake, a street in a town in which you've just arrived. Draw this setting in detail. Use the ideas suggested by your drawing for your story.

2. **Freewriting** Set a timer for five minutes, and write down as many story ideas as you can. Focus on getting down ideas rather than on spelling, grammar, or punctuation. At the end of five minutes, review your freewriting. Circle ideas to use in your story.

Writing Lab CD-ROM

For more help finding a topic, explore the activities and suggestions in the Choosing a Topic section of the Narration lesson.

Student Work
IN PROGRESS

Name: John Beamer
David Starr Jordan Middle School
Palo Alto, CA

Freewriting to Generate a Topic

John Beamer freewrote and then circled the phrases that led to his topic: "The Manitoba Monster." Because he was jotting notes only for himself, he used abbreviations and did not correct errors.

mystery story sci-fi something weird in the woods UFO? Loch Ness (monster)? Don't know Scotland change setting 2 where? (nr. Unc. Dave's house—that lake.) Something happens when kids are visiting thr uncle—swimming someone drowns gets sucked into water by monster? or water skiing or fshing. Guy like U Dave sees something. 2 guys, buddies, (ice fishing) cold cold old old guys? (no no just reg joes, argue a lot one of them sees something other guy doesn't believe him)

⏱ TIME AND RESOURCE MANAGER

Resources
Print: Writing Support Transparencies 5-A–C; *Writing Support Activity Book 5-1*
Technology: Writing Lab CD-ROM, Narration

In-Depth Coverage	Accelerated Pace
• Cover pp. 78–81 in class. • Use the Responding to Fine Arts Transparency to generate additional topics. • Do the Using a Conflict Map activity (p. 80) in class. **Option** Have students work independently or in small groups with the Writing Lab CD-ROM.	• Discuss strategies for generating topics. • Have students work independently to choose and narrow their topics. • Have students work with partners to focus on audience, purpose, and gathering details.

TOPIC BANK

If you're having trouble coming up with a topic, consider the following possibilities:

1. **Moving Day** Write a story about a person who moves to a new place. (Your story can be based on real life.) Include details about who or what your character misses most and about the surprises he or she finds in the new place.

2. **Be Careful What You Wish For** Many fairy tales feature a character who makes a foolish wish. Think of King Midas, who couldn't eat or drink because everything he touched turned to gold. Write a story about a human or animal character who is granted a wish that turns out to be a disaster.

Responding to Fine Art

3. This painting shows a scene from the story of Noah's ark. Write a story based on the painting. As you write, pretend you are one of the people or animals shown. Your story should answer these questions: Who are you? What events are taking place around you? How do you feel about them? What happens to you?

Responding to Literature

4. Read the story "Zlateh the Goat" by Isaac Bashevis Singer. Then, write your own story from Zlateh's point of view, telling what she was thinking and feeling—especially when she says "Maaa"! You can find "Zlateh the Goat" in *Prentice Hall Literature: Timeless Voices, Timeless Themes*, Copper.

☑ **Cooperative Writing Opportunity**

5. **Group Story** Working in a group, create a story. Brainstorm for a topic, and agree on a story plan. Decide on all of the events and characters in the story. Divide the following tasks: writing the story; illustrating the story and writing captions for the illustrations; and performing the story as a dramatic reading or skit.

Prewriting • 79

Noah's Ark, Aaron Douglas, Fisk University Fine Art Galleries, Nashville, Tennessee

---

Step-by Step Teaching Guide

Responding to Fine Art

Noah's Ark by Aaron Douglas

Teaching Resources: Writing Support Transparency 5-B

1. The story of Noah's ark may not be familiar to all students. Give a synopsis, presenting it as an adventure story (which it is): big flood, 40 days and 40 nights, all the animals two by two, ship on top of a mountain, survived.

2. Display the transparency and ask students to describe what they see.

Responding to Literature

In "Zlateh the Goat," Singer creates a character of both innocence and omniscience. This anthropomorphism is common in literature but works well only in the hands of a master. Encourage students to use their imaginations in fleshing out Zlateh's character, thoughts, and comments.

Spotlight on the Humanities

For additional topics, refer students to the Spotlight on the Humanities on page 94.

  TIME SAVERS!

Writing Support Transparencies
Use the transparency for Chapter 5 to teach these strategies.

Prewriting: Developing Narrative Elements

Teaching Resources: Writing Support Transparency 5-C; Writing Support Activity Book 5-1

1. Conflict is at the heart of every plot. Ask students to recall favorite stories or TV episodes and identify the conflict.

2. As students recount the conflict in stories, extend the discussion to external and internal conflicts. Help students see that external conflicts are more likely to appear in a story with a lot of action. Internal conflicts fit better in stories about a person's thoughts and feelings and relationships with other people.

3. Display the transparency. Review John's conflict map and help students create their own. Remind them that they need a main character, a goal, and an obstacle(s). Explore with students that the obstacles can be physical—landscape, weather—or they can be interpersonal—a rival or someone who doubts the main character's ability to succeed.

Real-World Connection

The real world is full of conflicts. To help students get started on their conflict map, partners can read a newspaper story (sports provides many easy examples) and draw a quick conflict map.

5.2

Developing Narrative Elements

Once you've come up with a topic, set your story in motion. A short story starts out as words lying on a page. In the best stories, though, the words start whisking by, pulling the reader along. Soon, the pages seem to turn themselves! The secret of all this commotion is the story's conflict. To set your story in motion, identify your conflict.

Identify the Conflict

A **conflict** is a struggle between two opposing forces. A race, for instance, is a conflict among runners. An **external conflict** occurs when a character is struggling against an outside force, such as another character or a natural event. An **internal conflict** takes place within a character, as when the character struggles to make a tough decision or to overcome fear.

Using a Conflict Map To identify the conflict in your story, ask yourself:

1. What does my main character want?
2. Who or what is getting in the way?

Create a conflict map like the one below (or one of your own design) to find the answers to these questions.

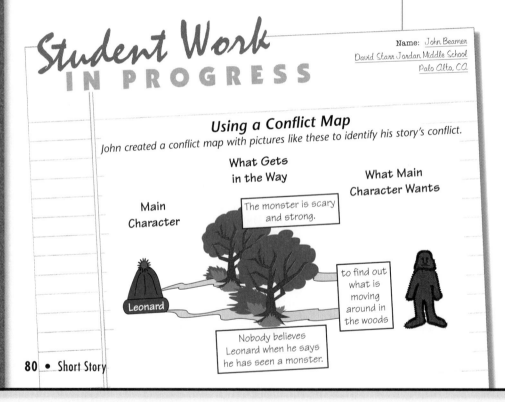

Student Work IN PROGRESS

Name: John Beamer
David Starr Jordan Middle School
Palo Alto, CA

Using a Conflict Map

John created a conflict map with pictures like these to identify his story's conflict.

What Gets in the Way

What Main Character Wants

Main Character

The monster is scary and strong.

Leonard

to find out what is moving around in the woods

Nobody believes Leonard when he says he has seen a monster.

80 • Short Story

⏱ **TIME SAVERS!**

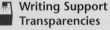 **Writing Support Transparencies**

Use the transparencies for Chapter 5 to facilitate teaching of strategies.

✓ **ONGOING ASSESSMENT: Monitor and Reinforce**

If some students are having difficulty completing the conflict map, use one of the following options:

Option 1 Drawing will not work for some students. They can use a combination of words, abbreviations, or symbols with direction lines or arrows to complete the conflict map.	**Option 2** Have students work with a partner and narrate the conflict as the partner writes it down.

Considering Your Audience and Purpose

The conflict in your story will keep your readers interested. Before you can start telling your story, though, you must know *who* your readers are—your **audience**—and *what* you want to do for them—your **purpose**. Knowing your audience and purpose will shape your writing, as in these examples:

If your audience is . . .

• **young children,** use simpler words than if you were writing a story for older readers.

• **people who don't go to your school,** remember that if you mention something particular to your school, such as a certain teacher, you must explain who or what you are talking about.

If your purpose is to . . .

• **make readers laugh,** select funny details to include.

• **give readers goosebumps,** include a couple of surprises.

• **present a theme (a question or message about life),** use events that illustrate the question or message.

Gathering Details

Your next step is to gather details to include in your story. Use the strategy of listing and itemizing.

List and Itemize

List ideas about your story topic. Then, circle the most interesting idea. Create another list about that circled item. Review your lists for details to include in your story. If you need more details, repeat the process. Here's an example:

set the story in the future—sci fi
(main character is a present-day kid from an average family)

kid finds a lamp with a genie who grants her a wish
(kid meets a strange man who grants her a wish)

she wishes she didn't have a little brother
(she wishes she could trade places with a wealthy friend)
(she trades places with her friend)
(the main character enjoys the limo rides to school and all the clothes)
(the other kids in school treat her funny, though)
(at dinner, the wealthy family hardly talks)
(she wishes she was back with her own family)

Writing Lab CD-ROM

For more help deciding on your audience and purpose, see the Considering Audience and Purpose section of the Narration lesson.

Considering Your Audience and Purpose

1. Determining audience and purpose are critical to a story's success. Discuss the examples given in the text and ask students to suggest some other examples.

2. Remind students that they can't always assume their audience is familiar with many things about their life. If the setting is important in the story, they need to describe it. If a game or some other activity is important and is not widely known (for example, the sport of cricket), it has to be described.

3. Discuss the importance of consistency of purpose. For example, in a scary story, it is hard to maintain the tone if the narrative is filled with wisecracks.

4. Review the listing and itemizing activity. Point out how the author builds on details.

Customize for
Less Advanced Students

Students may need help with the listing and itemizing. Work with students individually and have them tell the story orally, identifying the character, the conflict, and then begin making up a plot and setting. Write down what they tell you and have them use these results as the basis for beginning to draft the story.

Integrating Vocabulary Skills

Goosebumps Also known as *gooseflesh* or *goose pimples*, this condition is marked by a roughness to the skin. This roughness is caused when tiny muscles (known as *papillae*) on the surface of the skin and in hair shafts rise up in reaction to cold and fear.

Drafting: Using a Plot Diagram

Teaching Resources: Writing Support Transparency 5-D; Writing Support Activity Book 5-2

1. Discuss the nature of plot. Once more, ask students to think of the stories they mentioned earlier. Have a few volunteers describe the plot of a story or TV show and point out the shape of growing tension, climax, and resolution.

2. Display the transparency. Be sure that students understand the importance of each element. Discuss with students the linear nature of the plot diagram. Ask students to think of stories that begin seemingly in the middle of an action scene and then use flashback to set the scene. That is an effective narrative technique but a little more difficult to execute than the diagram in the text. Ask students to stick to the diagram for now, unless they show a well-developed plot sense.

3. To help students better understand the plot diagram, refer back to the Model From Literature. Show how Singer uses exposition to set the scene. The falling of snow and the moon in the barrel are the rising action. The conflict is how to preserve the snow. The climax is Gimpel on the table being taken around the village. The falling action is the discussion of how to spend the riches and the resolution is the Elders' idea of how to handle the next opportunity.

4. Give students copies of the blank organizer so that they can create their plot diagram. Circulate around the room to help where needed.

Critical Viewing

Analyze Students may say this is an external conflict between man and nature. At the climax, the drowning person may be rescued.

5.3 Drafting

Flight of the Thielens, Thomas Hart Benton, © T. H. Benton and R. P. Benton Testamentary Trusts

Shaping Your Writing

Now that you've decided on some of the key elements of your story, it's time to start structuring your ideas into a plot.

Create a Plot

A **plot** is the arrangement of events in the story. It is more than a simple sequence: "This happened, then this happened, then this happened." Instead, a plot is an arrangement of events designed to create interest, even excitement. Plots often follow this pattern:

- The **exposition** introduces the characters and their situation, including the central conflict.

- This **conflict** develops and intensifies during the **rising action,** which leads to the climax.

- The **climax,** or turning point of the story, might take the form of an argument or moment of decision.

- In the story's **falling action,** events start winding down, leading to the resolution.

- At the **resolution,** the conflict is resolved in some way and loose ends are tied up.

Using a Plot Diagram Map out the events in your story using a diagram like the one below. Refer to it as you draft.

▲ **Critical Viewing** Think about the force the people in this painting are struggling against. Then, describe the conflict taking place in the scene. What might happen at the climax? **[Analyze]**

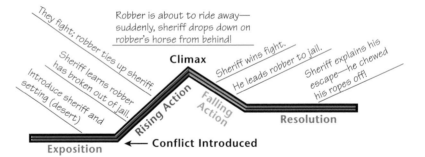

They fight; robber ties up sheriff.

Robber is about to ride away—suddenly, sheriff drops down on robber's horse from behind!

Sheriff learns robber has broken out of jail.

Introduce sheriff and setting (desert)

Climax

Sheriff wins fight.

He leads robber to jail.

Sheriff explains his escape—he chewed his ropes off!

Rising Action

Falling Action

Resolution

Exposition ← **Conflict Introduced**

82 • Short Story

Resources
Print: Writing Support Transparencies 5-D–E; Writing Support Activity Book 5-2–3
Technology: Writing Lab CD-ROM, Short Story

In-Depth Coverage	Accelerated Pace
• Cover pp. 82–83. • Work through the plot diagram with the entire class using the transparency. • Use the transparency to demonstrate how to create sensory sunbursts. • Have students write their own short story drafts in class. **Option** Have students work independently or in small groups with the Writing Lab CD-ROM.	• Have students review pp. 82–83 independently, then write their own short story drafts. • Respond to individual drafting issues as needed.

Providing Elaboration

Use Sensory Details

As you draft your story, make your characters and setting come alive by including sensory details—language that describes how things look, sound, feel, taste, and smell.

Livening Up Descriptions With Sensory Sunbursts

As you write, pause occasionally to find places where you can "burst" open your story, letting in more sights, sounds, textures, smells, and tastes. Circle any spot that could use some sensory pizzazz, and draw a sensory sunburst in the margin next to it. On each of the five rays of the sunburst, jot down details that appeal to a different one of the five senses. Later, review your draft, and add any words that will improve your description of the circled character, place, or thing.

Writing Lab CD-ROM

For more on adding details, use the Character Trait Word Bin in the Writer's Toolkit.

Student Work IN PROGRESS

Name: _John Beamer_
David Starr Jordan Middle School
Palo Alto, CA

Using Sensory Sunbursts

Here's an example of how John used sensory sunbursts to enliven his draft.

It was a (cold day) in the woods of Manitoba. *The wind was howling.* Snow covered all the trees, and the lake was crusted over with seven inches of ice at least. Leonard and Troy were out ice fishing. Leonard, a 60-year-old insurance salesman, was *chomping on* eating a *greasy chunk* strip of (salami.) Troy, a 48-year-old daytime gas station manager, was pulling out his week-old ham (sandwich.) *It didn't smell too good, but he took a bite anyway.*

Sunburst 1: feel: stinging wind; smell; sound: wind howling; taste; look

Sunburst 2: feel: greasy; smell: bad smell; sound: chomping; taste: salty; look

Sunburst 3: feel: dried out; smell: bad smell; sound: crinkly waxed paper; taste: moldy; look

Drafting • 83

☑ **ONGOING ASSESSMENT: Monitor and Reinforce**

If some students are having difficulty completing the sensory sunbursts, use one of the following options:

Option 1 Some students may do better without the visual cues of the sunburst. Have them write the headings *Look, Sound, Feel, Taste, Smell* on a piece of paper and write entries for each category.

Option 2 Have students close their eyes and think of the object or action they are trying to write about. Then have them write as many different words for each one. Direct them to go back and choose the most vivid ones for each sensory category.

Step-by-Step Teaching Guide

Drafting: Livening Up Descriptions With Sensory Sunbursts

Teaching Resources: Writing Support Transparency 5-E; Writing Support Activity Book 5-3

1. Discuss the value of sensory details. Read students the following sentences:

   The ice on the lake broke.

   With a loud crackling sound, the ice came ripping apart.

2. Elicit that the vivid details of the second sentence create more interest for the reader.

3. Display the transparency and review John's sensory sunbursts. Point out the power of the action verbs he uses: *howling, stings, chomping.* Vivid verbs make action come alive. Also point out the use of vivid adjectives such as *greasy* and *salty.*

4. Give students copies of the blank organizer to help them provide elaboration to details in their drafts.

 **TIME SAVERS!**

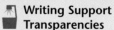 **Writing Support Transparencies**
Use the transparency for Chapter 5 to teach these strategies.

Writing Support Activity Book
Use the graphic organizers for Chapter 5 to facilitate these strategies.

Revising: Using a Bead Chart

Teaching Resources: Writing Support Transparency 5-F

1. Discuss the necessity of a story making sense. Remind them that making sense can mean many things. In the Model From Literature, everything the characters say and do makes little logical sense, but the story still makes perfect sense.

2. Display the transparency. Examine John's bead chart in detail. Be sure that students understand how he "connected the dots" by providing the motivation or reasons for what happens as well as assuring that the sequence is correct.

3. Direct students to make their own bead charts.

Revising

Revising Your Overall Structure
Create Logical Connections Between Events

The first step in revising your story is to make sure that your plot makes sense. Are the events you've included logically connected to one another and to the conflict? Have you left anything out that would explain your characters' actions? Use a bead chart to make sure events are logically connected.

▶ **REVISION STRATEGY**
Using a Bead Chart

Underline each major event in your story. Then, summarize each one in a "bead" on a chart like the one below. Show the connections between events by writing a simple word or phrase, such as *he is curious*, in the connector string. When one event simply happens to occur after another, you might write the word *next* in the connector.

Review your chart. If most of your connectors say *next*, consider adding events in between that explain *why*. If you can't think of a good connection between two events, one of them may not belong in the story. Consider eliminating it or reshaping it to fit better.

Language Lab CD-ROM

For more on writing dialogue, see the Writing Dialogue lesson in the Composing Unit.

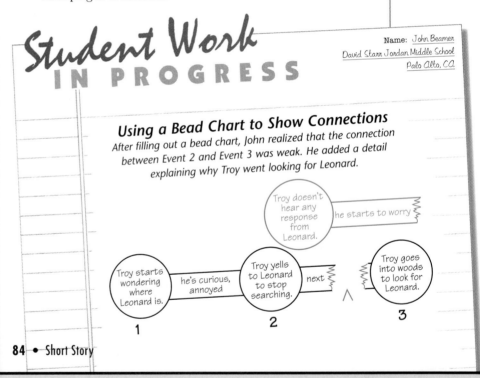

Student Work
IN PROGRESS

Name: *John Beamer*
David Starr Jordan Middle School
Palo Alto, CA

Using a Bead Chart to Show Connections
After filling out a bead chart, John realized that the connection between Event 2 and Event 3 was weak. He added a detail explaining why Troy went looking for Leonard.

⏱ **TIME SAVERS!**

🗂 **Writing Support Transparencies**
Use the transparencies for Chapter 5 to teach these strategies.

⏱ **TIME AND RESOURCE MANAGER**

Resources
Print: Writing Support Transparencies 5–F–H
Technology: Writing Lab CD-ROM, Narration

In-Depth Coverage	Accelerated Pace
• Cover pp. 84–88 in class. • Work through Revising strategy with entire class. • Use the relevant transparencies for creating a Bead Chart, Circling Direct Statements, and Using Dialogue Balloons.	• Assign students to review pp. 84–88 independently. • Have students revise their short stories independently.
Option Have students work independently or in small groups with the Writing Lab CD-ROM, focusing on revision activities and tools.	

Revising Your Paragraphs

Show, Don't Tell

As you revise, look for places where you can *show* instead of *tell*. For example, instead of telling readers "Matty felt afraid," show them her fear by describing the way she walks (quickly), her voice (trembling), and the way she laughs (nervously).

▶ REVISION STRATEGY
Circling Direct Statements

Circle every place in your story where you tell readers directly what a character, setting, or object is like. Then, go back and replace some of these "tellings" with "showings." Here is an example:

TELLING: Sam was an obnoxious know-it-all.

SHOWING: Whenever another kid answered a question, Sam rolled his eyes while frantically waving his hand.

Add Dialogue

To let your characters "show" themselves, add **dialogue**—words you've written as though the characters have said them. Realistic dialogue includes slang, trailing or interrupted speech, and spelling that reflects people's pronunciations.

EXAMPLE: "I dunno if I . . . Hey, wait a minute!" said Sid.

▶ REVISION STRATEGY
Using Dialogue Balloons

Review your draft for places to add dialogue. Using a glue stick, attach a dialogue balloon (a paper circle with a little tail, like those in comic strips) to every spot you find. You can add dialogue showing

1. a character's **answer** or response to another character.
2. **information** one character gives another.
3. an **order,** command, or instruction given by a character.
4. a **question** a character asks.
5. something a character says to express **feelings.**

As you attach a dialogue balloon, label it with reminder words—like *answer, information, order, question,* or *feelings.* After you have finished your draft, go back and add the appropriate kind of dialogue.

▲ Critical Viewing
Write one sentence that *tells* what you see in this picture. Now, "translate" your sentence into one that *shows* the same setting. Finally, write a line of dialogue that a parent might say after opening the door and seeing this room. [Describe]

⚙ Grammar ⚙ and Style Tip

When writing dialogue, you may write grammatically incorrect sentences, such as "I ain't got no pencil"—but only if they reflect the way the character would speak.

Revising • 85

Critical Viewing

Describe Possible response: The room is messy. The room looked as if a tornado had hit it. "What on earth happened to your room?"

Step-by-Step Teaching Guide

Revising: Circling Direct Statements, Using Dialogue Balloons

1. Review the examples of "showing" versus "telling." Elicit from students how much more interesting the showing example is than the telling. Point out that showing is a literary technique that is often absent from the verbal stories we tell each other, in which there is a tendency to tell everything.

2. Have students circle every direct statement in their drafts and replace some of these with more descriptive "show" statements.

3. Discuss the value of good dialogue, when a writer captures how his characters would actually speak. That is one of the best ways a writer can show instead of tell.

4. Review the five situations where students can add dialogue. Add to the list by telling students that we all talk to ourselves, either silently or out loud. Direct quotes of characters thoughts are another technique for showing rather than telling.

5. Have students add dialogue balloons with labels to their draft and select the best ones to include in their final draft.

Customize for
Interpersonal Learners

Students may benefit from working with peers at the revising stage. Pair students who you think will work well together and have them assist each other on the revision strategies to show instead of tell.

☑ ONGOING ASSESSMENT: Monitor and Reinforce

If some students are having difficulty completing the bead chart, use one of the following options:

Option 1 Have less visually minded students number 1–20 down the page and write each bead next to the number. In the left-hand column, have them supply the commentary.	**Option 2** Work individually with students needing special help. Have them narrate the plot and tell you why each event is happening. Record their narration in a bead chart.

Revising: Provide Transitions

*Teacher Resources: Writing Support
Transparency 5-G*

1. Ask students to scan their story, looking at their sentences. Do they notice any pattern?

2. Discuss with students the Transitional Words and Phrases chart. Point out how a transitional word accomplishes two tasks: it provides variety in sentence beginnings, and it provides connections and cues for the reader.

3. Display the transparency and examine John's use of transition boxes to show connections.

4. Direct students to use transition boxes on one paragraph of their story. If they are successful, encourage them to use it on other paragraphs as well.

5.4

Revising Your Sentences
Provide Transitions

As you revise, improve the flow of your sentences by adding **transitions**—words that show the connection between ideas.

TRANSITIONAL WORDS AND PHRASES			
Tell when or in what order	Show similarity	Show difference	Show cause and effect
after, during, finally, first, later, next, then, when	also, for example, for instance, similarly	although, despite, however, instead, nevertheless, yet	as a result, because, consequently, if, then, therefore

▶ **REVISION STRATEGY**
Using Transition Boxes

Try this strategy with one paragraph of your story:

1. Draw a box between every two sentences.
2. Place a check in the box if you think that the connection between the sentences is clear.
3. If the connection isn't clear enough, add a transition word or phrase above the line. (See the chart above for ideas.)

Student Work
IN PROGRESS

Name: John Beamer
David Starr Jordan Middle School
Palo Alto, CA

Using Transition Boxes to Show Connections
When John used transition boxes, he realized that he needed to add some transitions to clarify when events occurred.

Troy became pale and yelled, "Leonard—are ya all
right?" ☐ *Seconds later, a* A dark shadow fell over him, and everything

went black. . . . ☐
A few hours later, some
~~Some~~ campers found the two men wandering in the
woods and called the police. ☐ *After* Leonard and Troy told

their stories, ~~but~~ the authorities decided that the two

terrified men had imagined the whole thing. ☑

86 • Short Story

⏱ **TIME SAVERS!**

📄 **Writing Support Transparencies**
Use the transparencies for Chapter 5 to teach these strategies.

Revising Your Word Choice
Use Vivid Verbs

As you revise, replace boring, overused verbs like *said, was, had,* and *went* with colorful verbs that express your meaning more precisely. Review these examples:

OVERUSED: said
VIVID: chuckled, snorted
OVERUSED: was
VIVID: blossomed into, sounded
OVERUSED: went
VIVID: plodded, careened

▶ **REVISION STRATEGY**
Color-Coding Verbs

Using a green pencil, circle each verb in the first three and the last three paragraphs of your story. Then, go back and draw a red square around any verbs that sound boring or that you've overused (or even used twice in a row). Replace at least half of these weaklings with more exciting, unusual verbs.

⊚ Technology Tip

If you think you've used a word too many times, use your word-processing program's Find function to locate each appearance of the word in your draft. Consider replacing it in some cases with another word.

Grammar in Your Writing
Identifying Verbs

A **verb** is a word that shows either an action or a state of being. An **action verb** tells what action the subject of a sentence is doing. This action can be either physical *(run, dance, jump)* or mental *(think, believe, want)*. A **linking verb** connects the subject of a sentence with another word that identifies or describes the subject. The most common linking verb is *be* in all its forms. Other linking verbs are *feel, look, appear, become, remain, seem, grow, smell, sound, taste, stay,* and *prove.*

ACTION VERB: Samantha **rides** her bicycle to school.
LINKING VERB: Dan **seems** excited about going to camp.

If you use too many linking verbs, your writing will sound lifeless. If possible, use an action verb instead. (You might need to rewrite your sentence.)

Find It in Your Reading Find three action verbs and three linking verbs in "The Snow in Chelm" by Isaac Bashevis Singer on page 74.

Find It in Your Writing Underline five different action verbs in your story. If you can't find five, consider whether you've overused certain verbs or used too many linking verbs. If so, think of replacements for these verbs.

For more about verbs, see Chapter 15.

Step-by-Step Teaching Guide

Revising: Revising Your Word Choice

1. Review the comparison of overused with vivid verbs in the text. Discuss that since verbs supply the action, they are very much considered key words.
2. Review the Color-Coding Verbs strategy. Direct students to color-code the verbs in the first and last three paragraphs and try to replace overused verbs with more vivid ones.

Step-by-Step Teaching Guide

Grammar in Your Writing: Identifying Verbs

1. See that students understand that action verbs express physical or mental action, whereas linking verbs connect the subject to a word that describes it. Linking verbs do not describe any actual action.
2. Refer to the list of vivid verbs on the top of the page. Most are action verbs. Discuss how actions verbs provide energy and color to writing.

Find It in Your Reading

Among the many action verbs are the following occurring in the first paragraph: *spied, sealed, escape, moaned,* and *cried.* Linking verbs include many forms of the verb *be.*

Find It in Your Writing

If students have difficulty finding action verbs in their writing, ask them to think of what the characters are doing and then use those words. Too often, students unconsciously slip into the passive voice. Recommend that whenever they are faced with a choice, students should use action verbs rather than linking verbs.

☑ ONGOING ASSESSMENT: Prerequisite Skills

If students have difficulty identifying verbs, you may want to refer them to the following to assure coverage of prerequisite skills.

In the Textbook	Print Resources	Technology
Verbs, pp. 312–327	Grammar Exercise Workbook, pp. 13–20	On-Line Exercise Bank, Sections 15.1–2

Revising: Peer Review

*Teaching Resources: Writing Support
Transparency 5-H*

1. Discuss some good ground rules for peer review. It is best to tell what you like before offering criticism, which is best expressed as ways to improve the story rather than simply announcing that something is "wrong." Ask students to consider both how they want to be treated and the feelings of others in this exercise.

2. Review with students the peer review process.

3. Display the transparency. Examine John's highlighted excerpt and tell students to highlight the passages and specific comments specified by their peers.

5.4

Peer Review

Highlighting

Here are the steps for highlighting with a group of peers:

1. Read your revised draft aloud to a small group.
2. Next, ask the group to get ready to note parts they like and parts that need more details.
3. Read your story a second time while the group takes notes.
4. Afterward, ask group members to read back their notes and to explain their reactions.
5. In your draft, highlight the passages peers commented on. Write down specific comments in the margin.

You may use the group's comments to help you revise. Even if you don't accept every suggestion, these comments may help you come up with your own ideas.

**Writing Lab
CD-ROM**

For help working with a peer editor, use the Peer Evaluation Checklist in the Peer Review section of the Narration lesson.

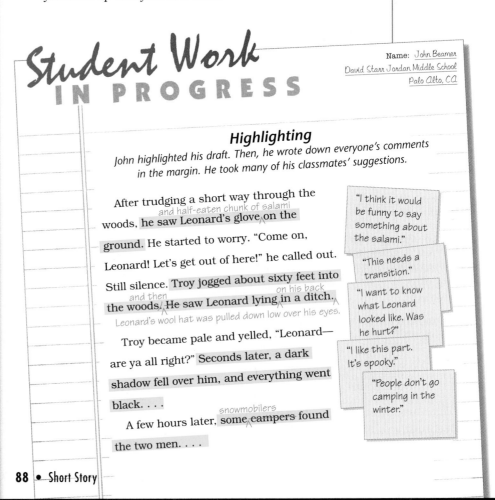

Student Work IN PROGRESS

Name: John Beamer
David Starr Jordan Middle School
Palo Alto, CA

Highlighting

John highlighted his draft. Then, he wrote down everyone's comments in the margin. He took many of his classmates' suggestions.

After trudging a short way through the
woods, he saw Leonard's glove on the
and half-eaten chunk of salami
ground. He started to worry. "Come on,
Leonard! Let's get out of here!" he called out.
Still silence. Troy jogged about sixty feet into
the woods. He saw Leonard lying in a ditch.
and then *on his back*
Leonard's wool hat was pulled down low over his eyes.
Troy became pale and yelled, "Leonard—
are ya all right?" Seconds later, a dark
shadow fell over him, and everything went
black. . . .
A few hours later, some campers found
snowmobilers
the two men. . . .

"I think it would be funny to say something about the salami."

"This needs a transition."

"I want to know what Leonard looked like. Was he hurt?"

"I like this part. It's spooky."

"People don't go camping in the winter."

88 • Short Story

☑ **ONGOING ASSESSMENT: Monitor and Reinforce**

Consider the following options in doing the peer review highlighting exercise:

Option 1 Pair students carefully according to ability and compatibility.	**Option 2** Allow students to select their own partners, but tell them that they will be evaluated on the quality of the feedback they give their peers.

5.5 Editing and Proofreading

Proofread your story carefully to catch errors in spelling, punctuation, capitalization, and grammar.

Focusing on Dialogue

Pay particular attention to proofreading your story's **dialogue**—speech that you've quoted exactly. Make sure you've punctuated it correctly.

Grammar in Your Writing
Punctuating and Formatting Dialogue

Dialogue is speech that is presented exactly as a character uttered it. Here are some guidelines that will help you punctuate, capitalize, and indent dialogue correctly:

1. Enclose dialogue in quotation marks.

   "I'm moving to California," Maria announced.
2. Don't use quotation marks when you simply report what a character said.

   Maria announced that she was moving to California.
3. If the dialogue comes *after* the "words of saying" in the rest of the sentence, use a comma before the quote.

   Arielle said, "My mom promised we could get a dog."
4. If the dialogue comes *before* the words of saying, use a comma, question mark, or exclamation mark—but not a period—at the end.

   "But now my dad says we have to wait a year," she complained.

   "I'm so annoyed!" she wailed.

   "Have you decided what kind of dog?" asked Abby.
5. Words of saying that interrupt the quote should be set off by punctuation marks and go outside the quotation marks.

   "We all want a poodle," explained Arielle, "except my mom."

Find It in Your Reading Skim "The Snow in Chelm" by Isaac Bashevis Singer on page 74, and find three examples of dialogue. For each, explain why it is punctuated correctly.

Find It in Your Writing Highlight each instance of dialogue in your story, and circle the "words of saying." Correct the punctuation if you find any mistakes.

For more on punctuating with quotation marks, see Chapter 26.

⏱ TIME AND RESOURCE MANAGER

Resources
Print: Scoring Rubrics on Transparency, Chapter 5; Writing Assessment: Scoring Rubric and Scoring Models for Short Story
Technology: Writing Lab CD-ROM, Narration

In-Depth Coverage	Accelerated Pace
• Review pp. 89–90 in class. • Have students edit and proofread their stories. • Analyze in class the Final Draft on pp. 91–92.	• Assign pp. 89–92 for independent review. • Have students independently edit and proofread their stories. • Respond to individual editing issues as needed.

Step-by-Step Teaching Guide

Editing and Proofreading

1. Remind students that no matter how funny or well written a story is, everyone will notice if it is full of misspellings and incorrect punctuation.
2. Tell students that dialogue presents more detailed and sometimes tricky punctuation problems that need to be examined carefully.

Step-by-Step Teaching Guide

Grammar in Your Writing: Punctuating and Formatting Dialogue

1. Review each dialogue situation individually, seeing that students understand the punctuation rules that apply.
2. Write the following sentences on the chalkboard (omitting the punctuation) and ask students to distinguish between the direct quotation and the indirect one. Then ask them to punctuate the direct quotation:

   Jimmy told me Jack said that he wasn't ready for the science test. (indirect)

   "If Jack is not ready, none of us stands a chance," said Maria. (direct)
3. Write the following sentences on the chalkboard (omitting the punctuation) and ask students to punctuate them:

   Jimmy said, "We need a miracle."

   "Let's just relax and give it our best shot," Maria answered.

   "I'll try hard," Jimmy said, "but it feels hopeless."
4. Confirm that students understand how to punctuate quotations with "words of saying."

Find It in Your Reading

Have students share their examples with the class.

Find It in Your Writing

After students have reviewed their writing, have them exchange papers with a partner so that each student can double-check his or her work.

89

Publishing and Presenting

1. Publishing and presenting are the reward for hard work. Urge students to seek out people to share their story with and other places to publish it.

2. Students who wrote in the same genre—adventure, fantasy, sci-fi—can work together to design a cover and combine their stories into a minibook.

3. Some stories may be appropriate for reading to a class of younger students.

4. Have students complete the Reflecting on Your Writing exercise, and encourage volunteers to share their reflections with the class.

ASSESS

Assessment

Teaching Resources: Scoring Rubrics on Transparency 5; Formal Assessment, Chapter 5

1. Display the Scoring Rubric transparency and review the criteria in class.

2. Before students proceed with self-assessment, you may wish to review the Final Draft of the Student Work in Progress on pages 91–92. Have students score the Final Draft in one or more of the rubric categories. For example, how would students score the essay in terms of audience and purpose?

3. In addition to student self-assessment, you may wish to use the following assessment options.

   • score student essays yourself, using the rubric and scoring models from Writing Assessment.

   • review the Standardized Test Preparation Workshop on pages 96–97 and have students respond to a persuasive writing prompt within a time limit.

   • administer the Chapter 5 Test from Formal Assessment in Teaching Resources to assess students' grasp of concepts presented.

5.6 Publishing and Presenting

Building Your Portfolio

Consider these suggestions for sharing your story:

1. **Submit Your Story** Submit your story to your school's literary magazine. You might also submit it to a national magazine, an e-zine, or a contest that publishes student writing. (Ask your teacher, librarian, or media specialist for suggestions.)

2. **Give a Reading** Get together with a group of classmates, and present a literary reading for an audience at your school. Tape your reading, and send copies to friends or family members who couldn't attend.

Reflecting on Your Writing

After you've finished writing your short story, jot down some of your thoughts about your writing experience. You might start by answering the following questions:

• Did you enjoy writing your story? What part of the process did you like most? What was the hardest part for you?

• The next time you write a story, what do you think you might do differently as a result of this experience?

Internet Tip

To see short stories scored with this rubric, visit **www.phschool.com**

Rubric for Self-Assessment

Evaluate your short story using the following criteria:

	Score 4	Score 3	Score 2	Score 1
Audience and Purpose	Contains an engaging introduction; successfully entertains or presents a theme	Contains a somewhat engaging introduction; entertains or presents a theme	Contains an introduction; attempts to entertain or to present a theme	Begins abruptly or confusingly; leaves purpose unclear
Organization	Creates an interesting, clear narrative; told from a consistent point of view	Presents a clear sequence of events; told from a specific point of view	Presents a mostly clear sequence of events; contains inconsistent points of view	Presents events without logical order; lacks a consistent point of view
Elaboration	Provides insight into character; develops plot; contains dialogue	Contains details and dialogue that develop character and plot	Contains details that develop plot; contains some dialogue	Contains few or no details to develop characters or plot
Use of Language	Uses word choice and tone to reveal story's theme; contains no errors in grammar, punctuation, or spelling	Uses interesting and fresh word choices; contains few errors in grammar, punctuation, and spelling	Uses some clichés and trite expressions; contains some errors in grammar, punctuation, and spelling	Uses uninspired word choices; has many errors in grammar, punctuation, and spelling

90 • Short Story

☑ ONGOING ASSESSMENT: Assess Mastery

Use one of the following options to assess final drafts of students' short stories.

Self-Assessment Ask students to score their essay, using the rubric provided. Then have students write a paragraph reflecting on the most valuable strategy they learned in completing this essay.

Teacher Assessment Use the rubric and the scoring models provided in Writing Assessment, Short Story to score students' work.

FINAL DRAFT

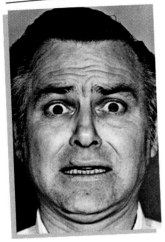

The Manitoba Monster

John Beamer
David Starr Jordan
Middle School
Palo Alto, California

It was a cold day in the woods of Manitoba. The wind was howling, snow covered all the trees, and the lake was crusted over with seven inches of ice at least. Leonard and Troy were out ice fishing. Leonard, a 60-year-old insurance salesman, was chomping on a greasy chunk of salami. Troy, a 48-year-old daytime gas station manager, was pulling out his week-old ham sandwich. It didn't smell too good, but he took a bite anyway.

Leonard and Troy went out ice fishing every January, but this time would be different. The two men were sitting next to their fishing hole. As Leonard chewed on his greasy salami, he occasionally wiped his chin on his jacket sleeve. "I'n it a cold day here in Manitoba?" he said. "You seen the northern pike Joe Hemal caught yesterday? I ain't never seen not'in' like it. So big!"

Troy started to complain, "We've been out here for three hours. I've started thinkin' lately—"

Suddenly looking startled, Leonard shouted, "Hey, did ya see that over to the left? I thought I saw somethin' over by those big trees!"

"It's that bad meat you're eatin', makin' ya see things. Just relax," Troy said with a laugh.

There was silence for two minutes, and then Leonard shouted again, "There it is! I saw it! It looked like a big guy comin' toward us from the trees over there. He was closer this time!"

Troy sighed, "I told you not to eat that garbage! You're seein' things."

◄ **Critical Viewing**
Pick two or three adjectives to describe the man in this picture. Then, find the part of the story that his expression fits. **[Connect]**

John's first sentence uses sensory details to introduce the setting— the woods of Manitoba, Canada.

The spelling of the dialogue shows how these characters actually talk. John also uses interrupted speech, another way to make dialogue sound realistic.

The conflict begins to develop. Leonard thinks he sees something, but Troy doesn't believe him.

Student Work in Progress • 91

Critical Viewing

Connect Students may say *surprised, shocked,* or *frightened.*

Step-by-Step Teaching Guide

Teaching from the Final Draft

1. Engage students in a discussion of "The Manitoba Monster," pointing out some of the strengths of the story that have been covered in the chapter. Use the margin notes to guide the discussion and cover the following points:

   • John's adventure story has a memorable setting.

   • The strong beginning tells the reader immediately where the story takes place and what the characters are up to.

   • The characters and setting are vividly described with words such as *greasy, howling,* and *crusted* and images such as *salami.*

   • Realistic, vernacular dialogue is combined with direct quotations.

   • The writer shows, not tells, what is happening.

   • There is a conflict between the characters, based on the plot map.

   • The story ends well, with the recurring image of the greasy salami and week-old ham sandwich.

continued

Language Highlight

Dialect Dialect is the particular form on a language that people from a certain geographical area or social group use. Writers can use dialect in their work to make dialogue seem more realistic.

✎ STANDARDIZED TEST PREPARATION WORKSHOP

Punctuating Dialogue Standardized test questions may require students to recognize correct punctuation for dialogue. Ask students to choose the correctly punctuated sentence below.

A "We want to go for a hike Sam said."

B We want to go for a hike, Sam said."

C "We want to go for a hike," Sam said.

D "We want to go for a hike", Sam said.

Choice **C** correctly uses quotations only around Sam's exact words and includes a comma inside the quotation marks.

Step-by-Step Teaching Guide
continued

2. Ask students for their opinion of the story. What did they like? What could have been improved?

3. Discuss how John mixes humor with suspense. Do students think he is successful? Or does the exaggerated humor undermine the suspense?

Customize for
More Advanced Students

Students can work together either to write a continuation of the story—a sequel—or to use the setting and characters but change elements of the plot to create a different story.

Customize for
Visual/Spatial Learners

Students can create a storyboard for the story to get a better sense of the use of plot.

Critical Viewing

Compare Students should note that both the monster in the picture and the monster in the story are tall and hairy. The one in the picture has brown fur, while the one in the story has "brown and black fur."

"I don't care," Leonard said. "I'm gonna have a look over there!" And with that, he went off. Troy ignored him and continued fishing while eating his week-old ham sandwich.

At the far side of the lake, Leonard called, "Hey you! I know you're here somewhere! What are ya doin', tryin' to scare us?"

Then he heard a rustling in the bushes, and out of the corner of his eye he saw a figure fleeing behind a tree.

"Ah ha!" he said. "I see ya over there! Why 'er you hidin' behind that tree? Ha ha!"

He ran to the tree where he thought he saw the figure. Then, he just stood frozen in shock. About forty feet away from him there was a tall creature. It stood like a man but was covered in wiry brown and black fur, with a long muzzle and small, beady eyes.

Leonard didn't want to show that he was scared, so he sort of joked, "You're a hairy lookin' fella!"

The creature galloped toward him, baring his long, sharp teeth. Leonard was too scared to move. He just stood there, clutching his greasy chunk of salami.

Meanwhile, Troy was starting to wonder about Leonard, and he yelled, "Hey, Leonard! Stop your searching—there's nothin' out there!" When he didn't hear a response, he got up and walked to where he thought he had seen his friend disappear. After trudging a short way through the woods, he saw Leonard's glove and half-eaten chunk of salami on the ground. He started to worry. "Come on, Leonard! Let's get out of here!" he called out. Still silence. Troy jogged about sixty feet into the woods and then saw Leonard lying on his back in a ditch. Leonard's wool hat was pulled down low over his eyes.

Troy became pale and yelled, "Leonard—are ya all right?" Seconds later, a dark shadow fell over him, and everything went black. . . .

A few hours later, some snowmobilers found the two men wandering in the woods and called the police. After Leonard and Troy told their stories, the authorities decided that the two terrified men had imagined the whole thing.

Deputy Dan told them, "You know, you two should take it easy, take a vacation, maybe see a doctor or somethin'."

Finally, Leonard and Troy began to believe that maybe they had just been seeing things. Maybe it was just something they'd eaten!

And the two continued with their lives as if nothing had happened—except that they never went ice fishing again . . . or ate old meat. But reports still come in of men who see large, dark, hairy creatures with long, sharp teeth in the woods of Manitoba—men like Troy and Leonard, who eat a bad diet of greasy salami and old ham sandwiches.

92 • Short Story

▲ **Critical Viewing**
Compare the monster in the picture to the one in the story. **[Compare]**

Specific sensory details about how the monster looks, and about how his hair might feel to the touch, add color to the story.

This is the story's climax, or turning point. The conflict—will anyone believe Leonard's story?—must be resolved.

At the resolution, the conflict is resolved. Troy now believes Leonard—but no one else believes either of them!

Connected Assignment *Drama*

Writing a short story is not the only way to tell a story. A **drama**, such as a play, uses actors to act out a narrative. Elements of drama include

- **dialogue**—or speech—for one or more characters.
- **stage directions** telling how the characters speak, where they are on stage, and what actions they perform.

MODEL

Grandpa and the Statue
Arthur Miller

Notice how sound effects, stage directions, and the identity of each speaker are set off from the spoken dialogue in this excerpt from a radio play:

[*High wind*]

CHILD MONOGHAN. [*Softly, as though* GRANDPA *is in bed*] Grampa?

MONOGHAN. [*awakened*] Heh? What are you doin' up?

Use the following strategies to write a radio script for a dialogue.

Prewriting Imagine two characters talking to each other about a problem. Write down important details about each character and about the problem they face.

Drafting Begin drafting by "listening" to your characters talk. After you write what one character says, imagine how the other character would respond. Then, write down his or her answer. Afterward, add directions that tell a reader how words are said, what characters are doing while they speak, or what sounds are heard in the background.

Revising and Editing Read the draft of your scene out loud. Rewrite lines that do not sound as if they would be said by the characters you have described.

Publishing and Presenting With a classmate, read your dialogue for the class. Have another partner produce the sound effects you need.

▲ **Critical Viewing**
What stage directions might this actor be following? **[Infer]**

▶ *Lesson Objectives*

1. To write a dialogue appropriate to audience and purpose.
2. To include appropriate stage directions.
3. To perform the dialogue for the class.

Step-by-Step Teaching Guide

Drama

1. Use the model to demonstrate the importance of stage directions. Copy the dialogue onto the chalkboard, eliminating the stage directions. Ask the class how the two versions of the dialogue differ. Point out that without the stage directions, the actor playing the child would not know to whisper his line and the actor playing Grampa would not know to mumble as though he had just awakened and was not fully lucid.

2. You might want to make this a partner activity. Partners can work together to agree on a scenario and then role-play a conversation between two characters. They can use this as the basis for their written dialogue.

3. Challenge students to perform their dialogues as radio plays, instead of reading or reciting them in front of the class. Students can tape-record their performances and play the tapes for the class. They should have fun devising the necessary sound effects. You might tell them that sound effects in real radio plays were very primitive; almost any solid objects could be banged on a table in rhythm to suggest a horse's hoofs trotting along, for example. Encourage students to use their imagination.

Critical Viewing

Infer Students may say the actor may be following stage directions for an action to perform.

93

Step-by-Step Teaching Guide

Comparing Themes Across the Arts

1. Choose a Spotlight element for class discussion, or have students work independently or in small groups on the element of their choice. Give students the initiative to find the necessary books and paintings.

2. Make a class list of the characteristics students associate with dragons, such as "breathing fire" or "evil-tempered." Be aware that students from different cultures may associate different qualities with these mythical beasts.

3. Have students compare stories they have read about dragons. Some students may have read *The Hobbit*, in which a dragon named Smaug, who has been hoarding the dwarves' treasure, attempts to destroy the nearby town when the dwarves threaten to take it back.

Viewing and Representing

Activity Students who have read novels or stories in which dragons appear may want to retell those stories from the dragon's point of view. Students may want to read their stories aloud to a class of kindergarten or first-grade students.

Critical Viewing

Draw Conclusions Students may say that if the lady were missing, there would be less of a sense of urgency for the knight to kill the dragon. If the dragon were missing, there would be no conflict. If the knight were missing, there would be no suspense or hope for a rescue.

Spotlight on the Humanities

Comparing Themes Across the Arts

Focus on Oral Traditions: Dragons

Perhaps the story started with a snake slithering away between two rocks. Perhaps it started with a curl of smoke rising from a mountain where nobody lived. No one is sure how the story of dragons got started. It seems as if the story has always been told.

Images of dragons appear in art as early as 2000 B.C. Dragon stories are familiar in Asia, Europe, and Africa. For the Chinese, the dragon symbolizes good fortune and wisdom. In Chinese mythology, dragons bring the rains from the sea. The ancient Greeks and Romans believed the dragon held great secrets. (The painting shown illustrates the battle between Perseus, a Greek hero, and a dragon-like creature.)

By the time the dragon appears in the tale of St. George, though, he is just an evil, scaly, firebreathing menace. In the legend, St. George saves a princess by battling a dragon who lives in Libya. St. George has appeared in artworks in Ethiopia, Egypt, and Britain.

Dragons make for good stories, in part because they create a strong conflict—they kidnap princesses, steal treasures, and burn towns. Dragon stories also remind us that princesses and treasures are often held captive by an old fear, coiled in a cave. Then, the only way to find the good things is to confront the bad.

Literature Connection The novel *Dragonfly* (1999) by Alice McLerran relates the story of a friendly dragon. Filled with humor and adventure, the novel tells the story of the friendship between a boy named Jason and the dragon "Drag."

Short Story Writing Activity: Story by a Dragon

Write a story from a dragon's point of view. First, decide whether your dragon is nice or nasty. Then, tell the story of his or her confrontation with a hero, with a princess, or with modern times.

94 • Short Story

Andromeda rescued from the monster by Perseus riding Pegasus, Christine de Pisan, British Library, London

▲ Critical Viewing Imagine that one of the three characters shown in this painting was missing. Explain why the story would be less interesting. **[Draw Conclusions]**

Media and Technology Skills

Analyzing Visual Meanings

Activity: Analyze Story Elements in Cartoons

Even the wackiest cartoon includes the same elements as a short story—character, setting, theme, and plot. To appreciate cartoons, learn about the storytelling elements they use.

Think About It Many cartoons feature the following elements:

Distinctive Characters You might remember one cartoon character for his ridiculous looks. You might remember another for her funny way of talking or the special phrases she always uses. For these reasons, viewers recognize cartoon characters easily. The characters quickly become like old friends.

Tricks With Reality Cartoonists often "bend the rules" of reality. Characters' limbs may stretch impossibly, then snap back into shape. People may fall a great distance—then bounce. Cartoonists use these tricks for humor and to show how a lively imagination can always get around reality.

Comic Pacing Think of a cartoon with a goofy hero and his foolish enemy. Each scene in the cartoon will show the hunter trying to capture the hero. Each scene grows more ridiculous than the last. If the hunter used a mousetrap in the first scene, he might use a cannon in the next. By the end of the cartoon, each scene may take place at high speed. In this way, a cartoonist sets up a certain rhythm or pacing, adding to the humor.

Pacing for Suspense In an action cartoon, the action may briefly slow down near the end. For example, just when the villain captures the hero, the cartoon may jump to the hero's friends eating lunch. Here, the pacing of events increases the viewer's suspense.

Analyze It As you watch a cartoon, record the storytelling elements it uses in a chart like the one shown. Referring to the details in your chart, write a paragraph explaining why you enjoyed or did not enjoy the cartoon.

Other Story Elements in Cartoons

- **Conflict** In action cartoons, the conflict concerns the hero's attempt to stop the villain from doing evil. In humorous cartoons, the conflict may be between a zany character and the character he or she is always annoying.

- **Theme** A basic theme of many action cartoons is simple: Good always wins over evil. A basic theme of many comic cartoons is also simple: It is foolish to trust even the best plans, because the world is unpredictable and mischievous.

Step-by-Step Teaching Guide

Analyzing Visual Meanings

Teaching Resources: Writing Support Transparency 5-I; Writing Support Activity Book 5-4

1. Ask students to describe the cartoons they watch. Have them discuss the qualities they like and dislike about different cartoons.

2. Show a variety of cartoons in the classroom if you have access to a VCR. You might show different types for contrast: a coyote/road runner cartoon, a Mickey Mouse adventure, and a Winnie the Pooh story. Use the transparency to demonstrate comparing and contrasting the story elements of the cartoons.

3. Give students copies of the blank organizer so that students can complete the activity.

Character Name	Distinctive Characteristics	Hero or Villain?	My Reaction to the Character

Conflict	My Reaction to the Conflict	Special Effects	My Reaction to the Effects

Media and Technology Skills • 95

Lesson Objectives

1. To analyze the narrative elements of a short story.
2. To use prewriting strategies to gather and organize details.
3. To draft, revise, and edit an analysis of a narrative.
4. To use correct grammar, spelling, and mechanics.

Step-by-Step Teaching Guide

Responding to Writing Prompts About Narratives

1. Have a student read aloud the writing prompt. Write the phrase *the author's opinion* on the chalkboard. Remind students not to discuss their own opinions of the Elders in the answer. Instead, they need to point out specific details in the story that show the author's opinion.

2. The author's attitude toward his or her subject is called *tone.* As students consider their answer in the prewriting stage of the essay, have them think about the tone of the story. How did it strike them? What did they think about the elders' decisions? Did the author want them to think this? Which clues in the story suggest that he did?

3. Remind students that when a question involves the interpretation of literature, there is often not one right answer. Students might have different, defensible opinions about the author's attitude toward the Elders. However, it is very important that they support their answers with specific details from the story. If an answer is not defended with evidence from the story, it will receive a low score.

Standardized Test Preparation Workshop

Responding to Writing Prompts About Narratives

Some standardized tests require you to write a short response to a story you have read. Learning how the elements of a short story work together will help you write about short stories. Before responding to a test prompt on a short story, think about how the following narrative elements shape the story:

- **Plot** is the sequence of events in the story, arranged in a way that will keep readers interested.
- **Characters** are the people, animals, or other beings that take part in the story's action.
- **Setting** is the time and place in which the story unfolds.
- **Theme** is the question or message about life that the story expresses.

As you read the story in a test-taking situation, think about how the writer uses each narrative device to create an effective short story.

To practice for such test questions, respond to the following prompt, using the suggestions on the next page. The clocks show what portion of your test-taking time to devote to each stage of the writing process.

Sample Writing Situation

Read "The Snow in Chelm" by Isaac Bashevis Singer on page 74. Then, answer the following question.

What is the author's opinion of the way the Elders of Chelm make their decisions? Use details and information from the story in your answer.

Test Tips

- To get a handle on narrative elements in a story or passage, first jot down the main characters and central events of the story or passage.
- If you are unsure whether you have made a grammar or spelling error in a sentence in your test essay, consider rewriting the sentence to eliminate the need to correct it.

 TEST-TAKING TIP

When they get a question like the one on this page that involves the interpretation of literature, students should look to see which of the four main short-story elements the question deals with. In this workshop, the question addresses character and possible theme. Thus, in the prewriting stages, students should make notes about important aspects of these two elements. Challenge students to identify the elements being addressed in the following writing prompts:

- In "To Build a Fire," how does Jack London make the Alaskan wilderness a character in the story? (Setting)
- In "The Cask of Amontillado," what is Edgar Allan Poe's attitude toward his narrator's vow of revenge? (Character, theme)

Encourage students to get into the habit of keeping a reader's response journal. After a student completes a reading assignment or reads a book or story for pleasure, the student should write a brief journal entry describing his or her reactions to the text. Journal entries should include whether the reader liked the text and why he or she did or did not. As students get into the habit of writing out their responses to literature, they will find it very easy to answer a literary-response question on a test.

Customize for
Less Advanced Students

Encourage students to choose partners with whom to work on reading assignments. Students should read on their own, then meet to discuss their assignments. In discussion, both partners should give their reactions to the assignment and give reasons for those reactions. As they get into the habit of articulating their responses, students will find that writing answers to test questions like the one on this page will get easier and easier.

Prewriting

Allow about one fourth of your time for prewriting.

Gather Details From the Story The prompt asks you to give the author's opinion on the Elders' way of solving problems. Scan the story for specific information about the Elders' decisions and their results. Note any comments the author makes about the Elders and their decisions.

Create a T-Chart As you gather details, enter them in a T-Chart. In one column, list the decisions the Elders make. In the other column, list the reasons they arrive at each decision, the results, and any opinion stated by the author about each.

Analyze Your Chart An author does not have to state his or her opinion on events in the story. Instead, the author can imply an opinion. Review your T-Chart. Evaluate each decision and its results. Ask such questions as the following: Were the results what the Elders intended? Did they look at the matter from a few different angles before deciding? Then, jot down on your chart the author's probable opinion on each decision.

Drafting

Allow approximately half of your time for drafting.

Write an Introduction In your introduction, clearly state what you will be covering in your response. Briefly summarize your conclusions.

Organize Details Outline the main points of your essay. Under each main point, list details from the story or from your own experience that support that point.

Include Story Details If you simply say that the author thinks the Elders are "foolish," you have not conveyed much about the story to your reader. Make sure that you support each statement about the author's opinion or about the Elders and their decisions with specific examples from the story. If you copy the exact words of the story to make a point, place them in quotation marks.

Revising, Editing, and Proofreading

Allow about twenty minutes for revising, editing, and proofreading.

Check Support Read through your response. Neatly draw a line through any details that do not support the main idea of your essay. For any main point you make about the story, be that sure you have supplied an example.

Clean It Up When you are satisfied with your answer, read your draft one last time for problems with spelling. Make all corrections neatly.

Standardized Test Preparation Workshop • 97

Time and Resource Manager

In-Depth Lesson Plan

	LESSON FOCUS	PRINT AND MEDIA RESOURCES
DAY 1	**Introduction to Description** Students learn key elements of descriptive writing and analyze the Model From Literature (pp. 98–101).	*Writers at Work* **Videotape**, Description *Writing Lab* **CD-ROM**, Description
DAY 2	**Prewriting** Students choose and narrow a topic, consider their audience and purpose, and gather information (pp. 102–105).	**Teaching Resources** *Writing Support Transparencies* 6-A–C; *Writing Support Activity Book* 6-1
DAY 3	**Drafting** Students organize their ideas and write their first drafts (pp. 106–107).	**Teaching Resources** *Writing Support Transparencies* 6-D
DAY 4	**Revising** Students revise their drafts in terms of overall structure, paragraphs, sentences, and word choice (pp. 108–112).	**Teaching Resources** *Writing Support Transparencies* 6-E–G
DAY 5	**Editing and Proofreading; Publishing and Presenting** Students check their work for accuracy and correctness and present their final drafts (pp. 113–114).	**Teaching Resources** *Scoring Rubrics on Transparency*, Ch. 6; *Formal Assessment*, Ch. 6

Accelerated Lesson Plan

	LESSON FOCUS	PRINT AND MEDIA RESOURCES
DAY 1	**Drafting** Students review characteristics of descriptive writing, select topics and write drafts (pp. 98–107).	**Teaching Resources** *Writing Support Transparencies* 6-A–D; *Writing Support Activity Book* 6-1 *Writers at Work* **Videotape**, Description *Writing Lab* **CD-ROM**, Description
DAY 2	**Revising to Presenting** Students work individually or with peers to revise, edit, and proofread their work for presentation (pp. 108–114).	**Teaching Resources** *Writing Support Transparencies* 6-E–G; *Scoring Rubrics on Transparency*, Chapter 6; *Formal Assessment* Ch. 6

Options for Adapting Lesson Plans

HOMEWORK
Have students complete any stage of the lesson for homework.

FEATURES
Extend coverage with the Connected Assignment (p. 118), Spotlight on the Humanities (p. 120), Media and Technology Skills (p. 121) and the Standardized Test Preparation Workshop (p. 122).

TECHNOLOGY
Students can complete any stage of the lesson on computer. Have them print out their completed work.

INTEGRATED SKILLS COVERAGE

Integrating Grammar
Adjectives SE p. 111
Commas with Adjectives SE p. 113

Reading/Writing Connection
Reading Strategy SE p. 100
Writing Application SE p. 101

Technology
SE pp. 111, 114, 121

Speaking and Listening
ATE p. 107

Viewing and Representing
Critical Viewing SE pp. 98, 100, 104, 106, 109, 112, 115, 116, 117, 120
ATE p. 120

BLOCK SCHEDULING

Pacing Suggestions
For 90-minute Blocks
• Have students complete the Prewriting and Drafting stages in a single period.
• Focus one class period on Revising and Editing and Publishing and Presenting. Allow at least 30 minutes for peer revision.

Resources for Varying Instruction
• *Writing Lab* **CD-ROM** If your students have access to hardware, a 90-minute block provides an ideal opportunity for students to work on computer.
• *Writers at Work* **Videotape** Show the Descriptive Essay segment in class.

Professional Development Support
• *How to Manage Instruction in the Block* This Teaching Resource provides management and activity suggestions.

ASSESSMENT SUPPORT

Standardized Test Preparation Workshop SE p. 122; ATE p. 110
Standardized Test Preparation Workbook, pp. 11–12
Scoring Rubrics on Transparency, Ch. 6
Formal Assessment, Ch. 6
Writing Assessment and Portfolio Management

MEDIA AND TECHNOLOGY

For the Student
• *Writing Lab* **CD-ROM**, Description

For the Teacher
• *Writers at Work* **Videotape**, Description
• *Resource Pro* **CD-ROM**

MEETING INDIVIDUAL NEEDS

Less Advanced Students ATE pp. 108, 123; See also Ongoing Assessments ATE pp. 99, 103, 104, 105, 107, 109, 111, 114
ESL Students ATE pp. 102, 103, 111
Visual/Spatial Learners ATE p. 106
Bodily/Kinesthetic Learners ATE p. 102
Interpersonal Learners ATE p. 106
Verbal/Linguistic Learners ATE p. 106

WRITING AND GRAMMAR WEB SITE

The Interactive Writing and Grammar Web site provides a wide array of support for students, teachers, and parents. Writing support includes:
• Interactive revision checkers
• Scoring rubrics with complete models

www.phschool.com

LITERATURE CONNECTIONS

Related selections from *Prentice Hall Literature: Timeless Voices, Timeless Themes,* Copper:
"The Sound of Summer Running," Ray Bradbury, SE p. 101
"Water," Helen Keller, SE p. 103

► *Lesson Objectives*

1. To define descriptive writing.
2. To identify four types of descriptive writing.
3. To read and interpret a descriptive excerpt from a novel.
4. To utilize strategies for choosing a topic.
5. To review strategies in the Topic Bank for choosing a topic.
6. To consider audience and purpose.
7. To use senses to gather details.
8. To use organizational plan to clarify ideas.
9. To use sensory details to elaborate.
10. To publish and present a descriptive essay.
11. To reflect on the experience of writing.

Critical Viewing

Apply Students may say the mountains look tall, the air smells fresh, the food tastes wonderful, the fruit feels ripe, and you can hear the wind outside.

Chapter 6 Description

Bok Choy and Apples, Patricia Chin Lee

Description in Everyday Life

"What kind of jacket are you looking for?" a sales clerk might inquire. "What does their music sound like?" a friend might ask. To answer these questions, you must describe what you are looking for or what you have heard.

Like your spoken words, a written description can show others what a person, thing, or scene is like. Descriptive writing is much harder than shopping, though! In a store, you can always point to the jacket you want. You can't point in writing. Words alone must do the job of showing what you have in mind.

Tap into the picture-making power of words: Develop your descriptive writing skills.

▲ Critical Viewing
Describe this scene, using one word from each of the five senses. [Apply]

98 • Description

⏱ TIME AND RESOURCE MANAGER

Resources
Technology: Writers at Work videotape

In-Depth Coverage	Accelerated Pace
• Cover pp. 98–101 in class. • Show the Descriptive Writing section of the Writers at Work videotape. • Discuss different types of descriptive writing. **Option** Have students work individually or in groups on the description section of the Writing Lab CD-ROM.	• Assign pp. 98–101 for independent student review. • Discuss definitions and types of descriptive writing.

What Is Descriptive Writing?

Descriptive writing creates a picture of a person, place, thing, or event. Description includes more than just the looks of a thing, however. It lets you hear the "shushing" sound of Grandpa's slippers outside the door. It gives you a sudden whiff of his icy aftershave and a woolly handful of his warm sweater—just like when you give him a hug! The elements of descriptive writing include

- vivid sensory details—details appealing to one or more of the five senses.
- a clear, consistent organization.
- a main impression to which each detail adds specific information.
- the use of figurative language, such as vivid comparisons.

To learn the criteria on which your description may be judged or graded, see the Rubric for Self-Assessment on page 114.

Types of Descriptive Writing

Your description may be one of several types:

- **Descriptions of people or places** portray the physical appearance and personality of a person or place and show readers why the subject is important or special.
- **Observations** describe an event the writer has witnessed.
- **Remembrances** recall a memorable experience in the writer's life; they may describe a specific moment or a longer period of time.
- **Vignettes** capture a single specific moment in the writer's life, painting a picture with words.

PREVIEW

Student Work
IN PROGRESS

Leann Goree, a student at Southside Fundamental Middle School in St. Petersburg, Florida, described the sensations and impressions of snow as she remembered them. You can see examples of the prewriting, drafting, and revising techniques she used to create her description. At the end of the chapter, you can read Leann's completed piece, "Snow Dance."

Writers in ACTION

Deborah Behler is a zoologist and wildlife writer. She writes about the animals at the Bronx Zoo—more than 4,000 of them! When Behler gathers details for her writing, she relies on her observation of the animals in their exhibits.

"Sensory language in descriptive writing is important because that's how people understand what's going on around them—what you see, what you hear, [what you] touch."

PREPARE and ENGAGE

Interest GRABBER Display a picture of an interesting object, such as a hot-air balloon, an octopus, the largest pumpkin ever grown. Ask students to suggest words that describe it. Write their words on the chalkboard and then look at what you have and how it might be assembled into a paragraph of description.

Activate Prior Knowledge

Ask students to think of an interesting or unusual experience they have had recently. It could be a place they visited, a movie they saw, a food they ate. Ask them to describe the experience in as much detail as possible.

✓ ONGOING ASSESSMENT: Diagnose

Use one of the following options to diagnose students' current level of proficiency in descriptive writing.

Option 1 Ask each student to select the strongest example of his or her descriptive writing from last year. Hold conferences to review each student's sample. Use the conferences to determine which students will need extra support in developing a descriptive essay.	**Option 2** Ask students to briefly describe either an object, experience, or memory. If students have difficulty with the exercise, you may need to devote more attention to the drafting phase of the writing process.

Reading\Writing Connection

Reading: Infer

Writers do not always state exactly what they mean. If they did, writing would be boring. Instead, they hint at meaning. Readers need to use their imagination and experience to "translate" or infer the meaning of those hints. What can be inferred from Yep's story about how to act in an emergency?

Teaching from the Model

Use the model to show the value of sensory descriptive writing. Furthermore, the author manages to integrate detailed description with a cliff-hanger plot. Be sure students notice the balance of detailed description with the tight, short declarative sentences, including the last one.

Step-by-Step Teaching Guide

Engage Students Through Literature

1. Read aloud "A Narrow Escape" or have volunteers read it.

2. After the reading, ask students to discuss the story, using the following questions as prompts.

   • What is the situation? (Three men are trapped in a cabin that is on fire.)

   • How do you know? Yep never says anything like, "The cabin caught fire. The three men couldn't get out." (Yep describes flames and the characters trying to break out.)

Critical Viewing

Comparison and Contrast
Students' responses will vary, but they may mention the movement or heat of the fire.

6.1 **Model From Literature**

In his novel The Tom Sawyer Fires, *Laurence Yep (1948–) recounts the adventures of a fireman named Tom Sawyer. In this excerpt, you can see how effective descriptive writing can create suspense and excitement as well as vivid images.*

Reading ◄ **Writing** ► **Connection**

Reading Strategy: **Infer**

A writer does not spell out all the information you need to understand characters or situations. To understand a situation or character fully, **make inferences,** or draw conclusions, based on the details the writer provides. For instance, at the end of the following excerpt, the writer does not tell you that the characters have broken through the roof. You can infer that they have broken through, however, when the narrator sees the sky and says, "You did it."

▲ Critical Viewing
Write a sentence comparing this fire to a specific kind of living thing. **[Comparison and Contrast]**

A Narrow Escape

Laurence Yep

Glass began tinkling all around us, and the smell of rotten eggs was overpowering. Flames crackled around the door and walls, small triangles at first, but they shot upward like bright weeds. The shack was already filling with smoke.

We began to swing the chair back and forth in rhythm, so that the legs hammered against the boards. By the sixth or seventh swing, a chair leg broke. And by the twelfth, the chair itself had caught fire.

We dropped it with a crash on the floor, and I got hold of a rag and whipped it against the burning chair leg. Now the boards of the cabin were outlined by fire—it seemed as if we were trapped inside a cell of glowing bars.

The author uses sensory details and a comparison to "bright weeds" to set the scene. The details tell readers what the characters hear, see, and smell.

Vivid sensory details such as "glowing bars" create strong images in the reader's mind.

100 • Description

"Those boards were nailed to stay there till doomsday," Tom said.

"Maybe someone will see the fire," I said, "and get the fire companies."

Mark was doubtful. "Even if they did, how would they know we were in here?"

Once the fire reached the roof, the shack was going to collapse. Tom looked up. "The roof. That's it."

He crouched, pointing his index finger toward a big brown stain in the center of the roof. "See that big patch of tin? Maybe we can knock it off and get out that way."

Tom and Mark had positioned the table underneath the tin patch. "Get Letty's shawl, will you?" Tom ordered. . . . "Come on, Your Grace." Mark got the pot of water and carefully poured it over the shawl.

Then Tom picked up the shawl and draped it over his head and shoulders. Water spattered down the wet fringes. "Stay close to the floor, Your Grace," he said. "More air there."

Tom swung a chair on top of the table and climbed up. "I think heaven is going to have to wait.". . .

Tom thrust the chair against the tin, and there was a hollow, bonging sound. "I think it's giving."

I beat at the flames on the floor, trying to keep them away from the table.

Tom was pounding at the tin, and the metal square boomed and echoed like we were in the middle of a thunderstorm. But by the tenth swing, we heard a crack.

"Was that a roof board?" Mark asked.

"No," Tom sounded grim, "it was a chair leg."

I was hopping around like a crazy frog as I flailed at the fire on the floor.

Tom swung again and I heard another chair leg crack and fall off. He began to batter frantically at the tin. Suddenly he gave a sharp yelp.

I looked up to see a little rectangle of glorious blue sky. "You did it."

Writing Application: Help Your Readers Make Inferences As you draft your description, include details that will help readers make inferences about the feelings you have about the person, place, or object that you are describing.

Words like then *show that this excerpt is organized chronologically: The author describes events in the order in which they occur.*

Sensory details such as boomed, echoed, *and* crack *let the reader hear what is happening.*

LITERATURE

For another example of vivid descriptive writing, read "The Sound of Summer Running" by Ray Bradbury. You can find this narrative in *Prentice Hall Literature: Timeless Voices, Timeless Themes,* Copper.

Responding to Literature

Have students create a chart that lists each of the five senses in one column and details that appeal to each of these senses in the other column.

More About the Author

Laurence Yep (born 1948) is a third-generation Chinese American who grew up in San Francisco. He sold his first story when he was 18 after being encouraged by his high school English teacher. He is the author of many books, including *Dragonwings.*

Reading\Writing Connection

Writing: Help Your Readers Make Inferences

Remind students that using details to imply things about the person, place, or thing about which they are writing can make reading their work more enjoyable for readers.

Prewriting: Drawing; Trigger Words

Teaching Resources: Writing Support Transparency 6-A

1. These activities are designed to stimulate students' thinking about choosing a topic. In getting students to generate topics for descriptive writing, the key is to think of things that hold interest and details that can be described.

2. The drawing activity will not appeal to all students. To get the widest coverage, remind students that the drawing is only a means to stimulate their imagination and memory, not an end in itself. It isn't supposed to be "art." Encourage them to sketch or draw in whatever detail works for them.

3. Display the transparency. Review Leann's trigger words. You might want to set up the activity by having students relax, close their eyes, and write down what comes into their minds.

Customize for
ESL Students

Urge students to try this activity in English, but let students freewrite using some words from their home language. The goal is quantity. Students can find the English equivalents afterward.

Customize for
Bodily/Kinesthetic Learners

Suggest that students use movement and gesture as a source for creating a topic. They could either apply movement or gesture to the Trigger Word activity or use it directly to recall something of interest they would like to use for a topic.

6.2 Prewriting

Choosing Your Topic

Almost any person, place, event, or object that you find interesting or that is important to you will make a good topic for descriptive writing. Use these strategies to select a topic:

Strategies for Generating a Topic

1. **Drawing** Think of a place, such as your grandparents' house or a park, that you visit. Draw the people and scenes that come to mind. After five minutes, review your drawings. Select your topic from among the people and events you have drawn, or from a memory your drawings bring to mind.

2. **Trigger Words** Think of three general words, such as *night, winter,* and *lunch*. For each word, write whatever pops into your mind. Write about each word for five minutes. Then, review your work, and circle the most interesting words. Select a topic related to these words.

Writing Lab CD-ROM

For more help finding a topic for a description, use the strategies and tips in the Choosing a Topic section of the Description Lesson.

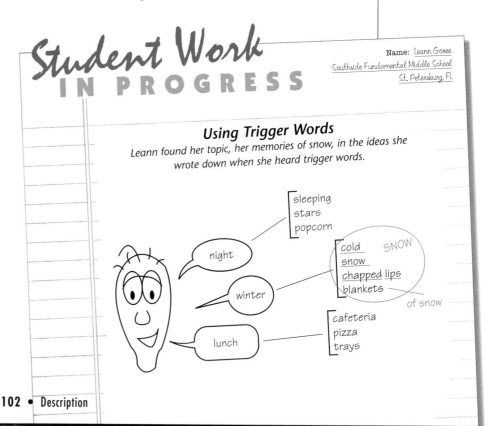

Student Work IN PROGRESS

Name: Leann Goree
Southside Fundamental Middle School
St. Petersburg, FL

Using Trigger Words
Leann found her topic, her memories of snow, in the ideas she wrote down when she heard trigger words.

night — sleeping / stars / popcorn

winter — cold / snow / chapped lips / blankets — SNOW / of snow

lunch — cafeteria / pizza / trays

102 • Description

⏱ TIME AND RESOURCE MANAGER

Resources
Print: Writing Support Transparencies 6-A–C; Writing Support Activity Book 6-I
Technology: Writing Lab CD-ROM, Description

In-Depth Coverage	Accelerated Pace
• Cover pp.102–105 in class. • Work through the Drawing and Trigger Words strategies with the class. • Use the Responding to Fine Art Transparency to generate additional topics. • Do the Audience Profile activity in class.	• Assign pp. 102–105 for independent student review. • Discuss strategies for generating topics. • Have students work independently to choose and narrow their topics. • Have students work with partners to focus on audience, purpose, and gathering details.

TOPICS

TOPIC BANK

If you're having trouble finding a topic, consider these possibilities:

1. **Description of Weather** Describe weather that is especially noticeable and creates a mood, such as a summer thunderstorm, a sunny day in early spring, a windy fall day, or a dreary, overcast winter afternoon.

2. **Observation of the Animal World** Take your cue from zoologist Deborah Behler, and choose an animal at the zoo or in your home as your topic.

Responding to Fine Art

3. Jot down notes about the scene in this painting. What objects do you see? What details is the painter able to capture? Write a description of the scene in this painting, or of a similar scene in your own life. Be sure to describe the sights, sounds, smells, and textures that belong to the scene.

Farberware Coffeepot, No. VI, Jeanette Pasin Sloan, National Museum of American Art, Washington, DC

Responding to Literature

4. Read "Water" by Helen Keller, paying special attention to the sensory details she uses. Then, write a description of an object. In the first part of your description, use just the senses that Keller uses. Then, describe the object using your other senses. You can find "Water" in *Prentice Hall Literature: Timeless Voices, Timeless Themes*, Copper.

☑ Cooperative Writing Opportunity

5. **Object Observation** With a group of classmates, create a grab bag. Each member should bring a small item from home—an object with an interesting shape, texture, or other sensory quality. Put the items in a bag. Individually, choose an item without looking, and then write a description of it. First, explain what the object felt like in the bag. Then, describe what it turned out to be. Together, organize your descriptions in a booklet.

Prewriting • 103

Step-by-Step Teaching Guide

Farberware Coffeepot, No. VI, by Jeanette Pasin Sloan

Responding to Fine Art

Teaching Resource: Writing Support Transparency 6-B

1. Display the transparency and have students describe the objects they see.

2. In addition to describing what they see in the picture, students can make up a story to go with it. For example, "The mug belongs to a young woman who has just gotten her own apartment . . ." or "There were two mugs on the counter, but the cat knocked one to the floor . . ."

Responding to Literature

Ask students to consider how hard it was for Helen Keller, deprived of sight and hearing, to learn language and the power of names for things. Does the breakthrough described in the well-house suggest any possible topics to them?

Customize for ESL Students

Helen Keller couldn't see, hear, or (until later) speak words. Students learning English at one time couldn't recognize, understand, or say English words. The challenges of having to learn a new language—and/or a new culture—may be fruitful topics for students' descriptions.

Spotlight on the Humanities

For additional topic suggestions, refer students to the Spotlight on the Humanities on page 120.

☑ ONGOING ASSESSMENT: Monitor and Reinforce

If some students are having difficulty coming up with a topic, use one of the following options.

Option 1 Suggest that students choose an idea from the Topic Bank. If many students have difficulty, work with them around one topic, modeling the process for them.	**Option 2** If the Topic Bank ideas seem too complex, suggest that students try one of the assignments from the Topic Bank for Heterogeneous Classes in the Teaching Resources.

⏱ TIME SAVERS!

Writing Support Transparencies
Use the transparencies for Chapter 6 to teach these strategies.

Prewriting: Narrowing Your Topic; Considering Your Audience and Purpose

1. Finding a topic that can be adequately described in a short essay takes some thinking. Students need to make notes on the amount of detail they can think of to determine the proper narrowness of the topic.

2. Write the following examples on the chalkboard for practice in distinguishing the proper range of a topic:

   Too broad: Animated Shows on TV

   Too narrow: Apu of *The Simpsons*

   Good range: Main characters of *The Simpsons*

3. Gauging audience is critical. If students are describing popular shows on TV, they can assume that most people will know what they are talking about. If, on the other hand, they are writing about shows that appeal to kids and are writing for a general audience, they need to provide some background.

4. Purpose is simple: What is the writer's goal in writing? If it is to entertain, is the topic in line with the purpose? If it is to express oneself in a serious way, will the topic allow the writer to do so successfully?

Critical Viewing

Analyze Students may say they can see someone pushing a child in a swing.

Narrowing Your Topic

Can you cover your entire topic in a brief description? If not, you must narrow your topic. Maybe your topic can be divided into subtopics. For instance, "the park" is a broad topic, but "the playground" is narrower, and "the swingset at the playground" is even more narrow. Decide which subtopic is most interesting to you. An index-card camera can help you zoom in to narrow your topic.

Zoom in to Narrow Your Topic

Use an index card as a "camera." Follow these steps:

1. Cut a small hole in the index card to make the camera's "lens."
2. Take your camera to the scene, object, or person you will describe. If you want to describe a past event or a place or person that is not nearby, find photographs or make drawings of your subject.
3. Look through the "camera lens" at your subject or at the photographs or drawings you have gathered.
4. Focus first on one part of your subject, and then on another. Look both closely and from a distance.
5. Take notes on the details that are particular to each part, and on the details that are common to the entire image.

Afterward, review your notes, and choose as your topic the most interesting aspect of your subject.

▲ **Critical Viewing** What new details can you see in the "close-up" view of this scene? **[Analyze]**

Considering Your Audience and Purpose

Who will read your description? How much do they know about your subject? If your **audience**—your intended reader—has never seen what you're describing, make sure you describe even the most basic details about your subject. If your readers are already familiar with your subject, focus on details that show how special it is.

Your **purpose** in writing a description is to share what you have experienced with readers. To achieve this purpose, include vivid sensory details in your writing. A **sensory detail** is a word, phrase, or sentence that gives precise information about the look, sound, taste, touch, or smell of something.

☑ ONGOING ASSESSMENT: Monitor and Reinforce

Students often fall into the habit of considering the teacher their audience. Use one of the following options to alter this pattern.

Option 1 Have students select a specific person as their audience, someone other than you. This will get them focused away from you and will also affect the level of detail, language, and formality that they put into the essay.	**Option 2** Have students identify a purpose in writing other than appealing to or impressing the teacher.

Gathering Details

Before you begin writing, gather details about your subject. Make sure you gather details for all of the senses. Sensory details are especially effective for creating a vivid picture for readers, as you can see in this example:

NO SENSORY DETAILS:	I got into the wagon for a hayride.
ADDED SENSORY DETAILS:	The hay crackled when I threw myself down, wrapping me in a cloud of sweet and sour smells and prickling me busily along my arms.

Use Each of Your Senses

Imagine your subject, along with all the sights, scents, textures, sounds, and tastes linked to it. Then, fill in a chart like the one below to help you gather details for each of the senses. Refer to your chart as you draft, using details from it in your description.

🔲 Research Tip

To use each of your senses as you gather details, try to use your senses separately. For instance, you might close your eyes and cover your ears as you taste a strawberry.

Student Work
IN PROGRESS

Name: *Leann Goree*
Southside Fundamental Middle School
St. Petersburg, FL

Using a Sensory Details Chart
To gather details from her memories of snow, Leann created a chart like the one below. Notice that she found details for each of the senses.

Sensory Details: Snow

sights	sounds	smells	tastes	sensations of touch
drifting	lips smacking	clean smell in the air	like a watery popsicle	chapped lips
flakes—tiny, white, frail	crisp crunch			soft blanket
sparkling and shining				melting from furry to wet
				tingling and cool

Step-by-Step Teaching Guide

Gathering Details from Each of the Senses

Teaching Resources: Writing Support Transparencies 6-C, Writing Support Activity Book 6-1

1. Descriptive writing relies on details. The key is using all the senses to gather details.
2. Display the transparency. Examine Leann's work in progress to see how she found sensory details for her topic.
3. Give students copies of the blank organizer and have them gather details for their topic.

☑ ONGOING ASSESSMENT: Monitor and Reinforce

If some students are having difficulty gathering sensory details, use one of the following options.

Option 1 Ask students to close their eyes and think individually of each sense, applying it to their topic, if appropriate. What are some visual details? How does it feel? Smell? Remind students that for some topics, not all senses will be appropriate.

Option 2 Remind students that they are describing what the topic means to them. A vivid memory might contain more mental images associated with the topic or event than sensory details.

⏲ TIME SAVERS!

📇 Writing Support Transparencies
Use the transparencies for Chapter 6 to teach these strategies.

📖 Writing Support Activity Book
Use the graphic organizers for Chapter 6 to facilitate these strategies.

105

Drafting: Organize to Make Your Ideas Clear; Create a Main Impression

1. Review the three organizational patterns. It is not a rule that writers must use chronological order to describe an event, and so on. These are general guidelines that may help students. They can use whatever order seems logical to them.

2. A main impression is an organizational tool too, since it provides the focus for the essay. The main impression can be a dominant characteristic of the subject; it can also be a feeling. In other words, students shouldn't look only at the topic or object they are describing for a main impression. They should also look internally at their own thoughts and feelings.

Critical Viewing

Apply Students may say that the ribbon is shiny and makes them feel excited because they like getting presents.

Customize for
Visual/Spatial Learners

Have students use sticky notes to arrange the details of their description in an organizational pattern before beginning to write.

Customize for
Interpersonal and Verbal/Linguistic Learners

Students may benefit from talking through details and a main impression. Have them take turns talking while the partner takes notes.

6.3 Drafting

Shaping Your Writing
Organize to Make Your Ideas Clear

Now that you've gathered details, arrange them in an order that readers can follow. Here are three types of order:

Chronological Order	• Present events in the order in which they occur. • Use for a remembrance or other description of an event.
Spatial Order 	• Present details from left to right, top to bottom, or back to front. • Use for descriptions of places or objects.
Order of Importance	• Present least important details at the beginning and the most important at the end. • Use to lead readers to your main impression.

Create a Main Impression

The descriptions that are most fun to read are those that create a **main impression**—an idea or feeling that ties the details about your subject together. Compare these examples:

NO MAIN IMPRESSION: The box is wrapped in shiny green paper. When I pull the ribbon, it comes free with a soft hissing sound. The top comes off. The object inside sits in light-green tissue paper.

MAIN IMPRESSION: The box keeps calling me. Its wrapping of shiny green paper glints and winks in the light, teasing me to guess what's inside. Finally, it is my turn to open a gift. The ribbon pulls free, sighing "Oh, all right, I'll tell!" The top falls off, revealing a shape nestled in light-green tissue paper.

The second description creates a main impression of suspense by comparing the box to a teasing friend. As you draft, choose details that will create a single main impression.

▼ Critical Viewing
Give a word from the senses to describe this object. Then, give a word describing a feeling you might associate with it. [Apply]

⏱ TIME AND RESOURCE MANAGER

Resources
Print: Writing Support Transparency 6-D
Technology: Writing Lab CD-ROM, Description

In-Depth Coverage	Accelerated Pace
• Cover pp. 106–107. • Work through the exercises on organizational patterns and creating a main impression with the entire class. • Have students write their own descriptive essay drafts in class. • Use the transparency to demonstrate using depth-charging.	• Have students review pp. 106–107 independently, then write their own descriptive drafts. • Respond to individual drafting issues as needed.

Providing Elaboration

Combine Details From Different Senses

The world offers a feast of sounds, scents, textures, and flavors. If your description tells only what things look like, the reader will feel hungry for more. It is as though you invited the reader to dinner and said, "All you get are potatoes!" Be generous—use "Depth-Charging" to share your sensory feast.

Using Depth-Charging As you draft, pause at the end of each paragraph. Then, follow these steps:

1. Circle an important item about which you can supply information from senses other than sight.
2. Draw an arrow from this circled word to a blank line.
3. Write a new sentence, giving details about the item. Use a sense other than the one you first used to describe it.
4. Circle the most interesting word in your new sentence.
5. Draw an arrow to a new line. Write a sentence using yet another sense.

Then, decide whether to use these sentences in your draft.

Collaborative Writing Tip

Get together with one or two classmates. Without identifying your subject, name details about it, one for each of the senses. Can your partners guess your subject from the details you give? If not, ask for suggestions for more precise details.

Drafting: Elaboration by Depth-Charging

Teaching Resources: Writing Support Transparency 6-D

1. Remind students of the importance of providing a "full menu" of sensory details.
2. Display the transparency. As you review Leann's work in progress and use the transparency to teach depth-charging, discuss the problem of a topic that may have details from only one or two senses. The solution to that problem is analogy or metaphor:

   The sculpture was the color of slightly cooked broccoli. You had the feeling you could pop it into boiling water and it would have that distinctive taste and snap of broccoli fresh from the garden.

Integrating Speaking and Listening Skills

In conversation, students use sensory details and figurative language without thinking about it. Have students work in small groups, describing a topic of their choice—a song, band, TV show, store. Appoint one member of the group as recorder to write any sensory details used in the descriptions.

Student Work IN PROGRESS

Name: Leann Goree
Southside Fundamental Middle School
St. Petersburg, FL

Depth-Charging to Use All the Senses

After Leann wrote this paragraph, she realized she had discussed only how the snow made things look. She added a few details from other senses.

The sun is out now! It spreads its cold, golden light along the new white ground. A few flakes still fall from the sky here and there, like they are hurrying to catch up with their friends. Every now and then, they get caught in a (sudden gust of chilly wind) and are whipped along. My friend Maria and I watch the flakes dancing and sparkling in the sun.

Each (gust) makes my ears turn to ice!   Touch

The wind and snow make the world smell new and clean.   Smell

Drafting • 107

ONGOING ASSESSMENT: Monitor and Reinforce

If some students are having difficulty using depth-charging, use one of the following options.

| **Option 1** Have students make a list of adjectives for each of the five senses and then review the list to see if they can use any as a depth charge. | **Option 2** Have those students experiencing difficulty work in pairs, offering each other suggestions of details they might use. |

⏱ **TIME SAVERS!**

 Writing Support Transparencies
Use the transparencies for Chapter 6 to teach these strategies.

Revising: Revising Your Overall Structure

Teaching Resources: Writing Support Transparency 6-E

1. An essay without an organizational plan, no matter how well done the descriptive details, will be confusing to the reader. An organizational plan provides structure and also acts as a guide for the reader.

2. Review the key words for each organizational plan. Be sure that students understand how to use these words as connectives and transitions in their essays.

3. Display the transparency. Examine Leann's coding for organization to see how she uses chronological order to structure her essay.

Customize for
Less Advanced Students

Help students find an organizational pattern best suited to their topic. If they are describing an event, chronological order might work best. If they are describing a place, spatial order is a good bet. If they are describing different sensory details for a memory or an experience, suggest order of importance.

6.4 Revising

After you complete your first draft, review it to make improvements. Start by looking at your overall structure.

Revising Your Overall Structure
Analyze Your Organization

To make sure you have organized your draft consistently, use the following coding strategy.

▶ **REVISION STRATEGY**
Coding for Organization

Highlight each sentence that introduces an aspect of your subject. For instance, you might highlight the sentence "My grandfather likes to rebuild cars." Write a key word next to each highlighted sentence to show its connection to the one before it. Select from these key words:

more important, less important

before, after, during

near, far, up, down, next to, across from

Then, look for out-of-sequence key words. For instance, the words "after . . . before" are out of sequence. Rearrange paragraphs or sentences to create a sensible order.

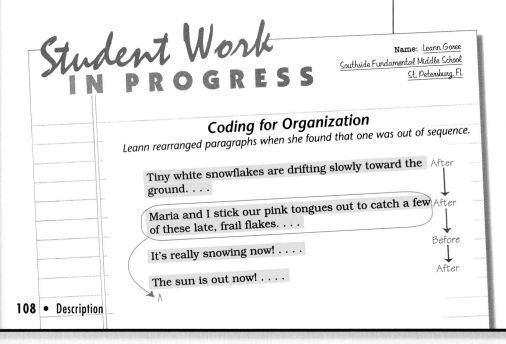

Student Work IN PROGRESS

Name: *Leann Goree*
Southside Fundamental Middle School
St. Petersburg, FL

Coding for Organization
Leann rearranged paragraphs when she found that one was out of sequence.

Tiny white snowflakes are drifting slowly toward the ground. . . .   *After*

Maria and I stick our pink tongues out to catch a few of these late, frail flakes. . . .   *After*

It's really snowing now! . . . .   *Before*

The sun is out now! . . . .   *After*

108 • Description

⏱ **TIME AND RESOURCE MANAGER**

Resources
Print: Writing Support Transparencies 6-E–G
Technology: Writing Lab CD-ROM, Description

In-Depth Coverage	Accelerated Pace
• Cover pp. 108–112 in class. • Work through the revising strategy with the entire class. • Use the relevant transparencies for coding for organization, adding functional paragraphs, color-coding pauses, and using precise adjectives.	• Assign students to review pages 108–112 independently. • Have students revise their descriptive essays independently.

Revising Your Paragraphs

Use Functional Paragraphs

Mechanics use different tools for different jobs. When you write, you can use different types of paragraphs to get the job done. **Functional paragraphs** perform specific functions. They may

- emphasize an idea.
- make a transition.
- add a special effect, such as dialogue.

A functional paragraph may be one sentence or a series of sentences. Here are a few examples:

Arouse or sustain interest:
Not everyone knows what life is like for a hunted man. Not everyone, but Luke Graywolf was an exception.

Present a special effect:
sssSSWOOSH! went the train.

Emphasize a point: Let me put it another way: I would rather move to another country than live in a place with such a law.

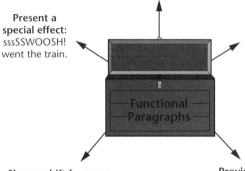

Functional Paragraphs

Show a shift from one speaker to another:
Next, Harriet chimed in with, "Oh, not another ice cream cone!"

Provide a transition:
It was only later that night that they got the news.

Add functional paragraphs to your description to get the job done.

▶ **REVISION STRATEGY**
Adding Functional Paragraphs

Reread your draft. Place brackets around sentences expressing the main idea of each paragraph. Then, evaluate the movement from one main idea to another. Add functional paragraphs where needed to make the movement clear.

▲ **Critical Viewing**
Write a one- or two-sentence functional paragraph introducing this scene.
[Apply]

Step-by-Step Teaching Guide

Revising: Use Functional Paragraphs

Teaching Resources: Writing Support Transparency 6-F

1. Students are used to paragraphs carrying main ideas and supporting details. Introduce the idea of the functional paragraph and review its various functions.

2. Functional paragraphs can add details or provide transitions between paragraphs. Have students review their drafts and find places where they can add a functional paragraph.

Critical Viewing

Apply Students may write *After the car broke down, we found a mechanic who said that he could fix it.*

☑ **ONGOING ASSESSMENT: Monitor and Reinforce**

If some students are having difficulty adding functional paragraphs, use one of the following options.

Option 1 Help students find places in their draft where they need to add additional detail or can flesh out an anecdote or comparison they have made.	**Option 2** Have students work in pairs, reading each other's drafts and suggesting places where a functional paragraph could be added.

109

Step-by-Step Teaching Guide

Revising: Color-Coding Pauses

Teaching Resources: Writing Support Transparency 6-G

1. There are other ways to correct a run-on sentence than the one shown.

   • **Semicolon:** My grandfather is a tall man; he's strong . . .

   • **Comma and conjunction:** My grandfather is a tall man, and he's strong. He can run . . .

   • **Add words:** My grandfather is a tall man who also is strong. He can run . . .

2. Display the transparency. Examine Leann's use of dot stickers to revise sentence length, eliminate run-ons, and establish a varied sentence pattern.

3. Have students review their drafts for sentence length, using stickers to mark the pauses.

Revising Your Sentences
Eliminate Run-on Sentences

When too many details collide in a sentence, the result may be a **run-on sentence**—two or more complete sentences written as though they were a single sentence.

RUN-ON: My grandfather is a tall man, he's strong, he can run three miles a day.

POSSIBLE CORRECTION: My grandfather is a tall man. He's strong, and he can run three miles a day.

Use this strategy to find and eliminate some run-ons.

▶ **REVISION STRATEGY**
Color-Coding for Comma Splices

Mark the first ten commas in your draft with yellow dot stickers. Review your yellow dots. If a yellow dot separates two complete ideas, consider the following changes:

EVALUATE	POSSIBLE REVISION
One idea simply adds to or contrasts with the other.	Add *and* or *but* after the comma. ("Bob is thirsty, and there is no water.")
The two ideas form a cause-and-effect relationship or show that a cause did not have an effect.	Replace the comma with a conjunction such as *because* or *although*. ("Bob is thirsty although I gave him water.")
The two ideas are not closely related.	Replace the comma with a period and capitalize the first letter of the next word.

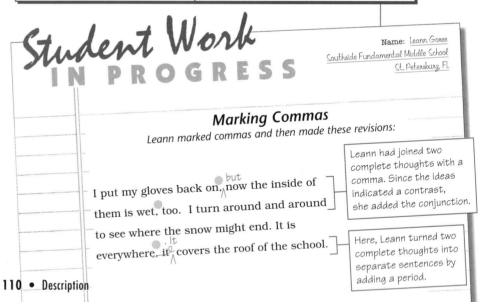

Student Work IN PROGRESS

Name: Leann Goree
Southside Fundamental Middle School
St. Petersburg, FL

Marking Commas
Leann marked commas and then made these revisions:

I put my gloves back on, but now the inside of them is wet, too. I turn around and around to see where the snow might end. It is everywhere, it covers the roof of the school.

> Leann had joined two complete thoughts with a comma. Since the ideas indicated a contrast, she added the conjunction.

> Here, Leann turned two complete thoughts into separate sentences by adding a period.

110 • Description

Language Lab CD-ROM

For additional practice avoiding run-on sentences, complete the Run-On Sentences lesson from the Sentence Errors unit.

⏱ TIME SAVERS!

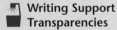 **Writing Support Transparencies**
Use the transparencies for Chapter 6 to facilitate teaching of strategies.

🎸 STANDARDIZED TEST PREPARATION WORKSHOP

Run-on Sentences Standardized test questions may require students to identify run-on sentences. Write the following examples on the chalkboard and ask students to select the run-on sentence:

A The clear blue sky was the color of the sea it made me think of last summer.

B Running through the fields and screaming at the top of our lungs, we had fun.

C When I was four years old, my mother and father took me to the zoo.

D None of the above

Item **A** is the run-on sentence because it contains two separate ideas that should be separated by a semicolon or period.

Revising Your Word Choice
Use Precise Words

When you use the right adjective, you create a vivid picture for a reader. That's why a vague adjective can be a disappointment. Just when a reader was hoping for a vivid word—*immense, sleek,* or *powerful*—a vague word like *great* stumbles in. Some readers may ask, "What makes this thing or person great?" Others simply yawn. Code adjectives and vague words in your draft to help you find more precise words.

▶ **REVISION STRATEGY**
Underlining Adjectives

Underline the first ten adjectives in your draft. For each, look for another adjective that explains why you chose it. For instance, you might call a car "great" because it is *powerful,* or because it is *sleek,* or both. Jot down new adjectives in the margins of your draft. Then, consider using these more precise adjectives to replace your original choices.

Technology Tip

Use the thesaurus tool of your word-processing program to find specific adjectives that will make your writing more precise.

Grammar in Your Writing
Adjectives

Adjectives are words that modify the meaning of a noun or pronoun by giving more information about it. (*Modify* means "change slightly.") In the phrase "red house," for example, the adjective *red* changes the meaning of *house* so it refers only to red houses. Adjectives answer one of four questions:

What Kind?	
cold sensation	*frail* flakes

Which One?	
your glove	*each* flake

How Many?	
two gloves	*several* flakes

How Much?	
deep snow	*more* wind

Find It in Your Reading Identify four adjectives in "A Narrow Escape" by Laurence Yep on page 100. For each, explain the question it answers.

Find It in Your Writing Identify five nouns in your draft. Consider whether you need to add an adjective to make your meaning more precise.

To learn more about nouns and adjectives, see Chapters 14 and 16.

Revising • 111

✓ **ONGOING ASSESSMENT: Prerequisite Skills**

If students have difficulty with adjectives, you may want to refer them to the following to assure coverage of prerequisite skills.

In the Textbook	Print Resources	Technology
Adjectives, pp. 330–339	Grammar Exercise Workbook, pp 21–28	On-Line Exercise Bank, Section 16.1

Step-by-Step Teaching Guide

Revising: Use Precise Words

1. Vivid, precise words are the hallmark of good writing. Vivid words paint a picture in the reader's mind. Vague, empty words such as *great, wonderful,* and *awesome* say little.

2. Read the following examples and discuss the difference:

    It was an amazing day. Bright sunshine and a blue sky made it altogether wonderful.

    This was a day that almost screamed at you to get out of bed. The sunlight was the color of the warmest smile, and the air kissed your skin. It was a day that carried its own exclamation point.

Step-by-Step Teaching Guide

Grammar in Your Writing: Adjectives

1. Review the questions answered by adjectives.

2. Write the following phrases on the chalkboard and have students identify which question the adjective is answering:

    light dusting (how much?)
    elegant tracings (what kind?)
    a dozen shovels (how many?)
    that storm (which one?)

Find It in Your Reading

Possible responses:
rotten (what kind?)
seventh (which one?)
those (which one?)
crazy (what kind?)

Find It in Your Writing

You may wish to have students work in pairs or small groups on this exercise.

Customize for
ESL Students

Students learning English may have difficulty finding vivid adjectives. Students can work in groups to brainstorm for synonyms. Suggest that they use a dictionary or thesaurus to come up with alternative wordings.

111

Revising: Peer Review

1. Students should not hesitate to express strong reactions to classmates' work. The only rule is that they be polite and specific. "I don't get it" is not helpful. "I understand what is special about your uncle's farm, but you don't make it clear what it means to you" is constructive criticism.

2. Remind students that the purpose of the peer review activity is to check essays for content.

Critical Viewing

Evaluate Students' responses will vary, but most will say that they would feel comfortable.

Peer Review

Although you have revised your draft thoroughly on your own, you can still benefit from listening to the suggestions of readers. Use the "Say Back" strategy to get the responses of classmates.

"Say Back"

Share your revised draft with a group of four or five of your classmates. Read your draft as the group listens. Then, ask the group to take notes as you read your draft a second time. Listeners should jot down two things:

• what they like
• what they want to know more about.

Afterward, ask group members to "say back" what they have written down. Use their comments as you complete your final revision. If appropriate, expand the sections that your listeners identified as strong. Add more details to clarify points about which listeners wanted to know more.

▲ Critical Viewing
Would you feel comfortable sharing your draft with peers such as these? Why or why not? **[Evaluate]**

112 • Description

6.5 Editing and Proofreading

Proofread your draft carefully for errors in spelling, grammar, and mechanics. Such errors may confuse or distract your readers.

Focusing on Commas

Commas signal readers when to pause. They are also used to prevent confusion. Use color-coding to find places in your draft where you may need to add commas.

Color-Code Clues for Commas

Using a colored pencil, circle adjectives wherever you use two or more of them in a row. Review these places to see whether you need to add commas. Refer to the rules in the box below.

Grammar in Your Writing
Using Commas With Two or More Adjectives

When two or more adjectives appear in front of the noun they modify, you may need to add a comma between them.

Adjectives of Equal Rank Adjectives are of equal rank when you can write them in any order before a noun without changing your meaning. Use a comma between adjectives of equal rank.

The tumbling, dancing snowflakes were swept along by the wind.
The dancing, tumbling snowflakes were swept along by the wind.

> Different order, same meaning

Adjectives That Must Stay in a Specific Order When adjectives must stay in a specific order, do not put a comma between them.

Several fragile (never Fragile several) snowflakes fell on my tongue.
A tiny white (rarely white tiny) snowflake landed on my head.

> Different order, different meaning

Find It in Your Reading Find two places where Laurence Yep uses two or more adjectives before a noun in "A Narrow Escape" on page 100. Explain why a comma should or should not be used between them.

Find It in Your Writing Find places in your draft where you use two or more adjectives before a noun. Make sure you have used commas correctly.

To learn more about commas, see Chapter 26.

Editing and Proofreading • 113

TIME AND RESOURCE MANAGER

Resources
Print: Scoring Rubrics on Transparency, Chapter 6; Writing Assessment: Scoring Rubric and Scoring Models for Descriptive Essay
Technology: Writing Lab CD-ROM, Description

In-Depth Coverage	Accelerated Pace
• Cover pp. 113–117 in class. • Have students edit and proofread their essays in class. • Analyze in class the Final Draft, pp. 115–117.	• Assign pp. 113–117 for independent review. • Have students independently edit and proofread their essays. • Respond to individual editing issues as needed.

Step-by-Step Teaching Guide

Editing and Proofreading

A common mistake is adding an unnecessary comma before *and,* as in *I went to the store, and bought milk, bread, and apples.* This is a simple sentence with a compound verb (*went, bought*), so the first comma is wrong. The items bought are in a series, so the last two commas are necessary.

Step-by-Step Teaching Guide

Grammar in Your Writing: Using Commas With Two or More Adjectives

1. See that students understand the rule: Adjectives of equal rank are separated by a comma; adjectives in specific order do not get separated by a comma.

2. Write the following additional examples on the chalkboard and ask students to make any corrections needed:

   A few large trees lay across the road.

   Magnificent[,] tall oak trees did not survive the storm.

   The sharp growl of chain saws could be heard all over.

   It was a hard[,] noisy job.

Find It in Your Reading

Possible responses: *big brown stain*—no comma because adjectives must stay in that order; *hollow, bonging sound*—comma because either adjective could come first; *glorious blue sky*—no comma; order can't change.

Find It in Your Writing

Have students list each example from their writing along with an explanation of why it does or does not require a comma.

Publishing and Presenting

1. If a video camera is not available, students can use an instant camera to take a photo, or they can draw an illustration to accompany their description.

2. Have students complete the Reflecting on Your Writing exercise and encourage volunteers to share their reflections with the class.

3. Have students use the rubric to self-assess their description.

ASSESS

Assessment

Teaching Resources: Scoring Rubrics on Transparency 6; Formal Assessment, Chapter 6

1. Display the Scoring Rubric transparency and review the criteria in class.

2. Before students proceed with self-assessment, you may wish to review the Final Draft of the Student Work in Progress on pages 115–117. Have students score the Final Draft in one or more of the rubric categories. For example, how would students score the essay in terms of audience and purpose?

3. In addition to student self-assessment, you may wish to use the following assessment options.

   • score student essays yourself, using the rubric and scoring models from Writing Assessment.

   • review the Standardized Test Preparation Workshop on pages 122–123 and have students respond to a persuasive writing prompt within a time limit.

   • administer the Chapter 6 Test from Formal Assessment in Teaching Resources to assess students' grasp of concepts presented.

6.6 Publishing and Presenting

Building Your Portfolio

Consider these ideas for publishing and presenting your work:

1. **Mail Your Description to a Friend or Relative**
   Mail your description to someone who also knows the subject of your description. Send a letter with it, asking the person to comment on your description.

2. **Videotape Your Description** If you have described a person or place accessible to you, videotape your subject while you read your description. Work with a friend or family member. Plan shots so that viewers will see what you are describing as you read. Rehearse before taping, and show your final "cut" to the class.

Reflecting on Your Writing

Jot down a few notes on your experience writing a description. To get started, answer these questions:

• As you wrote, what did you learn about the subject of your description? What more would you have liked to learn?

• Which writing strategies in this chapter worked best for you? Why? Which worked least well? Why?

Internet Tip

To read a descriptive essay scored according to this rubric, visit **www.phschool.com**

Rubric for Self-Assessment

Evaluate your description using the following criteria:

	Score 4	Score 3	Score 2	Score 1
Audience and Purpose	Creates a memorable main impression through effective use of details	Creates a main impression through use of details	Contains details that distract from main impression	Contains details that are unfocused and create no main impression
Organization	Is organized consistently, logically, and effectively	Is organized consistently	Is organized, but not consistently	Is disorganized and confusing
Elaboration	Contains rich sensory language that appeals to the five senses	Contains some rich sensory language	Contains some rich sensory language, but it appeals to only one or two of the senses	Contains only flat language
Use of Language	Uses vivid and precise adjectives; contains no errors in grammar, punctuation, or spelling	Uses some vivid and precise adjectives; contains few errors in grammar, punctuation, and spelling	Uses few vivid and precise adjectives; contains some errors in grammar, punctuation, and spelling	Uses no vivid adjectives; contains many errors in grammar, punctuation, and spelling

114 • Description

☑ ONGOING ASSESSMENT: Assess Mastery

Use one of the following options to assess final drafts of students' descriptive essays.

Self-Assessment Ask students to score their essay, using the rubric provided. Then have students write a paragraph reflecting on the most vauable strategy they learned in completing this essay.	**Teacher Assessment** Use the rubric and the scoring models provided in Writing Assessment, Descriptive Essay to score students' work.

Student Work IN PROGRESS

FINAL DRAFT

▲ **Critical Viewing**
Write a sentence describing this scene. Use two vivid sensory details. **[Apply]**

Snow Dance

Leann Goree
Southside Fundamental Middle School
St. Petersburg, Florida

It's 10 o'clock. I look up from my book of math exercises and turn to the window to check the weather. Gray clouds make a thick, heavy roof over the brown ground. I remember the hush in the air this morning. It felt as if, somewhere in the distance, something was waiting to happen.

It's 11 o'clock. I look up from my grammar book and turn to the window again. I notice the tiniest movement. One moment, the sky is absolutely still. In the next, like a camera coming into focus, the sky fills with a slow ballet. Tiny white snowflakes are drifting slowly toward the ground. Juanita shouts out, "It's

Leann begins by describing the feeling and look of the day of a snowfall as she remembered it.

Leann organizes her description chronologically (in time order). Her references to the time help her readers follow the order of events.

Teaching From the Final Draft

1. Read aloud the final draft of the student work in progress or have volunteers read it.

2. Point out the evocative introductory paragraph with its obvious but effective "something was waiting to happen."

3. Ask students what type of organization Leann used. (From the opening of each paragraph on this page, it is clear that she is using chronological order.)

4. Point out the use of similes: *like a camera, like a wet dog.*

continued

Critical Viewing

Apply Students may say that a snowy day makes them feel more cheerful than a rainy day.

5. Point out Leann's vivid language: *gust, tired flakes, frail flakes, crunch, clumps, furry.*

6. Discuss how Leann's use of details from taste and touch draws readers in. They can almost taste and feel the snow and the cold.

7. Point out the correct use of a comma with two adjectives of equal weight in the second paragraph: . . . *its cold, golden light.*

8. Leann uses effective images, such as *furry ball* and *watery popsicle.*

continued

Critical Viewing

Infer Students may say she is using her senses of touch and taste.

6.7

snowing!" and the class gathers around the window. To me, the snowflakes seem lonely. They make me think of skydivers leaving each other behind as they tumble through the sky.

It's 12 o'clock. We line up for the cafeteria. The hall smells like a wet dog from the snow tracked in by people. I look out the big windows facing the playground. It's really snowing now! The sky is lost in a white blur. Flakes come swirling out of the storm up to the window, then disappear back into the blur. They turn toward us, then jerk back in the wind, like a line of dancers taking turns. What a wild dance! The tired flakes lie still across the ground, making a peaceful white blanket.

It's 12:30, and it's time for recess. We get our coats on and march outside. The sun is out now! It spreads its cold, golden light along the new white ground. A few flakes still fall from the sky here and there, like they are hurrying to catch up with their friends. Every now and then, they get caught in a sudden gust of chilly wind and are whipped along. Each gust makes my ears turn to ice! The wind and snow make the world smell new and clean. My friend Maria and I watch the flakes dancing and sparkling in the sun.

Maria and I stick out our pink tongues to catch a few of these late, frail flakes. When a flake hits my tongue, I can just barely feel it. The snow tastes like a watery popsicle. We close our mouths and savor the cold sensation. Then, we smack our chapped lips at each other and laugh. My lips feel rough like leather.

After a while, we crunch our way across the blanket of snow toward the fence across the playground from the school. The snow has piled up in little clumps along the edges. We take our gloves off to feel the snow. The minute we grab a handful, it melts, turning from a furry ball into a trickle of ice-cold water. My hands turn red. First, it feels like my skin is

116 • Description

Vivid details of smell (like a wet dog) and sight (snow swirling out of the storm) help the reader envision the scene.

Leann's comparison of snowflakes to dancers helps create a main impression of the snowfall for readers.

Leann uses vivid details from the sense of taste (watery popsicle) and touch (rough like leather).

◀ Critical Viewing **Name** two senses the girl in the picture is using to experience the snow. **[Infer]**

9. Ask students to evaluate Leann's essay on two levels: the effectiveness of her descriptions and the overall effectiveness of the essay. Ask students to consider whether the essay held their interest and whether her voice sounded authentic.

◄ **Critical Viewing**
Compare this scene with the same scene as you imagine it would look in summer. **[Compare and Contrast]**

Critical Viewing

Compare and Contrast Students may say it would be more crowded since more people would be out enjoying the warm weather.

trying to pull inside me for warmth. Then, my hands start feeling like they belong to someone else.

I put my gloves back on, but now the inside of them is wet, too. I turn around and around to see where the snow might end. It is everywhere. It covers the roof of the school. Little heaps are piled up along the windowsills. Patches are caught in the gratings over the windows. Snow covers the trees on the other side of the schoolyard fence, making little caps for the branches. It has collected on the cars under the trees. I feel like we have been stranded in this cold wilderness forever!

"Get us out of here!" I shout.

Then, the teacher blows the whistle. Time to go back inside. We trudge along, dragging clumps of snow with us. Inside, the snow on my boots turns from pure white clusters of flakes into muddy gray slabs of ice. The merry, dancing flakes are gone. I kick a clump of snow off, and it plops onto the floor of the hallway.

Back in class, the heat starts to spread through my body. What a relief. Then I think: I can hardly wait to go home and start sledding!

Specific visual details, such as the "caps" made by the snow on the trees, bring this snowy scene to life.

Leann uses a functional paragraph—a single line of dialogue—to show her playfulness.

Lesson Objectives

1. To write a poem appropriate to audience and purpose.
2. To select and narrow a topic for a poem.
3. To choose a form for a poem.
4. To draft, revise, edit, and publish a poem.

Step-by-Step Teaching Guide

Poem

Teaching Resources: Writing Support Transparency 6-H; Writing Support Activity Book, 6-2

1. Write the word *poetry* on the chalkboard. Ask students what this word means to them. Have all students contribute to a class definition of poetry.

2. Use the transparency to demonstrate narrowing the topic of a poem. Give students copies of the blank organizer so that students can complete webs for themselves.

3. Remind students that even if a poem is in a set form such as a sonnet, the poet is still free to play with the rhythm and meter. Some lines may be longer or shorter than strictly required by the form. In "Ankylosaurus," for instance, some of the lines (1, 2, 8, 9, 11, 12) begin on a strong beat, others (3–7, 10) on a weak beat. Sometimes poets use variations in the expected rhythm or meter to achieve thematic or other effects.

continued

Connected Assignment
Poem

Vivid descriptive writing is often found in poems. Though you may not always hear it, poetry pulses through your life. From sing-alongs to skip-rope songs, from schoolyard raps to football chants—wherever words spark and dance, poetry is taking place.

A **poem** is a creation made of words chosen for their sounds and associations as well as their meaning. It uses words to suggest strong images and feelings. Many poems include

- words arranged for a rhythmical or musical effect (such as a rhyme).
- figures of speech such as
  - similes (comparisons of unlike things using *like* or *as*).
  - metaphors (comparisons of unlike things that do not use *like* or *as*).
  - personifications (descriptions of a nonhuman thing as though it were a person).
- a repeated pattern of lines and stanzas (groups of lines).

Prewriting Choose a topic to write a poem about. You might describe a person, place, thing, or animal, or you might tell a story.

Once you have chosen a topic, select part of it to focus on. For instance, if you choose to write about a birthday party, you might focus on the moment when the birthday person blows out the candles. Or, you might focus on the gifts.

After narrowing your topic, use a diagram like the one shown to gather details. Write your topic in the middle. Add related details in new circles.

Drafting Next, choose a form—the pattern of lines, beats, and rhymes you will use in your poem. Here are three forms from which you can choose:

- **Rhyming poems** are poems in which given lines rhyme with each other. Each line has a given number of accented syllables (beats). For instance, in "Ankylosaurus" (next page), each pair of lines rhymes. Each line has four beats.

- **Haiku** are three-line poems in a traditional Japanese form. The first line contains five syllables, the second contains seven syllables, and the third has five syllables.

- **Concrete poems** are poems in which the words form a shape—often, the shape of the thing the poem describes.

POETRY WEB

- delicious creamy filling awaits!
- candles make a glow in the dark
- birthday cake at party
- looks perfect, but will soon be cut into pieces
- frosting like a coat of snow

118 • Description

MODEL

Ankylosaurus
Jack Prelutsky

Clankity Clankity Clankity Clank!
Ankylosaurus was built like a tank,
its hide was a fortress as sturdy as steel,
it tended to be an inedible meal.

5   It was armored in front, it was armored behind,
there wasn't a thing on its minuscule mind,
it waddled about on its four stubby legs,
nibbling on plants with a mouthful of pegs.

Ankylosaurus was best left alone,
10 its tail was a cudgel of gristle and bone,
Clankity Clankity Clankity Clank!
Ankylosaurus was built like a tank.

> In the first line, the poet uses **onomatopoeia**—the use of words that sound like what they describe.

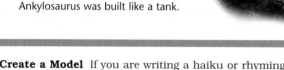

Create a Model If you are writing a haiku or rhyming poem, choose an example that you like. Make a photocopy and mark it up to show the pattern of rhyming and rhythm in the poem. Use this photocopy as a model for your own poem.

Use Poetic Effects As you draft, incorporate details from your diagram. Use figurative language, such as metaphors and similes, to create strong images. Create musical effects by using words beginning with the same sound.

Revising and Editing Once you have written your first draft, review each line of your poem.

Replace vague words Each word in your poem must pull its weight. A word like *nice* is too weak to do much for a reader. Replace such weak words with stronger, more precise words such as *tranquil, loving,* or *cuddly.*

Check your form Read your poem out loud, tapping as you go. Mark lines where there are too many or too few syllables or beats, or where the beats fall in the wrong place. Rewrite marked lines. For a rhyming poem, make sure the right lines rhyme. For a concrete poem, make sure the poem forms the right shape.

Publishing and Presenting Collect the poems of the class in a booklet. Place a copy of your own poem in your portfolio.

4. Show students an example of a concrete poem. As an exercise, have all students try writing short, simple concrete poems within a set amount of time. Don't require rhyme. When the time is up, have students copy their efforts on the chalkboard.

5. Use the model on the page to discuss imagery in poetry. Point out that the poem is full of military vocabulary: *tank, fortress, armored, cudgel.* This language evokes images of battle and fierceness, which forms a humorous contrast to what the Ankylosaurus is actually doing— waddling about and nibbling on plants. Urge students to use imagery in their poems.

Comparing Interpretations of Nature

1. Choose a Spotlight element for class discussion, or have students work independently or in small groups on the element of their choice. Give students the initiative to find the necessary books and photographs.

2. Ask students to compare black-and-white photography with color photography. Have them discuss their impressions of black-and-white movies as well as still photographs. Make a class list of the advantages, disadvantages, and special beauties of each type of photography.

3. Encourage students to go to the library and look at more of Adams's photographs and Bierstadt's paintings, either in art books or on the Internet. Students should try to get a sense of the identifying characteristics of each artist's style.

Viewing and Representing

Activity As an alternative, you might suggest that students choose partners and role-ply a discussion between Adams and Bierstadt. In the discussion, each man can give his opinion of the other's work. Remind students that their characters should give reasons for their comments.

Critical Viewing

Compare and Contrast Similarities: Both show flat-topped mounds of earth and rock. Both show fluffy white clouds. Differences: Only the painting shows trees and water. Only the photograph shows a dry canyon.

Spotlight on the Humanities

Comparing Interpretations of Nature

Focus on Photography: Ansel Adams

Descriptive writing uses vivid words to create an image. A photographer uses light. By experimenting with the camera, film, and lighting, a photographer can use light to vividly portray a scene—even in black and white.

American photographer Ansel Adams (1902–1984) was a noted master of black-and-white photography. He spent his career taking pictures of the American wilderness, and is most famous for his landscapes of the American West.

Canyon de Chelley, Ansel Adams

Adams's photographs do not just capture the look of a place. They create powerful patterns of texture and tone (shades of gray). An Adams photograph captures the eye with these patterns even as it "describes" the landscape. In this way, it achieves artistic effects similar to those found in paintings.

Art Connection The painter who most influenced Adams was the American Albert Bierstadt (1830–1902). During his travels, Bierstadt painted immense canvases of the scenery and people of the West, including the Rocky Mountains and Native Americans. Like Adams, Bierstadt experimented with light and tone to capture the beauty and grace of natural landscapes.

▲ **Critical Viewing** Name two similarities and two differences between Adams's photograph and Bierstadt's painting. [**Compare and Contrast**]

Descriptive Writing Application: Letter to Ansel Adams

Write a letter to Adams comparing his photograph to Bierstadt's painting. Describe both the photograph and the painting. Then, ask Adams any questions you might have about his work or about Bierstadt's influence on him.

120 • Description

Media and Technology Skills

Analyze Visual Representations

Activity: Analyze Camera Techniques in a Movie

You might describe a hunting cat as "a small, sleek panther" or as "a cruel captor." These two descriptions give very different pictures. Moviemakers can also shape our ideas of a thing. Learn to identify the techniques they use.

Think About It Here are some important camera techniques:

Dramatic Cutting One moment, the movie is showing you a high-speed car chase. The next, it is showing you a quiet scene by the fireplace in someone's living room. Dramatic "cuts" from one scene to another without a break can

- **build suspense.** When the movie interrupts one part of the story and turns to another, you wonder how the first part turns out.
- **create a fast pace for the movie.** One event can follow another quickly. The movie can easily include a few different stories.

Close-Up and Distance Shots When you look at the world, you see more detail in things close by and less detail in those farther away. Watching a movie is not like looking at the world. A camera can change how much detail you see in an instant. In a **close-up** shot,

- the person or thing filmed takes up most of the screen.
- something is emphasized. For example, a movie might use a close-up of the hero's face to emphasize his reaction to bad news.

In a **distance shot,**

- the person or thing filmed takes up little of the screen.
- the "big picture" of how things fit together is clear.

Watch It Watch a movie. Use a chart like this one to note examples of dramatic cutting, close-ups, and distance shots. Write a paragraph describing each.

Other Camera Techniques

"Zoom In" Shots In a zoom in shot, the image of a person or thing moves closer and closer. Like a close-up, a zoom shot tells you that you are looking at something important.

"Zoom Out" Shots In a zoom out shot, the image of a person or thing moves farther and farther away. Like a distance shot, a zoom out lets you see the "big picture."

Movie: _____

Dramatic Cutting		Close-up	Distance Shot
Scene 1: What happened?	**Scene 2:** What happened?	**Scene:** What happened?	**Scene:** What happened?
Who was involved?	Who was involved?	Who was involved?	Who was involved?
When did jump to next scene happen?		What did the close-up focus on?	What did the shot show?

▶ *Lesson Objectives*
- To analyze camera techniques in a movie.

Step-by-Step Teaching Guide

Analyze Visual Representations

Teaching Resources: Writing Support Transparency 6-I; Writing Support Activity Book 6-3

1. Remind students that filmmaking is a highly interpretive art. No shot in a film is accidental; every aspect of it has been planned, from the number of dishes on the table to the color of the heroine's dress to the weather conditions. A film crew can wait for hours for the sun to break through clouds, if the director insists on sunshine for a certain shot.

2. Explain that a film controls the audience's viewpoint. During a live stage performance, audience members are seated all over the theater, and a person sitting in the orchestra may have a completely different experience from someone in the balcony. At a movie, however, everyone in the audience sees the same thing.

3. Go over the camera techniques listed on the page. Ask students to give examples of these techniques from films they have seen. Have them describe the effects of the different types of shots. Use the transparency to demonstrate this, and then give students copies of the blank organizer so that they can complete the writing activity.

121

Lesson Objectives

1. To read a passage and analyze possible changes to it.
2. To choose the most logical sequence of ideas in a passage.
3. To determine the most appropriate language for the intended audience.

Step-by-Step Teaching Guide

Strategy, Organization, and Style

1. Remind students that in multiple-choice tests, two answers can often be eliminated immediately. Students may have some difficulty choosing between the remaining two. Remind students not to spend too much time on any one question. Their first instinct is usually correct; when in doubt, they should choose the answer they immediately thought was the right one.

2. Go over the sample test items with students. If any students have questions about the correct answers, explain why they are correct.

3. You may want to treat the test on the following page as a sample, working through each question with the whole class. Discuss and resolve any differences of opinion about the correct answers. As an alternative, you may wish to give students a set amount of time to complete the test on their own. Since this is a practice test, have them give a brief explanation of each answer they choose. This will help them be sure they have chosen the correct answer.

Standardized Test Preparation Workshop

Strategy, Organization, and Style

On standardized tests, some questions require you to read a passage and then choose improvements for it.

- *Strategy* questions ask whether a certain change fits the purpose of the passage.
- *Organization* questions ask you to choose the most logical sequence of ideas or sentences.
- *Style* questions ask you to find the most appropriate and effective language for the intended audience.

Practice for such questions with the following sample items.

Test Tip

Read each answer choice before responding to make sure you choose the best one.

Sample Test Items	Answers and Explanations

Directions Read the passage, and then answer the questions that follow.
 	
(1) It stopped at six. (2) The snow had started around midnight. (3) Eight inches had accumulated on the ground. (4) This morning, we awoke to a world blanketed in white.
 	
1 Choose the most logical sequence.
 	
  A 2, 4, 1, 3
  B 4, 2, 1, 3
  C 1, 2, 4, 3
  D Correct as is
	The correct answer is *B*. Part (2) must come before part (1) so events appear in the order they occurred.

2 Which of the following is the best way to write parts (1), (2), and (3)?
 	
  F It stopped at six after eight inches had accumulated on the ground; the snow started around midnight.
 	
  G It stopped at six but the snow had started at midnight. Eight inches had accumulated on the ground.
 	
  H The snow had started around midnight, and when it stopped at six, eight inches had accumulated.
 	
  J Correct as is
	The correct answer is *H*. This sentence most clearly expresses the order in which events occurred.

122 • Description

✏ TEST-TAKING TIP

Remind students of the *Correct as is* option. They should never hesitate to use this option; it will often be the correct answer. Students need to be able to recognize a logical sequence of ideas as much as they need to learn how to create one. You might write a few more sample questions for the passage on page 123, including the option *Correct as is* and making sure that this is the correct answer to some of the questions. Have students answer the questions and explain their answers. This will accustom them to choosing the option *Correct as is* without the fear that they must have missed a mistake in the passage.

▶ **Practice 1** **Directions:** Read the passage, and then answer the questions that follow. Choose the letter of the best answer.

(1) Each contestant was handed an envelope that contained a monetary gift and free lessons at a well-known cooking school. (2) When the <u>winners</u> were announced, they came up on stage to receive their prizes. (3) Some said a few words, but most just quietly exited the stage and went to <u>lunch</u>!

(4) The International Cooking Contest was a great success. (5) Early Saturday morning, a group of <u>people</u> converted our school cafeteria into an exhibition room. (6) I came extra early to supervise. (7) Every contestant had a small table on which he or she could display the international dish. (8) Judges circled the room trying every sample. (9) Many winners were there. (10) There were three big winners.

(11) First prize went to a hummus dish, a garlicky Middle Eastern chickpea dip. (12) It was accompanied by wedges of pita bread. (13) Second place was won by a man who made spanakopita, a Greek dish consisting of layers of spinach and feta cheese inside buttery phyllo pastry. (14) The recipe that won third place was the Spanish delicacy flan, a delicious caramel <u>custard</u>. (15) It was my favorite.

1 In which part should the underlined word be replaced by a more precise word?

A Part 2

B Part 3

C Part 5

D Part 14

2 Which of the following is the best order for the paragraphs?

F 2, 3, 1

G 1, 3, 2

H 3, 1, 2

J Correct as is

3 Which of the following would be the best way to write parts 9 and 10?

A Many winners were there, but there were only three big winners.

B There were three big winners of many.

C Many winners were there, and there were three big winners.

D Although the contest had many winners, three took top honors.

4 Which of the following sentences could be inserted between parts 8 and 9?

F My aunt was one of the judges.

G They were instructed to choose the best ten dishes.

H Every dish had to be approved and submitted with the application to the contest.

J One judge didn't like kielbasa.

5 Choose the most logical sentence sequence for paragraph 1.

A 3, 2, 1

B 2, 1, 3

C 3, 1, 2

D Correct as is

6 In paragraph 3, which of the following should be deleted as irrelevant?

F First prize went to a hummus recipe, a garlicky Middle Eastern chickpea dip.

G . . . a Greek dish consisting of layers of spinach and feta cheese inside buttery phyllo pastry.

H The recipe that won third place was the Spanish delicacy flan, a delicious caramel custard.

J It was my favorite.

▶ **Practice 1**

1. C
2. F
3. D
4. G
5. B
6. J

Customize for
Less Advanced Students

Encourage students to take practice tests. There are many such tests available in bookstores. Alternatively, you may want to develop your own practice tests. Have students take the tests at various times during the year. Students may want to work with tutors, or you may prefer to work with them yourself. Go over their test answer, discussing any problem areas. The more often students take practice tests, the more familiar and comfortable the format will grow.

Standardized Test Preparation Workshop • 123

123

In-Depth Lesson Plan

	LESSON FOCUS	PRINT AND MEDIA RESOURCES
DAY 1	**Introduction to Persuasive Essays** Students learn key elements of persuasive essays and analyze the Model From Literature (pp. 124–127).	*Writers at Work* **Videotape**, Persuasion *Writing Lab* **CD–ROM**, Persuasion
DAY 2	**Prewriting** Students choose and narrow a topic, consider their audience and purpose, and gather information (pp. 128–131).	**Teaching Resources** *Writing Support Transparencies, 7-A–B*
DAY 3	**Drafting** Students organize their ideas and write their first drafts (pp. 132–133).	**Teaching Resources** *Writing Support Transparencies, 7-C*
DAY 4	**Revising** Students revise their drafts in terms of overall structure, paragraphs, sentences, and word choice (pp. 134–138).	**Teaching Resources** *Writing Support Transparencies, 7-D–F; Writing Support Activity Book 7-1*
DAY 5	**Editing and Proofreading; Publishing and Presenting** Students check their work for accuracy and correctness and present their final drafts (pp. 139–140).	**Teaching Resources** *Scoring Rubrics on Transparency, Ch. 7; Formal Assessment, Ch. 7*

Accelerated Lesson Plan

	LESSON FOCUS	PRINT AND MEDIA RESOURCES
DAY 1	**Drafting** Students review characteristics for persuasive writing, select topics, and write drafts (pp. 124–133).	*Writers at Work* **Videotape**, Persuasion *Writing Lab* **CD–ROM**, Persuasion **Teaching Resources** *Writing Support Transparencies, 7-A–C*
DAY 2	**Revising to Presenting** Students work individually or with peers to revise, edit, and proofread their work for presentation (pp. 134–140).	**Teaching Resources** *Writing Support Transparencies, 7-D–F; Writing Support Activity Book 7-1; Scoring Rubrics on Transparency, Ch. 7; Formal Assessment, Ch. 7* *Writing Lab* **CD–ROM**, Persuasion

Options for Adapting Lesson Plans

HOMEWORK

Have students complete any stage of the lesson for homework.

FEATURES

Extend coverage with the Connected Assignment (p. 144), Spotlight on the Humanities (p. 146), Media and Technology Skills (p. 147), and the Standardized Test Preparation Workshop (p. 148).

TECHNOLOGY

Students can complete any stage of the lesson on computer. Have them print out their completed work.

INTEGRATED SKILLS COVERAGE

Integrating Grammar
Complete Sentences SE p. 137
End Marks SE p. 139

Reading/Writing Connection
Reading Strategy SE p. 126
Writing Application SE p. 127

Vocabulary
ATE pp. 138, 143

Workplace Skills
ATE pp. 127, 130, 145

Technology
ATE p. 145

Viewing and Representing
Critical Viewing SE pp. 124, 126, 141, 142, 143, 146
Viewing and Representing ATE p. 146

ASSESSMENT SUPPORT

Standardized Test Preparation Workshop SE p. 148; ATE p. 138

Standardized Test Preparation Workbook, pp. 13–14

Scoring Rubrics on Transparency, Ch. 7

Formal Assessment, Ch. 7

Writing Assessment and Portfolio Management

MEETING INDIVIDUAL NEEDS

Less Advanced Students ATE pp. 131, 149; see also Ongoing Assessments ATE pp. 129, 133, 135, 137, 140

More Advanced Students ATE p. 130

ESL Students ATE pp. 127, 129, 134, 149

Visual/Spatial Learners ATE p. 143

Verbal/Linguistic Learners ATE p. 133

BLOCK SCHEDULING

Pacing Suggestions
For 90-minute Blocks
• Have students complete the Prewriting and Drafting stages in a single period.
• Focus one class period on Revising and Editing and Publishing and Presenting. Allow at least 30 minutes for peer revision.

Resources for Varying Instruction
• *Writing Lab* **CD-ROM** If your students have access to hardware, a 90-minute block provides an ideal opportunity for students to work on computer.
• *Writers at Work* **Videotape** Show the Persuasion segment in class.

Professional Development Support
• *How to Manage Instruction in the Block* This Teaching Resource provides management and activity suggestions.

MEDIA AND TECHNOLOGY

For the Student
• *Writing Lab* **CD-ROM**, Persuasion

For the Teacher
• *Writers at Work* **Videotape**, Persuasion
• *Resource Pro* **CD-ROM**

WRITING AND GRAMMAR WEB SITE

The Interactive Writing and Grammar Web site provides a wide array of support for students, teachers and parents. Writing support includes:

• Interactive revision checkers
• Scoring rubrics with complete models

www.phschool.com

LITERATURE CONNECTIONS

Related selections from *Prentice Hall Literature: Timeless Voices, Timeless Themes*, Copper:

"Letter to Joan," C.S. Lewis, SE p. 127

"You've Got a Friend," Carole King, SE p. 129

Lesson Objectives

1. To recognize the distinguishing features of a persuasive essay.

2. To identify author's purpose when reading.

3. To generate and refine ideas and plans for writing by using the prewriting strategies.

4. To identify audience and purpose for writing a persuasive essay.

5. To gather support for ideas in a persuasive essay.

6. To develop a thesis statement.

7. To develop a draft by categorizing ideas, organizing them into paragraphs, and blending paragraphs within larger units of text.

8. To elaborate a draft by supporting each point.

9. To revise a draft by "interrogating" paragraphs to analyze organization and circling supporting evidence that supports main points.

10. To revise a draft to correct connecting words, eliminate sentence fragments, use precise persuasive language, and include correct end marks.

11. To "publish" a persuasive essay by creating an opinion board and writing a letter to a unit of government.

12. To evaluate a persuasive essay.

Critical Viewing

Hypothesize Students' responses will vary. Make sure students support their answers with details from the photographs.

Chapter 7 Persuasion
Persuasive Essay

▲ Critical Viewing
To persuade drivers to use their carwash, these young people might appeal to the value people put on cleanliness. Name another value to which they might appeal.
[Hypothesize]

Persuasion in Everyday Life

You've just finished lunch, but you're still hungry. Wait a minute—there's an extra apple on your friend's tray. What might you say to get your friend to share it?

You might use reason: "If you're not going to eat that apple, why not give it to me?" You might appeal to feelings: "Be a pal—share!" These words are examples of **persuasion**—words used to influence people's opinions or actions.

People don't just use persuasion to influence friends. Commercials, editorials, and speeches send persuasive messages. These messages appeal to shared values, such as logic. Learn to write persuasively, and learn more about the values that connect you with others.

124 • Persuasion

⏱ TIME AND RESOURCE MANAGER

Resources
Technology: Writers at Work videotape

In-Depth Coverage	Accelerated Pace
• Cover pp. 124–125 in class. • Show Persuasive Essay section of the Writers at Work videotape. • Bring in examples of various types of persuasive writing and discuss them. • Read the Model From Literature (pp. 126–127) in class and use it as a model to analyze the structure of a persuasive essay.	• Assign pp. 124–127 for independent student review. • Have students work independently to brainstorm techniques and word choices that might be effective in persuasive essays.

What Is a Persuasive Essay?

A **persuasive essay** is a brief work that presents the case for or against a particular position. An effective persuasive essay includes

- an issue with two sides.
- a clear statement of the writer's position.
- evidence supporting the writer's position.
- a clear organization, including an introduction, a body, and a strong conclusion.
- powerful images and language.

To learn the criteria on which your persuasive essay may be graded or judged, see the Rubric for Self-Assessment on page 140.

Types of Persuasive Writing

You might write any of the following types of persuasive writing:

- **Persuasive speeches,** such as one persuading students to elect you to the student council
- **Public service announcements,** such as a television commercial persuading people not to abandon their pets
- **Letters to the editor,** such as a letter you submit to your local paper asking people to attend more school games.

Writers in
ACTION

Doug Raboy writes many forms of advertisements, from television commercials to outdoor ads on billboards.

"The opportunity to influence an incredible number of people is just amazing to me and almost overwhelming."

PREVIEW
Student Work
IN PROGRESS

In this chapter, you'll follow the work of Donald Cleary, a student at Maplewood Middle School in Maplewood, New Jersey. You'll see how Donald used prewriting, drafting, and revising strategies to develop a persuasive letter addressed to the members of his town's city council. At the end of the chapter, you can read Donald's completed letter.

Persuasive Essay • 125

PREPARE and ENGAGE

Interest GRABBER Ask a couple of volunteers to give off-the-cuff persuasive speeches and have the rest of the class note and discuss the organization and techniques the speakers use. Consider topics that will require strong arguments, such as the following:

- *Why students should be required to wear uniforms*
- *Why school attendance should be voluntary*
- *Why the legal driving age should be raised to eighteen*

Activate Prior Knowledge

Help students realize that, unless they are sick and sleep the day away, they are exposed to persuasion every day: in commercials and advertisements, in letters to the editor and editorials, in their recreational reading, and in chats with families and friends. Have students recall the last written argument that struck them as particularly convincing. What qualities made the piece effective?

✓ ONGOING ASSESSMENT: Diagnose

Use this writing task to diagnose students' current level of proficiency in persuasive essay writing.

Ask students to choose an issue that would make a good persuasive essay and write a position sentence. If students have difficulty completing this exercise, clarify which sorts of topics make good persuasive essays as you work through the chapter.

Reading\Writing Connection

Reading: Understand a Writer's Purpose

Students may be puzzled about Richard Durbin's actual purpose in this speech: Was he really trying to persuade Congress to amend the Constitution? If not, what might his purpose have been? Discuss the heavy responsibilities and extensive speech to which members of Congress are subjected. Could Durbin's purpose have been to amuse his colleagues and display his oratorical skills a bit?

Teaching from the Model

Durbin's speech displays many characteristics of an effective persuasive essay in a concise form: It begins with a clearly stated topic sentence, includes appeals to logic and emotion, gains credibility through the writer's demonstrated knowledge of his subject, and concludes with a heartfelt restatement of the author's position.

Step-by-Step Teaching Guide

Engage Students Through Literature

1. Choose a student to practice Richard Durbin's speech until he or she can read it aloud convincingly and then proceed to read it to the class.

2. Ask students whether the speech includes the characteristics listed on page 125: an issue with two sides, a position statement supported by evidence, clear organization, and powerful language.

3. Have students point out words or phrases they find especially convincing or amusing. Why are phrases such as "heinous sacrilege" so funny? ("Heinous sacrilege" overstates the case a bit!)

4. Have students point out instances in which Durbin defuses potential arguments against his position.

Richard Durbin (1944–) was first elected to Congress from Illinois in 1982. On July 26, 1989, he gave the following humorous speech in the House of Representatives. In it, he warns against the idea that wooden baseball bats should be replaced by metal ones.

While Durbin is not entirely serious, his speech makes a convincing appeal to the idea of tradition. He also uses real persuasive devices, such as the repetition of words.

Reading Writing Connection

Reading Strategy: Understand a Writer's Purpose A writer's **purpose**—to inform, to entertain, to argue for a position—affects the facts, arguments, and images he or she uses. When reading, formulate an idea of the writer's purpose. Test whether it is effectively achieved as you read. For instance, Durbin's purpose is both to entertain and to persuade. With this in mind, you can evaluate his question: "What will be next? Teflon balls? Radar-enhanced gloves?"

▲ **Critical Viewing** Hank Aaron (1934–) was known as the "home run king." What tradition does this 1954 photograph of Aaron bring to mind? **[Relate]**

In his introduction, Durbin clearly introduces his topic and his position on it.

Preserving a Great American Symbol

Richard Durbin

Mr. Speaker, I rise to condemn the desecration of a great American symbol. No, I am not referring to flag burning; I am referring to the baseball bat.

Several experts tell us that the wooden baseball bat is doomed to extinction, that major league baseball players will soon be standing at home plate with aluminum bats in their hands.

Baseball fans have been forced to endure countless indignities

126 • Persuasive Essay

Critical Viewing

Relate Students may say that Aaron's wooden bat and woolen uniform represent the baseball tradition that Durbin wishes to uphold.

by those who just cannot leave well enough alone: designated hitters,[1] plastic grass, uniforms that look like pajamas, chicken clowns dancing on the baselines, and, of course, the most heinous sacrilege, lights in Wrigley Field.[2]

Are we willing to hear the crack of a bat replaced by the dinky ping? Are we ready to see the Louisville Slugger replaced by the aluminum ping dinger? Is nothing sacred?

Please do not tell me that wooden bats are too expensive, when players who cannot hit their weight are being paid more money than the President of the United States.

Please do not try to sell me on the notion that these metal clubs will make better hitters.

What will be next? Teflon baseballs? Radar-enhanced gloves? I ask you.

I do not want to hear about saving trees. Any tree in America would gladly give its life for the glory of a day at home plate.

I do not know if it will take a constitutional amendment to keep our baseball traditions alive, but if we forsake the great Americana of broken-bat singles and pine tar,[3] we will have certainly lost our way as a nation.

---

1. **designated hitter:** player who bats in place of the pitcher and does not play any other position. The position was created in 1973. Some fans argue it has changed the game for the worse.
2. **Wrigley Field:** historic baseball field in Chicago. It did not have lights for night games until 1988. Some fans regretted the change.
3. **broken-bat singles . . . pine tar:** When a batter breaks a wooden bat while hitting the ball and makes it to first base, it is a notable event in a baseball game. Pine tar is a substance used to improve the batter's grip on a wooden bat.

 **Writing Application: Help Readers Understand Your Purpose** To help readers understand the purpose of your essay, begin by introducing your issue and stating your position on it.

Durbin presents humorous "evidence" against metal bats: Other innovations in baseball have been bad, and a metal bat will not make the same satisfying noise as a wooden bat.

Durbin's organization is simple. He presents his "case" against metal bats. Next, in this paragraph, he dismisses arguments for metal bats. Finally, he concludes with a stirring call for support.

To read a persuasive letter, see C.S. Lewis's "Letter to Joan" in *C.S. Lewis: Letters to Children.* You can find an excerpt from the letter in *Prentice Hall Literature: Timeless Voices, Timeless Themes,* Copper.

More About the Speaker

Senator Durbin is committed to protecting children, and he used his persuasive skills in Congress as author of legislation that banned smoking on airline flights. He is currently fighting to protect kids from tobacco advertising and has introduced legislation to make adults responsible for storing guns away from children.

Customize for
ESL Students

Students from other countries may be puzzled by the tone of this speech unless they understand baseball's history as "the American pastime." Explain that, though baseball is no longer the most popular sport in the United States, for many years it was the sport that provided a point of identification for the children of immigrants from many different countries.

Integrating Workplace Skills

Persuasive Speech Politicians must be comfortable speaking before large groups and arguing their ideas convincingly. Since these are skills that successful lawyers possess, it should come as no surprise to students that many politicians are former lawyers.

Responding to Literature

Have students examine the persuasive techniques that Lewis uses, including his word choice and emotional appeals.

Reading\Writing Connection

Writing: Help Readers Understand Your Purpose

Explain to students that a clearly stated position will strengthen the persuasiveness of their writing. For example, if Durbin had not made his purpose for writing explicit, how would readers know that he was making an appeal to the notion of tradition?

Prewriting: Media Flip-through

1. If students keep writing notebooks, they can use them to jot down ideas inspired by TV shows or newspaper articles. If your students don't have notebooks, they may want to keep a pad of paper and a pencil next to the TV and use it every time they watch.

2. Remind students that suitable issues for a persuasive essay are ones that are open to debate. A scandal about neglected animals in a shelter, for example, probably would not make a good topic for a persuasive essay because no one is in favor of neglecting animals. On the other hand, an article or TV show about animal experimentation might suggest a very interesting topic for a persuasive essay because people have very strong beliefs for and against animal experimentation.

Prewriting: Round-Table Discussion

Teaching Resources: Writing Support Transparency 7-A

1. Display the transparency to show how Donald used a round-table discussion to help choose a topic for his essay.

2. Before students break into groups, you may want to discuss as a class examples of important people, places, and groups. If necessary, prompt students by asking questions such as *Who has changed your life? What places do you dream or daydream about? What groups do you belong to?*

3. Groups may wish to choose a scribe to summarize and record the discussions.

4. Bring the class back together to share the group lists. Then have students study the lists to see if any of the ideas suggest persuasive essay topics.

7.2 Prewriting

Choosing Your Topic

Your first step in persuasive writing is choosing an appropriate topic. The best topic may be one you feel strongly about. (Remember, the issue on which you write must have more than one side.) Use the following strategies to help you find a suitable topic:

Strategies for Generating a Topic

1. **Media Flip-Through** What's in the news? A blockbuster Hollywood movie has just flopped at the box office. The mayor has ordered all bike riders to wear helmets. You can learn about stories such as these every day in the news. Over the course of two or three days, skim through newspapers and listen to news programs. Write down any topics that interest you, and choose your topic from your list.

2. **Round-Table Discussion** Gather in a group with classmates, and list people, places, and groups that are important to you. Then, think of problems and issues that affect those you have listed. Have one student record on the board the ideas discussed. In your own notebook, jot down any that interest you, and choose a topic from your list.

Writing Lab CD-ROM

For more help finding a topic, see the activities and tips under Choosing a Topic in the Persuasion lesson.

Student Work IN PROGRESS

Name: Donald Cleary
Maplewood Middle School
Maplewood, NJ

Holding a Round-Table Discussion

To come up with topics, Donald and three other classmates held a round-table discussion. Donald selected his topic, a skating park, from his notes on the discussion.

Stray dogs and cats—a problem!

What about new computers for our class?

More choices in cafeteria lunch menu! Yes!

Where can my friends and I skate? A skating park.

128 • Persuasive Essay

⏱ TIME AND RESOURCE MANAGER

Resources
Print: Writing Support Transparencies 7-A–B
Technology: Writing Lab CD-ROM, Persuasion

In-Depth Coverage	Accelerated Pace
• Cover pp. 128–131 in class. • Have students work in pairs or small groups to generate topics, and work with the pairs or small groups as necessary. **Option** Have students use the Writing Lab CD-ROM.	• Assign pp. 128–131 for independent student review. • Have students brainstorm for and use alternate strategies to generate persuasive essay topics. • Ask students to discuss which topics suggest the most interesting persuasive essays.

TOPIC BANK

If you're having trouble finding a topic, consider the following possibilities:

1. **Editorial on Public Health** Write an editorial expressing your opinion about a problem related to people's health, such as pollution or exercise.

2. **Persuasive Essay on Pets** Take a stand on which kind of animal makes the best pet.

Responding to Fine Art

3. This painting shows the word "silence" in sign language, the language used by deaf people. It reminds us that, even in silence, people can communicate. Write a persuasive essay about a change that might be made to pay phones, at movie theaters, or in some other public place to better accommodate hearing-impaired people. Support your views with reasons.

Silence, collection of Elli Buk

Responding to Literature

4. Read or listen to the song "You've Got a Friend" by Carole King. Then, write a persuasive essay explaining what friends should do for one another. Also explain what even a friend should not have to do for a person (for instance, you might think it is wrong to tell a lie, even for a friend). Give reasons, examples, and other evidence supporting your views. You can read the lyrics to "You've Got a Friend" in *Prentice Hall Literature: Timeless Voices, Timeless Themes,* Copper.

☑ Cooperative Writing Opportunity

5. **Arts Campaign** In a group, create a brochure on your school's art and music programs. Each member should research a different aspect of the topic: What programs are currently available? What new programs do students want? What programs do other schools have? The group should assemble this research and vote on recommendations to make. Each member should then write or illustrate part of a brochure explaining the group's views.

Responding to Fine Art
Silence

Teaching Resources: Writing Support Transparency 7-B

1. Display the transparency. Have students respond freely to the art. A sign language textbook might include this same set of finger positions. Why is this art, but the textbook graphic not art? Or *is* this art? Are they both art?

2. Discuss sign language. Students who can sign may enjoy demonstrating signs for familiar words for the class.

3. Encourage students to use artwork or illustrations to suggest possible topics for their persuasive essays.

Responding to Literature

After students have listened to and/or read "You've Got a Friend" and discussed the qualities that the speaker in the song values in a friend, ask them to think of qualities they value in a friend. How would they persuade someone they like to become their friend?

Customize for
ESL Students

Students who are new to the United States have special problems and concerns. They may also see ways of solving these problems that elude tenth-generation Americans. This could lead to a topic, and the audience (discussed on page 130) could be local, state, or federal legislators.

Spotlight on the Humanities

For additional topic suggestions, refer students to the Spotlight on the Humanities on page 146.

☑ ONGOING ASSESSMENT: Monitor and Reinforce

For students who are still having difficulty choosing a topic, use one of the following options.

Option 1 Suggest that students discuss their dilemma with a partner and brainstorm ideas with that person.	**Option 2** If the Topic Bank ideas do not appeal, suggest that students select one of the suggestions from the Topic Bank for Heterogeneous Classes in the Teaching Resources.

Prewriting: Use Looping to Narrow Your Topic

1. Looping is an effective strategy for narrowing a topic, but students who know little about their chosen topic may find it difficult to write for five minutes. You can ask students to write for as long as they can, or you might ask them to do a bit of research about their topic before they begin writing.

2. You may want to model this strategy before students begin writing.

Prewriting: Considering Your Audience and Purpose

1. Have students ask and answer the questions about their topic.

2. Students might keep in mind other questions as they refine their topics. They might consider possible differences of opinion from the one they intend to support and provide counterarguments as Richard Durbin did in his speech about baseball bats.

Customize for
More Advanced Students

Students can consider choosing topics that are currently in the news, generate significant debate, and are meaningful to them. Urge them to go beyond simple topics, such as "Why Cats Make Better Pets than Dogs."

Integrating Workplace Skills

The ability to persuade in speech and writing is an essential workplace skill. Have students role-play persuading someone to hire them or convincing a boss that they deserve a raise.

7.2

Narrowing Your Topic

Once you've chosen a topic, trim it down to the right size. For instance, it could take you months to write on "children's rights." This topic includes many issues, such as children at work, children's health, and so on. It is too broad.

If your topic is too broad, narrow it down to the right size. Select one aspect to focus on. For instance, you might narrow "children's rights" to "the 'right' to a summer vacation." One way to narrow a topic is to use a strategy called looping.

Use Looping to Narrow Your Topic

Here's how to use looping to narrow your topic:
1. Write your topic at the top of a sheet of paper.
2. Set a timer for five minutes, and begin writing everything you can think of about your topic.
3. At the end of five minutes, review what you have written. Circle the most interesting idea you find.
4. Draw an arrow from the circle to a new blank line.
5. Write for another couple of minutes on your circled idea.
6. Review your new work. Circle the most interesting idea. If this idea is narrow enough to focus on in your essay, use it as your topic. If not, continue looping until you find a narrow topic.

Considering Your Audience and Purpose

Your purpose in a persuasive essay is to persuade your reader to share your opinion. To do so effectively, you must consider your reader. Ask yourself the following questions:

Are my readers older or younger than I am, or are they the same age? *If they are younger, use simple words. If you are writing for adults, express yourself in a formal way.*

How much does my reader know about the topic? *If the answer is "little," make sure you give enough background information. If the answer is "a lot," discuss your topic in depth.*

About what aspect of my topic are my readers most concerned? *Imagine you are writing about the length of your school's summer vacation. Your principal will care most about whether students will spend enough time learning. Your fellow students may care more about having enough time off. You might use different arguments for each audience!*

130 • Persuasive Essay

Gathering Support

After choosing a topic, gather support. When you present an opinion in an essay, readers will "try it on" to see whether it fits, like a suit of clothing. The reasons you give for your opinion are like buttons and zippers—if you don't use any, the "suit" will fall off as soon as the reader puts it on! Support includes:

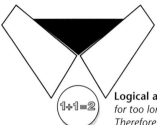

 Logical arguments: *If students are away from school for too long, they forget what they have learned. Therefore, schools should schedule only short breaks.*

 Facts: *Test scores have not gone up in schools that schedule shorter breaks.*

 Expert opinions: *Professor Edmund Havariti argues that a three-month summer vacation refreshes students' minds.*

Personal observations: *When I come back from summer vacation, I feel full of energy, ready to learn!*

Do research on your topic, and gather support using a T-chart.

Complete a T-Chart Fold a piece of paper in two. Jot down support for one side of your issue in one column and support for the other side in the other column. If you don't have an opinion yet, review your T-chart and choose a side.

 Research Tip

Ask your librarian to help you use guides to periodical literature to find magazine and newspaper articles on your topic.

Prewriting: Gathering Support; Complete a T-Chart

1. Have a volunteer read aloud the elements that students should include as support for their topics.

2. For each element, have students provide other examples.

3. Tell students to include a pro and con comment for each item on the T-Chart.

4. Students who are firmly entrenched in a position may find it difficult to imagine objections to it. These students can work with a partner to generate ideas.

5. When students have completed their T-Charts, they can trade them with a partner to see whether that person can come up with any additional ideas.

Customize for
Less Advanced Students

Students may have difficulty "seeing" potential arguments against their opinions. Have students work in pairs to complete their T-charts to allow for a greater range of possible counter-opinions and arguments.

Drafting: Develop a Position Statement

1. Make sure students understand that a thesis statement covers the entire persuasive essay. It differs from a topic sentence, which sums up each paragraph.

2. The directional statement is a restatement of the thesis that extends and amplifies it. Give the following examples of thesis statement and directional statement.

   - *No one should be allowed to build any more tall buildings across from the beach. Too much of the beautiful view is blocked already.*

   - *Kids who ride bikes should be required to take safety classes. Then maybe fewer children would get injured in accidents.*

7.3 Drafting

Shaping Your Writing

Develop a Position Statement

The evidence you have gathered will help support your position. To introduce your position to readers, develop a position statement. A **position statement** is a sentence naming the issue on which you are writing and expressing your position.

	POSITION	ISSUE
POSITION STATEMENT:	Schools should keep	a three-month summer vacation.

To develop your position statement, review all of your prewriting notes, and write down one or two sentences summing up your argument.

It is a good idea to follow your position statement with a "directional" statement explaining your main arguments.

	MAIN REASON
DIRECTIONAL STATEMENT:	Shortening the break will hurt students without helping their education.

Include these sentences in the introduction to your essay.

Organize for Clarity

Your essay does not come with a map, but you can still help keep your reader from getting lost. To help your reader follow your argument, organize your ideas clearly.

Introduction Your introduction should tell your readers what to expect in the rest of the essay. Include your position and directional statements in your introduction.

Body In the paragraphs following your introduction, explain each of your main points in turn. For each, provide evidence—facts, statistics, arguments, or expert opinions. Often, a main point and its support will make up one topical paragraph.

Conclusion Finally, write a strong conclusion that summarizes your arguments and restates your viewpoint in a memorable way.

Writing Lab CD-ROM

For more help organizing your essay, see the Organizing Details section of the Persuasion lesson.

132 • Persuasive Essay

⏱ TIME AND RESOURCE MANAGER

Resources
Print: Writing Support Transparency 7-B
Technology: Writing Lab CD-ROM, Persuasion

In-Depth Coverage	Accelerated Pace
• Cover pp. 132–133 in class. • Have students write their persuasive essay draft in class. **Option** Have students work independently or in small groups with the Writing Lab CD-ROM.	• Have students review pp. 132–133 independently and then write their first drafts. • Respond to questions as necessary.

Providing Elaboration

As you draft your essay, make sure you explain and support each of your main ideas fully. Elaborate as you draft by providing explanations and evidence, such as statistics, facts, expert opinions, and illustrations.

Support Each Point

To clarify and support your points, use any of the following techniques:

- Compare or contrast your topic with something else.
- Find an example.
- Make a specific observation.
- Use facts or statistics from books, magazines, or other media.

Some evidence comes from researching a topic in the library. Other evidence comes from personal experience and observation. Whatever support you provide must be accurate and clear.

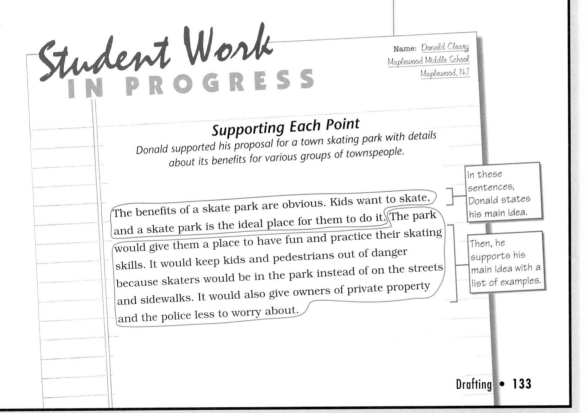

Student Work
IN PROGRESS

Name: Donald Cleary
Maplewood Middle School
Maplewood, NJ

Supporting Each Point

Donald supported his proposal for a town skating park with details about its benefits for various groups of townspeople.

The benefits of a skate park are obvious. Kids want to skate, and a skate park is the ideal place for them to do it. The park would give them a place to have fun and practice their skating skills. It would keep kids and pedestrians out of danger because skaters would be in the park instead of on the streets and sidewalks. It would also give owners of private property and the police less to worry about.

> In these sentences, Donald states his main idea.

> Then, he supports his main idea with a list of examples.

Drafting • 133

Step-by-Step Teaching Guide

Drafting: Providing Elaboration; Support Each Point

Teaching Resources: Writing Support Transparency 7-C

1. Discuss the various ways to elaborate on points in persuasive essays. Note that the elaboration techniques writers choose depend on their topics. If a writer is making a case against capital punishment, for instance, statistics showing that the threat of capital punishment does not deter crime would help build a powerful case against this kind of punishment.

2. Display the transparency. The skate park essay does not include statistics. Ask if the essay would be stronger if it did. How about quotes from skaters, pedestrians, or owners of private property?

3. Brainstorm with students techniques and sources of information that would be appropriate for their topics.

4. Have students examine their drafts and note places where additional information would help strengthen their arguments.

Customize for
Verbal/Linguistic Learners

Have students summarize their persuasive essays orally to partners. Have the listeners note statements that do not seem adequately supported by detailed evidence.

☑ **ONGOING ASSESSMENT: Monitor and Reinforce**

If students are not using the range of persuasive techniques, use the following strategy.

Have students underline comparisons and contrasts, examples, specific details, and facts or statistics in their papers, using a different color for each technique. Urge students who have relied on one method of elaboration to try several of the others.

 TIME SAVERS!

Writing Support Transparencies
Use the transparencies for Chapter 7 to teach these strategies.

Revising: "Interrogating Paragraphs" for Logical Order

Teaching Resources: Writing Support Transparency 7-D; Writing Support Activity Book 7-1

1. Explain to students that paragraphs in a persuasive essay must be in a logical order to build a convincing argument. If the paragraph order is confusing, readers will be confused about the argument the writer is trying to make. Transition words are important to clarify meaning, too, by linking one paragraph to the next.

2. Display the transparency and discuss the sorts of questions writers consider when they examine the order of their essays paragraph by paragraph.

3. Give students copies of the blank organizer. Have students examine their paragraphs and use the information they record in their charts to reorganize their paragraphs.

4. Remind students to add transition words to their essays as necessary. Suggest other possible transitions, such as *on the other hand, moreover,* and *besides.*

Customize for *ESL Students*

Students learning English as a second language are likely to omit transitions or rely on the same ones again and again. Review transitions such as *first, next, then,* and *last* and explain such phrases as *on one hand* and *in addition.* After students have added transition words to their essays, check to make sure they are appropriate and clarify the arguments presented.

7.4 Revising

Once you've written your first draft, find ways to improve it. Start by checking the overall structure of your essay. Then, move to smaller parts, like sentences and words.

Revising Your Overall Structure
Analyze Organization

Sometimes, it is difficult to see problems with structure until your draft is completed. Use the strategy of "Interrogating Paragraphs" to make sure your draft is logically organized.

▶ **REVISION STRATEGY**
"Interrogating Paragraphs" for Logical Order

Every paragraph is innocent until proven guilty—but occasionally one ends up in the wrong place at the wrong time! Draw a box around the main point in each paragraph in your draft. Use the following questions to determine whether your paragraph is in the right place:

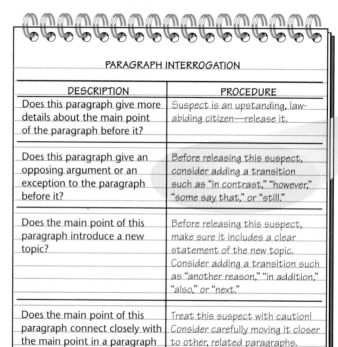

PARAGRAPH INTERROGATION	
DESCRIPTION	PROCEDURE
Does this paragraph give more details about the main point of the paragraph before it?	Suspect is an upstanding, law-abiding citizen—release it.
Does this paragraph give an opposing argument or an exception to the paragraph before it?	Before releasing this suspect, consider adding a transition such as "in contrast," "however," "some say that," or "still."
Does the main point of this paragraph introduce a new topic?	Before releasing this suspect, make sure it includes a clear statement of the new topic. Consider adding a transition such as "another reason," "in addition," "also," or "next."
Does the main point of this paragraph connect closely with the main point in a paragraph elsewhere in the essay?	Treat this suspect with caution! Consider carefully moving it closer to other, related paragraphs.

134 • Persuasive Essay

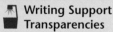 **TIME SAVERS!**

Writing Support Transparencies
Use the transparencies for Chapter 7 to teach these strategies.

Writing Support Activity Book
Use the graphic organizers for Chapter 7 to facilitate these strategies.

TIME AND RESOURCE MANAGER

Resources
Print: Writing Support Transparencies 7-D–F; Writing Support Activity Book 7-1
Technology: Writing Lab CD-ROM, Persuasion

In-Depth Coverage	Accelerated Pace
• Cover pp. 134–138 in class. • Use the relevant transparencies to demonstrate strategies for analyzing organization, supporting details (pp. 134–135), paragraph structure (p. 136), correcting incomplete sentences (p. 137), and using persuasive language (p. 138).	• Assign pp. 134–138 for independent student review. • Have students revise their persuasive essays independently.

Check Your Support

Now that your overall organization makes sense, take a look at the support you provide for each main point. You may have watched courtroom dramas on television. If so, you know that if there is too little evidence, a case can get kicked out of court! Each paragraph in your essay should provide a good amount of evidence for the case you are making. If it does not, evaluate whether you should strengthen it or eliminate it.

▶ **REVISION STRATEGY**
Circling Supporting Evidence

Review each of your main points. Circle the evidence that supports each one. Then, evaluate your circled support.

Strong Support If you find support that is especially strong, consider building on it. For instance, you might draw attention to a well-supported point by adding charged language or a colorful comparison.

No Support If you find a paragraph without circled sentences in it, review your prewriting notes for evidence and add support. If necessary, do extra research to find the support you need.

🔘 Technology Tip

If you are using a word-processing program, type in supporting details at the bottom of your document. Split the screen; then, scroll through your document in the top window while supporting details remain on view in the bottom. Find just the right spot to insert each detail.

Revising: Circle Supporting Evidence

Teaching Resources: Writing Support Transparency 7-E

1. Display the transparency. Ask students how the persuasiveness of Donald's essay would have been affected if he had not added this supporting evidence.

2. Have students underline the topic sentence in each paragraph and circle the sentences that give evidence to support the topic sentence.

3. Students should then add detail sentences to support any topic sentences that lack them. If students are unable to gather evidence to support some of their assertions, they should consider deleting these paragraphs. Emphasize that students' arguments must be convincing. A few well-supported arguments are more persuasive than lots of arguments that lack convincing support.

4. After students have revised their paragraphs to add supporting evidence, they should reread their essays to make sure each sentence they added supports the topic sentence of the paragraph in which it appears.

Student Work
IN PROGRESS

Name: Donald Cleary
Maplewood Middle School
Maplewood, NJ

Circling Supporting Evidence

After circling support, Donald found one paragraph without any circles. He added the missing support.

I know what you're thinking as you read this: cost, cost, and cost. Building a skate park will not be cheap, but it also won't be very expensive. Burlington built its park for only $18,000.

And if the jumps are under six feet, the insurance won't be too much.

> Donald found no support to circle in this paragraph. He called the Town Hall in Burlington and did a little more research into the cost of building a skate park. Then, he added these two details supporting the idea that a park might not be too expensive.

✓ ONGOING ASSESSMENT: Monitor and Reinforce

If students are having difficulty adding supporting sentences, try one of the following options.

Option 1 Suggest that students work in pairs. They can take turns reading aloud topic sentences that stump them and together brainstorm supporting evidence.

Option 2 Have students read editorials in magazines or newspapers and analyze the methods of persuasion employed by the writers. Students may be able to use some of these techniques in their essays.

135

Revising: Finding the "Glue" Between Sentences

Teaching Resources: Writing Support Transparency 7-F

1. Since the revision strategy comprises several steps, you may want to display the transparency and go through the steps one by one.

2. Then ask a volunteer to use his or her essay as an additional example of finding the "glue" between sentences. Write a paragraph or two from the essay on the chalkboard.

3. Choose students to come to the board and underline the connecting words (rather than highlighting them), circle, and draw arrows and rectangles following the model.

4. As students examine the transition words in boxes, encourage them to suggest alternatives for overused transition words.

5. Students should then be prepared to use this technique successfully as they revise the paragraphs in their essays.

7.4

Revising Your Paragraphs
Check Coherence

Now that you have improved the overall structure of your paper, check each paragraph. Every sentence in a paragraph should connect with the others in one of these ways:

- It should tell more about something in a previous sentence.

- It should contain a transition spelling out its connection with a previous sentence. Transitions include *first, however, next, then, for this reason,* and *by contrast.*

Check sentence connections by "Finding the 'Glue.'"

▶ **REVISION STRATEGY**
Finding the "Glue" Between Sentences

Follow these steps for three paragraphs in your draft:
1. In each sentence except the first, find a word that connects to a previous sentence. Highlight the word.
2. Circle the word or words in the earlier sentence to which the highlighted word connects.
3. Draw an arrow between the circled and the highlighted words.
4. For any sentence without a highlighted word, either
   - add words connecting back to the previous sentence, or
   - eliminate the sentence.

Writing Lab CD-ROM

For additional help revising paragraphs, use the Self-Revising section of the Persuasion lesson.

Student Work
IN PROGRESS

Name: *Donald Cleary*
Maplewood Middle School
Maplewood, NJ

Checking Coherence by Finding the "Glue"
Donald coded for the "glue" between sentences. He decided to eliminate a sentence that he could not connect back to previous sentences.

Another (problem) is where to put a (skate park.)

Well, I've already thought that through. It could

be built in (one of two places.) The first place is

just inside the South Mountain Reservation.

~~The best place for skateboarding is actually a~~

~~completely man-made environment with ramps,~~

~~like you see on television.~~

Donald could not connect words in this sentence with other sentences. He also found no transition words in the sentence. He decided the sentence did not belong in this paragraph and deleted it.

Revising Your Sentences

Eliminate Fragments

Sometimes the words explaining an idea drift off on their own—they become a sentence fragment.

FRAGMENT: Because we like him.

To eliminate fragments, use the following strategy:

▶ **REVISION STRATEGY**
Circling Sentence Beginnings to Eliminate Fragments

In your essay, circle sentences beginning with these words:

after	but	until
although	if	when
and	or	whenever
because	since	who
before	that	while

Then, read each circled sentence. Does it make sense on its own? If not, rewrite it, using the tips in the box below.

Grammar in Your Writing
Complete Sentences

A **sentence fragment** is a group of words that does not express a complete thought, even though it is punctuated as a sentence. Use these techniques to correct fragments:

Add a verb.

FRAGMENT: Many different endangered and rare animals at the zoo.
COMPLETE SENTENCE: Many different endangered and rare animals **live** at the zoo.

Add a subject.

FRAGMENT: Enjoy seeing all the animals there.
COMPLETE SENTENCE: **I** enjoy seeing all the animals there.

Join the fragment to a sentence that comes before or after it.

FRAGMENT: We visit the zoo. When we have guests from out of town.
COMPLETE SENTENCE: We visit the zoo when we have guests from out of town.

Find It in Your Reading Find two sentences beginning with the word *if* in the Student Model on page 141. Explain why they are not fragments.

Find It in Your Writing Read the last five sentences in your draft aloud. If any does not express a complete idea, rewrite it as a complete sentence.

For more on complete sentences, see Chapter 21.

Revising • 137

Step-by-Step Teaching Guide

Grammar in Your Writing: Complete Sentences

1. Discuss sentence fragments. Have volunteers define *subject* and *predicate* and reiterate that every sentence must have both—otherwise it isn't a sentence. Note that in one-word commands (such as "Halt!") the subject is understood to be *you*.

2. Students often assume that a long, involved series of words is a sentence, whereas two or three words are a fragment. Give the following example of a short sentence and a long fragment.
   Watch out!
   A great big scary snake 30 feet long, with fangs and a hungry look on its face.

3. Have partners trade papers, circle the sentence beginnings listed on this page, and note whether any of these words indicate sentence fragments. Are there any sentence fragments that do not begin with these words?

4. Students should retrieve their papers and correct any sentence fragments.

Find It in Your Reading

The fourth and fifth sentences both begin with *If*. They are sentences because each expresses a complete thought.

Find It in Your Writing

If students cannot find any incomplete sentences, challenge them to write two incomplete sentences and show how they can make them complete.

☑ ONGOING ASSESSMENT: Prerequisite Skills

If students have difficulty correcting sentence fragments, you may find it helpful to review the following to assure coverage of prerequisite knowledge.

In the Textbook	Print Resources	Technology
Basic Sentence Parts, pp. 378–413	Grammar Exercise Workbook, pp. 43–50	Language Lab CD-ROM, Problems with Sentences; On-Line Exercise Bank, Sections 19.1–4

Step-by-Step Teaching Guide

Revising: Using Thoughtshots

1. Talk about vague words—words such as *interesting* or *nice*—that make a reader ask *how?* and *in what way?*

2. Ask students to look for vague words in their essays and volunteer examples. Work together to think of replacement words for these examples.

3. Encourage students to use a dictionary or thesaurus or ask friends if they have difficulty thinking of precise words to replace some of the vague words in their essays.

4. Then pass out sticky notes and ask students to follow the procedure outlined on this page to identify vague words.

Step-by-Step Teaching Guide

Revising: Peer Review

1. Students may want to practice reading their essays aloud before they read them to the group so that reading difficulties don't get in the way of listeners' understanding.

2. Remind readers to read slowly and with expression and listeners to avoid negative comments and stick to noting the parts of the essays that puzzle them.

Integrating Vocabulary Skills

Synonyms Encourage students to use a thesaurus to find synonyms for overused words in their essays. Remind them that synonyms don't always carry precisely the same meaning. If students don't recognize the synonyms or understand their exact meanings, they should look up the words in a dictionary to make sure the words convey the exact meanings the writers intend.

Revising Your Word Choice
Use Precise, Persuasive Language

To persuade your reader, use words that point in a clear direction. Vague or general words, such as *good* or *bad*, will not give the best directions. Instead, choose precise words—words that give specific information—to let your reader know where you are headed.

For instance, if you say that your friend will make a "good class president," think of what you specifically mean by *good*. You might mean *intelligent*, *responsible*, or *honest*—or all three. You can better direct readers if you use these specific terms instead of the vague word *good*.

▶ **REVISION STRATEGY**
Using "Thoughtshots"

Circle words such as *good, bad, better, worse, nice, stupid, dumb,* and other vague words anywhere they appear in your draft. Next to each, place a sticky note. On each sticky note, write a sentence explaining the exact reasons the vague word applies, as in the following example:

| SENTENCE USING GENERAL WORD: | My friend will make a **good** class president. |
| WHY THE GENERAL WORD APPLIES: | My friend is **responsible**, **intelligent**, and **honest**. |

After you have finished marking your draft, review each Thoughtshot. Use specific words on the Thoughtshot to replace the general words you have circled in your draft.

Thoughtshot
responsible
intelligent
honest

Peer Review
"Say Back"

Once you have finished revising your essay on your own, you can still use the help of your classmates.

In a small group of four or five students, read your revised persuasive essay twice. Ask your listeners to listen the first time and respond the second time. To respond, listeners can jot down answers to these questions:

1. What details do I find persuasive?
2. What do I want to know more about?

After hearing from your classmates, consider using their suggestions to improve your essay.

138 • Persuasive Essay

Collaborative Writing Tip

Have a classmate circle vague words in your draft. For each one he or she finds, explain why you used it. Your classmate should take notes from your explanation. Review these notes for specific words you can use to replace the vague ones in your draft.

✍ STANDARDIZED TEST PREPARATION WORKSHOP

Synonyms Standardized tests may require students to choose synonyms. Ask them to identify the synonym of the underlined word in the following sentence.

Mr. Meijer is a <u>demanding</u> boss.

| A | mean | C | ugly |
| B | tough | D | good |

Item **B**, *tough*, is the most appropriate replacement for *demanding*. If necessary, discuss the difference between a tough boss and a mean one.

7.5 Editing and Proofreading

When you have finished revising your persuasive essay, you still have one more step to take. Correct any errors in spelling, punctuation, grammar, and usage. After all, your purpose is to persuade your reader of your opinion—not that you have difficulty spelling.

Focusing on End Marks

In persuasive writing, you use sentences to:

- make statements.
- ask questions.
- exclaim, expressing excitement.

Use the correct end mark for each kind of sentence.

⚙ Grammar and Style Tip

A good persuasive writer may build a case, then pose a question to readers asking what conclusions they draw. This strategy is persuasive because it makes readers feel that the author is asking them to make up their own minds.

Grammar in Your Writing
End Marks

Sentences must end with one of three **end marks**—the period (.), the question mark (?), or the exclamation point (!).

Use a period to end a statement of fact or opinion.

The bald eagle is the national bird of the United States.

Use a question mark to ask a direct question.

What can young people do to save the bald eagle?

Use an exclamation point to express strong feeling.

We must preserve the bald eagle!

Find It in Your Reading Find two different end marks used in "Preserving a Great American Symbol" by Richard Durbin on page 126. For each, explain why it is used correctly.

Find It in Your Writing Read your draft aloud with expression. If your voice rises at the end of a sentence, check whether you need a question mark. If you find your voice growing more excited, think about whether you might use an exclamation point.

To learn more on using end marks correctly, see Chapter 26.

Grammar in Your Writing: End Marks

1. Have volunteers explain the meaning and use of the three end marks. Make sure students understand that in some sentences both the exclamation mark and period are appropriate end marks, depending on how much feeling the writer intends to convey.

2. Caution students not to overuse exclamation marks. The logic and reasoning of the arguments in their persuasive essays should convince the reader—not the number of sentences that are exclamations.

Find It in Your Reading

Students should identify a period and a question mark. The periods in the first paragraph end statements of opinion. The question marks in the first full paragraph on page 127 end questions.

Find It in Your Writing

Remind students not to overuse exclamation marks. If they use one, make sure they can support their decision.

Revision Tips

Though students are polishing their writing by correcting errors at this stage, assure them that it is never too late to revise for elegance or clarity. Sometimes it takes writers several drafts to get their writing just the way they want it, and each time they read their pieces, students have another opportunity to refine their essays.

🕐 TIME AND RESOURCE MANAGER

Resources
Print: Scoring Rubrics on Transparency, Chapter 7; Writing Assessment: Scoring Rubric and Scoring Models for Persuasive Essay
Technology: Writing Lab CD-ROM, Persuasion

In-Depth Coverage	Accelerated Pace
• Cover pp. 139–140 in class. • Have students edit and proofread their essays in class. • Review Rubric for Self-Assessment in class. • Students present their final drafts.	• Assign pp. 139–140 for independent student review. • Students edit and proofread their essays as homework. • Students present their final drafts.

Publishing and Presenting

1. Help students identify the appropriate governmental body and individual to which to send their essay. Addresses may be obtained in a hurry by using an almanac or the Internet.

2. Letters sent to government officials should, if possible, be word processed, or at least typed. Students should double- and even triple-check their essays for errors.

3. If two or more students have written essays on related topics, they may want to combine them into one slightly longer essay. This is more effective than three similar letters.

4. Students should include a cover letter with their essay, introducing themselves and explaining their class project.

5. Have students consider adapting their essays as editorials for the student newspaper or letters to the editor of their local newspaper.

ASSESS

Assessment

Teaching Resources: Scoring Rubrics on Transparency 7; Formal Assessment, Chapter 7

1. Display the Scoring Rubric transparency and review the criteria in class.

2. Before the students proceed with self-assessment, you may wish to review the Final Draft of the Student Work in Progress on pages 141–143. Have students score the Final Draft in one or more of the rubric categories. For example, how would students score the essay in terms of audience and purpose?

3. In addition to student self-assessment, you may wish to use the following assessment options.

   • score student essays yourself, using the rubric and scoring models from Writing Assessment.

continued

7.6 Publishing and Presenting

Building Your Portfolio

Consider these ideas for publishing and presenting your persuasive essay:

1. **Create an Opinion Board** With a teacher's help, post student essays on a bulletin board in your school. Use art work and color to ensure that titles and topics stand out.

2. **Tell It to the Government** If you wrote about a political issue, send a neat copy of your essay with a cover letter to your mayor, state legislator, congressperson, or senator, or to the President. Share your essay and any response you receive with the class.

Reflecting on Your Writing

Jot down a few notes about your experience writing a persuasive essay. You might start off by answering the following questions:

• Did writing a persuasive essay change your feelings about the issue on which you wrote? How?

• Which writing strategy helped you the most? The least? Explain.

Internet Tip

To see examples of persuasive writing scored according to this rubric, visit **www.phschool.com**

Rubric for Self-Assessment

Use the following criteria to evaluate your persuasive essay:

	Score 4	Score 3	Score 2	Score 1
Audience and Purpose	Provides arguments, illustrations, and words that forcefully appeal to the audience and effectively serve persuasive purpose	Provides arguments, illustrations, and words that appeal to the audience and serve the persuasive purpose	Provides some support that appeals to the audience and serves the persuasive purpose	Shows little attention to the audience or persuasive purpose
Organization	Uses clear, consistent organizational strategy	Uses clear organizational strategy with occasional inconsistencies	Uses inconsistent organizational strategy	Shows lack of organizational strategy; writing is confusing
Elaboration	Provides specific, well-elaborated support for the writer's position	Provides some elaborated support for the writer's position	Provides some support, but with little elaboration	Lacks support
Use of Language	Uses transitions to connect ideas smoothly; shows few mechanical errors	Uses some transitions; shows few mechanical errors	Uses few transitions; shows some mechanical errors	Shows little connection between ideas; shows many mechanical errors

140 • Persuasive Essay

☑ ONGOING ASSESSMENT: Assess Mastery

Use one of the following options to assess final drafts of students' persuasive essays.

Self-Assessment Ask students to score their essay, using the rubric provided. Then have students write a paragraph describing one important lesson they learned in writing their persuasive essay.

Teacher Assessment You may want to use the rubric and the scoring models provided in Writing Assessment, Copper Level, to score the persuasive essays.

7.7 Student Work IN PROGRESS

FINAL DRAFT

Say "Yes!" to Skating!

Donald Cleary
Maplewood Middle School
Maplewood, New Jersey

Dear Council Members:

All through the streets of Maplewood, there are signs that read "No Skateboarding or Rollerblading." My friends and I enjoy freestyle skating. However, we have practically no place to do it. If we skate on the sidewalks, we are dangerous to pedestrians. If we skate on the streets, we could get hurt ourselves. We know that skating on private property, such as grocery store parking lots, is a bad idea, since sometimes the owners call the police to have skaters removed. Signs that say "No Skating" are not the answer to these problems. What this town needs is a skate park, and I am asking the council members to have one built.

The benefits of a skate park are obvious. Kids want to skate, and a skate park is the ideal place for them to do it. The park would give them a place to have fun and practice their skating skills. It would keep kids and pedestrians out of danger because skaters would be in the park instead of on the streets and sidewalks. It would also give owners of private property and the police less to worry about. And by building a skate park in Maplewood, you can and will make many frustrated kids happy.

There might be other advantages to the skate park. The skate park in Burlington gives skating lessons, and our skate park could, too. Our skate park could have competitions and family

▼ **Critical Viewing**
Give an opinion on the law represented by this sign.
[Evaluate]

Donald's introduction clearly states his topic: The need for a skate park in his town. The last sentence in this paragraph is Donald's thesis statement.

Donald's organization is logical. First, he gives his strongest arguments. He follows them with additional arguments.

- review the Standardized Test Preparation Workshop on pages 148–149 and have students respond to a persuasive writing prompt within a time limit.
- administer the Chapter 7 Test from Formal Assessment in Teaching Resources to assess students' grasp of concepts presented.

CLOSE

Step-by-Step Teaching Guide

Teaching from the Final Draft

1. As students read and analyze Donald Cleary's plea to his town's city council, ask them to pay close attention to the side notes. Students should be able to point out the following features included in an effective persuasive essay like this one:

- an issue with two sides (should or shouldn't a skate park be built)
- a thesis statement that clearly states the writer's position (the last sentence in the first paragraph)
- evidence supporting the writer's position (using a neighboring skate park as an example is particularly effective in this essay)
- clear organization including an introduction, a body, and a conclusion

continued

Critical Viewing

Evaluate Students may say that they disagree with the ban on skateboarding.

2. Which arguments in favor of building a skate park did students find most compelling? Why did they buy those arguments?

3. What other arguments or specific information might Donald have added to strengthen his thesis? (Example: He might have suggested ways a skate park could generate revenue to compensate for the cost of building it.)

4. Which words did students find persuasive? (Examples of persuasive buzz words include *benefits, advantages, not expensive, out of danger, less to worry about, make many frustrated kids happy.*)

5. Have students list what they liked and did not like about Donald's piece and consider making some last minute changes in their own essays based on their analyses of this model.

Critical Viewing

Apply Students may write *Skating is a great activity that provides physical exercise and allows kids to make new friends.*

7.7

◄ **Critical Viewing** Write a caption for this photo that might help persuade town council members to build a skate park in Donald's town. **[Apply]**

gatherings with snack stands. It would be a place where lots of people in the town could have fun.

I know what you're thinking as you read this: cost, cost, and cost. Building a skate park will not be cheap, but it also won't be very expensive. Burlington built its park for only $18,000. And if the jumps are under six feet, the insurance won't be too much.

Another problem is where to put a skate park. Well, I've already thought that through. It could be built in one of two places. The first place is just inside the South Mountain Reservation. It is very hilly, and it's a natural setting for fun skating. My friends and I really like lots of hills, and there is a lot of room to put just about anything in the Reservation. The other place is next to Waterlands soccer field, where the mulch center is. It would be good to have the skate park near the soccer field since the area is already used for sports. Why not make this a center for outdoor fun?

If you will consider this proposition now and vote to approve it, you could start building the park very soon, and it could be ready for us kids as soon as spring comes. Remember, the longer you

The main point in this paragraph is fully supported by detailed information. Donald is answering the arguments against his idea. In this way, he strengthens his own case.

Donald's conclusion clearly sums up his idea and his arguments for it.

142 • Persuasive Essay

wait, the more frustrated kids, property owners, pedestrians, and other citizens will become. I hope that you take this proposal into consideration and not turn it down. Thank you.

Sincerely,
Donald Cleary

▼ **Critical Viewing** Give a detail from Donald's proposal that might persuade this boy to support a skate park. **[Apply]**

Critical Viewing

Apply Students may mention Donald's point that skating on the sidewalk and in the street is dangerous.

Integrating Vocabulary Skills

Persuasive Words Have students analyze advertisements and commercials for persuasive language. Ask which of these words might be used to "sell" an idea. This exercise may help students vary the vocabulary they use to persuade readers of the strength of the arguments in their persuasive essays. However, caution students that ads and commercials may come on a bit stronger than effective arguments in a persuasive essay.

Customize for
Visual/Spatial Learners

Students can make graphic organizers such as webs to represent the information in Donald's essay. They can analyze the items on their webs by rating them with minus signs for arguments that they consider weak and one to three stars for arguments of increasing strength.

Student Work in Progress • 143

Lesson Objectives

1. To write an advertisement appropriate to audience purpose.

2. To analyze information as presented in various media.

3. To examine how visual techniques can be used to create an emotional response in viewers.

4. To evaluate the effectiveness of images used to add information to written text.

5. To publish and present an advertisement to an audience.

Step-by-Step Teaching Guide

Advertisement

Teaching Resources: Writing Support Transparency 7-G; Writing Support Activity Book 7-2

1. Bring sample advertisements to class, or suggest students find them in magazines and newspapers. Study several examples, including the model in the textbook, while going over the elements of advertisements. Ask students to look for a "hook" or "concept" in the sample advertisements.

2. Point out that advertisements are intended to act as pure persuasion and that they inform only to the degree that the advertiser thinks this will help sell a product or an idea. Explain that many advertisers spend a lot of time and money identifying their target audience and finding out what kinds of images and music will appeal to this group.

3. Display the transparency and use it to model how students can plan and create their own advertisements. Give students copies of the blank organizer, asking them to fill it out as they plan their advertisements alone or in groups.

4. Explain to students that identifying their intended audience ahead of time will help them organize and focus their own advertisements before they start creating them. Tell them that having identified a target audience they can choose a

Connected Assignment
Advertisement

You can find persuasive writing all around you. You can read it on a poster in the subway. You can hear it in a commercial on television. "20% less fat . . ." or "Cleans better, faster . . ."—these are the kinds of persuasive words you can find in advertisements.

An **advertisement** presents a persuasive message in print or broadcast form (on television or on radio). It is produced and paid for by an individual or a business to persuade you to do something or to form a certain opinion. Most advertisements try to persuade you to buy a product. Some try to change your opinion about an issue. Advertisements may include the following elements:

- the use of pictures, music, and skits

- a **"concept,"** or central theme (for instance, an advertiser might use the concept of *health* to promote a cereal by showing people working out)

- a **"hook,"** such as a catchy jingle, a memorable slogan, or an attention-grabbing image

Create your own print advertisement, following the strategies outlined here.

Prewriting First, make up a product or service you might sell. You might choose a topic like one of the following:

- **Sell a Product** Advertise a product your classmates might use, such as a pencil that erases words with the push of a button.

- **Advertise a Service** Advertise a service you might provide, such as baby-sitting or lawn-raking.

MODEL

*This advertisement is directed at a young audience. The **concept** is to create a friendly, fun atmosphere around the idea of reading. The **hook** is the cute dinosaur, Theo, and the whimsical slogan, "Read. Avoid Extinction." The ad implies that reading is not a chore. Only silly dinosaurs avoid reading, it seems to say—and look what happened to them!*

144 • Persuasive Essay

concept or a hook that will appeal to this group.

5. Encourage students to be creative as they develop their advertisements. Plan a class session in which students share their advertisements with each other or with other students in the school.

Once you have chosen something to advertise, focus your topic by creating a "concept" for your advertisement. You might use any of the following themes:

- **enjoying ease of use** (for example, show students happily working with your self-erasing pencil while others using old-style erasers rub away in frustration)

- **making smart choices** (for example, show students who use your pencil talking confidently about how much time they have saved)

- **fitting in with a trend** (for example, show a group of happy students showing off their self-erasing pencils to each other).

After you have developed a concept, brainstorm for a "hook"—a slogan or image—that will sum up your concept. Your hook should use easily understood, eye-catching images and colorful words so that even distracted readers will understand instantly. Gather ideas for your advertisement, using a chart like the one shown.

Product/Service: Self-Erasing Pencils

Concept	Hook	Image	Head
Follow the trend	All the popular kids are using self-erasing pencils: "I can't keep the pace without using my Self-Erase."	On left, kid stands, shrugging, with his pockets turned out, looking worried. On the right, a happy group of kids holding their self-erase pencils high walk by.	"I can't keep the pace without my Self-Erase!"

Drafting As you draft, use heads (words, phrases, or sentences set in large type) to grab the reader's eye. Feature your "hook" in these heads. The rest of the text should be short and to the point. When you have finished drafting, lay out your ad on the computer or by cutting and pasting on paper. Arrange pictures and text to create a neat, balanced effect.

Revising and Editing Review your draft. Circle the place where you present your concept most clearly. If necessary, revise to make your concept more easily understood by a reader. Delete any words or images that do not add to your message. Finally, proofread your work for any errors.

Publishing and Presenting Add a poster of your print advertisement to a class Advertising Gallery.

Integrating Technology and Workplace Skills

Explain to students that the Internet is the newest frontier for advertising. Tell them that an entire industry has grown around advertising on Web sites. Ask them if they have noticed, when doing research on the Internet or looking for items of interest, that many sites have advertising at the top and bottom of the page. Explain that a Web site attracts advertisers by guaranteeing a certain number of "hits" or visits. Advertisers are willing to pay for space on sites that attract a lot of visitors because it ensures that their ads will be seen.

1. To analyze how images communicate information.

2. To examine how visual techniques can be used to create an emotional response in viewers.

3. To use writing to respond to works of art.

4. To analyze the process that leads to the creation of works of art.

Step-by-Step Teaching Guide

Analyzing Visual Meanings

1. Choose one of the Spotlight elements for class discussion, or have students work individually or in groups on the element of their choice. Give students the initiative to find the necessary books, videotapes, or pictures.

2. Bring in reproductions of Michelangelo's paintings and photographs of his sculpture. If students view *The Agony and the Ecstasy,* ask them to think about the movie's themes. Have them compare and contrast Michelangelo's life to the life of one of the modern artists they have listed. Ask them if they think modern artists also experience the kind of agony and ecstasy portrayed in the movie.

3. Bring in a copy of "Lament on the Death of Lorenzo de' Medici" as well as a modern example of song written upon the death of a famous artist or public figure (e.g., Elton John's song for Princess Diana, which was an adaptation of his song "Candle in the Wind"). Ask students which artists we might still be hearing about in songs 100 years from now.

Viewing and Representing

Activity As students look at Michelangelo's work, ask them to think about what he conveyed in his art. Have them describe, in a small group or whole class discussion, what they see in his paintings and his sculpture.

Spotlight on the Humanities

Analyzing Visual Meanings

Focus on Art: Michelangelo

You can change people's minds with words, but how do you persuade a stone? Michelangelo Buonarroti (1475–1564) knew the secret of persuading rough stone to reveal the forms and figures hidden within. A master sculptor and painter, he is considered one of the world's greatest artists.

Born in Caprese, Italy, Michelangelo started studying painting and sculpture at age twelve. Michelangelo attracted the notice of Lorenzo de' Medici (1449–1492), the ruler of Florence, Italy. The Medici family became Michelangelo's patrons (supporters).

The ceiling of the Sistine Chapel is one of Michelangelo's masterworks. (The chapel is in the Vatican, the Pope's official residence in Vatican City, located within Rome.) Michelangelo filled the chapel's ceilings with thirty-three frescos (paintings on plaster) of subjects from the Bible. In the frescos, Michelangelo portrays human forms in a passionate, dynamic style. Among his other famous works, also noted for their expressive, dynamic figures, are the sculptures *David* and the *Pietà*.

Film Connection The film *The Agony and the Ecstacy* tells the story of Michelangelo, his painting of the Sistine Chapel, and his conflict over the project with Pope Julius II. Released in 1965 and starring Charlton Heston and Rex Harrison, the film received five Academy Award nominations.

Music Connection Michelangelo's patron Lorenzo de' Medici was called "Lorenzo the Magnificent" because of his statesmanship and support of the arts. When he died at age 43, Italian poet Angelo Poliziano (1454–1494) and Flemish composer Heinrich Isaac (1450–1517) composed a special funeral ode for him entitled "Lament on the Death of Lorenzo de' Medici." The song claims that music and poetry fell silent in the world due to his death. It reflected the profound influence he had on the culture of Florence.

Persuasive Writing Activity: "Artist for Hire" Poster
Choose a sculpture or painting by Michelangelo. Create a poster around it, advertising Michelangelo's services as an artist. Explain why a patron such as Lorenzo de' Medici or Pope Julius II should be eager to hire Michelangelo.

▲ Critical Viewing
Study the way David's head and shoulders are turned in Michelangelo's sculpture. Explain how this pose suggests movement, even though the sculpture is still. [Analyze]

Critical Viewing

Analyze Students may notice the tendons in David's neck, the shape and position of the muscles in his shoulders, and the direction of his gaze.

Media and Technology Skills

Analyzing How the Media Shape Perceptions

Activity: Recognizing Persuasion in Sitcoms

You can recognize the persuasive message of television commercials right away: "Buy this product!" Television entertainment programs may also contain persuasive messages. Instead of "Buy this!" these messages might say, "Act this way." Learn to recognize these persuasive messages in television programs such as sitcoms.

Think About It A television sitcom may send a persuasive message through its characters' words and actions. For instance, at the end of an episode, a sitcom character often makes a decision. Viewers may be persuaded that the decision is the best one. They are persuaded in part because the show presents the characters as likeable. Consider these examples of a sitcom story and its message:

- **Message: "Stick to your true friends."** Lance, a wealthy, popular student, starts making friends with one of the main characters of the show, Didi. When Lance makes fun of Didi's best friend, Gogo, Didi does not stand up for him. When Didi goes to Lance's party, though, she realizes Lance is just a snob. She leaves the party and apologizes to Gogo.

- **Message: "Anybody who acts like a snob deserves to be embarrassed."** When Didi goes to Lance's party, she sees that he is just a snob. Fed up with him, she tells the people at the party about the time Lance locked himself out of his house and was stopped by the police—in his pajamas! The kids laugh wildly as Lance runs from the room in embarrassment!

You may agree with the first message. If you think it is wrong to be mean to people, though, you might disagree with the second message.

Analyze It Watch an episode of a sitcom. Use a chart like the one shown to analyze its persuasive messages. Review your chart, and write a paragraph summarizing the show and explaining its message.

> ### How Persuasion Works in Sitcoms
>
> **Likeable Main Character**
> Because viewers like the main character, they tend to approve of what the main character does.
>
> **Foolish Main Character**
> On some shows, one character plays the fool. Viewers like him or her, but recognize that they are meant to laugh at many of the things the character does.

Title of Sitcom: _____

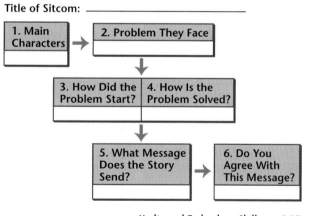

Media and Technology Skills • 147

▶ *Lesson Objectives*

1. To examine how visual techniques can be used to create an emotional response in television viewers.

2. To analyze how television affects audience perception.

3. To analyze messages as presented in various formats on television.

Step-by-Step Teaching Guide

Analyzing How the Media Shape Perceptions

Teaching Resources: Writing Support Transparency 7-H; Writing Support Activity Book, 7-3

1. Ask students if they can remember a time that something funny happened to them or someone else, which then led to a lesson being learned.

2. Point out that those situations which make an impression on us often convince us to see things differently. Explain that the people who create sitcoms and commercials on television know this and use it to send us persuasive messages. Tell students that being conscious of and identifying these messages can help them become more discriminating viewers.

3. Display the transparency and ask for one or two student volunteers to describe the plot of a sitcom that was recently on television. Fill out the transparency, using the plot described by the students. When students make suggestions about the message of the story, ask them if many other sitcoms send similar messages.

4. Point out that television has the power to strongly influence people's perceptions if many shows on television send similar messages to viewers every night.

5. Give students copies of the blank organizer and have them use it to take notes on an episode of a sitcom. Tell students to use these notes to summarize the plot and explain the message of the show.

Lesson Objectives

1. To write a persuasive essay appropriate to audience and purpose.

2. To use prewriting strategies to generate ideas.

3. To organize and present information to ensure support for ideas.

4. To use writing processes to develop and revise drafts.

5. To demonstrate control over grammatical elements.

Step-by-Step Teaching Guide

Persuasive Writing Prompts

1. Emphasize to students that, when writing persuasive essays in standardized tests, they should clearly identify their position before they start writing. Explain that if they develop their opinion as they write, as opposed to before they write, their essay will lack organization, and their supporting evidence may seem weaker.

2. Tell students that persuasive essays depend on their ability to clearly identify and understand their intended audience. Point out that, in the Sample Writing Situation, their intended audience is either the student body or the principal. Ask them how their responses to these two audiences might be different. What examples, facts, and arguments would they use if addressing fellow students that they might not use if addressing the principal?

3. Reassure students that, while neatness counts, examiners understand that time constraints prevent most standardized tests of this kind from being perfect finished products. Emphasize, however, that following the rules of grammar, punctuation, and spelling will make their persuasive essays clearer for their audience.

continued

Standardized Test Preparation Workshop

Responding to Persuasive Writing Prompts

Some writing prompts on standardized tests call on you to write persuasively about an issue. Your essay will be evaluated on how well you

- support your position, using examples, facts, and arguments that are appropriate to the purpose and audience named in the prompt.

- organize your points, using a consistent method suited to the topic.

- use correct grammar, spelling, and punctuation.

For practice on such tests, respond to the sample persuasive writing prompt below. The suggestions on the next page will help you to get started. The clocks represent the part of your test-taking time that you should devote to each stage of your writing.

Test Tip

When responding to a persuasive essay prompt, jot down a description of what your assigned audience cares about most in connection with your topic. Use this description to help gather details that your audience will find most convincing.

Sample Writing Situation

> The faculty and students at your school are being asked to vote on a logo for the school's Web page. The principal as well as many teachers believe that it should represent learning. They are considering an image of a book with the word *Sapientia*, the Latin word for *wisdom*, beneath it. Many students, on the other hand, want something more lively. They think the school mascot, a tiger, should be the logo. Choose one of the following prompts to which to respond.
>
> > State your position on the Web page logo in a letter to the editor of your school newspaper. Support your position with arguments, examples, and your own experiences.
>
> > State your position on the Web page logo in a letter to your school principal. Support your position with arguments, examples, and your own experiences.

 TEST-TAKING TIP

Tell students that one major similarity exists between writing a persuasive essay for class and during a standardized test: it helps if they really believe in the position about which they're writing. Explain that this may not always be possible during a standardized test because the writing prompt is chosen for them. Point out, however, that they may sometimes have choice about an intended audience or a particular perspective on the suggested topic.

Tell students that having chosen the exact position and intended audience for their essay, they should list as many arguments as they can. Point out that they may not have time to use them all, but that having a long list will allow them to choose the strongest supporting points. Explain that, because they must create their essay quickly, identifying their best arguments ahead of time will help them build a stronger draft.

Prewriting

One fourth of your time should be used for prewriting.

Consider Your Audience and Purpose Your purpose is to persuade your audience that your position on the Web page logo is the correct one. Your approach to this task depends on the audience specified in the prompt you have selected. For instance, the school principal cares about what is in the school's best interest. If you choose to write to the principal, focus your arguments on this point. The school newspaper is addressed to students. If you choose to write to the paper, address issues that most concern students, such as school pride or fun.

Gather Support Use a T-Chart to gather logical arguments, facts, and examples on both sides of the issue. Also, list strong images or phrases with which to present your case. Note any weak arguments against your position. You can answer them in your essay. (For instructions on making a T-Chart, see page 131.)

Drafting

Use almost half of your time for drafting.

Write an Introduction Start your letter with an interest-grabbing introduction. You might begin with a strong image or story that illustrates your position. Your introduction should also include a sentence that clearly states your position on the issue.

Develop Your Position In the body of your letter, develop support for your position. Refer to your T-Chart for details as you write. For each main idea, add supporting details. If you have found weak opposing arguments, prove them wrong. You might save your strongest argument for the end of your response.

Write a Conclusion In your conclusion, sum up your main points and restate your position.

Revising, Editing, and Proofreading

Use almost one fourth of your time to revise, edit, and proofread.

Strengthen Support As you revise, revise or eliminate sentences that do not help make your point. Note places in your paper where you have used vague words, such as *better*. Replace them with more precise words by answering the question, "Better in what way?" For example, you might argue that the school mascot is better because it is more colorful than the image of a book. In this case, you could replace *better* with *more eye-catching*.

Correct Errors When you have finished revising, check your work for errors in grammar, spelling, or punctuation. Place one line through any text you are deleting. Use a caret (^) to indicate where to add text.

4. As students review and revise their essays, encourage them to look for evidence and arguments that clearly support their position. Have they explained their position clearly? Finally, have they checked their drafts for grammar, punctuation, and spelling?

Customize for
ESL Students

Students who speak English as a second language may find it difficult to express their viewpoints in a persuasive essay because they don't have the vocabulary to explain exactly what they mean. Help students practice developing persuasive arguments by bringing in prompts and having students discuss them with each other and with the class. During these discussions, highlight the kinds of words and phrases that they might include in written versions of their persuasive arguments. Also, encourage students to notice how they organize their points. Some supporting examples may work more effectively at the beginning of an argument than at the end. Have a student volunteer to express his or her views persuasively to the class and then have a discussion about how that argument would be structured on paper.

Customize for
Less Advanced Students

Students may benefit from reading and reviewing other examples of persuasive writing. Point out that many essays and editorials are written around the basic structure of a persuasive argument. Ask students to find a persuasive article or essay and to analyze how the writer developed his or her arguments. Have them present their article to the class with their analysis of the viewpoint presented in it.

In-Depth Lesson Plan

	LESSON FOCUS	PRINT AND MEDIA RESOURCES
DAY 1	**Introduction to the Comparison-and-Contrast Essay** Students learn key elements of autobiographical writing and analyze the Model From Literature (pp. 150–153).	*Writers at Work* **Videotape**, Exposition: Making Connections *Writing Lab* **CD-ROM**, Exposition: Making Connections
DAY 2	**Prewriting** Students choose and narrow a topic, consider their audience and purpose, and gather information (pp. 154–157).	**Teaching Resources** *Writing Support Transparencies* 8-A–D; *Writing Support Activity Book* 8-1
DAY 3	**Drafting** Students organize their ideas and write their first drafts (pp. 158–159).	**Teaching Resources** *Writing Support Transparency* 8-E
DAY 4	**Revising** Students revise their drafts in terms of overall structure, paragraphs, sentences, and word choice (pp. 160–163).	**Teaching Resources** *Writing Support Transparencies* 8-F–G
DAY 5	**Editing and Proofreading; Publishing and Presenting** Students check their work for accuracy and correctness and present their final drafts (pp. 164–165).	**Teaching Resources** *Scoring Rubrics on Transparency*, Ch. 8; *Formal Assessment*, Ch. 8

Accelerated Lesson Plan

	LESSON FOCUS	PRINT AND MEDIA RESOURCES
DAY 1	**Drafting** Students review characteristics of Comparison-and-Contrast essays, select topics, and write drafts (pp. 150–159).	**Teaching Resources** *Writing Support Transparencies* 8-A–E; *Writing Support Activity Book* 8-1 *Writers at Work* **Videotape**, Exposition: Making Connections *Writing Lab* **CD-ROM**, Exposition: Making Connections
DAY 2	**Revising to Presenting** Students work individually or with peers to revise, edit, and proofread their work for presentation (pp. 160–165).	**Teaching Resources** *Writing Support Transparencies* 8-F–G; *Scoring Rubrics on Transparency*, Ch. 8; *Formal Assessment* Ch. 8

Options for Adapting Lesson Plans

HOMEWORK

Have students complete any stage of the lesson for homework.

FEATURES

Extend coverage with the Connected Assignment (p. 168), Spotlight on the Humanities (p. 170), Media and Technology Skills (p. 171), and the Standardized Test Preparation Workshop (p. 172).

TECHNOLOGY

Students can complete any stage of the lesson on computer. Have them print out their completed work.

INTEGRATED SKILLS COVERAGE

Integrating Grammar
Pronoun-Antecedent Agreement SE pp. 162, 164

Reading/Writing Connection
Reading Strategy SE p. 152
Writing Application SE p. 153

Speaking and Listening
ATE p. 156

Vocabulary
ATE pp. 157, 159

Viewing and Representing
Critical Viewing SE pp. 150, 152, 153, 156, 161, 166, 167, 168, 170
ATE p. 170

BLOCK SCHEDULING

Pacing Suggestions
For 90-minute Blocks
• Have students complete the Prewriting and Drafting stages in a single period.
• Focus one class period on Revising and Editing and Publishing and Presenting. Allow at least 30 minutes for peer revision.

Resources for Varying Instruction
• *Writing Lab* **CD-ROM** If your students have access to hardware, a 90-minute block provides an ideal opportunity for students to work on computer.
• *Writers at Work* **Videotape** Show the Comparison-and-Contrast segment in class.

Professional Development Support
• *How to Manage Instruction in the Block* This Teaching Resource provides management and activity suggestions.

ASSESSMENT SUPPORT

Standardized Test Preparation Workshop SE p. 172; ATE p. 163
Standardized Test Preparation Workbook, pp. 15–16
Scoring Rubrics on Transparency, Ch. 8
Formal Assessment, Ch. 8
Writing Assessment and Portfolio Management

MEDIA AND TECHNOLOGY

For the Student
• *Writing Lab* **CD-ROM,** Exposition: Making Connections

For the Teacher
• *Writers at Work* **Videotape,** Exposition: Making Connections
• *Resource Pro* **CD-ROM**

MEETING INDIVIDUAL NEEDS

Less Advanced Students ATE pp. 153, 173; See also Ongoing Assessments ATE pp. 155, 161, 162, 165
More Advanced Students ATE p. 169
ESL Students ATE pp. 153, 162
Visual/Spatial Learners ATE p. 158
Verbal/Linguistic Learners ATE p. 156

WRITING AND GRAMMAR WEB SITE

The Interactive Writing and Grammar Web site provides a wide array of support for students, teachers, and parents. Writing support includes:

• Interactive revision checkers
• Scoring rubrics with complete models

www.phschool.com

LITERATURE CONNECTIONS

Related selections from *Prentice Hall Literature: Timeless Voices, Timeless Themes,* Copper:
"The All-American Slurp," Lensey Namioka, SE p. 153
"He Lion, Bruh Bear, and Bruh Rabbit" retold by Virginia Hamilton, SE p. 155

Lesson Objectives

1. To recognize the distinguishing features of a comparison-and-contrast essay.

2. To determine a comparison-and-contrast essay's main idea and how that idea is supported by details.

3. To generate and refine ideas and plans for writing by using the prewriting strategies.

4. To identify audience and purpose for writing.

5. To develop a draft by categorizing ideas, organizing them into paragraphs, and blending paragraphs within larger units of text.

6. To revise a draft by checking organization and balance.

7. To revise and edit a draft for subject-verb and pronoun-antecedent agreement and variety in word choices.

8. To "publish" a comparison-and-contrast essay by illustrating with photographs or creating an audiotape.

9. To evaluate how well one's comparison-and-contrast essay achieves its purposes.

Critical Viewing

Compare and Contrast Students may say that they can tell identical twins apart by different hairstyles or clothes.

Chapter 8

Exposition
Comparison-and-Contrast Essay

▲ Critical Viewing
Identical twins look almost exactly alike. Do you know any identical twins? How can you tell them apart? **[Compare and Contrast]**

Comparison and Contrast in Everyday Life

Jump into the freezing water of a lake, and you may wish you were swimming in the warm ocean instead. Watch a great movie with your cousin, and later you may find yourself comparing it with the awful movie you saw last week. In both cases, you are comparing and contrasting.

We use comparisons and contrasts all the time. For instance, you might compare two shirts in the morning to decide which one to wear.

It's only the most interesting comparisons that are worth writing down, though. Whether it's a comparison of two vacation spots or of two works of art, a good written comparison shines new light on the things it compares.

150 • Exposition

⏱ TIME AND RESOURCE MANAGER

Resources:
Technology: Writers at Work videotape

In-Depth Coverage	Accelerated Pace
• Cover pp. 150–153 in class. • Show the Exposition: Making Connections section of the Writers at Work video. • Read literature excerpt (pp. 152–153) in class and use it to begin a discussion of comparison-and-contrast essays. • Discuss examples of comparison-and-contrast essays.	• Have students read pp. 150–153 on their own. • Pose and discuss this question with students: Which might make a more powerful subject of a comparison-and-contrast essay, like items or ideas or dissimilar items or ideas?

What Is a Comparison-and-Contrast Essay?

A **comparison-and-contrast essay** uses factual details to analyze the similarities and differences between two or more persons, places, or things. Comparison-and-contrast essays include

- a topic involving two or more things that are similar in some ways and different in other ways.

- an organized presentation of details that illustrate similarities and differences.

To learn the criteria on which your comparison-and-contrast essay may be graded or judged, see the Rubric for Self-Assessment on page 165.

Types of Comparison-and-Contrast Essays

In addition to comparison-and-contrast essays, some specialized types of essays also use comparison and contrast:

- A **product comparison** looks at two or more products and examines the advantages and disadvantages of purchasing each.

- A **comparison of literary works** looks at the similarities and differences among any number of elements—characters, setting, and so on—of two works of literature.

Writers in
ACTION

Kevin Powell writes reviews of entertainment and media events. Kevin enjoys his career as a writer. He says, "Writing is one of the freest things that you could ever do—[it let's you] express yourself on the written page."

Interest GRABBER Ask students if students could own only one CD, which one would they choose? Write students' favorites on the board. After you have accumulated a substantial list, ask some volunteers to sort the titles by musical genre and compare and contrast the different types of music.

Activate Prior Knowledge

Comparing and contrasting are important ways we come to understand the world. We compare and contrast sports teams, movies, and restaurants. Have students offer examples of comparisons or contrasts they've made recently. Then discuss how comparison-and-contrast essays build on this way of analyzing experience by reviewing the characteristics and types of comparison-and-contrast essays explained on this page of the textbook.

PREVIEW
Student Work
IN PROGRESS

This lesson will give you lots of sample strategies and tips for comparison-and-contrast writing. In this chapter, you will follow the progress of Brendan Barraclough, a student at Mountain School in Los Alamos, New Mexico. As you'll see, Brendan used the prewriting, drafting, and revising techniques taught in this chapter to develop the comparison-and-contrast essay "Cats and Frogs as Pets."

Comparison-and-Contrast Essay • 151

☑ **ONGOING ASSESSMENT: Diagnose**

Use this writing task to diagnose students' current level of proficiency in comparison-and-contrast essays.

Display two apples and two bananas (or two other kinds of fruit). Ask students to write several sentences comparing an apple and a banana and a few sentences contrasting two apples or two bananas. Provide students who have

difficulty completing this task models of comparisons and contrasts and repeat the difference between these concepts as you proceed through this chapter.

Reading\Writing Connection

Identify Main Points

Remind students that an author's main points may be stated in the text, or a reader may need to infer them. The fact that the Dead Sea and Great Salt Lake have different histories is stated explicitly in this essay, but the similar compositions of the two bodies of water must be inferred.

Teaching from the Model

Have students analyze the organization of this comparison-and-contrast essay. Make sure they notice that in the first, fourth, and fifth paragraphs are sentences that compare and contrast the Dead Sea and the Great Salt Lake. The second paragraph, however, discusses only the Dead Sea, and the third paragraph is concerned solely with the Great Salt Lake. Ask students to consider why the author chose this organization.

Step-by-Step Teaching Guide

Engage Students Through Literature

1. Ask students to preview the selection by reading the captions, title, and sidenotes.

2. Locate the Great Salt Lake and the Dead Sea on a map or globe.

3. Have students read "More Than a Pinch: Two Salt Lakes" silently, or choose a student to read the selection aloud.

4. Ask discussion questions such as the following:

   What do you think water as salty as the Great Salt Lake and Dead Sea would feel like?

   Were you surprised by anything you read?

   What is a comparison you recall from the excerpt? A contrast?

Critical Viewing

Compare and Contrast Students may say that they could not float in the pool or lake they have visited.

8.1 Model From Literature

Although there is only one Great Salt Lake, there is at least one other lake with which it compares—the Dead Sea. "More Than a Pinch: Two Salt Lakes" compares a number of geological features of these two unusual bodies of water, showing their striking similarities and differences.

Comparisons and contrasts are tools of the geologist's trade. Geology is the study of the Earth and its history, and geologists compare different kinds of rocks, climates, regions, and so on in their work. As this article shows, even geological features halfway around the globe from each other can have much in common.

▲ **Critical Viewing**
This woman is floating in the Dead Sea—without a float! Compare this picture to a similar scene at a pool or lake you have visited. **[Compare and Contrast]**

 **Reading Strategy: Identify Main Points** By identifying an author's main points—the points he or she wants you to remember—you can grasp the information he or she provides more easily. For instance, in "More Than a Pinch: Two Salt Lakes," you might identify one main idea as follows: Salt lakes started out as regular bodies of water and became salty as the result of changes over time.

More Than a Pinch: Two Salt Lakes

Douglas Amrine et al.

Holidaymakers on a first visit to the Dead Sea are invariably in for a surprise: those who enjoy swimming underwater in town pools at home have great difficulty in just staying below the surface. This is because the Dead Sea contains 25 to 30 percent

In the first paragraph, the writer introduces two things to be compared: the Dead Sea and the Great Salt Lake.

152 • Comparison-and-Contrast Essay

salt, compared to 4 to 6 percent in ocean water. Similar readings have been recorded at Utah's Great Salt Lake in the United States, where it is equally difficult to sink.

The two salt lakes have very different histories. The spectacular trench occupied by the Dead Sea and the Jordan River, which flows into it, was created some 26 million years ago by an upheaval on the seabed at a time when the Mediterranean covered the Holy Land. At 1300 feet below sea level, the Dead Sea is the lowest body of water on Earth.

The Great Salt Lake is of more recent origin, being the remnant of the glacial Lake Bonneville which came into existence 18,000 to 25,000 years ago. Having shrunk, through evaporation, to one-twentieth of its original size, it now, like the Dead Sea, has no outlet. But rivers still feed the lake, bearing minerals dissolved from surrounding rocks. As the water evaporates, the minerals remain—66 million tons of them, including magnesium, lithium, boron, and potash.

Salt lakes are conventionally seen as barren, because they support no fish, but the Dead Sea is not completely dead: certain algae and bacteria are adapted to its salt-rich environment. The Great Salt Lake, too, has its single-cell organisms, most noticeably the algae that color the northern part of the lake pink. There are also larger life forms: brine shrimps and flies, whose larvae develop in the water. The shrimps are eaten by gulls, and shrimp eggs are harvested for sale as tropical fish food.

This business is miniscule compared to trade in the lake's great mineral wealth, such as the valuable potash used for fertilizer. The Dead Sea also yields potash, and the Israelis run health spas where tourists can coat themselves in rich, black mineral mud.

The details of this selection are organized using the point-by-point method. First, the salt levels of the lakes are compared. Then, the writer discusses the history of each.

LITERATURE

To read a short story comparing and contrasting two families, see Lensey Namioka's "The All-American Slurp." You can find this story in *Prentice Hall Literature: Timeless Voices, Timeless Themes,* Copper.

▲ **Critical Viewing**
How does this scene of the Great Salt Lake compare with another body of water you know? **[Compare and Contrast]**

Reading\Writing Connection

Writing Application: Help Readers Identify Main Points As you draft your comparison-and-contrast essay, help your readers identify main points by introducing points with transition sentences and words. For instance, this essay introduces a point about the history of the two lakes with the following transition sentence: "The two salt lakes have very different histories."

Model From Literature • 153

Responding to Literature

Students may be amused by the challenges faced by a Chinese family in America in "The All-American Slurp," a lighthearted story by Lensey Namioka. Though the story cannot provide a direct model for students' comparison-and-contrast essays, the overall structure of the story is one students may consider.

Critical Viewing

Compare and Contrast Students' responses will vary depending on the body of water they choose.

Customize for
Less Advanced Students

Make sure students understand concepts that appear in the excerpt, such as *below sea level, evaporated, dissolved, salt-rich environment,* and *single-cell organisms.* Write the words on the board and discuss them before students begin reading. If the selection still seems too challenging for this group, read it aloud and stop as necessary to explain or provide synonyms.

Customize for
ESL Students

Go through the selection with students and replace difficult vocabulary words with simpler synonyms. The following are some suggestions:

invariably	*constantly*
spectacular	*amazing*
remnant	*remains*
conventionally	*usually*
minuscule	*tiny*

Reading\Writing Connection

Writing: Help Readers Identify Main Points

Explain to students that when they carefully identify the main points in their essays, readers will have an easier time understanding what they are reading.

Prewriting: Quicklist

1. If the prospect of listing words at random is daunting to students, you may want to have them brainstorm for general topic categories as a class or in small groups before they begin writing their own quicklists.

2. After the group has arrived at ten or so topics, individuals can choose one and begin writing a Quicklist of related words.

3. Reassure students that neat handwriting and accurate spelling don't matter here—writers of the quicklists will be the only ones to see them.

4. After students have finished their quicklists and identified related words, they need to decide whether these words suggest topics specific enough for a comparison-and-contrast essay. If not, the Looping strategy described on page 156 may help them.

Prewriting: Media Flip-Through

Teaching Resources: Writing Support Transparency 8-A

1. Have students jot down topic ideas based on their reading or television viewing over several days.

2. Encourage students to write freely; the more ideas they record, the more potential topics they will have to choose from.

3. Scanning magazine tables of contents, television guide listings, or newspaper headlines may help students generate abundant lists of potential topics.

4. Display the transparency to show students how Brendan did a media flip-through to generate a topic idea.

8.2 Prewriting

Choosing Your Topic

To write a comparison-and-contrast essay, you have to know a lot about your topic. Make sure that your subjects are in some ways similar and in other ways different. Use these strategies to help select a topic:

Strategies for Generating a Topic

1. **Quicklist** Make three columns on a piece of paper. Jot down a quick list of people, places, and things in the first column. List an adjective for each in the second column. Then, give a detail about each in the third column. Review your list for related ideas, such as *football* and *basketball*, that you can compare and contrast. Choose a pair of such ideas as your topic.

2. **Media Flip-Through** Keep paper and pencil handy while you read a magazine or watch television. Jot down ideas and stories that lend themselves to comparison. Review your notes, and choose the most interesting topic.

Writing Lab CD-ROM

For more help finding a topic, explore the activities and tips under Choosing a Topic in the Expository Writing: Making Connections lesson.

Student Work
IN PROGRESS

Name: Brendan Barraclough
Mountain School
Los Alamos, NM

Doing a Media Flip-Through

Brendan came across an article written by a veterinarian. Notice how he highlighted a section that interested him. Based on this article, he chose "pets" as the topic for his comparison-and-contrast essay.

Does your pet have to be cuddly? Dogs are friendly, loving, and loveable. Cats like to sit in your lap and be snuggled. But have you ever considered a lizard as a pet?

Lizards are reptiles and, unlike mammals, don't have fur. They are not cuddly. Neither are frogs, which are amphibians. But lizards and frogs can make great pets.

Visit your local vet's office to learn more about different kinds of pets. Your vet knows all about the animals. But what's also important is what you know about yourself and your family. What kind of pet is best for you? Only you know for sure.

154 • Comparison-and-Contrast Essay

⏱ TIME AND RESOURCE MANAGER

Resources
Print: Writing Support Transparencies 8-A–D; Writing Support Activity Book 8-1
Technology: Writing Lab CD-ROM, Exposition: Making Connections

In-Depth Coverage	Accelerated Pace
• Cover pp. 154–157 in class.	• Have the students brainstorm alternate strategies to generate comparison-and-contrast essay topics.
• Have students work in pairs or small groups to generate topics, and work with them as necessary.	• Ask students to discuss among themselves which sorts of topics seem to suggest the most manageable comparison-and-contrast essays.
Option Have students use the comparison-and-contrast essay section of the Writing Lab CD-ROM.	

TOPIC BANK

If you're having trouble finding a topic, consider the following possibilities:

1. **What's Cooking?** Burritos and tacos are two popular Mexican foods. Ravioli and lasagna are famous Italian dishes. Compare any two international food favorites.

2. **Musical Choice** In a large orchestra, there are many different kinds of instruments. To which instrument do you enjoy listening? Which would you like to play? Choose two instruments to compare.

Responding to Fine Art

3. Jot down notes on similarities and differences between the different parts of the landscape in this painting. Use your imagination to describe differences in touch, smell, sound, and even taste, as well as sight. Then, write an essay comparing this landscape to one you know.

Responding to Literature

4. Compare and contrast the characters of he Lion, Bruh Bear, and Bruh Rabbit in Virginia Hamilton's retelling of the folk tale "He Lion, Bruh Bear, and Bruh Rabbit." Look at similarities and differences in their strength, size, personality, and cleverness. Explain how the differences among them causes the story to end as it does. You can find the story in *Prentice Hall Literature: Timeless Voices, Timeless Themes*, Copper.

Black Mesa, 1982, Woody Gwyn, Courtesy of the artist

☑ Cooperative Writing Opportunity

5. **Consumer Guide** Work with your classmates to create a consumer guide on a related group of products. For example, you might write about new computer models or the latest video games. Each student should do a detailed analysis of two specific models, noting key features and their good and bad qualities. Then, work together to assemble the notes into a guide comparing and ranking various items.

Prewriting • 155

Responding to Fine Art

Black Mesa, by Woody Gwyn

Teaching Resources: Writing Support Transparency 8-B

1. Display the transparency and encourage students to respond freely to the painting. Then ask students to compare and contrast the highway in the foreground with the mesa in the background. Students should note contrasts of color, shape, and form. Are there any similarities?

2. Have the students suggest other dramatic landscapes that might be compared and contrasted. Challenge them to come up with places that seem very dissimilar but have subtle similarities, and vice versa.

Responding to Literature

Help students look at the different proportions in which strength, cleverness, and pride appear in the three characters. He Lion, for instance, is strong, but his pride is greater than his strength or intelligence. Bruh Rabbit lacks strength, but his intelligence leads to a kind of victory.

Integrating Workplace Skills

Many jobs require an ability to write comparisons and contrasts, for example, a movie or music reviewer, a supervisor who writes performance evaluations, a copywriter who analyzes competing advertisements. Ask students to think of other possibilities.

Spotlight on the Humanities

For additional topic suggestions, refer students to the Spotlight on the Humanities on page 170.

☑ ONGOING ASSESSMENT: Monitor and Reinforce

For students who are still having difficulty choosing or refining a topic, use one of the following options.

Option 1 Suggest that students discuss their dilemma with a partner and perhaps "borrow" a topic that the partner does not plan to use.	**Option 2** If the Topic Bank ideas do not appeal, suggest that students select one of the suggestions from the Topic Bank for Heterogeneous Classes in the Teaching Resources.

Prewriting: Looping

Teaching Resources: Writing Support Transparency 8-C

1. Display the transparency. Have a volunteer explain how Brendan used looping to narrow his topic.

2. To provide additional support, have students pause after they have written about their topics. Can students identify their most interesting or important ideas? Those who can easily identify aspects of their topics to connect should do so and continue writing by following steps 2 and 3.

3. Gather students who are puzzled about how to proceed and have them take turns reading their writing aloud. If the group is too large to be manageable, divide students into clusters of five or six. Feedback from group members about the aspects of topics that seem most generative may "unstick" student writers.

Integrating Listening and Speaking Skills

Before students work together in groups to read and comment on one another's writing, discuss close listening and considered responses. Remind listeners that restating what they've heard will help them improve their listening skills. Hearing their words restated will help writers make sure they've gotten across their intended meaning.

Customize for
Verbal/Linguistic Learners

Students will find the Looping strategy easier to accomplish if they work with partners and discuss what they know about their topics before they write.

Critical Viewing

Distinguish Students may say that both animals have fur, but that they live in very different habitats.

8.2

Narrowing Your Topic

Make sure your topic isn't too broad to cover thoroughly in a comparison-and-contrast essay. For example, you could write an entire book comparing two countries, such as Mexico and Spain. However, if you were to focus on a Mexican and a Spanish food, you would find that you had a perfect topic for a brief essay. Looping is a good strategy for narrowing your topic.

Looping

Looping is a strategy with several steps. Follow these instructions:

1. Write your topic at the top of a sheet of paper. Then, write for five or ten minutes on your topic. Read what you have written. What is your most important or interesting idea? What "tugs" at you? Circle it.

2. Draw a line connecting the idea you've circled to the next empty line on your paper. Then, write about the circled idea for five or ten minutes. You should find yourself going in a more specific direction. When you finish, circle again what "tugs" at you.

3. Keep repeating this process until you have circled a narrow, focused topic for your essay.

▲ **Critical Viewing**
In what ways are these animals similar? In what ways are they different? **[Distinguish]**

Student Work
IN PROGRESS

Name: *Brendan Barraclough*
Mountain School
Los Alamos, NM

Using Looping

Here is how Brendan used looping to narrow his broad topic, "pets."

Lots of animals can be pets. My dad had a pet goat when he was a kid. I used to have a dog. My mom won't let me get another dog because the big ones are too big, and we didn't want a little dog. Now I have a cat and a frog.

I like my cat because she is cuddly. The frogs are fun to watch and take care of. They are very different animals, but both make good pets.

156 • Comparison-and-Contrast Essay

Considering Your Audience and Purpose

Next, identify your **audience**—the people who will read your essay—and your **purpose**—what you hope to accomplish. Both your audience and your purpose will affect your choice of words and details, as shown in this chart:

Audience	Purpose	Language	Details
Young children	To instruct	Simple, informal	Basic—assume no knowledge of topic
Adults knowledgeable about topic	To inform, to persuade	Technical language, formal	Leave out the most basic details; offer opinions and back up with examples

Keep your audience and purpose in mind as you gather details, draft, and revise.

Gathering Details

Gather facts, descriptions, and examples that you can use to make comparisons and contrasts between the items about which you are writing. If necessary, consult reference sources. Then, use a Venn diagram to organize your details.

Use a Venn Diagram

Create a diagram like the one shown. Write down details about each item you are comparing in one of the circles. In the two outside sections, write how each is different. Write similarities in the part where the circles overlap.

DIFFERENT KINDS OF VETERINARIANS

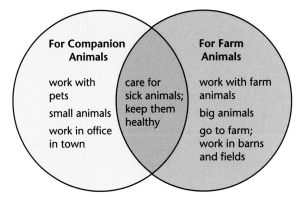

For Companion Animals

work with pets

small animals

work in office in town

care for sick animals; keep them healthy

For Farm Animals

work with farm animals

big animals

go to farm; work in barns and fields

Integrating Vocabulary Skills

Word Choice As students consider their audience and purpose, ask them to think about appropriate vocabulary for their essays. A comparison-and-contrast essay is a relatively formal piece of writing, so they should avoid slang. If they need to use technical language, they should define the terms an average sixth-grade student would not understand.

Step-by-Step Teaching Guide

Prewriting: Gathering Details

Teaching Resources: Writing Support Transparency 8-D; Writing Support Activity Book 8-1

1. To make their comparison-and-contrast papers more specific and interesting, urge students to consult outside sources even if they feel they can draw plenty of material from their own knowledge. Depending on the topic, these sources may include interviews with family members, magazine articles, or historical fiction, as well as reference books and the Internet.

2. Display the transparency and point out the three areas in which the comparisons and contrasts are made. Give students copies of the blank organizer for them to use as they gather details.

3. Remind students that they will need to summarize the comparisons and contrasts to fit them in their Venn diagrams. They need not, indeed should not, use complete sentences.

 TIME SAVERS!

Writing Support Transparencies
Use the transparencies for Chapter 8 to teach these strategies.

Writing Support Activity Book
Use the graphic organizers for Chapter 8 to facilitate these strategies.

Drafting: Block and Point-by-Point Organization

1. Make sure students understand the differences between the block and point-by-point methods of organization by going over the chart with them. To help students reinforce their understanding, you might ask a volunteer to explain the terms as if he or she were speaking to a younger student who had never heard of the terms.

2. Ask students to consult their Venn diagrams to draft outlines for their papers paragraph by paragraph using both methods, and then discuss with a partner or a small group which method seems to work best for their topic and why.

Customize for
Visual/Spatial Learners

Have students use index cards to write the main points they want to include about both items they are comparing and contrasting without regard to a specific organization. Then ask them to arrange the cards using the block and point-by-point methods. When they arrive at an organization that satisfies them, students can glue the sentences to a sheet of paper.

8.3 Drafting

Shaping Your Writing

Before you begin writing your first draft, decide how you want to organize your information.

Select an Appropriate Organization

Following are two methods for organizing your essay:

- **Block Method** To use the block method, present all details about one subject first. Then, present all details about the next. This method works well when you write about more than two things or cover many different types of details.

- **Point-by-Point Method** To use the point-by-point method, discuss each aspect of your subjects in turn. For example, if your topic is bicycling versus skating, you could first discuss the benefits of each, then the disadvantages, and finally the equipment necessary for each.

The following chart shows how each organization might be used for a paper comparing two types of dinosaurs:

1: Introduction
2: *Tyrannosaurus*—its diet, size, and mobility
3: *Velociraptor*—its diet, size, and mobility

1: Introduction
2: Feature—diet (*Tyrannosaurus* versus *Velociraptor*)
3: Feature—size and mobility (*Tyrannosaurus* versus *Velociraptor*)

Shape Your Introduction

Once you have chosen an organizational method, start writing. Begin with an introductory paragraph that

- introduces the subjects you are comparing.
- identifies the features or aspects you are comparing.
- states your conclusion about your subjects—for example, that there are more differences between them than similarities.

158 • Comparison-and-Contrast Essay

Writing Lab CD-ROM

For examples of good introductions, see the annotated Student Models in the Drafting section of the Exposition: Making Connections lesson.

⏱ TIME AND RESOURCE MANAGER

Resources:
Print: Writing Support Transparency 8-E
Technology: Writing Lab CD-ROM, Exposition: Making Connections

In-Depth Coverage	Accelerated Pace
• Cover pp. 158–159 in class. • Have students write their comparison-and-contrast essay draft in class. • Demonstrate adding specific details using the transparency. **Option** Have students work independently or in small groups with the Writing Lab CD-ROM.	• Have students review pp. 158–159 independently and then write their first drafts. • Respond to questions as necessary.

Providing Elaboration

Develop each main point of similarity or difference between your subjects by providing strong examples. For example, if you write that basketball is a faster game than baseball, you might cite the nonstop, end-to-end action in basketball and the long breaks in baseball.

Use Specific Details

Give details that are as specific as possible. The more specific your details are, the easier it will be for readers to see the similarities and differences. Look at the following examples:

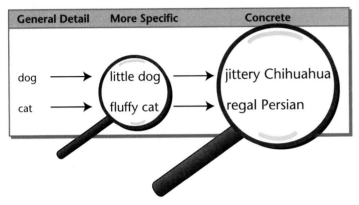

General Detail	More Specific	Concrete
dog	little dog	jittery Chihuahua
cat	fluffy cat	regal Persian

As you draft, pause now and then to make sure the details you are including are as specific as possible.

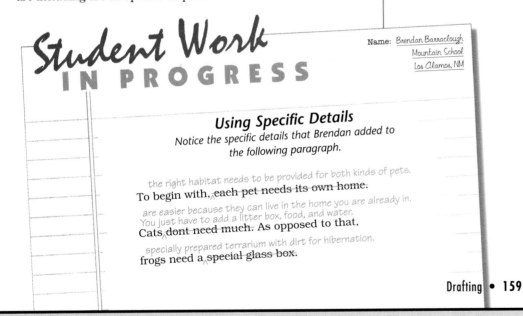

Student Work
IN PROGRESS

Name: *Brendan Barraclough*
Mountain School
Los Alamos, NM

Using Specific Details
Notice the specific details that Brendan added to the following paragraph.

the right habitat needs to be provided for both kinds of pets.
To begin with, ~~each pet needs its own home.~~

are easier because they can live in the home you are already in. You just have to add a litter box, food, and water.
Cats ~~dont need much.~~ As opposed to that,

specially prepared terrarium with dirt for hibernation.
frogs need a ~~special glass box.~~

Drafting: Use Specific Details

Teaching Resources: Writing Support Transparency 8-E

1. Engage students in a general discussion of the importance of specificity in writing. Make sure students note that specific details create pictures in a reader's mind and make writing interesting to read. They can have some fun suggesting additional replacement phrases for *little dog* and *fluffy cat.*

2. Display the transparency and have students look at changes Brendan made in his comparison-and-contrast essay. Make sure students notice that he replaced *home* with the more precise word *habitat.* The second sentence adds specific information. Brendan revised the last sentence to use the precise word *terrarium* in place of *special glass box* and also explained that a terrarium provides dirt for hibernation. Urge students to consider using both these types of details when they draft their essays.

Integrating Vocabulary Skills

Sensory Details Ask students to consider all the senses that fit their subjects as they write their comparison-and-contrast essays. Using the words *dog* and *cat* from the chart, ask students to list adjectives that describe what the animals might sound, look, smell, and feel like.

 TIME SAVERS!

 **Writing Support Transparencies**
Use the transparencies for Chapter 8 to teach these strategies.

159

1. If readers notice that a piece has far less information about one item that is being compared than another, they will assume the writer cares less or doesn't know as much about the item with less information. A successful comparison-and-contrast essay gives approximately equal weight and detail to its subjects.

2. Display the transparency to show how Brendan applied this strategy. Once students are familiar with this technique, have them color code their drafts.

3. As students review their color-coded drafts, they'll see clearly whether the information and structure of their essays are balanced.

4. Ask students also to note the content of the comparisons and contrasts in their essays. Is one item described more completely and colorfully than another? Urge students to keep a balanced tone in mind as they revise their essays.

8.4 Revising

When you revise, you strengthen your essay by eliminating unnecessary details and building on important ones.

Revising Your Overall Structure
Check Organization and Balance

Your essay should give equal space to each thing compared. For example, a comparison of baseball and football should give the same number of details about each, not two about baseball and ten about football. Your essay should also be organized consistently. Color-code to check organization and balance.

▶ **REVISION STRATEGY**
Color-Coding Details for Organization and Balance

Reread your essay. Use one color to highlight features of one of the things you're comparing, and another color to highlight features of the other. Review your draft. If you find:

- **more highlights of one color than of the other**—add more details about the subject with fewer highlights.

- **large chunks of a color and places where colors alternate**—reorganize your paper using either the block or the point-by-point method consistently.

Student Work
IN PROGRESS

Name: *Brendan Barraclough*
Mountain School
Los Alamos, NM

Coding for Organization and Balance
Brendan coded each detail about cats in yellow and each detail about frogs in green. He found a spot to create better balance by adding more details.

Cats are easier because they can live in the home you are already in. You just have to add a litter box, food, and water. As opposed to that, frogs need a specially prepared terrarium with dirt for hibernation. ∧
In addition, frogs need the air temperature controlled because they are coldblooded.

Brendan used point-by-point organization. Here, he included details about the habitats of both cats and frogs. He realized that he had included more than one detail about cats, so he added another detail about frogs.

160 • Comparison-and-Contrast Essay

⏱ TIME SAVERS!

🔖 **Writing Support Transparencies**
Use the transparencies for Chapter 8 to teach these strategies.

⏱ TIME AND RESOURCE MANAGER

Resources:
Print: Writing Support Transparencies 8-F–G
Technology: Writing Lab CD-ROM, Exposition: Making Connections

In-Depth Coverage	Accelerated Pace
• Work through pp. 160–163. • Have students check the organization and balance of their drafts. • Do the grammar in your writing activity on p. 162. **Option** Have students work independently or in small groups with the Writing Lab CD-ROM.	• Assign students to review the revising pages (pp. 160–163) independently. • Have students revise their comparison-and-contrast essays independently.

Revising Your Paragraphs

Check Your Paragraph Structure

A **topical paragraph** explains or illustrates one main idea. Most of the paragraphs in the body of your paper should be topical paragraphs. They should contain the following elements:

T: Topic sentence—a sentence summing up the main idea

R: Restatement—an expanded version of the idea found in the topic sentence

I: Illustration—one or more specific facts, images, anecdotes, or other details supporting or illustrating the main idea.

EXAMPLE: **T**   I like football better than baseball.

R   For one thing, football has more action.

I   Football teams must complete plays in a certain amount of time. Baseball pitchers can take long breaks.

Often, a paragraph with these elements has the structure **T-R-I**. However, in some instances, you might want to lead with the sentence that gives the illustration in order to hook your readers, making your pattern **I-T-R**.

▶ REVISION STRATEGY
Marking Paragraph Patterns

Go through your paper, and mark the pattern of each paragraph. Then, revise any paragraphs that are missing one or more of the **T-R-I** elements. For instance, add a topic sentence to any paragraph that is missing one.

Learn More

To learn more about the different kinds of paragraphs, see Chapter 3.

◀ **Critical Viewing**
Write a topic sentence for a paragraph comparing these two pictures. **[Apply]**

Revising: Marking Paragraph Patterns

1. Many students have difficulty writing restatements of topic sentences that go beyond reiteration. Review the difference between a topic sentence and a restatement and give examples, such as the following.

   People in all cultures want to be beautiful. (topic sentence)

   Even people who live at the heart of the Amazon rain forest enhance their natural appearance. (restatement)

   Food that is healthful does not have to be boring. (topic sentence)

   Some of the most delicious dishes are good for you—even desserts. (restatement)

2. Have volunteers read aloud paragraphs from magazines or books in the classroom. Listeners should identify topic sentences and restatements. Write one of the paragraphs that has a topic sentence, restatement, and details on the board. Choose students to mark **T** next to the topic sentence, **R** next to the restatement, and **I** next to the detail sentences, or illustrations.

3. Then ask students to follow this process to mark the paragraphs in their drafts.

Critical Viewing

Apply Students may write *Although different sports have their own specific rules, many of them require the same kinds of physical abilities.*

☑ ONGOING ASSESSMENT: Monitor and Reinforce

If some students are having difficulty writing restatements of their topic sentences, try one of the following options.

Option 1 Suggest that students work in pairs. Students should take turns reading aloud paragraphs that stump them and brainstorm restatement sentences together.

Option 2 Have small groups of students browse through magazines and underline restatement sentences. Check students' work and remind those who are still confused that a restatement goes beyond a topic sentence to amplify the topic sentence in some way.

Revising: Check Subject-Verb Agreement

1. Define a collective noun as a noun that names a group, such as *audience, band,* and *army.* Challenge students to think of others (hint: think of what groups of animals are called).

2. Make sure students understand that collective nouns generally take singular verbs.

   The <u>band</u> never <u>plays</u> in tune.

   The <u>army</u> <u>marches</u> to victory.

Grammar in Your Writing: Subject-Verb Agreement

1. Write the following sentence on the chalkboard:

   A hamster and a gerbil make good pets.

2. Have a volunteer underline the subject. Then challenge students to write other sentences with subjects linked by *and* and identify the subject of each.

3. Next, write the following:

   Does a hamster or a gerbil make a better pet?

4. Discuss the reason this sentence takes a singular verb. (A choice between two items is suggested.)

Find It in Your Reading

Students' responses will vary. Subjects and verbs in the first sentence are <u>Holidaymakers</u> <u>are,</u> <u>those</u> <u>have,</u> and <u>who</u> <u>enjoy.</u>

Find It in Your Writing

Encourage students to underline the subjects once and the verbs twice.

Customize for *ESL Students*

Subject-verb agreement can present quite a challenge for English-language learners, as regular verbs ending with *-s* in the singular do not occur in many languages. To provide practice, write five singular and five plural subjects (*A boy, Cows*) and five regular singular verbs and five plural verbs on separate index cards. Have students match the cards to form sentences.

8.4

Revising Your Sentences
Check Subject-Verb Agreement

In sentences comparing two things, pay special attention to the form of the verb you use. Whether you use the plural or singular form depends on how the subjects are joined:

PLURAL: Football and baseball *are* both fast-paced.
SINGULAR: Neither football nor baseball *is* an indoor game.

Check your draft to make sure your subjects and verbs agree.

▶ **REVISION STRATEGY**
Coding *and, nor,* and *or*

Review your use of the words *and, nor,* and *or.* Wherever they join two doers of an action or two things sharing a feature, underline the verb in the sentence.

EXAMPLE: Football <u>and</u> baseball <u>are</u> fun to watch.

Then, check your color-coded sentences for errors in agreement.

⚙ Grammar and Style Tip

You can make strong, direct comparisons using the comparative form of an adjective, such as "faster" or "furrier." (See Chapter 25 for instruction and practice in the proper use of comparative and superlative adjectives.)

Grammar in Your Writing
Subject-Verb Agreement

The **subject** of a sentence is the person or thing that performs the action of the sentence. The **verb** is the word expressing the action. Singular subjects take singular verbs. Plural subjects take plural verbs.

SINGULAR SUBJECT: a dog
SINGULAR VERBS: is, barks

PLURAL SUBJECT: dogs
PLURAL VERBS: are, bark

Subjects joined by *and* take a plural verb.
Dogs <u>and</u> cats are common pets.

Subjects joined by *or* or *nor* take a singular verb.
A dog <u>or</u> a cat is a common pet.
Neither a pony <u>nor</u> a pig is considered a good city pet.

Find It in Your Reading Review "More Than a Pinch: Two Salt Lakes" on page 152. Identify three subjects and their verbs. Do they agree?

Find It in Your Writing Identify three subjects and their verbs in your draft. Check to make sure they agree.

To learn more about subject-verb agreement, see Chapter 24.

162 • Comparison-and-Contrast Essay

✓ ONGOING ASSESSMENT: Prerequisite Skills

If students have difficulty with subject-verb agreement, you may find it helpful to review the following to assure coverage of prerequisite knowledge.

In the Textbook	Print Resources	Technology
Making Words Agree pp. 520–526	Grammar Exercise Workbook, pp. 115–120	Language Lab CD-ROM, Subject-Verb Agreement; On-Line Exercise Bank, Section 24.2

Revising Your Word Choice

Avoid Repetition

Repeated words or phrases will make your writing dull. Code and replace repeated words.

▶ REVISION STRATEGY
Highlighting Repeated Words

Reread your essay. Highlight nouns, verbs, adjectives, and phrases that you have used more than once. Then, use a thesaurus to find substitutes for repeated words.

Student Work
IN PROGRESS

Name: _Brendan Barraclough_
Mountain School
Los Alamos, NM

Highlighting Repeated Words

Brendan looked over his first paragraph and eliminated some repeated words.

Cats and frogs make great pets. Even though cats are mammals and frogs are amphibians, they are both lovable pets. Both kinds of pets _animals_ require a caretaker, or "parent." The pet needs the caretaker's time, responsibility, and money. There are some similarities and many differences _felines_ between cats and frogs as pets. _web-footed friends_

Peer Review

Pointing

Next, enlist the help of classmates to make additional refinements. Here's a strategy you can use:

1. Read your essay to the group of four or five students.
2. Pause, and ask group members to listen closely a second time, jotting down words, phrases, images—anything that really strikes them. Read your essay again.
3. Afterward, ask listeners to "point" to what they liked. Only positive comments are allowed.

Build on the strengths that classmates have identified. For instance, you might give more details about a point they liked.

Revising: Highlighting Repeated Words

Teacher Resources: Writing Support Transparency 8-G

1. Display the transparency and review Brendan's highlighted paragraph, noting the repeated words *kitten, see,* and *together* (which is repeated three times). Ask students to think of replacement words that will make the paragraph more interesting to read.

2. Ask students to reread their essays and highlight the repeated words. Emphasize that not every repeated word will necessarily have to be replaced. Urge them to search for repeated words that can be varied to add vivid details, specificity, and liveliness to their writing.

3. Students may want to read their drafts aloud. Hearing what they have written may help them decide which repeated words they want to replace.

4. After they have noted word changes, students can read their before and after drafts to a partner to see how a listener reacts to the word changes.

Revising: Peer Review

1. Have a group of four or five volunteers model the strategy for the class.

2. Read Brendan's paragraph on this page rapidly and with expression. Then reread it more slowly as the volunteers write comments.

3. Ask a few students to read their comments aloud. After each, discuss how the comment might affect revision choices for the remainder of the paper. For example, a comment that the last sentence is funny might lead the writer to include a bit more humor in the rest of a paper.

4. Remind students to read their drafts twice, once with maximum expression and a second time slowly so that listeners have time to jot down their comments.

⬥ STANDARDIZED TEST PREPARATION WORKSHOP

Agreement Standardized tests may require students to choose correct verbs and pronouns from among several choices. Ask students to choose the correct words to complete the following sentences:

1. Ken and Bob ___ best friends.
   A is   **C** are
   B was   **D** wasn't

2. Anna slammed shut ___ book.
   A her   **C** herself
   B hers   **D** theirs

C, because a plural subject takes a plural verb; A, because the singular subject takes a singular personal pronoun.

Editing and Proofreading

1. Ask a volunteer to define *pronoun*. (a word that takes the place of a noun) Explain that antecedents of pronouns are pronouns, common nouns, or proper nouns.

2. Review the pronoun chart. Make sure students understand that possessive pronouns indicate ownership.

Carla's hat	*her hat*
babies' bottles	*their bottles*

3. Have volunteers invent sentences that contain several of the pronouns.

Grammar in Your Writing: Pronoun-Antecedent Agreement

1. Discuss first, second, and third person briefly with students. Which pronoun indicates first person? (I) Second person? (you)

2. Have students turn back to page 152 and identify the person in which the article is written. (third person)

3. Explain that the word *those* in the first sentence of the selection is a pronoun. Ask students to identify its antecedent. (holidaymakers)

Find It in Your Reading

Possible answers: second paragraph, second sentence: *it*—antecedent is *Dead Sea*; fourth paragraph, first sentence: *they*—antecedent is *Salt lakes*; *its*—antecedent is *Dead Sea*. Note: In the first paragraph, last sentence *it* replaces "to sink."

Find It in Your Writing

If students cannot find at least three pronouns, have them revise their drafts to add more.

8.5

Editing and Proofreading

Once you've finished revising, check your essay for errors in spelling, grammar, punctuation, and usage.

Focusing on Pronouns

As you proofread, check pronoun-antecedent agreement, using the chart below and the information that follows.

SINGULAR		PLURAL	
PERSONAL	POSSESSIVE	PERSONAL	POSSESSIVE
I me	my, mine	we us	our, ours
you	your, yours	you	your, yours
he, she, it him, her, it	his, hers, its	they them	their, theirs

Grammar in Your Writing
Pronoun-Antecedent Agreement

A pronoun must agree with its antecedent in both person and number. **Person** indicates whether a pronoun refers to the person speaking (first person), the person spoken to (second person), or the person, place, or thing spoken about (third person). **Number** indicates whether a pronoun is singular (referring to one) or plural (referring to more than one).

A pronoun must agree with its antecedent in both person and number.

EXAMPLES: **Esther** is revising **her** essay about Susan B. Anthony. [third person singular]

The women are practicing for **their** debut performance. [third person plural]

Find It in Your Reading Review "More Than a Pinch: Two Salt Lakes" on page 152. Find two pronouns, and identify the antecedent of each.

Find It in Your Writing Circle in red three pronouns in your draft. Then, circle the antecedent of each in green. Revise any pronouns that do not agree with their antecedents.

To learn more about pronoun-antecedent agreement, see Chapter 24.

164 • Comparison-and-Contrast Essay

⏱ TIME AND RESOURCE MANAGER

Resources:
Print: Scoring Rubrics on Transparency, Chapter 8; Writing Assessment: Scoring Rubric and Scoring Models for Comparison-and-Contrast Essay
Technology: Writing Lab CD-ROM, Exposition: Making Connections

In-Depth Coverage	Accelerated Pace
• Cover pp. 164–167 in class. • Have students edit and proofread their essays in class. • Review the Rubric for Self-Assessment.	• Assign pp. 164–167 for independent student review. • Have students revise their comparison-and-contrast essays independently.

8.6 Publishing and Presenting

Building Your Portfolio

Once you've completed your final draft, consider these ideas for sharing it with a wider audience:

1. **Picture Essay** Find photographs to illustrate your essay. Then, share your illustrated essay with classmates.
2. **Create an Audiotape** Practice reading your essay aloud a few times. Read it slowly and clearly, emphasizing the strong points. Then, record it. You might present your reading to the class and share it with family and friends.

Reflecting on Your Writing

You have taken an idea through many different steps and created an essay. What have you learned? Write a few notes on your writing experience. Start by answering these questions:

- Do you view your topic differently now? If so, why and how?
- Do you think writing a comparison-and-contrast essay is difficult or easy for someone to learn? Why do you think so?

 Internet Tip

To view a comparison-and-contrast essay scored according to this rubric, visit **www.phschool.com**

Rubric for Self-Assessment

Evaluate your comparison-and-contrast essay using the following criteria:

	Score 4	Score 3	Score 2	Score 1
Audience and Purpose	Clearly attracts audience interest in the comparison-contrast analysis	Adequately attracts audience interest in the comparison-contrast analysis	Provides a reason for the comparison-contrast analysis	Does not provide a reason for a comparison-contrast analysis
Organization	Clearly presents information in a consistent organization well suited to the topic	Presents information using an organization suited to the topic	Chooses an organziation not suited to comparison and contrast	Shows a lack of organizational strategy
Elaboration	Elaborates ideas with facts, details, or examples; links all information to comparison and contrast	Elaborates most ideas with facts, details, or examples; links most information to comparison and contrast	Does not elaborate all ideas; does not link some details to comparison and contrast	Does not provide facts or examples to support comparison and contrast
Use of Language	Demonstrates excellent sentence and vocabulary variety; includes very few mechanical errors	Demonstrates adequate sentence and vocabulary variety; includes few mechanical errors	Demonstrates repetitive use of sentence structure and vocabulary; includes many mechanical errors	Demonstrates poor use of language; generates confusion; includes many mechanical errors

Publishing and Presenting • 165

☑ **ONGOING ASSESSMENT: Assess Mastery**

Use one of the following options to assess final drafts of students' comparison-and-contrast essays.

Self-Assessment Ask students to score their essay, using the rubric provided. Then have students write a paragraph explaining the most valuable thing they learned in writing their essay.

Teacher Assessment You may want to use the rubric and the scoring models provided in Writing Assessment, Comparison-and-Contrast Essay, to score students' work.

Publishing and Presenting

Discuss possible sources of photographs for students' essays.

- Magazines and photocopy machines are available at almost every library—with luck a library may even have a color copier.
- If time permits, students can telephone or write organizations for photographs. For example, to illustrate an essay comparing dog breeds, the American Kennel Club might be a source of photographs.
- Students can download photographs from the Internet. The quality of the reproductions may not be wonderful, but the results are nearly instantaneous.
- Depending on the subject of students' essays, they may be able to take their own photographs.

ASSESS

Assessment

Teacher Resources: Scoring Rubrics on Transparency 8; Formal Assessment, Chapter 8

1. Display the Scoring Rubric transparency and review the criteria in class.
2. Before students proceed with self-assessment, you may wish to review the Final Draft of the Student Work in Progress on pages 166–167. Have students score the Final Draft in one or more of the rubric categories. For example, how would students score the essay in terms of audience and purpose?
3. In addition to the student self-assessment, you may wish to use the following assessment options.
   - score student essays yourself, using the rubric and scoring models from Writing Assessment.
   - review the Standardized Test Preparation Workshop on pages 172–173 and have students respond to a writing prompt within a time limit.
   - administer the Chapter 8 Test from Formal Assessment in Teaching Resources to assess students' grasp of concepts presented.

Teaching from the Final Draft

Discuss Brendan's essay. List the reasons "Cats and Frogs as Pets" is a successful comparison-and-contrast essay.

- It compares and contrasts two items that are alike in some ways and different in others.

- It includes specific details about both cats and frogs.

- It gives approximately equal weight to both subjects.

- Paragraphs are well organized with topic sentences, frequent use of restatements, and detail sentences.

- Brendan writes for a general audience that knows little about cats or frogs, and he maintains the tone of the essay throughout.

- The essay uses point-by-point organization.

- It has an enticing opening sentence and a strong closing sentence.

Critical Viewing

Hypothesize Students may say there are more differences because of diet, grooming, and exercise.

8.7 *Student Work*
IN PROGRESS

FINAL DRAFT

▲ Critical Viewing
Are there more differences or more similarities between cats and frogs as pets? Explain. **[Hypothesize]**

Cats and Frogs as Pets

Brendan Barraclough
Mountain School
Los Alamos, New Mexico

Cats and frogs make great pets. Even though cats are mammals and frogs are amphibians, they are both lovable pets. Both kinds of animals require a caretaker, or "parent." The pet needs the caretaker's time, responsibility, and money. There are some similarities and many differences between felines and web-footed friends as pets.

To begin with, the right habitat needs to be provided for both kinds of pets. Cats are easier because they can live in the home you are already in. You just have to add a litter box, food, and water. As opposed to that, frogs need a specially prepared terrarium with dirt for hibernation. In addition, frogs need the air temperature controlled because they are coldblooded. An advantage of the terrarium is that frogs can be kept in one place easily.

By putting his topic sentence at the end of the first paragraph, Brendan makes a smooth transition to the next paragraph.

Note that Brendan uses specific examples with concrete details to give the readers precise information.

A big job as a pet owner is to protect the pets. Some pets, however, are easier to protect than others. It is harder to protect cats when they go outdoors, because in my neighborhood in northern New Mexico there are coyotes, mountain lions, rattlesnakes, owls, and cars that can kill cats. I keep my cat safe in our screened patio. In contrast, frogs just need their terrarium in a closed room protected from the mischievous house cats. This is important, because one time my naughty cat pushed the frog terrarium off my desk. Frogs and crickets were everywhere! My aunt, my mom, and I spent hours searching for the "liberated" frogs. From then on, the cats were banished from my room.

Cats are soft, like my favorite fuzzy blanket, while frogs are like a fragile toy that is fun to watch. Cats can be snuggled anytime. Unlike cats, frogs cannot be held because it will damage their protective mucus, and they might get an infection.

Another difference between cats and frogs as pets is that it is cheaper to take care of frogs. Cats need vaccinations and check-ups by a veterinarian once a year, while frogs never go to a vet. Frog food, which is usually live crickets, costs less than cat food. However, they both need fresh water all the time. In addition, cats require clean litter every few days. In general, neither pet is very expensive to take care of.

A disadvantage of having a cat as a pet is that some people are allergic to cat dander. This can limit the friends who can visit. This is not a problem with frogs.

One happy advantage of having a cat versus a frog is that cats usually live about five times longer than frogs do in captivity. Though I'm very sad when one of my pets dies, I remember all the happy times we had.

Unlike frogs, cats have distinctive personalities. Some cats are aloof, and some are affectionate, but they are all curious. This can be a disadvantage, because a cat's curiosity can result in some accidentally broken objects around the house.

Overall, cats and frogs make excellent pets in spite of their many similarities and differences. If cats are the furry couch potatoes of the pet world, frogs are the lean long-jumpers.

Brendan restates the topic of this paragraph in the second sentence. He gives a number of illustrations of the topic.

Brendan keeps his essay balanced by providing a detail about frogs for every detail he gives about cats.

Notice how Brendan successfully uses point-by-point organization, discussing each aspect of his pets in turn.

▼ **Critical Viewing**
Compare this cat to the one on the previous page. **[Compare and Contrast]**

Brendan ends his essay with two memorable figures of speech.

Teaching from the Model

1. Ask students to rethink their analyses of their own comparison-and-contrast essays, based on their discussion of the model in the textbook. What might they do differently next time?

2. Have students gather into groups of four or five to write some tips for aspiring comparison-and-contrast essay writers. After a few minutes of discussion, have each group's scribe jot down the suggestions. Gather as a class to share the lists.

Critical Viewing

Compare and Contrast Students may say that the cat on the previous page is younger and more lively than the cat on this page.

Lesson Objectives

1. To write a consumer report appropriate to audience and purpose.
2. To use prewriting strategies to choose and narrow a topic.
3. To gather and organize details.
4. To draft, revise, edit, and publish a consumer report.
5. To use correct grammar, spelling, and mechanics.

Step-by-Step Teaching Guide

Consumer Report

Teaching Resources: Writing Support Transparency 8-H; Writing Support Activity Book 8-2

1. Ask students whether anyone knows what a consumer report is. Show students a model. You may want to bring an issue of *Consumer Report* to class.

2. Point out that not all consumers have the same needs. A consumer report should compare the qualities of each competing product. It is not meant to urge a buyer to choose a particular product. For example, the model on the next page describes two restaurants. Each has different advantages and each will appeal to different diners.

3. Display the transparency and have a volunteer identify the similarities between the two dolls. Have another volunteer identify the differences. Then give students copies of the blank organizer to use for their own reports.

4. You may want to allow students to work together on their consumer reports, especially if students want to do a good deal of research or include numerous graphic organizers.

Connected Assignment
Consumer Report

Before people spend money, they often make a comparison and contrast among several products. By comparing different products, they can find the one that will best fit their needs. They can also find the best bargain. A consumer report can help.

A **consumer report** is a comparison of the strengths and weaknesses of different products. It draws conclusions about the advantages of using one over another. Useful consumer reports feature

• a detailed comparison of two or more similar products.

• a rating of the products, backed by facts.

Prewriting To choose a topic, consider topics such as these:

• **A Recent Purchase** Choose a purchase you or your family has made recently. Then, find a comparable product. Write a report comparing the product your family bought with the second product.

• **Report on a Toy** Choose two similar toys, such as toy cars, dolls or action figures, or board games. Identify the features people want in such a toy. Then, compare the two to find which one would best fulfill people's desires.

Narrow Your Topic After choosing your topic, make sure it is focused. For instance, if your topic is model cars, focus on two in the same price range.

Consider Your Audience Next, think about who will use your report. Will purchasers of the product be

• young people of your age?

• their parents?

• adults in general?

Then, determine the needs of your readers. In the case of model cars, you might ask

• whether they are looking for a car that will be fun to build.

• whether they are looking for a long-term project requiring patience and skill.

• how much money they have to spend.

▲ **Critical Viewing**
What might be puzzling the man in this cartoon? **[Infer]**

SOUTHSIDE SALLIE DOLL

• comes with three outfits
• comes in different hair colors
• has many fantasy setups, like the Southside Sallie Moon Walk

• pretty face
• many additional clothes available
• house available separately

MANHATTAN MARY DOLL

• comes with five outfits
• comes in one hair color
• has no fantasy setups

168 • Comparison-and-Contrast Essay

Critical Viewing

Infer Students may say that he is trying to decide what to do with his money.

Jot down a description of your audience and its needs on an index card. Refer to this card to make sure you are thinking of your audience as you gather details and draft your report.

Gathering Details To gather the details you need, consult brochures, user's guides, and magazine articles. Record details in a Venn diagram like the one shown.

Drafting After you've gathered information, begin drafting.

- Begin with an introduction clearly stating for whom and about what you are writing your report.
- In the body of your report, compare products point by point.
- Support each point with details about the product.
- Make your recommendation in a conclusion.

Revising and Editing After completing your first draft, check it against your audience description. Ask yourself:

- Is there information I have not included but that my audience needs? (If so, add the missing details.)
- Have I included information my audience doesn't need? (If so, consider deleting those details.)

Then, rearrange sentences to make sure that all those about a given feature appear near each other. Add transitions, such as *in contrast* and *likewise*, to clearly connect ideas.

Publishing and Presenting Create a consumer bulletin board in the school library for students to browse. Post your report on the board.

MODEL

Where to Eat

In this passage, notice that the writer compares the restaurants point by point. The conclusion makes a recommendation specifically meant for the writer's audience.

If you are looking for a lot of food on your plate and don't mind a lot of grease as well, Sloppy Joe's may be the restaurant for you. The cooking at Tartuffe's is a lot better, but the portions are a lot smaller. For prices, Joe's can't be beat. Tartuffe's is the kind of place you probably can afford only on special occasions.

In conclusion, I would recommend Joe's for any student with a little money and a big appetite.

Connected Assignment: Consumer Report • 169

Customize for
More Advanced Students

Have students go through a few back issues of *Consumer Report,* looking for a report on a product that interests them. Students should pay particular attention to the article's use of charts and diagrams. They can consider how they might use charts and diagrams in their own reports to add important information and visual interest. Challenge students to include at least one graphic organizer in their reports.

Lesson Objectives

1. To compare and contrast different stories on the same theme.

2. To write a paragraph that compares and contrasts musical ideas.

Step-by-Step Teaching Guide

Interpreting Themes in a Variety of Media

1. Choose a Spotlight element for class discussion, or have students work independently or in small groups on the element of their choice. Give students the initiative to find the necessary books, videotapes, and recordings.

2. Go around the room and have students tell the story of "Beauty and the Beast," each adding one sentence in turn. Repeat the activity for "Tam Lin." If students are not familiar with this story, locate a version of it and read it aloud in class.

3. Encourage interested students to organize a screening of Cocteau's film. Remind them that although the film is in French, it has English subtitles. Students who see the film may want to write their comparison-contrast paragraphs on Cocteau and Doré's visual interpretations of the story. Students can find Doré's illustrations in art books in the library.

4. The stage musical *Beauty and the Beast* is a live-action version of the animated film. Students may want to review the film before they begin the writing activity below.

Viewing and Representing

Activity Unless they have a strong music background, students may have difficulty with this activity. As an alternative, you might have them compare and contrast the stories of "Beauty and the Beast" and "Tam Lin"; compare and contrast Disney's version of Beauty's story with a written version such as Perrault's; compare and contrast the Disney and Cocteau films; or compare and contrast Cocteau and Doré's visual interpretations of the story as suggested in Step 2.

Spotlight on the Humanities

Interpreting Themes in a Variety of Media

Focus on Music: "The Ballad of Tam Lin"

One of the most beautiful comparison-and-contrast pieces is a fairy tale, "Beauty and the Beast." The story includes a strong contrast between a beautiful woman and the beast with whom she lives. The story also contrasts the beast with the handsome prince he turns into.

The fairy tale itself is the subject of comparisons. Many compare "Beauty and the Beast" to a Scottish ballad called "The Ballad of Tam Lin," which dates as far back as 1549. (A *ballad* is a long song or poem that tells a story.)

"Tam Lin" is about a young man who is a captive of the faeries, and about the young woman who rescues him. Like "Beauty and the Beast," the story of "Tam Lin" includes an enchanted forest where sacred roses grow. Trouble starts for both Beauty and Janet, the young woman in "Tam Lin," when they obtain one of these roses. In both stories, the spell on the man is broken only after the young woman expresses devotion to him.

Film Connection French director Jean Cocteau (1889–1963) created a classic film version of "Beauty and the Beast" in 1946. Cocteau was inspired to make this film after studying nineteenth-century artist Gustave Doré's illustrations for the story.

Theater Connection In 1994, a stage version of *Beauty and the Beast* arrived on Broadway. The musical won a Tony Award for Best Costumes in 1995.

Comparison-and-Contrast Writing Activity: Presenting Contrasts in Music

Listen to the songs from the Broadway version of *Beauty and the Beast*. Take notes on how the composer creates a contrast between Beauty and the Beast in music. Write your thoughts in a paragraph or two, and share them with the class. Play examples from the musical to help the class understand the contrast.

Scene from *Beauty and the Beast*, directed by Jean Cocteau.

▲ **Critical Viewing** Compare these two scenes from different versions of "Beauty and the Beast." List at least two similarities and two differences. [Compare and Contrast]

Critical Viewing

Compare and Contrast Students may say that the first image is a drawing; the second is a photograph. Both Beasts are dressed in human clothing; they both have human bodies and animal heads. In the first picture, Beauty is the dominant figure; in the second picture, the Beast is.

Media and Technology Skills

▶ **Lesson Objectives**

1. To watch a movie version of a familiar book.
2. To compare the two versions of the same story.

Comparing Stories in Different Media

Activity: Comparing Book and Movie Versions

The world's favorite stories can't stay put. People spread them around by retelling them in a variety of ways. For instance, movie makers often take a favorite book and turn the story into a film. Learn about some of the ways in which movie makers change stories when they film them.

Learn About It Here are some of the changes that take place when a story makes the transition from a book to a film:

- **Actions Versus Thoughts** Movie makers do not often include parts of a book that cannot be shown in actions. Long discussions between characters, or a character's deep thoughts, may not appear in the movie version of a story.

- **Time Limits** You can put a book down, and then pick it up again days later when you have more time to read. Most people, though, get restless if they sit in a movie theater for too long. For this reason, movie makers generally limit the length of movies to under two hours. To hold to this time, they may leave out events that appear in the book. They may even eliminate or combine characters.

- **Adding Image and Sound** Writers use only words to shape their story. In contrast, movie makers tell a story not just with words, but with visual images and sounds. They use actors, scenery, and special effects to create these images. Instead of a vivid description of a character's feelings, a movie maker might use yearning, romantic music, or take a close-up shot of a character's tear-streaked face.

   Words, though, can express important subtleties of meaning. By using words skillfully, you can show that a character feels fear and longing at the same time. A movie may show only a character's strongest feelings or only the most striking parts of the events in a story.

Watch It Watch a movie production of a book you have read. Take notes, using a chart like the one shown. Then, write a brief comparison of the two versions, noting the important differences between them.

Other Differences to Consider

Purpose
The purpose of a written story may not be the same as that of the movie version. The story's author might want to teach a lesson; the screenwriter might wish only to entertain.

Changing Times
In a modern version of an old story, a movie maker may appeal to current ideas and trends. For instance, the movie maker might add ideas about the rights of children that were not in the written version.

	Written Version	Movie Version
Events (Different/Similar)	1. Pete's dog gets lost. 2.	1. Pete's dog gets lost. 2.
Characters (Different/Similar)	1. Charlie – helps Pete look for his dog 2.	1. Charlie isn't in the movie. 2.
Words vs. Images (Written Descriptions vs. Acting, Scenery, Music, Camerawork)	1. Pete's reaction to missing dog: "like a chunk of ice in his stomach" 2.	1. Pete's reaction to missing dog: close-up of his shocked face; music sounds full of fear and danger 2.

Media and Technology Skills • 171

Step-by-Step Teaching Guide

Comparing Stories

Teaching Resources: Writing Support Transparency, 8-I; Writing Support Activity Book, 8-3

1. Ask students to list a few stories they have both read and seen dramatic presentations of. Have them list a few similarities and differences. Ask which version students preferred and why.

2. Point out that many films alter the endings of stories. Disney films in particular tend to change story endings that are at all dark or sad. Hans Christian Andersen's little mermaid dies at the end of the story; in the Disney version, she marries the prince. Ask students if they know of other Disney movies that alter their sources. Ask students why they think filmmakers tend to prefer "happy" endings.

3. You may want to have a video screening for the whole class of a story or book they have all read. If you wish, you can combine this activity with the *Beauty and the Beast* activity on the previous page. Students can read the fairy tale, then watch the Cocteau movie.

4. Use the transparency to demonstrate comparing and contrasting the two versions of the story. Then give students copies of the blank organizer so that they can complete the writing activity.

Lesson Objectives

1. To write a comparison-and-contrast essay.
2. To draft, revise, and edit a comparison-contrast essay.
3. To use correct grammar, spelling, and mechanics.

Step-by-Step Teaching Guide

Comparing and Contrasting

1. Review the terms *comparison* and *contrast*. Point out that this type of answer naturally falls into a two-part structure; one section discussing similarities and the other discussing differences. Students should find it very easy to organize their answers to this type of writing prompt.

2. Remind students of the importance of including specific details in their answers. Students should not only contrast the salt content of the two lakes, for example, but should also add some descriptive detail, such as listing the types of plants and animals that survive or flourish in this environment.

3. Remind students to vary their transitional words. Many of these words mean the same thing, but it is best not to use the same word over and over again. A reader will be irritated by too much repetition.

Standardized Test Preparation Workshop

Comparing and Contrasting in Response to Writing Prompts

The writing prompts of standardized tests often judge your ability to write an expository essay in which you compare and contrast things. Your test essay will be assessed on your ability to

- show the similarities and differences between subjects, following the requirements of the prompt exactly.
- use examples based on what you have read in the passage to support each point.
- use a consistent method of organization suited to the topic, such as the point-by-point method.
- unify your essay through the use of transitions.

Although on some tests you will not lose points for errors in spelling and grammar, always try to use correct English.

Some prompts ask you to write a short response. Others call for a long response. If you are given a short-response prompt, you should not go through the prewriting, drafting, and revising stages. The writing skills you have learned so far will be sufficient. However, a long-response prompt requires more attention. You can practice for such tests by responding to the sample expository writing prompt below. Use the suggestions on the next page to help you respond. The clocks represent the portion of your test-taking time that you should devote to each stage of your writing.

Test Tip

Pay special attention to key words in the prompt, such as *not, similarities,* and *differences.*

Sample Writing Situation

> Read "More Than a Pinch: Two Salt Lakes" on page 152, and then answer the prompt below.
>
> > In "More Than a Pinch: Two Salt Lakes," the writer compares the Great Salt Lake with the Dead Sea. Describe the ways the lakes are *alike* and *different,* using examples from the article.

TEST-TAKING TIP

If students have difficulty with Venn diagrams, suggest a two-column chart headed *Similarities* on the left and *Differences* on the right. Because a standardized test limits their time, students may not want to bother with drawing circles of the right size and trying to squeeze all relevant details inside them. Two-column charts are much easier to keep neat and organized when a student has one eye on the clock.

Customize for
Less Advanced Students

Students may find it difficult to articulate similarities and differences. Have each students find a topic in which he or she is interested, such as baseball, and have the students devise five comparison-contrast writing prompts relating to this topic (for example, *Compare and contrast Ty Cobb's and Babe Ruth's contributions to baseball.*). Go over students' lists to be sure that their writing prompts are appropriate for test practice. Then have each student complete an answer to one prompt every night for five nights. Students should soon show improvement in their ability to organize a comparison-contrast essay.

Prewriting

Allow close to one fourth of your time for prewriting.

Focus on Your Purpose Before you begin to gather details for your essay, keep in mind your purpose in writing. This is already decided by the prompt. For instance, in responding to the example prompt, you should focus on the similarities and differences between the two lakes, and avoid discussing details that do not lead to a comparison or a contrast.

Use a Venn Diagram Gather details for your essay, using a Venn diagram. Draw two overlapping circles. Write similarities in the section that overlaps, and list differences in the outer sections. (For an example of a Venn diagram, see page 157.)

Drafting

Allow nearly half of your time for drafting.

Organize Details Choose a method of organization. You may want to use the organization used in "More Than a Pinch," which is the point-by-point method. To use this method, discuss each aspect of both subjects in turn. After you have chosen a method, follow it in sketching an outline.

Introduction After organizing details, write an introductory paragraph in which you make a general statement comparing the lakes.

Use Examples Follow your organization in presenting necessary support from the model. For each feature that you write about—the level of salt, for instance—use examples from the text to explain how that feature is similar or different in the two lakes.

Use Transitions As you draft, use transitional words to show the connections between ideas. Words such as *but*, *however*, *yet*, *too*, and *likewise* show compare-and-contrast relationships.

Conclusion In your conclusion, sum up the differences and similarities between the lakes.

Revising, Editing, and Proofreading

Allow almost one fourth of your time for revising and editing. Use the last few minutes to proofread your work.

Review Organization of Ideas Check the organization of your essay against your outline. Rearrange sentences or paragraphs if necessary to put them in the best order. Also, make sure your ideas connect between sentences and paragraphs. If a connection seems to be missing between ideas, add an appropriate transitional word.

Make Corrections Check for spelling, grammar, and punctuation errors. When making changes, put one line through text that you are eliminating. Use a caret (^) to show where added text belongs.

Time and Resource Manager

In-Depth Lesson Plan

	LESSON FOCUS	PRINT AND MEDIA RESOURCES
DAY 1	**Introduction to Cause-and-Effect Essays** Students learn key elements of cause-and-effect essays and analyze the Model From Literature (pp. 174–177).	*Writers at Work* **Videotape**, Exposition: Making Connections
DAY 2	**Prewriting** Students choose and narrow a topic, consider their audience and purpose, and gather information (pp. 178–181).	**Teaching Resources** *Writing Support Transparencies,* 9-A–D; *Writing Support Activity Book* 9-1 **Writing Lab CD-ROM**, Exposition: Making Connections
DAY 3	**Drafting** Students organize their ideas and write their first drafts (pp. 182–183).	**Teaching Resources** *Writing Support Transparencies,* 9-E **Writing Lab CD-ROM**, Exposition: Making Connections
DAY 4	**Revising** Students revise their drafts in terms of overall structure, paragraphs, sentences, and word choice (pp. 184–187).	**Teaching Resources** *Writing Support Transparencies,* 9-F; *Writing Support Activity Book* 9-2 **Writing Lab CD-ROM**, Exposition: Making Connections
DAY 5	**Editing and Proofreading; Publishing and Presenting** Students check their work for accuracy and correctness and present their final drafts (pp.188–189).	**Teaching Resources** *Scoring Rubrics on Transparency,* Ch. 9; *Formal Assessment,* Ch. 9 **Writing Lab CD-ROM**, Exposition: Making Connections

Accelerated Lesson Plan

	LESSON FOCUS	PRINT AND MEDIA RESOURCES
DAY 1	**Drafting** Students review characteristics for cause-and-effect writing, select topics, and write drafts (pp. 174–183).	**Teaching Resources** *Writing Support Transparencies,* 9-A–E; *Writing Support Activity Book* 9-1 *Writers at Work* **Videotape**, Exposition: Making Connections
DAY 2	**Revising to Presenting** Students work individually or with peers to revise, edit, and proofread their work for presentation (pp. 184–189).	**Teaching Resources** *Writing Support Transparencies,* 9-F; *Scoring Rubrics on Transparency,* Ch. 9; *Formal Assessment,* Ch. 9 **Writing Lab CD-ROM**, Exposition: Making Connections

Options for Adapting Lesson Plans

HOMEWORK

Have students complete any stage of the lesson for homework.

FEATURES

Extend coverage with the Connected Assignment (p. 192), Spotlight on the Humanities (p. 194), Media and Technology Skills (p. 195), and the Standardized Test Preparation Workshop (p. 196).

TECHNOLOGY

Students can complete any stage of the lesson on computer. Have them print out their completed work.

INTEGRATED SKILLS COVERAGE

Integrating Grammar
Verb Tense SE p. 186
Using Prepositions SE p. 188

Reading/Writing Connection
Reading Strategy SE p. 176
Writing Application SE p. 177

Speaking and Listening
ATE p. 178

Technology
SE pp. 184, 189

Workplace Skills
ATE p. 179

Viewing and Representing
Critical Viewing SE pp. 174, 176, 177, 181, 185, 187, 190, 191, 192, 194, 195
ATE pp. 191, 194

ASSESSMENT SUPPORT

Standardized Test Preparation Workshop SE p. 196; ATE p. 187
Standardized Test Preparation Workbook, pp. 17–18
Scoring Rubrics on Transparency, Ch. 9
Formal Assessment, Ch. 9
Writing Assessment and Portfolio Management

MEETING INDIVIDUAL NEEDS

Less Advanced Students ATE pp. 177, 197; See also Ongoing Assessments ATE pp. 179, 183, 185, 186, 189
ESL Students ATE pp. 186, 188
Visual/Spatial Learners ATE p. 182
Verbal/Linguistic Learners ATE p. 182
Gifted/Talented Students ATE p. 197

BLOCK SCHEDULING

Pacing Suggestions
For 90-minute Blocks
• Have students complete the Prewriting and Drafting stages in a single period.
• Focus one class period on Revising and Editing and Publishing and Presenting. Allow at least 30 minutes for peer revision.

Resources for Varying Instruction
• *Writing Lab* **CD-ROM** If your students have access to hardware, a 90-minute block provides an ideal opportunity for students to work on computer.
• *Writers at Work* **Videotape** Show the Cause-and-Effect segment in class.

Professional Development Support
• *How to Manage Instruction in the Block* This Teaching Resource provides management and activity suggestions.

MEDIA AND TECHNOLOGY

For the Student
• *Writing Lab* **CD-ROM**, Exposition: Making Connections

For the Teacher
• *Writers at Work* **Videotape**, Exposition: Making Connections
• *Resource Pro* **CD-ROM**

WRITING AND GRAMMAR WEB SITE

The Interactive Writing and Grammar Web site provides a wide array of support for students, teachers, and parents. Writing support includes:

• Interactive revision checkers
• Scoring rubrics with complete models

www.phschool.com

LITERATURE CONNECTIONS

Related selections from *Prentice Hall Literature: Timeless Voices, Timeless Themes*, Copper:
"Breaker's Bridge," Laurence Yep, SE p. 177
"Space Shuttle Challenger," William Harwood, SE p. 179

Lesson Objectives

1. To analyze authors' uses of cause-and-effect relationships.

2. To write to inform or explain.

3. To generate and refine ideas and plans for writing by using the prewriting strategies Brainstorming, Browsing, and Topic Web.

4. To identify audience and purpose for writing.

5. To develop a draft by identifying cause-and-effect relationships and providing elaboration using the strategy Exploding the Moment.

6. To revise a draft by using the strategies Connecting the Steps and Finding the Tug.

7. To edit a draft for correct use of verb tenses.

8. To edit a draft for correct use of prepositions.

9. To publish a cause-and-effect essay by creating a class anthology and organizing a group reading.

10. To evaluate how well one's cause-and-effect essay achieves its purposes.

Critical Viewing

Hypothesize Students should say that all the gears will turn.

Chapter 9 Exposition
Cause-and-Effect Essay

▲ **Critical Viewing**
What will happen if one of these gears starts to turn? **[Hypothesize]**

Cause-and-Effect Explanations in Everyday Life

Through history, people have tried to understand why things happen. Why does it get dark at night? Why does it thunder and lightning? What causes the seasons to change?

People have tried to answer these questions in many ways. The ancient Greeks, for example, told stories of Zeus, the king of the gods, who hurled lightning bolts from the sky, and of Apollo, who drove a chariot pulling the sun.

The ancient Greeks used these myths to explain **causes**— the reasons behind events—and **effects**—the results produced by events. Today, we use science to explain many causes and effects. In this chapter, you will learn to explain causes and effects by writing a cause- and-effect essay.

174 • Exposition

⏱ TIME AND RESOURCE MANAGER

Resources
Technology: Writers at Work videotape, Exposition: Making Connections

In-Depth Coverage	Accelerated Pace
• Cover pp. 174–177 in class. • Show the Exposition: Making Connections section of the Writers at Work videotape. • Read the literature excerpt (pp. 176–177) in class and base a discussion of the characteristics of cause-and-effect essays on it. • Discuss examples of cause-and-effect essays from science or social studies textbooks or magazines.	• Assign pp. 174–177 for independent student review. • Challenge students to discuss these questions: Is it easier to analyze causes or effects? Can you still write a good cause-and-effect essay if you don't know a cause? An effect? • Assign the Model from Literature (pp. 176–177) for independent reading.

What Is a Cause-and-Effect Essay?

Exposition is writing that informs or explains. A **cause-and-effect essay** is a brief piece of expository writing that explains the circumstances leading to an event or a situation. It may also predict what will happen as a result of a current situation. Features of an effective cause-and-effect essay include

- a clear explanation of one or more causes and one or more effects.
- a thorough presentation of facts, statistics, and other details that support each explanation.
- a clear and consistent organization.
- transitions that clearly indicate the connections among the details.

To learn the criteria on which your essay may be judged or graded, see the Rubric for Self-Assessment on page 189.

Types of Cause-and-Effect Essays

Following are some of the specific types of writing that explain causes and effects:

- **History reports** explain the reasons behind past events.
- **Lab reports** explain the results of an experiment.
- **New reports** explain causes and effects of current events or developments.

Writers in
ACTION

Television news correspondent Gary Matsumoto often uses cause-and-effect explanations in his television news stories. He has only a short time to present information, but he realizes that it is important to give his audience background information:

"You can't cram too much into four minutes or ninety seconds. But you have to . . . have a sufficient amount of background information to make it clear why you're doing the story."

PREVIEW
Student Work
IN PROGRESS

Johnny Guo, a student at First Colony Middle School in Sugar Land, Texas, chose to write about the causes and effects of pollution. In this chapter, you will see how Johnny applied the featured strategies to compose his essay, "Saving Our Air." At the end of the chapter, you can read Johnny's completed essay.

PREPARE and ENGAGE

Interest GRABBER Ask students to get into a mental time machine and travel back 2,000 years. Have them make up myths to answer such questions as Why is the sky blue? Where does the sun go at night? What causes volcanoes? or other questions that perplexed ancient peoples.

Activate Prior Knowledge

From their very first days, as babies learn that crying causes parents to come to their aid, people analyze cause-and-effect relationships. Have students think of some other causes and effects of babies' behaviors. Then ask them to describe the effects of some of their behaviors on people. Next, lead from this discussion of causes and effects to a consideration of formal cause-and-effect essay features by going over the four features listed in the textbook.

☑ ONGOING ASSESSMENT: Diagnose

Use this writing task to diagnose students' current level of proficiency in writing cause-and-effect essays.

Do some simple action, such as pretending to trip over a string, and ask students to write a cause-and-effect sentence that describes what happened (the effect) and why it happened (the cause or causes). Provide students who have difficulty distinguishing between causes and effects additional examples of cause-and-effect relationships. Reiterate the difference between causes and effects as students complete this chapter.

175

Reading: Create a Cause-and-Effect Chart

Causes are not necessarily listed before effects in an essay. As students complete the chart, they may have to write an effect or effects on the right-hand side of their paper before they add a cause on the left-hand side. The overall effect, the topic of endangered manatees, can be inferred from the title. Point out that an effect of one action can be the cause of another.

Teaching from the Model

Students will find this a clear, easy-to-follow model of a cause-and-effect essay. Causes and effects are simple and stated explicitly. Specific details ("... 1,500 manatees ... scars from run-ins with propellers") bring vivid images to mind and help strengthen the arguments in the essay.

Step-by-Step Teaching Guide

Engage Students Through Literature

1. Have a volunteer read aloud the first paragraph. Ask students why the first sentence is a "hook" that entices readers. (Readers will want to learn how manatees can be endangered if they have no natural enemies.)

2. Make sure students can identify the "big effect" (manatees are endangered) and the "big cause" (people have endangered manatees) in the second sentence, as the remainder of the essay gives details that support this topic.

3. Ask the class to think about the reasons why the author wrote this essay. When they choose topics for their cause-and-effect essays, urge students to choose topics about which they feel strongly.

Critical Viewing

Speculate Students may say boat operators may know what to look for when operating their boats.

9.1 Model From Literature

Ross Bankson (1942–   ) is a former editor at National Geographic World. In this essay, he explains why West Indian manatees, large mammals that live in shallow tropical waters off North and South America, are threatened with extinction. Notice that Bankson outlines a variety of specific reasons that the manatee has become endangered.

Reading ◄ Writing Connection ►

Reading Strategy: Create a Cause-and-Effect Chart When you read a cause-and-effect essay, you may find it helpful to **create a cause-and-effect chart** in which you record each of the causes and effects a writer presents. List the causes along the left side of a sheet of paper. Then, list the effects on the right side. Draw arrows connecting related causes and effects.

▼ **Critical Viewing** Manatees are often harmed by speedboats. What effect might seeing this manatee up close have on a speedboat operator? **[Speculate]**

Gentle Giants in Trouble

Ross Bankson

They have no natural enemies, but they are in trouble anyway. West Indian manatees—large, gentle marine mammals—are in danger because of people. . . .

Some manatee feeding grounds have disappeared, filled in for construction projects. Other feeding grounds have been damaged by pollution, which becomes worse as the number of people grows. Discarded plastic objects floating in waterways can kill a manatee that swallows them.

Boaters create the greatest hazard for West Indian manatees in the shallow water that the animals prefer. The slow-moving manatees often cannot get away from speeding boats. In a collision with a boat, a manatee may be killed or injured by the force of the hit

The writer begins with an interesting "hook" that grabs the reader's interest.

Next, the writer presents the various reasons why the manatee is near extinction.

176 • Cause-and-Effect Essay

or by cuts from the propeller. Of some 1,500 manatees in Florida today, nearly all adults bear scars from run-ins with propellers.

The good news for the West Indian manatee is this: People can help as well as harm. Many in fact are working to save manatees. Some Florida car owners pay extra money for a "Save the Manatee" license plate. By doing so they help fund the state's manatee protection program and other programs for environmental education. Florida laws regulate boating in areas where manatees live. Other laws protect the animal as an endangered species.

Still, the experts say, even more safeguards are needed. The manatee population is shrinking. "With public support," says Judith Valee, "we can bring the species back from the brink of extinction."

Writing Application: Making Clear Connections Between Causes and Effects
Make it easy for readers to chart causes and effects. Use transitions such as *because of* and *as a result* to show the relationship between each cause and effect you discuss.

▼ Critical Viewing
These animals are in danger of extinction. Name something people might do to help the recovery of one of them. **[Apply]**

The last paragraphs encourage readers to support a solution—part of the writer's purpose.

LITERATURE

To read a fantasy involving causes and effects, see "Breaker's Bridge" by Laurence Yep. You can find the story in *Prentice Hall Literature: Timeless Voices, Timeless Themes,* Copper.

Clockwise from upper left: San Francisco rainbow garter snake, Florida panther, American bald eagle, orangutan

Model From Literature • 177

Critical Viewing

Apply Students may say people could pass laws to protect the habitat of the endangered animal.

Responding to Literature

Have students list the causes and effects they find as they read Yep's story.

Customize for
Less Advanced Students

Students may need further help analyzing the structure of the essay. Have volunteers sum up each paragraph. You might want to read the marginal notes aloud and make sure students understand what the notes mean and how to use them to gain meaning from the essay. Point out that this essay is organized following a "good news, bad news" structure. The first three paragraphs introduce the problem. The fourth and fifth paragraphs present some solutions. The last sentence is a call to action.

Reading\Writing Connection

Writing: Making Clear Connections Between Causes and Effects

Ask students to look for words Bankson uses in his essay to connect causes and effects. (*but, by doing so,* and so on) Brainstorm other phrases not mentioned in the textbook, such as *therefore, in order to,* and *thus.* Emphasize that transition phrases help readers link ideas in an essay.

Prewriting: Browsing, Brainstorming

Teaching Resources: Writing Support Transparency 9-A

1. Display the transparency. Have a volunteer read the topics that Johnny generated after browsing.

2. The browsing strategy works well in small groups. Begin by dividing the class into groups of three to six. Provide each group with some magazines or newspapers.

3. Have group members browse through the periodicals and jot down ideas the articles bring to mind.

4. Then have students read their lists aloud. Students should brainstorm other ideas the notes suggest. Students may be surprised to learn how many ideas the same article can suggest to different people, as well as how many more ideas a group can arrive at than can an individual working alone.

Integrating Listening Skills

Discuss the qualities of good listeners. These include focusing on the speaker—rather than waiting for him or her to finish so that the listener can begin speaking—and summarizing the speaker's words to make sure the listener understood what was said. Urge students to be good listeners as they brainstorm ideas with their classmates, not just to be polite but to get maximum benefit from brainstorming sessions.

9.2 Prewriting

Choosing Your Topic

If you have an interest in your topic, you are likely to write a lively and interesting essay on it. Start work on your cause-and-effect essay by choosing an event or situation that interests you. Use these strategies to stimulate ideas:

Strategies for Generating a Topic

1. **Brainstorming** In a group, discuss possible topics. You may wish to begin with a general idea such as "Historical Events" or a fill-in-the-blank exercise such as "What Causes ___?___" One member of the group should list all the ideas mentioned. Choose an idea from this list as your topic.

2. **Browsing** When you're looking for new clothes, you probably browse through the store. Browsing can also work when you need ideas for a piece of writing. Scan the morning newspaper, or look through magazines or books at the library. Skim for words, phrases, or ideas that concern causes and effects until you find just the right topic.

Writing Lab CD-ROM

For more help finding a topic, see the activities and tips in the Choosing a Topic section of the Exposition: Making Connections lesson.

Student Work IN PROGRESS

Name: Johnny Guo
First Colony Middle School
Sugar Land, TX

Browsing

After skimming through a number of magazines and browsing through a CD-ROM encyclopedia, Johnny became interested in writing about the causes and effects of pollution.

Ideas for Cause-and-Effect Essay

Television news story: Decrease in crime

Magazine article on the new dance crazes

Radio: air pollution in American cities

Conversation between Mom and Mr. Wexley: why lots of new people are moving to our town

178 • Cause-and-Effect Essay

⏱ **TIME SAVERS!**

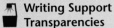 **Writing Support Transparencies**
Use the transparencies for Chapter 9 to teach these strategies.

⏱ **TIME AND RESOURCE MANAGER**

Resources
Print: Writing Support Transparencies 9-A–D; Writing Support Activity Book 9-1
Technology: Writing Lab CD-ROM, Exposition: Making Connections

In-Depth Coverage	Accelerated Pace
• Cover pp. 178–181. • Model the brainstorming strategy for the class. • Use the Writing Support transparency as you model browsing. • Brainstorm topic ideas with the class. Provide photocopies of a magazine article for students and browse through the article for topic ideas with them.	• Assign pp. 178–181 for independent student review. • Students who have unusual interests should think of ways they can present their favorite topics, no matter how complex, in cause-and-effect essays.

TOPIC BANK

If you're having trouble finding a topic, consider the following possibilities.

1. **Essay About Nature** Choose a natural event that interests you. It might be the blooming of a flower or the rumbling of thunder. Find out about the causes of this event, and write about them in a cause-and-effect essay.

2. **Essay About a Service** Every day people turn on lights, answer phones, and turn on the water. Each of these services—electricity, telephone service, and water—works only because of a series of causes and effects. Do research into one such service, and write about the causes and effects it involves.

Responding to Fine Art

3. In this painting, the people are creating soap bubbles. Think of what a soap bubble looks like. Then, formulate a question about what makes a soap bubble look or act as it does. Do research to answer your question, and write up the results in an essay.

Responding to Literature

4. Read an account of the space shuttle disaster. Write a cause-and-effect essay in which you examine either the causes behind the space shuttle crash or the effects the crash had on the space program. You can find an eyewitness account of the disaster, "Space Shuttle *Challenger*" by William Harwood, in *Prentice Hall Literature: Timeless Voices, Timeless Themes*, Copper.

Blowing Bubbles, John Kane, The Phillips Collection

☑ Cooperative Writing Opportunity

5. **Booklet of Causes and Effects** With a group of classmates, brainstorm for an event that has many causes and effects, such as a traffic jam, the opening of a new mall, or the passage of a law. Choose one topic. Then, have each student write a report on a single cause or effect related to the topic. Assemble the pieces of writing into a booklet with a cover, a table of contents, and illustrations.

Responding to Fine Art

Blowing Bubbles by John Kane

Teaching Resources: Writing Support Transparency 9-B

1. Display the transparency. Have students describe what the painting represents.

2. Ask students to suggest possible topics for an essay based on the art.

Responding to Literature

Before students write cause-and-effect essays on the space shuttle *Challenger* disaster, they need to research reasons the shuttle exploded and ways the disaster influenced the space missions that followed. You may have some student experts right in your classroom. If so, have space exploration buffs tell the class what they know about the disaster. The next step might be for students to consult NASA's Web page: www.nasa.gov.com

Integrating Workplace Skills

In jobs that put workers at serious risk, an analysis of what went wrong always follows a disaster. For instance, a thorough investigation occurs after firefighters lose their lives in a fire. Identifying and understanding causes and effects is a real-life skill that saves lives.

Spotlight on Humanities

For additional topic suggestions, refer students to the Spotlight on Humanities on page 194.

☑ ONGOING ASSESSMENT: Monitor and Reinforce

For students who are still having difficulty choosing or refining a topic, use one of the following options.

Option 1 Have students list places they like to visit or ways they like to spend their free time. Ask them to draw cause-and-effect essay topics from their lists.	**Option 2** If they are not interested in Topic Bank ideas, suggest that students select one of the suggestions from the Topic Bank for Heterogeneous Classes in the Teaching Resources.

Prewriting: Topic Web

Teaching Resources: Writing Support Transparency 9-C

1. Making a topic web will help students see at a glance whether the topic they have chosen for their essay is too broad.

2. Display the transparency. Use Johnny's topic web as a model, or use a student volunteer's topic and begin the topic web as a class.

3. Start by writing the topic on the chalkboard. To help the topic stand out visually as the web grows, write it in capital letters and draw a rectangle around it.

4. Have students suggest subtopics as indicated in the textbook. Continue for several minutes, and then choose one of the subtopics as the focus of a new topic web. Is this topic still too broad? Too narrow? The topic may be too narrow if students, even with your support, can think of few or no subtopics.

5. Students should follow this procedure as they develop topic webs for their own cause-and-effect essay.

9.2

Narrowing Your Topic

Before you begin gathering details about your topic, consider whether it is narrow enough to cover thoroughly. For example, the cause that brought the solar system into existence is too broad a topic. You might focus instead on the causes of Earth's rotation.

Use a Topic Web

Create a topic web to help you evaluate and narrow your topic. Follow these steps:

1. Draw a circle in the center of a blank page.
2. Write your topic inside the circle.
3. Write connected ideas inside new circles around your topic. Draw lines connecting them to your main topic.
4. Write additional ideas related to each one of your subtopics in new circles. Connect each to the appropriate subtopic.

When you've finished, review your completed web. To narrow your topic, focus on a single one of your subtopics.

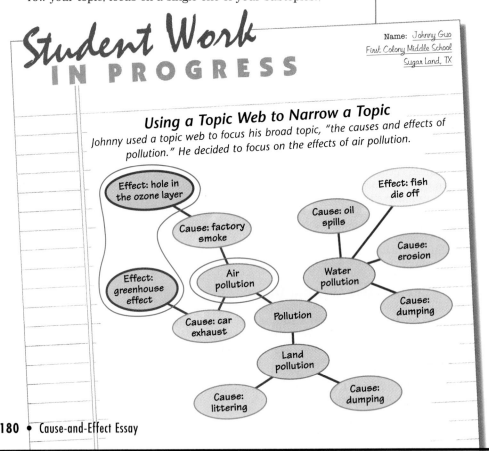

Student Work IN PROGRESS

Name: *Johnny Guo*
First Colony Middle School
Sugar Land, TX

Using a Topic Web to Narrow a Topic

Johnny used a topic web to focus his broad topic, "the causes and effects of pollution." He decided to focus on the effects of air pollution.

180 • Cause-and-Effect Essay

⏱ **TIME SAVERS!**

 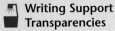 **Writing Support Transparencies**
Use the transparencies for Chapter 9 to facilitate teaching of strategies.

Considering Your Audience and Purpose

Your **audience** is the people for whom you are writing. How much they know and care about your topic will affect how you write your cause-and-effect essay. Jot down information about your audience for each of these categories:

- **Age** Young readers need explanations in simple language with much background; adults want more in-depth details.

- **Interest in Topic** Readers who are very interested will want as many details as you can provide; those who are less interested will feel swamped if you tell them too much.

- **Knowledge of Topic** Readers with little knowledge need background information; experts do not need this background.

Your **purpose**—what you hope to accomplish by writing—will also shape your writing. For instance, in "Gentle Giants in Trouble" on page 176, the writer's purpose is to persuade readers to join him in a cause as well as to explain a topic. To fulfill this purpose, he uses language and chooses details that will help readers see his point of view. Before writing, consider your purpose and how it will shape your writing.

Gathering Details

Research Your Topic

When you write your essay, you must use facts and examples to explain each cause-and-effect relationship you discuss. Gather this information through research in the library or on the Internet.

Using a T-Chart in Research A T-chart is a useful research tool. Use the example below as a model to help you create your own T-chart.

<table>
<tr><td colspan="2">Topic: <u>The May Flood</u></td></tr>
<tr><td>What caused the May flood?</td><td>What effects did the May flood have?</td></tr>
<tr><td>

• <u>Hurricane Barbara</u>

• <u>26" of rain</u>

• <u>Dam broke.</u>

• <u>Ground was already wet from earlier storms.</u>
</td><td>

• <u>$1.2 million in damages</u>

• <u>Schools and businesses closed for 7–10 days.</u>

• <u>35 families left town.</u>
</td></tr>
</table>

▲ **Critical Viewing**
What effects are these people trying to have on life in their city?
[Hypothesize]

Step-by-Step Teaching Guide

Prewriting: Considering Your Audience and Purpose

1. Review with students the three major categories that they should keep in mind when considering their audience.

2. Encourage students to jot down a few sentences that detail their purpose for writing. Have students refer to this as they write their essays.

Step-by-Step Teaching Guide

Using a T-Chart in Research

Teaching Resources: Writing Support Transparency 9-D; Writing Support Activity Book 9-1

1. Discuss how T-charts can help organize information. Students can write causes in the left-hand column of their T-chart and effects in the right-hand column.

2. Display the transparency to show students how to complete a T-chart.

3. Give students copies of the blank organizer. Students should label each sheet of their T-chart with their topic (or the title of their essay), but they may want to make a separate sheet for each subtopic they intend to include in their essay and add that subtopic under the title. For the topic shown in the textbook, the first three sheets might be headed The May Flood: When It Happened; The May Flood: Dam Construction; The May Flood: Unusual Weather Conditions.

Critical Viewing

Hypothesize Students may say that by planting a tree, these people are trying to make their city more beautiful.

Drafting: Shaping Your Writing

1. Before students review the information they have gathered for their cause-and-effect essays following the directions in the textbook, warn them to stop and think if they identify a simple cause and effect. If this is the case, do they have enough to write about? Will their paper be too simple and obvious? Will it include interesting and relevant details?

2. Have students consider the following organizational plans as they draft their essays: chronological order (what happened first, next, last), spatial order, and order of importance (with the most important cause or effect given first or last for emphasis).

3. Then have students follow the directions in the textbook. If they have several simple causes or effects, they may want to consider combining them in a single paragraph rather than devoting a separate paragraph to each.

Customize for
Visual/Spatial Learners

Students may find it helpful to write causes and effects in rectangles or ovals as shown in the textbook so that they can see the connections and organize their work.

Customize for
Verbal/Linguistic Learners

Students should read their lists aloud to themselves or to a partner. Hearing their words will help students add causes or effects they might otherwise forget. The inflection in their voice and natural pauses in speech may give aural clues to possible paragraph breaks and organizational possibilities.

9.3 Drafting

Shaping Your Writing
Organize Details

Review the information you've gathered, and organize it. Following are two common patterns for cause-and-effect essays. Select a suitable organization from among them, or devise your own, and follow it as you draft.

Many Causes/Single Effect If a number of unrelated events leads to a single result, focus one paragraph on each cause.

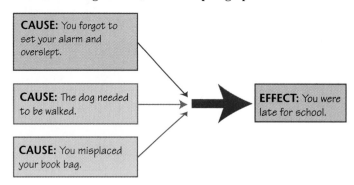

Single Cause/Many Effects If one cause produces several effects, focus one paragraph on each effect.

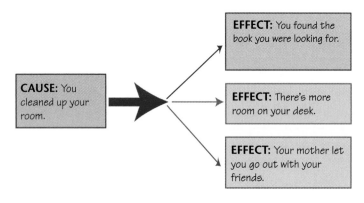

Find Your Focus

Review your information, and identify the main cause or the main effect involved in your topic. As you draft, connect each detail to this main focus.

182 • Cause-and-Effect Essay

⏱ TIME AND RESOURCE MANAGER

Resources
Print: Writing Support Transparency 9-E
Technology: Writing Lab CD-ROM, Exposition: Making Connections

In-Depth Coverage	Accelerated Pace
• Cover pp. 182–183 in class. • Have students write their cause-and-effect essay draft in class. **Option** Have students work independently or in small groups with the Writing Lab CD-ROM.	• Have students review pp. 182–183 independently and then write their first drafts. • Respond to questions as necessary.

Providing Elaboration

As you write your first draft, elaborate on each cause and effect by providing a thorough set of facts, statistics, description, and other information. Use the following strategy to help you develop layers of details.

"Explode the Moment"

As you draft, pause at the end of each paragraph. First, circle the most important event mentioned in it. Cut out a few sticky notes in the shape of starbursts. On your sticky notes, jot down notes about the events circled. (To help find details, imagine you are watching the event in slow motion. Note every part of the event as it unfolds.)

Attach each sticky note next to the pertinent paragraph of your draft. Consider adding details from your notes to the paragraph.

Writers in **ACTION**

As he writes, reporter Gary Matsumoto focuses on his viewer: "You have to grab your viewer right away. Then somewhere around the middle, you've got to think, 'What element of surprise can I offer? [What can] be a nice little kicker line at the end?'"

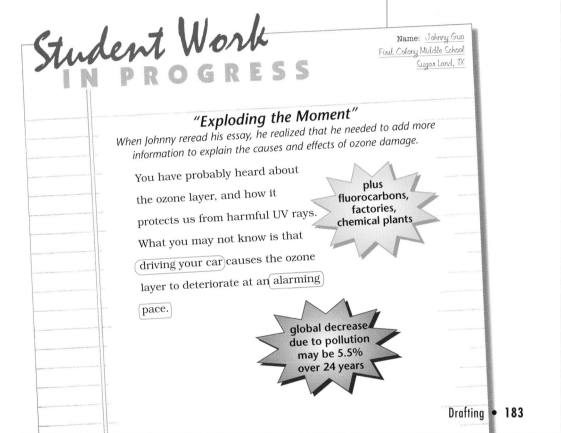

Student Work **IN PROGRESS**

Name: Johnny Guo
First Colony Middle School
Sugar Land, TX

"Exploding the Moment"

When Johnny reread his essay, he realized that he needed to add more information to explain the causes and effects of ozone damage.

You have probably heard about the ozone layer, and how it protects us from harmful UV rays. What you may not know is that (driving your car) causes the ozone layer to deteriorate at an (alarming) (pace.)

plus fluorocarbons, factories, chemical plants

global decrease due to pollution may be 5.5% over 24 years

Drafting • 183

Step-by-Step Teaching Guide

Drafting: "Explode the Moment"

Teaching Resources: Writing Support Transparency 9-E

1. Display the transparency. Review the Explode the Moment strategy and how to execute it. Students can use markers of various colors to draw bursts in the margin in which they write additional details.

2. Remind students to pause after they read each paragraph of their essay. Have them look for vague sentences, and caution them against generalities unsupported by facts.

3. Refer to Johnny's claim that "driving your car causes the ozone layer to deteriorate at an alarming pace." What proof is supplied? If a reader's response to a portion of an essay is "Why is that so?" or "How does that work?" then students need to provide additional information to support their assertions and explanations.

☑ **ONGOING ASSESSMENT: Monitor and Reinforce**

For students who are having difficulty organizing their essay, use one of the following options.

Option 1 Help students analyze the organization of cause-and-effect writing either by taking a look at papers from another class or by reviewing magazine articles you have photocopied for them.	**Option 2** Have partners go over both drafts, identifying causes and effects. Encourage them to cut and paste sentences as necessary, either on the computer or the old-fashioned way.

⏱ **TIME SAVERS!**

 Writing Support Transparencies
Use the transparencies for Chapter 9 to facilitate teaching of strategies.

Revising: Connecting the Steps

Teaching Resources: Writing Support Transparency 9-F

1. Display the transparency and carefully demonstrate how Johnny connected the steps in his essay. Ask students to identify any substeps that seem out of place.

2. Remind students that the steps in essays organized by spatial order or order of importance can be out of order also. The first step is still to circle each of the main causes and effects.

3. As students use this strategy to revise their drafts, make sure each student has a clear grasp of the strategy. Remind them as necessary that if they stick to one cause or effect per paragraph, details that don't fit will be easy to identify and move to where they belong.

9.4 Revising

Once you've completed your first draft, revise your work carefully. Start by looking at your overall structure.

Revising Your Overall Structure

Analyze Your Sequence of Details

To be effective, your essay should present a clear sequence of causes and effects. If any details are out of order, readers will not be able to follow your explanation. Use the following strategy to check the order of your details.

▶ **REVISION STRATEGY**
Connecting the Steps

As you review your draft, follow these steps:

1. Circle each main cause and each main effect.
2. Use a highlighter to mark each step that leads from a main cause to a main effect.
3. Draw arrows connecting the various steps in the order in which they logically occur.

If there are arrows crisscrossing the draft, consider rearranging details in a more logical order.

Technology Tip

If you are drafting in a word-processing program, you can bold-face or highlight main causes and effects. You can then cut and paste to make sure that sentences connecting them appear in the right order.

Student Work
IN PROGRESS

Name: *Johnny Guo*
First Colony Middle School
Sugar Land, TX

Connecting the Steps

Here is how Johnny marked a paragraph of his essay to check the logic of his cause-and-effect sequences.

CAUSE
An increase in the global temperature would change
CAUSE/EFFECT
climates everywhere. The polar icecaps would begin to melt, leading to a rising sea level. This is dangerous. Many islands such as those in the Caribbean would be submerged if the icecaps melted. The water would cover existing shorelines, causing many coastal cities to be submerged. Millions of
EFFECT
lives would be lost.

184 • Cause-and-Effect Essay

⏱ TIME SAVERS!

📋 Writing Support Transparencies

Use the transparencies for Chapter 9 to facilitate teaching of strategies.

🕐 TIME AND RESOURCE MANAGER

Resources
Print: Writing Support Transparency 9-F
Technology: Writing Lab CD-ROM, Exposition: Making Connections

In-Depth Coverage	Accelerated Pace
• Cover pp. 184–187 in class. • Work through the revising strategies with the entire class. • Do the Grammar in Your Writing activity on p. 186.	• Assign pp. 184–187 for independent student review. • Have students revise their cause-and-effect essays independently.

Revising Your Paragraphs

Every time you indent a new paragraph, you are signaling your reader, "Here comes a new idea!" This signal helps readers follow your essay. They can still grow confused, however, if you do not tell them what the new idea is. For this reason, many writers begin paragraphs with a topic sentence.

Topic Sentences

A **topical paragraph** is a paragraph that explains or illustrates one main idea. A sentence that states the main idea of a paragraph is called a **topic sentence.** In many cases, it is best to include a topic sentence in the paragraph. Readers will then know exactly what new idea the paragraph discusses.

PARAGRAPH: I didn't waterproof my treehouse. During the summer there were heavy thunderstorms. The rain started the wood rotting. When my cousin Sid climbed into the treehouse, you could feel some of the nails pulling free from the tree branch. One night, the treehouse finally fell to the ground.

TOPIC
SENTENCE: There were a few causes leading to my treehouse disaster.

▶ **REVISION STRATEGY**
Finding the "Tug"

Reread each paragraph in your draft. Decide which idea in the paragraph "tugs" at your attention. You can find this "tug" by imagining that someone has asked you, "What is this paragraph about?" Your answer would name the tug.

Summarize this tug in a few words in the margin. Then, check whether your paragraph includes a sentence that expresses this idea clearly. If not, craft a topic sentence explaining the tug.

ⓠ Learn More

To learn more about the different kinds of paragraphs and the placement of topic sentences, see Chapter 3.

◀ **Critical Viewing**
Write a short description of this picture. Then, write a topic sentence that identifies the "tug" of the group of sentences. **[Apply]**

Revising • 185

Step-by-Step Teaching Guide

Revising: Finding the "Tug"

1. Go over the procedure for finding the "tug" or topic sentences in students' paragraphs. First, direct students to read their essays paragraph by paragraph.

2. For each paragraph, ask them to jot down a phrase in the margin that sums up what the paragraph is all about. After that, they should check whether they have included a topic sentence that expresses the main idea clearly. If they have, they should go on to the next paragraph.

3. Students should add topic sentences to paragraphs that lack them. Then they can proceed to a task that may be more difficult—clarifying any unclear topic sentences.

Critical Viewing

Apply Students' descriptions and topic sentences will vary.

☑ **ONGOING ASSESSMENT: Monitor and Reinforce**

If students are having difficulty writing or clarifying topic sentences, try one of the following options.

Option 1 Have students work in pairs. Students should take turns reading aloud paragraphs for which they are having trouble writing topic sentences and brainstorm topic sentences together.	**Option 2** Ask small groups of students to browse through a history or science textbook to practice finding the "tug" in a paragraph or two. If they come up with different "tug" words, have them discuss their rationales for their choices.

Step-by-Step Teaching Guide

Revising: Circling Verbs in Different Tenses

Students who are writing about something that already happened (for example, a hurricane that caused various kinds of damage) will probably use past tense most frequently. If they are writing about something that has yet to happen (for example, the possible effects of further global warming), the main verb tense will be the future tense. Direct students to circle the verbs that differ from the principal verb tense in their essay.

Step-by-Step Teaching Guide

Grammar in Your Writing: Verb Tense

Students can mix and match verb tenses in their essays. A cause in the past can lead to an effect in the present: *Because so many manatees have died, there are few left today.* A cause in the present can lead to an effect in the future: *If we do not help the manatees today, there will be none left tomorrow.*

Find It in Your Reading

Ross Bankson used the present and past tenses to show how the situation today has roots in the past.

Find It in Your Writing

Have students reread the sentences in their essays in which they identified verb tenses. Do they need to correct any verbs? Students may want to read questionable sentences aloud. If the verbs sound right, chances are good that they are correct.

Customize for
ESL Students

Students learning English may find verb tenses difficult, as English has many irregular verbs. Have students work together to practice the essential irregular verbs *be, do,* and *have.* Write the first, second, and third person of these verbs in the present, past, and future tenses on the board. Students should practice reciting sentences to each other in the three persons and tenses.

Revising Your Sentences
Check Relationships Between Verb Tenses

In a cause-and-effect relationship, one event occurs after another. Changing verb tenses can make this sequence clear:

EVENTS AT
DIFFERENT TIMES: Because I **ran** over a nail with my bike, *(past)*

I **will not be able** to go on the bike trip. *(future)*

Using different tenses can also lead to errors, however. Use the following strategy to avoid mistakes in tense.

▶ **REVISION STRATEGY**
Circling Verbs in Different Tenses

Reread your draft, following these steps:

1. Identify your main tense (the tense of most of your verbs).
2. Circle any verbs in a different tense.
3. Review circled verbs. Are you using them to show a sequence? If not, change them to your main tense.

Grammar in Your Writing
Verb Tense

Verbs are words that express actions or conditions. An action may happen (or a condition may apply) in the past, the present, or the future. To express the time of an action or condition, verbs take different forms, called *tenses.* **Present tense** indicates an action or condition in the present. It may also indicate an action or condition that occurs regularly. **Past tense** shows that an action took place in the past. **Future tense** shows that an action will occur in the future.

PAST: My family and I **rode** our bikes on a hundred-mile trip this summer.

PRESENT: I **am riding** my bike right now.
              I **ride** my bike to school when the weather is good.

FUTURE: We **will ride** our bikes to the mall this weekend.

Find It in Your Reading   Review "Gentle Giants in Trouble" by Ross Bankson on page 176, and identify the tense of the first ten verbs. How many tenses has the writer used? Why has he used these tenses?

Find It in Your Writing   Review the first five verbs in your draft. Identify the tense of each verb and explain why you have used that tense. Correct any errors in tense that you find.

To learn more about verb tenses, see Chapter 22.

186 • Cause-and-Effect Essay

☑ **ONGOING ASSESSMENT: Prerequisite Skills**

If students have difficulty with verb tenses, you may find it helpful to review the following to assure coverage of prerequisite knowledge.

In the Textbook	Print Resources	Technology
Using Verbs, pp. 478–505	Grammar Exercise Workbook, pp. 87–106	Language Lab CD-ROM, Using Verbs; On-Line Exercise Bank, Sections 22.1–3

Revising Your Word Choice
Use Accurate Verbs

Good writers are careful with their selection of verbs because they know that verbs have the power to help readers visualize actions. Use the following strategy to help you choose strong verbs.

▶ **REVISION STRATEGY**
Highlighting Verbs

Highlight the verbs in several sentences in your draft. Revise any that are not specific enough to express your meaning clearly. For example, "Sarah went to school this morning" is clear. However, if you picture her moving slowly and dragging her feet as she goes, the verb *went* is not precise enough. Changing the sentence to "Sarah trudged to school this morning" gives readers a clearer sense of Sarah's mood.

Peer Review

Once you've finished revising on your own, enlist the help of classmates in making additional revisions. Use the following strategy:

Summarizing

Form a group of four or five classmates. Read your piece aloud. Pause for one minute. (Keep an eye on the clock—a minute can pass very slowly when you are anxious!) Read aloud again. During this second reading, listeners should focus on what they think is the main idea of your essay. When you have finished reading, each of your listeners should jot down

- the main idea.
- one word that expresses the main idea.
- a synonym for this word.
- a sentence that summarizes the main idea clearly.

Have your peers either give you their notes or read them to you. Check to see that their interpretation of your main idea matches what you had in mind. If not, revise your introduction to state the main idea of your essay more clearly.

▼ **Critical Viewing**
Write a sentence or two describing events that might have led to this scene. Use accurate verbs. **[Hypothesize, Apply]**

Revising • 187

Step-by-Step Teaching Guide

Revising: Highlighting Verbs

1. To demonstrate the importance of specific verbs to understanding, ask students to sketch what they imagine when you say the following sentence: *The dog made noise.*

2. Have several students display their drawings. Do the drawings vary? Was it easy for students to figure out what to draw? Help students understand that "made noise" is not very specific and therefore difficult to bring to mind and hard to draw.

3. Do the exercise again with this sentence: *The dog bared its teeth and growled.* Was it easier for students to create vivid pictures in their minds with this sentence than with the previous one? Why?

Step-by-Step Teaching Guide

Peer Review

1. Before groups begin the peer review activity, review the summarizing strategy.

2. Remind students to provide criticism in a constructive manner. Students should follow the strategy and not simply say "Your main idea doesn't make sense."

Critical Viewing

Hypothesize; Apply Students may say that the man lost his keys this morning or that he received a phone call on his way out of his apartment which made him late for his bus.

STANDARDIZED TEST PREPARATION WORKSHOP

Using Verbs Standardized test questions may require that students recognize synonyms for verbs. Ask students to identify the verb that is the best replacement for the underlined word in the following sentence.

The pup <u>tumbled</u> down the hill.

A ran　　C fell
B hopped　　D jumped

Item **C**, *fell*, has the closest meaning to the verb *tumbled*.

187

Grammar in Your Writing: Using Prepositions

1. Before students begin writing sentences with the prepositions listed in the textbook, explain that a preposition links a noun or pronoun to the rest of a sentence. A prepositional phrase is a preposition, its noun or pronoun, and any modifiers.

2. Have students think of some prepositions not mentioned, such as *to, for, through,* and *by.* Then have volunteers make up prepositional phrases with these prepositions.

Find It in Your Reading

Prepositional phrases include *in danger* (relates *danger* to *manatees*), *because of people* (names cause of danger), and *by pollution* (names source of damage).

Find It in Your Writing

If students choose to keep two prepositions, have them be prepared to explain their reasoning.

Customize for *ESL Students*

To practice using prepositions, students can do an activity that requires pennies and a stack of books. Students take turns moving the pennies and books and describing what they are doing: a penny might be placed *in front of* the stack, *between* two books, *behind* the books, *inside* a book, *under* the stack, and so on. To make sure students use a variety of prepositions, provide a list of prepositions and prepositional phrases you want them to practice.

9.5 Editing and Proofreading

Finally, review your work carefully for errors in grammar, usage, mechanics, and spelling. Focus extra attention on your use of prepositions.

Focusing on Prepositions

Review the prepositions you've used in your essay. Check to see that they express the exact relationship you intended. For example, you might be

- *in the truck* (ready to leave on a trip).
- *on the truck* (checking to see that the load is safely tied).
- *under the truck* (looking for an oil leak).

In each case, the preposition helps readers to picture the relationship between you and the truck. Check your draft to make sure you have used the right prepositions to give readers a good picture. In addition, make sure you have not used two prepositions where one will do.

Grammar in Your Writing
Using Prepositions

A **preposition** is a word that relates a noun or pronoun to another element of the sentence. A number of prepositions are listed below:

about	against	among	before	between	beyond
down	in	inside	inside of	into	off
on	onto	out of	outside	within	

Do not use two prepositions where one will do.

AVOIDABLE: He climbed **up on** the truck.

PREFERRED: He climbed **onto** the truck.

Find It in Your Reading Identify three prepositions in "Gentle Giants in Trouble" by Ross Bankson on page 176. What relationships do they show?

Find It in Your Writing Review your essay, and underline the first ten prepositions. If you have used two where one will do, replace them with a single preposition.

To learn more about prepositions, see Chapter 17.

188 • Cause-and-Effect Essay

⏱ TIME AND RESOURCE MANAGER

Resources
Print: Scoring Rubrics on Transparency, Chapter 9; Writing Assessment: Scoring Rubric and Scoring Models for Cause-and-Effect Essay
Technology: Writing Lab CD-ROM, Exposition: Making Connections

In-Depth Coverage	Accelerated Pace
• Cover pp. 188–191 in class. • Have students edit and proofread their essays in class. • Review the Rubric for Self-Assessment. • Students present their final drafts.	• Assign pp. 188–191 for independent student review. • Have students edit and proofread their cause-and-effect essays independently. • Students present their final drafts.

9.6 Publishing and Presenting

Building Your Portfolio

Here are some ideas for sharing your essay:

1. **Create a Class Anthology** Work with a group of classmates to create a class anthology of cause-and-effect essays. Work together to create a table of contents, a cover, and illustrations to accompany each essay.

2. **Organize a Group Reading** As a class, read and discuss your essays. Allow time for questions after each reading. Encourage listeners to come up with additional causes and effects related to each topic.

Reflecting on Your Writing

Jot down a few notes about writing your essay. Start by answering these questions:

- What new information did you learn about your topic?

- What was the biggest problem you encountered while writing this essay? How did you resolve it?

 Internet Tip

To read a cause-and-effect essay scored according to this rubric, visit **www.phschool.com**

Rubric for Self-Assessment

Evaluate your cause-and-effect essay using the following criteria:

	Score 4	Score 3	Score 2	Score 1
Audience and Purpose	Consistently targets an audience through word choice and details; clearly identifies purpose in introduction	Targets an audience through most word choice and details; identifies purpose in introduction	Misses a target audience by including a wide range of word choice and details; presents purpose unclearly	Addresses no specific audience or purpose
Organization	Uses a clear, consistent organizational strategy to show cause and effect	Uses a clear organizational strategy with occasional inconsistencies to show cause and effect	Uses an inconsistent organizational strategy; creates illogical presentation of causes and effects	Demonstrates a lack of organizational strategy; creates a confusing presentation
Elaboration	Successfully links causes with effects; fully elaborates connections among ideas	Links causes with effects; elaborates connections among most ideas	Links some causes with some effects; elaborates connections among some ideas	Develops and elaborates no links between causes and effects
Use of Language	Chooses clear transitions to convey ideas; presents very few mechanical errors	Uses transitions to convey ideas; presents few mechanical errors	Misses some opportunities for transitions; presents many mechanical errors	Demonstrates poor use of language; presents many mechanical errors

Publishing and Presenting • 189

☑ **ONGOING ASSESSMENT: Assess Mastery**

Use one of the following options to assess final drafts of students' cause-and-effect essays.

Self-Assessment Ask students to score their essay using the rubric provided on this page. Then have students write three tips for writers of cause-and-effect essays.

Teacher Assessment You may want to use the rubric and the scoring models provided in Writing Assessment, Copper Level, to score the cause-and-effect essays.

Publishing and Presenting: Create a Class Anthology

1. Interested students may form a committee to put together a class anthology of cause-and-effect essays.

2. The committee should gather essays from all contributors and figure out a sensible organization for the anthology. They may want to organize the essays into sections, such as natural phenomena, American history, and so on.

3. Then volunteers can write a table of contents, design a cover, and draw illustrations.

4. Place the class cause-and-effect essay anthology in the classroom library where students can consult it the next time they write about causes and effects.

ASSESS

Assessment

Teaching Resources: Scoring Rubric on Transparency 9; Formal Assessment, Chapter 9

1. Display the Scoring Rubric transparency and review the criteria in class.

2. Before students proceed with self-assessment, you may wish to review the Final Draft of the Student Work in Progress on pages 190–191. Have students score the Final Draft in one or more of the rubric categories. For example, how would students score the essay in terms of audience and purpose?

3. In addition to student self-assessment, you may wish to use the following assessment options.

   - score student essays yourself, using the rubric and scoring models from Writing Assessment.

   - review the Standardized Test Preparation Workshop on pages 196–197 and have students respond to a writing prompt within a time limit.

   - administer the Chapter 9 Test from Formal Assessment in Teaching Resources to assess students' grasp of concepts presented.

Teaching From the Final Draft

1. Work with students to analyze these features that make "Saving Our Air" a good cause-and-effect essay.

   • The introductory paragraph clearly states the topic: the effects of air pollution.

   • Each following paragraph covers one effect.

   • The final paragraph presents ways to solve the problem introduced in the first paragraph.

2. Have students identify the effect of air pollution discussed in each paragraph. Are there any sentences that are unclear? Can they think of ways to clarify these sentences?

3. Have students read their essays once again. Has their analysis of Johnny's essay inspired students to make changes in their own essays?

Critical Viewing

Speculate Students may say that using solar panels would cut down on the amount of industrial pollution.

9.7 *Student Work*
IN PROGRESS

FINAL DRAFT

Saving Our Air

Johnny Guo
First Colony Middle School
Sugar Land, Texas

With all the breakthroughs in this century, none has come close to solving the problem of air pollution. It has threatened us for the last 100 years. I believe that it's essential that we act now. To see why, just think about the effects of air pollution.

You have probably heard about the ozone layer, and how it protects us from harmful UV (ultraviolet) rays from the sun. What you may not know, however, is that fluorocarbons (found in aerosol-spray containers), cars, factories, and chemical plants all cause the ozone layer to deteriorate at an alarming pace. Some studies show that pollution may have caused a 5.5 percent decrease in ozone over a 24-year period. That is hazardous to

▲ **Critical Viewing**
Solar panels like the ones above generate electricity from sunlight. How might the use of such panels affect scenes like the one on the left? **[Speculate]**

In his introduction, Johnny identifies his topic, the effects of air pollution, and his purpose—to motivate readers to participate in a solution.

everyone's health and to the planet. Scientists predict that ozone layer damage will cause increases in skin cancer and cataracts (an eye disease) in both humans and animals. In addition, it will hurt certain crops and plankton, both important to the food web.

Air pollution may also lead to dangerous changes in the greenhouse effect. The greenhouse effect prevents Earth from being a frozen planet. Gases such as carbon dioxide, methane, and water vapor absorb energy from the sun and keep the planet warm. However, carbon dioxide has increased because of burning fossil fuels such as oil, gas, and coal. This causes more heat from the atmosphere to be trapped, resulting in global warming.

An increase in the global temperature would change climates everywhere. The polar icecaps would begin to melt, leading to a rising sea level. This is dangerous. Many islands such as those in the Caribbean would be submerged if the icecaps melted. The water would cover existing shorelines, causing many coastal cities to be submerged. Millions of lives would be lost.

These floods would also hurt people and animals in other ways as well. Lost land means less area for growing crops to feed both people and farm animals. In addition, lost land means lost habitats. Take away habitats and animals will die. Loss of habitat can endanger the survival of an entire species.

The disappearance of any species has many effects. The extinction of simple things like insects or worms can hurt the species that feed on insects or worms. To preserve the food chain, we must protect the ozone layer. To protect the ozone, we must start thinking about what we put into the air.

We can all fight air pollution. We can reduce the number of miles our family drives a car. We can walk, take public transportation, or ride our bikes instead of asking our parents to drive us short distances. We can help our parents carpool so they don't drive all over town. We can turn off lights and television sets when they are not in use.

A little help from each of us could add up to a lot. By caring for Earth, we can guarantee the children of tomorrow a safe place to live and a world they can love.

To organize his essay clearly, Johnny addresses each major effect of air pollution in turn. For each major cause, he explains the chain of causes and effects that leads to it.

▼ **Critical Viewing** Explain how this man may be contributing to an improvement in air quality. **[Connect]**

Student Work in Progress • 191

Integrating Viewing and Representing Skills

To demonstrate their understanding of "Saving Our Air" visually, have students incorporate the important information from the essay into anti-air pollution posters. Before they begin sketching their ideas, explain that posters require strong graphic elements because they need to be "read" at a glance. Challenge students to come up with graphic symbols (logos) that stand for the various effects of air pollution mentioned in the essay.

Critical Viewing

Connect Students may say that by skating to work (and not using any type of transportation that involves pollution from engine exhaust), the man is helping to cut down on pollution.

Lesson Objectives

1. To write a documentary video script appropriate to audience and purpose.

2. To organize and present information gathered from multiple sources.

3. To use writing processes to develop and revise drafts.

4. To publish and present a video documentary script to an audience.

Step-by-Step Teaching Guide

Documentary Video Script

Teaching Resources: Writing Support Transparency 9-G; Writing Support Activity Book, 9-2

1. Bring in a video tape of a short news segment that serves as a cause-and-effect explanation. Show it to students and ask them to identify the elements of the story. Who introduces it? How is information given to the audience? What is the main idea of the story? Which cause and which effect are the focus of the story?

2. Ask student volunteers to read the model script, "What's the Damage?" on the next page. Point out how each of the elements the class identified in the video sample is handled in a script. For example, highlight the listing of camera shots and their description. If students still feel uncertain about how to prepare a script, work with the class on turning the first few frames of the sample video segment into a script.

3. Encourage students to think about issues and stories that they would like to see presented in video documentary form on television. Tell them that conducting research for video documentaries is similar to conducting research for cause-and-effect essays. Point out, however, that if a particular interview subject is unavailable they can write a fictional set of responses. Remind them that their objective is to use the video documentary format to present a cause-and-effect explanation to viewers.

continued

Connected Assignment
Documentary Video Script

You don't just have to read cause-and-effect explanations: You can also watch them on television. Television documentaries feature **cause-and-effect explanations**—explanations showing how one event or situation leads to another. The writing for these shows does not appear on screen. Instead, it exists as a script.

A **documentary video script** outlines the words that are spoken on a television documentary. Some of these words are recorded from interviews. Others are spoken by a reporter or narrator. A video script also includes directions to the narrator, the camera operators, sound and lighting engineers, and the editor who will put the video together.

Write a documentary video script. Use the suggestions that follow to guide you.

Prewriting Watch a television newsmagazine show to see how documentary segments are organized.

Structure The following structure is common:

1. The anchor or host of the show introduces the segment.
2. The reporter who investigated the story gives a more detailed introduction.
3. The segment then alternates among
   • scenes from interviews,
   • scenes of events or places illustrating facts in the story, and
   • more scenes of the reporter giving explanations.
4. At the end, the reporter "wraps it up" with a conclusion.

Choose a Topic After taking notes on a television documentary, choose a topic that interests you—for example, a recent natural disaster.

Gather Details Next, conduct an investigation. Do research using various sources, such as newspapers and the Internet. Focus on the questions: What causes led to the event or situation in my documentary? What effects does it or will it have?

Then, if possible, conduct interviews with experts or eyewitnesses. (If you cannot perform actual interviews, write a fictional one based on what you learn in other sources.) Use an audio or video recorder, if available, to capture interviews and scenes illustrating your story.

▲ **Critical Viewing**
Explain what role news anchors such as these have in presenting a documentary. [**Connect**]

192 • Cause-and-Effect Essay

Critical Viewing

Connect Students may observe that news anchors provide an introduction to or an overview of news stories. Elicit that they may give a brief synopsis of the story, explaining both cause and effect in the process, in order to grab viewers' interest.

Documentary On: _____

SHOT 1	SHOT 2
Visual: *Host of show at desk.* **Camera Angle/Movement:** *Camera cuts to close-up of her face.* **Narration:** *If you've had "gnawing" doubts about your dog's health, the next story will interest you.* **Other Sound:** *Theme music fades as narration begins.*	**Visual:** _____ **Camera Angle/Movement:**__ **Narration:** _____ **Other Sound:** _____

Drafting To organize the facts, use a graphic organizer like the one shown. Then, include these elements:

• narration (interviews and the reporter's commentary)

• instruction for the use of visuals, including camera angles

• instructions for the use of sound (sound effects and music)

Revising and Editing Read your script aloud. Mark places where ideas seem disconnected or where transitions are not smooth. Revise to make the script flow better.

Publishing and Presenting If you have access to video equipment, produce your segment and show it to the class.

MODEL

What's the Damage?
News Documentary Segment

In this passage, notice how speakers are identified and how directions for visuals are presented.

[SHOT 10: Reporter standing before ruined house.]

REPORTER: As you can see, this was no small earthquake. Experts estimate that, by Tuesday morning, $10 million dollars worth of property had been damaged. The reason, they say, . . .

[CUT TO SHOT 11: Professor Mendicino in his office, shot from mid-distance.]

REPORTER [voice-over]: . . . was poor planning.

PROF. MENDICINO: . . . those buildings were built right over a major fault line.

[CAMERA MOVES IN ON MENDICINO'S FACE.]

Connected Assignment: Documentary Video Script • **193**

4. Ask for a volunteer to share a topic idea with the class. Display the transparency and give students copies of the blank organizer. Work with the class to begin filling out the graphic organizer transparency for the student volunteer's documentary topic. Encourage students to fill out the blank organizer for their own topic ideas, then have them use these notes to draft a script.

5. Review the model with students to help them understand the elements of a good script. The script is like a blueprint that contains all the necessary information to make shooting the material easier.

6. When students are finished revising and editing their scripts, encourage them to consider producing the scripts if they have access to video equipment. Suggest that they could also act out the scripts in front of the class.

Lesson Objectives

1. To interpret a variety of multimedia texts.
2. To analyze information as presented in various media.
3. To take notes from relevant sources.
4. To write a journal based on multimedia research.

Step-by-Step Teaching Guide

Interpreting Texts Using Varied Means

1. Choose one of the Spotlight elements for class discussion, or have students work individually or in groups on the element of their choice. Give students the initiative to find the necessary books, videotapes, or pictures.

2. Bring in a segment from Charlie Chaplin's movie *The Gold Rush* or another silent movie. Discuss with students the limitations and strengths of silent movies. Point out that silent film directors and actors had to depend on the visual to communicate information.

3. Ask students if they have ever read a story by Jack London or Will Hobbs. Encourage volunteers to briefly describe the stories they read. Interested students can choose to read one story by either author.

Viewing and Representing

Activity Help students find videos, books, and images about the causes and effects of the Klondike Gold Rushes. Encourage them to present their findings in a fictionalized journal with accompanying images to support their character's story, as well as to help their audience understand the challenges faced by this person.

Spotlight on the Humanities

Interpreting Texts Using Varied Means

Focus on Film: *The Gold Rush*

If you were writing a cause-and-effect paper on the Klondike Gold Rushes of 1897 and 1898, you might notice a surprising effect: The people who hurried west to find gold inspired many short stories, poems, and even movies.

Charlie Chaplin, one of the most beloved film personalities of all time, brought the Gold Rush to the screen in 1925. His film *The Gold Rush* tells the hilarious tale of a lone prospector who ventures into Alaska looking for gold. Along the way, he gets mixed up with some tough, burly characters and falls in love with the beautiful Georgia. Chaplin not only wrote and directed the film, but also starred as the charming, zany prospector.

Literature Connection Many authors of the day wrote about the experiences of those who searched for gold. In 1897, author Jack London (1876–1916) joined the rush to the Klondike. He did not turn up much gold, but he made another valuable find—he came to know the people of the Gold Rush. They served as models for his hard-driving heroes. His short stories of the Yukon portray the brutal, vigorous life of the Far North. London was one of the most popular short story writers of his day. He was one of the few writers at the time who were able to support themselves solely through writing.

The Gold Rush continues to inspire writers. In his 1999 novel *Jason's Gold*, author Will Hobbs (1947–   ) tells the story of a 15-year-old boy named Jason who embarks on a 10,000-mile journey to the Klondike to strike it rich. Along the way, he meets the not-yet-famous Jack London, and plenty of life-threatening adventures.

Cause-and-Effect Writing Activity: Gold Rush Journal

At your local library or on the Internet, research the causes and effects of the Klondike Gold Rushes. Then, write three entries from the journal of someone who experienced these events of the time. In one, record the person's decision to move. In the others, record some of the effects of the decision: What happens on the trip out west? Does the person find gold or go bust? Include details showing the thoughts and feelings of your character.

194 • Cause-and-Effect Essay

Charlie Chaplin in *The Gold Rush*

Jacket Illustration © 1999 by Derek James

▲ **Critical Viewing** Compare the two ideas of life in the Klondike presented in these images. **[Compare and Contrast]**

Critical Viewing

Compare and Contrast Students may note that Charlie Chaplin looks cold and worried or scared in the first image, while the man and dog in the second image look well-prepared and confident about being in the wintery landscape. Ask them to guess at some of the causes and effects behind the attitudes of the characters portrayed in each image.

Media and Technology Skills

Analyzing Images

Focus on Visual Arts: Photographs

One effect of a good photograph is to communicate information. It shows viewers what a person, event, or place looks like. A photograph can also shape your ideas about its subject. Learn about the elements that give an image its special meaning.

Think About It An effective photograph uses these elements:

- **A central point of interest** Most photographs focus on one main action, object, or person. In the photograph shown, the man's predicament, including the water and the telephone booth, is the focus.

- **Composition** The composition of a photograph involves the placement of objects and the use of space and of light. For instance, in the photograph shown:

  ▸ the telephone booth and the man inside are centered in the image.

  ▸ in the background, you can see the floodwaters, which helps you understand what is going on.

  ▸ the lighting is natural, so the photograph shows just what the weather looked like that day.

- **Emotional impact** By choosing the proper central point of interest, and by creating the right composition, a photographer can lead viewers to an emotional response. For instance, you may have laughed at the attempt by the man in this photograph to stay dry. You may also have sympathized with his difficulties.

Apply It Look through a newspaper or magazine for a photograph that catches your eye. Then, using the chart below, take notes on the photograph. Would you have chosen a different image for the story? Explain why or why not.

Source of Photograph: _____

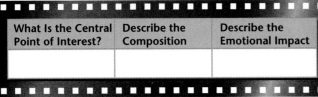

What Is the Central Point of Interest?	Describe the Composition	Describe the Emotional Impact

Media and Technology Skills • 195

Types of Photographs

- Candid—shows natural, unposed behavior
- Documentary—records an event
- Portrait—portrays people
- Abstract—evokes mood
- Landscape—shows a place

▼ **Critical Viewing** Describe your reaction to this image. **[Relate]**

Critical Viewing

Relate Students may consider this situation frightening or funny, or both. Ask them how they think the photographer got this picture. Have students guess what might have happened in the moments just after the photograph was taken.

▶ **Lesson Objectives**

1. To analyze how photographs communicate information.
2. To examine how visual techniques can be used to create an emotional response in viewers.
3. To evaluate the effectiveness of photographs used to add information to written texts.

Step-by-Step Teaching Guide

Analyzing Images

Teaching Resources: Writing Support Transparency 9-H; Writing Support Activity Book 9-3

1. Tell students that it has been said that a picture is worth a thousand words. Ask them whether or not they agree with this statement. Show the class an image from a newspaper or magazine and ask them to guess what is happening in the photograph. Lead a brief discussion about the kinds of information and meaning that a photograph can and cannot communicate when presented without explanatory text.

2. Review the elements of effective photography with students using the photograph provided as a model.

3. Ask students to think about other ways in which the photographer might have presented this image. For example, how would a close-up of the man's face have changed the meaning or focus of the photograph?

4. Using the list of effective photographic elements, have students imagine other variations on the photograph in their books. For example, what if the flood waters couldn't be seen in the background or the lighting were much darker?

5. Display the transparency and give students copies of the blank organizer. Provide a sample photograph and take notes about it with the class using the transparency.

195

1. To write an informative essay that describes and explains.

2. To develop writing by categorizing ideas and using effective transitions.

3. To use prewriting strategies to generate ideas.

4. To demonstrate control over grammatical elements.

Step-by-Step Teaching Guide

Cause-and-Effect Writing Prompts

1. Emphasize to students that when writing cause-and-effect essays in standardized tests they should clearly identify all the causes and their effects before they start writing. If the source of their essay is an article, as it is in the Sample Writing Situation, point out that they can identify the causes and effects by circling and connecting them in the article.

2. Point out that they may have to limit the number of causes-and-effects they can write about if they are taking a timed test. Explain that narrowing down their topic and organizing their main points carefully will save them time and help them remain focused as they write. Point out that they have been instructed to choose three main causes to write about in the Sample Writing Situation.

3. Reassure students that while neatness counts, examiners understand that time constraints prevent most standardized tests of this kind from being perfect finished products. Emphasize, however, that following the rules of grammar, punctuation, and spelling will make their cause-and-effect explanations clearer for their audience.

continued

Standardized Test Preparation Workshop

Using Cause-and-Effect Writing for Expository Writing Prompts

Some writing prompts on standardized tests require you to show the relationships between causes and their effects. You will be evaluated on the ability you show to

- respond directly to the prompt.

- make your writing thoughtful and interesting.

- organize ideas so they are clear and easy to follow.

- develop your ideas thoroughly by using appropriate details and precise language.

- stay focused on your purpose by making sure that each sentence contributes to your composition as a whole.

- use correct spelling, capitalization, punctuation, grammar, usage, and sentence structure.

Following is an example of an expository writing prompt. Respond using the suggestions on the following page. When taking a timed test, you should plan how much time you will devote to each part of the writing process. The clocks on the next page show the suggested percentage of time to devote to prewriting, drafting, revising and editing, and proofreading.

Test Tips

- Make sure that you get enough rest the night before the test.
- Come prepared with pencils, pens, and scrap paper.

Sample Writing Situation

West Indian manatees are not hunted by other animals, but they have come to be endangered. Read "Gentle Giants in Trouble" by Ross Bankson on page 176, in which he explains the causes of the manatee's problem. Then, respond to the following prompt:

Explain three main causes for the endangerment of manatees. In your response, use details from Ross Bankson's article.

✍ TEST-TAKING TIP

Point out that in the sample writing situation they are instructed to write about only three main causes of the manatee's problem. Explain that the narrow focus of the test question can be an advantage in two ways.

First of all, in most situations, the test question matches the chosen article closely. Therefore

they can guess, in this example, that the article is probably structured around three main causes.

Also, by identifying three main causes, usually the ones with the most supporting evidence in the article, they are demonstrating an understanding of the subject to test evaluators.

Prewriting

Allow close to one fourth of your time for prewriting.

Review Your Source Read "Gentle Giants in Trouble" by Ross Bankson on page 176. Each time he introduces a main cause for the endangerment of manatees, write it down. When you are done, review his essay to make sure you have correctly identified the three main causes.

Use a Cluster Diagram To create a cluster diagram, circle each cause you have noted. Then, review Bankson's essay. Next to each main cause in your notes, jot down related events and situations. Circle each new item and connect it with a line to the related main cause.

Review your diagram. Number all of the events associated with a main cause in order. If two or more take place at the same time, number each with the same number.

Drafting

Allow almost half of your time for drafting.

Organize Details The prompt asks you to discuss three main causes. Make an outline of these three causes, jotting down related events under each. Use the numbers on your cluster diagram to put events in chronological order—the order in which they occurred.

Elaborate As you write the body of your response, refer to your outline and explain how each main cause contributed to the manatee's problem. Make sure to explain the sequence of events that leads from a main cause to its effect on the manatees. Also, explain what other events added to each main cause.

Revising, Editing, and Proofreading

Allow almost one fourth of your time to revise and edit. Use the last few minutes to proofread your work.

Use Transitions Review your draft. Where needed, add transitional words, such as *as a result, because of, before,* and *after,* to indicate the cause-and-effect relationships between events.

Make Corrections Review your draft for errors in spelling, grammar, and punctuation. When making changes, neatly cross out text that you want eliminated and place it in brackets. Use a caret (^) to indicate the places at which you would like to add words.

4. As students review and revise their essays, encourage them to look for clear cause-and-effect explanations in their writing. Do the causes and effects match up? Have they explained the main points clearly? Finally, have they checked their drafts for grammar, punctuation, and spelling?

Customize for
Less Advanced Students

Students struggling to read the article and follow its most basic meaning may struggle in a high pressure situation such as the taking of a standardized test. Remind them to look for help with their responses in the original writing prompt. Tell students that they can underline words and phrases in the prompt that will help them look for specific information in the article. In the Sample Writing Situation, for example, the prompt begins by pointing out that the manatee is not hunted by other animals, but that it is endangered nonetheless. The phrase "not hunted by other animals" may give them a clue about what to look for in the article.

Customize for
Gifted and Talented Students

Tell students that developing cause-and-effect essays is an excellent way of practicing how to organize their writing. Point out that many essays and newspaper articles are written around the basic structure of a cause-and-effect argument. Ask students to find one such newspaper article or essay and to identify the main causes and effects analyzed by its author. Have them present their article to the class with a summary of the causes and effects presented in it.

In-Depth Lesson Plan

	LESSON FOCUS	PRINT AND MEDIA RESOURCES
DAY 1	**Introduction to How-To Essays** Students learn key elements of How-To essays and analyze the Model From Literature (pp. 198–201).	*Writers at Work* **Videotape**, Exposition: Giving Information *Writing Lab* **CD-ROM**, Exposition: Giving Information
DAY 2	**Prewriting** Students choose and narrow a topic, consider their audience and purpose, and gather information (pp. 202–205).	**Teaching Resources** *Writing Support Transparencies,* 10-A–C *Writing Lab* **CD-ROM**, Exposition: Giving Information
DAY 3	**Drafting** Students organize their ideas and write their first drafts (pp. 206–207).	**Teaching Resources** *Writing Support Transparencies,* 10-D–E *Writing Lab* **CD-ROM**, Exposition: Giving Information
DAY 4	**Revising** Students revise their drafts in terms of overall structure, paragraphs, sentences, and word choice (pp. 208–212).	**Teaching Resources** *Writing Support Transparencies,* 10-F–G *Writing Lab* **CD-ROM**, Exposition: Giving Information
DAY 5	**Editing and Proofreading; Publishing and Presenting** Students check their work for accuracy and correctness and present their final drafts (pp. 213–216).	**Teaching Resources** *Scoring Rubrics on Transparency,* Ch. 10; *Formal Assessment,* Ch. 10 *Writing Lab* **CD-ROM**, Exposition: Giving Information

Accelerated Lesson Plan

	LESSON FOCUS	PRINT AND MEDIA RESOURCES
DAY 1	**Drafting** Students review characteristics for how-to writing, select topics, and write drafts (pp. 198–207).	*Writers at Work* **Videotape**, Exposition: Giving Information *Writing Lab* **CD-ROM**, Exposition: Giving Information **Teaching Resources** *Writing Support Transparencies,* 10-A–E
DAY 2	**Revising to Presenting** Students work individually or with peers to revise, edit, and proofread their work for presentation (pp. 208–216).	**Teaching Resources** *Writing Support Transparencies,* 10-F–G; *Scoring Rubrics on Transparency,* Ch. 10; *Formal Assessment,* Ch. 10 *Writing Lab* **CD-ROM**, Exposition: Giving Information

Options for Adapting Lesson Plans

HOMEWORK

Have students complete any stage of the lesson for homework.

FEATURES

Extend coverage with the Connected Assignment (p. 217), Spotlight on the Humanities (p. 218), Media and Technology Skills (p. 219), and the Standardized Test Preparation Workshop (pp. 220–221).

TECHNOLOGY

Students can complete any stage of the lesson on computer. Have them print out their completed work.

INTEGRATED SKILLS COVERAGE

Integrating Grammar
Adverb Clauses and Phrases SE p. 211
Commas Separating Items in a Series SE p. 213

Reading/Writing Connection
Reading Strategy SE p. 200
Writing Application SE p. 201

Speaking and Listening
ATE p. 208

Technology
SE pp. 205, 219

Vocabulary
ATE p. 210

Workplace Skills
ATE pp. 201, 219

Viewing and Representing
Critical Viewing SE pp. 198, 200, 204, 209, 215, 217, 218
Viewing and Representing ATE p. 218

ASSESSMENT SUPPORT

Standardized Test Preparation Workshop, SE p. 220; ATE p. 212

Standardized Test Preparation Workbook, pp. 19–20

Scoring Rubrics on Transparency, Ch.10

Formal Assessment, Ch. 10

Writing Assessment and Portfolio Management

MEETING INDIVIDUAL NEEDS

Less Advanced Students ATE p. 204; See also Ongoing
Assessments ATE pp. 203, 207, 209, 211, 214
More Advanced Students ATE pp. 204, 221
ESL Students ATE pp. 201, 207, 221
Visual/Spatial Learners ATE p. 203
Logical/Mathematical Learners ATE p. 205
Bodily/Kinesthetic Learners ATE p. 216
Gifted/Talented Students ATE p. 216

BLOCK SCHEDULING

Pacing Suggestions
For 90-minute Blocks
• Have students complete the Prewriting and Drafting stages in
  a single period.
• Focus one class period on Revising and Editing and Publishing
  and Presenting. Allow at least 30 minutes for peer revision.

Resources for Varying Instruction
• *Writing Lab* **CD-ROM** If your students have access to
  hardware, a 90-minute block provides an ideal opportunity for
  students to work on computer.
• *Writers at Work* **Videotape** Show the Exposition: Giving
  Information segment in class.

Professional Development Support
• *How to Manage Instruction in the Block* This Teaching
  Resource provides management and activity suggestions.

MEDIA AND TECHNOLOGY

For the Student
• *Writing Lab* **CD-ROM**, Exposition: Giving Information

For the Teacher
• *Writers at Work* **Videotape**, Exposition: Giving Information
• *Resource Pro* **CD-ROM**

WRITING AND GRAMMAR WEB SITE

The Interactive Writing and Grammar Web site provides a wide
array of support for students, teachers and parents. Writing
support includes:

• Interactive revision checkers
• Scoring rubrics with complete models

www.phschool.com

LITERATURE CONNECTIONS

Related selections from *Prentice Hall Literature: Timeless Voices, Timeless Themes,* Copper:
"How to Write a Letter," Garrison Keillor, SE p. 201
"Old Ben," Jesse Stuart, SE p. 203

▶ *Lesson Objectives*

1. To recognize the distinguishing features of a how-to essay.

2. To identify author's purpose.

3. To generate and refine ideas and plans for writing by using the prewriting strategies Brainstorming and Blueprinting.

4. To write to explain how to do or make something.

5. To gather details for a how-to essay using the strategy Itemizing.

6. To develop a draft by organizing details in chronological order using a timeline.

7. To elaborate a draft by adding details using the Exploding the Moment strategy.

8. To revise a draft by adding an introduction and conclusion.

9. To revise a draft by adding transition words, varying sentence beginnings, and eliminating repeated words.

10. To proofread for punctuation.

11. To publish a how-to essay by giving a demonstration or creating a Web page.

12. To evaluate a how-to essay.

Critical Viewing

Speculate Students may say that following a recipe will help you avoid using the wrong ingredients or the wrong amounts of ingredients.

Chapter
10 **Exposition**
How-to Essay

▲ Critical Viewing
Name one mistake in baking that following a recipe can help you avoid. [Speculate]

How-to Essays in Everyday Life

When you were a young child, you learned how to do an amazing number of things—how to brush your teeth, how to tie your shoes, how to open a door, and so on. It was a very exciting time—especially when you learned to turn on a light! You probably clicked the switch over and over again.

Turning a light on and off gets a little boring after a while. You mastered one skill, however, that can never become dull: You learned to follow instructions. Using this skill, you can learn just about anything—how to program a VCR, play a new computer game, or make a chocolate cake. All you need is the right **how-to**—a user's guide, a manual, or a cookbook.

Now, you can learn a new skill—how to write your own how-to essay! It's even more exciting than turning the lights on.

⏱ **TIME AND RESOURCE MANAGER**

Resources
Technology: Writers at Work videotape

In-Depth Coverage	Accelerated Pace
• Cover pp. 198–201 in class. • Show How-to Essay section of the Writers at Work videotape. • Display various types of how-to writing, such as assembly instructions and users' manuals, and figure out together which directions are easiest to follow and why.	• Assign pp. 198–201 for independent student review. • Have students work independently in small groups to brainstorm for techniques and word choices they can use to clarify the steps in how-to essays.

What Is a How-to Essay?

Writing that explains or informs is called expository writing. A how-to essay is one common type of expository writing.

In a **how-to essay,** you explain how to do or make something. You break the process down into a series of logical steps. Then, you explain the steps in the order in which the reader should do them. The elements of a useful how-to essay include

- a specific result that the reader can make or accomplish by following the essay.
- a list of the materials needed.
- a series of steps explained in logical order.
- details that tell *when, how much, how often,* or *to what extent.*
- an introduction, a body, and a conclusion.

Types of How-to Essays

Following are some of the types of how-to essays you might write:

- How to do something ("How to Throw a Football")
- How to make something ("How to Bake a Cake")
- How to improve a skill ("How to Draw a Realistic Horse")
- How to achieve a desired effect ("How to Look Your Best")

Writers in ACTION

The ancient poet Horace (65–8 B.C.) wrote a how-to for writing poetry. He advised writers to make their work pleasing and even amusing, whatever their subject. The writer who succeeds, he said, does so "by delighting and instructing at the same time."

A how-to essay may be practical, but it need not be boring. Don't be afraid to add a little humor to your how-to essay!

PREVIEW *Student Work* IN PROGRESS

Jessica S. Lehman, a student at the Centre Learning Community in State College, Pennsylvania, wrote an essay giving directions. In this chapter, you will see how she used featured strategies to choose a topic, to gather details, to elaborate, and to revise. At the end of the chapter, you can read the final draft of Jessica's how-to essay.

How-to Essay • 199

PREPARE and ENGAGE

Interest GRABBER Invite volunteers to improvise a skit for the rest of the class. One person plays a Martian who has just landed on Earth and needs to learn the ways of Earthlings as quickly as possible. The second character tries to help the Martian by teaching him how to tie his shoes, use an ATM machine, order at a fast-food restaurant, or accomplish some other simple task. After the skit, discuss the reasons the Martian was or was not able to follow the directions.

Activate Prior Knowledge

It is a rare day when people don't read directions that explain how to do or make something. Ask students to recall directions that were easy to follow and give reasons why the directions were particularly clear. Then have them read the elements of a how-to essay listed on the page and compare the elements with their own ideas.

More About the Writer

Horace was a famous and influential Latin poet, whose benefactor Maecenas gave him a farm where Horace spent much of his later life writing about the beauty of the natural world. In ancient Rome, poets were respected. "If you include me among the lyric poets," Horace wrote, "I'll hold my head so high it'll strike the stars."

☑ **ONGOING ASSESSMENT: Diagnose**

Use this writing task to diagnose students' current level of proficiency in writing how-to essays.

Ask students to choose a topic for a how-to essay and write the first sentence of an introductory paragraph. If students have	difficulty completing this exercise, clarify the sorts of topics that make good how-to essays as you work through pp. 202–205 with the class.

Reading\Writing Connection

Reading: Identify Cause-and-Effect Relationships

The questions readers ask as they identify cause-and-effect relationships (such as, What is happening here? What made this happen?) help them understand and remember information. When they write, students should clarify causes and effects to provide as much support as possible for their readers.

Teaching from the Model

Learning how to make balloon animals will interest many students and may suggest possible how-to essay topics. The clear step-by-step directions in this essay provide a good model for students' own writing.

Step-by-Step Teaching Guide

Engage Students Through Literature

1. Have a volunteer read the introduction and then different students read each step of the directions. Explain that the notes in the margin point out the features of a successful how-to essay: introduction, required materials, steps listed in chronological order, and specific details.

2. If possible, provide a balloon for every student. As you read each step in the process, have students follow the directions.

3. Does everyone have a recognizable balloon dog by step 8? If not, ask students to reread the steps to figure out where they went astray.

4. After the balloon animals are complete, discuss the essay. Was the introduction enticing? Were the directions clear? Remind students that the directions in their how-to essays must be as clear as these—no critical details left out and no important steps assumed—if they expect readers to follow the directions successfully.

Critical Viewing

Evaluate Students' responses will vary.

Model From Literature

K. Wayne Wincey (1951–   ) wrote this article for Boys' Life *magazine. In it, he explains how to make a balloon animal.*

Reading Writing Connection

Reading Strategy: Identify Cause-and-Effect Relationships As you read, note **cause-and-effect relationships**—sequences in which one event brings about another event. In the following how-to essay, the author uses cause-and-effect relationships to explain certain instructions. For instance, he explains that a "locking twist" causes segments of the balloon to stick to each other permanently.

▲ **Critical Viewing** Judging from this essay, how easy was it to make the balloon hat in the picture? **[Evaluate]**

Twist and Shout

K. Wayne Wincey

A pinch here, a twist there, and you've made a balloon animal!

Creating balloon animals is easy. All you need is a bag of balloons and the desire to have some fun. You can usually master the basics in about a week.

The best part of balloon twisting is that most animal sculptures follow the same 10-step order: nose, ear, ear, neck, leg, leg, body, leg, leg, and tail. What varies is the size of the bubbles and the amount of uninflated balloon (tail) that you start with.

Supplies are cheap. A gross of animal balloons, that's 144 of 'em, costs about $10. Find the balloons (also called 260's, twisties, or pencil balloons) at party supply stores or magic shops. While there, consider paying about $4 for a palm pump that helps blow up the balloons. (It'll save time and heavy breathing.)

Start with an easy balloon animal, like the dog shown here. Experiment a little, and you'll soon have a whole zoo of critters!

1. Blow up a balloon, leaving about three inches uninflated. This is called the tail; the open end is the nozzle. Tie off the nozzle in an overhand knot.

Note: The more twists in your sculpture, the more uninflated the balloon must be.

Wincey begins with an attention-getting introduction that presents his subject.

Here, the author explains what materials are required and how to obtain them.

The writer organizes the essay logically. He presents steps in chronological order—the order in which the reader should perform them.

2. Using your thumb and forefinger, pinch or squeeze off three inches of the balloon from the nozzle for the dog's nose. Twist the body of the balloon around at least three times.

Don't worry about pops—they happen, but not often with this type of balloon.

3. Pinch off another three inches of balloon and twist. This will be one ear of your dog.

4. Fold the first two bubbles against the rest of the balloon. Squeeze the long segment against the twist of the two shorter segments. Keep a firm grip on all the bubbles at this point or they'll come undone.

Twist the long bubble and the two short bubbles together. Now your critter has two ears and a nose.

Note: This twist is called a split or locking twist, because it won't come undone.

5. Pinch off and twist three more inches for the neck, followed by three additional inches for one front leg.

6. Fold the long bubble over again and twist against the two new bubbles (another locking twist). Now you have two front legs.

7. Another three inches and a twist gives your dog a body. Squeeze and twist off three more.

8. Now give your canine one last locking twist with the rest of the balloon. You've got two hind legs, a tail, and finally, a dog!

By using words that tell how much, such as firm, the writer gives exact directions.

LITERATURE

To read another how-to essay, see "How to Write a Letter" by Garrison Keillor. You can find the essay in *Prentice Hall Literature: Timeless Voices, Timeless Themes, Copper.*

Reading Writing Connection

Writing Application: Help Readers Identify Cause-and-Effect Relationships As you write your how-to essay, explain the effects of following each step.

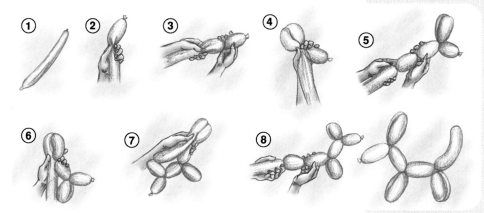

Responding to Literature

"How to Write a Letter" is a charming example of a how-to essay very different from the one here. Garrison Keillor's purpose is to present an eloquent case for letter writing, though he also gives letter-writing instructions and tips. Ask students to compare these two very different essays. Have them recall this discussion as they consider topics for their own essays and make sure they understand that the tone and emphasis of their essays will depend on the topic they choose.

Integrating Workplace Skills

Nearly every worker uses written directions many times a day, though the directions are unlikely to be essays with enticing introductions and restatements at the end. For instance, a graphic designer follows directions to install and run computer drawing programs. A truck driver follows directions to find addresses. A technical writer writes easy-to-follow directions for nonexperts.

Customize for *ESL Students*

To help them envision the steps clearly, students learning English will benefit from having some of the concepts in this essay demonstrated and some of the more challenging words defined. Using a balloon, point out its *tail* and *nozzle* and how to *inflate, pinch,* and *twist* it. As you work through the steps, show the *segments* and *bubbles.* Make sure students understand that a *gross* is 144 (12 times 12) and that a *canine* is a dog.

Reading\Writing Connection

Writing: Identify Cause-and-Effect Relationships

Tell students that making the connections between causes and their effects explicit will help readers follow what they are saying.

Prewriting: Brainstorming; Blueprinting

Teaching Resources: Writing Support Transparency 10-A

1. Some students will be able to brainstorm more readily if they narrow the focus from "Things I Like to Do" to "Sports I Like to Play," "Things I Know How to Make," or some other more specific category.

2. Display the transparency. Explain that blueprints are plans that architects and contractors make to help them construct buildings and that students' blueprints will help them build how-to essays.

3. Assure students that the blueprints of places they spend time need not be highly detailed. The purpose of the blueprints is to map ideas in order to jog their memories. Students can leave space at the margins of the maps to make notes, or they can write notes on a separate sheet of paper.

4. After students have finished their blueprints, suggest that partners trade blueprints to see which parts of their blueprint piques the partner's curiosity. Have them consider whether those areas bring to mind how-to essay topics.

Choosing Your Topic

Use one of the following strategies to choose a good topic for your how-to essay:

Strategies for Generating a Topic

1. **Brainstorming** Set a timer for five minutes. Think about things you like to do, and jot down every idea that comes to mind. At the end of five minutes, review your notes. Select an activity that you can teach a reader to do.

2. **Blueprinting** Draw a map of a place where you spend time, such as your home or a playground. Study your blueprint, and make notes of the activities you do in each area. Select one of these activities as your topic. (Make sure it is something you can teach a reader to do.)

Writing Lab CD-ROM

For more help finding a topic, see the activities and tips in the Choosing a Topic section of the Exposition: Giving Information lesson.

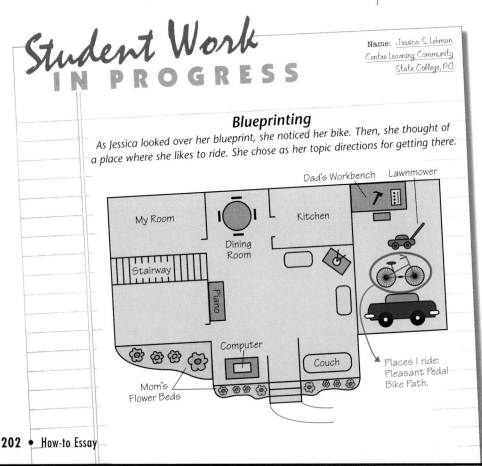

Student Work IN PROGRESS

Name: Jessica S. Lehman
Centre Learning Community
State College, PA.

Blueprinting

As Jessica looked over her blueprint, she noticed her bike. Then, she thought of a place where she likes to ride. She chose as her topic directions for getting there.

 **Writing Support Transparencies**

Use the transparencies for Chapter 10 to teach these strategies.

🕐 **TIME AND RESOURCE MANAGER**

Resources
Print: Writing Support Transparencies, 10-A–C
Technology: Writing Lab CD-ROM, Exposition: Giving Information

In-Depth Coverage	Accelerated Pace
• Cover pp. 202–205 in class. • Have students work in pairs or small groups to generate topics, and support the pairs or groups as necessary. **Option** Have students use the How-to essay section of the Writing Lab CD-ROM.	• Students may want to brainstorm for ideas in categories they feel strongly about, such as "Threats to Clean Water" or "Ways People Are Unfair to Teenagers." • Assign pp. 202–205 for independent student review. • Ask students to discuss ideas for making complicated topics accessible to readers.

TOPICS
TOPIC BANK

If you're having trouble finding a topic, consider these possibilities:

1. **How to Start a Hobby** Choose a hobby, such as stamp collecting or playing chess. Write an essay explaining how to get started in this hobby.

2. **How to Make a Meal** If you have a special sandwich, dessert, or shake that you make, write a how-to essay sharing your recipe and instructions with others.

Responding to Fine Art

3. Jot down a few notes about this painting. How many people are in it? What is each one doing? What is each one wearing? Then, think of a dance, music, or sports activity in which you participate. Write a how-to essay explaining the steps someone must take to get involved—signing up, buying special clothing or equipment, and so on.

Practice Session, Phoebe Beaseley. From the collection of Mr. and Mrs. E.C. Hanes, Winston-Salem, NC

Responding to Literature

4. Read the short story "Old Ben" by Jesse Stuart. Then, do some research into an unusual pet, and write an essay on how to take care of it. You can find this selection in *Prentice Hall Literature: Timeless Voices, Timeless Themes,* Copper.

☑ Cooperative Writing Opportunity

5. **How to Have a Fun Weekend** With a group, develop plans for a fun weekend in your community. Some students should research music, dance, and art events. Others should research amusement facilities, such as video arcades. Others should investigate restaurants. Assemble the results of your research, along with maps and pictures, into a step-by-step guide to having a fun weekend.

Prewriting • 203

Step-by-Step Teaching Guide

Responding to Fine Art

Practice Session by Phoebe Beaseley

Teaching Resources: Writing Support Transparency 10-B

1. Display the transparency. Have students respond freely to the mood and subject of the piece as well as the collage technique.

2. Ask students to think of how-to essay topics this artwork suggests. (how to do ballet positions, how to become a ballet dancer) Urge students to extend the range of possible topics by making a few suggestions, for example, how to look like a ballet dancer, how to help people love ballet, or how to make a collage.

3. Encourage students to study various kinds of art as a source of inspiration for how-to essay topics.

Responding to Literature

After students read the story "Old Ben," encourage students to relate any personal experiences they may have with unusual pets.

Customize for
Visual/Spatial Learners

To help them choose topics, students might do rough sketches that show the steps involved in doing or making something. When they draft their essays, sketches can help students make sure they haven't left out any steps.

Spotlight on the Humanities

For additional topic suggestions, refer student to the Spotlight on The Humanities on page 218.

☑ ONGOING ASSESSMENT: Monitor and Reinforce

For students who are still having difficulty choosing a topic, use one of the following options.

| **Option 1** Have students look through some tables of contents of favorite magazines to see whether any of the titles suggest possible how-to essay topics. | **Option 2** Ask students to select one of the suggestions from the Topic Bank for Heterogeneous Classes in the Teaching Resources. |

Prewriting: Considering Your Audience and Purpose

1. List the topics students have chosen on the chalkboard. Have the class respond to two questions about each topic: Is this topic too broad, too narrow, or on target? and Do you think most people know a lot or a little about this topic?

2. When his or her topic comes up for discussion, ask each student to take notes on classmates' answers to the questions.

3. Have students refer to their notes as they choose a how-to essay topic and decide how much explanation they will need to include in their essays.

Customize for
Less Advanced Students

Encourage students to choose simple and familiar topics that do not contain many steps or require extensive explanation, for example, how to peel a potato or how to dress for subzero weather.

Customize for
More Advanced Students

Students can use this assignment to learn more about topics that interest them. After they make tentative topic choices, they should research them to make sure the scope of the topics is not overly broad. One good way to do this is to consult experts in the topics they are considering.

Critical Viewing

Compare and Contrast Students may say that the audience in the photo on the left is in a less formal environment and is closer to the performer.

Narrowing Your Topic

Once you've chosen a topic, make sure it is not too general. Some topics start out too broad. For example, if your topic is "How to Dance," you will have a hard time figuring out how to explain every style of dance. A narrowed version of this topic would be "How to Dance Salsa" (one type of dance). For this narrowed topic, you can give your reader simple, step-by-step instructions. If your topic is too broad, focus on one manageable aspect. Considering your audience and purpose may also help you narrow your topic.

Considering Your Audience and Purpose

Your **purpose** in writing a how-to essay is to explain the steps in achieving a goal. To achieve this purpose, you should present complete, accurate information in an easy-to-follow form.

Your **audience**—the readers of your essay—should also influence what you write. Ask yourself the following questions:

- **How much does my audience know about the topic?** Do they need a little or a lot of information? Do I need to define terms so readers know what I am talking about?

- **What is the age of my audience?** Will I use simple vocabulary for young children, or can I use vocabulary appropriate for people my age or older?

- **What skills do my readers have?** If your readers know little about your topic, you will have to include many details to help them understand it. On the other hand, if your readers know something about your topic, you can present even complicated procedures or special alternative steps.

**Writing Lab
CD-ROM**

For tips and activities for narrowing a broad topic, go to the Narrowing a Topic section of Exposition: Giving Information lesson.

▶ Critical Viewing Name an important difference between the audiences in these pictures. Then, explain in what ways each audience affects how the performers dress and what they present. [**Compare and Contrast**]

Gathering Details

Now that you have a narrow topic and an audience, you have an idea of the details you need to include in your essay. To help gather your details, try the itemizing strategy.

Itemize to Gather Details

Begin with a simple list of the materials or the steps involved in your topic. Then, itemize each part of the list—break down each major step into the smaller steps it includes, or specify the kind, quantity, or preparation of each material required.

If your itemized list starts getting too long, consider whether your topic is still too broad or whether you are including more details than your audience needs.

Technology Tip

If you have access to a still camera or a video camera, perform the process you are explaining in your how-to essay while a partner takes pictures; then, switch places. Both of you can then review your visual records to identify details for your writing.

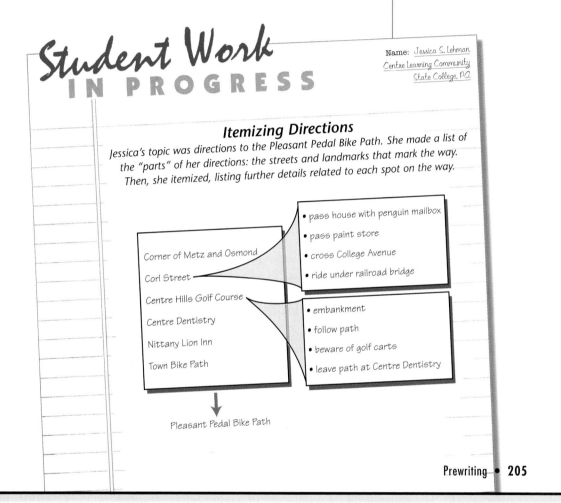

Student Work IN PROGRESS

Name: Jessica S. Lehman
Centre Learning Community
State College, PA

Itemizing Directions

Jessica's topic was directions to the Pleasant Pedal Bike Path. She made a list of the "parts" of her directions: the streets and landmarks that mark the way. Then, she itemized, listing further details related to each spot on the way.

Corner of Metz and Osmond
Corl Street
Centre Hills Golf Course
Centre Dentistry
Nittany Lion Inn
Town Bike Path

- pass house with penguin mailbox
- pass paint store
- cross College Avenue
- ride under railroad bridge

- embankment
- follow path
- beware of golf carts
- leave path at Centre Dentistry

Pleasant Pedal Bike Path

Prewriting: Itemize to Gather Details

Teaching Resources: Writing Support Transparency 10-C

1. Display the transparency. Using Jessica's list as a model, help students organize their own lists. Remind students first to list general categories that pertain to their topic.

2. Then have students consider each broad category and add critical details to each. For example, have they considered specialized equipment or protective gear in the materials category? Have they thought about conditions, such as temperature or humidity? Have they specified how long the process will take?

3. After students have organized and amplified their lists, they should reread them. Have they added details that readers would not need or want to know to accomplish the task? Students who find this task challenging can work in pairs or small groups to read their lists aloud and have group members help them include all the essential details and eliminate all the irrelevant ones.

Customize for
Logical/Mathematical Learners

Students may work more quickly and efficiently if they outline their how-to essays following a standard outline form. When they have completed their outlines, they should review them carefully to make sure they have included all the essential details.

 TIME SAVERS!

Writing Support Transparencies
Use the transparencies for Chapter 10 to teach these strategies.

205

Drafting: Organize Details in Chronological Order

Teaching Resources: Writing Support Transparency 10-D; Writing Support Activity Book 10-1

1. Emphasize the importance in a how-to essay of including all the essential steps in the order that they occur. Ask what would happen if the sugar was left out of a cake recipe. What would happen if the cake went into the oven before the flour was added?

2. Have students use their itemized and grouped lists to write the steps on cards or self-stick notes. Be sure they write only one step on each card.

3. After they place the steps in chronological order, urge students to ask a friend to read the steps to make sure nothing seems left out or ambiguous. This is the point at which students can easily reorder the cards or write additional steps.

4. When the steps are as clear and complete as they can make them, students number the cards or notes as specified in the textbook. Congratulate students on completing the most difficult part of writing a how-to essay!

Shaping Your Writing

Once you have gathered your details, you need to put them into some kind of order. The details for your how-to essay are like materials at a construction site. If the workers just start pouring concrete and pounding nails wherever they please, the building will be a disaster! On the other hand, if they follow a blueprint, the building will be sturdy and useful. Before you draft, make a plan in which you organize your details.

Organize Details in Chronological Order

Chronological order is the arrangement of steps in the order in which they take place. Since the reader of a how-to essay usually needs to complete one step before beginning the next, chronological order is the best order for most how-to essays. Organize your how-to steps chronologically by using a timeline.

Using a Timeline Write each step of your how-to topic on its own sticky note or note card. Lay out your notes in order on a table or on the floor. Read through them, and move any notes that are out of order into the right place. Once the steps are in the correct order, number your notes from start to finish.

STICKY NOTE TIMELINE

The lead takes her right hand and raises it until his arm makes an L.

The lead puts his right hand on his partner's back.

She rests her left hand on his shoulder.

He moves his right foot forward.

🔲 Research Tip

In slow motion, perform the process you are explaining. Note the individual steps and the exact order in which you complete them. Make sure the steps of your how-to essay are consistent with the way you complete the process yourself.

⏱ TIME AND RESOURCE MANAGER

Resources
Print: Writing Support Transparency 10-D
Technology: Writing Lab CD-ROM, Exposition: Giving Information

In-Depth Coverage	Accelerated Pace
• Work through the list with the entire class, using the list on the transparency as a model. • Have students write their how-to essay draft in class. • With the support of the transparency, demonstrate organizing a how-to essay using a timeline. **Option** Have students work independently or in small groups with the Writing Lab CD-ROM.	• Have students review pp. 206–207 independently and then write their first drafts. • Respond to questions as necessary.

Providing Elaboration

Remember, your reader needs your help! He or she is reading your essay to learn how to do something. Make sure you have sufficiently **elaborated** your explanation—that you have added enough details about *how much, how long,* and *to what extent.* The strategy of "Exploding the Moment" can help.

Add Details by "Exploding the Moment"

Follow these steps to explode the moment:

1. Cut out several "bursts," or "explosions," from colored paper.
2. Begin writing your draft. As you draft, pause at the end of each paragraph or step.
3. Circle words in the paragraph or step that indicate specific things, actions, times, or amounts.
4. For each circled word, think of details that give more specific information, answering *what kind? which one? how many? how much? in what way?* and *to what extent?*
5. Write additional details on the colored-paper explosions, and lightly paste them to your draft.

When you have finished drafting, review your explosions. Decide which details to add to your draft.

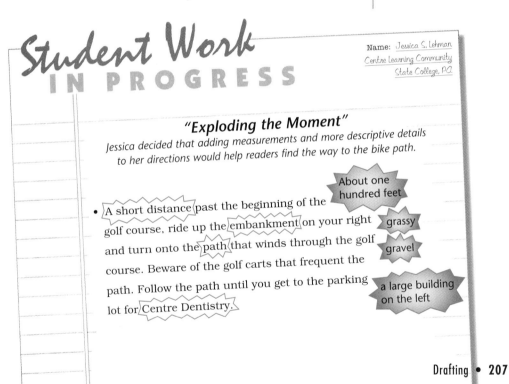

Student Work
IN PROGRESS

Name: *Jessica S. Lehman*
Centre Learning Community
State College, PA

"Exploding the Moment"

Jessica decided that adding measurements and more descriptive details to her directions would help readers find the way to the bike path.

- A short distance past the beginning of the golf course, ride up the embankment on your right and turn onto the path that winds through the golf course. Beware of the golf carts that frequent the path. Follow the path until you get to the parking lot for Centre Dentistry.

About one hundred feet

grassy

gravel

a large building on the left

Drafting • **207**

Step-by-Step Teaching Guide

Drafting: Add Details by "Exploding the Moment"

Teaching Resources: Writing Support Transparency 10-E

1. Display the transparency and choose someone to read aloud Jessica's paragraph. Discuss the revisions that Jessica plans to make. Do students agree that these will make the directions clearer?

2. As students begin drafting their how-to essays, remind them that each paragraph after the introduction will likely contain one step. They should make sure that each paragraph has a clearly stated topic sentence. After they write each paragraph, they should ask themselves whether readers have all the information they need to accomplish that step.

3. You may want students to complete their drafts before they go back and circle words that may need elaboration. If students have followed their chronological order timelines, they may find that only a few direction words need elaboration.

Customize for
ESL Students

Students will need to use order words, such as *first, next, after that, then, last, finally, in conclusion,* and so on in their how-to essays. Review these important abstract words and write them and others on the chalkboard. Act out simple actions, such as entering the room, sitting at a desk, and opening a book, and ask students to use order words to describe your actions. Leave the word list on the chalkboard and have students refer to it as they write their essays.

✓ ONGOING ASSESSMENT: Monitor and Reinforce

If the steps of some students' how-to essays are still not entirely clear, use the following strategy.

Have students read their essays aloud to a partner. If the partner is puzzled about a step, he or she should ask the reader to stop and explain. Writers should make a check next to the paragraphs that need elaboration and add to those paragraphs.

Revising: Writing a Strong Lead

Teaching Resources:
Writing Support Transparency 10-F

1. Discuss the importance of a strong first paragraph introduction. Point out that all the effort they have made writing clear steps will be wasted if readers don't proceed past the introductory paragraph. Have students consider the ways readers would benefit from learning about their topic and urge them to include some of these reasons in their introduction.

2. Display the transparency. Ask students to discuss how Jessica's revision improved her introduction.

3. Ask students to gather in small groups and take turns "selling" each other on their topics. After all the group members have spoken, they should decide which strategies proved most convincing.

4. Have students work individually to incorporate their most persuasive arguments in the introductions to their essays.

Integrating Speaking and Listening Skills

Before students break into small groups to "sell" their topics, review speaking skills, including the importance of speaking at a reasonable rate—neither too quickly nor too slowly—and speaking clearly and with conviction. Remind students to make eye contact with each member of the group.

10.4 Revising

You've finished your first draft—but you're just getting started! Now it's time to improve your work. Start by reviewing your essay's structure.

Revising Your Overall Structure

Add an Introduction

Start your essay with a strong introduction. The following strategy will help:

▶ **REVISION STRATEGY**
Writing a Strong Lead

To ensure your introduction is strong enough, ask yourself:

• Does it clearly define the topic?
• Does it make readers want to keep reading?
• Does it make a transition into the steps of the process?

If you answered "no" to any of these questions, think about what your introduction needs before you can answer "yes." Use your ideas to write a stronger lead.

Student Work
IN PROGRESS

Name: *Jessica S. Lehman*
Centre Learning Community
State College, PA.

Writing a Strong Lead
Jessica decided her introduction needed to do more to interest readers.

If you like to bicycle, you may be looking for a good place for a ride. The Pleasant Pedal Bike Path is a scenic route. Here are directions to get to it.

Jessica's first introduction accurately stated her topic. It also made a transition to her directions: "Here are directions to get to it." She decided, though, that it lacked the pizzazz needed to interest a reader.

Attention State College Area Bikers in the Holmes Foster Neighborhood area! Do you like paved paths? Do you like to ride where there is little traffic? Do you like to ride through scenic woodlands just blocks from downtown State College? If your answer to any of these questions is "yes," you'll love the Pleasant Pedal Bike Path. Getting there can be tricky, but if you follow these directions, you'll be pedaling along in no time at all.

208 • How-to Essay

⏱ TIME SAVERS!

📄 **Writing Support Transparencies**
Use the transparencies for Chapter 10 to teach these strategies.

⏱ TIME AND RESOURCE MANAGER

Resources
Print: Writing Support Transparencies 10-F–G
Technology: Writing Lab CD-ROM, Exposition: Giving Information

In-Depth Coverage	Accelerated Pace
• Cover pp. 208–212 in class. • Work through the revising strategies with the entire class.	• Assign pp. 208–212 for independent student review. • Have students revise their how-to essays independently.

Revising Your Paragraphs

Once you've improved your introduction and conclusion, examine the paragraphs in the body of your essay. Identify the purpose of each paragraph, and then add transition words and phrases to make your meaning clearer.

▶ **REVISION STRATEGY**
Identifying Steps, Stacks, Chains, and Balances

Reread each paragraph in your draft. Use the descriptions below to determine whether the paragraph is a "step," a "stack," a "chain," or a "balance." Then, consider adding the transition words listed in the description.

- **Steps** If the paragraph explains one or more steps for which time order is important, the sequence should be indicated. Use words such as *first, next,* and *finally.*

- **Stacks** If the paragraph explains how one part of a process adds to or contributes to another, point out the connection with words such as *and, furthermore,* and *for instance.*

- **Chains** If the paragraph shows the cause-and-effect relationship between steps, use words such as *so, because,* and *consequently.*

- **Balances** If the paragraph shows choice or contrast, use words or phrases such as *but, however, on the other hand,* and *rather.*

▶ Critical Viewing Based on details in this picture, what other things do bicyclists need to watch for besides landmarks? Does Jessica mention them in her introduction on the previous page? **[Deduce]**

Revising • 209

Step-by-Step Teaching Guide

Revising: Identifying Steps, Stacks, Chains, and Balances

1. Students may want to use markers of four different colors to draw stars or check marks in the margins to identify the four different types of paragraph organization.

2. If students notice that they use only step organization in their paragraphs, they may want to reorganize some of the paragraphs to use stack, chain, or balance organization.

3. Students should then circle the transition words as indicated in the textbook.

4. After students have revised their paragraphs to add transition words, they should reread their essays to make sure that they haven't omitted any words or changed the intended meaning of any sentences.

Critical Viewing

Deduce Most students will assume that since the man in the photograph is a bicyclist, he will be interested in Jessica's topic, so Jessica's task is to keep him interested. Knowing that the bike path described in the essay is an extension of a path with which he may already be familiar may do that. The bicyclist might also read on to find out how to get to the path as Jessica promises in the introduction.

☑ ONGOING ASSESSMENT: Monitor and Reinforce

If some students are having difficulty adding transition words, try one of the following options.

Option 1 Find an example of each type of paragraph organization, make copies for students, and have them underline the transition words.	**Option 2** To demonstrate the importance of transition words, write a short how-to paragraph on the chalkboard without transition words. Can students understand the paragraph easily? Ask them to add transition words to clarify meaning.

Revising: Using Clues to Vary Sentence Beginnings

Teaching Resources: Writing Support Transparency 10-G

1. Display the transparency and have students note the changes Jessica made in order to vary sentence beginnings. Can they think of any other ways she might have revised her sentences for variety and interest?

2. After discussing the model, ask students to write the first word of each sentence of their essays, as directed.

3. After everyone is finished, help volunteers figure out ways to revise repeated sentence beginnings to make their paragraphs more interesting.

4. After each student has gotten a couple of suggestions, everyone should be able to proceed independently to improve the sentences in their own essays by varying the sentence structures and choices of beginning words.

Integrating Vocabulary Skills

Technical Words Remind students that they may need to define technical words in their how-to essays. Review the various ways to gracefully insert definitions into writing, including defining words outright, defining them in apposition, and using examples.

10.4

Revising Your Sentences
Vary Your Sentence Beginnings

If every sentence in your how-to essay began with the word *the* or the word *you*, your readers wouldn't finish reading your instructions—they'd fall asleep first! Varying sentence beginnings—starting sentences in different ways—makes your writing more interesting and helps clarify your meaning.

▶ **REVISION STRATEGY**
Using Clues to Vary Sentence Beginnings

Fold a piece of lined loose-leaf paper into fourths, making a long strip. Place the strip on the side of your draft. On the strip, copy the first word of each sentence in your draft on its own line. Then, review this list of first words, and circle those that are repeated three times or more. Rewrite or combine some of the sentences that begin with the circled words so that they begin with a different word.

Language Lab CD-ROM

To help vary your sentences, complete the Combining Sentences lesson in the Sentence Style unit.

Student Work IN PROGRESS

Name: Jessica S. Lehman
Centre Learning Community
State College, PA

Varying Sentence Beginnings

In this paragraph, Jessica found that she had overused the words ride *and* you *as sentence beginnings. She rewrote some of these sentences to begin differently.*

Ride
Ride
You
You
You
You

Ride through the parking lot until you see the sign for the Town Bike Path. ~~Ride~~ ^Biking on this path, which runs alongside Atherton Street, ~~and~~ you will pedal up a hill and past the historic Nittany Lion Inn across the street on your left. You will be riding alongside Atherton Street. ~~You will see~~ ^there is a small dirt side path ~~just~~ ^Just before you get to the first intersection. ~~You~~ ^Take take this path, which branches out from the Town Bike Path and turns left. You will still be riding with the golf course on your left.

⏱ **TIME SAVERS!**

📋 **Writing Support Transparencies**
Use the transparencies for Chapter 10 to facilitate teaching of strategies.

Grammar in Your Writing
Using Adverb Clauses and Adverb Phrases

In a how-to essay, you tell readers exactly *how* to do something. To add information about *how*, you can use adverb phrases and adverb clauses. **Adverb phrases** and **adverb clauses** are groups of words that tell *how*, *where*, *when*, *why*, or *under what circumstances*. They act just like adverbs, giving more information about the verb in a sentence.

How: To climb the hill, pedal as hard as you can.

Where: There's a bike path in a scenic woodland.

When: After you turn the corner by the school, ride to Corl Street.

Why: Ride along Pleasant Pedal Bike Path to enjoy the scenery.

Under What Circumstances: If you take your time, you'll love the bike path.

When an adverb phrase or adverb clause comes before the main clause in the sentence, set it off with a comma. When the phrase or clause follows the main clause, do not set it off with a comma.

Phrase or clause that follows the main clause:
You'll be biking in no time if you follow these directions.

Phrase or clause that comes before the main clause:
After you turn the corner by the school, ride to Corl Street.

Find It in Your Reading Find two adverb phrases or adverb clauses in "Twist and Shout" by K. Wayne Wincey on page 200. Explain what information is added with each example you find.

Find It in Your Writing Find two adverb clauses or adverb phrases that you have used in your how-to essay. If you cannot find two, challenge yourself to add two adverb phrases or adverb clauses to provide more detail.

To learn more about adverb phrases and about clauses, see Chapter 20.

◄ **Critical Viewing**
Describe this scene in a sentence using either an adverb clause or an adverb phrase. **[Apply]**

Revising • 211

Grammar in Your Writing: Using Adverb Clauses and Adverb Phrases

1. An adverb phrase or clause need not—and usually does not—contain an adverb. All the examples here are prepositional phrases that act together to describe a verb.

2. Point out the adverb phrases in the Model From Literature.
   - *in about a week* modifies the verb *master*; it tells when
   - *at party supply stores or magic shops* modifies *Find*; it tells where
   - *against the two shorter segments* modifies *squeeze*; it tells how

3. Urge students to include adverb clauses and phrases in their how-to essays to strengthen readers' understanding of the directions.

Find It in Your Reading
Possible responses:

Paragraph 2—in about a week (tells when you can master the basics); paragraph 4—at party supply stores or magic shops (tells where to find balloons).

Find It in Your Writing
Have students explain what information is added for each example they find.

Critical Viewing
Apply Possible answer: The cyclists pass in a blur of bright colors and spinning wheels.

✓ **ONGOING ASSESSMENT: Prerequisite Skills**

If students have difficulty defining or understanding adverb clauses and phrases, you may find it helpful to review the following to assure coverage of prerequisite knowledge.

In the Textbook	Print Resources	Technology
Phrases and Clauses, pp. 414–435	Grammar Exercise Workbook, pp. 61–62	On-Line Exercise Bank, Section 20.1

Step-by-Step Teaching Guide

Revising: Highlighting Repeated Words

1. Students will have no difficulty highlighting repeated words in their essays, but they may need support figuring out which repeated words to replace.

2. Nouns can often be replaced with pronouns. Verbs, adjectives, and adverbs can often be replaced with more vivid synonyms. Emphasize that the writer's judgment is important—there are absolute rules for varying word choices.

3. Students may want to read their articles aloud to themselves or to a partner. Hearing their written words will make repeated words and boring passages stand out.

Step-by-Step Teaching Guide

Revising: Peer Review

1. Remind students to read their essays aloud twice, once for meaning and a second time so group members can take notes.

2. Caution listeners to be very detailed in their comments. You may want to give examples of vague versus specific comments, such as, *The second step doesn't tell readers what to do* versus *After I cut out the heart, I don't know which sheet of paper to paste it on.*

3. Each student should collect the notes taken on his or her essay and read them carefully. Ask students to pay particularly close attention to comments noted by more than one listener. Comments made by three or more listeners should definitely be addressed in their revised essays.

Revising Your Word Choice

Eliminate Repeated Words

Varying your word choice—avoiding the unnecessary repetition of words—is as important as varying your sentence beginnings. Variety is a quality of mature writing. Reread your essay, and look for overused words. One way to detect repetition is to highlight repeated words.

▶**REVISION STRATEGY**
Highlighting Repeated Words

Go through your essay, and highlight any nouns, verbs, or adjectives that you have used more than once. (You can ignore words that are commonly repeated, such as *the*, *and*, *of*, and *a*.) After marking repeated words, evaluate each use to determine whether you should replace the word with a synonym—another word with a similar meaning.

Peer Review

Getting feedback from your classmates is especially helpful when you revise a how-to essay. After all, your purpose in the essay is to show readers how to do something. Peer reviewers will be able to tell you how clear your explanation is and whether additional information is needed.

Asking a Group to Try It Out

Read your essay aloud to a small group while they listen. Then, read it aloud again. This time, the group should follow the steps of the process as you read your essay. As the group acts out each step, they should take notes on where they are confused or unsure of what to do. After you have finished the second reading, ask reviewers to respond to the following questions:

• Which step or steps could have been explained more clearly?

• What was confusing about those steps?

• In which sections was more or less information needed?

• What other questions or comments do you have?

Use your peers' responses to guide you as you make your final changes to your draft.

212 • How-to Essay

STANDARDIZED TEST PREPARATION WORKSHOP

Vocabulary Standardized test questions often require students to understand exact word meanings. Ask students which is the best replacement for the underlined word in the following sentence.

Adding more food coloring will make the colorful frosting even more <u>colorful</u>.

A pretty   **C** brilliant

B nice   **D** boring

Choice **C**, *brilliant* is the only word that relates directly to *colorful* in the sentence. *Pretty* and *nice* are both positive words, but they indicate nothing about color.

10.5 Editing and Proofreading

Your readers may run into trouble if you type *weight* when you mean *wait*—did you mean they should add some pounds, or that they should stick around for a while? Errors in spelling, punctuation, grammar, or usage can create confusion. Proofread your how-to essay to discover and eliminate misleading errors.

Focusing on Commas

In your how-to essay, you may list ingredients or materials. Whenever you list three or more items in a series, you must use commas. Check your essay for such series, and use the following rule to make sure you have used commas correctly.

Language Lab CD-ROM

For practice using commas, complete the Commas lesson in the Punctuation unit.

Grammar in Your Writing
Using Commas to Separate Items in a Series

A series consists of three or more similar items. Use commas to separate three or more words, phrases, or clauses in a series. The last comma goes before the conjunction (usually *or* or *and*) that precedes the last item. (Some writers prefer to do without this final comma unless it is needed to prevent confusion. Ask your teacher for his or her preference.)

Words in a Series: You'll see <u>flowers</u>, <u>trees</u>, <u>squirrels</u>, and <u>birds</u> as you ride.

Phrases in a Series: <u>Pedal through the intersection</u>, <u>past the paint store on your left</u>, and <u>along the golf course</u>.

Find It in Your Reading Identify a series in "Twist and Shout" by K. Wayne Wincey on page 200. Are the items in the series words or phrases?

Find It in Your Writing Review your essay, and circle any lists or series of items. Remember that the series can include either individual words or groups of words. Check that you have correctly used commas to separate the items in each series or list that you find.

For more on commas, see Chapter 26.

Grammar in Your Writing: Using Commas to Separate Items in a Series

1. To make sure students understand that a series is made up of three or more items, quiz them: *I have an apple and an orange. Do I have a series? I have an apple, an orange, and a plum. Do I have a series?*

2. To practice using serial commas correctly, have partners take turns writing sentences that include items in a series without commas and adding commas to the sentences.

3. Remind students that both words in a series and phrases in a series are separated by commas.

4. As students proofread their essays for correct use of serial commas, you might ask them to make tiny checks over the items they list in a sentence. If they don't count three or more check marks, students don't need commas in those sentences.

Find It in Your Reading

Students' responses will vary. Series include "nose, ear, ear, . . . leg, and tail" in paragraph 3, "260's, twisties, or pencil balloons" in paragraph 4, and "two hind legs, a tail, and finally, a dog!" in the final paragraph. All items in the series are words.

Find It in Your Writing

If students cannot find any examples in their own writing, challenge them to revise a sentence to incorporate items in a series.

⏱ TIME AND RESOURCE MANAGER

Resources
Print: Scoring Rubrics on Transparency, Chapter 10; Writing Assessment: Scoring Rubric and Scoring Model for How-to Essay
Technology: Writing Lab CD-ROM, Exposition: Giving Information

In-Depth Coverage	Accelerated Pace
• Cover pp. 213–216 in class. • Have students edit and proofread their essays in class. • Students present their final drafts.	• Assign pp. 213–216. • Have students edit and proofread their how-to essays independently. • Students present their final drafts.

1. If you can't schedule time for students to demonstrate their how-to essay topics at a school fair or event, they can do so for an audience of classmates.

2. Urge students to practice, practice, practice—by themselves and for family or friends. On the night before the demonstration, they should go over the list of ingredients or materials they need and gather everything together to bring to school the next morning.

3. After the demonstrations are complete, gather the class together to "decompress." Discuss the demonstrations and mention some strengths you noticed.

ASSESS

Assessment

Teaching Resources: Scoring Rubrics on Transparency 10; Formal Assessment, Chapter 10

1. Display the Scoring Rubric transparency and review the criteria in class.

2. Before students proceed with self-assessment, you may wish to review the Final Draft of the Student Work in Progress on pages 215–216. Have students score the final Draft in one or more of the rubric categories. For example, how would students score the essay in terms of audience and purpose?

3. In addition to student self-assessment, you may wish to use the following assessment options.

   • Score student essays yourself, using the rubric and scoring models from Writing Assessment.

   • Review the Standardized Test Preparation Workshop on pages 220–221 and have students respond to a writing prompt within a time limit.

   • Administer the Chapter 10 Test from Formal Assessment in Teaching Resources to assess students' grasp of concepts presented.

214

Publishing and Presenting

Building Your Portfolio

Consider the following possibilities for publishing or presenting your how-to essay:

1. **Give a Demonstration** Give a demonstration based on your essay in a "how-to" booth at a school fair. Consider creating visual aids to use with your presentation.

2. **How-to Web Page** Work with a teacher to design a Web page presenting the how-to essays of the class. If you don't have access to Internet technology, you can design a flow chart of screens for the site.

Reflecting on Your Writing

Write down a few thoughts about your experience writing a how-to essay. Start off by answering the following questions:

• As you wrote, did you learn more about the activity or skill you explained? Explain your answer.

• Do you think the part of the activity that was hardest to explain is the hardest to do? Explain your answer.

 **Internet Tip**

To read a how-to essay scored according to this rubric, visit **www.phschool.com**

Rubric for Self-Assessment

Evaluate your how-to essay using the following criteria:

	Score 4	Score 3	Score 2	Score 1
Audience and Purpose	Clearly focuses on the procedures necessary to accomplish a well-defined end	Presents procedures necessary to accomplish a well-defined end	Includes procedures related to an end, but presents some vaguely	Includes only vague descriptions of procedures and of the end result
Organization	Presents instructions as a sequence of logically ordered steps; lists all materials (if appropriate); subdivides complex actions	Presents instructions as a sequence of logically ordered steps; lists some materials (if appropriate)	Presents instructions in logical order, for the most part, but organization is poor in places	Presents instructions in a scattered, disorganized manner
Elaboration	Provides appropriate amount of detail; gives explanations or alternatives where useful	Provides appropriate amount of detail; gives some explanations	Provides some detail; gives few explanations	Provides few details; gives few or no explanations
Use of Language	Shows overall clarity and fluency; uses transitions to order steps clearly; contains few errors in spelling, punctuation, or usage	Shows good sentence variety; uses some transitions; contains some errors in spelling, punctuation, or usage	Uses awkward or overly simple sentence structures; contains many errors in spelling, punctuation, or usage	Contains incomplete thoughts and errors in spelling, punctuation, and usage that make the writing confusing

---

✓ ONGOING ASSESSMENT: Assess Mastery

Use one of the following options to assess final drafts of students' how-to essays.

Self-Assessment Ask students to score their essay using the rubric provided. Then have students write a paragraph describing one lesson they learned in writing their how-to essay.	**Teacher Assessment** You may want to use the rubric and the scoring models provided in Writing Assessment, Copper Level, to score the how-to essays.

FINAL DRAFT

Getting to the Pleasant Pedal Bike Path

Jessica S. Lehman
Centre Learning Community
State College, Pennsylvania

▲ Critical Viewing
Name three sights
these bicyclists will
see if they follow
Jessica's directions.
[Connect]

*Notice Jessica's
strong lead. Her
introduction grabs
readers' attention
and urges them to
take advantage of
her directions to get
to a great bike path.*

Attention State College Area Bikers in the Holmes Foster Neighborhood area! Do you like paved paths? Do you like to ride where there is little traffic? Do you like to ride through scenic woodlands just blocks from downtown State College? If your answer to any of these questions is "yes," you'll love the Pleasant Pedal Bike Path. Getting there can be tricky, but if you follow these directions, you'll be pedaling along in no time at all.

• Start at the corner of Metz Avenue and Osmond Street, near downtown State College. Cross Osmond Street and ride down the path through the Corl Street School playground. Turn left around the corner of the school and ride down the path that leads to Corl Street.

• Now you are facing Corl Street. Turn to the right and pedal for a few minutes until you get to the intersection of Corl Street and College Avenue. You will know you are on the right track when you see the house with the penguin mailbox on your right and the paint store to your left. At the intersection of Corl Street and College Avenue, cross College Avenue and continue down Corl Street, which is now unmarked.

*Jessica's directions
are arranged in
chronological order.
She explains what
the reader should do
first, then second,
and so on.*

CLOSE

Step-by-Step Teaching Guide

Teaching From the Final Draft

1. Draw students' attention to the margin notes that accompany Jessica's essay. These notes summarize the contents of the essay and point out its strengths.

2. Have students discuss the introduction. Is it inviting? Informative? Does it include a topic sentence?

3. Then review the conclusion. Make sure students notice that the last sentence relates to the final sentence of the introduction.

4. Finally, have students read the directions and follow along on the map. Have students consider making a visual aid such as a map to accompany their how-to essays.

Critical Viewing

Connect Students may mention the penguin mailbox, a railroad bridge, and the golf course.

Customize for
Bodily/Kinesthetic Learners

Students can make a large floor map copy of the map in their textbook and walk their way through the map as someone reads the directions aloud to them.

Customize for
Gifted/Talented Students

Have students design posters or advertisements promoting the Pleasant Pedal Bike Path.

Critical Viewing

Analyze Students may mention the golf course and the parking lot for Centre Dentistry. The map gives you a visual guide to help follow Jessica's directions.

• As you continue down Corl Street, one of the first landmarks is a railroad bridge you must ride under. You will notice that the landscape is changing from mostly houses to mostly fields. Soon you will see the Centre Hills Golf Course.

• About one hundred feet past the beginning of the golf course, ride up the grassy embankment on your right and turn onto the gravel path that winds through the golf course. Beware of the golf carts that frequent the path. Follow the path until you get to the parking lot for Centre Dentistry, a large building that you will see to your left.

• Ride through the parking lot until you see the sign for the Town Bike Path. Biking on this path, which runs alongside Atherton Street, you will pedal up a hill and past the historic Nittany Lion Inn across the street on your left. You will be riding alongside Atherton Street. Just before you get to the first intersection, there is a small dirt side path. Take this path, which branches out from the Town Bike Path and turns left. You will still be riding with the golf course on your left.

• When the path turns to pavement, you are well on your way. Soon you will see the sign for the Pleasant Pedal Bike Path.

You will be amazed at the beauty and tranquility of the Pleasant Pedal Bike Path. The flowers and trees are breathtaking in all seasons. Furthermore, you will be amused at the antics of the squirrels and birds that make the area surrounding the path their home. And don't forget, it took you only about 15 minutes to get to the bikeway.

▶ **Critical Viewing** Find two of the landmarks in Jessica's essay on this map. Explain how this map might help you follow her directions. [Analyze]

216 • How-to Essay

Jessica uses the adverb phrase as you continue down Corl Street to make a transition from one step to the next.

At each step, Jessica refers to landmarks and other sights so that someone following her directions will easily know whether they are on track or not.

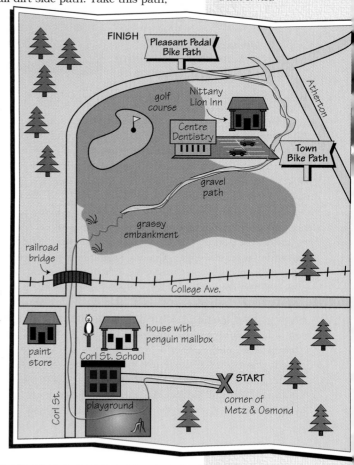

216

Connected Assignment
Problem-and-Solution Essay

A **problem-and-solution essay** explains a problem to readers. Then, it offers one or more solutions to the problem. Like a how-to essay, a problem-and-solution essay presents a set of steps to follow in order to achieve a result. An effective problem-and-solution essay

- clearly explains the problem.
- explains and defends the proposed solutions.

Prewriting Choose a topic by interviewing yourself. Ask yourself: What people, places, and organizations in my community are important to me? What problems do they face? If you have trouble finding answers, browse through local news sources for more information. Then, review your answers, and choose a problem that grabs your interest.

To gather details about your problem, use a cluster diagram like the one shown. Do research to find solutions, and collect the facts, expert opinions, and other evidence showing that the solutions will work.

Drafting After gathering information, begin drafting. In your introduction, clearly state the problem and the solutions you will cover in your essay. In your body paragraphs, explain your solutions in a well-organized, step-by-step manner. Provide evidence to show that your solutions will work.

Revising and Editing Review your draft. First, check the sequence of steps: If the order is not clear, rearrange details so readers will be able to follow their sequence. Then, check the connections between ideas. If necessary, add transition words such as *next, then, after,* and *for this reason* to show readers how one step or idea connects with another. Finally, proofread your essay to eliminate errors in spelling, grammar, or punctuation.

Publishing and Presenting Consider submitting your completed essay to a school or local newspaper.

Pay for racks by having bicyclists register.

Problem: There's no place to park a bike downtown.

Install bike racks.

Registered bikes would have stickers.

▼ **Critical Viewing** What problem are these students helping to solve? **[Analyze]**

Connected Assignment: Problem-and-Solution Essay • 217

1. To write a problem-and-solution essay appropriate to audience and purpose.
2. To organize and present information ensure support for ideas.
3. To use writing processes to develop and revise drafts.
4. To publish and present a problem-and-solution essay to an audience.

Step-by-Step Teaching Guide

Problem-and-Solution Essay

Teaching Resources: Writing Support Transparency 10-G; Writing Support Activity Book 10-1

1. Find examples of problem-and-solution essays in which problems of concern to sixth graders are addressed. School or local newspapers or essays written by other young people may provide good models for students as they try to generate their own topics. Help students identify the proposed solutions in each of the examples. Point out how the writer of each essay gives a detailed explanation of the proposed solution(s).

2. Help students generate topics through self-interviews by brainstorming a list of questions they can ask themselves. Give students some time to look through local news sources, school publications, or other journals of interest to them.

3. Ask for a volunteer to share a topic idea with the class. Display the transparency. Work with the class to begin filling out the cluster diagram transparency for the student volunteer's essay topic.

4. Give students copies of the blank organizer and encourage them to fill them out for their own essays. Then have them use these notes to draft a problem-and-solution essay.

continued

Step-by-Step Teaching Guide continued

5. When students are finished revising and editing their essays, encourage them to consider publishing their work in school or local newspapers. Point out that offering solutions to problems that affect their lives and communities is another of the ways in which writing can help them make a difference.

Critical Viewing

Analyze Students may note that the young people in this photograph are cleaning up the streets, dealing with the problem of pollution, or taking care of their environment. Encourage them to think about how the students in this image might have identified the problem and how they arrived at a possible solution.

1. To use writing to inform and teach.
2. To summarize information collected during research.
3. To take notes from relevant sources.
4. To analyze the process that leads to the creation of works of art.

Step-by-Step Teaching Guide

Organizing Information

1. Choose one of the Spotlight elements for class discussion, or have students work individually or in groups on the element of their choice. Give students the initiative to find the necessary books, videotapes, or pictures.

2. Bring in a recording of Aaron Copland's *Rodeo*, as well as some of his other work based on American folk music. Interested students may research the background of the American musical traditions from which Copland worked.

3. Discuss whether students think today's music could be incorporated into a ballet and encourage them to think about how this could be done. How would they tell dancers to incorporate modern dance moves into their work with the ballet score?

4. If students view *The Heiress*, ask them to find a scene from James's book and have them compare it to the film's presentation of it. Interested students can write a how-to essay about turning episodes from a book into scenes from a movie.

Spotlight on the Humanities

Organizing Information

Focus on Ballet: *Rodeo*

You can write a how-to essay that teaches someone how to find your favorite place. When a choreographer teaches performers dance steps, though, a big part of the how-to is a good piece of music!

Composer Aaron Copland (1900–1990) was asked to write the music for the ballet *Rodeo* in 1942. The choreographer (creator of dance) Agnes de Mille created the plot and the dance steps. Copland's music for *Rodeo* taught many toes how to tap. You can still hear one melody from Rodeo, "Hoedown," which is often played as background music for rodeos on television and in the movies.

Born in Brooklyn, New York, Copland was a landmark influence on American music. Many of his works, like *Rodeo*, incorporate melodies and musical styles from American folk music. He helped Americans take their own musical traditions more seriously.

Film Connection In 1949, Copland won an Academy Award for Best Dramatic Film Score for *The Heiress*. Directed by the legendary William Wyler, the film starred Olivia de Havilland, Montgomery Clift, and Sir Ralph Richardson. Based on a story by the famous author Henry James, *The Heiress* remains a classic American motion picture.

"How-to" Writing Activity: "How to Watch a Dance" Essay

Do some research into ballet or another form of dance performance. Take notes on what choreographers and dancers do to create a dance. Then, explain in a how-to essay what viewers should look for in this kind of dance. Present your essay to the class. If possible, show photographs or video clips to illustrate some of your points.

▲ **Critical Viewing**
Judging from these scenes from *Rodeo*, how is this ballet different from other ballets with which you may be familiar? **[Draw Conclusions]**

218 • How-to Essay

Viewing and Representing

Activity Help students find videos, books, and images about ballet and other dance performances. Encourage them to look for resources that show the rehearsal process that leads to a dance performance. Discuss with students what kinds of images will be helpful illustrations for their how-to presentations. Point out that focusing on particular kinds of steps or moves may help their audience understand what to look for in dance performances.

Critical Viewing

Draw Conclusions Students may notice that the dancers are wearing Western-style clothing and that the dancers are positioned as though they're square-dancing. Use the image to help students think about how ballet dancers and audience members learned about the traditions of the American West from Copland's music.

Media and Technology Skills

Getting "Help" On-line

Activity: Identifying Available Forms of Help

There is a "how-to" built right into most computer programs, a how-to called "Help." When you need to know how to do something as you work in the program, you can call up Help for instructions. By using Help, you can learn as you work.

Learn About It

Balloon Help You can turn Balloon Help on or off through a program's menu bar. With Balloon Help on, a balloon appears whenever you roll your mouse pointer over an active feature on the screen, such as a button or a dialogue box. The balloon contains a brief explanation of the feature on which the pointer is resting.

On-line Manuals When you select Help from the menu bar, you call up an on-line manual for the program. Typically, the manual lists topics by category under Contents. You can also check an alphabetical list by selecting Index. The manual may also have a Search feature that allows you to search for a particular subject.

Other Kinds of Help
Software also comes with a printed manual containing detailed information on using the program.

Explore It Choose an application, such as a word-processing program, to which you have access. Explore the program and the program manual to determine what types of Help the program includes. List these types in a chart like the one shown here.

> **Computer Help**
>
> **Built-in Help**
> • Balloon Help
> • On-line manuals
>
> **Other Kinds of Help**
> • Read Me files
> • Printed manuals

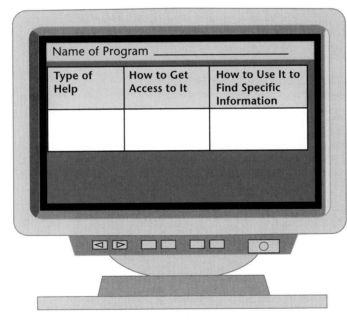

Name of Program _____		
Type of Help	**How to Get Access to It**	**How to Use It to Find Specific Information**

Integrating Workplace Skills

Point out to students that the number of jobs that require expertise in the use of media and technology is increasing rapidly. Explain that with frequent development of new or improved software in both of these areas their ability to adapt to and learn computer programs may be a deciding factor in their on-the-job success.

▶ *Lesson Objectives*

1. To use a variety of reference aids.
2. To become proficient at navigating electronic texts and other technology resources.
3. To evaluate the effectiveness and organization of technology resources.

Step-by-Step Teaching Guide

Getting "Help" On-Line

Teaching Resources: Writing Support Transparency 10-I; Writing Support Activity Book 10-3

1. Begin by asking students how often they use help on-line when working on computers. Ask for several student volunteers to give examples of situations in which they have sought help with a computer program while using it.

2. Encourage students to practice activating balloon help in class (if they have access to computers) or at home. Ask students to share their experiences using balloon help. In particular, ask them to share anything they learned about the program with which they received help. Explain that many people never use help within programs and therefore never learn about important shortcuts and features.

3. Have students open the on-line manual in a program they often use at school (if they have access to computers) or at home. Ask them to choose an area of this program about which they would like to learn more. Have them search for help with this area of the program in two ways: utilizing the index feature of the on-line manual, as well as the contents feature.

4. Display the transparency and give students copies of the blank organizer. Use students' experiences exploring balloon and on-line help to begin filling in the chart. Students can add to it as they continue working with help features on their own.

Lesson Objectives

1. To write an informative essay that describes and explains.

2. To develop writing by categorizing ideas and using effective transitions.

3. To use prewriting strategies to generate ideas.

4. To demonstrate control over grammatical elements.

Step-by-Step Teaching Guide

Expository Writing Prompts

1. Emphasize to students that when writing how-to essays in standardized tests they should identify all the steps of the process they are explaining before they start writing.

2. Tell students that the organization of their essay should follow the steps of the process clearly and logically. As an example, point out that they wouldn't start a how-to essay about tying one's shoes with instructions about tightening the knot.

3. Explain that frequently they can organize their ideas for a how-to essay by simply making a quick list of the steps required to complete the process about which they are going to write.

4. Reassure students that while neatness counts, examiners understand that time constraints prevent most standardized tests of this kind from being perfect finished products. Emphasize, however, that following the rules of grammar, punctuation, and spelling will make their how-to explanations clearer for their audience.

Standardized Test Preparation Workshop

Responding to Expository Writing Prompts

Some expository writing prompts on standardized tests measure your ability to write a "how-to"—to present clear instructions and explanations in writing. You will be evaluated on your ability to do the following:

- choose a logical, consistent organization
- provide the appropriate amount of detail for your specific audience and purpose
- use complete sentences and follow the rules of grammar
- use correct spelling and punctuation.

The process of writing for a test, or for any other kind of writing, can be divided into stages. Plan to use a specific amount of time for prewriting, drafting, revising, and proofreading.

Following is an example of one type of expository writing prompt you might find on a standardized test. Use the suggestions on the following page to help you respond. The clocks next to each stage show a suggested plan for organizing your time.

Sample Writing Situation

Imagine that you have been asked to help a group of kindergarteners learn how to tie their shoes.

As the basis for the lesson you will give, write a how-to for beginners on tying one's shoes.

Test Tip

When writing a how-to for a test, make sure you include every step necessary for the activity or process you are describing.

220 • How-to Essay

✎ TEST-TAKING TIP

Point out that following their own prescribed list of steps is one way of testing the soundness of their essay. Tell them that to test themselves properly, they must do exactly what they've written in their answers. By following their own words precisely, they will find any missing or incorrectly ordered steps in their how-to essays.

Tell students that if they are writing a how-to essay about a process they can't recreate in class as a self-check, they will have to picture the process in their minds. Point out that they can check the steps of the process by reading their essay and picturing the steps at the same time.

Prewriting

Allow one fourth of your time for jotting down the details you want to include.

Whom Are You Instructing? Since you already know how to tie a shoe, you do it automatically. However, that is not the case for a child who is just learning how to do it. Before writing anything, consider how well a young child will understand your instructions.

Take Notes on Tying Your Own Shoe Draw a picture in your mind of how you tie your shoe. As you think about it, consider the many steps that are involved in the process. List these steps.

Drafting

Allow about half of your time for drafting.

Create an Outline Begin your instructional essay by creating a timeline of steps. (See the example on page 206.) Since you are assuming that you are teaching a child who has never tied a shoe before, start by instructing the reader to put his or her shoes on.

Follow Your Outline As you draft, turn your outlined list of steps into sentences. Make sure that each sentence describes only one step. Take care to describe the technique simply, clearly, and completely in language that a child can understand.

Revising, Editing, and Proofreading

Allow almost one fourth of your time for revising. Allow several minutes to give your work one final check for errors in spelling and punctuation.

Put It to the Test Follow your own instructions, step by step. Observe any points where you get confused. Rewrite instructions at these points to make them clearer.

Add Missing Information Review your outline, and fill in any points you may have left out of your draft. Make sure that you connect one step to the next using transition words such as *next*, *then*, and *finally*.

Make Corrections Proofread your draft. Make sure that each sentence is complete, that your words are spelled correctly, and your use of punctuation is correct. If you have made any mistakes, cross them out neatly with a single line.

Customize for
ESL Students

Students who speak English as a second language may find it difficult to provide how-to explanations because they don't have the vocabulary to describe every step of a process. Tell them that this problem will be somewhat alleviated if they choose a process with which they are very familiar. Suggest that they focus on identifying the words that they'll need to describe the process (e.g. tie, pull, lace, etc.) Point out that if they can't think of the "right" word, they can find other, more familiar words with which to describe a step in a how-to process.

Customize for
More Advanced Students

Have students think of complicated processes with which they are familiar and give them the task of explaining them in an essay which they will share with the class. Point out that the art of the how-to essay lies in making complicated processes and ideas accessible to their audience. Interested students may want to look for essays and books that explain how to complete complex processes. Encourage them to notice how writers make their explanations clear and organized for their readers.

Time and Resource Manager

In-Depth Lesson Plan

	LESSON FOCUS	PRINT AND MEDIA RESOURCES
DAY 1	**Introduction to Research Reports** Students learn key elements of research reports and analyze the Model From Literature (pp. 222–225).	*Writers at Work* **Videotape**, Reports
DAY 2	**Prewriting** Students choose and narrow a topic, consider their audience and purpose, and gather information (pp. 226–229).	**Teaching Resources** *Writing Support Transparencies*, 11-A–C; *Writing Support Activity Book*, 11-1 *Writing Lab* **CD-ROM**, Reports
DAY 3	**Drafting** Students organize their ideas and write their first drafts (pp. 230–231).	**Teaching Resources** *Writing Support Transparencies*, 11-D *Writing Lab* **CD-ROM**, Reports
DAY 4	**Revising** Students revise their drafts in terms of overall structure, paragraphs, sentences, and word choice (pp. 232–235).	**Teaching Resources** *Writing Support Transparencies*, 11-E–F *Writing Lab* **CD-ROM**, Reports
DAY 5	**Editing and Proofreading; Publishing and Presenting** Students check their work for accuracy and correctness and present their final drafts (pp. 236–237).	**Teaching Resources** *Scoring Rubrics on Transparency*, Ch. 11; *Formal Assessment*, Ch. 11 *Writing Lab* **CD-ROM**, Reports

Accelerated Lesson Plan

	LESSON FOCUS	PRINT AND MEDIA RESOURCES
DAY 1	**Prewriting and Drafting** Students review characteristics for report writing, select topics, and write drafts (pp. 222–231).	**Teaching Resources** *Writing Support Transparencies*, 11-A–D; *Writing Support Activity Book*, 11-1 *Writing Lab* **CD-ROM**, Reports *Writers at Work* **Videotape**, Reports
DAY 2	**Revising to Presenting** Students work individually or with peers to revise, edit, and proofread their work for presentation (pp. 232–237).	**Teaching Resources** *Writing Support Transparencies*, 11-E–F; *Scoring Rubrics on Transparency*, Ch. 11; *Formal Assessment*, Ch. 11 *Writing Lab* **CD-ROM**, Reports

Options for Adapting Lesson Plans

HOMEWORK

Have students complete any stage of the lesson for homework.

FEATURES

Extend coverage with the Connected Assignment (p. 241), Spotlight on the Humanities (p. 242), Media and Technology Skills (p. 243), and the Standardized Test Preparation Workshop (pp. 244–245).

TECHNOLOGY

Students can complete any stage of the lesson on computer. Have them print out their completed work.

INTEGRATED SKILLS COVERAGE

Integrating Grammar
Participial Phrases SE p. 234
Quotation Marks and Underlining Titles SE p. 236

Reading/Writing Connection
Reading Strategy SE p. 224
Writing Application SE p. 225

Speaking and Listening
ATE p. 239

Language Highlight
ATE p. 233

Spelling
ATE p. 236

Workplace Skills
ATE p. 226

Technology
SE pp. 237, 243 ATE pp. 229, 234

Viewing and Representing
Critical Viewing SE pp. 222, 224, 228, 230, 232, 235, 238, 239, 240, 241, 242
ATE p. 242

ASSESSMENT SUPPORT

Standardized Test Preparation Workshop SE p. 244; ATE pp. 231, 233

Standardized Test Preparation Workbook, pp. 21–22

Scoring Rubrics on Transparency, Ch. 11

Formal Assessment, Ch. 11

Writing Assessment and Portfolio Management

MEETING INDIVIDUAL NEEDS

Less Advanced Students ATE pp. 223, 240; see also Ongoing Assessments ATE pp. 225, 227, 234, 237

ESL Students ATE pp. 225, 233, 245

Visual/Spatial Learners ATE p. 227

Logical/Mathematical Learners ATE p. 230

Gifted/Talented Students ATE p. 235

Interpersonal Learners ATE p. 230

BLOCK SCHEDULING

Pacing Suggestions
For 90-minute Blocks
- Have students complete the Prewriting and Drafting stages in a single period.
- Focus one class period on Revising and Editing and Publishing and Presenting. Allow at least 30 minutes for peer revision.

Resources for Varying Instruction
- *Writing Lab* **CD-ROM** If your students have access to hardware, a 90-minute block provides an ideal opportunity for students to work on computer.
- *Writers at Work* **Videotape** Show the Reports segment in class.

Professional Development Support
- *How to Manage Instruction in the Block* This Teaching Resource provides management and activity suggestions.

MEDIA AND TECHNOLOGY

For the Student
- *Writing Lab* **CD-ROM**, Reports

For the Teacher
- *Writers at Work* **Videotape**, Reports
- *Resource Pro* **CD-ROM**

WRITING AND GRAMMAR WEBSITE

The Interactive Writing and Grammar Web site provides a wide array of support for students, teachers and parents. Writing support includes:

- Interactive revision checkers
- Scoring rubrics with complete models

www.phschool.com

LITERATURE CONNECTIONS

Related selections from *Prentice Hall Literature: Timeless Voices, Timeless Themes,* Copper:
"A Backwoods Boy," Russell Freedman, SE p. 225
"The Wounded Wolf," Jean Craighead George, SE p. 227

Lesson Objectives

1. To recognize the elements of a research report.

2. To learn strategies, including browsing reference books and conducting self-interviews, to generate report topics.

3. To learn to use a Topic Web to narrow topics for a report.

4. To apply strategies for identifying a research report's purpose and audience.

5. To take notes on index cards as a strategy for gathering details.

6. To learn strategies for outlining.

7. To understand the technique of writing in layers to provide elaboration.

8. To check paragraph structure using the TRI pattern.

9. To revise sentences that are short and choppy.

10. To identify and define technical terms.

11. To practice the "say back" technique in peer reviews.

12. To learn how to cite sources of facts in a research report.

13. To present a report as a mini-lesson.

Critical Viewing

Infer Students may mention the difficulty of locating necessary information. A card or electronic catalog can help with this difficulty.

Chapter 11 Research
Research Report

Research in Everyday Life

Think about the facts you know about your friends and family: birthdays, names, ages; how your family first came to this country, or what happened when Grandpa moved North. These facts make up an important part of your picture of the world.

You probably picked up many of these facts here and there, at dinner or at a family gathering. Occasionally, though, you might go out of your way to find more information. Once you start asking questions, looking through photographs, or examining old papers, you are conducting research.

Research takes place when people search for facts on a subject. You can find the results of research in a magazine article about a scientific experiment or on a television program about a movie star. A good research writer helps others expand their picture of the world.

▲ **Critical Viewing**
What does this picture suggest about the difficulties of finding research sources? Name one library resource that can help with these difficulties. **[Infer]**

222 • Research Report

⏱ TIME AND RESOURCE MANAGER

Resources
Technology: Writers at Work videotape

In-Depth Coverage	Accelerated Pace
• Go over pp. 222–225 in class. • Show Reports section of the Writers at Work videotape. • Read the Model From Literature (pp. 224–225) in class and use it to demonstrate key techniques of research writing.	• Assign pp. 222–225 for independent student review.

What Is a Research Report?

A **research report** presents facts about a subject. The writer of a research report gathers these facts from credible **sources,** such as public records, experiments, reference books, and newspapers, and so can verify their truth. By citing these sources, a research writer lets readers check the facts for themselves. A research report includes

- a well-defined topic with an overall focus.
- information gathered from a variety of sources.
- a clear method of organization.
- facts and details supporting each main point.
- accurate, complete citations identifying sources.

To see the criteria on which your research report may be graded or judged, see the Rubric for Self-Assessment on page 237.

Types of Research Reports

The research reports you write might include the following:

- **Biographical sketches** report events in the life of a notable person.
- **Reports of scientific experiments** present the method and results of experiments.
- **Library research reports** present key facts about a topic gathered from library resources.

Writers in ACTION

The ancient Greek thinker and scientist Aristotle (384–322 B.C) thought research had its roots in human nature. In one work, he wrote:

"All men desire by nature to know."

In another, he wrote:

"Every science and every inquiry, and similarly every activity and every pursuit, is thought to aim at some good."

For centuries, Aristotle's own works were essential references for scholars.

PREVIEW Student Work IN PROGRESS

Christopher Sullivan, a student at Northborough Middle School in Northborough, Massachusetts, wrote a research report about the ancient Roman Colosseum. In this chapter, you will see how he used featured strategies to choose a topic, to gather information, to elaborate, and to revise. You can read his completed report at the end of the chapter.

☑ ONGOING ASSESSMENT: Diagnose

Use the following option to assess students' current level of proficiency in research writing.

Tell students that they are writing a research report on the history of their town or city. Have them generate a short list of questions they would like to address in their reports, as well as a list of places they might go to conduct their research. If students have difficulty with the exercise, you may need to devote more time on the prewriting phase of the process.

Interest GRABBER Have each student cut a small hole in an index card. Explain that students are going to survey the classroom, viewing it through these "cameras." Their mission is to find items in the room that could serve as topics for research papers. As students locate items, they should shout out the names as you (or a couple of students) record the items on the chalkboard. Allow about five minutes for this activity, then point out all the possibilities students have come up with for research reports. Leave this list on the chalkboard. (Possible topics: computer, hairstyle, flag, pen, sport shoes, hands)

Activate Prior Knowledge

Ask students to name as many types of reports as they can think of. Start them off with reports they've done themselves, including book reports, reports about what they did on summer vacation, and so on. Challenge them to think of reports adults make, including budget reports, traffic reports, progress reports on work projects.

More About the Writer

Aristotle, as the son of a physician, knew the importance of research and facts from an early age. In his career as a teacher and philosopher, Aristotle focused on ideas—ideas that were based on observable facts and events. His writings that still exist today present his ideas and research in several different formats, including a dictionary, lecture notes, and reports called "treatises" and "doctrines."

Customize for
Less Advanced Students

Bring in some examples of research reports to show students. Include magazine and newspaper articles, encyclopedia articles, and examples of student work. Invite students to locate and share examples of factual reports on topics that interest them.

Reading\Writing Connection

Reading: Question

Read aloud the first paragraph of "Sharks." Ask students to brainstorm for some questions this paragraph raises in their minds. Examples might include:

- *Do sharks deserve their bad reputation?*
- *What do experts say about sharks?*
- *Why is the author wondering if time is running out for sharks?*

Note the questions on the chalkboard, then follow up later with the Reading\Writing Connection on page 225.

Step-by-Step Teaching Guide

Engage Students Through Literature

1. Either have the class read the article "Sharks" to themselves, or ask students to take turns reading it aloud.

2. Lead a discussion based on these questions:

- What are some facts McGrath includes about sharks? (They're intelligent, with highly developed senses. Their ability to fight off infections might help doctors treat humans.)

- What is McGrath's conclusion about sharks' bad reputation? (They don't deserve it.)

- On what facts does McGrath base her conclusion? (Very few shark species attack humans, and then only under certain conditions.)

- Why does the author think sharks are in danger? (overfishing, "finning," net kills, slow reproduction rate, low survival rate)

- Does McGrath think sharks should be protected? (yes) Why? (They have an important role as top predators in the ocean.)

Critical Viewing

Analyze Most students will mention the shark's teeth.

11.1 Model From Literature

Many articles in magazines and newspapers, such as this article by Susan McGrath (1955–), are actually a type of research report: They give facts based on outside research.

Reading Writing Connection

Reading Strategy: Question To get the most out of reading research reports, **ask questions.** For instance, McGrath says that the bad reputation of sharks is based on misunderstandings. As you read further, you might ask, "What ideas about sharks are untrue?" As you read, you will learn the answer.

▼ **Critical Viewing** What features of this shark make it look dangerous? **[Analyze]**

Sharks

Susan McGrath

They're big, they're ugly, they're vicious, and the only good one is a dead one. That's what some people say about sharks. Is their bad reputation based on truth? "No!" say the experts. But is time running out for sharks?

The blue shark looks like any typical shark: streamlined, powerful, bluish gray—more fighter jet than fish. But shark experts are quick to tell you that, among the 370 species of sharks, there simply isn't a "typical" shark (Springer 52–53).

A whale shark is as long as a school bus, while a cigar shark would fit neatly in a pencil case. A frilled shark looks like an eel with a lacy collar. A Pacific angel shark is as flat as a pancake. And the megamouth shark's gums glow in the dark.

Not mindless monsters, sharks are more intelligent than once thought (Allen, *Shadows* 24). They possess highly developed senses, also (Parker 90–91). And a chemical compound that seems to help sharks fight off infections may someday help doctors treat humans (Springer 90).

As for their killer reputation, very few shark species attack humans, and then only under certain conditions (Taylor 50–51). Sharks have more reason to be afraid of people than the reverse. Surprised? Just look at the numbers. Sharks kill between five and

In her introduction, McGrath uses a question-and-answer combination to present the focus of her research: Sharks are more endangered than dangerous.

ten people a year (Allen, *Almanac* 44–46). People kill more than 100 *million* sharks a year (Perrine 17). Placed snout to tail fins, that many sharks would circle the Earth five times. So many sharks have been killed that scientists fear some species may be wiped out.

Why are sharks on the hit list? They are fished for food—shark steak has taken the place of more expensive tuna and swordfish on many menus (*Sharks* 144–148). Also, in a cruel practice called "finning," sharks are hooked; their fins are sliced off; and the animals are tossed back into the sea to die. The sail-shaped fins are used to make shark-fin soup (Allen, *Shadows* 240). Other sharks are killed after being trapped in nets intended for other fish (*Reader's* 133–134).

When you figure that many sharks don't breed until they are more than 12 years old and that only about half of all sharks born survive (Allen, *Shadows* 17–23), you can see how overfishing could eventually threaten sharks with extinction.

The oceans would be a very different place without sharks. As predators at the top of the oceans' food chain, large sharks play an important role in keeping the population of other species in check. Part of their job is to weed out weak and injured animals, leaving the healthiest to reproduce.

Concerned scientists are working with government officials to put reasonable limits on shark fishing (Taylor 35). If they succeed, sharks will survive and maintain a useful place in the oceans of the world.

Works Cited

Allen, Thomas B. *Shadows in the Sea.* New York: Lyons & Burford Publishers, 1999.
———. *The Shark Almanac.* New York: The Lyons Press, 1999.
Parker, Steve and Jane. *The Encyclopedia of Sharks.* Buffalo, NY: Firefly Books, 1999.
Perrine, Doug. *Sharks.* Stillwater, MN: Voyageur Press, Inc., 1995.
Reader's Digest Explores Sharks. Pleasantville, NY: Reader's Digest, 1998.
Sharks, Silent Hunters of the Deep. Pleasantville, NY: Reader's Digest, 1986–1995.
Springer, Victor G., and Joy P. Gold. *Sharks in Question: The Smithsonian Answer Book.* Washington, DC: Smithsonian Institution Press, 1989.
Taylor, Leighton, ed. *Sharks and Rays: The Nature Company Guides.* New York: Time-Life Books, 1997.

Reading Writing Connection

Writing Application: Help Readers Answer Questions As you draft your report, answer the questions readers are likely to ask.

McGrath discusses her topics in logical order. First, she shows that the bad reputation of sharks is not deserved. Then, she shows that humans are actually dangerous to sharks!

The writer uses facts and explanations to support her point that people are dangerous to sharks. She gives citations for each source she uses for this information.

McGrath supplies a complete list of the references she cites for her facts.

LITERATURE

To read another example of research writing, read *Lincoln: A Photobiography* by Russell Freedman. You can find "A Backwoods Boy," an excerpt from this book, in *Prentice Hall Literature: Timeless Voices, Timeless Themes,* Copper.

Teaching From the Model

Point out that McGrath's article is a type of research report because it presents facts about a subject. McGrath collected the facts through research.

More About the Author

Susan McGrath has chosen the world of nature as her subject for many fact-filled stories, articles, and books. Nature, of course, is a gigantic subject to write about. That's why McGrath narrows it down into more manageable topics such as sharks. In this article, she narrows her topic further to deal with just two aspects of sharks—their reputation and their future.

Responding to Literature

As students read "A Backwoods Boy," ask them to watch for these elements of research writing:

- factual sentences
- quotations
- interpretations of factual events

Customize for
ESL Students

Students may not know the words *frilled* and *snout.* The expressions *wiped out, hit list, in check,* and *weed out* may be new to them also. Have students look up the meanings of the unfamiliar words and use them in original sentences.

Reading\Writing Connection

Writing: Help Readers Answer Questions

Have students look again at the questions for which they brainstormed in the Reading\Writing Connection activity on page 224. Ask the class to evaluate how well McGrath addressed the questions. Remind students that they should make sure to provide information in their own essays to help readers answer the questions they have as they read.

☑ ONGOING ASSESSMENT: Monitor and Reinforce

The following strategies might be a helpful review of the difference between fact and opinion.

Option 1 If you wonder if a statement is a fact, ask this question: "Does the sentence describe something that really happened, that is known to exist, or that is known to be true?" If your answer is yes, you've got a fact.	**Option 2** Words in context can help you identify opinion statements: *It should, I think, in my opinion, in his opinion, she believed,* and so on.

Prewriting: Choosing Your Topic

Teaching Resources: Writing Support Transparency 11-A; Writing Support Activity Book 11-1

1. Ask students where they might get ideas for a research report (possible answers: looking through books or magazines, thinking up something that interests them, asking friends or family). Point out that these are all effective strategies and that students will now learn two ways to "sharpen" their strategies.

2. When students look through books or magazines, they're browsing. Browsing is even more effective when students use this technique: Jot down any interesting person, place, object, event, or fact you come across. It's helpful to note the source for later reference. After you've finished browsing, circle the two or three most interesting ideas. Do a little more browsing on each idea. Choose the one you find most interesting and which has information readily available about it.

3. Display the transparency and guide students through Christopher's self-interview. Point out how a self-interview can help students think creatively while at the same time focus their attention on likely topics.

Integrating Workplace Skills

Ask students to imagine they've been asked to write an article for a magazine called *All About Teens*. Have students create a self-interview chart with their own answers to come up with topics for their magazine articles. Invite students to share their topics with the class.

11.2 *Prewriting*

Choosing Your Topic

For a research report, you can choose almost any topic that interests you, as long as you can locate information about it. The following strategies can help you select a topic:

Strategies for Generating a Topic

1. **Browsing** Browse through reference books at the library— for example, a volume from an encyclopedia set, an almanac, or an atlas. Jot down each interesting person, place, object, or event that you come across. Then, scan your notes, and circle any words or phrases that suggest an interesting topic. Do a little more reading on each one, and then choose your topic from among them.

2. **Self-Interview** Create a chart like the one below, and answer the questions shown. Circle words and draw lines to show connections between items on your list. Choose a topic from among these linked items.

Writing Lab CD-ROM

For more help finding a topic, explore the activities and suggestions in the Choosing a Topic section of the Research lesson.

Student Work IN PROGRESS

Name: *Christopher Sullivan*
Northborough Middle School
Northborough, MA

Conducting a Self-Interview

Christopher conducted a self-interview to identify people, places, and things in which he was interested. He selected the Colosseum when he remembered a video on ancient Rome shown to the class by his history teacher, Mr. Sanchez.

People	Places	Things	Events
• What interesting people do I know or have I heard about?	• What interesting places have I been to or have I heard about?	• What interesting things do I know about or have I seen?	• What interesting events have happened to me or have I heard about?
Randy	Niagara Falls	soccer	Thanksgiving Day parade
Mr. Sanchez	library	dolphins	Migraine concert
Ayla	playground	Roman myths	debate in Social Studies
Paul	ancient Rome	aquarium	

226 • Research Report

⏱ TIME AND RESOURCE MANAGER

Resources
Print: Writing Support Transparencies 11-A–C; Writing Support Activity Book 11-1–2
Technology: Writing Lab CD-ROM, Reports

In-Depth Coverage	Accelerated Pace
• Cover pp. 226–229 in class. • Have students use the browsing and self-interview strategies to choose their topics for research reports. • Have students narrow their topics and gather information and purpose for writing.	• Have students read pp. 226–229 independently. • Have students submit their research report topics for your approval.

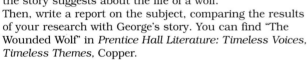

TOPIC BANK

If you're having trouble finding a topic, consider the following possibilities:

1. **Biographical Sketch** Select a person you admire, such as an athlete, a political figure, an artist, an explorer, or an inventor. Focus on one of the person's memorable achievements. Do research, and write a report explaining how the person was able to reach that achievement.

2. **Research Report on an Animal's Habitat** Choose an animal that interests you. Research the animal's characteristics and its habitat: the climate, vegetation, and other species that are present where the animal lives. Write a report explaining how the animal uses its habitat to survive.

Responding to Fine Art

3. Jot down a few notes about the painting on this page. What topics about technology, the environment, or life in the future does the painting suggest to you? Choose a topic from your notes, and write a report on it.

Responding to Literature

4. Read "The Wounded Wolf," a short story by Jean Craighead George. Think about what the story suggests about the life of a wolf. Then, write a report on the subject, comparing the results of your research with George's story. You can find "The Wounded Wolf" in *Prentice Hall Literature: Timeless Voices, Timeless Themes*, Copper.

New Man at the New Crossroads, Moses Ros

☑ Cooperative Writing Opportunity

5. **Effects of Pollution** In a group, do research on the forms of pollution. Then, assign each group member one type of pollution on which to report. Each report should discuss the causes and effects of the pollution and the ways it might be stopped. Members should review one another's work and suggest improvements. Illustrate the reports with charts, graphs, and drawings, and organize them in a binder.

Prewriting • **227**

Step-by-Step Teaching Guide

Responding to Fine Art
New Man at the New Crossroads
by Moses Ros

Teaching Resources: Writing Support Transparency 11-B

1. Display the transparency. Use the painting to prompt students to come up with topics.

2. Some students may mention topics such as nuclear war, the future of the oceans, new technologies, space travel, molecular research, and environmental concerns.

Responding to Literature

As students begin their research into wolves, suggest that they focus on the role of individual wolves within the pack.

Customize for
Visual/Spatial Learners

The strategy of browsing can apply to photos and graphic images as well as text. Students might have success finding a research topic by browsing for visual images in books, magazines, and other sources. After they come up with several topics suggested by the images, they can then browse related text for more information.

Spotlight on the Humanities

For additional topic suggestions, refer students to the Spotlight on the Humanities on page 242.

☑ ONGOING ASSESSMENT: Monitor and Reinforce

The following strategies might be helpful for students who have difficulty choosing a topic for a research report.

Option 1 Remind students to ask "I, me, and my" questions such as: "Do I like this topic? What does it have to do with me? How does it apply to my life?" If they find a personal connection with a research topic, it's more likely to keep their interest as they write their reports.

Option 2 As students browse or conduct a self-interview for a topic, have them notice topics that really interest them. Topics that grab their attention will help their research go faster and easier because they want to know more about them.

⏱ TIME SAVERS!

 Writing Support Transparencies
Use the transparencies for Chapter 11 to teach these strategies.

Prewriting: Narrowing Your Topic

Teaching Resources: Writing Support Transparency 11-C; Writing Support Activity Book 11-2

1. Display the transparency. Point out how Christopher started with his main topic in the top box. Then read the four questions Christopher asked himself to come up with the next row of boxes. Point out that Christopher circled the most interesting topics to evaluate if they were narrow enough to make a research paper topic.

2. Invite groups of students to create similar topic webs on the chalkboard, using a starter topic of their choice. Invite the groups to explain their webs to the class.

3. Give students copies of the blank organizer for them to use as they narrow their topics.

Critical Viewing

Analyze Students may say *types of reptiles, habitats,* and *diet.*

Narrowing Your Topic

Some topics are broader than others. For instance, "The Way Reptiles Live" is a broad topic. It includes everything from how pythons hunt to why lizards lose their tails. It might take years to write a report on this topic! The topic "How Horned Toads Survive in the Desert" is narrow. It covers a clearly limited set of facts.

To make sure that you cover your topic fully in your report, narrow your topic by "questioning" it.

Question Your Topic

Enter your topic in the top box of a web like the one below. Then, ask yourself the following questions:

• What different kinds of things does my topic include?

• What events are included in my topic?

• What places are included in my topic?

• Who is involved in my topic?

For each answer, enter an item in the second row of boxes in your web. Circle the most interesting of these subtopics. For each, consider whether it is narrow enough to make a good topic. If it isn't, repeat these steps for each subtopic until you reach a narrow topic.

▲ **Critical Viewing**
If you were writing a paper about reptiles for this audience, what subtopics might you include? **[Analyze]**

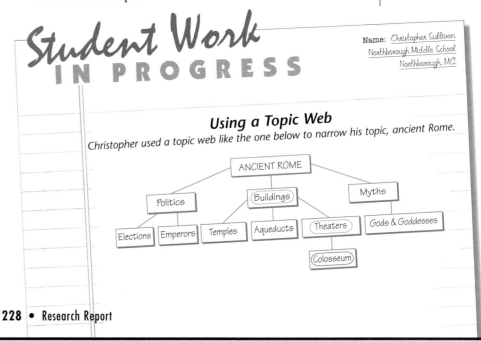

Student Work
IN PROGRESS

Name: Christopher Sullivan
Northborough Middle School
Northborough, MA

Using a Topic Web
Christopher used a topic web like the one below to narrow his topic, ancient Rome.

ANCIENT ROME
— Politics — Buildings — Myths
Elections · Emperors · Temples · Aqueducts · Theaters · Gods & Goddesses
Colosseum

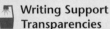 **Writing Support Transparencies**
Use the transparencies for Chapter 11 to teach these strategies.

📖 **Writing Support Activity Book**
Use the graphic organizers for Chapter 11 to facilitate these strategies.

Considering Your Audience and Purpose

The **purpose** of any research report is to clearly present facts on a topic. A report may be written for different groups of readers, or **audiences.** Your audience's background and interest in your topic will determine how much you say about each detail, as this chart suggests:

Audience:	Science teacher	A reader's club	Young children
Background in Subject:	Good	Fair	Little
Level of Detail:	Give detailed explanations of specialized facts (for example, the feeding habits of horned toads).	Give the most interesting facts (for example, the fact that horned toads squirt blood) and interesting explanations.	Thoroughly explain basic ideas (for example, the fact that horned toads are reptiles).

Gathering Details

Gather details from several different sources. By doing so, you make sure that your report will be accurate and balanced.

Take Notes

When you find information related to your topic, take notes on index cards. (You can also photocopy pages from sources, as long as you are using them just for research. Highlight the material you use.) Follow these guidelines for note taking:

- Use one card for each note. Give this card a key word.
- Double-check the spelling of names and technical terms.
- Use quotation marks when you copy words from a source.
- For each note, record the title of the book or article and the page number, or the name of the Web site or interviewee.
- Create a source card for each resource, listing the author, the title, the publisher, and the place and date of publication.

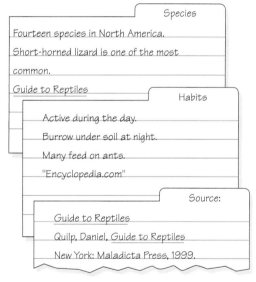

Species
Fourteen species in North America.
Short-horned lizard is one of the most common.
Guide to Reptiles

Habits
Active during the day.
Burrow under soil at night.
Many feed on ants.
"Encyclopedia.com"

Source:
Guide to Reptiles
Quilp, Daniel, Guide to Reptiles
New York: Maladicta Press, 1999.

Prewriting • 229

Step-by-Step Teaching Guide

Prewriting: Considering Your Audience; Gathering Details

1. Read through the chart at the top of the page, pointing out how the focus of the report changes to adapt to various audiences.

2. On the chalkboard, write an additional column for the chart and ask students to complete it:

   Audience: *Tourists*

   Background:

   Level of Detail:

   (Possible answers: Background: Little. Level of Detail: In-depth facts. Point out where to look for horned toads. Warn against touching, teasing, or bothering the animals.)

3. Ask students to read about the strategy of taking notes. Have students refer to the note cards to answer these questions:

   - What is an example of a key word? (history, parts, source)

   - What is the function of the source card? (to help locate the reference if you need to go back to it; to provide information for footnotes and the bibliography)

   - Why should you list the title of the source and the page number on each card? (so you can check for accuracy or additional information if you need to later)

Integrating Technology Skills

Today many people gather facts from the Internet. In this case, taking notes on note cards is not the most efficient way to gather details. Instead, people usually print out the information. Ask students to print out an example of information they find on the Internet. Point out how the printout even includes the source—usually the name of the publication or Web site as well as the site's URL address.

1. Have students display their note cards on their desks. Ask students to group the cards into categories. (The categories will vary according to the topics students have chosen.)

2. Review the descriptions of chronological order and ordering by type. Ask students to decide which method of organization better fits their topics.

3. Have each student make an outline that follows the type of organization chosen. Point out the two main types of outlines.

Customize for
Interpersonal Learners

Provide an area in the classroom where students can work in pairs, discussing their outlines as they work.

Customize for
Logical/Mathematical Learners

Students might appreciate writing their outlines on graph paper. A formal outline that uses Roman numerals takes on an orderly, geometric appearance, emphasized by the rules on graph paper.

Critical Viewing

Analyze Students may say "coloring," "body size," and "horns."

11.3 *Drafting*

Shaping Your Writing

When you think you have gathered enough information, decide how to organize your report.

Make an Outline

Choosing a Method of Organization Group your note cards by category. For instance, you might put all cards on what horned lizards eat in one group. You might put all cards on their habitats in another group. When you have finished, choose an organization that fits your topic.

- **Chronological order** organizes details according to their sequence in time. You might use chronological order when writing a report on a historical event.

- **Ordering by type** deals with each kind of thing included in your topic, discussing each in turn. It works well when your main ideas are of equal importance. For a report on the different kinds of horned lizards, for example, you might first discuss the desert horned lizard, then the regal horned lizard, and so on.

Next, make an outline following the order you have chosen. You can choose one of two ways of making an outline:

Making a Sentence Outline Jot down a sentence about each main idea in your report. Leave space between sentences. Then, write supporting details under each main idea.

Making a Formal Outline List each major part of your topic. Use Roman numerals (I, II, III) to number your most important points. Under each Roman numeral, list supporting details, labeling them with capital letters (A, B, C).

Horned Toads

I. Introduction

II. Horned toads are reptiles
   A. What is a reptile?
   B. Differences from other reptiles

III. Where do horned toads live?

▼ Critical Viewing Using details from this photograph, suggest headings for an outline of a report about the appearance of horned lizards. **[Analyze]**

⏱ TIME AND RESOURCE MANAGER

Resources
Print: Writing Support Transparency 11-D
Technology: Writing Lab CD-ROM, Reports

In-Depth Coverage	Accelerated Pace
• Cover pp. 230–231 in class. • Lead the class through the steps of choosing a method of organization and making an outline for their research reports. • You may want to choose one student's outline to demonstrate the strategy of writing in layers to elaborate.	• Have students review on pp. 230–231 independently. • Students draft their reports for homework.

Providing Elaboration

After you have mapped out the organization of your report, you are ready to start drafting. As you write, don't forget about your reader. Clearly explain everything your reader needs to know. Use the strategy below to ensure that you have included enough information.

Write in Layers

As you draft, leave space between sentences. At the end of each paragraph, pause and review your work. Ask yourself:

- Which words name people, things, or events about which I need to give a reader more information?
- Which words might confuse a reader?

Circle words that fit these descriptions. Then, using the space between sentences, add details that will give a more complete picture or that will keep a reader from growing confused.

Research Tip

As you draft, you may discover that you are missing details. Note such spots on your draft with sticky notes. Write your questions about missing information on note cards, do research to answer them, and add the information to your draft.

Student Work IN PROGRESS

Name: *Christopher Sullivan*
Northborough Middle School
Northborough, MA

Using Layers

Christopher wrote about the ancient Roman Colosseum. When he reviewed this paragraph, he realized that he could explain more about how the Colosseum was built. He also saw that unfamiliar names from ancient history could distract readers. He wrote a little bit more about each circled word.

Construction of the Colosseum started around A.D. 75 under the emperor Vespasian. The emperor ordered that a lake located between three of Rome's hills be drained for the project. The theater was named the Flavian Amphitheater. *in honor of Vespasian's family, the Flavians* Later, however, the building acquired its more familiar name, Colosseum, after a colossal statue of Nero, *an earlier emperor,* which stood nearby.

Drafting • 231

Step-by-Step Teaching Guide

Drafting: Write in Layers
Teaching Resources:
Writing Support Transparency 11-D

1. Write the following sentence on the chalkboard: Horned lizards are also called "horned toads." Ask students which words or concepts in this sentence could use further elaboration. (Students may respond: Why do they have two names? Do they have horns?) Circle the words suggested by students, e.g., horned, lizards, toads.

2. Explain that by circling the words, you've begun using a strategy called "writing in layers."

3. Display the transparency to demonstrate how Christopher used layers to elaborate details in his draft.

Revision Tip

After students have gathered details and included them in their draft, they should check to make sure they haven't "overdone" the facts. For each new detail, they should ask themselves: "Does this detail help clarify the facts, or does it detract from or confuse the facts? Does this detail belong in this paragraph?" Students can revise the draft based on their answers.

STANDARDIZED TEST PREPARATION WORKSHOP

Identifying Audience Standardized tests may require students to identify the audience for a piece of writing. Ask students for which audience was this text most likely written?

Drinking a glass of milk before bedtime can help you fall asleep. But eating a heavy meal late at night can do the opposite. Try to avoid reading in bed, so your body gets the idea that it should fall asleep—not stay awake—when you go to bed.

A heavy sleepers
B light sleepers
C nurses
D counselors

Item **B**, light sleepers, most likely need this tip. Nurses and counselors do not necessarily need this information for *themselves* (since the text is written as a direct address to the reader).

TIME SAVERS!

Writing Support Transparencies
Use the transparencies for Chapter 11 to teach these strategies.

Revising: Matching Your Draft to Your Outline

1. Ask students to refer to their drafts as you read through the process for matching a draft to its outline. Have students tag their paragraphs according to their outlines.

2. If students made a sentence outline instead of a formal outline, have them number the sentences in their outlines. They can use these numbers to tag the paragraphs in their drafts.

3. When students have tagged their paragraphs, review the bulleted questions in their textbooks. Give students time to respond to each question as you go through the questions.

Critical Viewing

Analyze Students should say that the photograph illustrates point I.B., different diets.

Revising Your Overall Structure

Analyze Your Organization

Now that you have completed a first draft, look over your report to analyze the organization of details.

▶ **REVISION STRATEGY**
Matching Your Draft to Your Outline

As you read through your report, stop at the end of each paragraph, and refer to your outline. Mark each paragraph with the Roman numeral and capital letter on your outline that designate the subject of the paragraph.

For example, the following might be part of your outline:

I. Horned toads
  A. Different habitats
  B. Different diets

In this case, you should mark a paragraph about the habitat of the desert horned toad "I.A." If your second paragraph explains that desert horned toads eat mainly ants, mark it "I.B." If your third paragraph explains that desert horned toads live in the southwestern United States, mark it "I.A.," and so on.

When you have finished labeling each paragraph, review your labels. Ask yourself the following questions:

- Are all the paragraphs that are labeled with the same Roman numeral-capital letter combination next to one another? If not, would the report make better sense if they were?

- Does the sequence of Roman numerals and capital letters in the report match the sequence on your outline? If not, is the change an improvement? Why or why not?

Reorganize the paragraphs in your draft to achieve the most effective organization.

▶ **Critical Viewing** What point on the outline shown on this page does this photograph illustrate? **[Analyze]**

Collaborative Writing Tip

Exchange drafts with a classmate. Check off paragraphs that are placed in a good order. Mark those that seem out of order with a red question mark.

⏱ TIME AND RESOURCE MANAGER

Resources
Print: Writing Support Transparencies 11-E–F
Technology: Writing Lab CD-ROM, Reports

In-Depth Coverage	Accelerated Pace
• Cover pp. 232–235 in class. • Do the Grammar in Your Writing on p. 234.	• Have students read pp. 232–235 independently. • Direct students to implement the strategy of matching a draft to its outline and marking paragraph patterns on their drafts, and then to show you their work.

Revising Your Paragraphs

Check Your Paragraph Structure

In a report, most paragraphs should include the following:

- a **topic** sentence **(T),** stating the main idea
- a **restatement (R)** of the main idea in the topic sentence
- an **illustration (I),** example, or explanation of the main idea

An effective topical paragraph uses at least one sentence of each kind. The order in which you organize them may vary.

EXAMPLE: **T**   Some horned lizards have risky feeding habits.

R   While feeding, their body temperature can reach dangerous levels.

I   They spend hours under the broiling hot desert sun waiting for or feeding on ants.

Use the following strategy to evaluate paragraph structure.

▶ **REVISION STRATEGY**
Marking Your Paragraph Patterns

Label each of your sentences a *T*, an *R*, or an *I*. Review your draft. If you find a group of *I*'s, make sure there is a *T* they support. If you find a *T* by itself, add an *I* sentence.

Student Work
IN PROGRESS

Name: *Christopher Sullivan*
Northborough Middle School
Northborough, MA

Analyzing Paragraph Patterns

Christopher analyzed paragraph patterns in his paper on the ancient Roman Colosseum. He realized that he needed to revise this paragraph.

The wild animal hunts in the Colosseum were elaborate and often extremely cruel shows. Spectators would occasionally get sick from the bloody sight.   **T R**

Sometimes, special scenery was built to add to the "realism" of the event. And the animals were not released into the arena any old way; they arrived through hand-operated trapdoors leading from underground cages. The animals either fought each other or were encouraged to attack unarmed slaves or criminals.   **I**   **I**   **I**

> Christopher noticed that his paragraph contained only "illustrations" (I)—details about a main idea—so he added a topic sentence (T) and a restatement (R) of the main idea of the paragraph.

Revising • **233**

Step-by-Step Teaching Guide

Revising: Marking Your Paragraph Patterns

Teaching Resources:
Writing Support Transparency 11-E

1. Display the transparency and lead students through Christopher's revisions. Point out that a paragraph structure can vary—TRI, ITR, TIR.

2. Have students mark each of the sentences in their drafts *T, R,* or *I.* Then have them check that each paragraph has at least one of each type of sentence.

Customize for
ESL Students

Encourage students to work in pairs to complete the activities on pages 232–233. You might consider asking more advanced students to serve as "coaches."

Language Highlight

The word *colossal* comes from the Greek word *kolossós.* The Greek historian Herodotus was the first to use *colossal* when he described several gigantic statues he saw in ancient Egypt. When Herodotus introduced the word in his homeland of Greece, *colossal* became the popular way to say that something was really, really big.

STANDARDIZED TEST PREPARATION WORKSHOP

Sentence Organization Standardized test questions may ask students to identify the best place to insert a new sentence into a paragraph.

(1) A horned lizard rests flat and motionless on the desert floor. (2) The lizard can puff up its body and squirt blood out of the corners of its eyes.

Ask where the following sentence would best fit into the paragraph:

But if it's bothered, watch out.

A Before sentence 1

B After sentence 1

C After sentence 2

D It doesn't fit in this paragraph

Choice **B** is the correct answer. The sentence serves as a transition between sentences 1 and 2.

 TIME SAVERS!

 **Writing Support Transparencies**
Use the transparencies for Chapter 11 to teach these strategies.

Step-by-Step Teaching Guide

Revising: Vary Your Sentence Structure

Challenge groups to search one another's papers to locate clusters of short, choppy sentences. Invite the group that first completes their search to share an example they found.

Step-by-Step Teaching Guide

Grammar in Your Writing: Participial Phrases

1. Review with students that participial phrases answer the questions *What kind? Which one? How many?* or *How much?*

2. Have students create participial phrases that answer the questions *What kind?* and *Which one?* for the following verbs:

   slithered

   tap-dancing

   growled

   hiccuping

Find It in Your Reading

Possible response: in a cruel practice called "finning"; it tells what kind of practice.

Find It in Your Writing

Have students identify the information added by the participial phrases they locate.

Integrating Technology Skills

Invite students to print out the home page of a Web site they have visited. Ask students to use their revising and editing skills to improve the text on the home page.

Revising Your Sentences

Vary Your Sentence Structure

"He did this . . . ." "He did that . . . ." No one likes to read one short, choppy sentence after another. Choppy writing often comes from stating each piece of information in its own sentence. Use the following strategy to combine sentences.

▶ **REVISION STRATEGY**

Adding to the Main Action in a Cluster

Select three paragraphs in your draft. In each, circle clusters of short sentences. In each cluster, find a verb that simply adds to the information about a person, thing, or event in another sentence. Use this verb to create a participial phrase (see the information in the box below). Add this phrase to the sentence about which it provides more information.

SHORT SENTENCES: The lizard ran away. It *shed* its tail first.

COMBINED: *Shedding* its tail, the lizard ran away.

Language Lab CD-ROM

For practice with different sentence structures, complete the Varying Sentence Structure lesson in the Sentence Style unit.

Grammar in Your Writing
Participial Phrases

A **participle** is a form of a verb that acts as an adjective. A present participle is the *-ing* form of a verb. A past participle is the past form of the verb, often ending in *-ed* or *-d*. A **participial phrase** combines a present or past participle with other words and phrases. The entire phrase acts as an adjective. It answers the questions *What kind? Which one? How many?* or *How much?* about something in a sentence.

By using participial phrases, you can combine sentences, as in these examples:

SHORT SENTENCES: The lizard crawled slowly. She vanished into her burrow.
COMBINED: Crawling slowly, the lizard vanished into her burrow.

SHORT SENTENCES: He found a reptile egg. It was buried in the desert.
COMBINED: He found a reptile egg buried in the desert.

Find It in Your Reading Find one participial phrase in "Sharks" by Susan McGrath on page 224. Explain what information it adds to the main action or point of the sentence.

Find It in Your Writing Identify two participial phrases that you have used in your research report. If you can't find two examples, find a place where you can combine two short sentences using a participial phrase.

To learn more about combining sentences, see Chapter 21.

234 • Research Report

☑ ONGOING ASSESSMENT: Prerequisite Skills

If students have difficulty with participial phrases, you may find it helpful to refer them to the following materials.

In the Textbook	Print Resources	Technology
Phrases and Clauses, pp. 416–431	Grammar Exercise Workbook, pp. 59–64	On-Line Exercise Bank, 20.1

Revising Your Word Choice

While writing your research report, you may have found new words, including technical terms such as *reticulated* ("marked with net-like patterns"). Code such terms, and consider adding their definitions to help readers understand their meaning.

▶ ## REVISION STRATEGY
Color-Coding Technical Terms

Highlight technical terms in your report. Check each term in a dictionary and in the source where you found it to make sure that you understand its use. Then, add a definition at the first place each new term appears in your draft.

▲ **Critical Viewing**
In what source might you find the name of the parts indicated? **[Apply]**

Student Work
IN PROGRESS

Name: *Christopher Sullivan*
Northborough Middle School
Northborough, MA

Defining Technical Terms

Christopher highlighted a few technical terms. He checked their meanings in his notes and in a dictionary, and then added their definitions.

the fighters trained for these shows,

Gladiators, were usually either slaves or prisoners.

(three-pronged spears, like giant forks)

A gladiator's weapons included tridents and swords. The men

with tridents were also equipped with nets.

Peer Review

"Say Back"

Join a group of three or four other classmates. Read your report aloud twice to the group. During the second reading, listeners should jot down strong points in your report and points about which they want to know more. Listeners should then "say back" these reactions to you. Consider the group's comments as you make your final revisions.

Revising • 235

Step-by-Step Teaching Guide

Revising: Color-Coding Technical Terms

Teaching Resources: Writing Support Transparency 11-F

1. Display the transparency. Ask students how Christopher's essay would have been different if he had not defined these terms for his readers.

2. Divide the class into small groups. Provide each group with an article or report that includes one or more technical terms.

3. Direct the groups to highlight the technical terms they find and note the definition provided in context. Have students share their results.

4. Have students follow this same procedure with their research reports. Have students double-check the definition of any terms they find.

Customize for
Gifted/Talented Students

After completing step 2 above, assign students the job of double-checking the technical definitions. In some cases, the sources of the definitions may be provided in footnotes in the article. In other cases, students will have to check dictionaries and other reference books.

Critical Viewing

Apply Students might suggest checking a dictionary of musical terms or the musical instruments or orchestra section of an encyclopedia.

⏱ TIME SAVERS!

📋 **Writing Support Transparencies**
Use the transparencies for Chapter 11 to teach these strategies.

235

Editing and Proofing: Focusing on Citations

1. Internal citations are necessary when:
   - stating an idea that is not your own
   - using a direct quotation
   - stating a fact (facts that are commonly known and available in numerous sources do not need internal citations)

2. Point out that Christopher's final draft on pages 238–240 includes both internal and external citations.

3. Students may wonder why newspaper articles do not use citations. Reporters must carefully document every fact, idea, and quotation they collect. The documentation remains in their notes for reference, but is not included with their newspaper articles because of space constraints.

Grammar in Your Writing: Quotation Marks and Underlining With Titles of Works

Ask students if they would use underlining (or italics) or quotation marks for the name of

- a movie (underline)
- a one-hour TV special (quotation marks)
- a TV soap opera (underline)
- a statue in an art museum (underline)

Find It in Your Reading

Have students explain why italics are used in the examples they find.

Find It in Your Writing

Have students share examples from their draft and explain why each is formatted as such.

Integrating Spelling Skills

Remind students that *page* and *pages* are abbreviated as *p.* and *pp.*, respectively, in internal citations.

11.5 Editing and Proofreading

Focusing on Citations

Cite sources for quotations, facts, and ideas that are not your own.

Internal Citations An internal citation appears in parentheses directly after the information you cited. It includes the author's last name and the page number on which the information appears.

> Although his writing could be savage and sarcastic, Jonathan Swift "was loved throughout Ireland as a defender of the underprivileged" (Sporre 379).

Works Cited List Provide full information about your sources in an alphabetical "Works Cited" list at the end of your report. The following is an example of the correct form:

> Sporre, Dennis J. *The Literary Spirit.* Englewood Cliffs, NJ: Prentice-Hall, 1988.

For each work cited, make sure that you write the author's last name first. Use a period after the author's name, after the title of the work, and at the end of the listing. Use a colon between the place of publication and the publisher. Use a comma between the publisher and the year of publication.

Learn More

For a full explanation of the form for citations, see the section on Citing Sources and Preparing Manuscript, page 722.

Grammar in Your Writing
Quotation Marks and Underlining With Titles of Works

Follow these guidelines for presenting the title of a work in your research report:

Underline (or italicize) the titles of long written works and the titles of periodicals. Also, underline or italicize the titles of movies, television series, and works of music and art.

Use quotation marks around the titles of short written works and Internet sites.

Find It in Your Reading Read the Works Cited list on page 225. Notice how italics are used for the titles of works.

Find It in Your Writing Review your essay to see whether you have used underlining and quotation marks correctly for the titles of works.

To learn more about the form for titles, see Chapters 26 and 27.

⏱ TIME AND RESOURCE MANAGER

Resources
Print: Scoring Rubrics on Transparency, Chapter 11; Writing Assessment: Scoring Rubric and Scoring Model for Research Report
Technology: Writing Lab CD-ROM, Reports

In-Depth Coverage	Accelerated Pace
• Cover pp. 236–240 in class.	• Have students read pp. 236–240 independently.
• Students edit and proofread their reports in class.	• Students edit and proofread their reports as homework.
• Students present their final drafts.	• Students present their final drafts.

11.6 Publishing and Presenting

Building Your Portfolio

Consider the following ways to publish and present your report:

1. **Present a Mini-lesson** Use your report as the basis for a mini-lesson on your topic. Plan a lesson that includes an activity related to the topic. Present your lesson to a group of classmates.

2. **Conduct a Round-Table Discussion** Form a group with others who have researched similar topics—for example, animals, music, or athletes. Each member should present his or her report. After each presentation, other members should ask questions, make comments, and compare the subjects.

Reflecting on Your Writing

Jot down a few notes on your experience writing a research report. To begin, you might answer the following questions:

- What was the most interesting thing you learned about your topic?

- Which strategy for prewriting, drafting, revising, or editing might you recommend to a friend?

Internet Tip

To see a research report scored according to this rubric, visit **www.phschool.com**

Rubric for Self-Assessment

Use the following criteria to evaluate your research report:

	Score 4	Score 3	Score 2	Score 1
Audience and Purpose	Focuses on a clearly stated topic, starting from a well-framed question; gives complete citations	Focuses on a clearly stated topic; gives citations	Focuses mainly on the chosen topic; gives some citations	Presents information without a clear focus; few or no citations
Organization	Presents information in logical order, emphasizing details of central importance	Presents information in logical order	Presents information logically, but organization is poor in places	Presents information in a scattered, disorganized manner
Elaboration	Draws clear conclusions from information gathered from multiple sources	Draws conclusions from information gathered from multiple sources	Explains and interprets some information	Presents information with little or no interpretation or synthesis
Use of Language	Shows overall clarity and fluency; contains few mechanical errors	Shows good sentence variety; contains some errors in spelling, punctuation, or usage	Uses awkward or overly simple sentence structures; contains many mechanical errors	Contains incomplete thoughts and mechanical errors that make the writing confusing

Publishing and Presenting • **237**

☑ **ONGOING ASSESSMENT: Assess Mastery**

Use one of the following options to assess final drafts of students' research reports.

Self-Assessment Ask students to score their essay using the rubric provided. Then have students write a paragraph reflecting on the most valuable strategy they learned in completing this essay.

Teacher Assessment Use the rubric and the scoring models provided in Writing Assessment, Research Report, to score students' work.

Step-by-Step Teaching Guide

Publishing and Presenting: Sharing Information

1. Research reports often contain information that other people would like to know. The writer of this type of report must decide which is the most effective way to get the information out there for others to learn about.

2. Lead students in thinking of the most effective ways they could let others know about the particular information in their research reports. (Possible answers: giving the information as a speech at a political rally, submitting it to a certain department of a newspaper or magazine for publication, printing it in the newsletter of a pertinent organization, publish it on the Internet or in the school newspaper)

ASSESS

Step-by-Step Teaching Guide

Assessment

Teaching Resources: Scoring Rubrics on Transparency 11; Formal Assessment, Chapter 11

1. Display the Scoring Rubric transparency and review the criteria in class.

2. Before students proceed with self-assessment, you may wish to review the Final Draft of the Student Work in Progress on pages 238–240. Have students score the Final Draft in one or more of the rubric categories. For example, how would students score the essay in terms of audience and purpose?

3. In addition to student self-assessment, you may wish to use the following assessment options.

   - score student essays yourself, using the rubric and scoring models from Writing Assessment.

   - review the Standardized Test Preparation Workshop on pages 244–245.

   - administer the Chapter 11 Test from Formal Assessment in Teaching Resources to assess students' grasp of concepts presented.

Teaching From the Final Draft

1. Have students read "The Ancient Roman Colosseum."

2. Lead a discussion in which students evaluate the report based on these questions:
   • Is the topic clearly stated?
   • How clear is the purpose of the report?
   • Is the method of organization clear?
   • Is the level of detail adequate?
   • Do most paragraphs follow the TRI principle?
   • How do the sentences flow?
   • Are technical terms defined?
   • Are all necessary citations provided?

3. Students might apply a scale of 1–10 (lowest to highest) to evaluate each criterion above.

Critical Viewing

Evaluate Students' responses will vary, but most will say that the ancient Romans lacked modern technology.

11.7 *Student Work*
IN PROGRESS

FINAL DRAFT

▲ Critical Viewing
What facts about the ancient Romans make the feat of building the Colosseum especially impressive? **[Evaluate]**

The Ancient Roman Colosseum

Christopher R. Sullivan
Northborough Middle School
Northborough, Massachusetts

The Colosseum, which may still be seen today in Rome, is one of the most remarkable entertainment centers ever built. Its history, the plan of the building, and the types of shows that were held there are all fascinating subjects.

Construction of the Colosseum started around A.D. 75 under the emperor Vespasian. The emperor ordered that a lake located between three of Rome's hills be drained for the project. The theater was named the Flavian Amphitheater in honor of Vespasian's

Christopher uses the first paragraph to introduce his research topic. He explains his main idea for the paper. He also gives the subtopics into which his report is organized.

family, the Flavians. Later, however, the building acquired its more familiar name, Colosseum, after a colossal statue of Nero, an earlier emperor, which stood nearby (Nardo 27–29).

Construction of this enormous building lasted for five years. The opening was celebrated with one hundred days of games, in which thousands of animals and numerous fighters were killed. The original spectators must have marveled at the building's dimensions. The outer walls were 157 feet high, and the central arena measured 290 feet by 180 feet (Quennell 36).

The seating plan was like the seating plan of a modern sports stadium. Extending all the way around the building, eighty entrances led to tiers of seats and standing areas. Each entrance was marked with a Roman numeral. The tickets or tokens that spectators needed for admission were probably marked with this section number (Macdonald 28–29).

Although admission to the Colosseum was free, rich, important people got to sit in the best seats. For example, the emperor had a personal entrance that led directly to his seat. Public officials and wealthy people occupied the lower rows of seats. The lower classes had to climb farther up to reach their seats. Finally, at the roof level were all the women. Overall, the Colosseum had a capacity of nearly 50,000 people (Mann 26).

The arena itself was the center of the stadium. It was made of wood and covered with sand. The most popular shows held there were gladiator fights and wild animal hunts (Nardo 38).

Gladiators, the fighters trained for these shows, were usually either slaves or prisoners. A gladiator's weapons included tridents (three-pronged spears, like giant forks) and swords. The men with tridents were also equipped with nets. They tried to cover and knock down the opposition. Fighters with swords wore armor and carried a shield (Connolly 212–215). Some fights ended with one gladiator's death. In cases of injury, however, the emperor, or sometimes the crowd, would decide whether the wounded gladiator would live or die. Some historians say that, contrary to popular belief, the crowd pointed their thumbs at their chests to vote "kill" and used a thumbs-down sign to vote "drop the sword" or "spare" (Nardo 63).

The wild animal hunts in the Colosseum were elaborate and often extremely cruel shows. Spectators would occasionally get sick from the bloody sight. Sometimes, special scenery was built to add to the "realism" of the event. And the animals were not released into

Notice that Christopher uses organization by type in his report, grouping related ideas together.

Christopher supports his point about the size of the Colosseum with precise measurements gathered during research.

Throughout his report, Christopher uses internal citations to refer to the sources of particular facts.

Christopher begins the third main section of the report, in which he discusses the types of shows held in the Colosseum.

Christopher knows readers may doubt his account of "thumbs down" because they have heard another popular but false account. He gives a citation so they can check the facts themselves.

◀ **Critical Viewing** Why might ancient Roman emperors have built buildings and had sculptures made of themselves? **[Hypothesize]**

Student Work in Progress • **239**

Integrating Speaking and Listening Skills

Invite students to read the research report aloud to the class. You might assign one student to read the introduction and the section on history, a second student to read the section on the building plan, and a third student to read the section on the types of shows as well as the conclusion.

Critical Viewing

Hypothesize Students may say emperors wanted to be remembered by future generations.

Customize for
Less Advanced Students

Invite students to reflect on the research report about the Colosseum by discussing these questions:

- What was the most interesting thing you learned about the topic?
- Did the report bring up anything you'd like to learn more about?
- If you could make a comment to Christopher, the report's author, what would you say?

Critical Viewing

Evaluate Students may say that the fights were fair.

▲ **Critical Viewing** This photograph shows a section of an ancient Roman mosaic (a picture made from small stone tiles). Judging from the mosaic, how fair were fights between gladiators? **[Evaluate]**

the arena any old way; they arrived through hand-operated trap-doors leading from underground cages. The animals either fought each other or were encouraged to attack unarmed slaves or criminals (Macdonald 31–33).

The Colosseum was used for centuries, but the violent shows staged there became less popular after Rome adopted Christianity as the official religion in the fourth century. For nearly two thousand years, the building has survived many natural disasters, including earthquakes and lightning strikes. The Colosseum still stands today as one of the most dramatic monuments of ancient Roman culture (Quennell 68–69).

In the last paragraph of the report, Christopher concludes with a sentence restating the main idea of the report as a whole.

At the end of his report, Christopher provides a complete list of the works he has cited. He uses the standard format for citing works.

Works Cited

Connolly, Peter, and Hazel Dodge. *The Ancient City*. New York: Oxford University Press, 1998.

Macdonald, Fiona, and Mark Bergin. *The Roman Colosseum*. New York: Peter Bedrick Books, 1996.

Mann, Elizabeth. *The Roman Colosseum*. New York: Mikaya Press, 1998.

Nardo, Don. *The Roman Colosseum*. San Diego: Lucent Books, Inc., 1998.

Quennell, Peter. *The Colosseum*. New York: Newsweek, 1971.

240 • **Research Report**

Connected Assignment *I-Search Report*

An **I-search report** is a personal exploration of a topic that especially interests you. It includes

- a topic you want to know more about, perhaps in order to do something.
- the story of why you are interested in the topic.
- the story of how you researched the topic.
- a report of what you learned.
- the use of the pronoun *I* to tell your story.

An I-search report is *similar* to a research report in that you use outside sources to gather information. It is *different* because it includes your own experiences. Write an I-search report using these suggestions:

Prewriting Choose a topic in which you have a real interest. For instance, you might be interested in building a model car or helping to clean up a local park. After choosing a topic,

- list the questions to which you want answers.
- choose those questions in which your interest is strong and to which you will be able to find answers.
- enter your questions in the "W" column of a K-W-L chart like the one shown.
- for each item in this column, list a possible source (a book, magazine, person, and so on) for the answer.
- fill in the chart as you gather details about your topic.

▲ **Critical Viewing**
This boy is doing research by phone. Cite details from the picture showing that he is well prepared. **[Analyze]**

Know	**W**ant to Know	**L**earned
The park is a mess! I can't even play Frisbee there without stepping on broken glass.	Who is supposed to clean it up? (source: I can look in the phonebook for the Parks Department number) Can volunteers help? (source: the Parks Department, or maybe the mayor's office)	The town can only afford two part-time workers to clean up.

Take separate notes on your research experiences.

Drafting Organize your details using an outline. Follow your outline as you draft. For each part of your story, explain exactly what you did and learned.

Revising and Editing Review your draft. Make sure that you present events and ideas in a clear sequence. Add transitions, such as *first*, *next*, and *for that reason*, to aid readers.

Publishing and Presenting After revising your I-Search report, consider posting it on a school Web site.

Connected Assignment: I-Search Report • **241**

Lesson Objectives

1. To write an I-search report appropriate to audience and purpose.
2. To organize and present information to ensure support for ideas.
3. To use writing processes to develop and revise drafts.
4. To publish and present an I-search report to an audience.

Step-by-Step Teaching Guide

I-Search Report

Teaching Resources: Writing Support Transparency 11-G; Writing Support Activity Book 11-3

1. Ask students to share their existing knowledge of how to write research reports. Students will probably say that they are supposed to focus on supporting or explaining the main topic using information gathered during their research. Point out, if students don't, that in research reports they are generally not encouraged to talk about their own experiences and interests.

2. Explain that I-search reports are different. Their own experiences, interests, and processes are as important as researched information in I-search reports.

3. Provide students with a model of an I-search report. After reading it through, ask students what kinds of information the writer provided about him or herself that would not be included in a research report.

4. Help students generate topics by encouraging them to make lists of topics that interest them. Students may benefit from hearing each other's lists.

continued

Step-by-Step Teaching Guide continued

5. Ask for a volunteer to share a topic idea with the class. Display the transparency and give students copies of the blank organizer. Work with the class to begin filling out the K-W-L chart transparency for the student volunteer's essay topic. Encourage students to fill out the blank organizer for their own topic ideas, then have them use these notes to begin drafting an I-search report.

Critical Viewing

Analyze Students may note that the boy has something to write with and a pad of paper. They may also see that he's wearing a watch, which is an important part of keeping interview appointments. Ask students what else the boy might have done in preparation for doing research over the phone.

Lesson Objectives

1. To analyze information as presented in various media.
2. To take notes from relevant sources.
3. To use a variety of reference aids.
4. To become proficient at navigating electronic texts and other technology resources.

Step-by-Step Teaching Guide

Select Visuals to Extend Meaning

1. Choose one of the Spotlight elements for class discussion, or have students work individually or in groups on the element of their choice. Give students the initiative to find the necessary books, videotapes, or pictures.

2. Bring in a video of *The African Queen*. Show a scene from the movie with the sound muted. Ask students to look for elements in the scene that give them clues about the personality of the characters or the direction of the storyline. Point out that every frame of a movie is an image that communicates information, so even small details must be carefully researched.

3. Ask students if they can think of any movies in addition to the *The African Queen* that have been made from books. Alternatively, ask them if they can think of any books they would like to see made into movies. Discuss the challenges film makers might face in adapting books for the screen.

4. Bring in images of vaudeville performers and images of scenes from silent movies. Ask students what they notice about the imagery from each of these forms of entertainment. Lead a discussion about the visual impact of these examples.

5. Interested students may want to do additional research about the relationship between these three forms of entertainment.

Spotlight on the Humanities

Select Visuals to Extend Meaning

Focus on Film: *The African Queen*

You might not guess it, but even an adventure-comedy film may be the result of research. When a film involves historical events, the writers, directors, costume makers, and scenery designers must do research into the period. They use this research to get story ideas and to portray details from the period accurately.

The *African Queen* is one such adventure-comedy. The film is set in Africa at the beginning of World War I. The creators of the film used research into the situation of the time to create a suspenseful story.

Released in 1951 and starring the legendary Humphrey Bogart (1899–1957) and Katharine Hepburn (1909–   ), *The African Queen* is a classic. Bogart won an Academy Award for his portrayal of Charlie Allnut, a tough steamboat captain, who meets the prim and proper Rose Sayer as war is brewing in Central Africa. Directed by John Huston (1906–1987), the exploits of this mismatched pair on the Ulonga-Bora River create a perfect mixture of comedy and adventure.

Literature Connection The British novelist C. S. Forester (1899–1966) wrote the novel *The African Queen*. Born in Africa, Forester grew up in London. He became famous for his eleven-book adventure series featuring Horatio Hornblower, a heroic naval officer.

Theater Connection Director John Huston's father was the stage actor Walter Huston (1884–1950). By 1905, Walter Huston was a successful vaudeville performer. (*Vaudeville* is a form of theater featuring dance, song, and comedy.) In 1924, Walter Huston showed the serious side of his acting ability, starring in Eugene O'Neill's play *Desire Under the Elms*.

Research Writing Activity: Picture Research on Africa
Choose a Central African nation. Imagine that you are doing research for a movie, and select visuals that give an accurate idea of the climate, landscapes, clothing, foods, and the important industries or trades of the country. Show different settings, such as as farms and cities.

242 • Research Report

▲ Critical Viewing
Using details from this movie still, explain how well the characters of Charlie Allnut and Rose Sayer got along at first in *The African Queen*. **[Draw Conclusions]**

Viewing and Representing

Activity Explain to students that many movies are not filmed where their stories take place. Filming a movie about a Central African nation may be less expensive, for example, in an American location as opposed to an African one. The film makers will therefore research the Central African nation, find an American location that looks similar and then build sets and costumes based on research.

Critical Viewing

Draw Conclusions Students may note the uncomfortable facial expressions of the two actors, the protective way in which Rose Sayer is holding onto her basket, or the fact that Charlie Allnut is reaching towards her from a distance. Ask them what other details of character and setting they notice in this movie still.

Media and Technology Skills

Using Available Technology for Research

Activity: Finding On-line Sources

When you turn on a computer, you open the door to a world of information. You can use this information as you do research for reports or for your own interests.

Learn About It The **Internet** is a a series of computers linked together across the world. A computer in this network can make information available to any user who logs on to the Internet. To log on and access information, you can use any computer with a Web browser and a connection to the Internet.

Web Sites A **Web site** is a set of connected images, words, and other information stored on a computer. People create Web sites on all sorts of subjects, from tarantulas to tooth decay.

Finding Specific Information You can travel to a particular Web site by typing in its URL (Uniform Resource Locator) address in your Web browser. Many times, though, you will not know of a specific Web site on your topic. To find one, use a search engine (click the "Search" button on your browser to call one up).

Using a Search Engine Enter a search term in the "Search" field of the engine and click "Search." The engine will then list Web pages containing words matching your search term. You are most likely to find the information you need on the pages listed first.

Choosing Good Search Terms A computer will not "know what you mean" if you misspell a term. Spell all search terms correctly. To start, use the most specific terms you can. For instance, *snakes* will bring up too many hits. Use a more specific term, such as *pythons*.

Apply It Come up with three specific questions on different topics. Use three different search engines to answer these questions. Record your results in a chart like the one shown. Then, use your notes to write a brief paragraph describing your Internet experience.

Tips for Using a Search Engine

Use Quotation Marks
If you are searching for information on a certain person or brand name, put quotation marks around your search term. The engine will focus on pages including exactly that name.

Use the Plus Sign
To cut down on the number of irrelevant "hits" in your search results, some search engines let you use the plus sign in your search term. For instance, if you want only information on birds in Africa, use "birds +Africa" as your search term. (Consult Help for more information on the engine you are using.)

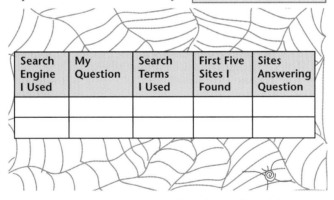

Search Engine I Used	My Question	Search Terms I Used	First Five Sites I Found	Sites Answering Question

Media and Technology Skills • 243

1. To use a variety of reference aids.
2. To become proficient at navigating electronic texts and other technology resources.
3. To evaluate the effectiveness and organization of technology resources.

Step-by-Step Teaching Guide

Using Available Technology for Research

Teaching Resources: Writing Support Transparency 11-H; Writing Support Activity Book 11-4

1. Begin by explaining to students that computers can be an excellent research tool if used correctly. Ask the class if any of them have ever tried to find something on the Internet and were unsuccessful. Point out that because there is so much information on the Internet they will need to learn how to find specific information efficiently.

2. Ask for a topic question about which the class wants to know an answer. Using the transparency, walk students through a sample search for this information. Students can follow the steps of the search on an overhead screen or on their own screens.

3. As the class moves through the steps of the sample search, have them review the definitions and explanations provided in their textbooks. For example, highlight the search terms used in the example, and use this as an opportunity to make sure they understand how to phrase or present their search subjects.

4. Give students copies of the blank organizer and have students choose three questions on three different topics. Have them fill out the chart as they conduct their searches, and then give them time to write a paragraph about their experience.

Lesson Objectives

1. To practice the elements of the revision process.
2. To practice editing drafts for specific purposes.
3. To demonstrate control over grammatical elements.

Revising and Editing

1. Explain to students that standardized test questions which test their ability to revise and edit a passage test the same skills they have been practicing when writing their own papers. The main difference is that optional revisions and edits are provided in test questions, and then they must choose between these options.

2. Ask for student volunteers to read the sample test item, the multiple choice question, and the answer and explanation. As students read, point out that the sample text is numbered so that the questions which follow it can target specific lines within the passage.

3. Explain that the question asks for the best answer, which means there may be other possible answers that they need to eliminate.

4. Tell them that questions of this sort may ask for appropriate titles or topic sentences for a test passage, good concluding sentences, or better word and sentence choices within the passage.

5. Give students time to practice on their own using the exercises on the next page.

Standardized Test Preparation Workshop

Revising and Editing

When writing a research report, you must strive to present information clearly. Revising your report to give it a strong, consistent organization is one key to clear writing. On a standardized test, you may be asked questions that test your ability to revise and edit a passage. The sample test item below shows one format for such questions.

Test Tip

When answering revising and editing questions, place each choice in the context of the passage before choosing an answer.

Sample Test Item

Read the passage below. Then, answer the multiple-choice question that follows.

1 The best way to protect against infectious
2 disease is to keep your body healthy. You
3 must eat nutritious food, as well as get
4 plenty of rest, fluids, and exercise. You can
5 also protect yourself by washing your
6 hands often and by not sharing eating
7 utensils or drink containers. You should
8 also make sure that you have all recom-
9 mended vaccinations. Storing food prop-
10 erly, keeping kitchen equipment and
11 surfaces clean, and cooking meats well
12 can prevent food poisoning.

1. Which of these sentences would make the **BEST** topic sentence for this paragraph?

  A Good health and a little caution are the best defense against disease.

  B Keeping your body healthy is the only real way to protect yourself from disease.

  C Food poisoning is a cause of disease.

  D Cleanliness is important to good health.

Answer and Explanation

The correct answer is *A*. *B* does not make a good topic sentence for the paragraph because the paragraph lists other steps for protecting yourself from disease in addition to keeping your body healthy. *C* does not make a good topic sentence because the main subject of the paragraph is what prevents disease, not what causes it. *D* does not make a good topic sentence because cleanliness is just one way to prevent infectious disease, and the paragraph talks about several preventive measures. *A* is the best choice because each sentence in the paragraph helps build support for this statement.

244 • Research Report

⬦ TEST-TAKING TIP

Tell students that they should read a test passage at least twice. Explain that the more familiar they are with the passage, the more easily they'll be able to substitute optional sentences, words, or phrases.

Suggest that they read sections of the passage to themselves when trying to fit in answer choices. To see if one of the multiple choice answers works in the sample passage, for example, they should probably read the sentences just before and after the one being questioned.

▶ **Practice**   **Directions:** Read the following passage. Then, answer the questions below, choosing the letter of the best answer.

1 Organisms may be composed of only
2 one cell or of many cells. Unicellular,
3 or single-celled, organisms include
4 bacteria, the most numerous organ-
5 isms on Earth. A bacterial cell carried
6 out all of the functions necessary for
7 the organism to stay alive.
8   Multicellular organisms are com-
9 posed of many cells. The cells of many
10 multicellular organisms are specialized
11 to do certain tasks. For example, you
12 are made of trillions of cells.
13 Specialized cells in your body such as
14 muscle and nerve cells work together to
15 keep you functioning. Nerve cells carry
16 messages from your surroundings to
17 your brain. Other nerve cells then
18 carry messages to your muscle cells,
19 making your body move.

1 What is the **BEST** change, if any, to make to the sentence in lines 5–7 (*"A . . . alive."*)?
  A Change *A bacterial cell* to **It**
  B Change *carried* to **carries**
  C Change *carried* to **carry**
  D Make no change.

2 Which of the following sentences would **BEST** fit after the sentence in lines 5–7 (*"A . . . alive."*)?
  F These functions include respiration and excretion.
  G In the twentieth century, scientists began studying bacteria for clues about how life began and maintains itself.
  H Bacteria are also classified by their shape.
  J The word *organism* is used to describe all living things.

3 What is the **BEST** change, if any, to make in the middle of the sentence in lines 8–9 (*"Multicellular . . . cells."*)?
  A Change *are composed of* to **are found in**
  B Change *are composed of* to **are contained in**
  C Delete *are composed of*
  D Make no change.

4 Which of these sentences would **BEST** fit the ideas in lines 9–11 (*"The . . . tasks."*)?
  F Your brain controls muscle movement.
  G Most single-cell organisms are not visible without the aid of a microscope.
  H Humans are considered multicellular organisms.
  J Multicellular organisms are more complex than single-cell organisms.

5 Which is the **BEST** change, if any, that should be made to the sentence in lines 13–15 (*"Specialized . . . functioning"*)?
  A Delete *such as muscle and nerve cells*
  B Change *such as muscle and nerve cells* to *. . ., such as muscle and nerve cells,*
  C Change *such as muscle and nerve* cells to **such as muscle-nerve cells**
  D Make no change.

6 Which of the following sentences would **BEST** conclude the passage?
  F From the simplest forms of life to the most complex, cells have many varied roles.
  G Organisms need nerves to survive.
  H Only the most complex organisms can use a large number of cells.
  J Large numbers of specialized cells are the key to life as we understand it.

Answer Key

▶ **Practice**
  1. B
  2. F
  3. D
  4. J
  5. B
  6. F

Customize for
ESL Students

Students who speak English as a second language may find it difficult to understand exactly what's being asked of them in standardized test questions, especially if they involve choosing between a number of possible sentences. Suggest that they carefully read and summarize the passage to themselves before looking at the questions. Then encourage them to look for certain phrases in the questions themselves. Review the questions modeled in their textbooks and help them find key words such as "BEST topic sentence," "BEST fits the ideas," and "BEST concludes the passage."

Chapter 12 — Time and Resource Manager

In-Depth Lesson Plan

	LESSON FOCUS	PRINT AND MEDIA RESOURCES
DAY 1	**Introduction to Response to Literature** Students learn key elements for response to literature and analyze the Model From Literature (pp. 246–249).	*Writers at Work* **Videotape,** Response to Literature
DAY 2	**Prewriting** Students choose and narrow a topic, consider their audience and purpose, and gather information (pp. 250–255).	**Teaching Resources** *Writing Support Transparencies,* 12-A–D; *Writing Support Activity Book,* 12-1–2 *Writing Lab* **CD-ROM,** Response to Literature
DAY 3	**Drafting** Students organize their ideas and write their first drafts (pp. 256–257).	**Teaching Resources** *Writing Support Transparencies,* 12-E *Writing Lab* **CD-ROM,** Response to Literature
DAY 4	**Revising** Students revise their drafts in terms of overall structure, paragraphs, sentences, and word choice (pp. 258–262).	**Teaching Resources** *Writing Support Transparencies,* 12-F–G *Writing Lab* **CD-ROM,** Response to Literature
DAY 5	**Editing and Proofreading; Publishing and Presenting** Students check their work for accuracy and correctness and present their final drafts (pp. 263–266).	**Teaching Resources** *Scoring Rubrics on Transparency,* Ch. 12; *Formal Assessment,* Ch. 12 *Writing Lab* **CD-ROM,** Response to Literature

Accelerated Lesson Plan

	LESSON FOCUS	PRINT AND MEDIA RESOURCES
DAY 1	**Introduction, Prewriting, and Drafting** Students review characteristics for response to literature writing, select topics, and write drafts (pp. 246–255).	**Teaching Resources** *Writing Support Transparencies,* 12-A–D; *Writing Support Activity Book,* 12-1–2 *Writing Lab* **CD-ROM,** Response to Literature *Writers at Work* **Videotape,** Response to Literature
DAY 2	**Revising to Presenting** Students work individually or with peers to revise, edit, and proofread their work for presentation (pp. 256–266).	**Teaching Resources** *Writing Support Transparencies,* 12-E–G; *Scoring Rubrics on Transparency,* Ch. 12; *Formal Assessment,* Ch. 12 *Writing Lab* **CD-ROM,** Response to Literature

Options for Adapting Lesson Plans

HOMEWORK

Have students complete any stage of the lesson for homework.

FEATURES

Extend coverage with the Connected Assignment (p. 267), Spotlight on the Humanities (p. 268), Media and Technology Skills (p. 269), and the Standardized Test Preparation Workshop (pp. 270–271).

TECHNOLOGY

Students can complete any stage of the lesson on computer. Have them print out their completed work.

INTEGRATED SKILLS COVERAGE

Integrating Grammar
Compound Sentences SE p. 261
Punctuating Quotations SE p. 263

Reading/Writing Connection
Reading Strategy SE p. 248
Writing Application SE p. 249

Language Highlight
ATE p. 259

Vocabulary
ATE p. 252

Workplace Skills
ATE p. 250

Real-World Connection
ATE p. 260

Viewing and Representing
Critical Viewing SE pp. 246, 248, 249, 253, 255, 256, 258, 262, 265, 267, 268
ATE p. 268

ASSESSMENT SUPPORT

Standardized Test Preparation Workshop SE p. 270; ATE p. 255

Standardized Test Preparation Workbook, pp. 23–24

Scoring Rubrics on Transparency, Ch. 12

Formal Assessment, Ch. 12

Writing Assessment and Portfolio Management

MEETING INDIVIDUAL NEEDS

Less Advanced Students ATE p. 251; See also Ongoing Assessments ATE pp. 251, 259, 261, 264

More Advanced Students ATE p. 271

ESL Students ATE pp. 248, 251, 253

Visual/Spatial Learners ATE pp. 254, 259

Logical/Mathematical Learners ATE p. 255

Bodily/Kinesthetic Learners ATE p. 250

Gifted/Talented Students ATE p. 264

BLOCK SCHEDULING

Pacing Suggestions
For 90-minute Blocks
- Have students complete the Prewriting and Drafting stages in a single period.
- Focus one class period on Revising and Editing and Publishing and Presenting. Allow at least 30 minutes for peer revision.

Resources for Varying Instruction
- *Writing Lab* CD-ROM If your students have access to hardware, a 90-minute block provides an ideal opportunity for students to work on computer.
- *Writers at Work* **Videotape** Show the Response to Literature segment in class.

Professional Development Support
- *How to Manage Instruction in the Block* This Teaching Resource provides management and activity suggestions.

MEDIA AND TECHNOLOGY

For the Student
- *Writing Lab* **CD-ROM**, Response to Literature

For the Teacher
- *Writers at Work* **Videotape**, Response to Literature
- *Resource Pro* **CD-ROM**

WRITING AND GRAMMAR WEB SITE

The Interactive Writing and Grammar Web site provides a wide array of support for students, teachers and parents. Writing support includes:

- Interactive revision checkers
- Scoring rubrics with complete models

www.phschool.com

LITERATURE CONNECTIONS

Related selections from *Prentice Hall Literature: Timeless Voices, Timeless Themes,* Copper:

"My Papa, Mark Twain," Suzy Clemens, SE p. 249

"Dragon, Dragon," John Gardner, SE p. 251

► Lesson Objectives

1. To recognize various types of responses to literature, such as book reviews and comparisons.

2. To learn the topic-generating strategies of interviewing yourself and participating in a literary roundtable.

3. To use self-questions to define the audience and clarify the purpose of the response to literature.

4. To learn and implement a variety of strategies for gathering details.

5. To learn strategies for drafting and revising an essay.

6. To measure sentences as a way of locating short and choppy sentences in a draft.

7. To focus on the proper use of clauses, coordinating conjunctions, and semicolons.

8. To participate in the strategy of pointing as a method of peer review.

9. To check quotations for accuracy and correct punctuation.

Critical Viewing

Apply Students may say that the girl could explain what she likes about the book.

Chapter 12 *Response to Literature*

▲ **Critical Viewing**
What might this girl tell someone to encourage him or her to read the book she is enjoying? **[Apply]**

Responding to Literature in Everyday Life

You can spend hours by yourself reading a good book. If you enjoyed it, the first thing you want to do is tell someone else about it: "The story was great—full of hair-raising suspense!" When you explain your reaction to a novel, play, short story, or poem, you are giving a **response to literature.** Book reviews and letters to authors are written responses to literature.

Writing down a response to literature takes a little more work than talking with a friend. Once you write about a work, however, more and more of it percolates through your brain. You will see more, and appreciate more, in it than before. To enrich your reading experiences, develop your skills writing a response to literature.

246 • Response to Literature

⏱ TIME AND RESOURCE MANAGER

Resources
Technology: Writers at Work videotape

In-Depth Coverage	Accelerated Pace
• Cover pp. 246–249 in class. • Show the Response to Literature Section of the Writers at Work videotape. • Read the Model From Literature (pp. 248–249) in class.	• Have students read pp. 246–249 on their own. • Discuss definitions and types of responses to literature in class. • Assign the Model From Literature for independent reading.

What Is a Response to Literature?

A **response to literature** expresses the writer's feelings and thoughts about a book, short story, essay, article, or poem. Using examples from the work, it explains why the writer reacted to the work as he or she did. The elements of a good response include

- a strong, interesting focus on some aspect of a novel, short story, drama, or poem.
- a clear organization.
- supporting details for each main idea.
- a summary of important features of the work.
- the writer's feelings about or judgment of the work.

To learn the criteria on which your response may be graded or judged, see the Rubric for Self-Assessment on page 264.

Types of Response to Literature

You might write one of the following types of response to literature:

- **Book reviews** give readers an impression of a book, encouraging them either to read it or to avoid reading it.
- **Letters to an author** let a writer know what a reader found enjoyable or disappointing in the writer's work.
- **Comparisons of works** highlight the features of two or more works by comparing them.

Writers in ACTION

Henry Wadsworth Longfellow (1807–1882), one of the most famous American poets of his day, thought that writers wish for a certain kind of response to their work:

"*What a writer asks of his reader is not so much to* like *as to* listen.*"*

PREVIEW
Student Work
IN PROGRESS

Erin Macdonald Roski, a student at Madison Middle School in Oceanside, California, wrote a response to a book retelling the story of the Trojan War. In this chapter, you can follow the strategies she used to choose a topic, draft, and revise her work. The final draft of her essay appears at the end of the chapter.

Response to Literature • 247

PREPARE and ENGAGE

Interest GRABBER Write the following words on the chalkboard:

yuck
wow
weird
heart-stopping
sad
sweet
real

Ask students to suggest movies they've seen that fit each word in the list. Explain that the words represent students' *responses* to the movies.

Activate Prior Knowledge

After completing the Interest Grabber, point out that movies are based on scripts—works of writing. Ask students to name any books, plays, stories, or poems they've read that have resulted in extremely strong personal responses, including the responses listed on the chalkboard.

More About the Writer

Henry Wadsworth Longfellow was a master at enticing his audience to "listen." His words were simple and clear, and his phrases flowed like the melodies of songs. For example, people who have read Longfellow's poem *Paul Revere's Ride* only once or twice can usually recall instantly its first two lines: "Listen my children, and you shall hear/Of the midnight ride of Paul Revere."

✓ **ONGOING ASSESSMENT: Diagnose**

Use the following option to diagnose students' current level of proficiency in responding to literature.

Ask students to brainstorm for a list of reactions to a piece of literature they have read in class recently. What did they like about it? What didn't they like? If students have difficulty completing this exercise, you will need to devote more time to the prewriting phase of the process.

Reading\Writing Connection

Reading: Identify Evidence

Read aloud the first paragraph of "Introducing Natty Bumppo." Ask students what the writer needs to "prove" in her essay, based on her introductory statement. (Natty Bumppo takes you completely into his time and place; Bumppo does this better than any other hero in American fiction.) Write students' responses on the chalkboard. Have students look for evidence that proves Becker's claims as they read her article.

Teaching From the Model

Point out that although Becker's article is a response to literature, it includes more than her feelings and opinions about *Leatherstocking Tales*. Responses to literature must also include facts, details, and other types of evidence.

Critical Viewing

Connect Students may say that from the man's expression and stance, he seems to have keen senses and cool nerve.

Customize for
ESL Students

Students may be unfamiliar with America's frontier period. They may also need more information about Native American culture and history to fully understand the article.

12.1 Model From Literature

May Lamberton Becker (1873–1958) was a critic and children's book author. A fan of James Fenimore Cooper's work, she wrote an introduction to his novel The Last of the Mohicans, *from which this excerpt is taken.*

Reading Writing Connection

Reading Strategy: Identify Evidence The writer of an essay or other piece of nonfiction should provide evidence to support each main point. **Identify the evidence** as you read for better understanding. For instance, Becker says that the character Natty Bumppo takes you "completely into his time and place." The evidence she gives for this claim are her summaries of his adventures: he lives with Indians, works as an army scout, and travels west. This evidence shows that Bumppo was involved in many aspects of the pioneer life of his time.

▲ **Critical Viewing** Explain what features of the man in this picture match the description of Natty Bumppo in the essay. **[Connect]**

In her introduction, Becker introduces her subject, a fictional character, and her enjoyment of him.

Introducing Natty Bumppo

May Lamberton Becker

There is no hero in American fiction who takes you with him into his time and place more completely than Natty Bumppo on his life journey through the five Leatherstocking Tales.

He strides into *The Deerslayer* a young hunter brought up among the Delaware Indians, getting experience in Indian warfare in the wilderness of northern New York State in the seventeen-forties. The perfect woodsman, he needs plenty of room; loving the forest, he has the keen senses and cool nerve needed to keep alive there.

In *The Last of the Mohicans: A Narrative of 1757* he is in the prime of life and at the top of his powers as a scout in the

248 • Response to Literature

campaign of Fort William Henry. In *The Pathfinder* he falls in love, but you remember that less than you do the defense of the block-house.

In *The Pioneers* civilization is beginning to catch up with the old scout. Leatherstocking, free hunter of the forest, is arrested for shooting deer out of season. In *The Prairie* he has retired still further to the western plains; frontiersman still, nearly ninety and still able to deal with forest fires and the buffalo stampedes, the last tremendous effort of his life is to rise from his sickbed as the sun goes down, answer "Here," and fall back, dead. Generous, resourceful, not so fond of traders as of Indians, his way through these five romances has been that of the pioneer through a period when America was taking shape. . . .

Few of us now take the adventures in order. We meet Natty Bumppo head-on in *The Last of the Mohicans* with Chingachgook and Uncas, holding our breaths from one escape to the other, hating to let the older men go on the last page, even if Uncas has gone beyond our reach. So when we find that Chingachgook is in another story, we read *The Deerslayer*. After that we take them any way they come, but *Mohicans* stays longest. All over the world this story has leaped out of the book and become part of the lives of boys. Reading it for the first time is an experience no one should miss. I never knew anyone who could quite forget it.

Writing Application: Provide Evidence
As you draft your own response to literature, provide your readers with evidence for each of your main points.

Becker uses a logical order, telling us about the development of Bumppo's character through the books in the Leatherstocking series.

Becker supports her picture of Bumppo as a true hero with details such as his death scene.

In this conclusion, Becker restates her response to Bumppo and the Tales in strong terms: She calls reading the books "an experience no one should miss."

LITERATURE

To read another response to literature, see Suzy Clemens's recollections of her father, Mark Twain. You can find her essay, "My Papa, Mark Twain," in *Prentice Hall Literature: Timeless Voices, Timeless Themes,* Copper.

◀ **Critical Viewing**
Briefly describe an adventure that might have led to this scene. **[Speculate]**

Model From Literature • **249**

Engage Students Through Literature

1. Lead the discussion described in the Reading\Writing Connection on page 248.

2. Read the rest of "Introducing Natty Bumppo" aloud to the class.

3. Then explain that you're going to read the article aloud again, but this time students will participate in a Time and Place Challenge.

4. Explain the rules:
   • When students hear a piece of evidence, they should raise their hands.
   • You will call on a student and ask "Time or place?"
   • The student should respond with the correct answer and the evidence to support it.
   • For example, when you read "among the Delaware Indians," students' hands should go up. You call on a student and ask, "Time or place?" The student responds, "Place: among the Delaware Indians."

Responding to Literature

Suzy Clemens wrote "My Papa, Mark Twain" as a journal entry when she was 13 years old. It includes her response to Mark Twain's *The Prince and the Pauper.*

Reading\Writing Connection

Writing: Provide Evidence

Referring to the Reading\Writing Connection on page 248, direct students' attention to their statements recorded on the chalkboard. Ask students to analyze whether Becker provided adequate evidence to support her claims. (Note: Becker's article is an excerpt. She undoubtedly provides additional evidence in her complete essay.)

Critical Viewing

Speculate Students' responses will vary.

Prewriting: Generating a Topic

Teaching Resources: Writing Support Transparency 12-A

1. Conduct an interview with a willing student, using the following questions.

   • Have you ever read a book or story that you just couldn't put down?

   • If you could read any type of story or book for a report, what kind would you choose? Thriller? True story? Biography? Mystery? Science fiction?

   • Of all the characters you've seen in books, movies, or TV shows, which character is most like you?

2. Point out that students can ask *themselves* interview questions like these to come up with literary topics to write about.

3. Similar interview questions can also get discussions started in a group of students called a *literary round table*. Group members can take notes during the discussion to identify topics that interest them.

4. Display the transparency. Direct students' attention to Erin's notes from a round table and some of the topics of interest that she identified.

Integrating Workplace Skills

Editors for newspapers, radio, and TV conduct round tables with their staff members to identify topics for news stories. Ask students to imagine participating in such a round table, knowing that not all story ideas will be selected. How would they "pitch" a topic to assure that it survives the cut?

Customize for
Bodily/Kinesthetic Learners

Invite students to role-play the literary round table discussion described in Integrating Workplace Skills. Before the role-play, have the students select topics to bring to the table.

250

Prewriting

Choosing Your Topic

Start off by choosing a good topic for your response to literature—a work to which you have a strong reaction. For help in finding such a work, use the following strategies:

Strategies for Generating a Topic

1. **Interview Yourself** Write down answers to the questions below. Review your answers, and then choose a work from among them as your topic.

   • What is my favorite type of reading? (Give examples.)

   • Which character from my reading would I like to be?

2. **Literary Round Table** In a group, discuss works you have enjoyed. Each person should give the title, author, and special qualities of a work. As the round table proceeds, jot down titles that sound interesting. Review your list, and choose your topic from these titles or from another work of which you were reminded.

Writing Lab CD-ROM

For more help choosing a topic, see the activities and tips in the Choosing a Topic section of the Response to Literature lesson.

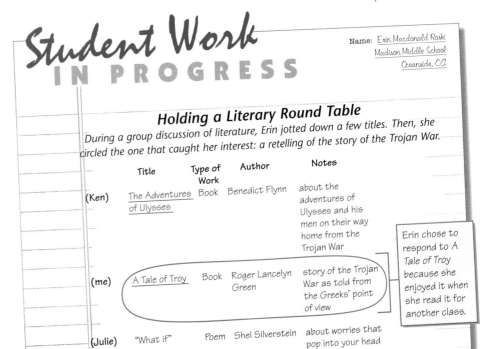

Student Work IN PROGRESS

Name: Erin Macdonald Roski
Madison Middle School
Oceanside, CA

Holding a Literary Round Table

During a group discussion of literature, Erin jotted down a few titles. Then, she circled the one that caught her interest: a retelling of the story of the Trojan War.

	Title	Type of Work	Author	Notes
(Ken)	The Adventures of Ulysses	Book	Benedict Flynn	about the adventures of Ulysses and his men on their way home from the Trojan War
(me)	A Tale of Troy	Book	Roger Lancelyn Green	story of the Trojan War as told from the Greeks' point of view
(Julie)	"What if"	Poem	Shel Silverstein	about worries that pop into your head at night

Erin chose to respond to A Tale of Troy because she enjoyed it when she read it for another class.

250 • Response to Literature

⏱ TIME AND RESOURCE MANAGER

Resources
Print: Writing Support Transparencies 12-A–D; Writing Support Activity Book 12-1–2
Technology: Writing Lab CD-ROM, Response to Literature

In-Depth Coverage	Accelerated Pace
• Cover pp. 250–255 in class. • Have students use either the self-interview or the literary round table strategy to generate a topic for writing a response to literature. • Students having difficulties may choose topics from the Topic Bank.	• Have students read pp. 250–255 independently. • Have students submit their topics for your approval. • Students narrow their topics and gather details.

TOPICS
TOPIC BANK

If you're having trouble finding a topic, consider the following possibilities:

1. **Advertising Poster** Choose a short story you liked or disliked. Create a poster for readers your own age, encouraging them to read or avoid the story. Use a strong visual image and slogan. Fill in details supporting your opinion about the work in a short essay attached to your poster.

2. **Letter** Write a letter to the author of a book you enjoyed. Give suggestions and ask questions about his or her writing, using examples from the work.

Responding to Fine Art

3. Jot down a few notes about this painting. What might happen during the game? How might it end? Where does the scene take place? Then, look over your notes and think of stories, books, or poems of which the scene reminds you. Choose one of these works as your topic.

Children's Round, Hans Thoma

Responding to Literature

4. John Gardner's short story "Dragon, Dragon" pokes fun at some of the ideas found in fairy tales. Read Gardner's story, and then read a fairy tale about three brothers—for example, "The Three Brothers" by Jacob and Wilhelm Grimm. Write an essay explaining which story you preferred reading. You can find Gardner's story in *Prentice Hall Literature: Timeless Voices, Timeless Themes,* Copper.

☑ Cooperative Writing Opportunity

5. **Literary Festival** With a group of other students, plan a series of activities to celebrate a book, story, or poem. Divide the following tasks: giving readings or acting out scenes from the work; creating art work based on the work, such as mural or an advertising poster; or creating a radio or television commercial. Then, prepare a panel discussion for the class in which group members discuss the work and give their opinions on it.

Prewriting • 251

Step-by-Step Teaching Guide

Responding to Fine Art

Children's Round, by Hans Thoma

Teaching Resources: Writing Support Transparency 12-B

1. Display the transparency and ask students to describe what is happening in the painting.

2. Have students suggest possible topics based on this painting.

Responding to Literature

As students read the two fairy tales, have them take notes of particular aspects and details of each story that help them decide which story they prefer.

Customize for
ESL Students

Erin's choice of the Trojan War is from Greek mythology. Suggest that students consider responding to a myth, legend, or folktale from their home culture.

Customize for
Less Advanced Students

Urge students to choose a piece of literature at their level, not something as challenging as the Trojan War, with names that are hard to pronounce. Jean Craighead George and Gary Paulsen should appeal to students who like animals. A mystery by Arthur Conan Doyle, a scary story by Edgar Allan Poe, or a funny story by James Thurber are other possibilities.

Spotlight on the Humanities

For additional topic suggestions, refer students to the Spotlight on the Humanities on page 268.

☑ ONGOING ASSESSMENT: Monitor and Reinforce

The following strategies might be helpful for students who have difficulty choosing a topic for their response-to-literature essays.

Option 1 Have students check with a librarian. They can explain the kinds of books and stories they like to read, and then ask for some recommendations.	**Option 2** Have students explore some Internet sources for topics. They might want to visit publishers' Web sites, homework-help Web sites, or student chat rooms.

⏱ TIME SAVERS!

 Writing Support Transparencies
Use the transparencies for Chapter 12 to teach these strategies.

Prewriting: Focusing Your Response

Teaching Resources: Writing Support Transparency 12-C; Writing Support Activity Book 12-1

1. Display the transparency. Refer students to the Literary Round Table chart on page 250. Point out that Erin chose *A Tale of Troy* as the topic of her essay.

2. Erin's next step was to use the pentad as a graphic organizer to narrow her topic. Ask students to review the pentad and figure out which episode of the book Erin is focusing on. (the episode of the Trojan horse)

3. On the chalkboard, write these questions:
   - Who did the action in this episode?
   - What did the actors do?
   - When or where did they do the action?
   - How did they do it?
   - Why did they do it?

4. Give students copies of the blank organizer. Help students match each of these questions to its label on the pentad. Have students answer the questions using the information noted on the pentad.

Integrating Vocabulary Skills

People often think of the word *agency* as a term that means "a company or a business." But *agency* can also mean "an operation, an action, or an activity." This is the meaning of *agency* as it is used in the pentad.

12.2

Focusing Your Response

After choosing a topic, focus your response. A story, poem, or play is like a town, with different streets to wander down. Focus on one "neighborhood" of your chosen work, such as the friendship of two characters. To focus your topic, fill in a pentad.

Use a Pentad

Fill in a star like the one shown by answering these questions:

- **Actors** Who performed the action?
- **Acts** What was done?
- **Scenes** When or where was it done?
- **Agencies** How was it done?
- **Purposes** Why was it done?

Highlight related details that interest you, and sum them up in a sentence to create a focused topic.

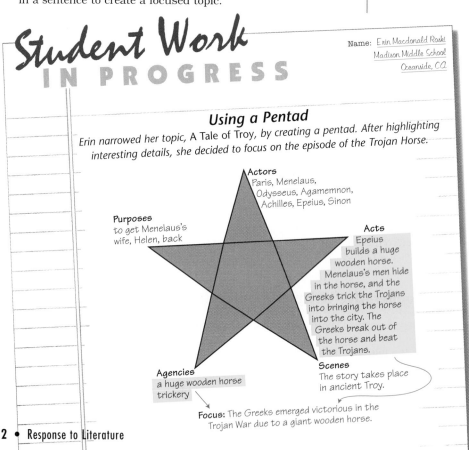

Student Work
IN PROGRESS

Name: Erin Macdonald Roski
Madison Middle School
Oceanside, CA

Using a Pentad

Erin narrowed her topic, A Tale of Troy, by creating a pentad. After highlighting interesting details, she decided to focus on the episode of the Trojan Horse.

Actors
Paris, Menelaus, Odysseus, Agamemnon, Achilles, Epeius, Sinon

Purposes
to get Menelaus's wife, Helen, back

Acts
Epeius builds a huge wooden horse. Menelaus's men hide in the horse, and the Greeks trick the Trojans into bringing the horse into the city. The Greeks break out of the horse and beat the Trojans.

Agencies
a huge wooden horse
trickery

Scenes
The story takes place in ancient Troy.

Focus: The Greeks emerged victorious in the Trojan War due to a giant wooden horse.

Considering Your Audience and Purpose

When you write about a work of literature, you must consider who your **audience**—your readers—will be. The nature of your audience will help determine what details you include in your response. Use questions like these to plan your writing:

- **Are my readers already familiar with this kind of work?** If so, give details showing what is unique about this work or how it differs from others of its kind.

- **Are my readers unfamiliar with this kind of work?** If so, explain the basic purpose of the work—to tell a suspenseful story, to make music with words, and so on.

You must also consider your **purpose** in writing. You should use questions like these to plan your writing:

- **Am I trying to persuade readers of something?** If your purpose is to persuade, concentrate on examples supporting your opinion.

- **Am I trying to enhance readers' appreciation of the work?** If your purpose is to enhance appreciation, point out qualities and patterns in the work that a reader might not see.

◀ **Critical Viewing**
Make a pentad for this photograph (see previous page). Describe the action shown. Describe the scene where the action is taking place. Who are the "actors" (those performing the action)? What is their purpose? Finally, by what "agency" are they performing the action? [Analyze]

Step-by-Step Teaching Guide

Prewriting: Considering Your Audience and Purpose

1. To help students identify the audience for their essays, you may need to clarify your expectations regarding the essays. For instance, will students turn in the essays to be graded? (You are the audience.) Or will students present their essays to the class? (The class is the audience.)

2. After students have identified their audience, have them briefly describe the audience on paper, such as, the students in my class. Ask students to write down answers to the first two bulleted questions on page 253, then provide the other information requested after each question.

3. To help students establish the purpose of their work, have them write answers to the last two bulleted questions and provide the information requested.

Customize for
ESL Students

Students may find it helpful to work in pairs or small groups to define the audience and purpose of their essays.

Critical Viewing

Analyze Students should say that the action involves skating. It is taking place outdoors. It is being "performed" by two girls and their purpose is to have fun. The agency by which they are performing is their skates.

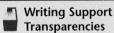

TIME SAVERS!

Writing Support Transparencies
Use the transparencies for Chapter 12 to teach these strategies.

Writing Support Activity Book
Use the graphic organizers for Chapter 12 to facilitate these strategies.

Prewriting: Gathering Details
Use Hexagonal Writing

Teaching Resources: Writing Support Transparency 12-D; Writing Support Activity Book 12-2

1. Create an oversized hexagon and display it on a bulletin chalkboard.

2. Display the transparency. Ask students to take turns reading the details that Erin included in her hexagon. Point out that the categories for the hexagon come from the list of strategies on page 255.

3. Give students copies of the blank organizer.

4. As students complete their hexagons, make copies and post the examples on the bulletin board, using your oversized hexagon as a colorful background.

Customize for
Visual/Spatial Learners

Suggest that students create a computer graphic that outlines the strategies. Students may want to distribute copies of their graphic or post it on the chalkboard or bulletin chalkboard as a helpful reminder for themselves and classmates.

12.2

Gathering Details

The reader of your response to literature will depend on you for a clear impression of your chosen work. Your reader will also look for evidence supporting your points. Write down details from the work that you will use to help your reader.

Hexagonal writing can help you gather details.

Use Hexagonal Writing

Obtain two different-colored sheets of construction paper. From each sheet, cut out three triangles of equal size. Alternating colors, arrange the triangles to form a hexagon (see the model below). Label each triangle as shown in the example. Then, fill in each triangle with details about your topic. (You can write additional details in a new hexagon or on separate note cards with the same labels.)

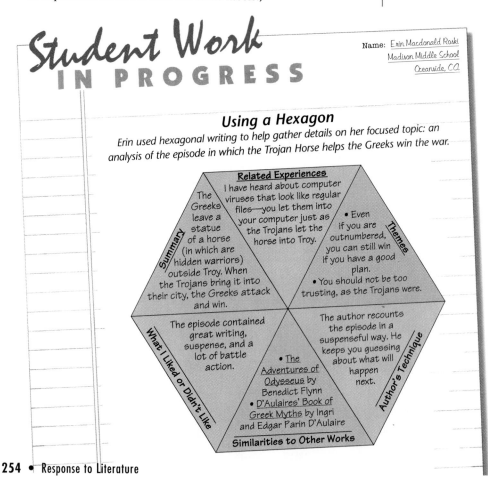

Student Work
IN PROGRESS

Name: Erin Macdonald Roski
Madison Middle School
Oceanside, CA

Using a Hexagon

Erin used hexagonal writing to help gather details on her focused topic: an analysis of the episode in which the Trojan Horse helps the Greeks win the war.

Related Experiences
I have heard about computer viruses that look like regular files—you let them into your computer just as the Trojans let the horse into Troy.

Summary
The Greeks leave a statue of a horse (in which are hidden warriors) outside Troy. When the Trojans bring it into their city, the Greeks attack and win.

Themes
• Even if you are outnumbered, you can still win if you have a good plan.
• You should not be too trusting, as the Trojans were.

What I Liked or Didn't Like
The episode contained great writing, suspense, and a lot of battle action.

Author's Technique
The author recounts the episode in a suspenseful way. He keeps you guessing about what will happen next.

Similarities to Other Works
• The Adventures of Odysseus by Benedict Flynn
• D'Aulaires' Book of Greek Myths by Ingri and Edgar Parin D'Aulaire

Details to Look For

To fill out your hexagonal, you will need to use the techniques listed below.

Write a Summary You need to familiarize readers with the work to which you are responding. Gather details you can use to summarize the work.

- List main events, ideas, or images.
- Indicate the connections among these details, such as the order in which events occur or a contrast between two images.
- List other background information, such as details about setting and characters.

Identify Related Experiences When you read a work of literature, part of the enjoyment comes from the way the work reflects real life. For each event or situation in a work, list a similar event or situation from real life.

Identify Themes Many works suggest a question or lesson about life—a **theme.** To find a theme, look for

- patterns of events—for instance, a happy ending for each good guy.
- contrasts between characters—for instance, one brother who is stubborn while the other is easygoing.

These patterns may suggest themes, such as "good people will be rewarded" or "stubbornness is a fault."

Note Examples of Author's Technique Writers use many different tricks and skills to create special effects:

- A short story writer may work hard to create suspense.
- A poet may skillfully use **figurative language** (words used for their associations or musical effects).

Gather examples of such techniques in the work.

Note Similarities to Other Works Books don't sit alone on the shelves. They jostle their neighbors, peek over one anothers' shoulders, and tell each other secrets. Compare the work about which you are writing with another, similar work. You will learn more about both works!

Evaluate and React A response to literature is not complete until you tell other readers what you thought of the book. Don't just tell them whether you did or didn't like it, however. Gather specific examples of the things you did or didn't appreciate in the work.

▲ **Critical Viewing** Summarize the predicament of this kitten. Identify a related experience of your own. Finally, give a theme this picture might illustrate. **[Apply]**

Step-by-Step Teaching Guide

Prewriting: Details to Look For

1. Have students write the first strategy (Write a Summary) near the top of a sheet of paper. As you explain this strategy, encourage students to note key words—such as *character, plot, ideas,* and *images*—that will prompt them to remember how to implement the strategy.

2. Repeat the process with each of the other strategies. Encourage students to refer to this list as they gather details for their essays.

Customize for *Logical/Mathematical Learners*

Invite students to create two-color hexagonals on the computer, then print them out to share.

Critical Viewing

Apply Students' responses will vary.

STANDARDIZED TEST PREPARATION WORKSHOP

Identifying Theme Standardized tests may require students to identify the theme of a poem. Ask which statement best describes the theme of this poem.

"Dust of Snow"
by Robert Frost

The way a crow
Shook down on me
The dust of snow
From a hemlock tree

Has given my heart
A change of mood
And saved some part
of a day I had rued.

A the habits of birds

B the beauty of snow

C small wonders of nature

D a wintry mood

Item **C** sums up the message of all aspects of the poem. The other three statements focus on just one aspect of the poem—birds, snow, or moods.

⏱ **TIME SAVERS!**

 **Writing Support Transparencies**
Use the transparencies for Chapter 12 to teach these strategies.

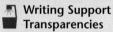 **Writing Support Activity Book**
Use the graphic organizers for Chapter 12 to facilitate these strategies.

1. Select an example of a pentad or hexagon from students' work to date. Display it on an overhead projector.

2. Ask the student whose work you've chosen to take notes on the chalkboard while you lead the class in the following activities:

   • Have students create one sentence about each main idea on the graphic organizer. Have the student at the chalkboard write down these sentences.

   • With direction from the class, have the student at the chalkboard draw arrows between sentences that:
     - concern the same aspect or part of the work
     - support the same point about the work

   • Have the class identify the order in which the ideas should be presented. The student at the chalkboard should number the paragraphs in this order.

3. The student writer can now create a new sentence list that will serve as the outline for his or her essay.

4. Direct students to the italicized text on the page for strategies that will help them add details to their outlines.

Drafting Tip

The introduction and conclusion of an essay usually consist of one paragraph each. The body of the essay, however, usually consists of several paragraphs.

Critical Viewing

Interpret Students should say the trunk of a tree.

12.3 Drafting

Shaping Your Writing

After gathering details, put them in order. These strategies can help you organize your writing:

Make a Sentence Outline

Review your notes. Write a sentence about each main idea you find. Leave plenty of space between sentences.

Review your main ideas. Ask yourself the following questions:

• Which ideas concern the same aspect or part of the work?
  Draw red arrows connecting these sentences, and consider grouping them together.

• Which ideas support the same point about the work?
  Draw green arrows connecting these sentences, and consider writing one sentence expressing the point that these sentences support. (For instance, one sentence might say, "Bart is a truly evil villain." Another might say, "Dudley is a wonderful hero." Both sentences support one point: "The characters are exciting.")

• Which ideas must readers understand before they can understand other ideas on your list?
  Label these ideas "Background." Consider moving them toward the beginning of your list.

Once you have marked up your list, rearrange and combine sentences according to your marks. Write each sentence on a separate line. Below each main idea, write related details.

Introduction, Body, and Conclusion

Like a sturdy tree with its roots, trunk, and branches, a well-organized draft has several different parts. As you draft, develop the following parts of your essay or letter:

• an **introduction** (usually a paragraph) in which you state your topic and focus, and give a preview of your main points

• a **body,** in which you set out your description of the literary work and develop your main ideas

• a **conclusion,** in which you forcefully restate your reactions to the work and your reasons for them.

You might write your introduction *after* writing the body. That is when you know exactly what you will say in your response.

256 • Response to Literature

▼ Critical Viewing
Which part of a tree might you compare to the body of a paper? **[Interpret]**

⏱ TIME AND RESOURCE MANAGER

Resources
Print: Writing Support Transparency 12-E
Technology: Writing Lab CD-ROM, Response to Literature

In-Depth Coverage	Accelerated Pace
• Cover pp. 256–257 in class. • Students can work in pairs or small groups to create their sentence outlines.	• Have students read pp. 256–257 independently. • Have students create sentence outlines and provide elaboration for their essays.

Providing Elaboration

Imagine rushing to tell a friend about an exciting book you just read. "It was really great!" you say. Your friend might reply, "Really? In what way?" As you draft, make sure you answer the question "In what way?" Add supporting details, such as summaries of the work, quotations, and comparisons, to back up each point.

Add Support

As you draft, pause at the end of each paragraph. Follow these steps:

1. Circle the main point of the paragraph.
2. Ask yourself, "Really? In what way?"
3. Below the paragraph, write supporting sentences that answer the question "In what way?" Review your prewriting notes for the details you need. If you have already given support, see whether you can add more.

(Keep in mind that a paragraph that sums up part of the story or poem may not need support of this kind.)

☑ Collaborative Writing Tip

Read a few of your main points to a partner. For each, your partner should ask, "Really? In what way?" Read any support you can find in your draft. If your partner is not satisfied with your answer, consider adding more support.

Drafting: Add Support

Teaching Resources: Writing Support Transparency 12-E

After students have drafted the bodies of their essays, display the transparency. Use Erin's work in progress to detail the following process:

- Circle the main point of the paragraph.

- Ask yourself if you've provided support within this paragraph for the main point. If you haven't, add support.

- If you have provided support for the main point, ask yourself if you should add more support.

Student Work
IN PROGRESS

Name: *Erin Macdonald Roski*
Madison Middle School
Oceanside, CA

Providing Support
After she drafted this paragraph, Erin circled the main point, and then decided to add more support.

(The story is full of suspense.) For instance, when the Trojans are talking about burning the horse, you are afraid the Greeks inside will be burned alive! Also, when Epeius builds the horse, he installs a trapdoor. The trapdoor is impossible to open from the outside. No one can open the lock except Epeius himself. Odysseus and other men squeeze inside with their armor and rations. There is barely room for Epeius. He has to be stuffed in somehow, though, for the plan to work! Again, the reader is in suspense until Epeius finally gets in.

Drafting • 257

⊘ TIME SAVERS!

🗐 **Writing Support Transparencies**
Use the transparencies for Chapter 12 to teach these strategies.

257

Revising: Color-Coding Related Details

1. Select two paragraphs from three or four students' essays. Make copies of the paragraphs on a separate sheet of paper for each student's work.

2. Display one set of paragraphs on an overhead projector. Lead the class in helping you color-code related details.

3. Display another set of paragraphs on the projector. This time, ask a student to be the scribe as the class directs the process.

4. Repeat the color-coding activity as time allows.

Critical Viewing

Evaluate Students may say that it does support the description because the horse is so massive and impressive.

12.4 Revising

Revising Your Overall Structure

A first draft is just your first step. Most of your ideas are on the page. Now, revise your draft to make sure your ideas will be clear to readers. Start by reviewing your organization.

Analyze Your Organization

Readers will have an easier time following your ideas if you group related details together. Use the strategy of color-coding to improve organization.

▶ **REVISION STRATEGY**
Color-Coding Related Details

As you read over what you have written, circle each of your main points in a different color. Underline the sentences supporting each main point in the same color as the main point.

When you have finished color-coding, review your draft. Use the following ideas for revision:

EVALUATE	REVISE
paragraph contains marks of a few different colors	Move sentences to the paragraph they support.
sentence is neither circled nor underlined	Delete the sentence, or use it in a new paragraph.

The Procession of the Trojan Horse, ©National Gallery Collection

◀ **Critical Viewing**
Erin explains in the excerpt on the next page that the Greeks made the Trojan Horse "impossible to resist." Does this picture of the horse support this description? Explain your answer. [**Evaluate**]

258 • Response to Literature

⏱ TIME AND RESOURCE MANAGER

Resources
Print: Writing Support Transparencies 12-F–G
Technology: Writing Lab CD-ROM, Response to Literature

In-Depth Coverage	Accelerated Pace
• Cover pp. 258–262 in class. • Do the Grammer in Your Writing on p. 261.	• Have students read the information on pp. 258–262 independently. • Provide colored pencils or highlighters and construction paper so students can implement the strategies independently.

Revising Your Paragraphs

Strengthen Support

Every point you make in a response to a literary work should be backed up by details from the work. The following strategy will help you provide support for your points:

▶ **REVISION STRATEGY**

Strengthening Support by Using Points to Illuminate

Make sure you have coded your draft, using the strategy on the previous page. Then, follow these steps to illuminate it:

1. Cut out a five-pointed construction paper star for each of your main points. Write the main idea in the center of the star, and label each point as shown in the model below.
2. Find support in your draft for each main idea. Add a check to the appropriate star point for each supporting detail.
3. Use the unchecked points on your star to assess support. For example, if the star for a main idea has no checkmarks, add support for that idea.

Writing Lab CD-ROM

For an example of revising to add support, see the annotated Student Model in the Revising and Editing section of the Response to Literature lesson.

Student Work IN PROGRESS

Name: *Erin Macdonald Roski*
Madison Middle School
Oceanside, CA

Using Points to Illuminate
Erin used the strategy of illuminating to describe the wooden horse.

The author describes the horse in the same poetic, elegant style he uses for the rest of the tale. Epeius ". . . fitted a neck to it with a purple fringed mane sprinkled with gold. . . . The cunningly fashioned head had blood-red eyes of amethyst surrounded with gems of sea-green beryl. . . . He fitted a flowing tail to it twisted with gold and hung with tassles. . . ."

They make the statue impossible to resist.

Then, the other Greeks pretend to sail away. A great cry rumbles through the streets of Troy when the Trojans see that the Greek fleet is gone....

Erin found no supporting details for her general statement about the horse. She reviewed her notes and added a quotation.

theme · quotation · character · figure of speech · event

Main Idea:
The statue is impossible to resist

Revising • 259

Step-by-Step Teaching Guide

Revising: Strengthening Support by Using Points to Illuminate

Teaching Resources: Writing Support Transparency 12-F

1. Display the transparency. Direct students' attention to Erin's draft and the labels on the star. Each label indicates a type of detail that can provide added support to a paragraph's main idea.
2. Direct students to locate circled sentences in their color-coded drafts. Tell them to place a star by each circled sentence, decide what type of detail needs to be added, and revise the paragraph accordingly.

Customize for *Visual/Spatial Learners*

Ask a "team" of students to figure out an efficient way to provide "points of illumination" stars for the class to use in revising their essays. Students might consider creating a master sheet of labeled stars on the computer, then making copies on colored paper. Or they may choose to use sticker stars, construction paper, or other materials. Have the team produce the stars before you lead the Step-by-Step activity below.

Language Highlight

The words *illuminate* ("to light up") and *enlighten* ("to inform") come from the same Latin prefix *(in-)* and root *(lumen)*. So when students enlighten readers by adding points of illumination, they are really adding sparkle . . .
glitter . . .
gleam . . .
and flash!

☑ **ONGOING ASSESSMENT: Monitor and Reinforce**

If students need help in identifying the main point of a paragraph, try one of the following options.

Option 1 After they read a paragraph, they should sum up what it says in one *short* sentence. Tell students that this is the main point.	**Option 2** The first and last sentences of a paragraph are good places to look for a main point. But tell students that they must sometimes draw a conclusion from all the sentences put together to find the main point.

⏱ **TIME SAVERS!**

📄 **Writing Support Transparencies**
Use the transparencies for Chapter 12 to teach these strategies.

Revising: Measuring Sentences

Teaching Resources: Writing Support Transparency 12-G

1. Display the transparency to model how Erin measured her sentences.

2. Ask a student to lend you a page from the latest draft of his or her essay. Display the page on an overhead projector.

3. Use a ruler to measure each sentence in one of the paragraphs. Circle the two shortest sentences. Ask the class to try combining the short sentences into one longer sentence.

4. Ask additional students to demonstrate the measuring technique with examples from their work.

Real-World Connection

Ask students to think of professions in which workers are required to respond to literature, art, and other creative works. Students will likely identify writers who review books, software, movies, or plays for magazines, newspapers, and Web sites. Point out that in many kinds of businesses, workers are required to write responses to software, training programs, and other products the company is considering purchasing.

⏱ **TIME SAVERS!**

 Writing Support Transparencies
Use the transparencies for Chapter 12 to teach these strategies.

12.4

Revising Your Sentences
Combine Sentences for Variety

In a first draft, you may have used many short sentences in your rush to get your ideas down. Too many short sentences in a row, though, create a monotonous beat. Don't bore your reader. To make your writing flow more smoothly, combine short sentences. The following strategy may help:

▶ **REVISION STRATEGY**
Measuring Sentences

The physical length of your sentences is not the key to good style, but it can help indicate places where you can vary your sentence structure. Using a ruler, measure each sentence in the first three paragraphs of your draft. Circle the two shortest sentences in each paragraph. See whether they can be combined with nearby sentences into longer, more interesting ones. For help combining sentences, see the ideas presented in the box on the next page.

Student Work
IN PROGRESS

Name: *Erin Macdonald Roski*
Madison Middle School
Oceanside, CA

Measuring Sentences
After Erin measured the sentences in this paragraph, she decided to combine the shortest two with other nearby sentences.

Also, when Epeius builds the horse, he installs a trapdoor. The trapdoor is impossible to open from the outside. *, and no* No one can open the lock except Epeius himself. Odysseus and other men squeeze inside with their armor and rations. There is barely room for Epeius. He *, but he* has to be stuffed in somehow, though, for the plan to work! Again, the reader is in suspense until Epeius finally gets in.

Grammar in Your Writing
Compound Sentences

To combine sentences and vary your sentence structure, you can combine clauses. A **clause** is a group of words with its own subject and a verb. An **independent clause** is a clause that expresses a complete thought. (An independent clause can stand on its own as a sentence.)

CLAUSES:	when he went to Troy	he stayed in his tent

INDEPENDENT CLAUSES:	the Trojans fought back	he attacked Troy

When a single sentence is made up of two or more independent clauses, it is called a **compound sentence.**

COMPOUND SENTENCE:
—— ind. clause —— —— ind. clause ——
He attacked Troy, but the Trojans fought back.

The clauses in a compound sentence may be connected in one of two ways: with a comma and a coordinating conjunction or with a semicolon.

There are seven coordinating conjunctions: *and, but, for, nor, or, so,* and *yet.* When you join two independent clauses with a coordinating conjunction, use a comma before the conjunction:

COMPOUND SENTENCE:
—— ind. clause ——
The Greeks left a wooden horse by the city, and
—— ind. clause ——
the Trojans took it inside.

You can also form a compound sentence with a semicolon (;).

COMPOUND SENTENCE:
—— ind. clause ——
The Trojans had been tricked;
—— ind. clause ——
the horse was filled with Greek warriors.

Types of Connections Between Clauses

When you use a coordinating conjunction, you can suggest the relationship between the ideas in the joined clauses. *And,* for instance, suggests that two similar ideas are being added together. *But* suggests that two opposing or contrasting ideas are being joined. A semicolon usually suggests addition or further explanation.

Find It in Your Reading Find one compound sentence in "Introducing Natty Bumppo" by May Lamberton Becker on page 248. Identify the independent clauses.

Find It in Your Writing Find four compound sentences in your response to literature. If you cannot find four, challenge yourself to combine sentences to create new compound sentences.

To learn more about compound sentences, see Chapter 20.

Revising • 261

Grammar in Your Writing: Compound Sentences

1. Write the following clauses on the chalkboard:

   when she studied hard
   she got good grades

   Ask students to identify the dependent clause (the first one) and the independent clause (the second one). Point out the difference between the two types of clauses. (An independent clause can stand on its own as a sentence; a dependent clause can't.)

2. Define a compound sentence as a sentence that contains two or more independent clauses.

3. Read aloud the information about coordinating conjunctions and the semicolon as types of connections between clauses.

4. Ask students to share examples of compound sentences from their essays. Clarify the correct punctuation for each sentence shared.

Find It in Your Reading

Possible responses: Independent clauses are bracketed. Paragraph 2: The perfect woodsman, [he needs plenty of room;] loving the forest, [he has the keen senses and cool nerve needed to keep alive there.] Last paragraph: After that, [we take them any way they come,] but [*Mohicans* stays longest.]

Find It in Your Writing

Once students have identified the compound statements, ask them to identify the independent clauses in each one.

☑ **ONGOING ASSESSMENT: Prerequisite Skills**

If students have difficulty creating compound sentences, you may want to refer them to the following materials to assure coverage of prerequisite skills.

In the Textbook	Print Resources	Technology
Effective Sentences, pp. 441–446	Grammar Exercise Workbook, pp. 71–72	On-Line Exercise Bank, Section 21.2

Step-by-Step Teaching Guide

Revising: Highlighting Value Words

1. Ask the class to list the names of popular TV shows. Choose one of the shows that most students have seen.

2. Ask students to share some words that describe the TV show. Write the words as students say them.

3. Circle any words that are general value words. Challenge students to provide more exact descriptions.

4. Point out how the more exact descriptions provide a clearer verbal picture of what the show is like.

Step-by-Step Teaching Guide

Revising: Peer Review

1. Display a page from a student's essay on the overhead projector. Read aloud a couple of paragraphs.

2. Ask students to raise their hands if they noticed something they especially liked in what they heard. Have these students come to the projector and point to the part(s) they liked.

3. Divide the class into small groups to practice this peer review strategy.

Critical Viewing

Analyze Students may say *luxurious*, *opulent*, and *immense*.

Revising Your Word Choice

Choose Precise Words for Evaluation

When you write about a literary work, you share your reactions with a reader. It doesn't give a reader much information, however, if all you write is "I didn't like it" or "I thought it was terrific." Use precise words to communicate your opinion clearly.

▶ **REVISION STRATEGY**
Highlighting Value Words

With a colored pencil, highlight words in your paper that express an opinion—words such as *good*, *bad*, or *exciting*. Rewrite the words to state your meaning clearly and exactly. Here are some examples of general and exact opinion words and expressions:

GENERAL	EXACT
great	well written, fast moving
bad	slow moving, unbelievable
unlikeable (characters)	bland, prim, two-dimensional

▲ Critical Viewing
Give three precise words you could use to describe this scene. **[Analyze]**

Peer Review

After you've finished revising on your own, it's a good idea to share your first draft with some of your classmates. You can learn whether you have clearly described the work and clearly expressed your opinions about it. Use the following strategy to gather comments about your work from classmates.

Pointing

Follow these steps for pointing:

1. Read what you have written to a small group of students.
2. Then, read it a second time.
3. During the second reading, the others in the group should jot down words and phrases that they find effective in some way—interesting, well put, or attention grabbing. No negative comments are allowed.
4. After you have finished reading, have your classmates point out the parts of your work that they liked.

As you write the final version of your paper, use what you learn from the group to build on, or say more about, the points that they liked.

12.5 Editing and Proofreading

After you have improved the organization and expression of your ideas, polish your work. Proofread for errors in spelling, punctuation, or grammar. In a response to literature, pay special attention to punctuating quotations.

Focusing on Punctuating Quotations

Check each quotation against the work quoted to make sure you have copied the words *exactly*. Then, make sure you have followed the rules for punctuating quotations.

Grammar in Your Writing
Rules for Punctuating Quotations

A **quotation** is a word, phrase, sentence, or passage from one work that is cited in another work. Follow these rules for punctuating quotations:

Brief quotations Use quotation marks and commas to separate the quotation from the rest of a sentence. Use single quotation marks for a quotation within the quotation:

> The writer then tells us, "Achilles retreated to his tent, saying, 'Let's see if they can beat the Trojans without me.' "

Long quotations If a quotation runs four lines or more, introduce it with a colon. Skip a line before the quotation and indent it on the left side.

> The author notes the different abilities of the heroes:

>> Achilles was the greatest warrior among them. (His mother had dipped him in the River Styx when he was a baby to make his body nearly invulnerable.) Odysseus, the crafty one, helped the Greeks plan and scheme. Agamemnon was a great leader.

Find It in Your Reading Find an example of a quotation in "Introducing Natty Bumppo" by May Lamberton Becker on page 248. Explain how its length affects its punctuation.

Find It in Your Writing Read over your response to literature, and check each quotation to make sure it is set off or punctuated correctly.

To learn more about punctuating quotations, see Chapter 26.

Grammar in Your Writing: Rules for Punctuating Quotations

1. Write these terms on the chalkboard.

   quotation
   brief quotation
   long quotation
   quotation mark
   single quotation mark

2. Ask students to tell everything they know about the first term on the chalkboard—without referring to their textbooks.

3. When you are satisfied with students' answers, move on to the subsequent terms and repeat the process.

Find It in Your Reading

In the first full paragraph on page 249, Becker quotes Natty Bumpo's last word. Because the quotation is short, quotation marks, not indentation, are appropriate. For another illustration, ask students to turn to page 266 and read the two quotations (one long and one brief) included in this section of Erin's final draft. Point out that Erin chose quotations that add "zing" to her essay. One paints a colorful word picture; the other conveys a crowd's excitement. Have students check the quotations they've used in their essays. Are they top quality? Do the quotations add something special to the essay?

Find It in Your Writing

Have students explain why their quotations are punctuated in the manner they are.

⏱ TIME AND RESOURCE MANAGER

Resources
Print: Scoring Rubrics on Transparency, Chapter 12; Writing Assessment: Scoring Rubric and Scoring Models for Response to Literature
Technology: Grammar CD-ROM, Response to Literature

In-Depth Coverage	Accelerated Pace
• Cover pp. 263–266 in class. • Have students edit and proofread their essays in class. • Review Rubric for Self-Assessment in class. • Students present their final drafts.	• Assign pp. 263–266 for independent student review. • Students edit and proofread their essays as homework. • Students present their final drafts.

Publishing and Presenting: Sharing Responses

1. The purpose of responses to literature is to "get the word out" about a particular piece of writing. This type of writing often causes a response in the reader—a desire to read a story for himself or herself, for example.

2. Ask the class to think of ways they could share their essays with others.

Customize for
Gifted/Talented Students

Have students create and implement a plan to share their essays. In addition, have them create a follow-up survey that would track responses in their audience. Students may want to publish their survey results on a Web site, in a report, or in a school newsletter.

ASSESS

Assessment

Teaching Resources: Scoring Rubrics on Transparency 12; Formal Assessment, Chapter 12

1. Display the Scoring Rubric transparency and review the criteria in class.

2. Before students proceed with self-assessment, you may wish to review the Final Draft of the Student Work in Progress on pages 265–266. Have students score the Final Draft in one or more of the rubric categories. For example, how would students score the essay in terms of audience and purpose?

3. In addition to student self-assessment, you may wish to use the following assessment options.

   • score student essays yourself, using the rubric and scoring models from Writing Assessment.

   • review the Standardized Test Preparation Workshop on pages 270–271 and have students respond to a writing prompt within a time limit.

continued

12.6 Publishing and Presenting

Building Your Portfolio

Consider these suggestions for publishing and presenting your response:

1. **Book Day** Arrange a Book Day on which students read their responses to literature and hold discussions about works they have enjoyed. Announce the day with posters and ads for literary works.

2. **Letter to the Author** If you have written a letter to an author, mail the letter to him or her, care of the publisher. If you have written a review, mail it to the author with a cover letter. Share your letter and any response you receive with the class.

Reflecting on Your Writing

Jot down a few notes on your experience writing a response to literature. Begin by answering the following questions:

• As you took notes, drafted, and revised, what did you learn about the work of literature about which you wrote?

• What aspects of the work did you not write about? Why did you decide to write about the aspect that you chose?

 **Internet Tip**

To see a response to literature scored according to this rubric, visit **www.phschool.com**

Rubric for Self-Assessment

Evaluate your response to literature using the following rubric:

	Score 4	Score 3	Score 2	Score 1
Audience and Purpose	Presents sufficient background on the work(s); presents the writer's reactions forcefully	Presents background on the work(s); presents the writer's reactions clearly	Presents some background on the work(s); presents the writer's reactions at points	Presents little or no background on the work(s); presents few of the writer's reactions
Organization	Presents points in logical order, smoothly connecting them to the overall focus	Presents points in logical order and connects many to the overall focus	Organizes points poorly in places; connects some points to an overall focus	Presents information in a scattered, disorganized manner
Elaboration	Supports reactions and evaluations with elaborated reasons and well-chosen examples	Supports reactions and evaluations with specific reasons and examples	Supports some reactions and evaluations with reasons and examples	Offers little support for reactions and evaluations
Use of Language	Shows overall clarity and fluency; uses precise, evaluative words; makes few mechanical errors	Shows good sentence variety; uses some precise evaluative terms; makes some mechanical errors	Uses awkward or overly simple sentence structures and vague evaluative terms; makes many mechanical errors	Presents incomplete thoughts; makes mechanical errors that create confusion

264 • Response to Literature

☑ ONGOING ASSESSMENT: Assess Mastery

Use one of the following options to assess final drafts of students' essays.

Self-Assessment Ask students to score their essay using the rubric provided. Then have students write a paragraph reflecting on the most valuable strategy they learned in completing this essay.	**Teacher Assessment** Use the rubric and the scoring models provided in Writing Assessment, Response to Literature, to score students' work.

12.7 Student Work IN PROGRESS

FINAL DRAFT

A Tale of Troy
by Roger Lancelyn Green

Erin Macdonald Roski
Madison Middle School
Oceanside, California

One of the most famous stories in the world is the ancient Greek tale of the Trojan War. In *A Tale of Troy*, Roger Lancelyn Green retells the tale in a suspenseful, enjoyable style. You can taste the excitement of his book in his retelling of the episode of the Trojan Horse, when the Greeks use trickery and a huge statue of a horse to finally beat the Trojans.

The cause of the Trojan War is mainly the beautiful Helen of Sparta. She is stolen from the Greeks by Paris, a prince in Troy. In a blind fury, her politically powerful husband Menelaus storms the seas, gathering a company of worthy heroes, including brave Odysseus, Agamemnon, and Achilles. Together, they charge their ships across the churning water and surround Troy. Bronze clashes on the windy plains outside the city. Swords ring. The wounded cry out. Despite the might of the Greeks, the war

In her introduction, Erin names the work to which she is responding. She also introduces her focus: the excitement of the episode of the Trojan Horse.

Erin's draft is well organized. First, she gives the reader necessary background information on the story. Then, she summarizes the episode of the Trojan Horse.

◀ **Critical Viewing**
This ancient Greek artwork shows a scene from the Trojan War. Draw two conclusions about the way wars were fought at the time. **[Draw Conclusions]**

Step-by Step Teaching Guide continued

- administer the Chapter 12 Test from Formal Assessment in Teaching Resources to assess students' grasp of concepts presented.

CLOSE

Step-by-Step Teaching Guide

Teaching From the Final Draft

1. Have students read the first two paragraphs of "A Tale of Troy."

2. Ask students to identify some words Erin uses that communicate the excitement, fear, and high drama of this story. (Possible answers: *suspenseful, trickery, beautiful Helen, blind fury, worthy heroes, charged their ships, churning water, bronze clashed*)

continued

Critical Viewing

Draw Conclusions Students may say that wars were fought with elaborate protection and in hand-to-hand combat.

265

3. After students have finished reading "A Tale of Troy," lead a discussion based on these questions:

- What precise value words did Erin use? (*victorious, wondrous, full of suspense, I love it,* and so on)

- Which paragraph supports Erin's claim that the story is suspenseful? (fifth)

- What type of detail does Erin use to support her point that the horse is "wondrous"? (long quotation)

- Does Erin leave any doubt about her feelings and opinions about the story? (no)

12.7

stretches on for ten long, draining years.

The Trojan horse wins the war for the Greeks. This victorious plan is concocted by Odysseus: Epeius, the shipbuilder, will build a sturdy, huge horse in which to hide a group of warriors. Once the Trojans bring the horse inside their city, the Greeks inside will leap out and open the gates to the other Greeks!

But one last thing is involved—how will they convince the Trojans to take the wondrous horse into the city? They make it impossible to resist. The author describes the horse in the same poetic, elegant style he uses for the rest of the tale. Epeius

> . . . fitted a neck to it with a purple fringed mane sprinkled with gold. . . . The cunningly fashioned head had blood-red eyes of amethyst surrounded with gems of sea-green beryl.
> . . . He fitted a flowing tail to it twisted with gold and hung with tassles. . . .

Then, the other Greeks pretend to sail away. A great cry rumbles through the streets of Troy when the Trojans see that the Greek fleet is gone. "We've won!! We've won!!" they cry and rush to the horse outside their city. Most people want to burn the horse or break it apart with their axes.

But a captive Greek named Sinon soon tells a fake story to save his people. And when two serpents crawl out of the sea and kill three of the people in favor of burning the dazzling horse, the Trojans immediately twine garlands of beautiful flowers around it and bring the giant horse into their city. Since it won't fit through the gates, the people take down part of their wall. Once the horse is inside, the Greeks scramble out. That night, great Troy falls. For those of you who are Trojan fans, this was a tragic night. But for friends of the Greeks, like myself, it was a time for rejoicing.

The story is full of suspense. For instance, when the Trojans are talking about burning the horse, you are afraid the Greeks inside will be burned alive! Also, when Epeius builds the horse, he installs a trapdoor. The trapdoor is impossible to open from the outside, and no one can open the lock except Epeius himself. Odysseus and other men squeeze inside with their armor and rations. There is barely room for Epeius, but he has to be stuffed in somehow, though, for the plan to work! Again, the reader is in suspense until Epeius finally gets in.

This book is for anyone who enjoys legends, fairy tales, and myths. I love it for its suspense and frequent cliffhangers. Read this book if you are ready to endure pain, sadness, anger, fear, and happiness under the magnificent pen of Roger Lancelyn Green.

266 • Response to Literature

Poetic and elegant are precise evaluative words describing the author's style.

Here, Erin uses a quotation to support two points. First, she supports her point that the book is well written. She also supports her point that the horse is "wondrous."

Erin supports her point that the story is suspenseful with a few examples from the story.

In her conclusion, Erin restates in strong terms her great enjoyment of the book.

Connected Assignment *Movie Review*

When you respond to a story, you explain whether you liked it or not, and why. When you write a movie review, you do the same for a film. A movie review features

- your reactions to the movie.
- details from the movie used to support your opinions.
- a recommendation to moviegoers about whether to see the movie.

Prewriting Choose a movie you have enjoyed. View it again. Write down your opinion of the movie, and collect details explaining your reaction in a Web like the one shown. Include notes on the story, acting, music, and special effects.

Drafting Begin by writing the introduction to your review. Your introduction should

- begin with a funny observation or interesting fact.
- include a sentence explaining your opinion of the film.

In the body of your review, you should

- give a brief summary of the story.
- explain your reaction to the movie.
- provide examples showing readers why you feel as you do.

Conclude your review with a recommendation.

Revising and Editing Read over your review. Add any information readers will need to follow your points. Replace vague words, such as *good* or *bad*, with forceful ones, such as *hilarious* or *sappy*.

Publishing and Presenting After revising your movie review, submit it to a school newspaper. Then, compare your review to professionally written reviews of the same movie.

▲ **Critical Viewing** What kind of movie do you think these people might enjoy seeing? [**Speculate**]

Movie: *Little Cabin in the Big Woods*

Main Opinion: I cared about the characters in this wilderness story.			
Special Effect: The fight scene with the grizzly is really scary.	**Plot:** The Bruder family is trying to survive the winter in their cabin in the woods.	**Acting:** When Matt Distaff comforts Lucy over her broken doll, he acts just like a real father.	**Colors:** The shots of the woods in the fall are a little faded.

Connected Assignment: Movie Review • 267

Critical Viewing

Speculate Students may note that the people in this image are teen-agers and therefore may like certain kinds of movies. Use student responses to discuss how movies are targeted for specific audiences and how film critics must be aware of the intended audience as they write their reviews.

▶ *Lesson Objectives*

1. To write a movie review appropriate to audience and purpose.
2. To organize and present information ensure support for ideas.
3. To use writing processes to develop and revise drafts.
4. To publish and present a movie review to an audience.

Step-by-Step Teaching Guide

Movie Review

Teaching Resources: Writing Support Transparency 12-H; Writing Support Activity Book 12-3

1. Bring sample movie reviews to class, or suggest that students find them in magazines and newspapers. Study one review with the students while going over the drafting notes in their textbooks. For example, ask students to look for a funny observation or interesting fact in the model review.

2. Point out that though movie reviews reflect an author's subjective opinions, readers still expect those opinions to be supported with detailed examples.

3. Explain that identifying their opinions ahead of time will help them organize and focus their review before they start writing. Display the transparency, and then use it to model how collecting details to support opinions can help students develop their reviews.

4. Give students copies of the blank organizer, asking them to fill it out with responses to the movie they've chosen to review.

5. Encourage students to revise their reviews and share them with an audience through a class read-around, publication in a school paper, or through submission to a magazine for young people.

Lesson Objectives

1. To use writing to respond to works of art.
2. To select visuals that have an impact on audience.
3. To evaluate how visual images influence an audience.

Comedy in Film

1. Choose one of the Spotlight elements for class discussion, or have students work individually or in groups on the element of their choice. Give students the initiative to find the necessary books, videotapes, or pictures.

2. Bring in a video of *You Can't Take It With You*. Show a scene from the movie and then ask students how that same scene might have been presented in a modern version of the movie. Encourage them to think about casting, costume, character, setting, and music.

3. Ask them to think about which elements of comedy might survive a transition into a modern context and which ones might not. For example, someone slipping on a banana peel might always be funny, whereas a specific reference to a popular band might not survive the passage of time.

4. Ask students how they think music and comedy are related. Point out that musical comedies provide another level of entertainment because they mix comic dialogue and action with music.

5. Have students research and view some classic comedies, with or without music. Ask students to compare and contrast the older films with recent comic films and television programs.

Spotlight on the Humanities

Understanding Comedy in Film
Focus on Film: *You Can't Take It With You*

There is one response to literature most writers would value—a Pulitzer Prize. This honor is an overwhelmingly positive response to a piece of literature or a theatrical production. In 1937, the Broadway comedy *You Can't Take It With You* won the Pulitzer Prize for Best New American Drama.

The play, considered a classic of American theater, was written by George S. Kaufman (1889–1961) and Moss Hart (1904–1961). It centers around an eccentric family and their funny capers.

The writer James Thurber called Kaufman "the man who was comedy." During his career, Kaufman wrote forty-three plays and had twenty-six hit shows.

Film Connection In 1935, Kaufman wrote the film *A Night at the Opera* for the Marx Brothers. A comedy team, the Marx Brothers—Groucho (born Julius, 1890–1977), Chico (born Leonard, 1886–1961), and Harpo (born Adolph, 1888–1964)—were masters of the art of slapstick, gags, and wisecracks.

Audiences still find *A Night at the Opera* a hilarious movie. The story is told that one of the lines in Kaufman's script was so funny, it had to be removed. When preview audiences heard the line, they laughed so hard that they could not hear the rest of the movie.

Music Connection In 1931, Kaufman collaborated with composer George Gershwin (1898–1937) on the musical *Of Thee I Sing*. This show was the first Broadway musical ever to win the Pulitzer Prize. Gershwin is perhaps best known for writing the first true American opera, *Porgy and Bess* (1935).

Response to Literature Writing Activity:
Comedy Journal Entry
View a Marx Brothers film. In a journal entry, note the three scenes in the movie that you found the funniest—or the dumbest! Explain your reaction to each.

▶ **Critical Viewing** Explain what is comical about each of the scenes on this page. [Analyze]

268 • Response to Literature

A scene from *You Can't Take It With You*

A scene from *A Night at the Opera*

Viewing and Representing

Activity Encourage students to take notes as they watch the movies, recording moments that they found especially humorous. Tell them to think about what made each of the scenes they chose funny or dumb. Was it a situation, a sight gag, or a particular line that made each of the scenes stand out for them?

Critical Viewing

Analyze Students may note that in the first image a woman is tickling or scratching a grown man as though he were a baby. In the second image, students may point out the facial expressions, clothing, or positioning of the three people in the picture. If they don't find either of the scenes comical, point out that humor is subjective and people laugh at different things.

Media and Technology Skills

Using Multimedia to Interpret Literature

Activity: Creating a Multimedia Presentation

You can respond to a story or poem by reading the work to others, accompanied by images, music, and sound effects. To create a multimedia presentation, follow these guidelines:

Learn About It

Plan Your Presentation Carefully Review the piece you have chosen to present. Mark up a photocopy to show which parts might be effectively illustrated with an image or where you might change from one kind of music to another. Referring to your "script," list all of the equipment, images, and music or sound effects you will need.

Learn How to Use Equipment Learn how to use the equipment you have listed—tape recorders, slide projectors, and so on. Read the manuals, and ask questions of experienced users.

Use Audio Elements Your reading of the work is the most important part of your presentation. Practice reading it slowly and with expression.

You may use a piece of music to accompany your reading. Choose pieces appropriate to the mood of the work—happy, sad, or suspenseful. Practice synchronizing your reading with a tape of the music. Consider adding other sound effects, as well.

Use Visual Elements

Consider including visuals in your presentation. You might run a slide show as you read the work. Or, you might videotape others acting out scenes and show the tape as you read. Work with a partner to time your reading with the slides or the video.

Apply It Choose a work of literature, and then plan a multimedia presentation of it using a storyboard organizer like this one.

Tips for Presenting Literature With Multimedia

- Choose a piece of literature you enjoy. It is easier to read such a work effectively.
- Practice your full presentation—reading while your images and sounds play—several times through.
- If you use background music, make sure that it is not so loud that it interferes with your reading.

Presentation of: "Change," Charlotte Zolotow

	Lines 1–4	Lines 5–8
Audio: Reading	"The summer / still hangs / heavy and sweet / with sunlight / as it did last year."	"The autumn / still comes / showering gold and crimson / as it did last year."
Audio: Music	cheery classical music	
Audio: Sound Effects		sound of wind blowing
Visual	slideshow: picture of people sunbathing; picture of big, orange, setting sun	slide show: two or three slides of trees in fall foliage

Media and Technology Skills • 269

▶ Lesson Objectives

1. To produce a multimedia presentation based on a work of literature.
2. To become proficient at using a variety of media to create desired effects.
3. To become proficient at navigating electronic texts and other technology resources.

Step-by-Step Teaching Guide

Using Multimedia to Interpret Literature

Teaching Resources: Writing Support Transparency 12-I; Writing Support Activity Book 12-4

1. Begin by asking students if they can think of any situations in which they've watched a multimedia presentation. Help them by listing some examples such as a planetarium show, a play in which special effects were used, or a speech in which the speaker used visuals or music to make a point or create a mood.

2. Encourage students to think of pieces of text that move them in some way and that will provide opportunities for the integration of images, music, and sound effects. Explain that these elements can be used to inform, create a mood, or evoke emotions in their intended audience.

3. Point out that one of the worst things that can happen to someone giving a multimedia presentation is that they don't know how to work the equipment and get stuck in the middle of the presentation. Encourage them to practice using any equipment that becomes part of their presentation.

4. Using the transparency, walk students through a sample plan for a multimedia presentation of a story, poem, or song that they have all read (perhaps in your class).

5. Give students copies of the blank organizer and have them use it while planning their own multimedia presentations.

Lesson Objectives

1. To write an essay in response to literatue.
2. To use prewriting strategies to generate ideas.
3. To develop writing by categorizing ideas and using effective transitions.
4. To demonstrate control over grammatical elements.

Responding to Prompts About Literature

1. Explain to students that standardized test questions which ask them to respond to literature require them first and foremost to have a thesis statement. Explain that all the evidence they will provide in their answers will flow from their thesis statement, therefore they should begin by writing a strong one.

2. Encourage them to develop thesis statements for which they will be able to find ample evidence in the piece of literature provided. Remind them that they may not have time to rewrite the entire essay, so having a thesis statement with clear, supporting evidence will be very important.

3. Point out that the selection in the Sample Writing Situation is numbered, so they can refer to specific lines as they draft their responses. Explain that specific references, as well as quotes from the piece of literature, can often strengthen the support for their thesis.

Standardized Test Preparation Workshop

Responding to Prompts About Literature

On standardized tests, you will frequently be asked to write in response to a literary work, or passage. When answering, you will need to comment on the work and support your analysis with examples. You will be evaluated on your ability to do the following:

- develop a clearly stated opinion
- present examples that effectively support your ideas
- organize ideas in a logical manner
- write in a style that flows smoothly
- produce an essay that is free of errors in grammar, usage, and mechanics.

Following is a sample standardized test writing prompt on literature. Use the suggestions on the next page to help you respond to the prompt. Note the clocks next to each stage. They represent suggestions for how much of your test-taking time you should devote to each stage.

Test Tip

When responding to a prompt about a poem, note figurative language in the poem, such as comparisons between unlike things, and repeated imagery. These devices are important effects in poems.

Sample Writing Situation

Read the following poem by Theodore Roethke.

"Child on Top of a Greenhouse"

[1] The wind billowing out the seat of my britches,
[2] My feet crackling splinters of glass and dried putty,
[3] The half-grown chrysanthemums staring up like accusers,
[4] Up through the streaked glass, flashing with sunlight,
[5] A few white clouds all rushing eastward,
[6] A line of elms plunging and tossing like horses,
[7] And everyone, everyone pointing and shouting!

"Child on Top of a Greenhouse" is a good example of the use of perspective, or point of view, in poetry. Write an essay in which you explain the point of view of the speaker in the poem. Answer these questions: Where is the speaker? What can the speaker see from this perspective? Then, explain how the poet uses details to help the reader share in this perspective.

270 • Response to Literature

TEST-TAKING TIP

Tell students that test questions will often provide a simple structure for their essays. In the Sample Writing Situation, for example, they can develop their thesis statement from the phrase, "explain the point of view of the speaker." Turn this phrase around or paraphrase it, and they have the beginning of a thesis statement: "The speaker's point of view is..."

In addition, the writing prompt provides specific questions that need to be answered. Each of these questions can represent a section or even a single paragraph of an essay. For example, "Where is the speaker?" can become the subject of one paragraph that contains all the supporting evidence for that part of their response to the prompt.

Customize for
More Advanced Students

For additional practice, provide students with other sample writing situations from past tests and encourage them to time themselves as they respond to them. If students express concern about a particular kind of literature that they find difficult to analyze (i.e., poetry), recommend that they practice with a question that focuses on that genre.

Prewriting

Allow about one fourth of your time for developing your response and noting supporting details.

Create a Thesis Statement The prompt is quite specific about your topic: You must explain the viewpoint of the speaker in the poem. Read the poem twice through. Then, write a thesis statement stating where the speaker is and how this affects what he can see. (A **thesis statement** is a sentence that explains the topic of an essay.)

Write a List After writing your thesis statement, list examples from the poem that support your thesis. Draw a line connecting each example to your thesis. Include in your list special uses of words that help you feel what it is like to be where the speaker is.

Drafting

Allow about half of your time for drafting. Remember to draft neatly and to allow space for revision changes.

Introduce Your Topic Start by writing a strong opening paragraph. This paragraph should include your thesis statement and summarize the details you will discuss.

Use Evidence for Support In the paragraphs following your introduction, discuss one of the examples you have collected in prewriting. Explain how each image shows something the speaker could see only from his point of view. Also, explain how the poet uses special language to convey what it feels like to see the world from that perspective. Include quotations from the poem to illustrate your points.

Conclude With a Summary In your last paragraph, summarize the points you have made.

Revising, Editing, and Proofreading

Allow almost one fourth of your time for revising. Spend any time remaining proofreading your essay.

Check Connections Reread your essay. For each point, ask yourself: What is the connection of this point with my thesis? Consider eliminating or rewording any point that is not well connected to your thesis statement.

Check Quotations Double-check the accuracy of your quotations from the poem. Also, make sure you have put quotation marks around quotations.

Make Corrections Correct errors in spelling, punctuation, and grammar. Neatly cross out mistakes with a single line. Indicate added words using a caret (^).

Time and Resource Manager

In-Depth Lesson Plan

	LESSON FOCUS	PRINT AND MEDIA RESOURCES
DAY 1	**Introduction to Writing for Assessment** Students learn key elements of writing for assessment (pp. 272–273).	
DAY 2	**Prewriting** Students choose and narrow a topic, consider their audience and purpose, and gather information (pp. 274–276).	**Teaching Resources** *Writing Support Transparencies, 13-A; Writing Support Activity Book* 13-1
DAY 3	**Drafting** Students organize their ideas and write their first drafts (pp. 277–278).	**Teaching Resources** *Writing Support Transparencies, 13-B*
DAY 4	**Revising** Students revise their drafts in terms of overall structure, paragraphs, sentences, and word choice (pp. 279–280).	**Teaching Resources** *Writing Support Transparencies, 13-C*
DAY 5	**Editing and Proofreading; Publishing and Presenting** Students check their work for accuracy and correctness and present their final drafts (pp. 281–284).	**Teaching Resources** *Scoring Rubrics on Transparency*, Ch. 13; *Formal Assessment*, Ch. 13

Accelerated Lesson Plan

	LESSON FOCUS	PRINT AND MEDIA RESOURCES
DAY 1	**Prewriting and Drafting** Students review characteristics for writing for assessment, select topics, and write drafts (pp. 272–278).	**Teaching Resources** *Writing Support Transparencies,*13-A–B; *Writing Support Activity Book* 13-1
DAY 2	**Revising to Presenting** Students work individually or with peers to revise, edit, and proofread their work for presentation (pp. 279–284).	**Teaching Resources** *Writing Support Transparencies, 13-C; Scoring Rubrics on Transparency*, Ch. 13; *Formal Assessment*, Ch. 13

Options for Adapting Lesson Plans

HOMEWORK

Have students complete any stage of the lesson for homework.

FEATURES

Extend coverage with the Connected Assignment (p. 285), Spotlight on the Humanities (p. 286), Media and Technology Skills (p. 287), and the Standardized Test Preparation Workshop (pp. 288–289).

TECHNOLOGY

Students can complete any stage of the lesson on computer. Have them print out their completed work.

INTEGRATED SKILLS COVERAGE

Integrating Grammar
Avoiding Comma Splices SE p. 281

Speaking and Listening
ATE pp. 274, 284

Technology
SE p. 287

Vocabulary
ATE p. 284

Real-World Connection
ATE p. 275

Viewing and Representing
Critical Viewing SE pp. 272, 273, 275, 277, 279, 283, 284, 285, 286
ATE p. 286

BLOCK SCHEDULING

Pacing Suggestions
For 90-minute Blocks
• Have students complete the Prewriting and Drafting stages in a single period.
• Focus one class period on Revising and Editing and Publishing and Presenting. Allow at least 30 minutes for peer revision.

Resources for Varying Instruction
• *Writing Lab* **CD-ROM** If your students have access to hardware, a 90-minute block provides an ideal opportunity for students to work on computer.

Professional Development Support
• *How to Manage Instruction in the Block* This Teaching Resource provides management and activity suggestions.

ASSESSMENT SUPPORT

Standardized Test Preparation Workshop SE p. 288
Standardized Test Preparation Workbook, pp. 25–26
Scoring Rubrics on Transparency, Ch. 13
Formal Assessment, Ch. 13
Writing Assessment and Portfolio Management

MEDIA AND TECHNOLOGY

For the Teacher
• *Resource Pro* **CD-ROM**

MEETING INDIVIDUAL NEEDS

Less Advanced Students ATE p. 277; See also Ongoing Assessments ATE pp. 273, 275, 278, 280, 282
ESL Students ATE pp. 273, 280
Verbal/Linguistic Learners ATE p. 276
Logical/Mathematical Learners ATE p. 279
Gifted/Talented Students ATE p. 278

WRITING AND GRAMMAR WEB SITE

The Interactive Writing and Grammar Web site provides a wide array of support for students, teachers and parents. Writing support includes:
• Interactive revision checkers
• Scoring rubrics with complete models

www.phschool.com

LITERATURE CONNECTIONS

Related selection from *Prentice Hall Literature: Timeless Voices, Timeless Themes,* Copper:
"The Wounded Wolf," Jean Craighead George, SE p. 283

▶ *Lesson Objectives*

1. To write narrative, persuasive, and expository writing for assessment.

2. To generate and refine ideas and plans for writing by using the prewriting strategies Choosing a Writing Prompt and Identifying Key Words.

3. To identify audience and purpose for writing.

4. To develop a draft by categorizing ideas, organizing them into paragraphs, and blending paragraphs within larger units of text.

5. To develop a draft by elaborating using the SEE strategy.

6. To revise a draft by using the strategies Checking Organization and Crossing Out Unnecessary Sentences.

7. To revise a draft by strengthening word choices.

8. To edit a draft to eliminate comma splices.

Critical Viewing

Drawing Conclusions Students may say that the students in a testing situation might be nervous, but that they can remember the strategies for test-taking situations to help themselves feel more comfortable.

Chapter 13 Writing for Assessment

Assessment in School

By now, you know that tests are an important part of life at school. You probably also know that there are many different types of tests, most of which include sections that call on you to do some writing.

Most people get a little nervous when they have to write in a test situation. Being prepared for this type of writing will help you do your best work even if you are nervous. This chapter provides tips, guidance, and practice to help you feel more confident and prepared when you write on tests.

▲ **Critical Viewing** Do you think the students in this situation might be nervous? What might they do to make themselves more comfortable? **[Draw Conclusions]**

🕐 **TIME AND RESOURCE MANAGER**

In-Depth Coverage	Accelerated Pace
• Cover pp. 272–273 in class. • Display and discuss essay sections from standardized tests.	• Assign pp. 272–273 for independent student review. • Have students discuss ways to assess writing skills and abilities. Students may want to design their own writing assessment vehicle.

What Is Writing for Assessment?

Writing for assessment is writing that takes place in a formal testing situation. Teachers use it to measure how much you've learned about a subject or how well your writing skills have progressed. This kind of writing usually involves

- one or more writing prompts that tell you what to write.
- a limited time in which to write.
- no chance to use textbooks or other reference books.

To learn the criteria on which your writing for assessment may be graded or judged, see the Rubric for Self-Assessment on page 282.

Types of Writing for Assessment

The writing prompts on tests may call for the following types of writing:

- **Narrative writing,** with which you tell a story about a personal experience that taught you something.
- **Persuasive writing,** with which you support an opinion or a position.
- **Expository writing,** with which you present information you have learned about a subject. Expository writing may include **cause-and-effect writing,** in which you show how one event or situation leads to others. It may also include **comparison-and-contrast writing,** in which you explore the similarities and differences between two or more things.
- **Response to literature,** normally to a specific passage that is provided on the test.

▲ Critical Viewing
Give an example showing how the object in the picture can help you do well on a test. [**Draw Conclusions**]

PREVIEW
Student Work
IN PROGRESS

In this chapter, you'll follow the work of John Grandy, a student at Holland Woods Middle School in Port Huron, Michigan, as he responds to a writing prompt for an essay test in his literature class. You'll see the strategies he used to narrow his topic, decide his purpose and audience, gather and organize details, draft a response, and revise his work.

Writing for Assessment • 273

PREPARE and ENGAGE

Interest GRABBER Have students work together to write a persuasive paragraph in which they try to convince the audience—you—that they deserve a special treat, for instance, time to play computer games. Give students ten minutes or so to come up with a coherent paragraph that includes several reasons why they deserve this bonus. Then read the paragraph, briefly discuss its organization and the information it contains, and, as the suspense builds, grant their request.

Activate Prior Knowledge

Students should have no difficulty recalling tests of various kinds they have taken. Tell students a story or two about memorable testing experiences you had when you were a student and ask them to share both enjoyable and unpleasant memories of taking tests. Then explain that students' writing will be assessed more often as they get older and that this chapter presents some strategies to help them write successfully for assessment.

Critical Viewing

Draw Conclusions Students should say that keeping track of time can help you do well on a test.

Customize for
ESL Students

The testing experiences of students from other countries may be of considerable interest to their classmates and can provide an opportunity for students learning English to practice speaking. In words or pictures, or a combination, have students share with the class some experiences taking tests.

☑ **ONGOING ASSESSMENT: Diagnose**

Use the following option to diagnose students' current level of proficiency in writing for assessment.

Give students 10 minutes to write about an experience they had taking a test. Students who can't write more than a sentence or two will need help committing to a topic and organizing thoughts quickly as they proceed through this chapter.

Prewriting: Choosing a Writing Prompt

1. Discuss the time constraints imposed on students' choice of a writing topic during a test. Ask, *If one topic interests you, but you know more about a second topic, which should you choose?* Then review the likenesses and differences between expository and persuasive writing (one explains or describes and the other persuades; both require an orderly progression of ideas).

2. Have a volunteer read aloud the three topics in the Topic Bank. Make a chart on the board, using the three topics as headings. Then ask each student which assignment he or she would choose. Record the responses on the chart. Which topic is the most popular? Why?

3. As students begin the assignment, have them build on the class discussion as they choose a topic.

Integrating Listening and Speaking Skills

As each student mentions a reason for choosing one of the topics in the Topic Bank, ask another student to restate the reason in his or her own words. Explain that a good test of understanding is paraphrasing, or repeating in their own words, what they have heard. This technique provides the listener an instant comprehension check and the speaker a chance to correct misunderstandings.

13.1 Prewriting

In most writing for assessment, you have a limited amount of time in which to complete your writing. Before you begin, you need to know how much time you have to work on your response. Plan to spend about one fourth of your total time preparing to write.

Choosing Your Topic

On most tests, you'll be given one or more specific topics on which to focus your writing. In some cases, however, you will be given a choice of topics. For example, you might be given three writing prompts and asked to choose one.

Choosing a Writing Prompt

When you are given a choice of writing prompts or questions, review each one. Before making a decision, carefully consider:

- how much you know about a topic.
- how much a topic interests you.
- how comfortable you are with the form of writing called for by a given prompt.

To practice writing for assessment, give yourself a limited amount of time to respond to one of these questions:

TOPIC BANK

1. **Historical Summary** Summarize three of the most important accomplishments of ancient Mesopotamian civilization. Explain the influence of each on the modern world.

2. **Describe Jobs of the Future** Your class is creating a magazine for students called *Jobs of the Future*. Write an article classifying three types of jobs you think will be important in the future. For each, tell what skills or knowledge workers will need.

3. **Persuasive Letter** Your school board has decided that your school must drop one after-school activity for students. Write a letter to the members of the school board persuading them to drop a specific activity and telling them why. Use convincing reasons and details to support your opinion.

274 • Writing for Assessment

⏱ TIME AND RESOURCE MANAGER

Resources
Print: Writing Support Transparency 13-A; Writing Support Activity Book 13-1

In-Depth Coverage	Accelerated Pace
• Cover pp. 274–276 in class. • Model the Choosing a Writing Prompt strategy by explaining which topic you would choose and giving detailed reasons why. • For each of the three topics, brainstorm for an idea or two to get writers started.	• Assign pp. 274–276 for independent student review. • Have students choose two of the three topics about which to write instead of just one.

Narrowing Your Topic

When you're writing for assessment, narrowing your topic means understanding and focusing in on exactly what the writing prompt is asking you to do.

Focus Your Topic

Carefully read the prompt you've chosen. You may find that it asks you to make choices. For example, the second prompt on the previous page calls on you to write about "jobs of the future." One of the first things you must do is decide which jobs fit that description.

You should also note whether a specific audience is identified in the question. The third prompt, for instance, targets the local school board. You should use appropriately formal language for this audience.

Identify Key Words

Most writing prompts also include one or more key words that indicate a specific purpose and organization. Note the key words in each of the sample questions:

1. In the first prompt, the key word is *summarize*, which means to provide the highlights or most important elements of a subject.
2. In the second prompt, the key word is *classifying*, which means grouping things into categories and defining these categories using facts and examples.
3. In the third prompt, the key word is *persuading*, which means providing convincing reasons to accept your position on an issue.

This chart shows other key words. When you identify a key word in a prompt, jot it down, and write notes next to it about the purpose and organization that the word dictates.

OTHER KEY WORDS	
Key Words	**What You Will Do**
explain	give a clear, complete account of how something works or why something happened
compare and contrast	provide details about how two or more things are alike and how they are different
describe	provide vivid sensory details to paint a word picture of a person, place, or thing
argue, convince	take a position on an issue and present strong reasons to support your side of the issue

▲ **Critical Viewing**
In what category would you classify this man's job? **[Classify]**

Prewriting: Identify Key Words

1. Read and discuss each key word on the chart. Have students suggest ways to organize writing that the key words suggest. The first key word, *explain*, for example, suggests that steps be listed in spatial or chronological order. Can students think of other words that may be key in writing prompts? (*inform, assess, sum up, argue, analyze,* and so on)

2. Then have students think of some general demands that all of the key words place on writers. Help students realize that all forms of analytic, persuasive, and informational writing require specific details presented in an orderly fashion.

Real-World Connection

Though the form of the assessment differs from the standardized tests students experience, journalists' writing is assessed every day for accuracy, clarity, completeness, and interest. Not only that, but reporters must meet strict deadlines and try to beat their competition with exclusive stories.

Critical Viewing

Classify Students may classify this man's job as a medical research job.

☑ **ONGOING ASSESSMENT: Monitor and Reinforce**

For students who are still having difficulty choosing one of the three topics, use the following option.

Have students list one plus (a good reason to choose that topic) and one minus (a reason the topic might prove difficult) for each of the topics. Then have them decide which reason is the strongest and write about that topic.

Prewriting: Using a Web to Gather Details

Teaching Resources: Writing Support Transparency 13-A; Writing Support Activity Book 13-1

1. To make sure students understand how creating a web will help them begin to organize a topic, display the transparency as a model. Have students identify the topic (Effects of Point of View), the subtopics (we experience his struggles first hand, makes readers care, affects what readers learn), and the details (the remainder of the of web).

2. Many students have difficulty thinking of subtopics, the most important points they want to make in their papers, and organizing them into categories, or chunks. You may want to choose one of the topics from the Topic Bank and work with students to begin a web about it.

3. Write the topic on the board and have students suggest subtopics. Discuss each subtopic. If the subtopic can be divided into many parts, it is too broad. If students can think of no details to support the subtopic, it is too narrow.

4. Give students copies of the blank organizer for them to use as they gather details for their topics.

Customize for
Verbal/Linguistic Learners

Have students work in small groups to discuss their topics and help each other think of subtopics. Direct each group member to come away from the discussion with at least three good ideas for subtopics.

⏱ TIME SAVERS!

Writing Support Transparencies
Use the transparencies for Chapter 13 to teach these strategies.

Writing Support Activity Book
Use the graphic organizers for Chapter 13 to facilitate these strategies.

276

13.1

Gathering Details

Once you have chosen a writing prompt, focused your topic, and identified your purpose, take a few minutes to collect some ideas by following these steps:

1. Divide your topic into subtopics or categories.
2. Jot down as many facts, quotations, and other types of details as you can for each subtopic.
3. Use a graphic organizer to record these details. If you are writing to classify, you might want to use a Venn diagram to find the similarities and differences between the items you are classifying. If you are writing to persuade, use a T-Chart to identify the pros and cons of the issue. If you are writing a narrative, order events using a timeline. If you are writing to explain, summarize, or inform, use a topic web.

John Grandy was writing to explain, so he used a topic web to organize his ideas.

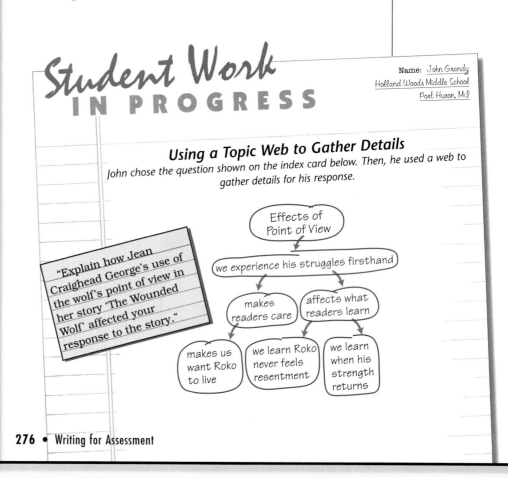

Student Work IN PROGRESS

Name: *John Grandy*
Holland Woods Middle School
Port Huron, MI

Using a Topic Web to Gather Details
John chose the question shown on the index card below. Then, he used a web to gather details for his response.

"Explain how Jean Craighead George's use of the wolf's point of view in her story 'The Wounded Wolf' affected your response to the story."

Effects of Point of View

we experience his struggles firsthand

makes readers care

affects what readers learn

makes us want Roko to live

we learn Roko never feels resentment

we learn when his strength returns

13.2 Drafting

Plan to spend half of your testing time writing a first draft of your response to the writing prompt.

Shaping Your Writing

Since you'll have little time to revise, it is important to make your first draft as organized and polished as possible.

Find a Focus

Regardless of the type of essay you're writing, it is essential that you have a main idea that provides a single focus for the entire piece. Review both the prompt and the details you have gathered, and write a single sentence that sums up your main point. For example, if you were describing jobs of the future, you might note: "All of the most important jobs of the future will be related to technology."

Use the focus sentence you've written as the center-piece of an introductory paragraph. Then, write supporting paragraphs that develop your main point.

Plan Your Organization

Consider the best plan for organizing your details. Generally, each type of essay dictates a specific organization. Consider the following suggestions:

For a **story, summary,** or **explanation,** organize your details in chronological order. Making a timeline is a simple way to do this.

For a **comparison-and-contrast essay,** present details about one subject first, then present details about the other; or, first present similarities, then present differences.

For a **persuasive essay** or a **classification,** organize your points by order of importance. Move from most to least important, or vice versa. In the example below, based on the second writing prompt on page 274, jobs are classified and organized from most to least important.

▲ Critical Viewing
What type of organization would be suitable for writing on the subject shown in the photograph? [Explain, Draw Conclusions]

JOBS OF THE FUTURE

(most important)	1. Careers in Health
	2. Careers in Computers
(least important)	3. Careers in Recreation

Drafting • 277

Drafting: Plan Your Organization

1. Make sure students understand which form of organization is appropriate for the topic they have chosen. If they are describing jobs of the future or persuading the school board, organizing their points in their essays in order of importance is the best choice. If they choose to write the yearbook essay, the most likely organization is chronological order.

2. Stress that least important does not mean unimportant. All their points in a persuasive essay should be important, but there is an order.

3. Ask students to use lists, outlines, or webs to organize their topics visually. Check to make sure that students are using graphic organizers to best advantage. You may want to have the students working on the same topic gather together to exchange ideas.

Critical Viewing

Explain; Draw Conclusions Students should say that chronological order is the best type of organization for writing about cooking.

Customize for
Less Advanced Students

Show students a timeline and explain that it shows significant dates in the order they occurred, that is, chronological order. Remind students that comparing is showing likenesses and contrasting is showing differences. Persuading is trying to convince people of something, and classifying is sorting.

⏱ TIME AND RESOURCE MANAGER

Resources
Print: Writing Support Transparency 13-B

In-Depth Coverage	Accelerated Pace
• Cover pp. 277–278 in class. • Work through the Plan Your Organization and SEE strategies with the class. • Have students write their drafts in class. • Demonstrate the SEE strategy using the transparency.	• Have students review pp. 277–278 independently and then write their first drafts. • Respond to questions as necessary.

Drafting: Layer Ideas Using SEE

Teaching Resources: Writing Support Transparency 13-B

1. Review the purpose of the SEE strategy and how to execute it. Make sure students understand that this strategy is used to develop paragraphs, and that each paragraph in their essay should include a sentence that states the main idea, a sentence that extends the idea, and several sentences that elaborate on the idea.

2. Display the transparency and go over John's paragraph carefully. Emphasize that all the other sentences in the paragraph flow from the main idea sentence, "Telling the story from the point of view of the wolf is much more effective than telling it from the point of view of a person."

3. For additional practice identifying main idea, elaboration, and extension sentences, select paragraphs from magazine articles or books. Have students identify sentences that state the main idea, as well as those that extend the idea and elaborate on it.

4. Even though many paragraphs don't include all three types of sentences, students are required to include all three types in their writing for assessment paragraphs.

Customize for
Gifted/Talented Students

Have students represent the layering strategy visually. They might show main ideas, extended ideas, and elaboration sentences in different colors or use transparent overlays. Challenge students to represent the SEE strategy in a new way.

⏱ **TIME SAVERS!**

🖋 **Writing Support Transparencies**

Use the transparencies for Chapter 13 to teach these strategies.

13.2

Providing Elaboration

Write your first draft following the organization you've selected. Use the strategy of SEE to develop each paragraph.

Layer Ideas Using SEE

To layer a paragraph, begin with the main idea. Then, create layer after layer to elaborate that idea. Follow these steps:

State the main idea for the paragraph.

Extend the idea. You might give your opinion on the idea, restate it with a new emphasis, or apply it to an example.

Elaborate on the idea in one or more sentences. If your idea explains something, show exactly what details it involves, giving examples and precise descriptions. If you are arguing for or against the idea, give supporting details for your opinion, such as facts and arguments.

Language Lab CD-ROM

For more practice building strong paragraphs, see the Main Idea and Topic Sentence lesson in the Building Paragraphs unit.

Student Work
IN PROGRESS

Name: *John Grandy*
Holland Woods Middle School
Port Huron, MI

Using the SEE Technique
John wrote this paragraph using the SEE technique.

Statement: This point of view also affects the amount that the reader learns about the wolf's experience. **Extension:** For example, we learn that Roko never feels anger or resentment toward the animals who are trying to eat him. **Elaboration:** In fact, at the end of the story he even shares with them the food that Kiglo brought him.

278 • Writing for Assessment

✓ **ONGOING ASSESSMENT: Monitor and Reinforce**

For students who are having difficulty including main idea, elaboration, and extension sentences in their essays, use one of the following options.

| **Option 1** Have students work in pairs. For both topics, have them answer these questions together to organize the paragraphs: What is the most important point? (main idea), Why is this important? (elaboration), and Prove it! (extension sentences) | **Option 2** Give students three paragraphs. The first should be missing a main idea statement, the second an elaboration sentence, and the third extension sentences. Ask students to write the missing parts of the paragraphs. |

13.3 Revising

Plan to spend one fourth of your testing time on revising your work. First, consider whether you'll have the time and space to copy a clean final draft, or whether you must make changes neatly in your first draft as you revise.

Revising Your Overall Structure

When teachers evaluate your writing on an essay test, they look for a logically organized piece of writing that clearly follows the directions in the writing prompt. As a result, probably the most important part of revising a test essay is to make sure that your writing presents an organized series of paragraphs that fully develop your topic.

▶ REVISION STRATEGY
Checking Your Organization

Follow these steps to check your organization and revise it if necessary:

1. Check to see that your opening paragraph clearly states your **main idea.** Try to improve the statement of your main idea to make it stronger and clearer.

2. Also check to see that your introduction presents your **subtopics.** If it does not, add a sentence that previews each subtopic.

3. Review each paragraph to ensure that it focuses on **a single subtopic.** Eliminate or refocus any that do not.

4. Review the **order** of your paragraphs to ensure that you have followed the organization you planned. If necessary, rearrange one or more paragraphs.

Revising Your Paragraphs

Review Paragraph Focus

Teachers will closely examine each paragraph of your response to the writing prompt. They expect to find a strong topic sentence and a focused set of supporting details.

▶ REVISION STRATEGY
Crossing Out Unnecessary Sentences

Identify the topic sentence within each paragraph. Review each sentence to see whether it focuses or develops the topic sentence. Cross out any sentences that do not. Then, read the paragraph, omitting the sentences you have crossed out, and consider what details you should add to support the topic sentence more thoroughly.

▲ **Critical Viewing**
What might this student be doing to prepare for a test? [Hypothesize]

Revising • 279

Step-by-Step Teaching Guide

Revising: Crossing Out Unnecessary Sentences

1. Sometimes writers have difficulty deleting unnecessary sentences in their work. Why do your students think this is so? Remind students that all the sentences in a paragraph should develop the topic sentence.

2. Have volunteers read paragraphs from their essays to the class. Can students identify any sentences that are redundant or irrelevant?

3. After identifying several examples of unnecessary sentences as a group, students should be able to revise their own papers independently. Remind them to reread each of the sentences in their paper and cross out sentences that do not extend or elaborate on the topic sentence. They may want to move those sentences to the paragraphs to which they relate and add sentences that are on target.

Customize for
Logical/Mathematical Learners

Ask students to design a template or grid that includes the required elements of their writing for assessment essays on one axis and the sentences in their paragraphs (assigned a number or letter) on the other. They can use the grid to check off each required element as they complete it.

Critical Viewing

Hypothesize Students may say he is researching a topic.

⏱ TIME AND RESOURCE MANAGER

Resources
Print: Writing Support Transparency 13-C

In-Depth Coverage	Accelerated Pace
• Cover pp. 279–280 in class. • Work through the Revising strategy with the entire class.	• Assign students to review pp. 279–280 independently. • Have students revise their writing for assessment essays independently.

Step-by-Step Teaching Guide

Revising: Adding Transitions

Teaching Resources: Writing Support Transparency 13-C

1. Remind students that by using a short, simple transition word, the connections between their ideas can be made more obvious to readers.

2. Display the transparency and have students discuss how John's changes improved his writing.

Step-by-Step Teaching Guide

Revising: Strengthen Word Choice to Achieve Your Purpose

1. Ask students to define the phrase *powerful words* and discuss how important choosing exactly the right words is to good writing.

2. Compile a class list of "tired words," imprecise and overused words that students should consider replacing as they revise their writing. Here are some suggestions to get you started: *nice, pretty, fun, bad, good, interesting.*

3. Ask students to refer to the list as they strengthen the word choices in their papers. Remind students that any word becomes tired if it is overused.

Customize for ESL Students

Students who are learning English may be struggling to express themselves clearly in their essays and may have considerable difficulty replacing words with more precise and colorful ones. Have students work with partners whose home language is English to arrive at replacement words.

Revising Your Sentences

Teachers will evaluate how well your writing hangs together and how easy it is to follow the flow of your ideas. They want to see a clear relationship between one sentence and the next.

▶ REVISION STRATEGY
Adding Transitions

To make sure your ideas are easy to follow, add transition words and phrases to your sentences. Transitions include words such as *first, for example, because,* and *for this reason.*

Student Work
IN PROGRESS

Name: *John Grandy*
Holland Woods Middle School
Port Huron, MI

Adding Transitions

John added a few transitions to his essay.

Telling the story from the point of view of the wolf is much more effective than telling it from the point of view of a person.
First of all,
∧Roko is in big trouble. . . .

This quote also demonstrates the author's use of the
For example,
present tense. ∧When it says in the story, "Roko pulls himself towards the sheltered rock," it gives the reader a sense of actually being there with Roko.

Revising Your Word Choice
Choose Precise and Vivid Words

On a test, you need to use words that say precisely what you mean. Follow this strategy to help revise your word choice:

▶ REVISION STRATEGY
Strengthening Word Choice to Achieve Your Purpose

Find general descriptive words, such as *great,* that cover many details. Revise by filling in those details, as in this example:

ORIGINAL SENTENCE: The band was *great.*
REVISED SENTENCE: The band *kept up an energetic groove that kept people dancing all night.*

280 • Writing for Assessment

☑ ONGOING ASSESSMENT: Monitor and Reinforce

If students are not revising their writing to replace imprecise and repetitive words, try one of these strategies.

Option 1 Have partners take turns reading their paragraphs aloud. Listeners should be able to suggest words that may need to be replaced.	**Option 2** Have students use a thesaurus to find synonyms for vague words or ones they have repeated frequently.

13.4 Editing and Proofreading

If you want teachers to take your ideas seriously, be sure to express yourself in complete, correctly punctuated sentences. Leave some time before you turn in your work to check that you have corrected any errors you have generated.

Focusing on Complete Sentences

If you have extra time before the test is over, use it to check your sentences. Use these questions to guide your review:

- Does each sentence express a complete thought and contain a subject and a verb?
- Does each sentence begin with a capital letter?
- Does each sentence end with a period, question mark, or exclamation point?
- Are the clauses in compound sentences joined correctly?

Make all corrections neatly.

Language Lab CD-ROM

For practice in the proper use of commas, complete the Commas lesson in the Punctuation unit.

Grammar in Your Writing
Avoiding Comma Splices

One of the most common sentence errors students make is trying to join two clauses with just a comma. This error is called a **comma splice.** Look for comma splices in your writing, and use the following techniques to correct them.

INCORRECT:	Nursing is a rewarding career, in the future we will need more nurses.

CORRECTED:

Add a Conjunction:	Nursing is a rewarding career, **and** in the future we will need more nurses.
Add a Semicolon:	Nursing is a rewarding career; in the future we will need more nurses.
Break Into Two Sentences:	Nursing is a rewarding career. In the future we will need more nurses.

To learn more about comma splices and other run-ons, see Chapter 21.

Step-by-Step Teaching Guide

Grammar in Your Writing: Avoiding Comma Splices

1. Write the following examples of comma splices on the chalkboard and discuss the three ways to correct them. Have volunteers correct the comma splices on the board in different ways.

   Nurses work in hospitals, they work in people's home too.

   Many men are becoming nurses, there will be more male nurses in the future.

   It is a rewarding career, you need to be willing to work hard.

2. Conjunctions that are added to correct comma splices must be coordinating conjunctions, such as *and, but, for, yet, or,* and *so.* Clauses linked by words such as *therefore, however, nevertheless, indeed, meanwhile,* and so on require a semicolon. Make two lists on the board: one in which the conjunctions follow a comma and the other in which the words (conjunctive adverbs) follow a semicolon.

3. Ask students to check the lists on the board as they correct comma splices by adding a conjunction or a semicolon.

⏱ TIME AND RESOURCE MANAGER

Resources
Print: Scoring Rubrics on Transparency, Chapter 13; Writing Assessment: Scoring Rubric and Scoring Models for Writing for Assessment

In-Depth Coverage	Accelerated Pace
• Cover pp. 281–284 in class. • Do the Grammar in Your Writing activity on p. 281.	• Assign pp. 281–284 for independent student review.

⏱ TIME SAVERS!

Writing Support Transparencies
Use the transparencies for Chapter 13 to teach these strategies.

Publishing and Presenting

1. For participating in the group discussion, have them take notes during the discussion. They can use these notes later when preparing for a test.

2. Reinforce the importance of reviewing past work, especially for test-taking situations. We can all learn from our past strengths and weaknesses.

ASSESS

Assessment

Teaching Resources: Scoring Rubrics on Transparency 13; Formal Assessment, Chapter 13

1. Display the Scoring Rubric transparency and review the criteria in class.

2. Before students proceed with self-assessment, you may wish to review the Final Draft of the Student Work in Progress on pages 283–284. Have students score the Final Draft in one or more of the rubric categories. For example, how would students score the essay in terms of audience and purpose?

3. In addition to student self-assessment, you may wish to use the following assessment options.

   • score the student essays yourself, using the rubric and scoring models from Writing Assessment.

   • review the Standardized Test Preparation Workshop on pages 288–289 and have students respond to a writing prompt within a time limit.

   • administer the Chapter 13 Test from Formal Assessment in Teaching Resources to assess students' grasp of concepts presented.

13.5 Publishing and Presenting

Building Your Portfolio

Consider the following suggestions for publishing and presenting your work:

1. **Group Discussion** Compare your work with that of classmates who have responded to the same question. Discuss the difficulties you encountered in answering the question and the solutions you found.

2. **Study for Other Exams** Next time you have a written test coming up, look over past test answers. Recall which strategies for writing worked well for you and which did not.

Reflecting on Your Writing

Note down some thoughts on writing for assessment. Start off by answering these questions:

• What do I usually do to prepare for a test? What might I do to prepare more fully?

• What strategy did I find most useful for preparing for a test?

 Internet Tip

To see a test essay scored according to this rubric, visit **www.phschool.com**

Rubric for Self-Assessment

Use the criteria below to evaluate your essay for assessment:

	Score 4	Score 3	Score 2	Score 1
Audience and Purpose	Uses word choices and supporting details appropriate to the specified audience; clearly addresses writing prompt	Mostly uses word choices and supporting details appropriate to the specified audience; adequately addresses prompt	Uses some inappropriate word choices and details; addresses writing prompt	Uses inappropriate word choices and details; does not address writing prompt
Organization	Presents a clear, consistent organizational strategy	Presents a clear organizational strategy with few inconsistencies	Presents an inconsistent organizational strategy	Shows a lack of organizational strategy
Elaboration	Adequately supports the thesis; elaborates each idea; links all details to the thesis	Supports the thesis; elaborates most ideas; links most information to the thesis	Partially supports the thesis; does not elaborate some ideas	Provides no thesis; does not elaborate ideas
Use of Language	Uses excellent sentence variety and vocabulary; includes very few mechanical errors	Uses adequate sentence variety and vocabulary; includes few mechanical errors	Uses repetitive sentence structure and vocabulary; includes some mechanical errors	Demonstrates poor use of language; includes many mechanical errors

282 • Writing for Assessment

☑ ONGOING ASSESSMENT: Assess Mastery

Use one of the following options to assess final drafts of students' writing for assessment.

Self-Assessment Ask students to score their essay using the rubric provided. Then have students write a paragraph reflecting on the most valuable strategy they learned in completing this essay.	**Teacher Assessment** Use the rubric and the scoring models provided in Writing Assessment, Writing for Assessment, to score students' work.

13.6 *Student Work* IN PROGRESS

FINAL DRAFT

John Grandy wrote his essay in response to the following test item: "Explain how Jean Craighead George's use of the wolf's point of view in her story 'The Wounded Wolf' affected your response to the story."

A Wolf's Point of View

John Grandy
Holland Woods Middle School
Port Huron, Michigan

In the story "The Wounded Wolf," a wolf is badly hurt and must find a way to reunite with his pack. His name is Roko, and in his weakened state, he is approached by many animals who want to feed on him. The unique factor of this story is that it is told from the perspective of the wolf.

Telling the story from the point of view of the wolf is much more effective than telling it from the point of view of a person.

◄ **Critical Viewing**
Do you have sympathy for this wolf? Read John's essay, and then explain how your feelings about the wolf have changed. **[Apply]**

The opening paragraph presents John's main idea: Telling the story from the wolf's point of view is more effective than telling it from the point of view of a person.

Student Work in Progress • 283

Step-by-Step Teaching Guide

Teaching from the Model

1. After students have had a chance to read "A Wolf's Point of View," have them react freely. Does John's essay make them want to read "The Wounded Wolf"?

2. Examine the structure of the essay together by analyzing paragraph by paragraph. Be sure students note that the main idea appears in the introductory paragraph, and the concluding paragraph reiterates the writer's argument: telling the story from the wolf's point of view makes "The Wounded Wolf" more powerful than it would have been if the story had been told from a human being's point of view.

3. Ask students whether every subtopic supports the topic sentence: "Telling the story from the point of view of the wolf is much more effective than telling it from the point of view of a person"? If not, which paragraphs or sentences could be deleted? (The third paragraph is interesting, but it has nothing to do with telling the story from the wolf's point of view.)

4. Urge students to reread their own essays once again and delete any subtopics—no matter how interesting—that don't support their topics.

Critical Viewing

Apply Students' responses will vary, but many of them will say that they do not have sympathy for the wolf. Many students' feelings may change after reading the essay.

Integrating Vocabulary Skills

Have students review strategies to use when they are not sure what a word they encounter in reading means. Have them provide "working definitions" of *reunite, unique, factor, effective, gristle, predator,* from "A Wolf's Point of View." Ask students to explain when readers should read on and when they should stop to look up a word in a dictionary or ask a friend what the word means.

Integrating Speaking Skills

Have a small group of students work together to figure out interesting ways to perform choral readings of the second paragraph of John's essay. They might recite sentences individually or as a group. They might have the girls recite some sentences together and the boys others. Challenge students to add to the meaning and strength of the paragraph by the way they choose to recite it. Students should perform their choral reading for the rest of the class.

Critical Viewing

Interpret Students' responses will vary.

First of all, Roko is in big trouble. The ravens, the grizzly bear, the fox, and the owl smell death, his death, and approach him. To these animals, Roko is just another meal to sustain them through the winter. This is really bad, but when you think about it, only moments earlier, Roko himself was busy bringing down a caribou, who would have liked to have been spared as well. So why do we even care about Roko? Well, we care because the story is told from his point of view. If the story were told from the point of view of a person, we might be just as likely to care about the caribou. We can imagine what it would be like to be in his place and we want him to survive. "Massive clouds blot out the sun. In their gloom Roko sees the deathwatch move in closer."

This quote also demonstrates the author's use of the present tense. For example, when it says in the story, "Roko pulls himself towards the sheltered rock," it gives the reader a sense of actually being there with Roko.

This point of view also affects the amount that the reader learns about the wolf's experience. For example, we learn that Roko never feels anger or resentment toward the animals who are trying to eat him. In fact, at the end of the story, he even shares with them the food that Kiglo brought him:

> Already Roko's wound feels better. He gulps at the food and feels his strength return. He shatters bone, flesh and gristle and shakes the scraps out on the snow. The hungry ravens swoop upon them. The white fox snatches up a bone. The snowy owl gulps down flesh and fur and Roko wags his tail and watches.

Notice how Roko doesn't hold a grudge for their earlier attempts to eat him. He even wags his tail because he is happy to see them eat! I don't know a lot of people who wouldn't want revenge on their predators.

In conclusion, telling the story in present tense, from Roko's point of view, allows the reader to (1) care about Roko's fate and (2) better understand a wolf's experience. These are reasons why it was very effective telling the story from the wolf's point of view.

John organizes his essay in order of importance, building to his most important point.

▼ **Critical Viewing** Does this picture capture the mood of Roko's story? Explain your answer. **[Interpret]**

Connected Assignment *Open-Book Test*

When taking most tests, you must work from what you remember of a subject. During an open-book test, you can refer to a textbook or to class notes as well. For such a test, your answer should

- include facts—such as specific names, dates, events, or formulas—from your books or notes.

- sum up your main idea.

- show a clear and logical organization.

Use these strategies to do your best on open-book tests:

Prewriting Organize your time well. Use a little more than one fourth of your time for prewriting.

Begin by outlining your answer to the question, as in the example on this page. Use the information that you remember first. Then, consult your reference materials to add details to each specific point of your outline. Use the index to locate information quickly in books.

Drafting Next, allow about one half of your time for drafting. Include the following elements in your draft:

- **Introduction** Include a sentence in your introduction that sums up your answer.

- **Body** In the body of your paper, develop each main point of your outline. Include the specific details you have gathered from your reference materials.

- **Conclusion** In your final paragraph, sum up your answer to the question and the details that support it.

Revising and Editing Allow one fourth of the test-taking time for revising.

Reread your essay. For each point you make, lightly underline details that explain or support the point. Then, look for paragraphs with few underlines. Add additional details from your reference materials to these paragraphs.

Publishing and Presenting Add your graded test to your portfolio.

▲ **Critical Viewing** What advice might you give this student for taking an open-book test? **[Analyze]**

```
TOPIC: Ancient Mesopotamia

I. Mesopotamia
   A. Location
      1. In the desert where Iran and
         ? are today              p. 10 – Iraq
      2. Two important rivers: Tigris and ? p. 10 – Euphrates
   B. Reasons for start of civilization
      1. Tigris and Euphrates allow trade
      2. Rivers flood, so farming is possible there
```

Connected Assignment: Open-Book Test • 285

Critical Viewing

Analyze Students may suggest that the student look for details to support his answer, manage his time carefully, avoid copying (plagiarizing) from the book, and that he makes sure his answers are correct by cross-checking information provided in the text.

▶ **Lesson Objectives**

1. To write an open-book test essay appropriate to audience and purpose.

2. To organize and present information to ensure support for ideas.

3. To use writing processes to develop and revise drafts.

Step-by-Step Teaching Guide

Open-Book Test

1. Find out how many students have experience with taking an open-book test. Lead a classroom discussion—hearing from those who have taken an open-book test as well as those who haven't—in which the students assess the advantages and disadvantages of this kind of evaluation.

2. As students explore this issue, elicit the following points:

   - can be confusing or time consuming to flip through the textbook looking for information

   - knowing the material well will save time during the test

   - organizing answers before writing them will also save time

   - teachers may expect better answers if students get to use their books so it's especially important to support all answers with detailed evidence

3. Review the outline with students. Point out that outlining their responses ahead of time will allow them to address many of the points listed above, especially those concerning organization and the gathering of details for their final drafts.

4. Have students practice taking an open book test by giving them a set amount of time and a topic. Ask them to outline their answer to the topic question before answering it.

Lesson Objectives

1. To use writing as a means of expressing personal opinion.

2. To make connections between a variety of artistic works and sources of information.

3. To compare and contrast related visual images.

Critical Viewing

Speculate Students may note that the cat is smiling while looking up with arms raised. They may observe that the cat looks happy, victorious, or welcoming. Ask students to think about which human traits or emotions we often attribute to cats and perhaps even to animals in general.

Themes Across Cultures

1. Choose one of the Spotlight elements for class discussion, or have students work individually or in groups on the element of their choice. Give students the initiative to find the necessary books, videotapes, or pictures.

2. Bring in a section of T.S. Eliot's more serious work, such as an excerpt from *The Wasteland* or a section of *The Lovesong of J. Alfred Prufrock,* as well as one or two poems from *Old Possum's Book of Practical Cats.* Have students compare the tone, language, and subject matter of these poems. Ask them what about cats might have inspired Eliot's playful side to come through in his poems.

3. If available, show students a video of the musical *Cats.* Compare the music and poetry of the musical with Eliot's original words. Ask students to think about other literature they have read that could be adapted for the stage.

4. Bring in images of cats to class, or have students research and find them. Try to have representations of cats from many cultures. Ask students to compare and contrast the ways in which cultures from different time periods and regions have represented the physical characteristics and personalities of cats.

Spotlight on the Humanities

Comparing Themes Across Cultures

Focus on Theater: *Cats*

In school, a teacher assesses your writing. When people write for the theater, their work is assessed by critics. The Broadway musical *Cats* got an "A" from audiences and critics alike. Based upon fourteen poems in T.S. Eliot's *Old Possum's Book of Practical Cats,* the musical *Cats* opened in London in 1981. It became one of the longest-running shows in London and on Broadway. Written by Andrew Lloyd Webber, *Cats* won seven Tony Awards and has played in more than 250 cities all across the world.

Literature Connection Born in St. Louis, Missouri, poet T. S. Eliot (1888–1965) became a citizen of Great Britain. He was one of the most prominent literary figures of the twentieth century. In his poems, Eliot often captured the sound of ordinary spoken language. He also gave poetry the nervous rhythms of the early twentieth century, a time of rapid change. Most of Eliot's work is serious in nature, including "The Wasteland" and "The Hollow Men." In *Old Possum's Book of Practical Cats,* though, he has fun exploring the quirky personalities and mysterious ways of cats.

Art Connection Cats have caught the attention of many artists through the ages. Ancient Egyptian civilization worshiped cats and included feline images in much of its art, especially on jars and urns.

There is a historical reason for the Egyptian celebration of cats. Around 2500 B.C., rats and mice threatened to eat up Egypt's grain. The wild cats of Egypt came from the woods to save the day. The grateful Egyptians welcomed cats into their society and mythology. Killing a cat in ancient Egypt was a serious crime.

Assessment Writing Application: Report Card on Cats

Create a set of requirements for an ideal pet. You might include categories such as "Shows Affection." Then, give cats a grade in each of your categories: Do they fulfill the requirement fully, somewhat, or not at all? Write a paragraph explaining the grades you have given.

▲ Critical Viewing
What does this photograph from the musical *Cats* suggest about the personality of this particular cat? Explain your answer. **[Speculate]**

◄ Critical Viewing
How does this sculpture convey the importance of cats in Egyptian culture? **[Evaluate]**

Viewing and Representing

Activity Ask students what formats have been used in the report cards they've received since they started going to school. Students may respond by describing report cards with letter grades, number grades, teacher comments, or evaluative words and phrases such as *Excellent, Satisfactory,* or *Needs Improvement.* Provide several models of these formats on the board, so that students can chose the format which will most effectively communicate their evaluation of cats as pets to others.

Critical Viewing

Evaluate Students may observe that cats' importance to Egyptian culture can be seen by the fact that they thought them important enough to be represented in statues. Students may also note the regal stance and distinguished facial features of the statue. Ask students how the image of this statue compares and contrasts with the photograph above it.

Media and Technology Skills

Using Available Technology

Activity: Exploring Computer Tests

You can take many kinds of tests on computer. On these tests, you can use many of the same test-taking skills you have developed for printed tests. To do well on a computer-based test, you should get comfortable with the computer test format.

Learn About It

Practice on the Computer If possible, practice using the computer on which the test will be given. For instance, if the test will be given in the school computer room, visit the room before the test. Start up the computer, use the mouse, and open and close applications. This practice will make you more comfortable during the actual test.

Read Instructions Carefully As on a printed test, make sure you read all test instructions carefully before taking a computer-based test. Pay special attention to instructions about using the computer to answer. For instance, you may not be able to change an answer once you have marked it. Or, you may have only a limited time to answer each question.

Take On-line Practice Tests To get comfortable with computer test-taking, practice. Take a few of the practice tests that are available on CD-ROM and on-line. Some of these tests can teach you more about a subject as well as give you practice in test-taking. These tests give you feedback after each answer to let you know why your answer is right or wrong. This feedback will help you learn more about the subject matter covered by the test.

Evaluate It With the help of a teacher or school librarian, locate a computer practice test. Take the test. Then, fill out a graphic organizer like the one shown with your thoughts on the experience. Write a letter to the computer-test maker commenting on the test.

Tips on Computer Test-Taking

• Read directions carefully. They will explain how to answer a question and then move to the next question.
• If you are having trouble with your computer, ask for help right away.

Were the Test Directions Easy to Understand?	Was it Easy to Get Around in the Program? Why?	Was it Easy to Enter Answers? Why?	Did the Program Give Feedback? Was It Helpful?

► **Lesson Objectives**

1. To analyze information as presented in various media.
2. To become proficient at navigating electronic texts and other technology resources.
3. To evaluate the effectiveness and organization of technology resources.

Step-by-Step Teaching Guide

Using Available Technology

Teaching Resources: Writing Support Transparency 13-D; Writing Support Activity Book 13-2

1. Begin by asking students if they can think of any advantages or disadvantages to taking tests on computers.

2. Explain to or elicit from students that computerized tests generally calculate their grades immediately, sometimes provide instant feedback when they answer a question, and can therefore be more interactive than tests given off-line. Point out that computerized tests on-line and on CD-ROM can also provide ideal opportunities to practice test-taking skills.

3. Using the transparency, walk students through the computer test evaluation form. Explain that evaluating a computer test will help them become more aware of how such on-line assessments work. Tell them that becoming familiar with a test's format is one excellent way to improve their scores and test-taking ability.

4. Give students copies of the blank organizer and tell them to use it after they find and practice using a computer test program on their own.

Lesson Objectives

1. To practice the elements of the proofreading process.
2. To practice capitalizing, spelling, and punctuating correctly to enhance meaning.
3. To demonstrate control over grammatical elements.

Proofreading

1. Explain to students that some standardized test questions assess their knowledge of spelling, capitalization, and punctuation.

2. Tell students that it's important for them to understand the format of a question before trying to answer it.

3. Ask for student volunteers to read the sample test items, the multiple-choice questions, and the answers and explanations.

4. As students read, point out that the sentence parts in question are numbered and that these numbers correspond to the questions below. Also emphasize that such questions often include an option like *No error,* which means that the sentence may be correct exactly as it's written.

5. Give students time to practice on their own using the exercises on the next page.

Standardized Test Preparation Workshop

Proofreading

On writing tests, you may be asked to demonstrate your proofreading skills by producing work that is error-free. Standardized tests also use a multiple-choice format to measure your ability to recognize errors in spelling, capitalization, and punctuation. Use these guidelines to help you answer such questions:

- When checking for punctuation errors, consider whether a mark is missing, unnecessary, or misplaced.
- Look closely at titles and proper nouns for mistakes in capitalization.
- When checking for spelling errors, be alert for homonyms—words that sound like the correct word but are spelled differently.

The following sample test items will help you become familiar with the format of these questions.

Test Tip

Don't assume that a word is spelled correctly because it looks familiar. On an open-book test, look it up in a dictionary or, on a computer-based test, use Spell Check.

Sample Test Items	Answers and Explanations
Read the following passage and decide which type of errors, if any, appear in the underlined sections. Mark the letters for your answer. I beleive that the poem *April Rain Song* (1) (2) was written by Langston Hughes.	

1 A Spelling error
  B Capitalization error
  C Punctuation error
  D No error
	The correct answer for item 1 is *A. Believe* is spelled incorrectly as it appears in the sentence.

2 F Spelling error
  G Capitalization error
  H Punctuation error
  J No error
	The correct answer for item 2 is *H.* The poem's title, "April Rain Song," is incorrectly punctuated as it appears in the sentence. The titles of poems are enclosed in quotation marks, not italicized.

288 • Writing for Assessment

✎ TEST-TAKING TIP

Tell students that they can check their own answers on proofreading questions by trying to remember the rules that govern spelling, capitalization, and punctuation. For example, the word *believe* is spelled incorrectly in the example above. Point out that remembering the *i* before **e** rule would help them answer this question.

Ask students to think about some other rules they've learned about spelling, capitalization, and punctuation. Point out that these kinds of generally applied rules—though they may have some exceptions—will help them when faced with proofreading questions on standardized tests.

Answer Key

▶ **Practice 1**

1 B
2. H
3. B
4. H
5. D

▶ **Practice 2**

1. B
2. F
3. B
4. H

▶ **Practice 1** **Directions:** Read the following passage and decide which type of errors, if any, appear in the under-lined sections. Mark the letters for your answer.

Antonio Vivaldi <u>was an italian composer</u> (1)
who wrote one of the <u>worlds most famous</u> (2)
<u>pieces</u> of music about the seasons. It

is called *The four Seasons*. <u>Its a collection</u> (3)   (4)
of four violin <u>concertos—one for each</u> (5)
<u>season.</u>

1 **A** Spelling error
    B Capitalization error
    C Punctuation error
    D No error

2 **F** Spelling error
    G Capitalization error
    H Punctuation error
    J No error

3 **A** Spelling error
    B Capitalization error
    C Punctuation error
    D No error

4 **F** Spelling error
    G Capitalization error
    H Punctuation error
    J No error

5 **A** Spelling error
    B Capitalization error
    C Punctuation error
    D No error

▶ **Practice 2** **Directions:** Read the following passage and decide which type of errors, if any, appear in the under-lined sections. Mark the letters for your answer.

We studied the poem <u>"April Rain Song" in</u> (1)
<u>our Language Arts class.</u> Langston

Hughes, like Vivaldi, <u>was intrested</u> in the (2)
seasons. The poem conveys his wonder at

the rain. It first appeared <u>in a magazine</u> (3)
<u>for African american children</u> in the <u>April,</u> (4)
<u>1912 issue.</u>

1 **A** Spelling error
    B Capitalization error
    C Punctuation error
    D No error

2 **F** Spelling error
    G Capitalization error
    H Punctuation error
    J No error

3 **A** Spelling error
    B Capitalization error
    C Punctuation error
    D No error

4 **F** Spelling error
    G Capitalization error
    H Punctuation error
    J No error

Lesson Objectives

1. To understand parts of speech and basic sentence patterns and to apply relevant concepts to their own writing.

2. To learn and apply key concepts governing usage of verbs.

3. To understand concepts of agreement relating to subjects and verbs and pronouns and antecedents, and to apply this understanding to their own writing.

4. To compose sentences of increasing sophistication and appropriateness.

5. To analyze works of literature as models of appropriate and effective English usage.

6. To recognize appropriate English usage in their own reading and writing.

7. To use "hands-on" strategies to reinforce understanding of grammar and usage concepts.

8. To master the conventions of capitalization, punctuation, and spelling, and to apply them accurately to their own writing.

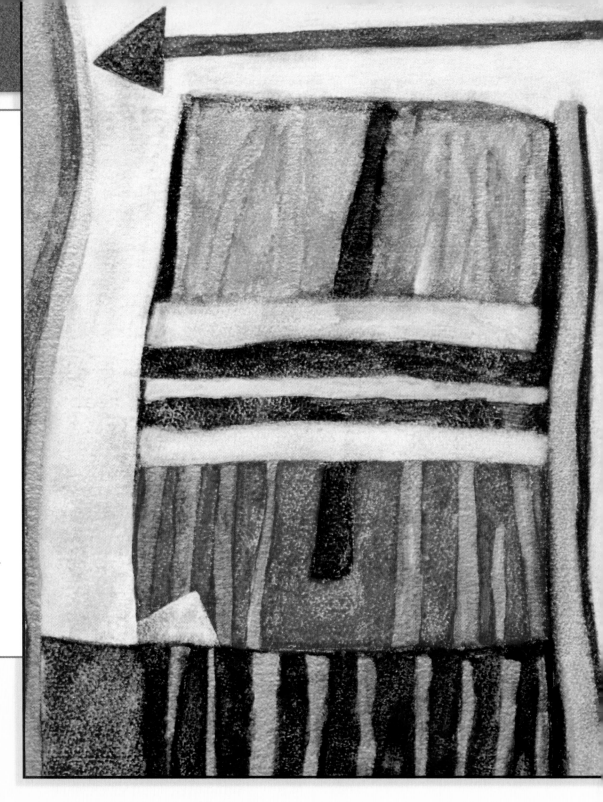

PART

2

Grammar, Usage, and Mechanics

Lucky for Us, Sandy Novak

Grammar, Usage, and Mechanics • **291**

Step-by-Step Teaching Guide

Responding to Fine Art
Lucky for Us
by Sandy Novak

Use this work of art to start a discussion about the functions of grammar, usage, and mechanics.

1. Have students examine the painting on pages 290–291. You might use the following questions to prompt discussion:

   What do you think this painting represents? What details can you use to help you?

   What words would you use to describe the feeling or mood of this painting? How does the artist's use of color create this feeling or mood?

2. Ask students why they think this painting was chosen for the section on grammar, usage, and mechanics. You can expect a wide range of descriptions about this painting from students. Encourage all responses, but make sure students support their ideas with details from the painting.

In-Depth Lesson Plan

	LESSON FOCUS	PRINT AND MEDIA RESOURCES
DAY 1	**Nouns** Students learn to identify different types of nouns (pp. 292–299).	**Teaching Resources** *Grammar Exercise Workbook,* pp. 1–6; *Grammar Exercises Answers on Transparencies,* Ch. 14 *Language Lab* **CD-ROM,** Using Nouns; **On-Line Exercise Bank,** Section 14.1
DAY 2	**Pronouns** Students learn to identify and use personal pronouns (pp. 300–303).	**Teaching Resources** *Grammar Exercise Workbook,* pp. 7–10; *Grammar Exercises Answers on Transparencies,* Ch. 14 *Language Lab* **CD-ROM,** Using Pronouns; **On-Line Exercise Bank,** Section 14.2
DAY 3	**Pronouns (continued)** Students learn to identify and use demonstrative pronouns and do the Hands-on Grammar activity (pp. 304–307).	**Teaching Resources** *Grammar Exercise Workbook,* pp. 11–12; *Grammar Exercises Answers on Transparencies,* Ch. 14; *Hands-on Grammar Activity Book,* Chapter 14 *Language Lab* **CD-ROM,** Using Pronouns; **On-Line Exercise Bank,** Section 14.2
DAY 4	**Review and Assess** Students review chapter and demonstrate mastery of use of nouns and pronouns (pp. 308–311).	**Teaching Resources** *Formal Assessment,* Ch. 14; *Grammar Exercises Answers on Transparencies,* Ch. 14 **On-Line Exercise Bank,** Sections 14.1–2

Accelerated Lesson Plan

	LESSON FOCUS	PRINT AND MEDIA RESOURCES
DAY 1	**Nouns** Students cover concepts and usage of nouns as determined by Diagnostic Test (pp. 292–299).	**Teaching Resources** *Grammar Exercise Workbook,* pp. 1–6; *Grammar Exercises Answers on Transparencies,* Ch. 14 *Language Lab* **CD-ROM,** Using Nouns; **On-Line Exercise Bank,** Section 14.1
DAY 2	**Pronouns** Students cover concepts and usage of pronouns as determined by Diagnostic Test (pp. 300–307).	**Teaching Resources** *Grammar Exercise Workbook,* pp. 7–12; *Grammar Exercises Answers on Transparencies,* Ch. 14; *Hands-on Grammar Activity Book,* Chapter 14 *Language Lab* **CD-ROM,** Using Pronouns; **On-Line Exercise Bank,** Section 14.2
DAY 3	**Review and Assess** Students review chapter and demonstrate mastery of use of nouns and pronouns (pp. 308–311).	**Teaching Resources** *Formal Assessment,* Ch. 14; *Grammar Exercises Answers on Transparencies,* Ch. 14 **On-Line Exercise Bank,** Sections 14.1–2

Options for Adapting Lesson Plans

HOMEWORK

Have students complete any section of the chapter for homework.

FEATURES

Extend coverage with the Grammar in Literature feature (pp. 298, 303), and the Standardized Test Preparation Workshop (p. 310).

TECHNOLOGY

Students can use the On-Line Exercise Bank to complete the exercises on computer. The Auto Check feature will grade their work.

INTEGRATED SKILLS COVERAGE

Grammar in Literature
SE pp. 298, 303

Reading
Find It in Your Reading SE pp. 299, 306, 307

Writing
Find It in Your Writing SE pp. 299, 306, 307
Writing Application SE pp. 299, 307, 309
Writing Skills ATE pp. 296, 301

Spelling
SE p. 296

Language Highlight
ATE p. 296

Workplace Skills
ATE p. 298

Real-World Connection
ATE p. 301

Viewing and Representing
Critical Viewing SE pp. 292, 295, 297, 301, 303, 305

ASSESSMENT SUPPORT

Standardized Test Preparation Workshop SE p. 310; ATE pp. 297, 302

Standardized Test Preparation Workbook, pp. 27–28

Formal Assessment, Ch. 14

MEETING INDIVIDUAL NEEDS

Less Advanced Students See Ongoing Assessments
ATE pp. 296, 301, 303, 305

ESL Students ATE pp. 297, 304

Visual/Spatial Learners ATE p. 294

Gifted/Talented Students ATE p. 302

BLOCK SCHEDULING

Pacing Suggestions
For 90-minute Blocks
- Administer the Diagnostic Test to students to determine instructional coverage.
- Have students complete the necessary exercises in class. Use the Hands-on Grammar activity to provide a change of pace.

Resources for Varying Instruction
- *Language Lab* CD-ROM If your students have access to hardware, a 90-minute block provides an ideal opportunity for students to work on computer.

Professional Development Support
- *How to Manage Instruction in the Block* This teaching Resource provides management and activity suggestions.

MEDIA AND TECHNOLOGY

For the Student
- *Language Lab* CD-ROM, Using Nouns, Using Pronouns
- *On-Line Exercise Bank,* Ch. 14

For the Teacher
- *Resource Pro* CD-ROM

WRITING AND GRAMMAR WEB SITE

The Interactive Writing and Grammar Web site provides a wide array of support for students, teachers, and parents. Grammar support includes:

- On-Line Exercise Bank with Auto Check scoring
- Diagnostic and assessment support

www.phschool.com

LITERATURE CONNECTIONS

Grammar in Literature selections from *Prentice Hall Literature: Timeless Voices, Timeless Themes,* Copper:
from "The Sound of Summer Running," Ray Bradbury, SE p. 298
from "Hard as Nails," Russell Baker, SE p. 303

Lesson Objectives

1. To identify common, proper, and compound nouns

2. To recognize pronouns, their functions, and their antecedents

3. To identify and correctly use personal and demonstrative pronouns

4. To answer different types and levels of questions such as open-ended, literal, and interpretive as well as test-like questions such as multiple choice, true-false, and short answer

5. To represent text information in different ways such as in outlines, timelines, and graphic organizers

6. To capitalize and punctuate correctly to clarify and enhance meaning such as capitalizing titles, using hyphens, semicolons, colons, possessives, and sentence punctuation

7. To use resources to find correct spellings

8. To employ standard English usage in writing for audiences, including subject-verb agreement, pronoun referents, and parts of speech

9. To proofread his/her own work and that of others

10. To describe how the illustrators' choice of style, elements, and media help to represent or extend the text's meanings

Critical Viewing

Identify Students may identify some of the following: nouns—men, woman, running shoes, socks, shirts, pants, hands, arms, and sand; pronouns—he, she, they, it.

Chapter 14 Nouns and Pronouns

▲ Critical Viewing
What nouns and pronouns can you use to describe the people in this picture? **[Identify]**

Runners know how the different parts of their bodies work together to help them move quickly and smoothly. In a similar way, writers know the parts of our language and how they work together to give sentences meaning. Words in English have eight different uses, or parts of speech. These are *nouns, pronouns, verbs, adjectives, adverbs, prepositions, conjunctions,* and *interjections.*

Just as runners stretch their muscles and practice their running technique, writers practice to improve their writing. Both work hard, and both exercise to become better.

This chapter will begin your practice with words. First, you will learn what makes nouns a special category of words and how to identify them. You will also learn about special kinds of nouns. Next, you will learn how pronouns can be used to take the place of nouns in sentences that you write. You will not only learn about nouns and pronouns, but you will also practice using them.

292 • Nouns and Pronouns

☑ **ONGOING ASSESSMENT: Diagnose**

If students miss more than one item in any category, direct them to the relevant pages of the text and assign exercises for practice and review.

Nouns and Pronouns	Diagnostic Test Items	Teach	Practice	Section Review	Chapter Review
Skill Check A					
Nouns	A 1–5	pp. 294–295	Ex. 1–2	Ex. 6	Ex. 26–28
Skill Check B					
Compound Nouns	B 6–10	p. 296	Ex. 3	Ex. 7, 9	Ex. 26, 28
Skill Check C					
Common and Proper Nouns	C 11–15	pp. 297–298	Ex. 4–5	Ex. 8–9	Ex. 27, 28, 32

Diagnostic Test

Directions: Write all answers on a separate sheet of paper.

Skill Check A. Identify each noun in the following sentences.
1. The decathlon includes ten different events.
2. Competition lasts for two days.
3. An athlete must use a variety of skills.
4. Speed and strength are tested in the decathlon.
5. Points are awarded for each event.

Skill Check B. Copy the sentences, underlining compound nouns.
6. The long jump and the shot put are on the first day.
7. The high jump takes place on that day also.
8. One event on the second day is the pole vault.
9. A timekeeper records each athlete's time in the footraces.
10. Finishing all of the events takes great willpower.

Skill Check C. Identify each underlined noun as *common* or *proper*.
11. The final <u>event</u> in the <u>decathlon</u> is the 1,500-meter <u>run</u>.
12. In 1912, <u>Jim Thorpe</u> won a <u>competition</u> in <u>Sweden</u>.
13. <u>Daley Thompson</u> of <u>Great Britain</u> was a two-time <u>winner</u>.
14. Another famous <u>champion</u> was <u>Bob Mathias</u>.
15. He won several gold <u>medals</u> in international <u>competitions</u> for the <u>United States</u>.

Skill Check D. Write each pronoun, and then write its antecedent.
16. The Greeks had the pentathlon in their competitions.
17. There were pentathlons for men and women, but they didn't compete against each other.
18. An athlete's points in each event would be added to his total.
19. Canada added a modern pentathlon to its track meets.
20. The first winner proudly displayed her medal around her neck.

Skill Check E. List the personal pronouns in the following sentences.
21. Do you know what events are in the pentathlon?
22. Two of them are fencing and swimming.
23. I think cross-country running is the most difficult.
24. They also include a horseback-riding event in most pentathlons.
25. We watched the riding on television.

Skill Check F. Write the demonstrative pronouns and the noun to which each refers.
26. The triathlon includes three events. These are very challenging.
27. Those are the participants in this event.
28. That is a distance I cannot run.
29. Many triathlons are held in Hawaii. That is a popular location.
30. This is a very difficult competition.

Nouns and Pronouns • **293**

Answer Key

Diagnostic Test

Each item in the diagnostic test corresponds to a specific section in the chapter on nouns and pronouns. This will enable you to tailor instruction to your students' particular needs. See "Ongoing Assessment: Diagnose" on the bottom of pages 292–293 for further details.

Skill Check A

1. decathlon, events
2. Competition, days
3. athlete, variety, skills
4. Speed, strength, decathlon
5. Points, event

Skill Check B

6. <u>long jump</u>, <u>shot put</u>
7. <u>high jump</u>
8. <u>pole vault</u>
9. <u>timekeeper</u>, <u>footraces</u>
10. <u>willpower</u>

Skill Check C

11. common, common, common
12. proper, common, proper
13. proper, proper, common
14. common, proper
15. common, common, proper

Skill Check D

16. their—Greeks
17. they—men and women
18. his—athlete's
19. its—Canada
20. her—winner, her—winner

Skill Check E

21. you   24. They
22. them   25. We
23. I

Skill Check F

26. These—events
27. Those—participants
28. That—distance
29. That—Hawaii
30. This—competition

✓ ONGOING ASSESSMENT: Diagnose *continued*

Nouns and Pronouns	Diagnostic Test Items	Teach	Practice	Section Review	Chapter Review
Skill Check D					
Pronouns and Their Antecedents	D 16–20	pp. 300–301	Ex. 13–14	Ex. 19	Ex. 30
Skill Check E					
Personal Pronouns	E 21–25	pp. 302–303	Ex. 15–16	Ex. 20, 22	Ex. 29, 30, 32
Skill Check F					
Demonstrative Pronouns	F 26–30	pp. 304–305	Ex. 17–18	Ex. 21–22	Ex. 31–32
Cumulative Review and Applications				Ex. 10–12, 23–25	Ex. 33–34

🕐 TIME SAVERS!

📄 **Answers on Transparency** Use the Grammar Exercises Answers on Transparencies for Chapter 14 to facilitate correction by students.

💻 **On-Line Exercise Bank** Have students complete the exercises on computer. The Auto Check feature will grade their work for you!

Ask students to look around the room and make a list of ten people, places, or things they see. Write some answers on the board. Then, point to each item and ask students whether it is a person, place, or thing. Explain that these words are nouns.

Activate Prior Knowledge

Ask students to describe their favorite places in a few sentences. For example: *I like Shea Stadium. The field has three bases and a pitcher's mound. My brother and I sit in the stands.* Write some of their sentences on the board and have volunteers point out the nouns in each one.

TEACH

Step-by-Step Teaching Guide

Nouns

1. Some students may have difficulty classifying words under the category of *things*. This category can be broken down into subcategories: living things, nonliving things, and things that cannot be seen, such as concepts, qualities, and conditions (for example: happiness, beauty, poverty).

2. Tell students that many nouns that cannot be seen can be identified by their suffixes, which include *-dom, -ism, -ment, -ness, -ship,* and *-tion.* (e.g., tourism, sadness, friendship)

3. Write the following sentences on the board and ask students to identify the nouns and label each as *person, place,* or *thing.*

   Javier went to college in Ohio.

   My mother believes that freedom is very important.

   Person: Javier, mother

   Place: Ohio

   Thing: college, freedom

Customize for
Visual/Spatial Learners

Have students look through magazines and newspapers to find images of people expressing emotion. Ask students to use nouns to name the emotions.

Section 14.1 **Nouns**

A *noun* is one of the eight parts of speech. It is a word that names something. Some nouns name people, some name places, and some name things. *Wilma Rudolph, Washington,* and *stopwatch,* for example, are all nouns.

▶ **KEY CONCEPT** A **noun** is the name of a person, place, or thing. ■

Nouns name both living and nonliving things. Some nouns name what can be seen, such as *elephant.* Others name ideas, such as *strength.* The nouns in the following chart are grouped under three headings: People, Places, and Things. Notice that the nouns in the third column name things you can see as well as ideas or feelings that you cannot see. Can you think of other nouns to add under each heading in the chart?

NOUNS		
People	**Places**	**Things**
runner	Ohio	movie
Mrs. Fisher	theater	hunger
Ann	stadium	race
sailor	Rocky Mountains	love

In order to find out whether a word is a noun, look at how it is used in a sentence. If the word names a person, place, or thing, it is a noun. The nouns in the following sentences are underlined.

EXAMPLES: Robert runs every day.
We raced in Canada.
Her breathing was loud.
Many outstanding runners come from Kenya, a country in Africa.

Almost every time you speak, you talk about people, places, or things. When you talk about them, you are using nouns.

Theme: Runners

In this section, you will learn to recognize different types of nouns. The examples and exercises are about running and track stars.

Cross-Curricular Connection: Physical Education

⏱ **TIME AND RESOURCE MANAGER**

Resources
Print: Grammar Exercise Workbook, pp. 1–6; Grammar Exercises Answers on Transparencies, Chapter 14
Technology: Language Lab CD-ROM, Using Nouns, On-Line Exercise Bank, Section 14.1

In-Depth Coverage	Accelerated Pace
• Work through all key concepts, pp. 294–298. • Assign and review Exercises 1–5. • Read and discuss Grammar in Literature, p. 298.	• Assign pp. 294–298 for independent student review. • Review common and proper nouns and assign Exercises 4–5. • Assign Section Review Exercises 6–9.

▶ **Exercise 1** Identifying Nouns List the nouns in each of the following sentences.

EXAMPLE: My favorite sprinter is Carl Lewis.
ANSWER: sprinter, Carl Lewis

1. Meets include many different events.
2. Edward runs the hurdles.
3. First, the runners wait for the signal to start.
4. They place their feet in starting blocks.
5. A loud bang signals the start of the race.
6. All runners race toward the finish line.
7. Ten barriers stand along the track.
8. Runners jump high over the hurdles.
9. Speed, flexibility, and coordination are important for success.
10. Hurdles are more complicated than the sprints.

▶ **Exercise 2** More Work With Nouns List the nouns in each sentence. Beside each noun, write whether it names a person, a place, or a thing.

EXAMPLE: The runner captured the gold medal in Seattle.
ANSWER: runner (person), medal (thing), Seattle (place)

1. The dashes are short races.
2. Runners competed in dashes at the Olympics in Atlanta.
3. Some competitors swing their arms and lean their bodies forward.
4. Each racer uses a different strategy.
5. Bursts of speed are combined with periods of coasting.

More Practice

Language Lab
CD-ROM
• Using Nouns lesson
On-line
Exercise Bank
• Section 14.1
Grammar Exercise
Workbook
• pp. 1–2

▼ **Critical Viewing**
Provide a noun that names something related to each runner in this picture.
[Distinguish]

Runners get ready for the start of a 50-yard dash.

Nouns • 295

Answer Key

▶ **Exercise 1**

1. Meets, events
2. Edward, hurdles
3. runners, signal
4. feet, blocks
5. bang, start, race
6. runners, finish line
7. barriers, track
8. Runners, hurdles
9. Speed, flexibility, coordination, success
10. Hurdles, sprints

▶ **Exercise 2**

1. dashes—thing, races—thing
2. Runners—person, dashes— thing, Olympics—thing, Atlanta—place
3. competitors—person, arms— thing, bodies—thing
4. racer—person, strategy—thing
5. Bursts—thing, speed—thing, periods—thing, coasting—thing

Critical Viewing

Distinguish Possible responses: boy, sneakers, shorts, tank top, T-shirt, etc.

TIME SAVERS!

Answers on Transparency Use the Grammar Exercises Answers on Transparencies for Chapter 14 to facilitate correction by students.

On-Line Exercise Bank Have students complete the exercises on computer. The Auto Check feature will grade their work for you!

Compound Nouns

1. Write the following words in two columns on the board and have students create compound nouns by joining a word from the first column with one from the second.

door	hander
table	room
dog	bell
left	house
bed	tennis

2. Tell students that not all compound nouns are written as one word. Have them look up the compound nouns from step one to learn how each is spelled. (doorbell, table tennis, doghouse, left-hander, bedroom) Remind students to use the dictionary if they are not sure if a compound noun is written as one word, as two words, or as a hyphenated word.

Integrating Writing Skills

Have students review a writing selection from their portfolios and check that they have correctly used and spelled compound nouns. If students have not used any compound nouns, encourage them to add to their work a few sentences that contain compound nouns.

Answer Key

▶ **Exercise 3**

1. sister-in-law, short story
2. footsteps, road runner
3. backpack, wristwatch, running shoes
4. mailbox, newsletters
5. doorbell
6. football, high school
7. weekends, countryside
8. cross-country, workout
9. baseball, basketball
10. roommate

Language Highlight

Explain to students that a *portmanteau word* is another type of word that is made by combining two different words. Unlike compound nouns, portmanteau words are spelled by blending the letters in the original words to create a completely new word (e.g. *smoke + fog = smog*). Have students think of other examples of portmanteau words.

296

14.1

Recognizing Compound Nouns

Some nouns are made up of two or more words. *Classroom* is a compound noun made up of *class* and *room*. *Homework* is a compound noun made up of the words *home* and *work*.

▶ **KEY CONCEPT** A **compound noun** is one noun made by joining two or more words. ■

Sometimes the meaning of a compound noun is more than just the meaning of two or more words put together. Words such as *drumstick*, *bookworm*, *boot camp*, and *housecoat* have meanings that are different from those of the individual words that have been combined.

EXAMPLES: Each runner wore a *headband*.
The entire meet ran like *clockwork*.

Check a dictionary when you are not sure of the meaning of a compound noun.

Compound nouns are written in three different ways. Some are written as single words, others as hyphenated words, and still others as two or more separate words.

COMPOUND NOUNS		
Single Words	Hyphenated Words	Separate Words
crossbar firefighter thunderstorm	shot-put right-hander middle-distance	dinner jacket pole vault pen pal

▶ **Exercise 3** Finding Compound Nouns Copy each sentence, underlining the compound nouns.

EXAMPLE: The race's <u>endpoint</u> was the <u>Brooklyn Bridge</u>.

1. My sister-in-law wrote a short story about jogging.
2. I hope to follow in her footsteps as a road runner.
3. Her backpack holds a wristwatch and her running shoes.
4. Her mailbox is always full of running newsletters.
5. The doorbell rings when fellow runners stop by.
6. A track circles the football stadium at our high school.
7. On the weekends, she runs in the countryside.
8. Running cross-country provides a great workout for her.
9. Baseball and basketball players also do a lot of running.
10. Her former roommate is a track star.

296 • Nouns and Pronouns

💡 Spelling Tip

Check your spelling of compound nouns that are single words. For example, in *pastime*, a combination of the words *past* and *time*, there is only one *t* in the compound form.

▶ **More Practice**

Language Lab CD-ROM
• Using Nouns lesson
On-line Exercise Bank
• Section 14.1
Grammar Exercise Workbook
• pp. 3–4

☑ **ONGOING ASSESSMENT: Monitor and Reinforce**

If students have difficulty with Exercise 1, 2, or 3, refer them to the following for additional practice.

In the Textbook	Print Resources	Technology
Section Review, Ex. 6–7, p. 299	Grammar Exercise Workbook, pp. 1–4	Language Lab CD-ROM Using Nouns; On-Line Exercise Bank, Section 14.1

Recognizing Common and Proper Nouns

Nouns can be grouped in several different ways. For example, all nouns are either *common nouns* or *proper nouns*. To decide whether a noun is common or proper, you must know whether it names something in a specific way or a general way.

▶ **KEY CONCEPT** A **common noun** names any one of a group of people, places, or things. ■

It is easy to recognize common nouns. Common nouns are not capitalized (except at the beginning of a sentence or in a title). Words such as *jogger, city,* and *race* are common nouns because they can apply to many different people, places, or things. In addition, a common noun can be a single word, such as *winner* or *track,* or a compound word, such as *muscle strain* or *finish line.*

▶ **KEY CONCEPT** A **proper noun** names a specific person, place, or thing. ■

Proper nouns, on the other hand, are always capitalized. *Mary Stewart, Chicago,* and *Monday* are proper nouns because they name specific people, places, and things. Proper nouns are often made up of more than one word. When a proper noun, such as *Avenue of the Americas,* contains words such as *a, an, the,* and *of,* these words are not capitalized unless they are the first word in the proper noun.

Jesse Owens competing in the 1936 Olympics in Berlin.

▲ **Critical Viewing** What are some important proper nouns that relate to the life of Jesse Owens? (See Exercise 5 for some ideas.) **[Identify; Support]**

COMMON NOUNS	PROPER NOUNS
scientist	Madam Curie
relative	Aunt Carol
city	Atlanta
state	Kentucky
book	*Julie of the Wolves*
bridge	Golden Gate Bridge
holiday	Columbus Day

Nouns • 297

Critical Viewing

Identify; Support Jesse Owens was a gifted athlete who attained uncommon success by winning four gold medals at the Berlin Olympics. He was also one of the first African Americans to go to the Olympics.

Step-by-Step Teaching Guide

Common and Proper Nouns

1. Some students may say that it is easy to recognize proper nouns—they are always capitalized. Remind them that any noun that begins a sentence is capitalized too. The key is recognizing a proper noun as a *specific* person, place, or thing.

2. Tell students that in most cases *specific* means a name, not a category. In other words, although a chemist is a specific kind of scientist, *chemist* is not a proper noun. However, the name Marie Curie, a chemist who discovered radium, is a proper noun.

3. Write the following examples on the board for more practice. Ask students to suggest an additional proper noun for each category.

Common Noun	Proper Noun
city	Chicago
basketball team	Boston Celtics
university	Duke University
baseball player	Pedro Martinez
country	France
language	English
ocean	Indian Ocean
lake	Lake Michigan
river	Missouri River

STANDARDIZED TEST PREPARATION WORKSHOP

Grammar and Usage Many standardized tests require students to identify errors in sentences. Problems with common and proper nouns are among the items included in these sentences. Ask students to identify the capitalization error in the following sentence.

A marathon is more than 26 miles long. The Boston Marathon is a great Race. It takes place every April.

A Boston   **B** Marathon
C Race   **D** April

The correct answer is item **C.** *Race* is a common, not a proper noun, so it should not be capitalized. The remaining capitalized words are all proper nouns because they name specific things.

Customize for
ESL Students

Not all languages follow the same capitalization rules. In fact, some do not incorporate the concept of capitalization at all. Encourage volunteers to give examples of capitalization rules in their home languages. For instance, have them write their names in their home languages. Discuss the contrast in capitalization.

Grammar in Literature

1. Have a volunteer read aloud the excerpt from "The Sound of Summer Running."

2. Discuss with students how the compound and proper nouns add detail and interest to the writing. Point out that if Bradbury had written *a place* instead of *California* and *sometime* instead of *September*, the passage would be less interesting and precise. Similarly, the word *shoes* in place of *tennis shoes* would also detract from the precision of the language.

More About the Author

Ray Bradbury is an American science-fiction writer who wrote such classics as *The Martian Chronicles* and *Fahrenheit 451*. Bradbury was an imaginative child who used to scare himself with his ideas. At age twelve he started writing stories, most of which were about space travel. He published his first story at age twenty-one, and he has been publishing novels, short stories, poems, and screenplays ever since.

Integrate Workplace Skills

Point out that Bradbury's use of the word *well* to start a sentence usually creates a casual tone. Tell students that in formal writing, such as business or cover letters, they should avoid beginning sentences with the word *well*.

Answer Key

Exercise 4

1. common
2. proper
3. proper
4. common
5. proper
6. common
7. proper
8. proper
9. common
10. common

Exercise 5

1. Jesse Owens, athlete
2. high school, Owens, Ohio
3. Ohio State University, broad jump, event
4. Owens, team
5. medals, Olympics, Berlin

14.1

GRAMMAR IN LITERATURE

from The Sound of Summer Running
Ray Bradbury

In the following passage, common nouns are shown in blue italics. Proper nouns are shown in red italics.

Well, he felt sorry for *boys* who lived in *California* where they wore *tennis shoes* all *year* and never knew what it was to get *winter* off your *feet*, peel off the iron leather *shoes* all full of *snow* and *rain* and run barefoot for a *day* and then lace on the first new *tennis shoes* of the *season*, which was better than barefoot. The *magic* was always in the new *pair* of *shoes*. The *magic* might die by the *first* of *September*, but now in late *June* there was still plenty of *magic*, and *shoes* like these could jump you over *trees* and *rivers* and *houses*.

Exercise 4 Recognizing Common and Proper Nouns On your paper, indicate whether each noun is common or proper.

EXAMPLES: building (*common*)
Cole Field House (*proper*)

1. runner
2. Penn Games
3. France
4. relay
5. Nile River
6. university
7. Gail Devers
8. Mercedes Lopez
9. judge
10. stadium

Exercise 5 Identifying Common and Proper Nouns Write these sentences on your paper. Circle the common nouns and underline the proper nouns.

1. Jesse Owens was a great track-and-field athlete.
2. In high school, Owens competed all around Ohio.
3. At Ohio State University, the broad jump was his top event.
4. Later, Owens made the United States track team.
5. He captured four gold medals at the Olympics in Berlin.

More Practice

Language Lab
CD-ROM
• Using Nouns lesson
On-line
Exercise Bank
• Section 14.1
Grammar Exercise
Workbook
• pp. 5–6

☑ ONGOING ASSESSMENT: Assess Mastery

Use the following resources to assess student mastery of nouns.

In the Textbook	Technology
Chapter Review, Ex. 26–28, p. 308	Language Lab CD-ROM, Using Nouns; On-Line Exercise Bank, Section 14.1

Section 14.1 Section Review

GRAMMAR EXERCISES 6–12

> **Exercise 6** Identifying Nouns
> Write the nouns in each sentence.

1. The team has practice every afternoon.
2. A whistle signals the start of practice.
3. Runners wear shorts, tank tops, and special shoes.
4. The team runs many short sprints.
5. The coach pays close attention.
6. His stopwatch times all the runners.
7. Some people do the high jump or the hammer throw.
8. The entire team drinks a lot of water.
9. The pulse measures the heartbeat.
10. Stretching is also important at the end of practice.

> **Exercise 7** Finding Compound Nouns Copy each sentence, underlining the compound nouns.

1. My family has footraces at the park on the weekends.
2. My brother gives me a head start.
3. Jeff runs track and field for the middle school.
4. I prefer field events like the shot put.
5. Another good exercise for runners is step aerobics.

> **Exercise 8** Revising Sentences by Adding Proper Nouns Rewrite the sentences below, replacing the underlined words with proper nouns of your choice.

1. The high school always hosts the county track meet.
2. The race was on a weekday.
3. Our team competed in another state.
4. The mayor made an opening speech.
5. A reporter from the newspaper came.
6. The reporter interviewed the top runner.
7. My friend finished first in one race.
8. A girl cheered the loudest.

9. The award was named for the principal.
10. First prize was dinner at a restaurant.

> **Exercise 9** Classifying Nouns
> Write the nouns in the following sentences, and label them *compound noun*, *common noun*, or *proper noun*.

1. Florence Griffith Joyner ran her races at high speeds.
2. She placed first at the Jesse Owens National Youth Games.
3. "FloJo" was a gold medalist.
4. She also wrote books and modeled.
5. Her husband starred in the triple jump.

> **Exercise 10** Find It in Your Reading List any proper nouns or compound nouns you find in this passage from "The Sound of Summer Running."

Old Mr. Sanderson moved through his shoe store as the proprietor of a pet shop must move through his shop where are kenneled animals from everywhere in the world. . . .

> **Exercise 11** Find It in Your Writing Look through your portfolio for a composition about a special person, place, or thing. Circle the proper nouns you used.

> **Exercise 12** Writing Application Write a brief description of a star athlete in your favorite sport. Label all of your nouns *common nouns*, *proper nouns*, or *compound nouns*.

Section Review • 299

Section Review

Each of these exercises correlates to the instruction on nouns, pages 294–298. These exercises may be used for more practice, for reteaching, or for review of the Key Concepts presented. Answers for all chapter exercises are available in *Grammar Exercises Answers on Transparencies* in your Teaching Resources.

Answer Key

> **Exercise 6**

1. team, practice, afternoon
2. whistle, start, practice
3. Runners, shorts, tank tops, shoes
4. team, sprints
5. coach, attention
6. stopwatch, runners
7. people, high jump, hammer throw
8. team, water
9. pulse, heartbeat
10. Stretching, end, practice

> **Exercise 7**

1. My family has footraces at the park on the weekends.
2. My brother gives me a head start.
3. Jeff runs track and field for the middle school.
4. I prefer field events like the shot put.
5. Another good exercise for runners is step aerobics.

> **Exercise 8**

Answers will vary. Samples are given.

1. Longfellow High School always hosts the Lake County track meet.
2. The race was on a Wednesday.
3. Our team competed in Vermont.
4. Mayor Suarez made an opening speech.
5. A reporter from the *Daily Tribune* came.
6. The reporter interviewed Joe Thompson.
7. Angela finished first in one race.
8. Sara cheered the loudest.
9. The award was named for Mr. Hanson.
10. First prize was dinner at Burger Barn.

> **Exercise 9**

1. Florence Griffith Joyner—proper; races—common; speeds—common

continued

Answer Key continued

2. Jesse Owens National Youth Games— proper
3. FloJo—proper; gold medalist—common, compound
4. books—common
5. husband—common; triple jump—common, compound

> **Exercise 10**

Find It in Your Reading
Mr. Sanderson, shoe store, pet shop, everywhere

> **Exercise 11**

Find It in Your Writing
Students also can search for common nouns and label the nouns they find as *proper* or *common.*

> **Exercise 12**

Writing Application
If possible, give students time to research their subjects in their school library or on the Internet. When they finish writing, students can combine their paragraphs into a class book about athletes.

Pronouns

PREPARE and ENGAGE

Interest GRABBER Have students converse in small groups for about 5 minutes. As they do so ask them to list all the pronouns they use. Then have them list pronouns by frequency of use. Be sure students include different types of pronouns. (subject, object, possessive, personal, demonstrative)

PREPARE and ENGAGE

Interest GRABBER Have students converse in small groups for about 5 minutes. As they do so ask them to list all the pronouns they use. Then have them list pronouns by frequency of use. Be sure students include different types of pronouns. (subject, object, possessive, personal, demonstrative)

Activate Prior Knowledge

Use student lists to generate conversation about pronouns. Help students classify various pronouns by how they function.

TEACH

Step-by-Step Teaching Guide

Pronouns

1. Pronouns help avoid awkward repetitions of nouns when we speak and write by replacing nouns that appear more than once:

   Maurice loves sports articles. Maurice reads sports articles every day.

   Maurice loves sports articles. *He* reads *them* every day.

2. Tell students that *antecedent* is derived from the Latin words *ante-* (before) and *cedere* (to go). This may help them remember that the antecedent is the noun that "goes before" the pronoun.

3. Have students identify the antecedents for *He* and *them* in the above example. (Maurice, sports articles)

Answer Key

Exercise 13

1. it
2. she, it
3. him
4. they, their
5. I, I, my, it

Pronouns are useful words because they can "stand in" for nouns. They prevent people from having to use the same nouns over and over again.

KEY CONCEPT A **pronoun** takes the place of a noun. ■

The noun that is replaced by a pronoun is called the *antecedent*. Usually, the antecedent comes before the pronoun. The antecedent is the name of a person, place, or thing.

PRONOUNS AND ANTECEDENTS	
Person	ANTECED PRON Marie said she would watch the news program.
Place	ANTECED PRON Florida is popular because it has a warm climate.
Thing	ANTECED Our old newspapers cannot be recycled PRON until they have been read.

A pronoun and its antecedent will often be in the same sentence, as they are in the examples above. Sometimes, however, a pronoun and its antecedent will be in different sentences.

EXAMPLES: Jane writes well. Many people have enjoyed reading her newspaper articles.

Michael collects magazines. He asks neighbors to save their old magazines for him.

Exercise 13 Recognizing Pronouns Identify the pronoun or pronouns in each of the following sentences.

EXAMPLE: I bought the newspaper and read it.
ANSWER: I, it

1. The editor read the article and corrected it.
2. The event interested the reporter, so she wrote an article about it.
3. The article was about the mayor and included a recent photo of him.
4. The delivery boys had bikes they could use for their paper routes.
5. I have a subscription to the newspaper. I read my copy every morning as soon as it arrives.

Theme: Media

In this section, you will learn how pronouns can be used to replace nouns in sentences. The examples and exercises are about different news media.

Cross-Curricular Connection: Social Studies

⏱ TIME AND RESOURCE MANAGER

Resources
Print: Grammar Exercise Workbook, pp. 7–12; Hands-on Grammar Activity Book, Chapter 14; Grammar Exercises Answers on Transparencies, Chapter 14
Technology: Language Lab CD-ROM, Using Pronouns; On-Line Exercise Bank, Section 14.2

In-Depth Coverage	Accelerated Pace
• Work through all key concepts, pp. 300–305. • Assign and review Exercises 13–18. • Read and discuss Grammar in Literature, p. 303. • Do the Hands-on Grammar Activity, p. 306.	• Assign pp. 300–305 for independent student review. • Review Demonstrative Pronouns and assign Exercises 17–18. • Assign Section Review Exercises 19–22.

> **Exercise 14** Identifying Pronouns and Their Antecedents
>
> Identify the pronouns in each of the following sentences. Then, identify each pronoun's antecedent.

EXAMPLE: The reporter made sure he got his facts right.

ANSWER: he (reporter), his (reporter)

1. Julius Caesar ordered the first news bulletins. They were posted for him every day.
2. Originally, newspapers were one page long, and they were about one event.
3. Johannes Gutenberg invented movable type. His invention made the modern newspaper industry possible.
4. In France, the magazine developed, but it was mainly a collection of literature and not a news source.
5. Each political group had a newspaper in which its leaders expressed their political views.
6. Daniel Defoe and Jonathan Swift were English journalists. They were involved with the struggle for freedom of the press.
7. Benjamin Harris published the first newspaper in the colonies. He was later imprisoned.
8. The publisher John Peter Zenger also got into trouble. A jury found him not guilty in a court trial about the freedom of the press.
9. The Alien and Sedition Acts were passed in 1798. They included laws about censorship.
10. Public education taught more people to read, and they soon demanded newspapers to supply them with the information they wanted to read.

More Practice

Language Lab
CD-ROM
• Using Nouns lesson
On-line
Exercise Bank
• Section 14.2
Grammar Exercise
Workbook
• pp. 7–8

◀ **Critical Viewing**
If you were writing about this picture, what pronouns would you use to replace *printer, printing press,* and *newsletters*? **[Analyze]**

Setting up a printing press to produce newsletters

Pronouns • **301**

Answer Key

▶ **Exercise 14**

1. They—bulletins; him—Julius Caesar
2. they—newspapers
3. His—Johannes Gutenberg
4. it—magazine
5. its—group, their—leaders
6. They—Daniel Defoe and Jonathan Swift
7. He—Benjamin Harris
8. him—John Peter Zenger
9. They—Alien and Sedition Acts
10. they—people, them—people, they—people

Integrating Writing Skills

Tell students that personal pronouns must have clear antecedents. For example, in the sentence "Jon lost his father when he was twenty," it is not clear whether *he* refers to Jon or to his father. When vague antecedents occur, students should rephrase the sentence: "When Jon was twenty, he lost his father."

Real-World Connection

Newspaper articles often have to fit in a very limited amount of space. One way journalists can save some space is by using pronouns to replace long nouns. This also makes their writing less clumsy and less repetitive. Have students read a newspaper article, underline the pronouns used, and then identify their antecedents.

Critical Viewing

Analyze Students should suggest some of the following pronouns: *he, him, it, they,* and *them.*

☑ ONGOING ASSESSMENT: Monitor and Reinforce

If students have difficulty with Exercise 13 or 14, refer them to the following for additional practice.

In the Textbook	Technology
Section Review, Ex. 19, p. 307	Language Lab CD-ROM, Parts of Speech; On-Line Exercise Bank, Section 18.2

⏱ TIME SAVERS!

🖨 **Answers on Transparency**
Use the Grammar Exercises Answers on Transparencies for Chapter 14 to facilitate correction by students.

🖥 **On-Line Exercise Bank**
Have students complete the exercises on computer. The Auto Check feature will grade their work for you!

Personal Pronouns

1. The antecedents of first- or second-person pronouns usually are not stated explicitly. Instead, they are implied because the person speaking or being spoken to is implicit in the sentence. In a sentence with third-person pronouns, the antecedent usually is stated explicitly.

2. Share the following sentences with students to illustrate the point made in step 1. Have them identify the personal pronouns and their antecedents, if any, in each.

   When we go to the zoo, can we take our dog with us? (we, we, our, us)

   Make sure you take your umbrella with you. (you, your, you)

   Jason wants his sister to help him with his homework. (his, him, his; antecedent: Jason)

Customize for
Gifted/Talented Students

Have students fill in the blanks with pronouns:

Jaime and I decided to give ___ dog a bath. ___ put the dog in the bathtub, but ___ tried to get out before ___ even turned the water on. Linda, Jaime's older sister, helped —— by holding the dog down. ___ wouldn't have been able to wash the dog without ___.

(Possible answers: my, We, he, I, us, We, her)

When they finish, have students write their own short paragraphs, replacing all personal pronouns with blank lines. Then have them exchange papers with partners and fill in the missing pronouns.

14.2

Recognizing Personal Pronouns

Personal pronouns refer to people who are speaking or the people they are speaking about.

KEY CONCEPT **Personal pronouns** refer to (1) the person speaking or writing, (2) the person listening or reading, or (3) the topic (person, place, or thing) being discussed or written about. ■

The first-person pronouns *I, me, my, mine, we, us, our,* and *ours* refer to the person speaking or writing.

EXAMPLE: *I* favor the new layout.
Give *me* the sports section.

The second-person pronouns *you, your,* and *yours* refer to the person spoken or written to.

EXAMPLE: <u>You</u> will see the photo.

The third-person pronouns *he, him, his, she, her, hers, it, its, they, them, their,* and *theirs* refer to the person, place, or thing being spoken or written about.

EXAMPLES: *He* wants to listen to the radio show.
They wrote letters to the editor.

Some personal pronouns show possession. Although they can function as adjectives, they are still identified as personal pronouns because they take the place of possessive nouns.

EXAMPLES: *Mary's* town paper comes out weekly.
Her town paper comes out weekly.
The following chart presents the personal pronouns.

PERSONAL PRONOUNS		
	Singular	Plural
First Person	I, me, my, mine	we, us, our, ours
Second Person	you, your, yours	you, your, yours
Third Person	he, him, his she, her, hers it, its	they, them, their, theirs

Grammar and Style Tip

In your writing, try not to use too many pronouns in each sentence. If there is more than one pronoun, your sentence may become confusing.

◇ STANDARDIZED TEST PREPARATION WORKSHOP

Analogies Standardized tests often measure students' ability to complete analogies. Share the following example with students:

Complete the following item by choosing the phrase that best completes the analogy:

EXCESS : WASTE : :

A heat : cold
B nourishment : growth
C fire : match
D king : power
E pen : writing

The correct answer is item **B**. *Excess* leads to *waste* as nourishment leads to growth.

GRAMMAR IN LITERATURE

from **Hard as Nails**
Russell Baker

Personal pronouns in this passage are printed in blue italics.

My mother started *me* in newspaper work in 1937 right after *my* twelfth birthday. *She* would have started *me* younger, but there was a law against working before age twelve. *She* thought *it* was a silly law, and said so to Deems.

Exercise 15 Recognizing Personal Pronouns Write the personal pronoun in each sentence.

1. Have you ever heard of William Randolph Hearst?
2. He established newspapers in many big cities.
3. *The San Francisco Examiner* was his first newspaper.
4. It featured glaring headlines and stories designed to excite readers.
5. We now consider sensational journalism to be normal.

Exercise 16 Classifying Personal Pronouns Identify whether the underlined pronouns in the sentences below are *first person, second person,* or *third person.*

EXAMPLE: I like to read.

ANSWER: first person

1. I read *The New York Times* every day.
2. Adolph Ochs bought it in 1896.
3. Stories backed by solid facts were his specialty.
4. You probably have seen the paper in the public library.
5. Its circulation is one of the largest in the world.
6. Writers and editors have their names listed in the paper.
7. The staff is much larger than that on our school paper.
8. There are only ten of us on staff here.
9. To me, reporting is the most exciting part.
10. They prefer to sell ads and assist the business manager.

Hundreds of daily and weekly newspapers are published in the United States.

▲ **Critical Viewing**
Think of a sentence about newspapers that can include pronouns in the first, second, and third person. **[Analyze]**

Pronouns • 303

More Practice

Language Lab CD-ROM
• Using Nouns lesson
On-line Exercise Bank
• Section 14.2
Grammar Exercise Workbook
• pp. 9–10

Step-by-Step Teaching Guide

Grammar in Literature

1. Have a volunteer read aloud the excerpt from "Hard as Nails."

2. Ask students to account for the high number of first-person pronouns. Elicit that writers use a lot of first-person pronouns when writing about themselves. This passage is an excerpt from an autobiographical memoir.

3. Ask students what type of pronouns they would expect to find in a biography an author writes about someone else. (third person)

More About the Author

Known for his dry sense of humor, journalist and author Russell Baker was a columnist for the *New York Times* for many years. He won two Pulitzer Prizes: the first for his newspaper column, and the second for his autobiography, *Growing Up.*

Answer Key

▶ **Exercise 15**

1. you	4. It
2. He	5. We
3. his	

▶ **Exercise 16**

1. I—first person
2. it—third person
3. his—third person
4. You—second person
5. Its—third person
6. their—third person
7. our—first person
8. us—first person
9. me—first person
10. They—third person

Critical Viewing

Analyze Encourage students to give a wide variety of sentences. One might be

I will give you a newspaper with an article by her.

✓ ONGOING ASSESSMENT SYSTEM: Monitor and Reinforce

If students have difficulty with Exercises 15–16, refer them to the following for additional practice.

In the Textbook	Print Resources	Technology
Section Review, Ex. 20, p. 307	Grammar Exercise Workbook, pp. 9–10	Language Lab CD-ROM, Using Pronouns; On-Line Exercise Bank, Section 14.2

Demonstrative Pronouns

1. The word *demonstrative* is related to *demonstrate,* which means "to show" or "to point out." Demonstrative pronouns therefore indicate or point to nouns.

2. Demonstrative pronouns can come either before or after their antecedents. Write the following examples on the board to reinforce this idea:

   That is a photo of my mother.

   The change jangled loudly. That was all I had in my pocket.

3. Have students use the pronouns *this, that, these,* and *those* to identify or describe things in the classroom, such as *That is the chalkboard* or *These are my shoes.*

Customize for
ESL Students

Word order is different in English and some other languages. In English, object pronouns usually follow verbs: *Sam ate it. Bonnie bought that. Franco likes this.* In other languages, such as Spanish, the object pronoun usually precedes the verb. English language learners may need extra practice in writing and speaking sentences with pronouns.

14.2

Recognizing Demonstrative Pronouns

Demonstrative pronouns point to people, places, and things, much as you point to them with your finger.

KEY CONCEPT A **demonstrative pronoun** points out a person, place, or thing. ■

There are four demonstrative pronouns. *This* and *that* are singular demonstrative pronouns; *these* and *those* are plural.

EXAMPLES: This is a new invention.

That is newsprint.

I brought some magazines. These are for you.

Those appear to be old papers.

This and *these* point to what is near the speaker or writer. *That* and *those* point to what is more distant.

NEAR: This is the desk where I sit.

Of all the books I own, these are my favorites.

FAR: Is that the computer to use?

Those are well-written articles.

A demonstrative pronoun can point to a noun in the same sentence or in a different one.

SAME SENTENCE: These are the reports I received.

DIFFERENT SENTENCE: You have a red pencil. That is what I need.

304 • Nouns and Pronouns

More Practice

Language Lab CD-ROM
• Using Nouns lesson
On-line Exercise Bank
• Section 14.2
Grammar Exercise Workbook
• pp. 11–12

Exercise 17 Recognizing Demonstrative Pronouns Find the demonstrative pronoun in each sentence. Write both the demonstrative pronoun and the noun to which it refers.

EXAMPLE: This is a new publication.
ANSWER: This (publication)

1. This is a magazine founded by Cyrus Curtis.
2. Isn't that called *Ladies' Home Journal?*
3. That is one of the many magazines that Curtis published.
4. Those were the first popular national magazines.
5. He made several attempts to start a newspaper. Those were not successful.
6. That is the same *Saturday Evening Post* I read today.
7. This is the magazine millions of people bought.
8. Those were record circulation figures in 1897.
9. Curtis printed *Young America* at the age of fifteen. That was his first weekly publication.
10. These are now collectors' items.

Exercise 18 More Work With Demonstrative Pronouns Identify the demonstrative pronouns in the following sentences. Then, identify each pronoun's antecedent.

1. This is the article I mentioned to you.
2. I was going to show you some others, but those weren't as interesting.
3. Early magazines pushed for social and political changes. These were sometimes adopted.
4. Some in the press helped bring reforms. Those were the journalists called "muckrakers."
5. Horace Greeley founded the *New York Tribune*. That was his outlet for sharing his opinions.

▼ Critical Viewing
Think of two sentences to describe this photo, starting one with *"That is . . ."* and the other with *"Those are . . ."*
[Analyze]

The *Saturday Evening Post* has been on newsstands for over 100 years.

Pronouns • 305

Answer Key

▶ **Exercise 17**

1. This—magazine
2. that—*Ladies' Home Journal*
3. That—one
4. Those—magazines
5. Those—attempts
6. That—*Saturday Evening Post*
7. This—magazine
8. Those—figures
9. That—*Young America*
10. These—items

▶ **Exercise 18**

1. This—article
2. those—others
3. These—changes
4. Those—Some
5. That—*New York Tribune*

Critical Viewing

Analyze Encourage students to provide sentences such as:

That is an old magazine.

Those are newer newspapers.

☑ **ONGOING ASSESSMENT: Monitor and Reinforce**

If students have difficulty with Exercises 17–18, refer them to the following for additional practice.

In the Textbook	Print Resources	Technology
Section Review, Ex. 21–22, p. 307	Grammar Exercise Workbook, pp. 11–12	Language Lab CD-ROM, Using Pronouns; On-Line Exercise Bank, Section 14.2

⏱ **TIME SAVERS!**

🗒 **Answers on Transparency**
Use the Grammar Exercises Answers on Transparencies for Chapter 14 to facilitate correction by students.

💻 **On-Line Exercise Bank**
Have students complete the exercises on computer. The Auto Check feature will grade their work for you!

Shape Up Your Pronouns

Teaching Resources: Hands-on Grammar Activity Book, Chapter 14

1. Have students refer to their Hands-on Grammar Activity Books or give them copies of the relevant pages.

2. Have students write the pronouns on the inside of the shapes leaving the covers clear for a label and a sentence.

3. Be sure students understand that they need to write both singular and plural pronouns for the second and third persons.

4. Challenge students to use several pronouns in sentences.

Find It in Your Reading

Some students may need to write the sentences they find on a separate paper.

Find It in Your Writing

Before students begin, ask them to identify the person for most of the personal pronouns they will use in autobiographies. (first person singular)

14.2

Hands-on Grammar

Shape Up Your Pronouns

To practice and remember the first-, second-, and third-person pronouns, do the following activity:

Fold pieces of different-colored construction paper in half. Cut out a large triangle shape, leaving a little space at the point so that when you open the paper you have two connected triangles. Next, cut out a double circle from another piece of construction paper by leaving a little of the circle uncut. Cut out a double square by cutting out a rectangle twice as long as it is wide and folding it in half.

On one triangle, write the first-person singular pronouns. On the other triangle, write the first-person plural pronouns. On the circles, write the second-person pronouns. On the squares, write the third-person pronouns. "Close" each shape and label the front.

Turn over your shapes. On the back side of each one, write a sentence using at least two of the pronoun forms on the reverse side in each of your sentences. Examples: *I gave my dog a bath.* or *We saw our neighbors' new dog.* Compare your sentences to those your classmates create.

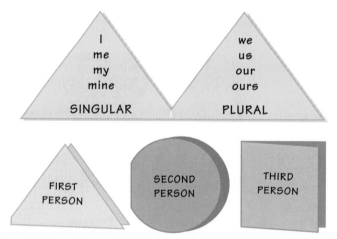

Find It in Your Reading Find sentences in your literature book that contain personal pronouns. Add these examples to your pronoun shapes.

Find It in Your Writing In a piece of autobiographical writing, find sentences that contain personal pronouns. Add them to your pronoun shapes. Look for places where replacing nouns with pronouns would make your writing less repetitive.

306 • Nouns and Pronouns

⏱ TIME SAVERS!

✋ **Hands-on Grammar Book**
Use the Hands-on Grammar activity sheet for Chapter 14 to facilitate this activity.

☑ ONGOING ASSESSMENT: Assess Mastery

Use the following resources to assess student mastery of nouns and pronouns.

In the Textbook	Print Resources	Technology
Chapter Review, Ex. 29–33, pp. 308–309	Formal Assessment, Chapter 14	Language Lab CD-ROM, Using Pronouns; On-Line Exercise Bank, Section 14.2

Section 14.2 Section Review

GRAMMAR EXERCISES 19–25

Exercise 19 Recognizing Pronouns and Antecedents Copy each sentence, underlining the pronouns and their antecedents. Then, draw an arrow connecting each pronoun and antecedent.

1. The telegraph was the first electric medium; it transmitted a message along a wire.
2. Several people invented the telegraph, and they applied for separate patents.
3. Samuel Morse sent the first message when he communicated from Washington, D.C., to Baltimore.
4. Morse was aware of the importance of his new invention.
5. Alexander Graham Bell invented the telephone, and it earned him fame.

Exercise 20 Recognizing Personal Pronouns Write the personal pronoun(s) in each sentence. Then, label the pronouns *first person, second person,* or *third person.*

1. Have you heard of Guglielmo Marconi?
2. He invented the wireless telegraph.
3. Marconi developed it for military and industrial uses.
4. We learned that he also helped invent radar.
5. During wartime, our government found many uses for his inventions.

Exercise 21 Recognizing Demonstrative Pronouns List the demonstrative pronouns that follow and the noun to which each refers.

1. KDKA and WGY—those were two early radio stations.
2. These were stations that attracted large audiences.

3. RCA developed home radios. These were in 10 million homes by 1929.
4. Broadcasters began selling advertising time. This was a new area for growth.
5. American stations had advertising, but British stations did not believe in that.

Exercise 22 Identifying All Kinds of Pronouns List each pronoun below, and label it *personal* or *demonstrative.*

1. Edward R. Murrow broadcast his reports live from London.
2. That was a first for war news.
3. President Roosevelt used the radio to broadcast his "fireside chats."
4. This gave his words a personal touch.
5. Leaders of other nations used the radio to influence their people.

Exercise 23 Find It in Your Reading Locate one personal pronoun and one demonstrative pronoun in this sentence from "Hard as Nails."

"Get that kick of pride that comes from knowing you are a newspaper man. That means something!"

Exercise 24 Find It in Your Writing Find a paragraph in your portfolio in which you used several pronouns. Draw arrows linking each pronoun with its antecedent.

Exercise 25 Writing Application Write a paragraph about your favorite radio station. Try to use several personal and demonstrative pronouns. Underline the pronouns that you use.

Section Review • 307

Section Review

Each of these exercises correlates to the instruction on pronouns, pages 300–306. These exercises may be used for more practice, for reteaching, or for review of the Key Concepts presented. Answers for all chapter exercises are available in *Grammar Exercises Answers on Transparencies* in your Teaching Resources.

Answer Key

Exercise 19

1. The <u>telegraph</u> was the first electric medium; <u>it</u> transmitted a message along a wire. (arrow from *it* to *telegraph*)
2. Several <u>people</u> invented the telegraph, and <u>they</u> applied for separate patents. (arrow from *they* to *people*)
3. <u>Samuel Morse</u> sent the first message when <u>he</u> communicated from Washington, D.C. to Baltimore. (arrow from *he* to *Samuel Morse*)
4. <u>Morse</u> was aware of the importance of <u>his</u> new invention. (arrow from *his* to *Morse*)
5. <u>Alexander Graham Bell</u> invented the <u>telephone</u>, and <u>it</u> earned <u>him</u> fame. (arrow from *it* to *telephone*; arrow from *him* to *Alexander Graham Bell*)

Exercise 20

1. you—second person
2. He—third person
3. it—third person
4. We—first person, he—third person
5. our—first person, his—third person

Exercise 21

1. those—KDKA and WGY
2. These—stations
3. These—radios
4. This—selling advertising time
5. that—advertising

Exercise 22

1. his—personal
2. That—demonstrative
3. his—personal
4. This—demonstrative, his—personal
5. their—personal

continued

Answer Key continued

versions.

Exercise 23

Find It in Your Reading
you—personal
That (third appearance)—demonstrative (Note that in its first appearance, *that* functions as an adjective modifying *kick*. In its second appearance, *that* functions as a relative pronoun, not a demonstrative one.)

Exercise 24

Find It in Your Writing
Suggest that students rewrite the paragraph without using pronouns and compare the two

CHAPTER REVIEW

Each of these exercises correlates to a section of the chapter on nouns and pronouns, pages 294–307. These exercises may be used for more practice, for reteaching, or for review of the Key Concepts presented.

Answer Key

▶ **Exercise 26**

1. broadcasts/airwaves
2. air time
3. homeowners, television sets, living rooms
4. prime time
5. station breaks

▶ **Exercise 27**

1. World War II—proper, government—common, regulations—common
2. Federal Communications Commission—proper, licenses—common, stations—common
3. stations—common
4. networks—common, television—common, United States—proper
5. years—common, Rupert Murdoch—proper, network—common
6. decade—common, networks—common
7. stations—common, advertisements—common
8. Public Broadcasting Act—proper, money—common, networks—common
9. stations—common, reruns—common, movies—common
10. events—common, World Series—proper, viewers—common

▶ **Exercise 28**

1. radio, inventors, attention, television—all common
2. teenager—compound, common; farm—common; Utah—proper; Philo Farnsworth—proper; work—common; television—common
3. patent—common
4. Companies, world, television—all common
5. London, British Broadcasting Company—both proper
6. America—proper; networks—compound, common; projects—common
7. people—common; television—common; New York World's Fair—proper
8. speech—common, President Roosevelt—proper

308

GRAMMAR EXERCISES 26–34

▶ **Exercise 26** Identifying Compound Nouns Write the compound nouns in each of the following sentences.

1. Local stations transmitted broadcasts over the airwaves.
2. Companies competed for air time for their commercial sales pitches.
3. Many homeowners purchased television sets and placed them in their living rooms.
4. The hours between 8:00 P.M. and 10:00 P.M. were considered prime time for families to watch television.
5. Advertising was featured during station breaks.

▶ **Exercise 27** Identifying Common and Proper Nouns List the nouns in the following sentences. Identify each noun as *common* or *proper*.

1. After World War II, the government established broadcast regulations.
2. The Federal Communications Commission would not issue licenses to new stations.
3. It made twelve stations available.
4. Three networks dominated television in the United States.
5. After thirty years, Rupert Murdoch started a fourth network.
6. In the following decade, two more networks were established.
7. These stations were funded through advertisements.
8. The Public Broadcasting Act provided money for educational networks.
9. Other independent stations played reruns and movies.
10. Sporting events, such as the World Series, were popular among viewers.

308 • Nouns and Pronouns

▶ **Exercise 28** Classifying All Kinds of Nouns List the nouns in each of the following sentences. Tell what kind of noun each one is.

1. After the radio, many inventors turned their attention toward television.
2. As a teenager on a farm in Utah, Philo Farnsworth began work on a television.
3. Later, he was granted the first patent.
4. Companies around the world were working to develop the television.
5. In London, the British Broadcasting Company was moving ahead.
6. In America, networks had development projects.
7. Many people first saw television at the New York World's Fair.
8. There was a live speech by President Roosevelt.
9. Visitors watched on monitors.
10. Experimentation slowed during World War II.

▶ **Exercise 29** Classifying Personal Pronouns Write the personal pronouns in each sentence. Then, label them *first person*, *second person*, or *third person*.

1. Do you have a favorite type of show?
2. My brother says his favorites are situation comedies.
3. When our parents get to pick the show we watch, they usually choose a show about family life.
4. I like talk shows more than you or your sister do.
5. The celebrity guests they feature appeal to me.

▶ **Exercise 30** Supplying Personal Pronouns Rewrite these sentences,

---

9. Visitors, monitors—both common
10. Experimentation—common, World War II—proper

▶ **Exercise 29**

1. you—second
2. My—first, his—third
3. our—first, we—first, they—third
4. I—first, you—second, your—second
5. they—third, me—first

supplying a personal pronoun to fill the blank. Then, circle the pronoun's antecedent.

1. The big networks dominated television so much that ___?___ controlled most programming.
2. Television changed the American way of life wherever ___?___ was watched.
3. Networks brought performers to audiences who hadn't seen ___?___ before.
4. One early star was Milton Berle. ___?___ show was very popular.
5. Cable television provided viewers with shows to match ___?___ interests.

▶ **Exercise 31** Recognizing Demonstrative Pronouns Find the demonstrative pronoun in each sentence. Write both the demonstrative pronoun and the noun to which it refers.

1. Television offered live images. Newspaper readers had never seen these.
2. That is one reason that newspapers changed their role.
3. Live drama and comedy in homes—these were innovations of radio.
4. One television network presented a news program in 1956. This was the first example of the evening news.
5. Presidential candidates participate in debates. Those are broadcast on national television.

▶ **Exercise 32** Classifying Nouns and Pronouns Write all the nouns and pronouns in the following sentences. Label each noun a *common noun* or a *proper noun*. Label each pronoun a *personal pronoun* or a *demonstrative pronoun*.

1. Broadcasting has been regulated since it began.
2. The Wireless Act was the first law to do this.
3. Laws about entertainment came later.
4. First, our legislators set up the Federal

Radio Commission.
5. That was then reorganized into the Federal Communications Commission.
6. This was how the government gained its power over broadcasting.
7. The president of the United States names five members to the commission.
8. These are the people responsible for licenses and regulations.
9. Its domain includes all technological media—from radio to the Internet.
10. My report mentions all of this.

▶ **Exercise 33** Revision Practice: Replacing Nouns With Pronouns Rewrite the following paragraph, replacing some repeated nouns with personal or demonstrative pronouns.

(1) Over the years, people have enjoyed watching different types of shows on the people's televisions. (2) Early on, variety shows were very popular. (3) Variety shows featured singers, comedians, dancers, and magicians. (4) One of the most popular variety show hosts was Ed Sullivan. (5) Ed Sullivan was a newspaper columnist; Ed Sullivan was not a performer. (6) Ed Sullivan did not really have any talent. (7) Yet millions of viewers tuned to Ed Sullivan's show every week. (8) Viewers enjoyed the performers Ed Sullivan presented, and viewers liked Ed Sullivan's funny way of introducing Ed Sullivan's guests. (9) Cheryl says Cheryl's grandfather does a great imitation of Ed Sullivan's way of speaking. (10) When Sal and I heard the imitation, Sal and I laughed.

▶ **Exercise 34** Writing Application Write a brief narrative based on a news story you have heard or read about. Include information about *who, what, where, when,* and *how* in your narrative, just as a reporter does. Underline all of the nouns and pronouns that you use.

▶ **Exercise 30**

1. they—networks
2. it—Television
3. them—performers
4. His—Milton Berle
5. their—viewers

▶ **Exercise 31**

1. these—images
2. That—reason
3. these—drama and comedy
4. This—program
5. Those—debates

▶ **Exercise 32**

1. Broadcasting—common noun, it—personal pronoun
2. Wireless Act—proper noun, law—common noun, this—demonstrative pronoun
3. Laws—common noun, entertainment—common noun
4. our—personal pronoun, legislators—common noun, Federal Radio Commission—proper noun
5. That—demonstrative pronoun, Federal Communications Commission—proper noun
6. This—demonstrative pronoun, government—common noun, its—personal pronoun, power—common noun, broadcasting—common noun
7. president—common noun, United States—proper noun, members—common noun, commission—common noun
8. These—demonstrative pronoun, people—common noun, licenses—common noun, regulations—common noun
9. Its—personal pronoun, domain—common noun, media—common noun, radio—common noun, Internet—proper noun
10. My—personal pronoun, report—common noun, this—demonstrative pronoun

continued

Answer Key continued

▶ **Exercise 33**

Possible answers:

1. their for people's
2. no change
3. They for Variety shows
4. no change
5. He for Ed Sullivan two times
6. He for Ed Sullivan
7. no change
8. They for viewers, his for Ed Sullivan's two times
9. her for Cheryl's
10. we for Sal and I

▶ **Exercise 34**

Writing Application
Have students exchange papers and check two things: first, that all five questions are answered; and second, that all nouns and pronouns have been properly identified.

Step-by-Step Teaching Guide

Completing Analogies

Teaching Resources:
Standardized Test Preparation
Workbook, Chapter 14

1. Have students make up some of their own analogies and specify the relationship using the list on page 310.

2. Encourage students to identify the relationship in the two examples before choosing the answer. (Example 1 antonyms, Example 2 synonyms)

3. Remind students to check for relationship and for part of speech when they encounter analogies.

Standardized Test Preparation Workshop

Completing Analogies

On standardized tests, analogies are test items that measure your understanding of the relationship between word meanings. The relationship between the words in the first pair is similar to the relationship between the words in the second pair.

Look for the following relationships between words in analogies:

synonyms—fondness : affection
antonyms—love : hate
part to whole or whole to part—
   member : club *or* club : member
cause and effect or effect and cause—ice : skid
functional—sewing : thread
degree—warm : sweltering

The following test items will give you practice with analogies. The two different formats used show the most common ways these items appear on tests.

Test Tips

- If the first pair of words are synonyms, eliminate answer pairs in which words seem related but are not synonyms. If the first pair are antonyms, eliminate answer pairs that have different characteristics but are not antonyms.
- Use the parts of speech as a clue. Make sure your answer choice consists of two nouns if the original pair are nouns.

Sample Test Items	Answers and Explanations
Directions: Complete each item by choosing the phrase that best completes the sentence. Glory is to dishonor as— (A) power is to energy. (B) honesty is to trickery. (C) knowledge is to books. (D) leader is to troops. (E) fame is to popularity.	The correct answer is *B*. The noun *glory* names the condition of being honored or praised, while the noun *dishonor* names the opposite condition—having lost honor or respect. In the same manner, the noun *honesty* names the condition of being truthful, while the noun *trickery* names the practice of being dishonest.
Each question below consists of a related pair of words, followed by five pairs of words labeled A through E. Select the pair that <u>best</u> expresses a relationship similar to that expressed in the original pair. ROOKIE : NEWCOMER :: (A) expert : apprentice (B) professional : amateur (C) freshman : senior (D) General : Chief (E) untrue : false	The correct answer is *D*. The noun *rookie* names a person who is just beginning a specific type of training, just as its synonym, *newcomer*, names a person who is new to some place or job. The nouns *General* and *Chief* both name persons in charge. The words in answer choices *A, B,* and *C* express relationships of antonyms or words that have opposite instead of similar meanings. Answer choice *E* presents two synonyms that are adjectives and not nouns, as in the original pair.

⬧ TEST-TAKING TIP

If students first identify the relationship between the two items given using the list above, they can eliminate some of the choices. Checking for part of speech may help them eliminate other choices.

Answer Key

> **Practice 1**

1. A
2. D
3. C
4. A
5. C

> **Practice 2**

1. D
2. E
3. D
4. E
5. B

> **Practice 1** **Directions:** Each question below consists of a related pair of words or phrases, followed by five pairs of words or phrases labeled A through E. Select the pair that <u>best</u> expresses a relationship similar to that expressed in the original pair.

1. HERO : VILLAIN ::
   (A) goodness : evil
   (B) guitar : instrument
   (C) teacher : school
   (D) triumph : evil
   (E) slide : toy

2. BEAUTY : ATTRACTIVENESS ::
   (A) pretty : nice
   (B) luck : loser
   (C) happiness : sorrow
   (D) affection : fondness
   (E) honesty : corruption

3. DESERT: SWAMP ::
   (A) jungle : lushness
   (B) forest : trees
   (C) dry : damp
   (D) land : ocean
   (E) humidity : weather

4. TALENT : SKILL ::
   (A) method : way
   (B) style : knowledge
   (C) library : readers
   (D) stylist : hair
   (E) coach : winner

5. WEALTH : POVERTY ::
   (A) television : entertainment
   (B) smart : intelligent
   (C) popularity : loneliness
   (D) store : purchases
   (E) apartment : building

> **Practice 2** **Directions:** Complete each item by choosing the phrase that best completes the sentence.

1. Expert is to beginner as —
   (A) middle is to outside.
   (B) sickness is to pain.
   (C) paper is to pen.
   (D) experience is to newness.
   (E) pianist is to musician.

2. Calmness is to peace as —
   (A) sorrow is to happiness.
   (B) silence is to a scream.
   (C) sight is to eyes.
   (D) fear is to anger.
   (E) rage is to conflict.

3. Feelings is to emotions as —
   (A) surf is to beach.
   (B) safety is to injury.
   (C) weakness is to power.
   (D) storm is to downpour.
   (E) snow is to sunshine.

4. Darkness is to light as —
   (A) garage is to car.
   (B) winter is to spring.
   (C) sun is to moon.
   (D) train is to transportation.
   (E) night is to day.

5. Vision is to sight as —
   (A) eye is to ear.
   (B) exhaustion is to tiredness.
   (C) train is to tracks.
   (D) airplane is to sky.
   (E) thirst is to water.

In-Depth Lesson Plan

	LESSON FOCUS	PRINT AND MEDIA RESOURCES
DAY 1	**Action and Linking Verbs** Students learn to identify and use action and linking verbs (pp. 312–319).	**Teaching Resources** *Grammar Exercise Workbook*, pp. 13–18; *Grammar Exercises Answers on Transparencies*, Ch. 15 **On-Line Exercise Bank**, Section 15.1
DAY 2	**Helping Verbs** Students learn to identify and use helping verbs and do the Hands-on Grammar activity (pp. 320–323).	**Teaching Resources** *Grammar Exercise Workbook*, pp. 19–20; *Grammar Exercises Answers on Transparencies*, Ch. 15; *Hands-on Grammar Activity Book*, Chapter 15 **On-Line Exercise Bank**, Section 15.2
DAY 3	**Review and Assess** Students review chapter and demonstrate mastery of use of verbs (pp. 324–327).	**Teaching Resources** *Formal Assessment*, Ch. 15; *Grammar Exercises Answers on Transparencies*, Ch. 15 **On-Line Exercise Bank**, Sections 15.1–2

Accelerated Lesson Plan

	LESSON FOCUS	PRINT AND MEDIA RESOURCES
DAY 1	**Verbs** Students cover concepts and usage of verbs as determined by Diagnostic Test (pp. 312–323).	**Teaching Resources** *Grammar Exercise Workbook*, pp. 13–20; *Grammar Exercises Answers on Transparencies*, Ch. 15; *Hands-on Grammar Activity Book*, Ch. 15 **On-Line Exercise Bank**, Sections 15.1–2
DAY 2	**Review and Assess** Students review chapter and demonstrate mastery of use of verbs (pp. 324–327).	**Teaching Resources** *Formal Assessment*, Ch. 15; *Grammar Exercises Answers on Transparencies*, Ch. 15 **On-Line Exercise Bank**, Sections 15.1–2

Options for Adapting Lesson Plans

HOMEWORK
Have students complete any section of the chapter for homework.

FEATURES
Extend coverage with the Grammar in Literature feature (p. 316), and the Standardized Test Preparation Workshop (p. 326).

TECHNOLOGY
Students can use the On-Line Exercise Bank to complete the exercises on computer. The Auto Check feature will grade their work.

INTEGRATED SKILLS COVERAGE

Grammar in Literature
SE p. 316

Reading
Find It in Your Reading SE pp. 319, 322, 323

Writing
Find It in Your Writing SE pp. 319, 322, 323
Writing Application SE pp. 319, 323, 325
Grammar and Style SE p. 315

Spelling
ATE p. 321

Language Highlight
ATE pp. 316

Real-World Connection
ATE p. 317

Viewing and Representing
Critical Viewing SE pp. 312, 314, 317, 318, 321

ASSESSMENT SUPPORT

Standardized Test Preparation Workshop SE p. 326;
ATE p. 322

Standardized Test Preparation Workbook, pp. 29–30

Formal Assessment, Ch. 15

MEETING INDIVIDUAL NEEDS

Less Advanced Students ATE p. 315; See also Ongoing
Assessments ATE pp. 318, 321
ESL Students ATE pp. 316, 317
Interpersonal Learners ATE p. 322

BLOCK SCHEDULING

Pacing Suggestions
For 90-minute Blocks
• Administer the Diagnostic Test to students to determine
instructional coverage.
• Have students complete the necessary exercises in class. Use
the Hands-on Grammar activity to provide a change of pace.

Resources for Varying Instruction
• *Language Lab* CD-ROM If your students have access to
hardware, a 90-minute block provides an ideal opportunity for
students to work on computer.

Professional Development Support
• *How to Manage Instruction in the Block* This teaching
Resource provides management and activity suggestions.

MEDIA AND TECHNOLOGY

For the Student
• *Language Lab* CD-ROM, Using Verbs
• *On-Line Exercise Bank,* Ch. 15

For the Teacher
• *Resource Pro* CD-ROM

WRITING AND GRAMMAR WEB SITE

The Interactive Writing and Grammar Web site provides a wide
array of support for students, teachers, and parents. Grammar
support includes:

• On-Line Exercise Bank with Auto Check scoring
• Diagnostic and assessment support

www.phschool.com

LITERATURE CONNECTIONS

Grammar in Literature selections from *Prentice Hall Literature: Timeless Voices, Timeless Themes,* Copper:
from *Orpheus,* Alice Low, SE p. 316

Lesson Objectives

1. To understand that a verb shows the action or condition of a person, place, or thing.
2. To identify action verbs.
3. To identify linking verbs.
4. To identify helping verbs.
5. To understand that a helping verb comes before the main verb.

Critical Viewing

Describe Encourage students to use both action and linking verbs in the present and past tense in their descriptions.

Chapter 15 Verbs

When you studied nouns and pronouns, you learned about words that name people, places, and things. To state your ideas, you also need words that express action or condition. Words that let you say what people are doing or what is happening are verbs. Verbs are necessary to tell about the events of the past. Verbs can relate the actions of Greek heroes, for example.

In this chapter, you will learn several things about verbs. First, you will learn how to recognize a verb. Then, you will learn about three different kinds of verbs—verbs that express action, verbs that link the parts of a sentence, and verbs that help other verbs.

▲ **Critical Viewing**
This photograph shows the ruins of a temple honoring the Greek goddess Athena. Describe how the temple looks today, and tell how you think the Greeks might have used the temple thousands of years ago. What verbs did you use and what purpose did they serve? [Describe]

☑ ONGOING ASSESSMENT: Diagnose

If students miss more than one item in any category, direct them to the relevant pages of the textbook and assign exercises for practice and review.

Verbs	Diagnostic Test Items	Teach	Practice	Section Review	Chapter Review
Skill Check A					
Action Verbs	A 1–10	pp. 314–315	Ex. 1–2	Ex. 7, 9	Ex. 23, 25
Skill Check B					
Linking Verbs	B 11–20	pp. 316–317	Ex. 3–4	Ex. 7–9	Ex. 24–25

Diagnostic Test

Directions: Write all answers on a separate sheet of paper.

Skill Check A. Identify the action verbs in the sentences below.

1. The ancient Greeks wondered about the causes of some events in nature.
2. They saw lightning between rain clouds.
3. They heard thunder soon after the lightning.
4. What caused these frightening occurrences?
5. Other questions also puzzled these early people.
6. As a result, they created myths.
7. The myths explained natural phenomena.
8. They described them as the acts of gods and goddesses.
9. People passed the stories down by word of mouth from one generation to the next.
10. Eventually, someone wrote down the stories.

Skill Check B. Copy the sentences below. Underline each linking verb, and draw a double-headed arrow to connect the words that are linked by the verb.

11. Thunder is an explosive noise.
12. It usually sounds very threatening.
13. A clap of thunder seems longer than a flash of lightning.
14. Thunder becomes evident after a lightning flash.
15. Zeus was the name given to the ruler of all the gods.
16. Perhaps thunder was the voice of this god.
17. Zeus grew angry at times.
18. He appeared more powerful than the other gods.
19. Mount Olympus became his home.
20. Hera was his wife.

Skill Check C. Label each underlined word a *linking verb* or an *action verb*.

21. Before the storm, the air <u>grew</u> quiet.
22. Massive black clouds <u>appeared</u> on the horizon.
23. The thunder <u>sounded</u> frightening.
24. Soon, we <u>felt</u> the first drops of rain.
25. Within minutes, the sky <u>looked</u> clear again.

Skill Check D. Write the verb phrase (main verb plus helping verbs) in each sentence below. Underline the helping verbs, and circle the main verbs.

26. Clouds are divided into four main groups.
27. These groups can be called families.
28. Low clouds might become rain or thunder clouds.
29. They would look thick, dark, and shapeless.
30. Clouds have been blocking the sun.

Verbs • **313**

Answer Key

Diagnostic Test

- Each item in the Diagnostic Test corresponds to a specific concept in the verbs chapter. This will enable you to tailor instruction to the particular needs of your students. See "Ongoing Assessment: Diagnose" at the bottoms of pages 312 and 313 for further details.
- Answers for the Diagnostic Test and all chapter exercises are available in *Grammar Exercises Answers on Transparencies* in your Teaching Resources.

Skill Check A

1. wondered
2. saw
3. heard
4. caused
5. puzzled
6. created
7. explained
8. described
9. passed
10. wrote

Skill Check B

11. Thunder <u>is</u> an explosive noise. (arrow between *Thunder* and *noise*)
12. It usually <u>sounds</u> very threatening. (arrow between *It* and *threatening*)
13. A clap of thunder <u>seems</u> longer than a flash of lightning. (arrow between *clap* and *longer*)
14. Thunder <u>becomes</u> evident after a lightning flash. (arrow between *Thunder* and *evident*)
15. Zeus <u>was</u> the name given to the ruler of all the gods. (arrow between *Zeus* and *name*)
16. Perhaps thunder <u>was</u> the voice of this god. (arrow between *thunder* and *voice*)
17. Zeus <u>grew</u> angry at times. (arrow between *Zeus* and *angry*)
18. He <u>appeared</u> more powerful than the other gods. (arrow between *He* and *powerful*)
19. Mount Olympus <u>became</u> his home. (arrow between *Mount Olympus* and *home*)
20. Hera <u>was</u> his wife. (arrow between *Hera* and *wife*)

Skill Check C

21. linking
22. action
23. linking
24. action
25. linking

Skill Check D

26. <u>are</u> (divided)
27. <u>can be</u> (called)
28. <u>might</u> (become)
29. <u>would</u> (look)
30. <u>have been</u> (blocking)

☑ ONGOING ASSESSMENT: Diagnose *continued*					
Verbs	Diagnostic Test Items	Teach	Practice	Section Review	Chapter Review
Skill Check C					
Linking Verbs and Action Verbs	C 21–25	p. 318	Ex. 5–6	Ex. 7–9	Ex. 23–25, 28–29
Skill Check D					
Helping Verbs, Main Verbs, and Verb Phrases	D 26–30	pp. 320–322	Ex. 13–16	Ex. 17–19	Ex. 26–27, 29
Cumulative Reviews and Applications				Ex. 10–12 20–22	Ex. 30–31

Divide the class into small groups. Give one student in each group a folded sheet of paper with a question written inside (see sample questions below). When you say "Go," each student with a paper reads the question aloud to the group, then writes as many answers as the group can think of in two minutes.

What can you do with water? (drink it, splash it, freeze it, and so on)

After the brainstorming, invite one group at a time to read aloud only its answers (e.g., drink it). Ask the other groups to guess the "it." (water) Conclude by pointing out that the answers are verbs.

What can you do with water? A pumpkin? An hour? $100?

Activate Prior Knowledge

Read aloud each statement below. Ask students to raise their hands if they think the statement is true. Point out the correct answer.

A sentence must have a verb. (T)

A verb is a person, place, or thing. (F)

A verb can express the subject's condition, such as, She was very tall. (T)

TEACH

Step-by-Step Teaching Guide

Verbs

1. Say and demonstrate these sentences for the class:
The pencil rolls across the desk.
The pencil feels sharp.

2. Ask students to identify the verb that shows an action. *(rolls)*

3. Point out that *feels* in the second sentence is a verb that shows a condition, not an action. The pencil does not have fingers that are actually feeling anything.

Critical Viewing

Describe Be sure students use both action and linking verbs in their descriptions.

Section 15.1

Action Verbs and Linking Verbs

A verb is an important part of every sentence. No sentence is complete without one. A verb tells what someone or something does or is. In other words, a verb shows action or condition.

KEY CONCEPT A **verb** expresses the action or condition of a person, place, or thing. ■

Many verbs express actions or activities that can be completed. In the following examples, the verbs showing action are underlined.

EXAMPLES: The archaeologist <u>digs</u>.
She <u>found</u> a shard of pottery.

Other verbs express condition, that is, they link a noun or pronoun with words that describe the condition of the noun or pronoun. In the examples below, the verbs expressing condition are underlined.

EXAMPLES: The ruins <u>were</u> spectacular.
This vase <u>feels</u> smooth.

▶ Critical Viewing
Describe your impressions of this famous ruin. What verbs did you use in your description? **[Describe]**

The Parthenon in Greece

314 • Verbs

Theme: Ancient Greece

In this section, you will learn about action verbs and linking verbs. All of the examples and exercises are about ancient Greece.

Cross-Curricular Connection: Social Studies

More Practice

Language Lab CD-ROM
• Using Verbs lesson
On-line Exercise Bank
• Section 15.1
Grammar Exercise Workbook
• pp. 13–14

⏱ TIME AND RESOURCE MANAGER

Resources
Print: Grammar Exercise Workbook, pp. 13–18; Grammar Exercises Answers on Transparencies, Chapter 15
Technology: Language Lab CD-ROM, Using Verbs; On-Line Exercise Bank, Section 15.1

In-Depth Coverage	Accelerated Pace
• Work through key concepts, pp. 314–318.	• Assign pp. 314–318 for independent student review.
• Assign and review Exercises 1–6.	• Assign Section Review Exercises 7–9.
• Review the chart on p. 316.	
• Read and discuss Grammar in Literature, p. 316.	

Using Action Verbs

There are several different kinds of verbs. One kind, *action verbs*, shows what someone or something does or did. *Rise, live, fall,* and *explode* are all action verbs.

KEY CONCEPT An **action verb** indicates the action of a person or thing. The action can be visible or mental. ■

Some action verbs show visible action:

EXAMPLES: The Parthenon <u>stands</u> on the Acropolis.
Homer <u>wrote</u> the poem.
Nancy <u>reads</u> history books.

Other verbs indicate mental actions. These actions cannot be seen or heard directly. They are thinking activities, but they are still actions.

EXAMPLES: The students <u>understand</u> the assignment.
Everyone <u>believes</u> you.

Exercise 1 Identifying Action Verbs Identify the action verb in each sentence below.

EXAMPLE: The audience applauded the performers.
ANSWER: applauded

1. The ancient Greeks called themselves Hellenes.
2. Their small states prized their independence.
3. Invading tribes from the north conquered new territories.
4. Kings replaced the tribal chiefs.
5. Then, noble families in the city-states acquired great wealth and power.
6. The nobility controlled the government completely.
7. They would not share any power.
8. Unhappy commoners disliked the rule of the aristocrats.
9. Tyrants seized political power by force.
10. Eventually, the system changed.

Exercise 2 Writing Sentences With Action Verbs Write a sentence using each of the following action verbs.
1. discover
2. wish
3. soothe
4. challenge
5. hide
6. announce
7. attempt
8. pursue
9. withdraw
10. scatter

Grammar and Style Tip

Remember that your verbs can add life to your descriptive writing. Choose verbs that add action and energy to your narratives and descriptions.

Action Verbs and Linking Verbs • 315

Step-by-Step Teaching Guide

Action Verbs and Linking Verbs

1. Write these sentences on the chalkboard:
   Jill scored a goal.
   Jack's hopes soared.

2. Select a student to underline the verb in each sentence.
   Jill <u>scored</u> a goal.
   Jack's hopes <u>soared</u>.

3. Ask students which verb shows a visible action *(scored)*, and which verb indicates an invisible action *(soared)*.

Exercise 1
1. called
2. prized
3. conquered
4. replaced
5. acquired
6. controlled
7. share
8. disliked
9. seized
10. changed

Exercise 2

Answers will vary. Samples are given.

1. Did you discover the treasure?
2. I wish summer were here.
3. They soothe crying children.
4. I challenge you to a game of tennis.
5. Hide the ball from the dog.
6. Did you announce who won?
7. We attempt to be fair.
8. Did you pursue the thief?
9. I'll withdraw my question.
10. Scatter the grass seed over here.

Customize for
Less Advanced Students

Some students may have difficulty understanding that some "action" verbs express nonvisible actions. Tell students that these verbs, such as *know, decide, wonder,* and so on, express mental *actions*. This will help them see that these kinds of verbs still involve some form of activity.

⏱ TIME SAVERS!

Answers on Transparency
Use the Grammar Exercises Answers on Transparencies for Chapter 15 to facilitate correction by students.

On-Line Exercise Bank
Have students complete the exercises on computer. The Auto Check feature will grade their work for you!

Grammar in Literature

1. Have a volunteer read aloud the excerpt from "Orpheus."

2. Ask students to name the highlighted action verbs in the excerpt. Which describe visible action? *(played, gathered)* Which describe invisible action? *(charmed, forgot)*

More About the Writer

Alice Low has been interested in drama since childhood, when she made puppets and performed plays. As an adult, she writes musical plays, magazine articles, and lively stories and myths. Low's use of action verbs in her writing helps readers visualize the action.

Linking Verbs

1. Write this sentence on the chalkboard:

   Kim is funny.

2. Circle the words *Kim* and *funny.* Point out how the verb *is* links the noun *(Kim)* and its descriptor *(funny).*

3. Explain that most linking verbs are forms of the verb *be.* Ask students to brainstorm for examples. *(am, are, is, was, were)*

4. To reinforce the concept of linking verbs, direct students to the Key Concept.

Customize for ESL Students

Some languages do not require a subject pronoun to be written with the verb. For example, in Spanish we can say: *¿El Sr. Salias? Es maestro.* (Mr. Salias? He is a teacher.) We know from the antecedent and from the noun *maestro* that we are talking about a singular, masculine noun, in this case, Mr. Salias. In addition, most verb endings tell us who is performing the action and we do not need a subject pronoun: *Tomamos café.* (We are drinking coffee.) Point out how this contrasts with English where we almost always have an expressed subject written in the sentence.

GRAMMAR IN LITERATURE

from Orpheus

translated by Alice Low

In the following excerpt from the Greek myth "Orpheus," the action verbs are highlighted in blue italics.

Orpheus *played* his lyre so sweetly that he *charmed* all things on earth. Men and women *forgot* their cares when they *gathered* around him to listen.

Using Linking Verbs

Linking verbs join nouns or pronouns with words that identify or describe them.

▶ **KEY CONCEPT** A **linking verb** connects a noun or pronoun to a word that identifies or describes the noun or pronoun. ■

The most common linking verbs are all forms of the verb *be: am, are, is, was,* and *were.*

EXAMPLES: Laura <u>is</u> the historian. (*Historian* identifies *Laura.*)

Elliot <u>was</u> ready. (*Ready* describes *Elliot.*)

Several other verbs also function as linking verbs. They work to connect the parts of a sentence in the same way as the forms of *be.*

EXAMPLE: The chief <u>remained</u> calm. (*Calm* describes *chief.*)

OTHER LINKING VERBS		
appear	look	sound
become	remain	stay
feel	seem	taste
grow	smell	turn

Language Highlight

Writing expert William Zinsser says that using vivid, descriptive verbs can make "the difference between life and death for a writer." Zinsser says to use verbs that burst with color and sound—*explode, twirl, glitter, dazzle, shriek.* And keep those verbs crisp and short. Zinsser points out that Abraham Lincoln, in his Second Inaugural Address, used only 701 words—505 words of one syllable and 122 of two syllables!

▶ **Exercise 3** Recognizing Linking Verbs Copy the sentences below onto a piece of paper. Underline each linking verb. Then, draw a double-headed arrow to connect the words that are linked by the verb.

EXAMPLE: The Greek philosophers <u>were</u> thoughtful.

1. The Greek language was understandable throughout the country.
2. All the dialects sounded similar.
3. Within each city-state, customs and religious practices were the same.
4. Four national festivals became traditional.
5. The Olympic Games were the most important.
6. The Greek city-states were very independent.
7. However, some unification seemed possible.
8. States and their weaker neighbors became leagues.
9. Athens and Sparta became the leading city-states.
10. Athens remained the best example of democracy in ancient Greece.
11. Sparta grew more powerful than any other state.
12. Sparta's rules appeared the strictest.
13. Its army was strong.
14. The Greek city-states became united during the Persian Wars.
15. Afterward, Athens was the center of culture in the Greek world.

▶ **Exercise 4** Writing Sentences With Linking Verbs For each pair of words below, write a sentence in which you use a linking verb to connect them.
1. Greek myths/entertaining
2. ruins/old
3. Greek food/delicious
4. tourists/tired
5. music/beautiful
6. weather/outstanding
7. Athens/larger
8. festivals/fun
9. air/cold
10. sculptures/exquisite

▶ **More Practice**

Language Lab
CD-ROM
• Using Verbs lesson
On-line
Exercise Bank
• Section 15.1
Grammar Exercise
Workbook
• pp. 17–18

▼ **Critical Viewing**
What two or three linking verbs might you use in describing this Greek mosaic? **[Describe]**

Action Verbs and Linking Verbs • **317**

Customize for
ESL Students

Pair students learning English with more fluent students. Let partners work together on Exercise 3. Have them take turns reading each sentence aloud before they copy the sentences and mark them.

Real-World Connection

Students often make posters for school events. Discuss with students which action verbs they might use on a poster for:

an upcoming play

a championship sports event

a chess tournament

Answer Key

▶ Exercise 3

1. The Greek language <u>was</u> understandable throughout the country. (arrow between *language* and *understandable*)
2. All the dialects <u>sounded</u> similar. (arrow between *dialects* and *similar*)
3. Within each city-state, customs and religious practices <u>were</u> the same. (arrow between *customs* and *same*; arrow between *practices* and *same*)
4. Four national festivals <u>became</u> traditional. (arrow between *festivals* and *traditional*)
5. The Olympic Games <u>were</u> the most important. (arrow between *Games* and *important*)
6. The Greek city-states <u>were</u> very independent. (arrow between *city-states* and *independent*)
7. However, some unification <u>seemed</u> possible. (arrow between *unification* and *possible*)
8. States and their weaker neighbors <u>became</u> leagues. (arrow between *States* and *leagues*; arrow between *neighbors* and *leagues*)
9. Athens and Sparta <u>became</u> the leading city-states. (arrow between *Athens* and *city-states*; arrow between *Sparta* and *city-states*)
10. Athens <u>remained</u> the best example of democracy in ancient Greece. (arrow between *Athens* and *example*)
11. Sparta <u>grew</u> more powerful than any other state. (arrow between *Sparta* and *powerful*)
12. Sparta's rules <u>appeared</u> the strictest. (arrow between *rules* and *strictest*)

continued

Answer Key continued

13. Its army <u>was</u> strong. (arrow between *army* and *strong*)
14. The Greek city-states <u>became</u> united during the Persian Wars. (arrow between *city-states* and *united*)
15. Afterward, Athens <u>was</u> the center of culture in the Greek world. (arrow between *Athens* and *center*)

▶ Exercise 4
Sample answers:
1. Greek myths are highly entertaining.

2. The Greek ruins appeared very old.
3. Greek food tastes delicious.
4. The tourists were tired.
5. The music was beautiful.
6. The weather was outstanding.
7. I think Athens was larger than Sparta.
8. The annual festivals were fun.
9. The air seemed cold.
10. The sculptures appeared exquisite.

Critical Viewing

Describe Students may suggest *seems*, *appears*, or forms of the verb *be*.

Action Verb or Linking Verb

1. Give students extra practice recognizing linking verbs.

2. Write the following sentences on the chalkboard. Ask students to explain why the verb is a linking verb, that is, why it does not show action here:

   Harry and Larry stayed friends after graduation. (They did not physically stay in one place.)

   Glue feels sticky. (The glue is not feeling anything.)

   Corn on the cob tastes good. (The corn is not doing the tasting.)

   The apples turned red on the tree. (The apples did not change their position.)

Critical Viewing

Describe Possible answers: The sculpture stares at the viewer—action. It seems both serious and scary—linking.

Answer Key

Exercise 5

1. felt—linking
2. felt—action
3. looked—linking
4. considered—action
5. seemed—linking
6. grew—linking
7. turned—action
8. felt—linking
9. felt—action
10. became—linking

Exercise 6

loved—action, were married—action, looked—action, stepped—action, died—action, roamed—action, singing—action, was—linking (Some words that look like verbs are participles (singing) and infinitives (to try, to overcome). Explain to students who circle those words that these verb forms can be used as nouns or modifiers.)

15.1

Distinguishing Between Action Verbs and Linking Verbs

Some verbs can be used as either linking verbs or action verbs.

LINKING:	The tyrant *felt* threatened. (*Felt* links *tyrant* and *threatened*.)
ACTION:	The tyrant *felt* the sword. (The tyrant performed an action.)
LINKING:	The people *grew* unhappy. (*Grew* links *people* and *unhappy*.)
ACTION:	The people *grew* poor crops. (The people performed an action.)

To test whether a verb is a linking verb or an action verb, replace the verb with *is, am,* or *are.* If a sentence still makes sense, then the verb is a linking verb.

EXAMPLE: The tyrant *is* threatened.

▲ Critical Viewing Think of two sentences to describe this sculpture—one using an action verb, the other using a linking verb. **[Describe]**

▶ **Exercise 5** Distinguishing Between Action Verbs and Linking Verbs Identify the verb in each sentence below. Label each one a *linking verb* or an *action verb.*
1. Athens felt most powerful after the Persian Wars.
2. During the war, the city felt great sorrow.
3. Afterward, the situation looked better.
4. Athens considered its former allies as subjects.
5. It seemed the strongest member of the Delian League.
6. The city-state of Athens grew dominant.
7. Pericles, its leader, turned his attention to the city's appearance.
8. He felt pleased with the city's prosperity and cultural accomplishments.
9. Many Greek writers felt the success of their dramas.
10. This period became the Golden Age of Greece.

▶ **Exercise 6** Identify Action Verbs and Linking Verbs in Literature Copy this passage from the Greek myth "Orpheus" into your notebook. Then, circle all of the verbs and identify each one as either a *linking verb* or an *action verb.*

Orpheus loved a young woman named Eurydice, and when they were married, they looked forward to many years of happiness together. But soon after, Eurydice stepped on a poisonous snake and died.

Orpheus roamed the earth, singing sad melodies to try to overcome his grief. But it was no use.

318 • Verbs

☑ **ONGOING ASSESSMENT: Monitor and Reinforce**

If students have difficulty with Exercises 1–6, refer them to the following resources for additional practice.

In the Textbook	Print Resources	Extended Resources
Section Review, Ex. 7–9, p. 319	Grammar Exercise Workbook, pp. 13–18	On-Line Exercise Bank, Section 15.1

Section 15.1 Section Review

GRAMMAR EXERCISES 7–12

Exercise 7 Distinguishing Between Action and Linking Verbs Identify the verb in each sentence below. Then, label each one a *linking verb* or an *action verb*.

1. The city-state of Athens led the Delian League.
2. The citizens of Sparta organized a separate league.
3. Sparta and Athens soon clashed in a war.
4. The conflict turned bitter.
5. Macedonia, to the north, became stronger.
6. With a Greek and Macedonian army, Alexander the Great grew very confident.
7. Later, the Greek world turned its interest to math and philosophy.
8. Many discoveries by Euclid and Archimedes remain correct today.
9. Other people felt the call of poetry.
10. Greek influence grew stronger in Syria and Egypt.

Exercise 8 Completing Sentences With Linking Verbs Complete each sentence below with an appropriate linking verb.

1. For many years, he __?__ dominant.
2. His army __?__ unbeatable.
3. His empire __?__ enormous.
4. Greek culture __?__ widely known.
5. The Greek culture and way of life __?__ still dominant.

Exercise 9 Completing Sentences With Action and Linking Verbs Complete two of the following sentences with action verbs and three with linking verbs. Label each verb *action* or *linking*.

1. Many city-states __?__ leagues.
2. They __?__ helpful for protection.
3. Some __?__ more powerful than others.
4. Sparta __?__ independent.
5. More conflicts __?__ .

Exercise 10 Find It in Your Reading Identify as *action* or *linking* each of the underlined verbs in the following excerpt from the Greek myth "Arachne," translated by Olivia Coolidge.

At last Arachne's fame <u>became</u> so great that people used to come from far and wide to watch her working. Even the graceful nymphs would <u>steal</u> in from stream or forest and <u>peep</u> shyly through the dark doorway, watching in wonder the white arms of Arachne as she <u>stood</u> at the loom and <u>threw</u> the shuttle from hand to hand between the hanging threads, or drew out the long wool, fine as a hair, from the distaff as she <u>sat</u> spinning.

Exercise 11 Find It in Your Writing Look through your portfolio to find a recent sample of descriptive writing. Go through at least two paragraphs and identify all the action verbs and linking verbs. Then, revise two sentences, replacing linking verbs with action verbs.

Exercise 12 Writing Application Write a brief summary of something you have learned about ancient Greece. Use at least three action verbs and three linking verbs. Underline the action verbs once and the linking verbs twice.

Section Review • 319

ASSESS

Section Review

Each of these exercises correlates to the instruction on action verbs and linking verbs, pages 314–318. The exercises may be used for more practice, for reteaching, or for review of the Key Concepts presented.

Answer Key

Exercise 7

1. led—action
2. organized—action
3. clashed—action
4. turned—linking
5. became—linking
6. grew—linking
7. turned—action
8. remain—linking
9. felt—action
10. grew—linking

Exercise 8

Possible answers:

1. remained
2. seemed
3. was
4. is
5. were

Exercise 9

Answers will vary. Samples are given.

1. Many city-states formed (action) leagues.
2. They were (linking) helpful for protection.
3. Some grew (linking) more powerful than others.
4. Sparta became (linking) independent.
5. More conflicts happened (action).

Exercise 10

Find It in Your Reading
linking, action, action, action, action, action

continued

TIME SAVERS!

Answers on Transparency
Use the Grammar Exercises Answers on Transparencies for Chapter 15 to facilitate correction by students.

On-Line Exercise Bank
Have students complete the exercise on computer. The Auto Check feature will grade their work for you!

Answer Key continued

Exercise 11

Find It in Your Writing
Have students draw arrows between the words linked by the verbs.

Exercise 12

Writing Application
Ask students if their action verbs show visible or mental action.

Interest GRABBER Ask students to add helping verbs to the following sentences:

He surfing today. (is, is going, was, went, and so on)

She gone surfing, too. (should have, might have, has, and so on)

Activate Prior Knowledge

Write the following brainstorm-starter on the chalkboard. Then challenge students to add helping verbs to the list. They can refer to the chart on the page for more examples.

Shoulda-Coulda-Woulda Verbs
should have
could have
would have

TEACH

Step-by-Step Teaching Guide

Helping Verbs

1. Write this sentence on the chalkboard:

   Hugo should have been an actor.

   Ask students to decide how many verbs are in the sentence, then vote for one of these options:

   one verb

   two verbs

   three verbs

2. Point out that when helping verbs appear with a main verb, all the verbs together are called a verb phrase.

3. Direct students to watch for verb phrases as they complete Exercises 13 and 14.

Answer Key

Exercise 13

1. had conquered
2. could ignore
3. might have worked
4. will study
5. have learned

Section 15.2

Helping Verbs

Verbs such as *jump, talk,* and *wait* are called *main verbs.* Sometimes, however, verbs are made up of several words, such as *had jumped, might have talked, would have understood,* and *could have been waiting.* In this case, the verbs that come before the main verb are called *helping verbs.* They help express the meaning of the main verb.

KEY CONCEPT A **helping verb** is a verb that comes before the main verb and adds to its meaning. ■

A main verb and one or more helping verbs form a *verb phrase.* In the sentences below, the helping verbs are underlined and the main verbs are boxed. Together, the two kinds of verbs make up verb phrases.

EXAMPLES: He <u>was</u> [leading] the Romans.

He <u>had</u> <u>been</u> [leading] the Romans.

He <u>should</u> <u>have</u> <u>been</u> [leading] the Romans.

The various forms of *be* and *have* are the most common helping verbs. The following chart includes some of the forms of *be* and *have,* as well as other helping verbs.

COMMON HELPING VERBS		
am	have	may
are	has	might
is	had	must
was	can	shall
were	could	should
be	do	will
being	does	would
been	did	

Exercise 13 Recognizing Verb Phrases Write each sentence below on your paper. Underline the verb phrase.
1. Rome had conquered many territories.
2. The emperors could ignore Greece.
3. Greek states might have worked together.
4. Next year, we will study more about Greece.
5. I have learned about Greece in several classes.

Theme: Ancient Greece

In this section, you will learn about helping verbs. The examples and exercises tell more about ancient Greece.

Cross-Curricular Connection: Social Studies

Grammar and Style Tip

In your own writing, be careful not to use very long strings of helping verbs. Sometimes they are necessary, but they can also make your sentence confusing. Ask a listener if the verbs in your sentences are clear.

⏱ TIME AND RESOURCE MANAGER

Resources
Print: Grammar Exercise Workbook, pp. 19–20; Hands-on Grammar Activity Book, Ch. 15; *Grammar Exercises Answers on Transparencies,* Chapter 15
Technology: On-Line Exercise Bank, Section 15.2

In-Depth Coverage	Accelerated Pace
• Work through the key concept, p. 320.	• Assign p. 320 for independent student review.
• Assign and review Exercises 13–16.	• Assign Section Review Exercises 17–19.
• Review the chart on p. 320.	
• Do the Hands-on Grammar Activity, p. 322.	

Exercise 14 Identifying Helping Verbs and Main Verbs

Copy the verb phrase in each sentence below. Then, underline the helping verbs and circle the main verbs.

EXAMPLE: Rome was intruding in Greek affairs.
ANSWER: was (intruding)

1. Macedonia had allied itself with Carthage.
2. The Romans were attaining a strong position in the Mediterranean area.
3. Rome had defeated the city-states.
4. All Greek territories would be placed under Roman rule.
5. Athens and Sparta could remain free states.
6. The political role of the city-state had declined.
7. In later years, Greece did experience a rebirth.
8. Trade and intellectual activities were thriving.
9. The emperor Hadrian had appreciated beauty.
10. He would restore the ruins of Athens.

Exercise 15 Writing Sentences With Helping Verbs

Using each of the following verb phrases, write five original sentences.
1. were going
2. must have known
3. should have been studying
4. had been listening
5. might rebound

Exercise 16 Revising Sentences to Include Helping Verbs

Revise each sentence below to include a verb phrase consisting of a helping verb and a main verb.
1. By 700 B.C., Greece organized itself into a loose collection of independent city-states.
2. By 508 B.C., a government formed in Athens that allowed citizens a say in the government.
3. When learning about the ancient Greeks, people study the arts and sciences as well as the government.
4. The story of Orpheus illustrates the Greek belief in the power of music.
5. An interest in Greek culture leads people to read Greek mythology.

More Practice

Language Lab CD-ROM
• Using Verbs lesson
On-line Exercise Bank
• Section 15.2
Grammar Exercise Workbook
• pp. 19–20

▼ **Critical Viewing** This is a photograph of the Roman Colosseum. How do you imagine it was used? What helping verbs did you use in answering this question? **[Infer]**

Helping Verbs • 321

Answer Key

▶ Exercise 14
1. had (allied)
2. were (attaining)
3. had (defeated)
4. would be (placed)
5. could (remain)
6. had (declined)
7. did (experience)
8. were (thriving)
9. had (appreciated)
10. would (restore)

▶ Exercise 15
Sample answers:
1. We were going to the movies.
2. Our friends must have known about our trip.
3. We should have been studying.
4. We had been listening to music.
5. The ball might rebound.

▶ Exercise 16
Possible answers.
1. had organized
2. was formed
3. would study
4. should illustrate
5. has led

Critical Viewing

Infer Encourage students to use at least two helping verbs in their answers. For example: The Colosseum may have been built to create a large arena.

Integrating Spelling Skills

Should've, would've, and *could've* are contractions for *should have, could have,* and *would have.* Students will frequently find these in their reading (usually in dialogue) as *should of, would of,* and *could of.* This confusion arises because the *ve* in the contractions is pronounced like *of.* Tell students to be sure to use *'ve* in their writing.

✓ ONGOING ASSESSMENT: Monitor and Reinforce

If students miss more than one item in Exercise 14 or 15, refer them to the following resources for additional practice.

In the Textbook	Print Resources	Technology
Section Review, Ex. 17–19, p. 323	Grammar Exercise Workbook, pp. 19–20	Language Lab CD-ROM, Using Verbs, On-Line Exercise Bank, Section 15.2

⏱ TIME SAVERS!

Answers on Transparency
Use the Grammar Exercises Answers on Transparencies for Chapter 15 to facilitate correction by students.

On-Line Exercise Bank
Have students complete the exercise on computer. The Auto Check feature will grade their work for you.

Helping-Verb Expander

Teaching Resources: Hands-on Grammar Activity Book, Chapter 15

1. Have students refer to their Hands-on Grammar activity books or give them copies of the relevant pages.

2. Remind students to look at the common helping verb chart on page 320 as they choose helping verbs for their verb expander.

3. Be sure students choose an appropriate form of the helping verb to fit the subjects of their sentences.

Find It in Your Reading

Ask students if they see any patterns in the meaning changes with certain helping verbs.

Find It in Your Writing

Work with your partner to find the helping verb that works best in your sentences for the meaning you intended.

Customize for
Interpersonal Learners

Collect the papers from the preceding activity in a container. Write the three verb categories on the chalkboard—action verbs, linking verbs, and helping verbs. Divide the class into small groups. Taking turns, a member of each group chooses a paper and reads the sentence to his or her group—without naming the verb category. The group decides which category the verb fits.

15.2

Hands-on Grammar

Helping-Verb Expander

To explore how helping verbs expand or change the meaning of a verb, create helping-verb expanders.

First, fan-fold a sheet of paper three times to create four "panels."

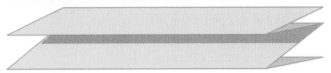

Then, with the paper folded, cut a basic shape, such as a diamond. Do not cut all the way to the folds, because the folds must stay connected, as when you cut a chain of paper dolls.

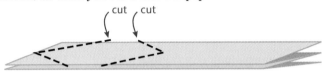

Set the extra paper aside. Unfold the shapes. Fold the outermost left shape inwards. Fold the outermost right shape inwards. The inside points of the end shapes should be next to each other and the middle shapes should be hidden. Write a simple sentence such as *The boat sailed.*

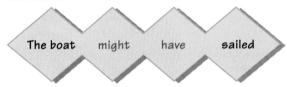

The boat   might   have   sailed

Unfold the helping-verb expander and fill in the blank spaces with helping verbs from the list on page 320. These verbs will "help" you get from the noun at the beginning of the expander to the verb at the end. Read the new sentence and contrast its meaning with the original sentence. Use the leftover paper to make more helping-verb expanders. With a partner, experiment with different numbers of folds and different verbs.

Find It in Your Reading Look in your literature anthology for sentences that contain verb phrases. Create helping-verb expanders for these sentences. Write the sentences with different helping verbs to see how the meaning changes.

Find It in Your Writing Find verb phrases in sentences in your writing. Discuss with a partner how the meaning of each sentence would change if you used different helping verbs.

322 • Verbs

⏱ TIME SAVERS!

✋ **Hands-on Grammar**
Use the Hands-on Grammar activity sheet for Chapter 15 to facilitate this activity.

🖌 STANDARDIZED TEST PREPARATION WORKSHOP

Grammar and Usage When taking standardized tests, students may be required to identify the words that make up a verb phrase. Write the following sentence on the chalkboard and ask students to identify the verb phrase.

By the 1980s, computers were becoming common in many types of businesses.

A were

B becoming

C were becoming

D were becoming common

The verb phrase is item **C**. Choices A and B are parts of the verb phrase. Choice D is the verb phrase plus an adjective.

Section 15.2 Section Review

GRAMMAR EXERCISES 17–22

Exercise 17 Identifying Helping Verbs and Main Verbs Copy the verb phrases in each sentence below. Then, underline the helping verbs and circle the main verbs.

1. Life in ancient Athens was structured differently from life today.
2. Women and men did occupy separate roles.
3. Girls were sheltered within their families.
4. Marriage may have been arranged very early.
5. White dresses would be worn for the ceremony.
6. Also, the girls would wear crowns.
7. Then, their childhood toys were given away.
8. Feasts of celebration could be offered for many days.
9. Both families must have enjoyed the wedding feasts.
10. Then, the bride would move into her new house.

Exercise 18 Completing Verb Phrases Complete each verb phrase below with one of the following: *was, were, would, would have, have been.* (Each will be used only once.)

1. The first Stone Age settlements ___?___ formed around 7000 B.C.
2. In 2500 B.C., the Bronze Age ___?___ just beginning.
3. The Olympic Games ___?___ held since 776 B.C.
4. The first Greek city-states ___?___ appeared between 800–600 B.C.
5. In 336 B.C., Alexander the Great ___?___ become king.

Exercise 19 Revising Sentences to Include Verb Phrases Rewrite each sentence below to include a helping verb and a main verb. Note that you may have to add a verb that changes the meaning of a given sentence.

1. Greek culture glorified the arts.
2. He read the *Iliad* and the *Odyssey*.
3. Hesiod and Alcman were great poets.
4. Lyric poetry achieved great popularity.
5. Thespis was the founder of Greek tragedy.
6. Sculptors and potters became famous.
7. Pythagoras created theories for mathematics.
8. Philosophers wrote many books.
9. Builders designed new buildings.
10. Writers recorded history.

Exercise 20 Find It in Your Reading Find a complete version of the Greek myth "Orpheus." Make a photocopy of it. Then, use a highlighter to identify all of the verb phrases it contains. Circle each helping verb.

Exercise 21 Find It in Your Writing Look through your writing portfolio. Find five sentences in which you have used verb phrases. Make sure that the helping verbs make your meaning clear. Revise any that could be improved.

Exercise 22 Writing Application Write a brief narrative relating an event that might have occurred at the Olympic Games in ancient Greece. Use helping verbs in some of your sentences, and underline all verb phrases.

Section Review • 323

ASSESS and CLOSE

Section Review

Each of these exercises correlates to the instruction on helping verbs, pages 320–322. The exercises may be used for more practice, for reteaching, or for review of the Key Concepts presented.

Answer Key

Exercise 17

1. was (structured)
2. did (occupy)
3. were (sheltered)
4. may have been (arranged)
5. would be (worn)
6. would (wear)
7. were (given)
8. could be (offered)
9. must have (enjoyed)
10. would (move)

Exercise 18

Answers will vary. Samples are given.

1. The first Stone Age settlements were formed around 7000 B.C.
2. In 2500 B.C., the Bronze Age was just beginning.
3. The Olympic Games have been held since 776 B.C.
4. The first Greek city-states would have appeared between 800–600 B.C.
5. In 335 B.C., Alexander the Great would become king.

Exercise 19

Sample answers:

1. did glorify
2. had read
3. have been called
4. would achieve

continued

Answer Key continued

5. would be called
6. could become
7. had created
8. were writing
9. were designing
10. had recorded

Exercise 20

Find It in Your Reading
You may want to divide the students into groups and assign parts of "Orpheus" to each group.

Exercise 21

Find It in Your Writing
If students decide that their writing cannot be improved, ask them to explain why it is good the way it is.

Exercise 22

Writing Application
Have students trade narratives with a partner who can check for awkward shifts of verb tense.

⏱ **TIME SAVERS!**

Answers on Transparency Use the Grammar Exercises Answers on Transparencies for Chapter 15 to facilitate correction by students.

On-Line Exercise Bank Have students complete the exercise on computer. The Auto Check feature will grade their work for you!

CHAPTER REVIEW

Each of these exercises correlates to a section of the chapter on verbs, pages 314–323. The exercises may be used for more practice, for reteaching, or for review of the key concepts presented.

Answer Key

Exercise 23

1. told
2. call
3. explained
4. thought, controlled
5. exhibited
6. had
7. lived
8. wielded
9. roamed
10. possessed
11. ruled
12. spent
13. led
14. controlled
15. lived

Exercise 24

1. The influence of mythology was apparent in all areas of Greek life. (arrow between *influence* and *apparent*)
2. Certain behavior grew unacceptable. (arrow between *behavior* and *unacceptable*)
3. People seemed wary of the gods' punishments. (arrow between *People* and *wary*)
4. The Greek gods remained well known through the poetry of the Greeks. (arrow between *gods* and *known*)
5. They were important in the arts. (arrow between *They* and *important*)
6. They became the inspiration for beautiful temples. (arrow between *They* and *inspiration*)
7. Worship at home was also common for the Greeks. (arrow between *Worship* and *common*)
8. Different places in the home were sacred for different reasons. (arrow between *places* and *sacred*)
9. The hearth became the place of honor for the goddess Hestia. (arrow between *hearth* and *place*)
10. Every person's rituals sounded unique. (arrow between *rituals* and *unique*)

Exercise 25

1. appeared—linking
2. appeared—action
3. looked—action
4. was thought to be—linking
5. was named—action
6. felt—action
7. appeared—linking
8. was—linking
9. looked—linking
10. sounded—action

GRAMMAR EXERCISES 23–31

Exercise 23 **Identifying Action Verbs** List the action verb(s) in each sentence below.

1. The Greeks told many stories and legends.
2. We call these stories myths.
3. The stories explained the mysteries of the world.
4. They thought Greek gods and goddesses controlled nature.
5. These characters in the stories exhibited human traits.
6. Like humans, they also had emotions and problems.
7. The mythological gods lived in their own society.
8. Some gods wielded more power than others.
9. They roamed freely around the world.
10. Gods and goddesses possessed immortality.
11. Each Greek god ruled in one part of the world.
12. The twelve chief gods and goddesses spent their time on Mount Olympus.
13. Zeus and Hera, his queen, led the gods in the sky.
14. Poseidon controlled the seas with his wife, Amphitrite.
15. Hades lived in the dark underworld.

Exercise 24 **Recognizing Linking Verbs** Copy the sentences below. Underline each linking verb. Then, draw a double-headed arrow to connect the words that are linked by the verb.

1. The influence of mythology was apparent in all areas of Greek life.
2. Certain behavior grew unacceptable.
3. People seemed wary of the gods' punishments.

4. The Greek gods remained well known through the poetry of the Greeks.
5. They were important in the arts.
6. They became the inspiration for beautiful temples.
7. Worship at home was also common for the Greeks.
8. Different places in the home were sacred for different reasons.
9. The hearth became the place of honor for the goddess Hestia.
10. Every person's rituals sounded unique.

Exercise 25 **Distinguishing Between Action Verbs and Linking Verbs** Identify the verb in each sentence below, and tell whether it is a *linking verb* or an *action verb*.

1. The temple at Delphi appeared holy to the ancient Greeks.
2. An oracle appeared to visitors.
3. She looked into the future.
4. The site was thought to be holy because of Apollo.
5. He was named the god of the sun.
6. The other gods felt the wrath of Zeus.
7. Zeus' strength appeared the greatest of all the gods.
8. Hermes was a messenger for the other mythological gods.
9. He looked graceful with his winged sandals.
10. A trumpet sounded his arrival.

Exercise 26 **Identifying Helping Verbs and Main Verbs** Copy the verb phrase in each sentence below. Underline the helping verbs, and circle the main verbs.

1. Greek mythology did develop from earlier ideas.
2. The Minoan civilization had developed on the island of Crete.

3. The legends of these people would have involved animals and nature.
4. According to their beliefs, all natural objects must have contained individual spirits.
5. These ideas have been included in Greek mythology.
6. Ancient Greeks could have explained events in nature differently.
7. Their heroes had been glorified frequently.
8. The mythological gods might have lived many years before.
9. Most will think them fantastic and unbelievable.
10. Maybe Greek rituals were adapted from Egyptian rituals.

Exercise 27 — Writing Sentences With Verbs and Verb Phrases

Write five sentences, each using one of the following verbs.

1. save
2. uncover
3. discover
4. attack
5. defeat

Exercise 28 — Revising Sentences With Verbs

Revise each of the following sentences to use an action verb instead of a linking verb. You may make other changes as needed.

EXAMPLE: The Titans were rulers of the Earth.

ANSWER: The Titans ruled the Earth.

1. Zeus was then in control of Mount Olympus.
2. Zeus is the one with lightning bolts for weapons.
3. In some stories, the gods were terrifying to humans.
4. In other stories, the mortal characters are able to trick the gods.
5. Reading mythology is something I like to do.

Exercise 29 — Identifying All Types of Verbs

Identify all the verbs and verb phrases in the following sentences. Then, tell whether each verb is an *action verb*, a *linking verb*, a *helping verb*, or a *main verb*.

1. Hercules was the son of Zeus.
2. He became the strongest man on Earth.
3. Single-handedly, he killed a lion.
4. This feat impressed a king.
5. Later, Hercules would marry the daughter of the king of Thebes.
6. For twelve years, Hercules was a servant to King Eurystheus of Tiryns.
7. He performed twelve difficult tasks.
8. He succeeded in killing a nine-headed swamp monster.
9. Then, Hercules was given immortality.
10. Hercules' story is still told today.

Exercise 30 — Writing Application

Write a short myth to explain an event in nature, such as lightning or a sunrise. Underline all verbs and verb phrases. Label each one *visible action*, *mental action*, or *linking verb*.

Exercise 31 — CUMULATIVE REVIEW Nouns, Pronouns, and Verbs

Identify all the nouns, pronouns, and verbs in this passage. Label each verb an *action verb* or a *linking verb*.

Zeus was the father of the gods. The ancient Greeks understood his strength. His wife, Hera, was often jealous of humans and other gods. Hermes carried messages for the gods. He traveled around the world. The goddess of love was Aphrodite. Many poets and musicians have based their works on myths. An opera retells the story of Orpheus. Shakespeare based some of his works on mythological characters. Myths still capture our imagination.

Chapter Review • 325

Exercise 26

1. did (develop)
2. had (developed)
3. would have (involved)
4. must have (contained)
5. have been (included)
6. could have (explained)
7. had been (glorified)
8. might have (lived)
9. will (think)
10. were (adapted)

Exercise 27

Possible answers:

1. I save stamps and coins.
2. Sometimes I uncover a valuable stamp.
3. Once I discovered a stamp worth $5.
4. On the stamp the soldiers were attacking a fort.
5. They had defeated the enemy.

Exercise 28

Possible answers:

1. Zeus controlled Mount Olympus.
2. Zeus used lightning bolts for weapons.
3. In some stories, the gods terrified humans.
4. In other stories the mortal characters tricked the gods.
5. I like to read mythology.

Exercise 29

1. was (linking)
2. became (linking)
3. killed (action)
4. impressed (action)
5. would (helping) marry (main action)
6. was (linking)
7. performed (action)
8. succeeded (action)
9. was (helping) given (main action)
10. is (helping) told (main action)

continued

Answer Key continued

Exercise 30

Writing Application

Students can compile their myths into a book, adding illustrations if they wish.

Exercise 31

Cumulative Review

1. Nouns: Zeus, father, gods; linking verb: was
2. Nouns: Greeks, strength; action verb: understood; pronoun: his
3. Nouns: wife, Hera, humans, gods; linking verb: was; pronoun: His
4. Nouns: Hermes, messages, gods; action verb: carried
5. Noun: world; action verb: traveled; pronoun: He
6. Nouns: goddess, love, Aphrodite; linking verb: was
7. Nouns: poets, musicians, works, myths; action verb: have based; pronoun: their
8. Nouns: story, Orpheus, opera; action verb: retells
9. Nouns: Shakespeare, works, characters; action verb: based; pronoun: his
10. Nouns: myths, imagination; action verb: capture; pronoun: our

---

 TIME SAVERS!

Answers on Transparency Use the Grammar Exercises Answers on Transparencies for Chapter 15 to facilitate correction by students.

On-Line Exercise Bank Have students complete the exercise on computer. The Auto Check feature will grade their work for you!

Step-by-Step Teaching Guide

Standard English Usage: Verbs

Teaching Resources: Standardized Test Preparation Workbook, Chapter 15

1. If two verb choices seem to indicate the correct timing, have students read each choice in the sentence to see which sounds better.

2. Determine whether each helping verb indicates past, present, or future.

3. Read each sentence mentally to see if your choice "sounds" correct.

Standardized Test Preparation Workshop

Standard English Usage: Verbs

Standardized tests of grammar and usage will usually include questions on verb usage. You will be asked to read a passage with numbered blanks. Then, you will have four choices for the best verb or verb phrase to complete each sentence. Often, the choice depends on the time of the action. Sometimes, you will need to evaluate how helping verbs affect the meaning of the completed sentence. The following sample and practice sets will give you practice responding to these types of items in a standardized test format.

Test Tips

• Look for word clues to determine when the action happens.
• Read the entire passage to determine the relationship between events that will be indicated by the verbs.

Sample Test Item	Answer and Explanation

Read the passage, and choose the letter of the word or group of words that belongs in the space.
 	
The American Red Cross ___(1)__ babysitting certification courses next year.
 	
1 A offers
   B did offer
   C will offer
   D offered
	The correct answer is *C*. The helping verb *will* indicates that the action occurs in the future. Since the action occurs next year, *will offer* best completes the sentence.

🖊 TEST-TAKING TIP

Encourage students to look for words that indicate time and list them in three categories: past, present, and future. This will help students determine the time frame of the passage. For example, in the sample test item, *next year* indicates that the verb needed to complete the sentence must be in the future tense form.

Answer Key

▶ **Practice 1**

1. A
2. G
3. C
4. G
5. B

▶ **Practice 2**

1. C
2. F
3. A
4. J
5. B

▶ **Practice 1** **Directions:** Read the passage, and choose the letter of the word or group of words that belongs in each space.

Last spring four rabbits ___(1)___ born in our backyard. When we saw them, we wondered if they ___(2)___ abandoned. The mother, however, ___(3)___ for them. Now, they ___(4)___ around the garden and soon ___(5)___ to climb through the fence.

1 A were
　 B is
　 C will be
　 D are being

2 F are
　 G had been
　 H were being
　 J will be

3 A did care
　 B would have cared
　 C cared
　 D might have been caring

4 F were hopping
　 G hop
　 H must have hopped
　 J will hop

5 A learned
　 B will have learned
　 C learns
　 D did learn

▶ **Practice 2** **Directions:** Read the passage, and choose the letter of the word or group of words that belongs in each space.

Early in 1874, the small family ___(1)___ their meager belongings into the wagon and set out for their new life in the west. Pa ___(2)___ the wagon while Ma ___(3)___ the family's belongings. The six children ___(4)___ impatiently while the preparations were going on. The whole family ___(5)___ excited about their adventure.

1 A loads
　 B did load
　 C loaded
　 D had been loading

2 F had prepared
　 G did prepare
　 H has prepared
　 J would have prepared

3 A packed
　 B will pack
　 C might have been packing
　 D packs

4 F did wait
　 G might wait
　 H should wait
　 J were waiting

5 A was being
　 B was
　 C would be
　 D will have been

Time and Resource Manager

In-Depth Lesson Plan

	LESSON FOCUS	PRINT AND MEDIA RESOURCES
DAY 1	**Adjectives** Students learn to recognize adjectives and the nouns they modify and to distinguish between definite and indefinite articles (pp. 330–333).	**Teaching Resources** *Grammar Exercise Workbook*, pp. 21–24; *Grammar Exercises Answers on Transparencies*, Ch. 16 *On-Line Exercise Bank*, Section 16.1
DAY 2	**Special Types of Adjectives** Students learn and apply concepts identifying nouns used as adjectives, and different types of adjectives (pp. 334–339).	**Teaching Resources** *Grammar Exercise Workbook*, pp. 25–28; *Grammar Exercises Answers on Transparencies*, Ch. 16 *On-Line Exercise Bank*, Section 16.1
DAY 3	**Adverbs** Students learn and apply concepts identifying and using adverbs, distinguishing between adjectives and adverbs and do the Hands-on Grammar activity (pp. 340–345).	**Teaching Resources** *Grammar Exercise Workbook*, pp. 29–32; *Grammar Exercises Answers on Transparencies*, Ch. 16; *Hands-on Grammar Activity Book*, Ch. 16 *On-Line Exercise Bank*, Section 16.2
DAY 4	**Review and Assess** Students review chapter and demonstrate mastery of use of adjectives and adverbs (pp. 346–349).	**Teaching Resources** *Formal Assessment*, Ch. 16; *Grammar Exercises Answers on Transparencies*, Ch. 16 *On-Line Exercise Bank*, Sections 16.1–2

Accelerated Lesson Plan

	LESSON FOCUS	PRINT AND MEDIA RESOURCES
DAY 1	**Adjectives** Students cover concepts and usage of adjectives as determined by Diagnostic Test (pp. 330–339).	**Teaching Resources** *Grammar Exercise Workbook*, pp. 21–28; *Grammar Exercises Answers on Transparencies*, Ch. 16 *On-Line Exercise Bank*, Section 16.1
DAY 2	**Adverbs** Students cover concepts and usage of adverbs as determined by Diagnostic Test (pp. 340–345).	**Teaching Resources** *Grammar Exercise Workbook*, pp. 29–32; *Grammar Exercises Answers on Transparencies*, Ch. 16; *Hands-on Grammar Activity Book*, Ch. 16 *On-Line Exercise Bank*, Section 16.2
DAY 3	**Review and Assess** Students review chapter and demonstrate mastery of use of adjectives and adverbs (pp. 346–349).	**Teaching Resources** *Formal Assessment*, Ch. 16; *Grammar Exercises Answers on Transparencies*, Ch. 16 *On-Line Exercise Bank*, Sections 16.1–2

Options for Adapting Lesson Plans

HOMEWORK
Have students complete any section of the chapter for homework.

FEATURES
Extend coverage with the Grammar in Literature feature (pp. 333, 341), and the Standardized Test Preparation Workshop (p. 348).

TECHNOLOGY
Students can use the On-Line Exercise Bank to complete the exercises on computer. The Auto Check feature will grade their work.

INTEGRATED SKILLS COVERAGE

Grammar in Literature
SE pp. 333, 341

Reading
Find It in Your Reading SE pp. 339, 344, 345

Writing
Find It in Your Writing SE pp. 339, 344, 345
Writing Application SE pp. 339, 345, 347
Writing Skills ATE p. 332
Grammar and Style SE pp. 336, 341

Spelling
SE pp. 334, 342

Real-World Connection
ATE p. 335

Viewing and Representing
Critical Viewing SE pp. 328, 331, 332, 333, 337, 340, 343

ASSESSMENT SUPPORT

Standardized Test Preparation Workshop SE p. 348; ATE pp. 334, 346
Standardized Test Preparation Workbook, pp. 31–32
Formal Assessment, Ch. 16

MEETING INDIVIDUAL NEEDS

Less Advanced Students ATE p. 338; See also Ongoing Assessments ATE pp. 333, 335, 337, 343
ESL Students ATE pp. 331, 332
More Advanced Students ATE pp. 334, 336, 342
Verbal/Linguistic Learners ATE p. 333
Bodily/Kinesthetic Learners ATE p. 341

BLOCK SCHEDULING

Pacing Suggestions
For 90-minute Blocks
• Administer the Diagnostic Test to students to determine instructional coverage.
• Have students complete the necessary exercises in class. Use the Hands-on Grammar activity to provide a change of pace.

Resources for Varying Instruction
• *Language Lab* **CD-ROM** If your students have access to hardware, a 90-minute block provides an ideal opportunity for students to work on computer.

Professional Development Support
• *How to Manage Instruction in the Block* This teaching Resource provides management and activity suggestions.

MEDIA AND TECHNOLOGY

For the Student
• *Language Lab* **CD-ROM**, Using Modifiers
• *On-Line Exercise Bank*, Ch. 16

For the Teacher
• *Resource Pro* **CD-ROM**

WRITING AND GRAMMAR WEB SITE

The Interactive Writing and Grammar Web site provides a wide array of support for students, teachers, and parents. Grammar support includes:

• On-Line Exercise Bank with Auto Check scoring
• Diagnostic and assessment support

www.phschool.com

LITERATURE CONNECTIONS

Grammar in Literature selections from *Prentice Hall Literature: Timeless Voices, Timeless Themes,* Copper:
from *The Pigman & Me,* Paul Zindel, SE p. 333
from "Mowgli's Brothers," Rudyard Kipling, SE p. 341

Lesson Objectives

1. To recognize adjectives.
2. To understand word order with adjectives and nouns.
3. To identify definite and indefinite articles.
4. To recognize and use proper adjectives.
5. To understand how suffixes can be added to nouns to make proper adjectives and adjectives.
6. To use pronouns as adjectives, including the demonstrative pronouns *this, that, these,* and *those.*
7. To recognize adverbs.
8. To recognize the function of adverbs when they modify adjectives or adverbs.
9. To understand the different functions of adjectives and adverbs.

Critical Viewing

Analyze Students might mention crystal-clear blue water and sounds of joy, surprise, or fear that the rafters make.

Chapter 16 Adjectives and Adverbs

▲ Critical Viewing
Identify words to describe the colors and sounds of the raft ride or to describe the way a rafter might feel while speeding down the river. **[Analyze]**

Some words make language come alive for a reader or listener in the same way that colors and sounds make some video games more exciting. The words that do this are called *modifiers.*

In this chapter, you will learn about *adjectives.* These are the words that help nouns create pictures. You might use adjectives to describe what kind of video game you are playing or how many games you have already played.

You will also learn about *adverbs.* Adverbs are the words that make verbs clear and exact. These words can describe how you are playing the game.

✓ ONGOING ASSESSMENT: Diagnose

If students miss more than one item in any category, direct them to the relevant pages of the text and assign exercises for practice and review.

Adjectives and Adverbs	Diagnostic Test Items	Teach	Practice	Section Review	Chapter Review
Skill Check A					
Identifying Adjectives and Modified Nouns	A 1–5	pp. 330–331	Ex. 1–2	Ex. 9	Ex. 28–29
Skill Check B					
Indefinite Articles	B 6–10	pp. 332–333	Ex. 3	Ex. 10	Ex. 30
Skill Check C					
Identifying Proper Adjectives	C 11–15	pp. 334–335	Ex. 4–5	Ex. 11	Ex. 31

Diagnostic Test

Directions: Write all answers on a separate sheet of paper.

Skill Check A. List the adjectives in the sentences below, and write the noun that each adjective modifies.

1. Bowlers wear special shoes.
2. Players sometimes wear colorful uniforms.
3. A bowling ball has two or three holes.
4. The white pins have narrow necks.
5. A player takes several running steps before releasing the ball.

Skill Check B. Write out each phrase. Replace the blank with the correct indefinite article (*a* or *an*).

6. ___?___ organized sport
7. ___?___ wooden runway
8. ___?___ high score
9. ___?___ unusual bowling style
10. ___?___ pair of strikes

Skill Check C. List the proper adjectives in each sentence. Then, list the noun each modifies.

11. European settlers brought these games to America.
12. Ninepin bowling, known as skittles, is a German game.
13. North American players prefer tenpin bowling.
14. Tenpins was originally a Dutch sport.
15. It quickly caught on among German immigrants in the Midwest.

Skill Check D. Write the possessive adjective in each sentence below. Then, write its antecedent and the noun it modifies.

16. Bowlers have enjoyed their game for hundreds of years.
17. King Edward III discouraged his troops from bowling.
18. Bowling increased its popularity under King Henry VIII.
19. American soldiers based in England during World War II taught British servicemen their version of the game.
20. Floretta McCutcheon gave clinics to teach women her sport.

Skill Check E. Write whether the underlined word is functioning as an *adjective* or a *pronoun*.

21. <u>This</u> was the early development of bowling.
22. Several pins stood at <u>that</u> end of the alley.
23. Variations emerged in <u>those</u> European countries.
24. Andy Varipapa taught me <u>this</u> bowling trick.
25. <u>That</u> is one of my fondest memories.

Skill Check F. Write the adverbs in the following sentences, and then write the word each adverb modifies.

26. Players roll the ball carefully down the alley.
27. They try hard to strike the first pin.
28. It is very difficult to knock down all of the pins.
29. A pinspotter automatically sets up the pins.
30. This invention quickly made bowling more enjoyable.

Adjectives and Adverbs • **329**

Answer Key

Diagnostic Test

- Each item in the Diagnostic Test corresponds to a specific section in the adjectives and adverbs chapter. This will enable you to tailor your instruction to your students' particular needs. See "Ongoing Assessment: Diagnose" on the bottom of pages 328–329 for further details.

- Answers for the Diagnostic Test and all chapter exercises are available in *Grammar Exercises Answers on Transparencies* in your Teaching Resources.

Skill Check A

1. special—shoes
2. colorful—uniforms
3. bowling—ball, two or three—holes
4. white—pins, narrow—necks
5. several—steps, running—steps

Skill Check B

6. an organized sport
7. a wooden runway
8. a high score
9. an unusual bowling style
10. a pair of strikes

Skill Check C

11. European—settlers
12. German—game
13. North American—players
14. Dutch—sport
15. German—immigrants

Skill Check D

16. their—Bowlers, game
17. his—King Edward III, troops
18. its—Bowling, popularity
19. their—American soldiers, version
20. her—Floretta McCutcheon, sport

Skill Check E

21. This—pronoun
22. that—adjective
23. those—adjective
24. this—adjective
25. That—pronoun

Skill Check F

26. carefully—roll
27. hard—try
28. very—difficult
29. automatically—sets, up—sets
30. quickly—made, more—enjoyable

☑ ONGOING ASSESSMENT: Diagnose *continued*

Adjectives and Adverbs	Diagnostic Test Items	Teach	Practice	Section Review	Chapter Review
Skill Check D, E, and F					
Identifying Possessive Adjectives and Their Antecedents	D 16–20	pp. 336–337	Ex. 6	Ex. 12	Ex. 32
Identifying Demonstrative Adjectives and Their Functions	E 21–25	p. 338	Ex. 7–8	Ex. 13	Ex. 33
Identifying Adverbs and the Words They Modify	F 26–30	pp. 340–344	Ex. 17–20	Ex. 21–24	Ex. 34–37
Cumulative Review and Applications				Ex. 14–16, 25–27	Ex. 38–39

Interest GRABBER Ask students to discuss favorite activities. Encourage them to describe what they like about these activities, asking questions such as: *What kinds of things do you like to do? Why do you like doing these activities? Tell students that many of the words they are using are adjectives.*

Activate Prior Knowledge

Let students know that song titles frequently consist of an adjective and a noun. Challenge students to list songs with an adjective and a noun.

TEACH

Step-by-Step Teaching Guide

Adjectives

1. Let students know that adjectives allow people, places, and things to be described in great detail.

2. Write the following phrases on the board. Have students provide adjectives:

   What kind of pepper? (red)

   Which dog? (that)

   How many students? (eleven)

   How much milk? (more)

3. Tell students to identify the noun in the sentence, and then to look for words that modify the noun by answering the questions What kind? Which one? How many? In what way?

Answer Key

> **Exercise 1**

1. table—What kind?, green—What kind?
2. white—What kind?
3. two or four—How many?, hollow—What kind?
4. wooden—What kind, oval—What kind?
5. proper—What kind?, each—Which?
6. One—How many?, five—How many?
7. This—Which one?, twenty-one—How many?
8. table—What kind?, winning—What kind?
9. every—How many?
10. Doubles—What kind?, these—Which ones?

> Section 16.1

Adjectives

Adjectives are words that make language more specific. For example, *car* is a general word, but a *red, two-door convertible* is far more specific. Adjectives such as *red* and *two-door* make nouns and pronouns clearer and more vivid.

> **KEY CONCEPT** An **adjective** is a word that describes something. ■

Adjectives are often called *modifiers*, because they modify, or change, the meaning of a noun or pronoun. Notice how *game* is modified by each set of adjectives below.

EXAMPLES: *old-fashioned* game
new video game
children's board game

Adjectives answer several questions about nouns and pronouns. They tell *What kind? Which one? How many?* or *How much?*

QUESTIONS ANSWERED BY ADJECTIVES		
What Kind?	*expensive* toys	*colorful* caps
Which One?	*this* man	*these* paddles
How Many? How Much?	*few* cars	*many* people

> **Exercise 1** Recognizing Adjectives Identify the adjectives in each sentence. Then, tell which question is answered by each adjective.

EXAMPLE: The amusement park has several rides.
ANSWER: amusement (*What kind* of park?)
          several (*How many* rides?)

1. Table tennis is played on green tables.
2. A white stripe runs down the center of the table.
3. Two or four players hit hollow balls over a net.
4. Their wooden racquets have an oval shape.
5. A proper serve bounces once on each side of the net.
6. One player will serve until five points are scored.
7. This game ended when I scored twenty-one points.
8. A shot that tips the table edge is usually a winning shot.
9. After every game, the players switch ends of the table.
10. Doubles games follow most of these rules.

330 • Adjectives and Adverbs

Theme: Sports and Games

In this section, you will learn that adjectives are used to describe nouns and pronouns. The examples and exercises in this section are about sports and games.

Cross-Curricular Connection: Physical Education

> **More Practice**

Language Lab CD-ROM
•Using Modifiers lesson
On-line Exercise Bank
• Section 16.1
Grammar Exercise Workbook
• pp. 21–22

⏱ **TIME AND RESOURCE MANAGER**

Resources
Print: Grammar Exercise Workbook, pp. 21–28; Grammar Exercises Answers on Transparencies, Chapter 16
Technology: Language Lab CD-ROM, Using Modifiers; On-Line Exercise Bank, Section 16.1

In-Depth Coverage	Accelerated Pace
• Work through all key concepts, pp. 330–338.	• Assign pp. 330–338 for independent student review.
• Assign and review Exercises 1–8.	• Review Pronouns as Adjectives and assign Exercises 6–8.
• Read and discuss Grammar in Literature, p. 333.	• Assign Section Review Exercises 9–13.

▶ **KEY CONCEPT** Adjectives usually come before the nouns they modify. They can come after nouns, but this order is less common. ■

BEFORE: Kevin owns three arcades.

Large, colorful graphics covered the screen.

AFTER: Kevin's arcades are busy.

Graphics, large and colorful, covered the screen.

In a similar way, one or more adjectives can come before or after a pronoun.

BEFORE: Intelligent and active, he won the tournament.

AFTER: She is talented.

▲ Critical Viewing
Name five adjectives you would use to describe your favorite video game.
[Analyze]

▶ **Exercise 2** Supplying Adjectives Add adjectives to each of the following sentences. Write the new sentences on a separate sheet of paper. You may need to change capitalization. Underline the adjective(s) you add and draw an arrow to the word each modifies.

EXAMPLE: The park has ___?___ rides.

ANSWER: The park has exciting rides.

1. Table tennis is a ___?___ game.
2. ___?___ people enjoy playing the game.
3. The ball is ___?___.
4. Paddles can be ___?___ or ___?___.
5. We had a ___?___ party at the arcade.
6. We each received ___?___ tokens.
7. Maurice was ___?___ at shooting baskets quickly.
8. Kara was ___?___ to play.
9. Everyone had a ___?___ time.
10. We were ___?___ when we had to leave.

Adjectives • 331

Customize for ESL Students

Be aware that Spanish-speaking students, as well as students speaking other languages, may not be accustomed to placing the adjective before the noun. In Spanish, for example, descriptive adjectives generally follow the noun. Adjectives placed before the noun tend to be evaluative rather than descriptive.

Critical Viewing

Analyze Answers will vary but may include *exciting, interesting, awesome, great, cool.*

Answer Key

▶ Exercise 2

Possible answers:

1. fascinating [arrow to *game*]
2. Intelligent [arrow to *people*]
3. white [arrow to *ball*]
4. green, red [arrows to *paddles*]
5. birthday [arrow to *party*]
6. seven [arrow to *tokens*]
7. best [arrow to *Maurice*]
8. happy [arrow to *Kara*]
9. great [arrow to *time*]
10. sad [arrow to *we*]

🕐 **TIME SAVERS!**

📄 **Answers on Transparency** Use the Grammar Exercises Answers on Transparencies for Chapter 16 to facilitate correction by students.

💻 **On-Line Exercise Bank** Have students complete the exercises on computer. The Auto Check feature will grade their work for you!

Articles

1. Tell students that *the* is called the definite article because it designates a specific noun: *the football team, the orange.* Indefinite articles, such as *a* and *an,* refer to any one of a category of persons, places, or things: *a football team, an orange.*

2. Let students know that there are exceptions to the rule for the use of the indefinite article. When a word begins with the letter *h,* if the *h* is pronounced, use the indefinite article *a.* If it is silent, use the indefinite article *an.* Also, before a long *u* or a word such as *one,* the indefinite article *a* is used:

a boat	*an iguana*
a radio	*an automobile*
a hotel	*an hour*
a union	*an unusual dog*
a one-time event	*an orange*

Customize for
ESL Students

Students learning English as a second language may be confused by definite and indefinite articles. Some languages, such as Russian and Chinese, have no articles. Other languages, such as Arabic, have no indefinite articles. In languages that do have articles, the usage rules are sometimes different. You may wish to place extra emphasis on the use of articles in English.

Critical Viewing

Identify; Support Students may mention the tall buildings, many trees, five players, small windows, white T-shirt.

Integrating Writing Skills

Ask students to review a piece of writing from their portfolios and determine where they used the definite article, and where they used indefinite articles. Do students see a pattern? Help them to see how the use of the definite article helps a reader determine which particular person, place, or thing the writer wants to describe.

332

16.1

Articles

Three frequently used adjectives are the words *a, an,* and *the.* They are called *articles.* Articles can be *definite* or *indefinite.* Both types indicate that a noun will soon follow.

KEY CONCEPT *The* is the **definite** article. It points to a specific person, place, or thing. *A* and *an* are **indefinite** articles. They point to any member of a group of similar people, places, or things. ■

DEFINITE: Mr. Ryan is <u>the</u> man to call. (a specific person)

Go into <u>the</u> gym. (a specific place)

INDEFINITE: I want to see <u>a</u> game. (any game)
Please take <u>an</u> apple. (any apple)

A is used before consonant sounds, and *an* is used before vowel sounds. The following chart gives several examples of the indefinite articles used correctly before consonant and vowel sounds.

HOW TO USE *A* AND *AN*	
A Before Consonant Sounds	*An* Before Vowel Sounds
a pineapple *a* useful item (*y* sound) *a* one-way street (*w* sound) *a* taxi *a* lamp	*an* ivory tusk *an* eraser *an* angry look *an* opportunity *an* umbrella

332 • Adjectives and Adverbs

▲ **Critical Viewing**
Find five people or things in the picture. Then, use an adjective to describe each person or thing. **[Identify; Support]**

🔲 **Research Tip**

When you are looking up titles in either print or electronic sources, ignore articles at the beginning. Titles are alphabetized by the first word that's not an article.

GRAMMAR IN LITERATURE

from The Pigman & Me
Paul Zindel

Notice how the adjectives—awful, one, another, first, gym, and school—*make the nouns they modify more specific.*

. . . Just when we think something *awful*'s going to happen *one* way, it throws you a curve and the something *awful* happens *another* way. This happened on the *first* Friday, during *gym* period, when we were allowed to play games in the *school* yard.

More Practice

Language Lab
CD-ROM
•Using Modifiers lesson
On-line
Exercise Bank
• Section 16.1
Grammar Exercise
Workbook
• pp. 23–24

▶ **Exercise 3** **Using Indefinite Articles** Copy each phrase. Replace the blank with the correct indefinite article.

EXAMPLE: __?__ red car
ANSWER: a red car

1. __?__ amazing track
2. __?__ driver
3. __?__ orange sign
4. __?__ steering wheel
5. __?__ unusual ride
6. __?__ international sport
7. __?__ exciting event
8. __?__ one-time champion
9. __?__ innocent mistake
10. __?__ two-lane track
11. __?__ original idea
12. __?__ amateur status
13. __?__ winning score
14. __?__ indoor activity
15. __?__ rubber bumper
16. __?__ instruction book
17. __?__ yellow stripe
18. __?__ successful attempt
19. __?__ additional invention
20. __?__ final outcome

▼ **Critical Viewing**
Use the articles *a, an,* and *the* with items in this photo. **[Apply]**

Adjectives • 333

✓ ONGOING ASSESSMENT: Monitor and Reinforce

If students miss more than two items in Exercises 1, 2, or 3, refer them to the following for additional practice.

In the Textbook	Print Resources	Technology
Section Review, Ex. 9–10, p. 339	Grammar Exercise Workbook, pp. 21–24	Language Lab CD-ROM, Using Modifiers; On-Line Exercise Bank, Section 16.1

Step-by-Step Teaching Guide

Grammar in Literature

1. Have a volunteer read aloud the Paul Zindel passage.
2. Ask students to identify the noun being modified by each adjective in the passage.
3. Discuss how these adjectives add color and detail to the passage.

More About the Author

Paul Zindel is a well-known author and playwright. He was born in Staten Island, New York, and worked as a teacher in the New York City public schools. His novel, *The Pigman*, was named an American Library Association Notable Book. His play, *The Effect of Gamma Rays on Man-in-the-Moon Marigolds*, won the Pulitzer Prize and the Drama Desk Critics Circle Award in 1971.

Customize for
Verbal/Linguistic Learners

Review with students when to use the indefinite article *a* or *an*. Use the following phrases to illustrate how some letters may change their sound at the beginning of a word. Encourage students to listen to how the word is pronounced before deciding whether to use *a* or *an*.

orange crayon (an)

once-in-a-lifetime chance (a)

unhappy baby (an)

union member (a)

happy puppy (a)

honest person (an)

Answer Key

▶ **Exercise 3**

1. an	11. an
2. a	12. an
3. an	13. a
4. a	14. an
5. an	15. a
6. an	16. an
7. an	17. a
8. a	18. a
9. an	19. an
10. a	20. a

Critical Viewing

Apply Be sure students use the articles *a, an,* and *the* correctly. Encourage them to pick items beginning with a vowel that has a consonant sound.

Proper Adjectives

1. Give students additional practice by asking them to identify the proper adjectives in the following examples:

   Florida sunshine

   Shakespearean verse

   A *Korean* grocery

2. There is no general rule for how endings are added to proper nouns. Caution students about making generalizations based on a few examples. It may appear that proper nouns ending in a vowel simply add an *-n*: *Californian* and *Colombian*. But there are also *Floridian* and *Canadian*.

3. Tell students that there are also irregular proper adjectives, such as *French*, *Scottish*, and *Japanese*. Challenge students to supply more examples.

Customize for
More Advanced Students

Have students work in small groups in a timed competition to come up with the most proper adjectives. You could give them themes, such as geography or people, to make the competition more interesting.

Answer Key

Exercise 4

1. German—game
2. European—countries
3. American—business people
4. French—companies
5. Texas—towns
6. Saturday—competitions
7. Canadian—trademarks
8. Oklahoma—city
9. Montana—competition
10. American—cities

16.1

Proper Adjectives

The words *African sunset*, *Siberian climate*, and *Korean Ping-Pong team* all have something in common. An adjective based on a proper noun begins each group of words. Such adjectives are called *proper adjectives*.

KEY CONCEPT A **proper adjective** is (1) a proper noun used as an adjective or (2) an adjective formed from a proper noun. ■

When a proper noun is used as an adjective, it answers the question *What kind?* or *Which one?* about the noun it modifies. The chart below lists proper nouns and shows how they can be used as proper adjectives.

Proper Nouns	Proper Nouns Used as Adjectives
Baltimore	<u>Baltimore</u> newspaper
April	<u>April</u> showers
Kennedy	<u>Kennedy</u> family

Exercise 4 Identifying Proper Adjectives Identify the proper adjective in each sentence. Then, tell which noun it modifies.

EXAMPLE: I went to the foosball arcade Sunday afternoon.
ANSWER: Sunday (afternoon)

1. Table soccer, or foosball, began as a German game.
2. In European countries, it was a popular arcade game.
3. American business people imported the idea.
4. Tables from French companies were shipped to the U.S.
5. Early tournaments were held in Texas towns.
6. Saturday competitions drew large crowds.
7. Canadian trademarks allowed companies to sell across the border.
8. An Oklahoma city hosted one of the first championship matches.
9. A Montana competition was one of the most exciting ever.
10. Now, many American cities host foosball tournaments.

334 • Adjectives and Adverbs

🖋 Spelling Tip

Be sure to make spelling changes when turning proper nouns into proper adjectives. However, don't assume that changes are always necessary. Check your dictionary to make the correct adjective form of the noun.

✏ STANDARDIZED TEST PREPARATION WORKSHOP

Grammar and Usage Standardized tests often measure students' ability to express themselves effectively using adjectives and adverbs.

Choose the letter of the word that best completes the sentence.

Kendra complained that the day was going ___.

A fast   C slowly

B lately   D quick

The correct answer is item **C**. An adverb is needed to complete the sentence, since the missing word modifies the verb *going*. The other adverbs, *lately* and *fast*, do not make sense in the context of the sentence.

> **KEY CONCEPT** Endings called suffixes are added to many proper nouns to make them into proper adjectives. ∎

Proper Nouns	Proper Adjective Forms
America	<u>American</u> jazz
Inca	<u>Incan</u> empire
Florida	<u>Floridian</u> sunset

Notice that an ending such as *-n* or *-ian* has been added to each of the proper nouns.

The following sentences give additional examples of proper adjectives.

EXAMPLES: <u>Colombian</u> players won the gold medal.
I played with a <u>Korean</u> partner.

> **Exercise 5** Creating Proper Adjectives Rewrite each sentence to use a proper adjective instead of the underlined proper noun. You may need to rearrange the words.

EXAMPLE: I learned to play a game from <u>Italy</u>.
ANSWER: I learned to play an Italian game.

1. *Croquet* is a word from <u>France</u>.
2. A doctor in <u>Paris</u> chose the name, which means "crooked stick."
3. Nobles in <u>Britain</u> played an earlier form of the game.
4. Golfers in <u>Scotland</u> played it indoors as a way to practice their putting.
5. Players in the <u>United States</u> took up croquet in the 1860's.
6. An office in <u>Florida</u> sets rules for the game in <u>North America</u>.
7. A group in <u>Arizona</u> organized an association for croquet players in the <u>United States</u>.
8. The sport in <u>North America</u> features hard rubber balls, nine narrow wickets, and short mallets.
9. The rules of croquet in <u>England</u> and <u>Egypt</u> call for six wickets and longer mallets.
10. The rules in <u>Australia</u> are the same as in England.

> **More Practice**

Language Lab
CD-ROM
• Adjectives lesson
On-line
Exercise Bank
• Section 16.1
Grammar Exercise
Workbook
• pp. 25–26

Adjectives • **335**

Real-World Connection

Give students the front page of a metropolitan newspaper, or have them read articles on a newspaper's Web site. Instruct them to assemble a list of proper adjectives they encounter. Students might work in small groups to analyze the different ways proper nouns are formed into proper adjectives.

Answer Key

> **Exercise 5**

1. *Croquet* is a French word.
2. A Parisian doctor chose the name, which means "crooked stick."
3. British nobles played an earlier form of the game.
4. Scottish golfers played it indoors as a way to practice their putting.
5. United States players took up croquet in the 1860's.
6. A Florida office sets North American rules for the game.
7. An Arizona group organized an association for United States croquet players.
8. The North American sport features hard rubber balls, nine narrow wickets, and short mallets.
9. The English and Egyptian rules of croquet call for six wickets and longer mallets.
10. The Australian rules are the same as in England.

☑ **ONGOING ASSESSMENT: Monitor and Reinforce**

If students miss more than two items in Exercise 4 or 5, refer them to the following for additional practice.

In the Textbook	Print Resources	Technology
Section Review, Ex. 11, p. 339	Grammar Exercise Workbook, pp. 25–26	Language Lab CD-ROM, Using Modifiers; On-Line Exercise Bank, Section 16.1

⏱ **TIME SAVERS!**

Answers on Transparency Use the Grammar Exercises Answers on Transparencies for Chapter 16 to facilitate correction by students.

On-Line Exercise Bank Have students complete the exercises on computer. The Auto Check feature will grade their work for you!

Pronouns as Adjectives

1. Pronouns act as adjectives when they modify a noun. They are known as either *possessive pronouns* or *possessive adjectives*. They are pronouns because they have antecedents, but they also modify nouns by answering the question *Which one?*

2. Offer students these additional examples. Remind them that in each case, the pronoun answers the question *Which one?*

   I love *my* dog.

   Ray painted *his* room.

   Franco fixed *their* car.

3. Explain to students that the pronoun *her* is both an objective and a possessive pronoun. *I gave the ball to her* uses *her* in the objective case. It does not modify a noun. Instead, it is the object of a preposition.

Customize for
More Advanced Students

Ask students to identify the antecedents to possessive pronouns in a piece of writing of their choice. Remind students that a pronoun's antecedent may be found in a previous sentence.

16.1

Pronouns as Adjectives

Not only can nouns be used as adjectives, but pronouns can also serve as adjectives. In the word pairs *my computer, our class,* and *its cover,* the personal pronouns are working as adjectives.

▶ **KEY CONCEPT** A **personal pronoun** can be used as an adjective if it modifies a noun. ■

The following examples show personal pronouns used as adjectives. Because they show possession, they are called *possessive adjectives.*

EXAMPLES:　　Eddie played <u>his</u> favorite game.
　　　　　　　Jane said, "<u>My</u> team is the Comets."
　　　　　　　The students hoped <u>their</u> team would win.

Notice that each underlined pronoun modifies the noun that follows it.

PERSONAL PRONOUNS USED AS POSSESSIVE ADJECTIVES	
Singular	**Plural**
my	our
your	your
his, her, its	their

Each pronoun in the examples above refers back to a noun, its antecedent. The next examples show that personal pronouns (1) work as adjectives and (2) take the place of nouns. The arrows point back to the antecedents and forward to the nouns modified.

EXAMPLES:　　All students can leave <u>their</u> games here.

　　　　　　　Ben predicted <u>his</u> score in the game.

　　　　　　　The club wants to increase <u>its</u> membership.

🔩 Grammar and Style Tip

Try not to use too many personal pronouns and possessive adjectives in one sentence. Your readers may have trouble understanding the antecedents, and the meaning of your sentence can become unclear.

336 • Adjectives and Adverbs

✏️ STANDARDIZED TEST PREPARATION WORKSHOP

Grammar and Usage Many standardized tests require students to complete sentences correctly. Problems with articles are among the usage errors that are tested. Ask students to choose the item that best completes the sentence.

　　That is ___ unusual way of putting things!

A　a
B　my

C　an
D　None of the above

The correct answer is item **C**. Item B is not an article, but a possessive pronoun. Item A is incorrect because the short *u* in *unusual* requires the indefinite article *an,* not *a.*

▶ **Exercise 6** Recognizing Possessive Adjectives Copy each sentence. Underline the possessive adjective. Then, draw one arrow connecting the possessive adjective to its antecedent, if any, and another arrow connecting it to the noun or pronoun it modifies.

EXAMPLE: Eric broke his record at the miniature-golf course.

1. We played miniature golf at our local golf course.
2. I used my club to hit the ball through the windmill.
3. Pam chose a pink ball because pink is her favorite color.
4. Mike says miniature golf is his favorite sport.
5. This course is well known because of its difficulty.
6. You probably don't enjoy competing against your brother.
7. Players must take their time and be patient.
8. Kayla and Serena were the leaders on their team.
9. My best shot ever was a hole-in-one.
10. The last hole on the golf course was its most challenging one.
11. The waterfall near the hole was its biggest obstacle.
12. Cheri hit her third shot right into the water.
13. Martin will show us his final scorecard.
14. Sam and I practiced for hours to improve our scores.
15. Sean promises that next year the championship will be his.

More Practice

Language Lab
CD-ROM
• Adjectives lesson
On-line
Exercise Bank
• Section 16.1
Grammar Exercise
Workbook
• pp. 27–28

◀ **Critical Viewing**
Using adjectives, tell how these table-tennis racquets are similar to and different from racquets used in other games. **[Compare and Contrast]**

Adjectives • 337

ONGOING ASSESSMENT: Monitor and Reinforce

If students miss more than two items in Exercise 6, refer them to the following for additional practice.

In the Textbook	Print Resources	Technology
Section Review, Ex. 12, p. 339	Grammar Exercise Workbook, pp. 27–28	Language Lab CD-ROM, Using Modifiers; On-Line Exercise Bank, Section 16.1

Answer Key

▶ **Exercise 6**

1. We played miniature golf at <u>our</u> local golf course. (arrow from *our* to *We*; arrow from *our* to *course*)
2. I used <u>my</u> club to hit the ball through the windmill. (arrow from *my* to *I*; arrow from *my* to *club*)
3. Pam chose a pink ball because pink is <u>her</u> favorite color. (arrow from *her* to *Pam*; arrow from *her* to *color*)
4. Mike says miniature golf is <u>his</u> favorite sport. (arrow from *his* to *Mike*; arrow from *his* to *sport*)
5. This course is well known because of <u>its</u> difficulty. (arrow from *its* to *course*; arrow from *its* to *difficulty*)
6. You probably don't enjoy competing against <u>your</u> brother. (arrow from *your* to *You*; arrow from *your* to *brother*)
7. Players must take <u>their</u> time and be patient. (arrow from *their* to *Players*; arrow from *their* to *time*)
8. Kayla and Serena were the leaders on <u>their</u> team. (arrow from *their* to *Kayla and Serena*; arrow from *their* to *team*)
9. <u>My</u> best shot ever was a hole-in-one. (arrow from *my* to *shot*; no antecedent)
10. The last hole on the golf course was <u>its</u> most challenging one. (arrow from *its* to *golf course*; arrow from *its* to *one*)
11. The waterfall near the hole was <u>its</u> biggest obstacle. (arrow from *its* to *hole*; arrow from *its* to *obstacle*)
12. Cheri hit <u>her</u> third shot right into the water. (arrow from *her* to *Cheri*; arrow from *her* to *shot*)
13. Martin will show us <u>his</u> final scorecard. (arrow from *his* to *Martin*; arrow from *his* to *scorecard*)
14. Sam and I practiced for hours to improve <u>our</u> scores. (arrow from *our* to *Sam and I*; arrow from *our* to *scores*)
15. Sean promises that next year the championship will be <u>his</u>. (arrow from *his* to *Sean*; arrow from *his* to *championship*)

Critical Viewing

Compare and Contrast Encourage students to compare these racquets to others with respect to size, handle length, and materials.

Demonstrative Adjectives

1. Like possessive adjectives, demonstrative adjectives are pronouns that modify nouns.

2. Write the following examples on the board for practice.

   That pitch was a strike. *(adj)*

   That was a strike. *(pron)*

   This is a great game. *(pron)*

   This game is great. *(adj)*

Customize for
Less Advanced Students

Clarify for students that *this* and *these* refer to things close to the speaker, or subject, while *that* and *those* commonly refer to things away from or other than the speaker or subject of the sentence. For example, *this book* refers to the book you are holding; *that book* refers to the book you are pointing to on the shelf.

Answer Key

> **Exercise 7**

1. That—adj	9. Those—pron
2. These—pron	10. That—pron
3. this—adj	11. these—adj
4. these—adj	12. These—pron
5. This—pron	13. this—pron
6. this—pron	14. those—adj
7. that—adj	15. this—adj
8. Those—adj	

> **Exercise 8**

Answers will vary. Samples are given.

1. This book is mine. This belongs to her.
2. That pencil is red. That writes better.
3. Those flowers are pretty. Those grow fast.
4. These cookies taste good. These cook faster.

16.1

Demonstrative Adjectives

The four demonstrative pronouns *this*, *that*, *these*, and *those* are often used as adjectives.

PRONOUN: That is difficult.

ADJECTIVE: That game is difficult.

PRONOUN: Try these.

ADJECTIVE: These darts are nicely balanced.

When *this*, *that*, *these*, or *those* appears immediately before a noun, that word is functioning as a *demonstrative adjective*.

> **Exercise 7** Classifying Demonstrative Pronouns and Adjectives On your paper, indicate whether the underlined word in each sentence is being used as an *adjective* or as a *pronoun*.

1. That game of darts looks like fun.
2. These are the arrows that players have found to be the most accurate.
3. Did you know this rule?
4. I learned that these rules were made more than a hundred years ago.
5. This is a fun game even today.
6. British rules say that this is the correct way to throw.
7. The distance to that target is approximately eight feet.
8. Those champions have great aim.
9. Those are the players who usually win.
10. That is not my best score.
11. Is there a way we can improve these scores?
12. These are the methods we have been taught.
13. When I reached for the dart, I noticed this.
14. I watched as those players practiced new ways to throw their darts.
15. I expect this date to go down in history as the day I won the club championship.

> **Exercise 8** Writing Sentences With Demonstrative Pronouns and Adjectives Using each word below, write two sentences. In the first sentence, use the word as an adjective before a noun. In the second sentence, use the word as a pronoun.

1. this   2. that   3. those   4. these

338 • Adjectives and Adverbs

More Practice

Language Lab
CD-ROM
• Adjectives lesson
On-line
Exercise Bank
• Section 16.1

☑ ONGOING ASSESSMENT: Assess Mastery

Use the following resources to assess student mastery of adjectives.

In the Textbook	Technology
Chapter Review, Ex. 28–33, pp. 346–347 Standardized Test Preparation Workshop, pp. 348–349	Language Lab CD-ROM, Using Modifiers; On-Line Exercise Bank, Section 16.1

Section 16.1 Section Review

GRAMMAR EXERCISES 9–16

Exercise 9 Identifying Adjectives
Identify the adjectives in each sentence, and tell the questions they answer.

1. Computer games are played in many homes.
2. These games fill store shelves.
3. The first games were simple.
4. Then, game technology advanced.
5. There are learning, adventure, and sports games.
6. A single player competes against the computer.
7. They have realistic sounds and special effects.
8. Modern games have detailed animation.
9. Some games feature virtual reality.
10. Computer games may improve hand-eye coordination.

Exercise 10 Using Indefinite Articles Write out each phrase. Replace the blank with the correct indefinite article.

1. ___?___ personal computer
2. ___?___ arcade game
3. ___?___ ice hockey competition
4. ___?___ new adventure series
5. ___?___ useful progam

Exercise 11 Identifying Proper Adjectives List the proper adjectives in these sentences and the nouns they modify.

1. Boccie is an Italian game.
2. Different versions are played in many European countries.
3. English settlers introduced the game in their colonies.
4. It was modified by American players.
5. There are also British and Australian varieties.

Exercise 12 Recognizing Possessive Adjectives Underline each possessive adjective, and draw arrows to its antecedent and to the word it modifies.

1. Shovel board was developed in England, where its popularity began.
2. The king banned it among his archers.
3. They spent too much of their time on it.
4. Shuffleboard got its name in 1924.
5. Travelers play it often on their cruises.

Exercise 13 Classifying Pronouns and Adjectives Label the underlined word *adjective* or *pronoun*.

1. These people are playing shuffleboard.
2. Those are the discs they will push.
3. The rules say this shot is your last.
4. That is the stick called a cue.
5. That disc is not a winner.

Exercise 14 Find It in Your Reading Read the excerpt from *The Pigman & Me* on page 333. Which adjectives answer the question *Which one?*

Exercise 15 Find It in Your Writing Look through your portfolio for a paragraph that describes a person or thing. Underline the adjectives you used.

Exercise 16 Writing Application Write a paragraph describing a game you like to play. Use adjectives to add interesting details to your description. Underline the adjectives.

Section Review • 339

ASSESS

Section Review

Each of these exercises correlates to the instruction on adjectives, pages 330–338. These exercises may be used for more practice, for reteaching, or for review of the Key Concepts presented. All chapter exercises are available in *Grammar Exercises Answers on Transparencies* in your Teaching Resources.

Answer Key

Exercise 9

1. Computer—What kind? many—How many?
2. These, store—Which ones?
3. first—Which one?, simple—What kind?
4. game—What kind?
5. learning, adventure, sports—What kind?
6. single—How many?
7. realistic, special—What kind?
8. Modern, detailed—What kind?
9. Some—How many?, virtual—What kind?
10. Computer—What kind? hand-eye—What kind?

Exercise 10

1. a personal computer
2. an arcade game
3. an ice hockey competition
4. a new adventure series
5. a useful program

Exercise 11

1. Italian—game
2. European—countries
3. English—settlers
4. American—players
5. British—varieties, Australian—varieties

Exercise 12

1. its (arrow from *its* to *Shovel board*; arrow from *its* to *popularity*)
2. his (arrow from *his* to *king*; arrow from *his* to *archers*)
3. their (arrow from *their* to *They*; arrow from *their* to *time*)
4. its (arrow from *its* to *Shuffleboard*; arrow from *its* to *name*)
5. their (arrow from *their* to *Travelers*; arrow from *their* to *cruises*)

continued

Answer Key continued

Exercise 13

1. These—adjective
2. Those—pronoun
3. this—adjective
4. That—pronoun
5. That—adjective

Exercise 14

Find It in Your Reading
one, another—answer the question *Which way?*, gym—answers the question *Which period?*, first—answers the question *Which Friday?*

Exercise 15

Find It in Your Writing
Also have students identify the word(s) each adjective modifies. Challenge students to substitute new adjectives for the ones they originally used.

Exercise 16

Writing Application
Students might trade their paragraphs with partners and suggest different adjectives.

Interest GRABBER Ask students *where, when,* or *in what way* they last played a sport such tennis or baseball. Point out that adverbs, like adjectives, help us to express ourselves more clearly.

Activate Prior Knowledge

Write the following two sentences on the board and ask students to note how two similar words, *grumpy* and *grumpily,* fulfill different purposes.

The grumpy dog growled at us.

The dog growled grumpily at us.

Lead students to see that in the first sentence, the adjective *grumpy* modifies the noun *dog,* while in the second sentence the adverb *grumpily* modifies the verb *growled.* Words that modify verbs are called *adverbs.*

Critical Viewing

Describe Students may suggest *clearly, frighteningly, loudly.*

TEACH

Step-by-Step Teaching Guide

Adverbs

1. Like adjectives, adverbs make language more specific. They answer the following questions: *When? Where? In what way?* or *To what extent?*

   The band played *wonderfully.*

   The concert started *late.*

   They played *here.*

2. Review commonly used adverbs. Write each question that adverbs answer as a heading on the board and ask students to suggest adverbs that fit in each column.

3. Point out to students that there are two components to the question *To what extent?: how much* and *how often.*

Answer Key

▶ Exercise 17

1. loudly
2. quickly
3. often
4. very
5. usually
6. frequently
7. most
8. closely
9. widely
10. early

340

Adverbs

Adverbs are words that modify other words, just as adjectives do. Adverbs most often modify verbs. The first word in each of the following phrases is an adverb: *slowly twisted, skillfully reads, quickly hides.*

Adverbs also modify adjectives and other adverbs. In the sentence *The game was very exciting,* the adverb *very* modifies the adjective *exciting.* In *They played extremely well,* the adverb *extremely* modifies the adverb *well.*

▶ **KEY CONCEPT** An **adverb** is a word that modifies a verb, an adjective, or another adverb. ■

Adverbs answer several questions when they modify verbs.

WHAT ADVERBS TELL ABOUT VERBS	
Where?	He lives <u>nearby</u>.
	I looked <u>inside</u>.
When?	Janice played <u>yesterday</u>.
	The message arrived <u>early</u>.
In What Way?	The musician performed <u>perfectly</u>.
	The dancers moved <u>gracefully</u>.
To What Extent?	Amy <u>fully</u> agrees with me.
	I am <u>totally</u> opposed to it.

▶ **Exercise 17** **Identifying Adverbs** Identify the adverb that modifies the underlined word in each sentence.

EXAMPLE: The wolves playfully <u>fought</u> with each other.

ANSWER: playfully

1. Wolves <u>howl</u> loudly to establish their territory.
2. The sounds <u>travel</u> quickly to other wolves.
3. They often <u>communicate</u> in this way.
4. Wolves have very <u>accurate</u> hearing.
5. Howling usually <u>expresses</u> their excitement as well.
6. Howling frequently <u>occurs</u> before a hunt.
7. Howls are one of the most <u>effective</u> ways to attract a mate.
8. Wolves <u>listen</u> closely and follow the howls.
9. Wolf habitats <u>range</u> widely in North America.
10. When wolves <u>awaken</u> early in the morning, they howl to greet the new day.

Theme: Wolves

In this section, you will learn that adverbs are used to describe verbs, adjectives, and other adverbs. The examples and exercises in this section are about wolves.

Cross-Curricular Connection: Science

▼ Critical Viewing Identify three adverbs that could tell in what way a wolf howls. [Describe]

⏱ TIME AND RESOURCE MANAGER

Resources
Print: Grammar Exercise Workbook, pp. 29–32; Hands-on Grammar Activity Book, Chapter 16; Grammar Exercises Answers on Transparencies, Chapter 16
Technology: Language Lab CD-ROM, Using Modifiers; On-Line Exercise Bank, Section 16.2

In-Depth Coverage	Accelerated Pace
• Work through all key concepts, pp. 340–343. • Assign and review Exercises 17–20. • Read and discuss Grammar in Literature, p. 341. • Do the Hands-on Grammar activity, p. 344.	• Assign pp. 340–343 for independent student review. • Review Adverb or Adjective? and assign Exercises 23–24. • Assign Section Review Exercises 21–24.

GRAMMAR IN LITERATURE

from **Mowgli's Brothers**
Rudyard Kipling

Notice in the following sentence that the adverbs down *and* clearly *modify the verb* lays. Down *tells where, and* clearly *tells in what way.* Very *modifies* clearly *by telling to what extent.*

. . . The Law of the Jungle lays *down very clearly* that any wolf may, when he marries, withdraw from the Pack. . . .

KEY CONCEPT When adverbs modify adjectives or adverbs, they answer the question *To what extent?*. ■

ADVERB MODIFYING A VERB:	The mother <u>tenderly</u> moved the pup.
ADVERB MODIFYING AN ADJECTIVE:	A <u>very</u> kind woman helped me.
ADVERB MODIFYING ANOTHER ADVERB:	The males hunt <u>extremely</u> well.

Exercise 18 Identifying Adverbs and the Words They Modify On your paper, identify the adverb(s) in each sentence. Then, write the word that each adverb modifies.

EXAMPLE: Wolves live socially in packs.
ANSWER: socially (live)

1. A double layer of fur effectively covers a wolf.
2. The underfur grows very thick in the cold months.
3. An outer layer fully repels snow and water.
4. A wolf often lies near trees or rocks during a storm.
5. This location shelters it very effectively from wind.
6. The wolf curls up tightly into a ball.
7. Its tail completely covers its nose.
8. During the spring, the underfur sheds quickly.
9. That way, the wolf survives the extremely hot months.
10. Wolves can live happily in almost any climate.

⚙ Grammar ⚙ and Style Tip

To keep your writing interesting, use adverbs to modify verbs, adjectives, and other adverbs. Just be sure not to overuse them.

More Practice

Language Lab CD-ROM
• Adjectives lesson
On-line Exercise Bank
• Section 16.2
Grammar Exercise Workbook
• Section 29–30

Adverbs • 341

Step-by-Step Teaching Guide

Grammar in Literature

1. Have a volunteer read aloud the Kipling passage.
2. Read aloud the passage to students—without the adverbs.

   The Law of the Jungle says that any wolf may, when he marries, withdraw from the Pack.

   Have students discuss what effect removing the adverbs has.

More About the Author

Rudyard Kipling (1865–1936) was a British writer of verse and short stories who won the Nobel Prize in 1907. Kipling was born in India, and many of his works are set in the great empire of Victorian Britain. He was a great patriot and advocate for the British Empire. Kipling's stories from *The Jungle Books* have entranced generations of children.

Answer Key

▶ **Exercise 18**

1. effectively—covers
2. very—thick; thick—grows
3. fully—repels
4. often—lies
5. very—effectively; effectively—shelters
6. tightly—curls
7. completely—covers
8. quickly—sheds
9. extremely—hot
10. happily—live

Customize for
Bodily/Kinesthetic Learners

Write some adverbs on slips of paper. Have students choose a slip and, one at a time, act out the adverb in front of the class. After sixty seconds, the rest of the class should try to guess the word. Guesses may be called out or written down. Help students ensure that their guesses take the form of adverbs.

Adverb or Adjective?

1. Since many adverbs and adjectives share the same form, students must determine the part of speech of the word being modified. Write the following examples on the board:

   It was a <u>long</u> class. (adjective, modifies noun class*)*

   The wolf howled all night <u>long</u>. (adverb, modifies verb howled*)*

2. Write the following phrases on the board and review with students for additional practice:

Adjectives	Adverbs
hard work	He works hard.
a late class	He arrived late.
a fast pitch	He pitched fast.
a slow song	Go slow.
an early bird	He arrived early.

3. Write these additional *-ly* adjectives on the board and review them with students.

   daily class

   kindly teacher

   lively child

   lovely park

   homely moose

Customize for
More Advanced Students

Have partners each write a brief paragraph in which the only modifiers (except for articles) that they use end in *-ly*. Then have them exchange papers and identify each modifier as either an adjective or adverb. They should support their identification by identifying the word and part of speech the word modifies.

16.2

Adverb or Adjective?

You may sometimes have to think carefully before identifying a word as an adverb or an adjective. The reason is that some words may be used as an adverb in one sentence and as an adjective in another.

> **KEY CONCEPT** If a noun or pronoun is modified by a word, that modifying word is an *adjective*. If a verb, adjective, or adverb is modified by a word, that modifying word is an adverb. ■

The next examples show how the word *right* is used as an adverb in the first sentence and as an adjective in the second.

ADVERB: When the wolves reached the clearing, they turned <u>right</u>.
(*Right* modifies the verb *turned*.)

ADJECTIVE: This is the <u>right</u> spot to view the wolves safely.
(*Right* modifies the noun *spot*.)

Adjectives and adverbs also answer different questions. Adjectives answer the questions *What kind? Which one? How many?* and *How much?* Adverbs answer the questions *Where? When? In what way?* and *To what extent?*

To decide whether a word is an adjective or an adverb, look at the part of speech of the word it modifies. Then, decide which question it answers about the word it modifies.

ADVERB: The pack stopped <u>short</u> outside the forest. (*Short* modifies the verb *stopped* and tells *in what way* the pack stopped.)

ADJECTIVE: The pack made a <u>short</u> stop outside the forest. (*Short* modifies the noun *stop* and tells *what kind* of stop.)

Note also that while many words that end in *-ly* are adverbs, some are not. Several adjectives also end in *-ly*. These adjectives are formed by adding *-ly* to certain nouns, such as *friend, prince,* or *shape.*

EXAMPLES: Wolves are not very <u>friendly</u> animals.
The leader of the pack had a <u>princely</u> attitude.

Spelling Tip

Some adjectives can be changed into adverbs by adding *-ly* to the end of the word. For example, in *I was careful, careful* is an adjective, but in *I looked carefully, carefully* is an adverb.

▶ **Exercise 19** Distinguishing Between Adverbs and Adjectives Tell whether each underlined word in the sentences below is an adverb or an adjective.

EXAMPLE: I saw a <u>wild</u> wolf.

ANSWER: adjective

1. Wolves travel <u>far</u> when they hunt.
2. Their prey takes them over the <u>far</u> horizons.
3. When they see prey, they move <u>near</u>.
4. The wolf failed at the hunt, but it was a <u>near</u> miss.
5. Wolves circle their prey and begin a <u>forward</u> movement.
6. As they inch <u>forward</u>, the wolves threaten their prey.
7. They try <u>hard</u> not to miss.
8. Hunting for food is a <u>hard</u> life.
9. Trying to find food is a <u>daily</u> event.
10. However, the wolves do not eat <u>daily</u>.

▶ **Exercise 20** Writing Sentences With Adverbs and Adjectives Use each numbered pair of words in a sentence. Write the sentence on a separate sheet of paper. Tell whether the underlined word is an adjective or adverb, and identify the word it modifies.

EXAMPLE: <u>wild</u> wolf

ANSWER: The <u>wild</u> wolf ran free in the woods. (adjective modifying *wolf*)

1. <u>distant</u> howling
2. move <u>close</u>
3. <u>close</u> call
4. <u>fast</u> rabbit
5. run <u>fast</u>

▶ **More Practice**

Language Lab CD-ROM
• Adjectives lesson
On-line Exercise Bank
• Section 16.2
Grammar Exercise Workbook
• pp. 31–32

◀ Critical Viewing
How would you distinguish between the wolf in this picture and the one on page 340? **[Compare and Contrast]**

Adverbs • **343**

Answer Key

▶ **Exercise 19**

1. adverb
2. adjective
3. adverb
4. adjective
5. adjective
6. adverb
7. adverb
8. adjective
9. adjective
10. adverb

▶ **Exercise 20**

Answers will vary. Samples are given.

1. The wolves' <u>distant</u> howling disturbed the sheep. (adjective modifying *howling*)
2. The wolves often move <u>close</u> at night. (adverb modifying *move*)
3. That was a <u>close</u> call. (adjective modifying *call*)
4. A <u>fast</u> rabbit outwits them. (adjective modifying *rabbit*)
5. The wolves run <u>fast</u>. (adverb modifying *run*)

Critical Viewing

Compare and Contrast Encourage students to compare the positions of the wolves and their actions.

☑ **ONGOING ASSESSMENT: Monitor and Reinforce**

If students have difficulty with Exercises 18–20, refer them to the following for additional practice.

In the Textbook	Print Resources	Technology
Section Review, Ex. 23–24, p. 345	Grammar Exercise Workbook, pp. 29–32	Language Lab CD-ROM, Using Modifiers; On-Line Exercise Bank, Section 16.2

⏱ **TIME SAVERS!**

Answers on Transparency Use the Grammar Exercises Answers on Transparencies for Chapter 16 to facilitate correction by students.

On-Line Exercise Bank Have students complete the exercises on computer. The Auto Check feature will grade their work for you!

Adjective or Adverb Slide

Teaching Resources: Hands-on Grammar Activity Book, Chapter 16

1. Have students refer to their Hands-on Grammar activity books or give them copies of the relevant pages.

2. Be sure students understand that many words can function as both adjectives and adverbs. The part of speech depends on what the word modifies.

3. After students identify adverbs that modify verbs, have them suggest adverbs that modify adjectives or other adverbs.

4. Have students use adjective-noun combinations and adverb-verb combinations in sentences.

Find It in Your Reading

Have students use these pairs in sentences also.

Find It in Your Writing

Have students attempt to use their adjectives as adverbs and their adverbs as adjectives.

16.2

Hands-on Grammar

Adjective or Adverb Slide

Create a three-window frame for sliding word strips, as in the model below. Then, create three word strips. The first word strip should list nouns, such as *job, decision, side, movement,* and *destination*. The second word strip should list a mix of adjectives and adverbs, including words that can function both as adjectives and as adverbs, such as *daily, hard, far,* and *forward*. The third strip should list verbs, such as *work, play,* and *move*. Leave enough blank space at the end of each strip to allow the strip to remain in the slots as it moves to the right and to the left. Label the front of the windows as shown.

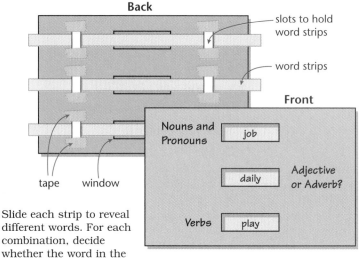

Slide each strip to reveal different words. For each combination, decide whether the word in the center window can modify the word in the upper window, the lower window, or both. Based on the part of speech each word modifies, determine whether it functions as an adverb or an adjective. (Although only verbs are used in the bottom window, remember that adverbs can also modify adjectives and other adverbs.)

Find It in Your Reading In your reading, find examples of words that can function both as adverbs and as adjectives. Create strips to challenge a partner to identify how these words function when they modify different parts of speech.

Find It in Your Writing Look through samples of your own writing to find words that modify other words. Identify the part of speech being modified, and then identify the modifier as an adjective or an adverb.

344 • Adjectives and Adverbs

⏱ TIME SAVERS!

✋ **Hands-on Grammar Book**
Use the Hands-on Grammar activity sheet for Chapter 16 to facilitate this activity.

☑ ONGOING ASSESSMENT: Assess Mastery

Use the following resources to assess student mastery of adverbs.

In the Textbook	Print Resources	Technology
Chapter Review, Ex. 34–37, p. 347 Standard Test Preparation Workshop, pp. 348–349	Formal Assessment, Chapter 16	Language Lab CD-ROM, Using Modifiers; On-Line Exercise Bank, Section 16.2

Section 16.2 Section Review

GRAMMAR EXERCISES 21–27

Exercise 21 Identifying Adverbs
On your paper, write the adverb that modifies each underlined word or phrase.

1. Wolves closely resemble other animals.
2. The coyote is very similar looking.
3. However, the coyote weighs much less.
4. Dogs and wild wolves are somewhat related.
5. No one has tamed wolves successfully.

Exercise 22 Identifying Adverbs and the Words They Modify Identify the adverb(s) in each sentence. Then, write the word or phrase each adverb modifies.

1. The gray wolf is sometimes called the timber wolf.
2. It was once found in North America, Europe, and Asia.
3. Wolves are equally comfortable in many environments.
4. During the winter, they travel together to find food.
5. In packs, wolves are very cooperative.
6. They live closely with their families.
7. Pups wrestle playfully to practice hunting skills.
8. Wolves usually hunt weak animals.
9. They run easily and rarely tire.
10. For small animals, wolves hunt alone.

Exercise 23 Distinguishing Between Adverbs and Adjectives Label each underlined word *adverb* or *adjective*.

1. Wolf puppies grow quickly.
2. New wolf mothers can be unfriendly.
3. The small wolves chew hard on bones.
4. Their hard teeth make a loud sound.
5. The pups nearly always stay close to their mother.

Exercise 24 Understanding Adverbs and Adjectives Copy each sentence. Underline the adverbs, and circle the adjectives, other than articles. Then, draw an arrow from each adjective or adverb to the word it modifies.

1. Each pack has a lead male.
2. Other males willingly obey him.
3. An alpha female firmly leads the others.
4. Every wolf is then ranked accordingly.
5. Leaders are strong and usually quite large.
6. The order often results in fewer fights.
7. A wolf snarls menacingly to show confidence.
8. The back fur rises automatically.
9. The other wolf hangs his head down.
10. He rolls over to avoid a fight.

Exercise 25 Find It in Your Reading Locate each adverb and the word it modifies in this sentence from "Mowgli's Brothers" by Rudyard Kipling.

Mowgli was still deeply interested in the pebbles, and he did not notice when the wolves came and looked at him. . . .

Exercise 26 Find It in Your Writing Look through your portfolio for a paragraph that describes how someone did something. Circle any adverbs you used. If you didn't use any adverbs, challenge yourself to add some.

Exercise 27 Writing Application Write a short description of an animal that you have observed or read about. Use modifiers to help describe how the animal behaves. Underline every adverb you use.

Section Review • 345

ASSESS and CLOSE

Section Review
Each of these exercises correlates with a concept covered in the section on using adverbs, pages 340–344. These exercises may be used for more practice, for reteaching, or for review of the Key Concepts presented. All chapter exercises are available in *Grammar Exercises Answers on Transparencies* in your teaching resources.

Answer Key

Exercise 21
1. closely 4. somewhat
2. very 5. successfully
3. much

Exercise 22
1. sometimes—called
2. once—found
3. equally—comfortable
4. together—travel
5. very—cooperative
6. closely—live
7. playfully—wrestle
8. usually—hunt
9. easily—run, rarely—tire
10. alone—hunt

Exercise 23
1. adverb 4. adjective
2. adjective 5. adverb
3. adverb

Exercise 24
1. Each pack has a lead male. (arrow from *Each* to *pack*; arrow from *lead* to *male*)
2. Other males willingly obey him. (arrow from *Other* to *males*; arrow from *willingly* to *obey*)
3. An alpha female firmly leads the others. (arrow from *alpha* to *female*; arrow from *firmly* to *leads*)
4. Every wolf is then ranked accordingly. (arrow from *Every* to *wolf*; arrow from *accordingly* to *ranked*)
5. Leaders are strong and usually quite large. (arrow from *strong* to *Leaders*; arrow from *usually* to *large*; arrow from *quite* to *large*; arrow from *large* to *Leaders*)
6. The order often results in fewer fights. (arrow from *often* to *results in*; arrow from *fewer* to *fights*)
7. A wolf snarls menacingly to show confidence. (arrow from *menacingly* to *snarls*)

continued

Answer Key continued

8. The back fur rises automatically. (arrow from *back* to *fur*; arrow from *automatically* to *rises*)
9. The other wolf hangs his head down. (arrow from *other* to *wolf*; arrow from *his* to *head*; arrow from *down* to *hangs*)
10. He rolls over to avoid a fight. (arrow from *over* to *rolls*)

Exercise 25
Find It in Your Reading
still—interested, deeply—interested, not—did notice

Exercise 26
Find It in Your Writing
Students can replace the existing adverbs with more descriptive ones.

Exercise 27
Writing Application
Suggest that students compare their descriptions with those of classmates who chose the same animal.

CHAPTER REVIEW

Each of these exercises correlates with a section of the chapter on adjectives and adverbs, pages 330–345. These exercises may be used for more practice, for reteaching, or for review of the Key Concepts presented. Answers for all chapter exercises are available in *Grammar Exercises Answers on Transparencies* in your Teaching Resources.

Answer Key

Exercise 28

1. close—relatives
2. larger—ears, shorter—muzzles
3. Their—habits, different—habits
4. social—groups
5. their—parents
6. Single—coyotes, unprotected—sheep
7. weak—animals, small—animals
8. North American—regions
9. eastern—expansion, Atlantic—coast
10. suburban—areas

Exercise 29

Possible answers.

1. excellent
2. thick
3. black, pointed
4. furry
5. hard

Exercise 30

1. a timber wolf
2. an abundant species
3. a large pack
4. an alpha female
5. a young animal

Exercise 31

1. Arctic wolves
2. Alaskan wolves
3. American states
4. North Carolinian coast
5. Mexican wolves

Chapter

16 Chapter Review

GRAMMAR EXERCISES 28–39

Exercise 28 Identifying Adjectives and the Words They Modify
On your paper, write the adjectives in each sentence and the word each modifies.

1. Coyotes are close relatives of wolves.
2. They have larger ears and shorter muzzles.
3. Their habits are also very different.
4. Coyotes do not live in social groups.
5. Pups leave their parents after they grow.
6. Single coyotes hunt unprotected sheep.
7. They also seek weak, small animals.
8. They live in many North American regions.
9. Their eastern expansion has reached the Atlantic coast.
10. Coyotes are seen in suburban areas.

Exercise 29 Supplying Adjectives
On your paper, supply an adjective to modify the underlined word. Use the pictures in the preceding section to help you.

1. Wolves are __?__ hunters.
2. They have __?__ fur.
3. A wolf has a __?__ nose and __?__ ears.
4. A wolf's tail is __?__.
5. The teeth are probably __?__.

Exercise 30 Using Indefinite Articles Write out each phrase, replacing the blank with the correct indefinite article.

1. __?__ timber wolf
2. __?__ abundant species
3. __?__ large pack
4. __?__ alpha female
5. __?__ young animal

Exercise 31 Revision Practice: Proper Adjectives Revise each sentence, replacing the underlined phrase with a proper adjective. You may need to rearrange some words in the sentence.

1. Wolves of the Arctic are usually white.
2. Some people call them wolves of Alaska.
3. States in America like Minnesota also have these wolves.
4. The coast of North Carolina is the habitat for red wolves.
5. Wolves of Mexico once had a much wider range than they do now.

Exercise 32 Supplying Possessive Adjectives Copy each sentence. Supply the possessive adjective to fill in the blank. Then, draw an arrow connecting the possessive adjective to the noun it modifies.

1. Coyotes do most of __?__ hunting at night.
2. A female has __?__ pups in the spring.
3. A wolf brings meat to __?__ den to feed the pups.
4. A father coyote helps raise __?__ pups.
5. A coyote stays with __?__ mate for life.

Exercise 33 Distinguishing Between Pronouns and Adjectives
Identify whether the underlined word is functioning as an adjective or a pronoun.

1. These are western coyotes.
2. This red color is one of their particular characteristics.
3. We consider those animals to be very similar.

Exercise 32

1. Coyotes do most of their hunting at night. (arrow from *their* to *hunting*)
2. A female has her pups in the spring. (arrow from *her* to *pups*)
3. A wolf brings meat to its den to feed the pups. (arrow from *its* to *den*)
4. A father coyote helps raise his pups. (arrow from *his* to *pups*)
5. A coyote stays with its mate for life. (arrow from *its* to *mate*)

Exercise 33

1. pronoun
2. adjective
3. adjective
4. pronoun
5. adjective

4. <u>This</u> is the bushy tail of a coyote.
5. It is different from <u>this</u> wolf tail.

Exercise 34   Recognizing Adverbs
Write the adverbs in each of the following sentences.

1. Foxes feed mostly on small rodents.
2. They often hunt alone, rather than in packs.
3. Swift runners, foxes are very agile.
4. They bravely defend their territory from intruders.
5. This territory usually measures about three square miles.

Exercise 35   Identifying Adverbs and the Words They Modify
Write down each adverb and the word it modifies.

1. The red fox is easily recognized.
2. Its tail often grows a white tip.
3. The black ears and feet are very noticeable.
4. Its reddish-brown coat is quite lovely.
5. Its range stretches widely across North America, Europe, and Asia.
6. Red foxes have even been seen in Africa and the Arctic.
7. They adapt to entirely new environments quickly.
8. The red fox lives easily near humans.
9. It uses its very keen senses to stay quite camouflaged.
10. Its food sources vary greatly.

Exercise 36   Distinguishing Between Adverbs and Adjectives
Tell whether each underlined word in the sentences below is an adverb or adjective.

1. Foxes spend the <u>early</u> spring near a den.
2. They fit <u>snugly</u> into enlarged groundhog holes.
3. The young stay in the den for <u>nearly</u> five weeks.
4. They are born with their eyes closed <u>fast</u>.

5. In the fall, the young make a <u>fast</u> trip away from the home territory.

Exercise 37   Revision Practice:
Adverbs and Adjectives Add adjectives and adverbs to the following paragraph. You may need to add words other than adjectives and adverbs for the new paragraph to make sense.

Wolves, dogs, foxes, and coyotes are all part of a family. They have habits and instincts. They travel to find food. When they hunt, they move. Eyes help them see prey, but the sense of smell helps them find prey. Fur keeps them warm when they can't be in a den. Wolves hunt as a pack, but foxes hunt alone.

Exercise 38   CUMULATIVE REVIEW
Nouns, Pronouns, and Verbs Copy the following paragraph onto your paper. Underline each noun once and each verb twice. Circle each personal or demonstrative pronoun.

(1) Three concerned naturalists formed the organization Wolf Help to help people better understand wolves. (2) They travel around the country, give lectures, and show photographs. (3) If you are worried about the survival of wolves, you might contact Wolf Help. (4) You may also enjoy a video called *Winter Wolf*. (5) This is about a fourteen-year-old Native American girl who learns what wolves meant to her ancestors.

Exercise 39   Writing Application
Write a descriptive paragraph about a pet that you have had or one that you would like. Give your reader a clear picture of the pet—how it looks and how it acts. Use at least one adjective and one adverb in each sentence. Underline the adverbs, and circle the adjectives that you use.

Chapter Review • **347**

Exercise 34
1. mostly
2. alone
3. very
4. bravely
5. usually

Exercise 35
1. easily—recognized
2. often—grows
3. very—noticeable
4. quite—lovely
5. widely—stretches
6. even—been seen
7. entirely—new, quickly—adapt
8. easily—lives
9. very—keen, quite—camouflaged
10. greatly—vary

Exercise 36
1. adjective
2. adverb
3. adverb
4. adverb
5. adjective

Exercise 37
Possible answer:

Wolves, dogs, foxes, and coyotes are all part of a scientific family. They have similar habits and instincts. They travel widely to find favorite foods. When they hunt, they often move quickly. Sharp eyes help them see their prey well, but their sense of smell helps them find desired prey easily. Soft fur keeps them very warm when they can't be in a safe den. Wolves hunt as a pack, but foxes usually hunt alone.

Exercise 38
Cumulative Review
(1) Three concerned <u>naturalists</u> <u>formed</u> the <u>organization</u> <u>Wolf Help</u> to help <u>people</u> better <u>understand</u> <u>wolves</u>. (2)(They)<u>travel</u> around the <u>country</u>, <u>give</u> <u>lectures</u>, and <u>show</u> <u>photographs</u>. (3) If(you)<u>are</u> <u>worried</u> about the <u>survival</u> of <u>wolves</u>,(you)<u>might</u> <u>contact</u> <u>Wolf Help</u>. (4)(You)<u>may</u> also <u>enjoy</u> a <u>video</u> called <u>Winter Wolf</u>. (5)(This)<u>is</u> about a fourteen-year-old Native American <u>girl</u> who <u>learns</u> what <u>wolves</u> <u>meant</u> to(her)<u>ancestors</u>.

Exercise 39
Writing Application
Students should trade paragraphs with partners to comment and correct.

Step-by-Step Teaching Guide

Using Adjectives and Adverbs

Teaching Resources: Standardized Test Preparation Workbook, Chapter 16

1. Be sure students understand that one way to decide whether a word is an adjective and an adverb is to identify the part of speech it modifies.

2. Encourage students to combine sentences like those in the second example on their own before checking the answers given.

3. Usually students should be able to eliminate some choices easily before analyzing the remaining choices.

Standardized Test Preparation Workshop

Using Adjectives and Adverbs

A knowledge of how adjectives and adverbs function will help you answer several types of standardized test questions that measure your ability to express yourself effectively. The following test items will give you practice with items that measure your ability to use adjectives and adverbs.

Test Tip

- Read through the answer choices, and eliminate the ones that would change the meaning of the sentence.

Sample Test Items	Answers and Explanations
Directions Read the passage, and choose the letter of the word or group of words that belongs in each space. Yesterday, the class took a _____ bus ride to the museum. 1 A slowly B very C hardly D long	The correct answer is *D*. Because the word in the blank space is meant to modify *bus ride*, a noun, the only correct choice is an adjective.
Directions Read the passage. Some sections are underlined. Choose the best way to write the underlined section. Last year, we also took a bus trip. <u>We took a bus ride to the zoo. The bus ride was short.</u> 1 A We took a short bus ride to the zoo. B We took a short ride on the bus to the zoo. C We took a bus ride to the zoo that was short. D We took a bus ride. Short was the bus ride.	The correct answer is *A*. *We took a short bus ride* is the clearest and most effective way to express the underlined sentences. This choice does not change the meaning of the passage, and it is more to the point than the original.

✎ TEST-TAKING TIP

Encourage students to eliminate choices based on part of speech, sense, and how they sound in the sentence. For example, in the first sample item, students should be looking for an adjective to modify the noun *bus ride*. This eliminates all choices but D.

▶ **Practice 1** **Directions:** Read the passage, and choose the letter of the word or group of words that belongs in each space.

All my relatives gather ___(1)___ to celebrate the Fourth of July. We choose a spot that is ___(2)___ for everyone, so that each person can get there ___(3)___ . ___(4)___ we meet in a park. When we get together as a group, my family can be ___(5)___ .

1 A year
  B yearly
  C some
  D silly

2 F nearly
  G outside
  H conveniently
  J convenient

3 A fair
  B fairly
  C easy
  D easily

4 F Some
  G Sometimes
  H Frequent
  J Rare

5 A lately
  B soon
  C loud
  D loudly

▶ **Practice 2** **Directions:** Read the passage. Some sections are underlined. Choose the best way to write each underlined section.

The guide told a story. The story
                    (1)
was humorous. We all enjoyed the
                (2)
tale. The tale was funny. Then he

asked us a question. He asked if any-

one was curious about the origins of
                    (3)
the tale. Although nobody raised a

hand, it was obvious that we hoped he

would tell us. He had our attention.
                    (4)
That was certain. We had lunch. We
                    (5)
had lunch later in the cafeteria.

1 A The humorous guide told a story.
  B Humorously, the guide told a story.
  C The guide told a humorous story.
  D The guide told a story humorously.

2 F We all enjoyed the tale that was funny.
  G We all enjoyed the tale.
  H Funny, we all enjoyed the tale.
  J We all enjoyed the funny tale.

3 A He asked if anyone was curious about the tale's origins.
  B He asked, curiously, if anyone wanted to know the origin of the tale.
  C He asked if anyone wanted to know the origin of the curious tale.
  D Curious, he asked if anyone wanted to know the origin of the tale.

4 F Certain he had our attention.
  G He certainly had our attention.
  H He had our certain attention.
  J He had our attention.

5 A We had lunch in the cafeteria.
  B We were late to lunch in the cafeteria.
  C We had a late lunch in the cafeteria.
  D Later, we had lunch in the cafeteria.

▶ **Practice 1**
1. B
2. J
3. D
4. G
5. C

▶ **Practice 2**
1. C
2. J
3. A
4. G
5. D

Time and Resource Manager

In-Depth Lesson Plan

	LESSON FOCUS	PRINT AND MEDIA RESOURCES
DAY 1	**Prepositions** Students learn to identify and correctly use prepositions and do the Hands-on Grammar activity (pp. 352–357).	**Teaching Resources** *Grammar Exercise Workbook*, pp. 33–36; *Grammar Exercises Answers on Transparencies*, Ch. 17; *Hands-on Grammar Activity Book*, Chapter 17 **On-Line Exercise Bank**, Section 17
DAY 2	**Review and Assess** Students review chapter and demonstrate mastery of use of prepositions (pp. 358–361).	**Teaching Resources** *Formal Assessment*, Ch. 17; *Grammar Exercises Answers on Transparencies*, Ch. 17 **On-Line Exercise Bank**, Section 17

Accelerated Lesson Plan

	LESSON FOCUS	PRINT AND MEDIA RESOURCES
DAY 1	**Prepositions** Students cover concepts and usage of prepositions as determined by Diagnostic Test (pp. 352–357).	**Teaching Resources** *Grammar Exercise Workbook*, pp. 33–36; *Grammar Exercises Answers on Transparencies*, Ch. 17; *Hands-on Grammar Activity Book*, Chapter 17 **On-Line Exercise Bank**, Section 17
DAY 2	**Review and Assess** Students review chapter and demonstrate mastery of use of prepositions (pp. 358–361).	**Teaching Resources** *Formal Assessment*, Ch. 17; *Grammar Exercises Answers on Transparencies*, Ch. 17 **On-Line Exercise Bank**, Section 17

Options for Adapting Lesson Plans

HOMEWORK

Have students complete any section of the chapter for homework.

FEATURES

Extend coverage with the Grammar in Literature feature (p. 353), and the Standardized Test Preparation Workshop (p. 360).

TECHNOLOGY

Students can use the On-Line Exercise Bank to complete the exercises on computer. The Auto Check feature will grade their work.

INTEGRATED SKILLS COVERAGE

Grammar in Literature
SE p. 353

Reading
Find It in Your Reading SE pp. 357, 359

Writing
Find It in Your Writing SE pp. 357, 359
Writing Application SE p. 359

Workplace Skills
ATE p. 355

Viewing and Representing
Critical Viewing SE pp. 350, 354, 355

ASSESSMENT SUPPORT

Standardized Test Preparation Workshop SE p. 360; ATE p. 354
Standardized Test Preparation Workbook, pp. 33–34
Formal Assessment, Ch. 17

MEETING INDIVIDUAL NEEDS

Less Advanced Students ATE p. 357; See also Ongoing
Assessment ATE p. 356
Bodily/Kinesthetic Learners ATE p. 352
Visual/Spatial Learners ATE p. 353

BLOCK SCHEDULING

Pacing Suggestions
For 90-minute Blocks
• Administer the Diagnostic Test to students to determine
instructional coverage.
• Have students complete the necessary exercises in class. Use
the Hands-on Grammar activity to provide a change of pace.

Resources for Varying Instruction
• *Language Lab* **CD-ROM** If your students have access to
hardware, a 90-minute block provides an ideal opportunity for
students to work on computer.

Professional Development Support
• *How to Manage Instruction in the Block* This teaching
Resource provides management and activity suggestions.

MEDIA AND TECHNOLOGY

For the Student
• *On-Line Exercise Bank*, Ch. 17

For the Teacher
• *Resource Pro* **CD-ROM**

WRITING AND GRAMMAR WEB SITE

The Interactive Writing and Grammar Web site provides a wide
array of support for students, teachers, and parents. Grammar
support includes:

• On-Line Exercise Bank with Auto Check scoring
• Diagnostic and assessment support

www.phschool.com

LITERATURE CONNECTIONS

Grammar in Literature selections from *Prentice Hall Literature: Timeless Voices, Timeless Themes*, Copper:
from "Lou Gehrig: The Iron Horse," Bob Considine, SE p. 353

Lesson Objectives

1. To recognize prepositions in a sentence.
2. To recognize the difference between a preposition and an adverb.

Critical Viewing

Interpret Students may include in their responses such prepositions as *on* the playing field, *around* the bases, *into* the outfield, *at* home plate, *in* the nineteenth century.

Chapter 17 Prepositions

A nineteenth-century baseball game in progress

Some words are important simply because they show how other words are related to each other. They may not provide as much meaning as these other words, but they make it possible for them to do their work.

Prepositions are one of the kinds of words that serve this necessary function. Although many prepositions are short words—*at, on, by*—they have a big effect on meaning. For example, would a baseball player rather be *at* the base, *on* the base, or *by* the base?

In this chapter, you will learn how to recognize prepositions. Then, you will learn how to tell whether a word is being used as a preposition or an adverb. Finally, you will practice using prepositions.

▲ **Critical Viewing**
Describe the setting and the action in the field. Use at least two prepositions in your description. **[Interpret]**

350 • Prepositions

ONGOING ASSESSMENT: Diagnose

If students miss more than one item in any category, direct them to the relevant pages of the text and assign exercises for practice and review.

Prepositions	Diagnostic Test Items	Teach	Practice	Chapter Review
Skill Check A				
Identifying Prepositions	A 1–5	pp. 352–353	Ex. 2	Ex. 6
Skill Check B				
Identifying Prepositions	B 6–10	pp. 352–353	Ex. 2	Ex. 6
Skill Check C				
Supplying Prepositions	C 11–15	pp. 352–353	Ex. 3	Ex. 7

Diagnostic Test

Directions: Write all answers on a separate sheet of paper.

Skill Check A. Write the preposition(s) in each of the following sentences.

1. Games like baseball were played in ancient Egypt.
2. They were played for recreation or for ceremonial purposes.
3. By the Middle Ages, these games were played in Europe.
4. Their popularity spread across many countries.
5. Europeans brought these games to the Americas.

Skill Check B. Write the preposition(s) in each of the following sentences.

6. Aristocrats had no interest in regular baseball.
7. They played the game of cricket.
8. A game called *rounders* was more like baseball.
9. Like baseball, it had a system of hits and outs.
10. Runners ran around the bases.

Skill Check C. Copy each sentence below, replacing the blank with a preposition.

11. The rules varied ___?___ place to place.
12. Baseball was very unorganized ___?___ 1842.
13. The *Knickerbocker Base Ball Club* moved ___?___ modern baseball.
14. They set up the field ___?___ a home plate and three bases.
15. The Knickerbockers made the rule ___?___ foul lines.

Skill Check D. Replace the underlined preposition in the following sentences with a different preposition.

16. The Knickerbockers' style of baseball spread <u>during</u> the 1850's.
17. Its popularity spread <u>beyond</u> New York.
18. People all <u>across</u> the country formed teams.
19. At first, they played other teams <u>inside</u> their own states.
20. Professional baseball started with a team <u>in</u> Ohio, the Cincinnati Red Stockings.

Skill Check E. Identify the underlined word in each sentence below as a *preposition* or an *adverb*.

21. In 1869, baseball teams traveled <u>around</u>, playing outside their own areas.
22. More teams came <u>out</u> following the formation of the National League in 1876.
23. The American League was organized soon <u>after</u>.
24. The leagues fought <u>over</u> the best baseball players.
25. They searched for players <u>around</u> the country.

Answer Key

Diagnostic Test

Each item in the Diagnostic Test corresponds to a specific section of the prepositions chapter. This will enable you to tailor instruction to the particular needs of your students. See "Ongoing Assessment: Diagnose" below for further details.

Skill Check A

1. like, in	4. across
2. for, for	5. to
3. By, in	

Skill Check B

6. in	9. Like, of
7. of	10. around
8. like	

Skill Check C

Answers may vary. Samples are given.

11. The rules varied <u>from</u> place to place.
12. Baseball was very unorganized <u>until</u> 1842.
13. The *Knickerbocker Base Ball Club* moved <u>toward</u> modern baseball.
14. They set up the field <u>with</u> a home plate and three bases.
15. The Knickerbockers made the rule <u>for</u> foul lines.

Skill Check D

Answers may vary. Samples are given.

16. in	19. around
17. past	20. from
18. over	

Skill Check E

21. adverb	24. preposition
22. adverb	25. preposition
23. adverb	

✓ **ONGOING ASSESSMENT: Diagnose** *continued*

Prepositions	Diagnostic Test Items	Teach	Practice	Chapter Review
Skill Check D				
Replacing Prepositions	D 16–20	pp. 352–353	Ex. 1, 4	Ex. 8
Skill Check E				
Recognizing Prepositions and Adverbs	E 21–25	pp. 354–355	Ex. 5	Ex. 9–10
Cumulative Review and Applications				Ex. 11–13

⏱ **TIME SAVERS!**

📄 **Answers on Transparency**
Use the Grammar Exercises Answers on Transparencies for Chapter 17 to facilitate correction by students.

💻 **On-Line Exercise Bank**
Have students complete the Diagnostic Test on computer. The Auto Check feature will grade their work for you!

PREPARE and ENGAGE

Interest GRABBER Ask students to write a short paragraph in which they describe their route from the front doors of their homes to school. Have volunteers read their paragraphs to the class. Point out the prepositions to students and ask them how their paragraphs would be different without the prepositions.

Activate Prior Knowledge

Share a story about getting bad directions, or getting lost, emphasizing how important even a single preposition can be in communicating specific information.

TEACH

Step-by-Step Teaching Guide

Using Prepositions

1. Write the following sentences on the chalkboard. Ask students why each underlined word functions as a preposition.

   The team practiced baseball after school in the park. (prepositions tell when and where)

   One player hit the ball over the field into the trees. (prepositions tell where)

2. Explain that some prepositions are made up of more than one word and can describe a specific relationship between one noun and another.

3. Write the following sentences on the board. Ask students how each shows a relationship.

   The team needs to find a new hitter because of the last hitter's injury. The game was canceled due to a loss of equipment.

Customize for
Bodily/Kinesthetic Learners

Have students write the appropriate preposition describing the location or movement of your hand as you place it above, beneath, behind, etc., a stationary object.

17

Using Prepositions

Prepositions help a reader or listener understand the relationship of one word to another.

> **KEY CONCEPT** A **preposition** relates a noun or pronoun to another word in the sentence. ■

In the examples below, notice how changing the preposition also changes the meaning.

EXAMPLES:
The ball was hit <u>over</u> the fence.
The ball was hit <u>toward</u> the fence.
The ball was hit <u>through</u> the fence.
The ball was hit <u>into</u> the fence.
The ball was hit <u>around</u> the fence.

Some frequently used prepositions are listed in the following chart.

FIFTY PREPOSITIONS				
about	behind	during	off	to
above	below	except	on	toward
across	beneath	for	onto	under
after	beside	from	opposite	underneath
against	besides	in	out	until
along	between	inside	outside	up
among	beyond	into	over	upon
around	but	like	past	with
at	by	near	since	within
before	down	of	through	without

A few prepositions are made up of more than one word.

EXAMPLES:
That is the score <u>according to</u> the umpire.
We need good pitching <u>in addition to</u> good hitting.
The fielder's glove is <u>next to</u> the ball.
Today, he bats first <u>instead of</u> batting cleanup.
The game was postponed <u>on account of</u> rain.

> **Exercise 1** Substituting Prepositions Write at least five prepositions from the preceding chart that could logically replace the underlined preposition in the following sentence.

The stadium is located <u>opposite</u> the school.

Theme: Baseball
In this chapter you will learn about prepositions. The examples and exercises are about baseball.
Cross-Curricular Connection: Physical Education

⏱ TIME AND RESOURCE MANAGER

Resources
Print: Grammar Exercise Workbook, pp. 33–36; Hands-on Grammar Activity Book, Ch. 17; Grammar Exercises Answers on Transparencies, Chapter 17
Technology: On-Line Exercise Bank, Section 17

In-Depth Coverage	Accelerated Pace
• Work through all key concepts, pp. 352–355. • Assign and review Exercises 1–5. • Read and discuss Grammar in Literature, p. 353. • Do the Hands-on Grammar Activity, pp. 356–357.	• Assign pp. 352–355 for independent student review. • Assign Chapter Review Exercises 6–10, pp. 358–359.

▶ **Exercise 2** Identifying Prepositions Copy each sentence below and underline the preposition(s).

EXAMPLE: Let's go to the ball game.

ANSWER: Let's go <u>to</u> the ball game.

1. Lou Gehrig was the son of German immigrants.
2. He grew up in New York City.
3. Gehrig went to Columbia University.
4. He was discovered by scouts while playing baseball in Hartford.
5. Then, he signed with the New York Yankees.

▶ **Exercise 3** Supplying Prepositions Copy each sentence below, replacing the blank with a preposition. Use the chart to help you.

EXAMPLE: I will meet you __?__ the stadium.

ANSWER: I will meet you outside the stadium.

1. Gehrig was a Yankee __?__ 1923 __?__ 1939.
2. __?__ thirteen seasons, he played every game.
3. Gehrig played __?__ eight championship teams.
4. He hit 493 homers __?__ the outfield fence.
5. His batting average was __?__ .300 twelve times.

GRAMMAR IN
LITERATURE

from **Lou Gehrig: The Iron Horse**
Bob Considine

In the following excerpt, the prepositions are highlighted in blue.

After a game *at* Yankee Stadium he told Shirley Povich *of* the Washington *Post* and me that a frightening thing had happened *to* him while pitching *against* Gehrig. Joe had uncorked his high inside fast ball *with* the expectation that Lou would move back and take it, *as* a ball. Instead, Krakauskas said, Lou—a renowned judge *of* balls and strikes—moved closer *to* the plate.

▶ **More Practice**

Language Lab CD-ROM
• Prepositional Phrases lesson
On-line Exercise Bank
• Section 17
Grammar Exercise Workbook
• pp. 33–34

Prepositions • 353

Answer Key

▶ **Exercise 1** (from page 352)

Possible answers include

behind, across, from, past, by, beyond, beside, near

▶ **Exercise 2**

1. Lou Gehrig was the son <u>of</u> German immigrants.
2. He grew up <u>in</u> New York City.
3. Gehrig went <u>to</u> Columbia University.
4. He was discovered <u>by</u> scouts while playing baseball <u>in</u> Hartford.
5. Then, he signed <u>with</u> the New York Yankees.

▶ **Exercise 3**

Answers may vary. Samples are given.

1. Gehrig was a Yankee <u>from</u> 1923 <u>until</u> 1939.
2. <u>During</u> 13 seasons, he played every game.
3. Gehrig played <u>on</u> eight championship teams.
4. He hit 493 homers <u>over</u> the outfield fence.
5. His batting average was <u>above</u> .300 twelve times.

Step-by-Step Teaching Guide

Grammar in Literature

1. Read aloud the passage from *Lou Gehrig: The Iron Horse.*
2. After reviewing the highlighted prepositions, ask students to identify what information each preposition adds to the passage.
3. Ask students to suggest different prepositions. Discuss how each replacement changes the meaning of the passage.

Customize for
Visual/Spatial Learners

Have students design a game similar to baseball but with a different-shaped field, different number of players, and so on. Have them draw their playing field on paper or poster board and write the rules using prepositions in each sentence.

Distinguishing Between Prepositions and Adverbs

1. Explain to students that many words can be used as both prepositions and adverbs. Here's how to tell the difference: Prepositions are always part of a prepositional phrase. A prepositional phrase includes a preposition and a noun or pronoun.

2. Write the sentences below on the board. Ask students to point out the prepositional phrases, naming the nouns that are included.

   The team practiced baseball every day <u>after</u> school <u>in</u> the park. (after school, school; in the park, park)

   Each player tried to hit the ball <u>over</u> the field <u>into</u> the trees. (over the field, field; into the trees, trees)

3. Explain that adverbs can stand alone and not be followed by a noun.

Critical Viewing

Describe Students' responses should contain such phrases as *through the air, across the plate,* and *toward the batter.*

17

Distinguishing Between Prepositions and Adverbs

Many words can be used either as prepositions or as adverbs. You must see how a word is being used in a sentence in order to know which part of speech it is.

▶ **KEY CONCEPTS** A *preposition* will always be followed by a noun or pronoun, forming a prepositional phrase. An *adverb* can stand alone. ■

PREPOSITION:	The ball rolled <u>outside the infield</u>.
ADVERB:	The game is played <u>outside</u>.

prepositional phrase (over "outside the infield")

Prepositional phrases always include a preposition followed by a noun or pronoun. They may also include words that modify the noun.

EXAMPLES: The "wave" started <u>in the bleachers</u>.
                 prep noun

The batter ran <u>along the base path</u>.
               prep modifiers noun

The phrases "in the bleachers" and "along the base path" are prepositional phrases. Adverbs, on the other hand, are used alone. They can end a sentence. Also, they answer questions that prepositions do not: *In what way?* and *To what extent?*

The following chart shows more examples of words that can be used as either prepositions or adverbs.

Prepositions	Adverbs
We played <u>before</u> a crowd.	I've played third <u>before</u>.
The ball rolled <u>down</u> the baseline.	The man sat <u>down</u>.
The ball bounced <u>off</u> the wall.	Harry walked <u>off</u>.
The umpire stands <u>behind</u> the catcher.	Barbara stayed <u>behind</u>.

⚲ Learn More

To review what you've learned about adverbs, see Chapter 16.

◀ **Critical Viewing** Use a prepositional phrase in a sentence that tells how or in what direction this ball moves. [Describe]

🖊 STANDARDIZED TEST PREPARATION WORKSHOP

Grammar and Usage Many standardized tests require students to identify parts of speech in the context of a passage. Use the following example to demonstrate.

The <u>tired</u> girls walked <u>slowly</u> <u>from</u> the baseball
     A   B   C
game carrying <u>their</u> gloves.
            D

Which word in the above passage is a preposition?

The correct answer is item **C**. The others are an adjective (tired), an adverb (slowly), and a possessive adjective (their).

▶ **Exercise 4** Revising Sentences With Prepositions Rewrite each sentence below, replacing the preposition with one that makes more sense.

1. Gehrig was good about everything—hitting and base-running.
2. When he stole home, he slid all the way with the plate.
3. On the end of the 1936 season, he had earned the Most Valuable Player award.
4. Lou Gehrig batted fourth, for Babe Ruth.
5. He was inducted after the Hall of Fame in 1939.

▶ **Exercise 5** Distinguishing Between Prepositions and Adverbs Tell whether each underlined word in the following sentences is a *preposition* or an *adverb*.

1. Satchel Paige was tested <u>before</u> he joined the Major Leagues.
2. He had already played for many years <u>before</u>.
3. Paige threw the ball <u>over</u> home plate.
4. His time in the Negro Leagues was <u>over</u>.
5. He played <u>past</u> his fifty-ninth birthday.

More Practice

Language Lab CD-ROM
• Prepositional Phrases lesson

On-line Exercise Bank
• Section 17

Grammar Exercise Workbook
• pp. 35–36

▼ **Critical Viewing** Use at least two prepositions in sentences that describe the action in this stadium. [**Describe**]

Answer Key

▶ **Exercise 4**

Answers may vary. Samples are given.

1. Gehrig was good <u>at</u> everything—hitting and base-running.
2. When he stole home, he slid all the way <u>across</u> the plate.
3. <u>By</u> the end of the 1936 season, he had earned the Most Valuable Player award.
4. Lou Gehrig batted fourth, <u>behind</u> Babe Ruth.
5. He was inducted <u>into</u> the Hall of Fame in 1939.

▶ **Exercise 5**

1. preposition
2. adverb
3. preposition
4. adverb
5. preposition

Integrating Workplace Skills

Many occupations involve giving and following directions. If firefighters don't know the fire is <u>above</u> the sixth floor, the result can be a disaster. If a shopper is not told that children's clothes are *behind* the shoe department, a sale can be lost. Have students practice writing precise prepositions to describe the route from one part of the school building to another.

Critical Viewing

Describe Students' responses may include sentences like "The scoreboard is beyond the outfield wall" and "The catcher crouches behind home plate."

Prepositions • 355

⏱ **TIME SAVERS!**

🖼 **Answers on Transparency** Use the Grammar Exercises Answers on Transparencies for Chapter 17 to facilitate correction by students.

💻 **On-Line Exercise Bank** Have students complete the exercises on computer. The Auto Check feature will grade their work for you.

Preposition Pop-Up Book

Teaching Resources: Hands-on Grammar Activity Book, Chapter 17

1. Have students refer to their Hands-on Grammar activity books or give them relevant pages for this activity.

2. Review the directions for constructing the pop-ups.

3. Be sure students use complete sentences to describe how the figure is being moved.

You may want to assign prepositions to students or let them refer to the chart on page 352.

Find It in Your Reading

Have students work in pairs to locate sentences with prepositions and use them with their pop-ups.

Find It in Your Writing

You may want to have students work with a partner to evaluate their use of prepositions.

17

Hands-on Grammar

Preposition Pop-Up Book

Create a preposition pop-up book to practice using prepositions and prepositional phrases.

Make one pop-up to illustrate *over, under,* and *through.* Fold a piece of colored paper in half, as shown below. Cut as shown in the diagram. Unfold the paper and pop out the step that is created. Glue or tape a piece of string to the base of your pop-up. To the other end of the string, attach a figure or shape.

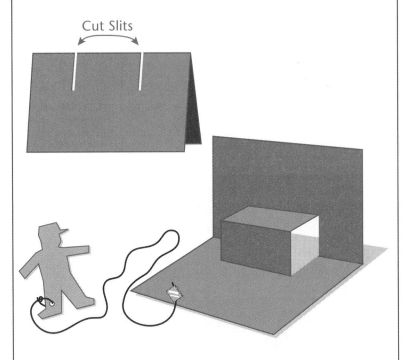

Cut Slits

Move the figure *over, under,* and *through* the step. Use complete sentences to describe how the figure is being moved in relation to the step. Write your sentences on the base of your pop-up. Find ways to demonstrate other prepositions with this pop-up. Use these prepositions in complete sentences that describe how the figure is being moved. Write the new sentences on the base of your pop-up.

356 • Prepositions

⏱ **TIME SAVERS!**

✋ **Hands-on Grammar**
Use the Hands-on Grammar activity sheet for Chapter 17 to facilitate this activity.

☑ **ONGOING ASSESSMENT: Assess Mastery**

Use the following resources to assess student mastery of prepositions.

In the Textbook	Print Resources	Technology
Chapter Review, Ex. 6–10, pp. 358–359 Standardized Test Preparation Workshop, pp. 360–361	Formal Assessment, Chapter 17	On-Line Exercise Bank, Chapter 17

Hands-on Grammar (cont.)

Make another pop-up to illustrate *with, after, before, in front of,* and *behind.* Fold a sheet of colored paper in fourths, lengthwise. On each of the three folds, draw four simple shapes, such as cats, snowmen, or geometric shapes, such as triangles. The bottom of each shape should rest on the fold. (Do not draw a row of cats on the outside edge.) Leave a space between the top of each shape and the next fold. Label each shape with a letter or a name. Carefully cut the outline of each shape, but do not separate the shape from the fold. Push each shape up so it stands up.

In complete sentences, use prepositions to describe the space or time relationship of one figure to another. For example, "A is *in front of* B." "I popped up B *after* popping up A." Use the pop-up to demonstrate as many prepositions as you can. Write the sentences that include the prepositions on a separate sheet of paper. Use one staple to attach the paper to the back of your pop-up.

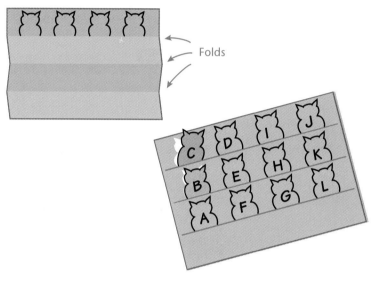

Folds

Find It in Your Reading In a short story or nonfiction work from your literature anthology, locate sentences that contain prepositions. Use one or both of your pop-ups to demonstrate the meaning of the prepositions. Add the sentences that you find to your pop-up list.

Find It in Your Writing Choose a piece of writing from your portfolio. Locate the prepositions you have used. Evaluate whether you have used the best preposition in each case.

Customize for
Less Advanced Students

Students may have difficulty seeing the connection between their actions and the prepositions they can use to describe the action. Have students work with more advanced students on this activity until they feel comfortable enough to work on their own.

Chapter Review

These exercises correlate to the instruction on pages 352–357. The exercises may be used for more practice, for reteaching, or for review of the Key Concepts presented. Answers for all chapter exercises are available in *Grammar Exercises Answers on Transparencies* in your Teaching Resources.

Answer Key

▶ Exercise 6

1. on
2. in
3. of
4. at, of
5. opposite
6. from
7. around
8. near, of
9. between
10. of, to, of

▶ Exercise 7

Answers may vary. Samples are given.

1. Base lines run <u>from</u> home plate to third and first base.
2. Foul lines run <u>along</u> the edges of the outfield.
3. The lines separate the field <u>into</u> fair and foul areas.
4. Base lines also mark the path <u>of</u> the runner.
5. The region <u>behind</u> the infield is the outfield.
6. Dugouts are shelters <u>on</u> each side of the field.
7. Players sit <u>under</u> the cover of the dugouts.
8. <u>Among</u> the field markings, there are several chalk boxes.
9. They show people where to stand <u>during</u> a game.
10. Players can walk <u>over</u> the various lines.

▶ Exercise 8

1. in
2. at
3. over
4. above
5. beneath
6. next to
7. toward
8. between
9. across
10. with

GRAMMAR EXERCISES 6–14

▶ Exercise 6 Recognizing **Prepositions** Write the prepositions in the following sentences.

1. Baseball is played on a level field.
2. The field is approximately two acres in size.
3. The infield area consists of a diamond shape.
4. There are canvas bases at three of the corners.
5. Home plate is opposite second base.
6. Batters hit the ball from home plate.
7. Then, they run around the bases.
8. The pitcher's mound is near the center of the diamond.
9. It is between home plate and second base.
10. A strip of rubber is nailed to the top of this mound.

▶ Exercise 7 Supplying Prepositions Copy each sentence below, replacing the blank with a preposition.

1. Base lines run __?__ home plate to third and first base.
2. Foul lines run __?__ the edges of the outfield.
3. The lines separate the field __?__ fair and foul areas.
4. Base lines also mark the path __?__ the runner.
5. The region __?__ the infield is the outfield.
6. Dugouts are shelters __?__ each side of the field.
7. Players sit __?__ the cover of the dugouts.
8. __?__ the field markings, there are several chalk boxes.
9. They show people where to stand __?__ a game.
10. Players can walk __?__ the various lines.

▶ Exercise 8 Revising Sentences With **Prepositions** Replace each underlined preposition with a different preposition.

1. Baseball is played <u>at</u> the stadium.
2. The game begins <u>with</u> the first pitch.
3. The pitcher throws the ball <u>toward</u> home plate.
4. A good pitch is <u>over</u> the knees.
5. Also, it must be <u>below</u> the shoulders.
6. The batter stands <u>beside</u> home plate.
7. He swings the bat <u>at</u> the pitched ball.
8. A good hit is <u>inside</u> the two foul lines.
9. Then, the batter runs <u>around</u> the bases.
10. The team hopes to win <u>by</u> many runs.

▶ Exercise 9 Distinguishing Between **Prepositions and Adverbs** Tell whether each underlined word below is a *preposition* or an *adverb*.

1. We cheer our favorite team <u>on</u>.
2. I'm rooting <u>for</u> the shortstop.
3. He runs quickly <u>after</u> the ball.
4. Then, he spins <u>around</u> and throws to first base.
5. The ball flies <u>across</u> the infield.
6. The throw beats the runner <u>to</u> the base.
7. He is out <u>by</u> one small step.
8. The runner looks <u>behind</u> to see the call.
9. He returns to the dugout and sits <u>down</u>.
10. <u>Inside</u> the dugout, he talks with the coach.
11. With two more outs, the inning is <u>over</u>.
12. They haven't gotten a hit <u>since</u> the sixth inning.
13. Our team has beaten this team <u>before</u>.
14. <u>After</u> the final play, they congratulate each other.
15. Then, the players take <u>off</u> and head for the showers.

▶ Exercise 9

1. adverb
2. preposition
3. preposition
4. adverb
5. preposition
6. preposition
7. preposition
8. adverb
9. adverb
10. preposition
11. adverb
12. preposition
13. adverb
14. preposition
15. adverb

> **Exercise 10** **Working With Prepositions and Adverbs** Identify each underlined word as a *preposition* or an *adverb*. If the word is a preposition, write the entire prepositional phrase.

1. Often, a stadium is built <u>outside</u> a city.
2. Old stadiums are being replaced <u>by</u> new ones.
3. When an old stadium closes, players <u>around</u> the league are sometimes sad.
4. Many new stadiums have been built <u>since</u> the 1980's.
5. Baseball fans are more comfortable than ever <u>before</u>.
6. Usually a stadium is named <u>for</u> its team, but not always.
7. A stadium's upper deck hangs <u>over</u> the lower deck.
8. Many times, players hit the ball <u>into</u> the stands.
9. Some home runs fly <u>to</u> the upper deck.
10. On the outfield wall, the scoreboard hangs <u>down</u>.
11. <u>In</u> one stadium, it was located <u>behind</u> the pitcher.
12. However, <u>in</u> that position, it interfered <u>with</u> the batter; so it was moved.
13. The dugouts are <u>along</u> the foul lines.
14. For the championship games, many fans come <u>out</u>.
15. When fans crowd the exits, guards move them <u>along</u>.

> **Exercise 11** **Find It in Your Reading** Identify the prepositions you find in the following excerpt from *Lou Gehrig: The Iron Horse.* Identify at least one word that is used here as an adverb but can also be used as a preposition.

Joe McCarthy started Gehrig at first base on opening day of the 1939 season, contemptuous of a fan who, a few days before in an exhibition game at Ebbets Field, had bawled, in earshot of both of them, "Hey Lou, why don't you give yourself up?". . .

Lou hobbled as far into the 1939 season as May 2. Then, on the morning of the first game of a series against Detroit, he called McCarthy on the hotel's house phone and asked to see him.

"I'm benching myself, Joe," he said, once in the manager's suite. McCarthy did not speak.

> **Exercise 12** **Find It in Your Writing** Look through your portfolio. Identify examples of prepositions and prepositional phrases in your own writing. Challenge yourself to improve a piece of writing by using prepositions to indicate relationships.

> **Exercise 13** **Writing Application** Write a brief description of a sport or activity that you enjoy. Identify the prepositions that you use.

> **Exercise 14** **CUMULATIVE REVIEW Nouns, Pronouns, Verbs, Adjectives, Adverbs, and Prepositions** Write these labels down the side of your paper, leaving two or three lines between one and the next: *Common Nouns, Proper Nouns, Personal Pronouns, Demonstrative Pronouns, Action Verbs, Linking Verbs, Adjectives, Adverbs, Prepositions.* Then, next to each label, write the appropriate words from the following paragraph.

I follow certain rituals at a baseball game. Do you? I always go to games on Saturday, when the stadium is full of excited fans. I usually buy two souvenirs—a cap for me and a pin for my friend Ellen. I buy a hot dog and a drink, and then I take my seat in the lower deck, near first base. This is the best seat!

Answer Key

> **Exercise 10**

1. preposition, outside a city
2. preposition, by new ones
3. preposition, around the league
4. preposition, since the 1980's
5. adverb
6. preposition, for its team
7. preposition, over the lower deck
8. preposition, into the stands
9. preposition, to the upper deck
10. adverb
11. preposition, In one stadium; preposition, behind the pitcher
12. preposition, in that position; preposition, with the batter
13. preposition, along the foul lines
14. adverb
15. adverb

> **Exercise 11**

Find It in Your Reading
Joe McCarthy started Gehrig <u>at</u> first base <u>on</u> opening day <u>of</u> the 1939 season, contemptuous <u>of</u> a fan who, a few days before <u>in</u> an exhibition game <u>at</u> Ebbets Field, had bawled, <u>in</u> earshot <u>of</u> both <u>of</u> them, "Hey Lou, why don't you give yourself up?" . . .

Lou hobbled <u>as</u> far <u>into</u> the 1939 season <u>as</u> May 2. Then, <u>on</u> the morning <u>of</u> the first game <u>of</u> a series <u>against</u> Detroit, he called McCarthy <u>on</u> the hotel's house phone and asked to see him.

"I'm benching myself, Joe," he said, once <u>in</u> the manager's suite. McCarthy did not speak.

Adverbs: a few days <u>before</u>, give yourself <u>up</u>

> **Exercise 12**

Find It in Your Writing
Students could also look for prepositions and prepositional phrases in each other's writings.

> **Exercise 13**

Writing Application
Ask volunteers to read their descriptions aloud. Listeners could raise their hands when they hear a preposition.

continued

Answer Key continued

> **Exercise 14**

Cumulative Review
Common Nouns: rituals, game, games, stadium, fans, souvenirs, cap, pin, friend, hot dog, drink, seat, deck, base, seat

Proper Nouns: Saturday, Ellen

Personal Pronouns: I, you, I, I, me, my, I, I, my

Demonstrative Pronouns: this

Action Verbs: follow, do, go, buy, take

Linking Verb: is, is

Adjectives: certain, a, baseball, the, full, excited, two, a, a, a, a, the, lower, first, the, best

Adverbs: always, usually, then
Prepositions: at, to, on, of, for, in, near

Lesson Objectives
- To revise and edit passages by connecting ideas using correct prepositional phrases
- To revise passages by combining and rearranging text

1. Explain to students that they should choose the answer that states the information in the passage in the most natural and grammatical way.

2. The sample passage conveys two items of information in two sentences: (1) There were shoemakers in the eighteenth century, and (2) every town had one. All the possible responses state this information in one sentence, but the one that states it most naturally is B. Choice B achieves this by using a prepositional phrase and by eliminating repeated words. B is the correct answer.

Standardized Test Preparation Workshop

Revising and Editing

One way standardized test questions evaluate your knowledge of standard grammar and usage is to test your ability to connect ideas using prepositional phrases. Before you answer this type of question, first read the entire passage. Then, choose the answer that best uses prepositional phrases to connect similar ideas and eliminate unnecessary words.

The following test item will give you practice with questions that measure your ability to use prepositional phrases.

Test Tip

Identify repeated ideas and words in the passages chosen. Combining those ideas with a prepositional phrase and eliminating unnecessary words will provide the best rewrite.

Sample Test Item

Directions Read the passage, and choose the letter of the best way to write the underlined sentences.

The eighteenth century was a time when there were shoemakers. Every town had a shoemaker.

1 A The eighteenth century was a time of shoemakers in every town.

  B During the eighteenth century, every town had a shoemaker.

  C The eighteenth century was a time when there were shoemakers in every town.

  D The eighteenth century was a time for every town to have a shoemaker.

Answer and Explanation

The best answer is *B*. Since both sentences provide information about shoemakers, the best way to rewrite the sentences is to combine similar ideas using the prepositional phrase, *during the eighteenth century.*

TEST-TAKING TIP

Point out that a possible response to a test item may sound grammatically correct but not accurately contain the information in the test item. After students have made their choices, encourage them to reread the passage and check it against their answer to be sure that their response accurately reflects the information in the passage.

Practice 1 **Directions:** Read the passage, and choose the letter of the best way to write the underlined sentences.

During the eighteenth century, men wore
(1)
shoes made of certain materials. Buckskin

or cowhide were those materials. Most
(2)
shoes were not fastened by laces. Buckles

fastened most shoes.

1 A During the eighteenth century, men wore shoes made of certain materials, and buckskin or cowhide were those materials.

B During the eighteenth century, men wore shoes made of buckskin or cowhide.

C During the eighteenth century, men wore shoes made of certain materials; buckskin or cowhide were those materials.

D Buckskin or cowhide were the materials of men's shoes during the eighteenth century when men wore shoes made of certain materials.

2 F Most shoes were not fastened by laces but with buckles.

G Most shoes were not fastened by laces but with buckles were most shoes fastened.

H With most shoes, laces were not used but instead buckles fastened most shoes.

J Most shoes were not fastened by laces or by buckles.

Practice 2 **Directions:** Read the passage, and choose the letter of the best way to write the underlined sentences.

Today, shoes can be fastened. They can be
(1)
 fastened by using laces. Some shoes don't
(2)
need to be fastened because they are made

in materials that stretch.

1 A Today, shoes can be fastened on laces.

B Today, shoes can be fastened in laces.

C Today, shoes can be fastened with laces.

D Today, shoes can be fastened for laces.

2 F Some shoes don't need to be fastened because they are made of materials that stretch.

G Some shoes don't need to be fastened because they are made around materials that stretch.

H Some shoes don't need to be fastened because they are made by materials that stretch.

J Some shoes don't need to be fastened because they are made for materials that stretch.

Answer Key

Practice 1

1. B
2. F

Practice 2

1. C
2. F

In-Depth Lesson Plan

	LESSON FOCUS	PRINT AND MEDIA RESOURCES
DAY 1	**Coordinating Conjunctions** Students learn and apply correct usage of coordinating conjunctions (pp. 364–366).	**Teaching Resources** *Grammar Exercise Workbook*, pp. 37–38; *Grammar Exercises Answers on Transparencies*, Ch. 18 *On-Line Exercise Bank*, Section 18.1
DAY 2	**Correlative Conjunctions** Students learn and apply correct usage of correlative conjunctions and do the Hands-on Grammar activity (pp. 366–369).	**Teaching Resources** *Grammar Exercise Workbook*, pp. 39–40; *Grammar Exercises Answers on Transparencies*, Ch. 18; *Hands-on Grammar Activity Book*, Ch. 18 *On-Line Exercise Bank*, Section 18.1
DAY 3	**Interjections** Students learn and apply correct usage of interjections (pp. 370–372).	**Teaching Resources** *Grammar Exercise Workbook*, pp. 41–42; *Grammar Exercises Answers on Transparencies*, Ch. 18 *On-Line Exercise Bank*, Section 18.2
DAY 4	**Review and Assess** Students review chapter and demonstrate mastery of use of conjunctions and interjections (pp. 373–377).	**Teaching Resources** *Formal Assessment*, Ch. 18; *Grammar Exercises Answers on Transparencies*, Ch. 18 *On-Line Exercise Bank*, Sections 18.1–2

Accelerated Lesson Plan

	LESSON FOCUS	PRINT AND MEDIA RESOURCES
DAY 1	**Conjunctions and Interjections** Students cover concepts and usage of conjunctions and interjections as determined by Diagnostic Test (pp. 364–372).	**Teaching Resources** *Grammar Exercise Workbook*, pp. 37–42; *Grammar Exercises Answers on Transparencies*, Ch. 18; *Hands-on Grammar Activity Book*, Ch. 18 *On-Line Exercise Bank*, Sections 18.1–2
DAY 2	**Review and Assess** Students review chapter and demonstrate mastery of use of conjunctions and interjections (pp. 373–377).	**Teaching Resources** *Formal Assessment*, Ch. 18; *Grammar Exercises Answers on Transparencies*, Ch. 18 *On-Line Exercise Bank*, Sections 18.1–2

Options for Adapting Lesson Plans

HOMEWORK

Have students complete any section of the chapter for homework.

FEATURES

Extend coverage with the Grammar in Literature feature (p. 365), and the Standardized Test Preparation Workshop (p. 375).

TECHNOLOGY

Students can use the On-Line Exercise Bank to complete the exercises on computer. The Auto Check feature will grade their work.

INTEGRATED SKILLS COVERAGE

Grammar in Literature
SE p. 365

Reading
Find It in Your Reading SE pp. 368, 369, 372

Writing
Find It in Your Writing SE pp. 368, 369, 372
Writing Application SE pp. 369, 372, 374
Grammar and Style SE p. 370

Spelling
SE p. 364

Vocabulary
ATE p. 370

Speaking
ATE p. 366

Viewing and Representing
Critical Viewing
SE pp. 362, 365, 367, 370, 371

ASSESSMENT SUPPORT

Standardized Test Preparation SE p. 375; ATE p. 366
Standardized Test Preparation Workbook, pp. 35–36
Formal Assessment, Ch. 18

MEETING INDIVIDUAL NEEDS

Less Advanced Students See Ongoing Assessments
ATE pp. 365, 367, 371
ESL Students ATE p. 371

BLOCK SCHEDULING

Pacing Suggestions
For 90-minute Blocks
• Administer the Diagnostic Test to students to determine instructional coverage.
• Have students complete the necessary exercises in class. Use the Hands-on Grammar activity to provide a change of pace.

Resources for Varying Instruction
• *Language Lab* **CD-ROM** If your students have access to hardware, a 90-minute block provides an ideal opportunity for students to work on computer.

Professional Development Support
• *How to Manage Instruction in the Block* This teaching Resource provides management and activity suggestions.

MEDIA AND TECHNOLOGY

For the Student
• *On-Line Exercise Bank,* Ch. 18

For the Teacher
• *Resource Pro* **CD-ROM**

WRITING AND GRAMMAR WEB SITE

The Interactive Writing and Grammar Web site provides a wide array of support for students, teachers, and parents. Grammar support includes:

• On-Line Exercise Bank with Auto Check scoring
• Diagnostic and assessment support

www.phschool.com

LITERATURE CONNECTIONS

Grammar in Literature selections from *Prentice Hall Literature: Timeless Voices, Timeless Themes,* Copper:
from *Greyling,* Jane Yolen, SE p. 365

1. To recognize and use coordinating conjunctions.
2. To recognize and use correlative conjunctions.
3. To recognize and use interjections.

Critical Viewing

Analyze Students' models should include one interjection per sentence.

Chapter 18 Conjunctions and Interjections

In this chapter, you will learn more about two important kinds of words: conjunctions and interjections. *Conjunctions* connect sentence parts and help you add information to your sentences. *Interjections* express feelings.

If you are writing about sea mammals, for example, you might have many interesting details to share. Conjunctions can help you add these pieces of information to your sentences. Interjections might help you express just how you feel.

In the following sections, you will learn how to identify conjunctions and interjections and how to use them properly in your sentences. When used correctly, conjunctions and interjections help hold sentences together and add emotion to your writing.

▲ **Critical Viewing** How do you feel when you look at the sea otter in this photograph? Express your feelings in a sentence with an interjection. **[Analyze]**

362 • Conjunctions and Interjections

☑ ONGOING ASSESSMENT: Diagnose

If students miss more than one item in any category, direct them to the relevant pages of the text and assign exercises for practice and review.

Conjunctions and Interjections	Diagnostic Test Items	Teach	Practice	Section Review	Chapter Review
Skill Checks A and C					
Coordinating Conjunctions	A 1–5 C 11–15	pp. 364–366	Ex. 1–2	Ex. 5, 7	Ex. 20, 22, 25–27
Skill Checks B and C					
Correlative Conjunctions	B 6–10 C 11–15	pp. 366–367	Ex. 3–4	Ex. 6–8	Ex. 21, 22, 25–27

Diagnostic Test

Directions: Write all answers on a separate sheet of paper.

Skill Check A. For each sentence, list the coordinating conjunction and the words or word groups it connects. Circle the conjunction.

1. Sea otters and river otters look very much alike.
2. The sea otters have thicker bodies, but they have shorter tails than the river otters.
3. There are four kinds of sea otters, yet most people cannot tell them apart.
4. Many live in the Pacific Ocean near the Americas or Asia.
5. Their front paws have five fingers, so they can hold on to food and seaweed.

Skill Check B. Copy each sentence below. Circle both parts of each correlative conjunction, and underline the words or word groups it connects.

6. Sea otter fur has not only brown but also silver in its coloring.
7. Their teeth are both large and strong.
8. They break open shells either with their teeth or with a rock.
9. Sea otters float on their backs whether they are eating or nursing their babies.
10. They neither swim very fast nor defend themselves very well.

Skill Check C. Write the conjunctions in the following sentences, and label them *coordinating* or *correlative.*

11. Sea otters dive deep under the water, for that is where they find clams and sea urchins.
12. They use both their paws and their forearms to gather food.
13. To keep warm, they not only eat lots of fish, but they also constantly clean their fur.
14. They don't have blubber, so the fur traps air against their skin.
15. This air protects them from the cold and helps them to maintain their warm body temperature.

Skill Check D. Identify the interjection in each sentence.

16. Wow! Can sea otters really stay underwater for four minutes?
17. Well, that is how they gather food.
18. Gosh! That is also how sea otters avoid danger.
19. Alas, they can't swim fast enough to escape.
20. Oh! What about baby sea otters?

Skill Check E. Supply an interjection to fill in the blank in each sentence. Properly punctuate the interjections with a comma or an exclamation mark.

21. _____ Baby sea otters are certainly adorable.
22. _____ they depend on their mothers for a long time.
23. _____ I didn't know they live in such large groups!
24. _____ They float in the same area most of the time.
25. _____ they hold onto the seaweed to keep from drifting away.

Conjunctions and Interjections • 363

ONGOING ASSESSMENT: Diagnose *continued*

Conjunctions and Interjections	Diagnostic Test Items	Teach	Practice	Section Review	Chapter Review
Skill Checks D and E					
Interjections	D 16–20 E 21–25	pp. 370–371	Ex. 12–13	Ex. 14–16	Ex. 23–24, 26–27
Cumulative Reviews and Applications				Ex. 9–11, 17–19	Ex. 28

Answer Key

Diagnostic Test

- Each item in the Diagnostic Test corresponds to a specific section in the chapter on conjunctions and interjections. This will enable you to tailor instruction to the particular needs of your students. See "Ongoing Assessment: Diagnose" below for further details.

- Answers for the Diagnostic Test and all chapter exercises are available in *Grammar Exercises Answers on Transparencies* in your Teaching Resources.

Skill Check A

1. (and) connects *sea otters* with *river otters*
2. (but) connects all words before with all words after
3. (yet) connects all words before with all words after
4. (or) connects *the Americas* with *Asia*
5. (so) connects all words before with all words after

Skill Check B

6. Sea otter fur has (not only) brown (but also) silver in its coloring.
7. Their teeth are (both) large (and) strong.
8. They break open shells (either) with their teeth (or) with a rock.
9. Sea otters float on their backs (whether) they are eating (or) nursing their babies.
10. They (neither) swim very fast (nor) defend themselves very well.

Skill Check C

11. for—coordinating; and—coordinating
12. both, and—correlative
13. not only, but also—correlative
14. so—coordinating
15. and—coordinating

Skill Check D

16. Wow
17. Well
18. Gosh
19. Alas
20. Oh

Skill Check E

Answers will vary. Samples are given.
21. Gosh!
22. Boy,
23. Wow!
24. Hey!
25. Aha,

Interest GRABBER Rewrite the first paragraph on the page without the conjunctions.

Conjunctions connect. They often join words in pairs, such as *Romeo Juliet, light sturdy, swimming running.* Conjunctions also connect larger word groups, such as phrases and sentences.

Ask students if the paragraph makes sense. Now have students read the paragraph in their books and compare both versions.

Activate Prior Knowledge

Ask volunteers to add a word to the following phrases.

warm ____ sunny (and)

chocolate ____ vanilla (or)

neither fish ____ fowl (nor)

slowly ____ surely (but)

Explain to students that the words they are using to connect the other words in each phrase are called *conjunctions.*

TEACH

Step-by-Step Teaching Guide

Coordinating Conjunctions

1. Go over the conjunctions and their definitions in the chart on this page with the whole class.

2. Call on volunteers to come to the chalkboard and write sample sentences with the different conjunctions. Student should circle the conjunctions in their sentences.

3. Ask the class to identify the words connected by the conjunctions.

Section 18.1

Conjunctions

Conjunctions connect. They often join words in pairs, such as *Romeo and Juliet, light but sturdy,* and *swimming or running.* Conjunctions also connect larger word groups, such as phrases and sentences.

▶ **KEY CONCEPT** **Conjunctions** connect words, groups of words, and whole sentences. ■

Using Coordinating Conjunctions

Coordinating conjunctions connect words or groups of words that are similar in form: noun with noun, phrase with phrase, sentence with sentence, and so on.

COORDINATING CONJUNCTIONS	
Conjunction	Function
and	Adds ideas of equal importance
or	Presents options, alternates, or substitutes for ideas of equal importance
but	Indicates a contrast or exception
nor	Presents an alternate negative idea
for	Connects ideas that follow logically
yet	Connects ideas that follow logically and are contrary
so	Shows the consequence of related ideas

In the following chart, each coordinating conjunction is boxed and each set of connected words is underlined.

USING COORDINATING CONJUNCTIONS	
Words Connected	Examples
Nouns	The seals and sea lions live there.
Pronouns	He or I will lead the nature talk.
Verbs	The scientists planned and practiced.
Adjectives	That photo is attractive but expensive.
Adverbs	He works quickly yet carefully.
Prepositional Phrases	The hikers followed the trail over the hill and to the beach.
Sentences	You should come soon, for next week we will be leaving.

Theme: Sea Mammals

In this section, you will learn how conjunctions connect words and phrases. The examples and exercises are about sea mammals.

Cross-Curricular Connection: Science

💡 **Spelling Tip**

When using *for* as a coordinating conjunction, remember that it looks like the preposition but that it is being used differently. Also, remember that the number *four* is spelled differently and has a completely different meaning.

⏱ TIME AND RESOURCE MANAGER

Resources
Print: Grammar Exercise Workbook, pp. 37–40; Grammar Exercises Answers on Transparencies, Ch. 18
Technology: On-Line Exercise Bank, Section 18.1

In-Depth Coverage	Accelerated Pace
• Work through all key concepts, pp. 364–367. • Assign and review Exercises 1–4. • Read and discuss Grammar in Literature, p. 365. • Do the Hands-on Grammar activity, p. 368.	• Assign pp. 364–367 for independent student review. • Assign Section Review Exercises 5–8, p. 369.

GRAMMAR IN LITERATURE

from **Greyling**
Jane Yolen

The coordinating conjunctions in this excerpt have been highlighted in blue italics.

Now the fisherman was also sad that they had no child. But he kept his sorrow to himself so that his wife would not know his grief *and* thus double her own. Indeed, he would leave the hut each morning with a breath of song *and* return each night with a whistle on his lips. His nets were full *but* his heart was empty, *yet* he never told his wife.

▶ **Exercise 1** **Recognizing Coordinating Conjunctions** For each sentence below, list the coordinating conjunction and the words or word groups it connects. Circle the conjunction.

EXAMPLE: Seals prefer to eat fish or shellfish.

ANSWER: fish (or) shellfish

1. Harbor seals cannot walk or travel on land with their hind flippers.
2. Sea lions and furred seals travel well on land.
3. These two water mammals are similar yet different.
4. Small sea lions are trained for circuses or for zoos.
5. Their fur is rich and silky.
6. The male seals' fur is mostly brown but also a little gray.
7. This large male has fought off its rivals, so it will keep its harem.
8. Immature males play together, for this is good practice for fighting.
9. The seal's fur is very valuable, so seals are hunted frequently.
10. Now, the population is protected and thriving.

▶ **Critical Viewing** Using coordinating conjunctions in sentences, describe the behavior of this elephant seal. **[Describe]**

▶ **More Practice**

Language Lab CD-ROM
• Subject-Verb Agreement lesson
On-line Exercise Bank
• Section 18.1
Grammar Exercise Workbook
• pp. 37–38

Conjunctions • **365**

Step-by-Step Teaching Guide

Grammar in Literature

1. Have a volunteer read aloud the excerpt from "Greyling," stressing the conjunctions.

2. *But* at the beginning of the second sentence is a special kind of adverb. It indicates the contrast between the idea in this sentence with the idea in the first sentence.

Connection With Literature

Have students read more of "Greyling." Encourage them to look for coordinating conjunctions and to identify the words they connect.

Answer Key

▶ **Exercise 1**

1. walk (or) travel
2. sea lions (and) furred seals
3. similar (yet) different
4. for circuses (or) for zoos
5. rich (and) silky
6. mostly brown (but) also a little gray
7. This large male has fought off its rivals, (so) it will keep its harem.
8. Immature males play together, (for) this is good practice for fighting.
9. The seal's fur is very valuable, (so) seals are hunted frequently.
10. protected (and) thriving

Critical Viewing

Describe Students may say that the sea lion is large and dominating.

☑ ONGOING ASSESSMENT: Monitor and Reinforce

If students have difficulty with Exercise 1 or 2, refer them to the following for additional practice.

In the Textbook	Print Resources	Technology
Section Review, Ex. 5–8, p. 369	Grammar Exercise Workbook, pp. 37–38	On-Line Exercise Bank, Section 18.1

Answers will vary. Samples are given.
1. nor
2. nor
3. and
4. so
5. but

Step-by-Step Teaching Guide

Correlative Conjunctions

1. Some of the individual words that make up the pairs of correlative conjunctions often appear alone.

   Both of you are to blame.

   Neither pitcher is ready to throw.

   Either answer is correct.

   I don't sing, nor do I dance.

2. Emphasize that the pairings shown in the chart are the only correct ones. If students want to use *whether* in a sentence that requires a correlative conjunction, they must use *or* with it. Correlative conjunctions cannot be mixed and matched. In order for sentences to make sense, the conjunctions must be paired as shown here. Write a few sentences with mixed pairings, such as *Neither the pitcher and the catcher claimed full credit for the perfect game,* to illustrate.

Integrating Speaking Skills

Pronunciation The diphthong *ei* in the conjunctions *either* and *neither* can be pronounced like the *ee* in *feet* or like the *i* in *ice*. Both pronunciations are correct. You might introduce students to this classic Ira Gershwin lyric as a reminder:

You say eether and I say eyether,
You say neether and I say nyther,
Eether, eyether, neether, nyther,
Let's call the whole thing off!

⏱ **TIME SAVERS!**

🖨 **Answers on Transparency**
Use the Grammar Exercises Answers on Transparencies for Chapter 18 to facilitate correction by students.

🖥 **On-Line Exercise Bank**
Have students complete the exercises on computer. The Auto Check feature will grade their work for you!

18.1

▶ **Exercise 2** Supplying Coordinating Conjunctions Write a coordinating conjunction to complete each sentence below. Make sure that the conjunction makes sense in the sentence.

1. True seals do not have ears ___?___ well-developed front flippers.
2. Their hind limbs do not bend forward, ___?___ do they work well on land.
3. When moving on land, seals wriggle ___?___ drag their bodies.
4. True seals do have claws, ___?___ they can climb on icebergs.
5. Once overhunted, the elephant seal has now slowly ___?___ steadily increased its population.

Using Correlative Conjunctions

Correlative conjunctions are conjunctions that are used in pairs. Like coordinating conjunctions, they connect similar types of words or word groups.

▶ **KEY CONCEPT** **Correlative conjunctions** are pairs of conjunctions that connect words or word groups. ■

There are five pairs of correlative conjunctions: *both . . . and, either . . . or, neither . . . nor, not only . . . but also,* and *whether . . . or.* They can connect nouns, pronouns, verbs, adjectives, adverbs, prepositional phrases, and sentences.

USING CORRELATIVE CONJUNCTIONS	
Words Connected	**Examples**
Nouns	Both seals and walruses are protected species.
Pronouns	Neither you nor I could have known.
Verbs	I'll either walk or jog to the beach.
Adjectives	Her aquarium is not only new but also custom-built.
Adverbs	He draws both skillfully and creatively.
Prepositional Phrases	Our team is not only in the playoffs but also in the division lead.
Sentences	Either we do the research here, or we will do it in Canada.

⚙ **Grammar and Style Tip**

When using the correlative conjunction *not only . . . but also,* you may separate the words. Sometimes, a noun comes between *but* and *also.* For example, "Not only seals eat fish, but walruses also."

✏ **STANDARDIZED TEST PREPARATION WORKSHOP**

Grammar and Usage Standardized tests measure students' knowledge of standard grammar and usage. Students might be asked to identify the problem in a sentence and rewrite it to correct that problem. Have students read the following and then choose the letter that shows the best rewrite.

Gosh lots of observers say they have seen flying saucers I bet they are seeing weather phenomena or satellites.

A Gosh, lots of observers say they have seen flying saucers, so I bet they are seeing weather phenomena or satellites.

B Gosh! Lots of observers say they have seen flying saucers. And I bet they are seeing weather phenomena or satellites.

C Gosh! Lots of observers say they have seen flying saucers, but I bet they are seeing weather phenomena or satellites.

The correct answer is **C**, because it punctuates the exclamation <u>Gosh</u> correctly and combines the two sentences in the run-on example with the conjunction <u>but</u>.

▶ **Exercise 3** Finding Correlative Conjunctions Copy each sentence below. Circle both parts of the correlative conjunction, and underline the words or word groups it connects.

EXAMPLE: Walrus skin is (both) thick (and) wrinkled.

1. Walruses are found not only in the Pacific Ocean but also in the Atlantic Ocean.
2. They are both large and agile.
3. Not only can they turn their hind limbs forward, but they can also move all four limbs to walk on land.
4. They are characterized not only by their long tusks but also by their massive size.
5. Their tusks are used either for fighting or for climbing.
6. They are neither hunting tools nor ornaments.
7. A walrus uses both its whiskers and its nose to find food.
8. Walruses live not only near the shore but also on ice floes.
9. They are popular animals—whether in zoos or in animal shows.
10. Their enemies are either polar bears or humans.

▶ **Exercise 4** Supplying Correlative Conjunctions Supply a correlative conjunction to complete each sentence below.

1. There are ___?___ seven thousand ___?___ eight thousand animals in that herd.
2. They ___?___ bellow loudly ___?___ can be heard for miles.
3. Walruses ___?___ pick fights ___?___ give up easily.
4. The group is very united, ___?___ while fighting ___?___ during socializing.
5. ___?___ the males ___?___ the females have extremely large bodies.
6. Walrus skin is ___?___ smooth ___?___ hairless.
7. Their heads are ___?___ small ___?___ covered in whiskers.
8. Their ears are ___?___ difficult to spot ___?___ marked by a fold of skin.
9. Walruses enjoy eating ___?___ mollusks ___?___ other shellfish.
10. Humans used to hunt the walrus ___?___ for its tusks ___?___ for its blubber.

More Practice

Language Lab
CD-ROM
• Subject-Verb
Agreement lesson
On-line
Exercise Bank
• Section 18.1
Grammar Exercise
Workbook
• pp. 39–40

▼ **Critical Viewing** Fill in the blanks in this sentence: These walruses are ____ and also ____. **[Describe]**

Conjunctions • 367

▶ **Exercise 3**

1. Walruses are found (not only) in the Pacific Ocean (but also) in the Atlantic Ocean.
2. They are (both) large (and) agile.
3. (Not only) can they turn their hind limbs forward (but) they can (also) move all four limbs to walk on land.
4. They are characterized (not only) by their long tusks (but also) by their massive size.
5. Their tusks are used (either) for fighting (or) for climbing.
6. They are (neither) hunting tools (nor) ornaments.
7. A walrus uses (both) its whiskers (and) its nose to find food.
8. Walruses live (not only) near the shore (but also) on ice floes.
9. They are popular animals — (whether) in zoos (or) in animal shows.
10. Their enemies are (either) polar bears (or) humans.

▶ **Exercise 4**

Answers will vary. Samples are given.

1. There are either seven thousand or eight thousand animals in that herd.
2. They both bellow loudly and can be heard for miles.
3. Walruses neither pick fights nor give up easily.
4. The group is very united, not only while fighting but also during socializing.
5. Both the males and the females have extremely large bodies.
6. Walrus skin is both smooth and hairless.
7. Their heads are both small and covered in whiskers.
8. Their ears are not only difficult to spot but also marked by a fold of skin.
9. Walruses enjoy eating both mollusks and other shellfish.
10. Humans used to hunt the walrus not only for its tusks but also for its blubber.

Critical Viewing

Describe Students may choose words that describe the animals' size, color, activity, or other characteristics.

☑ **ONGOING ASSESSMENT: Monitor and Reinforce**

If students miss more than two items in Exercises 3–4, refer them to the following for additional practice.

In the Textbook	Print Resources	Technology
Section Review, Ex. 6–8, p. 369	Grammar Exercise Workbook, pp. 39–40	On-Line Exercise Bank, Section 18.1

Conjunction Road Map

Teaching Resources: Hands-on Grammar Activity Book, Chapter 18

1. Have students refer to their *Hands-on Grammar Activity Book* or give them copies of relevant pages for this activity.

2. Have volunteers duplicate their roadmaps on the board and ask for responses from the rest of the class.

Find It in Your Reading

Have the class discuss which of the conjunctions they found most often and least often. Encourage them to continue to look for sentences using the conjunctions *for*, *yet*, and *so*.

Find It in Your Writing

Students may work with a partner to combine each other's short sentences.

18.1

Hands-on Grammar

Conjunction Road Map

Practice combining sentences with coordinating conjunctions using this road map. Draw a road map like the one in the illustration below. Then, on each road fill in one of the following sentences.

Mary wanted to buy those jeans.
She saved her allowance money.
Mary went to the store.
She could not find the jeans she wanted.
She bought a different pair.
She decided that she liked them better.

Decide which coordinating conjunction makes sense to join each sentence pair and write the conjunction at the junction of the roads. Choose from these conjunctions: *and, but, for, nor, or, so,* and *yet.*

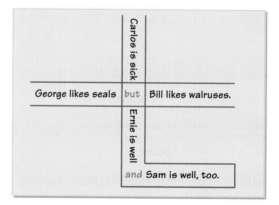

Find It in Your Reading Find examples of compound sentences joined with coordinating conjunctions in your reading. Map out those sentences.

Find It in Your Writing Look through your writing portfolio for examples of coordinating conjunctions. If you can't find any, challenge yourself to combine some shorter sentences with coordinating conjunctions.

⏱ **TIME SAVERS!**

✋ **Hands-on Grammar Book**
Use the Hands-on Grammar activity sheet for Chapter 18 to facilitate this activity.

Section 18.1 Section Review

GRAMMAR EXERCISES 5–11

▶ **Exercise 5** Recognizing **Coordinating Conjunctions** For each sentence below, list the coordinating conjunction and the words or word groups it connects. Circle the conjunction.

1. Manatees do not migrate very far, nor do they remain in the same place.
2. Some spend the winters in Florida but migrate north during the summer.
3. Others travel in the Gulf of Mexico to Louisiana or Texas.
4. The African manatee stays along the coast and in the rivers of Africa.
5. The Amazon manatee is not found in the ocean, for it lives in fresh water.

▶ **Exercise 6** Identifying Correlative **Conjunctions** Copy each sentence below. Circle both parts of each correlative conjunction, and underline the words or word groups it connects.

1. Manatees' mouths are well adapted both to gather and to chew plants.
2. Manatees not only have hard pads in their mouths but also have teeth that are constantly replaced.
3. They eat plants that are either under the water or on the surface.
4. Their front flippers are useful both for steering and for gathering food.
5. Manatees are neither fast moving nor able to defend themselves.

▶ **Exercise 7** Supplying Conjunctions Supply a coordinating or correlative conjunction to complete each sentence below.

1. The dugong ___?___ the manatee are similar water mammals.
2. Manatees are found in Florida ___?___ the Caribbean.
3. All manatees eat only plants, ___?___ they are vegetarians.
4. These animals are ___?___ gentle ___?___ curious.

5. Manatees enjoy playing ___?___ alone ___?___ in small groups.
6. Manatees' eyes are ___?___ small ___?___ protected by a thin layer of skin.
7. They can ___?___ hear well ___?___ use their bristles for feeling around.
8. Their nostrils are closed under the water ___?___ open at the surface.
9. Their need for air changes ___?___ they are playing ___?___ resting.
10. During the day, they rest ___?___ at the bottom ___?___ near the surface.

▶ **Exercise 8** Writing Sentences With **Conjunctions** Use each of the following conjunctions in a sentence.

1. and
2. both . . . and
3. or
4. either . . . or
5. not only . . . but also

▶ **Exercise 9** Find It in Your Reading In the excerpt from "Greyling" on page 365, identify the words or groups of words that each highlighted conjunction connects.

▶ **Exercise 10** Find It in Your **Writing** Find at least three examples of coordinating conjunctions in writing in your portfolio. Challenge yourself to add a correlative conjunction to a piece of your writing.

▶ **Exercise 11** Writing Application Write a description of something that lives or grows in the ocean. Use two correlative conjunctions and three coordinating conjunctions. Underline the conjunctions.

Section Review • 369

ASSESS

Section Review

Each of these exercises correlates to the instruction on conjunctions, pages 364–368. The exercises may be used for more practice, for reteaching, or for review of the Key Concepts presented. Answers for all chapter exercises are available in *Grammar Exercises Answers on Transparencies* in your Teaching Resources.

Answer Key

▶ **Exercise 5**

1. Manatees do not migrate very far, (nor) do they remain in the same place.
2. spend the winters in Florida (but) migrate north during the summer.
3. Louisiana (or) Texas
4. along the coast (and) in the rivers
5. The Amazon manatee is not found in the ocean, (for) it lives in fresh water.

▶ **Exercise 6**

1. Manatees' mouths are well adapted (both) to gather (and) to chew plants.
2. Manatees (not only) have hard pads in their mouths (but also) have teeth that are constantly replaced.
3. They eat plants that are (either) under the water (or) on the surface.
4. Their front flippers are useful (both) for steering (and) for gathering food.
5. Manatees are (neither) fast moving (nor) able to defend themselves.

▶ **Exercise 7**

Answers will vary. Samples are given.

1. and
2. and
3. for
4. both, and
5. both, and
6. both, and
7. both, and
8. but
9. whether, or
10. either, or

▶ **Exercise 8**

Answers will vary. Encourage students to create a variety of sentence structures.

continued

Answer Key continued

▶ **Exercise 9**

Find It in Your Reading
*would not know his grief **and** thus double her own; leave the hut each morning with a breath of song **and** return each night with a whistle on his lips; his nets were full **but** his heart was empty, **yet** he never told his wife*

▶ **Exercise 10**

Find It in Your Writing
Ask students to find examples of three different coordinating conjunctions.

▶ **Exercise 11**

Writing Application
Students may want to illustrate their descriptions and create an ocean bulletin-board display.

sentences on the chalkboard:

That is the biggest salami I've ever seen.

Don't put mustard all over it.

I dropped it on the rug.

Challenge students to add one word before each sentence that will indicate a certain strong feeling, such as surprise, disgust, or a mistake. (Possible answers: *Wow! Gee!; Ugh!; Oops!*) If none of students' suggestions are interjections, add an interjection of your own to one of the sentences as an example.

Activate Prior Knowledge

Students already have a good command of casual and slang expressions. Before they study the interjections in the chart on this page, ask them to list some words that show strong feeling. Then have them compare their list with the words in the chart.

TEACH

Step-by-Step Teaching Guide

Interjections

1. Go over the interjections in the chart with students, defining and giving examples of any that are new or unfamiliar to them.

2. Challenge students to add interjections to the list. (Possible answers: *Rats! Drat! Yikes! Awesome! Oy! Whoops! Cool!*)

3. Have students use these interjections in sentences.

Integrating Vocabulary Skills

Eureka is a Greek word meaning "I have found it." Legend has it that the ancient Greek mathematician Archimedes exclaimed "Eureka!" when he discovered the principle of displacement—any object lowered into water displaces its own weight in water. People exclaim "Eureka!" to signify triumph at discovering something.

Critical Viewing

Speculate Students might use the following interjections in their sentences: Wow!, Look out!, Great!

370

Section 18.2

Interjections

When you want to show strong feeling or excitement, you can use words that exclaim. In the sentence *Terrific! I will begin right now*, the word *terrific* shows strong feeling. *Terrific* is being used as an interjection.

▶ **KEY CONCEPT** **Interjections** are words that express sudden excitement or strong feeling. ■

Sometimes, an interjection is followed by an exclamation mark and is separated from the sentence that follows it.

EXAMPLES: Wow! That killer whale jumped very high.
Ouch! That belly flop must have hurt.

At other times, an interjection is followed by a comma and connected to a sentence. This occurs when the interjection expresses a mild feeling instead of a strong one.

EXAMPLES: My, that was an exciting trip.
Oh, I wish I could find it.

Interjections are used more in speech than in writing. They are informal, rather than formal, expressions. When you do see them in writing, they are often included in dialogue. The following chart lists words often used as interjections.

INTERJECTIONS				
ah	fine	huh	oops	ugh
aha	golly	hurray	ouch	well
alas	gosh	my	psst	what
boy	great	never	shh	whew
darn	heavens	nonsense	terrible	wonderful
eureka	hey	oh	terrific	wow

370 • Conjunctions and Interjections

Theme: Sea Mammals

In this section, you will learn how interjections add emotion to writing. The examples and exercises are about sea mammals.

Cross-Curricular Connection: Science

✿ Grammar and Style Tip

Try not to use interjections in your formal writing. They will make it sound too informal. In your casual writing, interjections can add interest and emotion.

◀ **Critical Viewing** What do you think the people in the front row say when the orca jumps out of—or reenters—the water? Use an interjection in a sentence in your response. **[Speculate]**

⏱ TIME AND RESOURCE MANAGER

Resources
Print: Grammar Exercise Workbook, pp. 41–42
Technology: On-Line Exercise Bank, Section 18.2

In-Depth Coverage	Accelerated Pace
• Work through all key concepts, p. 370. • Assign and review Exercises 12–13.	• Assign p. 370 for independent student review. • Assign Section Review Exercises 14–16, p. 372.

Exercise 12 Supplying Interjections Substitute an interjection for each of the blanks below. Use the interjections in the chart on page 370, or think of others.

EXAMPLE: ___?___! I'm very excited to learn about dolphins.

ANSWER: Boy! I'm very excited to learn about dolphins.

1. ___?___! There are 32 species of dolphins.
2. ___?___! We can go to see the dolphins.
3. ___?___! That will be an exciting trip.
4. ___?___! They won't let us swim with the dolphins.
5. ___?___, they are very gentle animals.
6. ___?___! Let's listen to the instructions.
7. ___?___! We can get so close to the dolphins!
8. ___?___! Did you know people once hunted dolphins?
9. ___?___, it sure is good they stopped.
10. ___?___, some are trapped in fishing nets accidentally.

Exercise 13 Choosing Appropriate Interjections Supply an interjection to fill in the blank in each sentence below, expressing the emotion indicated in brackets. Use the interjections listed in the chart on page 370, or think of others.

EXAMPLE: [excitement]___?___! I'm so happy we saw the dolphins.

ANSWER: Wow! I'm so happy we saw the dolphins.

1. [surprise] ___?___! Some dolphins eat one third of their body weight in fish each day.
2. [enthusiasm] ___?___! Spinner dolphins have more than 200 teeth.
3. [curiosity] ___?___, how do they breathe?
4. [mistake] ___?___! I didn't know that they don't breathe through the nose.
5. [realization] ___?___, the hole is on the top of the dolphin's head.
6. [excitement] ___?___! That's why they come to the surface every few minutes.
7. [agreement] ___?___, and they have specially adapted lungs.
8. [understanding] ___?___! That's how dolphins can dive so deep under the water.
9. [disagreement] ___?___! I don't know if that's true.
10. [secrecy] ___?___, you can read it right here in this book.

▲ **Critical Viewing** Use an interjection in a sentence to express the emotion you see on the face of this dolphin. [Infer]

More Practice
On-line Exercise Bank
• Section 18.2
Grammar Exercise Workbook
• pp. 41–42

Interjections • 371

ONGOING ASSESSMENT: Monitor and Reinforce

If students miss more than two items in Exercises 12–13, refer them to the following for additional practice.

In the Textbook	Print Resources	Technology
Section Review, Ex. 14–16, p. 372	Grammar Exercise Workbook, pp. 41–42	On-Line Exercise Bank, Section 18.2

Customize for ESL Students

Encourage students to make a list of foreign-language equivalents of all the interjections on page 370 and any others the class suggested. Students can teach classmates the Cambodian version of *oops,* the Spanish word for *drat,* and so on.

Answer Key

Exercise 12

Answers will vary. Samples are given.

1. Whew! There are 32 species of dolphins.
2. Hurray! We can go to see the dolphins.
3. Great! That will be an exciting trip.
4. Rats! They won't let us swim with the dolphins.
5. My, they are very gentle animals.
6. Ssh! Let's listen to the instructions.
7. Wonderful! We can get so close to the dolphins!
8. Heavens! Did you know people once hunted dolphins?
9. Boy, it sure is good they stopped.
10. Alas, some are trapped in fishing nets accidentally.

Exercise 13

Answers will vary. Samples are given.

1. Gosh! Some dolphins eat one third of their body weight in fish each day.
2. Wow! Spinner dolphins have more than 200 teeth.
3. Golly, how do they breathe?
4. Oops! I didn't know that they don't breathe through the nose.
5. Aha, the hole is on the top of the dolphin's head.
6. Oh! That's why they come to the surface every few minutes.
7. Yes, and they have specially adapted lungs.
8. Oh! That's how dolphins can dive so deep under the water.
9. Nonsense! I don't know if that's true.
10. Psst, you can read it right here in this book.

Critical Viewing

Infer Students' interjections should show their focus on the dolphin's face, including ah, boy, my, well, and so forth.

ASSESS and CLOSE

Section Review

Each of these exercises correlates to the instruction on interjections, pages 370–371. The exercises may be used for more practice, for reteaching, or for review of the Key Concepts presented. Answers for all chapter exercises are available in *Grammar Exercises Answers on Transparencies* in your Teaching Resources.

Answer Key

Exercise 14

Answers will vary. Samples are given.

1. Hey
2. Wow
3. What
4. Cool
5. My
6. Gosh
7. Boy
8. Hey
9. Hey
10. Wow

Exercise 15

Answers will vary. Samples are given.

1. Hey
2. Yes
3. Oops
4. Aha
5. Yes
6. Oh
7. Hey
8. Alas
9. Wow
10. Boy

Exercise 16

Answers will vary.

Exercise 17

Find It in Your Reading
Have students bring in some comics and have the class work together to identify interjections in them.

Exercise 18

Find It in Your Writing
Students may want to work with partners, adding interjections to each other's writing.

Exercise 19

Writing Application
Invite students to read their dialogues aloud with a partner, using appropriate inflection for the interjections.

Section 18.2 Section Review

GRAMMAR EXERCISES 14–19

Exercise 14 Supplying Interjections Substitute an interjection for each of the blanks below.

1. ___?___! Dolphins often make clicking noises.
2. ___?___, they also whistle.
3. ___?___! Dolphins can communicate?
4. ___?___! They use these noises to speak to each other.
5. ___?___, they also listen to the echoes from the noises.
6. ___?___! That is one way they navigate.
7. ___?___! Dolphins are very intelligent.
8. ___?___, I didn't know they had these abilities.
9. ___?___, in captivity some dolphins can learn human words.
10. ___?___! There is so much to learn about dolphins.

Exercise 15 Choosing Interjections Fill in each blank below with an interjection that expresses the emotion indicated in brackets.

1. [confusion] ___?___! Are porpoises the same as dolphins?
2. [agreement] ___?___, they are closely related.
3. [mistake] ___?___, porpoises are usually smaller than dolphins.
4. [understanding] ___?___! They sometimes surface four times a minute to breathe.
5. [agreement] ___?___, that is one of the main differences.
6. [surprise] ___?___, and they are rarely seen in the open ocean.
7. [excitement] ___?___! Don't they stay near rivers?
8. [sadness] ___?___, porpoises don't like to play near boats.
9. [surprise] ___?___, the Dall porpoise has such a white belly.

372 • Conjunctions and Interjections

10. [realization] ___?___! It doesn't travel very far during its lifetime.

Exercise 16 Writing Sentences With Interjections Write a sentence that expresses the emotion of each interjection below.

1. gosh
2. really
3. aha
4. wow
5. my
6. hurray
7. ouch
8. whew
9. never
10. ugh

Exercise 17 Find It in Your Reading Examine an adventure comic book or some comic strips in the newspaper. Find examples of interjections in the characters' conversations.

Exercise 18 Find It in Your Writing Choose a piece of writing from your portfolio that contains dialogue. Look for examples of interjections. If you can't find any, challenge yourself to find a spot where you can include an interjection.

Exercise 19 Writing Application Write a dialogue between two characters who are seeing the ocean for the first time. Include at least three interjections in your dialogue, and use appropriate punctuation.

✓ ONGOING ASSESSMENT: Assess Mastery

Use the following resources to assess student mastery of conjunctions and interjections.

In the Textbook	Print Resources	Technology
Chapter Review, Ex. 20–27, pp. 373–374 Standardized Test Preparation Workshop, p. 375	Formal Assessment, Chapter 18	On-Line Exercise Bank, Section 18

Chapter 18 Chapter Review

GRAMMAR EXERCISES 20–28

Exercise 20 Recognizing **Coordinating Conjunctions** For each sentence below, list the coordinating conjunction and the words or word groups it connects. Circle the conjunction.

1. Whales descended from land animals but developed in the water.
2. They are very streamlined, so they appear fishlike.
3. Whales don't have legs nor do they have any other structures for getting around on land.
4. Their tails are firm and flexible because they have elastic tissues.
5. Whale skin is without sweat glands or oil glands.
6. It feels smooth, for it is hairless.
7. Whales breathe through a single hole, yet they don't inhale water.
8. Muscles open the blowhole and then quickly close it.
9. The two types of whales are the toothed whales and the baleen whales.
10. The smallest toothed whales are dolphins or porpoises.

Exercise 21 Supplying Correlative **Conjunctions** Supply a correlative conjunction to complete each sentence below.

1. ___?___ do most whales live for twenty years ___?___ some ___?___ live eighty years.
2. However, they can fall victim ___?___ to predators ___?___ to diseases.
3. Predators are ___?___ other animals ___?___ humans.
4. Most whales are ___?___ aggressive ___?___ able to defend themselves.
5. ___?___ is their size a great advantage ___?___ they are able to dive very deep.
6. Babies are born ___?___ fully developed ___?___ ready to swim.
7. ___?___ the baby will rise to the surface ___?___ the mother pushes it.
8. Scientists are not certain ___?___ parents remain together ___?___ the father leaves.
9. Most baby whales ___?___ leave their mothers after two years ___?___ stay with the family forever.
10. Whales ___?___ breathe the air ___?___ stay underwater for long periods of time.

Exercise 22 Classifying **Conjunctions** Write the conjunctions in the following sentences, and label them *coordinating* or *correlative.*

1. Baleen whales eat krill or other small animals.
2. The pieces of baleen not only hang from the roof of the whale's mouth, but they also close like a gate.
3. Both gray whales and humpback whales are baleen whales.
4. Big whales may look slow, but they are fast swimmers.
5. The blue whale is the largest baleen whale, for it may be a hundred feet long.
6. Some toothed whales have only two teeth, yet others have more than fifty.
7. The teeth are uniform in both size and shape.
8. A few species are either in aquariums or in zoos.
9. The sperm whale is very large, and its head measures one third of its body.
10. It is not as large as some baleen whales, but it has a bigger throat.

Exercise 23 Identifying **Interjections** Write the interjection in each sentence below.

1. Wow! The killer whale is a very fast swimmer.
2. Gosh! It will attack such big whales.

Chapter Review • 373

CHAPTER REVIEW

Each of these exercises correlates to a section of the chapter on conjunctions and interjections, pages 364–372. The exercises may be used for more practice, for reteaching, or for review of the Key Concepts presented. Answers for all chapter exercises are available in *Grammar Exercises Answers on Transparencies* in your Teaching Resources.

Answer Key

Exercise 20

1. descended from land animals (but) developed in the water
2. They are very streamlined, (so) they appear fishlike.
3. Whales don't have legs (nor) do they have any other structures for getting around on land.
4. firm (and) flexible
5. sweat glands (or) oil glands
6. It feels smooth, (for) it is hairless.
7. Whales breathe through a single hole, (yet) they don't inhale water.
8. open the blowhole (and) then quickly close it
9. the toothed whales (and) the baleen whales
10. dolphins (or) porpoises

Exercise 21

1. Not only do most whales live for twenty years but some also live eighty years.
2. However, they can fall victim both to predators and to diseases.
3. Predators are either other animals or humans.
4. Most whales are not only aggressive but also able to defend themselves.
5. Not only is their size a great advantage but also they are able to dive very deep.
6. Babies are born both fully developed and ready to swim.
7. Either the baby will rise to the surface or the mother pushes it.
8. Scientists are not certain whether parents remain together or the father leaves.
9. Most baby whales either leave their mothers after two years or stay with the family forever.
10. Whales neither breathe the air nor stay underwater for long periods of time.

continued

Answer Key continued

Exercise 22

1. or—coordinating
2. not only, but also—correlative
3. both, and—correlative
4. but—coordinating
5. for—coordinating
6. yet—coordinating
7. both, and—correlative
8. either, or—correlative
9. and—coordinating
10. but—coordinating

Exercise 23

1. Wow
2. Gosh
3. My
4. Boy
5. Aha
6. Golly
7. Well
8. Well
9. Oops
10. Psst

Answer Key

Answers will vary. Samples are given.

1. Hey!
2. Well,
3. Yes,
4. Neat!
5. Wow,
6. Yay!
7. Uh,
8. Look!
9. Rats!
10. Nuts,

Exercise 25

1. Many whale species are considered rare and are endangered.
2. This not only includes the blue whale, but also includes many other species.
3. The International Whaling Commission is a group of both whaling and non-whaling nations.
4. Do they want to conserve and protect whales?
5. Well, whaling is easier these days, so we need stricter regulations.

Exercise 26

Answers will vary. Samples are given.

1. Not only do my parents like to hike, but they also like to swim.
2. Gosh! I didn't know you had an older brother.
3. We can eat either Japanese or Indian food.
4. I am not going to school, for I am sick.
5. Neither her parents nor my sister can come with us.

Exercise 27

Answers will vary. Samples are given.

I was in the ocean swimming and saw a fin in the distance coming toward me. Oh! My heart began to beat rapidly. I wanted to swim to shore or to grow wings and fly out of there. The fin came closer. Ah! I screamed and then woke up from the dream.

Exercise 28

Writing Application
Students can also identify the words connected by the conjunctions.

Chapter Review Exercises cont'd.

3. My, the killer whale will even eat walruses.
4. Boy! The teeth look pretty sharp.
5. Aha, they are in both its upper and lower jaws.
6. Golly! It's smaller than I expected.
7. Well, it is only twenty or thirty feet long.
8. Well, do they live alone or in groups?
9. Oops! I didn't know that they do both.
10. Psst! Those groups are called pods.

▶ **Exercise 24** Choosing
Interjections Fill in the blank in each sentence below with an interjection that expresses the emotion indicated in brackets. Add an appropriate punctuation mark.

1. [curiosity] ___?___ What is the big fin called?
2. [hesitation] ___?___ I think that's the dorsal fin.
3. [agreement] ___?___ it can be up to six feet tall.
4. [enthusiasm] ___?___ All of their flippers are oval.
5. [surprise] ___?___ that looks different from the other toothed whales.
6. [happiness] ___?___ Now we will be able to tell them apart.
7. [confusion] ___?___ isn't their coloring also different?
8. [excitement] ___?___ The black-and-white combination is very distinctive.
9. [frustration] ___?___ I knew I had forgotten something.
10. [unhappiness] ___?___ I don't think I can stay any longer.

▶ **Exercise 25** Combining Sentences
With Conjunctions Combine each pair of sentences below with the conjunction specified.

1. Many whale species are considered rare. Many are endangered. (and)
2. This includes the blue whale. It also includes many other species. (not only . . . but also)

3. The International Whaling Commission is a group of whaling nations. Non-whaling nations belong, too. (both . . . and)
4. Do they want to conserve whales? Do they want to protect whales? (and)
5. Well, whaling is easier these days. We need stricter regulations. (so)

▶ **Exercise 26** Writing Sentences
With Conjunctions and Interjections
Write an original sentence using each of the following conjunctions and/or interjections.

1. not only . . . but also
2. gosh
3. either . . . or
4. for
5. neither . . . nor

▶ **Exercise 27** Revising a Passage
With Conjunctions and Interjections
Revise the following passage, combining sentences where appropriate and inserting interjections to add emotion.

I was in the ocean swimming. I saw a fin in the distance coming toward me. My heart began to beat rapidly. I wanted to swim to shore. I wanted to grow wings and fly out of there. The fin came closer. I screamed. Then, I woke up from the dream.

▶ **Exercise 28** Writing Application
Write an account of an experience you had in or near the water. Use at least three interjections, three coordinating conjunctions, and two correlative conjunctions in your sentences. Underline these parts of speech.

374 • Conjunctions and Interjections

Standardized Test Preparation Workshop

Revising and Editing

Standardized test questions measure your knowledge of standard grammar and usage, such as when to use conjunctions. Conjunctions, such as *and, but, or,* and *for,* join closely related ideas together. When answering these types of questions, read the entire passage first. Then, note how using a conjunction could connect like ideas. Finally, choose the letter of the best rewrite of the underlined sentences.

Test Tip

When choosing the best rewrite of a sentence, make sure a comma is used before a conjunction connecting two independent clauses. If not, this choice is a run-on sentence and, therefore, incorrect.

Read the passage, and choose the letter of the best way to write the underlined sentences. If the underlined section needs no change, mark the choice "Correct as is."

(1) <u>Many people believe that the Loch Ness monster is a myth. Hundreds of people have reported sightings of the animal.</u>

1 A Many people believe that the Loch Ness monster is a myth. Wow! Hundreds of people have reported sightings of the animal.

B Many people believe that the Loch Ness monster is a myth, and hundreds of people have reported sightings of the animal.

C Many people believe that the Loch Ness monster is a myth, but hundreds of people have reported sightings of the animal.

D Correct as is

The best answer is *C.* The conjunction *but* joins contrasting ideas without changing the meaning.

> **Practice 1** **Directions:** Read the passage, and choose the letter of the best way to write the underlined sentences. If the underlined section needs no change, mark the choice "Correct as is."

The Loch Ness monster supposedly lives in Loch Ness, a lake in northern Scotland. (1) <u>It has been reported that the creature has flippers. It has one or two humps.</u> (2) <u>Many believe it looks like a dinosaur. It has a long, slender neck similar to a brontosaur's.</u>

1 A It has been reported that the creature has flippers and one or two humps.

B It has been reported that the creature has flippers but it has one or two humps.

C Yes! It has been reported that the creature has flippers. It has one or two humps.

D Correct as is

2 F Many believe it looks like a dinosaur, but it has a long, slender neck similar to a brontosaur's.

G Many believe it looks like a dinosaur and it has a long slender neck similar to a brontosaur's.

H Many believe it looks like a dinosaur, for it has a long slender neck similar to a brontosaur's.

J Correct as is

▶ Lesson Objectives

- To revise and edit sentences using conjunctions.
- To revise passages for coherence by using conjunctions.

Step-by-Step Teaching Guide

Revising and Editing

Teaching Resources: Standardized Test Preparation Workbook, Chapter 18

1. Encourage students to create simple charts that list conjunctions in one column and the relationship each conjunction expresses in the other. Students can refer to these charts as they answer the questions.

2. Have students carefully read the sentences in each passage and highlight any repeated information. This will help them determine how the sentences can be combined using conjunctions.

Answer Key

> **Practice 1**

1. A
2. H

⚒ TEST-TAKING TIP

Before students make a choice, encourage them to read all of the choices. Have them underline the conjunction used in each revised sentence. Students can immediately eliminate any choices that use conjunctions expressing the wrong relationship between ideas. For example, in the sample test item, students should see that the ideas expressed in the two sentences are contrasting. If the sentences are not joined by a conjunction showing contrast, it will seem as if the writer is contradicting him- or herself. They can immediately eliminate items A and D because they do not combine the sentences. They also can eliminate item B, because it uses *and,* which implies a similarity, not a contrast.

Answer Key

▶ **Exercise A**

1. element—common, singular; weather—common, singular; temperature—common, singular
2. day—common, singular; middle—common, singular; afternoon—compound, common, singular
3. It—personal pronoun; Tropics—proper, plural
4. North Pole—compound, proper, singular; South Pole—compound, proper, singular; temperatures—common, plural
5. Temperature—common, singular; latitude—common, singular; elevation—common, singular; season—common, singular
6. This—demonstrative pronoun; temperature—common, singular
7. These—demonstrative pronoun; scales—common, plural; temperature—common, singular
8. Scientists—common, plural; Kelvin—proper, singular; Celsius—proper, singular
9. That—demonstrative pronoun; countries—common, plural
10. United States—compound, proper, singular; Fahrenheit—proper, singular

▶ **Exercise B**

1. moves—action
2. are called—action
3. are included—action
4. lie—action
5. consist—action
6. travels—action
7. are—linking
8. are determined—action
9. is—linking
10. blow—action

▶ **Exercise C**

1. adjective, *crystals*
2. adverb, *are divided*
3. adverb, *rise*
4. adverb, *consist*
5. adverb, *are arranged*
6. adjective, *clouds*
7. adverb, *filters*
8. adjective, *puffs*
9. adverb, *are*
10. adjective, *clouds*

Cumulative Review

PARTS OF SPEECH

▶ **Exercise A** Classifying Nouns and Pronouns Identify the nouns and pronouns in the following sentences. Label each noun *compound*, *common*, or *proper*, and *singular* or *plural*. Label each pronoun *personal* or *demonstrative*.

1. One element of the weather is temperature.
2. Every day is warmest during the middle of the afternoon.
3. It is usually warmer in the Tropics.
4. The North Pole and the South Pole have the lowest temperatures.
5. Temperature varies with latitude, elevation, and season.
6. This means temperature can change suddenly.
7. These are the scales used for measuring temperature.
8. Scientists use Kelvin, or they use Celsius.
9. That is used in many countries.
10. The United States continues to use Fahrenheit.

▶ **Exercise B** Classifying Verbs Write the verbs in the following sentences, and label each *action* or *linking*. Include and underline all helping verbs.

1. Wind moves horizontally through the atmosphere.
2. Some winds are called "prevailing."
3. The trade winds are included in the prevailing winds category.
4. The doldrums lie within 10 degrees of the equator.
5. The horse latitudes, 30 degrees from the equator, consist of calm, light winds.
6. Surface air travels from the horse latitudes to the equator.

7. Those are the trade winds.
8. Seasonal winds are determined by air temperature.
9. The air over the continents is warmer in the summer than the air over the oceans.
10. Then winds from the colder ocean blow inland.

▶ **Exercise C** Recognizing Adjectives and Adverbs Label each underlined word in the following sentences as *adjective* or *adverb*. Then, write the word each one modifies.

1. Clouds are composed of small water droplets or <u>tiny</u> ice crystals.
2. They are <u>usually</u> divided into four families.
3. Cirrus clouds rise <u>higher</u> above the Earth.
4. They consist <u>mainly</u> of ice particles.
5. These feathery clouds are <u>commonly</u> arranged in bands.
6. <u>Thick</u> altostratus clouds may obscure the sun or moon.
7. Light <u>barely</u> filters through the bluish veil.
8. Altocumulus clouds resemble <u>dense</u> puffs.
9. Low clouds are <u>generally</u> less than one mile high.
10. Like <u>middle</u> clouds, they are composed of water droplets.

▶ **Exercise D** Recognizing Prepositions, Conjunctions, and Interjections Identify the underlined words in the following sentences as prepositions, conjunctions, or interjections. Write the object of the prepositions. Label the conjunctions *coordinating* or *correlative*.

▶ **Exercise D**

1. interjection; preposition (ground)
2. correlative conjunction
3. coordinating conjunction
4. interjection
5. coordinating conjunction

1. Wow! Did you see the hail falling to the ground?
2. It looks like a combination of both ice and snow.
3. Raindrops or snow pellets become hailstones as they collide with each other.
4. Gee, that requires the wind characteristic of thunderstorms.
5. They travel through the clouds but become too heavy.

Exercise E Supplying Interjections
In the following sentences, write an interjection that expresses the feeling shown in parentheses.

1. (surprise) Did you see that meteor shower last night?
2. (hesitation) I wasn't sure what that was.
3. (disappointment) did that happen while I was sleeping?
4. (amazement) I couldn't believe my eyes.
5. (agreement) it is a natural event.

Exercise F Identifying All the Parts of Speech
Write the part of speech of each underlined word in the following paragraph. Be as specific as possible.

Hey, those rainbows are an interesting sight. They can be seen after a shower or near a waterfall. The brightest rainbows show the spectrum colors with red on the outside. When the sun is low in the sky, rainbows appear relatively high.

Exercise G Supplying the Correct Part of Speech
In the following sentences, supply the part of speech indicated in parentheses.

1. Thunderstorms can be very (adjective).
2. Not only is there a lot of noise, (correlative conjunction) the lightning can be dangerous.
3. You should not stand under a (noun) during a thunderstorm.
4. The best place to be is (preposition) your house away from the windows.
5. (verb) not talk on the telephone during a storm.
6. Some thunderstorms also have (adverb) high winds.
7. Wind, rain, thunder, (conjunction) lightning are all elements of a storm.
8. Most thunderstorms (verb) in the spring and summer months.
9. (Adjective) tornadoes can accompany these storms.
10. (Interjection) It seems that every season has its (adjective) weather.

Exercise H Revising With Adjectives and Adverbs
Revise the following passage by adding adjectives and adverbs to modify nouns, verbs, and adjectives.

Some people enjoy winter. They like snow and cold winds. Snow covers everything and makes it look clean. There are a lot of outdoor activities that people enjoy in the winter: skiing, ice skating, and sledding. But some people just like to sit by a fire and watch through the window as the snow falls.

Exercise I Writing Application
Write a short narrative about a weather event that you have witnessed or learned about. Underline at least one noun, pronoun, verb, adjective, adverb, preposition, conjunction, and interjection. Then, label each word's part of speech as specifically as possible.

Exercise E
Answers will vary. Samples are given.
1. Wow!
2. Um,
3. Oh,
4. Gee!
5. Yes,

Exercise F
Hey—interjection; rainbows—plural, common noun; are—linking verb; They—personal pronoun; or—coordinating conjunction; near—preposition; brightest—adjective; show—action verb; colors—plural, common noun; with—preposition; on the outside—prepositional phrase (object is *outside*); in—preposition; relatively—adverb

Exercise G
Answers will vary. Samples are given.
1. dangerous
2. but also
3. tree
4. inside
5. Do
6. dangerously
7. and
8. occur
9. Strong
10. Wow!, bad

Exercise H
Answers will vary. Sample is given.
Some people really enjoy winter. They like heavy snow and cold winds. Snow quietly covers everything and makes it look very clean. There are a lot of fun outdoor activities that many people enjoy in the winter: skiing, ice skating, and sledding. But some people just like to quietly sit by a warm fire and watch through the window as the snow silently falls.

Exercise I
Writing Application
As an extension, have students remove the labels from their narratives and exchange them with a partner. Partners can then label the underlined words.

Time and Resource Manager

In-Depth Lesson Plan

	LESSON FOCUS	PRINT AND MEDIA RESOURCES
DAY 1	**The Basic Sentence** Students learn and apply concepts covering basic sentence parts (pp. 380–385).	**Teaching Resources** *Grammar Exercise Workbook*, pp. 43–44; *Grammar Exercises Answers on Transparencies*, Ch. 19 **On-Line Exercise Bank**, Section 19.1
DAY 2	**Subjects and Predicates** Students learn and apply concepts about complete and compound subjects and predicates (pp. 386–393).	**Teaching Resources** *Grammar Exercise Workbook*, pp. 45–48; *Grammar Exercises Answers on Transparencies*, Ch. 19 **Language Lab CD-ROM**, Sentence Style; **On-Line Exercise Bank**, Sections 19.2–3
DAY 3	**Hard-to-Find Subjects** Students learn and apply concepts about hard-to-find subjects (pp. 394–397).	**Teaching Resources** *Grammar Exercise Workbook*, pp. 49–50; *Grammar Exercises Answers on Transparencies*, Ch. 19 **On-Line Exercise Bank**, Section 19.4
DAY 4	**Direct and Indirect Objects** Students learn and apply concepts about direct and indirect objects and do the Hands-on Grammar activity (pp. 398–403).	**Teaching Resources** *Grammar Exercise Workbook*, pp. 51–54; *Grammar Exercises Answers on Transparencies*, Ch. 19; *Hands-on Grammar Activity Book*, Ch. 19 **On-Line Exercise Bank**, Section 19.5
DAY 5	**Predicate Nouns and Adjectives** Students learn and apply concepts about predicate nouns and adjectives (pp. 404–409).	**Teaching Resources** *Grammar Exercise Workbook*, pp. 55–58; *Grammar Exercises Answers on Transparencies*, Ch. 19 **On-Line Exercise Bank**, Section 19.6
DAY 6	**Review and Assess** Students review chapter and demonstrate mastery of use of basic sentence parts (pp. 410–413).	**Teaching Resources** *Formal Assessment*, Ch. 19; *Grammar Exercises Answers on Transparencies*, Ch. 19 **On-Line Exercise Bank**, Sections 19.1–6

Accelerated Lesson Plan

	LESSON FOCUS	PRINT AND MEDIA RESOURCES
DAY 1	**The Basic Sentence** Students cover concepts and usage of basic sentence parts as determined by Diagnostic Test (pp. 380–385).	**Teaching Resources** *Grammar Exercise Workbook*, pp. 43–44; *Grammar Exercises Answers on Transparencies*, Ch. 19 **On-Line Exercise Bank**, Section 19.1
DAY 2	**Subjects and Predicates** Students cover concepts and usage of subjects and predicates as determined by Diagnostic Test (pp. 386–397).	**Teaching Resources** *Grammar Exercise Workbook*, pp. 45–50; *Grammar Exercises Answers on Transparencies*, Ch. 19 **Language Lab CD-ROM**, Sentence Style; **On-Line Exercise Bank**, Sections 19.2–4
DAY 3	**Direct and Indirect Objects, Predicate Nouns and Adjectives** Students cover concepts and usage of direct and indirect objects, predicate nouns and adjectives as determined by Diagnostic Test (pp. 398–409).	**Teaching Resources** *Grammar Exercise Workbook*, pp. 51–58; *Grammar Exercises Answers on Transparencies*, Ch. 19; *Hands-on Grammar Activity Book*, Ch. 19 **On-Line Exercise Bank**, Sections 19.5–6
DAY 4	**Review and Assess** Students review chapter and demonstrate mastery of use of basic sentence parts (pp. 410–413).	**Teaching Resources** *Formal Assessment*, Ch. 19; *Grammar Exercises Answers on Transparencies*, Ch. 19 **On-Line Exercise Bank**, Sections 19.1–6

INTEGRATED SKILLS COVERAGE

Grammar in Literature
SE pp. 382, 388, 392, 399, 404

Reading
Find It in Your Reading SE pp. 385, 389, 393, 397, 402, 403, 409
Reading Skills ATE pp. 402, 407

Writing
Find It in Your Writing SE pp. 385, 389, 393, 397, 402, 403, 409
Writing Application SE pp. 385, 389, 393, 397, 403, 409, 411
Writing Skills ATE p. 392
Grammar and Style SE p. 382

Language Highlight
ATE p. 391

Technology
ATE p. 383

Real-World Connection
ATE p. 381

Viewing and Representing
Critical Viewing
SE pp. 378, 381, 383, 384, 387, 391, 395, 398, 401, 405, 406, 408
Representing Skills ATE p. 383

ASSESSMENT SUPPORT

Standardized Test Preparation SE pp. 412–413; ATE pp. 388, 405

Standardized Test Preparation Workbook, pp. 37–38
Formal Assessment, Ch. 19

MEETING INDIVIDUAL NEEDS

Less Advanced Students ATE p. 392. See also Ongoing
Assessments ATE pp. 383, 384, 387, 391, 395, 396, 399, 400, 406
ESL Students ATE pp. 395, 406
Verbal/Linguistic Learners ATE p. 401
Bodily/Kinesthetic Learners ATE p. 383
More Advanced Students ATE p. 408

BLOCK SCHEDULING

Pacing Suggestions
For 90-minute Blocks
- Administer the Diagnostic Test to students to determine instructional coverage.
- Have students complete the necessary exercises in class. Use the Hands-on Grammar activity to provide a change of pace.

Resources for Varying Instruction
- *Language Lab* CD-ROM If your students have access to hardware, a 90-minute block provides an ideal opportunity for students to work on computer.

Professional Development Support
- *How to Manage Instruction in the Block* This teaching Resource provides management and activity suggestions.

MEDIA AND TECHNOLOGY

For the Student
- *Language Lab* CD-ROM, Sentence Style
- *On-Line Exercise Bank,* Ch. 19

For the Teacher
- *Resource Pro* CD-ROM

WRITING AND GRAMMAR WEB SITE

The Interactive Writing and Grammar Web site provides a wide array of support for students, teachers, and parents. Grammar support includes:

- On-Line Exercise Bank with Auto Check scoring
- Diagnostic and assessment support

www.phschool.com

LITERATURE CONNECTIONS

Grammar in Literature selections from *Prentice Hall Literature: Timeless Voices, Timeless Themes,* Copper:
from "The Fun They Had," Isaac Asimov, SE pp. 382, 388, 392
from "Breaker's Bridge," Laurence Yep, SE pp. 399, 404

Lesson Objectives

1. To recognize subjects and predicates and understand their roles in sentences.

2. To locate simple and compound subjects and predicates within sentences.

3. To identify hard-to-find subjects.

4. To understand how direct and indirect objects complete the meanings of some sentences.

5. To recognize predicate nouns and predicate adjectives.

6. To establish and adjust purposes for reading such as reading to find out, to understand, to enjoy, and to solve problems.

7. To answer different types and levels of questions such as open-ended, literal, and interpretive as well as test-like questions such as multiple choice, true-false, and short answer.

8. To write in complete sentences, varying the types such as compound and complex, and use appropriately punctuated dependent clauses.

9. To use prepositional phrases to elaborate written ideas.

10. To employ standard English usage in writing for audiences, including subject-verb agreement, pronoun referents, and parts of speech.

Chapter 19 *Basic Sentence Parts*

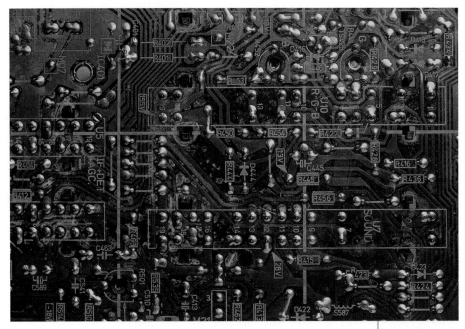

▲ Critical Viewing
Write a sentence explaining why a microchip is an important part of a computer. **[Analyze]**

Sentences help people explain what they mean when they speak or write. They make it possible for people to express a complete idea. Consider these two messages: *A test in science* and *We are having a test in science tomorrow*. The first is just a group of words. The second is a complete sentence. If you were getting ready to study, which message would you find more useful?

Computers have many different parts that help them work as quickly and as effectively as possible. In the same way, sentences are made up of many parts. All of these parts work together to express ideas and communicate meaning. In this chapter, you will learn more about the parts of sentences and how to use them.

Critical Viewing

Analyze Students may suggest that a microchip, although very small, is the "brain"of the computer.

☑ ONGOING ASSESSMENT: Diagnose

If students miss more than one item in any category, direct them to the relevant pages of the text and assign exercises for practice and review.

Basic Sentence Parts	Diagnostic Test Items	Teach	Practice	Section Review	Chapter Review
Skill Check A, B, C					
Simple Subjects and Predicates	A 1–5	pp. 380–384	Ex. 1–3	Ex. 4–6	Ex. 55
Complete Subjects and Complete Predicates	B 6–10	pp. 386–388	Ex. 10–13	Ex. 14–16	Ex. 55
Compound Subjects and Verbs	C 11–15	pp. 390–392	Ex. 20–22	Ex. 23–25	Ex. 57

Diagnostic Test

Directions: Write all answers on a separate sheet of paper.

Skill Check A. Copy the sentences below. Underline the simple subject once and the simple predicate twice.

1. Scientists invented miniature computer parts.
2. In the 1950's, they used silicon wafers.
3. Strong acids carved patterns into the silicon.
4. These patterns represent many larger parts.
5. Electricity flows through the patterns.

Skill Check B. Copy each sentence. Put a vertical line between the complete subject and the complete predicate. Underline the simple subject once and the simple predicate twice.

6. The pieces of silicon were called "integrated circuits."
7. Integrated circuits contain thousands of electronic parts.
8. These parts include diodes, resistors, and transistors.
9. A memory chip is a type of integrated circuit.
10. Most electronic equipment uses integrated circuits.

Skill Check C. Copy each sentence below, and then underline the subject once and the verb twice. Be sure to underline all the parts of compound subjects and verbs. Circle the conjunctions.

11. Scientists and researchers called the silicon pieces "chips."
12. Many circuits and other devices are on a chip.
13. Transistors either stop electrical current or allow its flow.
14. Scientists experimented and made even smaller chips.
15. Microchips are even tinier and perform many functions.

Skill Check D. Write the simple subject of each sentence.

16. There is another, more advanced computer.
17. Measure that in nanoseconds.
18. When was the first microchip used?
19. Here is a pocket calculator.
20. Use this calculator to find your answer.

Skill Check E. Write all direct objects and indirect objects on your paper, and then label them.

21. Engineers continually improve technology.
22. They offer the public new options all the time.
23. Computers perform both simple and complicated tasks.
24. We give computers essential tasks.
25. They give us more free time.

Skill Check F. Write all predicate nouns and predicate adjectives on your paper, and then label them.

26. The transistor was a new invention in 1947.
27. Three American physicists were responsible for its invention.
28. It was considered revolutionary in its time.
29. Transistors are essential parts of radios and television sets.
30. With transistors, circuits became smaller and more efficient.

Basic Sentence Parts • **379**

ONGOING ASSESSMENT: Diagnose *continued*

Basic Sentence Parts	Diagnostic Test Items	Teach	Practice	Section Review	Chapter Review
Skill Check D, E, F					
Hard-to-Find Subjects	D 16–20	pp. 394–396	Ex. 29–31	Ex. 32–34	Ex. 56
Direct and Indirect Objects	E 21–25	pp. 398–401	Ex. 38–39	Ex. 40–42	Ex. 58
Predicate Nouns and Predicate Adjectives	F 26–30	pp. 404–408	Ex. 46–47	Ex. 48–51	Ex. 59
Cumulative Reviews and Applications				Ex. 7–9, 17–19, 26–28, 35–37, 43–45, 52–54	Ex. 60–62

Answer Key

Diagnostic Test

Each item in the Diagnostic Test corresponds to a specific section in the chapter on basic sentence parts. This will enable you to tailor instruction to the particular needs of your students. See "Ongoing Assessment: Diagnose" on pages 378–379 for further details.

Skill Check A

1. <u>Scientists</u> <u>invented</u>
2. <u>they</u> <u>used</u>
3. <u>acids</u> <u>carved</u>
4. <u>patterns</u> <u>represent</u>
5. <u>Electricity</u> <u>flows</u>

Skill Check B

6. The <u>pieces</u> of silicon | <u>were</u> called "integrated circuits."
7. Integrated <u>circuits</u> | <u>contain</u> thousands of electronic parts.
8. These <u>parts</u> | <u>include</u> diodes, resistors, and transistors.
9. A memory <u>chip</u> | <u>is</u> a type of integrated circuit.
10. Most electronic <u>equipment</u> | <u>uses</u> integrated circuits.

Skill Check C

11. <u>Scientists</u> (and) <u>researchers</u> <u>called</u> the silicon pieces "chips."
12. Many <u>circuits</u> (and) other <u>devices</u> <u>are</u> on a chip.
13. <u>Transistors</u> (either) <u>stop</u> electrical current (or) <u>allow</u> its flow.
14. <u>Scientists</u> <u>experimented</u> (and) <u>made</u> even smaller chips.
15. <u>Microchips</u> <u>are</u> even tinier (and) <u>perform</u> many functions.

Skill Check D

16. computer
17. (you)
18. microchip
19. calculator
20. (you)

Skill Check E

21. technology—DO
22. public—IO, options—DO
23. tasks—DO
24. computers—IO, tasks—DO
25. us—IO, time—DO

Skill Check F

26. invention—predicate noun
27. responsible—predicate adjective
28. revolutionary—predicate adjective
29. parts—predicate noun
30. smaller, more efficient—predicate adjective

Give each of three students one of these tasks:

1. *Write "hello" on the board.*

2. *Walk toward the door.*

3. *Hold a book up for the class to see.*

Direct the class to observe as students perform their tasks in turn.

Write this chart on the board. Ask the class to complete it. Point out that students have identified the subjects and predicates in each sentence.

Subject	Predicate
Who	did what?
1.	
2.	
3.	

Activate Prior Knowledge

Remind students that subjects are nouns—people, places, or things—or pronouns—words that replace nouns. Ask students to use these words as subjects in sentences: *friend, class, I.* Remind students that predicates tell what the subject does or experiences. Then have students use these words as predicates in sentences: *like, run, is.*

TEACH

Step-by-Step Teaching Guide

The Subject

1. Ask students to suggest a variety of nouns—people, places, and things. Write several of their examples on the board.

2. Explain that any of these nouns could be the subject of a sentence. Some pronouns—*I, you, he, she, it, we,* and *they*—can also be used as subjects.

3. Help students identify the subject of a sentence. Write the following sentences on the board:

   Camp is a good place to swim.

   In the water, I have lots of fun.

   Ask a student to underline the subject in each sentence (camp, I).

4. Have students suggest simple sentences using the nouns written on the board.

The Basic Sentence

The sentence is a basic unit of speech and writing. By using sentences, particularly in writing, people make themselves understood. If you study the way sentences are put together, you will be able to recognize correct, well-formed sentences and learn which parts of a sentence are necessary and which parts are not.

KEY CONCEPT Every complete sentence contains a subject and a predicate. The **subject** tells who or what the sentence is about. The **predicate** tells something about the subject. ■

The Subject Sentences can be about anything. Any person, place, or thing can be a subject. The *simple subject* of a sentence is the main word or words in the subject part of the sentence. It answers the question *Who?* or *What?* in relation to the verb.

EXAMPLES: <u>He</u> asked me for help.
<u>China</u> was where the abacus was invented.
<u>Computers</u> are complicated machines.

Usually, the simple subject is a noun or pronoun found at the beginning of a sentence. However, there are some exceptions. First, there are simple subjects that consist of more than one word. These include titles, names, and compound nouns.

EXAMPLES: <u>Wilhelm Schikard</u> invented an early computer.
<u>Pen pals</u> can now use computers.

Second, subjects sometimes appear at the middle or the end of a sentence. Sometimes the subject can even appear after the verb. Notice the position of the subjects in the following examples:

EXAMPLES: After the debate, <u>Marion</u> sent an e-mail.
On the table sat the brand-new <u>monitor</u>.

Third, a sentence that makes a request or a command can have an unstated but understood subject. The subject *you* is not stated.

EXAMPLE: Type the word.
(The sentence is understood to mean "*You* type the word.")

Theme: Old and New Computers

In this section, you will learn how subjects and predicates are joined to create simple sentences. The examples and exercises are about old and new types of computers.

Cross-Curricular Connection: Math

⏱ TIME AND RESOURCE MANAGER

Resources
Print: Grammar Exercise Workbook, pp.43–44; Grammar Exercises Answers on Transparencies, Chapter 19
Technology: On-Line Exercise Bank, Section 19.1

In-Depth Coverage	Accelerated Pace
• Work through all key concepts, pp. 380–384. • Assign and review Exercises 1–3. • Read and discuss Grammar in Literature, p. 382.	• Assign pp. 380–384 for independent student review. • Assign Section Review Exercises 4–6, p. 385.

▶ **Exercise 1** Finding Simple Subjects Write the simple subject in each sentence below. If the subject is understood, write (*you*).

EXAMPLE: The students enjoyed the computer lesson.

ANSWER: students

1. Humans have always used numbers.
2. They counted objects around them.
3. In trading, numbers were important.
4. Two sheep might be traded for one goat.
5. Devices help us make calculations.
6. Use the abacus.
7. Inventors soon made better machines.
8. Eventually came computers.
9. Computers now solve math problems.
10. Imagine our world without computers.

▶ **More Practice**

On-line
Exercise Bank
• Section 19.1
**Grammar Exercise
Workbook**
• pp. 43–44

◀ Critical Viewing
Write two sentences about this picture. Use *boy* as the simple subject of one sentence, and *computer* as the simple subject of the other. **[Connect]**

Answer Key

▶ **Exercise 1**

1. Humans
2. They
3. numbers
4. sheep
5. Devices
6. [you]
7. Inventors
8. computers
9. Computers
10. [you]

Critical Viewing

Connect Possible sentences might be

The boy is using the computer.

The computer shows a game.

Real-World Connection

Explain to students that, as they go through school, they will encounter texts that are more and more challenging. Students often will be able to cut to the core meaning of sentences by finding simple subjects and predicates. Discuss situations in which this skill could help students, such as reading reference materials or reviewing textbooks before tests.

 TIME SAVERS!

▶ **Answers on Transparency**
Use the Grammar Exercises Answers on Transparencies for Chapter 19 to facilitate correction by students.

▶ **On-Line Exercise Bank**
Have students complete the exercises on computer. The Auto Check feature will grade their work for you!

Step-by-Step Teaching Guide

Grammar in Literature

1. Have a volunteer read aloud the passage from "The Fun They Had."

2. Ask students to rephrase the sentences so that the subject of the first sentence *(Margie)* is not the first word and so that the subject of the second sentence *(she)* is the first word.

3. Ask students if these changes affect the meaning of the passage. Explain that, though moving the subject doesn't change the meaning, it does change the flow of the sentence. Writers often put subjects where they do in order to highlight different things. For example, these sentences appear at the beginning of the story, and the date is very important.

More About the Writer

When Isaac Asimov was a boy, his father wouldn't allow him to read science fiction. Young Isaac finally convinced his dad that he could learn about science through the stories, even though they were fiction. Isaac eventually proved his point by becoming a science professor *and* a world-famous science fiction writer.

Step-by-Step Teaching Guide

The Predicate

1. Explain to students that finding the predicate usually will be easier if they identify the subject first.

2. Remind students that a simple predicate is always a verb. Once students know what the subject is, they can ask themselves which verb expresses the action or condition of the subject.

3. Write the following sentences on the board and have students identify the subjects *(Anna, flower)*:

   Anna walked to the store.

   The flower is beautiful.

4. Have students identify the verbs and tell if they relate an action or condition of the subject *(walked—action; is—condition)*. Tell students they have just identified the simple predicates.

382

GRAMMAR IN
LITERATURE

from The Fun They Had
Isaac Asimov

In the following passage, the simple subjects have been highlighted in blue italics.

Margie even wrote about it that night in her diary. On the page headed May 17, 2155, *she* wrote, "Today *Tommy* found a real book."

The Predicate The *simple predicate* is a verb that tells what the subject does, what is done to the subject, or what the condition of the subject is.

EXAMPLES: Connie <u>drew</u> the graphic for the cover.
The programs <u>were changed</u>.
Marvin <u>is</u> ready.

In the sentences shown in the next chart, the simple subjects are underlined once and the simple predicates are underlined twice.

SIMPLE SUBJECTS AND PREDICATES
<u>Donna</u> <u><u>types</u></u>.
The <u>plant</u> in the corner <u><u>blooms</u></u> every summer.
My new <u>keyboard</u> <u><u>is sitting</u></u> in the box.

It is easy to find the simple subject and simple predicate if you ask yourself the following questions:

SIMPLE SUBJECT: What noun or pronoun answers the question *Who?* or *What?* before the verb?

SIMPLE PREDICATE: What verb expresses action done by or to the subject or tells the condition of the subject?

✿ Grammar and Style Tip

Try to avoid sentence fragments in your writing. A fragment is a group of words that is punctuated as if it were a sentence, but it is incomplete. It is missing either a subject or a predicate, or it does not express a complete thought.

▶ **Exercise 2** Finding Simple Predicates Identify the simple predicate in each sentence below.

EXAMPLE: The computer program played the music beautifully.

ANSWER: played

1. Primitive people counted with their fingers.
2. This system works with small numbers.
3. Early Romans used pebbles for counting.
4. The pebbles were painted different colors.
5. Each color represented a different amount.
6. Some people tied knots in a cord.
7. Others made marks on wood.
8. Ancient Egyptian mathematics was very advanced.
9. The Egyptians developed formulas for area and volume.
10. They determined the size of their fields with these formulas.

▶ **More Practice**

On-line
Exercise Bank
• Section 19.1
Grammar Exercise
Workbook
• pp. 43–44

◀ Critical Viewing
Name four verbs you could use as simple predicates in sentences about this telephone keypad.
[Analyze]

The Basic Sentence • 383

Integrating Representing Skills

Have students create a visual representation of the relationship between subjects and predicates. Representations can be pictures, charts, diagrams, or mathematical symbols—anything that illustrates either action or condition of the subject (or both).

Customize for
Bodily/Kinesthetic Learners

Have students write the names of two or three classmates on the board. Then ask students whose names are on the board to do a simple activity, such as open a book or look out the window. Have the rest of the class write what was done after the name of the person who did it. Explain that the student named is the subject and what he or she did is the predicate.

Integrating Technology Skills

Have each student write an e-mail message to a classmate, relating something the student has done after school recently. Ask students to go through the e-mails they receive, using the electronic highlighter to mark simple subjects of sentences in blue and simple predicates in red.

Answer Key

▶ **Exercise 2**

1. counted
2. works
3. used
4. were painted
5. represented
6. tied
7. made
8. was
9. developed
10. determined

Critical Viewing

Analyze Verb choices might include *has, displays, is, shows.*

☑ **ONGOING ASSESSMENT: Monitor and Reinforce**

If students miss more than two items in Exercise 1 or 2, refer them to the following resources for additional practice.

In the Textbook	Print Resources	Technology
Section Review, Ex. 4–6, p. 385	Grammar Exercise Workbook, pp. 43–44	On-Line Exercise Bank, Section 19.1

Critical Viewing

Compare and Contrast Students may suggest that the abacus is mechanical and the calculator is electronic. The abacus uses beads or counters and the calculator displays numerals. The abacus uses wires and beads; the calculator has a number pad.

Answer Key

▶ **Exercise 3**

1. The next <u>system</u> <u><u>was</u></u> beads on wires.
2. The <u>wires</u> <u><u>were stretched</u></u> across a wooden frame.
3. Each <u>wire</u> <u><u>held</u></u> ten movable beads.
4. The <u>beads</u> <u><u>stood</u></u> for different quantities.
5. <u>They</u> <u><u>were pushed</u></u> from the left side to the right side.
6. This <u>device</u> <u><u>is called</u></u> an *abacus*.
7. The <u>Chinese</u> <u><u>were</u></u> among the first to use the abacus.
8. The <u>Japanese</u> <u><u>called</u></u> their version of the abacus the *soroban*.
9. <u>They</u> <u><u>solved</u></u> complex problems very quickly.
10. <u>People</u> <u><u>utilized</u></u> these devices until the 1950's.
11. <u>John Napier</u> <u><u>discovered</u></u> logarithms.
12. <u>Logarithms</u> <u><u>make</u></u> complicated problems much easier.
13. Then <u>he</u> <u><u>put</u></u> the multiplication tables onto rods.
14. <u>Multiplication</u> <u><u>became</u></u> much easier.
15. Some <u>people</u> <u><u>wanted</u></u> mechanical devices for counting.
16. <u>Blaise Pascal</u> <u><u>invented</u></u> the first mechanical calculator.
17. <u>It</u> <u><u>consisted</u></u> of several interlocking wheels.
18. The <u>machine</u> <u><u>made</u></u> calculations automatically.
19. This <u>invention</u> <u><u>was</u></u> the first adding machine.
20. <u>It</u> <u><u>performed</u></u> addition and subtraction.

⏱ TIME SAVERS!

🗂 **Answers on Transparency**
Use the Grammar Exercises Answers on Transparencies for Chapter 19 to facilitate correction by students.

💻 **On-Line Exercise Bank**
Have students complete the exercises on computer. The Auto Check feature will grade their work for you!

▶ **Exercise 3** Finding Simple Subjects and Simple Predicates

Copy the sentences below. Underline each simple subject once and each simple predicate twice. (Remember—the simple subject will be a noun or a pronoun that answers the question *Who?* or *What?* before the verb. The simple predicate will be a verb or verb phrase.)

1. The next system was beads on wires.
2. The wires were stretched across a wooden frame.
3. Each wire held ten movable beads.
4. The beads stood for different quantities.
5. They were pushed from the left side to the right side.
6. This device is called an *abacus*.
7. The Chinese were among the first to use the abacus.
8. The Japanese called their version of the abacus the *soroban*.
9. They solved complex problems very quickly.
10. People utilized these devices until the 1950's.
11. John Napier discovered logarithms.
12. Logarithms make complicated problems much easier.
13. Then, he put the multiplication tables onto rods.
14. Multiplication became much easier.
15. Some people wanted mechanical devices for counting.
16. Blaise Pascal invented the first mechanical calculator.
17. It consisted of several interlocking wheels.
18. The machine made calculations automatically.
19. This invention was the first adding machine.
20. It performed addition and subtraction.

▼ **Critical Viewing**
In two or three sentences, compare the workings and parts (such as these resistors) of a calculator with those of an abacus. **[Compare and Contrast]**

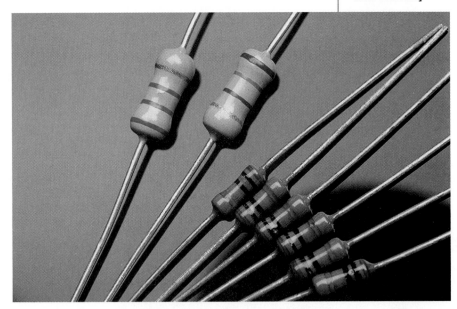

384 • Basic Sentence Parts

☑ ONGOING ASSESSMENT: Monitor and Reinforce

If students miss more than two items in Exercise 3, refer them to the following for additional practice.

In the Textbook	Print Resources	Technology
Section Review, Ex. 4–6, p. 385	Grammar Exercise Workbook, pp. 43–44	On-Line Exercise Bank, Section 19.1

Section 19.1 Section Review

19.1 THE BASIC SENTENCE

GRAMMAR EXERCISES 4–9

Exercise 4 Finding Simple Subjects and Simple Predicates Write the sentences below on your paper. Underline each simple subject once and each simple predicate twice.

1. Gottfried Leibniz designed a special mathematical system.
2. It made multiplication possible on a mechanical calculator.
3. Leibniz's model computed higher numbers.
4. It still solved only simple problems.
5. His calculator used a hand crank.
6. This device increased the speed of multiplication and division.
7. The science of astronomy required more advanced methods.
8. Astronomers studied orbits of planets.
9. Logarithm tables at that time often contained mistakes.
10. Scientists demanded very precise measurements.

Exercise 5 Supplying Simple Subjects and Simple Predicates Write the sentences below on your paper, filling each blank with a logical simple subject or verb.

1. A French ___?___ made a type of computer.
2. Joseph-Marie Jacquard ___?___ an automated loom.
3. ___?___ programmed the loom for different patterns.
4. The system ___?___ rigid cards with holes in them.
5. The different patterns of holes ___?___ different woven patterns.
6. The ___?___ of France rewarded Jacquard.
7. However, his invention ___?___ the jobs of workers.

8. The angry ___?___ chased him out of Paris.
9. In the city of Lyon, his looms ___?___ very popular.
10. Today, some fabric ___?___ still use this kind of loom.

Exercise 6 Revising to Eliminate Incomplete Sentences Revise this paragraph on your paper, adding missing sentence parts.

William Oughtred found a way to speed up calculations. Printed numbers on wooden rulers. The numbers were positioned according to their logarithms. Then, the rulers together. Called this device the "slide rule." A slide rule simple to use. Two numbers on the different rulers are lined up. Then, the product from the rulers. Before calculators were invented, many students slide rules.

Exercise 7 Find It in Your Reading In the excerpt from "The Fun They Had" on page 382, identify the simple predicate for each highlighted subject.

Exercise 8 Find It in Your Writing Choose a paragraph from your own writing. Identify the simple subject and the simple predicate in each sentence.

Exercise 9 Writing Application Write a description of some of the programs you use or activities you do on a computer. Underline simple subjects once and simple predicates twice.

Answer Key continued

Exercise 9

Writing Application
Have volunteers read aloud their descriptions. Ask other students to choose any sentence from the description and identify the subject and predicate of that sentence.

ASSESS

Section Review

Each of these exercises correlates to the instruction on simple subjects and simple predicates, pages 380–384. The exercises may be used for more practice, for reteaching, or for review of the Key Concepts presented. Answers for all chapter exercises are available in *Grammar Exercises Answers on Transparencies* in your Teaching Resources.

Answer Key

Exercise 4

1. <u>Gottfried Leibniz</u> <u>designed</u>
2. <u>It</u> <u>made</u>
3. <u>model</u> <u>computed</u>
4. <u>It</u> <u>solved</u>
5. <u>calculator</u> <u>used</u>
6. <u>device</u> <u>increased</u>
7. <u>science</u> <u>required</u>
8. <u>Astronomers</u> <u>studied</u>
9. <u>tables</u> <u>contained</u>
10. <u>Scientists</u> <u>demanded</u>

Exercise 5

1. inventor
2. invented
3. He
4. used
5. produced
6. emperor
7. threatened
8. workers
9. were
10. manufacturers

Exercise 6

Possible sentences

He printed . . .
Then he slid the . . .
He called . . .
A slide rule is . . .
Then you find the product . . .
. . . many students used . . .

Exercise 7

Find It in Your Reading
[Margie] wrote, [she] wrote, [Tommy] found

Exercise 8

Find It in Your Writing
Ask students to identify the parts of speech of the simple subjects and simple predicates.

continued

Ask students to supply a person's name as the subject of the following sentence:

__ is a great friend of mine.

Have students write the sentence about halfway down a sheet of paper. Point out that the name is the subject of the sentence. Tell students to give more information about the subject by providing adjectives that describe the person. Invite students to read their complete sentences to the class. Ask students to come up with a working definition of a "complete subject," e.g., "all the words that describe the subject."

Activate Prior Knowledge

Ask a volunteer to share a fact about himself or herself that the other students might not know (for example, I used to live on a farm). Invite the class to ask questions to find out more (Where was the farm? How old were you? Did you like it?). Point out that adding details to an idea makes it more *complete*.

TEACH

Step-by-Step Teaching Guide

Complete Subjects and Predicates

1. Write this sentence on the board, marking the simple subject and predicate:

   Students learn.

2. Ask students to share words they could add to the subject to make it more complete. Write students' answers on the board. (Possible responses: all students, sixth-grade students, all sixth-grade students in Texas)

3. Repeat step 2 with the predicate in the sentence. (Possible responses: on the Internet, at school, in Iowa)

4. Point out that a sentence often contains words that help *complete* the simple subject and simple predicate. All the words associated with the simple subject make up the complete subject, and those associated with the simple predicate make up the complete predicate.

Section 19.2

Complete Subjects and Predicates

Sentences can be expanded beyond a simple subject and simple predicate. A writer can add to both the subject and the predicate of a sentence.

▶ **KEY CONCEPTS** The **complete subject** of a sentence includes the simple subject and the words related to it. The **complete predicate** includes the verb (simple predicate) and the words related to it. ■

A sentence can have just a simple subject and a simple predicate. Such a sentence will usually be quite brief. In the following sentence, the vertical line separates the simple subject *people* from the simple predicate *type*.

EXAMPLE: People | type.

The sentence could be expanded by adding words to the subject and the predicate. The words would be part of the *complete subject* and the *complete predicate*.

EXAMPLE: Many people from different places | type on their computers and typewriters.

The following chart shows the complete subject and the complete predicate of several sentences. Each simple subject is underlined once, and each simple predicate is underlined twice.

COMPLETE SUBJECTS AND PREDICATES	
Complete Subjects	**Complete Predicates**
My old <u>friend</u>	<u>returned</u> my floppy disk
A new <u>model</u> of the computer	<u>sits</u> in the store window.
That strange <u>noise</u>	<u>frightened</u> my brother.
The skilled <u>technician</u>	quickly <u>repaired</u> the machine.

Theme: Computers and Their Inventors

In this section, you will learn to identify complete subjects and predicates in simple sentences. The examples and exercises are about the inventors of early computers.

Cross-Curricular Connection: Math

⏰ **TIME AND RESOURCE MANAGER**

Resources
Print: Grammar Exercise Workbook, pp. 45–46; Grammar Exercises Answers on Transparencies, Chapter 19
Technology: On-Line Exercise Bank, Section 19.2

In-Depth Coverage	Accelerated Pace
• Work through the key concepts, pp. 386–388. • Assign and review Exercises 10–13. • Read and discuss Grammar in Literature, p. 388.	• Assign pp. 386–388 for independent student review. • Assign Section Review Exercises 14–16, p. 389.

Exercise 10 Recognizing Complete Subjects Write the complete subject of each sentence below on your paper, and underline the simple subject.

EXAMPLE: A simple mechanical computer was invented during the 1820's.

ANSWER: A simple mechanical <u>computer</u>

1. A mathematician named Charles Babbage designed an early mechanical computer.
2. He called his invention the "Difference Engine."
3. The small parts were made precisely.
4. A working model was produced in 1822.
5. A steam engine provided power for the machine.
6. Babbage announced plans for a new machine ten years later.
7. This more powerful machine had more versatility.
8. The name for the new machine was the "Analytical Engine."
9. The Analytical Engine was able to solve any sort of mathematical problem.
10. The operator of the machine switched it from one kind of problem to another.

Exercise 11 Recognizing Complete Predicates Write the complete predicate of each sentence below on your paper, and underline the simple predicate twice.

EXAMPLE: A simple mechanical computer was invented during the 1820's.

ANSWER: <u>was invented</u> during the 1820's.

1. Charles Babbage built only working models of his calculating machines.
2. His ideas and detailed plans were later put to use by other inventors.
3. The clever Englishman was interested in economics, too.
4. He wrote a guide to the economics of manufacturing.
5. Babbage is still remembered today.

► **More Practice**

On-line
Exercise Bank
• Section 19.2
Grammar Exercise
Workbook
• pp. 45–46

British inventor Charles Babbage was a computer pioneer.

▲ Critical Viewing Write a sentence explaining what this man did or why he is still important today. Underline the complete subject once and the complete predicate twice. [Analyze]

Complete Subjects and Predicates • 387

Critical Viewing

Analyze Encourage students to use complete and interesting subjects and predicates, such as

<u>The British mathematician and inventor of the early mechanical computer Charles Babbage</u> <u>invented several calculating machines.</u>

Answer Key

► **Exercise 10**

1. A mathematician named <u>Charles Babbage</u>
2. <u>He</u>
3. The small <u>parts</u>
4. A working <u>model</u>
5. A steam <u>engine</u>
6. <u>Babbage</u>
7. This more powerful <u>machine</u>
8. The <u>name</u> for the new machine
9. The <u>Analytical Engine</u>
10. The <u>operator</u> of the machine

► **Exercise 11**

1. <u>built</u> only working models of his calculating machines.
2. <u>were</u> later <u>put</u> to use by other inventors.
3. <u>was interested</u> in economics, too.
4. <u>wrote</u> a guide to the economics of manufacturing.
5. <u>is</u> still <u>remembered</u> today.

☑ **ONGOING ASSESSMENT: Monitor and Reinforce**

If students have difficulty identifying complete subjects and complete predicates, refer them to the following sources for additional practice.

In the Textbook	Print Resources	Technology
Section Review, Ex. 14–16, p. 389	Grammar Exercise Workbook, pp. 45–46	On-Line Exercise Bank, Section 19.2

⏱ **TIME SAVERS!**

🖎 **Answers on Transparency** Use the Grammar Exercises Answers on Transparencies for Chapter 19 to facilitate correction by students.

💻 **On-Line Exercise Bank** Have students complete the exercises on computer. The Auto Check feature will grade their work for you!

Grammar in Literature

1. Have a volunteer read aloud the sentence from "The Fun They Had."

2. Ask students to identify the simple subjects and simple predicates. (screen/was, it/said, lesson/is)

Answer Key

▶ **Exercise 12**

1. <u>Babbage</u> | <u>imagined</u> a printing device for his machine.
2. Then the <u>machine</u> | <u>could</u> print the answers.
3. <u>Cards</u> with punched holes | <u>programmed</u> the Analytical Engine.
4. That <u>idea</u> | <u>was borrowed</u> from Jacquard's loom.
5. The punched <u>cards</u> | <u>stored</u> instructions.
6. <u>Babbage</u> | never <u>obtained</u> the funds for his machine.
7. A <u>student</u> of his named Augusta Ada Byron | <u>produced</u> detailed notes of Babbage's ideas.
8. This expert <u>mathematician</u> | <u>was</u> the daughter of the poet Lord Byron.
9. <u>Augusta Ada Byron</u> | also <u>devised</u> several programs for the Analytical Engine.
10. Her key <u>concepts</u>, such as memory and storage, | <u>are incorporated</u> in modern computers.

▶ **Exercise 13**

1. Wordprocessing software makes writing papers easier.
2. With a computer mouse, you can click on a menu item.
3. Computer games can require lots of memory.
4. Today's microcomputers can handle multiple tasks.
5. With the help of the internet, I researched a science topic.

19.2

GRAMMAR IN LITERATURE

from **The Fun They Had**
Isaac Asimov

In the following excerpt, the complete subject of the sentence in quotation marks is shown in red italics, and the complete predicate is shown in blue italics.

The screen was lit up, and it said: "Today's arithmetic lesson is on the addition of proper fractions. . . ."

▶ **Exercise 12** Recognizing Complete Subjects and Predicates Copy each sentence below. Put a vertical line between the complete subject and the complete predicate. Underline the simple subject once and the simple predicate twice.

1. Babbage imagined a printing device for his machine.
2. Then, the machine could print the answers.
3. Cards with punched holes programmed the Analytical Engine.
4. That idea was borrowed from Jacquard's loom.
5. The punched cards stored instructions.
6. Babbage never obtained the funds for his machine.
7. A student of his named Augusta Ada Byron produced detailed notes of Babbage's ideas.
8. This expert mathematician was the daughter of the poet Lord Byron.
9. Augusta Ada Byron also devised several programs for the Analytical Engine.
10. Her key concepts, such as memory and storage, are incorporated in modern computers.

▶ **Exercise 13** Matching Complete Subjects and Complete Predicates On your paper, combine a complete subject from the first column with a complete predicate from the second column to form a complete sentence.

1. Wordprocessing software — can click on a menu item.
2. With a computer mouse, you — can require lots of memory.
3. Computer games — researched a science topic.
4. Today's microcomputers — makes writing papers easier.
5. With the help of the Internet, I — can handle multiple tasks.

388 • Basic Sentence Parts

▶ **More Practice**

On-line
Exercise Bank
• Section 19.2
Grammar Exercise
Workbook
• pp. 45–46

✎ STANDARDIZED TEST PREPARATION WORKSHOP

Grammar and Usage Standardized tests often require students to identify parts of sentences. Ask students to identify the complete subject in the following sentence.

The tall apartment building towered over the neighborhood.

A building

B tall apartment building

C apartment building

D The tall apartment building

The correct answer is item **D**. Item A is the simple subject. Items B and C are only parts of the complete subject.

Section 19.2 Section Review

GRAMMAR EXERCISES 14–19

Exercise 14 Identifying Complete Subjects and Complete Predicates
Copy each of the following sentences onto your paper. Put a vertical line between the complete subject and the complete predicate. Underline the simple subject once and the simple predicate twice.

1. Herman Hollerith was an American inventor and businessman.
2. One of Hollerith's ideas combined punched-hole cards with an electric power source.
3. The 1890 census used some of Hollerith's inventions.
4. An operator of a tabulating machine placed cards in a slot of the machine.
5. Many pins pressed against the card.
6. The holes in the card allowed some pins through.
7. Those pins picked up an electrical current.
8. The current controlled dials on the face of the machine.
9. The operator read the dials on the machine carefully.
10. Hollerith's tabulator was the first electromechanical computing machine.

Exercise 15 Supplying Sentence Parts for Complete Subjects and Complete Predicates Copy each sentence below onto your paper, supplying a word or phrase to fill the blank. Identify whether the blank is part of the complete subject or the complete predicate.

1. My ___?___ writes e-mail messages to most of his friends.
2. On most mornings, he ___?___ at least a dozen replies.
3. Using e-mail, my brother ___?___ with friends all around the world.

4. Last week, a ___?___ from Portugal sent him a message.
5. My brother's friends often ___?___ digital photographs with their messages.

Exercise 16 Supplying Complete Subjects and Complete Predicates Add a complete subject or a complete predicate to each item to make a complete sentence.

1. My next project in science
2. looks like my machine at home
3. The newly designed keyboard
4. carried out a research project
5. A very useful Internet site

Exercise 17 Find It in Your Reading Identify the complete subject and complete predicate in each of these sentences from "The Fun They Had."

". . . Those things happen sometimes. I've slowed it up to an average ten-year level. Actually, the overall pattern of her progress is quite satisfactory." And he patted Margie's head again.

Exercise 18 Find It in Your Writing Choose a paragraph from your own writing. Draw a line between the complete subject and the complete predicate in each sentence. Underline the simple subjects once and the simple predicates twice.

Exercise 19 Writing Application Write an explanation of some ways that computers make life easier for us. Underline each complete subject once and each complete predicate twice.

ASSESS

Section Review

Each of these exercises correlates to the instruction on complete subjects and complete predicates, pages 386–388. The exercises may be used for more practice, for reteaching, or for review of the Key Concepts presented. Answers for all chapter exercises are available in *Grammar Exercises Answers on Transparencies* in your Teaching Resources.

Answer Key

Exercise 14

1. <u>Herman Hollerith</u> | <u><u>was</u></u> an American inventor and businessman.
2. One of Hollerith's <u>ideas</u> | <u><u>combined</u></u> punched-hole cards with an electric power source.
3. The 1890 <u>census</u> | <u><u>used</u></u> some of Hollerith's inventions.
4. An <u>operator</u> of a tabulating machine | <u><u>placed</u></u> cards in a slot of the machine.
5. Many <u>pins</u> | <u><u>pressed</u></u> against the card.
6. The <u>holes</u> in the card | <u><u>allowed</u></u> some pins through.
7. Those <u>pins</u> | <u><u>picked</u></u> up an electrical current.
8. The <u>current</u> | <u><u>controlled</u></u> dials on the face of the machine.
9. The <u>operator</u> | <u><u>read</u></u> the dials on the machine carefully.
10. Hollerith's <u>tabulator</u> | <u><u>was</u></u> the first electromechanical computing machine.

Exercise 15

Sample Answers

1. brother—subject
2. writes—predicate
3. corresponds—predicate
4. friend—subject
5. send—predicate

Exercise 16

Sample Answers

1. will be growing seeds in containers.
2. Your new computer
3. is very easy to use
4. My mother
5. is devoted to travel

continued

Answer Key continued

Exercise 17

Find It in Your Reading
complete subjects: *Those things, I, Actually, the overall pattern of her progress, And he*

complete predicates: *happen sometimes, [have] slowed it up to an average ten-year level, is quite satisfactory, patted Margie's head again*

Exercise 18

Find It in Your Writing
Have students trade papers with a partner to check each other's work.

Exercise 19

Writing Application
Ask students to pick one or two sentences with longer complete subjects or predicates. Have volunteers write their sentences on the board, then ask the class to identify complete and simple subjects and predicates.

Write the sentences on the board:

Sean uses the computer often.

Carla uses the computer often.

Ask students what these sentences have in common (their complete predicates). Have students suggest a way the sentences could be combined so that the predicates don't repeat. (Sean and Carla use the computer often.) Tell students they have just created a compound subject.

Activate Prior Knowledge

Ask students to think of "famous" combinations: salt and pepper, Laurel and Hardy, peanut butter and jelly, and so on. Put as many of these combinations as students suggest on the board. Point out that combinations like these make up much of our writing and conversation.

TEACH

Step-by-Step Teaching Guide

Compound Subjects and Predicates

1. Ask students how often they do things alone and how often they do things with friends or family members. Point out that actions sometimes happen in groups, too. Explain that, because they reflect the world around us, the subjects and predicates in sentences also sometimes are alone and are sometimes together.

2. Write these sentences on the board and point out the compound subject and compound predicate:

   Julia and I own a rabbit.

   I clean his cage and feed him.

3. Point out that sometimes students will need both a compound subject and a compound predicate to express an idea or relate a fact. Write the following sentence on the board, and have students identify the compound subject and compound predicate *Carlos and Martha are singing and dancing* in the spring talent show.

Section 19.3

Compound Subjects and Compound Predicates

A sentence can have more than one simple subject and more than one verb. When there is more than one subject, it is called a *compound subject*. When there is more than one verb related to the subject, it is called a *compound predicate*.

> **KEY CONCEPT** A **compound subject** includes two or more simple subjects that have the same verb. ■

Compound subjects are connected by conjunctions such as *and* or *or*.

EXAMPLES: <u>Bob</u> or <u>Sue</u> will go.
<u>Hockey</u> and <u>football</u> are my favorite sports.
<u>Anna</u>, <u>Steve</u>, and <u>Jane</u> are studying computer science.

> **Exercise 20** Identifying Compound Subjects Identify the compound subjects in each of the following sentences.
> 1. Businesses and schools use computers.
> 2. Neither government nor industry can function without them.
> 3. Words, pictures, and sounds are changed into numbers.
> 4. A memory and a processor are the basic parts.
> 5. Designers or artists may also use computers.

> **KEY CONCEPT** A **compound predicate** includes two or more verbs that relate to the same subject. ■

The following examples contain compound predicates. The verbs that make up each compound predicate are underlined twice.

EXAMPLES: At school, I <u>read</u> books, <u>made</u> friends, and <u>played</u> sports.

My friends <u>play</u> video games, <u>surf</u> the Internet, and <u>do</u> research on the computer.

Occasionally, a sentence may have both a compound subject and a compound predicate.

EXAMPLE: <u>Sandy</u> and <u>Marie</u> <u>called</u> and <u>asked</u> for help.

390 • Basic Sentence Parts

Theme: Uses of Computers

In this section, you will learn to recognize compound subjects or predicates in sentences. The examples and exercises are about different uses of computers.

Cross-Curricular Connection: Math

⏱ TIME AND RESOURCE MANAGER

Resources
Print: Grammar Exercise Workbook, pp. 47–48; Grammar Exercises Answers on Transparencies, Chapter 19
Technology: Language Lab CD-ROM, Sentence Style; On-Line Exercise Bank, Section 19.3

In-Depth Coverage	Accelerated Pace
• Work through the key concepts, pp. 390–392. • Assign and review Exercises 20–22. • Read and discuss Grammar in Literature, p. 392.	• Assign pp. 390–392 for independent student review. • Assign Section Review Exercises 23–25, p. 393.

Exercise 21 Identifying Compound Predicates Identify the compound predicate in each of the following sentences.

1. The memory of a computer receives data and stores it.
2. The processor changes data into useful information and performs calculations.
3. A computer operator uses a keyboard or manipulates a mouse.
4. That person normally inputs data or enters instructions.
5. People can think about problems and solve them with the help of a computer.
6. Computers manage and organize large amounts of information.
7. With their help, we create and display documents quickly.
8. Computers make models and simulate situations.
9. Scientists develop and test theories with the help of computers.
10. People even play games and compose music on computers.

> **More Practice**
>
> Language Lab
> CD-ROM
> • Sentence Style lesson
> On-line
> Exercise Bank
> • Section 19.3
> Grammar Exercise
> Workbook
> • pp. 47–48

▼ Critical Viewing
Write a sentence with a compound predicate describing two or more steps for getting inside a computer. **[Connect]**

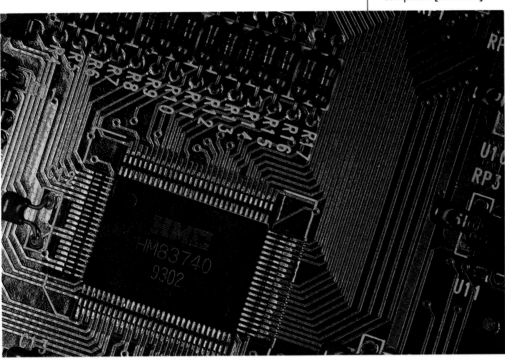

Compound Subjects and Compound Predicates • 391

Critical Viewing

Connect Encourage students to emphasize safety in their sentences, for example, *Before opening a computer, be sure to read the directions, unplug the electrical cord, and disconnect the phone line.*

Answer Key

Exercise 20 (page 390)

1. Businesses, schools
2. government, industry
3. Words, pictures, sounds
4. memory, processor
5. Designers, artists

Exercise 21

1. receives, stores
2. changes, performs
3. uses, manipulates
4. inputs, enters
5. can think, solve
6. manage, organize
7. create, display
8. make, simulate
9. develop, test
10. play, compose

Language Highlight

The word *compound* means "composed of two or more parts." It comes from the Old French *compondre*, which means "to put together." Explain to students that remembering what *compound* means can help them understand the concept of compound subjects and predicates. Explore additional uses of *compound*, such as:

• chemical compound—two or more elements bonded together

• compound organ—an organ, such as the brain, that serves many functions in the body

What additional uses of the word *compound* can students think of?

☑ **ONGOING ASSESSMENT: Monitor and Reinforce**

If students have difficulty identifying compound subjects and compound predicates, refer them to the following sources for additional practice.

In the Textbook	Print Resources	Technology
Section Review, Ex. 23–25, p. 393	Grammar Exercise Workbook, pp. 47–48	Language Lab CD-ROM, Sentence Style; On-Line Exercise Bank, Section 19.3

⊘ TIME SAVERS!

Answers on Transparency
Use the Grammar Exercises Answers on Transparencies for Chapter 19 to facilitate correction by students.

On-Line Exercise Bank
Have students complete the exercises on computer. The Auto Check feature will grade their work for you!

Grammar in Literature

1. Read the passage aloud to students.

2. Have a volunteer come to the board and rewrite the second sentence in the passage as three separate sentences.

3. Ask students which version they prefer and why. Explain to them that combining sentences to form compound predicates can help avoid choppy writing.

Customize for
Less Advanced Students

If students have difficulty identifying compound subjects and predicates, have them begin Exercise 22 by circling the conjunctions *and* and *or*. Explain that students can use the circled conjunctions as signals to locate the compound forms.

Integrating Writing Skills

Point out that using compound subjects and predicates can streamline a message. It eliminates the need for unnecessary repetition, and makes writing easier for both the writer and the reader. Have students compose a short paragraph about something they have done recently. Tell them to be sure to include one or more sentences with compound subjects and one or more with compound predicates.

Answer Key

Exercise 22

1. With word-processing programs, people <u>write</u> (and) <u>edit</u> various documents.
2. <u>Reports</u> (and) <u>letters</u> are just two examples of the ways people use word processors.
3. <u>Typing errors</u> (and) <u>misspellings</u> can be easily corrected on a computer.
4. A writer also <u>adds</u>, <u>moves</u>, (or) <u>deletes</u> copy easily before printing out a finished copy.
5. <u>Business people</u>, <u>students</u>, (and) <u>scientists</u> use word processors.
6. <u>Newsletters</u> (and) <u>other documents</u> can be created conveniently on computers.
7. Some computer programs <u>create</u> pictures (or) <u>draw</u> diagrams.

19.3

GRAMMAR IN LITERATURE

from The Fun They Had
Isaac Asimov

In the excerpt below, the parts of the compound predicate are highlighted in blue italics.

He was a round little man with a red face and a whole box of tools with dials and wires. He *smiled* at her and *gave* her an apple, then *took* the teacher apart.

▶ **Exercise 22** Recognizing Compound Subjects and Predicates Copy the sentences below. Underline the parts of each compound subject once and the parts of each compound predicate twice. Circle the conjunctions.

EXAMPLE: The <u>functions</u> (and) <u>uses</u> of computers seem endless.

1. With word-processing programs, people write and edit various documents.
2. Reports and letters are just two examples of the ways people use word processors.
3. Typing errors and misspellings can be easily corrected on a computer.
4. A writer also adds, moves, or deletes copy easily before printing out a finished copy.
5. Business people, students, and scientists use word processors.
6. Newsletters and other documents can be created conveniently on computers.
7. Some computer programs create pictures or draw diagrams.
8. Engineers and architects may also use these types of programs.
9. They may plan a bridge or design a building with special software.
10. A light pen and a mouse are useful tools for working on a computer.

More Practice

Language Lab
CD-ROM
• Sentence Style lesson
On-line
Exercise Bank
• Section 19.3
Grammar Exercise
Workbook
• pp. 47–48

---

8. <u>Engineers</u> (and) <u>architects</u> may also use these types of programs.
9. They may <u>plan</u> a bridge (or) <u>design</u> a building with special software.
10. A <u>light pen</u> (and) a <u>mouse</u> are useful tools for working on a computer.

Section 19.3 *Section Review*

GRAMMAR EXERCISES 23–28

Exercise 23 Identifying Compound Subjects or Predicates On your paper, write the parts of the compound subject or predicate in each sentence below.

1. Students and teachers use computers in the classroom.
2. The computer screen displays information and provides choices.
3. The keyboard or a mouse can highlight an item.
4. Maps, charts, graphs, and articles can be viewed on the computer.
5. Students can copy the information and save it or print it out.

Exercise 24 Supplying Parts of Compound Subjects and Compound Predicates Copy the sentences below on your paper, supplying a part of a compound subject or predicate to fill the blank. Underline the parts of each compound subject once and each compound predicate twice.

1. Computers guide students and ____?____ instruction.
2. Students and ____?____ use them on a daily basis.
3. The United States ____?____ and uses more computers than any other country.
4. Both European schools and Japanese ____?____ are also highly computerized.
5. Videos and animation provide information and ____?____ interaction.
6. Spreadsheets and databases organize and ____?____ data.
7. They ____?____ and transmit information.
8. ____?____ and instructors can communicate through a variety of programs.
9. Computer ____?____ and CD-ROMs store large amounts of data.
10. Computer learning is individual and ____?____ immediate answers.

Exercise 25 Revising a Paragraph by Creating Compound Subjects or Compound Predicates Revise the paragraph below by combining information in sentences to form compound subjects or compound predicates.

My family purchased a new computer. We signed up with an Internet provider. The computer has more memory than our old model. It also processes information more quickly than our old model. My brother set up his own password for the computer. I set up my own password for the computer, too. My father has asked me to help him use the computer. My mother has also asked me to help her use the computer.

Exercise 26 Find It in Your Reading Identify the compound verb in this excerpt from "The Fun They Had."

"A man? How could a man be a teacher?"
"Well, he just told the boys and girls things and gave them homework and asked them questions."

Exercise 27 Find It in Your Writing Look through your writing portfolio. Find an example of a compound subject or a compound verb.

Exercise 28 Writing Application Write a narrative about an activity that your entire class performed. Use compound subjects and compound predicates in your account. Underline the compound subjects once and the compound predicates twice.

Section Review • 393

ASSESS

Section Review

Each of these exercises correlates to the instruction on compound subjects and compound predicates, pages 390–392. The exercises may be used for more practice, for reteaching, or for review of the Key Concepts presented. Answers for all chapter exercises are available in *Grammar Exercises Answers on Transparencies* in your Teaching Resources.

Answer Key

Exercise 23

1. Students, teachers
2. displays, provides
3. keyboard, mouse
4. maps, charts, graphs, articles
5. can copy, save, print

Exercise 24

Possible answers:

1. Computers <u>guide</u> students (and) <u>provide</u> instruction.
2. <u>Students</u> (and) <u>teachers</u> use them on a daily basis.
3. The United States <u>buys</u> (and) <u>uses</u> more computers than any other country.
4. Both <u>European schools</u> (and) <u>Japanese schools</u> are also highly computerized.
5. <u>Videos</u> (and) <u>animation</u> <u>provide</u> information (and) <u>encourage</u> interaction.
6. <u>Spreadsheets</u> (and) <u>databases</u> <u>organize</u> (and) <u>collect</u> data.
7. They <u>analyze</u> (and) <u>transmit</u> information.
8. <u>Students</u> (and) <u>instructors</u> can communicate through a variety of programs.
9. Computer <u>disks</u> (and) <u>CD-ROMs</u> store large amounts of data.
10. Computer learning <u>is</u> individual (and) <u>gives</u> immediate answers.

Exercise 25

Possible answer given.

My family puchased a computer and signed up with an Internet provider. The computer has more memory and processes information more quickly than our old model. My bother and I set up our own passwords for the computer. My father and mother have asked me to help them use the computer.

continued

Answer Key continued

Exercise 26

Find It in Your Reading
told, gave, asked

Exercise 27

Find It in Your Writing
Ask students whether they have more compound subjects or more compound predicates in their writing. Have volunteers share the most complex combination they discovered. If students find no compounds, suggest that they try to find simple sentences they can combine or revise to form a compound subject or predicate.

Exercise 28

Writing Application
Let volunteers read their accounts to the class. Ask classmates to contribute their own recollections of the activity.

Ask for a volunteer to come to the front of the class. Face the volunteer and say "Please be seated." Write on the board the sentence you spoke. Ask the class to identify the subject of the sentence—who was doing the action (student's name). Ask how the student who sat down knew that he or she was the subject. Point out that the student *understood* what you meant.

Activate Prior Knowledge

Ask students to suggest simple sentences using the subjects "my friend," "the class," or "I" (or similar). Write a few of their sentences on the board. Point out that the verb follows the subject, and explain that this is considered normal order. If the verb and subject are reversed, the order is said to be inverted.

TEACH

Step-by-Step Teaching Guide

The Subject of a Command or Request

1. Explain that, as illustrated in the Interest Grabber, a subject is sometimes *understood* rather than stated.

2. Point out that, in situations where the subject is understood, one person directs another person or group.

3. Relate to students that occasions when *I* is understood occur (e.g., Thank you = I thank you), but they are not as common as situations where *you* is understood.

4. Have students each write two sentences with understood subjects, one of them with a name included.

Answer Key

Exercise 29

1. (you)	6. pony
2. Horses	7. (you)
3. (you)	8. *hand*
4. horses	9. (you)
5. (you)	10. hand

Hard-to-Find Subjects

This section shows how to identify simple subjects in three different kinds of sentences.

The Subject of a Command or Request When a sentence commands or requests someone to do something, the subject is often unstated.

▶ **KEY CONCEPT** The subject of a command or request is understood to be the word *you*. ■

Sentences	How the Sentences Are Understood
Stop!	You stop!
Begin at once.	You begin at once.
Audrey, make a list.	Audrey, you make a list.
Bob, get the tickets.	Bob, you get the tickets.

Even though a command or request may begin with the name of the person spoken to, the subject is still understood to be *you*.

▶ **Exercise 29** Recognizing Subjects in Commands or Requests List the simple subject of each sentence below. If the subject is understood as part of a command or request, write it in parentheses.

EXAMPLE: Jennifer, look out the window at the stables.
ANSWER: (you)

1. Show me the photo of the horse.
2. Horses live in family groups.
3. Look at the different sizes of the horses.
4. These wild horses have traveled great distances searching for food.
5. Emily, take a picture of the Shetland pony.
6. A pony is a small horse.
7. Listen to the sounds of the horses.
8. The *hand* is a measurement used for horses.
9. Take the measurement from the feet to the shoulders.
10. One hand is equal to four inches.

Theme: Horses
In this section, you will learn to identify hard-to-find subjects in commands, questions, and other sentences. The examples and exercises are about horses and horseback riding.

Cross-Curricular Connection: Science

▶ **More Practice**
On-line Exercise Bank
• Section 19.4
Grammar Exercise Workbook
• pp. 49–50

⏱ TIME AND RESOURCE MANAGER

Resources
Print: Grammar Exercise Workbook, pp. 49–50; Grammar Exercises Answers on Transparencies, Chapter 19
Technology: On-Line Exercise Bank, Section 19.4

In-Depth Coverage	Accelerated Pace
• Work through the key concepts, pp. 394–396. • Assign and review Exercises 29–31.	• Assign pp. 394–396 for independent student review. • Assign Section Review Exercises 32–34, p. 397.

The Subject of a Question If a sentence asks a question, the subject usually follows the verb. This is called *inverted order.*

KEY CONCEPT In questions, the subject often follows the verb or is located between a helping verb and the main verb. ■

EXAMPLES: How <u>can</u> <u>Claude</u> <u>ride</u> such an energetic horse?
<u>Is</u> there a good <u>movie</u> <u>playing</u> this evening?

If you are not sure of the subject of a question, turn the question into a statement. It will be easier to find the subject when the words are in normal order.

Questions	Questions Changed to Statements
<u>Has</u> <u>Ruth</u> <u>been practicing</u>?	<u>Ruth</u> <u>has been practicing</u>.
<u>Will</u> <u>David</u> <u>start</u> tomorrow?	<u>David</u> <u>will start</u> tomorrow.
<u>Can</u> this <u>horse</u> <u>hold</u> a mature rider?	This <u>horse</u> <u>can hold</u> a mature rider.

Exercise 30 **Finding the Subjects of Sentences That Ask Questions** Write the simple subject of each question below. Remember to change the question into a statement if you are not sure of the subject.

EXAMPLE: Why did Laura try the difficult jump?
ANSWER: Laura

1. What is the difference between a zebra and a horse?
2. In what ways do horses differ from donkeys?
3. When did you see the shire horse named King?
4. What was the horse's height?
5. How did you know about measuring horses?
6. Why is the Shetland pony so small?
7. Is it well adapted to its environment?
8. Do children ride that kind of pony?
9. Do horses live in Africa?
10. When did European travelers introduce domesticated horses?

▼ Critical Viewing
Write three questions you might ask about this horse before you ride it. Identify the subject in each sentence. **[Connect, Identify]**

Hard-to-Find Subjects • **395**

Step-by-Step Teaching Guide

The Subject of a Question

1. Write this question on the board:
   Why did she ride a skateboard?

2. Ask students to turn the question into a statement:
   She did ride a skateboard.

3. Ask students to underline the subject once and the predicate twice in both sentences:
   Why <u>did</u> <u>she</u> <u>ride</u> a skateboard?
   She <u>did</u> <u>ride</u> a skateboard.

4. Point out that, in current English usage, only a few verbs appear before the subject—primarily "helping verbs" like *can,* or forms of *to have, to do,* or *to be.* However, in older stories, students may encounter other verbs in inverted order, such as "How came you here?" or "Saw you anything new?" (You may want to ask if students have seen movies or read stories that use these inversions. In what time period were they set?)

5. Have volunteers make up questions and write them on the board. Ask other students to turn the questions into statements.

Critical Viewing

Connect, Identify Encourage students to ask questions that relate to their riding ability. Possible questions might be:

Is *it* a fast horse?
Do *beginners* usually ride it?
Does *it* like to be ridden?

Customize for
ESL Students

Discuss with students how questions are formed in their native languages. Invite them to write a statement in their language, then rewrite it as a question, to demonstrate. Have ESL students who are more fluent in English describe how their language differs from or is similar to English when forming questions.

Answer Key

▶ **Exercise 30**

1. difference
2. horses
3. you
4. height
5. you
6. Shetland pony
7. it
8. children
9. horses
10. travelers

✓ **ONGOING ASSESSMENT: Prerequisite Skills**

If students need to review commands or questions, refer them to the following sources for additional practice.

In the Textbook	Print Resources	Technology
Section Review, Ex. 32–33, p. 397	Grammar Exercises Workbook, pp. 49–50	On-Line Exercise Bank, Section 19.4

Subjects in Sentences That Begin with *There* or *Here*

1. Point out that questions are not the only sentences with inverted order of subjects and verbs. Often, when we want to direct attention to something, we use inverted order (e.g. Here it is. There it is.)

2. Explain that since *there* and *here* are never subjects, students should think of them as warning flags, to alert them to inverted order and hard-to-find subjects.

3. Suggest rewriting or restating as a good way to find subjects in sentences that begin with *there* or *here*.

4. Review the examples of rewritten sentences in the box. Point out that in the final example, *there* disappears in the rewritten version. Sometimes, *there* is just used to start a sentence.

5. Have students rewrite in normal order the four examples that follow the key concept.

Answer Key

▶ Exercise 31

1. people
2. [you]
3. statues
4. soldiers
5. horses
6. carvings
7. historians
8. article
9. [you]
10. drawings

The Subject of a Sentence Beginning With *There* or *Here*
There and *here* often begin sentences, but these words are never subjects.

▶ **KEY CONCEPT** The words *there* and *here* are never used as subjects. ■

Sometimes *there* and *here* are used as adverbs that answer the question *Where?* *There* can also be used as a sentence starter.

ADVERBS:	There <u>is</u> my <u>saddle</u>. Here <u>are</u> the <u>albums</u>.
SENTENCE STARTERS:	There <u>are</u> fifty <u>states</u> in the United States. There <u>was</u> a young <u>boy</u> here.

You can see that the order of subject and verb in each sentence above is inverted—that is, the subject follows the verb. If you have trouble finding the subject of sentences like these, rewrite the sentence so that it does not begin with *there* or *here*. When *there* is used as a sentence starter, it can safely be left out—the sentence will still make sense.

Sentences	Rewritten Sentences
Here <u>is</u> your <u>certificate</u>.	Your <u>certificate</u> <u>is</u> here.
There in the window <u>was</u> a tiny <u>monkey</u>.	A tiny <u>monkey</u> <u>was</u> there in the window.
There <u>are</u> two <u>senators</u> <u>elected</u> from every state.	Two <u>senators</u> <u>are</u> <u>elected</u> from every state. (*There* has been left out.)

▶ **Exercise 31** Identifying Hard-to-Find Subjects Write the simple subject of each of the following sentences.
1. When did people start riding horses?
2. Look in the museum.
3. There are statues of early horseback riders.
4. Did soldiers fight battles on horseback?
5. There were many horses in Genghis Khan's army.
6. Here are some carvings from 10,000 years ago.
7. What do historians think about the taming of the horse?
8. Here is an article about horses.
9. Read about their investigations.
10. There are cave drawings of horses.

▶ **More Practice**

On-line
Exercise Bank
• Section 19.4
Grammar Exercise
Workbook
• pp. 49–50

⏱ TIME SAVERS!

Answers on Transparency
Use the Grammar Exercises Answers on Transparencies for Chapter 19 to facilitate correction by students.

On-Line Exercise Bank
Have students complete the exercises on computer. The Auto Check feature will grade their work for you!

☑ ONGOING ASSESSMENT: Monitor and Reinforce

If students miss more than two items in Exercise 31, refer them to the following for additional practice.

In the Textbook	Print Resources	Technology
Section Review, Ex. 33–34, p. 397	Grammar Exercise Workbook, pp. 49–50	On-Line Exercise Bank, Section 19.4

Section 19.4 Section Review

GRAMMAR EXERCISES 32–37

Exercise 32 Rewriting Questions as Statements to Locate Their Subjects
On your paper, rewrite each question below as a statement. Then, underline each simple subject.

1. Is a bit needed in horseback riding?
2. Should all riders use this type of bridle?
3. Do you prefer an English saddle or a Western saddle?
4. Is the saddle too tight?
5. Was it uncomfortable to ride sidesaddle?

Exercise 33 Locating Hard-to-Find Subjects On your paper, write the simple subject of each sentence below.

1. Do you ever ride your horse in competitions?
2. Here is your formal riding jacket.
3. Wear a special helmet.
4. Which school teaches riding?
5. Use an English saddle.
6. When and where was the first jockey club founded?
7. There were races in Russia in 1775.
8. Have you ever seen a real racehorse?
9. There are several thoroughbreds near the track.
10. Go ahead and touch one.

Exercise 34 Supplying Subjects in Questions and Sentences Beginning with *Here* or *There* Rewrite the following sentences on your paper, supplying an appropriate simple subject for each blank. Then, underline the simple subject of your sentence once and the simple predicate twice.

1. Is this ___?___ easy to ride?
2. There are three ___?___ standing near the stables.

3. Have ___?___ ever wanted to gallop through the woods on a horse?
4. Here is my favorite ___?___ .
5. Is this ___?___ planning to ride that horse?
6. Where is the ___?___ going?
7. A short distance from here, there is a large ___?___ .
8. Can ___?___ see it from here?
9. Here are my ___?___ to help you.
10. Will the horse and ___?___ reach their destination on time?

Exercise 35 Find It in Your Reading Scan a sports article in a newspaper or magazine. Find at least one question and one sentence beginning with *here* or *there*. Name the subject of each sentence.

Exercise 36 Find It in Your Writing Look through your writing portfolio. Find a sentence that asks a question and one that begins with *here* or *there*. Write the subjects of those sentences.

Exercise 37 Writing Application Write a description of the picture on page 395. Include two sentences that begin with *here* or *there* and one question. Underline the simple subject of each sentence in your description.

Section Review • 397

☑ ONGOING ASSESSMENT: Assess Mastery

Use the following resources to assess student mastery of hard-to-find subjects.

In the Textbook	Technology
Chapter Review, Ex. 56, p. 410	On-Line Exercise Bank, Section 19.4

ASSESS

Section Review

Each of these exercises correlates to the instruction on hard-to-find subjects, pages 394–396. The exercises may be used for more practice, for reteaching, or for review of the Key Concepts presented.

Answer Key

Exercise 32

1. A <u>bit</u> is needed in horseback riding.
2. All <u>riders</u> should use this type of bridle.
3. <u>You</u> prefer an English saddle or a Western saddle.
4. The <u>saddle</u> is too tight.
5. <u>It</u> was uncomfortable to ride sidesaddle.

Exercise 33

1. you
2. riding jacket
3. [you]
4. school
5. [you]
6. club
7. races
8. you
9. thoroughbreds
10. [you]

Exercise 34

Possible answers:

1. <u>Is</u> this <u>horse</u> easy to ride?
2. There <u>are</u> three <u>ponies</u> <u>standing</u> near the stables.
3. <u>Have</u> <u>you</u> ever <u>wanted</u> to gallop through the woods on a horse?
4. Here <u>is</u> my favorite <u>saddle</u>.
5. <u>Is</u> this <u>girl</u> <u>planning</u> to ride that horse?
6. Where <u>is</u> the <u>trail</u> <u>going</u>?
7. A short distance from here, there <u>is</u> a large <u>lake</u>.
8. <u>Can</u> <u>you</u> <u>see</u> it from here?
9. Here <u>are</u> my <u>binoculars</u> to help you.
10. <u>Will</u> the <u>horse</u> and <u>rider</u> <u>reach</u> their destination on time?

Exercise 35

Find It in Your Reading
Students can explain to partners how they knew what the subject was.

Exercise 36

Find It in Your Writing
Let students trade sentences with a partner to check.

Exercise 37

Writing Application
Have students trade descriptions with a partner, who should try to find the subjects of the sentences.

PREPARE and ENGAGE

Interest GRABBER Write the following phrase on the board:

The shoppers spent

Ask students to identify the subject and verb. Then ask students if this is a complete sentence. (No, the sentence is incomplete.) Have volunteers complete the sentence.

Activate Prior Knowledge

Ask students to list three items that belong to them. Then tell students to imagine that they have to give these three items away. For each item, have the students complete this sentence:

I am giving [person's name] my [item].

On the board, write the indirect objects from students' sentences in one column and the direct objects in another.

TEACH

Step-by-Step Teaching Guide

Direct Objects

1. Explain that a direct object completes a sentence that contains an action verb. It tells who or what received the action of the verb. Point out if the verb is an action verb, students can state the verb, then ask the question *Whom?* or *What?* For example: *He threw the ball.* He threw what? *The ball.* If they cannot answer the question, the sentence does not have a direct object. For example: *He walked away* has no direct object, but *He walked the dog* does.

2. Write the following sentences on the board:

   My <u>dog</u> <u>chased</u> the squirrel.

   The <u>balloon</u> <u>floated</u> into the sky.

3. Point out that in the first sentence, *squirrel* is the direct object because it answers the question *Chased what?* The second sentence has no direct object because it gives no answer to the question *Floated what?*

Critical Viewing

Identify Students may write *The bike rider rode a <u>bike</u> in the city. The biker crossed the <u>bridge</u>. The rider saw lovely <u>homes</u>.*

398

Direct Objects and Indirect Objects

Identifying Direct Objects

You already know that a sentence must have two parts—a simple subject and a simple predicate. Some sentences need additional words to complete their meaning. These words are called *complements.* In the sentence *Jane gave a speech, speech* is a complement. It completes the meaning of *Jane gave.* It tells *what* Jane gave.

A *direct object* is one type of complement. It is used to complete many sentences that have action verbs.

▶ **KEY CONCEPT** A **direct object** is a noun or pronoun that appears with an action verb and receives the action of the verb. ■

A direct object answers the question *Whom?* or *What?* after an action verb.

EXAMPLE:	Mrs. Gomez picked <u>us</u>. (DO)
QUESTION:	Picked *whom?* Answer: *us*
EXAMPLE:	Fred asked a <u>question</u>. (DO)
QUESTION:	Asked *what?* Answer: *question*
EXAMPLE:	The detective drove <u>Abe</u> across the river. (DO)
QUESTION:	Drove *whom?* Answer: *Abe*

The following chart shows how simple subjects, simple predicates, and direct objects form complete sentences. As you can see, a direct object may be *compound.* That means that one verb can have two or more direct objects.

SENTENCES WITH DIRECT OBJECTS

My <u>sister</u> <u>draws</u> <u>pictures</u>. (DO)

Harry <u>invited</u> <u>you</u> and <u>me</u>. (DO) (DO)

Mr. Kelly <u>packed</u> <u>slacks</u>, <u>shirts</u>, and <u>ties</u>. (DO) (DO) (DO)

Theme: Bridges

In this section, you will learn to recognize two new sentence parts: direct and indirect objects. The examples and exercises are about bridges around the world.

Cross-Curricular Connection: Social Studies

▲ **Critical Viewing** Write three sentences about this picture using the verbs *rode, crossed,* and *saw.* What is the direct object in each sentence? **[Identify]**

⏱ TIME AND RESOURCE MANAGER

Resources
Print: Grammar Exercise Workbook, pp. 51–54; Hands-on Grammar Activity Book Chapter 19; Grammar Exercises Answers on Transparencies, Chapter 19
Technology: On-Line Exercise Bank, Section 19.5

In-Depth Coverage	Accelerated Pace
• Work through the key concepts, pp. 398–401. • Assign and review Exercises 38–39. • Do the Hands-on Grammar Activity, p. 402.	• Assign pp. 398–401 for independent student review. • Assign Section Review Exercises 40–42, p. 403.

GRAMMAR IN LITERATURE

From **Breaker's Bridge**

Laurence Yep

Notice the highlighted direct object in the following excerpt. What question does it answer?

. . . He could design a *bridge* to cross any obstacle. No canyon was too wide. No river was too deep. Somehow the clever man always found a way to bridge them all.

Exercise 38 **Finding Direct Objects** Copy each sentence below. Then, underline each direct object.

EXAMPLE: Ivan often crosses the Brooklyn Bridge.

1. The Pont Neuf crosses the Seine River in Paris.
2. It connects an island to the mainland.
3. The bridge has two arms.
4. The Pont Neuf replaced the older Pont Notre Dame.
5. Workers spent twenty-nine years building the bridge.
6. Religious wars interrupted the construction.
7. The plans for the bridge included space for shops.
8. Merchants displayed their goods in stalls on the bridge.
9. All levels of society visited the bridge for various reasons.
10. The Pont Neuf has played a big part in Parisian history.
11. Besides streets, Venice has canals.
12. The Rialto Bridge crosses the narrowest point of the Grand Canal.
13. Venetians have built several bridges at that spot.
14. They collected tolls on the Money Bridge.
15. The emperor Frederick III visited Venice.
16. A huge crowd watched him from the bridge.
17. The weight of the crowd caused the collapse of the bridge.
18. Eventually, Venetians built a larger stone bridge.
19. They lined it with shops.
20. Then, the Venetians changed its name to the Rialto Bridge.

More Practice

On-line
Exercise Bank
• Section 19.5
Grammar Exercise Workbook
• pp. 51–52

Direct Objects and Indirect Objects • 399

☑ **ONGOING ASSESSMENT: Monitor and Reinforce**

If students miss more than two items in Exercise 38, refer them to the following for additional practice.

In the Textbook	Print Resources	Technology
Section Review, Ex. 40–41, p. 403	Grammar Exercise Wookbook, pp. 51–52	On-Line Exercise Bank, Section 19.5

Step-by-Step Teaching Guide

Grammar in Literature

1. Have a volunteer read the passage aloud.

2. Remind students that the direct object should answer the question *Whom?* or *What?* In this case, the question should be *What could he design?*

3. Have students identify the direct object in the last sentence of the passage. (way)

Answer Key

Exercise 38

1. The Pont Neuf crosses the Seine River in Paris.
2. It connects an island to the mainland.
3. The bridge has two arms.
4. The Pont Neuf replaced the older Pont Notre Dame.
5. Workers spent twenty-nine years building the bridge.
6. Religious wars interrupted the construction.
7. The plans for the bridge included space for shops.
8. Merchants displayed their goods in stalls on the bridge.
9. All levels of society visited the bridge for various reasons.
10. The Pont Neuf has played a big part in Parisian history.
11. Besides streets, Venice has canals.
12. The Rialto Bridge crosses the narrowest point of the Grand Canal.
13. Venetians have built several bridges at that spot.
14. They collected tolls on the Money Bridge.
15. The emperor Frederick III visited Venice.
16. A huge crowd watched him from the bridge.
17. The weight of the crowd caused the collapse of the bridge.
18. Eventually, Venetians built a larger stone bridge.
19. They lined it with shops.
20. Then, the Venetians changed its name to the Rialto Bridge.

Indirect Objects

1. Explain that indirect objects are only found in sentences already containing direct objects. Indirect objects are only found after action verbs, but not after all action verbs. Verbs such as *bring, buy, give, lend, make, promise, sell, send, show, teach, tell,* or *write* (among others) commonly take an indirect object.

2. Write the following sentence on the chalkboard:

   Jorge gave me the CD.

3. Ask students to find the direct object first (gave what?—the CD). Then have them identify the indirect object by asking themselves the question *Gave the CD to whom?* (me)

4. Reinforce the rule that an indirect object is never the object of the preposition, such as *to* or *for,* and that an indirect object never follows a direct object. In the following sentence, *me* is not an indirect object:

   Jorge gave the CD to me.

19.5

Identifying Indirect Objects

A sentence that has a direct object can also have an indirect object. An indirect object is another type of complement. It also helps complete the meaning of a sentence.

▶ **KEY CONCEPT** An **indirect object** is a noun or pronoun usually located between an action verb and a direct object. It tells which person or thing something is being given to or done for. ■

An indirect object answers the question *To or for whom?* or *To or for what?* after an action verb.

EXAMPLE:	Yolanda sent [Marge] a [postcard].
QUESTION:	Sent *to whom?* Answer: *Marge*

EXAMPLE:	We gave the [magazine] a [title].
QUESTION:	Gave *to what?* Answer: *magazine*

You should not confuse an indirect object with an object of a preposition. An indirect object cannot be part of a prepositional phrase. In the sentence *Yolanda sent a postcard to Marge, Marge* is part of a prepositional phrase. It is the object of the preposition *to* and is not an indirect object.

Indirect objects can be compound. That is, a verb can be followed by two or more indirect objects.

EXAMPLES: Rose sold [John] and [Eric] the [tickets].

Sally sent [Stan] and [Martin] [photos] of the Tower Bridge .

SENTENCES WITH INDIRECT OBJECTS

Mrs. Lawton teaches [us] [engineering] .

The editor gave [Molly] and [Roy] an [assignment] .

A salesperson showed [Stan] a [watch] .

---

400 • Basic Sentence Parts

☑ **ONGOING ASSESSMENT: Monitor and Reinforce**

If students miss more than two items in Exercise 39, refer them to the following for additional practice.

In the Textbook	Print Resources	Technology
Section Review, Ex. 41–42, p. 403	Grammar Exercise Workbook, pp. 53–54	On-Line Exercise Bank, Section 19.5

▶ **Exercise 39** Identifying Indirect Objects Copy each
sentence below, and underline each indirect object. If a
sentence has no indirect object, write *none*.

EXAMPLE: I owe <u>Martin</u> a letter.

1. The Roman Empire built its citizens many bridges.
2. The Romans gave each bridge several arches.
3. Bridges with several tiers offered Romans many options.
4. The Pont du Gard at Nimes provided the area with much-needed water.
5. The aqueducts sent water to the cities.
6. They brought the citizens running water.
7. History tells us the benefits of the structure.
8. The Roman examples taught modern engineers much about bridge building.
9. I bought my friends postcards of the bridge.
10. I also sent my mother a photograph of the aqueducts.
11. In the Dark Ages, the monks built bridges for travelers.
12. The bridges saved the travelers a great deal of trouble.
13. Bridges offered them more protection from bandits.
14. Monks paid builders for their work.
15. The work also gave the builders training for other projects.
16. Some people taught themselves the skills to build bridges.
17. A shepherd boy promised the people of Avignon a bridge.
18. They granted him permission to build one.
19. A bishop lent the boy money for the project.
20. This book showed me the remaining four arches of the bridge.

An old stone bridge spans the Tarn Gorge in France.

▶ **More Practice**

On-line
Exercise Bank
• Section 19.5
Grammar Exercise
Workbook
• pp. 53–54

▼ **Critical Viewing**
In what ways can
you compare an
indirect object in
a sentence to a
bridge? [**Compare**]

Direct Objects and Indirect Objects • **401**

Customize for
Verbal/Linguistic Students

Direct students to create one sentence
that has a direct and indirect object
for each of the following verbs: *mailed,
draw, give, made.*

Critical Viewing

Compare Students may suggest that
a bridge goes from one side *to*
another and an indirect object
answers the question *to whom or
what?*

Answer Key

▶ **Exercise 39**

1. citizens
2. bridge
3. Romans
4. area
5. none
6. citizens
7. us
8. engineers
9. friends
10. mother
11. none
12. travelers
13. them
14. none
15. builders
16. themselves
17. people
18. him
19. boy
20. me

🕑 **TIME SAVERS!**

Answers on Transparency
Use the Grammar Exercises
Answers on Transparencies for
Chapter 19 to facilitate
correction by students.

On-Line Exercise Bank
Have students complete the
exercises on computer. The Auto
Check feature will grade their
work for you!

Indirect Object Spinner

Teaching Resources: Hands-on Grammar Activity Book, Chapter 19

1. Have students refer to their Hands-on Grammar activity books or give them copies of the revelant pages for this activity.

2. Encourage students to make up interesting direct objects to be *given, offered, sent,* etc. to them.

3. Remind students that a direct object is necessary for an indirect object, but that there can be a direct object without an indirect object.

Find It In Your Reading

Have students share their examples.

Find It In Your Writing

Remind students they must have direct objects if they change prepositional phrases to indirect objects.

Integrating Reading Skills

Challenge each student to find a sentence that contains a direct and indirect object in a math or science textbook. Students can write their examples on sentence strips, mark the direct and indirect objects, then post their sentences as part of a collection on a bulletin board.

19.5

Hands-on Grammar

Indirect Object Spinner

Sometimes you can use indirect objects instead of prepositional phrases in your sentences to add variety to your writing. To practice using indirect objects or prepositional phrases, try this activity:

Cut an index card in half. Fold each half to form an open rectangular box. You can do this by making a crease in the middle of the card piece and then folding in from the top and the bottom to your crease. (See the diagram below.) On each of the four creased areas of one of your index card halves, write a simple subject and predicate, using one of the following verbs: *sent, gave, made, offered, showed,* or *sent.* Examples: *My aunt gave* or *The teacher offered.* On the four creased areas of the other index card half, write two pairs of related endings for the sentence. One ending in each pair will contain the word *me* as an indirect object followed by a direct object. The other will contain the same direct object and a prepositional phrase ending with *me.* Examples: *me an alligator* and *an alligator to me.* Write the word *me* in one color when it is an indirect object and in another color when it is the object of a preposition.

Tape the edges of each card half together to form a box. Place your two boxes onto a pencil so that you can spin them around. Read each sentence opener with each pair of related endings. You will form sentences such as *My aunt gave me an alligator*

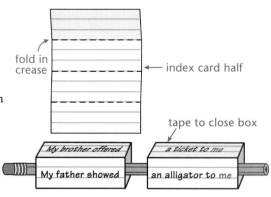

and *My aunt gave an alligator to me.* You can identify in which sentences *me* is functioning as an indirect object by its placement between the verb and the direct object in the sentence. The color coding will help you know whether you are right.

Find It in Your Reading Select a paragraph from a story in your literature book that contains a sentence with an indirect object. Make sure you can identify the indirect object and the direct object.

Find It in Your Writing Look for sentences in your own compositions that contain prepositional phrases beginning with *to* or *for.* Decide whether you should use an indirect object instead.

402 • Basic Sentence Parts

⏱ **TIME SAVERS!**

✋ **Hands-on Grammar**
Use the Hands-on Grammar activity sheet for Chapter 19 to facilitate this activity.

☑ **ONGOING ASSESSMENT: Assess Mastery**

Use the following resources to assess student mastery of direct and indirect objects.

In the Textbook	Technology
Chapter Review, Ex. 58, p. 410	On-Line Exercise Bank, Section 19.5

Section 19.5

Section Review

GRAMMAR EXERCISES 40–45

Exercise 40 **Identifying Direct Objects** Identify the direct object in each sentence below.

1. The Romans invented special arched bridges.
2. These aqueducts carried water from reservoirs to towns.
3. Modern builders make arches out of steel.
4. Sometimes cables attach the roadway to the framework.
5. Suspension bridges span the longest distances.

Exercise 41 **Identifying Direct and Indirect Objects** Write each sentence below on your paper. Underline the indirect object and circle the direct object. Write *none* after a sentence if it has no indirect object.

1. My grandparents took me on a tour of the Brooklyn Bridge.
2. The guide gave us a lecture on the history of the bridge.
3. The tour guide handed a brochure about the bridge to me.
4. We photographed the patterns of the cables.
5. Thousands of steel wires give each cable its strength.
6. Steel suspenders hold the roadway above the water.
7. Streetcars no longer take riders across the Brooklyn Bridge.
8. A walkway offers pedestrians a route to Brooklyn.
9. The bridge gives drivers a great view of the East River.
10. I sent my aunt and uncle postcards and photographs of the bridge.

Exercise 42 **Revising Sentences by Using Indirect Objects** Revise the sentences below by using an indirect object in place of a prepositional phrase.

1. My brother built a model of the Brooklyn Bridge for me.
2. I showed the model to my science teacher.
3. She thought that it gave a good idea to everyone of the complexity of the bridge.
4. My brother offered help to me in building a model of another famous bridge.
5. He gave advice on how to get started to me.

Exercise 43 **Find It in Your Reading** In the last sentence of the excerpt from "Breaker's Bridge" on page 399, find the direct object of the verb *found*.

Exercise 44 **Find It in Your Writing** In your own writing, find three examples of direct objects. Also, see whether you have used indirect objects in any of your sentences.

Exercise 45 **Writing Application** Write a postcard telling about a place you have visited or would like to visit. Include three direct objects and at least one indirect object. Circle the direct objects, and underline the indirect objects. You might want to use some of these verbs: *gave, made, told, bought, showed, sent.*

Section Review • 403

ASSESS and CLOSE

Section Review

Each of these exercises correlates to the instruction on direct objects and indirect objects, pages 398–402. The exercises may be used for more practice, for reteaching, or for review of the Key Concepts presented. Answers for all chapter exercises are available in *Grammar Exercises Answers on Transparencies* in your Teaching Resources.

Answer Key

Exercise 40

1. bridges
2. water
3. arches
4. roadway
5. distances

Exercise 41

1. me—direct, none
2. us—indirect, lecture—direct
3. brochure—direct, none
4. patterns—direct, none
5. cable—indirect, strength—direct
6. roadway—direct, none
7. riders—direct, none
8. pedestrians—indirect, route—direct
9. drivers—indirect, view—direct
10. aunt and uncle—indirect, postcards and photographs—direct

Exercise 42

1. My brother built me a model of the Brooklyn Bridge.
2. I showed my science teacher the model.
3. She thought it gave everyone a good idea of the complexity of the bridge.
4. My brother offered me help in building a model of another famous bridge.
5. He gave me advice on how to get started.

Exercise 43

Find It in Your Reading
way

Exercise 44

Find It in Your Writing
If students do not find indirect objects, challenge them to add indirect objects to a few of their sentences.

continued

Answer Key continued

Exercise 45

Writing Application
Ask volunteers to share their efforts with the class. After they have read their "post cards," have them select one sentence to write on the board, identifying the direct object and (if there is one) the indirect object.

PREPARE and ENGAGE

Interest GRABBER Ask students to list on a sheet of paper five roles they fulfill in life, such as *student, friend, daughter, soccer player, family comedian.* Ask students to write another list of at least five words that people would use to describe them, such as *tall, happy, smart, cool, funny.* Have students write their names at the top of each list. Read some of the lists aloud and point out how the nouns and adjectives give a more complete picture of each student.

Activate Prior Knowledge

Ask students to offer words that describe the following items in greater detail:

• book (dictionary, novel, paperback; blue, thick, lost)

• cat (lion, Siamese, calico; huge, small, noisy)

• tree (elm, spruce, pine; bare, old, fallen)

TEACH

Step-by-Step Teaching Guide

Predicate Nouns

1. Ask a volunteer to give examples of linking verbs.

2. Explain to students that when the word linked to the subject is a noun, it is called a predicate noun. It "identifies" the subject.

3. Write this sentence on the board:
   Miriam is a student.

4. Choose a student to underline the nouns in the sentence. *(Miriam, student)*

5. Ask which noun is the subject. *(Miriam)* Then ask them what the other noun is. (predicate noun)

Step-by-Step Teaching Guide

Grammar in Literature

1. Have a volunteer read the passage aloud.

2. Ask students to explain how they can tell that *place* is a predicate noun (It is a noun that follows a linking verb and identifies or renames the subject.)

Section 19.6

Predicate Nouns and Predicate Adjectives

In this section, you will learn about two sentence parts often found in a complete predicate. *Predicate nouns* and *predicate adjectives* are called *subject complements.* A predicate noun renames the subject. A predicate adjective describes the subject. Both subject complements add details about the subject.

Identifying Predicate Nouns

A subject and a linking verb will generally be followed by one or more words that are needed to form a complete sentence. Predicate nouns often follow linking verbs.

▶ **KEY CONCEPT** A **predicate noun** is a noun that appears with a subject and a linking verb. It renames or identifies the subject. ■

EXAMPLES: Robert is the [captain].
                                              PN

                     The bridge was a very old [structure].
                                                            PN

                     My dog is a [poodle].
                                       PN

All the verbs in the sentences above are linking verbs. They are forms of the verb *be*, the most common linking verb.

A linking verb functions like an equal sign. In the first sentence above, *Robert is the captain* means *Robert = the captain.* The word *is* links *Robert* and *the captain* by saying that the one equals the other.

GRAMMAR IN LITERATURE

from **Breaker's Bridge**
Laurence Yep

In the following excerpt, the predicate noun is shown in blue italics, and the word it identifies is in red italics.

Breaker became uneasy. "*This* is a *place* that doesn't like people very much."

⏱ **TIME AND RESOURCE MANAGER**

Resources
Print: Grammar Exercise Workbook, pp. 55–58; Grammar Exercises Answers on Transparencies, Chapter 19
Technology: On-Line Exercise Bank, Section 19.6

In-Depth Coverage	Accelerated Pace
• Work through the key concepts, pp. 404–408. • Assign and review Exercises 46–47. • Read and discuss Grammar in Literature, p. 404.	• Assign pp. 404–408 for independent student review. • Assign Section Review Exercises 48–51, p. 409.

Theme: Bridges
In this section, you will learn to recognize and use predicate nouns and predicate adjectives. The examples and exercises provide more information about bridges around the world.

Cross-Curricular Connection: Social Studies

> **KEY CONCEPT** Two or more nouns can be used after a linking verb to form a compound predicate noun. ∎

In the example below, two nouns are joined by the conjunction *and* to form a compound predicate noun. Both nouns identify or rename the same subject.

EXAMPLE: The <u>speakers</u> today <u>are</u> PN Jim and PN Rebecca .

> **KEY CONCEPT** A predicate noun is never part of a prepositional phrase. ∎

Predicate nouns, like other complements, can never be part of prepositional phrases.

EXAMPLE: <u>Engineering</u> <u>is</u> an interesting PN branch of science.

Branch is a predicate noun, but *science* is not. It is part of the prepositional phrase *of science.*

Built in 1870, this bridge in Waco, Texas, is one of the oldest suspension bridges in the United States.

▼ **Critical Viewing**
Think of three different predicate nouns to complete this sentence: *This old bridge is a (an) . . . .*
[Connect]

More About the Writer
Laurence Yep is a third-generation Chinese American. As a boy, he lived in an African-American neighborhood in San Francisco and went to school in Chinatown. Because of his experiences with different cultures, Yep's work often centers on the search for one's own identity.

Connections with Literature
Students can read about the struggles of one of Yep's characters in the folktale "Breaker's Bridge" in *Prentice Hall Literature: Timeless Voices, Timeless Themes,* Copper Level.

Critical Viewing
Connect Students should identify their answers such as:

an *example* of a suspension bridge.

a *place* to visit.

a *type* of bridge built frequently in the 1900's.

Predicate Nouns and Predicate Adjectives • **405**

STANDARDIZED TEST PREPARATION WORKSHOP

Appropriate Sentence Construction
Standardized tests frequently measure student's ability to identify a complete sentence. Ask students to choose the letter of the best way to rewrite the underlined section.

James and his sister are going to visit their grandmother. <u>Lives in Texas.</u>

A Who lives in Texas.

B She lives in Texas.

C Living in Texas all her life.

D Correct as is.

The underlined section is an incomplete sentence because it is missing a subject. Item **B** is the only complete sentence.

Customize for *ESL Students*

Students for whom English is a second language may have trouble with more complicated terms like *predicate noun* and *predicate adjective*. Break the terms down for them to make them easier to understand. First, review the complete predicate. Then point out that a predicate noun is just a type of noun that is sometimes found in the complete predicate and that identifies the subject.

Likewise, a predicate adjective is a type of adjective sometimes found in the complete predicate and that describes the subject.

Explain that it works a lot like translation: "means" is a linking verb, so if they say "buenos dias" means "good day," they have renamed the first word—they have used a predicate noun.

Critical Viewing

Identify Be sure students use nouns to identify the bridge rather than adjectives that describe it.

Answer Key

▶ **Exercise 47**

1. landmark
2. towers
3. drawbridge
4. requirement
5. Sir John Wolfe Barry
6. architect
7. walkway
8. spot
9. machines
10. elevators

▶ **Exercise 46** Identifying Predicate Nouns Identify the predicate noun in each sentence below.

EXAMPLE: Jane became a student.
ANSWER: student

1. Tower Bridge is a landmark in London.
2. Its supports are two Gothic-style towers.
3. The middle portion is a central drawbridge.
4. The design was a requirement of the government.
5. The engineer of the bridge was Sir John Wolfe Barry.
6. Sir Horace Jones was the architect.
7. The upper level is a pedestrian walkway.
8. The walkway became a popular tourist spot.
9. Devices in the towers are the machines that lift the drawbridge.
10. Other devices in the towers are elevators to the upper walkway.

▶ **More Practice**

On-line
Exercise Bank
• Section 19.6
**Grammar Exercise
Workbook**
• pp. 55–56

▼ Critical Viewing
Think of sentences that include predicate nouns to identify the bridge (named in the exercise above) and the boat passing under it. **[Identify]**

⏱ TIME SAVERS!

Answers on Transparency
Use the Grammar Exercises Answers on Transparencies for Chapter 19 to facilitate correction by students.

On-Line Exercise Bank
Have students complete the exercises on computer. The Auto Check feature will grade their work for you!

☑ ONGOING ASSESSMENT: Monitor and Reinforce

If students miss more than two items in Exercise 46, refer them to the following for additional practice.

In the Textbook	Print Resources	Technology
Section Review, Ex. 48, 50, p. 409	Grammar Exercise Workbook, pp. 55–56	On-Line Exercise Bank, Section 19.6

Identifying Predicate Adjectives

An adjective may also follow a linking verb. If it completes the sentence, it is called a *predicate adjective.*

> **KEY CONCEPT** A **predicate adjective** is an adjective that follows a subject and a linking verb. It describes or modifies the subject of the sentence. ■

Predicate adjectives always modify the subject of a sentence. The arrows in the examples below connect the boxed predicate adjectives with the subjects they modify.

EXAMPLES: The river appears deep .

Your hand feels cold .

Predicate adjectives follow linking verbs such as those in the examples above. Other linking verbs include *be, become, grow, look, smell, sound, stay,* and *turn.*

A sentence may also have a compound predicate adjective—two or more adjectives following a linking verb.

EXAMPLES: I felt tired and hungry after the long climb.

The room grew crowded and stuffy .

The following chart gives more examples of sentences with one or more predicate adjectives. An arrow connects each predicate adjective with the subject it modifies.

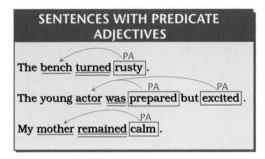

SENTENCES WITH PREDICATE ADJECTIVES

The bench turned rusty .

The young actor was prepared but excited .

My mother remained calm .

Step-by-Step Teaching Guide

Predicate Adjectives

1. Point out to students that since predicate nouns actually rename the subject, the linking verb one usually sees with a predicate noun is a form of *to be,* though *become, mean,* or *equal* are other possibilities. However, since predicate adjectives describe the subject, there are more linking verbs that can be used: *smell, appear, taste, grow,* etc.

2. Explain that the tricky part here is that some of these linking verbs can sometimes be action verbs. Write on the board:

   The rose smells good.

   Janet smells the rose.

   Ask students what *rose* is in the first sentence (subject). What is *good?* (predicate adjective) Then what is *rose* in the second sentence? (direct object).

3. Write this sentence on the board:

   You are super.

   Tell students that you are going to read a list of statements about the word *super* as used above. They should raise their hands whenever they hear a true statement.

   Super is an adjective.

   Super appears after the subject.

   Super appears after a linking verb.

   Super describes the subject.

4. Explain that students who raised their hands for each statement did a super job. Every statement is true. Together, the statements define a predicate adjective.

5. Ask students to create more sentences that use predicate adjectives.

Integrating Reading Skills

Ask students how identifying predicate nouns and predicate adjectives might help them in their reading. (helps them learn important details about the characters, places, and objects in a story) Ask students to suggest sentences with predicate nouns or predicate adjectives, either ones they remember from stories or ones they can imagine being used in a story. (Mike is a dog. The prince was handsome, etc.)

Critical Viewing

Analyze Be sure students use <u>covered</u> as a predicate adjective. Encourage students to use a wide variety of predicate adjectives.

Answer Key

▶ **Exercise 47**

1. Early bridges in New England were <u>wooden</u>. [*wooden* modifies *bridges*]
2. The supply of lumber was <u>abundant</u>. [*abundant* modifies *supply*]
3. Covered bridges may be <u>narrow</u> or <u>wide</u>. [*narrow* and *wide* modify *bridges*]
4. Even today they remain very <u>sturdy</u>. [*sturdy* modifies *they*]
5. The roof was <u>useful</u> for protecting the bridge from the elements. [*useful* modifies *roof*]
6. The sun and rain were <u>harmful</u> to the wood. [*harmful* modifies *sun and rain*]
7. With a roof, the plank floor would stay <u>strong</u>. [*strong* modifies *floor*]
8. The speed of horses and carriages seemed very <u>slow</u>. [*slow* modifies *speed*]
9. These bridges were <u>vulnerable</u> to fires. [*vulnerable* modifies *bridges*]
10. The truss system was <u>important</u> in the construction of covered bridges. [*important* modifies *system*]

Customize for
More Advanced Students

Have students use the additional verbs identified in the predicate adjective instruction to compose as many sentences as they can where the linking verb can be followed by either a predicate adjective or direct object. (For example: The room grew quiet. Gina grew tomatoes.)

19.6

▶ **Exercise 47** Identifying Predicate Adjectives Copy each of the sentences below. Underline each predicate adjective. Then, draw an arrow connecting it to the subject it modifies. Some compound predicate adjectives are included.

EXAMPLE: The bridge grew <u>crowded</u> with traffic.

1. Early bridges in New England were wooden.
2. The supply of lumber was abundant.
3. Covered bridges may be narrow or wide.
4. Even today, they remain very sturdy.
5. The roof was useful for protecting the bridge from the elements.
6. The sun and rain were harmful to the wood.
7. With a roof, the plank floor would stay strong.
8. The speed of horses and carriages seemed very slow.
9. These bridges were vulnerable to fires.
10. The truss system was important in the construction of covered bridges.

▶ **More Practice**

On-line
Exercise Bank
• Section 19.6
Grammar Exercise
Workbook
• pp. 57–58

▶ Critical Viewing
Think of several adjectives to describe this bridge. Use your words as predicate adjectives in sentences about the bridge. **[Analyze]**

408 • Basic Sentence Parts

⏱ TIME SAVERS!

🖼 **Answers on Transparency** Use the Grammar Exercises Answers on Transparencies for Chapter 19 to facilitate correction by students.

💻 **On-Line Exercise Bank** Have students complete the exercises on computer. The Auto Check feature will grade their work for you!

☑ ONGOING ASSESSMENT: Assess Mastery

Use the following resources to assess student mastery of basic sentence parts.

In the Textbook	Print Resources	Technology
Chapter Review, Ex. 55–61, pp. 410–411 Standardized Test Preparation Workshop, pp. 412–413	Formal Assessment, Chapter 19	On-Line Exercise Bank, Section 19.6

Section Review

GRAMMAR EXERCISES 48–54

Exercise 48 Recognizing
Predicate Nouns Identify the predicate
noun in each sentence below.

1. Charles Crocker was the originator of
   the idea.
2. Joseph Baermann Strauss was a well-
   known designer of bridges.
3. He was a believer in the plan.
4. The waterway in question was the
   Golden Gate Strait.
5. In 1930, the people in the area were
   supporters of the project.

Exercise 49 Identifying Predicate
Adjectives Copy each of the sentences
below. Underline each predicate adjective.
Then, draw an arrow connecting it to the
subject it modifies.

1. The bridge's color is orange.
2. Most modern bridges are black or
   gray.
3. The bridge is well maintained even
   today.
4. The Golden Gate Bridge has become
   irreplaceable.
5. It is useful for drivers and pedestrians.

Exercise 50 Identifying Predicate
Nouns and Adjectives Identify the
predicate nouns and the predicate adjectives in the following sentences. Label each
one PN or PA.

1. The study of bridges is fascinating.
2. Many bridges are wooden.
3. Concrete became a common material
   in combination with iron wire.
4. Ancient castles stayed safe behind
   drawbridges.
5. The movement of drawbridges is simple to understand.

6. The basic principles are the same as in
   other lift bridges.
7. A counterweight looks hard to move.
8. Actually, it becomes very useful in
   raising and lowering heavy bridges.
9. The small motors are powerful tools.
10. Bridges are important structures all
    around the world.

Exercise 51 Supplying Predicate
Nouns or Predicate Adjectives in
Sentences Copy the sentences below on
your paper, supplying an appropriate predicate noun or predicate adjective to fill
each blank. Underline the words you add,
and label them PN or PA.

1. This rope bridge seems ___?___.
2. Is it ___?___ enough to hold my weight?
3. The rope bridge was the only ___?___ to
   get across the ravine.
4. All of us were ___?___ as we crossed
   the bridge.
5. John was an expert ___?___, so he led
   the way.

Exercise 52 Find It in Your
Reading In the excerpt from "Breaker's
Bridge" on page 404, identify a predicate
adjective and the word it modifies.

Exercise 53 Find It in Your
Writing Look through your writing
portfolio. Find two predicate nouns and
two predicate adjectives in your writing.

Exercise 54 Writing Application
Write a description of a bridge that you
have seen. Use predicate nouns and predicate adjectives to tell more about your
subjects. Label each one PN or PA.

ASSESS and CLOSE

Section Review

Each of these exercises correlates to
the instruction on predicate nouns
and predicate adjectives, pages
404–408. The exercises may be used
for more practice, for reteaching, or
for review of the Key Concepts
presented. Answers for all chapter
exercises are available in *Grammar
Exercises Answers on Transparencies* in
your Teaching Resources.

Answer Key

Exercise 48

1. originator
2. designer
3. believer
4. Golden Gate Strait
5. supporters

Exercise 49

1. The bridge's color is <u>orange</u>.
   [*orange* modifies *color*]
2. Most modern bridges are <u>black</u>
   or <u>gray</u>. [*black* and *gray* modify
   bridges]
3. The bridge is well <u>maintained</u>
   even today. [*maintained* modifies
   bridge]
4. The Golden Gate Bridge has
   become <u>irreplaceable</u>.
   [*irreplaceable* modifies *Golden
   Gate Bridge*]
5. It is <u>useful</u> for drivers and
   pedestrians. [*useful* modifies *It*]

Exercise 50

1. fascinating—predicate adjective
2. wooden—predicate adjective
3. material—predicate noun
4. safe—predicate adjective
5. simple—predicate adjective
6. same—predicate adjective
7. hard—predicate adjective
8. useful—predicate adjective
9. tools—predicate noun
10. structures—predicate noun

Exercise 51

Possible answers:

1. sturdy, PA
2. strong, PA
3. way, PN
4. scared, PA
5. climber, PN

Exercise 52

Find It in Your Reading
uneasy modifies *Breaker*

Answer Key continued

Exercise 53

Find It in Your Writing
Ask volunteers to share the sentences they find
that contain predicate nouns and adjectives. If
any sentences have compound subjects,
predicate nouns, and/or predicate adjectives,
write them on the board and have the class
identify the sentence parts.

Exercise 54

Writing Application
Suggest that students trade their descriptions
with partners and check that predicate
adjectives and predicate nouns are correctly
used.

continued

CHAPTER REVIEW

Each of these exercises correlates to a section of the chapter on basic sentence parts, pages 380–409. The exercises may be used for more practice, for reteaching, or for review of the Key Concepts presented. Answers for all chapter exercises are available in *Grammar Exercises Answers on Transparencies* in your Teaching Resources.

Answer Key

▶ **Exercise 55**

1. The *Mayflower* | <u>sailed</u> across the Atlantic Ocean.
2. The <u>ship</u> | <u>was headed</u> for Virginia.
3. <u>It</u> | <u>carried</u> the Pilgrims to the New World.
4. Thrown off course, the <u>boat</u> | <u>reached</u> Massachusetts instead of Virginia.
5. The <u>Pilgrims</u> | <u>founded</u> Plymouth Colony.
6. All adult <u>males</u> | <u>gathered</u> in the cabin of the *Mayflower*.
7. Forty-one <u>men</u>, including John Alden and Miles Standish, | <u>signed</u> the Mayflower Compact.
8. The <u>compact</u> | <u>established</u> the rule of the majority.
9. <u>It</u> | <u>remained</u> their fundamental principle of government.
10. <u>Plymouth Colony</u> | <u>was absorbed</u> by the Massachusetts Bay Colony in 1691.

▶ **Exercise 56**

1. *Great Eastern*
2. steamship
3. [you]
4. route
5. ship
6. paddle wheel
7. [you]
8. it
9. [you]
10. *Great Eastern*

▶ **Exercise 57**

The *Merrimack* <u>was abandoned</u> (and) <u>was</u> then <u>sunk</u> by Union forces. Confederate workers <u>raised</u> it (and) <u>rebuilt</u> it as the *Virginia*. The *Virginia* <u>destroyed</u> two Union ships (and) then <u>engaged</u> the *Monitor* in battle. The two ironclad ships <u>faced</u> off against each other (and) <u>opened</u> fire. The *Virginia* (and) the *Monitor* sustained some damage. The battle at Hampton Roads was called a draw.

GRAMMAR EXERCISES 55–62

▶ **Exercise 55** Identifying Complete Subjects and Predicates and Simple Subjects and Predicates Copy each sentence below. Put a vertical line between the complete subject and the complete predicate. Underline the simple subject once and the simple predicate twice.

1. The *Mayflower* sailed across the Atlantic Ocean.
2. The ship was headed for Virginia.
3. It carried the Pilgrims to the New World.
4. Thrown off course, the boat reached Massachusetts instead of Virginia.
5. The Pilgrims founded Plymouth Colony.
6. All adult males gathered in the cabin of the *Mayflower*.
7. Forty-one men, including John Alden and Miles Standish, signed the Mayflower Compact.
8. The compact established the rule of the majority.
9. It remained their fundamental principle of government.
10. Plymouth Colony was absorbed by the Massachusetts Bay Colony in 1691.

▶ **Exercise 56** Identifying Hard-to-Find Subjects Write the simple subject of each sentence below.

1. There is the *Great Eastern*.
2. When was that steamship launched?
3. Look at the six masts!
4. Here is its route to Australia.
5. Could the ship carry enough coal?
6. There is a paddle wheel with an 18-meter diameter.
7. Start the paddle wheel.
8. Was it famous for its size?
9. Learn about the transatlantic cable.
10. Did the *Great Eastern* lay any other cables across the ocean?

▶ **Exercise 57** Revising a Paragraph by Forming Compound Subjects or Predicates Revise the paragraph below by combining information in sentences to form compound subjects or compound predicates.

The *Merrimack* was sunk by Union forces. The *Merrimack* was at first abandoned. Then, Confederate workers raised it. They rebuilt it as the *Virginia*. The *Virginia* destroyed two Union ships. It then engaged the *Monitor* in battle. The two ironclad ships faced off against each other. They opened fire. The *Virginia* sustained some damage. The *Monitor* also sustained some damage. The battle at Hampton Roads was called a draw.

▶ **Exercise 58** Identifying Direct and Indirect Objects Write the sentences below on your paper. Underline the indirect objects and circle the direct objects.

1. Our teacher showed the class pictures of caravels.
2. Caravels used the wind for power.
3. Traders sailed caravels on the Mediterranean Sea in the 1300's.
4. The town of Palos in Spain gave Christopher Columbus two caravels.
5. Columbus sailed these caravels and another ship west across the Atlantic.
6. The three ships carried ninety men.
7. Columbus paid the men monthly wages.
8. Cannons on the ships could fire large stones at enemies.
9. Queen Isabella gave the ships several flags to fly.
10. Columbus's journeys brought him fame.

▶ **Exercise 58**

1. direct: pictures; indirect: class
2. direct: wind; no indirect object
3. direct: caravels; no indirect object
4. direct: caravels; indirect: Christopher Columbus
5. direct: caravels, ship; no indirect object
6. direct: men; no indirect object
7. direct: wages; indirect: men
8. direct: stones; no indirect object
9. direct: flags; indirect: ships
10. direct: fame; indirect: him

▶ **Exercise 59** Identifying Predicate Nouns and Adjectives Write any predicate nouns or predicate adjectives you find in the following sentences. Label them *PN* or *PA*.

1. The *Niña* and the *Pinta* were caravels; the *Santa María* was much larger.
2. Caravels were smaller and lighter than galleons.
3. These ships were tiny compared to modern ships.
4. The *Santa María* was the slowest of the three ships.
5. Food, fuel, candles, and tools were important supplies.
6. "Bombards" were a type of cannon.
7. Other weapons were more accurate.
8. The trip across the Atlantic became very long.
9. The sailors grew tired.
10. Columbus was an experienced sailor.

▶ **Exercise 60** Identifying Basic Sentence Parts On your paper, indicate whether the underlined sentence part is a *subject, verb, direct object, indirect object, predicate noun,* or *predicate adjective.*

1. Today's cruise ships are <u>large</u> and luxurious.
2. They offer <u>passengers</u> fine food and accommodations.
3. The *Queen Mary* and *Queen Elizabeth* were early ocean <u>liners</u>.
4. Raging <u>fires</u> destroyed the *Queen Elizabeth* in 1972.
5. The *Andrea Doria* was very large and <u>fast</u>.
6. It <u>was called</u> the "Grande Dame of the Sea."
7. The ship provided swimming <u>pools</u> for all three classes.
8. Captain Calami <u>gave</u> the *Andrea Doria* a heading for New York.
9. The *Stockholm* and the <u>*Andrea Doria*</u> crossed paths.

10. Gunnar Nordensen was <u>captain</u> of the *Stockholm.*
11. How dense the <u>fog</u> was that night!
12. "<u>Pull</u> to the left!" the captain shouted.
13. Both boats maneuvered but still <u>collided</u>.
14. My father told <u>us</u> the story of the sinking of the *Andrea Doria.*
15. Today, most <u>passengers</u> cross the ocean in planes instead of ships.

▶ **Exercise 61** Revising by Adding Basic Sentence Parts Revise the following paragraph, adding subjects or predicates to any incomplete sentences as needed, forming compound subjects or predicates, or adding predicate nouns or predicate adjectives to provide details.

I saw a television documentary about the *Titanic.* Was a large luxury liner. Everyone thought it was. Nevertheless, it crashed. Sank quickly. The show included old newsreel films. The show featured interviews with survivors. Quite interesting. Provided many details about the disaster. Described the passengers' fates graphically. Many people lost their lives when sank. Some young, some old. The whole incident seemed so to me. I told my brother the story. He also felt about what happened.

▶ **Exercise 62** Writing Application Write a comparison of two means of transportation. Use some compound subjects and compound predicates in your writing. Also include some predicate nouns and predicate adjectives to add descriptive details.

▶ **Exercise 59**

1. caravels—predicate noun, larger—predicate adjective
2. smaller—predicate adjective, lighter—predicate adjective
3. tiny—predicate adjective
4. slowest—predicate adjective
5. supplies—predicate noun
6. type—predicate noun
7. accurate—predicate adjective
8. long—predicate adjective
9. tired—predicate adjective
10. sailor—predicate noun

▶ **Exercise 60**

1. PA: large
2. IO: passengers
3. PN: liners
4. subject: fires
5. PA: fast
6. verb: was called
7. DO: pools
8. verb: gave
9. subject: *Andrea Doria*
10. PN: captain
11. subject: fog
12. verb: Pull
13. verb: collided
14. IO: us
15. subject: passengers

▶ **Exercise 61**

Answers will vary. A sample is given.

I saw a television documentary about the *Titanic.* It was a large luxury liner. Everyone thought it was unsinkable. Nevertheless, it crashed and sank quickly. The show included old newsreel films and featured interviews with the survivors. The show was quite interesting, provided many details about the disaster, and described the passengers' fates graphically. Many people lost their lives when the *Titanic* sank. Some were young; some were old. The whole incident seemed so sad to me. I told my bother and he also felt sad about what happened.

▶ **Exercise 62**

Writing Application

If students need ideas, suggest they search the library or the Internet for ideas, as well as for details they can use to enrich their accounts. You may wish to ask volunteers to share their comparisons.

Recognizing Appropriate Sentence Construction

Teaching Resources:
Standardized Test Preparation Workbook, Chapter 19

1. Have students list the steps they should follow in checking a sentence for correctness and accuracy.

2. Point out that choices A and B in the sample also do not have a subject.

3. By the process of elimination students should choose C.

Standardized Test Preparation Workshop

Recognizing Appropriate Sentence Construction

Standardized tests that measure writing and communication skills often test your ability to identify a complete sentence. The following elements must be in place for a sentence to be complete and correct:

• **Subject**—the noun or pronoun that tells *who* or *what* performs the action;

• **Verb**—the action performed by or to the subject, or the condition of the subject.

All complete sentences must express a complete thought. If any of these elements is missing, the sentence is incomplete, a fragment.

When answering these test questions, check the numbered passages for the elements of a complete sentence. Then, choose the group of words that contains all the elements of a complete sentence and best fits in the context of the passage. The following sample test item will give you practice with the format used for testing your knowledge of basic sentence parts.

<table>
<tr><td colspan="2">Test Tip</td></tr>
</table>

Test Tip

Remember that not all verbs express action. A form of the verb *be* can be the main verb of a sentence, but it does not express action; instead, it links words together.

Sample Test Item	Answer and Explanation
Choose the letter of the best way to write the underlined section. If the underlined section needs no change, choose *Correct as is*. After school, several of the children walked home together. <u>Were very careful at the</u> (1) <u>crosswalks.</u>	
1 A Were very careful to look both ways at the crosswalks. **B** Careful at the crosswalks. **C** They were very careful at the crosswalks. **D** Correct as is	The underlined phrase consists of a linking verb, *were*, without a subject. It does not express a complete thought. The correct answer, C, adds a subject that is consistent with the rest of the passage, making the phrase a complete sentence.

✏ TEST-TAKING TIP

Encourage students to underline subjects once and verbs twice to see if a sentence has the necessary parts. For example, in the sample test item, if students were to underline the subject and verb of each sentence, they would see that the second sentence is incomplete because there is no subject.

> **Practice 1** **Directions:** Choose the letter of the best way to write each underlined section. If the underlined section needs no change, choose "Correct as is."

Seldom seen in modern offices. The ancestor
(1)
of today's wordprocessor. Although the
                                    (2)
typewriter has existed in its current form

only since 1873. In 1714, a patent was

requested for an early version. After over
                                    (3)
150 years of experimentation, the first

standard typewriter was introduced in 1873.

1 **A** Seldom seen in modern offices, the ancestor of today's word processor.
  B The typewriter is seldom seen in modern offices. The ancestor of today's word processor.
  C The typewriter, seldom seen in modern offices, is the ancestor of today's word processor.
  D Correct as is

2 **F** Although the typewriter has existed in its current form only since 1873, a patent was requested for an early version in 1714.
  G In 1714 a patent was requested. It was for an early typewriter.
  H The typewriter has existed in its current form since 1714, when a patent was requested for an early version.
  J Correct as is

3 **A** After over 150 years of experimentation, the first standard typewriter in 1873.
  B In 1873, the first standard typewriter was introduced. After over 150 years of experimentation,
  C After over 150 years of experimentation, the first standard typewriter in 1873.
  D Correct as is

> **Practice 2** **Directions:** Choose the letter of the best way to write each underlined section. If the underlined section needs no change, choose "Correct as is."

According to scientists, the involuntary
(1)
contraction of fifteen facial muscles.

This is caused by spontaneous laughter.

 This involuntary contraction accompanied
(2)
by changed breathing patterns. Both
                                    (3)
physical and mental. Events can cause

spontaneous laughter.

1 **A** According to scientists, the involuntary contraction of fifteen facial muscles produces spontaneous laughter.
  B According to scientists, spontaneous laughter produces the involuntary contraction of fifteen facial muscles.
  C According to scientists, spontaneous laughter contracts fifteen facial muscles.
  D Correct as is

2 **F** This involuntary contraction causes breathing patterns to change.
  G This involuntary contraction with accompanying changed breathing patterns.
  H Changed breathing patterns accompany this involuntary contraction.
  J Correct as is

3 **A** Both physical and mental events can cause. Spontaneous laughter.
  B Physical events can cause spontaneous laughter. Mental events can cause spontaneous laughter.
  C Both physical and mental events can cause spontaneous laughter.
  D Correct as is

> **Practice 1**

1. C
2. F
3. D

> **Practice 2**

1. B
2. H
3. C

Standardized Test Preparation Workshop • 413

Time and Resource Manager

In-Depth Lesson Plan

	LESSON FOCUS	PRINT AND MEDIA RESOURCES
DAY 1	**Phrases** Students learn and apply concepts about prepositional phrases and phrases that act as adjectives (pp. 416–419).	**Teaching Resources** *Grammar Exercise Workbook, pp. 59–60; Grammar Exercises Answers on Transparencies, Ch. 20* **On-Line Exercise Bank,** Section 20.1
DAY 2	**Phrases (continued)** Students learn and apply concepts about phrases that act as adverbs and appositive phrases (pp. 420–423).	**Teaching Resources** *Grammar Exercise Workbook, pp. 61–64; Grammar Exercises Answers on Transparencies, Ch. 20* **On-Line Exercise Bank,** Section 20.1
DAY 3	**Clauses** Students learn and apply concepts about independent and subordinate clauses and do the Hands-on Grammar activity (pp. 424–431).	**Teaching Resources** *Grammar Exercise Workbook, pp. 65–68; Grammar Exercises Answers on Transparencies, Ch. 20; Hands-on Grammar Activity Book, Ch. 20* **On-Line Exercise Bank,** Section 20.2
DAY 4	**Review and Assess** Students review chapter and demonstrate mastery of use of phrases and clauses (pp. 432–435).	**Teaching Resources** *Formal Assessment, Ch. 20; Grammar Exercises Answers on Transparencies, Ch. 20* **On-Line Exercise Bank,** Sections 20.1–2

Accelerated Lesson Plan

	LESSON FOCUS	PRINT AND MEDIA RESOURCES
DAY 1	**Phrases** Students cover concepts and usage of phrases as determined by Diagnostic Test (pp. 416–423).	**Teaching Resources** *Grammar Exercise Workbook, pp. 59–64; Grammar Exercises Answers on Transparencies, Ch. 20* **On-Line Exercise Bank,** Section 20.1
DAY 2	**Clauses** Students cover concepts and usage of clauses as determined by Diagnostic Test (pp. 424–431).	**Teaching Resources** *Grammar Exercise Workbook, pp. 65–68; Grammar Exercises Answers on Transparencies, Ch. 20; Hands-on Grammar Activity Book, Ch. 20* **On-Line Exercise Bank,** Section 20.2
DAY 3	**Review and Assess** Students review chapter and demonstrate mastery of use of phrases and clauses (pp. 432–435).	**Teaching Resources** *Formal Assessment, Ch. 20; Grammar Exercises Answers on Transparencies, Ch. 20* **On-Line Exercise Bank,** Sections 20.1–2

Options for Adapting Lesson Plans

HOMEWORK

Have students complete any section of the chapter for homework.

FEATURES

Extend coverage with the Grammar in Literature feature (pp. 419, 425), and the Standardized Test Preparation Workshop (p. 434).

TECHNOLOGY

Students can use the On-Line Exercise Bank to complete the exercises on computer. The Auto Check feature will grade their work.

INTEGRATED SKILLS COVERAGE

Grammar in Literature
SE pp. 419, 425

Reading
Find It in Your Reading SE pp. 423, 430, 431

Writing
Find It in Your Writing SE pp. 423, 430, 431
Writing Application SE pp. 423, 431, 433
Writing Skills SE p. 421
Grammar and Style SE pp. 421, 428
Journal SE p. 426

Language Highlight
ATE p. 427

Vocabulary
ATE p. 427

Real-World Connection
ATE p. 421

Viewing and Representing
Critical Viewing SE pp. 414, 417, 418, 420, 422, 424, 427, 429

BLOCK SCHEDULING

Pacing Suggestions
For 90-minute Blocks
• Administer the Diagnostic Test to students to determine instructional coverage.
• Have students complete the necessary exercises in class. Use the Hands-on Grammar activity to provide a change of pace.

Professional Development Support
• *How to Manage Instruction in the Block* This teaching Resource provides management and activity suggestions.

MEDIA AND TECHNOLOGY

For the Student
• *On-Line Exercise Bank,* Ch. 20

For the Teacher
• *Resource Pro* CD-ROM

ASSESSMENT SUPPORT

Standardized Test Preparation Workshop SE p. 434
Standardized Test Preparation Workbook, pp. 39–40
Formal Assessment, Ch. 20

MEETING INDIVIDUAL NEEDS

Less Advanced Students ATE p. 418; see also Ongoing Assessments ATE pp. 419, 421, 426, 428
ESL Students ATE pp. 418, 429
More Advanced Students ATE p. 421
Verbal/Linguistic Learners ATE p. 428
Bodily/Kinesthetic Learners ATE p. 427

WRITING AND GRAMMAR WEB SITE

The Interactive Writing and Grammar Web site provides a wide array of support for students, teachers, and parents. Grammar support includes:

• On-Line Exercise Bank with Auto Check scoring
• Diagnostic and assessment support

www.phschool.com

LITERATURE CONNECTIONS

Grammar in Literature selections from *Prentice Hall Literature: Timeless Voices, Timeless Themes,* Copper:
from "The Tiger Who Would Be King," James Thurber, SE p. 419
from "Becky and the Wheels-and-Brake Boys," James Berry, SE p. 425

Lesson Objectives

1. To apply standard grammar and usage to communicate clearly and effectively.
2. To use prepositional phrases to elaborate written ideas.
3. To use adjective, adverb, and appositive phrases to make writing vivid or precise.
4. To write compound and complex sentences.

Critical Viewing

Speculate Students may say that the elephant on the left has a broken tusk which might indicate that the animal has been in confrontations before.

Chapter 20 Phrases and Clauses

Two African elephants confront each other near a watering hole.

You have already learned about the parts of speech and the basic parts of a sentence: the simple subject and the simple predicate. This chapter will present two other grammatical structures: the *phrase* and the *clause*.

Phrases and clauses are groups of words that add information or create a complete thought. In sentences, they add details or bring pieces of information together. If you were writing about endangered animals, for example, you might include information about certain species that are protected by laws. The phrases and clauses in your writing might add information about habitats, lifestyles, and appearances of different animals. This information would help readers to understand your ideas better.

▲ **Critical Viewing**
What distinct difference do you see between these two elephants, and what might it indicate? **[Speculate]**

414 • Phrases and Clauses

✓ ONGOING ASSESSMENT: Diagnose					
Phrases and Clauses	Diagnostic Test Items	Teach	Practice	Section Review	Chapter Review
Skill Check A					
Adjective Phrases	A 1–5	pp. 416–419	Ex. 1–4	Ex. 8	Ex. 27, 29
Skill Check B					
Adverb Phrases	B 6–10	p. 420	Ex. 5	Ex. 9	Ex. 27, 29
Skill Check C					
Appositive Phrases	C 11–15	pp. 421–422	Ex. 6–7	Ex. 10	Ex. 28–29

Diagnostic Test

Directions: Write all answers on a separate sheet of paper.

Skill Check A. Copy the following sentences. Underline the prepositional phrases used as adjectives, and draw an arrow from each phrase to the word it modifies.

1. Have you read many articles about elephants?
2. The trunk is the most distinctive feature of the elephant.
3. It is a combination of a nose and an upper lip.
4. The fingerlike extensions on the end of the trunk hold objects.
5. Elephants in Africa are larger than those in Asia.

Skill Check B. Copy the following sentences. Underline the prepositional phrases used as adverbs, and draw an arrow from each phrase to the word it modifies.

6. An elephant does not actually drink water with its trunk.
7. Instead, it draws water through its nostrils.
8. Then, it squirts the water into its mouth.
9. Also, elephants smell with their trunks.
10. They can use their trunks as snorkels when they are swimming.

Skill Check C. Copy the following sentences. Underline the appositive phrases, and draw an arrow to the word each phrase identifies or explains.

11. Tusks, their enlarged incisor teeth, can grow up to 10 feet long.
12. Their molars, the grinding teeth, are on each side of both jaws.
13. Coarse plants, an elephant's main food, wear down its teeth.
14. Final molars, the largest ones, come in when the elephant is forty years old.
15. An aged elephant, one over sixty years old, may lose its teeth and be unable to eat.

Skill Check D. Label the following groups of words *independent clause* or *subordinate clause*.

16. the African elephant has larger ears
17. whereas the Asian elephant has only one "finger" on its trunk
18. both male and female African elephants have tusks
19. when the two kinds are side by side
20. the African will be somewhat larger and darker in color

Skill Check E. Identify each sentence below as *simple, compound,* or *complex.*

21. Elephant eyes are very small, and their eyesight is not very good.
22. In the water, elephants can swim for long distances.
23. When a baby cries, other elephants will gather to comfort it.
24. They frequently flap their ears, for this action cools them off.
25. When males reach about the age of fourteen, they leave the herd.

Phrases and Clauses • 415

✓ ONGOING ASSESSMENT: Diagnose *continued*

Phrases and Clauses	Diagnostic Test Items	Teach	Practice	Section Review	Chapter Review
Skill Check D					
Clauses	D 16–20	pp. 424–425	Ex. 14	Ex. 20	Ex. 30–31
Skill Check E					
Sentence Structure	E 21–25	pp. 426–430	Ex. 15–19	Ex. 21–23	Ex. 32
Cumulative Reviews and Applications				Ex. 11–13, 24–26	Ex. 33–34

Answer Key

Diagnostic Test

Each item in the Diagnostic Yest corresponds to a specific concept in the phrases and clauses chapter. Therefore, you can design instruction to support the individual needs of your students. See "Ongoing Assessment: Diagnose" below for further details.

Skill Check A

1. Have you read many articles <u>about elephants</u>? (arrow to *articles*)
2. The trunk is the most distinctive feature <u>of the elephant</u>. (arrow to *feature*)
3. It is a combination <u>of a nose and an upper lip</u>. (arrow to *combination*)
4. The fingerlike extensions <u>on the end</u> <u>of the trunk</u> hold objects. (arrow from *on the end* to *extensions*; arrow from *of the trunk* to *end*)
5. Elephants <u>in Africa</u> are larger than those <u>in Asia</u>. (arrows from *in Africa* to *Elephants;* arrow from *in Asia* to *those*)

Skill Check B

6. An elephant does not actually drink water <u>with its trunk</u>. (arrow to *drink*)
7. Instead, it draws water <u>through its nostrils</u>. (arrow to *draws*)
8. Then, it squirts the water <u>into its mouth</u>. (arrow to *squirts*)
9. Also, elephants smell <u>with their trunks</u>. (arrow to *smell*)
10. They can use their trunks <u>as snorkels</u> when they are swimming. (arrow to *trunks*)

Skill Check C

11. Tusks, <u>their enlarged incisor teeth</u>, can grow up to 10 feet long. (arrow to *Tusks*)
12. Their molars, <u>the grinding teeth</u>, are on each side of both jaws. (arrow to *molars*)
13. Coarse plants, <u>an elephant's main food</u>, wear down its teeth. (arrow to *plants*)
14. Final molars, <u>the largest ones</u>, come in when the elephant is forty years old. (arrow to *molars*)
15. An aged elephant, <u>one over sixty years old</u>, may lose its teeth and be unable to eat. (arrow to *elephant*)

Skill Check D

16. independent
17. subordinate
18. independent
19. subordinate
20. independent

Skill Check E

21. compound
22. simple
23. complex
24. compound
25. complex

415

Interest GRABBER On the chalkboard, write the following word puzzler. Have students fill in the blanks with words that make sense but are not verbs.

___ *the elephant* (on, with)

___ *the tiger* (of, beyond)

Activate Prior Knowledge

Ask students to look at their answers to the word puzzler and tell why they are not sentences. (They are not complete ideas; they do not contain a verb.) Now ask students to turn the phrases into complete sentences and read them aloud.

TEACH

Step-by-Step Teaching Guide

Using Prepositional Phrases

1. Explain that a phrase is two or more words. Phrases add details or tie together facts in a sentence. A writer uses phrases to make a sentence more interesting, descriptive, and informative.

2. Phrases are not complete sentences. A prepositional phrase has at least two parts: the preposition and the object of the preposition. The preposition shows the relationship between the object it modifies and another word in the sentence. Unlike complete sentences, phrases do not have both a subject and a verb.

3. Have students combine the following sentences into one, using a prepositional phrase:

   The elephant bathed. The elephant was in the water hole. (The elephant bathed in the water hole.)

Answer Key

Exercise 1

1. Tigers are members of the cat family.
2. They are related to lions and jaguars.
3. Bengal tigers are found in Asia.
4. They are well camouflaged by their stripes.
5. Tigers do not survive easily near people.

Section 20.1

Phrases

All phrases are alike in two ways. First, every phrase is made up of a group of words that do the work of a single part of speech. For example, a phrase can do the work of a single adverb or a single adjective. Second, a phrase never has a subject *and* a verb.

KEY CONCEPT A **phrase** is a group of words that functions in a sentence as a single part of speech. Phrases do *not* contain a subject and a verb. ■

Using Prepositional Phrases

By itself, a *prepositional phrase* is made up of at least two parts: a preposition and a noun or pronoun that is the *object* of the preposition.

EXAMPLE:
```
   PREP   OBJ
   near jungles
```

The object of the preposition may be modified by one or more adjectives:

EXAMPLE:
```
   PREP  ADJ    ADJ    OBJ
   near remote Asian jungles
```

The object may also be compound:

EXAMPLE:
```
   PREP  ADJ    ADJ     OBJ          OBJ
   near remote Asian grasslands and jungles
```

No matter how long a prepositional phrase is or how many different parts of speech it contains, a prepositional phrase always acts in a sentence as if it were a one-word adjective or adverb.

Exercise 1 Identifying Prepositional Phrases Copy each sentence below onto your paper. Underline each prepositional phrase, and circle the object of the preposition.

EXAMPLE: See the tiger waiting in the tall grass.

1. Tigers are members of the cat family.
2. They are related to lions and jaguars.
3. Bengal tigers are found in Asia.
4. They are well camouflaged by their stripes.
5. Tigers do not survive easily near people.

Theme: Endangered Species

In this section, you will learn how to use phrases to add details to the sentences you write. The examples and exercises are about endangered species of animals.

Cross-Curricular Connection: Science

More Practice

Language Lab CD-ROM
• Prepositional Phrases lesson
On-line Exercise Bank
• Section 20.1
Grammar Exercise Workbook
• pp. 59–60

⏱ TIME AND RESOURCE MANAGER

Resources
Print: Grammar Exercise Workbook, pp. 59–64; Grammar Exercises Answers on Transparencies, Chapter 20
Technology: On-Line Exercise Bank, Section 20.1

In-Depth Coverage	Accelerated Pace
• Introduce and practice all key concepts, pp. 416–422. • Assign Exercises 1–7 and review them in class. • Read and discuss Grammar in Literature, p. 419.	• Assign pp. 416–422 for independent or cooperative group learning. • Discuss Exercises 1–7 and have students complete them independently. • Assign Section Review Exercises 8–10, p. 423

Using Phrases That Act as Adjectives

A prepositional phrase that acts as an adjective in a sentence is called an *adjective phrase.*

KEY CONCEPT An **adjective phrase** is a prepositional phrase that modifies a noun or pronoun by telling *what kind* or *which one.* ■

Like a one-word adjective, an adjective phrase answers the question *What kind?* or *Which one?* While one-word adjectives usually come before nouns, adjective phrases usually come after nouns.

Adjectives	Adjective Phrases
The *tiger* story begins now.	The story *about tigers* begins now.
The *striped* tiger faced us.	The tiger *with the stripes* faced us.

▼ Critical Viewing Using adjective phrases, describe some of the differences between a tiger and a house cat. **[Distinguish]**

Step-by-Step Teaching Guide

Using Phrases That Act as Adjectives

1. Remind students that phrases are not complete sentences. Phrases do the job of a single part of speech.

2. An adjective phrase tells what kind or which one. An adjective phrase describes, or modifies, a noun.

3. Direct students' attention to the picture of the tiger. Have them brainstorm a list of words that describe the tiger.

4. Have students use the list to write a sentence using an adjective phrase. For example: *The tiger has black stripes on its face and back.*

Critical Viewing

Distinguish Students may say that a tiger, as opposed to a cat, has longer fangs in its mouth and larger paws with sharper claws.

⏱ **TIME SAVERS!**

🖨 **Answers on Transparency** Use the Grammar Exercises Answers on Transparencies for Chapter 20 to have students correct their own or one another's exercises.

💻 **On-Line Exercise Bank** Have students complete the exercises on computer. The Auto Check feature will grade their work for you!

417

Customize for
ESL Students

Make a list of common prepositions for display: *above, after, against, at, before, behind, below, down, for, from, in, inside, like, near, of, off, on, out, over, past, since, through, till, to, under, until, up, with, within, without.* Then model using a prepositional phrase while showing what it means. For example, hold up a pencil and put it on a desk as you say, *I put the pencil on the desk.* Have students model their demonstrations after yours.

Customize for
Less Advanced Students

The word *to* is not always a preposition; sometimes it is an infinitive. In *I want to fly to the moon, to fly* is an infinitive and *to the moon* is a prepositional phrase. Students should not underline *to hunt, to protect,* and *to help* in sentences 8, 9, and 10 below.

Answer Key

▶ Exercise 2

1. The tiger was a symbol <u>of power</u>. (arrow to *symbol*)
2. Now, tigers <u>around the world</u> are endangered species. (arrow to *tigers*)
3. Three subspecies <u>of tigers</u> have already become extinct. (arrow to *subspecies*)
4. Humans are the greatest threat <u>to the tiger</u>. (arrow to *threat*)
5. Tiger hunting was once a sport <u>for rich people</u>. (arrow to *sport*)
6. Many thousands <u>of tigers</u> were killed this way. (arrow to *thousands*)
7. Tiger body parts became ingredients <u>for Chinese medicines</u>. (arrow to *ingredients*)
8. Tiger hunting <u>in India</u> is now forbidden. (arrow to *Tiger hunting*)
9. Groups <u>of conservationists</u> promote laws protecting tigers. (arrow to *Groups*)
10. Did you help these tigers <u>in danger</u>? (arrow to *tigers*)

▶ Exercise 3

Answers will vary. Samples are given below.

1. China is the home of pandas.
2. I saw two pandas in the San Diego Zoo.
3. They were a gift from China.

▶ **Exercise 2** Identifying Adjective Phrases Copy the sentences below onto your paper. Underline each adjective phrase, and draw an arrow pointing from it to the word it modifies.

EXAMPLE: Pollution <u>from aircraft</u> may destroy

habitats <u>near busy urban airports.</u>

1. The tiger was a symbol of power.
2. Now, tigers around the world are endangered species.
3. Three subspecies of tigers have already become extinct.
4. Humans are the greatest threat to the tiger.
5. Tiger hunting was once a sport for rich people.
6. Many thousands of tigers were killed this way.
7. Tiger body parts became ingredients for Chinese medicines.
8. Tiger hunting in India is now forbidden.
9. Groups of conservationists promote laws protecting tigers.
10. Did you help these tigers in danger?

▶ **Exercise 3** Writing Sentences With Adjective Phrases Using the numbered items below, write sentences with prepositional phrases used as adjectives.

EXAMPLE: about giant pandas (news story)

ANSWER: Today, I read a news story about giant pandas.

1. of pandas (home)
2. in the San Diego Zoo (two pandas)
3. from China (gift)
4. around the panda enclosure (visitors)
5. on the increase (endangered species)

▶ Critical Viewing Where was the photographer in relation to this giant panda? Answer using an adjective phrase. **[Infer]**

4. There were many visitors around the panda enclosure.
5. Today, there are endangered species on the increase.

Critical Viewing

Infer Students may say that the photographer was at a location above the panda.

GRAMMAR IN LITERATURE

from The Tiger Who Would Be King
James Thurber

The phrases that act as adjectives are highlighted in the following excerpt.

It was a terrible fight, and it lasted until the setting *of the sun*. All the animals *of the jungle* joined in, some taking the side *of the tiger* and others the side *of the lion*.

▶ **Exercise 4** **Supplying Prepositions to Form Adjective Phrases** Rewrite the sentences below, supplying a preposition to complete each adjective phrase. Then, underline the adjective phrase, and draw an arrow pointing from it to the word it modifies.

1. There are many species ___?___ animals that are endangered and have a need ___?___ protection.
2. The giant panda is the subject ___?___ antihunting laws ___?___ China.
3. The snow leopard is the biggest threat ___?___ the panda's survival.
4. The panda's limited habitat ___?___ western China is very small.
5. Pandas prefer to eat the tender leaves and stems ___?___ only a few types ___?___ bamboo.
6. Researchers ___?___ the world admit that the lifestyle ___?___ the panda is not well known.
7. Valleys ___?___ flowers and bamboo are the panda's favorite areas to roam.
8. Their senses ___?___ smell and hearing are better than their eyesight.
9. Zoos around the world provide protection ___?___ small numbers ___?___ pandas.
10. We have read articles ___?___ pandas and seen television shows ___?___ them.

▶ **More Practice**

Language Lab CD-ROM
• Prepostional Phrases lesson
On-line Exercise Bank
• Section 20.1
Grammar Exercise Workbook
• pp. 59–60

Phrases • 419

Grammar in Literature

1. Read aloud the excerpt from "The Tiger Who Would Be King," without the adjective phrases: *It was a terrible fight, and it lasted until the setting. All the animals joined in, some taking the side and others the side.* Pause, then read the entire excerpt.

2. Ask students to describe how the adjective phrases change their response to the writing.

Answer Key

▶ **Exercise 4**

Answers may vary.

1. There are many species <u>of animals</u> that are endangered and have a need <u>for protection</u>. (arrow from *of animals* to *species*; arrow from *for protection* to *need*)
2. The giant panda is the subject <u>of antihunting laws</u> <u>in China</u>. (arrow from *of antihunting laws* to *subject*; arrow from *in China* to *laws*)
3. The snow leopard is the biggest threat <u>to the panda's survival</u>. (arrow to *threat*)
4. The panda's limited habitat <u>in western China</u> is very small. (arrow to *habitat*)
5. Pandas prefer to eat the tender leaves and stems <u>of only a few types</u> <u>of bamboo</u>. (arrows from *of only a few types* to *leaves, stems*; arrow from *of bamboo* to *types*)
6. Researchers <u>in the world</u> admit that the lifestyle <u>of the panda</u> is not well known. (arrow from *in the world* to *Researchers*; arrow from *of the panda* to *lifestyle*)
7. Valleys <u>with flowers and bamboo</u> are the panda's favorite areas to roam. (arrow to *Valleys*)
8. Their senses <u>of smell and hearing</u> are better than their eyesight. (arrow to *senses*)
9. Zoos around the world provide protection <u>for small numbers</u> of <u>pandas</u>. (arrow from *for small numbers* to *protection*; arrow from *of pandas* to *numbers*)
10. We have read articles <u>on pandas</u> and seen television shows <u>about them</u>. (arrow from *on pandas* to *articles*; arrow from *about them* to *shows*)

☑ **ONGOING ASSESSMENT: Monitor and Reinforce**

If students miss more than two items in Exercises 1–4, refer them to the following for additional practice.

In the Text	Print Resources	Technology
Section Review, Ex. 8, p. 423	Grammar Exercise Workbook, pp. 54–60	On-Line Exercise Bank, Section 20.1

Using Phrases That Act as Adverbs

1. An adverb phrase describes, or modifies, verbs, adjectives, and adverbs.

2. Refer students to the sentences they wrote about the tiger. Ask them to brainstorm for a list of words that describe, or modify, an adjective, verb, or adverb in their sentences.

3. Have students write a new sentence about the tiger or add a phrase to the sentence they wrote to make it more descriptive. For example, *The tiger has wide black stripes on its face and back.*

4. Ask students to describe how phrases are useful in writing sentences. By using phrases in their sentences, writers can create more descriptive and interesting sentences.

Answer Key

▶ **Exercise 5**

1. Grizzly bears hunt <u>for salmon during the summer</u>. (arrow from *for salmon* to *hunt;* arrow from *during the summer* to *hunt*)

2. They stay <u>near the stream</u> and hunt. (arrow to *stay*)

3. <u>During the winter</u> they hibernate <u>in a safe place</u>. (arrow from *During the winter* to *hibernate;* arrow from *in a safe place* to *hibernate*)

4. Most grizzlies dig their dens <u>on a hillside</u>. (arrow to *dig*)

5. Grizzlies rarely communicate <u>with one another</u> <u>through sounds</u>. (arrow from *with one another* to *communicate;* arrow from *through sounds* to *communicate*)

Critical Viewing

Speculate Students may say that the bear searched for fish with his eyes, and caught them with his paws and teeth.

420

20.1

Using Phrases That Act as Adverbs

One-word adverbs modify verbs, adjectives, and other adverbs. A prepositional phrase that acts as an adverb modifies the same parts of speech.

▶ **KEY CONCEPT** An **adverb phrase** is a prepositional phrase that modifies a verb, an adjective, or an adverb. Adverb phrases point out *where, when, in what way,* or *to what extent.* ■

Adverb phrases are used in the same way as one-word adverbs, but they are longer and sometimes provide more precise details.

Adverbs	Adverb Phrases
Bring your panda bear *here.*	Bring your panda bear *to the desk.*
The parade began *early.*	The parade began *at exactly eleven o'clock.*

▶ **Exercise 5** Identifying Adverb Phrases Copy the sentences below. Underline each adverb phrase, and draw an arrow from it to the word it modifies.

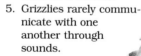

EXAMPLE: By chance, they always camped <u>near secluded bear preserves</u>.

1. Grizzly bears hunt for salmon during the summer.
2. They stay near the stream and hunt.
3. During the winter, they hibernate in a safe place.
4. Most grizzlies dig their dens on a hillside.
5. Grizzlies rarely communicate with one another through sounds.

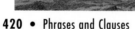

420 • Phrases and Clauses

▶ **More Practice**

Language Lab
CD-ROM
• Prepositional Phrases lesson
On-line
Exercise Bank
• Section 20.1
Grammar Exercise Workbook
• pp. 61–62

◀ Critical Viewing What actions do you think the bear took in order to catch this fish? Use adverb phrases in your answer. **[Speculate]**

Using Appositive Phrases

"One country, India, is home to the most tigers." In this sentence, the word *India* provides specific information about the *country*.

▶ **KEY CONCEPT** An **appositive** is a noun or pronoun placed after another noun or pronoun to *identify, rename,* or *explain* it. ■

Note the way appositives are used in the following chart:

APPOSITIVES
The naturalist *John James Audubon* identified several eagles.
The plains bison has a simple scientific name: *Bison bison.*
We visited the Empire State: *New York.*

An appositive can be expanded into a phrase by adding modifiers to it.

▶ **KEY CONCEPT** An **appositive phrase** is a noun or pronoun with modifiers. It stands next to a noun or pronoun and adds information or details. ■

The modifiers in the phrase are usually adjectives or adjective phrases.

APPOSITIVE PHRASES
The Asian water buffalo, *an animal similar to the American bison*, lives in Asia.
Willa Cather, *an American novelist*, wrote *My Antonia*.

Appositives and appositive phrases can be compound.

EXAMPLE: Two birds, *the hawk* and *the eagle*, are easily confused.

Grammar and Style Tip

You can use a variety of phrases with different functions or several of the same type of phrase to combine ideas and add interest to your writing.

Phrases • 421

Step-by-Step Teaching Guide

Using Appositive Phrases

1. Write the following pairs of words on the chalkboard: *bear/panda, cat/tiger, bird/eagle*. Ask students to name the part of speech of each word. (all nouns) Remind them that nouns name people, places, and things. Like adjectives and adverbs, nouns can be used in phrases.

2. An appositive is a noun or pronoun. When an appositive follows a noun in a sentence, it renames, identifies, or explains it. Phrases that rename or identify nouns are called appositive phrases.

3. Have students write sentences with appositive phrases using the word pairs on the chalkboard. For example, *The eagle, a majestic bird, soars across the sky.*

Customize for
More Advanced Students

Have students write a paragraph about an endangered animal that includes an example of each of the following phrases: adjective, adverb, and appositive. After students have written their paragraphs, have them circle and label each type of phrase.

Integrating Writing Skills

Phrases Phrases are one tool a writer uses to vary the length of sentences in a paragraph. Varying sentence length can make a paragraph more interesting and rhythmic for the reader.

Real-World Connection

Elaboration is adding details to writing to give readers the clearest picture of the ideas the writer is presenting. Writers in advertising elaborate when they describe a product or service they want to sell. They elaborate to create buyer interest. Have students browse through catalogs or magazines to locate examples of elaboration in advertising.

☑ ONGOING ASSESSMENT: Monitor and Reinforce

If students miss more than two items in Exercises 5–7, refer them to the following for additional practice.

In the Textbook	Print Resources	Technology
Section Review, Exercises 9–10, p. 423	Grammar Exercise Workbook, pp. 61–64	On-Line Exercise Bank, Section 20.1

Critical Viewing

Analyze Students may say that the plains, flat, grassy lands, are where the buffalo roam.

Answer Key

Exercise 6

1. This animal, <u>the American buffalo,</u> is one of the largest land mammals. (arrow to *animal*)
2. Cows, <u>the females,</u> live in small groups with their calves. (arrow to *Cows*)
3. One-year-old buffalo, <u>the yearlings,</u> practice survival skills by playing. (arrow to *buffalo*)
4. A related group, <u>the European bison,</u> is almost extinct. (arrow to *group*)
5. The American buffalo, <u>a threatened species,</u> now lives in protected areas. (arrow to *buffalo*)
6. The early buffalo population, <u>30 million animals,</u> had declined to 500 by 1900. (arrow to *population*)
7. The bull of the American buffalo, <u>*Bison bison,*</u> may weigh more than 2,000 pounds. (arrow to *buffalo*)
8. The Plains Indians used buffalo skins and bones, respectively, for these daily needs: <u>shelter, boots, and tools.</u> (arrow to *needs*)
9. The American buffalo, <u>an enduring symbol of power and strength,</u> is rich in Western imagery. (arrow to *buffalo*)
10. I'm learning about the buffalo in my social studies class, <u>American History I.</u> (arrow to *class*)

Exercise 7

Answers will vary. Samples are given.
1. America's national symbol, <u>the North American bald eagle,</u> is another threatened species.
2. Acid rain, <u>a form of pollution,</u> poisons their food supply.
3. A law passed by Congress, <u>the Endangered Species Act,</u> has guaranteed protection of the bald eagle.
4. Eagle recovery teams, <u>groups of scientists, conservationists, and volunteers,</u> study the eagles.
5. Raptor rehabilitation centers, <u>hospitals for sick and wounded eagles,</u> restore birds to health and then set them free.

20.1

▶ **Exercise 6** Identifying Appositive Phrases   Rewrite each sentence below, underlining the appositive or appositive phrase, and drawing an arrow from it to the noun it renames.

EXAMPLE: Buffalo, "wild cattle" to the early Spanish settlers, were present throughout North America.

1. This animal, the American buffalo, is one of the largest land mammals.
2. Cows, the females, live in small groups with their calves.
3. One-year-old buffalo, the yearlings, practice survival skills by playing.
4. A related group, the European bison, is almost extinct.
5. The American buffalo, a threatened species, now lives in protected areas.
6. The early buffalo population, 30 million animals, had declined to 500 by 1900.
7. The bull of the American buffalo, *Bison bison,* may weigh more than 2,000 pounds.
8. The Plains Indians used buffalo skins and bones, respectively, for these daily needs: shelter and boots, and tools.
9. The American buffalo, an enduring symbol of power and strength, is rich in Western imagery.
10. I'm learning about the buffalo in my social studies class, American History I.

▼ **Critical Viewing** Based on this photograph, where do the buffalo roam? Include an appositive phrase in your response. **[Analyze]**

▶ **Exercise 7** Revising to Combine Sentences With Appositive Phrases   Combine each pair of sentences below with an appositive phrase. Underline the appositive phrase.

EXAMPLE: Steller's sea eagle can be spotted at dusk. It is one of several eagles in the area.

ANSWER: Steller's sea eagle, one of several eagles in the area, can be spotted at dusk.

1. The North American bald eagle is another threatened species. It is America's national symbol.
2. Acid rain poisons their food supply. Acid rain is a form of pollution.
3. Congress passed the Endangered Species Act. This law has guaranteed protection of the bald eagle.
4. Groups of scientists, conservationists, and volunteers study the eagles. They are eagle recovery teams.
5. Hospitals for wounded eagles restore birds to health, and then set them free. They are raptor rehabilitation centers.

More Practice

Language Lab CD-ROM
• Prepositional Phrases lesson
On-line Exercise Bank
• Section 20.1
Grammar Exercise Workbook
• pp. 63–64

422 • Phrases and Clauses

☑ **ONGOING ASSESSMENT: Assess Mastery**

Use the following resources to assess students' mastery of phrases.

In the Textbook	Print Resources	Technology
Chapter Review, Ex. 27–29, p. 432	Formal Assessment, Chapter 20	On-Line Exercise Bank, Section 20.1

Section Review

GRAMMAR EXERCISES 8–13

Exercise 8 Supplying Prepositions in Adjective Phrases Copy each sentence below, and supply a preposition to complete the adjective phrase. Then, draw an arrow from it to the word it modifies.

1. There are fifty species ___?___ monkeys ___?___ South America.
2. Now, their habitats ___?___ the rain forest are being destroyed.
3. This destruction reduces the sources ___?___ food ___?___ the monkeys.
4. Marmosets and tamarins eat small animals ___?___ frogs and snails.
5. They also drink the gum ___?___ trees.

Exercise 9 Supplying Prepositions in Adverb Phrases Copy each sentence below and supply a preposition to complete the adverb phrase. Then, draw an arrow from it to the word it modifies.

1. Spider monkeys swing ___?___ the forest ___?___ the branches.
2. They can hang ___?___ branches ___?___ their tails.
3. Sometimes they drop twigs ___?___ their enemies.
4. Spider monkeys live ___?___ large groups.
5. These groups frequently split ___?___ smaller subgroups ___?___ the day.

Exercise 10 Combining Sentences With Appositive Phrases Combine each pair of sentences below with an appositive phrase.

1. Uakaris have short tails. They are mid-sized South American monkeys.
2. Uakaris are the best jumpers of all South American monkeys. They spend most of the year in the trees above flooded land.

3. Two species are the bald uakari and the black uakari. They look very different from each other.
4. The bald uakari's distinctive feature is its bright pink face. It is very noticeable.
5. Different shades of color may result from varying amounts of time each monkey spends in the sun. The shades are pale pinks and bright reds.

Exercise 11 Find It in Your Reading Find one adjective phrase and one adverb phrase in this opening sentence from "The Tiger Who Would Be King" by James Thurber.

One morning the tiger woke up in the jungle and told his mate that he was king of beasts.

Exercise 12 Find It in Your Writing Look through your portfolio to find examples of sentences that contain prepositional phrases used as adjectives, adverbs, or appositive phrases. Underline each phrase, and draw an arrow to the word it modifies.

Exercise 13 Writing Application Pick an animal that is endangered, such as the tiger, elephant, bald eagle, grizzly bear, panda, or uakari. Write the copy for an advertisement designed to interest people in helping to save the animal. Include adjective phrases, adverb phrases, and at least one appositive or appositive phrase to explain where the animal lives, how it looks, and why it needs to be protected.

ASSESS and CLOSE

Section Review

Each of these exercises correlates to the instruction on phrases, pages 416–422. They may be used for more practice, for reteaching, or for review of the key concepts presented. Answers for all chapter exercises are available in *Grammar Exercises Answers on Transparencies* in your Teaching Resources.

Answer Key

Exercise 8

1. There are fifty species <u>of monkeys in South America</u>. (arrow from *of monkeys* to *species*; arrow from *in South America* to *monkeys*)
2. Now, their habitats <u>in the rain forest</u> are being destroyed. (arrow to *habitats*)
3. This destruction reduces the sources <u>of food</u> <u>for the monkeys</u>. (arrow from *on to their enemies* to *of food* to *sources*; arrow from *for the monkeys* to *food*)
4. Marmosets and tamarins eat small animals <u>like frogs and snails</u>. (arrow to *animals*)
5. They also drink the gum <u>from trees</u>. (arrow to *gum*)

Exercise 9

1. Spider monkeys swing <u>through the forest</u> <u>below the branches</u>. (arrow from *through the forest* to *swing*; arrow from *below the branches* to *swing*)
2. They can hang <u>from branches with their tails</u>. (arrow from *from branches* to *hang*; arrow from *with their tails* to *hang*)
3. Sometimes they drop twigs <u>onto their enemies</u>. (arrow to *drop*)
4. Spider monkeys live <u>in large groups</u>. (arrow to *live*)
5. These groups frequently split <u>into smaller subgroups</u> <u>during the day</u>. (arrow from *into smaller subgroups* to *split*; arrow from *during the day* to *split*)

Exercise 10

1. Uakaris, <u>mid-sized South American monkeys</u>, have short tails.
2. Uakaris, <u>the best jumpers of all South American monkeys</u>, spend most of the year in the trees above flooded land.
3. Two species, <u>the bald uakari and the black uakari</u>, look very different from each other.
continued

Answer Key continued

4. The bald uakari's distinctive feature, <u>its bright pink face</u>, is very noticeable.
5. Different shades of color, <u>pale pinks and bright reds</u>, may result from varying amounts of time each monkey spends in the sun.

Exercise 11

Find It in Your Reading
adverb phrase: *in the jungle*
adjective phrase: *of beasts*

Exercise 12

Find It in Your Writing
Have students label each phrase adverb, adjective, or appositive.

Exercise 13

Writing Application
Students can visit Web sites of conservation organizations to get information on endangered animals. They may want to add illustrations to their advertisements.

On the chalkchalkboard, write the following clauses:

after the rock climber hammered the piton into the crack

the rock climber threaded rope through the piton

Ask students which is a complete sentence and why. (*The rock climber threaded rope through the piton* is a complete sentence because it has a subject and a verb, and it expresses a complete thought.) Encourage students to use the two ideas to write one complete sentence.

Activate Prior Knowledge

Write the word *skatechalkboarder* on the chalkboard. Ask students to brainstorm for a list of verbs to describe ways a skatechalkboarder moves. Record the list on the chalkboard. Ask students to write one complete sentence and one set of words that is not a sentence about a skatechalkboarder. Have them combine both to make one sentence.

TEACH

Step-by-Step Teaching Guide

Using Independent and Subordinate Clauses

1. Explain to students that a clause is a group of words that contains a subject and a verb.

2. If a clause expresses a complete idea, it is an independent clause. An independent clause acts like a complete sentence.

3. A subordinate clause does not express a complete idea. Even though it has a subject and a verb, it is not a sentence.

continued

Critical Viewing

Evaluate Students may say that the bike ride is bumpy.

Clauses

This section will deal with another important group of words—*clauses*.

KEY CONCEPT A **clause** is a group of words with its own subject and verb. ■

Using Independent and Subordinate Clauses

There are two basic kinds of clauses, and there is an important difference between them. The first kind is called an *independent clause.*

KEY CONCEPT An **independent clause** has a subject and a verb and can stand by itself as a complete sentence. ■

Independent clauses can be short or long. What is important is that the clause can express a complete thought and can stand by itself as a sentence.

INDEPENDENT CLAUSES:

The ski lift took us up the mountain.

In the morning, we practiced on the beginners' slope.

Lance Armstrong, an American cyclist, won the Tour de France.

424 • Phrases and Clauses

Theme: Extreme Sports

In this section, you will learn to recognize different types of clauses and to classify sentences according to their structure. The examples and exercises are about extreme sports.

Cross-Curricular Connection: Physical Education

◄ Critical Viewing
In a sentence with a single subject and verb, describe the quality of a bike ride on rocky terrain like that in the picture. [Evaluate]

☑ **ONGOING ASSESSMENT: Prerequisite Skills**

If students have trouble identifying independent and subordinate clauses, you may find it necessary to review the following to assure coverage of prerequisite knowledge.

In the Textbook	Print Resources	Technology
Nouns and Pronouns, pp. 294–307; Verbs, pp. 314–322	Grammar Exercise Workbook, pp. 1–20	Language Lab CD-ROM, Using Nouns, Using Pronouns, and Using Verbs; On-Line Exercise Bank, Sections 14.1–14.2, 15.1–15.2

GRAMMAR IN LITERATURE

from **Becky and the Wheels-and-Brake Boys**

James Berry

In the following excerpt, notice the two independent clauses joined together by the word but.

It was evening time, **but** *sunshine was still big patches in yards and on housetops.*

The second type of clause is called a *subordinate clause*. This type of clause also contains a subject and a verb, but it differs from an independent clause in one important way: By itself, it does *not* express a complete thought.

▶ KEY CONCEPT A **subordinate clause** has a subject and a verb but cannot stand by itself as a complete sentence. It is only *part* of a sentence. ■

Read the following examples. Do these clauses express complete thoughts, or do you need more information?

SUBORDINATE
CLAUSES: After she reached the top of the cliff

When the bicycle had a flat tire

As you can see, these subordinate clauses do have a subject and a verb. However, in each case something is missing; more information is needed. Consider the first clause. *After she reached the top of the cliff,* what happened or how did she feel? The thought is not complete, and the reader still has questions.

▶ Exercise 14 Identifying Independent and Subordinate Clauses Label each group of words below as an independent clause or a subordinate clause.
1. When mountain biking began in California.
2. Although regular bikes did not work very well.
3. Riders made their own bikes for their special needs.
4. Mountain bikes are made of strong, light metals.
5. Cyclists ride.

More Practice

Language Lab
CD-ROM
• Prepositional Phrases lesson
On-line
Exercise Bank
• Section 20.2
Grammar Exercise Workbook
• pp. 65–66

Step-by-Step Teaching Guide continued

4. Write the following clauses on the chalkboard.

    after the climber tied the rope to the piton

    she checked the knot

    Have students identify the independent and subordinate clauses, then write one complete sentence. (After the climber tied the rope to the piton, she checked the knot.)

Step-by-Step Teaching Guide

Grammar in Literature

1. Read aloud the excerpt from "Becky and the Wheels-and-Brake Boys."

2. Discuss why the author might have chosen to combine the independent clauses into a single sentence. (It sounds better than "It was evening time. Sunshine was still big patches in yards and on housetops.")

More About the Author

James Berry (born 1925) was born in Jamaica and now lives in England. Many of his stories capture and celebrate his West Indian heritage.

Answer Key

▶ Exercise 14

1. subordinate clause
2. subordinate clause
3. independent clause
4. independent clause
5. independent clause

⏲ TIME AND RESOURCE MANAGER

Resources
Print: Grammar Exercise Workbook, pp. 65–68; Hands-on Grammar Activity Book, Chapter 20; Grammar Exercises Answers on Transparencies, Chapter 20
Technology: On-Line Exercise Bank, Section 20.2

In-Depth Coverage	Accelerated Pace
• Introduce and practice all key concepts, pp. 424–429. • Assign Exercises 14–19 and review them in class. • Read and discuss Grammar in Literature, p. 425. • Do the Hands-on Grammar Activity, p. 430.	• Assign pp. 424–429 for independent or cooperative group learning. • Discuss Exercises 14–19 and have students complete them independently. • Assign Section Review Exercises 20–23, p. 431.

⏲ TIME SAVERS!

🖪 **Answers on Transparency**
Use the Grammar Exercises Answers on Transparencies for Chapter 20 to have students correct their own or one another's exercises.

🖳 **On-Line Exercise Bank**
Have students complete the exercises on computer. The Auto Check feature will grade their work for you!

Classifying Sentences by Structure

1. Ask students to dictate independent and subordinate clauses to describe the picture of the skier on page 429. Record the responses on the chalkboard.

2. Explain that a simple sentence is made up of one independent clause. Have students rewrite the independent clauses as simple sentences.

3. Ask students to make a single sentence out of two of the independent clauses. Explain that a sentence made up of two or more independent clauses is a compound sentence.

4. Have students make a single sentence using an independent clause and a subordinate clause. Explain that a sentence made up of both an independent clause and one or more subordinate clauses is a complex sentence.

5. Divide students into small groups. Have each group write a paragraph about the skier. Then have groups trade paragraphs and label the sentences as simple, complex, or compound.

Answer Key

▶ **Exercise 15**

1. Mountain <u>bikes</u> <u>have</u> fifteen to twenty-one gears.
2. <u>You</u> <u>pedal</u> with your feet and <u>shift</u> gears with your hands.
3. A <u>rider</u> <u>uses</u> high gears to keep the bike at speed during level riding.
4. <u>Low gears</u> <u>allow</u> quick acceleration and <u>help</u> on inclines.
5. <u>Flat levels</u> and <u>smooth surfaces</u> <u>are</u> the right terrains for using the middle and high gears.

20.2

Classifying Sentences by Structure

All sentences can be classified according to the number and kinds of clauses they contain. The three basic types of sentence structures are *simple*, *compound*, and *complex*.

The Simple Sentence

The *simple sentence* is the most common type of sentence structure.

▶ **KEY CONCEPT** A **simple sentence** consists of a single independent clause. ■

Simple sentences vary in length. Some are quite short; others can be several lines in length. All simple sentences, however, contain just one subject and one verb.

A simple sentence can have a compound subject, a compound verb, or both. Sometimes it may have other compound elements, such as a compound direct object or a compound phrase. All of the following sentences are simple sentences.

ONE SUBJECT AND VERB:	The <u>bell</u> <u>rang</u>.
COMPOUND SUBJECT:	<u>You</u> and <u>I</u> <u>need</u> some lessons.
COMPOUND VERB:	The <u>skier</u> <u>turned</u> and <u>jumped</u>.
COMPOUND SUBJECT AND VERB:	My <u>mother</u> and <u>father</u> <u>wished</u> me luck and <u>drove</u> me to the race.
COMPOUND DIRECT OBJECT:	I <u>tried</u> ski-jumping and snowboarding.
COMPOUND PREPOSITIONAL PHRASE:	<u>She</u> <u>rode</u> up the path to school.

▶ **Exercise 15** Recognizing Simple Sentences Copy each simple sentence below onto your paper, and underline the subject once and the verb twice. Notice that some of the subjects and verbs are compound.

EXAMPLE: <u>Jan</u> <u>opened</u> the catalog and <u>read</u> about the bikes.

1. Mountain bikes have fifteen to twenty-one gears.
2. You pedal with your feet and shift gears with your hands.
3. A rider uses high gears to keep the bike at speed during level riding.
4. Low gears allow quick acceleration and help on inclines.
5. Flat levels and smooth surfaces are the right terrains for using the middle and high gears.

Journal Tip

This section focuses on several kinds of outdoor sports. In your journal, note some of the facts that interest you. Then, review them later to find a writing topic—perhaps for a how-to essay.

▶ **More Practice**

Language Lab CD-ROM
• Varying Sentence Structure lesson
On-line Exercise Bank
• Section 20.2
Grammar Exercise Workbook
• pp. 65–66

☑ **ONGOING ASSESSMENT: Monitor and Reinforce**

If students miss more than two items in Exercises 14–15, refer them to the following for additional practice.

In the Textbook	Print Resources	Technology
Section Review, Ex. 20, p. 431	Grammar Exercise Workbook, pp. 65–66	On-Line Exercise Bank, Section 20.2

The Compound Sentence

A *compound sentence* is made up of more than one simple sentence.

▶ **KEY CONCEPT** A **compound sentence** consists of two or more independent clauses. ■

In most compound sentences, the independent clauses are joined by a comma and a coordinating conjunction *(and, but, for, nor, or, so,* or *yet).* The comma and conjunction come before the final independent clause. The independent clauses in a compound sentence may also be connected with a semicolon (;) if the clauses are closely related.

EXAMPLES: I <u>planned</u> to go to the hockey game, but <u>I</u> <u>could</u> not <u>get</u> tickets.
<u>Dorothy</u> <u>enjoys</u> white-water rafting; <u>she</u> also <u>likes</u> kayaking.
In the club triathlon, <u>Cara</u> <u>rode</u> her bike for ten miles, <u>she</u> <u>swam</u> for a mile, and then <u>she</u> <u>ran</u> for five miles.

Notice in the preceding examples that there are two or three separate and complete independent clauses. Each of the clauses has its own subject and verb. Like simple sentences, compound sentences never contain subordinate clauses.

▶ **Exercise 16** Recognizing Compound Sentences Copy each compound sentence below onto your paper. Then, underline the subject of each clause once, and the verb twice.

EXAMPLE: <u>Bridget</u> <u>ran</u> the first part, and <u>Tara</u> <u>biked</u> the second part.

1. Rock climbers concentrate on the climb, and they practice as often as possible.
2. Rock-climbing is a recreational sport, but it can be very dangerous.
3. Ropes and harnesses are used for safety, and climbers always wear helmets.
4. Climbers learn special words, and they use them to communicate during the climb.
5. One should always take lessons, for instructors teach many good techniques, and good techniques are necessary for a safe climb.

▼ **Critical Viewing** Of what childhood activity does this picture remind you? Respond using a complex sentence. **[Connect]**

Clauses • **427**

Answer Key

▶ **Exercise 16**

1. <u>Rock climbers</u> <u>concentrate</u> on the climb, and <u>they</u> <u>practice</u> as often as possible.
2. <u>Rock climbing</u> <u>is</u> a recreational sport, but <u>it</u> <u>can</u> <u>be</u> very dangerous.
3. <u>Ropes and harnesses</u> <u>are used</u> for safety, and <u>climbers</u> always <u>wear</u> helmets.
4. <u>Climbers</u> <u>learn</u> special words, and <u>they</u> <u>use</u> them to communicate during the climb.
5. <u>One</u> <u>should</u> always <u>take</u> lessons, for <u>instructors</u> <u>teach</u> many good techniques, and good <u>techniques</u> <u>are</u> necessary for a safe climb.

Critical Viewing

Connect Answers will vary. Make sure that the students are using an independent clause and a subordinate clause.

Language Highlight

Word History The word *ski* is a Norwegian word. It originates from the Old Norse *skidh,* which means "stick" or "snowshoe."

Integrating Vocabulary

Living Language Languages grow and change with the introduction of new ideas and inventions. These new words or phrases are adopted in spoken and written language. If the new word or phrase becomes commonly used, it is included in dictionaries. The phrase, "extreme sport" is growing in popularity, but it is not yet included in the dictionary. Have students look up the definitions of the words *extreme* and *sport,* then write a dictionary definition for the phrase.

Customize for
Bodily/Kinesthetic Learners

Have students work in pairs or small groups to take turns role-playing athletes performing extreme sports. After a student has performed the activity, have the partners or group write simple, compound, and complex sentences about what they saw and label each type of sentence.

Customize for
Verbal/Linguistic Learners

Have students revise or edit a piece of their own writing. Discuss how to change simple sentences into compound and complex sentences. Encourage students to read their work aloud so they can hear how the piece sounds with the changes. Encourage students to listen for changes in the rhythm of the piece and for clarity of ideas.

Answer Key

▶ **Exercise 17**

1. The <u>belayer</u> <u>stands</u> at the bottom of the cliff (while the <u>climber</u> <u>moves</u> up the rock face).
2. (If the <u>climber</u> <u>slips</u>,) the <u>belayer</u> <u>helps</u> prevent falls.
3. (After <u>it</u> <u>is anchored</u> at the top of the cliff,) the <u>rope</u> <u>is connected</u> to the belayer and the climber.
4. The <u>climb</u> <u>begins</u> (when the <u>commands</u> <u>have been exchanged</u>).
5. The <u>phrase</u> "on belay" <u>is spoken</u> (when the <u>climber</u> <u>is</u> ready).

20.2

The Complex Sentence

Complex sentences contain both independent and subordinate clauses.

▶ **KEY CONCEPT** A **complex sentence** consists of one independent clause and one or more subordinate clauses. ■

In a complex sentence, the independent clause is often called the *main clause*. The main clause has its own subject and verb, as does each subordinate clause.

EXAMPLES:

MAIN CLAUSE   SUBORD. CLAUSE
<u>This</u> <u>is</u> the event that <u>he</u> <u>describes</u> in the book.

SUBORD. CLAUSE
Because <u>Kayla</u> <u>has</u> so much climbing experience,

MAIN CLAUSE
<u>we</u> <u>asked</u> her to lead our group.

The preceding two examples are both complex sentences. Each has a main clause and a subordinate clause. In the first, the subordinate clause is an adjective clause that modifies the noun *event*. In the second, the subordinate clause is an adverb clause that modifies the verb *asked*.

In the next example, the complex sentence is more complicated because the main clause is split by an adjective clause.

EXAMPLE:

MAIN CLAUSE   MAIN CLAUSE
┌─ SUBORD. CLAUSE ─┐
<u>Andrea</u>, who <u>plays</u> basketball, <u>won</u> a trophy.

▶ **Exercise 17** Recognizing Complex Sentences Copy each complex sentence below onto your paper. Underline the subject of each clause once and the verb twice. Then, put parentheses around each subordinate clause.

EXAMPLE: <u>Alan</u> <u>is</u> stronger (than <u>we</u> <u>realized</u>).

1. The belayer stands at the bottom of the cliff while the climber moves up the rock face.
2. If the climber slips, the belayer helps prevent falls.
3. After it is anchored at the top of the cliff, the rope is connected to the belayer and the climber.
4. The climb begins when the commands have been exchanged.
5. The phrase "on belay" is spoken when the climber is ready.

✿ Grammar and Style Tip

Many words that introduce subordinate clauses are called **subordinating conjunctions.** They include *after, although, because, before, if, since, than, until, when,* and *while.* Other words that introduce subordinate clauses are called **relative pronouns.** They include *which, that who, whoever, whom,* and *whose.*

▶ **More Practice**

Language Lab CD-ROM
• Varying Sentence Structure lesson

On-line Exercise Bank
• Section 20.2

Grammar Exercise Workbook
• pp. 67–68

☑ ONGOING ASSESSMENT: Monitor and Reinforce

If students miss more than two items in Exercises 16–19, refer them to the following for additional practice.

In the Textbook	Print Resources	Technology
Section Review, Ex. 21–23, p. 431	Grammar Exercise Workbook, pp. 67–68	On-Line Exercise Bank, Section 20.2

Exercise 18 Distinguishing Between Compound and Complex Sentences Label each sentence below *compound* or *complex.*

1. As busy resorts show, skiing is very popular.
2. Unless a person practices, however, his or her skills won't improve.
3. I took lessons from a pro, and I learned excellent techniques.
4. After I conquered beginners' slopes, I took on the higher slopes.
5. Suddenly, a tree appeared in front of me, and I swerved to avoid it.
6. You can rent equipment, unless you prefer to buy your own.
7. Follow the rules, and stay on the designated trails.
8. Before you travel, you should check the weather.
9. My brother likes cross-country skiing, but I prefer downhill.
10. He won't try downhill skiing, nor will he snowboard.

Exercise 19 Writing Simple, Compound, and Complex Sentences Write sentences on the topics given below, using the type of sentence structure indicated. Then, underline each subject once and each verb twice.

EXAMPLE: snow (compound sentence joined by *but*)
ANSWER: My dad likes snow, but he does not like to shovel the driveway.

1. ice skating (compound sentence joined by *and*)
2. sledding (complex sentence with a subordinate clause beginning with *because*)
3. figure skating competitions on television (complex sentence with a subordinate clause beginning with *whenever*)
4. snowcapped mountains (simple sentence)
5. a winter vacation (compound sentence joined by *or*)
6. a parka and warm gloves (complex sentence with a subordinate clause beginning with *before*)
7. snowboarding competitions on television (simple sentence with a compound verb)
8. a snowman (compound sentence joined by *nor*)
9. a head cold (simple sentence with a compound subject)
10. a warm climate (complex sentence with a subordinate clause beginning with *if*)

▲ **Critical Viewing** What is the possible effect of this ski jump into the air? Answer using a complex sentence. [**Analyze; Cause and Effect**]

Clauses • **429**

Critical Viewing

Analyze; Cause and Effect Students may say that unless the skier keeps his balance, he will take a nasty fall.

Customize for
ESL Students

Discuss the meanings of the words *compound* and *complex*. Explain that both words refer to a whole that is made up of more than one part. However, the word *complex* implies a more complicated relationship between the parts of the whole.

Answer Key

▶ **Exercise 18**

1. complex	6. complex
2. complex	7. compound
3. compound	8. complex
4. complex	9. compound
5. compound	10. compound

▶ **Exercise 19**

Answers will vary. Samples are given.

1. I went ice skating, and I broke my ankle.
2. Because he has a cold, Tom could not go sledding with us.
3. Whenever I see figure skating competitions on television, I dream of going to the Olympics.
4. We saw snowcapped mountains.
5. A winter vacation can be a visit to a ski slope, or it might involve basking on a tropical beach.
6. Before she left the house, she put on a parka and warm gloves.
7. Snowboarding competitions on television are fun and exciting to watch.
8. She won't build a snowman nor will she participate in a snowball fight.
9. Tom and his sister each have a head cold.
10. If we lived in a warm climate, we could not ski.

⏱ TIME SAVERS!

Answers on Transparency Use the Grammar Exercises Answers on Transparencies for Chapter 20 to have students correct their own or one another's exercises.

On-Line Exercise Bank Have students complete the exercises on computer. The Auto Check feature will grade their work for you!

Complex Sentence Shifter

Teaching Resources: Hands-on Grammar Activity Book, Chapter 20

1. Have students refer to their Hands-on Grammar activity books or give them copies of the relevant pages.

2. Review the instructions for constructing the sentence shifters.

3. As students create sentences, have them record each one to keep track of the variations.

4. You may want to have students complete this activity in small groups so they can help each other.

Find It in Your Reading

Have students copy the sentences they find and present them to the class.

Find It in Your Writing

If students cannot find an adequate number of sentences, have them write complex sentences that they can add to their writing.

20.2

Hands-on Grammar

Complex Sentence Shifter

Make and use a Complex Sentence Shifter to help you learn ways to use subordinate clauses to vary your sentences. Fold a piece of plain paper (or construction paper) in half lengthwise, and then in half again; now, unfold it. You will have three equally spaced creases down the length of the paper. Then, mark and cut six 1" slits across each crease at equal intervals. Flatten the paper. (See illustration A.)

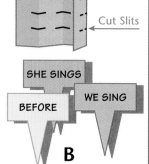

Next, using colored paper, cut out 12 T-shaped pieces—the top measuring 1-1/2" x 1", and the stem tapering from 1/2" to a point. Cut out 6 more Ts in a contrasting color. (See illustration B.) Now, on each of the original 12 Ts, print a short sentence to pair with another sentence. Examples: HE CAME—SHE WENT / WE SING—THEY SING / THEY WATCH TV—SHE STUDIES / I RIDE MY BIKE—YOU WALK / MY FRIEND WORKS—HE PLAYS / I HIT THE BALL—THEY WAIT.

Then, print one of these subordinating conjunctions on each of the other 6 Ts: AFTER, BECAUSE, ALTHOUGH, BEFORE, IF, WHEN.

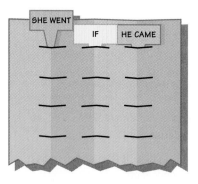

Now, begin making complex sentences by inserting the Ts into the slitted paper. A sentence might read, "Before he came, she went," or "She went because he came," or "After he plays, my friend works." Revise each sentence several different ways, changing the word order and using different subordinating conjunctions. Notice how many variations you can make.

Find It in Your Reading Look through a story or essay for several examples of complex sentences. Notice how the writer varied the position of the subordinate clauses, and the effect.

Find It in Your Writing Review the complex sentences in a piece of your writing. Try changing the position of some subordinate clauses to give your sentences variety.

430 • Phrases and Clauses

⏱ TIME SAVERS!

✋ **Hands-on Grammar Book**
Use the Hands-on Grammar activity sheet for Chapter 20 to facilitate this activity.

☑ ONGOING ASSESSMENT: Assess Mastery

Use the following resources to assess student mastery of phrases and clauses.

In the Textbook	Print Resources	Technology
Chapter Review, Ex. 30–32, pp. 432–433 Standardized Test Preparation Workshop, pp. 434–435	*Formal Assessment*, Chapter 20	On-Line Exercise Bank, Chapter 20

Section Review

GRAMMAR EXERCISES 20–26

> **Exercise 20** Recognizing Independent and Subordinate Clauses in Sentences Copy each sentence below. Underline each independent clause twice, and each subordinate clause once.

1. After diving sports became popular, the United States created an underwater national park.
2. Divers can see animals, fishes, and coral while they use the underwater signs to find their way around.
3. Some divers search for treasure, while other divers explore nature.
4. When divers visit shipwrecks, they use modern devices to find artifacts.
5. There is much to explore underwater because the ocean is so vast.

> **Exercise 21** Recognizing Compound Sentences Copy each sentence below. In each independent clause, underline the subject once and the verb twice.

1. Some people have trouble breathing through a snorkel, but it becomes easier with practice.
2. Lessons are given in swimming pools, so the students feel comfortable and safe.
3. Divers enter the water from a boat, and they go in feet first or backward.
4. One should take a deep breath first, for water may get in the snorkel tube.
5. It is easy to swim with the fins on, and the flutter kick helps you go faster.

> **Exercise 22** Revising to Create Compound Sentences Rewrite the simple sentences below as compound sentences by adding a conjunction and another independent clause to each one.

1. Divers and snorkelers must swim well.
2. Rubber fins fit securely on your feet.
3. The mask is rubber with a plastic face.
4. Teeth grip the snorkel's mouthpiece.
5. People often dive in groups for safety.

> **Exercise 23** Recognizing Subordinate Clauses in Complex Sentences Copy each sentence below, and put parentheses around the subordinate clause.

1. While they are under the water, divers are in a new and silent world.
2. Unless divers are careful, motor boats could pose a danger.
3. Boaters have difficulty seeing divers when divers are under the water.
4. Some fish, since they are so curious and unafraid, will follow divers.
5. When a diver wants to surface, she should swim up slowly.

> **Exercise 24** Find It in Your Reading Identify each type of sentence in this excerpt from James Berry's "Becky and the Wheels-and-Brake Boys."

I ride into town with the Wheels-and-Brake Boys now. When she can borrow a bike, Shirnette comes too.

> **Exercise 25** Find It in Your Writing Look through your portfolio to find examples of simple, compound, and complex sentences. Label each type.

> **Exercise 26** Writing Application Imagine that you are exploring an underwater park. Write a paragraph about the animals and things you see. Use all three types of sentences in your paragraph.

Section Review • 431

ASSESS and CLOSE

Section Review

Each of these exercises correlates to the instruction on clauses, pages 424–430. They may be used for practice, for reteaching, or for review of the key concepts presented. Answers for all chapter exercises are available in *Grammar Exercises Answers on Transparencies* in your Teaching Resources.

Answer Key

> **Exercise 20**

1. <u>After diving sports became popular</u>, <u><u>the United States created an underwater national park</u></u>.
2. <u><u>Divers can see animals, fishes, and coral</u></u> <u>while they use the underwater signs to find their way around</u>.
3. <u><u>Some divers search for treasure</u></u>, <u>while other divers explore nature</u>.
4. <u>When divers visit shipwrecks</u>, <u><u>they use modern devices to find artifacts</u></u>.
5. <u><u>There is much to explore underwater</u></u> <u>because the ocean is so vast</u>.

> **Exercise 21**

1. Some <u>people</u> <u><u>have</u></u> trouble breathing through a snorkel, but <u>it</u> <u><u>becomes</u></u> easier with practice.
2. <u>Lessons</u> <u><u>are given</u></u> in swimming pools, so the <u>students</u> <u><u>feel</u></u> comfortable and safe.
3. <u>Divers</u> <u><u>enter</u></u> the water from a boat, and <u>they</u> <u><u>go</u></u> in feet first or backwards.
4. <u>One</u> <u><u>should take</u></u> a deep breath first, for <u>water</u> <u><u>may get</u></u> in the snorkel tube.
5. <u>It</u> <u><u>is</u></u> easy to swim with the fins on, and the <u>flutter kick</u> <u><u>helps</u></u> you go faster.

> **Exercise 22**

Answers will vary. Make sure the students are using independent clauses.

> **Exercise 23**

1. (While they are under the water,) divers are in a new and silent world.
2. (Unless divers are careful,) motor boats could pose a danger.
3. Boaters have difficulty seeing divers (when divers are under the water).
4. Some fish, (since they are so curious and unafraid,) will follow divers.
5. (When a diver wants to surface,) she should swim up slowly.

continued

Answer Key continued

> **Exercise 24**

Find It in Your Reading
first sentence: simple; second sentence: complex

> **Exercise 25**

Find It in Your Writing
If students cannot find at least one of each type of sentence, they should write additional sentences.

> **Exercise 26**

Writing Application
Suggest that students read aloud their completed paragraphs.

Each of the exercises correlates to a concept in the chapter on phrases and clauses, pages 416–430. They may be used for more practice, for reteaching, or for review of the key concepts presented. Answers for all chapter exercises are available in *Grammar Exercises Answers on Transparencies* in your Teaching Resources.

Answer Key

Exercise 27

1. adjective
2. adjective
3. adjective; adverb; adverb
4. adverb
5. adjective; adjective; adjective
6. adverb
7. adjective
8. adverb
9. adverb; adverb
10. adjective

Exercise 28

1. The results of the super giant slalom, <u>a combination of downhill and giant slalom</u>, are decided after only one run.
2. Another kind of skiing, <u>cross-country</u>, is performed on rolling courses.
3. The cross-country stride, <u>a kickoff step and then a glide step</u>, propels the skier.
4. Ski jumping, <u>a part of Nordic competition</u>, is judged for distance and style.
5. Freestyle skiing, <u>an event including ballet and aerials</u>, tests different abilities.

Exercise 29

1. A kick turn is a special turn <u>for flat ground</u>. (arrow to *turn*)
2. Sidestepping moves a skier successfully <u>up a hill</u>. (arrow to *moves*)
3. The herringbone step, <u>another way to move uphill</u>, makes marks like fishbones. (arrow to *step*)
4. The inside edges <u>of the skis</u> dig <u>into the snow</u>. (arrow from *of the skis* to *edges*; arrow from *into the snow* to *dig*)
5. The chairlift carries skiers <u>to the top</u> of the mountain. (arrow from *to the top* to *carries*; arrow from *of the mountain* to *top*)

GRAMMAR EXERCISES 27–34

Exercise 27 Distinguishing Between Adjective and Adverb Phrases Identify whether the underlined prepositional phrase in each sentence below functions as an *adjective* or as an *adverb*.

1. Skis are strips <u>of wood, metal, or plastic</u>.
2. The front tips <u>of all skis</u> curve upward.
3. Boots <u>with flat soles</u> are attached tightly <u>to the skis</u> <u>by bindings</u>.
4. Ski poles provide skiers <u>with a way</u> to balance themselves.
5. The disk <u>at the bottom</u> <u>of the pole</u> allows a firm hold <u>in the snow</u>.
6. Alpine skiing races vary <u>in distance</u>.
7. Gates mark courses <u>for downhill races</u>.
8. The racer passes <u>through these gates</u> quickly.
9. Slalom skiers zigzag <u>across the slope</u>, moving <u>between flags</u>.
10. A skier's total time is a combination <u>of two runs</u>.

Exercise 28 Revising to Combine Sentences Using Appositive Phrases Combine each pair of sentences below with an appositive phrase.

1. The results of the super giant slalom are decided after only one run. The super giant slalom is a combination of downhill and giant slalom.
2. Cross-country is another kind of skiing. It is performed on rolling courses.
3. The cross-country stride is a kickoff step and then a glide step. This stride propels the skier.
4. Ski jumping is a part of Nordic competition. This competition is judged for distance and style.
5. Freestyle skiing is an event that includes ballet and aerials. It tests different abilities.

Exercise 29 Recognizing Phrases and the Words They Modify Copy the sentences below. Underline all the adjective, adverb, and appositive phrases. Then, draw an arrow from each phrase to the word it modifies or explains.

1. A kick turn is a special turn for flat ground.
2. Sidestepping moves a skier successfully up a hill.
3. The herringbone step, another way to move uphill, makes marks like fishbones.
4. The inside edges of the skis dig into the snow.
5. The chairlift carries skiers to the top of the mountain.

Exercise 30 Classifying Compound and Complex Sentences Copy each sentence below and identify it as *compound* or *complex*. Then, underline each independent clause once and each subordinate clause twice.

1. Stretching exercises warm up your body before you hit the slopes.
2. While you warm up, it is also good to check all your equipment.
3. You should examine the two edges of your snowboard, so you will understand your braking system.
4. If you practice jump turns, you can get a good feel for your board.
5. First, you can maneuver on flat ground, where only one foot needs to be attached to the board.
6. Since you may have to take some steps up the slope, it is good to practice walking uphill.
7. "Skating" is a series of small steps, but it is a good skill to practice.
8. Because everyone falls while snow-

Exercise 30

1. <u>Stretching exercises warm up your body</u> <u>before you hit the slopes.</u> (complex)
2. <u>While you warm up</u>, <u>it is also good to check all your equipment.</u> (complex)
3. <u>You should examine the two edges of your snowboard</u>, <u>so you will understand your breaking system.</u> (compound)
4. <u>If you practice jump turns</u>, <u>you can get a good feel for your board.</u> (complex)
5. First, <u>you can maneuver on flat ground</u>, <u>where only one foot needs to be attached to the board.</u> (complex)
6. <u>Since you may have to take some steps up the slope</u>, <u>it is good to practice walking uphill.</u>
7. <u>"Skating" is a series of small steps</u>, <u>but it is a good skill to practice.</u> (compound)
8. <u>Because everyone falls while snowboarding</u>, <u>the ability to fall safely is important.</u> (complex)
9. Also, <u>the board can help you get up from the ground</u>, <u>and you should practice falling and rising.</u> (compound)
10. <u>Sideslipping helps control the board's movement</u> <u>until you become more experienced.</u> (complex)

boarding, the ability to fall safely is important.
9. Also, the board can help you get up from the ground, and you should practice falling and rising.
10. Sideslipping helps control the board's movement until you become more experienced.

Exercise 31 Classifying Phrases and Clauses
Label the following sentences as *simple*, *complex*, or *compound*. List the adjective phrases, adverb phrases, and appositives or appositive phrases.

1. When you learn tricks, beginning ones form the basis for more advanced skills.
2. A tail slide, a variation of the basic slide, is the first level of tricks.
3. As you gain skill, you can experiment with tricks like nose slides.
4. Ollies, a kind of jump, carry you over small obstacles.
5. Safe jumping is important, so you should check your landing area for rocks or other obstacles.
6. Snowboard racers use special boards, and they wear special boots for extra speed and control.
7. Racing competitions are arranged for all levels.
8. Protective helmets and arm guards provide safety.
9. The board is more controllable with your feet when your boots fit well.
10. After you master turning, slalom races can test your abilities on the slopes.

Exercise 32 Revising to Expand Simple Sentences
Expand each simple sentence below into a compound sentence—adding another independent clause—or into a complex sentence—adding a subordinate clause.

1. Mountain weather is often very cold and snowy, but . . .

2. Waterproof gloves and pants are good clothing choices because . . .
3. When . . . , a hat will warm your head and keep body heat from escaping.
4. Padding can protect you if . . .
5. Snowboarding boots are bulky but comfortable, and . . .

Exercise 33 Writing Application
Write a paragraph giving advice to someone about how to do well in your favorite sport. Underline any adjective or adverb phrases you include in your paragraph. Vary your sentence structure, and put parentheses around subordinate clauses.

Exercise 34 CUMULATIVE REVIEW
Basic Sentence Parts and Phrases and Clauses
On your paper, write whether each underlined word is a *subject, verb, direct object, indirect object, predicate noun,* or *predicate adjective*. Then, identify each sentence as simple, compound, or complex. Circle five prepositional phrases.

(1) Mogul skiing is a difficult sport. (2) You maneuver over and around bumps of snow as you move down a mountain. (3) When you begin mogul skiing, several tips are important. (4) Your speed should remain constant, and you should remember to keep your head up and look down the mountain. (5) Make a plan for yourself. (6) Do not keep your attention just on one turn, but focus on several turns. (7) If one of your knees feels tired, you may be putting too much weight on one side of your body. (8) Lack of good balance can also give you a sore knee. (9) One key to successful skiing is rhythm; another is balance. (10) Follow these tips, and you will improve your skills and have a terrific time.

Answer Key continued

Exercise 34
Cumulative Review
1. is—verb; sport—predicate noun; simple
2. maneuver—verb; you—subject; move—verb; complex
3. you—subject; begin—verb; mogul skiing—direct object; tips—subject; important—predicate adjective; complex
4. speed—subject; constant—predicate adjective; should remember—verb; compound
5. plan—direct object; simple

6. keep—verb; attention—direct object; compound
7. one—subject; feels—verb; tired—predicate adjective; weight—direct object; complex
8. lack—subject; you—indirect object; knee—direct object; simple
9. key—subject; rhythm—predicate noun; another—subject; balance—predicate noun; complex
10. tips—direct object; skills—direct object; time—direct object; compound

Prepositional phrases will vary.

Exercise 31
1. complex; for more advanced skills—adjective phrase
2. simple; a variation of the basic slide—appositive phrase; of the basic slide—adjective phrase; of tricks—adjective phrase
3. complex; with tricks—adverb phrase; like nose slides—adjective phrase
4. simple; a kind of jump—appositive phrase; of jump—adjective phrase; over small obstacles—adverb phrase
5. compound; for rocks or other obstacles—adverb phrase
6. compound; for extra speed and control—adverb phrase
7. simple; for all levels—adverb phrase
8. simple
9. complex; with your feet—adverb phrase
10. complex; on the slopes—adverb phrase

Exercise 32
Answers will vary. Samples are given.
1. Mountain weather is often very cold and snowy, but skiers love this kind of weather. (independent clause; compound)
2. Waterproof gloves and pants are good clothing choices because it's not a good idea to get wet in such cold weather. (independent clause; compound)
3. When you are outside for a long time, a hat will warm your head and keep body heat from escaping. (subordinate clause, complex)
4. Padding can protect you if you fall in rocky areas. (subordinate clause, complex)
5. Snowboarding boots are bulky but comfortable, and many people wear them for protection. (independent clause; compound)

Exercise 33
Writing Application
Have students exchange paragraphs with partners to check each other's work. Make sure students revise their paragraphs to correct any errors.
continued

Lesson Objectives

- To revise and edit passages based on standard rules of grammar.

Step-by-Step Teaching Guide

Revising and Editing

Teaching Resources: Standardized Test Preparation Workbook, Chapter 20

1. Have a volunteer read aloud the strategies for answering questions that require revising and editing.

2. Tell students to read each choice carefully. Not only should the best choice offer a grammatically correct revision, but it should also not change the meaning of the original sentence(s).

Standardized Test Preparation Workshop

Revising and Editing

Knowledge of grammar is tested on standardized tests. Questions that measure your ability to use phrases and clauses reveal your understanding of basic sentence construction and style. Remember that a *phrase* is a group of words, without a subject and a verb, that acts as a unit. A *clause* is a group of words that contains a subject and a verb. Use the following strategies when answering these types of questions:

- First, read the entire passage to get an idea of the author's purpose.

- Focus on the underlined groups of words, and note any similarities, or ways they can be combined with a phrase or clause without changing meaning.

- Then, choose a revision that uses a phrase or clause to combine like ideas without changing the meaning.

The following sample test item will give you practice with the format of questions that test standard rules of grammar.

Test Tip

Make sure the answer you've chosen is a complete sentence. Other choices may seem correct, but there is only one correct answer. Read them all carefully.

Sample Test Item	Answer and Explanation
Choose the letter of the best way to write each underlined section. If the underlined section needs no change, choose "Correct as is." Bacteria are microorganisms. Bacteria belong (1) to the kingdom Monera. **1 A** Bacteria are microorganisms, and they belong to the kingdom Monera. **B** Bacteria are microorganisms belonging to the kingdom Monera. **C** Microorganisms, which belong to the kingdom Monera, are bacteria. **D** Correct as is	The correct answer is *B*. This is the best rewrite of the two sentences because it combines related ideas and eliminates extra words without changing the meaning. Changing the second sentence into a phrase eliminates the repetition of the word *bacteria*. Choice *A* combines the sentences but does not eliminate extra words. Choice *C* changes the original meaning.

TEST-TAKING TIP

Remind students that even though a given sentence can be improved, sometimes it is best to choose "correct as is." Tell students that they should choose a revision only if it improves the sentence(s) and is grammatically correct. For example, in item 2 of Practice 1, the sentences could be improved. However, none of the choices are appropriate, so the original version is the correct answer.

Practice 1 **Directions:** Choose the letter of the best way to write each underlined section. If the underlined section needs no change, choose "Correct as is."

Bacteria appear in many shapes and sizes.
(1)
You may not know this. Some bacteria
                          (2)
look like spheres. They are called cocci.

Other bacteria are shaped like corkscrews.
(3)
Bacteria shaped like corkscrews are known

as spirilla.

1 A Bacteria appear in many shapes and sizes, and you may not know this.

 B You may not know this: There are many shapes and sizes of bacteria.

 C You may not know that bacteria appear in many shapes and sizes.

 D Correct as is

2 F Some bacteria with a spherical shape are called cocci.

 G There are some sphere bacteria, and they are called cocci.

 H Some of the bacteria that are called cocci look like spheres.

 J Correct as is

3 A Other bacteria are shaped like corkscrews, which are known as spirilla.

 B There are other corkscrew bacteria, which are known as spirilla.

 C Other bacteria, which are known as spirilla, are shaped like corkscrews.

 D Correct as is

Practice 2 **Directions:** Choose the letter of the best way to write each underlined section. If the underlined section needs no change, choose "Correct as is."

Although some bacteria are dangerous,
(1)
others are quite useful. Good bacteria
                          (2)
digest organic matter, they break down

organic matter. Good bacteria can also be
                          (3)
found in food. Foods such as cheese or

yogurt contain bacteria.

1 A Bacteria are dangerous and also quite useful.

 B Some bacteria are dangerous although some others are useful.

 C Some bacteria are dangerous; other bacteria are quite useful.

 D Correct as is

2 F Good bacteria digest and break down organic matter.

 G Good bacteria digest organic matter and then it break it down.

 H Good bacteria digest organic matter. Then it break down organic matter.

 J Correct as is

3 A Good foods such as cheese or yogurt contain bacteria.

 B Good bacteria can also be found in foods such as cheese or yogurt.

 C Also found in food, such as cheese and yogurt, are good bacteria.

 D Correct as is

Answer Key

Practice 1
1. C
2. J
3. C

Practice 2
1. D
2. F
3. B

In-Depth Lesson Plan

	LESSON FOCUS	PRINT AND MEDIA RESOURCES
DAY 1	**Four Functions of a Sentence and Combining Sentences** Students learn and apply concepts of the four functions of a sentence. Students learn and apply concepts for combining sentences and do the Hands-on Grammar activity (pp. 438–447).	**Teaching Resources** *Grammar Exercise Workbook*, pp. 69–72; *Grammar Exercises Answers on Transparencies*, Ch. 21; *Hands-on Grammar Activity Book*, Ch. 21 *Language Lab* **CD-ROM**, Problems With Sentences; *On-Line Exercise Bank*, Sections 21.1–2
DAY 2	**Varying Sentences** Students learn and apply concepts for varying sentences (pp. 448–453).	**Teaching Resources** *Grammar Exercise Workbook*, pp. 73–76; *Grammar Exercises Answers on Transparencies*, Ch. 21 *Language Lab* **CD-ROM**, Problems With Sentences; *On-Line Exercise Bank*, Section 21.3
DAY 3	**Avoiding Sentence Problems** Students learn and apply concepts for avoiding such sentence problems as fragments, run-ons and misplaced modifiers (pp. 454–471).	**Teaching Resources** *Grammar Exercise Workbook*, pp. 77–86; *Grammar Exercises Answers on Transparencies*, Ch. 21 *Language Lab* **CD-ROM**, Problems With Sentences; *On-Line Exercise Bank*, Section 21.4
DAY 4	**Review and Assess** Students review chapter and demonstrate mastery of use of Effective Sentences (pp. 472–477).	**Teaching Resources** *Formal Assessment*, Ch. 21; *Grammar Exercises Answers on Transparencies*, Ch. 21 *On-Line Exercise Bank*, Sections 21.1–4

Accelerated Lesson Plan

	LESSON FOCUS	PRINT AND MEDIA RESOURCES
DAY 1	**Sentence Functions, Combining, and Varying Sentences** Students cover concepts and usage of sentence functions and combining sentences as determined by Diagnostic Test (pp. 438–453).	**Teaching Resources** *Grammar Exercise Workbook*, pp. 69–76; *Grammar Exercises Answers on Transparencies*, Ch. 21; *Hands-on Grammar Activity Book*, Ch. 21 *Language Lab* **CD-ROM**, Problems With Sentences; *On-Line Exercise Bank*, Sections 21.1–3
DAY 2	**Avoiding Sentence Problems** Students cover concepts and usage of avoiding sentence problems as determined by Diagnostic Test (pp. 454–471).	**Teaching Resources** *Grammar Exercise Workbook*, pp. 77–86; *Grammar Exercises Answers on Transparencies*, Ch. 21 *Language Lab* **CD-ROM**, Problems With Sentences; *On-Line Exercise Bank*, Section 21.4
DAY 3	**Review and Assess** Students review chapter and demonstrate mastery of use of Effective Sentences (pp. 472–477).	**Teaching Resources** *Formal Assessment*, Ch. 21; *Grammar Exercises Answers on Transparencies*, Ch. 21 *On-Line Exercise Bank*, Sections 21.1–4

Options for Adapting Lesson Plans

HOMEWORK

Have students complete any section of the chapter for homework.

FEATURES

Extend coverage with the Grammar in Literature feature (pp. 441, 449), and the Standardized Test Preparation Workshop (pp. 474–575).

TECHNOLOGY

Students can use the On-Line Exercise Bank to complete the exercises on computer. The Auto Check feature will grade their work.

INTEGRATED SKILLS COVERAGE

Grammar in Literature
SE pp. 441, 449

Reading
Find It in Your Reading SE pp. 440, 446, 447, 453, 471

Writing
Find It in Your Writing SE pp. 440, 446, 447, 453, 471
Writing Application SE pp. 440, 447, 453, 471, 473, 477
Writing Skills ATE p. 452

Language Highlight
ATE p. 438

Real-World Connection
ATE p. 442

Viewing and Representing
Critical Viewing SE pp. 436, 439, 442, 445, 448, 449, 450, 452, 455, 456, 459, 461, 463, 465, 469

ASSESSMENT SUPPORT

Standardized Test Preparation Workshop SE pp. 474–475; ATE pp. 442, 462, 467

Standardized Test Preparation Workbook, pp. 41–42

Formal Assessment, Ch. 21

MEETING INDIVIDUAL NEEDS

Less Advanced Students ATE pp. 438, 442, 444; see also Ongoing Assessments ATE pp. 444, 449, 450, 455, 457, 459, 460, 465, 466, 468

ESL Students ATE p. 464

Logical/Mathematical Learners ATE p. 450

Auditory Learners ATE p. 448

BLOCK SCHEDULING

Pacing Suggestions
For 90-minute Blocks
• Administer the Diagnostic Test to students to determine instructional coverage.
• Have students complete the necessary exercises in class. Use the Hands-on Grammar activity to provide a change of pace.

Resources for Varying Instruction
• *Language Lab* **CD-ROM** If your students have access to hardware, a 90-minute block provides an ideal opportunity for students to work on computer.

Professional Development Support
• *How to Manage Instruction in the Block* This teaching Resource provides management and activity suggestions.

MEDIA AND TECHNOLOGY

For the Student
• *Language Lab* **CD-ROM**, Problems With Sentences
• *On-Line Exercise Bank,* Ch. 21

For the Teacher
• *Resource Pro* **CD-ROM**

WRITING AND GRAMMAR WEB SITE

The Interactive Writing and Grammar Web site provides a wide array of support for students, teachers, and parents. Grammar support includes:

• On-Line Exercise Bank with Auto Check scoring
• Diagnostic and assessment support

www.phschool.com

LITERATURE CONNECTIONS

Grammar in Literature selections from *Prentice Hall Literature: Timeless Voices, Timeless Themes,* Copper:
from "Space Shuttle *Challenger,*" William Harwood, SE p. 441
from *Parade,* Rachel Field, SE p. 449

Lesson Objectives

1. To recognize and distinguish among declarative, interrogative, imperative, and exclamatory sentence types.

2. To recognize and use compound subjects, verbs, and objects in sentences.

3. To use *and, but, or, nor,* or a semicolon and two independent clauses to make compound sentences.

4. To recognize and use subordinating conjunctions and phrases to make compound sentences.

5. To vary sentences.

6. To recognize and correct sentence fragments.

7. To avoid capitalizing and punctuating phrases as sentences.

8. To recognize and avoid using run-on sentences.

9. To correct run-on sentences.

10. To recognize and correct misplaced modifiers.

11. To recognize and correct double negatives.

12. To recognize and correct fifteen common usage problems.

Critical Viewing

Describe Students may write an exclamatory sentence about the moon's brightness or apparent size, and then rewrite it as a declarative.

Chapter 21 Effective Sentences

▲ Critical Viewing
Write an exclamatory sentence describing this photograph. Then, change it into a declarative sentence. [Describe]

We use sentences every day. We ask questions, make statements, express emotion, or share information, all of which require sentences. Therefore, we rely on sentences as our basic unit of communication. Without sentences, we would be unable to convey our thoughts and needs effectively.

In writing, putting words together in effective sentences is the first step to clear communication. In this chapter, you will learn basic sentence functions and structures, ways in which you can vary sentence structures to make your writing clearer, and some common pitfalls that hinder clear communication.

436 • Effective Sentences

☑ ONGOING ASSESSMENT: Diagnose

If students miss more than one item in each category, direct them to the relevant pages of the textbook and assign the following exercises for practice and review.

Effective Sentences	Diagnostic Test Items	Teach	Practice	Section Review	Chapter Review
Skill Check A					
Four Functions of a Sentence	A 1–5	pp. 438–439	Ex. 1–2	Ex. 3–6	Ex. 53
Skill Check B					
Sentence Combining	B 6–10	pp. 441–446	Ex. 10–13	Ex. 14–16	Ex. 54
Skill Check C					
Fragments and Run-Ons	C 11–15	pp. 454–459	Ex. 31–33	Ex. 43	Ex. 56

Diagnostic Test

Directions: Write all answers on a separate sheet of paper.

Skill Check A. Identify each sentence below by its sense as *declarative, interrogative, imperative,* or *exclamatory.*

1. The entire class became interested in comets
2. In what year will Halley's Comet be visible again
3. Ask Carla if she knows the date
4. She has spent nearly two weeks collecting facts
5. That's amazing

Skill Check B. Combine the following sentences, using the construction given in parentheses.

6. (compound verb) From early times, people have been fascinated with the stars. People have wondered about their meaning.
7. (comma and coordinating conjunction *but*) The sun is only a medium-sized star. Its diameter is more than 100 times that of the Earth.
8. (semicolon) Some stars look yellow. Others glow blue or red.
9. (comma and coordinating conjunction *and*) During the day, sunlight brightens the sky. We cannot see the stars.
10. (comma and compound direct objects) Space exploration has aided science. It has aided medicine. It has aided industry.

Skill Check C. Change each of the following items into a complete sentence.

11. So far away.
12. When stars twinkle.
13. We do not see the sun every day I miss it when it does not come out.
14. A microscope is usually smaller than a telescope, we have both at my school.
15. Visiting the planetarium.

Skill Check D. Rewrite the following sentences to eliminate sentence problems such as misplaced modifers and double negatives.

16. I lost the ticket to the planetarium that my uncle bought.
17. I wanted to see the mountains at the planetarium on Mars.
18. Jim, Alex, and I are not going on no trip to the planetarium.
19. We can't find none of the tickets.
20. Nobody doesn't feel as bad as I do about it.

Skill Check E. For each of the following sentences, choose the correct form in parentheses.

21. You should not stare directly into the sun because it can (effect, affect) your vision.
22. It must be (kind of, rather) frightening to travel into space.
23. Do you know where the Milky Way (is at, is)?
24. (Their, There, They're) must be a large telescope at the university.
25. The reason I am interested is (because, that) I would like to become an astronaut.

☑ ONGOING ASSESSMENT: Diagnose *continued*

Effective Sentences	Diagnostic Test Items	Teach	Practice	Section Review	Chapter Review
Skill Check D					
Misplaced Modifiers	D 16–17	pp. 461–463	Ex. 36–37	Ex. 46	Ex. 58
Double Negatives	D 18–20	pp. 464–465	Ex. 38–39	Ex. 47	Ex. 58
Skill Check E					
Usage Problems	E 21–25	pp. 466–469	Ex. 40–42	Ex. 44–49	Ex. 59–60
Cumulative Reviews and Applications				Ex. 7–9, 17–19, 28–30, 50–52	Ex. 61

Answer Key

Diagnostic Test

Each item in the Diagnostic Test corresponds to a specific section in the chapter on effective sentences. See "Ongoing Assessment: Diagnose" below for further details.

Skill Check A

1. declarative
2. interrogative
3. imperative
4. declarative
5. exclamatory

Skill Check B

6. From early times, people have been fascinated with the stars and have wondered about their meaning.
7. The sun is only a medium-sized star, but its diameter is more than 100 times that of the Earth.
8. Some stars look yellow; others glow blue or red.
9. During the day, sunlight brightens the sky, and we cannot see the stars.
10. Space exploration has aided science, medicine, and industry.

Skill Check C

Answers may vary. Samples are given.

11. The stars are so far away.
12. When stars twinkle, we see them.
13. We do not see the sun every day, and I miss it when it does not come out.
14. A microscope is usually smaller than a telescope. We have both at my school.
15. Visiting the planetarium, the class viewed the night sky.

Skill Check D

16. I lost the ticket that my uncle bought to the planetarium.
17. I wanted to see the mountains on Mars at the planetarium.
18. Jim, Alex, and I are not going on any trip to the planetarium.
19. We can't find any of the tickets.
20. Nobody feels as bad as I do about it.

Skill Check E

21. affect
22. rather
23. is
24. There
25. that

The Four Functions of a Sentence

Interest GRABBER Have students read their favorite comic strips. Ask them to use four colors to highlight each of the sentence categories: declarative, exclamatory, interrogative, and imperative. Have students tally up their sentences and compare notes as to which kind appears most frequently. (Tell students to save the comics, and collect some more.)

Activate Prior Knowledge

Students may be able to guess three of the four functions of sentences based on their punctuation. Ask students to write three sentences, punctuated with an exclamation point, a question mark, and a period, then exchange with a partner. Have the partner guess what kinds of sentences they are, based on their punctuation. Then have each partner check the written sentences against the kinds of sentences described in the textbook.

TEACH

Step-by-Step Teaching Guide

The Four Functions of a Sentence

1. Sentences fall into four categories: declarative, interrogative, imperative, or exclamatory.

2. Kinds of sentences can be determined from context. A simple, factual comment is usually a declarative sentence. A sentence that asks a question is an interrogative. Sentences that give orders or directions are imperative. Sentences that express emotion and end in exclamation points are exclamatory.

Customize for

Less Advanced Students

Divide students into four groups in each corner of the room. Have each group write sentences according to their sentence "corner": declarative, interrogative, imperative, or exclamatory.

Sentences can be classified according to what they do. The four types of sentences in English are *declarative, interrogative, imperative,* and *exclamatory.*

Declarative sentences are the most common type. They are used to "declare" or state facts.

▶ **KEY CONCEPT** A **declarative sentence** states an idea and ends with a period. ■

DECLARATIVE: Space travel is very exciting.

Interrogative means "asking." An *interrogative sentence* is a question.

▶ **KEY CONCEPT** An **interrogative sentence** asks a question and ends with a question mark. ■

INTERROGATIVE: Which planet is closest to Earth?

The word *imperative* comes from the Latin word *imperare,* which means "to command." Imperative sentences give commands.

▶ **KEY CONCEPT** An **imperative sentence** gives an order or a direction and ends with either a period or an exclamation mark. ■

Most imperative sentences start with a verb. In this type of imperative sentence, the subject is understood to be *you.*

IMPERATIVE: Follow the directions carefully.
                Wait for me!

Notice the punctuation at the end of these examples. In the first sentence, the period suggests that a mild command is being given in an ordinary tone of voice. The exclamation mark at the end of the second sentence suggests a strong command, one given in a loud voice.

To *exclaim* means to "shout out." *Exclamatory sentences* are used to "shout out" emotions such as happiness, fear, delight, and anger.

▶ **KEY CONCEPT** An **exclamatory sentence** conveys strong emotion and ends with an exclamation mark. ■

EXCLAMATORY: She's not telling the truth!
                What an outrage that is!

438 • Effective Sentences

Theme: The Earth and Moon

In this section, you will learn about the four functions of sentences. The examples and exercises are about the Earth and moon.

Cross-Curricular Connection: Science

⏲ TIME AND RESOURCE MANAGER

Resources
Print: Grammar Exercises Workbook, pp. 69–70; Grammar Exercises Answers on Transparencies, Chapter 21
Technology: Language Lab CD-ROM, Problems With Sentences; On-Line Exercise Bank, Section 21.1

In-Depth Coverage	Accelerated Pace
• Work through all key concepts, p. 438.	• Assign p. 438 for independent student review. • Assign Chapter review Exercise 53, p. 472.

Exercise 1 Identifying the Four Types of
Sentences Read each of the following sentences carefully, and identify it as *declarative*,
interrogative, *imperative*, or *exclamatory*. Then,
write the appropriate end mark.

EXAMPLE: How do you say "moon" in Italian
ANSWER: interrogative (?)

1. The Italian word for "moon" is *luna*
2. Wow, that's how you say it in Spanish, too
3. What words in English do you know with
   the *luna* root
4. I have heard the words *lunatic* and *lunacy*
5. Tell me what they mean
6. *Lunatic* means "insane" and *lunacy* means
   "insanity"
7. Does that make sense to you
8. Well, the word *moonstruck* means "crazy"
   or "insane," so it makes sense to me
9. Oh, look at the time
10. Don't be late

Exercise 2 Writing the Four Types of Sentences Rewrite
each sentence below to fit the type of sentence specified in
parentheses. Be sure to use the correct end mark.
1. The moon travels around the Earth in an elliptical orbit.
   (interrogative)
2. The moon travels at more than 2,300 miles per hour.
   (exclamatory)
3. Does the gravitational pull of the Earth keep the moon in
   orbit? (declarative)
4. We have been studying the moon in science class this
   year. (imperative)
5. Measure time by the phases of the moon. (interrogative)
6. Does the word *Monday* come from the word *moon*?
   (declarative)
7. Look at the man in the moon! (interrogative)
8. Some people thought the moon was made out of green
   cheese. (exclamatory)
9. If you look out this window, you can see the full moon.
   (imperative)
10. How beautiful that moon is! (declarative)

▲ Critical Viewing
Write one each of
the four types of
sentences about this
photograph of the
moon. [**Describe**]

More Practice
Language Lab
CD-ROM
• Punctuation: End
  Marks lesson
On-line
Exercise Bank
• Section 21.1
Grammar Exercise
Workbook
• pp. 69–70

The Four Functions of a Sentence • 439

Critical Viewing
Describe Students may suggest
sentences like the following:

*Much of the moon's surface is lighted
by the sun.*

When was this picture taken?

*Wow, look at all the craters on the
surface of the moon!*

*Compare this photo with the real
moon tonight.*

Answer Key

Exercise 1

1. declarative (.)
2. exclamatory (!)
3. interrogative (?)
4. declarative (.)
5. imperative (.)
6. declarative (.)
7. interrogative (?)
8. declarative (.)
9. exclamatory (!)
10. imperative (.)

Exercise 2

1. Does the moon travel around
   the Earth in an elliptical orbit?
2. Hey, the moon travels at more
   than 2,300 miles per hour!
3. The gravitational pull of the
   Earth keeps the moon in orbit.
4. Be sure to study the moon in
   science class this year.
5. Can you measaure time by the
   phases of the moon?
6. The word *Monday* comes from
   the word *moon*.
7. Can you find the man in the
   moon?
8. Neat, some people thought the
   moon was made out of green
   cheese!
9. Look out this window and see
   the full moon.
10. The moon is beautiful.

⏱ **TIME SAVERS!**

🎞 **Answers on Transparency**
Use the Grammar Exercises
Answers on Transparencies for
Chapter 21 to have students
correct their own or one another's
exercises.

💻 **On-Line Exercise Bank**
Have students complete the
exercises on computer. The Auto
Check feature will grade their
work for you.

ASSESS and CLOSE

Section Review

Each of these exercises correlates to the instruction on the four types of sentences, pages 438–439. These exercises may be used for more practice, for reteaching, or for review of the key concepts presented. Answers to all chapter exercises are available in *Grammar Exercises Answers on Transparencies* in your Teaching Resources.

Answer Key

> **Exercise 3**

1. imperative
2. interrogative
3. imperative
4. declarative
5. exclamatory

> **Exercise 4**

1. On July 20, 1969, for the first time in history, humans landed on the moon. (dec.)
2. Who was the first human to walk on the moon? (inter.)
3. Was it Neil Armstrong or was it Edwin E. Aldrin? (inter.)
4. Look it up in your book. (imp.)
5. It was Armstrong, of course! (ex.)

> **Exercise 5**

Answers may vary. Samples are given.

1. Was Galileo Galilei the first person to look at the moon through a telescope?
2. He noticed the light areas and dark areas on the surface.
3. Look at the moon on the second or third day after the first-quarter phase.
4. Did you know that at this time the moon is in a good position in the evening sky and many surface features are clearly visible?
5. Incredible, the length of a day on the moon equals about fourteen Earth days!

> **Exercise 6**

Answers will vary.

> **Exercise 7**

Find It in Your Reading

Sentence 1—declarative
Sentence 2—declarative
Sentence 3—interrogative
Sentence 4—declarative

> **Exercise 8**

Find It in Your Writing

Have students share their writing with a partner and check each other's identification of the different types of sentences.

> **Exercise 9**

Writing Application

Have volunteers read their descriptions to the class and ask for feedback.

Section 21.1 Section Review

GRAMMAR EXERCISES 3–9

> **Exercise 3** Identifying the Four Types of Sentences Read each of the following sentences carefully, and identify it as *declarative, interrogative, imperative,* or *exclamatory.*

1. Open your books to page 45 and begin reading.
2. How many have finished reading the assignment?
3. Raise your hands.
4. This week's topic is the solar system.
5. I can't wait for class to be over!

> **Exercise 4** Punctuating the Four Types of Sentences Copy the sentences below onto your paper, adding the appropriate end mark. Then, label each sentence by its type.

1. On July 20, 1969, for the first time in history, humans landed on the moon
2. Who was the first human to walk on the moon
3. Was it Neil Armstrong or was it Edwin E. Aldrin
4. Look it up in your book
5. It was Armstrong, of course

> **Exercise 5** Revising Sentences to Vary Type Rewrite each sentence below to fit the function indicated in parentheses. Add the appropriate end mark.

1. Galileo Galilei was the first person to look at the moon through a telescope. (interrogative)
2. Did he notice the light areas and dark areas on the surface? (declarative)
3. You should look at the moon on the second or third day after the first-quarter phase. (imperative)

4. At this time, the moon is in a good position in the evening sky and many surface features are clearly visible. (interrogative)
5. Did you know that the length of a day on the moon equals about fourteen Earth days? (exclamatory)

> **Exercise 6** Writing the Four Types of Sentences For each subject listed below, write a declarative, an interrogative, an imperative, and an exclamatory sentence.

1. the moon   4. a star
2. the sun   5. an astronaut
3. the Earth

> **Exercise 7** Find It in Your Reading Read the following excerpt from "If I Forget Thee, Oh Earth . . ." by Arthur C. Clarke. Identify the type of each sentence.

Well, *he* knew what the stars were. Whoever asked that question must have been very stupid. And what did they mean by "twinkle"? You could see at a glance that all the stars shone with the same steady, unwavering light.

> **Exercise 8** Find It in Your Writing Look through your portfolio for examples of all four types of sentences. If you can't find examples of each, challenge yourself to revise a piece of writing to vary your sentence types.

> **Exercise 9** Writing Application Write a brief description of the sky on the night of a full moon. Use all four types of sentences in your description.

440 • Effective Sentences

Section 21.2 Combining Sentences

Books written for very young readers present information in short, direct sentences. While this method makes the book easy to read, it doesn't make it enjoyable or interesting to older readers. Writing that is to be read by mature readers should include sentences of varying lengths and complexity to create a flow of ideas. One way to achieve sentence variety is to combine sentences.

EXAMPLE: We went to the planetarium. We saw planets.
COMBINED: We went to the planetarium and saw planets. We saw planets at the planetarium.

Sentences can be combined by using a compound subject, a compound verb, or a compound object.

EXAMPLE: Mori enjoyed watching the sky.
                      Tatiana enjoyed watching the sky.

COMPOUND
SUBJECT: *Mori* and *Tatiana* enjoyed watching the sky.

EXAMPLE: Leelee assembled the telescope.
                      Leelee watched the stars.

COMPOUND
VERB: Leelee *assembled* the telescope and *watched* the stars.

EXAMPLE: Martin likes the sun.
                      Martin likes the moon.

COMPOUND
OBJECT: Martin likes the *sun* and the *moon*.

GRAMMAR IN LITERATURE

from "Space Shuttle *Challenger*"
William Harwood

This sentence uses a compound subject. The simple subjects are highlighted in blue italics.

A veteran shuttle reporter with an encyclopedic memory for space trivia, *Rob* and *I* had covered fourteen straight missions together.

Theme: Planets and Stars

In this section, you will learn about combining sentences to give your writing smoothness and variety. The examples and exercises are about planets and stars.

Cross-Curricular Connection: Science

Combining Sentences • 441

PREPARE and ENGAGE

Interest GRABBER Ask students to go back to their comics. All the sentences are short. Ask students to combine some to make longer sentences. If the content makes this awkward, students can add their own words to make more interesting sentences.

Activate Prior Knowledge

Ask students to write a brief paragraph about what they did this morning before school. Then have them go back and see how many sentences they began with "I did . . ." or "Then I did . . ." Ask them to rewrite their paragraphs, using compound verbs. Have students underline the compound verbs.

TEACH

Step-by-Step Teaching Guide

Grammar in Literature

1. Have a volunteer read the sentence from "Space Shuttle *Challenger*"

2. Ask the class to identify the two simple subjects that make up the compound subject of the sentence (*Rob, I*).

Connection with Literature

Have students read "Space Shuttle *Challenger*" and find compound subjects, verbs, and objects.

Step-by-Step Teaching Guide

Combining Sentences

1. Three easy ways to combine sentences involve making compound subjects, verbs, or objects.

2. Review the different ways to make compound subjects, verbs, and objects as described on the page.

continued

⏲ TIME AND RESOURCE MANAGER

Resources
Print: Grammar Exercises Workbook, pp. 71–72; Hands-on Grammar Activity Book, Chapter 21; Grammar Exercises Answers on Transparencies, Chapter 21
Technology: Language Lab CD-ROM, Problems With Sentences; On-Line Exercise Bank, Section 21.2

In-Depth Coverage	Accelerated Pace
• Work through all key concepts, pp. 441–445. • Assign and review Exercises 10–13.	• Assign pp. 441–445 for independent student review. • Assign Section Review Exercises 14–16, p. 447.

3. In addition to using compound subjects, verbs, and objects to vary their writing and combine sentences, students can use conjunctions and forms of punctuation.

4. The conjunctions *and, but, or,* and *nor* work like glue to attach two independent clauses together.

5. The semicolon also works to combine sentences. Explain that it should be used occasionally to link two sentences with very closely related ideas.

continued

Customize for
Less Advanced Students

Review subject, verb, and object. Then review the way compound subjects, compound verbs, and compound objects function in sentences. Ask students to practice writing sentences that use compound subjects, verbs, and objects.

Critical Viewing

Apply Students may form compound subjects such as *Saturn and its rings* or *The planet and its rings* and a compound verb such as *orbit the sun and reflect its light.*

Real-World Connection

Whether applying for a summer job or writing a résumé, students will need to compress what they have accomplished into a small space. One way to fit in more information is to write sentences that use active compound verbs. Compound verbs not only showcase the student's linguistic abilities but also impress employers, who will notice immediately the activities and work of an applicant.

21.2

▲ **Critical Viewing**
Write a sentence about Saturn and its rings using a compound subject and a compound verb. **[Apply]**

▶ **Exercise 10** **Combining Sentences** Combine each pair of sentences below by using a compound subject, a compound verb, or a compound object. Identify what you have done to combine them.

EXAMPLE: Frank stared at the full moon.
              Bertha stared at the full moon.

ANSWER: Frank and Bertha stared at the full moon.
              (compound subject)

1. Elliot went to P.S. 101. Melvin went to P.S. 101.
2. They were in the sixth grade. They liked science class.
3. They studied the planets. They studied the stars.
4. The teacher assigned Melvin a written project. The teacher assigned Elliot a written project.
5. Melvin decided to write about Mars. Elliot decided to write about Mars.
6. They studied the planet. They studied its moons.
7. They researched separately. They wrote their papers separately.
8. The teacher read their papers. The teacher thought they had worked together.
9. Melvin said he had liked the subject. Elliot said he had liked the subject.
10. The teacher praised them. The teacher gave them good grades.

442 • Effective Sentences

🎸 STANDARDIZED TEST PREPARATION WORKSHOP

Sentence Construction Standardized tests often evaluate students' ability to recognize effective sentences. Students might be asked to rewrite a sentence to correct a problem in the original. Ask students if the sentence below is written correctly. If not, which choice is the best way to rewrite the sentence?

The trapeze artist hung in the air and seemed about to fall her partner caught her gracefully at the final moment.

A No change

B The trapeze artist hung in the air, and seemed about to fall, and her partner caught her gracefully at the final moment.

C The trapeze artist hung in the air; her partner caught her gracefully at the final moment, but she seemed about to fall.

D The trapeze artist hung in the air and seemed about to fall, but her partner caught her gracefully at the final moment.

The correct answer is **D**, because it combines two correctly written run-on sentences by using the conjunction *but.*

KEY CONCEPT Sentences can be combined by using *and, but, or, nor,* or a semicolon. These combined sentences are called **compound sentences.** ∎

EXAMPLE: The moon was full. It illuminated the night.

COMPOUND
SENTENCE: The moon was full, **and** it illuminated the night.

EXAMPLE: The sun shone brightly. Its rays beat down on the pavement.

COMPOUND
SENTENCE: The sun shone brightly; its rays beat down on the pavement.

Exercise 11 Combining Independent Clauses to Form Compound Sentences Combine the following pairs of sentences, using the method given in parentheses.

EXAMPLE: The planet Venus is very hot. Lead, tin, and zinc would easily melt on its surface. (semicolon)

ANSWER: The planet Venus is very hot; lead, tin, and zinc would easily melt on its surface.

1. Mercury is the planet closest to the sun. Consequently, it is the hottest. (semicolon)
2. It is about 36 million miles from the sun. That is close enough for the sun's rays to scorch its surface. (comma and coordinating conjunction)
3. Mercury does not reflect much sunlight. Its surface is rough, dark-colored rock. (semicolon)
4. Its volume is much less than Earth's. Its density is about equal to Earth's. (comma and coordinating conjunction)
5. Temperatures vary wildly on Mercury. They range from 810° Fahrenheit on the sunlit side to –290° Fahrenheit on the dark side. (semicolon)
6. Mercury revolves around the sun in about 88 days. It takes only 59 days for it to rotate on its axis. (comma and coordinating conjunction)
7. Cliffs crisscross Mercury's surface. They may have been created when the planet was formed. (semicolon)
8. The *Mariner 10* spacecraft passed Mercury in 1974 and 1975. It sent pictures of the planet back to Earth. (comma and coordinating conjunction)
9. Vast sheets of ice were discovered in 1991 by powerful telescopes. These areas were not covered by *Mariner 10.* (semicolon)
10. Space exploration has advanced tremendously in the past twenty-five years. What we know about Mercury is limited. [comma and coordinating conjunction]

More Practice
**Language Lab
CD-ROM**
• Sentence Style: Combining Sentences lesson
**On-line
Exercise Bank**
• Section 21.2
Grammar Exercise Workbook
• pp. 71–72

Combining Sentences • **443**

Answer Key

Exercise 10 (page 442)

1. Elliot and Melvin went to P.S. 101. (compound subject)
2. They were in sixth grade and liked science class. (compound verb)
3. They studied the planets and the stars. (compound object)
4. The teacher assigned Melvin and Elliot a written project. (compound object)
5. Melvin and Elliot decided to write about Mars. (compound subject)
6. They studied the planet and its moons. (compound object)
7. They researched and wrote their papers separately. (compound verb)
8. The teacher read their papers and thought they had worked together. (compound verb)
9. Melvin and Elliot said they had liked the subject. (compound subject)
10. The teacher praised them and gave them good grades. (compound verb)

Exercise 11

1. Mercury is the planet closest to the sun; consequently, it is the hottest.
2. It is about 36 million miles from the sun, and that is close enough for the sun's rays to scorch its surface.
3. Mercury does not reflect much sunlight; its surface is rough, dark-colored rock.
4. Its volume is much less than Earth's, but its density is about equal to Earth's.
5. Temperatures vary wildly on Mercury; they range from 810 degrees Fahrenheit on the sunlit side to –290 degrees Fahrenheit on the dark side.
6. Mercury revolves around the sun in about 88 days, but it takes only 59 days for it to rotate on its axis.
7. Cliffs criss-cross Mercury's surface; they may have been created when the planet was formed.
8. The *Mariner 10* spacecraft passed Mercury in 1974 and 1975, and it sent pictures of the planet back to Earth.

continued

Answer Key continued

9. Vast sheets of ice were discovered in 1991 by powerful telescopes; these areas were not covered by *Mariner 10.*
10. Space exploration has advanced tremendously in the past twenty-five years, but what we know about Mercury is limited.

6. Another way to combine sentences involves changing one of the sentences to make it dependent on the other for meaning.

7. By turning one complete sentence into a subordinate clause, students can more clearly show the links between their sentences.

continued

Answer Key

▶ **Exercise 12**

1. Venus is known as Earth's twin because the two planets are similar in size.
2. Although Venus is nearly the same size as Earth, it has a completely different surface.
3. Venus is brighter than any other planet because it is the second planet from the sun.
4. Scientists learned about the surface of Venus after they used radar and radio astronomy equipment.
5. Although Venus has a bright color, its surface can never be seen with the unaided eye.

Customize for
Less Advanced Students

Review the differences between subordinate clauses and complete sentences. Because some students may find it challenging to change complete sentences into clauses, review what is required for a subordinate clause and what is required for a sentence. Have students practice combining sentences by making one sentence a subordinate clause dependent on another.

21.2

▶ **KEY CONCEPT** Sentences can be combined by changing one of them into a subordinate clause. ■

Use a complex sentence when you are combining sentences to show the relationship between ideas. The subordinating conjunctions will help your readers understand the relationship.

EXAMPLE: We were frightened. We thought an asteroid would hit Earth.

COMBINED WITH A SUBORDINATE CLAUSE: We were frightened *because* we thought an asteroid would hit Earth.

▶ **Exercise 12** Combining Sentences Using Subordinating Conjunctions and Subordinate Clauses Combine the following sentences, using the conjunction given in parentheses.

EXAMPLE: (although) Neptune's volume is 57.4 times that of Earth. Its mass is only seventeen times Earth's mass.

ANSWER: Although Neptune's volume is 57.4 times that of Earth, its mass is only seventeen times Earth's mass.

1. (because) Venus is known as Earth's twin. The two planets are similar in size.
2. (although) Venus is nearly the same size as Earth. It has a completely different surface.
3. (because) Venus is brighter than any other planet. It is the second planet from the sun.
4. (after) Scientists learned about the surface of Venus. They used radar and radio astronomy equipment.
5. (although) Venus has a bright color. Its surface can never be seen with the unaided eye.

▶ **KEY CONCEPT** Sentences can be combined by changing one of them into a phrase. ■

EXAMPLE: The space shuttle will be launched tomorrow. It will orbit Earth.

COMBINED: The space shuttle will be launched tomorrow *to orbit Earth.*

EXAMPLE: The space shuttle will be launched tomorrow to orbit Earth. The space shuttle is the most advanced vehicle in the world.

COMBINED: The space shuttle, *the most advanced vehicle in the world,* will be launched tomorrow to orbit Earth.

444 • **Effective Sentences**

▶ **More Practice**

Language Lab CD-ROM
• Sentence Style: Combining Sentences lesson
On-Line Exercise Bank
• Section 21.2
Grammar Exercise Workbook
• pp. 71–72

☑ ONGOING ASSESSMENT: Monitor and Reinforce

If students miss more than two items in Exercises 12–13, refer them to the following for additional practice.

In the Textbook	Print Resources	Technology
Section Review, Ex. 15–16, p. 447	Grammar Exercise Workbook, pp. 71–72	Language Lab CD-ROM, Sentence Style; On-Line Exercise Bank, Section 21.2

► **Exercise 13** Combining Sentences Using Phrases

Combine the following pairs of sentences by changing one of them into a phrase.

EXAMPLE: Pluto is the outermost known member of the solar system. Pluto is the ninth planet from the sun.

ANSWER: Pluto, the ninth planet from the sun, is the outermost known member of the solar system.

1. The search for Pluto was begun by Percival Lowell. He was an American astronomer.
2. The search ended in 1930. The search was finished by the members of the Lowell Observatory staff.
3. Clyde William Tombaugh found Pluto where Lowell had predicted. Tombaugh was also an American astronomer.
4. Pluto orbits around the sun once in almost 250 Earth years. It is at a distance of almost 4 billion miles from the sun.
5. Sometimes Pluto is closer to the sun than Neptune. Neptune is Pluto's neighbor.
6. Pluto appears to have a yellowish color. It is visible only through very large telescopes.
7. In 1978, astronomers discovered Pluto's moon. It is named Charon.
8. Pluto was discovered to have a thin atmosphere. The atmosphere is probably methane gas.
9. The Hubble Space Telescope was launched in 1990. It allowed astronomers to learn a great deal about Pluto and Charon.
10. Pluto is made of rockier material than the other planets of the solar system. It has a density twice that of water.

▼ **Critical Viewing**
Write two sentences about this image of the Milky Way galaxy. Then, combine the two sentences by making one of them a phrase. **[Draw Conclusions]**

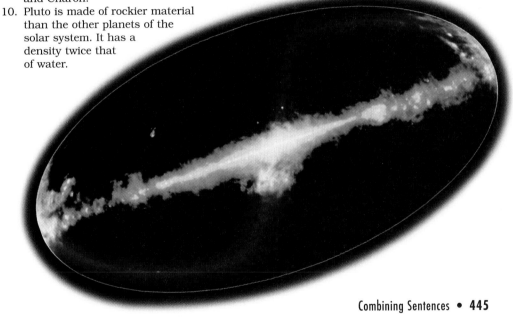

Combining Sentences • 445

8. Review the differences between phrases and sentences. A sentence expresses a complete thought; it has a subject and a verb.

9. Explain that, as two sentences can be combined by changing one of the sentences to a subordinate clause, they can also be combined by changing one of the sentences to a phrase.

10. Divide students into small groups. Using the key concepts on page 444 as their guide, students should write sentences and combine them by changing sentences into phrases or subordinate clauses.

Answer Key

► **Exercise 13**

1. The search for Pluto was begun by Percival Lowell, an American astronomer.
2. Ended in 1930, the search was finished by the members of the Lowell Observatory staff.
3. Clyde William Tombaugh, an American astronomer, found Pluto where Lowell had predicted.
4. Pluto, at a distance of almost 4 billion miles from the sun, orbits around the sun once in almost 250 Earth years.
5. Sometimes Pluto is closer to the sun than Neptune, its neighbor.
6. Pluto, visible only through very large telescopes, appears to have a yellowish color.
7. In 1978, astronomers discovered Pluto's moon, Charon.
8. Pluto was discovered to have a thin atmosphere, probably methane gas.
9. The Hubble Space Telescope, launched in 1990, allowed astronomers to learn a great deal about Pluto and Charon.
10. Pluto, made of rockier material than the other planets of the solar system, has a density twice that of water.

Critical Viewing

Draw Conclusions Answers will vary.

☑ **ONGOING ASSESSMENT: Prerequisite Skills**

If students have difficulty combining sentences, you may find it necessary to review the following to assure coverage of prerequisite knowledge.

In the Textbook	Print	Technology
Phrases and Clauses, pp. 414–435	Grammar Exercise Workbook, pp. 59–68	On-Line Exercise Bank, Sections 20.1–2

Conjunction Pop-up

Teaching Resources: Hands-on Grammar Activity Book, Chapter 21

1. Have students refer to their *Hands-on Grammar Activity Book* or give them copies of relevant pages for this activity.

2. Be sure students use a variety of conjunctions and don't keep reusing *and* or *but*. Give suggestions for sentences using *or, so, because,* and *although,* if necessary.

Find It in Your Reading

Have volunteers write examples on the board of sentences that could be combined in more than one way.

Find It in Your Writing

Ask some students to read aloud their writing examples and ask for feedback from the class.

21.2

Hands-on Grammar

Conjunction Pop-up

Practice combining sentences with conjunctions.

Fold a piece of paper so that there is a pocket, as shown in the illustration. Write the first sentence of each pair on the left side of the pocket and the second sentence of each pair on the right.

The moon was full.
The sky was bright.

The moon was full.
It lit up the night sky.

The moon was full.
I could see things clearly in the yard.

You might want to write them more than once and join them by using different conjunctions.

In the pocket between each pair of sentences, write a conjunction —such as *and, or, but, so, because,* or *although*—that can be used to join the sentences. When you "pop" the pocket open, you will see a complete sentence joined by the conjunction. On a separate sheet of paper, write the new sentence with the correct punctuation.

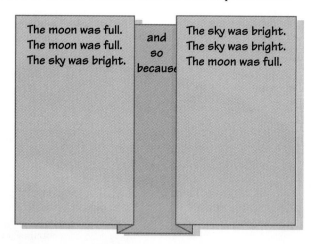

Find It in Your Reading Look through a story or essay for several examples of sentences that have been combined using conjunctions. See if the sentences could be joined in any other way.

Find It in Your Writing Look through your writing portfolio. See if you can smooth out the style of your writing and add interest to it by combining some of the sentences.

446 • Effective Sentences

⏱ TIME SAVERS!

✋ **Hands-on Grammar Book**
Use the Hands-on Grammar activity sheet for Chapter 21 to facilitate this activity.

☑ ONGOING ASSESSMENT: Assess Mastery

Use the following resources to assess student mastery of combining sentences.

In the Textbook	Technology
Chapter Review, Ex. 54, p. 472	On-Line Exercise Bank, Section 21.2

Section
21.2 *Section Review*

Section Review

Each of these exercises correlates to the instruction on sentence combining, pages 441–446. These exercises may be used for more practice, for reteaching, or for review of the key concepts as presented. Answers to all chapter exercises are available in *Grammar Exercises Answers on Transparencies* in your Teaching Resources.

GRAMMAR EXERCISES 14–19

▶ **Exercise 14** Combining Sentences Combine the following pairs of sentences, using the method given in parentheses.

1. Venus is one of the planets of the solar system. It is second from the sun. (comma and coordinating conjunction)
2. The sun and the moon are the brightest objects in Earth's sky. Venus is almost as bright. (comma and coordinating conjunction)
3. Venus is known as the morning star when it appears in the east at sunrise. It is called the evening star when it is in the western sky at sunset. (semicolon)
4. In ancient times, the evening star was called Hesperus. The morning star was referred to as Phosphorus. (comma and coordinating conjunction)
5. The phases of Venus repeat about every 18 months. Venus is brightest in the crescent phase. (semicolon)

▶ **Exercise 15** Combining Sentences Using Subordination Combine the following sentences, using the subordinating conjunction given in parentheses.

1. (although) It may seem strange. Ninety-seven percent of Venus's atmosphere is carbon dioxide.
2. (because) The moon appears to give light. It reflects the light of the sun.
3. (even though) The cloud cover of Venus is very dense. Features can be seen from the cloud tops.
4. (which) Venus is encircled by high-altitude winds. The winds can be gauged by the cloud patterns.
5. (because) The upper-level winds remain above the planet's surface. The atmosphere at ground level is still.

▶ **Exercise 16** Combining Sentences Using Phrases Combine the following pairs of sentences by changing one of them into a phrase.

1. Saturn is the sixth planet from the sun. Saturn is the second largest planet in the solar system.
2. Saturn's most noticeable feature is its rings. The rings are a collection of rock, frozen gases, and ice.
3. The rings were first seen in 1610 by the Italian scientist Galileo. He saw them through his primitive telescope.
4. Galileo described them incorrectly. He described them as handles.
5. In 1655, Christian Huygens became the first to describe the rings of Saturn correctly. Huygens was Dutch.

▶ **Exercise 17** Find It in Your Reading Read the following sentence from "An Astronaut's Answers" by John Glenn. On a separate sheet of paper, write the two sentences that were combined to make this sentence.

In 1962, I looked down from an orbit high above our planet and saw our beautiful Earth and its curved horizon against the vastness of space.

▶ **Exercise 18** Find It in Your Writing Select a piece of your writing. Use a comma and a coordinating conjunction to combine two related sentences.

▶ **Exercise 19** Writing Application Write an expository paragraph providing information you know about some part of the solar system. Be sure that some of your sentences use coordination and that others use subordination.

Answer Key

▶ **Exercise 14**

1. Venus is one of the planets of the solar system, and it is second from the sun.
2. The sun and the moon are the brightest objects in Earth's sky, and Venus is almost as bright.
3. Venus is known as the morning star when it appears in the east at sunrise; it is called the evening star when it is in the western sky at sunset.
4. In ancient times the evening star was called Hesperus, and the morning star was referred to as Phosphorus.
5. The phases of Venus repeat about every 18 months; Venus is brightest in the crescent phase.

▶ **Exercise 15**

1. Although it may seem strange, ninety-seven percent of Venus's atmosphere is carbon dioxide.
2. The moon appears to give light because it reflects the light of the sun.
3. Even though the cloud cover of Venus is very dense, features can be seen from the cloud tops.
4. Venus is encircled by high-altitude winds, which can be gauged by the cloud patterns.
5. Because the upper-level winds remain above the planet's surface, the atmosphere at ground level is still.

▶ **Exercise 16**

1. Saturn, the second largest planet in the solar system, is the sixth planet from the sun.
2. Saturn's most noticeable feature is its rings, a collection of rock, frozen gases, and ice.
3. The rings were first seen in 1610 by the Italian scientist Galileo through his primitive telescope.

continued

Answer Key continued

4. Galileo described them incorrectly as handles.
5. In 1655 Christian Huygens, a Dutchman, became the first to describe the rings of Saturn correctly.

▶ **Exercise 17**

Find It in Your Reading
In 1962, I looked down from an orbit high above our planet.

I saw our beautiful Earth . . . vastness of space.

▶ **Exercise 18**

Find It in Your Writing
Have students share their writing with a partner and review their use of a coordinating conjunction and a comma.

▶ **Exercise 19**

Writing Application
Students can assemble their paragraphs into a book about the solar system.

447

Ask students to think of a time in which a few words made all the difference. They may have come in the form of advice: "Just do it!" or a warning: "Look out!" or even a joke. Have them tell about an experience in which just a few words made a difference in their lives.

Activate Prior Knowledge

Remind students that one way writers keep readers interested is by changing the style or flow of information. Encourage students to think of their writing like a kind of music—if it's the same pattern over and over again, it might put someone to sleep! Ask them to think of varying their writing in the same way that they vary their diet or their activities with friends.

TEACH

Step-by-Step Teaching Guide

Vary Sentence Length

1. Remind students of the old saying: "Variety is the spice of life." The same is true in writing.

2. Ask students to ask themselves if they are writing sentences that are repetitive. If the answer is yes, encourage them to rephrase and rewrite in order to keep the interest of their readers.

Critical Viewing

Infer Write the following on the board as models:

The marchers celebrate an American holiday.

With flags flying and horns blowing, the marchers parade through the streets of town.

Customize for
Auditory Learners

Have partners read their sentences aloud to each other. If listeners notice that all the sentences tend to be about the same in length, they can work together to break up some of the longer sentences into short, to-the-point sentences.

Section 21.3 *Varying Sentences*

Vary your sentences to create a rhythm, to achieve an effect, or to emphasize the connections between ideas. There are several ways you can create variety in your sentences.

Varying Sentence Length

You have already learned that you can combine several short, choppy sentences to create a longer, more fluid, and stylistically mature sentence. However, too many long sentences in a row is as uninteresting as too many short sentences. When you want to emphasize a point, or surprise a reader, insert a short, direct sentence to interrupt the flow of long sentences. Read the following example.

EXAMPLE: Veteran's Day is a holiday that is observed in the United States to honor all those who served in the armed forces in time of war. It is celebrated in most states on November 11 and in some states on the fourth Monday of October. *However, it was first known as Armistice Day.*

Some sentences contain only one idea and can't be broken up. It may be possible, however, to state the idea in a shorter sentence. Other sentences contain two or more ideas and may be shortened by breaking up the ideas.

EXAMPLE: This holiday was proclaimed in 1919 by President Woodrow Wilson to commemorate the ending of World War I, which occurred on November 11, 1918.

SHORTER
SENTENCES: This holiday was proclaimed in 1919 by President Woodrow Wilson. It commemorated the ending of World War I, which was November 11, 1918.

▶ Critical Viewing What do you think is the occasion for this parade? Write two sentences about it—one that is short and choppy, the other long and flowing. [Infer]

448 • Effective Sentences

Theme: Festivals

In this section, you will learn about varying the length of your sentences. The examples and exercises are about festivals and holidays.

**Cross-Curricular Connection:
Social Studies**

⏱ TIME AND RESOURCE MANAGER

Resources
Print: Grammar Exercises Answers on Transparencies, Chapter 21; Grammar Exercise Workbook, pp. 73–76
Technology: Language Lab CD-ROM, Problems With Sentences; On-Line Exercise Bank, Section 21.3

In-Depth Coverage	Accelerated Pace
• Work through all key concepts, pp. 448–452. • Assign and review Exercises 20–24.	• Assign pp. 448–452 for independent student review. • Assign Section Review Exercises 25–27, p. 453.

Exercise 20 Varying Sentence Length In the following items, break up long sentences into two or more simple sentences, or restate long sentences more simply.

EXAMPLE: Millions of people in the United States celebrate the Fourth of July by gathering together with family and friends for picnics and fireworks and by watching or participating in parades.

ANSWER: Millions of people in the United States celebrate the Fourth of July. Family and friends gather together for picnics and fireworks. Some watch or participate in parades.

1. One important holiday is the Fourth of July, or Independence Day, when people often get together to watch fireworks displays.
2. Some people celebrate the Fourth of July by sharing a simple picnic of hot dogs and hamburgers with family and friends in the backyard.
3. Others look forward to seeing one of the many huge, public fireworks displays, often staged in city and town parks, which seem to bring the excitement of the day to life.
4. Leaving fireworks to the experts is a good idea because the private use of fireworks is illegal in many states.
5. Most states have passed laws restricting the private use of fireworks to protect people from the many injuries that can happen when people handle these explosives.

GRAMMAR IN LITERATURE

from **Parade**
Rachel Field

Note how several details (in blue) are combined in this long, fluid, poetic sentence.

This is the day the circus comes / With blare of brass, with beating drums, / And clashing cymbals, and with roar / Of wild beasts never heard before / Within town limits.

▲ **Critical Viewing** In one long and one short sentence, tell what this photograph of fireworks makes you think of. **[Describe]**

Varying Sentences • 449

Answer Key

▶ **Exercise 20**

Answers may vary. Samples are given.

1. One important holiday is the Fourth of July, or Independence Day. People often get together to watch fireworks displays.
2. Some people celebrate the Fourth of July with family and friends. They share a simple backyard picnic of hot dogs and hamburgers.
3. Others look forward to seeing one of the many huge, public fireworks displays often staged in city and town parks. These displays seem to bring the excitement of the day to life.
4. Leaving fireworks to the experts is a good idea. The private use of fireworks is illegal in many states.
5. To protect people from the injuries that happen when they handle explosives, most states have passed laws restricting the private use of fireworks.

Step-by-Step Teaching Guide

Grammar in Literature

1. Have a volunteer read aloud the excerpt from "Parade."
2. Ask the class to identify the variety of details that make up the parade (circus, brass, drums, cymbals, wild beasts).
3. Now have students read the excerpt and try to catch the meter of the poetic lines.

Critical Viewing

Describe Students may use sentences with the words *bright, explode, colorful, booming,* and so forth.

☑ **ONGOING ASSESSMENT: Monitor and Reinforce**

If students miss more than two items in Exercise 20, refer them to the following for additional practice.

In the Textbook	Print	Technology
Section Review, Ex. 25, p. 453	Grammar Exercise Workbook, pp. 73–76	Language Lab CD-ROM, Problems with Sentences; On-Line Exercise Bank, Section 21.3

▶ **Exercise 21**

Answers will vary. Samples are given.

Among the most popular festivals in the United States are the state, county, or local fairs. Usually held in the summer months, most of these fairs have amusement park rides, game booths, and food courts. Some fairs also have contests. The contests may include beauty pageants, bake-offs, automobile races, horse shows, and 4-H club events, in which boys and girls show off the animals they have raised. Politicians often attend local and state fairs, giving speeches and talking to voters about various issues. If you have never been to a state, county, or local fair, find out if one is being held in your community. Plan to go this summer.

Step-by-Step Teaching Guide

Vary Sentence Beginnings

1. Varying the parts of speech that begin sentences makes writing more interesting.

2. Have students think about (or look at) their comics. If there were no pictures, all those short sentences one after the other would be boring.

continued

Customize for
Logical/Mathematical Learners

Have students analyze the opening sentences of paragraphs in a newspaper or magazine article. Ask students to tally the parts of speech used to begin paragraphs. Then have them create a bar or circle graph showing their findings.

Critical Viewing

Deduce Have students compare their three-sentence descriptions by identifying each other's parts of speech.

21.3

▶ **Exercise 21** Varying Sentence Length Read the following paragraph. Then, rewrite it, breaking up long sentences into two or more simple sentences or restating long sentences more simply.

Among the most popular festivals in the United States are the state, county, or local fairs, which are usually held in the summer months. Most of these fairs have amusement park rides, game booths, and food courts, but some fairs also have contests. The contests may include beauty pageants, bake-offs, automobile races, horse shows, and 4-H club events, in which boys and girls show off the animals they have raised. Politicians often attend local and state fairs and give speeches and talk to the voters about various issues. If you have never been to a state, county, or local fair, find out if one is being held in your community, and plan to go this summer.

▲ Critical Viewing In two or three sentences, tell what makes this clown funny. Use a different part of speech to begin each sentence. **[Deduce]**

450 • Effective Sentences

☑ **ONGOING ASSESSMENT: Monitor and Reinforce**

If students miss more than two items in Exercises 21–23, refer them to the following for additional practice.

In the Textbook	Print Resources	Technology
Section Review, Ex. 25–27, p. 453	Grammar Exercise Workbook, pp. 73–76	Language Lab CD-ROM, Problems With Sentences; On-Line Exercise Bank, Section 21.3

Varying Sentence Beginnings

Another way to create sentence variety is to start sentences with different parts of speech.

NOUN:	Carnivals are excellent fund-raisers.
ADVERB:	Often, carnivals are excellent fund-raisers.
PARTICIPIAL PHRASE:	Having helped with many carnivals, I know they are excellent fund-raisers.
PREPOSITIONAL PHRASE:	For large churches or small communities, carnivals are excellent fund-raisers.

Exercise 22 Writing Sentences With Varied Beginnings
Write sentences following the instructions given below.
1. Begin with the noun *Holidays.*
2. Begin with the adverb *Usually.*
3. Begin with the present participial phrase *Watching the people.*
4. Begin with the past participial phrase *Excited by the events.*
5. Begin with the prepositional phrase *After the celebration.*

Exercise 23 Revising Sentences by Varying Sentence Beginnings Follow the instructions in parentheses to revise each sentence below.

EXAMPLE: Clowns are very popular. (Start with an adverb.)
ANSWER: Not surprisingly, clowns are very popular.

1. Clowns wear bright-colored makeup. (Start with an adverb.)
2. The high wire looks very frightening. (Start with a prepositional phrase.)
3. I know that training lions is very difficult. (Start with a participial phrase.)
4. Living on the road can be hard. (Start with a prepositional phrase.)
5. Some circuses no longer have live animals. (Start with an adverb.)
6. Some people are worried that the animals suffer. (Start with a participial phrase.)
7. Animal trainers make sure that the animals are well cared for. (Start with an adverb.)
8. Elephants are used by circus workers to help with heavy lifting. (Start with a prepositional phrase.)
9. I have been to the circus three times this year. (Start with a participial phrase.)
10. The popcorn and peanuts taste good. (Start with an adverb.)

More Practice

On-line
Exercise Bank
• Section 21.3
Grammar Exercise
Workbook
• pp. 73–76

Learn More

To learn more about participles, see Chapter 22.

Answer Key

Exercise 22

Answers will vary. Samples are given.

1. Holidays are days that honor people or annual celebrations.
2. Usually, we do not have school on holidays.
3. Watching the people, I enjoy a parade.
4. Excited by the events, they make it a festive day for everyone.
5. After the celebration, it's back to work as usual.

Exercise 23

Answers will vary. Samples are given.

1. Usually clowns wear bright-colored makeup.
2. From the audience's perspective, the high-wire looks very frightening.
3. Having worked at a circus, I know that training lions is very difficult.
4. For the participants, living on the road can be hard.
5. Currently, some circuses no longer have live animals.
6. Concerned about conditions, some people are worried that the animals suffer.
7. Almost universally, the animal trainers make sure that the animals are well cared for.
8. Before the circus begins, elephants are used by circus workers to help with heavy lifting.
9. Enjoying the excitement, I have been to the circus three times this year.
10. Undeniably, the popcorn and peanuts taste good.

TIME SAVERS!

Answers on Transparency
Use the Grammar Exercises Answers on Transparencies for Chapter 21 to have students correct their own or one another's exercises.

On-Line Exercise Bank
Have students complete the exercises on computer. The Auto Check feature will grade their work for you.

3. Most sentences begin with a subject and follow with a verb, but sometimes this pattern is reversed.

4. Reversing sounds complicated, but it really isn't. Have students read the first paragraph in the right column of page 47 in *Prentice Hall Literature: Timeless Voices, Timeless Themes,* Copper. The sentences begin with different parts of speech, but the paragraph is not awkward or strange. Students probably do this in their own writing without even thinking about it.

Integrating Writing Skills

Have students write a short letter to a friend. Then ask them to rewrite the letter, reversing the traditional order of subjects and verbs wherever possible to make their writing fresh and unexpected. Have volunteers read their letters aloud to the class.

Answer Key

▶ **Exercise 24**

1. First comes the opening procession.
2. Around the ring parade the animals and performers.
3. In the ring tumble the clowns.
4. Loudly plays the music.
5. Announcing the acts is the ringmaster.
6. Through the hoops jump the lions.
7. Into the net falls the acrobat.
8. With excitement roars the crowd.
9. After the acrobats, enter the jugglers.
10. Home we go.

Critical Viewing

Infer Have students work in pairs to assess each other's inverted sentences.

21.3

▶ **KEY CONCEPT** You can also vary sentence beginnings by inverting the traditional subject-verb order. ■

EXAMPLE: The clowns are here.
          (S) (V)

INVERTED: Here are the clowns.
          (V) (S)

EXAMPLE: The acrobats soared through the air.
          (S)   (V)   (Prep. Phrase)

INVERTED: Through the air soared the acrobats.
          (Prep. Phrase)   (V)   (S)

▶ **Exercise 24** Inverting Sentences for Variety Invert the subject-verb order in the following sentences.

EXAMPLE: The circus is in town.
ANSWER: In town is the circus.

1. The opening procession comes first.
2. The animals and performers parade around the ring.
3. The clowns tumble in the ring.
4. The music plays loudly.
5. The ringmaster is announcing the acts.
6. The lions jump through the hoops.
7. The acrobat falls into the net.
8. The crowd roars with excitement.
9. The jugglers enter after the acrobats.
10. We go home.

452 • Effective Sentences

▲ **Critical Viewing**
What would you expect to find inside the big tent? Use sentences with inverted word order in your response. **[Infer]**

▶ **More Practice**

On-line
Exercise Bank
• Section 21.3
Grammar Exercise
Workbook
• pp. 73–76

☑ **ONGOING ASSESSMENT: Assess Mastery**

Use the following resources to assess student mastery of varying sentences.

In the Textbook	Technology
Chapter Review, Ex. 55, p. 472	On-Line Exercise Bank, Section 21.3

Section Review

GRAMMAR EXERCISES 25–30

▶ **Exercise 25** Revising Long
Sentences Rewrite the following sentences by breaking each into two sentences, or by forming a simpler, more direct sentence.

1. One of the oldest types of clown is the whiteface, which dates back to the eighteenth century; the white color of the face was originally achieved with flour.
2. White lead later replaced flour, but after the 1880's, when lead was discovered to be toxic, safer greasepaints were introduced.
3. The whiteface clown evolved from earlier whiteface entertainers, and one of the most popular whiteface characters in history is Harlequin.
4. English actor John Rich, who performed in the eighteenth century, was the most famous Harlequin of his time.
5. The clown gradually replaced the Harlequin character; English entertainer Joseph Grimaldi is considered the most famous clown.

▶ **Exercise 26** Varying Sentence
Beginnings Rewrite each sentence below, following the instructions in parentheses.

1. Modern clowns are performers who have turned away from traditional clown acts. (Start with an adverb.)
2. Some wear no makeup. (Start with a participle.)
3. They interact closely with their audiences. (Start with a prepositional phrase.)
4. Some of the new clowns perform with circuses. (Start with an adverb.)
5. Others make their mark in the theater. (Start with a participle.)

▶ **Exercise 27** Inverting Subject-
Verb Order Invert the subject-verb order in the following sentences.

1. The Ferris wheel spins around and around.
2. We whirl through the darkness.
3. The sticky cotton candy clings to our clothes.
4. The child desired a green stuffed bear.
5. The band is here.

▶ **Exercise 28** Find It in Your
Reading Reread the excerpt from "Parade" by Rachel Field on page 449. On your paper, write the phrases that appear in the sentence.

▶ **Exercise 29** Find It in Your
Writing Choose a piece of writing from your portfolio, and make the following changes to three sentences.

1. Start with an adverb.
2. Start with a participle.
3. Start with a prepositional phrase.

▶ **Exercise 30** Writing Application
On your paper, write a descriptive paragraph of ten sentences about an entertainment event that you have watched. Include details about the location and the performers. Then, on the same paper, rewrite the paragraph by varying the lengths of your sentences. Be sure to vary the beginnings of your sentences as well as the phrases and clauses.

Section Review • **453**

ASSESS and CLOSE

Section Review

Each of these exercises correlates to the instruction on varying sentences, pages 448–452. These exercises may be used for more practice, for reteaching, or for review of the key concepts presented. Answers for all exercises are available in *Grammar Exercises Answers on Transparencies* in your Teaching Resources.

Answer Key

▶ **Exercise 25**

Answers will vary. Samples are given.

1. One of the oldest types of clown is the whiteface, originally achieved with flour, which dates back to the eighteenth century.
2. White lead later replaced flour. Safer greasepaints were introduced after the 1880s, when lead was discovered to be toxic.
3. The whiteface clown evolved from earlier whiteface entertainers. One of the most popular whiteface entertainers in history is Harlequin.
4. The most famous Harlequin of his time was English actor John Rich, who performed in the eighteenth century.
5. The clown gradually replaced the Harlequin character. English entertainer Joseph Grimaldi is considered the most famous clown.

▶ **Exercise 26**

Answers will vary. Samples are given.

1. Usually, modern clowns are performers who have turned away from traditional clown acts.
2. Performing, some wear no makeup.
3. During their act, they interact closely with their audiences.
4. Unsurprisingly, some of the new clowns perform with circuses.
5. Thrilled by the exposure, others make their mark in the theater.

▶ **Exercise 27**

1. Around and around spins the Ferris wheel.
2. Through the darkness whirl the riders.
3. To our clothes clings the sticky cotton candy.

continued

Answer Key continued

4. Desired the child a green stuffed bear.
5. Here is the band.

▶ **Exercise 28**

Find It in Your Reading
with blare of brass, with beating drums and clashing cymbals, with roar of wild beasts, never heard before, within town limits

▶ **Exercise 29**

Find It in Your Writing
Have students work in pairs and share their revisions with a partner. Ask the partner to identify the opening adverb, participle, and prepositional phrase in the revised sentences.

▶ **Exercise 30**

Writing Application
Suggest that students who wrote about the same subject compare their paragraphs in terms of content and types of sentences.

Have students write two or three sentences in pencil. Ask them to erase one or two words from each sentence. Then have them share the fragments with the class. Ask the class to guess what the sentences are about. Then have the writer explain the actual meaning.

Activate Prior Knowledge

Students should be familiar with incomplete ideas and sentences. Have them suggest complete sentences. Then ask them to identify the parts of sentences that make the sentence complete. Have them suggest fragments and identify what parts of speech need to be added to make the fragments complete sentences.

TEACH

Step-by-Step Teaching Guide

Avoiding Fragments

1. The key parts of a sentence are simple: subject and verb.

2. The difference between a sentence and a fragment is not length. Read students the following short sentence and long fragment.

   The kitten played.

   played with a ball of yarn, hitting it with a paw from one side of the room to the other and running after it

---

| Section 21.4 | **Avoiding Sentence Problems** |

Being able to recognize the parts of sentences can help you avoid certain errors in your writing.

Avoiding Fragments

Some groups of words, even though they have a capital letter at the beginning and a period at the end, are not complete sentences. They are *fragments*.

▶ **KEY CONCEPT** A fragment is a group of words that does not express a complete thought but is punctuated as a sentence. ■

A fragment is only *part* of a sentence.

FRAGMENTS
In the center ring.
Felt happy and excited.
The man on the trapeze.
The elephants coming into the tent.
When she smiled.

You will usually be able to tell whether a group of words expresses a complete thought. One trick is to read the words aloud. This will help you hear whether or not some part is missing.

In the following chart, words have been added to the preceding fragments to make complete sentences. Read each italicized fragment; then, read the complete sentence. Can you hear the difference?

COMPLETE SENTENCES
The clowns arrived *in the center ring.*
I *felt happy and excited.*
The man on the trapeze is agile.
The elephants are *coming into the tent.*
When she smiled, the clowns were pleased.

Each of the preceding examples needed one or more new parts. The first needed both a subject and a verb. The second needed only a subject. The third became complete when a verb and an adjective were added. The fourth became complete when a helping verb was added. The final example needed a complete main clause to go with the subordinate clause.

Theme: Circuses
In this section, you will learn how to avoid sentence errors, including fragments, run-on sentences, misplaced modifiers, and some common usage errors. The examples and exercises are about circuses.
Cross-Curricular Connection: Social Studies

⏱ **TIME AND RESOURCE MANAGER**

Resources
Print: Grammar Exercise Workbook, pp. 77–86; Grammar Exercises Answers on Transparencies, Chapter 21
Technology: Language Lab CD-ROM, Problems With Sentences; On-Line Exercise Bank, Section 21.4

In-Depth Coverage	Accelerated Pace
• Work through all key concepts, pp. 454–469. • Assign and review Exercises 31–42.	• Assign pp. 454–469 for independent student review. • Assign Section Review Exercises 43–49, pp. 470–471.

> **Exercise 31** Recognizing Sentence Fragments Each of the following numbered items is either a sentence or a fragment. Write *F* if it is a fragment and *S* if it is a complete sentence.

EXAMPLE: Clowns climbing ladders.

ANSWER: F

1. Lights dimmed.
2. With three rings.
3. Painted beautiful colors.
4. Waiting for her cue.
5. Clowns tumbled.
6. When the horse rode by.
7. The tiger in its cage.
8. Before the clown tripped.
9. The acrobats are here.
10. On the flying trapeze.

Phrase Fragments   A phrase by itself is a fragment. It cannot stand alone because it does not have a subject and a verb.

> **KEY CONCEPT** A phrase should not be capitalized and punctuated as though it were a sentence. ∎

Three types of phrases—prepositional, participial, and infinitive—are often mistaken for sentences. A *phrase fragment* can be changed into a sentence in either of two ways.

FRAGMENT: The circus began this evening. *In the arena.*

You can correct this fragment simply by attaching it to the preceding sentence.

ADDED TO
NEARBY SENTENCE: The circus began this evening *in the arena.*

You can correct other fragments simply by attaching them to the beginning of a sentence.

FRAGMENT: *Arriving in the center ring.* The clowns were greeted by cheers.

ADDED TO
NEARBY SENTENCE: *Arriving in the center ring,* the clowns were greeted by cheers.

Sometimes, however, you may not be able to correct a phrase fragment by adding it to a nearby sentence. Correct the fragment by adding to the phrase whatever is needed to make it a complete sentence. Often, this method requires adding a subject and a verb.

More Practice

Language Lab CD-ROM
• Sentence Fragments lesson

On-line Exercise Bank
• Section 21.4

Grammar Exercise Workbook
• pp. 77–80

▼ Critical Viewing
Turn the fragments *with a goose* and *wearing bright clothing* into complete sentences that describe this photograph. [Describe]

Avoiding Sentence Problems • 455

Answer Key

> **Exercise 31**
1. S
2. F
3. F
4. F
5. S
6. F
7. F
8. F
9. S
10. F

Step-by-Step Teaching Guide

Phrase Fragments

1. Three types of phrases— prepositional, participial, and infinitive—are prone to confusion because they sound like sentences, but they lack subjects.

2. Write the following phrases on the chalkboard and ask students to turn them into complete sentences:

   above the audience

   spinning high in the air

   to fall gracefully

3. Point out the difference between an infinitive and a prepositional phrase beginning with *to:*

   I want to go to the circus.

   An infinitive is always a *to* verb, in this sentence, *to go*. A prepositional phrase has a preposition, *to*, and an object, *circus.*

Critical Viewing

Describe Students may write sentences like the following:

A clown entered the ring with a goose.

The clown was wearing bright clothing.

☑ **ONGOING ASSESSMENT: Monitor and Reinforce**

If students miss more than two items in Exercise 31, refer them to the following for additional practice.

In the Textbook	Print	Technology
Section Review, Ex. 43, p. 470	Grammar Exercise Workbook, pp. 77–78	Language Lab CD-ROM, Problems With Sentences; On-Line Exercise Bank, Section 21.4

⏲ **TIME SAVERS!**

🖵 **Answers on Transparency** Use the Grammar Exercises Answers on Transparencies for Chapter 21 to have students correct their own or one another's exercises.

💻 **On-Line Exercise Bank** Have students complete the exercises on computer. The Auto Check feature will grade their work for you.

Answer Key

Answers will vary. Samples are given.

1. This week we went to the circus.
2. We were in town last weekend.
3. I was having a great time.
4. It was my first time at the circus.
5. Taking in all the colors and sounds, I was rapt with attention.
6. I didn't want it to be over.
7. After the show, we ate ice cream.
8. I wanted to learn how to use the flying trapeze.
9. My friend enjoyed the circus too.
10. The cunning lion tamer was brave.

Critical Viewing

Respond Students may suggest

When the acrobat did a handstand on a tall pole, I was on the edge of my seat.

21.4

CHANGING PHRASE FRAGMENTS INTO SENTENCES	
Phrase Fragment	**Complete Sentence**
Near the old clown.	The silly puppy flopped down *near the old clown.*
Taking a bow.	*Taking a bow,* the ringmaster had tears in his eyes.
To ask nicely.	She planned *to ask nicely* to go to the circus.

▶ **Exercise 32** Changing Phrase Fragments Into Sentences

Use each of the following phrase fragments in a sentence. You may use the phrase at the beginning, at the end, or in any other position in the sentence. Check to see that each of your sentences contains a subject and a verb.

EXAMPLE: Before the show started.

ANSWER: Before the show started, the performers got ready.

1. To the circus.
2. In town last weekend.
3. Having a great time.
4. My first time at the circus.
5. Taking in all the colors and sounds.
6. To be over.
7. After the show.
8. To learn to use the flying trapeze.
9. Enjoyed the circus.
10. The cunning lion tamer.

Clause Fragments All clauses have subjects and verbs, but some cannot stand alone as sentences.

Subordinate clauses do not express complete thoughts. Although a subordinate clause has a subject and a verb, it cannot stand by itself as a sentence. (See Chapter 20 for more information about subordinate clauses and the words that begin them.)

▼ Critical Viewing
How do you feel looking at the balancing act in this photograph? Change the phrase fragment *on the edge of my seat* into a sentence. **[Respond]**

KEY CONCEPT A subordinate clause should not be capitalized and punctuated as though it were a sentence. ∎

Like phrase fragments, *clause fragments* can usually be corrected in either of two ways: by attaching the fragment to a nearby sentence, or by adding whatever words are needed to make the fragment into a sentence.

Notice how the following clause fragments are corrected using the first method.

FRAGMENT: The class enjoyed the poem. *That I recited to them as part of my oral report.*

ADDED TO   The class enjoyed the poem *that I recited to*
NEARBY SENTENCE: *them as part of my oral report.*

To change a clause fragment into a sentence by the second method, you must add an independent clause to the fragment.

CHANGING CLAUSE FRAGMENTS INTO SENTENCES

Clause Fragment	Complete Sentence
That you described.	I saw the show *that you described.* The show *that you described* was in town.
After he knocked.	A pie hit him *after he knocked.* *After he knocked*, a pie hit him.

Exercise 33 Changing Clause Fragments Into Sentences
Use each of the clause fragments below in a sentence. Make sure that each sentence contains an independent clause.

EXAMPLE: That we saw last week.
ANSWER: We enjoyed the circus that we saw last week.

1. That they wear in the show.
2. When it is time to go on.
3. When they are in the ring.
4. Because they make children laugh.
5. While they are on.
6. That they are funny.
7. As long as there is an audience.
8. That they wear.
9. Because they travel often.
10. That I'll be a clown.

▶ **More Practice**

Language Lab CD-ROM
• Sentence Fragments lesson
On-line Exercise Bank
• Section 21.4
Grammar Exercise Workbook
• pp. 77–80

Step-by-Step Teaching Guide

Clause Fragments

Clauses are similar to sentences in that a clause also has a subject and a verb. The difference is that a subordinate clause does not express a complete thought.

Answer Key

▶ **Exercise 33**

Answers will vary. Samples are given.

1. The costumes that they wear in the show are beautiful.
2. A bell rings when it is time to go on.
3. They smile when they are in the ring.
4. Because they make children laugh, clowns like performing.
5. While they are on, they enjoy themselves.
6. They know that they are funny.
7. As long as there is an audience, they will perform.
8. I like the costumes that they wear.
9. Because they travel often, they visit interesting places.
10. I think that I'll be a clown.

☑ ONGOING ASSESSMENT: Monitor and Reinforce

If students miss more than two items in Exercises 32–33, refer them to the following for additional practice.

In the Textbook	Print	Technology
Section Review, Ex. 43, p. 470	Grammar Exercise Workbook, pp. 79–80	Language Lab CD-ROM, Problems With Sentences; On-Line Exercise Bank, Section 21.4

⏱ TIME SAVERS!

🖼 **Answers on Transparency**
Use the Grammar Exercises Answers on Transparencies for Chapter 21 to have students correct their own or one another's exercises.

💻 **On-Line Exercise Bank**
Have students complete the exercises on computer. The Auto Check feature will grade their work for you.

Step-by-Step Teaching Guide

Two Kinds of Run-ons

1. A sentence can have a compound subject, a compound verb, or a compound object—or two, or all three. A compound subject (or verb, or object) functions as a unit: *Tilly and Lily went to the beach.*

2. The problem with the run-on with no punctuation in the box is that it has two separate subjects (*I, arts and crafts*) and two verbs (*go, are*). That makes it two sentences.

3. Ask students to think of the end of each sentence as a stop sign. They should stop and look around to make sure that the end is properly complete. If it is not punctuated, they need to add punctuation.

Answer Key

> **Exercise 34**

1. R-O
2. S
3. R-O
4. R-O
5. S

21.4

Avoiding Run-ons

A *run-on sentence* contains two or more complete sentences that have been improperly combined.

> **KEY CONCEPT** A **run-on** is two or more complete sentences that are not properly joined or separated. ■

Run-ons are usually the result of haste. Learn to check your sentences carefully to see where one sentence ends and the next one begins.

Two Kinds of Run-ons There are two kinds of run-ons: One kind is made up of two or more sentences run together without any punctuation between them; the other consists of two or more sentences separated only by a comma.

RUN-ONS	
With No Punctuation	**With Only a Comma**
I go to the fair often the arts and crafts are my favorite part.	Fireworks and parades mark July 4th in the United States, family picnics are also a feature.

A good way to distinguish between a run-on and a sentence is to read the words aloud. Your ear will tell you whether you have one or two complete thoughts.

> **Exercise 34** Recognizing Run-ons On your paper, write *S* if an item below is a sentence and *R-O* if it is a run-on.

EXAMPLE: The clowns are silly and fun to watch they wear colorful suits.

ANSWER: R-O

1. A circus is usually held in a round theater it usually has tiers of seats for the audience.
2. It may be held in the open air, but it is usually under a tent.
3. The first modern circus was staged in London in 1768, a former cavalry rider performed tricks on his horse.
4. Philip Astley, the rider, brought his show to Paris, it soon spread throughout Europe.
5. By the nineteenth century, there were many permanent circuses in Europe; small caravans of traveling performers also gave shows.

> **More Practice**

Language Lab CD-ROM
• Run-on Sentences lesson
On-line Exercise Bank
• Section 21.4
Grammar Exercise Workbook
• pp. 81–84

⏱ TIME SAVERS!

Answers on Transparency
Use the Grammar Exercises Answers on Transparencies for Chapter 21 to have students correct their own or one another's exercises.

On-Line Exercise Bank
Have students complete the exercises on computer. The Auto Check feature will grade their work for you.

Correcting Run-ons There are three easy ways to correct a run-on.

Using End Marks *End marks* are periods, question marks, and exclamation marks.

▶ **KEY CONCEPT** Use an end mark to separate the parts of a run-on into two sentences. ■

Properly used, an end mark splits a run-on into two shorter but complete sentences. Which end mark you use depends on the function of the sentence.

RUN-ON: Every year we celebrate Independence Day with fireworks, a circus comes to town, too.

CORRECTED: Every year we celebrate Independence Day with fireworks. A circus comes to town, too.

RUN-ON: Have you found my tickets, I lost them yesterday.

CORRECTED: Have you found my tickets? I lost them yesterday.

▶ Critical Viewing Who is this man and what do you think he is saying? Make sure to avoid run-ons in your response. [**Deduce**]

Avoiding Sentence Problems • **459**

Using End Marks

Have students practice correcting run-ons by making each of the following into two sentences:

I like Independence Day we have a barbecue.

Hot dogs are my favorite I like hamburgers too.

Is that a clown in the parade I love clowns!

Critical Viewing

Deduce Students may suggest that this man is the ringmaster, or announcer, and that he is introducing a circus act.

☑ **ONGOING ASSESSMENT: Monitor and Reinforce**

If students miss more than two items in Exercise 34, refer them to the following for additional practice.

In the Textbook	Print	Technology
Section Review, Ex. 45, 48, pp. 470–471	Grammar Exercise Workbook, pp. 81–84	Language Lab CD-ROM, Problems With Sentences; On-Line Exercise Bank, Section 21.4

Using Commas and Coordinating Conjunctions

1. Introduce semicolons. Like a period, a semicolon separates two independent clauses. Use a semicolon when the ideas in the clauses are very closely connected.

2. In a well-written paragraph, the ideas in all the sentences are connected. There are two reasons to use a semicolon rather than a period, and both are the writer's choice.

   • The writer may want to emphasize how the ideas in two sentences are related. The sample answer in Exercise 35 could use a semicolon if the writer wanted to show a clear cause and effect relationship: sister is afraid of clowns (cause), so she hates the circus (effect).

   • Writers can add variety with sentences of different lengths. Connecting two short sentences with a semicolon now and then makes writing more interesting to read.

3. Students should use semicolons rarely. A period or a comma with a conjunction is usually a better choice.

▶ Exercise 35

Answers will vary. Samples are given.

1. Traveling shows were quite simple. They usually had a fiddler, a juggler, a rope dancer, and an acrobat.
2. These early circuses performed in open spaces. The performers took up a collection for pay.
3. Later, the performers used an enclosed area, and they began to charge admission.
4. Permanent, indoor, European circuses staged elaborate shows, and they specialized in horse tricks.
5. The circus was introduced to the United States in 1793; John Bill Ricketts brought his circus to Philadelphia.

21.4

Using Commas and Coordinating Conjunctions Sometimes the two parts of a run-on are related and should stay in the same sentence.

▶ **KEY CONCEPT** Use a comma and a coordinating conjunction to combine two independent clauses into a compound sentence. ■

RUN-ON: The lions and the tigers are roaming around the ring they look scary.

CORRECTED: The lions and the tigers are roaming around the ring, *and* they look scary.

Using Semicolons You can sometimes use a semicolon to punctuate the two parts of a run-on.

▶ **KEY CONCEPT** Use a semicolon to connect two closely related ideas. ■

Do not overuse the semicolon. Remember, semicolons should be used only when the ideas in both parts of the sentence are closely related.

RUN-ON: The circus begins at 7:30, I don't want to be late.
CORRECTED: The circus begins at 7:30; I don't want to be late.

▶ **Exercise 35** Revising to Correct Run-ons Correct each of the following run-on sentences using any of the three methods described in this section. Write the corrected sentences on a separate sheet of paper.

EXAMPLE: My sister hates the circus she is afraid of clowns.
ANSWER: My sister hates the circus. She is afraid of clowns.

1. Traveling shows were quite simple they usually had a fiddler, a juggler, a rope dancer, and an acrobat.
2. These early circuses performed in open spaces the performers took up a collection for pay.
3. Later, the performers used an enclosed area, they began to charge admission.
4. Permanent, indoor European circuses staged elaborate shows, they specialized in horse tricks.
5. The circus was introduced to the United States in 1793 John Bill Ricketts brought his circus to Philadelphia.

▶ More Practice

Language Lab CD-ROM
• Run-on Sentences lesson
On-line Exercise Bank
• Section 21.4
Grammar Exercise Workbook
• pp. 81–84

☑ ONGOING ASSESSMENT: Monitor and Reinforce

If students miss more than two items in Exercise 35, refer them to the following for additional practice.

In the Textbook	Print	Technology
Section Review, Ex. 45, 48, pp. 470–471	Grammar Exercise Workbook, pp. 81–84	Language Lab CD-ROM, Problems With Sentences; On-Line Exercise Bank, Section 21.4

Correcting Misplaced Modifiers

A phrase or clause that acts as an adjective or adverb should be placed close to the word it modifies. Otherwise, the meaning of the sentence may be unclear.

KEY CONCEPT A modifier should be placed as close as possible to the word it modifies. ■

Misplaced Modifiers A modifier placed too far away from the word it modifies is called a *misplaced modifier.* Because they are misplaced, such phrases and clauses seem to modify the wrong word in a sentence.

MISPLACED
MODIFIER: The circus featured an acrobat on
              the high wire *with an umbrella.*

The misplaced modifier is the phrase *with an umbrella.* In the sentence, it sounds as though the high wire has an umbrella. The sentence needs to be reworded slightly to put the modifier closer to *acrobat.*

CORRECTED: The circus featured an acrobat *with an umbrella* on the high wire.

Below is a somewhat different type of misplaced modifier.

MISPLACED
MODIFIER: *Balancing on her toes,* the net seemed far away.

In this sentence *balancing on her toes* should modify a person. Instead, it incorrectly modifies *net.*

CORRECTED: *Balancing on her toes,* the acrobat thought the net seemed far away.

◀ Critical Viewing
Tell what would happen if one of these acrobats were in the wrong position.
[Infer]

Step-by-Step Teaching Guide

Misplaced Modifiers
Write examples of misplaced modifiers on the chalkboard. Have students identify each one and correct it.

  The cat in the house with the black tail ate fish.

  Hopping across the field, Sheila saw a rabbit.

  Suki gave a cookie to her brother with chocolate chips.

  Kai received a bike for his birthday that had three speeds.

Critical Viewing

Infer Students might suggest that one acrobat in the wrong position could cause the act to fail or make someone fall.

1. MM
2. C
3. MM
4. MM
5. MM

Step-by-Step Teaching Guide

Revising Sentences With Misplaced Modifiers

1. Explain to students that misplaced modifiers—no matter what kind—can be corrected by placing the modifier closer to the noun it modifies.

2. Encourage students to isolate the noun being modified, then revise sentences accordingly.

21.4

Read each sentence below carefully, and check the placement of the modifiers. If the sentence is correct, write *C* on your paper. If the sentence contains a misplaced modifier, write *MM*.

EXAMPLE: My brother bought tickets at the box office for the front row.

ANSWER: MM

1. Born in Bethel, Connecticut, the circus was made famous by Phineas Taylor Barnum.
2. Beginning his career in New York, Barnum made a name for himself as a showman.
3. Claiming to be 161 years old, he exhibited a woman named Joice Heth.
4. Also in his show, Tom Thumb was presented by Barnum.
5. Always looking for new acts, Barnum's shows were a big success.

Revising Sentences With Misplaced Modifiers
Among the most common misplaced modifiers are prepositional phrases, participial phrases, and adjective clauses. All are corrected in the same way—by placing the modifier as close as possible to the word it modifies.

MISPLACED PREPOSITIONAL PHRASE:	Uncle Max took me to the circus *on the train*.
CORRECTED:	Uncle Max took me *on the train* to the circus.
MISPLACED PARTICIPIAL PHRASE:	*Waiting for his turn on the trapeze*, the crowd seemed to be engrossed by the acrobat.
CORRECTED:	The crowd seemed to be engrossed by the acrobat *waiting for his turn on the trapeze*.
MISPLACED ADJECTIVE CLAUSE:	I found the tickets after several months of searching *that my grandmother gave me*.
CORRECTED:	After several months of searching, I found the tickets *that my grandmother gave me*.

⏱ TIME SAVERS!

Answers on Transparency
Use the Grammar Exercises Answers on Transparencies for Chapter 21 to have students correct their own or one another's exercises.

On-Line Exercise Bank
Have students complete the exercises on computer. The Auto Check feature will grade their work for you.

✎ STANDARDIZED TEST PREPARATION WORKSHOP

Grammar and Usage Many standardized tests require students to recognize correct use of modifiers and punctuation within the context of a passage. Ask students if the sentence below is written and punctuated correctly. If not, which choice is the best way to write the sentence?

The girl was enchanted with the blue pony waiting in line for her ride on the merry-go-round.

A No change

B The girl was enchanted with the blue pony, waiting in line for her ride on the merry-go-round.

C Waiting in line for her ride on the merry-go-round, the girl was enchanted with the blue pony.

D Waiting in line for her ride on the merry-go-round, the blue pony was enchanted with the girl.

The correct answer is **C** because it eliminates the misplaced modifier and punctuates the sentence with a comma.

▶ **Exercise 37** **Correcting Misplaced Modifiers** Rewrite the following sentences to eliminate the misplaced modifiers. In each rewritten sentence, underline the modifier that was misplaced in the original. Then, draw an arrow pointing from the modifier to the word it modifies.

EXAMPLE: My brother Rikard bought a box of cereal at the local supermarket that had clown shapes in it.

ANSWER: At the local supermarket, my brother Rikard

bought a box of cereal <u>that had clown shapes in it.</u>

1. The multi-ring circus is an American development that accommodates thousands of spectators.
2. In 1869, a huge show was organized by William Cameron Coup that gave two performances at once.
3. Advertised as "The Greatest Circus," Coup formed a partnership with P. T. Barnum in 1871, and they opened a huge circus in Brooklyn, New York.
4. Ten years later, Barnum joined American showman James Anthony Bailey and two other businessmen, a tremendous promoter and organizer.
5. Their new circus was so large that it staged shows in three rings, in which Barnum and Bailey eventually became sole partners.
6. *Eisteddfod* is a national festival held every summer in Wales, which means "a sitting of learned men" in Welsh.
7. A week-long celebration, language, literature, and music are celebrated during Eisteddfod.
8. Now known as storytellers, the ceremony brings back the Welsh custom of bards and minstrels.
9. Candidates were once licensed at Eisteddfod for the position of bard.
10. After working hard, a prize should be awarded to the best storyteller or bard.

▶ **Critical Viewing** Jenny Lind, also known as the "Swedish Nightingale," toured under the management of famous circus owner P. T. Barnum. What modifiers would you expect people to use when describing her voice? [Infer]

Avoiding Sentence Problems • 463

Answer Key

▶ **Exercise 37**

1. The multi-ring circus <u>that accommodates thousands of spectators</u> is an American development. (arrow to *circus*)
2. In 1869 William Cameron Coup organized a huge show <u>that gave two performances at once</u>. (arrow to *show*)
3. Coup formed a partnership with P. T. Barnum in 1871, and they opened a huge circus in Brooklyn, New York, <u>advertised as "The Greatest Circus."</u> (arrow to *circus*)
4. Ten years later Barnum, <u>a tremendous promoter and organizer</u>, joined American showman James Anthony Bailey and two other businessmen. (arrow to *Barnum*)
5. Their new circus, in <u>which Barnum and Bailey eventually became sole partners</u>, was so large that it staged shows in three rings. (arrow to *circus*)
6. *Eisteddfod*, <u>which means "a sitting of learned men" in Welsh</u>, is a national festival held every summer in Wales. (arrow to *Eisteddfod*)
7. Language, literature, and music are celebrated during *Eisteddfod*, <u>a week-long celebration</u>. (arrow to *Eisteddfod*)
8. The ceremony brings back the Welsh custom of bards and minstrels, <u>now known as storytellers</u>. (arrow to *minstrels*)
9. Candidates were once licensed <u>for the position of bard</u> at *Eisteddfod*. (arrow to *licensed*)
10. A prize should be awarded to the best storyteller or bard <u>after working hard</u>. (arrow to *storyteller or bard*)

Critical Viewing

Infer Students may suggest modifiers such as <u>soaring to the rafters</u>, <u>transfixing her audience</u>, and so forth.

Step-by-Step Teaching Guide

Double Negatives

1. List negatives on the chalkboard: *no, not, never, none, no one, nobody, nothing.*

2. Ask students to make up sentences using two negatives, so the class can hear the errors. Have other students correct the sentences.

Customize for
ESL Students

Encourage students to look through their portfolios and circle negatives in sentences. If they find double negatives, they should correct them and say the new sentences aloud to hear that they make sense.

Solving Special Problems

Many mistakes in speaking and in writing involve words and expressions that are sometimes used in very informal conversation but are considered nonstandard for most writing and speaking. Other problems involve words that are easily confused because they are spelled almost alike. In the following sections, note those problems that occur in your speaking or writing.

Double Negatives

Negative words, such as *nothing* and *not,* are used to deny or to say *no.* At one time, it was customary to use two or more negative words in one clause to add emphasis. Today, only one negative word is used to give a sentence a negative meaning.

▶ **KEY CONCEPT** Do not write sentences with two negative words when only one is needed. ■

INCORRECT   My parents *never* take me *nowhere.*
CORRECT: My parents *never* take me *anywhere.*
             My parents take me *nowhere.*

The sentences on the left in the following chart contain double negatives. Notice on the right how each can be corrected in either of two ways. Usually, either negative word can be changed to a positive to correct the sentence.

Double Negatives	Corrected Sentences
Shelly did*n't* invite *nobody.*	Shelly did*n't* invite anybody. Shelly invited *nobody.*
I have*n't no* time now.	I have*n't* any time now. I have *no* time now.
She *never* told us *nothing* about her party.	She *never* told us anything about her party. She told us *nothing* about her party.

More Practice

Language Lab
CD-ROM
• Avoiding Double
  Negatives lesson
**On-Line
Exercise Bank**
• Section 21.4
**Grammar Exercise
Workbook**
• pp. 85–86

TIME SAVERS!

Answers on Transparency
Use the Grammar Exercises Answers on Transparencies for Chapter 21 to have students correct their own or one another's exercises.

On-Line Exercise Bank
Have students complete the exercises on computer. The Auto Check feature will grade their work for you.

▶ **Exercise 38** Correcting Double Negatives

The following sentences contain double negatives, which are underlined. Correct each sentence in *two* ways.

EXAMPLE: I <u>didn't</u> see <u>no</u> clowns.
ANSWER: I didn't see any clowns.
     I saw no clowns.

1. We <u>couldn't</u> go to <u>no</u> circus.
2. I <u>haven't no</u> money to buy tickets.
3. Father <u>wouldn't</u> let me bring <u>nobody</u>.
4. Stella <u>doesn't</u> like <u>no</u> lions.
5. The lion tamer <u>didn't</u> get scared by <u>no</u> lions.
6. The clowns <u>never</u> played with <u>no</u> lions.
7. We <u>never</u> get to see <u>nothing</u> like the circus.
8. When the clown opened the fake door, there <u>wasn't no one</u> there.
9. The trapeze artists <u>weren't</u> scared of <u>no</u> heights.
10. They <u>didn't</u> work with <u>no</u> net.

▶ **Exercise 39** Writing Negative Sentences Write ten negative sentences, following the instructions given below.

EXAMPLE: Use *ever* in a negative sentence about going up in a hot-air balloon.
ANSWER: My sister hasn't ever gone up in a hot-air balloon.

1. Use *nothing* in a sentence about the contents of a box.
2. Use *no one* in a sentence about the people who had seen a certain movie.
3. Use *anything* in a negative sentence about what your friend did wrong.
4. Use *anyone* in a negative sentence about whom you saw at the movies.
5. Use *none* in a sentence about cake left over after a birthday party.
6. Use *never* in a sentence about walking a tightrope.
7. Use *ever* in a negative sentence about seeing a comet.
8. Use *nobody* in a sentence about knowing a password.
9. Use *somebody* in a negative sentence about liking loud noises.
10. Use *everyone* in a negative sentence about voting.

▲ Critical Viewing
Write two negative sentences about something these trapeze artists should never do. [Draw Conclusions]

Avoiding Sentence Problems • 465

Answer Key

▶ Exercise 38

1. We could not go to the circus. We could go to no circus.
2. I have no money to buy tickets. I haven't any money to buy tickets.
3. Father let me bring nobody. Father wouldn't let me bring anybody.
4. Stella likes no lions. Stella doesn't like any lions.
5. The lion tamer got scared by no lions. The lion tamer didn't get scared by any lions.
6. The clowns played with no lions. The clowns never played with any lions.
7. We get to see nothing like the circus. We never get to see anything like the circus.
8. When the clown opened the fake door, there was no one there. When the clown opened the fake door, there wasn't anyone there.
9. The trapeze artists were scared of no heights. The trapeze artists weren't scared of any heights.
10. They worked with no net. They didn't work with a net.

▶ Exercise 39

Answers will vary. Samples are given.

1. There is nothing in the box.
2. The people who saw the movie saw no one they knew at the theater.
3. My friend didn't do anything right in her math homework.
4. I didn't see anyone I knew at the movies.
5. None of the birthday cake was left at the end of the party.
6. I would never want to walk on a tightrope.
7. I haven't ever seen a comet.
8. Nobody else knows my password.
9. Somebody on our street doesn't like loud noise.
10. Not everyone can vote.

Critical Viewing

Draw Conclusions Students might write sentences that include "should never look down," "should not lose their balance," and so forth.

If students miss more than two items in Exercises 38–39, refer them to the following for additional practice.

In the Textbook	Print	Technology
Section Review, Ex. 47, 49, p. 471	Grammar Exercise Workbook, pp. 85–86	Language Lab CD-ROM, Problems With Sentences; On-Line Exercise Bank, Section 21.4

Fifteen Common Usage Problems

Divide students into ten groups and assign each group one or two of these usage problems: 1, 2, 3, 6, 8, 9, 12, 13, 14, 15. Have the groups create memory aids for their problem(s), such as "I went to the library farther from my home so I could do further research." Have students share their memory aids with the class.

21.4

Fifteen Common Usage Problems

This section contains fifteen common usage problems in alphabetical order. Some of the problems are expressions that you should avoid in both your speaking and your writing. Others are words that are often confused because of similar spellings or meanings.

As you read through the list, note the problems that may have caused you difficulty in the past. Then, use the exercises for practice in recognizing and avoiding those problems.

Later, when you write and revise your compositions, this section can help you check your work. If you do not find the explanation of a problem in this section, check for it in the index at the back of the book.

(1) accept, except Do not confuse the spelling of these words. *Accept,* a verb, means "to take (what is offered)" or "to agree to." *Except,* a preposition, means "leaving out" or "other than."

VERB: She willingly *accepted* responsibility for the others.
PREPOSITION: Everyone *except* him will be at the party.

(2) advice, advise Do not confuse the spelling of these related words. *Advice,* a noun, means "an opinion." *Advise,* a verb, means "to give an opinion to."

NOUN: My mother gave me *advice* about how to answer the letter.
VERB: My mother *advised* me to accept the invitation to the dance.

(3) affect, effect *Affect,* almost always a verb, means "to influence" or "to bring about a change in." *Effect,* usually a noun, means "result."

VERB: The rainy weather *affected* the outdoor wedding.
NOUN: What *effect* does the Mardi Gras celebration have on the city of New Orleans?

(4) at Do not use *at* after *where.*

INCORRECT: Do you know *where* the circus is *at?*
CORRECT: Do you know *where* the circus is?

(5) because Do not use *because* after *the reason.* Eliminate one or the other.

INCORRECT: *The reason* I am late is *because* the bus broke down.
CORRECT: *The reason* I am late is *that* the bus broke down.

▶ **Exercise 40**

▶ **Exercise 40** Avoiding Usage Problems For each of the following sentences, choose the correct word or phrase from the choices in parentheses, and write it on your paper.

1. effect
2. advised
3. that
4. is
5. except

EXAMPLE: I can't (accept, except) these tickets to the circus.
ANSWER: accept

1. What (effect, affect) will clown college have on my future?
2. My father (advised, adviced) me that I should not be a clown.
3. The reason I want to be a clown is (because, that) it looks like fun.
4. I don't know where the clown college (is at, is).
5. Everyone (accept, except) me thinks clown college is a bad idea.

(6) beside, besides These two prepositions have different meanings and cannot be interchanged. *Beside* means "at the side of" or "close to." *Besides* means "in addition to."

EXAMPLES: The clown sat down *beside* the child.
No one *besides* us was there.

(7) different from, different than *Different from* is generally preferred over *different than.*

EXAMPLE: The clown's routine was *different from* what I had expected.

(8) farther, further *Farther* is usually used to refer to distance. *Further* means "additional" or "to a greater degree or extent."

EXAMPLES: Haven't we walked much *farther* than a mile?
I need *further* advice.
When he began raising his voice, I listened no *further.*

(9) in, into *In* refers to position. *Into* suggests motion.

POSITION: The ringmaster is *in* the big top.
MOTION: The ringmaster stepped *into* the center ring.

(10) kind of, sort of Do not use *kind of* or *sort of* to mean "rather" or "somewhat."

INCORRECT: The new CD that I brought home sounds *sort of* interesting.
CORRECT: The new CD that I brought home sounds *rather* interesting.

▶ **More Practice**

On-line
Exercise Bank
• Section 21.4

Avoiding Sentence Problems • **467**

🖊 **STANDARDIZED TEST PREPARATION WORKSHOP**

Grammar and Usage Standardized tests often ask students to identify misused words in sentences. Ask students which choice makes the following sentence correct.

No one except the lion tamer is allowed to go into the lions' cages.

A Change *except* to *accept.*
B Change *to* to *two.*
C Change *into* to *in.*
D No change is needed.

The correct choice is **D**. The sentence is correct as written.

⏱ **TIME SAVERS!**

🖨 **Answers on Transparency**
Use the Grammar Exercises Answers on Transparencies for Chapter 21 to have students correct their own or one another's exercises.

🖥 **On-Line Exercise Bank**
Have students complete the exercises on computer. The Auto Check feature will grade their work for you.

1. besides
2. different from
3. farther
4. into
5. rather

21.4

► **Exercise 41** Avoiding Usage Problems For each of the following sentences, choose the correct word or phrase from the choices in parentheses, and write it on your paper.
1. No one (beside, besides) the acrobat has the courage to go on the trapeze.
2. The circus is very (different from, different than) the opera.
3. There is no one who can tumble (farther, further) than Lucinda.
4. The lion tamer put his head (in, into) the lion's mouth.
5. A ringmaster is (kind of, rather) like an orchestra conductor.

(11) like *Like,* a preposition, means "similar to" or "in the same way as." It should be followed by an object. Do not use *like* before the subject and verb of a clause. Use *as* or *that* instead.

PREPOSITION: The rubbing alcohol felt *like* ice on my feverish skin.

INCORRECT: The stew that I ordered doesn't taste *like* it should.

CORRECT: The stew that I ordered doesn't taste *as* it should.

(12) that, which, who *That* can be used to refer to either things or people. *Which* should be used to refer only to things. *Who* should be used to refer only to people.

THINGS: The dress *that* I designed won first prize.
PEOPLE: The dancer *that* (or *who*) performed is my brother.

(13) their, there, they're Do not confuse the spelling of these three words. *Their,* a possessive adjective, always modifies a noun. *There* is usually used either as a sentence starter or as an adverb. *They're* is a contraction for *they are.*

POSSESSIVE
ADJECTIVE: The team won all of *their* games.

SENTENCE
STARTER: *There* are no easy answers to the problem of prejudice.

ADVERB: Move the chair over *there.*

CONTRACTION: *They're* trying to set new track records.

► **More Practice**

On-line
Exercise Bank
• Section 21.4

⏱ **TIME SAVERS!**

📠 **Answers on Transparency**
Use the Grammar Exercises Answers on Transparencies for Chapter 21 to have students correct their own or one another's exercises.

🖥 **On-Line Exercise Bank**
Have students complete the exercises on computer. The Auto Check feature will grade their work for you.

(14) to, too, two Do not confuse the spelling of these words. *To*, a preposition, begins a prepositional phrase or an infinitive. *Too*, with two *o*'s, is an adverb and modifies adjectives and other adverbs. *Two* is a number.

PREPOSITION:	*to* the store	*to* Maine
INFINITIVE:	*to* meet	*to* see
ADVERB:	*too* sad	*too* quickly
NUMBER:	*two* buttons	*two* apples

(15) when, where, why Do not use *when*, *where*, or *why* directly after a linking verb such as *is*. Reword the sentence.

INCORRECT:	In the evening *is when* I do my homework.
	The gym *is where* the acrobats practice.
	To see the circus *is why* we came to New York City.
CORRECT:	I do my homework in the evening.
	The acrobats practice in the gym.
	We came to New York City to see the circus.

> **Exercise 42** Proofreading to Correct Usage Problems
Rewrite the following sentences, correcting any usage problems.
1. The carnival is coming together like it should.
2. At the carnival is where there will be games.
3. It is almost to exciting at Mardi Gras.
4. Do you know all the people which are coming to the party?
5. They're will be a lot of delicious food at the carnival.

▼ Critical Viewing
How does a ride like this affect you? Respond using the word *effect* (not *affect*) correctly. **[Analyze]**

Avoiding Sentence Problems • **469**

Answer Key

> **Exercise 42**
1. The carnival is coming together as it should.
2. There will be games at the carnival. Or: At the carnival there will be games.
3. It is almost too exciting at Mardi Gras.
4. Do you know all the people who are coming to the party?
5. There will be a lot of delicious food at the carnival.

Critical Viewing

Analyze Students may suggest that the ride has a dizzying effect, a nauseating effect, a frightening effect, and so forth.

✓ **ONGOING ASSESSMENT: Assess Mastery**	
Use the following resources to assess student mastery of effective sentences.	
In the Textbook	**Technology**
Chapter Review, Ex. 53–60, pp. 472–473 Standardized Test Preparation Workshop, pp. 474–475	On-Line Exercise Bank, Section 21.4

ASSESS and CLOSE

Section Review

Each of these exercises correlates to the instruction on sentence problems, pages 454–469. These exercises may be used for more practice, for reteaching, or for review of the key concepts presented. Answers for all chapter exercises are available in *Grammar Exercises Answers on Transparencies* in your Teaching Resources.

Answer Key

▶ **Exercise 43**

Answers will vary. Samples are given.

1. They brought the animals into the big top.
2. Before the show started, I got a bag of peanuts.
3. Feeling excited, I ate them in a minute.
4. When the lion roared, my dad jumped.
5. The tightrope walker was in the air.
6. Staring at the fire-eater, I became hungry.
7. Following the bareback rider, an elephant danced.
8. Although there was a net, the trapeze act looked scary to me.
9. The elephants, which were the most fascinating, walked with slow dignity.
10. They must have been so tired!

▶ **Exercise 44**

1. affect
2. Their
3. different from
4. who
5. that
6. except
7. advised
8. that
9. is
10. into

▶ **Exercise 45**

Answers will vary. Samples are given.

1. After George Washington attended a Ricketts circus, he sold the company a horse.
2. The Ricketts circus, which changed its name several times, existed through the early nineteenth century.
3. As the circus evolved throughout the nineteenth century, the programs became more elaborate.

▶ **Exercise 43** Writing Sentences From Fragments Use each of the following fragments in a sentence.

1. Into the big top.
2. Before the show started.
3. Feeling excited.
4. When the lion roared.
5. In the air.
6. Staring at the fire-eater.
7. Following the bareback rider.
8. Although there was a net.
9. Which were the most fascinating.
10. Have been so tired!

▶ **Exercise 44** Avoiding Usage Problems For each of the following sentences, choose the correct word or phrase in parentheses, and write it on your paper.

1. The rainy weather will (effect, affect) the barbecue.
2. (Their, There, They're) picnic will be ruined.
3. This picnic will be a lot (different from, different than) last year's.
4. The man (which, who) runs the barbecue will be late.
5. The reason he is late is (because, that) he has a flat tire.
6. No one showed up on time for the dress rehearsal (accept, except) the trapeze artist.
7. The ringmaster (advised, adviced) the other performers that attendance at rehearsals was important.
8. The reason the lion tamer was late was (because, that) he tripped on a chair.
9. "Do you know where the first aid kit (is at, is)?" he asked.
10. "I put it (in, into) the box in the cupboard," said the ringmaster.

▶ **Exercise 45** Revising to Eliminate Run-Ons Correct the following run-ons, using any of the three methods described in this section.

1. George Washington attended a Ricketts circus, he sold the company a horse.
2. The Ricketts circus existed through the early nineteenth century, it changed its name several times.
3. The circus evolved throughout the nineteenth century the programs became more elaborate.
4. Horse tricks dominated circuses at first, clowning, acrobats, juggling, and the like were soon introduced.
5. Tents were not used until the 1820's, the flying trapeze was not invented until 1859.

▶ **Exercise 46** Revising to Eliminate Misplaced Modifiers Rewrite the following sentences to eliminate misplaced modifiers.

1. Although usually used as pack animals, circuses often feature camels or dromedaries.
2. Having only one hump, the characteristics of dromedaries are that they are intelligent and easy to train.
3. Making them more gentle, some trainers bottle-feed baby dromedaries.
4. Dromedaries are rewarded with carrots learning to respond to commands.
5. So that its mouth doesn't get irritated, the bit in the bridle must be put in upside down in the dromedary.

---

4. Horse tricks dominated circuses at first; clowning, acrobats, juggling, and the like were soon introduced.
5. Tents were not used until the 1820's. The flying trapeze was not invented until 1859.

▶ **Exercise 46**

1. Circuses often feature camels or dromedaries, usually used as pack animals.
2. The characteristics of dromedaries, which have only one hump, are that they are intelligent and easy to train.

3. Some trainers bottle-feed baby dromedaries, making them more gentle.
4. Learning to respond to commands, dromedaries are rewarded with carrots.
5. The bit in the bridle must be put in upside down in the dromedary so that its mouth doesn't get irritated.

Exercise 47 Revising to Eliminate Double Negatives The following sentences contain double negatives, which are underlined. Correct each sentence in two ways.

1. We <u>won't</u> be going to <u>no</u> carnival.
2. My sister <u>doesn't</u> have <u>no</u> time to take us.
3. I <u>never</u> played <u>none</u> of the games at the carnival.
4. I <u>can't</u> get <u>nobody</u> to take me.
5. My friend <u>won't</u> tell me <u>nothing</u> about the fun he has.
6. The lion tamer <u>won't</u> let <u>none</u> of the audience see his fear.
7. I have <u>never</u> seen <u>no</u> courage like that.
8. We have <u>never</u> seen <u>nobody</u> tame lions.
9. I <u>don't</u> think I can learn to do <u>nothing</u> like that.
10. The lion tamer <u>hardly</u> spent <u>no</u> time training the animals.

Exercise 48 Revising a Passage to Eliminate Run-ons Rewrite the following paragraph to eliminate the run-on sentences. Use end marks, commas and coordinating conjunctions, and semicolons.

Many circuses feature trained animals they play an important part in the circus. Clowns in funny clothes provide the comedy for the show the circus band adds to the excitement. A colorful parade begins the show animals and circus performers march around the arena the circus band plays music.

Exercise 49 Revising a Passage to Eliminate Sentence Errors Rewrite the following paragraph to correct sentence fragments, run-ons, misplaced modifiers, double negatives, and usage problems.

In the mid-nineteenth century, the arrival of the circus was a huge event in a small town. Many people lived on farms. Isolated from neighbors with few entertainments. There wasn't no television or movies, or even radio. The circus brought drama and mystery, for example it often featured sword swallowers. Also wild animals such as lions and tigers. Posters advertised the arrival of the circus, people lined the streets to watch the animals and performers parade through town. Local townspeople, serving like circus staff, helped set up the tent. Sideshows entertained people before the show started with unusual sights. Such as a sheep with three heads. No one had never seen such things on the farm.

Exercise 50 Find It in Your Reading Read the following excerpt from Rachel Field's "Parade," and explain why her use of the word *like* instead of *as* is correct.

. . . There will be floats / in shapes like dragons, thrones and boats. . . .

Exercise 51 Find It in Your Writing Choose a piece of writing from your portfolio. Find and correct two examples of run-on sentences, using end marks or commas and coordinating conjunctions. If you are unable to find run-on sentences, challenge yourself to add a sentence that uses a comma and a coordinating conjunction to combine two independent clauses into a compound sentence.

Exercise 52 Writing Application Write a brief narrative about a performance you once gave. (It can be imaginary or real.) In addition to including information about the place and the audience, relate the events as they occurred. Avoid fragments and run-ons in your writing, and include the words *effect*, *they're*, and *further* in your narrative.

Section Review • 471

Exercise 47
1. We will be going to no carnival. We won't be going to any carnival.
2. My sister has no time to take us. My sister doesn't have any time to take us.
3. I played none of the games at the carnival. I never played any of the games at the carnival.
4. I can get nobody to take me. I can't get anybody to take me.
5. My friend will tell me nothing about the fun he has. My friend won't tell me anything about the fun he has.
6. The lion tamer will let none of the audience see his fear. The lion tamer won't let any of the audience see his fear.
7. I have seen no courage like that. I have never seen courage like that.
8. We have seen nobody tame lions. We have never seen anybody tame lions.
9. I think I can learn to do nothing like that. I don't think I can learn to do anything like that.
10. The lion tamer spent no time training the animals. The lion tamer hardly spent any time training the animals.

Exercise 48
Many circuses feature trained animals that play an important part in the circus. Clowns in funny clothes provide the comedy for the show, and the circus band adds to the excitement. A colorful parade begins the show. Animals and circus performers march around the arena while the circus band plays music.

Exercise 49
In the mid-nineteenth century, the arrival of the circus was a huge event in a small town. Isolated from neighbors, and with few entertainments, many people lived on farms. There wasn't any television, movies, or even radio. The circus brought drama and mystery; it often featured sword swallowers and wild animals such as lions and tigers. Posters advertised the arrival of the circus. People lined the streets to watch the animals and performers parade through town. Serving like circus staff, local townspeople helped set up the tent. Sideshows with unusual sights such as a sheep with

continued

Answer Key continued

three heads entertained people before the show started. No one had ever seen such things on the farm.

Exercise 50

Find It in Your Reading
Like is a preposition that means "similar to" or "in the same way as," and should be followed by an object (as it is in this example). *As* should be used before the subject and verb of a clause.

Exercise 51

Find It in Your Writing
Have students explain to partners the reasons for their corrections.

Exercise 52

Writing Application
Ask students to read their narratives aloud to the class.

Each of these exercises correlates to the instruction on effective sentences, pages 438–471. These exercises may be used for more practice, for reteaching, or for review of the key concepts presented. Answers for all exercises are available in *Grammar Exercises Answers on Transparencies* in your Teaching Resources.

Answer Key

Exercise 53

1. interrogative ?
2. imperative .
3. declarative .
4. exclamatory !
5. declarative .
6. interrogative ?
7. imperative .
8. declarative .
9. interrogative ?
10. exclamatory !

Exercise 54

1. A clown is a performer who plays the fool and also performs practical jokes.
2. Because clowns do tricks to make people laugh, they are also called buffoons, jesters, fools, and harlequins.
3. Although we often think all clowns are alike, each clown develops a unique face or performance personality.
4. It takes years for a clown to establish a face; it eventually becomes the clown's unique personal property.
5. Clowning techniques are taught in specialized clown schools, and the most famous clown school is in Florida.

Exercise 55

Answers will vary. Samples are given.

1. Annually, Canadians celebrate Canada Day on July 1.
2. With parades and fireworks, the country marks the anniversary of the unification of Upper and Lower Canada.
3. Created through passage of the British North American Act, the union took place on July 1, 1867.
4. Formerly, the celebration was known as Dominion Day.
5. For its display of patriotism, Canada Day is quite similar to America's Independence Day.

Chapter 21 Chapter Review

GRAMMAR EXERCISES 53–61

Exercise 53 Identifying Types of Sentences Identify each sentence below as *declarative, interrogative, imperative,* or *exclamatory.* Then, write the end mark for each sentence.

1. Will you take me to the circus
2. Ask Nancy whether she wants to go, too
3. Nancy can go if she saves her allowance
4. What fun it will be
5. The circus will be in town for a month
6. May I have cotton candy and peanuts
7. Tell the clown he is funny
8. The ringmaster is a busy man
9. Do the elephants sleep in the big top
10. Wow—I can't wait to go

Exercise 54 Combining Sentences Combine the following sentences, using the construction given in parentheses.

1. A clown is a performer who plays the fool. He also performs practical jokes. (compound verb)
2. Clowns do tricks to make people laugh. They are also called buffoons, jesters, fools, and harlequins. (subordinate conjunction *because*)
3. We often think all clowns are alike. Each clown develops a unique face, or performance personality. (subordinate conjunction *although*)
4. It takes years for a clown to establish a face. It eventually becomes the clown's unique personal property. (semicolon)
5. Clowning techniques are taught in specialized clown schools. The most famous clown school is in Florida. (comma and conjunction *and*)

Exercise 55 Varying Sentence Beginnings Reorder the words in the following sentences according to the instructions in parentheses.

1. (Start with an adverb.) Canadians celebrate Canada Day annually on July 1.
2. (Start with a prepositional phrase.) The country marks with parades and fireworks the anniversary of the unification of Upper and Lower Canada.
3. (Start with a participle.) The union, created through passage of the British North American Act, took place on July 1, 1867.
4. (Start with an adverb.) The celebration was formerly known as Dominion Day.
5. (Start with a prepositional phrase.) Canada Day, for its display of patriotism, is quite similar to America's Independence Day.

Exercise 56 Writing Sentences From Fragments Use each of the following fragments in a sentence.

1. On the Ferris wheel.
2. Above the carnival.
3. Eating cotton candy.
4. Spending money on the games.
5. That I won at the carnival.

Exercise 57 Revising to Eliminate Run-ons Rewrite the following sentences to eliminate run-ons, using any of the three methods described in Section 21.4.

1. The Circus Maximus was an arena of ancient Rome it was located between the Palatine and Aventine hills.
2. It was the main amusement place of the city from 600 B.C. to the early days of the Roman Empire, it was enlarged by Julius Caesar.

Exercise 56

Answers will vary. Samples are given.

1. I rode on the Ferris wheel.
2. We looked out above the carnival.
3. I like eating cotton candy.
4. Spending money on the games was fun.
5. I love the toy that I won at the carnival.

Exercise 57

Answers will vary. Samples are given.

1. Located between the Palatine and Aventine hills, the Circus Maximus was an arena of ancient Rome.
2. It was the main amusement place of the city from 600 B.C. to the early days of the Roman Empire, and it was enlarged by Julius Caesar.
3. The Circus Maximus had three tiers of seats and room for almost 200,000 spectators.
4. An adaptation of the Greek hippodrome, it was the scene of athletic contests and chariot races.
5. In the center was a low wall that ran lengthwise. Riders or charioteers rode around it.

3. The Circus Maximus had three tiers of seats it had room for almost 200,000 spectators.
4. It was the scene of athletic contests and chariot races, it was an adaptation of the Greek hippodrome.
5. In the center was a low wall that ran lengthwise, riders or charioteers rode around it.

Exercise 58 Revising to Eliminate Errors

Rewrite the following sentences to eliminate the misplaced modifiers and double negatives.

1. Balancing on the wire, the audience gasped at the tightrope walker.
2. The ringmaster shouted at the elephants and jugglers above the din.
3. The juggler won't drop none of his pins.
4. I have never seen no pins like that.
5. We have never seen nobody juggle like that!
6. We finally went to the circus that was advertised on the radio with the terrific clowns.
7. The man on the flying trapeze reached for the second swing with a free hand.
8. Circling the ring, we were excited to watch the tigers.
9. I don't think I can learn to do nothing like that.
10. I don't have no time to learn.

Exercise 59 Writing Sentences Using Difficult Words Correctly

Write a sentence illustrating the correct usage of each word listed below.

1. effect, affect
2. advise, advice
3. because, that
4. farther, further
5. accept, except
6. to, two, too
7. that, which, who
8. they're, their, there
9. like
10. in, into

Exercise 60 Revision Practice: Writing Effective Sentences

Rewrite the following paragraphs to make the entire piece more effective. Vary the openers and the structures of sentences, vary sentence lengths, and correct fragments, run-ons, and other problems in word usage.

The first modern circus performance. It occurred in 1768 in London, England. It consisted of trick horseback riding by Philip Astley. He was a former cavalry officer he later took his circus to Paris and other cities. The circus came to America in George Washington's time, introduced in the United States by an English rider, John Ricketts. He opened a show in Philadelphia in 1793. The circus gradually evolved. It evolved throughout the nineteenth century. In the beginning, horse shows and riding. They dominated circuses. Juggling, acrobatic and trapeze acts, and wild animal shows were gradually added, sideshows and parades did not appear until the end of the century.

Exercise 61 Writing Application

Write a brief persuasive essay to convince your readers to watch your favorite show or a special performance. In addition to including good reasons, use effective sentences to hold your reader's attention. Use a variety of sentence openers and structures, and vary the length of your sentences.

Exercise 58

1. The audience gasped at the tightrope walker balancing on the wire.
2. The ringmaster shouted above the din at the elephants and jugglers.
3. The juggler will drop none of his pins.
4. I have never seen any pins like that.
5. We have never seen anybody juggle like that!
6. We finally went to the circus with the terrific clowns that was advertised on the radio.
7. The man on the flying trapeze reached with a free hand for the second swing.
8. We were excited to watch the tigers circling the ring.
9. I don't think I can learn to do anything like that.
10. I don't have any time to learn.

Exercise 59

Answers will vary. Allow students who have difficulty creating sentences to consult the Usage Problems instruction, pages 466–469.

Exercise 60

Answers will vary. Samples are given.

The first modern circus performance occurred in 1768 in London, England. It consisted of trick horseback riding by Philip Astley, a former cavalry officer, who later took his circus to Paris and other cities.

Introduced in the United States by an English rider, John Ricketts, the circus came to America in George Washington's time. Ricketts opened a show in Philadelphia in 1793. The circus gradually evolved throughout the nineteenth century. In the beginning, horse shows and riding dominated circuses. While juggling, acrobatic and trapeze acts, and wild animal shows were gradually added, sideshows and parades did not appear until the end of the century.

Exercise 61

Writing Application
Ask students to share their essays in small groups. The listeners can tell if they were persuaded, and why.

Step-by-Step Teaching Guide

Recognizing Appropriate Sentence Construction

1. Review with students the types of errors that they will encounter.

2. As students read each passage, encourage them to revise and edit, as well as to highlight any errors that will help them choose the correct answer.

Standardized Test Preparation Workshop

Recognizing Appropriate Sentence Construction

Standardized tests often evaluate your ability to recognize effective sentences. Sometimes, these items require you to identify a problem and choose the best way to rewrite to eliminate the problem. First, read the passage. Some sections are underlined. The underlined sections may be one of the following:

- incomplete sentences

- run-ons

- correctly written sentences that should be combined

- correctly written sentences that do not need to be rewritten

Test Tip

First, try reading each answer silently to yourself. Although some answers may seem correct at first glance, review them carefully. Make sure your choice does not change the original meaning of the sentence.

Sample Test Item	Answer and Explanation
Directions: Choose the best way to write the underlined section, and mark the letter for your answer. If the underlined section needs no change, mark "Correct as is." Connie made a silly face. It was by sticking her tongue out.	
1 A Connie made a silly face with her tongue out. **B** Connie made a silly face by sticking her tongue out. **C** Connie made a silly face, it was by sticking out her tongue. **D** Correct as is	The correct answer is *B*. Choice *B* correctly combines the important elements of both sentences to form one complete sentence.

 TEST-TAKING TIP

Tell students that after reading the passage, they should carefully read the choices to eliminate any incorrect ones. This will help them make their final choices. For example, in the sample text item, students can eliminate item C because it has inappropriate sentence construction.

Answer Key

▶ **Practice 1**

1. B
2. G
3. A

▶ **Practice 2**

1. B
2. G
3. C

▶ **Practice 1** **Directions:** Choose the best way to write each underlined section, and mark the letter for your answer. If the underlined section needs no changes, mark "Correct as is."

The parade lasted all morning, the band
(1)
went on. The floats were colorful and
          (2)
the floats were imaginative. The band
                                  (3)
played marching music, the music was by

John Philip Sousa.

1 A The parade lasted all morning it went on.

   B The parade lasted all morning and then the band went on.

   C The parade lasted all morning.

   D Correct as is

2 F The floats were colorful, imaginative floats.

   G The floats were imaginative and colorful.

   H The floats were colorful, and the floats were imaginative.

   J Correct as is

3 A The band played marching music by John Philip Sousa.

   B The band played John Philip Sousa's marching music.

   C The band played music, the marching was by John Philip Sousa.

   D Correct as is

▶ **Practice 2** **Directions:** Choose the best way to write each underlined section, and mark the letter for your answer. If the underlined section needs no changes, mark "Correct as is."

We went to the street fair that took
(1)
place after the parade was over then.

The handicrafts sold there were from
(2)
everywhere all over the world.

My favorite was a marionette, the
(3)
marionette was from Thailand.

1 A We went to the street fair which was after the parade was over then.

   B After the parade was over we went to the street fair.

   C Then, we went to the street fair that took place after the parade was over then.

   D Correct as is

2 F The handicrafts sold there were from everywhere all over.

   G The handicrafts sold there were from all over the world.

   H Everywhere, the handicrafts sold were from all over the world.

   J Correct as is

3 A My favorite was a marionette, and it was from Thailand.

   B My favorite was a Thailand marionette.

   C My favorite was a marionette from Thailand.

   D Correct as is

Answer Key

> **Exercise A**

1. Does <u>Matt</u> or <u>Jeremy</u> <u>enjoy</u> figure (skating) or speed (skating)? (direct object; interrogative)
2. <u>Speed skating</u> <u>is</u> good (exercise). (predicate nominative, declarative)
3. There <u>are</u> <u>races</u> against the clock and against other skaters. (declarative)
4. <u>Speed skaters</u> <u>use</u> (skates) with long straight edges. (direct object; declarative)
5. Wow! The <u>blades</u> <u>are</u> so (long) and <u>look</u> so (sharp)! (predicate adjectives, exclamatory)
6. (You) <u>Try</u> that (pair) of skates. (direct object, imperative)
7. <u>I</u> <u>gave</u> (Danielle) figure skating (lessons). (indirect object, direct object, declarative)
8. <u>She</u> and <u>Hannah</u> <u>were</u> (eager) and (attentive). (predicate adjectives, declarative)
9. <u>We</u> <u>practiced</u> (cross-overs) and snowplow (stops). (direct objects, declarative)
10. <u>Can</u> <u>you</u> <u>do</u> any (jumps)? (direct object, interrogative)

> **Exercise B**

1. <u>Ice hocky</u> <u>is</u> a winter (sport) and a rough (game).
2. Hockey-playing <u>countries</u> <u>include</u> Russia, where it is a big sport, and Canada.
3. <u>Defense</u> and <u>offense</u> <u>are</u> important (parts) of the game.
4. The <u>players</u> <u>use</u> hockey (sticks) and <u>wear</u> protective (pads).
5. <u>Goaltenders</u> <u>wear</u> face (masks) and other protective (equipment).
6. Two <u>areas</u> on the ice <u>are</u> the (neutral zone) and the (attacking zone).
7. <u>Substitution</u> of players <u>is</u> (frequent) and <u>occurs</u> during the game.
8. Hockey skate <u>blades</u> <u>are</u> (thin) and (short).
9. <u>Teams</u> <u>pass</u> the (puck) and <u>shoot</u> (it) with their sticks.
10. Ancient <u>Egyptians</u> and <u>Persians</u> <u>played</u> (games) similar to hockey.

Cumulative Review

PHRASES, CLAUSES, AND SENTENCES

> **Exercise A** Recognizing Basic
Sentence Parts Copy the following sentences, underlining each simple subject once and each simple predicate twice. Circle the complements and label each one *direct object*, *indirect object*, *predicate nominative*, or *predicate adjective*. Then, identify each sentence as *declarative*, *imperative*, *interrogative*, or *exclamatory*.

1. Does Matt or Jeremy enjoy figure skating or speed skating?
2. Speed skating is good exercise.
3. There are races against the clock and against other skaters.
4. Speed skaters use skates with long straight edges.
5. Wow! The blades are so long and look so sharp!
6. Try that pair of skates.
7. I gave Danielle figure skating lessons.
8. She and Hannah were eager and attentive.
9. We practiced cross-overs and snow-plow stops.
10. Can you do any jumps?

> **Exercise B** Using Basic Sentence
Parts Rewrite the following sentences according to the directions in parentheses. In your new sentences, underline each simple subject once and each simple predicate twice. Circle each complement.

1. Ice hockey is a winter sport. It is a rough game. (Combine by creating a compound predicate nominative.)
2. Hockey-playing countries include Canada. Hockey is a big sport in Russia. (Combine by creating a compound direct object.)
3. Defense is an important part of the game, and so is offense. (Rewrite by creating a compound subject.)

4. The players use hockey sticks. They wear protective pads. (Rewrite by creating a compound predicate.)
5. Goaltenders wear face masks. They wear other protective equipment. (Combine by creating a compound direct object.)
6. One area on the ice is the neutral zone. Another is the attacking zone. (Combine by creating a compound predicate nominative.)
7. Substitution of players is frequent. It occurs during the game. (Combine by creating a compound predicate.)
8. Hockey skate blades are thin. They are also short. (Combine by creating a compound predicate adjective.)
9. Teams pass the puck, shooting it with their sticks. (Rewrite by creating a compound predicate.)
10. Ancient Egyptians played games similar to hockey, and so did the Persians. (Rewrite by creating a compound subject.)

> **Exercise C** Identifying Phrases and
Clauses Label each phrase in the following sentences an *adjective prepositional phrase*, an *adverb prepositional phrase*, or an *appositive phrase*. Identify and label each clause.

1. Skiing is a popular winter sport in many countries.
2. Boots, flexible or rigid, are important pieces of equipment.
3. Ski poles that vary in length are used for balance.
4. There are three kinds of skiing that have been developed.
5. One type, Alpine skiing, involves racing down steep, snow-covered slopes.
6. Skiers descend in the fastest time possible.

> **Exercise C**

1. in many countries—adverb phrase; whole sentence is an independent clause
2. flexible or rigid—appositive phrase; whole sentence is an independent clause
3. in length—adverb phrase; for balance—adverb phrase; that vary in length—subordinate clause; Ski poles . . . are used for balance—independent clause
4. of skiing—adjective phrase; that have been developed—subordinate clause; There are three kinds of skiing—independent clause

5. Alpine skiing—appositive phrase; down steep, snow-covered slopes—adverb phrase; whole sentence is an independent clause
6. in the fastest time possible—adverb phrase; whole sentence is an independent clause
7. by a series—adverb phrase; of gates—adjective phrase; of poles and flag markers—adverb phrase; which are made of poles and flag markers—subordinate clause; A course is defined by a series of gates—independent clause

7. A course is defined by a series of gates, which are made of poles and flag markers.
8. The racer passes through these gates.
9. This downhill racing includes the slalom, in which the course is made of many turns.
10. The super giant slalom, a combination of downhill and slalom, is decided after one run.

Exercise D Using Phrases and Clauses Rewrite the following sentences according to the instructions in parentheses.

1. Cross-country skiing is called Nordic skiing and is practiced in many parts of the world. (Rewrite by creating an appositive phrase.)
2. It is performed on longer courses. These courses are also flatter than downhill courses. (Combine by creating a clause.)
3. Nordic skiing emphasizes two things. Those are endurance and strength. (Combine by creating a clause.)
4. A side-to-side motion is the way cross-country skiers move. (Rewrite by creating an adverb prepositional phrase.)
5. Cross-country skiing developed to fill a need. That need was for transportation. (Combine by creating an adjective prepositional phrase.)

Exercise E Revising Sentences to Eliminate Errors and Create Variety Rewrite the following sentences according to the instructions in parentheses.

1. Bobsledding was first developed in Saint Moritz, Switzerland, the first competition was held there. (Correct the run-on sentence.)
2. Teams of two or four people descend an icy run in bobsledding. (Vary the sentence by beginning with a prepositional phrase.)
3. The part of a bobsled run most critical is its start. (Correct the misplaced modifier.)

4. The captain occupies the front position in the sled. This person is also called the driver. (Combine the sentences by creating a phrase.)
5. The crew members lean backward and forward in unison and accelerate the speed of the sled. (Vary the sentence by beginning with a participial phrase.)
6. Bobsledding is different than the luge. (Correct the common usage problem.)
7. Lie on their backs with their feet at the front of the luge sled. (Correct the sentence fragment.)
8. Luge courses aren't constructed for nothing other than this sport. (Correct the double negative.)
9. These courses feature turns. Courses also feature straight stretches. (Combine by creating a compound direct object.)
10. The reason it looks dangerous is because luges travel at high speeds. (Correct the common usage problem.)

Exercise F Revision Practice: Sentence Combining Rewrite the following passage, combining sentences where appropriate.

Most children are delighted when it snows. They wake up early. They listen for school cancellations on the radio. If school is cancelled, the children are excited. The parents say "Oh, no!" It means the schedule is off. The day has to be rearranged. They get out the boots and warm clothes. They get out the sleds. An unexpected vacation day.

Exercise G Writing Application
Write a description of a winter activity that you enjoy. Vary the lengths and beginnings of your sentences. Underline each simple subject once and each simple verb twice. Then, circle at least three phrases and three clauses. Avoid fragments, run-ons, double negatives, misplaced modifiers, and common usage problems.

8. through these gates—adverb phrase; whole sentence is an independent clause
9. of many turns—adverb phrase; in which the course is made of many turns—subordinate clause; This downhill racing includes the slalom—independent clause
10. a combination of downhill and slalom—appositive phrase; of downhill and slalom—adjective phrase; after one run—adverb phrase; The super giant slalom . . . is decided after one run—independent clause

Exercise D

1. Nordic skiing, cross-country skiing, is practiced in many parts of the world.
2. It is performed on courses which are longer and flatter than downhill courses.
3. Nordic skiing emphasizes two things, which are endurance and strength.
4. Cross-country skiers move in a side-to-side motion.
5. Cross-country skiing developed to fill a need for transportation.

Exercise E

1. Bobsledding was first developed in Saint Moritz, Switzerland, where the first competition was held.
2. In bobsledding, teams of two or four people descend an icy run.
3. The most critical part of a bobsled run is its start.
4. The captain, also called the driver, occupies the front position in the sled.
5. Accelerating the speed of the sled, the crew members lean backward and forward in unison.
6. Bobsledding is different from the luge.
7. Luge competitors lie on their backs with their feet at the front of the luge sled.
8. Luge courses aren't constructed for anything other than this sport.
9. These courses feature turns and straight stretches.
10. The reason it looks dangerous is that luges travel at high speeds.

continued

Answer Key continued

Exercise F

Most children are delighted when it snows. They wake up early to listen for school cancellations on the radio. If school is cancelled, the children are excited, but the parents say, "Oh, no!" It means the schedule is off and the day has to be rearranged. They get out the boots, warm clothes, and sleds for an unexpected vacation day.

Exercise G

Descriptions will vary.

In-Depth Lesson Plan

	LESSON FOCUS	PRINT AND MEDIA RESOURCES
DAY 1	**Four Principal Parts of Verbs** Students learn and apply concepts about the four principal parts of verbs (pp. 480–487).	**Teaching Resources** *Grammar Exercise Workbook*, pp. 87–94; *Grammar Exercises Answers on Transparencies*, Ch. 22 *Language Lab* **CD-ROM**, Using Verbs; **On-Line Exercise Bank**, Section 22.1
DAY 2	**Verb Tenses** Students learn and apply concepts about verb tenses (pp. 488–493).	**Teaching Resources** *Grammar Exercise Workbook*, pp. 95–100; *Grammar Exercises Answers on Transparencies*, Ch. 22 *Language Lab* **CD-ROM**, Using Verbs; **On-Line Exercise Bank**, Section 22.2
DAY 3	**Troublesome Verbs** Students learn and apply concepts about troublesome verbs and do the Hands-on Grammar activity (pp. 494–501).	**Teaching Resources** *Grammar Exercise Workbook*, pp. 101–106; *Grammar Exercises Answers on Transparencies*, Ch. 22; *Hands-on Grammar Activity Book*, Ch. 22 *Language Lab* **CD-ROM**, Using Verbs; **On-Line Exercise Bank**, Section 22.3
DAY 4	**Review and Assess** Students review chapter and demonstrate mastery of use of verbs (pp. 502–505).	**Teaching Resources** *Formal Assessment*, Ch. 22; *Grammar Exercises Answers on Transparencies*, Ch. 22 **On-Line Exercise Bank**, Sections 22.1–3

Accelerated Lesson Plan

	LESSON FOCUS	PRINT AND MEDIA RESOURCES
DAY 1	**Four Principal Verb Parts and Verb Tenses** Students cover concepts and usage of verbs as determined by Diagnostic Test (pp. 480–493).	**Teaching Resources** *Grammar Exercise Workbook*, pp. 87–100; *Grammar Exercises Answers on Transparencies*, Ch. 22 *Language Lab* **CD-ROM**, Using Verbs; **On-Line Exercise Bank**, Sections 22.1–2
DAY 2	**Troublesome Verbs** Students cover concepts and usage of troublesome verbs as determined by Diagnostic Test (pp. 494–501).	**Teaching Resources** *Grammar Exercise Workbook*, pp. 101–106; *Grammar Exercises Answers on Transparencies*, Ch. 22; *Hands-on Grammar Activity Book*, Chapter 22 *Language Lab* **CD-ROM**, Using Verbs; **On-Line Exercise Bank**, Section 22.3
DAY 3	**Review and Assess** Students review chapter and demonstrate mastery of use of verbs (pp. 502–505).	**Teaching Resources** *Formal Assessment*, Ch. 22; *Grammar Exercises Answers on Transparencies*, Ch. 22 **On-Line Exercise Bank**, Sections 22.1–3

Options for Adapting Lesson Plans

HOMEWORK

Have students complete any section of the chapter for homework.

FEATURES

Extend coverage with the Grammar in Literature feature (pp. 482, 492), and the Standardized Test Preparation Workshop (p. 504).

TECHNOLOGY

Students can use the On-Line Exercise Bank to complete the exercises on computer. The Auto Check feature will grade their work.

INTEGRATED SKILLS COVERAGE

Grammar in Literature SE pp. 482, 492

Reading
Find It in Your Reading SE pp. 487, 493, 496, 500, 501

Writing
Find It in Your Writing SE pp. 487, 493, 500, 501
Writing Application SE pp. 487, 493, 501, 503

Spelling
SE p. 483, ATE p. 497

Viewing and Representing
Critical Viewing SE pp. 478, 480, 485, 486, 489, 490, 491, 492, 495, 497, 499

ASSESSMENT SUPPORT

Standardized Test Preparation Workshop SE p. 504; ATE p. 490
Standardized Test Preparation Workbook, pp. 43–44
Formal Assessment, Ch. 22

MEETING INDIVIDUAL NEEDS

Less Advanced Students ATE pp. 480, 494; see also Ongoing Assessments ATE pp. 484, 491, 498
ESL Students ATE pp. 485, 488, 496, 498
Verbal/Linguistic Learners ATE p. 481

BLOCK SCHEDULING

Pacing Suggestions
For 90-minute Blocks
- Administer the Diagnostic Test to students to determine instructional coverage.
- Have students complete the necessary exercises in class. Use the Hands-on Grammar activity to provide a change of pace.

Resources for Varying Instruction
- *Language Lab* **CD-ROM** If your students have access to hardware, a 90-minute block provides an ideal opportunity for students to work on computer.

Professional Development Support
- *How to Manage Instruction in the Block* This teaching Resource provides management and activity suggestions.

MEDIA AND TECHNOLOGY

For the Student
- *Language Lab* **CD-ROM,** Using Verbs
- *On-Line Exercise Bank,* Ch. 22

For the Teacher
- *Resource Pro* **CD-ROM**

WRITING AND GRAMMAR WEB SITE

The Interactive Writing and Grammar Web site provides a wide array of support for students, teachers, and parents. Grammar support includes:

- On-Line Exercise Bank with Auto Check scoring
- Diagnostic and assessment support

www.phschool.com

LITERATURE CONNECTIONS

Grammar in Literature selections from *Prentice Hall Literature: Timeless Voices, Timeless Themes,* Copper:
from "Overdoing It," Anton Chekhov, SE p. 482
from "Count That Day Lost," George Eliot, SE p. 492

Lesson Objectives

1. To identify the four principal parts of a verb.
2. To know how to form the past and past participle of regular verbs.
3. To know how to form the past and past participle of irregular verbs.
4. To understand the meaning of verb tenses.
5. To demonstrate understanding and use of the present, past, and future tense.
6. To demonstrate understanding and use of the perfect tenses.
7. To understand correct usage of *did* and *done* as the past tense and past participle of *do*.
8. To understand correct usage of *lay* and *lie* as the past tense and past participle of *lie*.
9. To understand correct usage of *set* and *sit* as the past tense and past participle of *sit*.

Critical Viewing

Identify Students may suggest verbs such as *glowing, gleaming, sparkling, flying, fluttering, looming,* and *standing*.

Chapter 22 Using Verbs

The Kremlin, a former royal palace, has been the headquarters of Russia's government since 1918.

▲ **Critical Viewing**
Name verbs to describe actions or conditions of the lights, flag, and building in this picture. **[Identify]**

Usage refers to the way a word or expression is used in a sentence. The rules in this and the following chapters are those of standard English. You will apply these rules in most of your writing and speaking.

If you wanted to write an essay about Russia, you would use many different verbs to show actions or conditions of the people, the cities, the landforms, and anything else. Just like a large country, verbs have different parts; you will learn about those parts in this chapter. Also, a country like Russia has a past, a present, and a future, so the verbs you would use in your essay would need to show whether an action takes place in the past, the present, or the future.

In this chapter, you will learn rules about using verbs correctly. Some rules will teach you about the parts of verbs. Other rules will help you use the different tenses. Finally, there are rules that will help you solve verb problems.

478 • Using Verbs

☑ ONGOING ASSESSMENT: Diagnose

If students miss more than one item in each category, direct them to the relevant pages of the text and assign exercises for practice and review.

Using Verbs	Diagnostic Test Items	Teach	Practice	Section Review	Chapter Review
Skill Check A					
Principal Parts of Regular and Irregular Verbs	A 1–5 B 6–10	pp. 480–486	Ex. 1–5	Ex. 6–9	Ex. 36–37
Skill Check B					
Principal Parts of Regular and Irregular Verbs	A 1–5 B 6–10	pp. 480–486	Ex. 1–5	Ex. 6–9	Ex. 36–37

Diagnostic Test

Directions: Write all answers on a separate sheet of paper. (The sentences that follow are not intended to be in the same verb tense. Read each sentence as though it stood alone.)

Skill Check A. Label the principal part of each underlined verb *present, present participle, past,* or *past participle.*

1. Yesterday, Katerina <u>saw</u> a Russian film from the 1940's.
2. She has <u>seen</u> many foreign films.
3. Her friends <u>enjoy</u> these films with her.
4. She is <u>planning</u> to study filmmaking.
5. She has <u>heard</u> of a good film school in Moscow.

Skill Check B. Write the present participle, past, and past participle forms of the following verbs.

6. earn
7. laugh
8. drink
9. have
10. ride

Skill Check C. In each sentence below, choose the correct verb in parentheses.

11. My friend Vladimir (grew, growed) up in Russia.
12. He and his family (come, came) to this country last year.
13. They (saw, seen) many new things when they arrived.
14. He has (spoke, spoken) often about his life back in Moscow.
15. Vladimir has (wrote, written) beautiful stories about his grandparents in Moscow.

Skill Check D. Rewrite each sentence below, changing the tense of the underlined verb to the tense indicated in parentheses.

16. I <u>have studied</u> Russian for two years. (future)
17. It <u>is</u> one of the most difficult languages to learn. (past)
18. Earlier, I <u>studied</u> Spanish. (past perfect)
19. Studying the Russian language <u>helped</u> me to appreciate Russian culture better. (present perfect)
20. This summer, my family <u>visited</u> Russia. (present)

Skill Check E. In each sentence below, choose the correct verb in parentheses.

21. We (did, done) several things to prepare for our trip to Russia.
22. First, my father (set, sat) a map of Russia on the kitchen table, and we studied it.
23. We noted that Moscow (lies, lays) in the western part of the country.
24. The Kremlin in Moscow (sits, sets) alongside the Moscow River.
25. The map has (lain, laid) on the table ever since, so we can look at it whenever we pass.

Answer Key

Diagnostic Test

Each item in the Diagnostic Test corresponds with a specific concept in the using verbs chapter. This will enable you to tailor instruction to the particular needs of your students. See "Ongoing Assessment: Diagnose" below for further details.

Skill Check A

1. past
2. past participle
3. present
4. present participle
5. past participle

Skill Check B

6. earn, earning, earned, earned
7. laugh, laughing, laughed, laughed
8. drink, drinking, drank, drunk
9. have, having, had, had
10. ride, riding, rode, ridden

Skill Check C

11. grew
12. came
13. saw
14. spoken
15. written

Skill Check D

16. I will study Russian for two years.
17. It was one of the most difficult languages to learn.
18. Earlier, I had studied Spanish.
19. Studying the Russian language has helped me to appreciate Russian culture better.
20. This summer, my family visits Russia.

Skill Check E

21. did
22. set
23. lies
24. sits
25. lain

✓ ONGOING ASSESSMENT: Diagnose *continued*

Using Verbs	Diagnostic Test Items	Teach	Practice	Section Review	Chapter Review
Skill Check C					
Irregular Verbs	C 11–15	pp. 483–486	Ex. 3–5	Ex. 6, 8	Ex. 36, 37
Skill Check D					
Tenses of Verbs	D 16–20	pp. 488–492	Ex. 13–17	Ex. 18–20	Ex. 38–40, 43
Skill Check E					
Forms of Troublesome Verbs	E 21–25	pp. 494–500	Ex. 24–29	Ex. 30–32	Ex. 41–42
Cumulative Reviews and Applications				Ex. 10–12, 21–23, 33–35	Ex. 44

⏱ TIME SAVERS!

🗐 **Answers on Transparency** Use the Grammar Exercises Answers on Transparencies for Chapter 22 to facilitate correction by students.

🖥 **On-Line Exercise Bank** Have students complete the Diagnostic Test on computer. The Auto Check feature will grade their work for you!

I feed my hamster twice a day.

I fed him this morning.

I will feed him again tonight.

Ask students to identify the verbs in each sentence. Then ask students to discuss the difference between these verbs. Lead them to see that the verbs tell the time when the action happens.

Activate Prior Knowledge

Ask students to describe activities they did last weekend. Then ask them to describe what they hope to do next weekend. Ask them why they think the English language has different verb tenses.

TEACH

Step-by-Step Teaching Guide

The Four Principal Parts of Verbs

1. Make sure that students understand the basic function of verbs: to express the action in a sentence.

2. Review the four principal parts of a verb. Note the helping verbs with the participles and point out that helping verbs combined with participles form verb phrases.

3. Write the following sentences on the board and ask students to identify the verbs.

   He talks too much.

   He was talking to the teacher.

   We talked yesterday.

   We have talked about this before.

Customize for
Less Advanced Students

Review helping verbs and verb phrases. Go over the list of common helping verbs, principal parts of *have, be, do* with students, and have them combine helping verbs with participles to form verb phrases.

Critical Viewing

Describe Answers will vary. Students may suggest sentences such as "The bear is hungry. The bear was hungry. The bear will be hungry."

480

The Four Principal Parts of Verbs

Verbs have different forms to express time. The form of the verb *walk* in the sentence "They *walk* very fast" expresses action in the present. In "They *walked* too far," the form of the verb shows that the action happened in the past. In "They *will walk* home," the verb expresses action in the future. These forms of verbs are known as *tenses*. To use the tenses of a verb correctly, you must know the *principal parts* of the verb.

▶ **KEY CONCEPT** A verb has four **principal parts:** the *present*, the *present participle*, the *past*, and the *past participle*. ■

Here, for example, are the four principal parts of the verb *walk*:

THE FOUR PRINCIPAL PARTS OF *WALK*			
Present	Present Participle	Past	Past Participle
walk	(am) walking	walked	(have) walked

The first principal part, called the *present*, is the form of the verb that is listed in a dictionary. Sometimes, the present tense has an *s* on the end when it is used with a singular subject. Notice also the helping verbs in parentheses before the second and fourth principal parts in the chart. These two principal parts must be combined with helping verbs before they can be used as verbs in sentences. The result will always be a *verb phrase*.

Following are four sentences, each using one of the principal parts of the verb *walk*:

EXAMPLES: He *walks* slowly through the Moscow Zoo.
A large bear *was walking* around in its cage.
My parents *walked* to the Belorussian Station.
We *have walked* all through this part of Moscow.

The way the last two principal parts of a verb—the past and past participle—are formed shows whether the verb is regular or irregular.

Theme: Russia

In this section, you will learn about the four principal parts of regular and irregular verbs. The examples and exercises are about Russia's history, geography, and culture.

Cross Curricular Connection: Social Studies

▼ Critical Viewing Write a sentence about this bear. Then, rewrite it in the past tense and in the future tense. **[Describe]**

⏱ TIME AND RESOURCE MANAGER

Resources
Print: Grammar Exercise Workbook, pp. 87–94; Grammar Exercises Answers Transparencies, Chapter 22
Technology: Language Lab CD-ROM, Using Verbs; On-Line Exercise Bank, Section 22.1

In-Depth Coverage	Accelerated Pace
• Work through all key concepts, pp. 480–486. • Assign and review Exercises 1–5. • Read and discuss Grammar in Literature, p. 482.	• Assign pp. 480–482 for independent student review. • Review Irregular Verbs, pp. 483–486. • Assign Section Review Exercises 6–9, p. 487.

Using Regular Verbs

Most verbs are *regular*, which means that the past and past participle of these verbs are formed according to a predictable pattern.

> **KEY CONCEPT** With **regular verbs**, the past and past participle are formed by adding *-ed* or *-d* to the present form. ■

To form the past and past participle of a regular verb, such as *talk* or *look*, you simply add *-ed* to the present tense. With regular verbs that already end in *e*—verbs such as *move* and *charge*—you simply add *-d* to the present tense. ■

PRINCIPAL PARTS OF REGULAR VERBS			
Present	Present Participle	Past	Past Participle
talk	(am) talking	talked	(have) talked
look	(am) looking	looked	(have) looked
move	(am) moving	moved	(have) moved
charge	(am) charging	charged	(have) charged

> **Exercise 1** Recognizing the Principal Parts of Regular Verbs
Identify the principal part used to form each underlined verb or verb phrase in the following sentences.

EXAMPLE: Mia is painting a portrait of the Russian
                       president.

ANSWER: present participle

1. Our class is reading about Russia.
2. Every Friday, we look at videos about Russian cities and culture.
3. The country has served as a bridge between Europe and Asia for many centuries.
4. From the sixteenth century to the early part of the twentieth century, an emperor ruled over Russia.
5. In 1917, a revolution occurred in Russia.
6. A new government was established there.
7. We are studying the Russian Revolution in our social studies class.
8. Our teacher describes it as a major event of the twentieth century.
9. For more than seventy years, Communist leaders controlled the government.
10. Today, elected officials are governing the people of Russia.

> **More Practice**
Language Lab
CD-ROM
• Using Verbs lesson
On-line
Exercise Bank
• Section 22.1
Grammar Exercise
Workbook
• pp. 87–88

The Four Principal Parts of Verbs • 481

Step-by-Step Teaching Guide

Using Regular Verbs

1. Regular verbs are easy: add *-ed* to form the past and past participle. For verbs ending in *e*, such as *hope, fumble, notice*, add *-d*.

2. For verbs that end in *e*, drop the *e* before adding *-ing* to form the present participle. Write the following verbs on the board and ask students to form the present participle.

   store *(storing)*

   create *(creating)*

   charge *(charging)*

Customize for
Verbal/Linguistic Learners

Let a small group of students work together to list participles that double the final consonant before adding *-ed* or *-ing*. Have students use the list to attempt to generalize some rules about doubling the final consonant.

Answer Key

> **Exercise 1**

1. present participle
2. present
3. past participle
4. past
5. past
6. past participle
7. present participle
8. present
9. past
10. present participle

✓ **ONGOING ASSESSMENT: Prerequisite Skills**

If students have difficulty forming the principal parts of regular verbs, you may find it necessary to review the following to assure coverage for prerequisite knowledge.

In the Textbook	Print Resources	Technology
Verbs, pp. 312–327	Grammar Exercise Workbook, pp. 13–14	Language Lab CD-ROM, Using Verbs; On-Line Exercise Bank, Section 15.1

⏱ **TIME SAVERS!**

🖥 **Answers on Transparency**
Use the Grammar Exercises Answers on Transparencies for Chapter 22 to facilitate correction by students.

💻 **On-Line Exercise Bank**
Have students complete the exercises on computer. The Auto Check feature will grade their work for you!

▶ **Exercise 2**

1. I am giving an oral report on Peter I of Russia.
2. He has often been called Peter the Great.
3. Peter inherited the throne as czar of Russia in 1682.
4. He wanted to make Russia more modern.
5. Peter disguised himself as a ship's carpenter.
6. He traveled in disguise to England and Holland.
7. Peter actually labored in shipyards in those countries.
8. He was impressed with the industrial development he had observed in Western Europe.
9. He modeled changes in his country after things he had learned during his travels.
10. I am planning to show several portraits of Peter during my report.

Step-by-Step Teaching Guide

Grammar in Literature

1. Have a volunteer read aloud the passage from "Overdoing It."

2. Put the verbs in the passage into different tenses and ask students to name the tense. For example, *stretch*—present; *tried*—past.

More About the Author

In his short life (1860–1904), Russian playwright and short story writer Anton Chekhov wrote three plays considered classics today—*The Seagull, Uncle Vanya,* and *The Cherry Orchard*—and hundreds of short stories. He was also a physician who wrote a pioneering study of health conditions in Siberian prisons.

▶ **Exercise 2** Supplying the Principal Parts of Regular Verbs

Copy each of the following sentences onto your paper, writing the correct form of the verb in parentheses.

EXAMPLE: We have (visit) the famous art museum in St. Petersburg.

ANSWER: We have visited the famous art museum in St. Petersburg.

1. I am (give) an oral report on Peter I of Russia.
2. He has often been (call) Peter the Great.
3. Peter (inherit—past) the throne as czar of Russia in 1682.
4. He (want—past) to make Russia more modern.
5. Peter (disguise—past) himself as a ship's carpenter.
6. He (travel—past) in disguise to England and Holland.
7. Peter actually (labor—past) in shipyards in those countries.
8. He was (impress) with the industrial development he had (observe) in Western Europe.
9. He (model—past) changes in his country after things he had (learn) during his travels.
10. I am (plan) to show several portraits of Peter during my report.

GRAMMAR IN LITERATURE

from **Overdoing It**
Anton Chekhov

The verbs in this excerpt are printed in blue italics. Stretched, merged, *and* disappeared *are in the past tense.* Try *and* come *are in the present tense.* Was sinking *is made up of the past tense of the verb* be *and the present participle of the verb* sink.

. . . To the right of the surveyor *stretched* the dark, frozen plain—broad and endless. *Try* to cross it and you'll *come* to the end of the world. On the horizon, where the plain *merged* with the sky and *disappeared*, the autumn sun *was* lazily *sinking* in the mist.

Using Irregular Verbs

Many common verbs are *irregular*. These are the verbs that tend to cause the most problems.

> **KEY CONCEPT** With **irregular verbs**, the past and past participle are *not* formed by adding *-ed* or *-d* to the present. ■

The third and fourth principal parts of irregular verbs are formed in various ways. You should memorize them.

IRREGULAR VERBS WITH THE SAME PAST AND PAST PARTICIPLE			
Present	Present Participle	Past	Past Participle
bring	(am) bringing	brought	(have) brought
build	(am) building	built	(have) built
buy	(am) buying	bought	(have) bought
catch	(am) catching	caught	(have) caught
fight	(am) fighting	fought	(have) fought
find	(am) finding	found	(have) found
get	(am) getting	got	(have) got *or* (have) gotten
hold	(am) holding	held	(have) held
lay	(am) laying	laid	(have) laid
lead	(am) leading	led	(have) led
lose	(am) losing	lost	(have) lost
pay	(am) paying	paid	(have) paid
say	(am) saying	said	(have) said
sit	(am) sitting	sat	(have) sat
spin	(am) spinning	spun	(have) spun
stick	(am) sticking	stuck	(have) stuck
swing	(am) swinging	swung	(have) swung
teach	(am) teaching	taught	(have) taught

> **Exercise 3** **Using Irregular Verbs** Rewrite each sentence below, replacing the underlined verb with the principal part shown in parentheses. Refer to the chart above if you need help.

EXAMPLE: I <u>buy</u> a painting from a gallery in Moscow. (past)

ANSWER: I bought a painting from a gallery in Moscow.

1. Russians <u>fight</u> many wars on the site that is now the city of St. Petersburg. (past participle)
2. In 1240, Russians <u>hold</u> off the Swedes there. (past)
3. In 1703, Peter I <u>lay</u> out plans for his new capital there. (past)
4. He <u>bring</u> in architects to build palaces and factories. (past)
5. We are <u>study</u> Russia in social studies. (present participle)

✒ Spelling Tip

Pay particular attention to the word *paid*. Make sure you do not spell it *payed*.

> **More Practice**
> Language Lab CD-ROM
> • Using Verbs lesson
> On-line Exercise Bank
> • Section 22.1
> Grammar Exercise Workbook
> • pp. 89–94

The Four Principal Parts of Verbs • 483

Step-by-Step Teaching Guide

Using Irregular Verbs

1. Irregular verbs do not follow rules. There are no shortcuts for remembering the correct principal parts. The best way to remember irregular verbs is to use them in speech and writing.

2. Review the list of irregular verbs individually, going over each principal part. Point out that each irregular verb on this list has the same past and past participle.

Answer Key

> **Exercise 3**

1. Russians have fought many wars on the site that is now the city of St. Petersburg.
2. In 1240, Russians held off the Swedes there.
3. In 1703, Peter I laid out plans for his new capital there.
4. He brought in architects to build palaces and factories.
5. We are studying Russia in social studies.

⏱ **TIME SAVERS!**

🎞 **Answers on Transparency** Use the Grammar Exercises Answers on Transparencies for Chapter 22 to facilitate correction by students.

💻 **On-Line Exercise Bank** Have students complete the exercises on computer. The Auto Check feature will grade their work for you!

Using Irregular Verbs

1. Continue the review of irregular verbs. Point out that in this list, each verb has the same present, past, and past participle, with only the present participle taking a different form.

2. Point out that *bid*, *put*, and *set* follow the pattern of doubling the final consonant before *-ing*.

3. Write the following verbs on the board and ask students to form the past and past participle.

cut *(cut, cut)*

hit *(hit, hit)*

let *(let, let)*

shut *(shut, shut)*

Answer Key

Exercise 4

1. Moscow has burst forth as a major tourist attraction in recent years.
2. The city set itself apart from other Russian cities with its beautiful architecture.
3. As in most metropolises, things have cost more in Moscow than in rural regions of Russia.
4. The high prices are hurting tourism only slightly.
5. Despite the high cost of housing, people set up homes in all parts of the city.
6. The increase in population put great strain on the city of Moscow.
7. The population is spreading out rapidly to the surrounding regions.
8. Many of the city's residents are setting up new shops and businesses.
9. Construction companies bid on contracts to build new office buildings and factories in the city.
10. Many Russians have put their life savings into a new house or business in Moscow.

22.1

IRREGULAR VERBS WITH THE SAME PRESENT, PAST, AND PAST PARTICIPLE			
Present	Present Participle	Past	Past Participle
bid	(am) bidding	bid	(have) bid
burst	(am) bursting	burst	(have) burst
cost	(am) costing	cost	(have) cost
hurt	(am) hurting	hurt	(have) hurt
put	(am) putting	put	(have) put
set	(am) setting	set	(have) set

▶ **Exercise 4** Revising Sentences With Irregular Verbs Copy each sentence below, replacing the underlined verb with the principal part indicated in parentheses. Refer to the chart above if you need help.

EXAMPLE: I set the delicate Russian doll on the store counter. (past participle)

ANSWER: I have set the delicate Russian doll on the store counter.

EXAMPLE: The clerk put it in a box. (present participle)

ANSWER: The clerk is putting it in a box.

1. Moscow burst forth as a major tourist attraction in recent years. (past participle)
2. The city has set itself apart from other Russian cities with its beautiful architecture. (past)
3. As in most metropolises, things cost more in Moscow than in rural regions of Russia. (past participle)
4. The high prices hurt tourism only slightly. (present participle)
5. Despite the high cost of housing, people have set up homes in all parts of the city. (present)
6. The increase in population has put great strain on the city of Moscow. (past)
7. The population spread out rapidly to the surrounding regions. (present participle)
8. Many of the city's residents have set up new shops and businesses. (present participle)
9. Construction companies have bid on contracts to build new office buildings and factories in the city. (past)
10. Many Russians put their life savings into a new house or business in Moscow. (past participle)

More Practice

Language Lab CD-ROM
• Using Verbs lesson
On-line Exercise Bank
• Section 22.1
Grammar Exercise Workbook
• pp. 89–94

☑ **ONGOING ASSESSMENT: Monitor and Reinforce**

If students miss more than two items in Exercises 1–5, refer them to the following for additional practice.

In the Textbook	Print Resources	Technology
Section Review, Ex. 6–10, p. 487	Grammar Exercise Workbook, pp. 87–94	Language Lab CD-ROM, Using Verbs; On-Line Exercise Bank, Section 22.1

Critical Viewing

Infer Responses will vary. Students' sentences should contain past tense verbs.

◀ **Critical Viewing**
Red Square in Moscow, Russia, does not look very red or very square in this photograph. Imagine that you have just returned from a trip to Moscow, and write three sentences about what you saw in Red Square while you were there. **[Infer]**

Step-by-Step Teaching Guide

Irregular Verbs

1. Review the list of irregular verbs that change in other ways. It should be clear to students that in this list there are no patterns. Each form of the verb is different.

2. As a whole-class activity, have students take turns using each form of a verb on the chart in sentences.

3. Reinforce the directions about checking a dictionary when students are unsure of a verb. Again, remind them that the best way to learn irregular verbs is to memorize and use them.

⚙ Grammar and **Style Tip**

The past participle of *dream* is *dreamed* or *dreamt*. Both are correct, and both are used.

Customize for
ESL Students

Review the principal parts of verbs with students, making sure they understand how parts are formed and their functions. Encourage them to talk about how tenses are formed in their home language.

IRREGULAR VERBS THAT CHANGE IN OTHER WAYS

Present	Present Participle	Past	Past Participle
be	(am) being	was	(have) been
begin	(am) beginning	began	(have) begun
choose	(am) choosing	chose	(have) chosen
come	(am) coming	came	(have) come
do	(am) doing	did	(have) done
draw	(am) drawing	drew	(have) drawn
drink	(am) drinking	drank	(have) drunk
drive	(am) driving	drove	(have) driven
eat	(am) eating	ate	(have) eaten
fly	(am) flying	flew	(have) flown
give	(am) giving	gave	(have) given
go	(am) going	went	(have) gone
know	(am) knowing	knew	(have) known
lie	(am) lying	lay	(have) lain
ring	(am) ringing	rang	(have) rung
rise	(am) rising	rose	(have) risen
see	(am) seeing	saw	(have) seen
sing	(am) singing	sang	(have) sung
speak	(am) speaking	spoke	(have) spoken
swim	(am) swimming	swam	(have) swum
take	(am) taking	took	(have) taken
tear	(am) tearing	tore	(have) torn
throw	(am) throwing	threw	(have) thrown
write	(am) writing	wrote	(have) written

Check a dictionary whenever you are in doubt about the correct form of an irregular verb.

🕐 TIME SAVERS!

📄 **Answers on Transparency**
Use the Grammar Exercises Answers on Transparencies for Chapter 22 to facilitate correction by students.

🖥 **On-Line Exercise Bank**
Have students complete the exercises on computer. The Auto Check feature will grade their work for you!

1. Many Russian novelists wrote about their country and its people.
2. Russia has given the world many memorable writers.
3. One of the most famous Russian writers is Leo Tolstoy.
4. Tolstoy began his career in 1852 with the autobiographical novel *Childhood*.
5. We are choosing a short story to read in class.
6. We have begun to study Tolstoy's life.
7. Nearly everyone in the world knows Tolstoy's epic novel *War and Peace* (1865–1869).
8. My brother has spoken to me about that book.
9. He did a college paper on *War and Peace*.
10. Numerous students have chosen to study Tolstoy's novels.

Critical Viewing

Analyze Students' responses should contain verbs such as *wear, grow, hoed, sit,* and *get*.

22.1

► **Exercise 5** Revising Sentences With Other Irregular Verbs
Copy each sentence below, replacing the underlined verb with the principal part indicated in parentheses. Refer to the chart on the previous page if you need help.

EXAMPLE: We <u>take</u> a tour of the Kremlin. (present participle)
ANSWER: We are taking a tour of the Kremlin.

1. Many Russian novelists <u>have written</u> about their country and its people. (past)
2. Russia <u>gave</u> the world many memorable writers. (past participle)
3. One of the most famous Russian writers <u>was</u> Leo Tolstoy. (present)
4. Tolstoy <u>begins</u> his career in 1852 with the autobiographical novel *Childhood*. (past)
5. We <u>choose</u> a short story to read in class. (present participle)
6. We <u>begin</u> to study Tolstoy's life. (past participle)
7. Nearly everyone in the world <u>knew</u> Tolstoy's epic novel *War and Peace* (1865–1869). (present)
8. My brother <u>speaks</u> to me about that book. (past participle)
9. He <u>has done</u> a college paper on *War and Peace*. (past)
10. Numerous students <u>choose</u> to study Tolstoy's novels. (past participle)

► **More Practice**

Language Lab CD-ROM
• Using Verbs lesson
On-line Exercise Bank
• Section 22.1
Grammar Exercise Workbook
• pp. 89–94

◄ Critical Viewing
What details in this photograph of Leo Tolstoy tell you that he lived in a different time period? Respond with sentences using irregular verbs in different tenses. [Analyze]

486 • Using Verbs

⏱ **TIME SAVERS!**

🔦 **Answers on Transparency**
Use the Grammar Exercises Answers on Transparencies for Chapter 22 to facilitate correction by students.

💻 **On-Line Exercise Bank**
Have students complete the exercises on computer. The Auto Check feature will grade their work for you!

☑ **ONGOING ASSESSMENT: Assess Mastery**

Use the following resources to assess student mastery of the principal parts of regular and irregular verbs.

In the Textbook	Technology
Chapter Review, Ex. 36–37, p. 502	On-Line Exercise Bank, Section 22.1

Section Review

GRAMMAR EXERCISES 6–12

> **Exercise 6** Identifying Regular and Irregular Verbs Specify whether the following verbs are *regular* or *irregular*.

1. put
2. drink
3. stop
4. inform
5. lose
6. ring
7. hurt
8. turn
9. do
10. visit

> **Exercise 7** Recognizing Principal Parts of Regular Verbs Identify the principal part used to form the underlined regular verb(s) in each sentence below.

1. Russians have <u>enjoyed</u> the works of many outstanding native poets.
2. In their writings, the poets <u>are</u> <u>expressing</u> strong emotions.
3. The writings of Aleksandr Pushkin are still <u>cherished</u> today.
4. Pushkin <u>is considered</u> by some to be Russia's greatest poet.
5. Composers <u>combined</u> their music with his dramatic poems to create operas.

> **Exercise 8** Recognizing Principal Parts of Regular and Irregular Verbs Identify the principal part used to form each underlined verb below. Then, specify whether the verb is *regular* or *irregular*.

1. Many outstanding composers have <u>come</u> from Russia.
2. Most music lovers <u>know</u> the works of Peter Ilich Tchaikovsky.
3. Tchaikovsky <u>created</u> many masterpieces during the nineteenth century.
4. He <u>studied</u> music in St. Petersburg.
5. People around the world are still <u>listening</u> to his music.
6. Have you ever <u>heard</u> *The Nutcracker*?
7. Tchaikovsky <u>began</u> that ballet in 1891 and <u>finished</u> it in 1892.

8. Numerous ballet companies around the world are <u>performing</u> the ballet.
9. Many music lovers have <u>flown</u> to Russia and <u>visited</u> Tchaikovsky's home.
10. They are <u>impressed</u> with his music.

> **Exercise 9** Revising to Eliminate Errors in Verb Usage Rewrite the following sentences, correcting all misused principal parts of verbs.

1. Russia has did much for the development of motion pictures.
2. Have you ever saw any films by the Russian director Sergei Eisenstein?
3. Eisenstein winned recognition for *The Battleship Potemkin* in 1925.
4. The film becomed an international hit.
5. Critics have gave this film much praise.

> **Exercise 10** Find It in Your Reading Identify the four principal parts of each underlined verb in this excerpt from Anton Chekhov's "Overdoing It."

It <u>grew</u> dark. The wagon suddenly <u>creaked</u>, <u>squeaked</u>, <u>shook</u>, and, as though against its will, <u>turned</u> left.

> **Exercise 11** Find It in Your Writing Look through your writing portfolio. Find examples of sentences with regular and irregular verbs. Identify which principal part of each verb you used.

> **Exercise 12** Writing Application On your paper, write a descriptive paragraph about a foreign city or country. Try to use all four principal parts of verbs in your sentences. Include both regular and irregular verbs.

Section Review • 487

ASSESS and CLOSE

Section Review

Each of these exercises correlates with the instruction on the principal parts of verbs, pages 480–486. These exercises may be used for more practice, for reteaching, or for review of the key concepts presented. Answers for all chapter exercises are available in *Grammar Exercises Answers on Transparencies* in your Teaching Resources.

Answer Key

> **Exercise 6**

1. irregular
2. irregular
3. regular
4. regular
5. irregular
6. irregular
7. irregular
8. regular
9. irregular
10. regular

> **Exercise 7**

1. past participle
2. present participle
3. past participle
4. past participle
5. past

> **Exercise 8**

1. past participle—irregular
2. present—irregular
3. past—regular
4. past—regular
5. present participle—regular
6. past participle—irregular
7. past—irregular, past—regular
8. present participle—regular
9. past participle—irregular, past participle—regular
10. past participle—regular

> **Exercise 9**

1. Russia has done much for the development of motion pictures.
2. Have you ever seen any films by the Russian director Sergei Eisenstein?
3. Eisenstein won recognition for *The Battleship Potemkin* in 1925.
4. The film became an international hit.
5. Critics have given this film much praise.

continued

Answer Key continued

> **Exercise 10**

Find It in Your Reading

grow, growing, grew, grown

creak, creaking, creaked, creaked

squeak, squeaking, squeaked, squeaked

shake, shaking, shook, shaken

turn, turning, turned, turned

> **Exercise 11**

Find It in Your Writing

Ask students to label the verbs *regular* and *irregular*.

> **Exercise 12**

Writing Application

Students can trade papers with a partner to label the principal part of each verb.

PREPARE and ENGAGE

Interest GRABBER Write the following sentences on the board and ask students to put them in the past and future tenses.

The elegant elephant eats eclairs.

Six sleepy salamanders sing silly songs.

An amorous alligator acts alluring.

Fragrant flamingos fly freely.

Activate Prior Knowledge

Ask students to choose one action—walking, talking, running, sleeping—and write three sentences about performing that action yesterday, today, and tomorrow.

TEACH

Step-by-Step Teaching Guide

Verb Tenses

1. Briefly review the six tenses, being sure that students fully understand the definition of tense as telling the time of an action.

2. Review the present tense. See that students understand the addition of -s when used with third-person singular nouns or pronouns.

3. Introduce the past tense, reminding students that most verbs form the past by adding -ed or -d, except for irregular verbs, which form the past in different ways.

Customize for
ESL Students

Students learning English may have memorized the rule that adding -s to a word makes it plural: one *horse*, two *horses*. Now they encounter a contradiction to the "s means more than one" rule: *he* [one person] *walks*, but *they* [more than one person] *walk*. Stress that the rule applies to (regular) nouns. Verbs do not follow that rule.

Section 22.2

Verb Tenses

English verbs have six basic tenses: *past, present, future, past perfect, present perfect,* and *future perfect.* The tenses are formed by using the principal parts of verbs along with helping verbs.

▶ **KEY CONCEPT** A **verb tense** tells whether the time of an action or condition is in the past, the present, or the future. ■

Using Present, Past, and Future Tenses

Refer to this chart as you learn how the six basic tenses are formed.

PRINCIPAL PARTS OF FOUR COMMON VERBS			
Base	Present Participle	Past	Past Participle
look	looking	looked	(have/had) looked
eat	eating	ate	(have/had) eaten
speak	speaking	spoke	(have/had) spoken
wait	waiting	waited	(have/had) waited

Present Tense The *present tense* shows actions that happen in the present. This tense is also used to show actions that occur regularly (every day, every week, all the time). The present tense is formed with the base form of the verb.

EXAMPLES: We *help.*
　　　　　　The firefighters *race* to the burning building.

When a present tense verb follows a singular noun or the pronoun *he, she,* or *it,* add -s or -es to the base of the verb.

EXAMPLES: Amelia *speaks* to the nurses.
　　　　　　She *hopes* to become a nurse someday.

Past Tense The *past tense* shows actions that have already happened. Regular verbs form the past tense by adding -ed or -d to the present form. Irregular verbs form the past tense in a variety of ways.

EXAMPLES: We *helped.*
　　　　　　The firefighters *raced* to the burning building.
　　　　　　Amelia *spoke* to the nurses.

488 • Using Verbs

Theme: Helping Jobs

In this section, you will learn to recognize and use the six tenses of verbs. The examples and exercises are about careers of people who help others.

Cross-Curricular Connection: Social Studies

⏱ TIME AND RESOURCE MANAGER

Resources

Print: Grammar Exercise Workbook, pp. 95–100; Grammar Exercises Answers on Transparencies, Chapter 22

Technology: Language Lab CD-ROM, Using Verbs; On-Line Exercise Bank, Section 22.2

In-Depth Coverage	Accelerated Pace
• Work through all key concepts, pp. 488–492. • Assign and review Exercises 13–17. • Read and discuss Grammar in Literature, p. 492.	• Assign pp. 488–492 for independent student review. • Assign Section Review Exercises 18–20, p. 493.

Future Tense The *future tense* shows actions that will take place in the future. The future tense is formed by using the helping verb *will* with the base of the verb.

EXAMPLES: We *will help.*
The firefighters *will race* to the burning building.
Amelia *will speak* to the nurses.

▶ **Exercise 13** Identifying the Present, Past, and Future Tenses On your paper, write the tense of each underlined verb in the following sentences.

EXAMPLE: The chauffeur <u>raced</u> through the traffic.
ANSWER: past

1. Ambulances <u>bring</u> sick or injured people to hospitals.
2. The first ambulances <u>carried</u> wounded soldiers in wartime.
3. Until the twentieth century, animals <u>pulled</u> ambulances.
4. Sick or injured people usually <u>went</u> to crude hospitals.
5. Today, an engine <u>propels</u> an ambulance.
6. Paramedics <u>ride</u> in ambulances to treat the injured.
7. Fast action by paramedics <u>will save</u> many lives.
8. In the twenty-first century, engineers <u>will make</u> even better ambulances.
9. New equipment <u>offers</u> hope that more lives will be saved.
10. My brother <u>brought</u> his paramedic equipment aboard the ambulance.

▶ **Exercise 14** Supplying Verbs On your paper, complete each sentence with a verb from the list below. Then, indicate whether the verb is in the *present, past,* or *future tense.* Use each verb only once.

managed	occur	will be
occurred	arrived	walked

1. Accidents rarely __?__ in my neighborhood.
2. However, one __?__ as I __?__ home from school yesterday.
3. The police __?__ first and, soon afterward, a rescue helicopter.
4. The helicopter team __?__ to get the victims to a hospital quickly.
5. The victims __?__ grateful to the emergency workers for a long time to come.

▶ **More Practice**

Language Lab
CD-ROM
• Using Verbs lesson
On-line
Exercise Bank
• Section 22.2
Grammar Exercise
Workbook
• pp. 95–96

▼ **Critical Viewing**
Describe this skateboarder's accident using past tense verbs. Describe the police officer's actions using present tense verbs. **[Analyze]**

Verb Tenses • 489

Future Tense

1. Introduce the future tense. See that students understand that it expresses action that has not happened yet and is formed with the helping verb *will.*

2. Write the following sentences on the board, asking students to identify the tense of each verb.

   I will run home to get the book. (future)

   I left my homework on the table. (past)

   My mother drives me to school. (present)

Answer Key

▶ **Exercise 13**

1. present
2. past
3. past
4. past
5. present
6. present
7. future
8. future
9. present
10. past

▶ **Exercise 14**

1. occur—present
2. occurred—past, walked—past
3. arrived—past
4. managed—past
5. will be—future

Critical Viewing

Analyze Students' responses should contain the past tense of verbs such as *fall, trip, stumble, hurt,* and *cut,* and present tense of verbs such as *kneel, help, ask,* and *take.*

☑ **ONGOING ASSESSMENT: Prerequisite Skills**

If students have trouble identifying verbs in six tenses, you may find it necessary to review the following to assure coverage for prerequisite knowledge.

In the Textbook	Print Resources	Technology
Verbs, pp. 312–327	Grammar Exercise Workbook, pp. 13–14	Language Lab CD-ROM, Using Verbs; On-Line Exercise Bank, Section 15.1

⏱ **TIME SAVERS!**

🗚 **Answers on Transparency**
Use the Grammar Exercises Answers on Transparencies for Chapter 22 to facilitate correction by students.

💻 **On-Line Exercise Bank**
Have students complete the exercises on computer. The Auto Check feature will grade their work for you!

Exercise 15

1. The forest ranger gave us a tour of the state park.
2. The ranger shows us many strange plants.
3. She also taught us how to recognize poison ivy.
4. Touching poison ivy will cause a painful rash.
5. Calamine lotion took away the itch.
6. Now we will know how to avoid poison ivy.
7. The ranger carefully tore off a leaf from a tree.
8. She warns us to avoid poison sumac.
9. Forest rangers will assist travelers to state parks.
10. I wrote her a note of thanks for her help.

Step-by-Step Teaching Guide

Using Perfect Tenses

1. The present perfect tense expresses action that takes place at no particular time in the past. It is formed using the helping verb *has* or *have. Seeing Eye dogs have helped people who cannot see* means that the dogs are still helping people.

2. The past perfect tense expresses action completed in the past before some other action. It is formed using *had. The dogs had learned their jobs before being assigned to help people* means that learning came before helping.

Critical Viewing

Infer Possible answer: The ranger has focused her magnifying glass on a small object.

22.2

Exercise 15 Using the Basic Forms of Verbs Rewrite each sentence below, changing the tense of the underlined verb to the one indicated in parentheses.

EXAMPLE: The nurse <u>checks</u> his temperature. (future)
ANSWER: The nurse will check his temperature.

1. The forest ranger <u>gives</u> us a tour of the state park. (past)
2. The ranger <u>showed</u> us many strange plants. (present)
3. She also <u>teaches</u> us how to recognize poison ivy. (past)
4. Touching poison ivy <u>causes</u> a painful rash. (future)
5. Calamine lotion <u>will take</u> away the itch. (past)
6. Now, we <u>knew</u> how to avoid poison ivy. (future)
7. The ranger carefully <u>tears</u> off a leaf from a tree. (past)
8. She <u>warned</u> us to avoid poison sumac, too. (present)
9. Forest rangers <u>assist</u> travelers to state parks. (future)
10. I <u>will write</u> her a note of thanks for her help. (past)

Using Perfect Tenses

Present Perfect Tense The *present perfect tense* shows actions that began in the past and continue to the present. It also shows actions that began in the past and ended in the past. The present perfect tense is formed by using *have* or *has* with the past participle.

EXAMPLES: We *have helped.*
Amelia *has spoken* to the nurses.

Past Perfect Tense The *past perfect tense* shows a past action or condition that ended before another past action began. The past perfect tense is formed by using *had* with the past participle.

EXAMPLES: We *had helped* her before today.
Amelia *had spoken* to the nurses. Then, she wrote her report.

▲ Critical Viewing Use verbs in the present perfect tense to describe what the forest ranger is doing. **[Infer]**

STANDARDIZED TEST PREPARATION WORKSHOP

Grammar and Usage Standardized tests often require students to identify tense errors in sentences. Ask students to choose the correct verb for the following sentence:

Karen ___ her homework before she went to Luann's house.

A has finished
B had finished
C will have finished
D will finish

The correct choice is item **B**, the only choice that agrees with the past-tense *went*.

Future Perfect Tense The *future perfect tense* shows a future action or condition that will have ended before another begins. It uses *will have* with the past participle.

EXAMPLES: By the end of this week, we *will have helped* her five times.

Amelia *will have spoken* to the nurses before she begins her report.

Exercise 16 Identifying Perfect Verb Tenses Identify the perfect tense of each underlined verb in the following sentences.

EXAMPLE: My brother <u>has</u> already <u>learned</u> how to perform CPR.

ANSWER: present perfect

1. People <u>have written</u> letters for hundreds of years.
2. Postal workers <u>have delivered</u> mail for nearly as long.
3. Before the telephone was invented, people <u>had written</u> more letters to each other.
4. They <u>have had</u> few other means of communication.
5. By the late twenty-first century, people <u>will have turned</u> to other forms of communication.
6. Since last year, we <u>have</u> often <u>corresponded</u> by e-mail.
7. Nevertheless, before the year has ended, mail carriers <u>will have placed</u> millions of letters in people's mailboxes.
8. We <u>have</u> always <u>relied</u> on postal workers to handle our important correspondence.
9. They <u>have been</u> able to meet our needs.
10. <u>Had</u> you ever <u>thought</u> of becoming a postal worker before?

► **More Practice**

Language Lab CD-ROM
• Using Verbs lesson

On-line Exercise Bank
• Section 22.2

Grammar Exercise Workbook
• pp. 95–98

◄ **Critical Viewing** Does it appear that a mail carrier has visited these mailboxes recently? Tell why or why not, using verbs in the present and past perfect tenses in your response. **[Speculate]**

Verb Tenses • 491

Step-by-Step Teaching Guide

Future Perfect Tense

The future perfect tense is used to express an action in the future that will be completed before some other action. It is formed using *shall have* or *will have*. *By the end of the week, Selma will have written her essay* means that the essay will be written before the week ends.

Answer Key

► **Exercise 16**

1. present perfect
2. present perfect
3. past perfect
4. present perfect
5. future perfect
6. present perfect
7. future perfect
8. present perfect
9. present perfect
10. past perfect

Critical Viewing

Speculate Students may say that a mail carrier has not visited the mailboxes lately; that if she or he had delivered mail, the boxes would be clear of snow.

☑ ONGOING ASSESSMENT: Monitor and Reinforce

If students miss more than two items in Exercises 13–17, refer them to the following for additional practice.

In the Textbook	Print Resources	Technology
Section Review, Ex. 18–20, p. 493	Grammar Exercise Workbook, pp. 95–98	Language Lab CD-ROM, Using Verbs; On-Line Exercise Bank, Section 22.2

⏱ TIME SAVERS!

Answers on Transparency Use the Grammar Exercises Answers on Transparencies for Chapter 22 to facilitate correction by students.

On-Line Exercise Bank Have students complete the exercises on computer. The Auto Check feature will grade their work for you!

Exercise 17

1. Firefighters have saved thousands of lives.
2. There were firefighters in the seventeenth century.
3. Until recently, most firefighters had been volunteers.
4. Salaried firefighters usually have worked in large cities.
5. Until some time ago, volunteer firefighters had served small communities.
6. Some things have remained the same.
7. Before their first real fire experience, firefighters will have trained for six months to learn firefighting and livesaving techniques.
8. They often will risk their lives to protect people.
9. Firefighters also have taught fire prevention methods.
10. Within just a few years, smoke alarms had prevented thousands of fires and deaths.

Critical Viewing

Infer Students may say he has been battling forest fires and he saved a person last week.

Step-by-Step Teaching Guide

Grammar in Literature

1. Have a volunteer read aloud the passage from "Count That Day Lost."
2. Challenge students to change *have done* to the present, past, and present participle. *(do, did, are doing)*

More About the Author

George Eliot (1819–1880) was the pseudonym of the English writer Mary Ann Evans. Her novels documented life across class lines, carefully describing relationships of families and lovers. Her greatest novels include *Middlemarch, The Mill on the Floss, Adam Bede,* and *Silas Marner.*

Exercise 17 Revising Sentences With Verb Forms

On your paper, rewrite each sentence below, changing the tense of the underlined verb to the one indicated in parentheses.

EXAMPLE: That lifeguard <u>rescued</u> three swimmers. (present perfect)

ANSWER: That lifeguard has rescued three swimmers.

1. Firefighters <u>save</u> thousands of lives. (present perfect)
2. There <u>are</u> firefighters in the seventeenth century. (past)
3. Until recently, most firefighters <u>were</u> volunteers. (past perfect)
4. Salaried firefighters usually <u>worked</u> in large cities. (present perfect)
5. Until some time ago, volunteer firefighters <u>served</u> small communities. (past perfect)
6. Some things <u>remain</u> the same. (present perfect)
7. Before their first real fire experience, firefighters <u>train</u> for six months to learn firefighting and lifesaving techniques. (future perfect)
8. They often <u>risk</u> their lives to protect people. (future)
9. Firefighters also <u>teach</u> fire prevention methods. (present perfect)
10. Within just a few years, smoke alarms <u>prevent</u> thousands of fires and deaths. (past perfect)

GRAMMAR IN LITERATURE

from **Count That Day Lost**
George Eliot

Notice the highlighted verbs in this poem stanza. Present tense verbs are highlighted in blue, past tense verbs in green, and present perfect tense verbs in red.

If you *sit* down at set of sun
And *count* the acts that you *have done,*
 And, counting, *find*
One self-denying deed, one word
That *eased* the heart of him who *heard,*
 One glance most kind
That *fell* like sunshine where it *went*—
Then you *may count* that day well spent.

492 • Using Verbs

▲ Critical Viewing
This firefighter appears to have been working hard. Describe some of his actions in the past. [Infer]

More Practice

Language Lab CD-ROM
• Using Verbs lesson
On-line Exercise Bank
• Section 22.2
Grammar Exercise Workbook
• pp. 95–98

☑ **ONGOING ASSESSMENT: Assess Mastery**

Use the following resources to assess student mastery of the six tenses of verbs.

In the Textbook	Technology
Chapter Review, Ex. 38–40, pp. 502–503	On-Line Exercise Bank, Section 22.2

Section 22.2 Section Review

GRAMMAR EXERCISES 18–23

Exercise 18 Recognizing Verb Tenses Write the tense of each underlined verb in the sentences below.

1. A flight attendant <u>serves</u> an important role on an airplane flight.
2. Until the 1980's, most airlines <u>had hired</u> only female flight attendants.
3. This trend <u>began</u> to change.
4. Most people <u>have welcomed</u> the change.
5. Male and female flight attendants now <u>work</u> together on many flights.
6. They <u>will help</u> you during a flight.
7. They <u>have made</u> flying safer and more comfortable for passengers.
8. Before the plane <u>takes</u> off, flight attendants <u>will present</u> safety instructions.
9. By the time they <u>have worked</u> for several years, flight attendants <u>will have repeated</u> the instructions many times.
10. By the end of your ride, a flight attendant <u>will have worked</u> hard to assure that your trip <u>has been</u> pleasant.

Exercise 19 Forming Verb Tenses Write the tense indicated for each verb below.

1. go (present)
2. hurt (past)
3. become (future perfect)
4. take (past perfect)
5. teach (future)

Exercise 20 Recognizing Correct Verb Forms Choose the correct verb from each pair in parentheses below. Then, identify the tense of the verb or verb phrase.

1. In the past, many accident victims had (suffer, suffered) because they could not receive medical care in time.
2. The modern EMT, or emergency medical technician, has (did, done) much to change that situation.
3. An EMT has (chose, chosen) to work in emergency situations.
4. EMTs will (arrived, arrive) at the scene of an accident and know exactly what to do.
5. During training, EMTs will have (went, gone) over many first-aid techniques.
6. They will have (became, become) familiar with emergencies by practicing on volunteers and specialized dummies.
7. Hospitals have (put, putted) a lot of responsibility on EMTs.
8. During one recent year, EMTs (gave, gived) emergency medical care to more than 25,000 people in our city.
9. Often, EMTs will (begin, began) treating victims on the way to the hospital.
10. Some EMTs have even (flew, flown) by helicopter to help injured people.

Exercise 21 Find It in Your Reading On your paper, rewrite the first four lines of the stanza from "Count That Day Lost" on page 492. Change each present tense verb to past tense and each present perfect tense verb to past perfect.

Exercise 22 Find It in Your Writing Look through your writing portfolio. Find examples of sentences with verbs in different tenses. Circle each verb or verb phrase, and identify its tense.

Exercise 23 Writing Application Imagine that you are a medical doctor at a busy hospital. On your paper, write five sentences describing a case you had recently. Use the verbs listed below.

1. past perfect of *catch*
2. past of *become*
3. present perfect of *have*
4. future of *be*
5. future perfect of *receive*

Section Review

Each of these exercises correlates with the instruction on verb tenses, pages 488–492. These exercises may be used for more practice, for reteaching, or for review of the key concepts presented. Answers for all chapter exercises are available in *Grammar Exercises Answers on Transparencies* in your Teaching Resources.

Answer Key

Exercise 18

1. present
2. past perfect
3. past
4. present perfect
5. present
6. future
7. present perfect
8. present, future
9. present perfect, future perfect
10. future perfect, present perfect

Exercise 19

1. go <u>or</u> goes
2. hurt
3. will have become
4. had taken
5. will teach

Exercise 20

1. suffered—past perfect
2. done—present perfect
3. chosen—present perfect
4. arrive—future
5. gone—future perfect
6. become—future perfect
7. put—present perfect
8. gave—past
9. begin—future
10. flown—present perfect

Exercise 21

Find It in Your Reading

If you sat down at set of sun
And counted the acts that you had done,
And, counting, found
One self-denying deed, one word

Exercise 22

Find It in Your Writing
Students can rewrite sentences containing present, past, and future tenses using the perfect forms of the verbs.

continued

Answer Key continued

Exercise 23

Writing Application
1. had caught
2. became
3. have had
4. will be
5. will have received

PREPARE and ENGAGE

Interest GRABBER Write the following sentences on the board.

Fifi did her homework. Didi has done her homework, too. "We're done!" the girls exclaimed.

Ask students to describe the underlined words in terms of their tenses and parts of speech. (*did*—past tense verb, *has done*—present perfect verb, *done*—adjective)

Activate Prior Knowledge

Ask students to write three sentences about activities they like to do, in each sentence using a form of the verb *do*.

TEACH

Step-by-Step Teaching Guide

Glossary of Troublesome Verbs

1. Review the use of *did* as the past form of *do*, going over the conjugation chart.

2. Make sure students understand that *done* is the past participle form of *do* and always is used with a helping verb.

3. Discuss the frequent error of using *done* as the past form of *do* without a helping verb: *I done my homework.* Review the present perfect tense chart on this page.

4. Write the following additional examples on the board and review with students.

   You have done a good job.

   They have done nothing with this project.

Customize for
Less Advanced Students

Review the key concepts and conjugation charts with students. First make sure they know the four principal parts of a verb. Then work with them to write a conjugation chart for the past perfect and future perfect tenses of *do* and have them make up sentences with each form.

494

Section 22.3 — Troublesome Verbs

Using *Did* and *Done*

Did and *done* are both forms of the frequently used verb *do*.

> **KEY CONCEPT** *Did* is the past form of *do*. It is used without a helping verb for actions that began and ended in the past. ■

EXAMPLE: She *did* the drawing of Tom Sawyer, and I *did* the painting of Huck Finn.

> **KEY CONCEPT** *Done* is the past participle of *do*. It is always used with a helping verb, such as *have* or *has*. ■

EXAMPLES: We *have done* all the research for Mark Twain's biography.
Dylan *has done* all of the illustrations for this book.

The following chart shows the conjugation of two of the tenses of *do*:

CONJUGATION OF TWO TENSES OF *DO*	
Past Tense	**Present Perfect Tense**
I did	I have done
you did	you have done
he, she, it did	he, she, it has done
we did	we have done
you did	you have done
they did	they have done

If a sentence contains the past participle *done* without a helping verb, it is incorrect. To correct it, add a helping verb or change *done* to *did*.

INCORRECT: We *done* the assignment.
CORRECT: We *have done* the assignment.
We *did* the assignment.

Theme: Mark Twain's Mississippi

In this section, you will learn the correct uses of several verbs that sometimes give people trouble. The examples and exercises are about the author Mark Twain and the Mississippi River he loved.

Cross-Curricular Connection: Social Studies

> **More Practice**

Language Lab CD-ROM
• Using Verbs lesson
On-Line Exercise Bank
• Section 22.3
Grammar Exercise Workbook
• pp. 101–102

⏱ TIME AND RESOURCE MANAGER

Resources
Print: Grammar Exercise Workbook, pp. 101–106; Hands-on Grammar Activity Book, Chapter 22; Grammar Exercises Answers on Transparencies, Chapter 22
Technology: Language Lab CD-ROM, Using Verbs; On-Line Exercise Bank, Section 22.3

In-Depth Coverage	Accelerated Pace
• Work through all key concepts, pp. 494–498.	• Assign pp. 494–498 for independent student review.
• Assign and review Exercises 24–29.	• Review *set* and *sit*. Assign Exercises 28–29.
• Do the Hands-on Grammar Activity, p. 500.	• Assign Section Review Exercises 30–32, p. 501.

▶ **Exercise 24** Using *Did* and *Done* On your paper, write the correct verb from the choices in parentheses.

EXAMPLE: We have (did, done) a biography of Mark Twain.

ANSWER: done

1. Mark Twain was once asked to name his favorite job of all of those he had (did, done).
2. He said he most enjoyed the work he (did, done) as a riverboat pilot on the Mississippi River.
3. However, he is best known for what he (did, done) as a writer.
4. His stories (did, done) much to make him rich and famous.
5. People have (did, done) many studies of Mark Twain's work.
6. Thanks to this research, we have a better appreciation of what Mark Twain (did, done) in the nineteenth century.
7. Not many people knew what Twain had (did, done) before he became a famous writer.
8. Before his writing career, he (did, done) many odd jobs.
9. Piloting a riverboat was just one job he had (did, done).
10. He also (did, done) stints as a printer and prospector.

▲ **Critical Viewing** Write three sentences about some things you know Mark Twain did. Use the verb *do* in your sentences. **[Connect]**

▶ **Exercise 25** Supplying the Correct Principal Part of *Do* Rewrite the following sentences on your paper, filling in the blank with the correct form of the verb *do*.

EXAMPLE: They have ___?___ what we asked them to do.

ANSWER: done

1. Our class is ___?___ oral reports on Mark Twain.
2. I am going to tell what Twain ___?___ as a riverboat pilot on the Mississippi River.
3. I have ___?___ most of my research.
4. Twain's work on the Mississippi was ___?___ before the Civil War began.
5. Many of the things Twain ___?___ on the Mississippi are described in his novels and stories.

Troublesome Verbs • **495**

Answer Key

▶ **Exercise 24**

1. done
2. did
3. did
4. did
5. done
6. did
7. done
8. did
9. done
10. did

▶ **Exercise 25**

1. Our class is doing oral reports on Mark Twain.
2. I am going to tell what Twain did as a riverboat pilot on the Mississippi River.
3. I have done most of my research.
4. Twain's work on the Mississippi was done before the Civil War began.
5. Many of the things Twain did on the Mississippi are described in his novels and stories.

Critical Viewing

Connect Students may say that Twain did work as a writer, that he did many odd jobs; and that most of his work on the Mississippi was done before the Civil War.

⏱ **TIME SAVERS!**

🗃 **Answers on Transparency** Use the Grammar Exercises Answers on Transparencies for Chapter 22 to facilitate correction by students.

💻 **On-Line Exercise Bank** Have students complete the exercises on computer. The Auto Check feature will grade their work for you!

Using *Lay* and *Lie*

1. *Lay* and *lie* make every troublesome verb list. First, clarify the meaning of each verb. *Lay* means "to put or place something." *Lie* means "to rest in a reclining position."

2. Review the chart and examples for *lay*. Ask students to use each principal part of the verb in a sentence. Point out that *lay* takes a direct object, but *lie* does not.

Customize for ESL Students

Lay and *lie* are confusing even for native speakers. Work with a small group of students to clarify their knowledge of principal parts of each verb. Work through a conjugation chart providing sentences for each example in all six tenses.

22.3

Using *Lay* and *Lie*

Lay and *lie* are two different verbs with different meanings.

▶ **KEY CONCEPT** *Lay* means "to put or place something." ■

PRINCIPAL PARTS OF *LAY*			
Present	Present Participle	Past	Past Participle
lay	(am) laying	laid	(have) laid

When the verb *lay* is used in a sentence, it takes a direct object.

EXAMPLES: Sue usually *lays* her bags in the hallway.

The workers *are laying* the foundation for the house.

The captain *laid* the navigation map on the table.

I *have laid* my glasses on the desk.

▶ **KEY CONCEPT** *Lie* means "to rest in a reclining position." Another meaning for *lie* is "to be situated." ■

PRINCIPAL PARTS OF *LIE*			
Present	Present Participle	Past	Past Participle
lie	(am) lying	lay	(have) lain

Lie does not take a direct object. It can, however, be followed by an adverb or a prepositional phrase.

EXAMPLES: The city *lies* at the mouth of the Mississippi River.
Your atlas *is lying* on my desk.
I *lay* down on the raft and fell asleep.
This Mark Twain novel *has lain* in the attic for years.

Exercise 26 Using the Correct Form of *Lay* or *Lie*

On your paper, write the correct verb from the choices in parentheses.

EXAMPLE: The riverboat captain is (lying, laying) in his cabin.

ANSWER: lying

1. Mississippi (lies, lays) west of Alabama.
2. The beauty of Mississippi has (laid, lain) in its rivers and meadows.
3. Following the hurricane, many tree branches (lay, laid) along the shore of the Gulf of Mexico.
4. Some Mississippi families have (laid, lain) plans for new homes along the state's many rivers.
5. For years, many Mississippians have (laid, lain) under magnolia trees on warm spring days.
6. Jackson, the capital of Mississippi, (lies, lays) on the Pearl River in southwest central Mississippi.
7. Jackson's planners (lay, laid) the city out on the site of an old trading post.
8. The Mississippi River (lies, lays) at the western border of Mississippi.
9. Many residents of Mississippi have (laid, lain) their roots within the state.
10. At this very moment, people are (laying, lying) the foundations for new homes and businesses throughout the state.

▲ Critical Viewing Using *lie* or *lay* correctly in a sentence, tell what might be around the bend of the river in this photograph of a riverboat. **[Speculate]**

Exercise 27 Proofreading for Errors With *Lay* and *Lie*

Read the following sentences. If the verb form is correct, write *correct*. If it is incorrect, rewrite the sentence with the correct form.
1. Mark Twain lain type before writing books.
2. The joy of childhood lays at the heart of many of Mark Twain's books.
3. His characters often spend days lying on the banks of the Mississippi River.
4. You may enjoy his books while laying in a quiet place.
5. He laid to rest his dreams of gold.
6. Small towns that laid throughout the West were depicted in Twain's books.
7. Before that time, Twain lay his stories of the West aside while he prospected for gold.
8. His humor lays at the heart of every story.
9. It is clear to modern readers that important messages are lying in his stories.
10. Yesterday, I lay my copy of *Tom Sawyer* on the table, but someone must have borrowed it.

More Practice

Language Lab CD-ROM
• Using Verbs lesson
On-line Exercise Bank
• Section 22.3
Grammar Exercise Workbook
• pp. 103–104

Critical Viewing

Speculate Students may say that a large town lies around the bend or that a huge log lies in the boat's path.

Answer Key

Exercise 26
1. lies
2. lain
3. lay
4. laid
5. lain
6. lies
7. laid
8. lies
9. laid
10. laying

Exercise 27
1. laid
2. lies
3. correct
4. lying
5. correct
6. lay
7. laid
8. lies
9. correct
10. laid

Integrating Spelling

Multiple-Meaning Words The word *capitol* has only one meaning: the actual building that is the seat of government. *Capital*, however, has several meanings: the capital city of a state or country, an uppercase letter, the top of a column in architecture, money.

TIME SAVERS!

Answers on Transparency Use the Grammar Exercises Answers on Transparencies for Chapter 22 to facilitate correction by students.

On-Line Exercise Bank Have students complete the exercises on computer. The Auto Check feature will grade their work for you!

Using *Set* and *Sit*

1. Review the two key concepts and examples.
2. Point out that *set* takes a direct object. Have students use each form in a sentence.
3. Point out that *sit* does not take a direct object. Have students use each form in a sentence.
4. Write the following additional examples on the board.

   We are sitting in our assigned seats.

   The dog had sat in front of the salami for two hours without moving.

   We will sit in the bleachers.

Customize for *ESL Students*

Reassure students that *did/done, lay/lie,* and *set/sit* confuse people who have spoken English all their lives. It is all right if students are still not 100 percent sure when to use each word. If they just remember that these three word pairs are confusing, then they will know to ask for help or refer to the dictionary.

22.3

Using *Set* and *Sit*

Set and *sit* look and sound similar, but their meanings are different.

▶ **KEY CONCEPT** *Set* means "to put something in a certain place." ■

PRINCIPAL PARTS OF *SET*			
Present	Present Participle	Past	Past Participle
set	(am) setting	set	(have) set

Set is followed by a direct object.

EXAMPLES: I *set* the book on top of the shelves. (DO)

Our class *is setting* all our poems in notebooks. (DO)

The boys *set* the raft afloat. (DO)

Mark Twain *had set* this novel in Europe. (DO)

▶ **KEY CONCEPT** *Sit* means "to be seated" or "to rest." ■

PRINCIPAL PARTS OF *SIT*			
Present	Present Participle	Past	Past Participle
sit	(am) sitting	sat	(have) sat

Sit does not take a direct object. Instead, it is often followed by an adverb or a prepositional phrase, as in the following sentences.

EXAMPLES: We *sit* at tables in our English class.
Paul *is sitting* with Tim and Jackie.
Carmen and Claudia *sat* quietly in the library.
We *have sat* here for more than three hours.

498 • Using Verbs

☑ ONGOING ASSESSMENT: Monitor and Reinforce

If students miss more than two items in Exercises 24–29, refer them to the following for additional practice.

In the Textbook	Print Resources	Technology
Section Review, Ex. 30–32, p. 501	Grammar Exercise Workbook, pp. 101–106	Language Lab CD-ROM, Using Verbs; On-Line Exercise Bank, Section 22.3

▶ **Exercise 28** Using *Set* and *Sit* In the sentences below, choose the correct verb from the pair in parentheses.

EXAMPLE: Felicia usually (sits, sets) in the first row.

ANSWER: sits

1. I am (sitting, setting) here reading a story by Mark Twain.
2. Soon, I must (set, sit) the book down and do my other homework.
3. Believe it or not, this book (set, sat) in the library for two years before anyone checked it out.
4. I would love to (sit, set) a place at our dinner table for Mark Twain.
5. I could (set, sit) for hours and listen to him talk.
6. Until Mark Twain came along, most American writers had (sat, set) their stories in New England or other eastern states.
7. Unlike them, Twain (sat, set) many of his stories in small towns along the Mississippi River.
8. My small town (sits, sets) in the center of our state.
9. If you wanted, you could probably (sit, set) many of the characters in Twain's stories right in my town.
10. If you had (set, sat) down near Main Street in our town in 1870, you would have met similar people.

▼ **Critical Viewing**
Using *set* or *sat* correctly in a sentence, describe what the frog in this picture is doing. **[Describe]**

▶ **Exercise 29** Supplying Forms of *Set* or *Sit* in Sentences
Rewrite the following sentences on your paper, filling in each blank with the proper form of *set* or *sit*.
1. Twain's books have ___?___ a high standard for American literature.
2. Thousands of people are ___?___ and reading these American classics every day.
3. Twain's many novels have ___?___ prominently on library shelves all over the world.
4. Twain ___?___ humor and satire into his stories.
5. Almost everyone who has ___?___ down to read one of his novels has started to laugh.
6. Twain ___?___ *The Adventures of Huckleberry Finn* (1884) along the Mississippi River.
7. During much of the novel, Huck and Jim ___?___ on a raft and discuss life.
8. In the daytime, they ___?___ the raft near the shore and hide from slave catchers.
9. They must ___?___ quietly so that Jim will not be caught.
10. Where should I ___?___ this biography of Mark Twain that I checked out of the library?

▶ **More Practice**
**Language Lab
CD-ROM**
• Using Verbs lesson
**On-line
Exercise Bank**
• Section 22.3
**Grammar Exercise
Workbook**
• pp. 105–106

▶ **Exercise 28**

1. sitting
2. set
3. sat
4. set
5. sit
6. set
7. set
8. sits
9. set
10. sat

▶ **Exercise 29**

1. Twain's books have set a high standard for American literature.
2. Thousands of people are sitting and reading these American classics every day.
3. Twain's many novels have sat prominently on library shelves all over the world.
4. Twain set humor and satire into his stories.
5. Almost everyone who has sat down to read one of his novels has started to laugh.
6. Twain set *The Adventures of Huckleberry Finn* (1884) along the Mississippi River.
7. During much of the novel, Huck and Jim sit on a raft and discuss life.
8. In the daytime they set the raft near the shore and hide from slave catchers.
9. They must sit quietly so that Jim will not be caught.
10. Where should I set this biography of Mark Twain that I checked out of the library?

Critical Viewing

Describe Students may say that the frog is sitting and waiting for a fly.

Stop-and-Go Verb Game

Teaching Resources: Hands-on Grammar Activity Book, Chapter 22

1. Have students refer to their Hands-on Grammar activity books or give them copies of relevant pages for this activity.

2. Be sure students use the nouns on the board as direct objects. You may want to specify that a player who uses the verb incorrectly does not advance.

Find It in Your Reading

Have students list the verbs and their tenses.

Find It in Your Writing

You may want to have students complete this activity in pairs so they can check each other's work.

22.3

Hands-on Grammar

Stop-and-Go Verb Game

Practice forming sentences with those troublesome verbs *set*, *sit*, *lay*, and *lie* by playing the following game.

Create a game board as illustrated in the picture below. Write a variety of nouns in the squares. Cut paper into twenty 2 1/2" x 1 1/2" pieces. With a green crayon or marker, write *lay* on five pieces of paper; then, write *set* in green on five pieces. With a red crayon or marker, write *lie* on five pieces of paper; then, write *sit* in red on five pieces. These are your verb cards. Write *verb* on the back of each card. Shuffle the cards together and set them in the middle of the board.

The object of the game is to move all the way around the board from start to finish by creating sentences with the noun on the board as the direct object.

(2 1/2" x 1 1/2" cards)

1. Place a token, such as a coin or a pebble, in the start square.

2. The first player draws a card. If there is a green verb on the card, the player must form a sentence using the noun in the square as a direct object. After forming an appropriate sentence, the player moves to the next square. If there is a red verb on the card, the player stops and waits until his or her next turn. The next player then takes a turn. The first player to reach the finish square is the winner.

Find It in Your Reading Find examples of the proper use of these troublesome verbs in your reading.

Find It in Your Writing Look through your writing portfolio for examples of how you have used *sit*, *set*, *lay*, and *lie*. Make sure that you have used these verbs correctly. If not, rewrite the sentences that are incorrect.

500 • Using Verbs

⏱ **TIME SAVERS!**

✋ **Hands-on Grammar**
Use the Hands-on Grammar activity sheet for Chapter 22 to facilitate this activity.

☑ **ONGOING ASSESSMENT: Assess Mastery**

Use the following resources to assess student mastery of using verbs.

In the Textbook	Print Resources	Technology
Chapter Review, Ex. 41–43, p. 503	Formal Assessment, Chapter 22	On-Line Exercise Bank, Chapter 22

Section 22.3 Section Review

GRAMMAR EXERCISES 30–35

▶ **Exercise 30** Revising Sentences to Eliminate Errors in Verb Usage
Rewrite each incorrect sentence below, eliminating errors in verb usage. If a sentence contains no errors, write *correct*.

1. Many beautiful states are laying along the Mississippi River.
2. Missouri lies west of the Mississippi.
3. Jefferson City, the capital of Missouri, sets in the center of the state.
4. The people of Missouri done many things to preserve the state's charm.
5. State workers sat beds of flowers along state highways.
6. A state agency set rules to preserve caves and natural springs.
7. Everything they done has helped.
8. These steps have did much to preserve Missouri's environment.
9. Today, we are setting in a park near Columbia, Missouri.
10. The University of Missouri lays in the center of the city.

▶ **Exercise 31** Using Troublesome Verbs For each of the following sentences, write the correct verb from the pair in parentheses.

1. Mark Twain's birthplace (lies, lays) in Hannibal, Missouri.
2. Town leaders (set, sat) a marker in the center of the town to honor Twain.
3. Mark Twain (did, done) much to make Hannibal a popular tourist site.
4. The house where he grew up still (sits, sets) in the town.
5. Many nights, Twain had (laid, lain) awake in that house, thinking up stories.
6. The cave where he (set, sat) part of *Tom Sawyer* (lies, lays) nearby.
7. Volunteers have (did, done) a good job of preserving these landmarks.

8. They (did, done) this as an act of love and respect.
9. If you (set, sit) in Mark Twain's home, you can imagine that he is (setting, sitting) there with you.
10. When we (lay, laid) in Mark Twain Cave, we felt that Tom Sawyer was (lying, laying) next to us.

▶ **Exercise 32** Writing Sentences With *Set* and *Lay* Write a sentence for each numbered item below, using the verb tense and the direct object given.

1. lay (present perfect), the package
2. set (past), the flowers
3. lay (present), the books
4. set (past perfect), the groceries
5. lay (past), the pencil

▶ **Exercise 33** Find It in Your Reading Look through magazines and newspapers to find sentences in which the troublesome verbs in this section are used correctly.

▶ **Exercise 34** Find It in Your Writing Look through your writing portfolio. Find examples of sentences in which you used *did, done, lie, lay, sit,* or *set*. Make sure that you have used them correctly.

▶ **Exercise 35** Writing Application Imagine that you are sitting on a riverboat gliding down the Mississippi River. Write a brief description of your trip. Include the following verbs or verb phrases in your description: *have done, set, have sat, laid, lay* (past tense).

ASSESS and CLOSE

Section Review

Each of these exercises correlates with the instruction on troublesome verbs, pages 494–500. These exercises may be used for more practice, for reteaching, or for review of the key concepts presented. Answers to all chapter exercises are available in *Grammar Exercises Answers on Transparencies* in your Teaching Resources.

Answer Key

▶ **Exercise 30**

1. Many beautiful states lie along the Mississippi River.
2. correct
3. Jefferson City, the capital of Missouri, sits in the center of the state.
4. The people of Missouri did many things to preserve the state's charm.
5. State workers set beds of flowers along state highways.
6. correct
7. Everything they did has helped.
8. These steps have done much to preserve Missouri's environment.
9. Today, we are sitting in a park near Columbia, Missouri.
10. The University of Missouri lies in the center of the city.

▶ **Exercise 31**

1. lies
2. set
3. did
4. sits
5. lain
6. set, lies
7. done
8. did
9. sit, sitting
10. lay, lying

▶ **Exercise 32**

1. I have laid the package on the counter.
2. She set the flowers in the vase.
3. He lays the books on the shelf.
4. We had set the groceries in the refrigerator.
5. He laid the pencil beside the notepad.

continued

Answer Key continued

▶ **Exercise 33**

Find It in Your Reading
Students may also find these verbs used incorrectly (more often in quotations). Suggest that they cut them out and make a bulletin board display titled "Mistakes <u>We</u> Don't Make."

▶ **Exercise 34**

Find It in Your Writing
If students find any mistakes in their verb use, they should correct them.

▶ **Exercise 35**

Writing Application
Students can read their descriptions aloud to the class.

CHAPTER REVIEW

Each of these exercises correlates with a section of the chapter on using verbs, pages 480–501. These exercises may be used for more practice, for reteaching, or for review of the key concepts presented. Answers for all chapter exercises are available in *Grammar Exercises Answers on Transparencies* in your Teaching Resources.

Answer Key

1. want—regular
2. travel—regular
3. read—irregular
4. lie—irregular
5. describe—regular
6. think—irregular
7. write—irregular
8. begin—irregular
9. replace—regular
10. sail—regular

1. present
2. past
3. past; past participle
4. past
5. past participle

1. arrived
2. traveled
3. come
4. drew
5. began
6. gave
7. correct
8. made
9. bought
10. became

1. present perfect
2. past
3. past
4. past
5. past perfect
6. present
7. present perfect
8. present perfect
9. future
10. future perfect

▶ **Exercise 36** Classifying Regular and Irregular Verbs List the verbs below on your paper. Then, label each verb *regular* or *irregular*.

1. want
2. travel
3. read
4. lie
5. describe
6. think
7. write
8. begin
9. replace
10. sail

▶ **Exercise 37** Identifying Principal Parts of Regular and Irregular Verbs On your paper, write the principal part used to form each underlined verb below.

1. Mark Twain <u>is</u> only one famous person from Missouri.
2. President Harry Truman <u>grew</u> up there.
3. He <u>became</u> president in 1945, after Franklin Roosevelt had <u>died</u>.
4. Inventor George Washington Carver also <u>spent</u> his early years in Missouri.
5. His parents had <u>been</u> slaves.

▶ **Exercise 38** Supplying the Correct Verb Form Revise the following passage by writing the correct form of each underlined verb. If the correct form of the verb has been used, write *correct* on your paper.

The first Europeans <u>arrive</u> in Missouri in the late 1600's. In 1673 two French explorers, Marquette and Joliet, had <u>travel</u> down the Mississippi River. They had <u>came</u> to where the Mississippi and Missouri rivers met. They <u>drawed</u> a map of the area. Soon, other French explorers and trappers <u>begin</u> arriving in the area. They <u>give</u> the area the name *Missouri*, after a Native American word that means "canoe owner." In 1764, the city of St. Louis was <u>established</u> there. When

Thomas Jefferson <u>maked</u> the Louisiana Purchase in 1803, Missouri was included in the purchase. Jefferson had <u>buyed</u> millions of acres of new territory for the United States. In 1821, Missouri <u>become</u> the twenty-fourth state to join the Union.

▶ **Exercise 39** Classifying Verb Tenses On your paper, write the tense of each underlined verb in the following sentences.

1. Many people <u>have dreamed</u> of traveling down a river on a makeshift raft.
2. In the 1800's, steamboats <u>ferried</u> people up and down American rivers.
3. People <u>flocked</u> to the Mississippi River to ride on steamboats.
4. Many steamboats <u>had</u> luxurious cabins and dining halls.
5. Until the early 1900's, steamboats <u>had dominated</u> transportation along the nation's rivers.
6. Today, people <u>travel</u> mostly on airplanes and in automobiles.
7. For the most part, that era of steamboat travel <u>has come</u> to an end.
8. Improvements in transportation and highways <u>have pushed</u> steamboats out of existence.
9. Transportation <u>will improve</u> even more in the near future.
10. By the next century, most people <u>will have forgotten</u> what it was like to travel on a steamboat.

▶ **Exercise 40** Supplying the Correct Verb Form On your paper, rewrite the following sentences, replacing the underlined verb with the tense indicated in parentheses.

1. Mark Twain's stories <u>inspire</u> many

readers and writers. (present perfect)

2. This be true even when Mark Twain was alive. (past)
3. By the early 1900's, thousands of Twain's fans see the Mississippi River for themselves. (past perfect)
4. Many admirers of Mark Twain's stories make trips to towns along the Mississippi River. (past perfect)
5. Many do so to see the places that inspired Twain. (past)
6. They continue to do so in the future. (future)
7. Missouri always welcomes its visitors warmly. (present perfect)
8. For many years, cities and towns throughout Missouri hold festivals for visitors. (present perfect)
9. By the end of each year, thousands of visitors take part in these festivals. (future perfect)
10. By the end of next year, even more Mark Twain fans set off on journeys along the Mississippi. (future perfect)

▶ **Exercise 41** Revising Sentences With Troublesome Verbs Rewrite the following sentences, correcting the verbs. If a sentence is correct, write *correct*.

1. When the first French explorers came to Missouri, they did not know what riches laid beneath the soil.
2. A rich deposit of lead had lain in Missouri's hills for thousands of years.
3. In the 1770's, adventurous people who were setting in their homes in the East heard about the lead deposits.
4. Many sat all of their belongings into wagons and proceeded west.
5. Some who had done poorly in other parts of the country done quite well for themselves in Missouri.

▶ **Exercise 42** Revising a Paragraph to Eliminate Errors in Verb Usage Rewrite the following paragraph, correcting all errors in verb usage.

The Mississippi River has play a key role in United States history. Today, many important cities lay along the river. New Orleans, Memphis, St. Louis, and Minneapolis are just a few of the cities that set along the river's banks. During the 1600's, the Mississippi becomed a vital transportation route for trappers. They sat furs upon rafts and ship them up or down the river. Later, settlers move into these areas. Steamboats make the river an even more important trade route. You may have thunk the Mississippi was a southern river. However, it actually begun in Minnesota and flows southward. If you travel down the entire river, you will have went 2,340 miles.

▶ **Exercise 43** Writing Sentences With Different Verb Tenses On your paper, write a sentence using each verb below in the tense specified.

1. notice (present perfect)
2. bring (past)
3. create (past perfect)
4. write (future perfect)
5. begin (past)
6. remember (future)
7. continue (present)
8. get (present perfect)
9. remark (present perfect)
10. set (past perfect)

▶ **Exercise 44** Writing Application Write a description of an interesting trip you have taken. Use both regular and irregular verbs in different tenses. Circle the verbs you use. Use each of the following verbs at least once.

1. did
2. set
3. had sat
4. lay
5. had lain

Chapter Review • 503

Answer Key continued

(9) However, it actually begins in Minnesota and flows southward. (10) If you travel down the entire river, you will have gone 2,340 miles.

▶ **Exercise 43**

1. has or have noticed
2. brought
3. had created
4. will have written
5. began

6. will remember
7. continue or continues
8. has or have gotten
9. has or have remarked
10. had set

▶ **Exercise 44**

Writing Application
Students could write instead about a trip they would like to take. Have them label the verbs *regular* and *irregular*.

▶ **Exercise 40** *(page 502)*

1. Mark Twain's stories have inspired many readers and writers.
2. This was true even when Mark Twain was alive.
3. By the early 1900's, thousands of Twain's fans had seen the Mississippi River for themselves.
4. Many admirers of Mark Twain's stories had made trips to towns along the Mississippi River.
5. Many did so to see the places that inspired Twain.
6. They will continue to do so in the future.
7. Missouri always has welcomed its visitors warmly.
8. For many years cities and towns throughout Missouri have held festivals for visitors.
9. By the end of each year, thousands of visitors will have taken part in these festivals.
10. By the end of next year, even more Mark Twain fans will have set off on journeys along the Mississippi.

▶ **Exercise 41**

1. When the first French explorers came to Missouri, they did not know what riches lay beneath the soil.
2. correct
3. In the 1770's, adventurous people who were sitting in their homes in the East heard about the lead deposits.
4. Many set all of their belongings into wagons and proceeded west.
5. Some who had done poorly in other parts of the country did quite well for themselves in Missouri.

▶ **Exercise 42**

(1) The Mississippi River has played a key role in United States history. (2) Today, many important cities lie along the river. (3) New Orleans, Memphis, St. Louis, and Minneapolis are just a few of the cities that sit along the river's banks. (4) During the 1600's, the Mississippi became a vital transportation route for trappers. (5) They set furs upon rafts and shipped them up or down the river. (6) Later, settlers moved into these areas. (7) Steamboats made the river an even more important trade route. (8) You may have thought the Mississippi was a southern river.

continued

Standard English Usage: Verb Tenses

Teaching Resources: Standardized Test Preparation Workbook, Chapter 22

1. Explain to students that they should look for clues in the sentence that tell them when the action takes place. This will help them choose the correct verb tense or form.

2. Dinosaurs are the subject of the first sentence. The sentence contrasts the conditions on Earth during the time of the dinosaurs with conditions today. Both of these clues indicate that the missing verb is in the past tense, narrowing the choices to C and D. Choice D, which is in the past perfect tense, does not fit the sentence. The correct answer is **C**.

3. Have a volunteer explain her or his reasoning for question 2.

Standardized Test Preparation Workshop

Standard English Usage: Verb Tenses

Your knowledge of verb usage is frequently measured on standardized tests. Your ability to determine the correct tense of a verb—present, present perfect, past, past perfect, future, and future perfect—is tested when you must choose a verb or verb phrase to complete a sentence. When choosing a verb, first read the sentence to yourself and determine when the action is taking place. Then, choose a verb in the tense that indicates the time of the action.

The following sample test items will give you practice with the format of questions that test verb usage.

Test Tip

Read the sentence to yourself several times, substituting each answer choice in place of the blank. Eliminate those choices that sound awkward or change the meaning of the sentence.

Sample Test Items

Directions Read the passage, and choose the letter of the word or group of words that belongs in each space.

Dinosaurs _____(1)_____ in an Earth much different from today. In this chapter, you _____(2)_____ about the major differences.

1 A live
  B are living
  C lived
  D had lived

2 F have learned
  G is learning
  H are learning
  J will learn

Answers and Explanations

The correct answer is *C*. The passage indicates an action that took place in the past. Therefore, the past tense verb form *lived* is the correct choice for completing the sentence.

The correct answer is *J*. The passage indicates an action that will occur in the future. Therefore, the future tense verb *will appear* is the correct choice for completing the sentence.

✎ TEST-TAKING TIP

Remind students that the clues used to determine the correct response to the first sample item are called context clues. Point out that many context clues have meaning because of a person's general knowledge and life experiences. For example, the context clue "dinosaurs" would be of no help to a person who did not know that dinosaurs lived in the past. Remind students to draw on all their knowledge when taking a test.

Answer Key

> **Practice 1**

1. D
2. G
3. A
4. F
5. A

> **Practice 2**

1. D
2. H
3. C
4. H
5. D

> **Practice 1** **Directions:** Read the passage, and choose the letter of the word or group of words that belongs in each space.

Many scientists ___(1)___ that present-day continents were once a single land mass. During the Mesozoic Era, the continents slowly ___(2)___ apart. Before this occurred, dinosaurs ___(3)___ over land connections between the continents. As the continents drifted apart, however, their climates ___(4)___ more and more. One theory to explain the disappearance of dinosaurs ___(5)___ this change in climate.

1 A have believed
  B are believing
  C believed
  D believe

2 F is drifting
  G drifted
  H have drifted
  J drift

3 A had wandered
  B wander
  C has wandered
  D are wandering

4 F changed
  G are changing
  H was changing
  J will change

5 A concerns
  B concern
  C concerned
  D was concerned

> **Practice 2** **Directions:** Read the passage, and choose the letter of the word or group of words that belongs in each space.

Today, in science class, we ___(1)___ the theories as to why dinosaurs died out. Many scientists ___(2)___ their theories on a change in climate—from tropical to cold. Other experts believe that plant-eating dinosaurs ___(3)___ the new plants that developed and starved. Another theory ___(4)___ that a large asteroid ___(5)___ into Earth, thus creating billions of tons of dust that blocked out the sun for three to six months.

1 A was investigating
  B are investigating
  C investigate
  D investigated

2 F had based
  G will base
  H base
  J were basing

3 A ate
  B are not eating
  C could not eat
  D cannot have eaten

4 F are suggesting
  G had suggested
  H suggests
  J will suggest

5 A crash
  B are crashing
  C were crashing
  D crashed

In-Depth Lesson Plan

	LESSON FOCUS	PRINT AND MEDIA RESOURCES
DAY 1	**Using Subject, Objective, and Possessive Pronouns** Students learn and apply concepts covering subject, objective, and possessive pronouns (pp. 508–511).	**Teaching Resources** *Grammar Exercise Workbook*, pp. 107–112; *Grammar Exercises Answers on Transparencies*, Ch. 23 *Language Lab* **CD-ROM**, Using Pronouns; **On-Line Exercise Bank**, Section 23
DAY 2	**Using Different Pronoun Cases** Students learn and apply concepts covering pronoun cases and do the Hands-on Grammar activity (pp. 511–513).	**Teaching Resources** *Grammar Exercise Workbook*, pp. 113–114; *Grammar Exercises Answers on Transparencies*, Ch. 23; *Hands-on Grammar Activity Book*, Ch. 23 *Language Lab* **CD-ROM**, Using Pronouns; **On-Line Exercise Bank**, Section 23
DAY 3	**Review and Assess** Students review chapter and demonstrate mastery of use of pronouns (pp. 514–517).	**Teaching Resources** *Formal Assessment*, Ch. 23; *Grammar Exercises Answers on Transparencies*, Ch. 23 **On-Line Exercise Bank**, Section 23

Accelerated Lesson Plan

	LESSON FOCUS	PRINT AND MEDIA RESOURCES
DAY 1	**Pronouns** Students cover concepts and usage of pronouns as determined by Diagnostic Test (pp. 508–513).	**Teaching Resources** *Grammar Exercise Workbook*, pp. 107–114; *Grammar Exercises Answers on Transparencies*, Ch. 23; *Hands-on Grammar Activity Book*, Ch. 23 *Language Lab* **CD-ROM**, Using Pronouns; **On-Line Exercise Bank**, Section 23
DAY 2	**Review and Assess** Students review chapter and demonstrate mastery of use of pronouns (pp. 514–517).	**Teaching Resources** *Formal Assessment*, Ch. 23; *Grammar Exercises Answers on Transparencies*, Ch. 23 **On-Line Exercise Bank**, Section 23

Options for Adapting Lesson Plans

HOMEWORK

Have students complete any section of the chapter for homework.

FEATURES

Extend coverage with the Grammar in Literature feature (p. 512), and the Standardized Test Preparation Workshop (p. 516).

TECHNOLOGY

Students can use the On-Line Exercise Bank to complete the exercises on computer. The Auto Check feature will grade their work.

INTEGRATED SKILLS COVERAGE

Grammar in Literature
SE p. 512

Reading
Find It in Your Reading SE p. 513

Writing
Find It in Your Writing SE p. 513
Writing Application SE p. 515

Spelling
SE p. 510, ATE p. 510

Viewing and Representing
Critical Viewing SE pp. 506, 509, 510, 512

ASSESSMENT SUPPORT

Standardized Test Preparation SE p. 516; ATE p. 512
Standardized Test Preparation Workbook, pp. 45–46
Formal Assessment, Ch. 23

MEETING INDIVIDUAL NEEDS

Less Advanced Students See Ongoing Assessment
ATE p. 511
Verbal/Linguistic Learners ATE p. 508
Bodily/Kinesthetic Learners ATE p. 509

BLOCK SCHEDULING

Pacing Suggestions
For 90-minute Blocks
- Administer the Diagnostic Test to students to determine instructional coverage.
- Have students complete the necessary exercises in class. Use the Hands-on Grammar activity to provide a change of pace.

Resources for Varying Instruction
- *Language Lab* **CD-ROM** If your students have access to hardware, a 90-minute block provides an ideal opportunity for students to work on computer.

Professional Development Support
- *How to Manage Instruction in the Block* This teaching Resource provides management and activity suggestions.

MEDIA AND TECHNOLOGY

For the Student
- *Language Lab* **CD-ROM**, Using Pronouns
- *On-Line Exercise Bank*, Ch. 23

For the Teacher
- *Resource Pro* **CD-ROM**

WRITING AND GRAMMAR WEB SITE

The Interactive Writing and Grammar Web site provides a wide array of support for students, teachers, and parents. Grammar support includes:

- On-Line Exercise Bank with Auto Check scoring
- Diagnostic and assessment support

www.phschool.com

LITERATURE CONNECTIONS

Grammar in Literature selections from *Prentice Hall Literature: Timeless Voices, Timeless Themes,* Copper:
from "The Shutout," Patricia C. McKissack and Frederick McKissack, Jr., SE p. 512

Lesson Objectives

1. To identify subject pronouns and use them correctly in sentences.
2. To recognize object pronouns as direct objects, indirect objects, and objects of prepositions in sentences.
3. To use and identify possessive pronouns in sentences.
4. To recognize the different kinds of personal pronouns and their uses.

Critical Viewing

Infer Students may say of the players that they are running onto the field and that the fans are watching them.

Chapter 23 Using Pronouns

▲ **Critical Viewing**
What are the football players and fans doing or about to do? Use the pronouns *they* and *them* in your answer. **[Infer]**

Personal pronouns have different forms, such as *he, his,* and *him,* that tell how the pronouns are being used. Personal pronouns can be subjects *(he),* objects *(him),* or words showing ownership *(his).*

You must use different forms of pronouns to make your ideas clear. For instance, without pronouns you might write *Jack caught the football. Jack then ran Jack's fastest to score a touchdown.* Using the correct forms of pronouns, however, you can write this:

Jack caught the football. He then ran his fastest to score a touchdown.

This chapter will tell you more about the three types of personal pronouns. Each type does a different job when used in a sentence. In this chapter, you will learn about each type. Then, you will practice using the pronouns correctly.

506 • Using Pronouns

☑ ONGOING ASSESSMENT: Diagnose

If students miss more than one item in each category, direct them to the relevant pages of the text and assign exercises for practice and review.

Using Pronouns	Diagnostic Test Items	Teach	Practice	Chapter Review
Skill Check A				
Subject Pronouns	A 1–5	p. 508	Ex. 1	Ex. 5–7
Skill Check B				
Objective Pronouns	B 6–10	p. 509	Ex. 2	Ex. 5, 8

Diagnostic Test

Directions: Write all answers on a separate piece of paper.

Skill Check A. Write the correct subject pronoun from the choices in parentheses.

1. The coach and (they, them) decided on the play.
2. The quarterback and (he, him) discussed several options.
3. Either the fullback or (I, me) will run with the ball.
4. (He, Him) and the other linemen will block for us.
5. The fans and (we, us) will hope for a touchdown.

Skill Check B. Select the correct objective pronoun from the pair in parentheses, and tell whether it functions as a *direct object*, an *indirect object*, or an *object of a preposition*.

6. Knute Rockne taught (we, us) many lessons about the game of football.
7. His innovations to the game made (it, its) much more exciting.
8. The forward pass was pioneered by Charles Dorais and (he, him).
9. Football fans regard (they, them) as legends.
10. Rockne's determination inspires my friends and (me, I).

Skill Check C. Select the correct possessive pronoun from the choices in parentheses.

11. Are these tickets to the baseball game (yours, your's)?
12. These seats are (ours, ours').
13. (Hers, Hers') are the ones near first base.
14. Our team is in first place in (it's, its) league.
15. Our second baseman and shortstop are known for (their, there) speed.

Skill Check D. Label each underlined pronoun *nominative*, *objective*, or *possessive*.

16. During the 1950s, the city of Cleveland had <u>its</u> sports hero.
17. Running back Jim Brown was terrific, in <u>our</u> opinion.
18. Opposing players could not stop <u>him</u> from advancing.
19. Brown managed to run past <u>them</u> or through <u>them</u>.
20. <u>He</u> scored 126 touchdowns during <u>his</u> career.

Skill Check E. Select the correct pronoun from the choices in parentheses.

21. Bill Russell is (her, hers) choice for the most valuable professional basketball player ever.
22. The tall, thin center changed how (his', his) position was played.
23. Opponents feared (him, he) and the other players on his team.
24. During his career, (he, him) and his teammates won eleven league titles.
25. (He, him) gave my friends and (I, me) many exciting moments during (he, his) career.

Answer Key

Diagnostic Test

Each item in the Diagnostic Test corresponds to a specific section in the chapter on using pronouns. This will enable you to tailor instruction to the particular needs of your students. See "Ongoing Assessment: Diagnose" below for further details.

Skill Check A

1. they
2. he
3. I
4. He
5. we

Skill Check B

6. us—indirect object
7. it—direct object
8. him—object of a preposition
9. them—direct object
10. me—direct object

Skill Check C

11. yours
12. ours
13. Hers
14. its
15. their

Skill Check D

16. possessive
17. possessive
18. objective
19. objective; objective
20. nominative; possessive

Skill Check E

21. her
22. his
23. him
24. he
25. He; me; his

✓ ONGOING ASSESSMENT: Diagnose *continued*

Using Pronouns	Diagnostic Test Items	Teach	Practice	Chapter Review
Skill Check C				
Possessive Pronouns	C 11–15	pp. 510–511	Ex. 3	Ex. 9–10
Skill Check D				
Different Pronoun Cases	D 16–20	pp. 511–512	Ex. 4	Ex. 5, 7
Skill Check E				
Different Pronoun Forms	E 21–25	p. 511–512	Ex. 4	Ex. 6, 11
Cumulative Reviews and Applications				Ex. 12–13

⏱ TIME SAVERS!

📽 **Answers on Transparency** Use the Grammar Exercises Answers on Transparencies for Chapter 23 to facilitate correction by students.

💻 **On-Line Exercise Bank** Have students complete the Diagnostic Test on computer. The Auto Check feature will grade their work for you!

PREPARE and ENGAGE

Interest GRABBER Have students brainstorm lyrics from radio or television jingles that use pronouns. Have them write the lyrics on the chalkboard and circle the pronouns.

Activate Prior Knowledge

Have partners each make a list of five nouns. Then have students trade lists, writing sentences that replace the nouns with singular and plural pronouns.

TEACH

Step-by-Step Teaching Guide

Using Subject Pronouns

1. Subject pronouns behave like subjects in sentences. Subject pronouns are modified by adjectives, and they are singular and plural.

2. Students may have difficulty using pronouns grammatically in compound subjects. Urge students to memorize the rule for compound subjects: When in doubt about which pronoun to use with a subject, say the sentence aloud with the pronoun as the only subject. Choose the pronoun that sounds better.

Answer Key

Exercise 1

1. we	6. she
2. they	7. he
3. she	8. she
4. he	9. I
5. I	10. He; I

Customize for
Verbal/Linguistic Learners

Encourage students to read the sentences in Exercise 1 (and elsewhere) aloud quietly. Often, they will instinctively choose the correct answer because it "sounds right." Then, have them go back and make sure their answers agree with the chart of subject pronouns on page 508.

Using Subject Pronouns

Pronouns have different forms to show how they are being used.

▶ **KEY CONCEPT** A *subject pronoun* is used as the subject of a sentence. ■

SUBJECT PRONOUNS	
Singular	**Plural**
I, you, he, she, it	we, you, they

When a sentence has a single subject, it is easy to select the correct subject pronoun. However, when a sentence has a compound subject, it is more difficult to choose the right pronoun.

EXAMPLES: Fred and *I* [not *me*] agreed to block for Matthew.
The coach and *he* [not *him*] led the parade.

To choose the correct pronoun when the subject is a compound, say the sentence to yourself with only the pronoun as the subject. Omit the other words in the subject. Say the sentence with each pronoun you think might be correct. Choose the one pronoun that sounds correct.

EXAMPLE: Ken and (I, me) organized the pep rally.

Omit the words *Ken and.* Try each of the pronouns with the rest of the sentence. "*Me* organized the pep rally" does not sound correct. "*I* organized the pep rally" does.

▶ **Exercise 1** Identifying the Correct Subject Pronoun On your paper, write the correct subject pronoun from the choices in parentheses.

EXAMPLE: My friends and (I, me) like football.
ANSWER: I

1. The kids down the street and (us, we) often play football.
2. Our team members and (them, they) are the same age.
3. Derrick and (her, she) will be the team captains.
4. Franklin and (him, he) brought their footballs.
5. Julie and (I, me) run faster than anyone else.
6. Terry or (her, she) will receive the kickoff.
7. Bill and (he, him) blocked our opponents.
8. Robert and (she, her) tackled him.
9. John and (I, me) scored a touchdown.
10. (Him, He) and (I, me) celebrated.

508 • Using Pronouns

Theme: Team Sports

In this chapter, you will learn how to use three different forms of pronouns. The examples and exercises are about team sports and famous players.

Cross-Curricular Connection: Physical Education

▶ **More Practice**

Language Lab CD-ROM
• Pronoun Case lesson
On-line Exercise Bank
• Chapter 23
Grammar Exercise Workbook
• pp. 107–108

⏱ TIME AND RESOURCE MANAGER	
Resources	

Print: Grammar Exercise Workbook, pp. 107–114; Grammar Exercises Answers on Transparencies, Chapter 23
Technology: Language Lab CD-ROM, Using Pronouns; On-Line Exercise Bank, Section 23

In-Depth Coverage	Accelerated Pace
• Work through all key concepts, pp. 508–512.	• Assign pp. 508–512 for independent student review.
• Assign and review Exercises 1–4.	
• Do the Hands-on Grammar Activity, p. 513.	• Assign Chapter Review Exercises 5–11.

Using Objective Pronouns

The objective pronouns are *me, you, him, her, it, us, you* (plural), and *them*.

▶ **KEY CONCEPT** *Objective pronouns* are used as (1) direct objects, (2) indirect objects, and (3) objects of prepositions. ■

Direct Object An objective pronoun used as a direct object appears with an action verb and answers the question *Whom?* or *What?*

EXAMPLE: The referee penalized *her.*

Indirect Object An objective pronoun used as an indirect object appears with an action verb and a direct object. It answers the question *To or for whom?* or *To or for what?*

EXAMPLE: My friend gave *me* highlights of the game.

Object of a Preposition An objective pronoun can also be the object of a preposition.

EXAMPLE: Our team captain voted for *him.*

Sometimes, objective pronouns are part of a compound object. To determine the correct pronoun, use the pronoun by itself without the rest of the compound.

EXAMPLE: The player asked the coach and (he, him) for help.

First, try the pronoun *he* without the words *the coach and.* "The player asked *he* for help" does not sound right. Now, try the pronoun *him.* "The player asked *him* for help" does sound right.

▶ **Exercise 2** Identifying Objective Pronouns Choose the correct pronoun(s). Then, tell how each pronoun is being used.

EXAMPLE: The two teams gave (we, us) a great game.
ANSWER: us (indirect object)

1. Tim invited (I, me) to a soccer game.
2. Just above (he and I, him and me) were some rowdy fans.
3. Zoe visited (we, us) before the game started.
4. She brought Tim and (I, me) a game program.
5. Between you and (I, me), it was a fantastic day.

▼ Critical Viewing
Why might these fans be shouting? Use at least one objective pronoun in your response. **[Speculate]**

More Practice

Language Lab
CD-ROM
• Pronoun Case lesson
On-line
Exercise Bank
• Chapter 23
Grammar Exercise
Workbook
• pp. 109–110

Using Pronouns • **509**

Step-by-Step Teaching Guide

Using Objective Pronouns

1. Explain to students that objective pronouns *(me, you, him, her, it, us, you* [plural], and *them)* are different from subject pronouns because they are used as direct objects, indirect objects, and objects of prepositions—not as subjects.

2. Review direct object, indirect object, and object of a preposition.

3. Write subject pronouns and objective pronouns at random on the chalkboard, and ask students to select a pronoun and label it subject or objective.

4. Ask students to use the objective pronouns in sentences as direct objects, indirect objects, and objects of a preposition.

Answer Key

▶ **Exercise 2**

1. me (direct object)
2. him and me (object of preposition)
3. us (direct object)
4. me (indirect object)
5. me (object of preposition)

Customize for
Bodily/Kinesthetic Learners

Have students work in pairs, using a common object (pencil, piece of paper, ruler). Ask them to "lend" the object to the partner and write a sentence about the exchange, using a subject pronoun and an objective pronoun. Have students identify whether the objective pronoun is used as a direct object, an indirect object, or an object of a preposition.

Critical Viewing

Speculate Students may say that the fans are shouting for their team, rooting for them to score.

☑ **ONGOING ASSESSMENT SYSTEM: Prerequisite Skills**

If students have difficulty with subject pronouns, you may find it necessary to review the following to assure coverage of prerequisite knowledge.

In the Textbook	Print Resources	Technology
Nouns and Pronouns, pp. 292–311	Grammar Exercise Workbook, pp. 7–8	Language Lab CD-ROM, Using Nouns; On-Line Exercise Bank, Sections 14.1–2

Using Possessive Pronouns

1. Ask students to define the word *possessive*. Then ask them to infer why certain pronouns might be called possessive. (They show ownership.)

2. Possessive pronouns modify nouns (or the objects possessed) or are used by themselves.

3. Refer students to the chart on page 510. Ask them to write 14 sentences using each possessive pronoun once.

Integrating Spelling Skills

To make a noun possessive, *'s* is added: *the dog's bone.* A possessive pronoun is already possessive, so it never changes: *The dog chewed her bone* (not *her's bone*).

Critical Viewing

Connect Students may say, "I would write my name on the inside of my mitt."

Using Possessive Pronouns

Possessive pronouns have a special job in sentences.

▶ **KEY CONCEPT** Use the *possessive* forms of personal pronouns to show ownership. ■

Some possessive pronouns come before nouns.

EXAMPLES: I left *my* sneakers at home.
             Their team is in first place.

Other possessive pronouns are used by themselves to show ownership. These pronouns do not come before nouns.

EXAMPLES: These sneakers are *mine.*
             The trophy will be *theirs.*

Never use an apostrophe when writing a possessive pronoun.

POSSESSIVE PRONOUNS	
Used Before Nouns	**Used by Themselves**
my its	mine its
your our	yours ours
his their	his theirs
her	hers

INCORRECT: *Their's* is the best infield in the league.

CORRECT: *Theirs* is the best infield in the league.

INCORRECT: The baseball mitt lying on the chair is *her's.*

CORRECT: The baseball mitt lying on the chair is *hers.*

A common error with possessive pronouns is to use an apostrophe after *it.* The possessive form of *it* is *its.* *It's* is a contraction that means "it is."

CONTRACTION: I know *it's* an important game, so don't be late.

POSSESSIVE
PRONOUN: Be sure to hold the bat with *its* label toward you.

✔ Spelling Tip

Don't confuse the spelling of the possessive pronoun *their* with the adverb *there.* Also, avoid confusing the possessive pronouns *their* and *theirs* with the contractions *they're* (they are) and *there's* (there is).

▼ **Critical Viewing**
How would you personalize a piece of sports equipment, such as a baseball mitt, a hockey stick, or a tennis racquet? Answer using at least one possessive pronoun. **[Connect]**

Exercise 3 Using Possessive Pronouns Supply a possessive pronoun to fill in each blank correctly.

EXAMPLE: From what I know of Canadian fans, hockey is
             __?__ favorite sport.

ANSWER: From what I know of Canadian fans, hockey is
             their favorite sport.

1. Wayne Gretzky was one of the greatest hockey players of __?__ time.
2. I have several posters of Gretzky on __?__ wall.
3. I even had a poster with __?__ autograph.
4. That one is missing from __?__ frame.
5. If you find it, remember that it is __?__ and not __?__.

Using Different Pronoun Cases

The different forms of subject pronouns, objective pronouns, and possessive pronouns are called *cases*. Each case has different uses.

KEY CONCEPT Use the *cases* of pronouns correctly. ■

Subject pronouns, which are said to be in the *nominative case*, are used as *subjects* and *predicate pronouns*. Predicate pronouns generally appear after some form of the linking verb *be*. They help identify the subjects of sentences.

PREDICATE
PRONOUNS: The *centers* in the face-off circle are Sue and *she*.

             The *hero* was *I*.

The chart below summarizes what you have learned so far.

THE THREE CASES OF PERSONAL PRONOUNS AND THEIR USES		
Cases	Pronoun Forms	Uses
Nominative	I, you, he, she, it we, you, they	Subject of a Verb Predicate Pronoun
Objective	me, you, him, her, it us, you, them	Direct Object Indirect Object Object of a Preposition
Possessive	my, mine, you, yours, his, her, hers, its, our, ours, your, yours, their, theirs	To Show Ownership

More Practice

Language Lab
CD-ROM
• Pronoun Case lesson
On-line
Exercise Bank
• Chapter 23
Grammar Exercise
Workbook
• pp. 111–112

Using Pronouns • 511

Answer Key

Exercise 3

1. Wayne Gretzky was one of the greatest hockey players of <u>our</u> time.
2. I have several posters of Gretzky on <u>my</u> wall.
3. I even had a poster with <u>his</u> autograph.
4. That one is missing from <u>its</u> frame.
5. If you find it, remember that it is <u>mine</u> and not <u>yours</u>.

Step-by-Step Teaching Guide

Using Different Pronoun Cases

1. Review the three different cases of pronouns discussed so far: subject, objective, and possessive.

2. Explain that subject pronouns (*I, you, she, he, it, we, you, they*) are in the nominative case, which means they are used as subjects and as **predicate pronouns**, pronouns that help identify the subjects of sentences using the verb *be*.

3. Predicate pronouns may sound strange, but the wording of the sentence can be altered to verify that the pronoun is used correctly. Write examples of correct predicate pronouns in sentences on the chalkboard for student practice. Then, tell them to write eight subject pronouns they know in sentences as subjects and then as predicate pronouns.

☑ **ONGOING ASSESSMENT: Monitor and Reinforce**

If students miss more than two items in Exercise 3, refer them to the following for additional practice.

In the Textbook	Print Resources	Technology
Chapter Review, Ex. 9–10, p. 515	Grammar Exercise Workbook, pp. 111–112	Language Lab CD-ROM, Using Pronouns; On-Line Exercise Bank, Section 23

⏱ **TIME SAVERS!**

📃 **Answers on Transparency** Use the Grammar Exercises Answers on Transparencies for Chapter 23 to facilitate correction by students.

💻 **On-Line Exercise Bank** Have students complete the exercises on computer. The Auto Check feature will grade their work for you!

Grammar in Literature

1. Have a volunteer read aloud the passage from "The Shutout."

2. After discussing the annotation about the use of *it* as a subject of a clause and the use of *them* as the object of a preposition, ask students whether *them* could be used as the subject of a clause. (No, because *them* is an objective pronoun.)

3. Discuss the differences between subject and objective pronouns.

Answer Key

▶ Exercise 4

1. <u>It's</u> a fact that Sam Jethroe was one of the fastest men ever to play baseball.
2. However, many baseball fans have never heard of <u>him</u>.
3. My aunt, who loves baseball history, gave my sister and <u>me</u> all the facts about Jethroe.
4. Her friends and <u>she</u> spend a lot of time discussing baseball.
5. correct
6. correct
7. In 1945, Jackie Robinson and <u>he</u> tried out for a major league team.
8. Despite <u>their</u> talent, the team rejected them.
9. In 1950, Jethroe finally joined a National League team and quickly showed <u>his</u> skills.
10. As he stole base after base, fans raised <u>their</u> voices in cheers.
11. <u>They</u> and the sports writers were impressed by him.
12. My aunt, my sister, and <u>I</u> are very impressed, too!

Critical Viewing

Compare and Contrast Students may say, "My view was not as good as his view" and "I could barely see their numbers."

GRAMMAR IN LITERATURE

from The Shutout
Patricia C. McKissack and Frederick McKissack, Jr.

In this passage, the pronoun it, *in blue italics, is used as the subject of a clause. The objective pronoun* them, *in red italics, is used as the object of the preposition* of.

The history of baseball is difficult to trace because *it* is embroidered with wonderful anecdotes that are fun but not necessarily supported by fact. There are a lot of myths that persist about baseball—the games, the players, the owners, and the fans—in spite of contemporary research that disproves most of *them*.

▶ **More Practice**

Language Lab CD-ROM
• Pronoun Case lesson
On-line Exercise Bank
• Chapter 23
Grammar Exercise Workbook
• pp. 113–114

▶ **Exercise 4** **Revising to Correct Pronoun Errors** Revise the following paragraph, correcting the pronouns as necessary. (Not every sentence contains an error.)

Its a fact that Sam Jethroe was one of the fastest men ever to play baseball. However, many baseball fans have never heard of his. My aunt, who loves baseball history, gave my sister and I all the facts about Jethroe. Her friends and her spend a lot of time discussing baseball. Jethroe spent most of his career in the Negro Leagues. He was its leader in batting and base stealing. In 1945, Jackie Robinson and him tried out for a major league team. Despite there talent, the team rejected them. In 1950, Jethroe finally joined a National League team and quickly showed his' skills. As he stole base after base, fans raised they're voices in cheers. Them and the sports writers were impressed by him. My aunt, my sister, and me are very impressed too!

▼ **Critical Viewing** Compare your view from this place in the stands to that of a friend sitting closer to the field. Use possessive pronouns such as *my, our, his, her,* and *their.* **[Compare and Contrast]**

512 • Using Pronouns

STANDARDIZED TEST PREPARATION WORKSHOP

Grammar and Usage Many standardized tests require students to recognize correct usage in a passage. Ask students if the underlined word in the sentence below is correct or should be changed.

She opened <u>mine</u> door to enter my house.

A No change	C my
B me	D its

The correct choice is item **C**, because this is the possessive pronoun that agrees with the word *door*.

Hands-on Grammar

Nominative and Objective Pronoun People

Use Pronoun People to help you practice the nominative and objective case pronouns. First, cut out your people from construction paper—four single people and three groups of two or three people. Starting with each of the single people, label one side with a nominative pronoun: *I, you, he,* or *she.* On the other side, write the corresponding objective pronoun: *me, you, him, her.* Then, label one side of each group of people *we, you (pl.),* or *they*; label the other side *us, you (pl.),* or *them.* Now, each person or group is labeled with a nominative pronoun on one side and its corresponding objective form on the other.

Next, with a partner, take turns moving and flipping your Pronoun People as you use them in sentences. Build your sentences from the following sentence parts:

- *sat next to*
- *walked between*
- *The next in line is/are*
- *invited*
- *gave some pizza*

Write each sentence as you create it. One partner may not duplicate the other's sentences. Check each other's work to make sure you have used your Pronoun People correctly. When you have finished, you should have used all your people as subjects, predicate pronouns, direct and indirect objects, and objects of prepositions. (See illustration.)

He and she sat next to us.

We walked between you and her.

The next in line are he and I.

They invited him to the party.

You and I gave them some pizza.

Find It in Your Reading Read an advice column in a newspaper or a magazine. Note the number of pronouns in each of the three cases.

Find It in Your Writing Review a piece of personal writing, and check to make sure that you have used all personal pronouns correctly. Correct those that are in the wrong case.

Nominative and Objective Pronoun People

Teaching Resources: Hands-on Grammar Activity Book, Chapter 23

1. Have students refer to their Hands-on Grammar activity books or give them copies of relevant pages for this activity.

2. Be sure students understand that there is more than one way to use the pronoun *people* correctly and that their sentences will not be alike.

Find It in Your Reading

Have students underline the pronouns and then list them on a separate sheet of paper.

Find It in Your Writing

You may want to have students work with a partner to evaluate their use of pronouns.

⏱ **TIME SAVERS!**

Hands-on Grammar
Use the Hands-on Grammar activity sheet for Chapter 23 to facilitate this activity.

513

Answer Key

Exercise 5

1. you (nominative)
2. It (nominative)
3. their (possessive)
4. they (nominative)
5. They, their, them (nominative, possessive, objective)
6. you, he (nominative, nominative)
7. you, your (nominative, possessive)
8. you (nominative)
9. My, his (possessive, possessive)
10. His, he (possessive, nominative)
11. My, I, his (possessive, nominative, possessive)
12. We, him (nominative, objective)
13. he, us (nominative, objective)
14. he, his (nominative, possessive)
15. them (objective)

Exercise 6

1. My brother and I read about the history of rugby.
2. Legend says it got its start at Rugby School in England in 1823.
3. Two teams of students were playing soccer on their school field.
4. One boy picked up the ball and ran with it in his hands.
5. correct
6. They and his own teammates told him he was breaking the rules.
7. Their warnings didn't bother him.
8. Soon, he and the other boys developed rules for a new game.
9. Their new game caught on at other British schools, too.
10. correct

Chapter 23 Chapter Review

GRAMMAR EXERCISES 5–13

Exercise 5 Identifying Personal Pronouns and Case On your paper, list the personal pronouns in the sentences below. Label each pronoun *nominative*, *objective*, or *possessive*.

1. Have you ever seen a rugby match?
2. It is a sport that requires strength and speed.
3. Two teams try to kick, pass, or carry a ball across their opponent's goal.
4. Players often run into each other as they attempt to advance the ball.
5. They try to tackle their opponents and steal the ball from them.
6. However, you are not allowed to tackle someone if he doesn't have the ball.
7. If you cross the goal line and throw the ball down, your team gets four points.
8. Then, you can place-kick or drop-kick the ball to score two more points.
9. My brother and his friend play on a rugby team.
10. His friend and he have been playing rugby for two years.
11. My mom and I often go to his games.
12. We cheer loudly for him.
13. Today, he looked up and gave us a smile.
14. Then, he turned and grabbed an opponent by his legs.
15. Both of them tumbled to the ground.

Exercise 6 Revising to Correct Pronoun Errors Revise each of the sentences below, correcting all pronoun errors. If a sentence contains no error, write *correct*.

1. My brother and me read about the history of rugby.
2. Legend says it got it's start at Rugby School in England in 1823.
3. Two teams of students were playing

soccer on there school field.
4. One boy picked up the ball and ran with it in his' hands.
5. The opposing team chased after him.
6. Them and his own teammates told him he was breaking the rules.
7. They're warnings didn't bother him.
8. Soon, him and the other boys developed rules for a new game.
9. There new game caught on at other British schools, too.
10. Watching rugby is a lot of fun for my friends and me.

Exercise 7 Determining the Use of Nominative Pronouns On your paper, identify whether the underlined pronoun is being used as the *subject* of a verb or as a *predicate pronoun*.

1. We often play basketball in gym class.
2. The best shooter in the class is he.
3. Today, he made ten shots in a row.
4. Our teacher was impressed, and she said so.
5. The first players chosen were Jim and I.
6. Sara's next picks were Alan and she.
7. We scored the first six points.
8. Then, they scored the next eight.
9. In the end, the winners were we.
10. Talia hopes that she will play better.

Exercise 8 Determining the Use of Objective Pronouns On your paper, identify how the underlined objective pronoun is used in each sentence below.

1. The coach showed Eric and them the new play.
2. He worked with us for two hours.
3. The assistant coach encouraged me from the sidelines.
4. She also applauded for Andy and him.

Exercise 7

1. subject
2. predicate pronoun
3. subject
4. subject
5. predicate pronoun
6. predicate pronoun
7. subject
8. subject
9. predicate pronoun
10. subject

Exercise 8

1. indirect object
2. object of a preposition
3. direct object
4. object of a preposition
5. indirect object
6. object of a preposition
7. direct object
8. indirect object
9. object of a preposition
10. direct object

5. Darryl handed <u>her</u> the damaged ball.
6. She threw a new ball to <u>him</u>.
7. The coach instructed Todd and <u>me</u>.
8. The team manager handed Billy and <u>them</u> cups of water.
9. <u>They</u> were grateful to <u>her</u> for the refreshing drinks.
10. The coach rewarded <u>us</u> for our hard work.

▶ **Exercise 9** Revising to Correct Possessive Pronouns Revise the following sentences, correcting possessive pronouns as necessary.

1. The quarterback called his' team into the huddle.
2. The players gathered together to hear there leader's plan.
3. He called a favorite play of there's.
4. The outcome of the game depended on it's success.
5. Fortunately, the element of surprise was our's.

▶ **Exercise 10** Supplying Possessive Pronouns Supply a possessive pronoun to fill in each blank logically.

1. Aunt Pat was on the edge of ___?___ seat.
2. ___?___ whole family was glued to the television screen.
3. My cousin Sean was playing in ___?___ first televised game.
4. ___?___ parents cheered excitedly.
5. The loudest cheers were ___?___.

▶ **Exercise 11** Revising Incorrect Pronoun Usage Rewrite each sentence below, correcting any pronoun errors. If there is no pronoun error, write *correct*.

1. Em's best sport is soccer; my is volleyball.
2. Tim and her are playing on my team.
3. Tim returns almost every shot that is hit toward he.

4. Its not often that he misses the ball.
5. The first player chosen is usually he.
6. When the ball was hit between Connie and I, I got to it first.
7. I lifted the ball up, and she smacked it over the net.
8. The ball sailed untouched on it's flight.
9. The point was our's.
10. Connie and me work well together.

▶ **Exercise 12** Writing Application
Imagine that you are a sports announcer. Write a play-by-play description of an event during a game. Use at least three nominative pronouns, three objective pronouns, and four possessive pronouns.

▶ **Exercise 13** CUMULATIVE REVIEW
Problems With Verbs and Pronouns
Revise the following paragraph, correcting errors in verb or pronoun usage.

(1) Baseball fans have always went to games to cheer for home-run hitters. (2) In 1927, Babe Ruth wallops sixty home runs. (3) No one ever done that before. (4) The nickname "The Sultan of Swat" was gave to him. (5) The Babe finished his' career with a record 714 homers. (6) Both of Babe's records have since been broke. (7) In 1961, Roger Maris and Mickey Mantle hitted home runs in almost every game. (8) Mantle knowed that either Roger or him would top sixty. (9) On the last day of the season, Maris had drove home run number sixty-one over the fence. (10) Babe's other record laid unbroken for thirteen more years. (11) In 1974, fans in Atlanta cheered for there hero, Henry Aaron, when he hit his 715th homer. (12) That homer sat his name in the record books. (13) Aaron goes on to hit 755 home runs before he retired. (14) By the end of the 1998 season, two players, Mark McGwire and Sammy Sosa, had became the first two players to smash Roger Maris's record. (15) Hitting seventy homers, McGwire showed that the greatest home-run hitter ever may be him.

Exercise 9
1. his
2. their
3. theirs
4. its
5. ours

Exercise 10
Answers will vary. Samples are given.
1. her
2. My
3. his
4. His
5. mine

Exercise 11
1. Em's best sport is soccer; mine is volleyball.
2. Tim and she are playing on my team.
3. Tim returns almost every shot that is hit toward him.
4. It's not often that he misses the ball.
5. correct.
6. When the ball was hit between Connie and me, I got to it first.
7. correct
8. The ball sailed untouched on its flight.
9. The point was ours.
10. Connie and I work well together.

Exercise 12
Writing Application
Have students work in pairs and locate the nominative, objective, and possessive pronouns in their partner's play-by-play description.

Exercise 13
Cumulative Review
(1) Baseball fans have always gone to games to cheer for home run hitters. (2) In 1927, Babe Ruth walloped sixty home runs. (3) No one had ever done that before. (4) The nickname "The Sultan of Swat"
continued

Answer Key continued

was given to him. (5) The Babe finished his career with a record 714 homers. (6) Both of Babe's records have since been broken. (7) In 1961, Roger Maris and Mickey Mantle hit home runs in almost every game. (8) Mantle knew that either Roger or he would top sixty. (9) On the last day of the season, Maris drove home run number sixty-one over the fence. (10) Babe's other record lay unbroken for thirteen more years. (11) In 1974, fans in Atlanta cheered for their hero, Henry Aaron, when he hit his 715th homer. (12) That homer set his name in the record books. (13) Aaron went on to hit 755 home runs before he retired. (14) By the end of the 1998 season, two players, Mark McGwire and Sammy Sosa, had become the first two players to smash Roger Maris's record. (15) Hitting seventy homers, McGwire showed that the greatest home run hitter ever may be he.

⏱ **TIME SAVERS!**

📋 **Answers on Transparency** Use the Grammar Exercises Answers on Transparencies for Chapter 23 to facilitate correction by students.

💻 **On-Line Exercise Bank** Have students complete the exercises on computer. The Auto Check feature will grade their work for you!

Step-by-Step Teaching Guide

Standard English Usage: Pronouns

Teaching Resources: Standardized Test Preparation Workbook, Chapter 23

1. Explain to students that in the sample test items, the first missing word's position in the sentence indicates that it is a subject pronoun.

2. Choice B is the only subject pronoun, so it is the correct answer.

3. Point out that the second blank calls for a possessive pronoun that refers to the subject of the sentence, Ryan and I. F is the correct answer, because the other possessive pronoun among the choices, *ours*, stands alone and would not be used before *mom*.

Standardized Test Preparation Workshop

Standard English Usage: Pronouns

Standardized tests measure your knowledge of the rules of standard grammar, such as correct pronoun usage. Questions test your ability to use the three cases of personal pronouns correctly. When answering these questions, determine what type of pronoun is needed in the sentence—nominative case pronouns are used as subjects or predicate pronouns; objective case pronouns are used as direct objects, indirect objects, or objects of prepositions; and possessive case pronouns are used to show ownership.

The following test items will give you practice with the format of questions that test your knowledge of pronoun usage.

Test Tip

When an object or subject is compound, check to see whether the case is correct by using only the pronoun in the compound construction.

Example: *Karen and I/me went to the bike store.*

Incorrect: *Me went to the bike store.*

Correct: *I went to the bike store.*

Sample Test Items

Read the passage, and choose the letter of the word or group of words that belongs in each space. Ryan and __(1)__ couldn't believe that __(2)__ mom bought new bikes.	

1 A me
    B I
    C my
    D mine
2 F our
    G us
    H we
    J ours
	The correct answer is *B*. Since the sentence calls for a subject, a pronoun in the nominative case is required. Choice *A* is in the objective case, and choices *C* and *D* are in the possessive case.
	
	The correct answer is *F*, since the sentence calls for a pronoun in the possessive case that comes before the noun it modifies. Choice *J* is also in the possessive case, but it stands alone.

Answers and Explanations

TEST-TAKING TIP

Remind students that they should check their answers by trying out the other choices to see how they sound in the sentence. Often their ear for language will tell them when an answer is correct.

Practice 1 **Directions:** Read the passage, and choose the letter of the word or group of words that belongs in each space.

Karen, Ryan, Mike, and __(1)__ went bike riding on Block Island last summer. Mike's and Ryan's bikes are the smallest, and __(2)__ have training wheels. Surprisingly, the boys kept up pretty well with Karen and __(3)__ . Karen and Mike forgot to bring __(4)__ helmets so __(5)__ rented one for each of them

1 **A** me
  B I
  C my
  D mine

2 **F** they
  G they're
  H their
  J there's

3 **A** mine
  B me
  C I
  D my

4 **F** they're
  G their
  H there
  J theirs

5 **A** our
  B us
  C ours
  D we

Practice 2 **Directions:** Read the passage, and choose the letter of the word or group of words that belongs in each space.

All of __(1)__ rode ahead of me for a few miles. The chain had fallen off __(2)__ bike. When I finally caught up to them, __(3)__ and Ryan said it was time for our picnic. Afterward, the boys looked tired, so Karen asked Mike, "Don't __(4)__ think it's time to head home?"

1 **A** their
  B them
  C they
  D theirs

2 **F** me
  G our
  H mine
  J my

3 **A** him
  B she
  C I
  D me

4 **F** you and him
  G you and he
  H yours and his
  J you're and he

Answer Key

Practice 1
1. B
2. F
3. B
4. G
5. D

Practice 2
1. B
2. J
3. B
4. G

In-Depth Lesson Plan

	LESSON FOCUS	PRINT AND MEDIA RESOURCES
DAY 1	**Subject and Verb Agreement** Students learn and apply concepts covering simple and compound subjects and verbs (pp. 520–523).	**Teaching Resources** *Grammar Exercise Workbook*, pp. 115–118; *Grammar Exercises Answers on Transparencies*, Ch. 24 *Language Lab* **CD-ROM**, Subject-Verb Agreement; *On-Line Exercise Bank*, Section 24.1
DAY 2	**Subject and Verb Agreement (continued)** Students learn and apply concepts covering pronoun subjects and verbs and do the Hands-on Grammar activity (pp. 524–527).	**Teaching Resources** *Grammar Exercise Workbook*, pp. 119–120; *Grammar Exercises Answers on Transparencies*, Ch. 24; *Hands-on Grammar Activity Book*, Chapter 24 *Language Lab* **CD-ROM**, Subject-Verb Agreement; *On-Line Exercise Bank*, Section 24.1
DAY 3	**Pronoun and Antecedent Agreement** Students learn and apply concepts covering pronoun and antecedent agreement (pp. 528–531).	**Teaching Resources** *Grammar Exercise Workbook*, pp. 121–122; *Grammar Exercises Answers on Transparencies*, Ch. 24 *Language Lab* **CD-ROM**, Subject-Verb Agreement; *On-Line Exercise Bank*, Section 24.2
DAY 4	**Review and Assess** Students review chapter and demonstrate mastery of use of adjectives and adverbs (pp. 532–535).	**Teaching Resources** *Formal Assessment*, Ch. 24; *Grammar Exercises Answers on Transparencies*, Ch. 24 *On-Line Exercise Bank*, Sections 24.1–2

Accelerated Lesson Plan

	LESSON FOCUS	PRINT AND MEDIA RESOURCES
DAY 1	**Subject and Verb Agreement** Students cover concepts and usage of subject and verb agreement as determined by Diagnostic Test (pp. 520–527).	**Teaching Resources** *Grammar Exercise Workbook*, pp. 115–120; *Grammar Exercises Answers on Transparencies*, Ch. 24; *Hands-on Grammar Activity Book*, Chapter 24 *Language Lab* **CD-ROM**, Subject-Verb Agreement; *On-Line Exercise Bank*, Section 24.1
DAY 2	**Pronoun and Antecedent Agreement** Students cover concepts and usage of pronoun and antecedent agreement as determined by Diagnostic Test (pp. 528–531).	**Teaching Resources** *Grammar Exercise Workbook*, pp. 121–122; *Grammar Exercises Answers on Transparencies*, Ch. 24 *Language Lab* **CD-ROM**, Subject-Verb Agreement; *On-Line Exercise Bank*, Section 24.2
DAY 3	**Review and Assess** Students review chapter and demonstrate mastery of use of adjectives and adverbs (pp. 532–535).	**Teaching Resources** *Formal Assessment*, Ch. 24; *Grammar Exercises Answers on Transparencies*, Ch. 24 *On-Line Exercise Bank*, Sections 24.1–2

Options for Adapting Lesson Plans

HOMEWORK

Have students complete any section of the chapter for homework.

FEATURES

Extend coverage with the Grammar in Literature feature (pp. 524, 530), and the Standardized Test Preparation Workshop (p. 534).

TECHNOLOGY

Students can use the On-Line Exercise Bank to complete the exercises on computer. The Auto Check feature will grade their work.

INTEGRATED SKILLS COVERAGE

Grammar in Literature
SE pp. 524, 530

Reading
Find It in Your Reading SE pp. 526, 527, 531

Writing
Find It in Your Writing SE pp. 526, 527, 531
Writing Application SE pp. 527, 531, 533

Language Highlight
ATE pp. 522, 529

Vocabulary
ATE p. 520

Real-World Connection
ATE p. 521

Workplace Skills
ATE p. 328

Viewing and Representing
Critical Viewing SE pp. 518, 521, 523, 525, 529, 530

BLOCK SCHEDULING

Pacing Suggestions
For 90-minute Blocks
• Administer the Diagnostic Test to students to determine instructional coverage.
• Have students complete the necessary exercises in class. Use the Hands-on Grammar activity to provide a change of pace.

Resources for Varying Instruction
• *Language Lab* **CD-ROM** If your students have access to hardware, a 90-minute block provides an ideal opportunity for students to work on computer.

Professional Development Support
• *How to Manage Instruction in the Block* This teaching resource provides management and activity suggestions.

ASSESSMENT SUPPORT

Standardized Test Preparation Workshop SE p. 534; ATE p. 524
Standardized Test Preparation Workbook, pp. 47–48
Formal Assessment, Ch. 24

MEDIA AND TECHNOLOGY

For the Student
• *Language Lab* **CD-ROM**, Subject-Verb Agreement
• *On-Line Exercise Bank*, Ch. 24

For the Teacher
• *Resource Pro* **CD-ROM**

MEETING INDIVIDUAL NEEDS

Less Advanced Students See Ongoing Assessments ATE pp. 522, 523, 525, 526, 530
Verbal/Linguistic Learners ATE p. 525
Logical/Mathematical Learners ATE p. 524

WRITING AND GRAMMAR WEB SITE

The Interactive Writing and Grammar Web site provides a wide array of support for students, teachers, and parents. Grammar support includes:

• On-Line Exercise Bank with Auto Check scoring
• Diagnostic and assessment support

www.phschool.com

LITERATURE CONNECTIONS

Grammar in Literature selections from *Prentice Hall Literature: Timeless Voices, Timeless Themes,* Copper:
from *The Phantom Tollbooth,* screenplay by Susan Nanus, SE p. 524
from "The King of Mazy May," Jack London, SE p. 530

Lesson Objectives

1. To employ standard English usage in writing for audiences, including subject-verb agreement and pronoun-antecedent agreement.

2. To select verbs that agree with compound, hard-to-find subjects, collective nouns, indefinite pronouns, and other potentially confusing subjects.

3. To write with increasing accuracy when using pronoun case.

Critical Viewing

Connect Students might suggest:

Abraham Lincoln is the president shown in this memorial.

Tourists enjoy visiting the Lincoln Memorial.

The first sentence needs a singular verb; the second a plural verb.

Chapter 24 Making Words Agree

During a visit to Washington, D.C., you might jot down the following sentences on the back of a postcard of the Lincoln Memorial:

> I love Washington. It is a great city. The Lincoln Memorial is my favorite monument. I like the other monuments, too. All of them are worth visiting.

You probably wouldn't have to think too much about how to word these sentences. However, without even realizing it, you would be following the rules of agreement—both subject-verb agreement and pronoun-antecedent agreement. In this chapter, you'll learn *why* the sentences above are correct, and you will discover how to apply rules of agreement to sentences that are much more complex.

▲ **Critical Viewing**
Write two sentences about this monument, one with *Abraham Lincoln* as the subject and the other with *tourists* as the subject. Which sentence needs a singular verb? Which one needs a plural verb? [**Connect**]

518 • Making Words Agree

☑ ONGOING ASSESSMENT: Diagnose

If students miss more than one item in each category, direct them to the relevant pages of the text and assign exercises for practice and review.

Making Words Agree	Diagnostic Test Items	Teach	Practice	Section Review	Chapter Review
Skill Check A					
Subject-Verb Agreement	A 1–15	pp. 520–526	Ex. 1–6	Ex. 7–10	Ex. 22–24
Skill Check B					
Pronouns and Antecedents	B 16–25	pp. 528–530	Ex. 14–16	Ex. 17–18	Ex. 25–26
Cumulative Reviews and Applications				Ex. 11–13, 19–21	Ex. 27–28

Diagnostic Test

Directions: Write all answers on a separate sheet of paper.

Skill Check A. Choose the verb in parentheses that agrees with the subject of each sentence below.

1. Washington, D.C., (is, are) the capital of the United States.
2. National landmarks (is, are) found throughout the city.
3. The Lincoln Memorial (contain, contains) a 19-foot statue of Abraham Lincoln, the sixteenth president of the United States.
4. In spring, visitors to the Jefferson Memorial (enjoy, enjoys) seeing the cherry trees that surround the monument.
5. When tourists (see, sees) the 555-foot Washington Monument, they wonder whether they will have to climb to the top.
6. Stairs and elevators (is, are) available to those who wish to reach the top of the Washington Monument.
7. Either the Natural History Museum or the Museum of American History (take, takes) hours to tour.
8. Neither my parents nor my brother (want, wants) to miss seeing the Air and Space Museum.
9. The Vietnam Veterans Memorial and the Korean War Veterans Memorial (honor, honors) the men and women who gave their lives during these conflicts.
10. My sister and brother (want, wants) to see as much of Washington, D.C., as possible.
11. Every visitor to Washington, D.C., (is, are) impressed with its national landmarks and museums.
12. None of the national museums (charge, charges) admission.
13. Few people (leave, leaves) the city disappointed.
14. Many visitors (come, comes) back more than once.
15. Most tourists (stay, stays) in hotels.

Skill Check B. Copy each sentence below, filling in the blank with a pronoun that agrees with its antecedent.

16. My parents enjoyed __?__ trip to Washington, D.C.
17. We girls were excited about __?__ trip to the nation's capital.
18. Ruth used __?__ camera to take pictures of the monuments.
19. The Washington Monument had __?__ exterior walls covered with scaffolding.
20. Either Adam or Keith took __?__ journal on the trip.
21. The President and the First Lady were having __?__ breakfast when we toured the White House.
22. When the First Lady stepped out of the door, we waved to __?__ and she waved back.
23. Rachel and Donald told about __?__ trip to Washington, D.C.
24. My brother lost __?__ hat while visiting the Lincoln Memorial.
25. Neither John nor Peter remembered __?__ camera.

Answer Key

Diagnostic Test

Each item in the Diagnostic Test corresponds to a specific section in the chapter on agreement. This will enable you to tailor instruction to the particular needs of your students. See "Ongoing Assessment: Diagnose" below for further details.

Skill Check A

1. is
2. are
3. contains
4. enjoy
5. see
6. are
7. takes
8. wants
9. honor
10. want
11. is
12. charges
13. leave
14. come
15. stay

Skill Check B

16. My parents enjoyed their trip to Washington, D.C.
17. We girls were excited about our trip to the nation's capital.
18. Ruth used her camera to take pictures of the monuments.
19. The Washington Monument had its exterior walls covered with scaffolding.
20. Either Adam or Keith took his journal on the trip.
21. The President and the First Lady were having their breakfast when we toured the White House.
22. When the First Lady stepped out of the door, we waved to her and she waved back.
23. Rachel and Donald told about their trip to Washington, D.C.
24. My brother lost his hat while visiting the Lincoln Memorial.
25. Neither John nor Peter remembered his camera.

TIME SAVERS!

Answers on Transparency
Use the Grammar Exercises Answers on Transparencies for Chapter 24 to facilitate correction by students.

On-Line Exercise Bank
Have students complete the Diagnostic Test on computer. The Auto Check feature will grade their work for you!

On an overhead projector, display the painting *Stairway* (*Prentice Hall Literature: Timeless Voices, Timeless Themes,* Copper, page 325). Ask students to tell what they see, using sentences. Write the sentences on the chalkboard and circle the subjects and underline the verbs. Ask whether the subjects are singular or plural.

Activate Prior Knowledge

Have each student write six subjects, three singular and three plural. Then have students exchange papers and write sentences using those subjects.

TEACH

Step-by-Step Teaching Guide

Subject-Verb Agreement

1. The guiding rule of subject-verb agreement: If the subject is singular, the verb must be singular. If the subject is plural, the verb must be plural.

2. Remind students that *singular* means "one" and *plural* means "more than one."

Integrating Vocabulary Skills

The plural form of some nouns is irregular and not formed by adding -*s* or -*es*. These words include *deer* (singular and plural), *fish* (singular and plural), *focus/foci,* and *alumnus/alumni.* Discuss other irregular plural nouns students know.

Section 24.1

Subject and Verb Agreement

Simple Subjects and Verbs

Subjects are either singular or plural in number. Singular subjects refer to one person, place, or thing; plural subjects refer to more than one. Verbs, too, are either singular or plural. Singular subjects take singular verbs. Plural subjects take plural verbs.

Singular and Plural Subjects

Many subjects are nouns. Most singular nouns can be made plural by adding *s* or *es.* Some nouns, like *woman* and *mouse,* form their plurals differently.

SINGULAR NOUNS: bell, canyon, tax, city, woman, mouse
PLURAL NOUNS: bells, canyons, taxes, cities, women, mice

Singular and Plural Verbs

Present-tense verbs have both singular and plural forms. Third-person singular verbs end in *s,* while plural verbs do not. This is just the opposite of nouns that form their plurals by adding *s.*

The chart below shows how an *s* is added to the third-person singular form of the verb *look:*

PRESENT TENSE VERB FORMS	
Singular	**Plural**
I look	we look
you look	you look
he, she, it looks	they look

Agreement The subject and verb in a sentence must agree in number.

▶ **KEY CONCEPT** Use a **singular** subject with a singular verb. Use a **plural** subject with a plural verb. ■

SINGULAR SUBJECT AND VERB: Terry visits the Statue of Liberty once a year.

PLURAL SUBJECT AND VERB: They visit the Statue of Liberty once a year.

Theme: Landmarks of the United States

In this section, you will learn how to make sure that verbs in sentences agree in number with their subjects. The examples and exercises are about different United States landmarks.

••••••••••••••••••••••

Cross-Curricular Connection: Social Studies

⏰ TIME AND RESOURCE MANAGER

Resources
Print: Grammar Exercise Workbook, pp. 115–120; Hands-on Grammar Activity Book, Chapter 24; Grammar Exercises Answers on Transparencies, Chapter 24
Technology: Language Lab CD-ROM, Subject-Verb Agreement; On-Line Exercise Bank, Section 24.1

In-Depth Coverage	Accelerated Pace
• Work through all key concepts, pp. 520–525. • Assign and review Exercises 1–6. • Do the Hands-on Grammar Activity, p. 531.	• Assign pp. 520–525 for independent student review. • Assign Section Review Exercises 7–10, p. 527.

◄ **Critical Viewing**
Use *Statue of Liberty* and *buildings* as the subjects of two sentences about this photo. Which subject would agree with the verb *stand*? Which would agree with the verb *stands*? **[Connect]**

Exercise 1 Making Subjects and Verbs Agree For each sentence below, write the verb that agrees with the subject.
1. The Statue of Liberty (is, are) located on Liberty Island, near the southern tip of Manhattan.
2. Ferries (take, takes) passengers to the island.
3. Visitors (is, are) always amazed at the size of the statue.
4. The statue (measure, measures) 151 feet and 1 inch tall.
5. The stone pedestal (add, adds) another 154 feet to the height of the statue.

Exercise 2 Revising a Paragraph to Correct Errors in Subject-Verb Agreement Rewrite the following paragraph, correcting errors in subject-verb agreement.

The Statue of Liberty is a symbol of freedom. Some visitors weep as they approach the statue. They remembers that the statue was the first thing their great-grandparents saw when they arrived at the United States. In one hand, the Statue of Liberty holds the Tablet of Law bearing the date July 4, 1776. The date is the United States Independence Day. In the other hand, the statue hold a torch. The torch light the way for immigrants to the United States. Many visitors climb the 354 steps to the statue's crown. They gazes out to view the New York City skyline. Others climb just to the top of the pedestal and enjoys the view from there.

More Practice

Language Lab CD-ROM
• Agreement in Number lesson
On-line Exercise Bank
• Section 24.1
Grammar Exercise Workbook
• pp. 115–116

Subject and Verb Agreement • 521

Answer Key

▶ **Exercise 1**
1. is
2. take
3. are
4. measures
5. adds

▶ **Exercise 2**
(1) The Statue of Liberty is a symbol of freedom. (2) Some visitors weep as they approach the statue. (3) They remember that the statue was the first thing their great-grandparents saw when they arrived at the United States. (4) In one hand, the Statue of Liberty holds the Tablet of Law bearing the date July 4, 1776. (5) The date is the United States Independence Day. (6) In the other hand, the statue holds a torch. (7) The torch lights the way for immigrants to the United States. (8) Many visitors climb the 354 steps to the statue's crown. (9) They gaze out to view the New York City skyline. (10) Others climb just to the top of the pedestal and enjoy the view from there.

Critical Viewing

Connect Students may suggest:

The Statue of Liberty stands proudly in the New York harbor.

Buildings in lower Manhattan stand opposite it.

Singular verb with statue; plural with buildings.

Real-World Connection

Journalists often report events as they occur. Because accuracy is vital, the accounts of events must rely on subject-verb agreement that is unambiguous. If a journalist wrote, "The President have arrived in Paris," there would be confusion—are there two presidents who have arrived, or one president who has arrived? In the same way, subject-verb agreement in our speaking and writing is essential.

☑ **ONGOING ASSESSMENT: Prerequisite Skills**

If students have difficulty with subject-verb agreement, you may find it necessary to review the following to assure coverage of prerequisite knowledge.

In the Textbook	Print Resources	Technology
Nouns and Pronouns, pp. 292–311 Basic Sentence Parts, pp. 378–413	Grammar Exercise Workbook, pp. 1–20, 43–46	Language Lab CD-ROM, Using Nouns, Using Pronouns, Using Verbs; On-Line Exercise Bank, Sections 14.1, 14.2, 19.2

Compound Subjects and Verbs

1. Compound subjects are two or more subjects that share the same verb. It might be useful to compare compound subjects to two oxen yoked together—in the case of the compound subjects, they are yoked together by the same verb.

2. Show students the following key rules regarding compound subjects and their corresponding verbs. You may want to leave the rules on display.

Subject	Verb
singular **and** singular	= plural
plural **and** plural	= plural
singular **or** singular	= singular
plural **or** singular	= singular
singular **or** plural	= plural

3. The last two examples are the trickiest. The verb agrees with the subject closer to it (the third key concept).

Language Highlight

In chemistry, a *compound* is a substance made up of two or more elements held together by chemical bonds. In language, a *compound* subject is two or more subjects held together by a verb. The word *compound* is derived from the Latin *componere*, which means "to put more, to put together."

24.1

Compound Subjects and Verbs

A *compound subject* refers to two or more subjects that share the same verb. They are connected by conjunctions such as *and, or,* or *nor.*

COMPOUND SUBJECTS
<u>Robert</u> and <u>Jennifer</u> enjoy visiting Philadelphia.
The <u>museums</u> or <u>historical sites</u> interest many visitors.
Neither the <u>Liberty Bell</u> nor <u>Independence Hall</u> disappoints tourists.

A number of rules can help you choose the right verb to use with a compound subject.

▶ **KEY CONCEPT** When a compound subject is connected by *and*, the verb that follows is usually plural. ∎

EXAMPLE: <u>Washington, D.C.,</u> and <u>Philadelphia</u> <u>are</u> my favorite cities.

There is an exception to this rule: If the parts of a compound subject are thought of as one person or thing, the subject is singular and takes a singular verb.

EXAMPLE: <u>Spaghetti</u> and <u>meatballs</u> <u>is</u> my favorite meal.

▶ **KEY CONCEPT** When two singular subjects are joined by *or* or *nor,* use a singular verb. When two plural subjects are joined by *or* or *nor,* use a plural verb. ∎

SINGULAR: A <u>car</u> or a <u>train</u> <u>provides</u> good transportation to Washington, D.C.

PLURAL: Neither <u>children</u> nor <u>adults</u> <u>like</u> to wait in line to enter the White House.

▶ **KEY CONCEPT** When a compound subject is made up of one singular and one plural subject joined by *or* or *nor,* the verb agrees with the subject closer to it. ∎

SINGULAR SUBJECT CLOSER: Either the <u>monuments</u> or the <u>White House</u> <u>is</u> interesting to see.

PLURAL SUBJECT CLOSER: Either the <u>White House</u> or the <u>monuments</u> <u>are</u> interesting to see.

💡 Spelling Tip

If you suspect that the plural form of a noun is irregular, use a dictionary to help you find the noun's plural form.

☑ **ONGOING ASSESSMENT: Monitor and Reinforce**

If students miss more than two items in Exercises 1–2, refer them to the following for additional practice.

In the Textbook	Print Resources	Technology
Section Review, Ex. 7, p. 527	Grammar Exercise Workbook, pp. 115–116	Language Lab CD-ROM, Subject-Verb Agreement; On-Line Exercise Bank, Section 24.1

Exercise 3 Making Compound Subjects and Verbs Agree
Write the verb that correctly completes each sentence.
1. The White House and the Capitol Building (is, are) sites all visitors to Washington, D.C., should see.
2. Neither my brother nor my sister (has, have) ever visited the White House before.
3. In the White House, the Green Room, the Red Room, and the Blue Room (is, are) open to public touring.
4. The East Room and the State Dining Room (is, are) also open to tours.
5. Neither the President nor the other members of his family (was, were) home when we toured the White House.
6. Uniformed police and plainclothes Secret Service agents (patrol, patrols) the White House.
7. Neither adults nor a child (is, are) permitted to touch anything in the White House.
8. The Senate and the House of Representatives (meet, meets) in the Capitol Building.
9. Either the Senate or the House of Representatives (has, have) its offices in the south wing.
10. Corned beef and cabbage (is, are) a dish the cafeteria in the Capitol Building sometimes serves.

Exercise 4 Revising Sentences With Compound Subjects and Verbs Revise the following paragraph, correcting errors in subject-verb agreement.

Either Martha or Irene visit Independence Hall often. The Declaration of Independence and the U.S. Constitution was signed there. Philadelphia's Old City Hall and Congress Hall sit on either side of Independence Hall. Neither Independence Hall nor Philadelphia's museums charges high entrance fees. Macaroni and cheese are the dish Martha and Irene usually order at a restaurant near Independence Hall.

▶ Critical Viewing Write a sentence about this picture, beginning *Neither the dome atop the hall nor the clock. . . .* Does your sentence need a singular verb or a plural one? [**Make a Judgment**]

More Practice

Language Lab CD-ROM
• Agreement With Compound Subjects lesson
On-line Exercise Bank
• Section 24.1
Grammar Exercise Workbook
• pp. 117–118

Independence Hall in Philadelphia

Subject and Verb Agreement • **523**

Answer Key

Exercise 3
1. are
2. has
3. are
4. are
5. were
6. patrol
7. is
8. meet
9. has
10. is

Exercise 4
(1) Either Martha or Irene visits Independence Hall often. (2) The Declaration of Independence and the U.S. Constitution were signed there. (3) Philadelphia's Old City Hall and Congress Hall sit on either side of Independence Hall. (4) Neither Independence Hall nor Philadelphia's museums charge high entrance fees. (5) Macaroni and cheese is the dish Martha and Irene usually order at a restaurant near Independence Hall.

Critical Viewing

Make a Judgment Students may suggest:

Neither the dome atop the hall nor the clock needs help attracting visitors. (singular verb)

ONGOING ASSESSMENT: Monitor and Reinforce

If students have difficulty with Exercise 3 or 4, refer them to the following for additional practice.

In the Textbook	Print Resources	Technology
Section Review, Ex. 8, p. 527	Grammar Exercise Workbook, pp. 117–118	Language Lab CD-ROM, Subject-Verb Agreement; On-Line Exercise Bank, Section 24.1

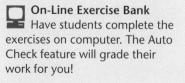 **TIME SAVERS!**

Answers on Transparency Use the Grammar Exercises Answers on Transparencies for Chapter 24 to facilitate correction by students.

On-Line Exercise Bank Have students complete the exercises on computer. The Auto Check feature will grade their work for you!

Pronoun Subjects and Verbs

1. Indefinite pronouns that function as subjects must agree with the verb.

2. Pronoun subjects follow the same rules as any subject of a sentence: A singular subject takes a singular verb; a plural subject takes a plural verb.

3. When an indefinite pronoun can be singular or plural, students need to consider the noun to which the pronoun refers in order to determine the correct verb to use.

Customize for
Logical/Mathematical Learners

Have students make a simple Venn diagram of the indefinite pronouns, with singular pronouns on the left side, plural pronouns on the right side, and singular or plural pronouns in the middle. Hang the diagram on the chalkboard during the lesson for reinforcement.

Grammar in Literature

1. Have a volunteer read aloud the excerpt from *The Phantom Tollbooth.*

2. Ask students to identify whether each verb is singular or plural.

3. Ask students to identify the indefinite pronoun in the excerpt. *(Everything)*

24.1

Pronoun Subjects and Verbs

Indefinite pronouns refer to people, places, or things in a general way.

KEY CONCEPT When an indefinite pronoun is the subject of a sentence, the verb must agree in number with the pronoun. ■

INDEFINITE PRONOUNS				
Singular			Plural	Singular or Plural
anybody	everyone	nothing	both	all
anyone	everything	one	few	any
anything	much	other	many	more
each	neither	somebody	others	most
either	nobody	someone	several	none
everybody	no one	something		some

Indefinite Pronouns That Are Always Singular
Indefinite pronouns that are always singular are used with singular verbs.

EXAMPLE: Everyone is ready.

Indefinite Pronouns That Are Always Plural Indefinite pronouns that are always plural are used with plural verbs.

EXAMPLE: Both of my suitcases are in the closet.

GRAMMAR IN LITERATURE

from **The Phantom Tollbooth**
Based on the book by Norton Juster
Screenplay by Susan Nanus

The singular indefinite pronoun (in red italics) used as a subject in this passage agrees in number with its verb (in blue italics).

CLOCK. . . . Wherever he is, he wants to be somewhere else—and when he gets there, so what. *Everything is* too much trouble or a waste of time. . . . Unless he bothers to notice a very large package that happened to arrive today.

524 • Making Words Agree

More Practice
Language Lab CD-ROM
• Agreement in Number lesson
On-line Exercise Bank
• Section 24.1
Grammar Exercise Workbook
• pp. 119–120

STANDARDIZED TEST PREPARATION WORKSHOP

Grammar and Usage Many standardized tests require students to recognize correct usage. Ask students if the underlined word is used correctly. If not, choose the correct usage.

Either the lion or the tiger lives in Asia.

A no change   **C** have lived
B live   **D** were living

The correct answer is item **A**. The singular verb *lives* agrees with the singular subject.

Indefinite Pronouns That Are Either Singular or Plural

Some indefinite pronouns can be either singular or plural. To decide on the number, look for the noun to which the pronoun refers. If the noun is singular, the pronoun is singular. If the noun is plural, the pronoun is plural.

EXAMPLES: <u>All</u> of my money <u>is</u> gone.
<u>All</u> of these souvenirs <u>are</u> for you.

► **Exercise 5** **Choosing Verbs That Agree With Indefinite Pronouns** Write the form of the verb that agrees with the subject in the following sentences.
1. Everyone who visits the Grand Canyon in Arizona (is, are) impressed.
2. Many (stand, stands) in awe as they gaze into the canyon.
3. Some (is, are) able to hike from the South Rim of the canyon to the North Rim.
4. Either of the rims (offer, offers) visitors spectacular views of the canyon.
5. Much of the day (is, are) spent hiking around the canyon's rim.
6. No one in our group (want, wants) to hike to the bottom of the canyon.
7. All of us (agree, agrees) that the hike back up will be difficult.
8. More of our time (was, were) spent hiking back up the trail than hiking down into the canyon.
9. If someone (wish, wishes) to ride a mule into the canyon, he or she must make a reservation in advance.
10. Others (prefer, prefers) to reach the bottom by foot.

► **Exercise 6** **Revising to Eliminate Errors in Agreement** Look closely at each sentence below. If the subject and verb agree, write *correct*. If a sentence is not correct, revise it to eliminate agreement errors.
1. Many visits the Alamo to learn about its history.
2. Nearly everyone know that the Alamo is in San Antonio, Texas.
3. Anyone in a tour group finds out that Texans defended the fort in 1836 during the Texas War for Independence.
4. Several in our group was not aware that most of the Alamo's defenders died during the battle.
5. Few of the Alamo's original buildings stands today.

An aerial view of the Grand Canyon

▲ **Critical Viewing** Write two sentences about this photo. Begin one with *Most of the clouds . . .* and the other with *Most of the day . . . .* Are the verbs in the two sentences the same or different in number? **[Compare]**

Subject and Verb Agreement • 525

Answer Key

► **Exercise 5**
1. is
2. stand
3. are
4. offers
5. is
6. wants
7. agree
8. was
9. wishes
10. prefer

► **Exercise 6**
1. Many visit the Alamo to learn about its history.
2. Nearly everyone knows that the Alamo is in San Antonio, Texas.
3. correct
4. Several in our group were not aware that most of the Alamo's defenders died during the battle.
5. Few of the Alamo's original buildings stand today.

Critical Viewing

Compare Students may suggest:

Most of the clouds are on the left side of the picture.

Most of the day was cloudy.

The verbs differ in number.

Customize for
Verbal/Linguistic Learners

Allow students to leave their books open to the chart on page 524. Call on each student, choosing a pronoun at random from the chart. Ask him or her to invent a sentence out loud, using a verb that agrees with the indefinite pronoun.

☑ **ONGOING ASSESSMENT: Monitor and Reinforce**

If students miss more than two items in Exercises 5–6, refer them to the following for additional practice.

In the Textbook	Print Resources	Technology
Section Review, Ex. 9 and 10, p. 527	Grammar Exercise Workbook, pp. 119–120	Language Lab CD-ROM, Subject-Verb Agreement; On-Line Exercise Bank, Section 24.1

⏱ **TIME SAVERS!**

Answers on Transparency Use the Grammar Exercises Answers on Transparencies for Chapter 24 to facilitate correction by students.

On-Line Exercise Bank Have students complete the exercises on computer. The Auto Check feature will grade their work for you!

Lining Up Pronouns and Verbs

Teaching Resources: Hands-on Grammar Activity Book, Chapter 24

1. Have students refer to their Hands-on Grammar Activity Books or give them copies of the relevant pages for this activity.

2. Have students identify in which corner they will always find plural verbs; (upper right) singular verbs (lower right).

3. Repeat with additional index cards and different pronouns and verbs.

Find It In Your Reading

Work with a partner. Choose two of each other's sentences to check whether pronouns were correctly identified.

Find It In Your Writing

List four of your pronouns and tell whether their verbs should be singular or plural.

24.1

Hands-on Grammar

Lining Up Pronouns and Verbs

Make three stacks of index cards. On each card in one stack, draw a diagonal line with a pencil from the lower left corner to the upper right corner. On the left above the line, write a singular indefinite pronoun (Examples: *anybody, each, everyone, either, one*). On the right below the line, write a singular verb (Examples: *arrives, carries, does, has, tries, wants*).

On each card in the second stack, draw a diagonal line from the upper left corner to the lower right corner. This time, write a plural indefinite pronoun (Examples: *all, both, few, some*) on the left below the line and a plural verb on the right above the line (Examples: *arrive, do, have, try, want*).

Use the third stack of cards for pronouns that can be either singular or plural. Draw a diagonal line from the lower left to the upper right on one side. Then, flip the card over and draw a line from the upper left to the lower right. The two lines should match back-to-back. Write a pronoun on the left part of each side of the card. Write a singular verb on the right above the line on one side and a plural verb on the right below the line on the other side. Cut the cards with scissors along the diagonal lines.

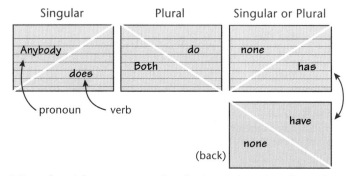

Mix and match pronouns and verbs to create rectangles and two-word sentences. The shape of the card will prevent matching a singular indefinite pronoun with a plural verb.

Find It in Your Reading In your reading, find examples of sentences that contain indefinite pronouns used as subjects. Write the sentences on your paper, and indicate whether the pronouns are singular or plural.

Find It in Your Writing Look through samples of your writing to find sentences in which you have used personal and indefinite pronouns as subjects. Check to see that the pronouns agree in number with their verbs.

526 • *Making Words Agree*

⏰ **TIME SAVERS!**

✋ **Hands-on Grammar**
Use the Hands-on Grammar activity sheet for Chapter 24 to facilitate this activity.

☑ **ONGOING ASSESSMENT: Assess Mastery**

Use the following resources to assess mastery of subject and verb agreement.

In the Textbook	Technology
Chapter Review, Ex. 22–24, pp. 532–533	Language Lab CD-ROM, Subject-Verb Agreement; On-Line Exercise Bank, Section 24.1

Section 24.1 Section Review

GRAMMAR EXERCISES 7–13

Exercise 7 Making Subjects and Verbs Agree For each sentence below, write the verb that agrees with the subject.

1. The Boston National Historical Park (contain, contains) seven sites that are on Boston's Freedom Trail.
2. These places (include, includes) Bunker Hill Monument, the U.S.S. *Constitution*, and Old North Church.
3. The sites on the trail (is, are) places where historic events occurred.
4. Faneuil Hall (was, were) used as a marketplace and a place for Boston town meetings during the 1700's.
5. The Bunker Hill Monument (commemorate, commemorates) the first major battle in the American Revolution.

Exercise 8 Supplying Verbs That Agree With Compound Subjects Write each sentence below, filling in the blank with a verb that agrees with the subject.

1. Muir Woods and Golden Gate Park ___?___ located in northern California.
2. Giant redwood and Douglas Firs ___?___ in Muir Woods.
3. Neither redwood nor sequoia roots ___?___ more than six feet underground.
4. Plants and animals ___?___ in Muir Woods.
5. Neither overnight campers nor fire ___?___ permitted in Muir Woods.

Exercise 9 Making Pronoun Subjects and Verbs Agree Write the verb that agrees with each subject below.

1. Both of my parents (wish, wishes) to visit Utah's Arches National Park.
2. Most of the tourists (visit, visits) the park to see the strange rock formations.
3. All who visit (photograph, photographs) the unusual rock formations.
4. Neither of my brothers (own, owns) a camera.
5. Much of the park's grounds (is, are) filled with natural stone arches, windows, spires, and pinnacles.

Exercise 10 Revising to Eliminate Errors in Subject-Verb Agreement Revise each sentence below, correcting errors in subject-verb agreement.

1. People enjoys hearing how lanterns hung in the Old North Church's steeple warned colonists that the British soldiers was coming.
2. One of the oldest U.S. ships afloat are the U.S.S. *Constitution*, which sit in Boston Harbor.
3. Either surfers or a bather enjoy the beaches in Golden Gate Park.
4. Often, fog or mist surround the Golden Gate Bridge.
5. Nothing in the world compare to Arches National Park.

Exercise 11 Find It in Your Reading Identify the four verbs used with the pronoun *he* in the passage on page 524. Are all of the verbs singular, to agree with a singular subject?

Exercise 12 Find It in Your Writing Review a piece of writing from your portfolio. Identify and correct any errors in subject-verb agreement.

Exercise 13 Writing Application Write a description of a landmark or site of interest in your area. Include compound subjects and indefinite pronouns.

Section Review • 527

ASSESS and CLOSE

Section Review

Each of these exercises correlates with the instruction on subject-verb agreement, pages 520–525. These exercises may be used for more practice, for reteaching, or for review of the key concepts presented. Answers for all chapter exercises are available in *Grammar Exercises Answers on Transparencies* in your Teaching Resources.

Answer Key

Exercise 7

1. contains
2. include
3. are
4. was
5. commemorates

Exercise 8

Answers will vary. Samples are given.
1. are
2. grow
3. extend
4. live
5. is

Exercise 9

1. wish
2. visit
3. photograph
4. owns
5. is

Exercise 10

1. People enjoy hearing how lanterns hung in the Old North Church's steeple warned colonists that the British soldiers were coming.
2. One of the oldest U.S. ships afloat is the U.S.S. *Constitution*, which sits in Boston Harbor.
3. Either surfers or a bather enjoys the beaches in Golden Gate Park.
4. Often, fog or mist surrounds the Golden Gate Bridge.
5. Nothing in the world compares to Arches National Park.

Exercise 11

Find It in Your Reading

is, wants, gets, bothers

All are singular.

continued

Answer Key continued

Exercise 12

Find It in Your Writing
Have students exchange papers with a partner for a review of agreement.

Exercise 13

Writing Application
Students can use the Internet or reference books to find interesting details about the place they choose.

Pronoun and Antecedent Agreement

PREPARE and ENGAGE

Interest GRABBER Explain that an antecedent is something that comes before something else. The two things are related, and you can't have the second thing unless there is an antecedent. This applies to the real world as well as to grammar. Have students suggest the missing antecedents or things that follow in the following chart.

Antecedent	Object
(record)	CD
fan	(air conditioner)
(typewriter)	computer
pony express	(postal service)

Activate Prior Knowledge

Ask students to name some pronouns and write them on the chalkboard. Then ask students to suggest nouns the pronouns could refer to. For example, the pronoun *they* could refer to the noun *rabbits*.

TEACH

Step-by-Step Teaching Guide

Pronoun and Antecedent Agreement

1. Errors occur when the antecedent is an indefinite pronoun (page 524). When a singular indefinite pronoun is the subject of the sentence, the later pronoun that refers to it must be singular.

2. Write the following sentences on the chalkboard and have students choose the correct pronoun.

   Has anyone lost (his/their) umbrella?

   Somebody forgot (his/their) textbook.

Integrating Workplace Skills

Jobs often require workers to provide their employers with reports of what they have accomplished. By using pronoun and antecedent agreement, these reports will enable an employee to explain precisely what he or she has done, because the pronouns will refer directly back to the task or project completed.

An *antecedent* is the word to which a pronoun refers.

> **KEY CONCEPT** Use a singular pronoun with a singular antecedent. ■

SINGULAR PRONOUNS AND ANTECEDENTS

The Yukon takes <u>its</u> name from the Native American word Yu-kun-ah.

Melissa planned <u>her</u> trip to Canada's Yukon last month.

Tom will lend Melissa <u>his</u> suitcase.

> **KEY CONCEPT** Use a plural pronoun with a plural antecedent. ■

PLURAL PRONOUNS AND ANTECEDENTS

Hikers will have <u>their</u> pick of trails in the Yukon.

The boys have all brought <u>their</u> hiking boots.

The girls knew <u>they</u> had to bring coats and hats.

Two special rules are used for compound antecedents:

> **KEY CONCEPT** Use a singular pronoun with two or more singular antecedents joined by *or* or *nor.* ■

EXAMPLE: Andrew or Keith gives <u>his</u> report about the Klondike Gold Rush today.

> **KEY CONCEPT** Use a plural pronoun with two or more singular antecedents joined by *and.* ■

EXAMPLE: Joyce and Robert showed <u>their</u> father the drawing of the Yukon River.

Theme: The Yukon

In this section, you will learn how to make pronouns agree in number with their antecedents. The examples and exercises are about the Yukon Territory in Canada.

Cross-Curricular Connection: Social Studies

528 • Making Words Agree

⏱ TIME AND RESOURCE MANAGER

Resources
Print: Grammar Exercise Workbook, pp. 121–122; Grammar Exercises Answers on Transparencies, Chapter 24
Technology: Language Lab CD-ROM, Using Pronouns; On-Line Exercise Bank, Section 24.2

In-Depth Coverage	Accelerated Pace
• Work through all key concepts, pp. 528–530. • Assign and review Exercises 14–16.	• Assign pp. 528–530 for independent student review. • Assign Section Review Exercises 17–18 p. 531.

▶ **Exercise 14** Identifying Pronouns That Agree With Their Antecedents In the sentences below, write the pronoun in parentheses that agrees with its antecedent.

1. The gold prospectors packed up (his, their) supplies and headed toward the Yukon.
2. A man and wife kept a journal of (her, their) travels.
3. Either Claude or his brother hopes to make (his, their) fortune prospecting in the Yukon.
4. Claude's wife and daughter looked sad as (she, they) watched him leave.
5. The Yukon is noted for (its, their) harsh winters.

▶ **Exercise 15** Supplying Pronouns That Agree With Antecedents Copy each sentence below, filling in the blank with a pronoun that agrees with its antecedent.

EXAMPLE: Jake trained ___?___ sled dog to do tricks.

ANSWER: Jake trained his sled dog to do tricks.

1. Fred and Tony are preparing ___?___ report about Canada's Yukon Territory.
2. Neither boy knows what ___?___ will say about the Yukon.
3. Perhaps Tony will ask ___?___ parents to help.
4. Joan has loaned the boys ___?___ book about the Yukon.
5. The book is missing some of ___?___ pages.

More Practice

Language Lab CD-ROM
• Pronouns and Antecedents lesson
On-line Exercise Bank
• Section 24.2
Grammar Exercise Workbook
• pp. 121–122

◀ Critical Viewing Include a pronoun in a sentence about one of the dogs in this picture. Include a different pronoun in a sentence about both dogs. Make sure your pronouns agree with their antecedents. **[Analyze]**

▶ Exercise 14

1. their
2. their
3. his
4. they
5. its

▶ Exercise 15

1. Fred and Tony are preparing their report about Canada's Yukon Territory.
2. Neither boy knows what he will say about the Yukon.
3. Perhaps Tony will ask his parents to help.
4. Joan has loaned the boys her book about the Yukon.
5. The book is missing some of its pages.

Critical Viewing

Analyze Students might suggest

One of the dogs has its eyes closed.

Both of the dogs seem to like to have their picture taken.

Language Highlight

When the gender of the subject of a sentence is not specified, it used to be customary to use a masculine pronoun: *Each child ate his lunch.* This is no longer acceptable. The sentence must read *Each child ate his or her lunch.* If this construction is too awkward, the sentence can be rewritten as *All children ate their lunches.*

Pronoun and Antecedent Agreement • 529

☑ ONGOING ASSESSMENT: Prerequisite Skills

If students have difficulty with pronoun and antecedent agreement, you may find it necessary to review the following to ensure coverage of prerequisite knowledge.

In the Textbook	Print Resources	Technology
Nouns and Pronouns, pp. 292–311	Grammar Exercise Workbook, pp. 7–12	Language Lab CD-ROM, Using Pronouns; On-Line Exercise Bank, Section 14.2

▶ **Exercise 16**

1. When tourists visit the Yukon, they must respect the wilderness.
2. If the Yukon's natural beauty is spoiled, its wilderness areas will be gone forever.
3. correct
4. correct
5. Rescue workers carried their equipment to the place where Ben had fallen.
6. The rescue workers told Ben that he was lucky that his ankle was not broken.
7. Ben's sister Betsy came to see him at the hospital.
8. Either Betsy or Ben's wife, June, plans to spend her time visiting Ben at the hospital.
9. Despite his accident, Ben decided that he would try to climb Mt. Logan, Canada's highest peak, during his next vacation.
10. Located in the Yukon, Mt. Logan measures 19,524 feet from sea level to its summit.

Step-by-Step Teaching Guide

Grammar in Literature

1. Have a volunteer read aloud the passage from "The King of Mazy May."

2. It is not unusual for antecedents to occur far from the pronouns that rename them. *His* in the second sentence refers all the way back to *Walt* in the first sentence. *Them* and *their* in the last sentence refer to the antecedent *they and several others* early in the sentence. Be sure students can match each pronoun and antecedent.

3. There are some difficult blue/red matches in this passage. The blue *they* in the fourth line refers to the blue and red *his father and he* in the third line.

Critical Viewing

Analyze, Identify Students may say: *My parents took this photo on their Alaskan cruise* (antecedent is *parents*). *The mountain reaches its highest point here* (antecedent is *mountain*).

24.2

▶ **Exercise 16** Revising Sentences to Correct Errors in Pronoun-Antecedent Agreement Revise the following sentences, correcting errors in pronoun-antecedent agreement. If a sentence has no errors, write *correct.*

1. When tourists visit the Yukon, he or she must respect the wilderness.
2. If the Yukon's natural beauty is spoiled, his wilderness areas will be gone forever.
3. Ben and Joe chose to take their vacation in the Yukon last summer.
4. While hiking, Ben slipped and sprained his ankle badly.
5. Rescue workers carried her equipment to the place where Ben had fallen.
6. The rescue workers told Ben that he was lucky that their ankle was not broken.
7. Ben's sister Betsy came to see them at the hospital.
8. Either Betsy or Ben's wife, June, plans to spend their time visiting Ben at the hospital.
9. Despite their accident, Ben decided that they would try to climb Mt. Logan, Canada's highest peak, during his next vacation.
10. Located in the Yukon, Mt. Logan measures 19,524 feet from sea level to their summit.

GRAMMAR IN LITERATURE

from **The King of Mazy May**
Jack London

In this passage from a story about the Yukon, the personal pronouns, highlighted in blue italics, agree in number with their antecedents, highlighted in red italics.

Walt was born a thousand miles or so down the Yukon, in a trading post below the Ramparts. After *his* mother died, *his father* and *he* came up on the river, step by step, from camp to camp, till now *they* are settled down on the Mazy May Creek in the Klondike country. Last year *they* and several *others* had spent much toil and time on the Mazy May, and endured great hardships; the *creek*, in turn, was just beginning to show up *its* richness and to reward *them* for *their* heavy labor.

530 • Making Words Agree

▶ **More Practice**

Language Lab CD-ROM
• Pronouns and Antecedents lesson
On-line Exercise Bank
• Section 24.2
Grammar Exercise Workbook
• pp. 121–122

▲ **Critical Viewing** Use the pronouns *their* and *its* in two sentences about this photo. What is the antecedent of each pronoun? **[Analyze, Identify]**

☑ **ONGOING ASSESSMENT: Monitor and Reinforce**

If students miss more than two items in Exercises 14–16, refer them to the following for additional practice.

In the Textbook	Print Resources	Technology
Section Review, Ex. 17–19, p. 531	Grammar Exercise Workbook, pp. 121–122	Language Lab CD-ROM, Using Pronouns; On-Line Exercise Bank, Section 24.2

Section 24.2 Section Review

GRAMMAR EXERCISES 17–21

> **Exercise 17** Supplying Pronouns That Agree With Their Antecedents

Copy each sentence below, filling in the blank with a pronoun that agrees with its antecedent.

1. In the late 1890's, prospectors took ___?___ chances and headed off to the Yukon in search of gold.
2. Men and women hoped to make ___?___ fortunes by finding gold nuggets.
3. Neither men nor women knew what to expect the first time ___?___ decided to journey into the Northwest Territory.
4. One woman, Ethel Bush Berry, went to the Yukon with ___?___ husband.
5. Together, Mr. and Mrs. Berry made ___?___ way along Chilkoot Pass.
6. The second time the Berrys went there, Mrs. Berry's sister went with ___?___.
7. Many gold seekers went to Dawson because ___?___ is located near the Klondike River.
8. When Edith Feero Larson was ten years old, ___?___ family went to the Yukon and the Klondike.
9. Edith's mother and father and ___?___ children left for the Yukon in 1897.
10. Mrs. Larson remembered ___?___ youth in the Klondike with fondness.

> **Exercise 18** Revising to Eliminate Errors in Pronoun-Antecedent Agreement

Revise the following paragraphs, correcting errors in pronoun-antecedent agreement. If the sentence is correct as is, write *correct*.

Dawson City, located where the Yukon and Klondike rivers meet, is known for its role in the gold rush of the late 1890's. Today, Dawson is a popular place for tourists to go on his or her vacations. Nearly 60,000 people crowd into Dawson each summer, making tourism their biggest industry. Some residents make its living by raising sled dogs. In mid-February, participants in the annual sled-dog race stream through Dawson on her way to Fairbanks, Alaska. The roads into Dawson are known for its scenery. In Dawson, visitors can see how the city has restored its oldest buildings.

When my family visited Dawson during our vacation, the city was lively. Neither my sister nor my mother forgot to bring their camera. My brother and my father wanted us to take his picture near Bonanza Creek, where the first gold nuggets were found. Both my brother and father tried his luck finding gold in the creek.

> **Exercise 19** Find It in Your Reading

Find the antecedent for each underlined pronoun in this passage from "The King of Mazy May." Indicate whether the antecedent is singular or plural.

Walt has walked all the fourteen years of <u>his</u> life in suntanned, moose-hide moccasins, and <u>he</u> can go to the Indian camps and "talk big" with the men, and trade calico and beads with <u>them</u> for <u>their</u> precious furs.

> **Exercise 20** Find It in Your Writing

Review a piece of writing from your portfolio. Identify and correct any errors in pronoun-antecedent agreement.

> **Exercise 21** Writing Application

Write a summary of a short story you have read about a character in conflict with natural forces. Use at least five different pronouns. Draw arrows from each pronoun to its antecedent.

Answer Key continued

> **Exercise 21**

Writing Application
Have students write one sentence from their paragraphs on the chalkboard (without the arrows). Then have students go up to the chalkboard and choose a sentence (not their own) and draw an arrow connecting one pronoun and its antecedent.

ASSESS and CLOSE

Section Review

Each of these exercises correlates to the instruction on pronoun-antecedent agreement, pages 528–530. These exercises may be used for more practice, for reteaching, or for review of the key concepts presented. Answers for all exercises are available in *Grammar Exercises Answers on Transparencies* in your Teaching Resources.

Answer Key

> **Exercise 17**

1. their
2. their
3. they
4. her
5. their
6. them
7. it
8. her
9. their
10. her

> **Exercise 18**

(1) correct (2) Today, Dawson is a popular place for tourists to go on their vacations. (3) Nearly 60,000 people crowd into Dawson each summer, making tourism its biggest industry. (4) Some residents make their living by raising sled dogs. (5) In mid-February, participants in the annual sled dog race stream through Dawson on their way to Fairbanks, Alaska. (6) The roads leading into Dawson are known for their scenery. (7) correct
(8) correct (9) Neither my sister nor my mother forgot to bring her camera. (10) My brother and my father wanted us to take their picture near Bonanza Creek, where the first gold nuggets were found. (11) Both my brother and father tried their luck finding gold in the creek.

> **Exercise 19**

Find It in Your Reading
Walt—singular; *Walt*—singular; *men*—plural; *men*—plural

> **Exercise 20**

Find It in Your Writing
Students should especially check for agreement with indefinite pronoun antecedents.

continued

Each of these exercises correlates to a section of the chapter on agreement, pages 520–531. These exercises may be used for more practice, for reteaching, or for review of the key concepts presented. Answers for all exercises are available in *Grammar Exercise Answers on Transparencies* in your Teaching Resources.

Answer Key

▶ Exercise 22

1. is
2. is
3. live
4. shares
5. provide
6. is
7. are
8. are
9. participates
10. cares
11. are
12. is
13. have
14. looks
15. draws

▶ Exercise 23

1. live
2. visit
3. serves
4. resides
5. needs
6. include
7. brings
8. ranks
9. swim
10. commemorates

▶ Exercise 24

1. The Yukon River flows through Alaska into the Bering Sea.
2. The Yukon lies in the subarctic climate zone.
3. Bears and some other mammals hibernate when winter comes.
4. correct
5. In summer, however, temperatures have reached as high as 95°F.
6. Eight sled dogs and a driver come down this road quite often.
7. correct

continued

GRAMMAR EXERCISES 22–28

▶ **Exercise 22** Identifying Verbs That Agree With Subjects For each sentence below, write the verb in parentheses that agrees with the subject.

1. The Yukon (is, are) a Canadian territory.
2. It (is, are) located in the northwest corner of Canada.
3. Moose, wolves, and many other animals (live, lives) in the Yukon.
4. Yukon Territory (share, shares) more than 650 miles of border with Alaska.
5. The forests or the mountains (provide, provides) shelter for the Yukon's wildlife.
6. Much of the Yukon (is, are) forest land.
7. Most of the Native Americans in the Yukon (is, are) of the Athabascan language family.
8. Some (is, are) Tlingit-speaking people.
9. Nearly everyone (participate, participates) in the annual Native American festival at Moosehide.
10. No one (care, cares) whether festival goers are Native American or not.
11. Mountains (is, are) a dominant feature of the Yukon's landscape.
12. The Yukon's major mountain range (is, are) the St. Elias in the southwest corner of the territory.
13. Miners and loggers (has, have) left their mark on the land.
14. Each tourist or Yukon resident (look, looks) for signs of wildlife.
15. Either swimming or boating (draw, draws) tourists in the summer.

▶ **Exercise 23** Supplying Verbs That Agree With Subjects Copy each sentence below, supplying the correct form of the verb in parentheses.

1. Because of its harsh climate and terain, very few people (live) in the Yukon.

2. However, thousands of tourists (visit) the region each year.
3. The small city of Whitehorse (serve) as the capital of the Yukon Territory.
4. Most of the Yukon's population (reside) in Whitehorse.
5. If a person anywhere in the Yukon (need) to see a dentist, he or she must go to Whitehorse or Dawson City.
6. Other Yukon communities (include) Watson Lake, Faro, and Ross River.
7. Mining (bring) in much of the Yukon's income.
8. Either tourism or manufacturing (rank) second in economic importance.
9. Salmon, whitefish, and trout (swim) in the Yukon River.
10. A popular museum in Whitehorse (commemorate) the great gold rush in the 1890's.

▶ **Exercise 24** Revising Sentences to Eliminate Errors in Subject-Verb Agreement Revise the following sentences, correcting errors in subject-verb agreement. If a sentence is correct as is, write *correct*.

1. The Yukon River flow through Alaska into the Bering Sea.
2. The Yukon lie in the subarctic climate zone.
3. Bears and some other mammals hibernates when winter comes.
4. Extremely cold temperatures mark the Yukon's climate for much of the year.
5. In summer, however, temperatures has reached as high as 95° F.
6. Eight sled dogs and a driver comes down this road quite often.
7. Either the dogs or the driver makes a great deal of noise.
8. The Yukon's location near the Arctic affect how many daylight hours it receives.

9. Today, more tourists are visiting the Yukon.
10. More of the region's money are coming from "adventure tourism."
11. A trip to the Yukon offer tourists an authentic outdoor experience.
12. In summer in the Yukon, daylight last as long as twenty hours.
13. In winter, the time of daylight is very short.
14. Neither freezing temperatures nor snow keep people from enjoying themselves in the Yukon.
15. Neither bad weather nor icy conditions prevents tourists from exploring the Yukon.

▶ **Exercise 25** Supplying Pronouns That Agree With Their Antecedents
Copy each sentence below, filling in the blank with a pronoun that agrees with its antecedent.

1. My brother and ___?___ friend will travel to the Yukon this summer.
2. The two friends are planning to spend much of ___?___ time in Kluane National Park.
3. Kluane is a huge park. ___?___ is Canada's fourth largest park.
4. Visitors to Kluane will get ___?___ fill of the outdoors.
5. It is important that visitors bring all the equipment ___?___ will need.

▶ **Exercise 26** Revising a Paragraph to Eliminate All Agreement Errors
Revise the following paragraph, correcting any errors in agreement.

Most of the Yukon's economy is based on mining. Many people in the Yukon mines lead, zinc, copper, or gold. My Aunt Jane moved with their family to the Yukon. Each of my aunt's sons are miners. Either my cousin Theo or his two brothers works in a copper mine. He wrote me about a camping trip he and his mother recently

took. During the trip Aunt Jane and Theo was confronted by a bear. The bear stuck their paw out at them. Both Aunt Jane and Theo stood still as she watched the bear lumber away. Each of them feel lucky to have survived that adventure.

▶ **Exercise 27** Writing Application
Write a diary entry about a memorable trip that you took with other members of your family. Include compound subjects, and use personal and indefinite pronouns in your writing. Proofread carefully to avoid any agreement errors.

▶ **Exercise 28** CUMULATIVE REVIEW
Using Verbs and Pronouns Correctly
Rewrite the paragraph below on your paper, correcting any errors in verb or pronoun usage.

In the 1840's, Robert Campbell, a British fur trapper, become the first European to explore the Yukon. He build a trading post near the Pelly River, which laid in the southern part of the region. The Chilkat Indians were distrustful of Campbell, and them burn down their trading post a short time later. For the next fifty years, few other Europeans come into the area. Then, in 1896, three men was prospect on Bonanza Creek, when he spotted flecks of gold setting in the creek bed. Word about them gold strike quickly spread. During the next two years, more than 35,000 people rushed to the Yukon. They was hope to get rich. As the wealth of the region increased, their political importance increased as well. In 1898, the Yukon were named an official Canadian territory.

8. The Yukon's location near the Arctic affects how many daylight hours it receives.
9. correct
10. More of the region's money is coming from "adventure tourism."
11. A trip to the Yukon offers tourists an authentic outdoor experience.
12. In summer in the Yukon, daylight lasts as long as 20 hours.
13. correct
14. Neither freezing temperatures nor snow keeps people from enjoying themselves in the Yukon.
15. Neither bad weather nor icy conditions prevent tourists from exploring the Yukon.

▶ **Exercise 25**

1. My brother and his friend will travel to the Yukon this summer.
2. The two friends are planning to spend much of their time in Kluane National Park.
3. Kluane is a huge park. It is Canada's fourth largest park.
4. Visitors to Kluane will get their fill of the outdoors.
5. It is important that visitors bring all the equipment they will need.

▶ **Exercise 26**

1. correct
2. Many people in the Yukon mine lead, zinc, copper, or gold.
3. My Aunt Jane moved with her family to the Yukon.
4. Each of my aunt's sons is a miner.
5. Either my cousin Theo or his two brothers work in a copper mine.
6. correct
7. During the trip Aunt Jane and Theo were confronted by a bear.
8. The bear stuck its paw out at them.
9. Both Aunt Jane and Theo stood still as they watched the bear lumber away.
10. Each of them feels lucky to have survived that adventure.

▶ **Exercise 27**

Writing Application
Exchange entries with a partner. Check each other's writing for agreement errors.

continued

▶ **Exercise 28**

Cumulative Review
In the 1840's, Robert Campbell, a British fur trapper, became the first European to explore the Yukon. He built a trading post near the Pelly River, which lay in the southern part of the region. The Chilkat Indians were distrustful of Campbell, and they burnt down his trading post a short time later. For the next fifty years, few other Europeans came into the area. Then, in 1896, three men were prospecting on Bonanza Creek, when they spotted flecks of gold sitting in the creek bed. Word about their gold strike quickly spread. During the next two years, more than 35,000 people rushed to the Yukon. They were hoping to get rich. As the wealth of the region increased, its political importance increased as well. In 1898, the Yukon was named an official Canadian territory.

Standard English Usage: Agreement

Teaching Resources: Standardized Test Preparation Workbook, Chapter 24

1. Share with students the chart in step 2 of the Step-by-Step Teaching Guide on page 522 of this Teacher's Edition.

2. Ask which rule sample test item 1 uses. (singular or plural = plural)

3. Ask which rule sample test item 2 uses. (plural or singular = singular)

4. Remind students to review the rules when dealing with compound subjects.

Standardized Test Preparation Workshop

Standard English Usage: Agreement

Standardized tests frequently test your knowledge of the rules of subject and verb agreement. When checking a sentence for errors, first identify the subject. Next, identify the type of subject: singular, plural, or compound. Then, apply the rules of agreement to make sure that the verb in the sentence agrees with the subject.

The following questions will give you practice with different formats used for items that test knowledge of subject-verb agreement.

Test Tip

Remember, the singular or plural form of the subject in the sentence will dictate which form the verb takes.

Sample Test Items	Answers and Explanations
Identify the underlined word or phrase that contains an error in the following sentence. Either Simon or the Caseys knows the 　(A)　　　　(B)　　　　(C) correct answer. No errors. 　(D)　　　　(E)	The correct answer is *C*. The compound subject of the sentence is *Either Simon or the Caseys*. When singular and plural subjects are joined by *or* or *nor*, the verb must agree with the subject closer to it. In this case, the closer subject, *the Caseys*, is plural, so the plural verb *know* should be used in the sentence.
Choose the revised version of the following sentence that eliminates all errors in grammar, usage, and mechanics. Either the Caseys or Simon know the correct answer. **A** Neither the Caseys nor Simon know the correct answer. **B** Either the Caseys or Simon knows the correct answer. **C** The Caseys and Simon knows the correct answer. **D** The correct answers is known by the Caseys or Simon.	The correct answer is *B*. The compound subject of the sentence is *Either the Caseys or Simon*. When singular and plural subjects are joined by *or* or *nor*, the verb must agree with the subject closer to it. In this case, the closer subject, *Simon*, is singular, so the singular verb *knows* should be used in the sentence. Answer choice *C* is incorrect because the two parts of the compound subject are joined by *and*. Therefore, the plural verb *know* should be used. Answer choice *D* introduces a new agreement problem between the plural subject *answers* and the singular verb *is*.

◇ TEST-TAKING TIP

When reading test items like those in the first sample, be sure to read the entire item carefully. Often parts in themselves are correct but are not correct in the whole sentence. For example, without the B section in the first Sample Test Item, <u>knows</u> would be the correct verb.

> **Practice 1**

1. B
2. B
3. E
4. D
5. B

> **Practice 2**

1. A
2. J

> **Practice 1** **Directions:** Identify the underlined word or phrase that contains an error in each of the following sentences.

1 *Romeo and Juliet* are known as one of
       (A)   (B)
the most popular plays
      (C)
by Shakespeare. No error.
  (D)   (E)

2 Every student have won a prize
     (A)   (B)
in this year's science fair. No error.
   (C)   (D)   (E)

3 My cat and dog are always
  (A)   (B)   (C)
teasing each other. No error.
    (D)   (E)

4 Jason's best friend, Jimmy, is carrying
       (A)   (B)
his notebook in their bookbag.
   (C)   (D)
No error.
  (E)

5 Neither Stanley nor their friend Ramon
     (A)   (B)
thinks the picnic is
    (C)
this Saturday. No error.
  (D)   (E)

> **Practice 2** **Directions:** Choose the revised version of each numbered sentence below that eliminates all errors in grammar, usage, and mechanics.

1 The Massachusetts 54th Regiment, made up of 1,000 African American soldiers, were form in 1863.

  A The Massachusetts 54th Regiment, made up of 1,000 African American soldiers, was formed in 1863.

  B The Massachusetts 54th Regiment, made up of 1,000 African American soldiers, were formed in 1863.

  C The Massachusetts 54th Regiment, made up of 1,000 African American soldiers, was form in 1863.

  D The Massachusetts 54th Regiment, make up of 1,000 African American soldiers formed in 1863.

2 Although more than 50,000 African American soldiers who fought during the Civil War come from the northern states, more than 90,000 was from the South.

  F Although more than 50,000 African American soldiers who fought during the Civil War come from the northern states, more than 90,000 were from the South.

  G Although more than 50,000 African American soldiers who fought during the Civil War came from the northern states, more than 90,000 was from the South.

  H Although more than 50,000 African American soldiers who fight during the Civil War came from the northern states, more than 90,000 were from the South.

  J Although more than 50,000 African American soldiers who fought during the Civil War came from the northern states, more than 90,000 were from the South.

Time and Resource Manager

In-Depth Lesson Plan

	LESSON FOCUS	PRINT AND MEDIA RESOURCES
DAY 1	**Comparisons Using Adjectives** Students learn and apply concepts of using adjectives in comparisons (pp. 538–540).	**Teaching Resources** *Grammar Exercise Workbook*, pp. 123–124; *Grammar Exercises Answers on Transparencies*, Ch. 25 *Language Lab* **CD-ROM**, Using Modifiers; *On-Line Exercise Bank*, Section 25.1
DAY 2	**Comparisons Using Adverbs** Students learn and apply concepts of using adverbs in comparisons and do the Hands-on Grammar activity (pp. 541–545).	**Teaching Resources** *Grammar Exercise Workbook*, pp. 125–130; *Grammar Exercises Answers on Transparencies*, Ch. 25; *Hands-on Grammar Activity Book*, Ch. 25 *Language Lab* **CD-ROM**, Using Modifiers; *On-Line Exercise Bank*, Section 25.1
DAY 3	**Troublesome Modifiers** Students learn and practice correct degrees of comparison for troublesome modifiers (pp. 546–549).	**Teaching Resources** *Grammar Exercise Workbook*, pp. 131–134; *Grammar Exercises Answers on Transparencies*, Ch. 25 *Language Lab* **CD-ROM**, Using Modifiers; *On-Line Exercise Bank*, Section 25.2
DAY 4	**Review and Assess** Students review chapter and demonstrate mastery of use of adjectives and adverbs (pp. 550–555).	**Teaching Resources** *Formal Assessment*, Ch. 25; *Grammar Exercises Answers on Transparencies*, Ch. 25 *On-Line Exercise Bank*, Section 25.1

Accelerated Lesson Plan

	LESSON FOCUS	PRINT AND MEDIA RESOURCES
DAY 1	**Comparisons Using Adjectives and Adverbs** Students cover concepts and usage of adjectives and adverbs as determined by Diagnostic Test (pp. 538–545).	**Teaching Resources** *Grammar Exercise Workbook*, pp. 123–130; *Grammar Exercises Answers on Transparencies*, Ch. 25; *Hands-on Grammar Activity Book*, Chapter 25 *Language Lab* **CD-ROM**, Using Modifiers; *On-Line Exercise Bank*, Section 25.1
DAY 2	**Troublesome Modifiers** Students cover concepts and correct usage of troublesome modifiers as determined by Diagnostic Test (pp. 546–549).	**Teaching Resources** *Grammar Exercise Workbook*, pp. 131–134; *Grammar Exercises Answers on Transparencies*, Ch. 25 *Language Lab* **CD-ROM**, Using Modifiers; *On-Line Exercise Bank*, Section 25.2
DAY 3	**Review and Assess** Students review chapter and demonstrate mastery of use of adjectives and adverbs (pp. 550–555).	**Teaching Resources** *Formal Assessment*, Ch. 25; *Grammar Exercises Answers on Transparencies*, Ch. 25 *On-Line Exercise Bank*, Section 25.1

Options for Adapting Lesson Plans

HOMEWORK

Have students complete any section of the chapter for homework.

FEATURES

Extend coverage with the Grammar in Literature feature (p. 543), and the Standardized Test Preparation Workshop (p. 552).

TECHNOLOGY

Students can use the On-Line Exercise Bank to complete the exercises on computer. The Auto Check feature will grade their work.

INTEGRATED SKILLS COVERAGE

Grammar in Literature
SE p. 543

Reading
Find It in Your Reading SE pp. 544, 545, 549

Writing
Find It in Your Writing SE pp. 544, 545, 549
Writing Application SE pp. 545, 549, 551

Language Highlight
ATE p. 539

Speaking
ATE p. 539

Viewing and Representing
Critical Viewing SE pp. 536, 540, 542, 547

ASSESSMENT SUPPORT

Standardized Test Preparation Workshop SE p. 552–553;
ATE p. 547

Standardized Test Preparation Workbook, pp. 49–50

Formal Assessment, Ch. 25

MEETING INDIVIDUAL NEEDS

Less Advanced Students See Ongoing Assessments ATE pp. 539,
542, 548

ESL Students ATE p. 540

More Advanced Students ATE p. 548

BLOCK SCHEDULING

Pacing Suggestions
For 90-minute Blocks
• Administer the Diagnostic Test to students to determine
instructional coverage.
• Have students complete the necessary exercises in class. Use
the Hands-on Grammar activity to provide a change of pace.

Resources for Varying Instruction
• **Language Lab CD-ROM** If your students have access to
hardware, a 90-minute block provides an ideal opportunity for
students to work on computer.

Professional Development Support
• **How to Manage Instruction in the Block** This teaching
Resource provides management and activity suggestions.

MEDIA AND TECHNOLOGY

For the Student
• **Language Lab CD-ROM,** Using Modifiers
• **On-Line Exercise Bank,** Ch. 25

For the Teacher
• **Resource Pro CD-ROM**

WRITING AND GRAMMAR WEB SITE

The Interactive Writing and Grammar Web site provides a wide
array of support for students, teachers, and parents. Grammar
support includes:

• On-Line Exercise Bank with Auto Check scoring
• Diagnostic and assessment support

www.phschool.com

LITERATURE CONNECTIONS

Grammar in Literature selections from *Prentice Hall Literature: Timeless Voices, Timeless Themes,* Copper:
from "The Loch Ness Monster," George Laycock, SE p. 543

Lesson Objectives

1. To recognize and use the positive, comparative, and superlative forms of adjectives.

2. To use adjectives with *more* and *most*.

3. To recognize and use the positive, comparative, and superlative forms of adverbs.

4. To distinguish between *bad* and *badly*.

5. To distinguish between *good* and *well*.

Critical Viewing

Compare and Contrast Students may suggest the stingray is brighter than the ocean bottom or that the ocean bottom is darker. Encourage them to use comparative forms of colors also.

Chapter 25 Using Modifiers

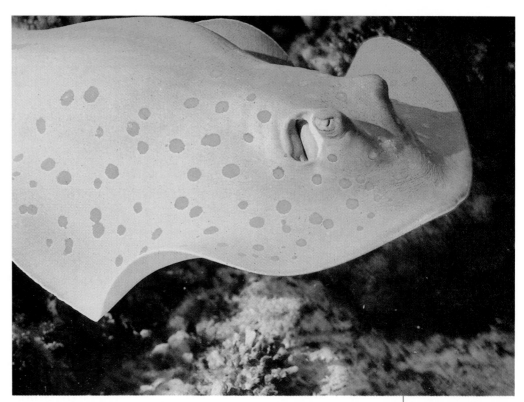

▲ Critical Viewing
Compare the colors of this stingray with the colors of the ocean bottom. Use comparative forms of adjectives in the sentences of your response. [**Compare and Contrast**]

Many choices are made after comparing one thing with another. For example, a fish may select one hiding spot because it looks darker than another. A sea turtle may eat a particular type of sea grass because it looks more appetizing than the other types.

As a writer, you must choose the correct forms of modifiers. Adjectives, for instance, have different forms for making comparisons. You might describe one fish as *more colorful* than another. You might also use different forms of adverbs to make comparisons. For instance, you can describe how one fish swims *fast*, another swims *faster*, and a third swims *fastest* of all.

In this chapter, you will discover more about using adjectives and adverbs to make comparisons. You will learn about the three degrees of comparison: positive, comparative, and superlative.

536 • Using Modifiers

☑ ONGOING ASSESSMENT: Diagnose

If students miss more than one item in each category, direct them to the relevant pages of the text and assign exercises for practice and review.

Using Modifiers	Diagnostic Test Items	Teach	Practice	Section Review	Chapter Review
Skill Checks A and C					
Using Adjectives to Compare	A 1–5 C 11–15	pp. 538–541	Ex. 1–5	Ex. 9–11	Ex. 25–27
Skill Checks B and C					
Using Adverbs to Compare	B 6–10 C 11–15	pp. 540–543	Ex. 5–8	Ex. 10–11	Ex. 25–27

Diagnostic Test

Directions: Write all answers on a separate sheet of paper.

Skill Check A. Make three columns on your paper, labeling them *positive*, *comparative*, and *superlative*. Then, write the appropriate forms of the following adjectives in each column.

1. salty
2. warm
3. tiny
4. flexible
5. noticeable

Skill Check B. Make columns for the positive, comparative, and superlative forms of each adverb below. Write the appropriate forms in each column.

6. playfully
7. near
8. deep
9. rapidly
10. calmly

Skill Check C. Rewrite the sentences below, changing each adjective or adverb in parentheses to the correct comparative or superlative form.

11. Some sea cucumbers live in the (deep) part of the ocean.
12. They often prefer to live in the (dark) spot they can find.
13. Some, however, live in (sunny) areas.
14. Although these look like cucumbers, they (closely) resemble sea stars and sea urchins.
15. They eat animals much (tiny) than themselves.

Skill Check D. Choose the correct modifier in parentheses to complete each sentence that follows.

16. Compared with their colorful cousins in the sea, garden snails look (bad, badly).
17. Cone snails shoot poison darts that stun their prey (bad, badly).
18. Once the prey feels (bad, badly) and can't move, the cone snail scoops it up.
19. Most snails are (bad, badly) when it comes to swimming.
20. They crawl along the ocean floor because they swim (bad, badly).

Skill Check E. Choose the correct modifier—*good* or *well*—to complete each sentence.

21. Moray eels can swim really ___?___ .

22. They are ___?___ at catching their prey.

23. Their sense of smell also seems ___?___ .

24. This moray eel doesn't seem to feel ___?___ .

25. It has not been eating ___?___ .

Answer Key

Diagnostic Test

Each item in the Diagnostic Test corresponds to a specific concept in the chapter on using modifiers. This will enable you to tailor instruction to the particular needs of your students. See "Ongoing Assessment: Diagnose" below for further details.

Skill Check A

1. salty, saltier, saltiest
2. warm, warmer, warmest
3. tiny, tinier, tiniest
4. flexible, more flexible, most flexible
5. noticeable, more noticeable, most noticeable

Skill Check B

6. playfully, more playfully, most playfully
7. near, nearer, nearest
8. deep, deeper, deepest
9. rapidly, more rapidly, most rapidly
10. calmly, more calmly, most calmly

Skill Check C

11. Some sea cucumbers live in the deepest part of the ocean.
12. They often prefer to live in the darkest spot they can find.
13. Some, however, live in sunnier areas.
14. Although these look like cucumbers, they more closely resemble sea stars and sea urchins.
15. They eat animals much tinier than themselves.

Skill Check D

16. bad
17. badly
18. bad
19. bad
20. badly

Skill Check E

21. well
22. good
23. good
24. well
25. well

✓ ONGOING ASSESSMENT: Diagnose *continued*					
Using Modifiers	**Diagnostic Test Items**	**Teach**	**Practice**	**Section Review**	**Chapter Review**
Skill Check D					
Bad and *Badly*	D 16–20	pp. 546–547	Ex. 15, 17	Ex. 18, 20–21	Ex. 28–29
Skill Check E					
Good and *Well*	E 21–25	pp. 547–548	Ex. 16–17	Ex. 19–21	Ex. 28–29
Cumulative Reviews and Applications				Ex. 12–14, Ex. 22–24	Ex. 32

Interest GRABBER Write the following sentences on the board and ask students to identify the comparison words.

The biggest animal in the sea is the giant squid at 50 feet long.

No, a blue whale is bigger, at 100 feet.

An electric eel isn't the biggest, but it is the scariest.

Activate Prior Knowledge

Review that adjectives are words that describe nouns. Ask students to look at your desk and suggest as many adjectives as they can to describe it. (*metal, ugly, gray, messy, neat*)

TEACH

Step-by-Step Teaching Guide

Using Adjectives to Compare; Using Adjectives with *More* and *Most*

1. Go over the three degrees of comparison in the chart. Ask students to suggest other adjectives and give their comparative and superlative forms.

2. Write the adjectives *good* and *bad* on the chalkboard. Ask students to supply the comparative and superlative forms of each. (*better, best; worse, worst*) Explain that these are the most common irregular adjectives. Almost all others follow the pattern in the chart on this page. Other irregularities include the occasional doubling of a final consonant (*sad, sadder, saddest; wet, wetter, wettest*) and the dropping of a final e (*little, littler, littlest*).

3. Tell students that adjectives with certain endings such as *-ing* or *-ful* always take *more* or *most* rather than adding *-er* and *-est*.

4. Remind students that *more* is used when comparing or contrasting two things. *Most* is used when choosing the outstanding one of a group of three or more.

Using Adjectives to Compare

Adjectives are often used to compare people, places, or things. The form of the adjective to use depends on the kind of comparison.

▶ **KEY CONCEPT** There are three degrees of comparison: *positive, comparative,* and *superlative.* ■

POSITIVE:	The hermit crab moved into a *large* shell.
COMPARATIVE:	Soon, it will need a *larger* shell.
SUPERLATIVE:	The crab is living in its *largest* shell yet.

The *positive degree* is used when no comparison is being made. This form is listed in a dictionary. The *comparative degree* is used when two items are being compared. The *superlative degree* is used when three or more items are being compared. When the superlative degree is used, the article *the* is often added.

▶ **KEY CONCEPTS** To form the comparative of most one- and two-syllable adjectives, add *-er.* To form the superlative, add *-est.* ■

DEGREES OF COMPARISON FORMED BY ADDING -*ER* AND -*EST*		
Positive	Comparative	Superlative
clear	clearer	clearest
cool	cooler	coolest
bright	brighter	brightest
slimy	slimier	slimiest

▶ **Exercise 1** Forming the Degrees of Comparison of One- and Two-Syllable Adjectives Make a chart showing the positive, comparative, and superlative form of each adjective listed below.

EXAMPLE: steep

ANSWER:
Positive	Comparative	Superlative
steep	steeper	steepest

1. sandy
2. scary
3. little
4. sharp
5. young

538 • Using Modifiers

Theme: Ocean Life

In this section, you will learn how adjectives and adverbs are used as modifiers in their comparative and superlative forms. The examples and exercises are about animals that live in the ocean.

Cross-Curricular Connection: Science

⏱ **TIME AND RESOURCE MANAGER**

Resources
Print: Grammar Exercise Workbook, pp. 123–130; Hands-on Grammar Activity Book, Chapter 25; Grammar Exercises Answers on Transparencies, Chapter 25
Technology: Language Lab CD-ROM, Using Modifiers; On-Line Exercise Bank, Section 25.1

In-Depth Coverage	Accelerated Pace
• Work through all key concepts, pp. 538–543. • Assign and review Exercises 1–8. • Read and discuss Grammar in Literature, p. 543. • Do the Hands-on Grammar activity, p. 544.	• Assign pp. 538–543 for independent student review. • Assign Section Review Exercises 9-11, p. 545.

▶ **Exercise 2** Identifying Positives, Comparatives, and Superlatives Label each adjective form below *positive*, *comparative*, or *superlative*. Then, write the other two forms of each word.

1. muddy
2. hardiest
3. most
4. cloudy
5. longest
6. grander
7. hardest
8. roomy
9. narrowest
10. shorter

Using Adjectives With *More* and *Most*

Besides adding *-er* and *-est* to adjectives, there is another way to change them to show comparison.

▶ **KEY CONCEPT** *More* and *most* can be used to form the comparative and superlative degrees of many adjectives. ■

Although *-er* and *-est* are usually used to change the degree of short adjectives, *more* and *most* may also be used. *More* and *most* should not be used when they sound awkward, as in *He is more tall than I.* With some adjectives, only *more* and *most* are used.

▶ **KEY CONCEPT** *More* and *most* can be used with many one- and two-syllable adjectives. ■

EXAMPLE: This dolphin is *more playful* than that one.

When you are unsure about how a modifier forms its degrees of comparison, check a dictionary.

▶ **KEY CONCEPT** Use *more* and *most* to form the comparative and superlative degrees of adjectives with three or more syllables. ■

EXAMPLES: Ocean animals are *more interesting* than plants.
Sharks often eat the *most debilitated* fish.

SOME ADJECTIVES REQUIRING *MORE* AND *MOST*		
Positive	Comparative	Superlative
playful	more playful	most playful
careful	more careful	most careful
devious	more devious	most devious
terrifying	more terrifying	most terrifying

More Practice
Language Lab CD-ROM
• Using Modifiers lesson
On-line Exercise Bank
• Section 25.1
Grammar Exercise Workbook
• pp. 123–124

Answer Key

▶ **Exercise 1** *(page 538)*

1. sandy, sandier, sandiest
2. scary, scarier, scariest
3. little, littler, littlest
4. sharp, sharper, sharpest
5. young, younger, youngest

▶ **Exercise 2**

1. positive; muddier, muddiest
2. superlative; hardy, hardier
3. superlative; many, more
4. positive; cloudier, cloudiest
5. superlative; long, longer
6. comparative; grand, grandest
7. superlative; hard, harder
8. positive; roomier, roomiest
9. superlative; narrow, narrower
10. comparative; short, shortest

Language Highlight

Some adjectives cannot be qualified by the words *more* and *most*. One example is the adjective *dead*. A noun or pronoun can be described as dead or not dead; there are no degrees of death. One person or thing cannot be more or less dead than another. Other adjectives that cannot be qualified include *unique, complete, flawless,* and *perfect.*

☑ **ONGOING ASSESSMENT: Monitor and Reinforce**

If students miss more than two items in Exercise 1 or 2, refer them to the following for additional practice.

In the Textbook	Print Resources	Technology
Section Review, Ex. 9, p. 545	Grammar Exercise Workbook, pp. 123–124	Language Lab CD-ROM, Using Modifiers; On-Line Exercise Bank, Section 25.1

⏱ **TIME SAVERS!**

📊 **Answers on Transparency**
Use the Grammar Exercises Answers on Transparencies for Chapter 25 to have students correct their own or one another's exercises.

🖥 **On-Line Exercise Bank**
Have students complete the exercises on computer. The Auto Check feature will grade their work for you!

Integrating Speaking Skills

Awkward Sounds Read the last key concept on page 539 aloud to students. Have them try adding *-er* and *-est* to a variety of polysyllabic adjectives, such as *delicious, important, modest, hyperactive, necessary,* and *luxurious.* Students will soon grasp the idea that these words are too long to be comfortably spoken. This exercise will help them remember to use *more* and *most* with long adjectives, rather than change their endings.

Answer Key

> **Exercise 3**

1. most frightening
2. more skillful
3. most respectable
4. most delicious
5. more important

> **Exercise 4**

1. most fearsome
2. correct
3. more docile
4. likelier
5. plainer

Customize for
ESL Students

Students may find new or unfamiliar words among the adjectives in Exercise 4. Have students write down any adjectives they don't know. Then have partners compare their lists. They can teach one another as many words as possible, then work together to define the rest. Students can continue this activity throughout this chapter.

Critical Viewing

Speculate Students may suggest sentences such as:

It would be <u>scarier</u> than I had imagined in my most <u>terrifying</u>

⏱ **TIME SAVERS!**

🎞 **Answers on Transparency**
Use the Grammar Exercises Answers on Transparencies for Chapter 25 to have students correct their own or one another's exercises.

💻 **On-Line Exercise Bank**
Have students complete the exercises on computer. The Auto Check feature will grade their work for you!

Note About *Double Comparisons:* Avoid double comparisons. Never use both *-er* or *-est* and *more* or *most* to form the comparative and superlative degrees in the same sentence.

▶ **Exercise 3** Using Adjectives With *More* and *Most* Use *more* or *most* to form the comparative or superlative form of each adjective shown in parentheses.

1. Because people thought sharks were the (frightening) animals in the ocean, they believed it was all right to kill them.
2. People trapped sharks because the sharks were often (skillful) fishers than humans.
3. Commercial fishers sold the shark meat to some of the (respectable) restaurants in the world.
4. Now, many people think shark is one of the (delicious) meals.
5. Other people, however, feel it is (important) to study the lives and habits of sharks than to eat them.

▶ **Exercise 4** Revising Sentences With Adjectives Read the following sentences. If the modifier in the sentence is correct as written, write *correct.* If the modifier is in the wrong degree or if it is formed incorrectly, rewrite the sentence, correcting it.

1. Of all the underwater animals, sharks have the more fearsome reputation.
2. Some of the most spine-tingling movies involve shark attacks on humans.
3. But many sharks are dociler than their movie counterparts.
4. In fact, sharks are much likeliest to leave humans alone.
5. Some sharks are plain in color than others.

Memorizing Irregular Adjectives and Adverbs

A few adjectives and adverbs are *irregular.* Their comparative and superlative degrees must be memorized.

▶ **KEY CONCEPT** Memorize the irregular comparative and superlative forms of certain adjectives and adverbs. ■

The chart on the next page lists the most common irregular modifiers.

▲ **Critical Viewing** Using one comparative adjective and one superlative adjective in a sentence, describe how you might feel if you were swimming next to this shark. **[Speculate]**

DEGREES OF IRREGULAR ADJECTIVES AND ADVERBS

Positive	Comparative	Superlative
bad	worse	worst
badly	worse	worst
far (distance)	farther	farthest
far (extent)	further	furthest
good	better	best
well	better	best
many	more	most
much	more	most

▶ **Exercise 5** Recognizing the Degree of Irregular Modifiers
On your paper, indicate the degree of the underlined word in each of the following sentences.
1. The bite of a shark is <u>worse</u> than the bite of a dog.
2. Who found the <u>most</u> shells on the beach?
3. I believe that I found <u>more</u> shells than you did.
4. Which do you like <u>better</u>, my drawing or his?
5. This is the <u>worst</u> day of my life!

Using Adverbs to Compare

Adverbs also have three degrees of comparison.

POSITIVE: The fish swims *fast.*

COMPARATIVE: The eel swims *faster* than the fish.

SUPERLATIVE: The shark swims the *fastest* of the three.

The *positive* degree is used to describe only one action. The *comparative* degree is used when two actions are being compared. The *superlative* degree is used when three or more actions are being compared.

▶ **KEY CONCEPTS** To form the comparative of most one-syllable adverbs, add *-er.* To form the superlative, add *-est.* ■

The chart below shows a number of these adverbs.

DEGREES OF COMPARISON FORMED BY ADDING -ER OR -EST

Positive	Comparative	Superlative
hard	harder	hardest
early	earlier	earliest
late	later	latest
far	farther	farthest

More Practice

Language Lab
CD-ROM
• Using Modifiers lesson
On-line
Exercise Bank
• Section 25.1
Grammar Exercise
Workbook
• pp. 125–126, 129–130

Comparisons Using Adjectives and Adverbs • **541**

Answer Key

▶ **Exercise 5**
1. comparative
2. superlative
3. comparative
4. comparative
5. superlative

Step-by-Step Teaching Guide

Using Adverbs to Compare

1. Review adverbs as words that describe or modify verbs, adjectives, or other adverbs. Comparative and superlative adverbs can compare verbs, adjectives, or adverbs.

2. Remind students that many adverbs end in *-ly.* These adverbs change their final *y* to *i* when the comparative and superlative endings are added.

☑ **ONGOING ASSESSMENT Prerequisite Skills**

If students have difficulty with comparative and superlative degrees, you may find it necessary to review the following to assure coverage of prerequisite knowledge.

In the Textbook	Print Resources	Technology
Adjectives and Adverbs, pp. 328–349	Grammar Exercise Workbook, pp. 21–32	Language Lab CD-ROM, Using Modifiers; On-Line Exercise Bank, Sections 16.1–16.2

1. often, more often, most often
2. deep, deeper, deepest
3. carefully, more carefully, most carefully
4. tightly, more tightly, most tightly
5. soon, sooner, soonest
6. fully, more fully, most fully
7. playfully, more playfully, most playfully
8. low, lower, lowest
9. frantically, more frantically, most frantically
10. smoothly, more smoothly, most smoothly

Critical Viewing

Compare and Contrast Students may suggest that the shark moves or swims more smoothly than the squid. Their comparisons should use comparative forms.

25.1

▶ **KEY CONCEPT** With most adverbs of two or more syllables, especially those ending in *-ly*, use *more* to form the comparative and *most* to form the superlative. ■

DEGREES OF COMPARISON FORMED BY ADDING *MORE* OR *MOST*		
Positive	**Comparative**	**Superlative**
quickly constantly loudly	more quickly more constantly more loudly	most quickly most constantly most loudly

To form the comparative and superlative of some two-syllable adjectives, such as *early*, use *-er* and *-est*. Check a dictionary if you are not sure whether to use these endings or *more* and *most*.

▶ **Exercise 6** Forming the Comparative and Superlative Degrees of Adverbs Make a chart showing the positive, comparative, and superlative degrees of each adverb listed below. Add *-er* or *-est* to the adverbs whenever possible. When necessary, use *more* and *most*.

1. often
2. deep
3. carefully
4. tightly
5. soon
6. fully
7. playfully
8. low
9. frantically
10. smoothly

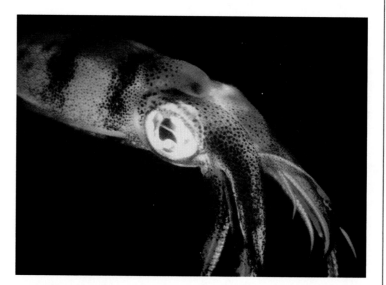

◀ Critical Viewing Compare the way a squid moves with the way a shark moves. Use adverbs in your sentences. **[Compare and Contrast]**

⏱ **TIME SAVERS!**

🖨 **Answers on Transparency** Use the Grammar Exercises Answers on Transparencies for Chapter 25 to have students correct their own or one another's exercises.

💻 **On-line Exercise Bank** Have students complete the exercises on computer. The Auto Check feature will grade their work for you!

☑ **ONGOING ASSESSMENT: Monitor and Reinforce**

If students miss more than two items in Exercises 6–7, refer them to the following for additional practice.

In the Textbook	Print Resources	Technology
Section Review, Ex. 9–11, p. 545	Grammar Exercise Workbook, pp. 127–128	Language Lab CD-ROM, Using Modifiers; On-Line Exercise Bank, Section 25.1

GRAMMAR IN LITERATURE

from **The Loch Ness Monster**
George Laycock

In the following passage, the comparative forms of adjectives are highlighted in blue italics.

. . . The hiding places made the whole story of Nessie *more believable.* Nessie, it was agreed, could cruise about down there among those dark caves without sending a ripple to the surface.

This is also the area in which one *earlier* investigator heard strange underwater sounds the year before, tapping sounds that no biologist has yet been able to successfully identify.

Exercise 7 Using the Comparative and Superlative Degrees of Adverbs In the following sentences, use *-er* or *-est* or *more* or *most* to form the comparative or superlative of each adverb in parentheses.

1. Some sea creatures behave (playfully) than others.
2. Of all the animals that performed in the water show, the dolphins swam the (masterfully).
3. Sharks are found in warm waters (commonly) than in cold waters.
4. Because of their keen senses, sharks can compete (successfully) for prey than many other fish.
5. The shark swims (smoothly) than these fish because of its streamlined shape.

Exercise 8 Writing Sentences With Comparative and Superlative Degrees of Adverbs On your paper, write two sentences for each of the following modifiers. One sentence should use the comparative degree; the other should use the superlative degree.

1. softly
2. hard
3. suddenly
4. briefly
5. badly

More Practice

Language Lab CD-ROM
• Using Modifiers lesson
On-line Exercise Bank
• Section 25.1
Grammar Exercise Workbook
• pp. 127–128

Comparisons Using Adjectives and Adverbs • 543

Grammar in Literature

1. Have volunteers read aloud the excerpt from "The Loch Ness Monster."

2. Have students identify the positive and superlative degrees of the comparative adjectives in the passage. (*believable, most believable; early, earliest*)

Responding to Literature

Have students locate and read more of "The Loch Ness Monster." Have them identify other comparative adjectives and practice writing the positive and superlative forms of these adjectives.

Answer Key

Exercise 7

1. more playfully
2. most masterfully
3. more commonly
4. more successfully
5. more smoothly

Exercise 8

Possible answers.

1. The drums played more softly than the cymbals.
   The violins play most softly of all the instruments.
2. The cellists practiced harder than the violinists.
   The trombone player practiced hardest of all.
3. The audience left Friday's concert more suddenly than Saturday's.
   The audience left Sunday's concert most suddenly.
4. The first violin played more briefly during the first piece than the second.
   The first violin played most briefly in the last piece.
5. The cellist played worse than the violinist.
   Actually, he played worst of all.

Adjective and Adverb Window Shutters

Teaching Resources: Hands-on Grammar Activity Book, Chapter 25

1. Have students refer to their Hands-on Grammar activity books or give them copies of the relevant pages for this activity.

2. Have students keep lists of all the adjectives and adverbs and their forms that they test.

3. Ask students if they find more examples using *more* and *most* or using *-er* and *-est*.

Find It in Your Writing

Work with a partner. Check each other's comparatives and superlatives.

Find It in Your Reading

Pick several examples of adjectives and adverbs that form comparatives and superlatives in each way.

25.1

Hands-on Grammar

Adjective and Adverb Window Shutters

Practice forming the comparative and superlative degrees with the following activity.

Cut a piece of paper approximately 3" x 7". Fold two sides in (as shown in the illustration), leaving a space in the middle. Cut two slots as shown. Under the left shutter, write *more* and *most*. Under the right shutter, write *-er* and *-est*.

On a strip of paper about 1" wide, list adjectives and adverbs, such as *cold, hard, beautiful, slowly, fast, colorful, muddy, early,* and *quickly*. Feed the strip of paper through the slots, as shown, making sure that a word shows in the window.

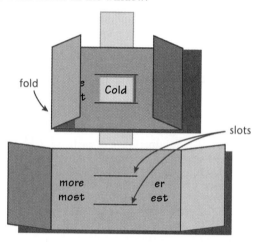

Now, decide whether the modifier forms its comparative and superlative degrees with *more* and *most* or with *-er* and *-est*. First, close the right shutter to cover up *-er* and *-est* and say the word with *more* and *most*. Then, close the left shutter and try the word with *-er* and *-est*. By always closing one shutter, you avoid forming a double comparison. Decide how the comparative and superlative degrees are formed. If you are unsure, consult a dictionary.

Find It in Your Writing Look through your portfolio to find examples of adjectives and adverbs in the positive degree. Write them down on a strip of paper that you can feed through your window shutter. See how they form their comparative and superlative degrees.

Find It in Your Reading In a short story or in a textbook, pick out examples of adjectives and adverbs. Add them to your list of modifiers to test.

544 • Using Modifiers

⏱ **TIME SAVERS!**

✋ **Hands-on Grammar**
Use the Hands-on Grammar activity sheet for Chapter 25 to facilitate this activity.

☑ **ONGOING ASSESSMENT: Assess Mastery**

Use the following resources to assess student mastery of the use of positive, comparative, and superlative adjectives and adverbs.

In the Textbook	Technology
Chapter Review, Ex. 25–27, p. 550	Language Lab CD-ROM, Using Modifiers; On-Line Exercise Bank, Section 25.1

Section 25.1 Section Review

GRAMMAR EXERCISES 9–14

Exercise 9 Forming Comparative and Superlative Degrees of Adjectives and Adverbs Make columns for the positive, comparative, and superlative degrees. Write the correct forms of each adjective or adverb below in the appropriate columns.

1. red
2. happy
3. scaly
4. firmly
5. fresh
6. sensible
7. outrageous
8. recently
9. good
10. confidently

Exercise 10 Using Modifiers Correctly Write the sentences below, using the correct comparative or superlative form of the adjective or adverb in parentheses.

(1) Animals that live in the sea must protect themselves because there is always a (big) animal trying to eat them. (2) Some fish escape their captors by swimming (quickly) than the hunters. (3) Swimming in a school with many other fish can scare away predators who might think that the school is just one animal that is much (large) than itself. (4) Also, the predator might get confused trying to decide which of the fish in the school is the (easy) prey and thus not catch any at all. (5) Other animals protect themselves by hiding in the (dark) places they can find. (6) That way, it doesn't matter if they swim (slowly) than the hunters. (7) Colors can also help animals to protect themselves from the (ferocious) predators. (8) Some fish change color, becoming (dark) or (light) to match their backgrounds. (9) The (bright) the color is, the (poisonous) or distasteful the fish. (10) Although these survival techniques are very helpful, animals still must move (carefully) than their predators.

Exercise 11 Revising to Eliminate Errors in Comparisons Rewrite the following sentences, correcting any errors in comparisons that you find.

1. That is the most happiest dog that I have ever seen.
2. The situation could not be more worse.
3. She can throw even further than I can.
4. My worse fears have been realized.
5. Jan enjoys writing poetry more better than I do.

Exercise 12 Find It in Your Reading In addition to the adjectives highlighted in the excerpt from "The Loch Ness Monster" on page 543, the author also used the adjectives *dark* and *strange* and the adverb *successfully*. List the comparative and superlative forms of these modifiers.

Exercise 13 Find It in Your Writing Look through your writing portfolio. Find one comparative form and one superlative form of an adjective and an adverb. If you cannot find examples, choose an adjective and an adverb in the positive degree and write the comparative and superlative forms.

Exercise 14 Writing Application Write a brief description of an imaginary sea monster. Include the comparative and the superlative forms of an adjective and an adverb.

Section Review • 545

ASSESS and CLOSE

Section Review

Each of these exercises correlates to the instruction on comparisons using adjectives and adverbs, pages 538–544. The exercises may be used for more practice, for reteaching, or for review of the key concepts presented. Answers for all chapter exercises are available in *Grammar Exercises Answers on Transparencies* in your Teaching Resources.

Answer Key

Exercise 9

1. red, redder, reddest
2. happy, happier, happiest
3. scaly, scalier, scaliest
4. firmly, more firmly, most firmly
5. fresh, fresher, freshest
6. sensible, more sensible, most sensible
7. outrageous, more outrageous, most outrageous
8. recently, more recently, most recently
9. good, better, best
10. confidently, more confidently, most confidently

Exercise 10

(1) Animals that live in the sea must protect themselves because there is always a bigger animal trying to eat them. (2) Some fish escape their captors by swimming more quickly than the hunters. (3) Swimming in a school with many other fish can scare away predators who might think that the school is just one animal that is much larger than itself. (4) Also, the predator might get confused trying to decide which of the fish in the school is the easiest prey and thus not catch any at all. (5) Other animals protect themselves by hiding in the darkest places they can find. (6) That way, it doesn't matter if they swim more slowly than the hunters. (7) Colors can also help animals to protect themselves from the most ferocious predators. (8) Some fish change color, becoming darker or lighter to match their backgrounds. (9) The brighter the color is, the more poisonous or distasteful the fish. (10) Although these survival techniques are all very helpful, animals still must move more carefully than their predators.

continued

Answer Key continued

Exercise 11

1. happiest
2. worse
3. farther
4. worst
5. better

Exercise 12

Find It in Your Reading
darker, darkest; stranger, strangest; more successfully, most successfully

Exercise 13

Find It in Your Writing
Suggest that students choose two modifiers, one that takes *-er* and *-est* and one that takes *more* and *most*.

Exercise 14

Writing Application
Students may want to illustrate their descriptions.

Write the following sentences on the board and ask students to write *good, well, bad,* or *badly* in each blank.

A spiny sea urchin doesn't feel ___ if you grab it. (good)

Your foot will feel ___ if you step on a Portuguese man-of-war. (bad)

Sea turtles are good swimmers, but they walk ___. (badly)

I wish I swam as ___ as a porpoise! (well)

Activate Prior Knowledge

Ask students which words they wrote in the Interest Grabber are adjectives and which are adverbs. (adjectives: *good, bad*; adverbs: *well, badly*)

TEACH

Step-by-Step Teaching Guide

Using *Bad* and *Badly*

1. Remind students that since linking verbs do not show action, they cannot be modified by adverbs. They describe the condition of a subject (always a noun or pronoun). Therefore, the subject can be modified only by adjectives. These are called predicate adjectives. The linking verb links the subject with the adjective. If students use a linking verb, they should use an adjective to modify it.

2. The suffix *-ly* is a common ending for adverbs. This will help students remember that *badly* is an adverb and *bad* is an adjective.

3. The comparative and superlative degrees of *bad* and *badly* are *worse* and *worst*. These two words can be either adjectives or adverbs.

   Adjective: I feel worse than you do about our quarrel.

   Adverb: I draw worst of all my classmates.

Troublesome Modifers

You probably use most adjectives and adverbs with little difficulty. Using modifiers is important, because they add detail to speaking and writing. They help make communication clear. For example, if a fish hides in the sea grass, does it hide *well* or *badly*? Such modifiers can add important details.

Some frequently used modifiers can be troublesome. For instance, is it correct to say *It hides bad* or *It hides badly*? (In this case, the answer is *It hides badly. Badly* is an adverb, and an adverb is needed to modify the verb *hide.*)

To understand troublesome modifiers, you must learn which word in each pair is an adjective and which word is an adverb. Then, when a sentence requires either an adjective or an adverb, you will know which word to use.

In this section, two pairs of troublesome modifiers are presented. First, the modifiers *bad* and *badly* are explained. Then, the modifiers *good* and *well* are discussed. The exercises will give you practice in using all of these modifiers.

Using *Bad* and *Badly*

You will not confuse *bad* and *badly* if you remember that *bad* is an adjective and *badly* is an adverb.

> **KEY CONCEPT** *Bad* is an adjective. It is used with linking verbs. ■

The two examples that follow show *bad* used correctly.

EXAMPLES:
The bite of an alligator is <u>bad</u>. (LV)

Your cough sounds <u>bad</u>. (LV)

In the sentences above, the adjective *bad* is used following a linking verb to describe the subject of the sentence. Other linking verbs that are used with *bad* are *appear, become, feel, grow, remain, seem, smell, stay, taste,* and *turn.*

> **KEY CONCEPT** *Badly* is an adverb. It is used with action verbs. ■

EXAMPLES:
The seal performed <u>badly</u> because it was hurt. (AV)

Jim draws animals <u>badly</u>. (AV)

To summarize, if the modifier follows a linking verb and describes the subject, use *bad.* If the modifier follows an action verb and describes the action, use *badly.*

Theme: Ocean Life

In this section, you will learn how to tell the difference between *bad* and *badly* and *good* and *well.* The examples and exercises are about the animals that live in and near the ocean.

Cross-Curricular Connection: Science

Grammar and Style Tip

Keep your modifiers as close as possible to the words they modify. For example, "He played the game badly that afternoon" is better than "He played the game that afternoon badly."

⏱ **TIME AND RESOURCE MANAGER**

Resources
Print: Grammar Exercise Workbook, pp. 131–134; Grammar Exercises Answers on Transparencies, Chapter 25
Technology: Language Lab CD-ROM, Using Modifiers; On-Line Exercise Bank, Section 25.2

In-Depth Coverage	Accelerated Pace
• Work through all key concepts, pp. 546–548. • Assign and review Exercises 15–17.	• Assign pp. 546–548 for independent student review. • Assign Section Review Exercises 18–21, p. 549.

Exercise 15 Using *Bad* and *Badly* Choose the correct modifier—*bad* or *badly*—to complete each sentence below.

1. The ocean environment is (bad, badly) for hatching their young, so sea turtles lay their eggs on sandy beaches.
2. Because their flippers are made for swimming, they crawl along the beaches (bad, badly).
3. On the land, they protect themselves (bad, badly), but in the sea, they can rely on their size and strength.
4. Their large flippers ensure that they do not swim (bad, badly).
5. As parents, sea turtles may seem (bad, badly) because they don't return to take care of the eggs.
6. The survival rate of baby sea turtles looks (bad, badly).
7. The number of sea turtles in the world has decreased (bad, badly).
8. They are treated (bad, badly) by humans, who hunt them and their eggs for food.
9. The outlook appears (bad, badly) unless people do more to protect the sea turtles.
10. Turtles are called coldblooded because they are (bad, badly) at regulating their body temperature.

Using *Good* and *Well*

Good and *well* are used differently in sentences. *Good* is always an adjective, but *well* can be either an adjective or an adverb. To decide which word to use, you must think about the meaning of the sentence and how the word is being used.

KEY CONCEPT *Good* is an adjective. It is used with linking verbs. ■

EXAMPLES: The quality of the water has been <u>good</u>.
LV

The sea air smells <u>good</u>.
LV

We felt <u>good</u> after our swim.
LV

> **More Practice**

Language Lab CD-ROM
• Using Modifiers lesson
On-line Exercise Bank
• Section 25.2
Grammar Exercise Workbook
• pp. 131–132

▼ Critical Viewing
Using the words *bad* and *badly* in a sentence, discuss how a sea turtle moves on land. **[Infer]**

Troublesome Modifiers • 547

Answer Key

> **Exercise 15**

1. bad
2. badly
3. badly
4. badly
5. bad
6. bad
7. badly
8. badly
9. bad
10. bad

Critical Viewing

Infer Students may write sentences such as:

I feel bad when I see how badly the sea turtle moves on land.

STANDARDIZED TEST PREPARATION WORKSHOP

Using Modifiers Standardized tests often measure students' ability to use modifiers to correctly complete a given sentence. Ask students to choose the letter of the word(s) that best completes the following sentence:

She skated so _____ that she knew she would not win the competition.

A badder
B more bad
C badly
D bad

The correct answer is **C**. The missing word modifies the verb *skated*, so the adverb *badly* is needed to complete the sentence.

⏱ **TIME SAVERS!**

📇 **Answers on Transparency**
Use the Grammar Exercises Answers on Transparencies for Chapter 25 to have students correct their own or one another's exercises.

🖥 **On-line Exercise Bank**
Have students complete the exercises on computer. The Auto Check feature will grade their work for you!

Using *Good* and *Well*

1. *Better* and *best* are the comparative and superlative degrees of both *good* and *well*. *Better* and *best* can be either adverbs or adjectives, depending on the sentence. These two modifiers behave the same way as *worse* and *worst*.

2. In English, the common question about a person's health is "How are you?" This question has to be answered with an adjective because it includes a linking verb. In this case <u>well</u> would be an adjective.

Customize for
More Advanced Students

Good, bad, well, and *badly* are fairly vague descriptive words. They give readers and listeners no specific information. Challenge students to take the sentences in Section Review Exercises 20 and 21 and substitute other adverbs and adjectives for these four modifiers. The only rule is that they should not alter the basic meaning of the sentence. For example, a rewrite of sentence 5 in Exercise 20 might be, "The wound looks serious enough to prevent it from flying."

Answer Key

▶ **Exercise 16**

1. well
2. well
3. good
4. good
5. well

▶ **Exercise 17**

1. looked bad
2. sings well
3. looks good
4. correct
5. How well
6. draws badly
7. correct
8. correct
9. printed badly
10. felt bad

25.2

▶ **KEY CONCEPT** *Well* can be an adverb or an adjective. When *well* is an adverb, it is used with an action verb. ■

WELL AS AN ADVERB: Many water birds can swim and fly <u>well</u>.

Other types of animals also live <u>well</u> both in the water and on land.

Loons dive <u>well</u> because their feet, which propel them, are set far back on their bodies.

When *well* is an adjective, it is used with a linking verb and usually refers to a person's health.

WELL AS AN ADJECTIVE: The fish looked <u>well</u> after the attack by the eel.

The eel seems <u>well</u>, too, but he looks hungry.

Are you <u>well</u> enough to travel?

▶ **Exercise 16** Using *Good* and *Well* Choose the correct modifier—*good* or *well*—to complete each sentence below.
1. Mallard ducks live (good, well) in any type of water—salty, brackish, or fresh.
2. They adapt (good, well) to new environments.
3. Their webbed feet are (good, well) as paddles.
4. It was (good, well) to see the mother protecting the babies.
5. I'm afraid that one baby is not (good, well).

▶ **Exercise 17** Revising Sentences With Troublesome Modifiers Read each of the following sentences. If the modifier is used correctly, write *correct*. If the modifier is used incorrectly, rewrite the sentence, correcting the modifier.
1. During his illness, Henry looked badly.
2. Tony is very talented; he sings good.
3. For a campsite, this spot looks well.
4. It was good to hear that song again.
5. How good do you know him?
6. Paul draws bad.
7. This new soap smells good.
8. Are you feeling well enough to go?
9. Because she was in a hurry, she printed bad.
10. I felt badly because I forgot your birthday.

▶ **More Practice**
Language Lab CD-ROM
• Using Modifiers lesson
On-line Exercise Bank
• Section 25.2
Grammar Exercise Workbook
• pp. 133–134

548 • Using Modifiers

☑ **ONGOING ASSESSMENT: Monitor and Reinforce**

If students miss more than two items in Exercises 15–16, refer them to the following for additional practice.

In the Textbook	Print Resources	Technology
Section Review, Ex. 18–21, p. 549	Grammar Exercise Workbook, pp. 131–134	Language Lab CD-ROM, Using Modifiers; On-Line Exercise Bank, Section 25.2

Section 25.2 Section Review

GRAMMAR EXERCISES 18–24

Exercise 18 Using *Bad* and *Badly*
Write the correct modifier—*bad* or *badly*—to follow each verb below.

1. sings
2. appears
3. seems
4. limps
5. runs

Exercise 19 Using *Good* and *Well*
Write the correct modifier—*good* or *well*—to follow each verb below. (Assume that none of the verbs refer to a person's health.)

1. dashes
2. sounds
3. skitters
4. floats
5. becomes

Exercise 20 Using Troublesome Modifiers Choose the correct modifier to complete each sentence below.

1. Gulls used to live only near the seashore, but now they can survive (good, well) near inland bodies of water, too.
2. They eat (good, well) off animals that live in the water, although they live on land themselves.
3. Gulls are (good, well) at waiting and will patiently search for locations with many fish.
4. That gull injured its wing (bad, badly) when it flew into the window.
5. The wound looks (bad, badly) enough to prevent it from flying.

Exercise 21 Revising a Passage to Eliminate Problems With Modifiers On a separate sheet of paper, rewrite the passage below, correcting any modifier errors.

The spines along the top of a stingray's tail work good as a form of protection. They protect the stingray well from anything that approaches from above. If you step on a resting stingray, you can cut your foot bad. Not all stingrays behave bad. At "Stingray City" in the Cayman Islands, the relationship between stingrays and scuba divers is well. They play good together. This is good for tourism. People learn that stingrays are not bad. I feel badly that stingrays are misunderstood. It seems good that people are learning more about these animals.

Exercise 22 Find It in Your Reading Skim through a magazine to find examples of *bad, badly, good,* and *well.* Explain why each usage is correct.

Exercise 23 Find It in Your Writing Review the compositions in your portfolio for examples of the troublesome modifiers discussed in this section. Check to make sure that you have used each modifier correctly.

Exercise 24 Writing Application Write a brief description of an animal that has a bad reputation. Explain why you think this reputation is or is not deserved. Use *bad, badly, good,* and *well* in your description.

Section Review • 549

ASSESS and CLOSE

Section Review
Each of these exercises correlates to the instruction on troublesome modifiers, pages 546-548. The exercises may be used for more practice, for reteaching, or for review of the key concepts presented.

Answer Key

Exercise 18

1. badly
2. bad
3. bad
4. badly
5. badly

Exercise 19

1. well
2. good
3. well
4. well
5. good

Exercise 20

1. well
2. well
3. good
4. badly
5. bad

Exercise 21

1. The spines along the top of a stingray's tail work well as a form of protection.
2. correct
3. If you step on a resting stingray, you can cut your foot badly.
4. Not all stingrays behave badly.
5. At "Stingray City" in the Cayman Islands, the relationship between stingrays and scuba divers is good.
6. They play well together.
7. correct
8. correct
9. I feel bad that stingrays are misunderstood.
10. correct

Answer Key continued

Exercise 22

Find It in Your Reading
Have students bring in some magazines and have the class discuss examples of troublesome modifiers.

Exercise 23

Find It in Your Writing
Have students exchange papers with partners to double-check their use of modifiers.

Exercise 24

Writing Application
Have volunteers read their paragraphs aloud. Ask the class if they were persuaded.

TIME SAVERS!

Answers on Transparency Use the Grammar Exercises Answers on Transparencies for Chapter 25 to have students correct their own or one another's exercises.

On-Line Exercise Bank Have students complete the exercises on computer. The Auto Check feature will grade their work for you!

Each of these exercises correlates to a section of the chapter on using modifiers, pages 538–549. The exercises may be used for more practice, for reteaching, or for review of the key concepts presented.

Answer Key

▶ Exercise 25

1. sad, sadder, saddest
2. eagerly, more eagerly, most eagerly
3. probable, more probable, most probable
4. unlikely, more unlikely, most unlikely
5. lightly, more lightly, most lightly
6. humid, more humid, most humid
7. wild, wilder, wildest
8. suddenly, more suddenly, most suddenly
9. cranky, crankier, crankiest
10. powerfully, more powerfully, most powerfully

▶ Exercise 26

1. Queen conches can grow larger than a child's head.
2. Young conches live in sea grass; here, of all places, they can most easily hide from hungry predators.
3. When they grow bigger, they move out of the grass to the sand.
4. Their most common food is plant matter that they find along the ocean floor.
5. Some people think conch chowder is more delicious than clam chowder.
6. Those earrings made from conch shells are more beautiful than these.
7. Older civilizations, such as the Mayan, treasured the shells of queen conches.
8. From the shells, people crafted jewelry and spoons, which they considered their most prized possessions.
9. Overfishing of conches is one of the most serious problems for Caribbean countries, in whose waters conches live.
10. Governments have made laws to protect the conches from their most fearsome enemies: humans.

GRAMMAR EXERCISES 25–32

▶ **Exercise 25** Charting Degrees of Comparison Make a chart showing the positive, comparative, and superlative forms of each adjective or adverb below.

1. sad
2. eagerly
3. probable
4. unlikely
5. lightly
6. humid
7. wild
8. suddenly
9. cranky
10. powerfully

▶ **Exercise 26** Using Comparative and Superlative Forms of Adjectives and Adverbs Rewrite the sentences below, using the comparative or superlative form of the adjective or adverb in parentheses.

1. Queen conches can grow (large) than a child's head.
2. Young conches live in sea grass; here, of all places, they can (easily) hide from hungry predators.
3. When they grow (big), they move out of the grass to the sand.
4. Their (common) food is plant matter that they find along the ocean floor.
5. Some people think conch chowder is (delicious) than clam chowder.
6. Those earrings made from conch shells are (beautiful) than these.
7. (Old) civilizations, such as the Mayan, treasured the shells of queen conches.
8. From the shells, people crafted jewelry and spoons, which they considered their (prized) possessions.
9. Overfishing of conches is one of the (serious) problems for Caribbean countries, in whose waters conches live.
10. Governments have made laws to protect the conches from their (fearsome) enemies: humans.

▶ **Exercise 27** Supplying Comparative and Superlative Forms of Adjectives and Adverbs Use the comparative or superlative form of an adjective or adverb from the list to fill each blank below. Use each word only once.

wet   close   slowly   loud   comfortable   slow   large   strong   similar   tiny

1. The ___?___ instinct of most frogs is to live in a moist area.
2. The frog laid its eggs near the river because it is ___?___ there than in the woods.
3. Some tree frogs lay their eggs on the bottom sides of leaves. They choose the leaves that are the ___?___ to the water.
4. Tadpoles resemble fish ___?___ than they do frogs.
5. They are ___?___ in water than on land.
6. Frogs are carnivorous and will eat animals, insects, worms, and spiders that are ___?___ than themselves.
7. However, they may also eat animals that are ___?___ than they.
8. A tadpole may change into a frog in a few months, but some go through the process ___?___.
9. Snakes and turtles are ___?___ than frogs, but they still feed on them.
10. That frog croaks the ___?___ of all.

▶ **Exercise 28** Using Troublesome Modifiers Write the correct modifier from those in parentheses when you copy each sentence below.

1. Crabs discard their old shells just as we discard old clothes that fit (bad, badly).
2. A crab's soft, new shell is not (good, well) for protection.

▶ Exercise 27

1. strongest
2. wetter
3. closest
4. more
5. more comfortable
6. tinier
7. larger
8. more slowly
9. slower
10. loudest

3. Soon, the new shells harden, and they protect the crabs (good, well) once again.
4. This crab looks (good, well) in a shell abandoned by another animal.
5. Crabs are (good, well) scavengers.
6. They also hunt (good, well) for food.
7. Their claws work (good, well) when grabbing worms and tiny animals.
8. The claws of fiddler crabs aren't used for hunting, but they don't function (bad, badly) as warning flags to other fiddler crabs.
9. The porcelain crabs have claws that are (bad, badly) for grabbing food.
10. As a result, they use a method that seems (good, well) for them: They spread a net made of mucus between their two claws to entrap food floating by.

▶ **Exercise 29**   Recognizing the Correct Modifier Choose the correct modifier from those in parentheses to complete each sentence.

1. Crocodilians, the word used for both alligators and crocodiles, are (more advanced, most advanced) than the fish, frogs, and salamanders that developed before them.
2. They survive on land (more easily, most easily) than any other animal did before them.
3. They can also breathe (good, well) while they are in the water, as long as their nostrils remain above water.
4. Crocodiles have (narrow, narrower, narrowest) snouts than alligators have.
5. Because they are coldblooded, however, they cannot regulate their body temperatures and do not survive (well, good) in very hot or very cold conditions.

▶ **Exercise 30**   Revising a Paragraph With Modifiers Some sentences in the following paragraph contain modifier errors. Rewrite the sentences correctly.

American alligators are found in freshwater lakes, rivers, and swamps most often than crocodiles are. The American alligator is the more famous type of crocodilian. Spanish explorers told stories that portrayed alligators bad. They said alligators were the more ferocious beasts alive. The explorers said that alligators had bulletproof skin and made the loud noises they had ever heard. For the first year or two of their lives, alligators are bad at protecting themselves. Because they are defenseless, they have to rely on most strategic ways to discourage their enemies. Their high-pitched sounds scare away attackers good. The fate of crocodilians does not look good. Crocodilians need humans' help bad to get them off the endangered species list.

▶ **Exercise 31**   Writing Sentences With Modifiers Write five sentences, using each of the following modifiers in the degree indicated.

1. slowly (comparative)
2. beautiful (superlative)
3. fast (superlative)
4. tall (comparative)
5. loud (comparative and superlative)

▶ **Exercise 32**   Writing Application Write a description of some things you might find during a walk on the beach. Include two comparative forms and two superlative forms of adjectives or adverbs.

▶ **Exercise 28**
1. badly
2. good
3. well
4. good
5. good
6. well
7. well
8. badly
9. bad
10. good

▶ **Exercise 29**
1. more advanced
2. more easily
3. well
4. narrower
5. well

▶ **Exercise 30**
1. more often
2. most famous
3. badly
4. most ferocious
5. loudest
6. correct
7. more strategic
8. well
9. correct
10. badly

▶ **Exercise 31**
Sample answers
1. I write more slowly than Joe.
2. He has the most beautiful handwriting in the class.
3. He is also the fastest writer.
4. Tom is taller than Joe.
5. Mario is louder than Sue, but Carlos is loudest in the class.

▶ **Exercise 32**
Writing Application
Students can combine their descriptions into a book, *A Walk on the Beach.*

⏱ **TIME SAVERS!**

📺 **Answers on Transparency** Use the Grammar Exercises Answers on Transparencies for Chapter 25 to have students correct their own or one another's exercises.

💻 **On-line Exercise Bank** Have students complete the exercises on computer. The Auto Check feature will grade their work for you!

Step-by-Step Teaching Guide

Using Modifiers

Teaching Resources: Standardized Test Preparation Workbook, Chapter 25

1. Encourage students to decide if no, two items, or more than two things are being compared before they choose a form of the modifier.

2. Most students will find the first sample easier because the modifier is regular.

Standardized Test Preparation Workshop

Using Modifiers

Standardized test questions often measure your ability to use modifiers correctly. One way this is done is by testing your ability to choose the correct form of comparison to complete a sentence. Use the following strategies to help you determine which form to use in a sentence:

- If no comparison is being made, use the positive form of the modifier.

- If one thing or action is compared with another thing or action, use the comparative form of the modifier—ending in *-er* or preceded by *more*.

- If one thing or action is being compared with more than one other thing or action, use the superlative form of the modifier—ending in *-est* or preceded by *most*.

The following sample items will give you practice in answering these types of standardized test questions.

Test Tip

Avoid using double comparisons, such as *most happiest*, to complete a sentence. The correct forms are *most happy* or *happiest*.

Sample Test Items	Answers and Explanations

Directions Read the passage, and choose the letter of the word or group of words that belongs in each space.
 	
Today was the __(1)__ day of the entire year. Although yesterday was uncomfortable, today is even __(2)__ because it is so windy.
 	
1 A cold
   B colder
   C coldest
   D most coldest
	The correct answer for item 1 is *C*. The comparison is being made between today and all the other days of the year, so the superlative form *coldest* should be used to complete the sentence.

2 F bad
   G badder
   H worse
   J worst
	The correct answer for item 2 is *H*. The comparison is being made between two days, so the comparative form *worse* should be used to complete the sentence.

⬥ TEST-TAKING TIP

After students choose a modifier to complete a sentence, encourage them to read over the sentence silently with the modifier in place to "hear" how it sounds. They may be able to catch mistakes with this technique.

▶ **Practice 1** **Directions:** Read the passage, and choose the letter of the word or group of words that belongs in each space.

During the winter, there is nothing __(1)__ than a big snowstorm. Even the __(2)__ weather can still be enjoyed. A snowstorm can be __(3)__ than a summer thunderstorm. During the storm, we all huddle around the fire, and have a contest to see who can tell the __(4)__ story. After the storm is over, there is no sight __(5)__ than a world covered in a beautiful white blanket.

1 **A** exciting
  B more excited
  C most exciting
  D more exciting

2 **F** bad
  G badder
  H worse
  J worst

3 **A** fun
  B funner
  C more fun
  D funnest

4 **F** good
  G better
  H best
  J more better

5 **A** spectacular
  B spectacularer
  C most spectacular
  D more spectacular

▶ **Practice 2** **Directions:** Read the passage, and choose the letter of the word or group of words that belongs in each space.

Winter sports are among the __(1)__ challenging. Downhill skiing takes __(2)__ than many sports, and using snowshoes is __(3)__ than hiking in the woods. Walking or gliding on snow or ice requires your body to work its __(4)__ while keeping every muscle moving and maintaining your balance. __(5)__ times, you can push your body too far without even knowing it. Take it easy and have fun!

1 **A** physical
  B more physically
  C physically
  D most physically

2 **F** coordination
  G more coordination
  H most coordination
  J more coordinated

3 **A** exhausted
  B exhausting
  C more exhausting
  D most exhausting

4 **F** harder
  G hardest
  H most hardest
  J more hard

5 **A** Much
  B Many
  C More
  D Most

▶ **Practice 1**
1. D
2. J
3. C
4. H
5. D

▶ **Practice 2**
1. D
2. G
3. C
4. G
5. B

Answer Key

> **Exercise A**

1. brought, past, past
2. laid, past participle, past (passive voice)
3. did, past, past
4. caught, ate, past, past
5. set, present, present
6. leading, present participle, past progressive
7. began, past, past
8. built, past, past
9. is, present, present
10. knew, past, past

> **Exercise B**

1. nom.
2. obj.
3. poss.
4. obj.
5. nom.
6. poss.
7. obj.
8. obj.
9. poss.
10. poss.

> **Exercise C**

1. we, its
2. their
3. its
4. his
5. their
6. his
7. their
8. their
9. my
10. him

Cumulative Review

USAGE

> **Exercise A**   **Using Verbs** Choose the correct verb or verb phrase in parentheses to complete each sentence below. Identify its principal part and tense.

1. Several Native American groups (brung, brought) their culture to what is now Texas.
2. The foundations of early dwellings were found where they were (lain, laid).
3. The Karankawa (did, done) a great deal of fishing in the Gulf of Mexico.
4. The Apache and the Comanche (caught, catched) and (eat, ate) the buffalo.
5. Alonzo Álvarez de Piñeda (set, sat) foot in Texas in 1519.
6. He was (leading, led) a group around the mouth of the Rio Grande.
7. Cabeza de Vaca (began, begun) to explore more of inland Texas.
8. In 1682, the Spanish (built, builded) the first mission in Texas.
9. That was near where present-day El Paso (is, was).
10. Spain (knew, known) that France was claiming the area.

> **Exercise B**   **Identifying the Case of Pronouns** Identify the case of each pronoun in the following sentences as *nominative, objective,* or *possessive.*

1. One French explorer was La Salle. He built a fort near Matagorda Bay.
2. La Salle named it Fort Saint Louis.
3. France claimed the Mississippi River and its tributaries.
4. In 1716, the Spanish established missions, founding them throughout the territory.
5. They include the city of San Antonio.
6. However, the Spanish found that their hold on the province of Texas was weak.
7. Expeditions of adventurers from the United States had been traveling through it.
8. Philip Nolan led one invasion, but the Spanish captured him.
9. In 1820, Moses Austin, a United States citizen, made his request to settle in Texas.
10. His son, Stephen F. Austin, carried out the plan.

> **Exercise C**   **Using Agreement** Fill in each blank below with a pronoun that agrees with its antecedent.

1. In our social studies class, __?__ are studying Texas and __?__ fight for independence.
2. Texans decided that they wanted to make __?__ own laws.
3. The Mexican government wanted settlers in Texas to obey __?__ laws.
4. General Santa Anna gathered __?__ troops together to crush the rebellious Texans.
5. Texans declared __?__ independence from Mexico on March 2, 1836, in Washington-on-the-Brazos.
6. Either Oleg or Sam will give __?__ report on the Alamo today.
7. Fewer than 200 Texans tried to defend __?__ territory against Santa Anna's army there.
8. Jim Bowie, Davey Crockett, and William B. Travis lost __?__ lives at the Alamo.
9. I hope that I will do well on __?__ test about the Alamo.
10. Texans captured Santa Anna and forced __?__ to sign a treaty.

Exercise D — Using Verb

Agreement Write the form of the verb in parentheses that agrees with the subject of each sentence below.

1. All of our reports (be) about the settling of the West.
2. Many students (want) to write about California.
3. No one (know) more about the early days in California than Rudy.
4. Everybody in our class (love) to look at the maps of the trails heading west.
5. Each of the students (have) to pick a trail to report on.
6. Julie and Thomas (ask) to read about the Oregon Trail.
7. Neither Sam nor Randy (have) picked a topic yet.
8. Tanya and I (hope) to do our report on the Santa Fe Trail.
9. Either the Santa Fe Trail or the Oregon Trail (be) interesting.
10. According to the map, each of the trails (appear) to begin in Independence, Missouri.

Exercise E — Using Modifiers

In the sentences below, write the form of the adjective or adverb indicated in parentheses.

1. A Texan army gathered (quickly—comparative) than expected.
2. After taking San Antonio, (many—superlative) soldiers left the city.
3. They believed that Santa Anna, the Mexican dictator, would wait until (late—positive) spring.
4. Santa Anna's army was (large—comparative) than that of the settlers.
5. The (small—superlative) of all Texan forces withdrew to the Alamo.
6. (Brave—comparative) than expected, the Texans fought for thirteen days.
7. (Many—superlative) of the Texan forces were defeated in other battles.
8. Then, a group of Texans declared independence (cautiously—comparative) than they had earlier.
9. They attacked, (probably—superlative) surprising the Mexican Army.
10. Santa Anna (soon—positive) recognized Texas's independence.

Exercise F — Correcting Usage

Mistakes Rewrite the following sentences, correcting any errors in usage.

1. The Republic of Texas continued their existence for almost ten years.
2. The more prominent of all Texas's problems was finances.
3. There was disputes about the new country's boundaries.
4. More immigrants came to Texas, and the troubles did not prevent they from settling.
5. Sam Houston will be one who wanted the United States to annex the republic.
6. After Sam Houston wins in the battle of San Jacinto, Texas had become independent.
7. These two groups, the Cherokee and the Mexicans, brought its concerns into battle.
8. However, the Cherokee and them were arrested by the Texas army.
9. A new president of Texas, Mirabeau Lamar, were elected in 1838.
10. The Cherokee resist his orders, but they were defeated and moved to what is now Oklahoma.

Exercise G — Writing Application

Write a short description of the state in which you live or one that you have visited. Be sure that the words in your sentences follow the rules of agreement and that your modifiers are used correctly. Then, list the verbs and verb phrases, identifying their tenses. Make a list of pronouns, and identify their case.

> **Exercise D**

1. are
2. want
3. knows
4. loves
5. has
6. ask
7. has
8. hope
9. is
10. appears

> **Exercise E**

1. more quickly
2. most
3. late
4. larger
5. smallest
6. Braver
7. Most
8. more cautiously
9. most probably
10. soon

> **Exercise F**

1. its
2. most
3. were
4. them
5. was
6. won, became
7. their
8. they
9. was
10. resisted

> **Exercise G**

Writing Application
Have students exchange descriptions with partners and check for correct usage and identification.

Time and Resource Manager

In-Depth Lesson Plan

	LESSON FOCUS	PRINT AND MEDIA RESOURCES
DAY 1	**End Marks** Students learn and apply the concepts of the correct usage of end marks and do the Hands-on Grammar activity (pp. 558–563).	**Teaching Resources** *Grammar Exercise Workbook*, pp. 135–140; *Grammar Exercises Answers on Transparencies*, Ch. 26; *Hands-on Grammar Activity Book*, Ch. 26 *Language Lab* **CD-ROM**, Punctuation; **On-Line Exercise Bank**, Section 26.1
DAY 2	**Commas, Semicolons, and Colons** Students learn and apply the concepts of the correct usage of commas, semicolons, and colons (pp. 564–577).	**Teaching Resources** *Grammar Exercise Workbook*, pp. 141–156; *Grammar Exercises Answers on Transparencies*, Ch. 26 *Language Lab* **CD-ROM**, Punctuation; **On-Line Exercise Bank**, Sections 26.2–3
DAY 3	**Quotation Marks, Underlining, Hyphens, and Apostrophes** Students learn and apply the concepts of the correct usage of quotation marks, underlining, hyphens, and apostrophes (pp. 578–595).	**Teaching Resources** *Grammar Exercise Workbook*, pp. 157–174; *Grammar Exercises Answers on Transparencies*, Ch. 26 *Language Lab* **CD-ROM**, Punctuation; **On-Line Exercise Bank**, Sections 26.4–5
DAY 4	**Review and Assess** Students review chapter and demonstrate mastery of use of punctuation (pp. 596–599).	**Teaching Resources** *Formal Assessment*, Ch. 26; *Grammar Exercises Answers on Transparencies*, Ch. 26 **On-Line Exercise Bank**, Sections 26.1–5

Accelerated Lesson Plan

	LESSON FOCUS	PRINT AND MEDIA RESOURCES
DAY 1	**End Marks and Commas** Students cover concepts and usage of end marks and commas as determined by Diagnostic Test (pp. 558–573).	**Teaching Resources** *Grammar Exercise Workbook*, pp. 135–152; *Grammar Exercises Answers on Transparencies*, Ch. 26; *Hands-on Grammar Activity Book*, Ch. 26 *Language Lab* **CD-ROM**, Punctuation; **On-Line Exercise Bank**, Sections 26.1–2
DAY 2	**Other Punctuation** Students cover concepts and usage of semicolons and colons, quotation marks and underlining, hyphens, and apostrophes as determined by Diagnostic Test (pp. 574–595).	**Teaching Resources** *Grammar Exercise Workbook*, pp. 153–174; *Grammar Exercises Answers on Transparencies*, Ch. 26 *Language Lab* **CD-ROM**, Punctuation; **On-Line Exercise Bank**, Sections 26.3–5
DAY 3	**Review and Assess** Students review chapter and demonstrate mastery of use of punctuation (pp. 596–599).	**Teaching Resources** *Formal Assessment*, Ch. 26; *Grammar Exercises Answers on Transparencies*, Ch. 26 **On-Line Exercise Bank**, Sections 26.1–5

Options for Adapting Lesson Plans

HOMEWORK

Have students complete any section of the chapter for homework.

FEATURES

Extend coverage with the Standardized Test Preparation Workshop (pp. 598–599).

TECHNOLOGY

Students can use the On-Line Exercise Bank to complete the exercises on computer. The Auto Check feature will grade their work.

INTEGRATED SKILLS COVERAGE

Grammar in Literature
SE pp. 565, 592

Reading
Find It in Your Reading SE pp. 562, 563, 573, 577, 585, 595

Writing
Find It in Your Writing SE pp. 562, 563, 573, 577, 585, 595
Writing Application SE pp. 563, 573, 577, 585, 595, 597

Language Highlight
ATE p. 586

Vocabulary
ATE pp. 569, 590

Speaking and Listening
ATE p. 561

Technology
ATE p. 582

Viewing and Representing
Critical Viewing SE pp. 556, 559, 560, 566, 568, 571, 574, 576, 580, 583, 584, 587, 588, 590, 593, 594

ASSESSMENT SUPPORT

Standardized Test Preparation Workshop SE p. 598; ATE pp. 580, 593

Standardized Test Preparation Workbook, pp. 51–52

Formal Assessment, Ch. 26

MEETING INDIVIDUAL NEEDS

Less Advanced Students See Ongoing Assessments ATE pp. 566, 568, 570, 575, 576, 582, 586, 588

ESL Students ATE pp. 560, 589

Gifted/Talented Students ATE p. 583

BLOCK SCHEDULING

Pacing Suggestions
For 90-minute Blocks
- Administer the Diagnostic Test to students to determine instructional coverage.
- Have students complete the necessary exercises in class. Use the Hands-on Grammar activity to provide a change of pace.

Resources for Varying Instruction
- *Language Lab* **CD-ROM** If your students have access to hardware, a 90-minute block provides an ideal opportunity for students to work on computer.

Professional Development Support
- *How to Manage Instruction in the Block* This teaching Resource provides management and activity suggestions.

MEDIA AND TECHNOLOGY

For the Student
- *Language Lab* **CD-ROM,** Punctuation
- *On-Line Exercise Bank,* Ch. 26

For the Teacher
- *Resource Pro* **CD-ROM**

WRITING AND GRAMMAR WEB SITE

The Interactive Writing and Grammar Web site provides a wide array of support for students, teachers, and parents. Grammar support includes:

- On-Line Exercise Bank with Auto Check scoring
- Diagnostic and assessment support

www.phschool.com

LITERATURE CONNECTIONS

Grammar in Literature selections from *Prentice Hall Literature: Timeless Voices, Timeless Themes,* Copper:
from "Why Monkeys Live in Trees," Julius Lester, SE p. 565
from "The Spring and the Fall," Edna St. Vincent Millay, SE p. 592

Lesson Objectives

1. To end every sentence with an appropriate punctuation mark.

2. To use commas to separate basic sentence elements and in a series.

3. To use commas to set off introductory and interrupting words and phrases, and in numbers.

4. To use semicolons to connect independent clauses.

5. To use colons correctly.

6. To use quotation marks around direct quotations and dialogue.

7. To identify when to use quotation marks in titles and when to underline them.

8. To use hyphens correctly in numbers, words, and sentences.

9. To use apostrophes in contractions and to show possession.

Critical Viewing

Connect Students may say that a monkey's eyes and limbs help it to move. Punctuation helps readers know where to pause and stop as they read.

Answer Key

Diagnostic Test *(page 557)*

• Each item in the Diagnostic Test corresponds to a specific concept in the chapter on punctuation. This will enable you to tailor instruction to the particular needs of your students. See "Ongoing Assessment: Diagnose" at right for further details.

• Answers for the Diagnostic Test and all chapter exercises are available in *Grammar Exercises Answers on Transparencies* in your Teaching Resources.

Chapter 26 Punctuation

▲ Critical Viewing
What physical characteristics help this monkey move successfully through the jungle? How do punctuation marks help readers move successfully through written compositions? **[Connect]**

How would you punctuate the following string of words? *Please deliver the tomato soup chicken salad corn bread and fruit I ordered.* The sentence needs punctuation to get its meaning across.

Correct punctuation helps make the meaning of a sentence clear. It does this by telling the reader when to pause briefly and when to come to a full stop. It also tells whether a sentence is meant to make a statement, ask a question, give a command, or show surprise or strong emotion.

This chapter tells about five different groupings of punctuation marks: end marks; commas; semicolons and colons; quotation marks and underlining; and hyphens and apostrophes. You should read, study, and practice using all these marks. Notice how they are used in the books, newspapers, and magazines you read.

556 • Punctuation

☑ ONGOING ASSESSMENT: Diagnose

If students miss more than one item in any category, direct them to the relevant pages of the text and assign exercises for practice and review.

Punctuation	Diagnostic Test Items	Teach	Practice	Section Review	Chapter Review
Skill Check A					
End Marks	A 1–5	pp. 558–562	Ex. 1–3	Ex. 4–6	Ex. 63
Skill Check B					
Commas	B 6–10	pp. 564–572	Ex. 10–19	Ex. 20–22	Ex. 64
Skill Check C					
Semicolons and Colons	C 11–15	pp. 574–576	Ex. 26–29	Ex. 30–31	Ex. 65

Diagnostic Test

Directions: Write all answers on a separate sheet of paper.

Skill Check A. Write the correct end mark for each sentence below.
1. What is the difference between a rain forest and a jungle
2. A jungle is like a rain forest but is not as moist or dark
3. Rain forests get more than one hundred inches of rain a year
4. Trees in the rain forest form a canopy over the forest floor
5. Wow That means there's not as much sunlight in a rain forest

Skill Check B. Rewrite the following sentences, adding commas where needed. If a sentence is correct, write *correct*.
6. However due to the heavy forestation all rain forests are jungles.
7. Most of the world's rain forests and jungles are in South and Central America Africa and Southeast Asia.
8. Jamaica is 4244 square miles and it was once mostly rain forest.
9. Many jungles and rain forests are shrinking for the local governments allow the land to be destroyed.
10. The forest can't support life once the trees and plants are gone.

Skill Check C. Rewrite the following sentences, adding colons and semicolons where necessary.
11. Rain forests produce more vegetation than any other land on Earth the tropical sun and heavy rain encourage rapid growth.
12. Trees are the foundation of any jungle they provide shelter for other plants and animals, produce flowers that feed insects and birds, and bear fruits that feed animals and insects.
13. Rain forests shelter three creatures that eat ants the slow loris, the tamandua anteater, and the giant pangolin.
14. It isn't easy to explain rain forests and jungles within each, there is a wide variety of environments.
15. Caitlin posted a sign in her room that read Caution Rain Forests and Jungles Disappearing.

Skill Check D. Add quotation marks to the sentences below.
16. How can the jungles and rain forests be saved? asked my sister.
17. Well, my mother said, we must learn their value to Earth.
18. I read an article last week about Peruvian rain forests.
19. Jim asked, Where can I find out about rain forests and jungles?
20. There's information on the Internet and on television, said Mother.

Skill Check E. Rewrite the following sentences, adding hyphens and apostrophes where necessary.
21. In the 1970s attention began to be focused on saving nature.
22. Many people thought this was somehow anti American.
23. The truth is that conservationists just wanted to defend people, places, and animals that couldnt defend themselves.
24. Without the worlds rain forests, Earth would suffer.
25. Its a problem that is everyones responsibility.

✓ ONGOING ASSESSMENT: Diagnose *continued*

Punctuation	Diagnostic Test Items	Teach	Practice	Section Review	Chapter Review
Skill Check D					
Quotation Marks	D 16–20	pp. 578–584	Ex. 35–41	Ex. 42–43	Ex. 66–67
Skill Check E					
Hyphens and Apostrophes	E 21–25	pp. 586–594	Ex. 47–55	Ex. 56–59	Ex. 68–70
Cumulative Reviews and Applications				Ex. 7–9, 23–25, 32–34, 44–46, 60–62	Ex. 71

Skill Check A
1. ?; 2. .; 3. .; 4. .; 5. !.

Skill Check B
6. However, due to the heavy forestation, all rain forests are jungles.
7. Most of the world's rain forests and jungles are in South and Central America, Africa, and Southeast Asia.
8. Jamaica is 4,244 square miles, and it was once mostly rain forest.
9. Many jungles and rain forests are shrinking, for the local governments allow the land to be destroyed.
10. correct

Skill Check C
11. Rain forests produce more vegetation than any other land on Earth; the tropical sun and heavy rain encourage rapid growth.
12. Trees are the foundation of any jungle: they provide shelter for other plants and animals, produce flowers that feed insects and birds, and bear fruits that feed animals and insects.
13. Rain forests shelter three creatures that eat ants: the slow loris, the tamandua anteater, and the giant pangolin.
14. It isn't easy to explain rain forests and jungles; within each, there is a wide variety of environments.
15. Caitlin posted a sign in her room that read Caution: Rain Forests and Jungles Disappearing.

Skill Check D
16. "How can the jungles and rain forests be saved?" asked my sister.
17. "Well," my mother said, "we must learn their value to Earth."
18. no quotation marks needed
19. Jim asked, "Where can I find out about rain forests and jungles?"
20. "There's information on the Internet and on television," said Mother.

Skill Check E
21. correct
22. anti-American
23. couldn't
24. world's
25. It's, everyone's

End Marks

PREPARE and ENGAGE

Interest GRABBER Write the following sentences on the chalkboard and have volunteers come up and add punctuation:

Help I'm trapped

Will I ever escape

I hope someone rescues me soon

Activate Prior Knowledge

Review the four types of sentences—declarative, interrogative, imperative, and exclamatory. Have students define each type of sentence and give an example. Ask students which end punctuation mark (or marks) appears with each type of sentence.

TEACH

Step-by-Step Teaching Guide

Periods

1. Point out several declarative sentences on the page. All these statements end in periods.

2. A statement of fact or opinion can be spoken forcefully enough to end with an exclamation point rather than a period. Such a sentence is called an exclamatory sentence. Students will read more about this type of sentence on page 561.

3. If a person makes a one-word statement, it should end with a period. "Yes" does not appear to be a sentence, but the rest of the sentence (the question to which the speaker is answering "yes") is understood.

   Are you coming with me?

   Yes. (Understood: Yes, I am coming with you.)

Answer Key

Exercise 1

1. .
2. in. .
3. .
4. Blvd. .
5. in. .

Using Periods

A period indicates the end of a sentence or an abbreviation.

▶ **KEY CONCEPT** Use a period to end a declarative sentence—a statement of fact or opinion. ■

DECLARATIVE SENTENCE: Ocean water is always moving.

▶ **KEY CONCEPT** Use a period to end an imperative sentence—a direction or command. ■

IMPERATIVE SENTENCE: Finish reading the chapter.

▶ **KEY CONCEPT** Use a period to end a sentence that contains an indirect question. ■

An *indirect question* reports a question but does not ask it. It does not give the speaker's exact words.

INDIRECT QUESTION: Mae asked me whether I could stay.

▶ **KEY CONCEPT** Use a period after most abbreviations and after initials. ■

ABBREVIATIONS: Gov. Mrs. St. Rd. in. Jr.
INITIALS: E. B. White Robin F. Brancato

WHEN TO USE A PERIOD	
With a Declarative Sentence	Many types of owls live in the desert.
With an Imperative Sentence	Do not carve holes in the cactus.
With an Indirect Question	Carl asked if rattlesnakes can swim.
With an Abbreviation	Mr. Jackson guides tours of the desert.

▶ **Exercise 1** Using Periods Copy the following sentences, adding periods where necessary.

1. Coyotes are related to dogs and are smaller than wolves
2. A full-grown coyote measures about 47 in long
3. Coyote babies, called pups, are born in April and May
4. A coyote was once seen near Lester Blvd in our town
5. The tail of a coyote is 11–16 in long

Theme: Deserts

In this section, you will learn which punctuation marks to use to end different types of sentences. The examples and exercises are about desert animals and plants.

Cross-Curricular Connection: Science

▶ **More Practice**

Language Lab CD-ROM
• End Marks lesson
On-line Exercise Bank
• Section 26.1
Grammar Exercise Workbook
• pp. 135–138

⏱ TIME AND RESOURCE MANAGER

Resources
Print: Grammar Exercises Workbook, pp. 135–140; Hands-on Grammar Activity Book, Chapter 26; Grammar Exercises Answers on Transparencies, Chapter 26
Technology: Language Lab CD-ROM, Punctuation; On-Line Exercise Bank, Section 26.1

In-Depth Coverage	Accelerated Pace
• Work through all key concepts, pp. 558–561. • Assign and review Exercises 1–3. • Do the Hands-on Grammar activity, p. 562.	• Assign pp. 558–561 for independent student review. • Assign Section Review Exercises 4–6, p. 563.

Using Question Marks

A question mark follows a word, phrase, or sentence that asks a question.

KEY CONCEPT Use a question mark after an interrogative sentence—one that asks a direct question. ■

INTERROGATIVE
SENTENCES:
Do snakes hatch from eggs?
Are there ever floods in the desert?

Sometimes, a single word or brief phrase is used to ask a direct question. Such a question is punctuated as though it were a complete sentence because the words left out are easily understood.

KEY CONCEPT Use a question mark after a word or phrase that asks a question. ■

EXAMPLES:
Many small birds build false nests. Why?
(Understood: Why do small birds build false nests?)
It can be risky to walk alone in the desert. In what way?
(Understood: In what way is it risky to walk alone?)

Do not use a question mark with an *indirect question*—a sentence that is really a statement but relates to a question.

EXAMPLE:
I asked how coyotes raise their young.

▲ Critical Viewing
Write a question concerning the ways these coyotes resemble dogs, then write the answer. Make sure that you use the correct end mark with each sentence. **[Compare]**

QUESTIONS AND HOW TO PUNCTUATE THEM	
Direct Question in a Complete Sentence	Use a question mark. (How old is Steven?)
Direct Question in an Incomplete Sentence	Use a question mark. (How tall?)
Indirect Question	Use a period. (I asked Steven where he was born.)

Step-by-Step Teaching Guide

Question Marks

1. Students can often recognize interrogative sentences by the words they begin with. Often, a question will begin with *how, what, when, where, who,* or *why.*

2. Have students take turns reading aloud some of the questions on this page while the rest of the class listens. Point out that the pitch of a person's voice usually rises at the end of an interrogative sentence. Remembering this will help students recognize interrogative sentences in plays, dramas, speeches, and other works they are listening to.

Critical Viewing

Compare Coyotes are about the same size as medium-sized dogs, and their bodies are much the same shape. They walk on four legs like dogs. Their faces and teeth are sharper, and their ears and paws are larger.

559

Critical Viewing

Analyze Students may say *I asked how a cactus can survive in the desert.* A period is needed.

Answer Key

▶ **Exercise 2**

1. Where are the four desert areas of the United States located?
2. Is a desert defined by the amount of rain it gets each year?
3. The Great Basin, a cold desert, is mostly in Nevada and Utah.
4. People ask whether it can snow in a cold desert.
5. In the Mojave Desert lives an animal called a cave myotis. Does it fly?
6. Are the plants, animals, and insects in the Chihuahuan Desert different from those at the beach?
7. Some of the plants in the desert are cactus and wildflowers.
8. The rainbow cactus is found in W. Texas and S. Arizona. Can a cactus bloom?
9. In the very hot Sonoran Desert, the rabbits sometimes dig holes. Why?
10. One desert reptile, the Texas horned lizard, is also found in Oklahoma and Kansas.

Customize for
ESL Students

Spanish uses question marks and exclamation points before and after questions and exclamations. Remind students that English uses only one mark, at the end.

26.1

▶ **Exercise 2** **Using Question Marks and Periods** Copy the sentences below, adding question marks and periods where necessary.

EXAMPLE:	Are all the deserts in the US located between the Rocky Mts and the Sierra Nevada range
ANSWER:	Are all the deserts in the U.S. located between the Rocky Mts. and the Sierra Nevada range?

1. Where are the four desert areas of the United States located
2. Is a desert defined by the amount of rain it gets each year
3. The Great Basin, a cold desert, is mostly in Nevada and Utah
4. People ask whether it can snow in a cold desert
5. In the Mojave Desert lives an animal called a cave myotis Does it fly
6. Are the plants, animals, and insects in the Chihuahuan Desert different from those at the beach
7. Some of the plants in the desert are cactus and wildflowers
8. The rainbow cactus is found in W Texas and S Arizona Can a cactus bloom
9. In the very hot Sonoran Desert, the rabbits sometimes dig holes Why
10. One desert reptile, the Texas horned lizard, is also found in Oklahoma and Kansas

▲ **Critical Viewing**
Write an indirect question about the ability of a cactus to survive in the dry desert climate. Which end mark is needed for your sentence? **[Analyze]**

560 • Punctuation

🖳 **Answers on Transparency**
Use the Grammar Exercises Answers on Transparencies for Chapter 26 to facilitate correction by students.

💻 **On-Line Exercise Bank**
Have students complete the exercises on computer. The Auto Check feature will grade their work for you!

☑ **ONGOING ASSESSMENT: Prerequisite Skills**

If students have difficulty with different types of sentences, you may find it necessary to review the following to assure coverage of prerequisite knowledge.

In the Textbook	Print Resources	Technology
Effective Sentences, pp. 436–445	Grammar Exercise Workbook, pp. 69–72	Language Lab CD-ROM, Sentence Style; On-Line Exercise Bank, Section 21.1–2

Using Exclamation Marks

An exclamation mark indicates strong feeling or emotion, including surprise.

KEY CONCEPT Use an exclamation mark to end an exclamatory sentence. ■

EXCLAMATORY SENTENCES:　　Look at that huge vulture!
　　　　　　　　　　　　　　The sagebrush smells great!
　　　　　　　　　　　　　　There's a red-tailed hawk!

KEY CONCEPT Use an exclamation mark after an imperative sentence that gives a forceful or urgent command. ■

IMPERATIVE SENTENCES:　　Be careful not to sit on the cactus!
　　　　　　　　　　　　　Don't spill the water!

Remember: Only imperative sentences containing *forceful* commands are followed by an exclamation mark. Mild imperatives are followed by a period: Please sit down.

KEY CONCEPT Use an exclamation mark after an interjection expressing strong emotion. ■

INTERJECTIONS:　　Wow! That was a great throw.
　　　　　　　　　Oh! Look what I found.

Exercise 3 Using Exclamation Marks and Periods Copy the sentences below on your paper, adding the necessary exclamation marks and periods.

1. Giant scorpions can be 5 ½ in long That's pretty big
2. The great horned owl lives in deserts It really seems to have horns
3. Conservationists work to protect deserts and desert creatures It's a very important job
4. A slider sounds like it should be a snake, but it's a turtle
5. Get too close and the Western diamondback rattlesnake will rattle its tail and bite
6. Desert candles don't really burn They're wildflowers
7. Turkey vultures live in the Sonoran Desert They don't look like turkeys at all
8. The white-winged dove is so beautiful However, it sometimes makes an annoying sound
9. The common nighthawk hunts mainly at night, of course
10. You don't wear the desert inky cap on your head It's a mushroom

More Practice

Language Lab
CD-ROM
• End Marks lesson
On-line
Exercise Bank
• Section 26.1
Grammar Exercise
Workbook
• pp. 139–140

End Marks • 561

Integrating Speaking and Listening Skills

Tone Ask a student to read aloud the three example exclamatory sentences at the top of this page. Then you read them as if they were declarative sentences. Discuss the difference in sound between an exclamation and a statement. All three of these sentences make just as much sense read one way as the other. The attitude of the speaker toward what he or she is saying determines whether a sentence is exclamatory.

Step-by-Step Teaching Guide

Exclamation Marks

1. Use the second example sentence to demonstrate that exclamatory sentences often make statements of fact or opinion, just as declarative sentences do. The difference is not in the sentence itself but in the speaker's feeling about what he or she is saying. If the speaker feels strong emotion, a sentence stating a fact or opinion should end with an exclamation point. If he or she is perfectly calm, the sentence should end in a period.

   She wrinkled her nose, commenting, "This water tastes awful."

   "This water tastes awful!" he exclaimed, choking.

2. Interjections are exclamations that show emotion, such as surprise, pleasure, or excitement. Challenge students to list some interjections on the chalkboard. (Possible answers: Whee! Gosh! Rats! Shoot! Aha!)

Answer Key

Exercise 3

1. Giant scorpions can be $5\frac{1}{2}$ in. long! That's pretty big!
2. The great horned owl lives in deserts. It really seems to have horns!
3. Conservationists work to protect deserts and desert creatures. It's a very important job.
4. A slider sounds like it should be a snake, but it's a turtle.
5. Get too close and the Western diamondback rattlesnake will rattle its tail and bite!
6. Desert candles don't really burn. They're wildflowers.
7. Turkey vultures live in the Sonoran Desert. They don't look like turkeys at all!
8. The white-winged dove is so beautiful! However, it sometimes makes an annoying sound.
9. The common nighthawk hunts mainly at night, of course.
10. You don't wear the desert inky cap on your head! It's a mushroom.

561

Rounding Up End Marks

Teaching Resources: Hands-on Grammar Activity Book, Chapter 26

1. Have students refer to their Hands-on Grammar activity book or give them copies of the relevant pages for the activity.

2. Review the instructions for constructing the spinners.

3. Have each pair write down the sentences they use with the appropriate end marks.

Find It in Your Reading

Have students share their examples with the class.

Find It in Your Writing

If students cannot find adequate examples of each type of end mark, have them rewrite some sentences so that they require these end marks.

26.1

Hands-on Grammar

Rounding Up End Marks

The punctuation mark you use at the end of a sentence lets a reader know whether you are making a statement, asking a question, giving an order, or showing strong emotion. Practice using the right end marks for your sentences with the following activity.

Make a spinner out of cardboard or index cards. Cut out two circles, one somewhat smaller than the other. With a pencil, press a hole in the center of each circle. Then, connect the two circles with a paper fastener pushed through the two center holes.

Write the three end marks two times each, evenly spaced around the outside of the larger circle, in an alternating pattern.(See model.) Then, draw three lines across the smaller circle, so that it is divided into six even "pie slices." In each slice, write a simple sentence or question with no end mark. Examples: *Will you open the door / The forest is beautiful / The moon seems very bright tonight / Can you see a rattlesnake over there / The fire did destroy the building / This is exciting /*

Work with a partner. One partner spins the inner circle and lines up the sentences with the end marks. Then, work around the circle, reading each sentence exactly as it is or rewording it slightly so that it fits the end mark. For example, you may need to add an interjection to make the sentence an exclamation, or you may have to invert some words to change a question to a statement or a statement to a question. Spin again to line up the sentences with different end marks, and repeat the exercise.

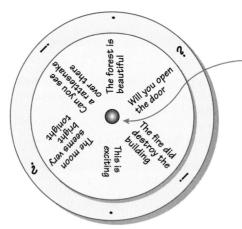

Use a paper fastener to attach wheel

Find It in Your Reading In a story or article, find examples of sentences with all three end marks. Read the sentences aloud to see how the punctuation mark affects the meaning of the sentence.

Find It in Your Writing Look through samples of your own writing to find statements, questions, and exclamations. Check to be sure that you have punctuated them correctly.

⏱ TIME SAVERS!

✋ **Hands-on Grammar Book** Use the Hands-on Grammar activity sheet for Chapter 26 to facilitate this activity.

☑ ONGOING ASSESSMENT: Assess Mastery

Use the following resources to assess student mastery of end punctuation.

In the Textbook	Technology
Chapter Review, Ex. 63, p. 596	Language Lab CD-ROM, Punctuation; On-Line Exercise Bank, Section 26.1

Section 26.1 Section Review

GRAMMAR EXERCISES 4–9

Exercise 4 Writing Abbreviations
Write an abbreviation for each of the following items. Check a dictionary if you need help.

1. Post Office
2. Commander
3. September
4. each
5. yard

Exercise 5 Supplying Correct End Marks Copy each sentence or group of sentences below, adding appropriate end marks.

1. Bats fly at night How do they keep from crashing into cactuses
2. Wolves and coyotes don't live together in groups, do they
3. Should desert plants and animals be protected Yes
4. The beavertail cactus has attractive flowers Be careful of its hidden spines
5. I asked where golden eagles nest if there are no trees
6. The Great Basin has fewer cactuses and yuccas than other deserts
7. The elephant tree has beautiful leaves Its flowers are small, but stinky
8. The lowest elevation in the U.S. is in the Mojave Desert What is it called
9. When the zebratail lizard runs, does it hold its tail in the air
10. The Sonoran Desert is home to the tiniest owl on earth Wow The elf owl is only 5–6 in long

Exercise 6 Identifying Declarative, Imperative, Interrogative, or Exclamatory Sentences Label each sentence below *declarative, imperative, interrogative,* or *exclamatory*. Then, indicate the appropriate end mark.

1. Is there enough water anywhere in a desert for fish to live
2. The cactus wren lives in the desert
3. Don't bother the badgers
4. The skin of a few North American frogs releases a fluid harmful to humans
5. I know a shrike eats insects, but does it eat anything else
6. Wow A thunderstorm in the desert is very beautiful
7. Don't leave your trash in the desert
8. Be safety conscious Never sit down in the desert without looking first
9. Never go into the desert without water and the proper tools to survive
10. In which three North American deserts does the desert gold plant grow

Exercise 7 Find It in Your Reading
Read the following excerpt from "Why Monkeys Live in Trees." Explain why the writer has used three different end marks.

. . . At that exact moment, one of Leopard's children ran up to him. "Daddy! Daddy! Are you going to be in the contest?"

Exercise 8 Find It in Your Writing
Look through your portfolio for sentences that you have ended with a period, a question mark, or an exclamation mark. Explain why each end mark is appropriate.

Exercise 9 Writing Application
Write five sentences to a friend in which you identify animals you would like to see. Include the following items, and be sure to use the correct end marks.

1. a direct question
2. a forceful imperative sentence
3. a sentence with an interjection
4. an abbreviation
5. an exclamation

ASSESS and CLOSE

Section Review
Each of these exercises correlates to the instruction on end marks, pages 558–562. The exercises may be used for more practice, for reteaching, or for review of the key concepts presented. Answers for all chapter exercises are available in *Grammar Exercises Answers on Transparencies* in your Teaching Resources.

Answer Key

Exercise 4
1. P.O.
2. Cmdr.
3. Sept.
4. ea.
5. yd.

Exercise 5
1. Bats fly at night. How do they keep from crashing into cactuses?
2. Wolves and coyotes don't live together in groups, do they?
3. Should desert plants and animals be protected? Yes!
4. The beavertail cactus has attractive flowers. Be careful of its hidden spines!
5. I asked where golden eagles nest if there are no trees.
6. The Great Basin has fewer cactuses and yuccas than other deserts.
7. The elephant tree has beautiful leaves. Its flowers are small, but stinky.
8. The lowest elevation in the U.S. is in the Mojave Desert. What is it called?
9. When the zebratail lizard runs, does it hold its tail in the air?
10. The Sonoran Desert is home to the tiniest owl on earth. Wow! The elf owl is only 5–6 in. long!

Exercise 6
1. interrogative ?
2. declarative .
3. imperative !
4. declarative .
5. interrogative ?
6. exclamatory ! (both sentences)
7. imperative !
8. imperative . (both sentences)
9. imperative .
10. interrogative ?

continued

Answer Key continued

Exercise 7
Find It in Your Reading
The first sentence ends in a period because it states a fact. The exclamation marks after "Daddy" indicate the child's excitement. The question mark shows that he or she is asking a question.

Exercise 8
Find It in Your Writing
Have students explain their punctuation choices to a partner.

Exercise 9
Writing Application
Students can use reference books or the Internet to find facts about animals they would like to see.

the following sentence. Ask students why it is so confusing. (no commas)

Well as anyone knew the hills around town were wild with friends putting cows to riot playing barometer to the atmospheric changes taking sun peeling like calendars each day to take more sun.

Students can read the punctuated sentence in *Prentice Hall Literature: Timeless Voices, Timeless Themes,* Copper, page 6, right column. It has commas after *riot* (line 3) and *changes* (line 4).

Activate Prior Knowledge

Ask students to tell situations in which they would use commas. Challenge them to give sample sentences that illustrate their answers.

TEACH

Step-by-Step Teaching Guide

Commas

1. Read aloud Sentence 1 in Exercise 10 as written, with no pauses. Then reread it, pausing where the comma belongs. Students will hear that it is easier to follow the logic of a long sentence when appropriate commas are inserted.

2. A compound sentence contains two independent clauses, each with a subject and a verb. If these were two sentences, a period would separate them. Written together, they still need punctuation in between, in this case a comma.

Answer Key

Exercise 10

1. species, but
2. other, for
3. Ethiopia, yet
4. mangos, or
5. larger, yet

Commas

Using Commas to Separate Basic Elements

End marks signal a full stop. Commas signal a brief pause. A comma may be used to separate elements in a sentence or to set off part of a sentence.

Commas in Compound Sentences A comma is used to separate two independent clauses that are joined by a coordinating conjunction to form a *compound sentence.*

▶ **KEY CONCEPT** Use a comma before the conjunction to separate two independent clauses in a compound sentence. ■

The comma in a compound sentence is followed by one of the following conjunctions: *and, but, for, nor, or, so,* or *yet.*

COMPOUND SENTENCE:	Chimpanzees are grown at age five, but their mothers still take care of them.

Do not use a comma when there is just a word, phrase, or subordinate clause on either side of the conjunction.

WORDS:	We saw *chimpanzees* and *gorillas.*
PHRASES:	Light was reflected *from the road* and *off the car's hood.*
SUBORDINATE CLAUSES:	Choose someone *who has experience* but *who can also follow directions.*

▶ **Exercise 10** Using Commas in Compound Sentences A comma has been left out of each of the following sentences. On your paper, write the word before the comma, the comma, and the conjunction following the comma.

EXAMPLE:	Monkeys are in the animal family called primates and apes and humans are, too.
ANSWER:	primates, and

1. Collared brown lemurs are protected as an endangered species but they continue to be killed for food.
2. Olive baboons communicate well with each other for they make more than fifteen different vocal sounds.
3. Geladas live in families of about twenty in Ethiopia yet as many as four hundred may sleep in a group for safety.
4. Orangutans eat soft fruit like figs and mangos or they will eat insects and birds if fruit is not plentiful.
5. Male baboons are larger yet the females carry the young.

Theme: The Jungle

In this section, you will learn how to use commas correctly in your writing. The examples and exercises are about different jungle animals and plants.

Cross-Curricular Connection: Science

▶ **More Practice**

Language Lab CD-ROM
• Commas lesson
On-line Exercise Bank
• Section 26.2
Grammar Exercise Workbook
• pp. 141–142

⏱ TIME AND RESOURCE MANAGER

Resources
Print: Grammar Exercises Workbook, pp. 141–152; Grammar Exercises Answers on Transparencies, Chapter 26
Technology: Language Lab CD-ROM, Punctuation; On-Line Exercise Bank, Section 26.2

In-Depth Coverage	Accelerated Pace
• Work through all key concepts, pp. 564–572. • Assign and review Exercises 10–19. • Read and discuss Grammar in Literature, p. 565.	• Assign pp. 564–572 for independent student review. • Assign Section Review Exercises 20–22, p. 573.

GRAMMAR IN LITERATURE

from **Why Monkeys Live in Trees**

Julius Lester

In these sentences, the writer has used commas to separate items in a series, making the information easier to read.

Monkey went to the mound, took a tiny bit of pepper on his tongue, swallowed, and went into the tall grasses. A few minutes later, Monkey came out, took a little more, swallowed it, and went into the tall grasses.

Exercise 11 Proofreading Sentences for Commas Copy each of the sentences below, adding commas where needed. If no comma is needed, write *none.*

1. Gorillas and chimpanzees do not have tails but most monkeys do.
2. There are three types of gorillas and mountain gorillas are the rarest.
3. Chimpanzees may use sticks in a humanlike manner to get termites for food but gorillas don't do that.
4. Adult male mountain gorillas weigh four hundred pounds and they stand six feet tall.
5. One would think the mountain gorilla's size would guarantee survival yet in 1997 only six hundred remained in the wild.
6. Leave immediately if a gorilla begins to grunt and beat its chest.
7. A gorilla is too big to live in trees and it cannot swing from branch to branch like a monkey.
8. The fat-tailed dwarf lemur stores fat in its tail so it can hibernate six months each year.
9. The black-capped capuchin monkey lives in trees yet it will hop down to catch frogs for dinner.
10. Primates are generally defenseless against humans and they deserve our help.

Commas • 565

Grammar in Literature

1. A comma is both a visual and an aural pause in a sentence. Read the opening sentence of the excerpt aloud, pausing at each comma. When a person reads the sentence silently, the commas show where to pause and how the different parts of the sentence relate to one another. When a person speaks the sentence aloud, the listener can hear the commas, with the same effect.

2. Use the literature excerpt to review what students have learned about end punctuation. Have them identify the types of sentences and explain why they end in periods. (They are declarative sentences; they state facts.)

Answer Key

Exercise 11

1. Gorillas and chimpanzees do not have tails, but most monkeys do.
2. There are three types of gorillas, and mountain gorillas are the rarest.
3. Chimpanzees may use sticks in a humanlike manner to get termites for food, but gorillas don't do that.
4. Adult male mountain gorillas weigh four hundred pounds, and they stand six feet tall.
5. One would think the mountain gorilla's size would guarantee survival, yet in 1997 only six hundred remained in the wild.
6. none
7. A gorilla is too big to live in trees, and it cannot swing from branch to branch like a monkey.
8. The fat-tailed dwarf lemur stores fat in its tail, so it can hibernate six months each year.
9. The black-capped capuchin monkey lives in trees, yet it will hop down to catch frogs for dinner.
10. Primates are generally defenseless against humans, and they deserve our help.

☑ ONGOING ASSESSMENT: Prerequisite Skills

If students have difficulty with commas in compound sentences, you may find it necessary to review the following to assure coverage of prerequisite knowledge.

In the Textbook	Print Resources	Technology
Compound Subjects and Compound Predicates, pp. 390–397	Grammar Exercise Workbook, pp. 47–50	Language Lab CD-ROM, Styling Sentences; On-Line Exercise Bank, Section 19.3

Commas in Series

1. Point out the parallel grammatical structure in both series of phrases examples. In the first sentence, each phrase begins with an infinitive: *to have, to find, to make, to play.* In the second, each phrase begins with a verb: *chase, hide, throw, wrestle.* Phrases in a series should always have parallel grammatical structure. It makes the sentence stronger, more balanced, and easier to follow.

2. Even a long series with conjunctions does not need commas. Show students this correct sentence without commas.

   For dessert I will have cake or pie or cookies or ice cream.

Answer Key

> **Exercise 12**

1. Snow monkeys are found in northern Africa, India, or Southeast Asia.
2. The aye-aye has big ears, long fingers, and an oversized tail.
3. Pileated gibbons have an eight- to ten-hour day spent sleeping, feeding, and calling to one another.
4. Uakaris live in the Amazon Basin and have bare red faces, bald heads, and shaggy white fur.
5. correct

Critical Viewing

Identify Students may suggest that a gorilla will find roots, stems, and leaves.

26.2

Using Commas in Series

Sometimes, a sentence lists a number of items. When three or more items are listed, the list is called a *series*. The items in the series are separated by commas.

> **KEY CONCEPT** Use commas to separate a series of words or a series of phrases. ■

The items in a series may be single words or groups of words.

SERIES OF WORDS: A gorilla's diet includes roots, stems, leaves, and bamboo. Many primates make human-like gestures, sounds, and faces.

SERIES OF PHRASES: All primates have the instincts to have families, to find food, to make safe nests, and to play with one another. When primates play, they may chase one another, hide behind trees, throw things at one another, or wrestle together.

Notice that each of the items except the last one in these series is followed by a comma. The conjunction *and* or *or* is added after the last comma.

If each item in a series is followed by a conjunction, commas are not needed; the conjunctions separate the items.

EXAMPLE: I visited castles and museums and forts.

> **Exercise 12** Using Commas With Items in a Series Copy each sentence below, adding commas where they are needed.

EXAMPLE: Redwoods pines and firs are all needleleaf trees.
ANSWER: Redwoods, pines, and firs are all needleleaf trees.

1. Snow monkeys are found in northern Africa India or Southeast Asia.
2. The aye-aye has big ears long fingers and an oversized tail.
3. Pileated gibbons have an eight- to ten-hour day spent sleeping feeding and calling to one another.
4. Uakaris live in the Amazon Basin and have bare red faces bald heads and shaggy white fur.
5. Snow monkeys will eat fruit and insects and small animals.

▲ Critical Viewing
Write a sentence listing three different foods this gorilla might find in the jungle. Make sure that you use commas and a conjunction correctly in your sentence. [Identify]

☑ ONGOING ASSESSMENT: Monitor and Reinforce

If students miss more than two items in Exercises 10–13, refer them to the following for additional practice.

In the Textbook	Print Resources	Technology
Section Review, Ex. 20–21, p. 573	Grammar Exercise Workbook, pp. 141–144	Language Lab CD-ROM, Punctuation; On-Line Exercise Bank, Section 26.2

> **Exercise 13** Proofreading Sentences for Commas   Copy each sentence below, adding or removing commas as needed.

1. The Kayapo Indians have lived in the rain forest for centuries, but are losing their land to ranching mining and farming.
2. The tribe depends on the forest to provide food medicine from plants and housing.
3. The Yanomami in the Amazon gather hundreds of plants for food as well as fish fruit and even insects.
4. Native peoples the world over use wild plants as medicine, to heal wounds dull pain and cure fevers.
5. Other uses of plants include fuels dyes and insecticides.
6. The insects eat plants the birds eat insects and other animals eat birds, and plants.
7. The forest's careful balance has sustained the people plants animals and insects for millions of years.
8. We will never know what valuable element might be lost, if these areas are not protected from wasteful, mining logging and farming.
9. Each day a hundred species, including lizards birds snakes and insects are lost forever.
10. We must strive to respect plants, and wildlife.

Using Commas With Introductory Words and Phrases

When a sentence begins with an introductory word or phrase, that word or phrase is generally separated from the rest of the sentence by a comma.

> **KEY CONCEPT** Use a comma after an introductory word or phrase. ■

EXAMPLES: Yes, nightjars come out only at night.
Under a full moon, nightjars will sing all night!

The chart below gives additional examples of commas used after introductory words and phrases.

USING COMMAS WITH INTRODUCTORY WORDS AND PHRASES	
Introductory Words	<u>Well</u>, how shall we begin? <u>Jane</u>, please read that page aloud. <u>No</u>, we already have too many magazines.
Introductory Phrase	<u>Besides camping and hiking</u>, Dave also canoes.

> **More Practice**

Language Lab CD-ROM
• Commas lesson
On-line Exercise Bank
• Section 26.2
Grammar Exercise Workbook
• pp. 143–144

Commas • 567

---

1. The Kayapo Indians have lived in the rain forest for centuries but are losing their land to ranching, mining, and farming.
2. The tribe depends on the forest to provide food, medicine from plants, and housing.
3. The Yanomami in the Amazon gather hundreds of plants for food, as well as fish, fruit, and even insects.
4. Native peoples the world over use wild plants as medicine to heal wounds, dull pain, and cure fevers.
5. Other uses of plants include fuels, dyes, and insecticides.
6. The insects eat plants, the birds eat insects, and other animals eat birds and plants.
7. The forest's careful balance has sustained the people, plants, animals, and insects for millions of years.
8. We will never know what valuable element might be lost if these areas are not protected from wasteful mining, logging, and farming.
9. Each day a hundred species, including lizards, birds, snakes, and insects, are lost forever.
10. We must strive to respect plants and wildlife.

> **Step-by-Step Teaching Guide**

Commas With Introductory Words and Phrases

Have volunteers read the sample sentences aloud. Have the rest of the class listen for the natural pauses at the ends of the introductory words and phrases.

⏱ TIME SAVERS!

🖺 **Answers on Transparency** Use the Grammar Exercises Answers on Transparencies for Chapter 26 to have students correct their own or one another's exercises.

🖥 **On-Line Exercise Bank** Have students complete the exercises on computer. The Auto Check feature will grade their work for you!

1. At birth, parrots have no feathers and cannot see.
2. A beautiful bird, the African gray parrot is a good talker.
3. Like most parrots, the African gray nests in tree cavities.
4. Yes, gray parrots can be noisy.
5. At 13 inches, the African gray is the largest parrot in Africa.

1. To protect themselves, many plants in the jungle give off chemicals harmful to insects.
2. This keeps the insects from attacking, devouring, and eventually destroying certain types of trees and smaller plants.
3. Most trees have bad-tasting chemicals in their leaves, roots, bark, and flowers.
4. Over the centuries, a few insects have been able to overcome some of the trees' defenses.
5. For instance, some caterpillars are not affected by the toxic cycad leaf.
6. In fact, these caterpillars use the toxin to make their bodies red and yellow to ward off their own predators!
7. Because of these natural chemicals, insects are forced to eat a variety of plants.
8. In this way, no one plant or tree is wiped out by hungry insects or animals.
9. Natural characteristics make it possible for all living things to have a chance to survive.
10. Amazingly, this is just a tiny portion of what there is to know about the jungles and forests of the world.

Critical Viewing

Infer Students may suggest that like many bird species, the macaw's colors act as camouflage against potential predators.

568

26.2

Using Commas With Introductory Words and Phrases Copy the sentences below, placing a comma after the introductory words and phrases.

EXAMPLE: After gathering other birds' feathers the African palm swift builds a nest.

ANSWER: After gathering other birds' feathers, the African palm swift builds a nest.

1. At birth parrots have no feathers and cannot see.
2. A beautiful bird the African gray parrot is a good talker.
3. Like most parrots the African gray nests in tree cavities.
4. Yes gray parrots can be noisy.
5. At 13 inches the African gray is the largest parrot in Africa.

Proofreading a Passage for Commas Copy the paragraph below on your paper, adding or removing commas as needed.

To protect themselves many plants, in the jungle give off chemicals harmful to insects. This keeps the insects from attacking, devouring and eventually destroying certain types of trees, and smaller plants. Most trees have bad-tasting chemicals in their leaves roots bark, and flowers. Over the centuries a few insects have been able to overcome some of the trees' defenses. For instance some caterpillars are not affected, by the toxic cycad leaf. In fact these caterpillars use the toxin to make their bodies red and yellow to ward off their own predators! Because of these natural chemicals insects are forced to eat a variety of plants. In this way no one plant or tree is wiped out by hungry insects, or animals. Natural characteristics make it possible for all living things to have a chance to survive. Amazingly this is just a tiny portion of what there is to know about the jungles and forests of the world.

▶ **Critical Viewing** Write a sentence with an introductory phrase to explain how this macaw's colors help protect it in the jungle. Make sure that you have used commas correctly in your sentence. [Infer]

More Practice

Language Lab
CD-ROM
• Commas lesson
**On-line
Exercise Bank**
• Section 26.2
**Grammar Exercise
Workbook**
• pp. 145–146

☑ ONGOING ASSESSMENT: Monitor and Reinforce

If students miss more than two items in Exercises 14–15, refer them to the following for additional practice.

In the Textbook	Print Resources	Technology
Section Review, Ex. 22, p. 573	Grammar Exercise Workbook, pp. 145–146	Language Lab CD-ROM, Punctuation; On-Line Exercise Bank, Section 26.2

Using Commas With Interrupting Words and Phrases

Some sentences contain words or phrases that interrupt the flow of the sentence. They should be set off from the rest of the sentence by commas.

KEY CONCEPT Use commas to set off interrupting words and phrases from the rest of the sentence. ■

The commas indicate that these words could be left out, and the sentence would still make sense.

Words That Name a Person Being Addressed
Interrupting words tell who is being spoken to.

EXAMPLES: Look, Nat, at what we did last week.

Well, Sarah, have you cleaned the parrot's cage?

Words That Rename a Noun   Words that rename a noun give additional information about it.

EXAMPLES: His present, a camera, is just what he wanted.

My uncle, an expert on chimpanzees, will address the class next week.

Common Expressions   Writers often use certain expressions to indicate that they are expressing an opinion, a conclusion, or a summary.

EXAMPLES: The game, I believe, starts at three o'clock.

The answer, in my opinion, lies in the bird's protective coloration.

The following chart presents several more examples of how commas are used to set off interrupting words, phrases, and expressions.

USING COMMAS WITH INTERRUPTING WORDS AND PHRASES	
To Name a Person Being Addressed	Why, Mr. Kane, are you doing that?
To Rename a Noun	Daniel Boone, an American pioneer, helped build the Wilderness Trail.
To Set Off a Common Expression	The forecast, for once, was accurate.

Commas • 569

Step-by-Step Teaching Guide

Commas With Interrupting Words and Phrases

1. In grammar as in real life, an interruption does not add anything crucial to what was being said.

2. Have volunteers read the example sentences aloud. Listeners will hear that the readers pause slightly at the commas.

Integrating Vocabulary Skills

Latin Roots Write the word *interrupt* on the chalkboard and underline the root *rupt*. This is from the Latin verb meaning "to break." List other words with this root, such as *corrupt, disrupt,* and *rupture.* Students should think of an interrupting word or phrase in grammar as a word or phrase that breaks up the sentence. Since it breaks the sentence, it must be set off with commas.

⏲ TIME SAVERS!

🗐 **Answers on Transparency** Use the Grammar Exercises Answers on Transparencies for Chapter 26 to have students correct their own or one another's exercises.

🖳 **On-Line Exercise Bank** Have students complete the exercises on computer. The Auto Check feature will grade their work for you!

1. There are many other ways, Kevin, for plants, seeds, and pollen to be dispersed in the jungle.
2. Animals and birds, for instance, may spread seeds or pollen to other areas of the forest.
3. Once deposited, the seeds, likely as not, will sprout and grow new plants.
4. Not all of the seeds, certainly, will grow into mature plants.
5. Yet, obviously, enough do mature to feed future generations.
6. The agouti, a large Brazilian rodent, sometimes hoards seeds from fruit found on the ground.
7. Later, the seeds, long forgotten, will sprout.
8. Anything, even a raindrop, can cause a plant to be pollinated.
9. The puffball, a jungle fungus, will release spores into the air that can be carried far away.
10. Can you think of other ways, Tommy, that the jungle has to re-create itself every day?

Step-by-Step Teaching Guide

Commas in Letters

1. In the address of a friendly letter, the commas simply make reading easier. They mark a visual separation between elements of the address.
2. A colon rather than a comma is used after the salutation of a business letter.

26.2

▶ **Exercise 16** Using Commas With Interrupting Words and Phrases Copy each sentence, adding commas where necessary.

1. There are many other ways Kevin for plants, seeds, and pollen to be dispersed in the jungle.
2. Animals and birds for instance may spread seeds or pollen to other areas of the forest.
3. Once deposited, the seeds likely as not will sprout and grow new plants.
4. Not all of the seeds certainly will grow into mature plants.
5. Yet obviously enough do mature to feed future generations.
6. The agouti a large Brazilian rodent sometimes hoards seeds from fruit found on the ground.
7. Later, the seeds long forgotten will sprout.
8. Anything even a raindrop can cause a plant to be pollinated.
9. The puffball a jungle fungus will release spores into the air that can be carried far away.
10. Can you think of other ways Tommy that the jungle has to re-create itself every day?

Using Commas With Addresses and in Letters

Commas are also used in addresses, salutations of friendly letters, and closings of friendly or business letters.

▶ **KEY CONCEPT** Use a comma after each item in an address made up of two or more parts. ■

EXAMPLE: She is writing to her friend Helen Wilson, 1402 Croydon Street, Apt. 2B, Princeton, New Jersey 08540.

Notice, however, that when the same address is written on an envelope, several of the commas are eliminated.

EXAMPLE: Helen Wilson
1402 Croydon Street, Apt. 2B
Princeton, NJ 08540

▶ **KEY CONCEPT** Use a comma after the salutation in a friendly letter. ■

SALUTATION: Dear Helen,

▶ **KEY CONCEPT** Use a comma after the closing of every letter. ■

CLOSINGS: Sincerely yours,   With warm regards,

570 • Punctuation

▶ **More Practice**

Language Lab CD-ROM
• Commas lesson
On-line Exercise Bank
• Section 26.2
Grammar Exercise Workbook
• pp. 147–150

☑ ONGOING ASSESSMENT: Monitor and Reinforce

If students miss more than two items in Exercises 16–19, refer them to the following for additional practice.

In the Textbook	Print Resources	Technology
Section Review, Ex. 22, p. 573	Grammar Exercise Workbook, pp. 147–152	Language Lab CD-ROM, Punctuation; On-Line Exercise Bank, Section 26.2

Describe Possible answer: This landscape, a dense section of rain forest, seems to have plants growing from every surface.

Answer Key

▶ **Exercise 17**

1. 1525 Porter Street,
   New Kingston, NY 12459
2. Very truly yours,
3. Dear Louis,
4. Best regards,
5. 719 Desert Rim Ave., Apt. 6D,
   Phoenix, AZ 85001

▶ **Exercise 18**

Ms. Joan Conklin
42 Ralston Beach Road, Apartment 5
Chicago, Illinois 60660

Dear Ms. Conklin,

Thank you for sending the slides of your trip to the Kenyan wildlife reserve. Your work, I must say, is very important, and your slides are fascinating to view. You must feel a sense of reward knowing that your photos document progress and that your work has saved human as well as animal lives. Over the next few weeks, we will complete our planning for the new book on wildlife preservation. Your photos, certainly, will be an important part of the book. Thank you for the fine work.

Warm regards,

Melissa Smithson
New World Books

▶ **Exercise 17** Supplying Commas With Addresses and in Letters Copy each address, salutation, and closing below. Add commas where necessary.

1. 1525 Porter Street New Kingston NY 12459
2. Very truly yours
3. Dear Louis
4. Best regards
5. 719 Desert Rim Ave. Apt. 6D Phoenix AZ 85001

▶ **Exercise 18** Revising a Letter by Adding Needed Commas
Copy the following letter, adding commas where necessary.

Ms. Joan Conklin
42 Ralston Beach Road Apartment 5
Chicago Illinois 60660

Dear Ms. Conklin:

Thank you for sending the slides of your trip to the Kenyan wildlife reserve. Your work I must say is very important and your slides are fascinating to view. You must feel a sense of reward knowing that your photos document progress and that your work has saved human as well as animal lives. Over the next few weeks we will complete our planning for the new book on wildlife preservation. Your photos certainly will be an important part of the book. Thank you for the fine work.

Warm regards

Melissa Smithson
New World Books

▲ **Critical Viewing**
Use the phrase *a dense section of rain forest* as an interrupter in a sentence about this photo. Where should commas be used in your sentence? **[Describe]**

☑ **ONGOING ASSESSMENT: Assess Mastery**

Use the following resources to assess student mastery of commas.

In the Textbook	Print Resources	Technology
Chapter Review, Ex. 64, p. 596	Formal Assessment, Chapter 26	Language Lab CD-ROM, Punctuation; On-Line Exercise Bank, Section 26.2

 **TIME SAVERS!**

📄 **Answers on Transparency**
Use the Grammar Exercises Answers on Transparencies for Chapter 26 to have students correct their own or one another's exercises.

💻 **On-Line Exercise Bank**
Have students complete the exercises on computer. The Auto Check feature will grade their work for you!

Commas in Numbers

1. Large numbers are usually written in numerals rather than words because they are easier to read. A person can comprehend 8,463 much more quickly and easily than eight thousand four hundred sixty-three.

2. To avoid confusion in a series of large numbers, a semicolon is used to separate the items. Write the following examples on the chalkboard to show why:

   The votes for senator were 23,891, 87,422, 100,665.

   The votes for senator were 23,891; 87,422; 100,665.

Answer Key

> **Exercise 19**

1. Information can be found on pages 322, 323, and 324.
2. The Amazon River, mostly in Brazil, is about 4,080 miles long.
3. correct
4. The Amazon rain forest has over 1,500 species of fish.
5. The population of Brazil was 158,739,257 in 1995.

26.2

Using Commas in Numbers

Numbers of one hundred or less and numbers made up of two words (for example, three thousand) are generally spelled out. Other large numbers (for example, 8,463) are written in numerals. Commas make large numbers easier to read.

▶ **KEY CONCEPT** Use commas with numbers of more than three digits. ■

To place the comma correctly, count from the right: Commas are placed before every third digit.

EXAMPLES: a population of 247,867
             an area of 3,615,122 square miles

Commas are also used with a series of numbers.

▶ **KEY CONCEPT** Use commas with three or more numbers written in a series. ■

EXAMPLE: Read pages 123, 124, and 125 carefully.

▶ **KEY CONCEPT** Do not use a comma with ZIP Codes, telephone numbers, page numbers, years, serial numbers, or house numbers. ■

NUMBERS WITHOUT COMMAS
ZIP Code: Jamaica, NY 11432
Telephone number: (617) 532-7593
Page number: page 1002
Year: the year 2010
Serial number: 026 35 7494
House number: 1801 Houston Street

▶ **Exercise 19** Using Commas in Numbers Copy each sentence below, adding commas where necessary. If no commas are needed, write *correct*.

1. Information can be found on pages 322 323 and 324.
2. The Amazon River mostly in Brazil is about 4080 miles long.
3. The Amazon has over one thousand tributaries, or secondary streams.
4. The Amazon rain forest has over 1500 species of fish.
5. The population of Brazil was 169806557 in 1998.

▶ **More Practice**

Language Lab
CD-ROM
• Commas lesson
On-line
Exercise Bank
• Section 26.2
Grammar Exercise
Workbook
• pp. 151–152

⏱ TIME SAVERS!

🖹 **Answers on Transparency**
Use the Grammar Exercises Answers on Transparencies for Chapter 26 to have students correct their own or one another's exercises.

🖥 **On-Line Exercise Bank**
Have students complete the exercises on computer. The Auto Check feature will grade their work for you!

Section Review

GRAMMAR EXERCISES 20–25

Exercise 20 Supplying Commas in Compound Sentences Write the following sentences on your paper, adding commas where needed.

1. Nature is a partnership so flowers and their pollinators work closely together.
2. This might seem mysterious but birds are attracted to bright colors.
3. The rafflesia is the largest flower in the world and it grows in Southeast Asia.
4. It grows mostly underground so only the bloom is visible.
5. You can read about colorful plants but you should really see them up close.

Exercise 21 Using Commas With Items in a Series Write the following sentences on your paper, inserting commas where needed. If no comma is needed, write *none*.

1. Can only birds or insects pollinate jungle plants?
2. Will snakes monkeys or bats do the job?
3. Frogs, toads and squirrels are also good pollinators.
4. Bats locate trees and flowers using sonar at night.
5. They have long tongues big appetites and furry wings for quick pollen pickup.

Exercise 22 Proofreading Sentences for Commas Copy these sentences, adding or removing commas as needed. If a sentence is correct, write *correct*.

1. Not only plants, Jessie but animals must have special qualities to survive.
2. Without bright feathers of course many male birds would never attract a mate.
3. The dappled coat, of the jaguar, helps it hide in the forest, so it can remain unnoticed, until its prey draws near.

4. The coat may hide the jaguar from other animals, but the cat has not successfully escaped human hunters.
5. Unbeknownst to humans moths butterflies and some other insects give off odors to attract mates.
6. Male baboons yawn oddly enough and toss their heads to show off big teeth to potential rivals.
7. Black howler monkeys shout so loudly that explorers once thought they were jaguars.
8. No matter, how frightening their howl it is meant only to defend their territory.
9. Part of the moth caterpillar its tail looks like a poisonous snake's head.
10. The mandrill a West Central African monkey has inflated blue face markings, that look like a permanent snarl.

Exercise 23 Find It in Your Reading Read a paragraph from your favorite magazine that contains at least three commas. With a friend, explain the use of the commas in the paragraph.

Exercise 24 Find It in Your Writing Look through your portfolio to find a paragraph that includes several commas. Explain the purpose of each comma.

Exercise 25 Writing Application Write a paragraph of at least five sentences describing plants or animals that you might see in a jungle. Include the following items and use commas correctly.

1. a compound sentence
2. a list of items in a sentence
3. an introductory phrase
4. an interrupting word or expression
5. a number of at least four digits

ASSESS and CLOSE

Section Review

Each of these exercises correlates to a concept in the section on commas, pp. 564–572. The exercises may be used for more practice, for reteaching, or for review of the key concepts presented. Answers for all chapter exercises are available in *Grammar Exercises Answers on Transparencies* in your Teaching Resources.

Answer Key

Exercise 20

1. Nature is a partnership, so flowers and their pollinators work closely together.
2. This might seem mysterious, but birds are attracted to bright colors.
3. The rafflesia is the largest flower in the world, and it grows in Southeast Asia.
4. It grows mostly underground, so only the bloom is visible.
5. You can read about colorful plants, but you should really see them up close.

Exercise 21

1. none
2. Will snakes, monkeys, or bats do the job?
3. Frogs, toads, and squirrels are also good pollinators.
4. none
5. They have long tongues, big appetites, and furry wings for quick pollen pickup.

Exercise 22

1. Not only plants, Jessie, but animals must have special qualities to survive.
2. Without bright feathers, of course, many male birds would never attract a mate.
3. The dappled coat of the jaguar helps it hide in the forest so it can remain unnoticed until its prey draws near.
4. correct
5. Unbeknownst to humans, moths, butterflies, and some other insects give off odors to attract mates.
6. Male baboons yawn, oddly enough, and toss their heads to show off big teeth to potential rivals.
7. correct

continued

Answer Key continued

8. No matter how frightening their howl, it is meant only to defend their territory.
9. Part of the moth caterpillar, its tail, looks like a poisonous snake's head.
10. The mandrill, a West Central African monkey, has inflated blue face markings that look like a permanent snarl.

Exercise 23

Find It in Your Reading
Have students read some of their choices aloud so the class can discuss the use of commas.

Exercise 24

Find It in Your Writing
Have students correct any comma errors they find.

Exercise 25

Writing Application
Students can trade papers with partners to check the punctuation.

Write the following sentences on the chalkboard. Ask students which needs a colon and which needs a semicolon. Where?

Freddy learned about dangerous rain forest animals[:] poisonous snakes, poisonous frogs, poisonous insects, and poisonous fish.

Freddy learned about dangerous rain forest animals[;] he had nightmares for a week.

Activate Prior Knowledge

Ask students to tell in their own words why the first sentence in the Interest Grabber needs a colon and the second sentence needs a semicolon.

TEACH

Step-by-Step Teaching Guide

Semicolons

1. A semicolon should be used to connect independent clauses only when one follows the other. If the second clause extends and develops the same thought that was expressed in the first clause, then a semicolon is appropriate. Remind students that a semicolon does not mark the end of a sentence; the clause beginning after a semicolon is not capitalized.

2. To avoid confusion, semicolons are used to separate items in a series if those items have commas within them.

   I picked out two shirts, which were red; a cap, which was blue; and several pairs of socks, all white.

Critical Viewing

Infer Students may suggest that the tree frog's coloring, brown, is used as camouflage against predators; its senses of sight, smell, and hearing also help it to survive.

Answer Key

▶ **Exercise 26**

1. protective; they are
2. warning; they
3. use; it
4. toxin; such
5. leaves; their

Section 26.3

Semicolons and Colons

Using Semicolons

Sometimes two independent clauses are so closely connected in meaning that they make up a single sentence, rather than two separate sentences.

▶ **KEY CONCEPT** Use a semicolon to connect two independent clauses that are closely connected in meaning. ■

If the two independent clauses do not make up a single sentence, they should be punctuated separately, with periods.

EXAMPLES: Bill enjoys exploring jungle areas; Betsy is more interested in deserts. (two independent clauses closely connected in meaning)

Bill and Betsy don't agree. Betsy is working on a paper about newts. (two separate sentences)

The following chart gives more examples of independent clauses so closely connected in meaning that a semicolon should be used between them.

INDEPENDENT CLAUSES PUNCTUATED BY SEMICOLONS
The rain forest has no marked trails; don't forget your compass.
The river has many hazards; it's full of snakes.
Every inch of the forest is valuable; watch where you walk.

▶ **Exercise 26** Using Semicolons Copy the sentences below, adding semicolons where necessary.

1. The green algae growing on sloths are protective they are good camouflage in the trees.
2. The colors of black and yellow insects are a warning they say leave me alone.
3. The poison in poison-arrow frogs has more than one use it contains antibiotics that protect the frogs against infections.
4. The pitohui bird and the poison frog emit the same toxin such a similarity is rare in nature.
5. Glass frogs can cling to leaves their bodies blend in.

Theme: The Jungle

In this section, you will learn when to use semicolons and colons in your writing. The examples and exercises focus on additional jungle animals and plants.

Cross-Curricular Connection: Science

▼ **Critical Viewing** Write two independent clauses connected by a semicolon to identify characteristics that help the giant tree frog survive in the rain forest. [Infer]

⏱ **TIME AND RESOURCE MANAGER**

Resources
Print: Grammar Exercises Workbook, pp. 153–156; Grammar Exercises Answers on Transparencies, Chapter 26
Technology: Language Lab CD-ROM, Punctuation; On-Line Exercise Bank, Section 26.3

In-Depth Coverage	Accelerated Pace
• Work through all key concepts, pp. 574–576. • Assign and review Exercises 26–29.	• Assign pp. 574–576 for independent student review. • Assign Section Review Exercises 30–31, p. 577.

Exercise 27 Using Semicolons Copy each sentence below, adding a semicolon where necessary.

1. The parrot snake bluffs with a wide open mouth it has no venom.
2. Shield bugs use color to ward off predators they also form large groups for protection.
3. One shield bug may be sampled by a bird the remaining bugs are safe after that.
4. Thorn bugs look like parts of branches from afar up close, their red stripes discourage birds.
5. Chameleons are said to change color to conceal themselves in fact, they are responding to temperature changes.

Using Colons

A colon (:) is a punctuation mark with a number of uses.

KEY CONCEPT Use a colon after an independent clause to introduce a list of items. Use commas to separate three or more items. ■

The independent clause that comes before the colon often includes the words *the following, as follows, these,* or *those.*

EXAMPLES: The rain forest is home to many beautiful birds: scarlet macaws, black-necked red cottingas, and bowerbirds.

Some orchids grow only in the following countries: Costa Rica, Peru, and Brazil.

Olaf's favorite orchids are the ones in these colors: red, pale pink, and purple.

Do not use a colon after a verb or a preposition.

INCORRECT: Veronica always orders: soup, salad, and dessert.
CORRECT: Veronica always orders soup, salad, and dessert.

SOME ADDITIONAL USES OF THE COLON	
To Separate Hours and Minutes	3:15 P.M., 9:45 A.M.
After the Salutation in a Business Letter	Gentlemen: Dear Miss Robinson:
On Warnings and Labels	Warning: The ice is thin. Note: Shake before using. Caution: Children Playing

More Practice

On-line
Exercise Bank
• Section 26.2
Grammar Exercise
Workbook
• pp. 153–154

Answer Key

Exercise 27

1. mouth; it
2. predators; they
3. bird; the
4. afar; up
5. themselves; in

Step-by-Step Teaching Guide

Colons

1. A colon is like an arrow. It points to examples of whatever comes before it.

2. The example sentences show correct uses of colons. These sentences could also be written with other punctuation.

   The rain forest is home to many beautiful birds, such as . . .

   Some orchids grow only in Costa Rica, . . .

   Olaf's favorite orchids are the red, . . .

The use of different kinds of punctuation will make students' writing more varied and interesting.

☑ **ONGOING ASSESSMENT: Monitor and Reinforce**

If students miss more than two items in Exercises 26–29, refer them to the following for additional practice.

In the Textbook	Print Resources	Technology
Section Review, Ex. 30–31, p. 577	Grammar Exercise Workbook, pp. 153–156	Language Lab CD-ROM, Punctuation; On-Line Exercise Bank, Section 26.3

⏱ **TIME SAVERS!**

🗔 **Answers on Transparency**
Use the Grammar Exercises Answers on Transparencies for Chapter 26 to have students correct their own or one another's exercises.

🖵 **On-Line Exercise Bank**
Have students complete the exercises on computer. The Auto Check feature will grade their work for you!

Answer Key

Exercise 28

1. Many types of jungle creatures build nests: ants, wasps, and monkeys.
2. Frogs will nurture their eggs in several places: under leaves, in plants, or on their backs.
3. correct
4. The river tour leaves three times each day: 11:00 A.M., 2:00 P.M., and 4:00 P.M.
5. Marty fears these jungle aminals: snakes, jaguars, and poison frogs.

Exercise 29

1. correct
2. "Danger: No Swimming Allowed," read the sign by the river.
3. Jungle plants provide medicines to treat several ailments: malaria, heart disease, and leukemia.
4. correct
5. The Yanomami succeed in harvesting many crops: plantains, sugar cane, and maize.

Critical Viewing

Infer Students may suggest that the jaguar survives in the jungle because of these characteristics: speed and coloring.

26.3

▶ **Exercise 28** **Supplying Colons in Sentences** Rewrite each of the sentences below, adding colons where needed. If a sentence is correct, write *correct*.

EXAMPLE: We visited three Canadian cities Calgary, Edmonton, and Winnipeg.

ANSWER: We visited three Canadian cities: Calgary, Edmonton, and Winnipeg.

1. Many types of jungle creatures build nests ants, wasps, and monkeys.
2. Frogs will nurture their eggs in several places under leaves, in plants, or on their backs.
3. Items that could be made from unknown plants include waxes, oils, and perfumes.
4. The river tour leaves three times each day 1100 A.M., 200 P.M., and 400 P.M.
5. Marty fears these jungle animals snakes, jaguars, and poison frogs.

▶ **Exercise 29** **Proofreading for Colons** Rewrite the sentences below on your paper, adding colons as needed. If a sentence is correct, write *correct*.

1. Lynn will not eat ants, monkeys, or sloths.
2. "Danger No Swimming Allowed," read the sign by the river.
3. Jungle plants provide medicines to treat several ailments malaria, heart disease, and leukemia.
4. To flourish, termites need darkness, decaying matter, and moisture.
5. The Yanomami succeed in harvesting many crops plantains, sugar cane, and maize.

▶ **More Practice**

Language Lab CD-ROM
• Colons lesson
On-line Exercise Bank
• Section 26.3
Grammar Exercise Workbook
• pp. 155–156

◀ **Critical Viewing** Write a sentence with a colon to introduce a list of characteristics that enable a jaguar to survive in the jungle. **[Infer]**

☑ ONGOING ASSESSMENT: Assess Mastery

Use the following resources to assess student mastery of semicolons and colons.

In the Textbook	Technology
Chapter Review, Ex. 65, p. 596	Language Lab CD-ROM, Punctuation; On-Line Exercise Bank, Section 26.3

Section 26.3 Section Review

GRAMMAR EXERCISES 30–34

▶ **Exercise 30** Using Semicolons to Connect Independent Clauses Add a semicolon to connect clauses in each sentence below. On your paper, write the word before each semicolon, the semicolon, and the word following the semicolon.

1. The native people of the rain forest don't want to leave development is driving them out.
2. Industries that produce income from the forest can seem helpful however, they deplete the resources forever.
3. Laws have been made to protect the native people it is very difficult to enforce them.
4. Some African peoples work for timber companies their low wages cannot replace their vanishing forest.
5. Many governments feel that they must exploit their rain forests they owe huge debts to other countries.

▶ **Exercise 31** Using Colons Add colons where appropriate in the following sentences. On your paper, write the word before the colon, the colon, and the word following the colon.

1. Much of New Zealand's rain forest has protected species that evolved there the kiwi, a flightless bird; the kakapo, one of the largest parrots in the world; and the saddleback bird.
2. New Zealand's agricultural development sustains itself and allows for exportation lamb and wool provided by sheep, butter and beef from cattle, and fruits and vegetables from farms.
3. The terrain of New Zealand is diverse and beautiful the snow-covered Mt. Cook, the Tasman Glacier, and the flooded valleys of Fiordland.

4. New Zealand has several overseas territories Rarotonga, Tokelau, and Niue Island, among others.
5. The California Monterey pine was introduced to New Zealand and contributes to the export of many products paper, pulp, timber, and woodchips.
6. Dear Captain Cook
7. At 1230 P.M. today, we board the ship.
8. Caution No Alcohol Allowed Inside.
9. To Whom It May Concern
10. Be ready to leave at 600 A.M.

▶ **Exercise 32** Find It in Your Reading Read the following excerpt from the Greek myth "Arachne." Explain why the writer used a semicolon in this sentence.

. . . Before the group that was gathered there she [Arachne] would not give in; so pressing her pale lips together in obstinacy and pride, she led the goddess to one of the great looms and set herself before the other.

▶ **Exercise 33** Find It in Your Writing Look through your portfolio for passages containing compound sentences or a list of items. Rewrite the passages using semicolons or colons correctly.

▶ **Exercise 34** Writing Application Write a brief paragraph explaining the preparation necessary for taking a trip into a forest. Use semicolons at least twice to connect related ideas, and use colons at least three times.

Section Review • 577

ASSESS and CLOSE

Section Review

Each of these exercises correlates to a concept in the section on semicolons and colons, pp. 574–576. The exercises may be used for more practice, for reteaching, or for review of the key concepts presented. Answers for all chapter exercises are available in *Grammar Exercises Answers on Transparencies* in your Teaching Resources.

Answer Key

▶ **Exercise 30**

1. leave; development
2. helpful; however
3. people; it
4. companies; their
5. rain forests; they

▶ **Exercise 31**

1. there: the
2. exportation: lamb
3. beautiful: the
4. territories: Rarotonga
5. products: paper
6. Cook:
7. 12:30
8. Caution: No
9. Concern:
10. 6:00

▶ **Exercise 32**

Find It in Your Reading
The semicolon indicates a pause between two related complete thoughts. The second thought follows up on the first, continuing and explaining it.

▶ **Exercise 33**

Find It in Your Writing
Have students explain to partners why they used each punctuation mark.

continued

Answer Key continued

▶ **Exercise 34**

Writing Application
Invite students to read their paragraphs aloud to the class.

⏱ TIME SAVERS!

Answers on Transparency Use the Grammar Exercises Answers on Transparencies for Chapter 26 to have students correct their own or one another's exercises.

On-Line Exercise Bank Have students complete the exercises on computer. The Auto Check feature will grade their work for you!

Quotation Marks and Underlining

PREPARE and ENGAGE

Interest GRABBER Write the following sentences on the chalkboard and ask volunteers to come up and add quotation marks.

The spaceship hovered over Earth. What is that? asked the Martian commander, pointing.

I don't know, said a crew member. I see people hitting something round with a stick. And then they run.

It must be some kind of punishment, the commander announced. No one would do that for fun.

Activate Prior Knowledge

Ask students why quotation marks were needed in the Interest Grabber. (to show someone's exact words)

Step-by-Step Teaching Guide

Quotation Marks

1. Correct capitalization with direct quotations can cause problems, because capital letters do not appear in the middle of a sentence unless they begin proper nouns.

2. In the first example, Jennifer's quote is a sentence, and that is why the first word is capitalized.

3. In the second example, Mark's entire quote is one sentence. If *Mark said* were removed, *or* would not be capitalized. So it is not capitalized in this context either.

Answer Key

▶ **Exercise 35**

1. "A herbivore," said Matt, "is any animal that eats vegetation."
2. "Insects eat plants too," said Chuck.
3. "Yes, insects can be herbivores as well," Matt answered.
4. Berry said, "A scavenger is any creature that eats dead meat or decayed matter."
5. "Vultures are scavengers," said Chuck.

Using Quotation Marks With Direct Quotations

A *direct quotation* conveys the exact words that a person wrote, said, or thought.

▶ **KEY CONCEPT** Use quotation marks to enclose a person's exact words. ■

A direct quotation is often accompanied by words such as *he said* or *she replied*. These words, which may fall at the beginning, middle, or end of a quotation, identify the speaker.

Introductory Words When words that identify the speaker come right before a direct quotation, they are followed by a comma.

EXAMPLE: Jennifer said, "The acorn is one of the most important sources of food in the woods."

Interrupting Words When words that identify the speaker come in the middle of a quoted sentence, each part of the interrupted quotation is enclosed in quotation marks. The first part of the quotation ends with a comma followed by quotation marks. The interrupting words are also followed by a comma.

EXAMPLE: "Don't forget the hickory nuts," Mark said, "or the walnuts and pecans."

Concluding Words If the words that identify the speaker are placed at the end of a direct quotation, the quoted material is followed by a comma, a question mark, or an exclamation mark placed inside the final quotation marks.

EXAMPLE: "Did you know that one oak tree can produce 30,000 acorns in a year?" the ranger asked.

▶ **Exercise 35** Using Quotation Marks With Direct Quotations Copy each sentence below, adding commas and quotation marks where necessary.

1. A herbivore said Matt is any animal that eats vegetation.
2. Insects eat plants too said Chuck.
3. Yes insects can be herbivores as well Matt answered.
4. Barry said A scavenger is any creature that eats dead meat or decayed matter.
5. Vultures are scavengers said Chuck.

Theme: North American Animals

In this section, you will learn when to use quotation marks with direct quotations and when to use either quotation marks or underlining with titles. The examples and exercises are about animals native to the United States.

Cross-Curricular Connection: Science

⏱ TIME AND RESOURCE MANAGER

Resources
Print: Grammar Exercises Workbook, pp. 157–164, 173–174; Grammar Exercises Answers on Transparencies, Chapter 26
Technology: Language Lab CD-ROM, Punctuation; On-Line Exercise Bank, Section 26.4

In-Depth Coverage	Accelerated Pace
• Work through all key concepts, pp. 578–584. • Assign and review Exercises 35–41.	• Assign pp. 578–584 for independent student review. • Assign Section Review Exercises 42–43, p. 585.

▶ **Exercise 36** Punctuating Quotations With the Speaker
Introduced at Different Locations Use each direct quotation
below in a sentence. Supply a verb and the name of a speaker
in the location indicated in parentheses. Add the necessary
commas and quotation marks.

1. A tree bears a nut, a squirrel eats it, and then a predator
   eats the squirrel. (introductory words)
2. I know what that's called. It's the food chain. (concluding
   words)
3. Correct. (concluding words)
4. When food chains form a network, all connected in the forest, it's a food web. (interrupting words)
5. You are absolutely right. (introductory words)

Using Quotation Marks
With Other Punctuation Marks

Commas, periods, question marks, and exclamation marks
are often used with quotation marks.

▶ **KEY CONCEPT** Place commas and periods inside final
quotation marks. ■

EXAMPLES: "Our class trip is this Tuesday," said Janet.
Matthew added, "We are leaving very early."

Place a question mark or exclamation mark inside the final
quotation marks if it is part of the quotation.

EXAMPLES: Retha asked, "What animal eats the most leaves?"
Peter said to Andy, "Help me get this raccoon out
of my car!"

Each sentence above is declarative. That is, each makes a
statement by reporting what someone said. Nevertheless, neither ends with a period. Since a sentence cannot have two
final punctuation marks, the punctuation needed for the
direct quotation stands alone, inside the quotation marks.

INCORRECT: Dan asked, "When can I get a pet"?
CORRECT: Dan asked, "When can I get a pet?"

Place a question mark or exclamation mark outside the
final quotation marks if the mark is not part of the quotation.

EXAMPLES: Who said, "We have nothing to fear but fear itself"?
Don't say, "I doubt that it will work"!

More Practice

**Language Lab
CD-ROM**
• Quotation Marks
  lesson
**On-line
Exercise Bank**
• Section 26.4
**Grammar Exercise
Workbook**
• pp. 157–158

⚙ **Grammar
and Style Tip**

Sometimes, for the sake of
clarity, quotation marks
are used to refer to words
that are out of context, as
in these sentences:

Every time he wrote
"dog," he should have
written "cat."

The sign said "Private
Party," so we left.

Answer Key

▶ **Exercise 36**

1. Ms. Crandall said, "A tree bears a
   nut, a squirrel eats it, and then a
   predator eats the squirrel."
2. "I know what that's called. It's
   the food chain," exclaimed
   Rhoda.
3. "Correct," said Ms. Crandall.
4. "When food chains form a
   network, all connected in the
   forest," said Rhoda, "it's a food
   web."
5. Ms. Crandall replied, "You are
   absolutely right."

Step-by-Step Teaching Guide

Quotation Marks With Other
Punctuation Marks

Emphasize that students should look
at an entire sentence before deciding
whether the question mark or
exclamation point goes inside or
outside the quotation marks.

⏱ **TIME SAVERS!**

 **Answers on Transparency**
Use the Grammar Exercises
Answers on Transparencies for
Chapter 26 to have students
correct their own or one
another's exercises.

▭ **On-Line Exercise Bank**
Have students complete the
exercises on computer. The Auto
Check feature will grade their
work for you!

Critical Viewing

Apply Answers will vary. Make sure that students are using quotation marks correctly.

Answer Key

▶ **Exercise 37**

1. "Do you know what bird Benjamin Franklin wanted as our national bird?" asked Lucy.
2. Beth exclaimed, "I would imagine it was the duck!"
3. "No!" laughed Lucy. "Franklin wanted the wild turkey to be the national bird."
4. "Why?" asked Beth.
5. "Because," explained Lucy, "he thought that the bald eagle was the wrong choice because it eats carrion, as do vultures."
6. "Turkeys are stupid, aren't they?" asked Beth.
7. "Some Native American people thought so, too," Lucy agreed, "but they are smart enough to sleep in branches over water so nothing can catch them during the night."
8. "Are there very many wild turkeys left in the forests?" asked Chuck.
9. "Not as many as there used to be," Lucy explained, "but they can still be found across the East and Southeast, down into Florida, and up to New York State."
10. Chuck asked, "Do they gobble like turkeys on a farm?"

26.4

▶ **Critical Viewing** With a partner, exchange observations about the appearance of this turkey. Write your statements as correctly punctuated dialogue. [Apply]

▶ **Exercise 37** Using Quotation Marks With Other Punctuation Marks Copy each sentence below, adding commas, periods, question marks, and exclamation marks where needed.

EXAMPLE: I was annoyed when you yelled I'm staying here
ANSWER: I was annoyed when you yelled, "I'm staying here!"

1. Do you know which bird Benjamin Franklin wanted as our national bird asked Lucy
2. Beth exclaimed I would imagine it was the duck
3. No laughed Lucy Franklin wanted the wild turkey to be the national bird
4. Why asked Beth
5. Because explained Lucy he thought that the bald eagle was the wrong choice because it eats carrion, as do vultures
6. Turkeys are stupid, aren't they asked Beth
7. Some Native American people thought so, too Lucy agreed but they are smart enough to sleep in branches over water so nothing can catch them during the night
8. Are there very many wild turkeys left in the forests asked Chuck
9. Not as many as there used to be Lucy explained but they can still be found across the East and Southeast, down into Florida, and up to New York State
10. Chuck asked Do they gobble like turkeys on a farm

More Practice

Language Lab
CD-ROM
• Quotation Marks
lesson
On-line
Exercise Bank
• Section 26.4
Grammar Exercise
Workbook
• pp. 159–160

STANDARDIZED TEST PREPARATION WORKSHOP

Punctuation Standardized tests frequently require students to proofread a passage for punctuation errors. Share the following sample test item with students:

Choose the letter of the best way to rewrite the sentence.

Why cant you go to the park, asked Philip.

A "Why can't you go to the park," asked Philip?
B "Why can't you go to the park? asked Philip.
C "Why can't you go to the park?" asked Philip.
D Correct as is

The correct answer is item **C**. The sentence requires quotation marks and a question mark to end the speaker's question.

Using Quotation Marks for Dialogue

A dialogue is talk between two or more people. A new paragraph signals that a different person is speaking.

KEY CONCEPT In dialogue, start a new paragraph to signal a change of speaker. ∎

EXAMPLE: "William!" Erica shouted to her brother. "You'd better get up and feed the dog."

               "All right," William groaned, "I'm coming."

               "And hurry. Champ looks mighty hungry."

               "I said all right, Erica," William snapped. "C'mon, Champ, breakfast time."

GUIDELINES FOR WRITING DIALOGUE

1. Follow the general rules for using quotation marks, capital letters, end marks, and other punctuation marks.
2. Start a new paragraph with each change of speaker.
3. When a speaker utters two or more sentences without an interruption, put quotation marks at the beginning of the first sentence and at the end of the last sentence.

Guideline 3 is illustrated in the following examples:

INCORRECT: Martha said, "I think I heard a screech owl."
                    "Let's go outside and see."

CORRECT: Martha said, "I think I heard a screech owl. Let's go outside and see."

Exercise 38   Supplying Quotation Marks in a Dialogue
Rewrite the dialogue below on your paper, adding punctuation and quotation marks where needed.

That, said Corey, sounded like a wolf howling! Let's open the window in case it howls again!

I replied, I don't think we're in the right part of the country to hear a wolf.

Oh, yes, Corey insisted northern Washington has wolves.

Well, I said, open the window, but not too much. I'd like to hear it howl, but I don't want to meet it!

Don't be silly Corey said impatiently. Wolves are really shy.

Really I asked.

Oh, yes, Corey insisted as he opened the window. They stick close to their pack and do not generally attack people.

So wolves are actually peaceful and family oriented. I didn't know, I said softly.

Step-by-Step Teaching Guide

Quotation Marks for Dialogue

1. Have students look at the last paragraph on page 284 and the first paragraph on page 285 of *Prentice Hall Literature: Timeless Voices, Timeless Themes,* Copper. These two paragraphs are one long quotation by the same speaker. Students should note that the first paragraph begins with quotation marks; the second paragraph also begins with quotation marks, to show that the quotation continues. Only at the end of the quote—the end of the second paragraph—are there closing quotation marks.

2. Remind students to indent each new paragraph of dialogue.

Answer Key

Exercise 38

"That," said Corey, "sounded like a wolf howling! Let's open the window in case it howls again!"

I replied, "I don't think we're in the right part of the country to hear a wolf."

"Oh, yes," Corey insisted, "northern Washington has wolves."

"Well," I said, "open the window, but not too much. I'd like to hear it howl, but I don't want to meet it!"

"Don't be silly," Corey said impatiently. "Wolves are really shy."

"Really?" I asked.

"Oh, yes," Corey insisted as he opened the window. "They stick close to their pack and do not generally attack people."

"So wolves are actually peaceful and family oriented. I didn't know," I said softly.

⏱ TIME SAVERS!

📑 **Answers on Transparency** Use the Grammar Exercises Answers on Transparencies for Chapter 26 to have students correct their own or one another's exercises.

💻 **On-Line Exercise Bank** Have students complete the exercises on computer. The Auto Check feature will grade their work for you!

1. "My goodness! What is that creature?" cried Mother.
2. "Do you mean the hump-backed, cat-sized, dinosaur-like thing beside the tree?" Josh asked.
3. "I certainly do," Mother said. "What is it? Will it bite?"
4. "No," Josh assured her. "It's an armadillo. The thing it wants most is to find a full trash can or some baby birds."
5. "Then can I pet it?" Mother asked.
6. "Mother, make up your mind!" Josh laughed. "Are you afraid of it, or do you want to take it home?"
7. "A little of both," Mother replied. "It is cute, with its bands of armor and tiny little feet. I like its pointy little face and long tail."
8. "If you get close to it, it will do one of two things, Mother," said Josh.
9. "And those two things are what?" asked Mother.
10. "That armadillo will either roll up into a ball or tunnel into the ground so quickly you'll hardly be able to see it go!"

Step-by-Step Teaching Guide

Underlining and Quotation Marks in Titles

1. The basic difference between underlined titles of written works and those enclosed in quotation marks is length. This rule is not invariable, but it is a good rule to go by when in doubt.
2. Point out that while complete written works are underlined, the sections that comprise them are enclosed in quotation marks.

   "The Adventure of the Empty House" is the first story in <u>The Return of Sherlock Holmes</u>.

   "A Game of Chess" is the second section of the long poem <u>The Waste Land</u>.

Technology Tip

On the computer, students should use the italics function, not underlining, for titles of books, movies, and so on.

26.4

▶ **Exercise 39** Revising Punctuation and Paragraphing in a Dialogue Rewrite the numbered sentences below as a dialogue. Add any missing punctuation marks, and start a new paragraph whenever the speaker changes.

(1) My goodness! What is that creature cried Mother. (2) Do you mean the hump-backed, cat-sized, dinosaur-like thing beside the tree? Josh asked. (3) I certainly do Mother said What is it? Will it bite? (4) No Josh assured her. It's an armadillo. The thing it wants most is to find a full trash can or some baby birds. (5) Then can I pet it? Mother asked. (6) Mother, make up your mind Josh laughed. Are you afraid of it, or do you want to take it home? (7) A little of both Mother replied. It is cute, with its bands of armor and tiny little feet. I like its pointy little face and long tail (8) If you get close to it, it will do one of two things Mother said Josh. (9) And those two things are what asked Mother. (10) That armadillo will either roll up into a ball or tunnel into the ground so quickly you'll hardly be able to see it go!

Underlining and Quotation Marks in Titles

Many titles and names are either underlined or enclosed in quotation marks. Underlining is used only in handwritten or typewritten material. In printed material, italic (slanted) print is used instead of underlining.

▶ **KEY CONCEPT** Underline the titles of long written works, movies, television and radio series, paintings, and sculptures. Also underline the names of specific vehicles. ■

KINDS OF TITLES THAT ARE UNDERLINED

Written Works	
Books	<u>The Outsiders</u>, <u>The Good Earth</u>
Plays	<u>The Miracle Worker</u>, <u>Pygmalion</u>
Magazines and Newspapers	<u>Newsweek</u>, <u>USA Today</u>
Other Artistic Works	
Movies	<u>Gone With the Wind</u>, <u>Star Wars</u>
Television Series	<u>Hill Street Blues</u>
Paintings and Sculptures	<u>Christina's World</u>, <u>The Thinker</u>
Names of Specific Vehicles	
Aircraft	<u>Spirit of St. Louis</u>
Ships	<u>Queen Mary</u>
Trains	<u>Yankee Clipper</u>
Spacecraft	<u>Discovery</u>

▶ **More Practice**

Language Lab CD-ROM
• Quotation Marks and Writing Dialogue lesson
On-line Exercise Bank
• Section 26.4
Grammar Exercise Workbook
• pp. 161–162

☑ **ONGOING ASSESSMENT: Monitor and Reinforce**

If students miss more than two items in Exercises 35–40, refer them to the following for additional practice.

In the Textbook	Print Resources	Technology
Section Review, Ex. 42–43, p. 585	Grammar Exercise Workbook, pp. 157–164, 173–174	Language Lab CD-ROM, Punctuation; On-Line Exercise Bank, Section 26.4

◄ **Critical Viewing**
Write a sentence noting that this picture is described on pages 48–49 in a book entitled *The Historic Hudson.* What words should be underlined in your sentence? [**Identify**]

▶ **Exercise 40** **Underlining Titles and Names** On your paper, write the items that should be underlined, and then underline them.

1. Henry Hudson explored the Hudson River in the Half Moon.
2. In 1976, Viking I landed on Mars.
3. J.R.R Tolkien's novel The Hobbit is a classic.
4. The Venus de Milo is in the Louvre Museum in Paris.
5. Cats was the longest-running play on Broadway.

▶ **KEY CONCEPT** Use quotation marks around titles of short written works and other short artistic works. ■

KINDS OF TITLES THAT ARE ENCLOSED IN QUOTATION MARKS

Written Works	
Stories Chapters Articles	"The Most Dangerous Game" "The First Americans" "Meet a Mystery Writer"
Other Artistic Works	
Episodes	"Foreign Territory" (the second episode of <u>To Serve Them All My Days</u>)
Songs	"Memories"

Answer Key

▶ **Exercise 40**

1. <u>Half Moon</u>
2. <u>Viking I</u>
3. <u>The Hobbit</u>
4. <u>Venus de Milo</u>
5. <u>Cats</u>

Customize for
Gifted/Talented Students

Challenge students to come up with at least one more title of each type listed in the charts on these two pages. Remind them to capitalize titles correctly. Students should write each title on an index card, without quotation marks or underlining. Students can then gather the cards together and play a game. The first player draws a card, identifies the work, and tells whether it should be underlined or enclosed in quotation marks. If the answer is wrong, the next player gets a try at the same card. Players get one point for each correct answer.

Critical Viewing

Identify Make sure that the students underline *The Historic Hudson.*

TIME SAVERS!

Answers on Transparency
Use the Grammar Exercises Answers on Transparencies for Chapter 26 to have students correct their own or one another's exercises.

On-Line Exercise Bank
Have students complete the exercises on computer. The Auto Check feature will grade their work for you!

Critical Viewing

Identify Answers will vary. Make sure that students identify the chapter titles as parts of the book to be enclosed in quotation marks.

Answer Key

▶ **Exercise 41**

1. "America the Beautiful."
2. "To Serve Man"; <u>The Twilight Zone</u>.
3. <u>Misty of Chincoteague</u>
4. <u>Romeo and Juliet</u>
5. "The Open Window,"
6. <u>Revenge of the Pink Panther</u>.
7. <u>Cleveland Plain Dealer</u>; <u>The Miracle Worker</u>?
8. "The Lottery,"
9. "The Road Not Taken,"
10. <u>Nova</u>

26.4

▶ **Exercise 41** Using Underlining and Quotation Marks

Copy each sentence below, adding underlining, quotation marks, and correct punctuation where necessary.

EXAMPLE: In our English class we are reading the novel Call of the Wild.

ANSWER: In our English class, we are reading the novel <u>Call of the Wild</u>.

1. Her favorite patriotic song was Katharine Lee Bates's America the Beautiful.
2. To Serve Man is one of the episodes in the famous series The Twilight Zone.
3. Misty of Chincoteague is Leah's favorite book from her childhood.
4. Carter is reading Romeo and Juliet for the first time this week.
5. I have always remembered the story The Open Window by Saki.
6. My father's favorite movie is Revenge of the Pink Panther.
7. Did you see the review in the Cleveland Plain Dealer of the play The Miracle Worker?
8. Rick just read The Lottery a short story by Shirley Jackson.
9. Chloe's favorite poem is The Road Not Taken by Robert Frost.
10. My grandmother loves the television series Nova on the Public Broadcasting System station.

▶ **More Practice**

Language Lab CD-ROM
• Quotation Marks lesson
On-line Exercise Bank
• Section 26.4
Grammar Exercise Workbook
• pp. 173–174

◀ **Critical Viewing** If you were listing the titles of these medical books, which titles would you underline? For which parts of the books would you need to use quotation marks? **[Identify]**

⏱ TIME SAVERS!

Answers on Transparency Use the Grammar Exercises Answers on Transparencies for Chapter 26 to have students correct their own or one another's exercises.

On-Line Exercise Bank Have students complete the exercises on computer. The Auto Check feature will grade their work for you!

☑ ONGOING ASSESSMENT: Assess Mastery

Use the following resources to assess student mastery of quotation marks.

In the Textbook	Print Resources	Technology
Chapter Review, Ex. 66–67, pp. 596–597 Standardized Test Preparation Workshop, pp. 598–599	*Formal Assessment*, Chapter 26	Language Lab CD-ROM, Punctuation; On-Line Exercise Bank, Section 26.4

Section Review

Section Review

Each of these exercises correlates to a concept in the section on quotation marks and underlining, pages 578–584. The exercises may be used for more practice, for reteaching, or for review of the Key Concepts presented.

GRAMMAR EXERCISES 42–46

▶ **Exercise 42** Supplying Correct Punctuation in Direct Quotations Copy each of the following sentences, inserting the proper quotation marks, commas, and end punctuation. (It may help to read the sentences silently to yourself if you have trouble understanding their meanings.)

1. Go now cried Sheila and get the milk before these baby squirrels starve
2. Don't be so upset, honey, said Sheila's mother You are doing your best
3. Remember the ranger said most wild infants can't live outside their natural habitat said Rick trying to calm Sheila.
4. I once raised a baby jackrabbit Grandma claimed loudly.
5. Then please, Grandma, said Sheila desperately help me do this
6. Grandma said Well, they might be big enough to survive on their own Sheila
7. I know said Sheila but a dog might get them if I leave them under the tree
8. Yes said Grandma gently that might happen But they're big enough to climb a tree
9. It's too risky I can't do that shouted Sheila
10. Mother said calmly All right then, dear. We'll call the veterinarian and ask her what we should feed them.

▶ **Exercise 43** Revising Dialogue for Punctuation and Paragraphing Write the following dialogue on your paper, starting a new paragraph each time a different person speaks. Insert quotation marks, commas, periods, question marks, and exclamation marks where needed. Be sure to capitalize where necessary.

Katie asked what is a lynx and why is Steven so excited about seeing one Roger replied the lynx is a big cat. It's endangered and lives in the forest It stays mostly under ledges said Steven and waits for prey to come by. Then it pounces Kevin read aloud from the encyclopedia: the lynx has big, furry feet that enable it to walk easily in the snow They live in a few states, but only in the extreme northern parts of those states explained Roger. How big are they Katie inquired. Dad says they are about forty inches long when fully grown Kevin replied. The long tufts of fur in their ears are used like antennae to help them hear Kevin continued. bobcats are bigger according to Dad Kevin finished. Where do they live Katie asked Kevin.

▶ **Exercise 44** Find It in Your Reading Look at a dialogue from a short story you have recently read to find examples of a statement, a question, and an exclamation. Notice how the writer uses end punctuation with quotation marks.

▶ **Exercise 45** Find It in Your Writing Look through your portfolio to find a composition that includes at least one direct quotation. Make sure that you used quotation marks correctly with other punctuation marks.

▶ **Exercise 46** Writing Application Write a brief narrative including dialogue in which two people try to identify an animal by its characteristics. You might use one of the photos from this chapter for ideas. Use quotation marks correctly. In your dialogue, mention at least two book or article titles (which you can make up). Proofread to make sure that you have punctuated your narrative correctly.

Answer Key

▶ **Exercise 42**

1. "Go now," cried Sheila, "and get the milk before these baby squirrels starve!"
2. "Don't be so upset, honey," said Sheila's mother. "You are doing your best."
3. "Remember, the ranger said that most wild infants can't live outside their natural habitat," said Rick, trying to calm Sheila.
4. "I once raised a baby jackrabbit," Grandma claimed loudly.
5. "Then please, Grandma," said Sheila desperately, "help me do this."
6. Grandma said, "Well, they might be big enough to survive on their own, Sheila."
7. "I know," said Sheila, "but a dog might get them if I leave them under the tree."
8. "Yes," said Grandma gently, "that might happen. But they're big enough to climb a tree."
9. "It's too risky! I can't do that!" shouted Sheila.
10. Mother said calmly, "All right then, dear. We'll call the veterinarian and ask her what we should feed them."

▶ **Exercise 43**

1. Katy asked, "What is a lynx and why is Steven so excited about seeing one?"
2. Roger replied, "The lynx is a big cat. It's endangered and lives in the forest."
3. "It stays mostly under ledges," said Steven, "and waits for prey to come by. Then it pounces."
4. Kevin read aloud from the encyclopedia: "The lynx has big, furry feet that enable it to walk easily in the snow."
5. "They live in a few states, but only in the extreme northern parts of those states," explained Roger.

continued

Answer Key continued

6. "How big are they?" Katy inquired.
7. "Dad says they are about forty inches long when fully grown," Kevin replied.
8. "The long tufts of fur in their ears are used like antennae to help them hear," Kevin continued.
9. "Bobcats are bigger, according to Dad," Kevin finished.
10. "Where do they live?" Katy asked Kevin.

▶ **Exercise 44**

Find It in Your Reading
Have students bring in examples for class discussion.

▶ **Exercise 45**

Find It in Your Writing
If students can't find a quotation, they can write one to add to the composition.

▶ **Exercise 46**

Writing Application
Students can work with partners to write and read aloud their dialogue.

Write the following paragraph on the chalkboard. Ask students to add six hyphens and four apostrophes.

At Marigolds family reunion, there were forty three people, including her sister in law, her great grandfather, her ex husbands brother, and the twins brand new puppy, which kept trying to eat everyones food.

(Marigold's, forty-three, sister-in-law, great-grandfather, ex-husband's, twins' brand-new, everyone's)

Activate Prior Knowledge

Ask students to explain why they inserted apostrophes and hyphens in the Interest Grabber.

Step-by-Step Teaching Guide

Hyphens

1. The basic purpose of a hyphen is to link two words together. Words joined by hyphens generally count as one part of speech.

   The three-year-old children got tired easily.

   The bright-eyed squirrel winked at me.

   My brother-in-law called last night.

   Three-year-old is an adjective modifying *children*. *Bright-eyed* is an adjective modifying *squirrel*. *Brother-in-law* is a noun.

2. Hyphens clarify meaning. Have students compare the *three-year-old children* with the *three year-old children*.

Language Highlight

From Hyphen to Compound Many English words that began as hyphenated words are now written as one word. *Baseball* is an example. When the game was introduced after the Civil War, it was spelled *base-ball*. When the game became so popular and the word was used so often, the hyphen was eventually dropped. The more common a hyphenated term becomes, the more likely it is that it will lose its hyphen eventually.

Section 26.5
Hyphens and Apostrophes

Hyphens have many uses with numbers and words.

Using Hyphens in Numbers

▶ **KEY CONCEPT** Use a hyphen when you write two-word numbers from *twenty-one* through *ninety-nine*. ■

EXAMPLES: seventy-eight thirty-five forty-six

▶ **KEY CONCEPT** Use a hyphen when you use a fraction as an adjective but not when you use a fraction as a noun. ■

EXAMPLES: This glass is two-thirds full. (adjective)
Two thirds of the members were present. (noun)

Using Hyphens in Words

Hyphens are also used to separate certain words from the prefixes and suffixes attached to them.

▶ **KEY CONCEPT** Use a hyphen after a prefix followed by a proper noun or a proper adjective. ■

EXAMPLES: pre-Columbian pro-British mid-August

▶ **KEY CONCEPT** Use a hyphen in words with the prefixes *all-*, *ex-*, and *self-* and the suffix *-elect*. ■

EXAMPLES: all-American   ex-president
self-conscious   mayor-elect

▶ **KEY CONCEPT** Use a hyphen when you write certain compound nouns. ■

Compound nouns are written in three different ways: as single words, as separate words, or as hyphenated words. When in doubt, check a dictionary.

SINGLE WORDS:	flashlight	passageway
SEPARATE WORDS:	rocking chair	time clock
HYPHENATED WORDS:	ten-year-old	mother-in-law

Theme: Forest Life

In this section, you will learn when to use hyphens and apostrophes in your writing. The examples and exercises focus on forest animals and plants.

Cross-Curricular Connection: Science

⏱ TIME AND RESOURCE MANAGER

Resources
Print: Grammar Exercises Workbook, pp. 163–172; Grammar Exercises Answers on Transparencies, Chapter 26
Technology: Language Lab CD-ROM, Punctuation; On-Line Exercise Bank, Section 26.5

In-Depth Coverage	Accelerated Pace
• Work through all key concepts, pp. 586–594. • Assign and review exercises 47–55. • Read and discuss Grammar in Literature, p. 592.	• Assign pp. 586–594 for independent student review. • Assign Section Review Exercises 56–59, p. 595.

> **Exercise 47** Using Hyphens in Numbers and Words
Rewrite each of the sentences below, adding hyphens where necessary. If no hyphens are needed, write *correct*.

EXAMPLE: We plan to arrive at the Big Thicket forest in the pre dawn hours.

ANSWER: We plan to arrive at the Big Thicket forest in the pre-dawn hours.

1. Mid January is not the most interesting time to visit the Big Thicket forest in southeastern Texas.
2. Once teeming with a wide variety of plants and animals, the Big Thicket had a pre twentieth century total area of 3,500,000 acres.
3. Hurricanes, fires, and natural plagues have contributed to a ninety percent reduction of the forest.
4. Careful preservation and a current pro forest attitude now protect the thicket's remaining 84,550 acres.
5. Once the most lush forest north of Central America, the thicket takes on a mystical appearance as mist rises from the ground following a midafternoon rain shower.

> **Exercise 48** Proofreading a Passage for Hyphens Rewrite the paragraphs below, adding hyphens as needed.

The Big Thicket forest of southeast Texas was partly consumed by post World War II development. Even prior to that, during fifty four years from 1876 to 1930, railroads began to crisscross the thicket. The area was the site of a post Depression oil boom. Proud of their state's beauty, most inhabitants would think it un Texan to act in a way that threatens their environment.

As a nine year old, Gwen used to go with her father on photography expeditions to the thicket. The pine trees, dense undergrowth, and faint stirring of unseen creatures intrigued the youngster. Many times, especially at the height of spring in mid May, she would stand quietly and absorb the stillness of the deep forest. She never felt self conscious about her all consuming interest in the forest.

The jaguar, mountain lion, and red wolf are gone, but twenty four different mammals still live in the Big Thicket. One hundred different types of soil lie under the deep carpet of pine needles. Far from being a wasteland, the Big Thicket today has seventy nine types of reptiles and amphibians.

More Practice
Language Lab CD-ROM
• Apostrophes and Hyphens lesson
On-line Exercise Bank
• Section 26.5
Grammar Exercise Workbook
• pp. 163–164

▼ **Critical Viewing** In the middle of which month do you think this photo was taken? Write your answer in a sentence that includes the prefix *mid* and a hyphen. [**Make a Judgment**]

Hyphens and Apostrophes • 587

Exercise 47
1. Mid-January is not the most interesting time to visit the Big Thicket forest in southeastern Texas.
2. Once teeming with a wide variety of plants and animals, the Big Thicket had a pre-twentieth-century total area of 3,500,000 acres.
3. correct
4. Careful preservation and a current pro-forest attitude now protect the thicket's remaining 84,550 acres.
5. correct

Exercise 48
1. The Big Thicket forest of southeast Texas was partly consumed by post-World War II development.
2. Even prior to that, during fifty-four years, from 1876 to 1930, railroads began to crisscross the thicket.
3. The area was the site of a post-Depression oil boom.
4. Proud of their state's beauty, most inhabitants would think it un-Texan to act in a way that threatens their environment.
5. As a nine-year-old, Gwen used to go with her father on photography expeditions to the thicket.
6. correct
7. Many times, especially at the height of spring in mid-May, she would stand quietly and absorb the stillness of the deep forest.
8. She never felt self-conscious about her all-consuming interest in the forest.
9. The jaguar, mountain lion, and red wolf are gone, but twenty-four different mammals still live in the Big Thicket.
10. correct
11. Far from being a wasteland, the Big Thicket today has seventy-nine types of reptiles and amphibians.

Critical Viewing

Make a Judgement Students may suggest that the picture was taken in mid-January.

☑ **ONGOING ASSESSMENT: Prerequisite Skills**

If students have difficulty with hyphenation, you may find it necessary to review the following to assure coverage of prerequisite knowledge.

In the Textbook	Print Resources	Technology
Adjectives, Proper Adjectives, pp. 330–339	Grammar Exercise Workbook, pp. 21–22, 25–26	Language Lab CD-ROM, Using Modifiers; On-Line Exercise Bank, Section 16.1

Hyphens at the Ends of Lines

1. Students cannot rely on pronunciation to determine syllables in a word. Is *flower* syllabicated *flow-er* or *flo-wer*? The answer is *flow-er*, but the only way to know is to use the dictionary.

2. As a rule of thumb, words break between consonants: *stan-dard*. But this rule has many exceptions, such as *stand-ing*.

Critical Viewing

Identify Students should say *or-chid*, *blos-som*, and *flow-er*.

Answer Key

▶ **Exercise 49** *(page 589)*

1. mag-nol-ia
2. oc-e-lot
3. her-ba-ceous
4. lily
5. snake
6. white-breasted nut-hatch
7. Antarctica
8. acorn
9. Mexican
10. hur-ri-cane

26.5

Using Hyphens at the Ends of Lines

When you cannot avoid dividing a word at the end of a line, the following is the chief rule to follow:

▶ **KEY CONCEPT** Divide a word only between syllables. ∎

EXAMPLE:　　Marcia seems to have taken my advice most seri- ously.

Check in a dictionary if you are unsure how a word is divided into syllables. Looking up the word *seriously*, for example, you would find that its syllables are *se-ri-ous-ly*.

The following chart presents four other rules for dividing words.

FOUR OTHER RULES FOR WORD DIVISION
1. Never divide a one-syllable word.
2. Never divide a word so that one letter stands alone at the end of a line or at the beginning of the next.
3. Never divide proper nouns or proper adjectives.
4. Divide a hyphenated word only after the hyphen.

If the rules make it impossible for you to fit a word at the end of a line, simply move the word down to the next line.

The following examples illustrate the rules in the chart.

INCORRECT:　Karen wanted to take home an orchid fr- om the forest.

CORRECT:　　Karen wanted to take home an orchid from the forest.

INCORRECT:　Rusty has many photographs of a- zaleas in bloom.

CORRECT:　　Rusty has many photographs of aza- leas in bloom.

INCORRECT:　The man scared the bear away on Wed- nesday.

CORRECT:　　The man scared the bear away on Wednesday.

INCORRECT:　Students today are taking an ever-in- creasing interest in the environment.

CORRECT:　　Students today are taking an ever- increasing interest in the environment.

588 • Punctuation

▲ **Critical Viewing** Where should you divide *orchid*, *blossom*, or *flower* if the word does not fit completely at the end of a line in your writing? **[Identify]**

💡 **Spelling Tip**

In words of two or more syllables that contain double consonants, you can usually place a hyphen between those consonants. Always check in a dictionary if you are unsure. Examples: *col-lar*, *mil-len-nium*, and *begin-ning*.

⏱ **TIME SAVERS!**

🖥 **Answers on Transparency** Use the Grammar Exercises Answers on Transparencies for Chapter 26 to have students correct their own or one another's exercises.

💻 **On-Line Exercise Bank** Have students complete the exercises on computer. The Auto Check feature will grade their work for you!

☑ **ONGOING ASSESSMENT: Monitor and Reinforce**

If students miss more than two items in Exercises 47–49, refer them to the following for additional practice.

In the Textbook	Print Resources	Technology
Section Review, Ex. 56–57, p. 595	Grammar Exercise Workbook, pp. 163–166	Language Lab CD-ROM, Punctuation; On-Line Exercise Bank, Section 26.5

Exercise 49 Using Hyphens to Divide Words Hyphenate each word listed below as though it appeared at the end of a line. If a word should not be broken, simply rewrite the word. If you are not sure how to divide a word, look up the word in a dictionary.

1. magnolia
2. ocelot
3. herbaceous
4. lily
5. snake
6. white-breasted nuthatch
7. Antarctica
8. acorn
9. Mexican
10. hurricane

Using Apostrophes to Show Ownership

An apostrophe is used with singular or plural nouns to show ownership or possession.

KEY CONCEPT To form the possessive of a singular noun, add an apostrophe and an *s*. ■

EXAMPLES: the doctor's advice   Nat's decision

Some singular nouns already end in *s*. With a few exceptions, add an apostrophe and an *s*.

KEY CONCEPT To form the possessive of a singular noun that ends in *s*, add an apostrophe and an *s*. ■

EXAMPLES: James's jacket   his boss's idea

The exceptions are names from classical literature or ancient times. For example, *Ulysses'* and *Moses'*.
Most plural nouns already end in *s*. Form the possessive of these nouns by simply adding an apostrophe.

KEY CONCEPT To form the possessive of plural nouns that end in *s*, add an apostrophe. ■

EXAMPLES: the officers' club   the witnesses' testimonies

Some plural nouns do not end in *s*. Form the possessive in the same way as for singular nouns.

KEY CONCEPT To form the possessive of a plural noun that does not end in *s*, add an apostrophe and an *s*. ■

EXAMPLES: the men's store   the women's committee

More Practice

Language Lab
CD-ROM
• Apostrophes and
  Hyphens lesson
On-line
Exercise Bank
• Section 26.5
Grammar Exercise
Workbook
• pp. 165–166

Step-by-Step Teaching Guide

Apostrophes Used to Show Ownership

1. Apostrophes are never used to indicate plurals. If a noun is plural without being possessive, it requires no apostrophe.

   Incorrect The Garcia's moved in.

   Correct The Garcias moved in.

2. Singular nouns get *'s* to form the possessive, even if the noun already ends in *s* or *ss*. The exception is names from ancient times (*Ulysses* in the text): These words get an apostrophe only.

3. All plural nouns that end in *-s* get only an apostrophe to show possession.

4. Mistakes frequently arise with the plural possessive of proper names that end in *s*. Use these examples and any students' last names that end in *s* (the more examples the better).

Singular	Plural	Plural Possessive
Wiliams	Williamses	Williamses'
Jones	Joneses	Joneses'
Hopkins	Hopkinses	Hopkinses'
Burns	Burnses	Burnses'

Customize for
ESL Students

Spanish-speaking students may have difficulty with apostrophes to show possession, because the rules in Spanish are different. In Spanish, one says "the dog of Juan," not "Juan's dog." Give students extra practice. For instance, you might have students give the possessive forms of each of the nouns in Exercise 49 at the top of the page. Work with students if they still need help.

Integrating Vocabulary Skills

Derivations The whippoorwill got its name from its call, which sounds like, "Whip poor Will!"

Answer Key

▶ **Exercise 50**

1. whippoorwill's
2. car's
3. Tess's
4. wolves'
5. campers' or camper's

▶ **Exercise 51**

1. deer's
2. kingsnakes'
3. correct
4. treehopper's
5. flies'
6. correct
7. maple's
8. girls'
9. class's
10. bees'

Critical Viewing

Describe Students may say that the deer's antlers have many points.

26.5

▶ **Exercise 50** Using Apostrophes to Show Ownership

Write the possessive form of each underlined noun below.

EXAMPLE: The judge remarks were lengthy.
ANSWER: judge's

1. The whippoorwills cry was lovely.
2. The prairie warbler flew very close to the car windshield.
3. Tess idea for planting baby oak trees was popular.
4. At the bridge, the wolves trail seemed to fade.
5. The campers plan was to be quiet and not disturb the deer.

▶ **Exercise 51** Proofreading for Apostrophes That Show Ownership Rewrite the sentences below, adding or correcting apostrophes to show ownership. If a sentence is correct, write *correct*.

1. No one wanted to disturb the white-tailed deer serene stroll.
2. Certainly, no one thought of disturbing those kingsnakes's nests intentionally.
3. When Rose found several daddy-longlegs' webs, she was fascinated.
4. A buffalo treehoppers' eggs take all winter to hatch.
5. The deer flies goal was to bite all the deer they could in one day.
6. There was trash at the base of the sycamore's trunk.
7. A sugar maples' leaves turn deep red or orange in the fall.
8. The girls club decided to spend the night in the cabin at the edge of the pine barrens.
9. A great place for a biology class' field trip is a swamp.
10. All of the bee's nests are filled with honey.

▶ **More Practice**

Language Lab
CD-ROM
• Apostrophes and Hyphens lesson
On-line
Exercise Bank
• Section 26.5
Grammar Exercise Workbook
• pp. 167–168

◀ Critical Viewing
Write a sentence describing the antlers of this white-tailed deer, using an apostrophe to show ownership. [Describe]

Using Apostrophes in Contractions

A *contraction* is a word, or a combination of two separate words, written in a contracted (shortened) form.

KEY CONCEPT Use an apostrophe in a contraction to show where one or more letters have been omitted. ■

Contractions are used in informal speech and writing. You can often find contractions in the dialogue of stories and plays. Contractions create the feeling of real-life speech.

EXAMPLES: "I'll bring in all the packages."
              "Fine. I'd help, but I'm late already."
              "Wait 'til you see this!"

The following chart lists commonly used contractions.

COMMONLY USED CONTRACTIONS	
aren't (are not)	couldn't (could not)
isn't (is not)	didn't (did not)
wasn't (was not)	don't (do not)
weren't (were not)	doesn't (does not)
hasn't (has not)	shouldn't (should not)
haven't (have not)	won't (will not)
hadn't (had not)	wouldn't (would not)
can't (cannot)	
I'll (I will)	she'll (she will)
you'll (you will)	we'll (we will)
he'll (he will)	they'll (they will)
I'm (I am)	we're (we are)
you're (you are)	they're (they are)
he's (he is)	who's (who is)
she's (she is)	where's (where is)
it's (it is)	Patty's (Patty is)

Exercise 52 Using Apostrophes in Contractions Write the contractions that can be used in place of the underlined words in the sentences below.

1. The table mountain pine <u>does not</u> grow in New Mexico.
2. The red wolf <u>has not</u> ever returned to the Big Thicket.
3. The raccoon <u>will not</u> grow big ears.
4. Wolverines <u>are not</u> very big, but they can scare bears away from their meals.
5. An ermine is similar to a weasel, but <u>it is</u> smaller.

Step-by-Step Teaching Guide

Apostrophes in Contractions

1. *Contract* means "to shrink" or "to grow smaller." A contraction is a shortened form of two words.
2. Although more than one letter may be dropped to create a contraction, only one apostrophe is ever used: *cannot/can't*.

Answer Key

▶ **Exercise 52**

1. doesn't
2. hasn't
3. won't
4. aren't
5. it's

⏱ **TIME SAVERS!**

 **Answers on Transparency** Use the Grammar Exercises Answers on Transparencies for Chapter 26 to have students correct their own or one another's exercises.

🖥 **On-Line Exercise Bank** Have students complete the exercises on computer. The Auto Check feature will grade their work for you!

Step-by-Step Teaching Guide

Grammar in Literature

Read aloud the excerpt from "The Spring and the Fall." Have students listen to the rhythm of the lines. Then reread it, this time substituting *There is* and *that is* for the contractions in the third line. Ask students to discuss the difference and why the poet might have used contractions. (for the sake of the rhythm; for the sound of the words)

More About the Writer

When she was 20, Edna St. Vincent Millay published "Renascence," a poem about a heroic first-person narrator in the rugged outdoors. The poem was signed "E. St. Vincent Millay." Millay was amused when readers assumed the poet was a man! She sent two of her readers a photograph of herself, signed "The brawny male sends his picture."

Answer Key

Exercise 53

1. don't, winter's
2. wouldn't
3. It's, they'll
4. They've
5. aren't, trappers'
6. shouldn't, people's
7. it'll, it's
8. they'll, enemy's
9. They're, America's
10. wouldn't

GRAMMAR IN LITERATURE

from **The Spring and the Fall**

Edna St. Vincent Millay

The contractions the poet has used are highlighted in blue italics. They give the poem a conversational tone.

> Year be springing or year be falling,
> The bark will drip and the birds be calling.
> *There's* much *that's* fine to see and hear
> In the spring of a year, in the fall of a year.

▶ **Exercise 53** Using Apostrophes in Contractions and Possessives Rewrite the sentences below on your paper, adding needed apostrophes.

EXAMPLE: I wasnt listening and didnt hear Helens question.

ANSWER: I wasn't listening and didn't hear Helen's question.

1. Beavers dont hibernate to avoid the winters cold.
2. They wouldnt hesitate to work during the day, but they are mostly nocturnal.
3. Its known that theyll build a burrow along riverbanks.
4. Theyve usually built dams, with lodges, in streams, ponds, and lakes.
5. Beavers arent in danger of extinction because of trappers activities.
6. However, many people think beaver skins shouldnt be used for peoples coats.
7. If an opossum is frightened, itll sometimes pretend that its dead.
8. More often, theyll hiss and show their teeth to ward off an enemys attack.
9. Theyre North Americas only marsupial.
10. A marsupial wouldnt keep its infants anywhere but in its fur-lined stomach pouch.

▶ **More Practice**

Language Lab CD-ROM
• Apostrophes and Hyphens lesson
On-line Exercise Bank
• Section 26.5
Grammar Exercise Workbook
• pp. 169–170

🕐 **TIME SAVERS!**

🎨 **Answers on Transparency** Use the Grammar Exercises Answers on Transparencies for Chapter 26 to have students correct their own or one another's exercises.

💻 **On-Line Exercise Bank** Have students complete the exercises on computer. The Auto Check feature will grade their work for you!

Avoiding Problems With Apostrophes

Even good writers must sometimes pause to figure out whether to write *its* or *it's*, *theirs* or *there's*, *whose* or *who's*, or *your* or *you're*. It is helpful to remember the following guideline: *It's, there's, who's,* and *you're* are contractions for *it is, there is, who is,* and *you are.*

EXAMPLES: It's now seven o'clock. (*It is* now seven o'clock.)

There's Fred. (*There is* Fred.)

Who's bringing the food? (*Who is* bringing the food?)

You're a good sport. (*You are* a good sport.)

Its, theirs, whose, and *your* (all without apostrophes) are possessive forms of *it, they, who,* and *you.*

EXAMPLES: Uncle Bert's old car stalled when its engine overheated.

Is it our turn or theirs?

Whose dog is that?

Your friend Tom just phoned.

KEY CONCEPT Do not use an apostrophe with any possessive personal pronouns. ■

Notice in the chart below that no apostrophes are used with *your, hers, its, ours,* and *theirs.*

POSSESSIVE PERSONAL PRONOUNS					
my	your	his	hers	our	their
mine	yours	her	its	ours	theirs

▲ Critical Viewing
What do you see in this picture? Start your answer with a contraction for *it is* and include a possessive form of *it* later in the sentence. **[Identify]**

Step-by-Step Teaching Guide

Avoiding Problems With Apostrophes

Have students try this trick when they have finished writing anything that includes a number of contractions. Go back over the text, substituting the full phrase for each contraction (such as *he will* for *he'll*). Students should then look at the contraction and decide whether they used the right one.

Critical Viewing

Identify Answers will vary. Students may suggest: It's a beaver at its dam.

STANDARDIZED TEST PREPARATION WORKSHOP

Standardized tests often ask students to choose which sentences contains a particular grammatical error. Ask students which sentence below contains an incorrect use of an apostrophe.

A The bears' lived in a cave deep in the woods.

B The bears' cave was their winter home.

C They curled up together in the cave's shelter and slept through the winter.

D The same cave might make a perfect wolves' den.

Item **A** is incorrect. The word *bears* is a plural, not a possessive. It should have no apostrophe.

Exercise 54

1. The southern flying squirrel is the smallest squirrel; it's only ten inches long.
2. They have loose folds of skin between their front and hind legs.
3. Bob said, "Is that cat yours? It might try to catch the squirrels when they fly by!"
4. Ann answered, "It's ours, and squirrels don't really fly!"
5. "True," said Bob, "a flying squirrel will leap with its legs outstretched and glide up to eighty yards."

Exercise 55

1. Whose carrots are these?
2. Ann said that the carrots are hers.
3. Ann brought carrots to tempt the snowshoe hares out of their warrens.
4. correct
5. Because snowshoe hares have big, furry feet, you'll always know which footprints are theirs.
6. Gary said there's no way to follow the hare unless you're able to see the tracks.
7. correct
8. It's hard to see the hares against the snow because in winter they're white.
9. correct
10. If you don't have a camera, you can borrow ours.

Critical Viewing

Describe Answers will vary. Students may say there's a raccoon. Its body is positioned on a dead log.

⏱ TIME SAVERS!

Answers on Transparency
Use the Grammar Exercises Answers on Transparencies for Chapter 26 to have students correct their own or one another's exercises.

On-Line Exercise Bank
Have students complete the exercises on computer. The Auto Check feature will grade their work for you!

594

26.5

▶ **Exercise 54** Avoiding Problems With Apostrophes
Rewrite each sentence below, using the correct word in parentheses.

EXAMPLE: May I borrow (you're, your) pencil?
ANSWER: May I borrow your pencil?

1. The southern flying squirrel is the smallest squirrel; (it's, its) only ten inches long.
2. They have loose folds of skin between (they're, their) front and hind legs.
3. Bob said, "Is that cat (yours, your's)? It might try to catch the squirrels when they fly by!"
4. Ann answered, "It's (ours, our's), and squirrels don't really fly!"
5. "True," said Bob, "a flying squirrel will leap with (its, it's) legs outstretched and glide up to eighty yards."

▶ **Exercise 55** Proofreading for Apostrophes Rewrite the sentences below to correct problems with the use of apostrophes. If a sentence contains no errors, write *correct*.

1. Who's carrots are these?
2. Ann said that the carrots are her's.
3. Ann brought carrots to tempt the snowshoe hares out of they're warrens.
4. She tracked the hare by following its footprints in the snow.
5. Because snowshoe hares have big, furry feet, you'll always know which footprints are there's.
6. Gary said there's no way to follow the hare unless your able to see the tracks.
7. He said that sometimes the sound and vibration of your footsteps scare them away.
8. Its hard to see the hares against the snow because in winter their white.
9. Ann asked, "Who's going to go with me to photograph the baby rabbits in their warren?"
10. If you dont have a camera, you can borrow our's.

▶ Critical Viewing Write a question and answer about this raccoon, including a contraction and a possessive personal pronoun in each sentence. [Describe]

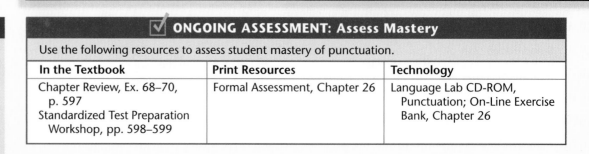

594 • Punctuation

More Practice

Language Lab CD-ROM
• Apostrophes and Hyphens lesson
On-line Exercise Bank
• Section 26.5
Grammar Exercise Workbook
• pp. 171–172

☑ ONGOING ASSESSMENT: Assess Mastery

Use the following resources to assess student mastery of punctuation.

In the Textbook	Print Resources	Technology
Chapter Review, Ex. 68–70, p. 597 Standardized Test Preparation Workshop, pp. 598–599	Formal Assessment, Chapter 26	Language Lab CD-ROM, Punctuation; On-Line Exercise Bank, Chapter 26

Section 26.5 *Section Review*

GRAMMAR EXERCISES 56–62

> **Exercise 56** Using Hyphens in Words at the End of a Line Insert hyphens in the proper places to divide the words below. If a word cannot be divided, write the word.

1. knowledge
2. raft
3. closure
4. instinct
5. winner
6. robust
7. extremity
8. overture
9. parliamentarian
10. quote

> **Exercise 57** Using Hyphens in Words in Sentences Read each sentence below to find a word that needs a hyphen. On your paper, write that word with a hyphen. If no word in a sentence needs a hyphen, write *correct*.

1. The salt in desert spring water is often eighty eight parts per thousand, more than twice as salty as sea water.
2. In North America, there are thirty one endangered species of fish.
3. Twenty three of the endangered species of fish are found in the south-western American deserts.
4. One threat to the endangered fish has been the appearance of nonnative fish in their habitat.
5. The food supply in the delicate desert springs is threatened by these uninvited guests.

> **Exercise 58** Using Apostrophes to Show Ownership Write the possessive form of the underlined singular and plural nouns below, placing the apostrophe correctly.

1. There were no signs we were near the mother <u>bear</u> den.
2. My sister wanted to whisper in the stuffed <u>chipmunk</u> ear.

3. The <u>leaves</u> edges were sharp and scratched our hands.
4. I was wary of the <u>skunk</u> behavior as it rushed toward me.
5. Some kind of sap had fallen on the <u>foxes</u> tails.

> **Exercise 59** Using Apostrophes in Contractions On your paper, write the contractions for the following words. Be sure to place the apostrophe correctly.

1. is not
2. did not
3. they are
4. have not
5. we are
6. do not
7. where is
8. should not
9. I will
10. it is

> **Exercise 60** Find It in Your Reading Look at an article in a news-magazine. Make a list of words that break at the ends of lines, and show where they have been broken.

> **Exercise 61** Find It in Your Writing Look through your portfolio to find a composition that includes possessive nouns and pronouns. Make sure that you used apostrophes correctly.

> **Exercise 62** Writing Application Write a narrative about a walk in the woods. Include a hyphenated word and number in your narration, as well as several possessive nouns and pronouns. Proofread carefully to make sure that you have used hyphens and apostrophes correctly.

Section Review • **595**

Answer Key continued

> **Exercise 62**

Writing Application
Students can rewrite the sentences without hyphens and apostrophes and trade with a partner to correct.

ASSESS and CLOSE

Section Review

Each of these exercises correlates to a concept in the section on hyphens and apostrophes, pages 586–594. The exercises may be used for more practice, for reteaching, or for review of the key concepts presented. Answers for all chapter exercises are available in *Grammar Exercises Answers on Transparencies* in your Teaching Resources.

Answer Key

> **Exercise 56**

1. knowl-edge
2. raft
3. clo-sure
4. in-stinct
5. win-ner
6. ro-bust
7. ex-trem-i-ty
8. over-ture
9. par-lia-men-tar-i-an
10. quote

> **Exercise 57**

1. eighty-eight
2. thirty-one
3. Twenty-three
4. non-native
5. correct

> **Exercise 58**

1. bear's
2. chipmunk's
3. leaves'
4. skunk's
5. foxes'

> **Exercise 59**

1. isn't
2. didn't
3. they're
4. haven't
5. we're
6. don't
7. where's
8. shouldn't
9. I'll
10. it's

> **Exercise 60**

Find It in Your Reading
Have students bring in examples for class discussion.

> **Exercise 61**

Find It in Your Writing
Challenge students to write the plural possessive of any singular possessives they find.

continued

Answer Key

▶ **Exercise 63**

1. Deserts can have mountains with snow on them.
2. Most of the animals in the desert survive without much water. How?
3. Wow! Don't ask me to go to a desert town called Death Valley.
4. Martin asked if we had ever heard of it.
5. Is Death Valley the lowest point below sea level in the United States?

▶ **Exercise 64**

1. My favorite gorilla, which is named Koko, knows human sign language.
2. Koko never stops talking, nor is talking her only form of communication.
3. Koko, who has never lived in the wild, has a daily life a lot like ours.
4. The fully mature gorilla has used painting to express herself for years, and she always captures the image of the items she's painting.
5. There are other gorillas who use sign language living with Koko, so she is not lonely for animal companionship.
6. Jenny, who had never seen a gorilla, had a stuffed toy chimpanzee at home.
7. correct
8. Gorillas, it is known, are quite intelligent.
9. Strict laws, armed guards, and ground patrols keep endangered species safe.
10. A secure habitat, regular observation, and emergency food can keep endangered species surviving in the wild.
11. Jane Goodall, Dian Fossey, and Joy Adamson all added to the study of wild animals by living with their subjects.
12. Yes, if you corner a wild animal it will bite you.
13. In the summer of 1960, Jane Goodall went to Tanzania, East Africa.
14. The population of Tanzania is 31,270,820.
15. Jane Goodall was born at 22 Grosvenor Square, London, England in 1934.

GRAMMAR EXERCISES 63–71

▶ **Exercise 63**   Using End Marks

Copy each sentence below, adding end marks where necessary.

1. Deserts can have mountains with snow on them
2. Most of the animals in the desert survive without much water How
3. Wow Don't ask me to go to a desert town called Death Valley
4. Martin asked if we had ever heard of it
5. Is Death Valley the lowest point below sea level in the United States

▶ **Exercise 64**   Using Commas

Rewrite the sentences below, adding commas where necessary.

1. My favorite gorilla which is named Koko knows human sign language.
2. Koko never stops talking nor is talking her only form of communication.
3. Koko who has never lived in the wild has a daily life a lot like ours.
4. The fully mature gorilla has used painting to express herself for years and she always captures the image of the items she's painting.
5. There are other gorillas who use sign language living with Koko so she is not lonely for animal companionship.
6. Jenny who had never seen a gorilla had a stuffed toy chimpanzee at home.
7. I worried that the apes that were in the zoo were too crowded.
8. Gorillas it is known are quite intelligent.
9. Strict laws armed guards and ground patrols keep endangered species safe.
10. A secure habitat regular observation and emergency food can keep endangered species surviving in the wild.
11. Jane Goodall Dian Fossey and Joy Adamson all added to the study of wild animals by living with their subjects.

12. Yes if you corner a wild animal it will bite you.
13. In the summer of 1960 Jane Goodall went to Tanzania East Africa.
14. The population of Tanzania is 31270820.
15. Jane Goodall was born at 22 Grosvenor Square London England in 1934.

▶ **Exercise 65**   Using Semicolons and Colons   Rewrite each sentence below, adding semicolons and colons where necessary.

1. Some cheeses are made from cow's milk others are made from goat's milk.
2. Mary chose three poets to study Dickinson, Frost, and Sandburg.
3. The trees bear leaves and fruit the leaves and fruit fall on the ground.
4. I saw a sign that said "Caution Guard Dogs on Duty."
5. This glass lens is concave the other is convex.
6. Grate a small amount of cheese over the spaghetti don't smother it.
7. Forest creatures eat the fruit and leaves they eventually die and their bodies feed the fungi.
8. The whistle blew three minutes early it was only 557 P.M.
9. The letter began "Gentlemen I am writing to inform you that your lease has expired."
10. The train leaves at 900 A.M.

▶ **Exercise 66**   Revising Punctuation and Paragraphing in a Dialogue

Rewrite the following paragraph as a dialogue, adding quotation marks and other punctuation marks where necessary. Make sure that you start a new paragraph for each new speaker.

▶ **Exercise 65**

1. Some cheeses are made from cow's milk; others are made from goat's milk.
2. Mary chose three poets to study: Dickinson, Frost, and Sandburg.
3. The trees bear leaves and fruit; the leaves and fruit fall on the ground.
4. I saw a sign that said "Caution: Guard Dogs On Duty."
5. This glass lens is concave; the other is convex.
6. Grate a small amount of cheese over the spaghetti; don't smother it.
7. Forest creatures eat the fruit and leaves; they eventually die and their bodies feed the fungi.

8. The whistle blew three minutes early; it was only 5:57 P.M.
9. The letter began "Gentlemen: I am writing to inform you that your lease has expired."
10. The train leaves at 9:00 A.M.

▶ **Exercise 66**

The river guide said, "Don't put your hands in the water; the fish bite."

"Is the weather always this hot?" Peter asked. "Or did we just get lucky?"

"The Amazon rain forest temperature is fairly constant," said Dr. Franklin.

continued

The river guide said Don't put your hands in the water the fish bite Is the weather always this hot Peter asked Or did we just get lucky The Amazon rain forest temperature is fairly constant said Dr. Franklin I think said Robert that the canopy of trees over the river here is very beautiful The guide was looking ahead down the river There are lots of snakes out today he said because of the rain last night

Exercise 67 Supplying Quotation Marks and Underlining
Write the titles in the sentences below, adding quotation marks or underlining as needed.

1. We read A Separate Peace by John Knowles in class last semester.
2. At age seven, Rita performed The Star Spangled Banner at a baseball game, and her mother cried.
3. My grandmother loves to watch the movie Casablanca, but we're tired of seeing it.
4. The Lady or the Tiger is one of my favorite stories.
5. Some people think that reading The Power of Positive Thinking can change their lives.

Exercise 68 Using Hyphens and Apostrophes in Sentences
Copy the following sentences, inserting the hyphens and apostrophes where needed.

1. Our ex chairmans daughter studies the biology of the worlds deserts.
2. Often, well receive emails about her midweek observations on a project.
3. Her fathers proud of her self reliance, as shes frequently alone in the desert.
4. When she returns from the desert, theres always a post expedition party.
5. Its interesting to know someone whose all encompassing goal is to assure the deserts survival, in spite of civilizations missteps.

Exercise 69 Supplying Punctuation Marks in Sentences
Copy each sentence below, punctuating as needed.

1. Mother thought the sand dunes were near Yuma Arizona
2. Jason asked Do you know what makes a Mexican jumping bean jump
3. Scorpions arent out much during the day but youd better watch out at night
4. Some books we have about nature include The Earth and Explore Nature
5. With the proper effort said Kitty many endangered species wont have to die

Exercise 70 Proofreading Sentences for Punctuation
Proofread the following sentences to correct any punctuation errors. If a sentence is correct, write *correct*.

1. The baboon called the mandrill has I think a very attractive face?
2. Dear Mr Sartain Well plant the flower seeds the tomato seeds and the bean seeds that you sent us last week!
3. Our ex landlords ranch has 1000 sq miles of desert it must have cactus
4. There are many ducks in our marsh grebes wood ducks and mallards?
5. The Calypso still sails the world, yet its captain, Jacques Cousteau, isn't alive.
6. Dont you wish youd lived in the 1,800's.
7. Dear John the letter began and we knew that shed gone
8. Look George theres a bat in your den?
9. The Broadway Limited leaves Chicago at 900 P.M.
10. Sam my younger brother enjoys skateboarding hockey and baseball!

Exercise 71 Writing Application
Write a brief letter to the tourist bureau of a country you would like to visit. (You may invent names and addresses.) Use each of the punctuation marks you have studied.

Answer Key continued

"I think," said Robert, "that the canopy of trees over the river here is very beautiful."
The guide was looking ahead down the river. "There are lots of snakes out today," he said, "because of the rain last night."

Exercise 67
1. We read A Separate Peace by John Knowles in class last semester.
2. At age seven, Rita performed "The Star Spangled Banner" at a baseball game, and her mother cried.
3. My grandmother loves to watch the movie Casablanca, but we're tired of seeing it.
4. "The Lady or the Tiger" is one of my favorite stories.
5. Some people think that reading The Power of Positive Thinking can change their lives.

Exercise 68
1. Our ex-chairman's daughter studies the biology of the world's deserts.
2. Often, we'll receive e-mails about her mid-week observations on a project.
3. Her father's proud of her self-reliance, as she's frequently alone in the desert.
4. When she returns from the desert, there's always a post-expedition party.
5. It's interesting to know someone whose all-encompassing goal is to assure the desert's survival, in spite of civilization's missteps.

Exercise 69
1. Mother thought the sand dunes were near Yuma, Arizona.
2. Jason asked, "Do you know what makes a Mexican jumping bean jump?"
3. Scorpions aren't out much during the day, but you'd better watch out at night!
4. Some books we have about nature include The Earth and Explore Nature.
5. "With the proper effort," said Kitty, "many endangered species won't have to die."

continued

Answer Key continued

Exercise 70
1. The baboon, called the mandrill, has, I think, a very attractive face.
2. Dear Mr. Sartain: We'll plant the flower seeds, the tomato seeds, and the bean seeds that you sent us last week.
3. Our ex-landlord's ranch has 1,000 sq. miles of desert; it must have cactus.
4. There are many ducks in our marsh; grebes, wood ducks, and mallards.
5. correct
6. Don't you wish you'd lived in the 1800's?
7. "Dear John," the letter began, and we knew that she'd gone.
8. Look, George, there's a bat in your den.
9. The Broadway Limited leaves Chicago at 9:00 P.M.
10. Sam, my younger brother, enjoys skateboarding, hockey, and baseball.

Exercise 71
Writing Application
Encourage students to rewrite some of their sentences to use a variety of punctuation marks.

Lesson Objectives

- To proofread a passage for errors in punctuation.

Step-by-Step Teaching Guide

Proofreading

Teaching Resources: Standardized Test Prepaation Workbook, Chapter 26

1. Review with students the basic rules they can use to help them identify punctuation errors.

2. Tell students to read each choice carefully. If students read too quickly, they may make careless mistakes by misreading an answer.

3. As students carefully read each choice, they should immediately eliminate any answers that contain errors in punctuation.

Standardized Test Preparation Workshop

Proofreading

Some standardized tests ask you to proofread a passage for errors in punctuation. Remember these basic rules to help you identify such errors:

- End marks denote the end of a sentence and identify the type of sentence.
- Commas are used to separate items in a series; after introductory words, phrases, or clauses at the beginning of a sentence; and to set off elements from the rest of the sentence.
- Colons introduce a list of items, and semicolons connect independent clauses that are closely related.
- Review the rules for using quotation marks and underlining, hyphens, and apostrophes.

The following sample test items will give you practice in identifying punctuation errors.

Test Tip

Scan written passages first for an overview, and then reread carefully, looking for punctuation errors.

Sample Test Items	Answers and Explanations
Choose the best way to write each underlined section. If the underlined section needs no change, mark the choice "Correct as is." "Hey! Mr Tucker shouted, You can't park (1) (2) there after 700 A.M."	
1 A "Hey"! Mr. Tucker shouted, **B** "Hey!" Mr Tucker shouted, **C** "Hey!" Mr. Tucker shouted, **D** Correct as is	The correct answer for item 1 is *C*. Quotation marks are needed to end the direct quotation, *Hey!*, and they come after the exclamation mark. Also, the title *Mr.* requires a period at the end.
2 F "You can't park there after 7:00 A.M." **G** You can't park, there after 7:00 A.M." **H** "You can't park there after 700 A.M." **J** Correct as is	The correct answer for item 2 is *F*. A colon is needed to separate hours and minutes in expressions of time, and quotation marks are needed before the second part of the quotation.

⬦ TEST-TAKING TIP

Call students' attention to the Test Tip above. Tell them that they can add any missing punctuation to the passage when they reread it and correct any errors in punctuation. Students can then use their handwritten corrections to help them answer each question.

▶ **Practice 1** **Directions:** Choose the best way to write each underlined section. If the underlined section needs no change, mark the choice "Correct as is."

After swim team practice on Tuesday I
(1)
finally received the letter Mom! I shouted.
(2)
It's here! Mom and I opened the letter
(3)
from Blythewood Academy and we

nervously read the brief note inside!

1 A After swim team practice on Tuesday I finally received the letter!

B After swim team practice on Tuesday, I finally received the letter.

C After swim team practice. On Tuesday. I finally received the letter.

D Correct as is

2 F "Mom! I shouted. It's here!".

G "Mom!" I shouted. "Its here!"

H "Mom!" I shouted. "It's here!"

J Correct as is

3 A Mom, and I, opened the letter, from Blythewood Academy, and we nervously read the brief note inside.

B Mom and I opened the letter from: Blythewood Academy and we nervously read the brief note inside!

C Mom and I opened the letter from Blythewood Academy, and we nervously read the brief note inside.

D Correct as is

▶ **Practice 2** **Directions:** Choose the best way to write each underlined section. If the underlined section needs no change, mark the choice "Correct as is."

When Mom and Dad took Wesley to the train
(1)
Sara and her sisters were left alone for the

first time They lived on a farm near
(2)
Lincoln, and raised cows chickens, and

sheep. The farm couldn't be left unattended,
(3)
even for a few days, so the four girls were

left to run it themselves.

1 A When Mom and Dad took Wesley to the train, Sara and her sisters were left alone for the first time.

B When Mom and Dad took Wesley to the train; Sara and her sisters were left alone for the first time.

C When Mom and Dad took Wesley to the train Sara and her sisters were left alone for the first time?

D Correct as is

2 F They lived on a farm near Lincoln and raised cows chickens, and sheep.

G They lived on a farm near Lincoln and raised: cows, chickens, and sheep.

H They lived on a farm near Lincoln and raised cows, chickens, and sheep.

J Correct as is

3 A The farm couldn't be left unattended, even for a few days; so the four girls were left to run it themselves.

B The farm couldnt be left unattended, even for a few days, so the four girls were left to run it themselves.

C The farm couldn't be left unattended even for a few days so the four girls were left to run it themselves.

D Correct as is

▶ **Practice 1**
1. B
2. H
3. C

▶ **Practice 2**
1. A
2. H
3. D

In-Depth Lesson Plan

	LESSON FOCUS	PRINT AND MEDIA RESOURCES
DAY 1	**Capitals in Sentences and the Word *I*** Students learn and apply the concepts for using capitals in sentences and for the word *I* (pp. 602–604).	**Teaching Resources** *Grammar Exercise Workbook*, pp. 175–176; *Grammar Exercises Answers on Transparencies*, Ch. 27 **Language Lab** CD-ROM, Capitalization; **On-Line Exercise Bank**, Section 27
DAY 2	**Capitals for People, Places, and Names of Specific Things** Students learn and apply concepts for using capitals for people, places and names of specific things (pp. 605–608).	**Teaching Resources** *Grammar Exercise Workbook*, pp. 177–182; *Grammar Exercises Answers on Transparencies*, Ch. 27 **Language Lab** CD-ROM, Capitalization; **On-Line Exercise Bank**, Section 27
DAY 3	**Capitals for Titles of People and Things; Using Capitals in Letters** Students learn and apply concepts for using capitals for titles of people, things and in letters and do the Hands-on Grammar activity (pp. 609–613).	**Teaching Resources** *Grammar Exercise Workbook*, pp. 183–186; *Grammar Exercises Answers on Transparencies*, Ch. 27; *Hands-on Grammar Activity Book*, Ch. 27 **Language Lab** CD-ROM, Capitalization; **On-Line Exercise Bank**, Section 27
DAY 4	**Review and Assess** Students review chapter and demonstrate mastery of use of capitalization (pp. 614–619).	**Teaching Resources** *Formal Assessment*, Ch. 27; *Grammar Exercises Answers on Transparencies*, Ch. 27 **On-Line Exercise Bank**, Section 27

Accelerated Lesson Plan

	LESSON FOCUS	PRINT AND MEDIA RESOURCES
DAY 1	**Capitalization** Students cover concepts and usage of capitalization as determined by Diagnostic Test (pp. 602–613).	**Teaching Resources** *Grammar Exercise Workbook*, pp. 175–186; *Grammar Exercises Answers on Transparencies*, Ch. 27; *Hands-on Grammar Activity Book*, Chapter 27 **Language Lab** CD-ROM, Capitalization; **On-Line Exercise Bank**, Section 27
DAY 2	**Review and Assess** Students review chapter and demonstrate mastery of use of capitalization (pp. 614–619).	**Teaching Resources** *Formal Assessment*, Ch. 27; *Grammar Exercises Answers on Transparencies*, Ch. 27 **On-Line Exercise Bank**, Section 27

Options for Adapting Lesson Plans

HOMEWORK
Have students complete any section of the chapter for homework.

FEATURES
Extend coverage with the Standardized Test Preparation Workshop (p. 616).

TECHNOLOGY
Students can use the On-Line Exercise Bank to complete the exercises on computer. The Auto Check feature will grade their work.

INTEGRATED SKILLS COVERAGE

Reading
Find It in Your Reading SE p. 613

Writing
Find It in Your Writing SE p. 613
Writing Application SE p. 615

Technology
ATE p. 611

Viewing and Representing
Critical Viewing SE pp. 600, 603, 604, 606, 608, 611

BLOCK SCHEDULING

Pacing Suggestions
For 90-minute Blocks
- Administer the Diagnostic Test to students to determine instructional coverage.
- Have students complete the necessary exercises in class. Use the Hands-on Grammar activity to provide a change of pace.

Resources for Varying Instruction
- *Language Lab* **CD-ROM** If your students have access to hardware, a 90-minute block provides an ideal opportunity for students to work on computer.

Professional Development Support
- *How to Manage Instruction in the Block* This teaching Resource provides management and activity suggestions.

ASSESSMENT SUPPORT

Standardized Test Preparation Workshop SE pp. 616, 617; ATE p. 605

Standardized Test Preparation Workbook, pp. 53–54

Formal Assessment, Ch. 27

MEDIA AND TECHNOLOGY

For the Student
- *Language Lab* **CD-ROM**, Capitalization
- *On-Line Exercise Bank*, Ch. 27

For the Teacher
- *Resource Pro* **CD-ROM**

MEETING INDIVIDUAL NEEDS

Less Advanced Students See Ongoing Assessment ATE pp. 604, 606, 608, 611, 612

ESL Students ATE pp. 603, 610

More Advanced Students ATE p. 607

WRITING AND GRAMMAR WEB SITE

The Interactive Writing and Grammar Web site provides a wide array of support for students, teachers, and parents. Grammar support includes:

- On-Line Exercise Bank with Auto Check scoring
- Diagnostic and assessment support

www.phschool.com

Lesson Objectives

1. To capitalize the first word of any sentence.
2. To capitalize the personal pronoun *I*.
3. To capitalize names of people and places.
4. To capitalize names of specific things.
5. To capitalize titles of people and things.
6. To capitalize certain words in friendly letters.

Critical Viewing

Support Students may say that the names of the person, the mountain, and the river should begin with capital letters because they name specific people and places.

Chapter 27 *Capitalization*

Zion National Park in Southern Utah

Several words are capitalized in the following sentence: *During the winter, Nancy, Marie, Hal, and I skate on Lake Placid and Lake Champlain.* Some of these words name specific people. Other words name specific places. The capital letters indicate that these are important words in the sentence.

Another use of capital letters is to signal the beginning of a sentence. When several sentences follow one another in a paragraph, capital letters can help to separate them. Capital letters indicate when you can pause in your thinking and reading to sort out ideas.

Capital letters have a number of different uses. Besides indicating the beginning of sentences and the names of specific people and places, capital letters are used to point out specific things, such as a holiday—Mother's Day—or a document—the Constitution. Capital letters are also used to show the specific titles of people, such as President Roosevelt, or of things, such as the book *My Side of the Mountain.*

In addition, capital letters are used in parts of letters. This chapter gives information about each of these uses of capital letters.

▲ **Critical Viewing**
Name three things in this picture that should be spelled with a capital letter. Explain your reasoning. **[Support]**

600 • Capitalization

☑ **ONGOING ASSESSMENT: Diagnose**

If students miss more than one item in each category, direct them to the relevant pages of the text and assign exercises for practice and review.

Capitalization	Diagnostic Test Items	Teach	Practice	Chapter Review
Skill Check A				
Capitalizing Sentence Beginnings and *I*	A 1–5	pp. 602–604	Ex. 1–3	Ex. 13, 17
Skill Check B				
Capitalizing Personal Names and Place Names	B 6–10	pp. 605–606	Ex. 4–5	Ex. 14, 17

Diagnostic Test

Directions: Write all answers on a separate sheet of paper.

Skill Check A. Rewrite each sentence below, using capital letters where necessary.

1. i have never traveled very far from home.
2. hundreds of years ago, travel was difficult.
3. two americans led an expedition to the west.
4. do you know the names of those two men?
5. tell me if you know.

Skill Check B. In the following sentences, list the names of people and places, and capitalize them as needed.

6. meriwether lewis and william clark traveled northwest.
7. Commissioned by president thomas jefferson, they made the first exploration of the louisiana territory.
8. They traveled from st. louis, missouri, to the pacific ocean.
9. They crossed montana to reach the snake river.
10. The interpreter toussaint charbonneau and his wife, sacajawea, joined the party.

Skill Check C. List each specific thing that should be capitalized in the sentences below, adding the necessary capital letters.

11. The traveling group was officially called the corps of discovery.
12. Sacajawea, a native american woman, helped as a peacemaker.
13. She was a shoshone.
14. spanish officials felt threatened by american ambitions.
15. Since the american revolution, they feared, correctly, that the americans would spread across the continent.

Skill Check D. Copy the following items, adding capital letters as needed for titles of people and things and for parts of a letter.

16. This american expedition was president jefferson's idea.
17. He was influenced by the journeys of captain james cook and captain george vancouver.
18. captain meriwether lewis selected his friend, lieutenant william clark, to serve as co-commander.
19. history of the expedition . . . of captains lewis and clark
20. "appalachian spring"
21. the pioneers
22. "oh, susanna"
23. "song of the open road"
24. 86 kirkland street / portland, oregon 97223 / june 15, 1987
25. my dear meriwether,

Answer Key

Diagnostic Test

Each item in the Diagnostic Test corresponds to a specific section in the chapter on capitalization. This will enable you to tailor instruction to the particular needs of your students. See "Ongoing Assessment: Diagnose" below for further details.

Skill Check A

1. I have never traveled very far from home.
2. Hundreds of years ago, travel was difficult.
3. Two Americans led an expedition to the West.
4. Do you know the names of those two men?
5. Tell me if you know.

Skill Check B

6. Meriwether Lewis, William Clark
7. President Thomas Jefferson, Louisiana Territory
8. St. Louis, Missouri, Pacific Ocean
9. Montana, Snake River
10. Toussaint Charbonneau, Sacajawea

Skill Check C

11. Corps of Discovery
12. Native American
13. Shoshone
14. Spanish, American
15. American Revolution, Americans

Skill Check D

16. This American expedition was President Jefferson's idea.
17. He was influenced by the journeys of Captain James Cook and Captain George Vancouver.
18. Captain Meriwether Lewis selected his friend, Lieutenant William Clark, to serve as co-commander.
19. History of the Expedition . . . of Captains Lewis and Clark
20. "Appalachian Spring"
21. The Pioneers
22. "Oh, Susanna"
23. "Song of the Open Road"
24. 86 Kirkland Street / Portland, Oregon 97223 / June 15, 1987
25. My dear Meriwether,

ONGOING ASSESSMENT: Diagnose *continued*				
Capitalization	**Diagnostic Test Items**	**Teach**	**Practice**	**Chapter Review**
Skill Check C				
Capitalizing Names of Specific Things	C 11–15	pp. 607–608	Ex. 6	Ex. 15, 17
Skill Check D				
Capitalizing Titles	D 16–23	pp. 609–611	Ex. 7–10	Ex. 16–17
Capitalizing in Letters	D 24–25	p. 612	Ex. 11–12	Ex. 18
Cumulative Reviews and Applications				Ex. 19

PREPARE and ENGAGE

Interest GRABBER Write the following paragraph from Ray Bradbury's "The Sound of Summer Running" on the board or show it on an overhead projector. Ask students what is wrong.

"first, i know just what you want to buy," said mr. sanderson. "second, i see you every afternoon at my window; you think i don't see? you're wrong. third, to give it its full name, you want the royal crown cream-sponge para litefoot tennis shoes. fourth, you want credit."

Activate Prior Knowledge

Ask volunteers to correct the mistakes in the Bradbury paragraph. Then ask students to tell any rules they know about when to use capital letters.

TEACH

Step-by-Step Teaching Guide

Using Capitals for Sentences and the Word *I*

1. The first word of every sentence is capitalized, even if it begins with a word that would not be capitalized elsewhere—*a, you, cat,* and the like.

2. *I* is the only pronoun that gets capitalized. All other personal pronouns, including the object pronoun *me,* are capitalized only when they begin sentences.

Using Capitals for Sentences and the Word *I*

One important use of capital letters is to indicate the beginning of a sentence.

> **KEY CONCEPT** Always capitalize the first word of a sentence. ■

EXAMPLE: <u>H</u>e visited the historical landmark.

Some sentences include a person's exact words. These words are called a *direct quotation.*

> **KEY CONCEPT** Capitalize the first word of a direct quotation when it is used as part of a larger sentence. ■

EXAMPLES: He said, "<u>H</u>ere is the road map."
"<u>H</u>awaii," she said, "is made up of islands."

When a quotation is interrupted, the last part of the quotation is not capitalized. In the second example above, the words *she said* interrupt the direct quotation "Hawaii is made up of islands." Notice that the word *is,* in the second part of this quotation, is not capitalized.

When a quotation continues with a new sentence, however, a capital is required.

EXAMPLES: "<u>L</u>ook at the road map," he said. "<u>W</u>e have about 120 miles to go."
"<u>H</u>awaii is made up of lush volcanic islands," she sighed dreamily. "<u>T</u>hey are so beautiful!"

> **KEY CONCEPT** The word *I* is always capitalized. ■

EXAMPLE: The librarian knows <u>I</u> am interested in geology.

EXAMPLES OF CAPITALS FOR SENTENCES AND *I*

<u>N</u>ancy enjoys Western adventure novels and stories. (Capitalize the first word of a sentence.)

Ed asked, "<u>W</u>ho brought the shovels?" (Capitalize the first word of a direct quotation within a larger sentence.)

<u>I</u> know <u>I</u> can learn to ski well if <u>I</u> practice enough. (*I* is always capitalized.)

Theme: American History

In this chapter, you will learn about many different uses of capitalization. The examples and exercises are about people in American history and the exploration of the American wilderness.

Cross-Curricular Connection: Social Studies

602 • Capitalization

⏱ TIME AND RESOURCE MANAGER

Resources
Print: Grammar Exercise Workbook, pp. 175–186; Grammar Exercises Answers on Transparencies, Chapter 27
Technology: Language Lab CD-ROM, Capitalization; On-Line Exercise Bank, Section 27

In-Depth Coverage	Accelerated Pace
• Work through all key concepts, pp. 602–612. • Assign and review Exercises 1–12.	• Assign pp.602–612 for independent student review. • Assign Chapter Review Exercises 13–18, pp. 614–615.

Customize for
ESL Students

In Spanish, only the formal second-person pronouns are capitalized when using their abbreviated forms *Ud.* and *Uds.*, while *yo* (the Spanish pronoun for *I*) is not. Have students write the subject and object pronouns in both English and their home language. Have them compare capitalization rules. Remind them that the rule is very simple: In English, *I* is always capitalized.

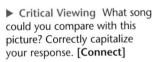

▶ **Exercise 1** **Supplying Capital Letters** Rewrite each sentence below, using capital letters where necessary.

EXAMPLE: the two rival groups were in the election.

ANSWER: The two rival groups were in the election.

1. all parts of the country have unique landforms.
2. in some places, rivers have shaped the ground.
3. glaciers have carved ravines and scattered rocks.
4. "have you ever seen a desert?" i asked.
5. "yes!" he replied, "when i traveled across the country."
6. i exclaimed, "that must have been so exciting!"
7. then i asked, "what was your favorite sight?"
8. "the snowcapped mountains were very dramatic," he replied.
9. he continued, "there was great skiing and snowboarding."
10. "i can't wait to travel to other parts of our country," i said.

▶ **Exercise 2** **Writing Sentences With Capital Letters** Write sentences on the topics listed below. Make sure to capitalize the first word of each sentence and the word *I*.

EXAMPLE: a friend: quotation

ANSWER: My friend Milly shouted, "Don't be late for the party!"

1. a favorite activity
2. a recent news event
3. the season of the year
4. something you know how to build or fix
5. direction from a teacher: interrupted quotation

▶ **More Practice**

Language Lab CD-ROM
• Capitalization in Sentences lesson
On-line Exercise Bank
• Chapter 27
Grammar Exercise Workbook
• pp. 175–176

Yosemite National Park

▶ **Critical Viewing** What song could you compare with this picture? Correctly capitalize your response. **[Connect]**

Answer Key

▶ **Exercise 1**

1. All parts of the country have unique landforms.
2. In some places, rivers have shaped the ground.
3. Glaciers have carved ravines and scattered rocks.
4. "Have you ever seen a desert?" I asked.
5. "Yes!" he replied. "When I traveled across the country."
6. I exclaimed, "That must have been so exciting!"
7. Then I asked, "What was your favorite sight?"
8. "The snowcapped mountains were very dramatic," he replied.
9. He continued, "There was great skiing and snowboarding."
10. "I can't wait to travel to other parts of our country," I said.

▶ **Exercise 2**

Answers will vary. Encourage students to create sentences that illustrate all of the key concepts on page 602.

Critical Viewing

Connect Students may say

"America, the Beautiful."

Capitalization • 603

⏱ **TIME SAVERS!**

📄 **Answers on Transparency**
Use the Grammar Exercises Answers on Transparencies for Chapter 27 to facilitate correction by students.

💻 **On-Line Exercise Bank**
Have students complete the exercises on computer. The Auto Check feature will grade their work for you!

27

1. I had a conversation with my history teacher about the early pioneers who traveled west.
2. "The pioneers discovered new land formations," he told me. "The hunters and trappers followed paths in the mountains."
3. He continued, "Wagon trails crossed rivers and circled around buttes and plateaus."
4. "How long were these trips? I asked.
5. "The pioneers traveled on foot and by horse," he replied. "It was very slow. They spent months traveling to their new homes."
6. "I bet they stayed close to rivers," I guessed, "because water is scarce in some western areas."
7. "You're right," he said.
8. Then he went on, "Sometimes, people surveyed the land by climbing rocks and outcroppings."
9. "I don't know if I would have the courage to make that trip," I said.
10. Then I said, "It must have been a great relief to cross the mountains and start a new home."

Critical Viewing

Infer Students may suggest such quotations as "O my gosh!" and "That is beautiful!"

Exercise 3 Proofreading for Capitalization of Sentences

Proofread the following dialogue, adding capital letters where necessary. Copy the dialogue, with corrections, into your notebook.

i had a conversation with my history teacher about the early pioneers who traveled west.

"the pioneers discovered new land formations," he told me. "the hunters and trappers followed paths in the mountains."

he continued, "wagon trails crossed rivers and circled around buttes and plateaus."

"how long were these trips?" i asked.

"the pioneers traveled on foot and by horse," he replied. "it was very slow. they spent months traveling to their new homes."

"i bet they stayed close to rivers," i guessed, "because water is scarce in some western areas."

"you're right," he said.

then he went on, "sometimes, people surveyed the land by climbing rocks and outcroppings."

"i don't know if i would have the courage to make that trip," i said.

then i said, "it must have been a great relief to cross the mountains and start a new home."

Bryce Canyon National Park

Language Lab
CD-ROM
• Proper Nouns lesson
On-line
Exercise Bank
• Chapter 27
Grammar Exercise
Workbook
• pp. 175–176

◄ Critical Viewing
Coming upon this sight for the first time, how might a person react? Answer with a quotation, correctly capitalized. [Infer]

604 • Capitalization

☑ **ONGOING ASSESSMENT: Monitor and Reinforce**

If students miss more than two items in Exercises 1, 2, or 3, refer them to the following for additional practice.

In the Textbook	Print Resources	Technology
Chapter Review, Ex. 13, p. 614	Grammar Exercise Workbook, pp. 175–176	Language Lab CD-ROM, Capitalization; On-Line Exercise Bank, Section 27

Using Capitals for Names of People and Places

A capital letter indicates the name of a specific person—John Muir—or a specific place—Denver.

KEY CONCEPT Capitalize the name of a specific person. ■

EXAMPLES: John L. Lewis, Clara Barton

Notice that a person's initials are also capitalized.
The names of specific places also begin with capital letters.

KEY CONCEPT Capitalize the name of a specific place. ■

The chart below shows some of the kinds of specific places that are capitalized.

EXAMPLES OF CAPITALS FOR SPECIFIC PLACES	
Streets	Warren Street, Carlton Avenue, Interstate 10
Cities	Baltimore, London, Memphis, Tokyo
States	Arizona, Florida, Hawaii, Idaho
Nations	Italy, Canada, Kenya, France, Peru, Korea
Continents	North America, Asia, Africa, Antarctica
Deserts	Sahara, Negev, Mojave
Mountains	Mount Everest, Rocky Mountains
Regions	Great Plains, Appalachian Highlands
Islands	Canary Islands, Fiji Islands
Rivers	Mississippi River, Amazon River
Lakes	Lake Michigan, Great Salt Lake, Lake Erie
Bays	Hudson Bay, Baffin Bay, Biscayne Bay
Seas	Black Sea, Mediterranean Sea, North Sea
Oceans	Atlantic Ocean, Arctic Ocean

Exercise 4 Using Capital Letters in Sentences About Places Write sentences on the topics given below, using capitals where needed.

EXAMPLE: amusement park and location
ANSWER: Disney World is located in Orlando, Florida.

1. your street or the street on which your school is located
2. your city or town and state
3. your neighbors
4. a body of water in or near your town or city
5. directions from one place in town to another, using street names

---

STANDARDIZED TEST PREPARATION WORKSHOP

Grammar and Usage Standardized tests often ask students to identify which sentence in a passage contains a certain kind of grammatical error. Ask students which of the following sentences contains an error in capitalization.

(A) Baseball was first played in the 1840's.
(B) The first professional team was the cincinnati
Red Stockings. (C) It was organized in 1869 by Harry Wright. (D) In 1871, the National Association of Professional Baseball Players chartered nine teams as the first league.

Students should choose sentence **B.** Cincinnati is the name of a city, and it is also part of the name of the team.

Step-by-Step Teaching Guide

Using Capitals for Names of People and Places

1. The simple rule to capitalize a person's first, middle, and last name—Louisa May Alcott—has exceptions. People can spell and capitalize their names any way they wish.

   Eamon De Valera

   Leonardo da Vinci

   Vincent van Gogh

   Mark Van Doren

   The only way students can be sure is to look up the names of well-known people in a dictionary or an encyclopedia.

2. Internal letters similarly follow no rule.

   MacDonald

   macdonald

3. *Mc* and *O'* are usually followed by a capital letter.

   Mark McGwire

   Sandra Day O'Connor

Answer Key

Exercise 4

Answers will vary. Have students exchange papers to be sure their capitalization is correct.

⏱ **TIME SAVERS!**

🖨 **Answers on Transparency** Use the Grammar Exercises Answers on Transparencies for Chapter 27 to facilitate correction by students.

💻 **On-Line Exercise Bank** Have students complete the exercises on computer. The Auto Check feature will grade their work for you!

605

Exercise 5

1. In 1535, Francisco de Coronado arrived in New Spain, the old name for Mexico.
2. Four years later, he became governor of Nueva Galicia.
3. That territory included the modern Mexican states of Aguascalientes, Jalisco, and Zacatecas.
4. He listened to stories about the Spanish explorer Cabeza de Vaca and the Seven Golden Cities of Cibola.
5. Coronado set out to conquer these regions for Spain.
6. He traveled with Spanish soldiers and Native Americans.
7. They followed the Sierra Madre to what is now Arizona.
8. Members of his group were the first Europeans to see the Grand Canyon and the Colorado River.
9. They were also the first Europeans to see and describe the American buffalo.
10. They spent the winter near what is now Santa Fe, New Mexico.
11. Heading eastward, they crossed the Rio Grande and the Great Plains of northern Texas.
12. In 1541, they crossed the Canadian and Arkansas rivers into Kansas.
13. Then, in 1869, the American geologist John Wesley Powell led the first passage through the Grand Canyon.
14. He and his party observed the northern rim, the Kaibab Plateau, and the southern rim, the Coconino Plateau.
15. The Colorado River carved a canyon through the Colorado Plateau.
16. The Glen Canyon Dam in Arizona was built on the Colorado River in 1963.
17. Powell, born in New York, later moved to Illinois.
18. His interest in geography and geology drew him to the Ohio River.
19. After the Grand Canyon, he studied the Green River Canyon.
20. Between 1870 and 1871, he surveyed much of the Rocky Mountain region.

27

Exercise 5 Proofreading for Capitals for Names of People and Places Proofread each sentence below, copying it into your notebook and adding capital letters where needed.

EXAMPLE: francisco de coronado was born in salamanca, spain.

ANSWER: Francisco de Coronado was born in Salamanca, Spain.

1. In 1535, francisco de coronado arrived in new spain, the old name for mexico.
2. Four years later, he became governor of nueva galicia.
3. That territory included the modern mexican states of aguascalientes, jalisco, and zacatecas.
4. He listened to stories about the spanish explorer cabeza de vaca and the seven golden cities of cibola.
5. coronado set out to conquer these regions for spain.
6. He traveled with spanish soldiers and native americans.
7. They followed the sierra madre to what is now arizona.
8. Members of his group were the first europeans to see the grand canyon and the colorado river.
9. They were also the first europeans to see and describe the american buffalo.
10. They spent the winter near what is now santa fe, new mexico.
11. Heading eastward, they crossed the rio grande and the great plains of northern texas.
12. In 1541, they crossed the canadian and arkansas rivers into kansas.
13. Then, in 1869, the american geologist john wesley powell led the first passage through the grand canyon.
14. He and his party observed the northern rim, the kaibab plateau, and the southern rim, the coconino plateau.
15. The colorado river carved a canyon through the colorado plateau.
16. The glen canyon dam in arizona was built on the colorado river in 1963.
17. powell, born in new york, later moved to illinois.
18. His interest in geography and geology drew him to the ohio river.
19. After the grand canyon, he studied the green river canyon.
20. Between 1870 and 1871, he surveyed much of the rocky mountain region.

606 • Capitalization

More Practice

Language Lab CD-ROM
• Proper Nouns lesson
On-line Exercise Bank
• Chapter 27
Grammar Exercise Workbook
• pp. 177–178

▼ Critical Viewing
Why might photographers enjoy visiting this park? [Infer]

Powell Memorial Point, Grand Canyon National Park

☑ **ONGOING ASSESSMENT: Monitor and Reinforce**

If students have difficulty with Exercise 4 or 5, refer them to the following for additional practice.

In the Textbook	Print Resources	Technology
Chapter Review, Ex. 14, p. 614	Grammar Exercise Workbook, pp. 177–178	Language Lab CD-ROM, Capitalization; On-Line Exercise Bank, Section 27

Using Capitals for Names of Specific Things

In addition to capitalizing the names of specific persons and places, you should also capitalize the names of specific things.

> **KEY CONCEPT** Capitalize the names of specific things. ■

The chart below lists a number of categories of specific things that should be capitalized.

CAPITALS FOR SPECIFIC THINGS	
Historical Periods and Events	Renaissance, Battle of Lexington
Historical Documents	Constitution
Days and Months	Monday, December
Holidays	Memorial Day, Arbor Day
Organizations and Schools	Antique Airplane Club, Central High School
Government Bodies	Senate, Congress
Political Parties	Democratic Party
Ethnic Groups	Latinos, African Americans
Nationalities and Languages	Colombian, Spanish
Monuments and Memorials	Washington Monument, Lincoln Memorial
Buildings	World Trade Center
Religious Faiths	Christianity, Judaism, Islam, Hinduism
Awards	Nobel Prize
Air and Sea Craft	*China Clipper, Old Ironsides*
Space and Land Craft	*Apollo 2,* Metroliner

Unlike special holidays, such as Thanksgiving Day, the names of the seasons of the year are not capitalized. Write *spring, summer, fall* (or *autumn*), and *winter* when you are discussing those times of year. When a season is part of a title, however, it should be capitalized.

EXAMPLES: If <u>w</u>inter's here, can <u>s</u>pring be far behind?

We always look forward to seeing the scarecrows and the pumpkins at the <u>F</u>all Fun Fair and the ice sculptures at the <u>W</u>inter Carnival.

Step-by-Step Teaching Guide

Using Capitals for Names of Specific Things

1. Go over the chart on this page with the whole class. Explain that each proper noun listed is like a personal name. It is the specific name of an individual time period, item, building, or vehicle. This is the reason to capitalize it.

2. One category of proper nouns not included in the chart is brand names. Kodak, Heinz, Reebok, Kleenex, Band-Aids, Xerox, and so on, are always capitalized.

3. Point out that the names of ships and spacecraft are italicized or underlined in addition to being capitalized.

Customize for
More Advanced Students

Challenge students to find two more items for each category of proper nouns listed in the chart on this page. Students can use dictionaries or other reference books if necessary. Have students exchange papers and compare their items.

Critical Viewing *(page 606)*

Infer Students may say that photographers might enjoy photographing the beautiful and dramatic colors and shapes of this natural landscape.

607

1. January, Nantucket, Massachusetts
2. Society, Friends
3. American Anti-slavery Society
4. July, Women's Rights Convention, Seneca Falls, New York
5. Declaration, Sentiments, Declaration, Independence
6. Fugitive Slave Act
7. Underground Railroad
8. American Civil War, National Woman Suffrage Association
9. November, American Woman Suffrage Association
10. Wyoming
11. Fifteenth Amendment, Constitution, African American
12. World War, August, Nineteenth Amendment
13. Women's Rights National Historic Park
14. Montana, Congress
15. American, Election Day, Tuesday, Monday, November

Critical Viewing

Compare and Contrast Students may suggest the name of a charitable organization such as The United Way or that of a labor organization such as the AFL-CIO.

27

Exercise 6 Proofreading for Capitals for Names of **Specific Things** In your notebook, copy the sentences below, adding capital letters where they are needed.

EXAMPLE: Lucretia Coffin Mott was educated at nine partners, a quaker boarding school.

ANSWER: Nine Partners, Quaker

1. Lucretia Coffin Mott was born on january 3, 1793, in nantucket, massachusetts.
2. After 1817, she became active in the society of friends.
3. Lucretia and her husband, James Mott, helped to organize the american anti-slavery society.
4. In july of 1848, she and Elizabeth Cady Stanton organized the women's rights convention in seneca falls, new york.
5. Stanton wrote the declaration of sentiments, similar to the declaration of independence.
6. The fugitive slave act was passed in 1850.
7. Then, the Motts made their house a stop on the underground railroad.
8. After the american civil war, Carrie Chapman Catt formed the national woman suffrage association.
9. In november of 1869, other suffragists formed the american woman suffrage association.
10. The territory of wyoming gave women the right to vote in 1869.
11. The fifteenth amendment to the constitution gave african american men the vote.
12. After world war I, on august 18, 1920, the nineteenth amendment gave women the right to vote.
13. There are statues of Susan B. Anthony, Lucretia Mott, and Elizabeth Cady Stanton at the women's rights national historic park.
14. Jeannette Rankin of montana was the first woman elected to congress.
15. For all american citizens, election day is the first tuesday after the first monday in november.

More Practice

Language Lab
CD-ROM
• Proper Nouns lesson
On-line
Exercise Bank
• Chapter 27
Grammar Exercise
Workbook
• pp. 179–182

▲ Critical Viewing Name an organization that sometimes marches for a cause today, and tell how its marches differ from this suffragist march. [**Compare and Contrast**]

✓ ONGOING ASSESSMENT: Monitor and Reinforce

If students miss more than two items in Exercise 6, refer them to the following for additional practice.

In the Textbook	Print Resources	Technology
Chapter Review, Ex. 15, p. 614	Grammar Exercise Workbook, pp. 179–182	Language Lab CD-ROM, Capitalization; On-Line Exercise Bank, Section 27

Using Capitals for Titles of People

Whether or not a title of a person is capitalized often depends on how it is used in a sentence.

KEY CONCEPT Capitalize a social or professional title before a person's name or in direct address, but not at other times. ■

BEFORE A NAME: Governor Brown spoke about taxes.

DIRECT ADDRESS: Tell us, Governor, about the new program.

SOME OTHER SOCIAL AND PROFESSIONAL TITLES	
Social	Sir, Mister, Miss, Madame, Mesdames
Professional	Congresswoman, Senator, Governor, Mayor, Secretary of the Treasury, Attorney General, Professor, Doctor, Attorney, Judge, Reverend, Father, Rabbi, Bishop, Sister, Private, Lieutenant, Sergeant, Corporal

KEY CONCEPT Capitalize a title showing a family relationship when used before a person's name or in direct address. ■

BEFORE A NAME: I sent a postcard to Aunt Alexandra.

DIRECT ADDRESS: I mailed you an invitation, Grandpa.

KEY CONCEPT Capitalize a title showing a family relationship when it refers to a specific person, except when it follows a possessive noun or a possessive pronoun. ■

A SPECIFIC PERSON: Ask Grandmother her opinion.

AFTER A POSSESSIVE: I'll ask my grandmother.

Exercise 7 Using Capitals for Titles of People Copy the following sentences, adding capital letters where necessary.

EXAMPLE: Last summer, doctor Martin traveled to Florida.

ANSWER: Last summer, Doctor Martin traveled to Florida.

1. A school visitor, professor Travis, taught us about Florida.
2. Florida was discovered by explorer juan ponce de León.
3. We learned about chief Osceola.
4. He fought against general Andrew Jackson.
5. "Many Seminoles hid in the Everglades," said mrs. Everett.

Technology Tip

When your spell-check tool identifies a name as unrecognized, choose the "ignore all" option. If the name is one that you use often—such as your town—add it to your customized dictionary.

Step-by-Step Teaching Guide

Using Capitals for Titles of People

1. People's titles are capitalized when they are part of the person's name or when they are used in place of a person's name. The first two examples on the page illustrate this.

2. In the example *Ask Grandmother her opinion, Grandmother* could be replaced by her name: *Ask Sharon her opinion.* In *I'll ask my grandmother,* the replacement would not make sense: *I'll ask my Sharon.* In this example, *grandmother* is not used instead of the person's name, so it is not capitalized.

Answer Key

Exercise 7

1. A school visitor, Professor Travis, taught us about Florida.
2. Florida was discovered by exploror Juan Ponce de Leon.
3. We learned about Chief Osceola.
4. He fought against General Andrew Jackson.
5. "Many Seminoles hid in the Everglades," said Mrs. Everett.

TIME SAVERS!

Answers on Transparency Use the Grammar Exercises Answers on Transparencies for Chapter 27 to facilitate correction by students.

On-Line Exercise Bank Have students complete the exercises on computer. The Auto Check feature will grade their work for you!

Using Capitals for Titles of Things

Many books are divided into chapters, plays into acts, and long poems into various types of sections. These sections of written works are capitalized (and put inside quotation marks).

Answer Key

> **Exercise 8**

1. <u>Life on the Mississippi</u>
2. "Sweet Home Alabama"
3. "I Hear America Singing"
4. American History 102
5. <u>The Ox-Bow Incident</u>

Customize for
ESL Students

The rules of capitalization vary greatly from one language to the next. For example, in Spanish and French, only the first word and any proper nouns in a title are capitalized. When in doubt, students should always capitalize the key words of titles in English.

27

Using Capitals for Titles of Things

Capitals are used for the titles of things.

> **KEY CONCEPT** Capitalize the first word and all other key words in the titles of books, newspapers, magazines, short stories, poems, plays, movies, songs, and artworks. ■

Do not capitalize articles (*a, an, the*) or prepositions and conjunctions that are only two or three letters long unless they begin a title.

TITLES OF WRITTEN WORKS AND WORKS OF ART	
Books	*O! Pioneers*
Newspapers	Fort Worth *Star-Telegram*
Magazines	*National Geographic*
Short Stories	"The Bet"
Poems	"Birches"
Plays	*Death of a Salesman*
Movies	*The Sting*
Songs	"Singin' in the Rain"
Paintings	*Three Musicians*
Sculptures	*Bird in Space*

Note that in titles, verbs and personal pronouns, no matter how short, are always capitalized.

EXAMPLES: "Why the Tortoise's Shell Is Not Smooth"
by Chinua Achebe

"Overdoing It" by Anton Chekhov

> **KEY CONCEPT** Capitalize the title of a school course when it is followed by a number or it refers to a language. Otherwise, do not capitalize school subjects. ■

EXAMPLES: <u>F</u>rench; <u>H</u>istory 420; <u>A</u>lgebra II

I have <u>s</u>ocial <u>s</u>tudies and <u>m</u>usic this morning.

> **Exercise 8**   Using Capitals for Titles of Things   Rewrite each title, adding capital letters where necessary. Keep the underlining and quotation marks as shown.

1. <u>life on the mississippi</u>
2. "sweet home alabama"
3. "I hear america singing"
4. american history 102
5. <u>the ox-bow incident</u>

> **More Practice**

Language Lab
CD-ROM
• Proper Nouns lesson
On-line
Exercise Bank
• Chapter 27
Grammar Exercise
Workbook
• pp. 183–184

Exercise 9 Proofreading for Capitalization of Titles of **Things** Copy the titles in these sentences, adding capital letters as necessary. Keep the underlining and quotation marks as shown.

EXAMPLE: I like to read the <u>rocky mountain news</u>.

ANSWER: I like to read the <u>Rocky Mountain News</u>.

1. Laura Ingalls Wilder wrote about many parts of the country in books such as <u>little house in the big woods</u>.
2. Some of her books, such as <u>farmer boy</u> and <u>by the shores of silver lake</u>, are set in Wisconsin, Kansas, and Iowa.
3. The television show <u>little house on the prairie</u> takes place in Walnut Grove, Minnesota.
4. In the second episode, "country girls," Laura and Mary go to their first day of school.
5. We learned about this historic episode in social studies II.

Exercise 10 Proofreading for Capitalization of Titles of **People and Things** Proofread each sentence below, rewriting it in your notebook and adding capital letters where necessary. Write *correct* if no additional capital letters are needed.

1. The monroe doctrine was written by secretary of state John Quincy Adams.
2. It encouraged foreign leaders, emperors, presidents, and dictators to leave their former colonies alone.
3. When Santa Anna, the Mexican dictator, tried to crush the Texas government, he faced the settlers at the Alamo.
4. Young colonel William Travis commanded the Texas troops.
5. Former congressman Davy Crockett and Jim Bowie were two of the 189 men who defended the Alamo.

▲ **Critical Viewing** Name a book or movie in which a rustic cottage like this one might appear. Capitalize the title correctly. **[Connect]**

Answer Key

> **Exercise 9**

1. <u>Little House in the Big Woods</u>
2. <u>Farmer Boy,</u> <u>By the Shores of Silver Lake</u>
3. <u>Little House on the Prairie</u>
4. "Country Girls"
5. Social Studies II

> **Exercise 10**

1. The Monroe Doctrine was written by Secretary of State John Quincy Adams.
2. correct
3. correct
4. Young Colonel William Travis commanded the Texas troops.
5. Former Congressman Davy Crockett and Jim Bowie were two of the 189 men who defended the Alamo.

Critical Viewing

Connect Students may suggest titles such as <u>Little House on the Prairie</u> and <u>O Pioneers</u>!

Technology Tip

To make their word-processed work look professional, students can use these two tips. Use the italic function, not the underline, for the titles of books, movies, plays, newspapers, magazines, and artwork. Use "smart quotes" for titles of short stories, poems, and songs. Smart quotes are the curly quotation marks, not straight up-and-down ones (" ").

☑ **ONGOING ASSESSMENT: Monitor and Reinforce**

If students miss more than one item in Exercise 7, 8, 9, or 10, refer them to the following for additional practice.

In the Textbook	Print Resources	Technology
Chapter Review, Ex. 16–17, pp. 614–615	Grammar Exercise Workbook, pp. 181–184	Language Lab CD-ROM, Capitalization; On-Line Exercise Bank, Section 27

Using Capitals in Letters

1. The rules for friendly letters apply to business letters also.

   Dear Mr. Schumacher:

   Dear Senator Zinn:

   Yours sincerely,

   Very truly yours,

2. When addressing letters, most people do not write out the name of the state. Instead, they use the two-letter postal code: TX for Texas, NH for New Hampshire, and so on. Both letters of a postal code are always capitalized. If students are uncertain of the postal code for a specific state, they can find this information in a telephone book or ZIP code directory.

Answer Key

▶ **Exercise 11**

1. 25 Lakeside Avenue / Somerville, Missouri 63344 / October 28, 20--
2. Dear Sarah and Edward,
3. Fondly,
4. 5112 Brady Green / San Antonio, Texas 78200 / September 4, 20--
5. Sincerely,

▶ **Exercise 12**

1. 15 Webster Avenue / Hanover, New Hampshire 03755 / December 5, 20--
2. My dear Therese,
3. 245 Indian Trail Road / Chapel Hill, North Carolina 27514 / October 13, 20--
4. Dear Aunt Ricki,
5. Your friend,

27

Using Capitals in Letters

Several parts of personal letters are capitalized.

▶ **KEY CONCEPT** In the heading, capitalize the street, city, and state, as well as the month of the year. ■

HEADING:	17 Vanderburg Street
	Newton, Massachusetts 02162
	May 29, 20--

▶ **KEY CONCEPT** In the salutation, capitalize the first word, any title, and the name of the person or group mentioned. ■

SALUTATIONS: My dear Susan,   Dear Uncle Steve,

▶ **KEY CONCEPT** In the closing, capitalize the first word. ■

CLOSINGS: Your friend,   Yours truly,   Love,

▶ **Exercise 11** Proofreading for Capitalization in Letters
Proofread the parts of letters shown below, copying them into your notebook and adding capital letters as needed.

EXAMPLE: dear arnold
ANSWER: Dear Arnold

1. 25 lakeside avenue / somerville, missouri 63344 / october 28, 20--
2. dear sarah and edward,
3. fondly,
4. 5112 brady green / san antonio, texas 78200 / september 4, 20--
5. sincerely,

▶ **Exercise 12** More Practice Proofreading for Capitalization in Letters Proofread the parts of letters shown below, copying them into your notebook with capital letters as needed.

1. 15 webster avenue / hanover, new hampshire 03755 / december 5, 20--
2. my dear therese,
3. 245 indian trail road / chapel hill, north carolina 27514 / october 13, 20--
4. dear aunt ricki,
5. your friend,

▶ **More Practice**

Language Lab CD-ROM
• Proper Nouns lesson
On-line Exercise Bank
• Chapter 27
Grammar Exercise Workbook
• pp. 185–186

612 • Capitalization

☑ **ONGOING ASSESSMENT: Monitor and Reinforce**

If students miss more than one item in Exercise 11 or 12, refer them to the following for additional practice

In the Textbook	Print Resources	Technology
Chapter Review, Ex. 18, p. 615	Grammar Exercise Workbook, pp. 185–186	Language Lab CD-ROM, Capitalization; On-Line Exercise Bank, Section 27

Hands-on Grammar

Capitalization Car

Take a ride in a Capitalization Car to help you remember the categories of words that need to be capitalized. To begin, cut out a simple car about 6" long and 3" high. Draw the doors, windows, headlights, trunk, passengers, and so on. Next, draw a road lengthwise across a piece of construction paper. Then, glue or tape down the car in the middle of the road. Around the car and on the road, print these questions:

What are the make and model of the car? **W**ho is the driver? **W**ho is the front-seat passenger? **W**hat is he or she reading? **W**ho are in the back seat? **W**hat are the brands of things in the trunk? **W**hat song is playing? **W**hat is the name of the street or highway? **W**here are they going? **F**rom where are they coming? **On** what date did they leave? **On** what date will they arrive? **W**hat landmarks will they pass along the way?

Under each question, use a ruler to draw an appropriate number of short lines for answers to the questions. (See illustration.)

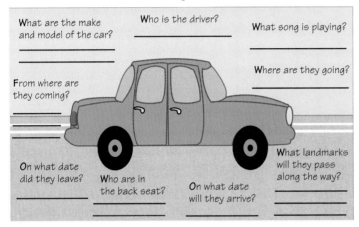

Finally, on the lines, print an answer to each of the questions, using names of specific people, things, and places. Capitalize all the words correctly, and review the categories when you need to know what kinds of words to capitalize.

Find It in Your Reading Read a few paragraphs of a travel article in a magazine or newspaper. Use some of the place names on your Capitalization Car.

Find It in Your Reading Review a piece of writing in your portfolio. Check to see that you have begun each sentence with a capital letter, and that you have capitalized names of specific people, places, and things. Insert capital letters where they are needed.

Capitalization • 613

Step by Step Teaching Guide

Capitalization Car

Teaching Resources: Hands-on Grammar Activity Book, Chapter 27

1. Have students refer to their Hands-on Grammar activity books or give them copies of relevant pages for this activity.

2. Be sure students select names of specific people, things, and places to write on the lines. You may want to let them make up some of the names.

Find It in Your Reading

Have students underline the place names they find.

Find It in Your Writing

You may want to have students exchange pieces of writing so they can check each other's work.

☑ ONGOING ASSESSMENT: Assess Mastery

Use the following resources to assess student mastery of capitalization.

In the Textbook	Print Resources	Technology
Chapter Review, Ex. 13–18, pp. 614–615 Standardized Test Preparation Workshop, pp. 616–617	Formal Assessment, Chapter 27	On-Line Exercise Bank, Chapter 27

⏱ TIME SAVERS!

✋ **Hands-on Grammar** Use the Hands-on Grammar Activity Sheet for Chapter 27 to facilitate this activity.

Chapter Review

Each of these exercises correlates to the instruction on capitalization, pages 602–613. The exercises may be used for more practice, for reteaching, or for review of the key concepts presented. Answers for all chapter exercises are available in *Grammar Exercises Answers on Transparencies* in your Teaching Resources.

Answer Key

Exercise 13

1. I traveled north through the mountains and saw thousands of lakes.
2. In the fall, all of the leaves were orange and red.
3. He asked, "Have you visited this part of the country before?"
4. "I have never seen a waterfall that size before," I replied.
5. "Everywhere I go," I replied, "there are new sights to see."

Exercise 14

1. In 1607 Henry Hudson sailed to Greenland and the Svalbard Islands.
2. Hudson sailed past Nova Scotia and down the coast of North America.
3. He believed that the Pacific Ocean was connected to the Atlantic Ocean.
4. Then in 1609, he explored what was later named the Hudson River.
5. He sailed from New York Bay to the present site of Albany.
6. The river flows past the Catskill Mountains and the Hudson Highlands.
7. Near its mouth, it forms the border between New York and New Jersey.
8. Several canals link the Hudson to Lake Champlain, the Great Lakes, and the Saint Lawrence River.
9. Giovanni da Verrazzano, from Italy, had been the first to explore the river.
10. Robert Fulton launched one of his first steamboats on the Hudson River in 1807.

Chapter 27 Chapter Review

GRAMMAR EXERCISES 13–19

Exercise 13 Supplying Capital Letters in Sentences Rewrite each sentence below, using capital letters where necessary.

1. i traveled north through the mountains and saw thousands of lakes.
2. in the fall, all of the leaves were orange and red.
3. he asked, "have you visited this part of the country before?"
4. "i have never seen a waterfall that size before," i replied.
5. "everywhere i go," i replied, "there are new sights to see."

Exercise 14 Proofreading for Capitals for Names of People and Places Proofread each sentence below, copying it into your notebook and adding capital letters where needed.

1. In 1607, henry hudson sailed to greenland and the svalbard islands.
2. hudson sailed past nova scotia and down the coast of north america.
3. He believed that the pacific ocean was connected to the atlantic ocean.
4. Then, in 1609, he explored what was later named the hudson river.
5. He sailed from new york bay to the present site of albany.
6. The river flows past the catskill mountains and the hudson highlands.
7. Near its mouth, it forms the border between new york and new jersey.
8. Several canals link the hudson to lake champlain, the great lakes, and the saint lawrence river.
9. giovanni da verrazzano, from italy, had been the first to explore the river.
10. robert fulton launched one of his first steamboats on the hudson river in 1807.

Exercise 15 Proofreading for Capitals for Names of Specific Things Proofread each sentence below, copying it into your notebook and adding capital letters where needed.

1. Huey Long was educated at the university of oklahoma and tulane university.
2. In 1928, he won the nomination of the democratic party and ran for governor of louisiana.
3. During the great depression, the american people supported him.
4. He won a seat in the senate in 1932.
5. From his seat in the capitol building, Long fought President Roosevelt.
6. He sought to delay the passage of new deal measures.
7. Long was assassinated just after labor day in 1935.
8. His wife, Rose McConnell Long, completed his term in the senate.
9. In 1947, Robert Penn Warren won the pulitzer prize for his novel <u>All The King's Men</u>.
10. The book is about a southern governor resembling Huey Long.

Exercise 16 Proofreading for Capitals for Titles of People and Things Proofread each sentence below, copying it into your notebook and adding capital letters where needed.

1. The mountain now called Pikes Peak was discovered by lieutenant Zebulon Pike.
2. It is located near Colorado Springs, which was founded as a resort by general William Palmer.
3. "Is it true, mr. O'Brien," I asked, "that the pony express was operated by the Pikes Peak Express Company?"

Exercise 15

1. University of Oklahoma, Tulane University
2. Democratic Party, Louisiana
3. Great Depression, American
4. Senate
5. Capitol Building
6. New Deal
7. Labor Day
8. Senate
9. Pulitzer Prize
10. correct

Exercise 16

1. Lieutenant
2. General
3. Mr.
4. President
5. Postmaster General
6. <u>The Expeditions of Zebulon Montgomery Pike</u>
7. <u>The Great Pikes Peak Gold Rush</u>
8. <u>Colorado Geographic's</u>, "Pikes Peak or Bust"
9. "Colorado Springs & Pikes Peak Trail Map"
10. <u>Vacationing in Pikes Peak Country</u>

4. "Yes," he replied, "the pony express helped spread the news of president Lincoln's election."

5. Then, in 1863, postmaster general Montgomery Blair established free mail delivery.

6. The expeditions of zebulon montgomery pike is a fascinating book, edited by Elliot Coues from Pike's diaries.

7. Pikes Peak eventually became a mining area; Robert L. Brown brings this era to life in his book the great pikes peak gold rush.

8. colorado geographic's travel brochure entitled "pikes peak or bust" describes the area's attractions for hikers and campers.

9. Present-day hikers can purchase Kent Schulte's "colorado springs & pikes peak trail map."

10. There's even a video available: vacationing in pikes peak country.

Exercise 17 Proofreading to Follow All the Rules of Capitalization

Proofread the following passage, looking for errors in capitalization. On your paper, rewrite the passage, adding or eliminating capitals as necessary.

in the last of the mohicans, james fenimore cooper describes the hurons, a tribe of native americans. the hurons allied themselves with the french against the british during the american revolution. living near lake ontario and in the st. lawrence river valley, the hurons first met the french explorer jacques cartier in 1534. the meeting was the beginning of a long-lasting friendship between the hurons and the french. You can learn more about this tribe in a book from the junior library of american indians: huron indians by martin and martha schwabacher.

Exercise 18 Proofreading Letters

Practice Rewrite the following friendly letter, adding capital letters as needed.

10773 mckenzie avenue
victoria, british columbia
canada
december 5, 20––

dear dominic,

i am so excited to write to you about my new favorite author. i just finished reading some books by the american author john steinbeck. he was from salinas, california, and was educated at stanford university. his first novel, cup of gold, is about the infamous welsh pirate sir henry morgan. many of steinbeck's other novels are about farmers and workers in california. his book the grapes of wrath is about the joad family as they migrate from the oklahoma dust bowl to california during the great depression. steinbeck won a pulitzer prize for that book, and it was made into a successful movie. do you remember when we drove across the country? steinbeck wrote a book, travels with charley, about his drive across the united states with his pet poodle.

also, i found an interesting article by steinbeck in the new york times from 1943. the article, "the making of a new yorker," is about the first time he moved to new york city. although steinbeck had lived in san francisco, mexico city, and paris, he felt that new york city was unique. he said many of the things you had told me about living in the city. i am enclosing a copy of the article and a list of steinbeck's novels.

i miss you very much. please write back soon.

love,
maggie

Exercise 19 Writing Application

Write a letter to a friend. Include a heading, salutation, and closing. Describe an interesting place in the United States. Try to include the names of people and places. Use proper capitalization throughout your letter.

Chapter Review • 615

Answer Key continued

Exercise 19

Writing Application
Encourage students to mail or e-mail their letters.

Exercise 17

(1) In <u>The Last of the Mohicans</u>, James Fenimore Cooper describes the Hurons, a tribe of Native Americans. (2) The Hurons allied themselves with the French against the British during the American Revolution. (3) Living near Lake Ontario and in the St. Lawrence River Valley, the Hurons first met the French explorer Jacques Cartier in 1534. (4) The meeting was the beginning of a long-lasting friendship between the Hurons and the French. (5) You can learn more about this tribe in a book from the Junior Library of American Indians: <u>Huron Indians</u> by Martin and Martha Schwabacher.

Exercise 18

(1) 10773 McKenzie Avenue
Victoria, British Columbia
Canada
December 5, 20––
(2) Dear Dominic,
(3) I am so excited to write to you about my new favorite author. (4) I just finished reading some books by the American author John Steinbeck. (5) He was from Salinas, California, and was educated at Stanford University. (6) His first novel, <u>Cup of Gold</u>, is about the infamous Welsh pirate Sir Henry Morgan. (7) Many of Steinbeck's other novels are about farmers and workers in California. (8) His book <u>The Grapes of Wrath</u> is about the Joad family as they migrate from the Oklahoma Dust Bowl to California during the Great Depression. (9) Steinbeck won a Pulitzer Prize for that book, and it was made into a successful movie. (10) Do you remember when we drove across the country? (11) Steinbeck wrote a book, <u>Travels with Charley</u>, about his drive across the United States with his pet poodle. (12) Also, I found an interesting article by Steinbeck in <u>The New York Times</u> from 1943. (13) The article, "The Making of a New Yorker," is about the first time he moved to New York City. (14) Although Steinbeck had lived in San Francisco, Mexico City, and Paris, he felt that New York City was unique. (15) He said many of the things you had told me about living in the city. (16) I am enclosing a copy of the article and a list of Steinbeck's novels.
(17) I miss you very much. (18) Please write back soon.
(19) Love,
Maggie

continued

Step-by-Step Teaching Guide

Proofreading

Teaching Resources: Standardized Test Preparation Workbook, Chapter 27

1. Explain to students that each numbered, underlined section is made up of a single sentence. They should read each sentence carefully and compare it with the possible errors.

2. When they compare the first sentence with possible error A, spelling, they should see that it does indeed contain a spelling error—*gymnazium*. The only possible choice is item A.

3. Have a volunteer explain how she or he arrived at the answer for question 2.

Standardized Test Preparation Workshop

Proofreading

Standardized tests often measure your understanding of the rules of capitalization, spelling, and punctuation. You may be expected to recognize errors within the context of a written passage. You will be asked to identify the type of error, if any, in the passage. The following sample test items will give you practice in responding to these types of questions.

Test Tip

Some tests count more points off for wrong answers than they do for unanswered items. Find out how the test you are taking is scored.

Sample Test Items	Answers and Explanations
Read the passage, and decide which type of error, if any, appears in each underlined section. Excitedly, the class race-walked down the (1) school corridor to the gymnazium. Today was the first day of the mini-course, (2) and dr. Cooke would be presenting the program.	

1   A   Spelling error
 	
      B   Capitalization error
 	
      C   Punctuation error
 	
      D   No error
	The correct answer is *A*. The word *gymnazium* is spelled incorrectly with a *z* instead of an *s*.

2   F   Spelling error
 	
      G   Capitalization error
 	
      H   Punctuation error
 	
      J   No error
	The correct answer is *G. Dr.,* the abbreviation for *doctor*, should be capitalized because it is a professional title used with a person's name.

616 • Capitalization

⬦ TEST-TAKING TIP

Point out to students that multiple-choice questions such as the one in the sample have only one correct answer. This means that after they have chosen an answer, they can check it by reviewing the other choices. If in item 1, for example, they cannot find a capitalization or punctuation error, they can be even more confident that their choice of response A is correct.

Answer Key

> **Practice 1**

1. A
2. G
3. C
4. G

> **Practice 2**

1. C
2. F
3. B
4. H

> **Practice 1** **Directions:** Read the passage, and decide which type of error, if any, appears in each underlined section.

With a large bucket of fresh flowers in
(1)
hand, Ms. Casella entered the clasroom.

The members of the Eastlake middle
(2)
school service club had assembled to

make nosegays—small floral bouquets—

for their monthly project. In Elizabethan
                                      (3)
England, nosegays had been used to ward

off disease but these nosegays would

bring color and cheer to the Residents of
(4)
the Golden Glen Retirement Center.

1   **A** Spelling error
    B Capitalization error
    C Punctuation error
    D No error

2   **F** Spelling error
    G Capitalization error
    H Punctuation error
    J No error

3   **A** Spelling error
    B Capitalization error
    C Punctuation error
    D No error

4   **F** Spelling error
    G Capitalization error
    H Punctuation error
    J No error

> **Practice 2** **Directions:** Read the passage, and decide which type of error, if any, appears in each underlined section.

Colonists clashed with British soldiers
(1)
in Lexington Massachusetts on April 19,

1775. From 1775 to 1783, the Continental
                    (2)
Army waged the American Revolution

agianst Great Britain. The leader of the
                              (3)
Continental Army was general George

Washington. A few years later in 1789, he
                        (4)
became President George Washington.

1   **A** Spelling error
    B Capitalization error
    C Punctuation error
    D No error

2   **F** Spelling error
    G Capitalization error
    H Punctuation error
    J No error

3   **A** Spelling error
    B Capitalization error
    C Punctuation error
    D No error

4   **F** Spelling error
    G Capitalization error
    H Punctuation error
    J No error

Answer Key

▶ **Exercise A**

1. What was your favorite toy when you were young?
2. My little brother has a rattle and a teething ring.
3. Hey, I *really* miss my baby toys!
4. Do you still sleep with a favorite stuffed animal?
5. Maybe they will be collectible items one day.

▶ **Exercise B**

1. Every summer at the beach, we make sand castles using sand, seashells, and water.
2. I play catch with my cousins, who visit us for several weeks each year.
3. Last summer, I learned a new sport: volleyball.
4. When we first started playing, the net seemed so high.
5. Then I learned how to hit the ball; it wasn't very difficult.
6. I enjoyed volleyball; in fact, we played from noon until about 5:30 P.M.
7. Some people don't play sports at the beach. They read, listen to music, or just lie in the sun.
8. After a full, enjoyable day, we like to have a barbecue.
9. We cook many of my favorite foods: hamburgers, hot dogs, and corn on the cob.
10. When the sun sets, the temperature drops, but we still stay outside.

▶ **Exercise C**

1. Did you know that there are three types of kites?
2. The most well-known type is the diamond-shaped kite.
3. There are also box kites, delta kites, and bowed kites.
4. Paper or cloth is used for the kite; however, the frame can be wood or metal.
5. During the 1800's, kites served an important purpose: weather forecasting.
6. When Benjamin Franklin flew a kite, he proved his theory about electricity.
7. Alexander Graham Bell, the inventor of the telephone, also created kites.
8. "Let's Go Fly a Kite" is a great song.

Cumulative Review

MECHANICS

▶ **Exercise A** Using End Marks Copy the following sentences, inserting the appropriate end marks.

1. What was your favorite toy when you were young
2. My little brother has a rattle and a teething ring
3. Hey, I *really* miss my baby toys
4. Do you still sleep with a favorite stuffed animal
5. Maybe they will be collectible items one day

▶ **Exercise B** Using Commas, Semicolons, and Colons Copy the following sentences, inserting the appropriate commas, semicolons, and colons.

1. Every summer at the beach we make sand castles using sand seashells and water.
2. I play catch with my cousins who visit us for several weeks each year.
3. Last summer I learned a new sport volleyball.
4. When we first started playing the net seemed so high.
5. Then I learned how to hit the ball it wasn't very difficult.
6. I enjoyed volleyball in fact we played from noon until about 530 p.m.
7. Some people don't play sports at the beach They read listen to music or just lie in the sun.
8. After a full enjoyable day we like to have a barbecue.
9. We cook many of my favorite foods hamburgers hot dogs and corn on the cob.
10. When the sun sets the temperature drops but we still stay outside.

▶ **Exercise C** Using All the Rules of Punctuation Copy the following sentences, inserting the appropriate end marks, commas, semicolons, colons, quotation marks, underlining, hyphens, and apostrophes.

1. Did you know that there are three types of kites
2. The most well known type is the diamond shaped kite
3. There are also box kites delta kites and bowed kites
4. Paper or cloth is used for the kite however the frame can be wood or metal
5. During the 1800s kites served an important purpose weather forecasting
6. When Benjamin Franklin flew a kite he proved his theory about electricity
7. Alexander Graham Bell the inventor of the telephone also created kites
8. Let's Go Fly a Kite is a great song
9. Remember the line Lets go fly a kite up to the highest height
10. Its from a famous movie Mary Poppins

▶ **Exercise D** Using All the Rules of Capitalization Copy the following sentences, inserting the appropriate capital letters.

1. people throughout north america, south america, and europe ride bicycles.
2. around 1790, count divrac of france invented a wooden scooter.
3. a german inventor, baron drais, improved upon that model.
4. his version had a steering bar attached to the front wheel.
5. then, a scottish blacksmith, kirkpatrick macmillan, added foot pedals.

9. Remember the line: "Let's go fly a kite up to the highest height"?
10. It's from a famous movie: <u>Mary Poppins</u>.

▶ **Exercise D**

1. People throughout North America, South America, and Europe ride bicycles.
2. Around 1790, Count Divrac of France invented a wooden scooter.
3. A German inventor, Baron Drais, improved upon that model.
4. His version had a steering bar attached to the front wheel.
5. Then a Scottish blacksmith, Kirkpatrick MacMillan, added foot pedals.
6. In 1866, Pierre Lallement, a French carriage maker, took out the first U.S. patent on a pedal bicycle.
7. Mr. J.K. Starley of England produced the first commercially successful bicycle.
8. By 1897, more than four million Americans were riding bikes.
9. There are many road races like the Tour de France.
10. Other races, called BMX, are held on bumpy dirt tracks.

6. in 1866, pierre lallement, a french carriage maker, took out the first u.s. patent on a pedal bicycle.
7. mr. j.k. starley of england produced the first commercially successful bicycle.
8. by 1897, more than four million americans were riding bikes.
9. there are many road races like the tour de france.
10. other races, called bmx, are held on bumpy dirt tracks.

Exercise E Proofreading Dialogue for Punctuation and Capitalization

Copy the following dialogue, adding the proper punctuation and capitalization.

1. isnt that a new yo-yo asked pam i've never seen it before
2. no ive had it awhile replied joe i found it underneath my bed
3. i bet you dont know how yo-yos were invented
4. joe answered sure i do arent they toys for children
5. no pam said they originated in the philippines
6. right as toys joe insisted
7. they were weapons and toys pam corrected
8. ok well i know what the word yo-yo means
9. pam said so do i tell me and ill see if you're correct
10. well joe said im pretty sure it means come back
11. thats right pam said
12. its a toy that has been around for more than 3,000 years joe continued
13. it wasnt until the 1920s pam added that they were developed in the united states
14. who was donald duncan asked joe
15. he was the man who improved upon the design of the yo-yo and made it a popular toy in the united states

Exercise F Writing Sentences With Correct Punctuation and Capitalization

Write five sentences following the instructions given below. Be sure to punctuate and capitalize correctly.

1. Write a sentence about your favorite board game or video game.
2. Describe what you like about it.
3. Write a sentence about a favorite outdoor game.
4. Tell what time of year you play it, and name some of the friends who join in.
5. Write an exclamatory sentence about a great play in a game.

Exercise G Proofreading Paragraphs for Punctuation and Capitalization

Proofread the following paragraphs, copying them into your notebook and adding punctuation and capitalization as needed.

Do children still play board games I wonder. perhaps tv and video games have begun to replace checkers and chess.

There was a time you know when i excitedly hoped for board games as gifts on certain special occasions birthdays and holidays. one birthday when my twin sister, lily, and i received our first checkers set we were thrilled we couldn't wait to begin playing i think we played for hours. when aunt dotti and uncle larry came over with our cousins joanie and mark we all took turns playing. wow what a great time we had.

Exercise H Writing Application

Write a brief dialogue between you and a friend about your favorite toy from childhood. Be sure to include proper punctuation, capitalization, and indentation.

1. "Isn't that a new yo-yo?" asked Pam. "I've never seen it before."
2. "No, I've had it awhile," replied Joe. "I found it underneath my bed."
3. "I bet you don't know how yo-yos were invented."
4. Joe answered, "Sure I do. Aren't they toys for children?"
5. "No," Pam said. "They originated in the Philippines."
6. "Right. As toys," Joe insisted.
7. "They were weapons and toys," Pam corrected.
8. "OK. Well, I know what the word yo-yo means."
9. Pam said, "So do I. Tell me and I'll see if you're correct."
10. "Well," Joe said, "I'm pretty sure it means 'come back.'"
11. "That's right," Pam said.
12. "It's a toy that has been around for more than 3,000 years," Joe continued.
13. "It wasn't until the 1920's," Pam added, "that they were developed in the United States."
14. "Who was Donald Duncan?" asked Joe.
15. "He was the man who improved upon the design of the yo-yo and made it a popular toy in the United States."

Exercise F

Answers will vary. Encourage students to exchange papers and use chapters 26 and 27 to resolve any disagreements about correct capitalization and punctuation.

Exercise G

Do children still play board games, I wonder? Perhaps TV and video games have begun to replace checkers and chess.

There was a time, you know, when I excitedly hoped for board games as gifts on certain special occasions: birthdays and holidays. One birthday when my twin sister, Lily, and I received our first checkers set, we were thrilled. We couldn't wait to begin playing. I think we played for hours. When Aunt Dotti and Uncle Larry came over with our cousins Joanie and Mark, we all took turns playing. Wow, what a great time we had!

Exercise H

Answers will vary. Briefly review the rules for punctuating, capitalizing, and indenting dialogue.

1. Iron | rusts

2. Jeffrey | will be coming

3. it | Is moving

4. Cyclones | move

5. (you) | Begin

6. language | Will change

7. we | Must leave

8. Congress | has been meeting

9. (you) | Decide

10. Crickets | jump

Sentence Diagraming Workshop

When you study sentences, it is often helpful to draw diagrams of them.

KEY CONCEPT A diagram shows how the parts of a sentence are related. ■

Sentence diagrams begin with two lines—one horizontal and one vertical. The horizontal line is called a base line and the vertical line is called a bar.

FORM OF A DIAGRAM:

Diagraming Simple Subjects and Simple Verbs

The simple subject of a sentence is written to the left of the bar. The simple verb is written to the right. No punctuation is used in diagrams.

DECLARATIVE SENTENCE: Dogs bark.

Dogs | bark

Put the subject on the left—even when the sentence begins with a verb.

INTERROGATIVE SENTENCE: Did he remember?

he | Did remember

To diagram an imperative sentence, you must remember that the subject *you* is understood. Put it on the base line in parentheses.

IMPERATIVE SENTENCE: Wait!

(you) | Wait

DIAGRAMING A SENTENCE

1. Draw two lines, the base line and the bar.
2. Write the simple subject on the left and the verb on the right.
3. Capitalize the first word of the sentence.
4. If the sentence is imperative, write the subject as (*you*).

Exercise 1 **Making Sentence Diagrams** Diagram each of the sentences below, following the explanation on the preceding page.

EXAMPLE: Aunt Deborah called.

ANSWER:

Aunt Deborah	called

1. Iron rusts.
2. Jeffrey will be coming.
3. Is it moving?
4. Cyclones move.
5. Begin.
6. Will language change?
7. Must we leave?
8. Congress has been meeting.
9. Decide!
10. Crickets jump.

Exercise 2 **More Practice Diagraming Sentences** Diagram each of the following sentences.
1. Karen has been waiting.
2. Did he understand?
3. Opportunities come.
4. Try!
5. Robert was pretending.
6. Concentrate.
7. Shall we try?
8. Mrs. Young hesitated.
9. Has Shelly decided?
10. Finish.

Exercise 2

1. Karen | has been waiting

2. he | Did understand

3. Opportunities | come

4. (you) | Try

5. Robert | was pretending

6. (you) | Concentrate

7. we | Shall try

8. Mrs. Young | hesitated

9. Shelly | Has decided

10. (you) | Finish

Answer Key

1.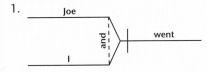

2.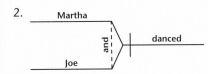

3.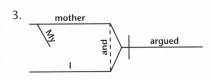

4.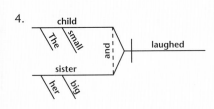

5.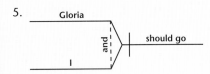

6.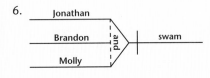

7.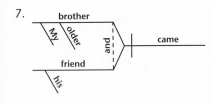

8.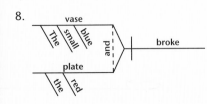

9.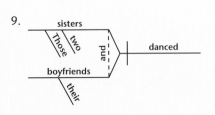

10.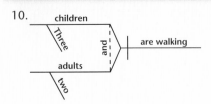

Diagraming Compound Subjects

When there is more than one subject in a sentence, split the base line on the left, or the subject side, so that each subject has its own line. The conjunction joining the subjects goes on a vertical dotted line between the subject lines.

EXAMPLE: She and I ate.

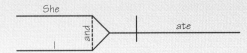

If the subjects have modifiers, put them beneath each noun on slanted lines.

EXAMPLE: The black dog and the gray cat ate.

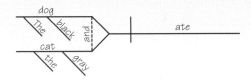

Exercise 3 Diagraming Compound Subjects Diagram each of the sentences below,

EXAMPLE: Mike and Ralph were fighting.

ANSWER:

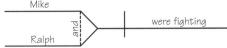

1. Joe and I went.
2. Martha and Joe danced.
3. My mother and I argued.
4. The small child and her big sister laughed.
5. Gloria and I should go.
6. Jonathan, Brandon, and Molly swam.
7. My older brother and his friend came.
8. The small blue vase and the red plate broke.
9. Those two sisters and their boyfriends danced.
10. Three children and two adults are walking.

Diagraming Compound Verbs

When there is more than one verb in a sentence, split the base line on the right, or the verb side, so that each verb has its own line. The conjunction joining the verbs goes on a vertical dotted line between the verb lines.

EXAMPLE: Martha dances and sings.

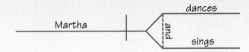

If there is a modifier in the sentence and it modifies both verbs, it goes on a diagonal line beneath the main base line. This shows that it applies to both verbs.

EXAMPLE: Martha dances and sings well.

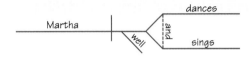

If each verb has its own modifier, each modifier goes on a diagonal line beneath the verb it modifies.

EXAMPLE: Nancy dances well but sings poorly.

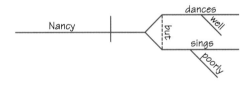

▶ **Exercise 4** Diagraming Compound Verbs Diagram each of the sentences below.
1. We swam and canoed.
2. Gerald speaks quietly but sings loudly.
3. My mother ate and drank slowly.
4. Sam walks and runs fast.
5. Katie talks fast but walks slowly.

▶ **Exercise 4**

1.
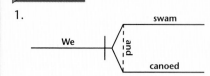

2.
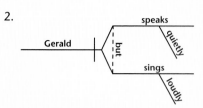

3.
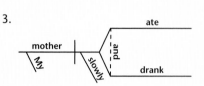

4.
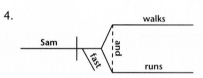

5.
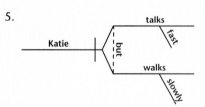

Exercise 5 *(page 625)*

1.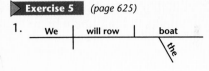

2.

3.

4.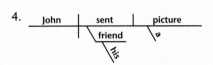

5.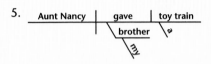

Diagraming Sentences
With Direct and Indirect Objects

Because objects complete the meaning of a verb, they are diagramed on the verb side of the sentence. Direct objects sit on the same line as the subject and the verb and are separated from the verb by a short vertical line. Indirect objects are placed on a horizontal line extending from a slanted line directly beneath the verb.

EXAMPLES: The dog ate its dinner.

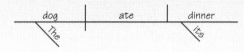

My friend sent me a letter.

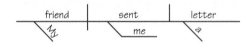

The boy gave the girl a ring.

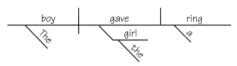

Exercise 5 Diagraming Sentences With Direct and Indirect Objects Diagram each of the sentences below.

EXAMPLE: I sent Charles a message.

ANSWER:

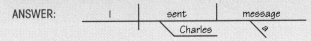

1. We will row the boat.
2. Randy gave me a book.
3. The large dog licked the little kitten.
4. John sent his friend a picture.
5. Aunt Nancy gave my brother a toy train.

Exercise 6 Diagraming Sentences Diagram each of the following sentences. There are compound subjects, compound verbs, and/or complements in the sentences.

EXAMPLE: Bees and wasps stung the children.

ANSWER:

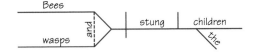

1. Jack and Joan ate ice cream.
2. My brother and my sister laughed and ran.
3. My younger brother and my older sister laughed loudly and ran quickly.
4. Jeri and David sent their friend a present.
5. Thomas and his brother argued.
6. Molly ate cookies and drank lemonade.
7. Jonathan and Brandon rode their bicycles.
8. The yellow dog chased the black cat.
9. My mother and father gave me a new coat.
10. The student wrote a wonderful paper.

Sentence Diagraming Workshop • 625

10.
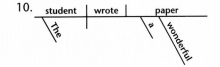

Exercise 6

1.
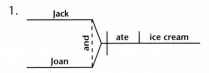

2.
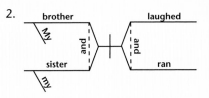

3.
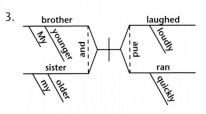

4.
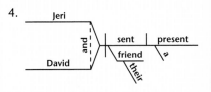

5.
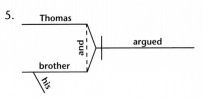

6.
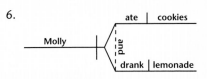

7.
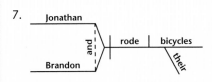

8.
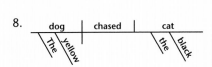

9.
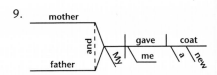

1.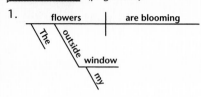

2.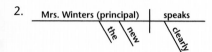

3.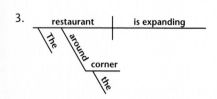

4.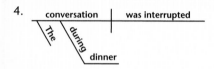

5.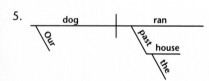

6.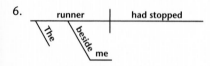

7.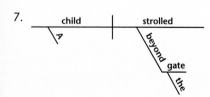

8.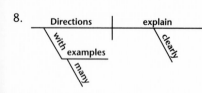

9.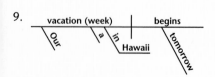

10.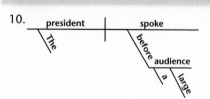

Diagraming Phrases

Prepositional Phrases To diagram a prepositional phrase, draw a slanted line for the preposition and a horizontal line for the noun. Put modifiers on slanted lines beneath the noun.

EXAMPLES: near the red barn

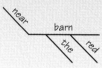

under the old oak tree

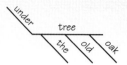

Adjective Phrases A prepositional phrase that acts as an adjective is placed beneath the noun or pronoun it modifies.

EXAMPLES: Our neighbor *down the road* jogs often.

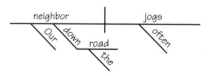

The bridge *over the fast river* collapsed.

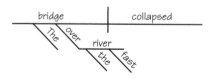

Adverb Phrases A prepositional phrase that acts as an adverb is placed beneath the verb, adjective, or adverb it modifies.

EXAMPLES: The plane flew *over the runway.*

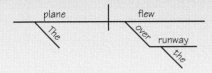

He finished the book *after dinner.*

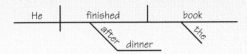

Appositive Phrases To diagram an appositive phrase, put the most important noun in the phrase in parentheses, and place it next to the noun it renames, identifies, or explains. Place the modifiers beneath the noun.

EXAMPLES: Sam, *the manager of a store*, works hard.

Molly, *my niece*, plays basketball.

▶ **Exercise 8** *(page 628)*

1.
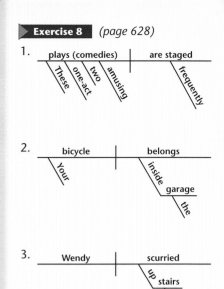

2.
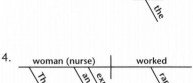

3.
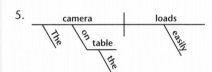

4.

5.

Exercise 9 (page 629)

1.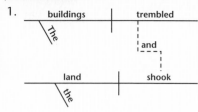

2.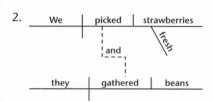

3.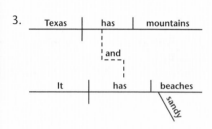

4.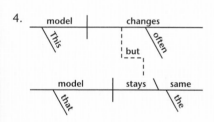

5.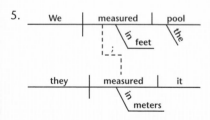

6.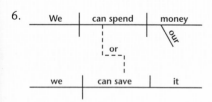

7.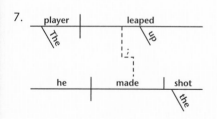

Exercise 7 Diagraming Phrases

Diagram the sentences below. Each one contains at least one prepositional or appositive phrase.

EXAMPLE: Poe, the author of the story, was born in Boston.

ANSWER:

1. The flowers outside my window are blooming.
2. Mrs. Winters, the new principal, speaks clearly.
3. The restaurant around the corner is expanding.
4. The conversation during dinner was interrupted.
5. Our dog ran past the house.
6. The runner beside me had stopped.
7. A child strolled beyond the gate.
8. Directions with many examples explain clearly.
9. Our vacation, a week in Hawaii, begins tomorrow.
10. The president spoke before a large audience.

Exercise 8 More Practice Diagraming Phrases

Diagram the following sentences. Each one contains a prepositional or appositive phrase.

EXAMPLE: Our president, Georgia Smith, will speak now.

ANSWER:

1. These one-act plays, two amusing comedies, are staged frequently.
2. Your bicycle belongs inside the garage.
3. Wendy scurried up the stairs.
4. The woman, an experienced nurse, worked rapidly.
5. The camera on the table loads easily.

Diagraming Compound Sentences

The clauses of a compound sentence are diagramed separately, one under the other. They are connected by a dotted line that looks like a step. The coordinating conjunction or semicolon that connects them is written on the "step."

EXAMPLES:

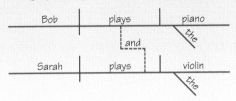

Bob plays the piano, and Sarah plays the violin.

Simon wrote the story, but Ted read it aloud.

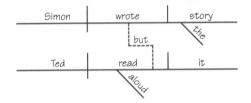

Exercise 9 Diagraming Compound Sentences Diagram each of the following compound sentences.

1. The buildings trembled, and the land shook.
2. We picked fresh strawberries, and they gathered beans.
3. Texas has mountains, and it has sandy beaches.
4. This model changes often, but that model stays the same.
5. We measured the pool in feet; they measured it in meters.
6. We can spend our money, or we can save it.
7. The player leaped up; he made the shot.
8. Some members came by plane, but others arrived by bus.
9. The blizzard could hit the city, or it could move east.
10. She told a story, and I listened attentively.
11. Michael received the message, but his older brother wrote a reply.
12. Amy can plant her seeds now, or she can wait until June.
13. The children arrived early, and they stayed late.
14. Mark hit a home run, but the visiting team still lost the game.
15. I tried hard, but some questions stumped me.

8.
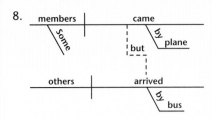

9.
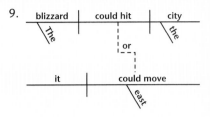

10.
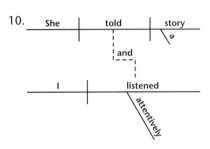

11.
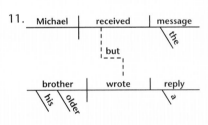

12.
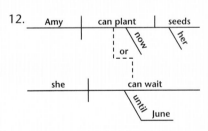

13.
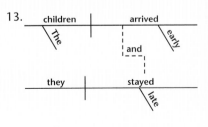

14. 15.
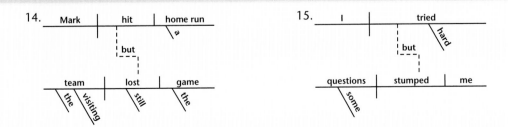

Lesson Objectives

1. To develop critical listening and effective speaking skills and apply them to various types of presentations.

2. To understand and evaluate visual images and messages in a variety of media.

3. To produce visual images, messages, and meanings that communicate with others.

4. To expand vocabulary through reading and listening and by developing skills in using context, word structure, word origins, and reference tools to determine word meanings.

5. To develop and apply reading strategies for a variety purposes and texts.

6. To develop study and research skills and become familiar with reference tools and the resources of libraries and the Internet.

7. To develop skills in taking tests in various formats.

8. To learn and apply specific communication and procedural skills of the workplace, including the problem-solving and managing time and money.

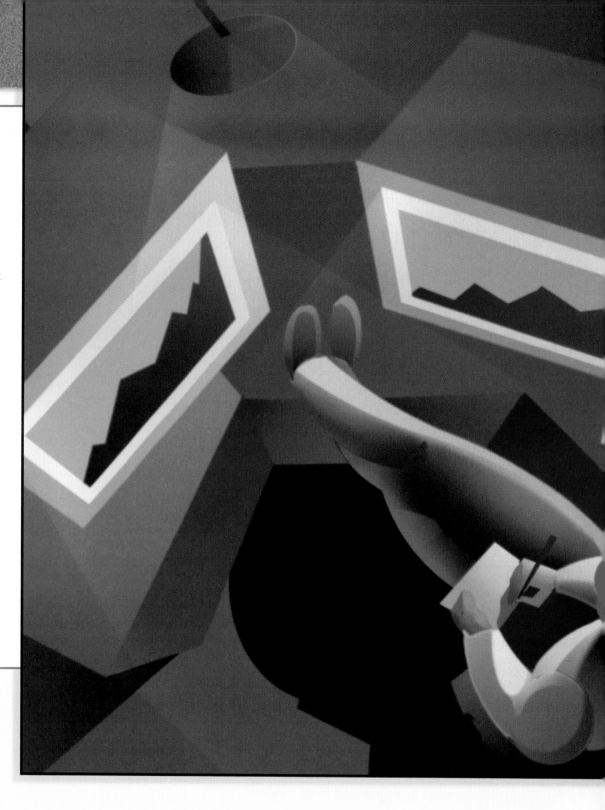

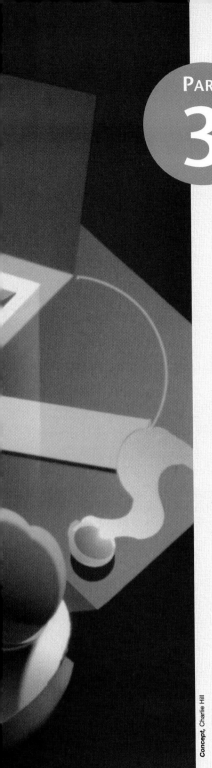

Concept, Charlie Hill

PART 3

Academic and Workplace Skills

Step-by-Step Teaching Guide

Responding to Fine Art

Concept
by Charlie Hill

Use this painting to start a discussion about the definition of academic and workplace skills.

1. Have students examine the painting on pages 630–631. You might use the following questions to prompt discussion:

   What is happening in this painting? How can you tell?

   Describe how the artist uses shapes and color to create the scene. How would you describe the mood of this painting?

2. Ask students what they think the figure in the painting is writing. Have students discuss what they think this person does for a living. Ask students how they think this person uses writing in his work. Lead students into a discussion of their own experiences of academic and workplace writing. Encourage students to identify the skills they need in school and at the workplace (for those who may have after-school jobs). Ask students why writing and other communicative skills are important to almost every type of work.

In-Depth Lesson Plan

	LESSON FOCUS	PRINT AND MEDIA RESOURCES
DAY 1	**Speaking Skills** Students learn and apply speaking skills (pp. 632–636).	**Teaching Resources** *Academic and Workplace Skills Activity Book,* pp. 1–5
DAY 2	**Listening Skills** Students learn and apply the skills of effective and critical listening (pp. 637–638).	**Teaching Resources** *Academic and Workplace Skills Activity Book,* pp. 1–5
DAY 3	**Viewing Skills** Students learn and apply viewing skills (pp. 639–644).	**Teaching Resources** *Academic and Workplace Skills Activity Book,* pp. 6–16
DAY 4	**Representing Skills** Students learn and apply representing skills such as creating graphic organizers, multimedia presentations, videos, and performing (pp. 645–651).	**Teaching Resources** *Academic and Workplace Skills Activity Book,* pp. 6–16

Accelerated Lesson Plan

	LESSON FOCUS	PRINT AND MEDIA RESOURCES
DAY 1	**Speaking and Listening Skills** Students learn and apply speaking skills and the skills of effective and critical listening (pp. 632–638).	**Teaching Resources** *Academic and Workplace Skills Activity Book,* pp. 1–5
DAY 2	**Viewing and Representing Skills** Students learn and apply viewing skills and representing skills such as creating graphic organizers, multimedia presentations, videos, and performing (pp. 639–651).	**Teaching Resources** *Academic and Workplace Skills Activity Book,* pp. 6–16

Options for Adapting Lesson Plans

HOMEWORK

Have students complete any section of the chapter for homework.

FEATURES

Extend coverage with the Standardized Test Preparation Workshop (p. 652).

TECHNOLOGY

Students can use the On-Line Exercise Bank to complete the exercises on computer. The Auto Check feature will grade their work.

INTEGRATED SKILLS COVERAGE

Workplace Skills
Integrating Workplace Skills ATE p. 651

Viewing and Representing
Critical Viewing SE pp. 632, 635, 639, 640, 641, 646, 650

ASSESSMENT SUPPORT

Standardized Test Preparation Workshop SE p. 652; ATE p. 652

Standardized Test Preparation Workbook, pp. 55–56

Formal Assessment, Ch. 28

MEETING INDIVIDUAL NEEDS

Less Advanced Students ATE p. 634; see also Ongoing Assessments ATE pp. 636, 638, 640, 643

ESL Students ATE pp. 633, 636, 650

More Advanced Students ATE p. 651

Logical/Mathematical Learners ATE p. 640

Visual/Spatial Learners ATE pp. 644, 650

Musical/Rhythmic Learners ATE p. 650

BLOCK SCHEDULING

Pacing Suggestions
For 90-minute Blocks
- Administer the Diagnostic Test to students to determine instructional coverage.
- Have students complete the necessary exercises in class. Use the Hands-on Grammar activity to provide a change of pace.

Professional Development Support
- *How to Manage Instruction in the Block* This teaching Resource provides management and activity suggestions.

MEDIA AND TECHNOLOGY

For the Teacher
- *Resource Pro* CD-ROM

WRITING AND GRAMMAR WEB SITE

The Interactive Writing and Grammar Web site provides a wide array of support for students, teachers, and parents. Grammar support includes:

- On-Line Exercise Bank with Auto Check scoring
- Diagnostic and assessment support

www.phschool.com

Lesson Objectives

1. To participate in class discussions.
2. To give accurate directions.
3. To greet people and make introductions.
4. To prepare and deliver speeches.
5. To listen effectively and critically.
6. To interpret maps, graphs, and photographs.
7. To view informative media critically.
8. To view fine art critically.
9. To create graphic organizers.
10. To present information in an effective format.
11. To develop a multimedia presentation.
12. To perform and interpret.

Critical Viewing

Analyze; Extend She is using an overhead projector and a model. Students may suggest posters, charts, graphs, or photographs.

Chapter 28 Speaking, Listening, Viewing, and Representing

How much of your day do you spend talking to friends? Listening to the radio? Watching movies or television? Presenting your ideas through pictures, videos, and other visual media? In today's world, speaking, listening, and viewing are a vital part of everyday life, and the ability to communicate through the visual media is becoming more important than ever. In this chapter, you'll learn all of the skills you need to be an effective communicator in the multimedia age.

▲ **Critical Viewing**
What visual medium is this girl using in her presentation? What other options would she have for presenting visual aids? **[Analyze; Extend]**

⏱ TIME AND RESOURCE MANAGER

Resources
Print: Academic and Workplace Skills Activity Book, pp. 1–5

In-Depth Coverage	Accelerated Pace
• Cover pp. 633–638 in class. • Assign and review Exercises 1–8.	• Assign pp. 633–638 for independent student review. • Have students complete Exercises 1–8.

Section 28.1

Speaking and Listening Skills

In school, you use speaking and listening skills every day. You listen to your teachers and friends. You give reports and presentations to your classmates. These *formal* activities involve special skills. You also use *informal* skills in your everyday life, in conversations with friends and family members and when you meet new people.

Using Informal Speaking Skills

You use informal speaking skills without thinking about it—on the phone with a friend, or talking to a family member. This section will help you apply these skills to other situations, such as class discussions and introductions.

Participate in Class Discussions Participating in class discussions will help you become a successful student. It not only enables you to ask questions that will help you better understand material, but also allows you to contribute your own ideas.

> **KEY CONCEPT** By preparing thoroughly for class discussions and practicing your discussion skills, you will develop the confidence and the comfort level you need to be a strong contributor to class discussions. ■

TIPS FOR PARTICIPATING IN CLASS DISCUSSIONS

- Establish a goal for class participation. For example, you might aim to make a minimum of one contribution to every discussion.
- Do whatever studying and homework is required, so that you come to class prepared to participate.
- Listen attentively, not only to your teacher but also to the questions and answers of your classmates.
- Ask questions when you are unclear about something, or when you want to learn more about something.
- When your teacher asks a question that you can answer, raise your hand and, if called on, give your answer.

> **Exercise 1** Improving Class Participation Skills Set a goal of answering or asking a question in each subject every day. Keep a record in your notebook of each question you ask or contribution you make. Take notes about which questions were most helpful and which comments were most effective.

> **More Practice**
> Academic and Workplace Skills Activity Book
> • p. 1

Speaking, Listening, Viewing, and Representing • **633**

Answer Key

> **Exercise 1**

Students' responses will vary. Make sure students keep a record of their progress.

PREPARE and ENGAGE

Interest GRABBER Choose the class clown or another extrovert to come to the front of the room and give a speech that re-creates what he or she was busy saying to friends before you called the class to order. Then ask the audience to tell the main points of the speech.

Activate Prior Knowledge

Ask students what kinds of things they listen to. (school lectures, friends' anecdotes, parents' instructions, TV, radio, and so on) Ask them to tell how they listen differently to each, and why.

TEACH

Step-by-Step Teaching Guide

Participate in Class Discussions

1. Emphasize that there is no such thing as a "stupid" question. The purpose of a class discussion is to share ideas and information. If no one asks questions, there can be no discussion. No student should ever hesitate to ask a question for fear that any other student will laugh. The worst thing a student can do is keep silent when he or she is confused about anything. This ensures that the confusion will not be solved.

2. Remind students that everyone's point of view is valid, especially in a discussion on a subjective topic such as literature. Every person in the class has his or her own unique viewpoint to contribute, and everyone's views deserve respect.

Customize for
ESL Students

Students who are uncomfortable speaking English may be especially reluctant to contribute to class discussion. Encourage them to take their time when speaking. Their classmates are often supportive and patient. Remind students that the more they speak English, the easier it will get.

Give Directions; Greet New People and Make Introductions

1. Ask students to share stories of times when they have been given inaccurate or confusing directions. What were the results? Were they annoyed? Suggest that a fifth step in the list on this page might be to have the listener read the directions back. This way the person giving the directions can clarify questions and correct any mistakes.

2. Go over the list of instructions for introducing people. It is polite to introduce a younger person to an older one first. If students introduce friends of their own age to parents, teachers, or older people, they should always speak first to the older person.

   "Aunt Rosa, this is my friend Tom. Tom, this is my aunt, Mrs. Garcia."

Customize for
Less Advanced Students

Have everyone in the class write out the directions from his or her home to the school. Read some examples aloud (anonymously). Have the class comment on whether the directions are easy to follow. If they are not, have students suggest changes and improvements. Make sure students explain why they might have difficulty following a particular direction.

Answer Key

Exercise 2

Have students rewrite their directions after they have been evaluated by a partner.

Exercise 3

You may want to have students complete this activity in class with students role-playing the parts of strangers.

28.1

Give Directions You have probably given people directions for how to get to your house or apartment. You may also have given someone directions on how to complete an activity. In either case, you probably found that the more specific and accurate details you were able to provide, the easier your directions were to follow.

TIPS FOR GIVING DIRECTIONS

- Think through your directions before you share them. You may even find it helpful to write them down.

- Provide as much detail as possible. Make sure that all of your details are accurate. Just one inaccurate detail can send someone off track.

- Speak slowly and clearly. Pause after each key detail to make sure that your listener comprehends it.

- When you have finished, ask your listener if he or she has been able to understand everything. Answer any questions.

Greet New People and Make Introductions Throughout your life, you will meet many people, and you will often be asked to introduce people you already know to each other.

TIPS FOR GREETING NEW PEOPLE AND MAKING INTRODUCTIONS

- Say the person's name when you greet him or her for the first time. You'll find that it will help you to remember it.

- Ask the person questions about himself or herself, and try to make frequent eye contact.

- Repeat the person's name when your first meeting ends.

- When making introductions, pronounce the person's full name clearly and correctly.

- Add something of interest about the person you're introducing. For example, you might describe that person's hobby.

Exercise 2 Giving Directions Write a set of accurate directions to a place you like to visit. Then, share these directions with someone who has never been there. Have your listener evaluate whether you have provided enough detail.

Exercise 3 Greeting People and Making an Introduction Introduce two people you know who have never met one another. Greet each person properly, and follow the checklist for making introductions.

Using Formal Speaking Skills

Formal speaking refers to speeches and presentations delivered to an audience. At this point in your life, most of the formal speaking you do will be at school. As you grow older, however, you may very well find yourself in other situations in which you are called on to deliver a speech or presentation. Following are some of the situations outside school in which you may deliver speeches and presentations:

Occasions for Formal Speeches

- Speeches at weddings and formal parties
- Presentations in the workplace
- Speeches at town meetings, board of education meetings, and other public forums
- Speeches to clubs or sports teams

Understand Different Kinds of Speeches Following are the three main kinds of speeches:

- An **explanatory** speech explains a situation or event. It presents facts without attempting to sway the audience.
- A **persuasive** speech attempts to convince an audience to agree with a point of view or to take some course of action. It may use techniques such as repetition of key points to capture the attention of an audience.
- An **entertaining** speech is given to amuse the audience and may be included in other kinds of speeches. Often, a good speaker will use informal language (such as humor) to relax the audience.

The kind of speech you give will depend on your audience, your purpose, and the occasion on which you are delivering your speech. For example, if you are giving a speech to friends to add to the enjoyment of a party, it will most likely be an entertaining speech.

> **Exercise 4** Listing Kinds of Speeches Give two topic examples for each kind of speech described above. Then, identify appropriate audiences for each.

> **More Practice**
> Academic and Workplace Skills Activity Book
> • p. 2

▼ Critical Viewing
Tiger Woods is a popular and extremely successful professional golfer. What nonverbal communication skills is Woods displaying in this photograph? **[Analyze]**

Step-by-Step Teaching Guide

Understand Different Kinds of Speeches

Go over the different types of speeches. Have students try to match the occasions for formal speeches with the types of speeches described below. Ask if students can think of other types of speeches and whether they can describe occasions on which such speeches would be given.

Critical Viewing

Analyze Students may suggest such nonverbal communication skills as his facial expression, or smile, and his posture.

Answer Key

> **Exercise 4**

Answers will vary. Samples are given.

Explanatory: How to do a swan dive/swimmers; The reasons for the Civil War/historians

Persuasive: The need for more after-school programs/students, school personnel; Why Yellowstone Park is more fun than Disneyland/travelers

Entertaining: How I taught my cat to do tricks/cat owners; Ten ways to avoid eating vegetables without your mother noticing/friends

635

Prepare and Deliver a Speech

1. Go over the preparatory steps. Clarify any step students do not fully understand. Explain that even speakers who are giving talks on topics with which they are very familiar prepare. People are often nervous about speaking in front of audiences and can get flustered and lose track of what they meant to say. If speakers have prepared good notes and practiced delivering their speeches beforehand, the process will seem more comfortable and familiar, and the speaker is less likely to be nervous.

2. Emphasize the benefits of speaking from notes rather than reading a written-out text. A speaker who has to read a speech cannot make eye contact with the audience. Eye contact is very important, because audiences respond to a speaker's attitude and personality. Written text can also sound artificial and dull when read aloud. A speech given from notes usually has much more flow and spontaneity.

Customize for
ESL Students

Students may be worried that they will mispronounce some words in their speech. Suggest that their note cards contain pronunciations to help them. They should use phonetics, not dictionary symbols, for example, prez-en-TAY-shun.

Answer Key

▶ **Exercise 5**

Have students present their speeches in class. Make sure that they have prepared note cards.

28.1

Prepare and Deliver a Speech After deciding on your topic and type of speech, plan your speech carefully.

▶ **KEY CONCEPT** Use an organized plan to prepare and present your speech. ■

Gather Information Research the subject for reliable information by using the library and other sources. Take careful notes, quoting the author's exact words where helpful. Record the source of each piece of information.

Outline Main Points and Supporting Details Create an outline using the information you have gathered. Group your information into main points or subtopics and provide supporting details for each. Look at this sample outline.

> **The Land and Climate of California**
>
> A. Landscape
>   1. two mountain ranges
>   a. coast ranges—along coast
>   b. Sierra Nevada—borders Nevada and Arizona
>   2. fertile central valley
>
> B. Climate
>   1. lots of rain in the north
>   2. desert in the south
>   3. mild temperature except in mountains

Prepare Note Cards Jot down each main point with its accompanying details on a separate index card. You can glance at your cards while speaking to help you remember each point. Use few words and write them in large letters.

Practice Your Speech Practice your speech using *verbal* and *nonverbal language* to emphasize your points. *Verbal* techniques include altering the loudness of your voice and the rate at which you speak. *Nonverbal* techniques include your use of movements, posture, facial expressions, and gestures to reinforce your meaning.

Deliver Your Speech Use your note cards to guide you as you speak. Use your examples to illustrate each point. Conclude your speech with a restatement of your main idea.

▶ **Exercise 5** Preparing and Presenting a Speech Prepare and deliver a brief speech on a topic that interests you.

⦿ Learn More

For tips on writing a persuasive speech, review the elements of persuasive writing in Chapter 7. For help writing an explanatory speech, review the guidelines for writing a how-to essay in Chapter 10.

💿 Technology Tip

Practice your speech by recording it on tape. Play it back to hear how you sound.

☑ ONGOING ASSESSMENT: Monitor and Reinforce

If students have trouble preparing for and giving class presentations, try one of the following options.

Option 1 Have each student write a paragraph or two of text and prepare a speech on the same topic from notes. Have the student read the speech, then give it from the notes. Compare and contrast the styles of delivery and effect on the audience.	**Option 2** Encourage students to choose topics they are interested in and already know something about. They should not worry about classmates' reactions to their topics. Make it clear that listeners in the classroom are required to listen with the same respect they hope to be shown when they are speaking.

Listening Effectively

To become a good listener, you must get involved in what you are hearing. Concentrate on the speaker's words. Listen for his or her main points, and evaluate what he or she is saying. You will understand more, and you will better enjoy the time you spend listening.

KEY CONCEPT Listening is a two-step process consisting of identifying and then evaluating a speaker's message. ■

Active Listening Active listening means getting involved in what you hear—the more involved you become, the more you will learn.

Determine Your Purpose for Listening The way you listen depends upon what you are listening for. There are three main purposes for listening:

- **To gain information:** Listen for main ideas and major details.
- **To solve problems:** Listen and ask questions to clarify problems so a solution can be found.
- **To enjoy and appreciate:** Listen for artistic elements, such as rhyme, imagery, and descriptive language.

Eliminate Barriers Prepare to listen by putting away all distracting material (books, magazines, homework). Block out all disruptive noises, inside and outside the classroom, so you can concentrate on the speaker and his or her message.

Summarize Main Ideas and Supporting Details Summarizing a speaker's message forces you to listen attentively and to make decisions about what is important. Use the suggestions below to summarize a speaker's message:

- In your own words, write only main ideas and supporting details—the information you want to remember.
- Underline main ideas so they are easy to locate when you want to refer back to them.
- Write notes in short phrases, not complete sentences.

Exercise 6 Becoming an Active Listener For one week, practice active listening techniques in one of your classes. Remember to decide on your purpose, block out all distractions, and take notes on important information. Track your progress after each class by reviewing how well you listened. Analyze whether or not you accomplished your purpose for listening.

▶ **More Practice**
Academic and Workplace Skills Activity Book
- p. 4

Speaking and Listening Skills • **637**

Active Listening

1. Suggest that students always position their seats in a class or audience so that they can see the speaker. This will help them to concentrate on the speaker.

2. Taking notes while listening guarantees that the listener's attention will not wander and that he or she will not miss important points. Some speakers (such as classroom teachers) do not mind stopping to repeat a point or to answer a question. Other speakers prefer to have listeners hold all their questions until the end of the presentation.

Answer Key

▶ **Exercise 6**

Students' responses will vary. Make sure students record their progress.

Listening Critically

As students approach Exercises 7 and 8, remind them that all political speeches are persuasive. A political speaker uses any techniques at his or her command to convince listeners of a particular point of view. It is necessary to be especially careful when listening to political speeches.

Answer Key

Exercise 7

You may want to bring in a videotape of a political speech so that students can focus on the same event.

Exercise 8

Have students present their findings to the class. Make sure that they have tested their understanding by restating parts of the speaker's message.

28.1

Listening Critically

KEY CONCEPT Do not accept all that you hear at face value. Analyze and evaluate as you listen to draw your own conclusions about a speaker's message. ■

Use these techniques to become a critical listener:

Analyze Persuasive Techniques Speakers often use techniques like these to persuade you to think a certain way:

- **Emotional Appeals** The speaker uses emotional words to persuade you to agree with a certain point of view.

- **Propaganda** The speaker presents selected information to promote a particular set of ideas.

Interpret Verbal and Nonverbal Gestures Paying attention to verbal and nonverbal gestures can enhance your comprehension of a speaker's message.

- **Verbal Gestures** Pay attention to when speakers choose to raise or lower, or slow down or speed up, their voices.

- **Nonverbal Gestures** Notice a speaker's movements, such as arm-waving or head-nodding.

Evaluate Your Listening To find ways to improve your listening skills, take time to evaluate yourself.

- **Monitor Your Understanding** You can test your understanding of the speaker's message by restating parts of it to the speaker. Does the speaker agree with your restatement?

- **Compare and Contrast Interpretations** Write your interpretation of a speaker's message, and use a chart such as a Venn diagram to compare and contrast it with a peer's interpretation.

Exercise 7 Listening Critically Listen to a political speech. Note each of the speaking techniques the speaker uses. Analyze and interpret the content of the message, and then compare your view with a peer's.

Exercise 8 Evaluating Your Listening Skills Listen to a political speech and take note of the speaker's use of persuasive techniques and gestures. Report your findings to the class.

More Practice

Academic and Workplace Skills Activity Book
• p. 5

☑ ONGOING ASSESSMENT: Monitor and Reinforce

If students have trouble listening critically, try the following options.

Option 1 Have students choose partners and listen to a news broadcast or a speech together. After listening, students can compare their impressions. This will help show each student which aspects of listening he or she needs to work on.	**Option 2** Have students take notes during a speech or lecture. Then challenge them to try to reconstruct the speech from the notes. This will help students with both their note-taking and listening skills.

Section 28.2

Viewing and Representing Skills

You are surrounded by visual images: A fire truck screaming across the television screen, a painting pouring out colors on a museum wall, a page bristling with buttons on a Web site—these are all visual images. In this section, you will learn how to interpret and create images.

Interpreting Maps, Graphs, and Photographs

Maps, graphs, and photographs can convey as much information as written texts—sometimes more.

KEY CONCEPT Learn the key features of maps, graphs, and photographs to learn how to interpret them properly. ■

When you interpret any type of visual aid, follow these steps:

1. **Determine your purpose** for viewing. What information do you hope to gain?
2. **Study the title, caption, and labels.** What information do they add?
3. **Examine all symbols.** Use a key if one is provided.
4. **Connect the visuals to the written text** they accompany.

Read Maps

Different kinds of maps give different information. **Political** maps show boundaries, cities, towns, and capital cities of a particular place. **Physical** maps show the different land and water forms, such as mountains, deserts, farmland, rivers, lakes, and oceans. **Climate** maps and **population** maps give information on these topics for a particular region.

Use these steps to help you interpret maps:

1. Determine the type and purpose of the map.
2. Examine the map's distance scale and any symbols.
3. Relate the map's information to any accompanying written information.

▼ **Critical Viewing**
This map shows the territorial extent of an ancient culture. What information does the map convey? What do the symbols on the map represent? [**Analyze, Extend**]

Silver
Gold
Iron
Marble
Timber

Mt. Olympus

PINDUS MTS.

Delphi
GREECE
Corinth
Olympia
Mycenae
Athens
PELOPONNESUS
Sparta

Aegean Sea

ASIA MINOR
Ephesus

Milos

Rhodes

Mediterranean Sea

Albers Equal Area Projection
0   50   100 Miles
0   50   100 Kilometers

Crete

N
W   E
S

Mycenaean world about 1300 B.C.   ▪ Centers of ancient Greek civilization

Viewing and Representing Skills • 639

Interpreting Maps

1. Use an atlas to show students historical, political, physical, climate, population, and solar system maps.
2. Be sure that students can identify and interpret different map features: distance scale, compass rose, national boundaries, rivers, mountains, capital cities, and so on.

Critical Viewing

Analyze; Extend The map shows the cities and cultural centers that comprised the ancient Greek civilization during a particular period. it also shows a boundary between Greece proper and its holdings in Asia Minor. Students may suggest that the symbols represent the natural resources of the ancient Greek culture.

⊘ TIME AND RESOURCE MANAGER

Resources
Print: Academic and Workplace Skills Activity Book, pp. 6–16

In-Depth Coverage	Accelerated Pace
• Cover pp. 639–651 in class. • Assign and review Exercises 9–18.	• Assign pp. 639–651 for independent student review. • Have students complete Exercises 9–18.

Interpreting Graphs

1. A line graph shows the change of something (in this case, world population) over time. Ask the following questions to provide practice in reading a line graph.

   What was the world population in 1600? (less than 1 billion)

   What was the increase in population between 1700 and 1900? (2 billion)

2. A bar graph compares amounts of similar things (in this case, life expectancies). Ask:

   Which country has the highest life expectancy? The lowest? (Italy; India)

   In which countries is life expectancy the same? (Brazil and Egypt)

Customize for
Logical/Mathematical Learners

Have a small group of students extend Exercise 9 on page 641 by finding information and representing it on graphs. The group should create three graphs, one of each type. Let students find their own topics. Suggest an almanac as a good place to find statistics that can be represented graphically. Have students explain to the class what their graphs represent and why the type of graph they chose is appropriate.

Critical Viewing

Analyze, Draw Conclusions
Students may suggest that the world's population in 2000 is roughly 6 billion. Moreover, much of the population's growth has taken place in the nineteenth and twentieth centuries. Students should identify the life expectancy of the people living in the countries represented in the graph.

Critical Viewing

Analyze, Draw Conclusions
Students should suggest that the numbers refer to years of age.

Read Graphs

Graphs provide a visual comparison of related information.

Line Graph A line graph shows change over a period of time. It features a line that connects points. The points represent numbers. To interpret a line graph: (1) Read the labels on the outermost horizontal and vertical lines (called axes) to determine what information is shown. (2) Match each point on the line to the point straight across and the point straight down from it on each axis. (3) Combine the information for these two points to determine what was happening at a given time.

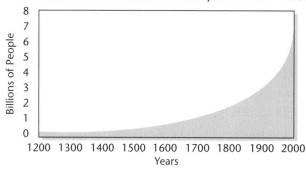

WORLD POPULATION GROWTH, A.D. 1200–2000

Bar Graph A bar graph compares and contrasts amounts. To interpret a bar graph: (1) Look at the lengths of the bars. (2) Match the subject that goes with the bar to the number the bar reaches. (3) Compare and contrast the size of the bars.

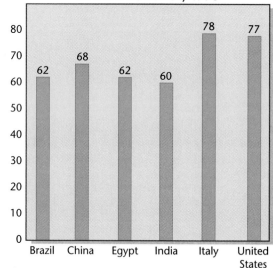

LIFE EXPECTANCY, 1995

640 • Speaking, Listening, Viewing, and Representing

◄ **Critical Viewing**
The numbers on the vertical axis represent the population in billions; the numbers on the horizontal axis represent years. What conclusion can you draw about the world's population based on this graph? [**Analyze, Draw Conclusions**]

◄ **Critical Viewing**
Based on the title of this graph, what do the numbers on the vertical axis represent? [**Analyze, Draw Conclusions**]

☑ **ONGOING ASSESSMENT: Monitor and Reinforce**

If students have trouble reading maps, try one of the following options.

Have each student find a map (historical map, street map, or any other kind of map) and write a paragraph explaining how to read it. Remind them to explain what the different colors and symbols stand for and to give the map's scale. Explain and correct their mistakes.

Use a pull-down classroom map to go over map-reading skills with the whole class. Point to different elements of the map (scale, compass rose, key) and ask students to identify them and explain how they are used.

Pie Graph A pie graph is shaped like a circle divided into parts. The graph shows how each part is related to the whole circle. The circle stands for 100 percent of something. Each part stands for a certain portion, or percentage, of the whole. To interpret a pie graph: (1) Look at the numbers that go with the individual parts. (2) Match the parts to the key. (3) Use the numbers and parts to make comparisons.

POPULATION DIVIDED BY AGE GROUP

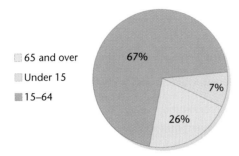

■ 65 and over
■ Under 15
■ 15–64

67%

7%

26%

▶ **Exercise 9** Working With Others to Interpret Maps and Graphs Working with three other classmates, find a map, a line graph, a bar graph, and a pie graph. Assign one group member to find each map or graph. After you find your assigned map or graph, use the appropriate steps mentioned above to acquire information. Then, share the information and how you found it with the other members of the group. Ask them whether they can find any additional information you may have overlooked.

Analyze Photographs

Photographs can also contribute to your understanding of books, magazines, and Web sites. Follow these steps to help you get the most out of photographs:
1. Look carefully at the details to make sure that you are viewing the picture correctly. Sometimes, when you take a quick glance at a picture, you may be misled.
2. Carefully read any accompanying captions.
3. Connect the photograph to the accompanying text.

▶ Critical Viewing If this photograph appeared in a school brochure, what would it imply about interaction in classrooms? **[Interpret]**

◀ Critical Viewing According to this pie graph, which age group makes up the largest proportion of the population? The smallest? Why would this information be useful for a social scientist? **[Analyze, Draw Conclusions, Speculate]**

▶ **More Practice**

Academic and Workplace Skills Activity Book
• pp. 6–7

Viewing and Representing Skills • 641

Pie Graph; Analyze Photographs

1. A pie graph equals a whole, that is, 100%. Make sure students understand that this graph does not say there are 67 people between 15 and 64. It says that 67% of all the people are 15 to 64 years old.

2. Ask students what they can learn from photographs that text alone cannot tell them. (exact appearance of a place or person; his or her mood; qualities of personality that are difficult to convey in words) Point out that verbal descriptions interpret photographs. When students can look directly at a photograph, they can draw their own conclusions without being affected by a writer's interpretations.

3. Bring in some photographs, a history book with photographs in it, or even a current magazine. Have students look at the photographs and talk about the different kinds of information the photographs give them.

Critical Viewing

Analyze; Draw Conclusions; Speculate Students should say that the age 15 to 64 group makes up the largest proportion of the population, while the age 65 and over makes up the smallest.

Answer Key

▶ **Exercise 9**

Students' responses will vary.

Critical Viewing

Interpret Students may say that it would imply that teachers directly interact with students on a one-on-one basis.

Viewing Information Media Critically

1. Go over the types of media listed in the chart. Ask students whether they watch any of these programs, how often, and so on. Try to get a profile of the class viewing habits. Since students at this age may not have much interest in national or international news, spend the majority of your time discussing the types of news they are most familiar with and interested in.

2. Remind students that most news stories they see have been edited. After a newsmagazine such as *60 Minutes* has interviewed a person, the studio edits the interview to make it the proper length for the television show. The editing process also gives the story a particular slant. Students should always keep in mind that they are seeing and hearing only what the editors decided to show them. Live television interviews, of course, are not edited.

continued

Answer Key

> **Exercise 10**

Students' responses will vary.

28.2

Viewing Information Media Critically

You view some form of information every day—television programs, newspaper or magazine articles, and Internet Web sites. Learn to evaluate the information you are viewing for content, quality, and importance.

> **KEY CONCEPT** Become a critical viewer by learning to identify and evaluate different types of visual media and images. ∎

Kinds of Information Media Technology provides different kinds of information media. Knowing how to tell them apart will help you to understand the information and points of view conveyed by each.

This chart shows several forms of information media.

TYPES OF INFORMATION MEDIA

Television News Program	Television Newsmagazine
• Covers current news events • Gives information objectively	• Covers variety of topics • Entertains and informs
Editorial	**Commercial**
• Covers current issues • Expresses an opinion	• Presents products, people, or ideas • Persuades people to buy or take action

> **Exercise 10** Classifying Information Media Identify at least three examples of each of the following:
> 1. Television newsmagazines
> 2. Internet news sources
> 3. Nightly news programs
>
> For what types of information would you use each of these sources? Why?

> **🗂 Research Tip**
>
> Many television news organizations have Web sites with in-depth coverage of current events.

> **More Practice**
>
> Academic and Workplace Skills Activity Book
> • p. 8

642 • Speaking, Listening, Viewing, and Representing

Evaluate Information From the Media Once you understand the different types of media, become a critical viewer. Do this by carefully analyzing and evaluating everything you see and hear.

- **Distinguish facts and opinions**. A *fact* is a statement that can be proved to be true. An *opinion* is what someone believes and may not have been proven to be true. Avoid mistaking opinions for facts.

- **Look for emotional words (also known as *loaded language*) and pictures.** By appealing to our emotions through words and images, programs can persuade us to see things in a certain way without giving us real reasons for that viewpoint. Rely on evidence, such as facts and expert opinions, when making up your mind about an issue.

- **Identify bias.** Bias occurs when a subject is looked at from only one viewpoint. To be fair, all viewpoints should be presented.

TIPS FOR EVALUATING INFORMATION MEDIA

- Be aware of the kind of program you are watching, its purpose, and its limitations.
- Sort out facts from opinions.
- Be aware of any loaded language or sensationalist images that might cause you to react in a certain way.
- Listen for bias and note any points of view not discussed.
- Check surprising or questionable information in other sources.
- View the complete program before reaching a conclusion.
- Develop your own views on the issues, people, and information.

Exercise 11 Analyzing Information Media Watch a television program that provides information, such as a news program, a documentary, or an interview. Pay attention to the commercials as well. Then, write a few paragraphs in which you identify the type of program and describe the topics covered. In addition, comment on what the commercials were selling. Finally, evaluate the information on each topic in the program and in the commercials, using the strategies listed above.

Learn More

For more information about methods of persuasion, see Chapter 7, Persuasion.

3. All sources of news compete with one another for viewers. If a news show does not get enough regular viewers, it will have to go off the air. This is a powerful incentive for news shows to be first with a story, to show what they think are the most gripping images, and to present their information in the way they think will interest the greatest number of people. Make sure students understand that the primary purpose of any news show is to stay on the air, not to inform viewers. Encourage students to listen critically to any newscast.

4. Newspapers are an excellent supplement to a television newscast. A newscast must cover all the news stories in a brief time, but a newspaper can always add pages and devote any number of pages to a particular story. A half-hour news broadcast can show only a brief excerpt of a speech by the president. Newspapers, however, often print the entire text of the speech.

5. The purpose of commercials is to sell products. Advertisers generally buy time on programs whose viewers are more likely to buy their products. Have students watch for this as they complete Exercise 11.

Answer Key

Exercise 11

Have students present their findings to the class.

☑ ONGOING ASSESSMENT: Monitor and Reinforce

If students have trouble viewing information media critically, try the following option.

Have partners watch a news broadcast together. Students may want to take notes during the broadcast. Afterward, they can compare their impressions and discuss whether they think the stories on the broadcast were reliable, and why they think so. You might extend this exercise by assigning a particular broadcast for the entire class to watch and then discuss the following day.

Viewing Fine Art Critically

1. Encourage students to visit museums and to look at actual works of art whenever they have the opportunity. Most museums have free days and admit students for lower fees on other days. Paintings look very different on the wall. Size, color, texture, and other characteristics are more obvious.

2. Encourage students to look at the art before they read any accompanying captions or text. This way they can come to their own conclusions about what the art "means"—and more important, what it means to them.

Customize for
Visual/Spatial Learners

Organize a trip to a local art museum, or have students make their own arrangements to visit it. Have each student choose one painting or statue at the museum and spend a few minutes observing it closely, looking at every detail. If it is a statue, encourage them to walk around it and observe it from different angles. Afterward, have students discuss the experience in a group. Questions for them to consider: What was the artist trying to communicate? Why do you think so? Why do you think the artist made certain choices about color, perspective, and style?

Answer Key

▶ **Exercise 12**

Students' responses will vary.

28.2

Viewing Fine Art Critically

Fine art, such as painting and sculpture, can show you fascinating scenes and beautiful objects. A painting is not just a picture of a thing, though. It is a creation of colors, lines, and shapes that express a mood, idea, or energy all its own. Using these elements, an artist shares what he or she sees or feels.

▶ **KEY CONCEPT** It is important to learn about some of the basic elements of art so that you can understand what the artist is trying to express. ■

Following are some of the elements of painting:

1. **Color** Artists choose specific colors to convey a mood or atmosphere.
2. **Perspective** The same scene or object can be viewed from different angles or perspectives. Why did the artist choose the one he or she used?
3. **Style** Some works are painted in a realistic style; others look far different from a photograph. What is the artist trying to convey through choice of style?

Parkville, Main Street (Missouri), 1933, Gale Stockwell, National Museum of American Art, Washington, D.C.

▶ **Exercise 12** Interpreting Fine Art Have a class discussion about the painting above, *Parkville Main Street* by Gale Stockwell. How has the artist used color, perspective, and style? Remember that some students will likely have differing ideas. Respect everyone's opinion.

644 • Speaking, Listening, Viewing, and Representing

💿 **Technology Tip**

There are many art museums to visit online. For example, you can take a tour of The National Gallery of Art in Washington, D.C., by visiting their Web site: **www.nga.gov**

🔲 **Research Tip**

Browse in the library for books of fine art. Spend some time looking at paintings, sculptures, and photographs in these books to discover your favorites.

▶ **More Practice**

Academic and Workplace Skills Activity Book
• p. 9

Creating Graphic Organizers

Graphic organizers are an excellent tool for breaking down the main ideas in what you read and see and for understanding how those ideas are related.

KEY CONCEPT Putting information into visual form makes ideas easy to identify and comprehend. ■

Follow these steps to help you use graphic organizers:

- **Identify Your Purpose** Are you making the graphic organizer to help you study and remember ideas? Will you present your graphic organizer to other people in a report or presentation?

- **Use Organizing Elements in the Text** Textbooks and other information sources, such as encyclopedias, usually have information organized under headings and subheadings. Use these headings and subheadings to identify main points for your graphic organizer.

- **Decide on the Type of Graphic Organizer** The type of graphic organizer you create depends on how the information is organized in the text you use.

  1. If the text compares and contrasts two or more things, you might want to make a T-chart or a Venn diagram. Both of these graphic organizers can be used to show similarities and differences.
  2. If you want to show cause-and-effect relationships, a flowchart might be the best way to illustrate them.
  3. For main ideas and details, you might make an outline.
  4. A timeline is a good way to show events over a period of time.
  5. A drawing can show what a thing or place looks like.
  6. A diagram can show how a process works.

Use graphic organizers and other visual aids, like those described on the pages that follow, to enhance oral and written presentations.

⊘ Learn More

For more information about comparing and contrasting, see Chapter 8, Exposition: Comparison-and-Contrast Essay. For more information on cause-and-effect relationships, see Chapter 9, Exposition: Cause-and-Effect Essay.

💿 Technology Tip

Use the computer to make charts, graphs, and tables. Look in the computer manual or use the Help function to find out how you can draw diagrams and illustrations on screen.

Creating Graphic Organizers

1. Have a class discussion about the various types of graphic organizers students have seen in different textbooks. Make sure that everyone can recognize a flow chart, Venn diagram, and the other graphic organizers mentioned on this page.

2. Ask students to comment on the usefulness of graphic organizers. Do students find them helpful as illustrations, or do they often outline and summarize what they read by making graphic organizers, or both? Are graphic organizers more useful as a study tool or as a supplement to reading?

continued

3. As a homework assignment, have each student locate and bring in a newspaper or magazine article that includes a graphic organizer. It can be any of the types described in this chapter. Use these articles for a class discussion about how the graphic organizers help readers understand the information in each article.

Critical Viewing

Analyze; Draw Conclusions
Students may suggest that this map was created to report on a geographical area. The student who drew the map may wish to convey a visual representation of the school's main buildings and athletic facilities in relation to each other.

Answer Key

▶ **Exercise 13**

Students' responses will vary.

28.2

Charts, Graphs, and Tables Charts can show numbers, words, or pictures. An example of a picture chart is a seating plan for a classroom. A graph can be a bar, line, or circle graph. Graphs show how things change over time. Tables help you organize information so that facts can be found quickly and easily. An example of a table is a bus or train schedule.

Diagrams and Illustrations Diagrams are simple line drawings. They may show what something looks like, such as the parts of a computer. A set of diagrams might show how to put together the computer. Illustrations may show an object in more detail than a diagram. Both diagrams and illustrations use labels to identify objects and their parts.

Maps It is useful to make a map when you are giving someone directions to get to a place. You might also make a map for a report, showing the geographical area you are writing about. A map can show many kinds of information besides location. It can also show population, climate, and so on.

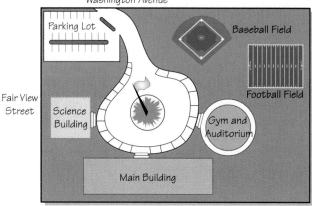

MAP OF MY MIDDLE SCHOOL CAMPUS

▶ **Exercise 13** Creating a Visual Representation To present some information from your science or social studies textbook, create a graphic organizer. Choose a chart, graph, table, diagram, or map. Share your graphic organizer with the class, and explain why you chose that form to present your information.

📖 Research Tip

The reference section of your library has encyclopedias and almanacs that provide a variety of information presented in graph, map, diagram, and chart form.

◀ **Critical Viewing** For what purpose might a student have created this map? What information might he or she wish to convey? [**Analyze, Draw Conclusions**]

▶ **More Practice**

Academic and Workplace Skills Activity Book
• pp. 10–11

646

Formatting to Create an Effect

Use basic word-processing formatting features to enhance written work. Following are some formatting features and tips for creating effective visual enhancements to your text:

- **Capitals** Use capital letters in headings for key ideas.
- **Boldface** Use boldface to highlight ideas.
- **Italics** To give words special emphasis, use italics.
- **Numbered Lists** Use numbered lists to show a sequence.
- **Bulleted Lists** Items that can be presented in any order can go in a bulleted list.

Icy Sunshine in a Cup
Fresh homemade lemonade

12 oz. cup for only $1
Two glasses for $1.50

- Freshly squeezed lemons
- Bottled spring water
- Sweetened and chilled to perfection
- Refreshment guaranteed!!!

*Every Saturday in July
From noon to 2 P.M.
227 Grove Ave.
Between Chestnut
and Oak Streets*

Stop by and cool off!

Technology Tip

Find out how to use these formatting techniques on your computer. Experiment with other formatting options, such as page borders and shading, colors, different fonts (type styles), and special effects on type, such as outlines and shadows. Use software to add pictures.

▶ **Exercise 14** Using Formatting to Create a Timeline
Create a timeline using formatting to clarify your work. First, choose an author, artist, or historical figure you would like to research. Next, gather data about your subject. Organize your material into chronological order and create your timeline. Use the tips on formatting to create an easy-to-follow timeline.

▶ **More Practice**
Academic and Workplace Skills Activity Book
• p. 12

Step-by-Step Teaching Guide

Formatting to Create an Effect
Have students analyze the lemonade poster. Ask them to point out the various features: boldface and italic type, capital letters, bulleted list, and art. Have them discuss whether the poster is effective, and why or why not. What changes, if any, would they make to it?

Answer Key

▶ **Exercise 14**

Student's timelines will vary.

647

Developing a Multimedia Presentation

1. Write a list of sample topics on the chalkboard, such as "the history of rock and roll" and "dogs: from workers to pets." Ask students to suggest different types of media they might use in a presentation on the topics. Students should explain their choices. For example, a presentation on rock and roll should include sound recordings.

2. Remind students not to get too carried away when planning a multimedia presentation. They should remember to keep within the time limit set for their presentation. They may not be able to use every idea they have in one presentation. Many presentations are more effective if they use only a few visual or audio aids besides whatever the students have to say.

Answer Key

▶ **Exercise 15**

Students' responses will vary.

28.2

Developing a Multimedia Presentation

An oral report can be made more effective with the use of slides, videos, and audiotapes, as well as charts, maps, and graphs. These forms of media can help illustrate the main points of your report and make them more understandable to your listeners.

▶ **KEY CONCEPT** Multimedia presentations supply information through a variety of media, including text, slides, videos, music, maps, charts, and artwork. ■

Tips for Preparing a Multimedia Presentation

- First, make an outline of your report. Look for parts you would like to illustrate through the use of media.

- Choose a form of media that fits your topic. For example, if your report is about another country, you might show slides of important sites and play a tape of that country's music. If you report on becoming a veterinarian, or animal doctor, you might videotape your veterinarian examining your pet.

- Don't put all your media presentations at the beginning or end of your report. Space them out.

- Make your posters, maps, or slides big enough for the audience to see.

- Check all your equipment before you give your presentation. Make sure the cassette player, overhead projector, or slide projector is working properly. It's a good idea to ask a friend to be your media helper. He or she can run the equipment while you speak.

- Always have a backup plan in case something goes wrong with the equipment. For example, you might have photographs to pass around in case the slide projector doesn't work.

- Rehearse with the equipment (and your helper) before the day of your presentation.

▶ **Exercise 15** Preparing a Multimedia Presentation Look through your writing portfolio. Choose a piece of writing that you could make into a multimedia presentation. Make a list of some ideas for media you might use to illustrate the topic.

🎧 Research Tip

Your school or public library may have slides, videos, and audiocassettes you can use in your multimedia presentation.

▶ **More Practice**

Academic and Workplace Skills Activity Book
• pp. 13–14

Creating a Video

Telling a story or reporting on a topic by using images, sound, and dialogue is a powerful way to communicate. Video allows your viewers to see a particular subject matter, event, or story just as *you* see it. Videos can be informative, humorous, or dramatic.

KEY CONCEPT Create a video to communicate information, to entertain, or to do both. ∎

Organization is the component most essential to making a video. Follow these basic steps when making your video:

Step-by-Step Guide to Video Production

1. Create a shooting script that contains
   - any lines of spoken dialogue.
   - directions about camera angles.
   - descriptions of settings, costumes or wardrobe, and props.
2. Use your shooting script to map out a storyboard, a cartoonlike map of the key events in your video.
3. Choose the locations in which you'll shoot your video.
4. Get permission to use these locations and identify when you'll use them.
5. Choose crew members and assign tasks.
6. Cast the roles and rehearse.
7. Write out a shooting schedule (listing each scene and who is in it) and distribute it.
8. Film the scenes.
9. Review your scenes and edit them together to make a completed video.

Tips for Filming

- Hold the camera steady.
- Avoid quick actions, such as zooming in or out too fast.
- Shoot as much footage as possible. It is easier to edit out footage than to add it later.
- Make sure you have good lighting at your locations.

Exercise 16 Creating a Video Report Choose a place in your town that interests you or a local event that you have always enjoyed. Capture this place or event in a video. Work with a team of classmates, with each of you assuming different roles. Follow the step-by-step tips above.

Creating a Video

1. Ask students to discuss their reactions to videos, films, and filmstrips as they are used in the classroom. How do videos and films help them learn?

2. If it is not practical for students to make videos of their own, organize them into groups to plan videos. Students can discuss ideas, write scripts and map out story boards, and complete all other preparatory steps. They can present their video proposals to the class.

Answer Key

Exercise 16

If your class does not have access to video equipment, have students prepare plans, including scripts and storyboards, that they would use for a video report.

Performing and Interpreting

1. Organize students into groups of three, two actors and one director. Each group can find a scene for two actors and prepare it for a class performance. All three students should contribute ideas on how the scene should be performed and presented.

2. During the rehearsal period, meet with members of each group. Discuss any concerns they have and give them any guidance they need.

Critical Viewing

Speculate Students may suggest that like the audience, the performers must watch and listen to each other. One major difference between the audience's experience and that of the performers' is that the performers do all the talking.

Customize for
Visual/Spatial and Musical/Rhythmic Learners

For Exercise 17, students may want to prepare scenery or musical accompaniment.

Customize for
ESL Students

For Exercise 18, encourage students to find a library book that includes poems in their home language and English. They can present the poem in both languages. Suggest that they read the poem first in the other language. Even though the class won't understand the words, the rhythm and sound of the words may convey a feeling. Then they can listen to the English version and see if their original "vibes" were correct.

28.2

Performing and Interpreting

Everyone has experienced the thrill of watching a live performance in a theater or an auditorium. Actors, singers, instrumentalists, and dancers are all performing artists.

▶ **KEY CONCEPT** Experience what it is like to perform in a dramatic scene or to deliver a monologue by following the steps listed below. ■

1. Write down the text you will read out loud. Think about its meaning. Then, highlight the most important words and ideas.
2. Read the text out loud several times. Try different ways to express the meaning with your voice. You can use the tone, pitch (high or low), and loudness or softness of your voice to communicate your meaning.
3. Practice gestures that help express the meaning of the words. Consider what your posture and movements will express to your audience.
4. You might have background music that adds to the mood you want to create. You might also want to wear a costume.

▲ Critical Viewing
How do you think the experience of the performers is similar to and different from the experience of the audience in this photograph? [Speculate]

🛈 Research Tip

The plays of William Shakespeare (1564–1616) have given many actors a chance to perform at their very best. You can learn about how theater plays were performed in Shakespeare's time by doing research on the Globe Theater.

5. Rehearse the text in front of a mirror and with an audience of friends and family. Be comfortable before you perform, but remember, even experienced performers feel a little nervous!

6. While you perform, speak more slowly than you think necessary. Avoid fidgeting, and make a conscious effort to make eye contact with your audience from time to time. ■

Exercise 17 Presenting a Skit Work with a group of classmates to create a humorous skit. Assume roles of characters. Then, practice acting out the skit. Focus on speaking naturally, as you do in everyday life. When you have rehearsed several times, present your skit to the class. Following the performance, allow time for comments and discussion.

Exercise 18 Dramatic Reading Select a poem that has an especially pleasing rhythm or rhyme scheme. Copy it, and highlight the most important words and ideas. Work on your own or with a partner to practice delivering dramatic readings of the poem. Vary the tone and volume of your voice to emphasize key words. Pause only where punctuation indicates that you should. Deliver your reading to the class.

> **More Practice**
> Academic and
> Workplace Skills
> Activity Book
> • pp. 15–16

Reflecting on Your Speaking, Listening, Viewing, and Representing Skills

Review all the different kinds of strategies and suggestions discussed in this chapter. Write a journal entry discussing these experiences. Begin your inquiry by asking yourself these questions:

• What are my strengths and weaknesses as a speaker and as a listener? Which skills need further improvement?

• In what situations do I listen most effectively? In what situations can I improve my listening skills?

• What viewing experiences gave me the most information?

• What representing experiences did I find the most enjoyable? Why?

• What school clubs or potential careers might I explore in which I can use and develop my speaking, listening, viewing, and representing skills?

Integrating Workplace Skills

Many professions require the ability to speak easily, fluently, and well. These include acting, politics, broadcasting, teaching, lecturing, and marketing. Have students discuss what kind of chance a person would have to succeed in any of these professions if he or she did not work hard to perfect speaking skills.

Customize for
More Advanced Students

Student can create an extra-credit project. For example, two students might watch a film and then review it for the class in the style of a typical film reviewer. This project will test their informal speaking, critical viewing, and listening skills.

Answer Key

> **Exercise 17**

Remind students to keep their skits short. You may want to review each group's script before they perform for the class.

> **Exercise 18**

You may want to review the poems students have selected before they begin practicing their dramatic readings.

Interpreting Graphic Aids

Teaching Resources: Standardized Test Preparation Workbook, Chapter 28

1. Emphasize to students that their key to success in most standardized essay tests is for them to address the question being asked. Students should read the question carefully and confine their answers to the topic area indicated.

2. Remind students to study the title, caption and labels of the graphic aid because they provide vital information necessary for a proper interpretation.

3. Remind students to examine all symbols, using a key if one is provided, and to connect the visuals to the written text they accompany. Again, key features such as symbols provide vital information necessary for a proper interpretation.

4. Remind students that line graphs show a change over a period of time, bar graphs compare and contrast amounts, and pie graphs show the relation of a particular to the whole.

Standardized Test Preparation Workshop

Interpreting Graphic Aids

Some standardized tests contain questions measuring your ability to gather details and draw conclusions from maps, charts, graphs, and other graphic aids. The following sample item will help you become familiar with these types of questions.

Test Tip
As you examine each graphic aid, ask yourself what each part of the graphic means or represents in relation to the whole.

Sample Test Item

Answer and Explanation

Directions: Read the passage and answer the question that follows.

Feudalism was a system of rule by local lords who were bound to a king by ties of loyalty. Under feudalism in Europe, everyone had a well-defined place in society. The king granted estates to powerful lords. These lords owed military service to the king. The lords divided their estates among vassals (lesser lords). The estates were then subdivided among knights, or mounted warriors. Finally, there were the common people, or serfs. Although they were not slaves, serfs were not free to leave the land. They lived on lands owned by lords and worked the land in return for protection.

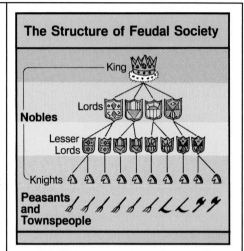

1 Which class of the population had more power than the lords?

A Peasants

B Lesser lords

C King

D Knights

The correct answer is C. The chart indicates that the lords are second in rank according to the feudal system.

Colonists From Many Lands

English	French
Scotch-Irish	Dutch
Scottish	Swedish
German	African (free and slave)

```
0    100    200 Miles
0    100    200 Kilometers
```

ME. (part of Mass.)

N.H.

Boston

MASS.

L.Ontario

N.Y.

CONN. R.I.

Huron

L.Erie

PA.

New York

N.J.

Philadelphia

Pittsburgh

MD. Baltimore

DEL.

ATLANTIC OCEAN

Richmond

Norfolk

VA.

N.C.

S.C.

Charleston

Augusta

GA.

Savannah

Practice **Directions:** Read the passage and answer the questions that follow.

Colonists from all over the new world came to the American colonies. From the beginning, the United States has been a melting pot of cultures. The English were strongly represented in the original thirteen colonies, while many other groups settled outside of the English areas.

1 Which group settled in all the colonies?
  A Scotch-Irish
  B German
  C African
  D English

2 Which group was represented the least?
  F French
  G Swedish
  H Dutch
  J Scottish

3 Why might certain groups of people decide to live outside of predominately English areas?
  A This would enable them to preserve their own culture.
  B They were battling with the English.
  C The English enforced harsh rules and regulations.
  D The English were unfair business associates.

Answer Key

▶ **Practice**

1. D
2. G
3. A

In-Depth Lesson Plan

	LESSON FOCUS	PRINT AND MEDIA RESOURCES
DAY 1	**Developing Vocabulary** Students learn and apply vocabulary-building skills such as conversation, reading, and using context clues (pp. 655–658).	**Teaching Resources** *Academic and Workplace Skills Activity Book,* pp. 17–18
DAY 2	**Studying Words Systematically** Students learn and apply such vocabulary-building skills as keeping a vocabulary notebook, and using a dictionary and other reference aids (pp. 659–661).	**Teaching Resources** *Academic and Workplace Skills Activity Book,* pp. 19–21
DAY 3	**Studying Word Parts and Origins** Students learn and apply the skills of studying word parts and origins (pp. 662–665).	**Teaching Resources** *Academic and Workplace Skills Activity Book,* pp. 22–25
DAY 4	**Improving Your Spelling** Students learn and apply spelling rules (pp. 666–670).	**Teaching Resources** *Academic and Workplace Skills Activity Book,* pp. 26–33
DAY 5	**Improving Your Spelling (continued)** Students learn and apply spelling aids such as understanding other cultural influences and forming plurals (pp. 671–675).	**Teaching Resources** *Academic and Workplace Skills Activity Book,* pp. 26–33

Accelerated Lesson Plan

	LESSON FOCUS	PRINT AND MEDIA RESOURCES
DAY 1	**Vocabulary** Students learn and apply vocabulary-building skills (pp. 654–665).	**Teaching Resources** *Academic and Workplace Skills Activity Book,* pp. 17–25
DAY 2	**Spelling** Students learn and apply spelling rules (pp. 666–675).	**Teaching Resources** *Academic and Workplace Skills Activity Book,* pp. 26–33

Options for Adapting Lesson Plans

HOMEWORK

Have students complete any section of the chapter for homework.

FEATURES

Extend coverage with the Standardized Test Preparation Workshop (pp. 676–677).

TECHNOLOGY

Students can use the On-Line Exercise Bank to complete the exercises on computer. The Auto Check feature will grade their work.

INTEGRATED SKILLS COVERAGE

Language
Language Highlight ATE p. 661

Spelling
ATE pp. 663, 664

Social Studies
ATE p. 657

Technology
ATE p. 661

Test Taking
ATE p. 663

Real-World Connection
ATE p. 660

Viewing and Representing
Critical Viewing SE pp. 654, 659, 663, 669

MEDIA AND TECHNOLOGY

For the Student
• *On-Line Exercise Bank,* Ch. 29

For the Teacher
• *Resource Pro* CD-ROM

ASSESSMENT SUPPORT

Standardized Test Preparation Workshop, SE pp. 676–677; ATE p. 668
Standardized Test Preparation Workbook, pp. 57–58
Formal Assessment, Ch. 29

MEETING INDIVIDUAL NEEDS

Less Advanced Students See Ongoing Assessments ATE pp. 658, 660, 664
ESL Students ATE pp. 656, 674
Verbal Linguistic Students ATE p. 660
Visual/Spatial Learners ATE p. 656
Musical Learners ATE p. 665

WRITING AND GRAMMAR WEB SITE

The Interactive Writing and Grammar Web site provides a wide array of support for students, teachers, and parents. Grammar support includes:

• On-Line Exercise Bank with Auto Check scoring
• Diagnostic and assessment support

www.phschool.com

▶ **Lesson Objectives**

1. To develop vocabulary through broad reading, conversation, and reading aloud.

2. To use context clues and content areas to determine the meanings of unknown vocabulary words.

3. To keep a vocabulary notebook.

4. To use flashcards and a tape recorder to practice new vocabulary words.

5. To use dictionaries and other reference sources to learn the meanings of new words.

6. To study roots and origins of words.

7. To use prefixes and suffixes to establish word meaning.

8. To analyze word origins.

9. To develop a list of frequently misspelled words.

10. To review spelling words systematically and apply spelling rules.

11. To understand the influences of other cultures on spelling.

12. To form regular and irregular plurals according to common spelling rules.

13. To proofread for common spelling errors.

Critical Viewing

Infer Students may say that a reader of literature has a great or expansive vocabulary because reading is vital to the development of a good vocabulary.

Chapter 29 Vocabulary and Spelling

Still Life: Shelf with books, Master of the Aix Annunciation (15th century, French)

One of the most useful parts of your education is the development of good vocabulary and spelling. By learning new words, you will improve your reading, writing, and speaking—and even your thinking. Not only will you be better at these activities, you will also enjoy them more.

Expanding your vocabulary and your knowledge of spelling will help you in many ways. Vocabulary and spelling mistakes, for example, will lower your grades. A narrow vocabulary will limit what you are trying to say or write. However, with a little effort, you can greatly improve your vocabulary and spelling skills.

▲ **Critical Viewing**
What kind of vocabulary might the reader of books like these have? **[Infer]**

654 • Vocabulary and Spelling

⏱ **TIME AND RESOURCE MANAGER**

Resources
Print: Academic and Workplace Skills Activity Book, pp. 17–18

In-Depth Coverage	Accelerated Pace
• Work through all key concepts, pp. 655–658. • Assign and review Exercises 1–3.	• Assign pp. 655–658 for independent student review.

Section 29.1 *Developing Vocabulary*

Developing Vocabulary Through Listening

Taking part in conversations, listening to works read aloud, and reading many types of works are three of the most common ways to increase your vocabulary.

Conversation

From the time you were born, you have been listening to the words of others. In these conversations, you learned—and continue to learn—the meanings and pronunciations of new words. You can improve your vocabulary even more if you take note of unfamiliar words in your conversations, especially those with people whose life experiences and ideas are different from your own. Learn the meanings of unfamiliar words by asking or by looking them up in a dictionary.

Works Read Aloud

Listening to works of literature read aloud is another important way to build your vocabulary. Nearly all types of literature —including plays, poems, and short stories—are available on audiocassette or compact disc. By listening to these works, you will learn the pronunciations of unfamiliar words. You will also hear the context—the words and sentences around the unfamiliar word that help give it meaning. Read along as you listen so you can see unfamiliar words as you hear them.

Wide Reading

Among the many benefits of reading is developing your vocabulary. As you read, you encounter new words and their meanings. The more you read, the more familiar many of these new words will become. Wide reading—reading a variety of books, newspapers, magazines, Internet articles, and so on—will expose you to many new words and their different uses.

> ▶ **More Practice**
>
> Academic and Workplace Skills Activity Book
> • p. 17

PREPARE and ENGAGE

Interest GRABBER Have students listen to the news on the radio or watch it on television. Ask them to write down unfamiliar words from the broadcast. Then have them use a dictionary to define the words and write sentences that use them in context.

Activate Prior Knowledge

Have partners tell each other a brief story or anecdote. Then have the students write what they just heard. Have students write another paragraph about any new information or facts they learned.

TEACH

Step-by-Step Teaching Guide

Developing Vocabulary Through Listening

1. Play the Listening to Literature Audiocassette for the first (long) paragraph of William Bradford's "The Pilgrims' Landing and First Winter." Play it twice, having students note new vocabulary.

2. As homework, have students find definitions for those words and report back to the class. Students can use the textbook (*Timeless Voices, Timeless Themes*, Copper, pages 163–164) to help with context.

3. Have students visit the school library and find a book on a subject that is completely new to them. Then have them write down the new words they learn on their "vocabulary expedition." Encourage them to read widely to discover new vocabulary words.

Using Context

1. Have students work in groups to write ten sentences that use language figuratively. Then ask students to write some of their sentences on the board for class discussion.

2. Ask partners to write down as many idioms as they can think of. Write the following idioms on the board to aid their brainstorming.

   It was raining cats and dogs outside.

   She knew it was no use crying over spilled milk.

3. Some students may know of idioms in other languages. Encourage them to ask their families or friends for additional idioms.

Customize for
Visual/Spatial Learners

Because idioms are often colorful or even amusing ways of expressing an idea figuratively, students may enjoy illustrating them. Have students draw some of their favorite idioms and have their classmates guess what idiom they have illustrated.

Customize for
ESL Students

Students learning English may find figurative language and idioms especially difficult because they seem illogical or (in some cases) irrelevant. Cats and dogs aren't *really* falling out of the sky. Encourage them to think of idioms in their home languages and translate them into English. Or analyze idioms with students in ways that make the meaning of the idiom clear.

29.1

Using Context Clues

Every word you hear or see has a context. The context goes a long way toward giving meaning to a word.

KEY CONCEPT The **context** of a word means the group of words—the sentence or passage—that surrounds it. ■

In the example below, you can figure out two different meanings of *bear* by looking at the surrounding words.

EXAMPLES: I could no longer <u>bear</u> the pain. ("endure")
The shelf cannot <u>bear</u> a huge
number of books. ("support")

USING CONTEXT CLUES

1. Read the sentence carefully and focus on the overall meaning.

2. Look for clues in nearby words.

3. Guess the meaning of the unfamiliar word.

4. Reread the sentence and see whether your guess seems to fit.

5. Check your guess in a dictionary.

Figurative Language Figurative language is language used to mean something different from its ordinary meaning. It often involves unusual comparisons or familiar words in unfamiliar ways. For instance, consider this sentence: "The suffering engine groaned as the train climbed the steep hill." Engines cannot literally suffer or groan. You can tell from context that *suffering* and *groaned* are used figuratively to show that the engine was straining to pull the train.

Idioms Idioms are common expressions that are not meant literally. For example, in the sentence "David went home early, explaining that he was feeling under the weather," there is no literal meaning for *feeling under the weather*. The context of this sentence, however, makes it clear that David was not feeling well.

Research Tip

Look in a geography book or an atlas, and find three unfamiliar words. Check their meanings in a dictionary.

656 • Vocabulary and Spelling

Use Context Clues in All of Your Reading Very often, you can figure out the meaning of a word from its context, whether you are reading literature or articles, or even instructions or directions for making or fixing something.

Use "Possible Sentences" This strategy can help you to increase your vocabulary and your understanding of words in context. Try using this method to learn and reinforce the meanings of unfamiliar words.

STEPS FOR USING "POSSIBLE SENTENCES"

1. Find an unfamiliar word in your reading, and use context clues to try to figure out its meaning.

2. Write a sentence for the unfamiliar word in your vocabulary notebook.

3. Check the actual meaning of the word in a dictionary.

4. Evaluate your sentence to see whether you have used the word correctly.

5. Revise your sentence to make it correct.

Exercise 1 Using Context Clues Explain how context clues help determine the meanings of the underlined words below.
1. Fencing is a sport that requires speed and agility.
2. Dad bought some fencing for our vegetable garden.
3. My mother will book a hotel room with an ocean view.
4. You will need a book of matches to light this campfire.
5. The book I read last night kept me awake for hours.

Exercise 2 Using the "Possible Sentences" Strategy With Words in Context Find a story or an article of interest to you. Read through it, and identify five words that are unfamiliar to you. Then, use the "Possible Sentences" strategy to try to determine the definitions of the words. Enter the words and their correct meanings in a vocabulary notebook.

More Practice
Academic and Workplace Skills Activity Book
• p. 18

Answer Key

Exercise 1

Answers will vary. Samples are given.
1. Fencing is a kind of sport for athletes who are quick.
2. Fencing is something used by gardeners.
3. Book is something you do to reserve a room in a hotel.
4. A book is a collection or assortment, based on the description in the sentence.
5. A book is long written work.

Exercise 2

After students have completed this exercise, have them discuss their findings with a partner. Ask students to discuss the way the context of a sentence helps them gather meaning for words that are unfamiliar to them.

Integrating Social Studies

Have students keep a record of unfamiliar words that pertain to particular countries, such as *río* ("river" in Spanish-speaking countries) or *mont* ("mountain" in French-speaking countries). These keys to foreign words in other disciplines will help them better understand the context of what is being said.

Developing Vocabulary • 657

Studying Meanings in Content Areas

1. Have students keep an unofficial dictionary of words that they've learned or want to learn. Each month, offer an extra credit opportunity to students who research their "dictionaries" and define unfamiliar words or write sentences that put the words into context.

2. Ask students to make a list of prefixes and suffixes of words that they use in science class. Ask students to guess what words beginning with the prefix *hydro-* might mean. Then ask them to guess what words ending with the suffix *-itis* might mean. Encourage them to think of other common prefixes and suffixes and words that use them.

Answer Key

> **Exercise 3**

Answers will vary.

> **Exercise 4** *(page 659)*

Answers will vary.

Have students pair up and use the words in conversation. Students may need to refer to their vocabulary notebooks for help in using these words in context.

29.1

Studying Meanings in the Content Areas

Use a Notebook and a Glossary

During your school studies, you will encounter many unfamiliar words related to specific subjects. While context can help you determine the meanings of some of them, you should record and study any unfamiliar words related to the topic you are learning in class. For each subject area, write the meanings and pronunciations of new words in a special section of your notebook. Use the glossary at the back of your textbook to find the subject-specific meanings of unfamiliar words.

Social Studies Words that you are likely to encounter in social studies deal with types of government, political activity, history, society, and geography. To aid your studying, group new words under these categories.

Science Many terms in science textbooks have Latin or Greek origins. Categorize new science words by their prefixes, suffixes, or roots. For example, you could group *atmosphere* with *biosphere* because they both end with *-sphere*. Once you have learned that *-sphere* means "something resembling a sphere, or globe" you will more easily remember the meanings of both words.

Current Events Whenever you listen to the news or read a newspaper, it is likely that you will encounter words you have learned in science and social studies. Remember—the more times you hear or see a word used, the greater your command of the word. Use current event topics as a source of vocabulary reinforcement.

> **Exercise 3** Studying Words in the Content Areas Compile a list of unfamiliar words from a chapter of your social studies or science book. Then, read newspaper or newsmagazine articles over a period of a week, identifying passages in which these words appear. In your notebook, write the sentence or paragraph from the article in which the word appears. Compare the word's meaning in the article with its meaning in your textbook.

 **Internet Tip**

Find a short entry about any history or science topic in an on-line encyclopedia. Find an unfamiliar word, look it up in a dictionary, and add it to your notebook.

> **More Practice**

Academic and Workplace Skills Activity Book
• pp. 19–20

✓ ONGOING ASSESSMENT: Monitor and Reinforce

If students miss more than two items in Exercises 1–3, use one of the following options.

Option 1 Have students try to identify the meaning of an unfamiliar word by saying it aloud and using it in another sentence. If students are still unsure of the meaning of the word, have them identify other words in the sentence that help in understanding the meaning of the unknown word.

Option 2 Encourage students to keep an ongoing list of unfamiliar words. As an exercise, have students work in teams, sharing their unfamiliar words and trying to determine their meanings from the contexts in which they find them.

Section 29.2 — Studying Words Systematically

Keeping a Vocabulary Notebook

Use a vocabulary notebook to help you learn new words from textbook reading or from reading for pleasure.

KEY CONCEPT Study and review new words in your vocabulary notebook a few times each week. ■

Create a Vocabulary Notebook Keep a notebook to list new words. On the page, write the source of the word. Then, list the word, its definition, and examples of how to use it.

VOCABULARY NOTEBOOK		
Chapter 3: Europeans Explore America		
Words	Definitions	Examples
navigate	1. to steer or direct a ship	The Prince used the instruments
	2. to travel through or over water	to navigate the ship into safe waters.

Exercise 4 Using a Vocabulary Notebook
Look up the following words, and add them, their definitions, and an example of your own to your vocabulary notebook.

1. bleach
2. hangar
3. germinate
4. indigent
5. literate
6. patriot
7. parched
8. manipulate
9. acceleration
10. instill

▶ Critical Viewing What kinds of words would you expect to be defined in the glossary of a geography book? **[Relate]**

Studying Words Systematically • 659

⏱ **TIME AND RESOURCE MANAGER**

Resources
Print: Academic and Workplace Skills Activity Book, pp. 19–21

In-Depth Coverage	Accelerated Pace
• Work through all key concepts, pp. 659–661. • Assign and review Exercises 4–6.	• Assign pp. 659–661 for independent student review.

PREPARE and ENGAGE

✹ **Interest GRABBER** Students may be interested to know that two famous writers of English dictionaries—Samuel Johnson and Noah Webster—kept personal dictionaries. Johnson's *Dictionary* (1755) reveals his sense of humor. His definition for a net was "a series of holes held together by string." Noah Webster's *An American Dictionary of the English Language* (1828) is notable for its insistence on American spellings. Encourage students to make their dictionaries accurate and personal by writing descriptive and meaningful sentences to help define words.

Activate Prior Knowledge

Have students look at a children's book or children's dictionary to see the ways words are used to reinforce their meaning. Then have them write sentences for new or unfamiliar words that use context to reinforce the definition.

TEACH

Step-by-Step Teaching Guide

Keeping a Vocabulary Notebook

1. Have students spend a few minutes each week writing down new words they have learned from assignments or reading.

2. Ask students to treat their dictionary as an ongoing assignment and remind them that improving their vocabulary will help them in test-taking, writing, reading comprehension, and everyday interactions.

3. Encourage students to update their vocabulary notebooks as soon as they hear an unfamiliar word or phrase.

Critical Viewing

Relate Answers will vary. Students may suggest words related to landforms, land use, and cultures, for example.

Studying New Words

1. Students may find writing sentences for new vocabulary words difficult. Encourage them to refer to their definitions and the words' parts of speech.

2. Encourage students to treat vocabulary words as they do multiplication tables or a math equation: They need to memorize the way these words are used.

   Have them use flashcards for words that are especially difficult.

3. Some students might find that recording the definitions of words on audiocassettes helps them learn or remember vocabulary words.

4. Have partners write "practice tests" containing sentences with blanks for correct vocabulary words. Then have them make a list of vocabulary words to be put into the blanks. Have students trade tests, then trade them back to check the answers.

Customize for
Verbal/Linguistic Learners

Students who learn new vocabulary can reinforce it by using it regularly. Ask students to prepare short statements to recite aloud to the class that use some of the new vocabulary words that they have learned.

Real-World Connection

The average person knows many thousands of vocabulary words but uses fewer than 10,000 words with any regularity. Having a large vocabulary can be an advantage in any number of social situations. Students should challenge themselves to learn new words and to use them regularly in conversation. The more they use them, the more likely it is that they will retain them.

Answer Key

> **Exercise 5**

After students have finished this exercise, you may want to have them practice with a partner in class. Or ask them to review their flashcards or tapes and have a friend test them on their knowledge.

29.2

Studying New Words

It is important to set a regular time to review new vocabulary words, such as just before you begin your daily homework assignments. Use one or more of the following methods to review new words.

Use Your Notebook

To help you remember the meaning of each new word in your notebook, cover its definition with your hand. Then, look at the word and the example sentence and define the word. Check your definition against the definition in your notebook. Finally, write a sentence using the new word.

Write Sentences With Vocabulary Words When you write a sentence using a new vocabulary word, include the word's definition in the sentence. This will help you remember the word by reinforcing its meaning.

EXAMPLE: He *acquired* a college loan, *getting* it by working out a deal with the bank.

Use Flashcards

Make a flashcard for each new word from your notebook. Write the word on the front of an index card. On the back, write the word's definition and, if necessary, the subject to which it relates. Consider including the word's pronunciation and a sentence using the word. Working with a partner, test your knowledge of the new words.

Use a Tape Recorder

Record a vocabulary word, pronouncing it carefully. Then, after a pause, record its definition. To review, play the tape. During the pause, recall the word's definition. Listen to the recorded definition to check yourself and to reinforce the word's meaning.

▶ **Exercise 5** Making Flashcards or Tapes Make a set of flashcards or tapes to study the following words. Add words from your own reading or from assigned vocabulary lists.
1. prodigy
2. conspired
3. uncanny
4. intrigue
5. eminent

660 • Vocabulary and Spelling

🔲 **Research Tip**

Find a science book in the library. Locate a few sentences in the book that suggest the meaning of a word through context clues. Add the new word to your notebook.

More Practice

Academic and Workplace Skills Activity Book
• pp. 21–22

✓ ONGOING ASSESSMENT: Monitor and Reinforce

Depending on how students respond to Exercises 4–6 and how successfully they enhance their vocabularies, use one of the following options for reinforcement.

Option 1 Have students keep a chart of the new vocabulary words they've learned. When they learn a new word successfully, have them "retire" that word and put it on a list of "retired" words in their notebook.

Option 2 Have students insert new vocabulary words into a mixed letter puzzle. Then have them write synonyms as clues and exchange their puzzles with a classmate.

```
j  k  u  v  y  (i
b  s  f  n  q  (l
t  d  g  e  v  (k)
```

The word the student would have to recognize in the puzzle is *ilk*. The synonym would be "kind" or "family."

Using a Dictionary

When you want to find the exact meaning of a word, consult a dictionary. Besides giving the definition of a word, a dictionary will also tell you the word's pronunciation, part of speech, and history. Words in a dictionary are listed alphabetically.

▶ **KEY CONCEPT** Use a **dictionary** to find meanings of words you do not know. ■

Using Other Reference Aids

Thesaurus Use a thesaurus to find synonyms (words with similar meanings) and sometimes antonyms (words with opposite meanings) to a given word. A thesaurus is useful for finding more precise words for your writing.

Synonym Finder If you are drafting with a word-processing program, check to see whether it includes a synonym finder in one of the pull-down menus. If so, highlight a word for which you want to find a synonym, and the synonym finder will check for alternative words.

Glossary Many textbooks include a glossary of terms and definitions. The terms are specific to the field of study covered in the textbook. The glossary lists the words you need to learn and know in the subject area.

Software In addition to being available in book form, most references, including dictionaries and thesauruses, are available as software. You can purchase some of these programs, while others are available for free on the Internet.

▶ **KEY CONCEPT** Use **references**, such as thesauruses, synonym finders, or glossaries, to find the exact words you need when writing. ■

▶ **Exercise 6** Using Vocabulary Reference Aids Look up the words below in the references indicated. Compare and contrast the information found in each source. Then, look up each word in a thesaurus, and write down three similar words.
1. cerebral (science textbook glossary, dictionary)
2. patriot (dictionary, social studies textbook glossary)
3. eccentric (dictionary, synonym finder)
4. synthesis (science text book, on-line dictionary)
5. cabinet (social studies textbook glossary, dictionary)

DICTIONARY
1. Have a dictionary nearby when you are reading or writing.
2. Look up any word whose meaning you do not know or are not sure about.

THESAURUS
1. Use a thesaurus when you cannot think of a word that expresses just what you want to say. Look up a word that is close in meaning to what you want to say.
2. Use a thesaurus to replace words you have overused in a piece of writing.

⟳ Learn More

To find more detailed information about reference aids, and to see an annotated dictionary entry, turn to Chapter 31.

Using Other Reference Aids

1. Ask students to look up unfamiliar words in a thesaurus. Have them add a list of similar words to their vocabulary dictionaries to remind them of the meaning of new words.

2. If students are comfortable using word processors, have them look up the meanings of unfamiliar words on their computer's built-in thesaurus. Ask them to write two sentences for new vocabulary words: one that uses the unfamiliar word and another that uses a synonym.

3. Acquaint students with glossaries and other spelling and vocabulary resources.

Language Highlight

Students may be interested to know that the word *thesaurus* comes from the Greek *thesauros*, meaning "a treasure or storehouse." The modern-day thesaurus is literally a treasury or storehouse of words, because it provides synonyms for thousands of words.

Integrating Technology

Students who prefer to use technology to update their vocabularies can also use the "search engines" on the Internet to seek out Web sites that use the unfamiliar words they are attempting to define. By visiting specific Web sites that use new language, they may be able to gather the meanings of the words they don't know from context.

Answer Key

▶ **Exercise 6**

Answers may vary.

Interest GRABBER

Students may be unfamiliar with the concept of roots in language. Ask them to consider other kinds of roots. How do roots work in plants, for instance, or what does it mean when we say "Let's get to the root of the problem" or "It's in my roots"? Then have them consider roots in language.

Activate Prior Knowledge

Students use roots all the time without realizing it. Ask how many words they can think of that contain the root *graph,* Greek for "write." *(photograph, phonograph, autograph, paragraph, telegraph, graphics,* and so on)

TEACH

Step-by-Step Teaching Guide

Studying Word Parts and Origins

Ask students to think of other words that use the roots in the box. (Possibilities: *capture, dictate, dynamo, motion, antonym, inspect, retain, reverse, television*)

Answer Key

Exercise 7

1. f
2. d
3. a
4. j
5. b
6. i
7. c
8. e
9. h
10. g

Section 29.3

Studying Word Parts and Origins

Using Word Roots

The root of a word is the word part containing the word's basic meaning. The chart below contains ten common roots whose meanings you should know.

▶ **KEY CONCEPT** A **root** is the base of a word. ■

Roots have come into the English language from many sources. In the first column below, additional spellings for each word root are in parentheses. The origins of the roots are indicated by the abbreviations *L., Gr.,* and *A.S.* (Latin, Greek, and Anglo-Saxon).

TEN COMMON ROOTS		
Root and Origin	Meaning	Example
-cap- (-capt-) [L.]	to take, seize	*captivate* (to take hold of)
-dic- (-dict-) [L.]	to say in words	pre*dict* (to say before)
-dyna- [Gr.]	to be strong	*dynasty* (a state of strength)
-mov- (-mot-) [L.]	to move	*movable* (able to be moved)
-nym- [Gr.]	to name	anto*nym* (to name as an opposite)
-pon- (-pos-) [L.]	to put, place	com*pose* (to put together)
-spec- (-spect-) [L.]	to see	*spectator* (one who sees)
-ten (-tain-) [L.]	to hold	de*tain* (to hold back)
-vert- (-vers-) [L.]	to turn	in*vert* (to turn upside down)
-vid- (-vis-) [L.]	to see	*visible* (able to be seen)
-heal- [A.S.]	sound, whole	*health* (physical and mental well-being)

▶ **Exercise 7** Using Roots to Define Words Match the words in the first column below with their definitions in the second column.

1. prospect	a. way of using words
2. inversion	b. sounding alike
3. diction	c. a strong explosive
4. mobility	d. a turning upside down
5. homophonic	e. oversee
6. transpose	f. future outlook
7. dynamite	g. someone taken as a prisoner
8. supervise	h. reach
9. attain	i. change places
10. captive	j. ease of movement

662 • Vocabulary and Spelling

▶ **More Practice**

Academic and Workplace Skills Activity Book
• pp. 23–24

⏱ TIME AND RESOURCE MANAGER

Resources
Print: Academic and Workplace Skills Activity Book, pp. 22–25

In-Depth Coverage	Accelerated Pace
• Work through all key concepts, pp. 662–665. • Assign and review Exercises 7–11.	• Assign pp. 662–665 for independent student review.

Using Prefixes

Knowing only a small number of prefixes can help you understand thousands of words.

▶ **KEY CONCEPT** A **prefix** is one or more syllables added to the beginning of a word to form a new word. ■

Learn the prefixes in the chart below to create new words and to enlarge your vocabulary. The origins of the roots are indicated by the abbreviations *L.*, *Gr.*, and *A.S.* (Latin, Greek, and Anglo-Saxon).

TEN COMMON PREFIXES		
Prefix and Origin	**Meaning**	**Example**
anti- [Gr.]	against	*anti*social (against society)
dis- [L.]	away, apart	*dis*grace (to lose favor)
ex- [L.]	from, out	*ex*port (to send out)
mis- [A.S.]	wrong	*mis*lead (to lead in a wrong direction)
mono- [Gr.]	one, alone	*mono*rail (a single rail)
non- [L.]	not	*non*profit (not trying to earn a profit)
pre- [L.]	before	*pre*view (to view beforehand)
re- [L.]	back, again	*re*view (to view again)
trans- [L.]	over, across	*trans*mit (to send across)
un- [A.S.]	not	*un*known (unable to be determined)

▶ **Exercise 8** **Working With Prefixes** On a piece of paper, combine the prefix in parentheses with each word below to create a new word. In your notebook, write the definition next to each word. Use a dictionary to check your answers.

1. appear (dis-)
2. historic (pre-)
3. behave (mis-)
4. aircraft (anti-)
5. available (un-)
6. vocal (non-)
7. syllable (mono-)
8. form (trans-)
9. claim (re-)
10. act (ex-)

▼ Critical Viewing
If he is studying *before* a test, what will this boy be? If he studies well, what will he avoid? Use words with the prefixes *pre-* and *mis-* in your answer. **[Draw Conclusions]**

Studying Word Parts and Origins • 663

Using Prefixes

1. Have students memorize the list of prefixes and their meanings. Ask them to write them in their vocabulary notebooks.

2. Ask students to brainstorm other words that use the ten common prefixes. Have them write sentences that use those words.

3. Have students work in teams to prepare presentations that use as many common prefixes as possible. Or ask students to brainstorm other common prefixes that are used in everyday conversation. Have students present their lists to the class.

Critical Viewing

Draw Conclusions Students may say that the boy will be prepared and that he will avoid mistakes.

Answer Key

▶ **Exercise 8**

1. disappear: to go out of sight
2. prehistoric: before written history
3. misbehave: act badly
4. antiaircraft: for use against enemy planes
5. unavailable: not handy
6. nonvocal: unspoken
7. monosyllable: a word with one syllable
8. transform: change
9. reclaim: take back
10. exact: demand with force

Integrating Spelling

Adding a prefix to a word never changes the spelling of the base word: *misspell, reexamine, nonnative, anti-inflammatory*. Sometimes when it results in a double vowel, a hyphen is used after the prefix for clarity.

Integrating Test Taking

Students will be familiar with tests that require their knowledge of a word's meaning. Explain that prefixes are helpful clues to the meaning of a word. If students memorize common prefixes and their meanings, they may be able to determine the meaning of a word without understanding the context.

Using Suffixes

1. Have students memorize the common suffixes and their meanings. Ask them to write them in their vocabulary notebooks.

2. Ask students to brainstorm other words that use the ten common suffixes. Have them write sentences that use those words.

3. Have students work in teams to prepare presentations that use as many common suffixes as possible. Or ask students to brainstorm other common suffixes that are used in everyday conversation. Have students present their lists to their classmates.

Answer Key

> **Exercise 9**

Have students check each other's answers.

> **Exercise 10**

After students have completed this exercise, they may want to try out their new sentences on their classmates. Have each student write one new sentence on the board. Then have a class discussion about the way the suffixes are functioning in each sentence.

Integrating Spelling

The addition of a suffix may alter the spelling of the base word, for example, *literacy = literate + -cy; reaction = react + -tion.*

29.3

Using Suffixes

> **KEY CONCEPT** A **suffix** is one or more syllables added to the end of a word to form a new word. ■

Suffixes can change both the meaning and the part of speech of a word. For instance, the noun *color* becomes the adjective *colorless* when the suffix *-less* is added. In the following chart, five common suffixes are listed. Alternative spellings are in parentheses. The abbreviations *L., Gr.,* and *A.S.* mean Latin, Greek, and Anglo-Saxon, the origins of the suffixes.

TEN COMMON SUFFIXES		
Suffix and Origin	**Meaning**	**Example**
-able (-ible) [L.]	capable of being	laugh*able* (capable of being laughed at)
-cy (-acy) [Gr.]	quality of	democra*cy* (quality of being democratic)
-ful [A.S.]	full of	hope*ful* (full of hope)
-ism [Gr.]	idea, belief, act	national*ism* (belief in a nation)
-ist [Gr.]	believer, doer	violin*ist* (player of the violin)
-ity [L.]	state of being	char*ity* (state of being charitable)
-less [A.S.]	without, lacking	sound*less* (without sound)
-ly [Gr.]	in a certain way	local*ly* (in a local way)
-ment [L.]	result or act of	state*ment* (result of stating)
-tion (-ion, -sion) [L.]	act of, state of being	crea*tion* (act of creating)

> **Exercise 9** Working With Suffixes Divide a piece of paper into two columns. In the first column, write two new examples for each suffix listed above. In the second column, write their definitions. Check your answers in a dictionary.

> **Exercise 10** Changing Suffixes to Make New Words
Define each word below; then, change the suffix as indicated, and define the new word. Write a sentence for every word. Check the meanings in a dictionary if necessary.
1. helpful (change *-ful* to *-less*)
2. prediction (change *-tion* to *-[t]able*)
3. realism (change *-ism* to *-ity*)
4. consistency (change *-cy* to *-[t]ly*)
5. purity (change *-ity* to *-ist*)

> **More Practice**
Academic and Workplace Skills Activity Book
• pp. 25–26

☑ ONGOING ASSESSMENT: Monitor and Reinforce

If students have difficulty with Exercises 7–11, use one of the following options.

Option 1 Have students write the common roots, prefixes, and suffixes from the charts on pages 662–664. Have them work in pairs to write words that use the roots, prefixes, and suffixes.

Option 2 Ask students to review a newspaper or magazine article and circle all the prefixes, suffixes, or roots they see. Then have them define what these prefixes, suffixes, and roots mean if they are unclear.

Examining Word Origins

You may not ever have thought about it, but English is one of a family of languages with a very long history. English is part of the Indo-European family of languages. Its closest relatives are other Germanic languages, such as Dutch and German. English is the most widely spoken language in the Western world. It has also borrowed words from more languages than any other. In fact, more than 70 percent of the words we call English are borrowed from other languages.

Understanding Historical Influences

Throughout its history, English has been exposed to many other languages. Events and circumstances—such as wars and trade with other nations, new inventions, and emerging technologies—have contributed to the growth and change of the language.

INFLUENCES ON THE GROWTH OF ENGLISH		
Conquest	Throughout history, invasion and conquests of Great Britain added many words to English.	earth (Anglo-Saxon) secure (Latin) avenue (French)
Travelers	Travelers, including merchants, explorers, and soldiers, added words to English from languages and cultures they encountered around the world.	moose (North America) banjo (Africa) calico (India) boondocks (Malayan) tea (China)
New Words	New words were coined to describe new inventions and technologies.	automobile photography movie Internet suburb

> **Exercise 11** **Analyzing Word Origins** Write the words below on a separate sheet of paper, and look them up in a print or electronic dictionary. Then, write the language from which each word comes.
> 1. balcony
> 2. piano
> 3. mustard
> 4. encyclopedia
> 5. nickel

 Internet Tip

To find Internet sites containing information about how English developed with influences from other languages, type "origins of English" in the query field of your search engine.

Step-by-Step Teaching Guide

Examining Word Origins

1. Have students be word detectives, researching the etymologies or origins of words.

2. Most dictionaries provide brief etymologies of words, but some dictionaries, like the *Oxford English Dictionary (OED)* are devoted to extensive histories of words in the English language.

3. Encourage students to investigate the histories of at least ten words. If they have access to an *OED*, ask them to present their most interesting discoveries to their classmates.

Answer Key

▶ **Exercise 11**

1. balcony—Italian < Langobardic < Old High German
2. piano—Italian
3. mustard—Middle English < Old French < Latin
4. encyclopedia—Latin < Greek
5. nickel—Swedish < German

Customize for *Musical Learners*

Have students look up the origins of 20 (or more) musical instruments: banjo, guitar, oboe, harmonica, and so on.

Have students look through local newspapers or magazines for spelling mistakes. Ask them to look in advertisements, and on packaging for common spelling mistakes, such as "Eat-Inn Diner" or "Febuary." Have them cut out these errors and keep them in a "bloopers" section of their vocabulary notebooks.

Activate Prior Knowledge

Have students look back at their writing and find spelling errors from past assignments. Have them write the word again, correctly spelled, in their vocabulary notebooks. Ask them to write new sentences using the correctly spelled words.

TEACH

Step-by-Step Teaching Guide

Improving Your Spelling

1. Divide the class into small groups to play Hangman. Have one student in each group choose a secret word from a list of difficult-to-spell words. Group members take turns guessing a letter that might be in the mystery word. Any student who correctly guesses a word writes that word in a vocabulary notebook and writes a sentence to accompany the word.

2. Ask students to give themselves spelling tests by thinking of difficult words they have heard, writing them as they think they are spelled, then looking them up in a dictionary to confirm their spelling.

Answer Key

Exercise 12

1. correct	11. potato
2. complete	12. correct
3. encouragement	13. tomato
4. correct	14. correct
5. nineteenth	15. correct
6. correct	16. escape
7. religion	17. medicine
8. correct	18. correct
9. ninety	19. correct
10. correct	20. Wednesday

Section 29.4

Improving Your Spelling

Whether you are writing for a teacher, a friend, or someone you haven't met, your writing makes an impression on the reader. You want that impression to be positive. Anyone can learn to eliminate nearly all spelling errors by using a dictionary, keeping a spelling list, and observing some basic rules.

Using a Spelling List

▶ **KEY CONCEPT** When selecting the words for your spelling list, focus on words you frequently misspell. Enter the spelling and pronunciation of each word in your notebook, and study your list regularly. ■

SPELLING NOTEBOOK

Words	Definitions
necessary	essential
Mississippi	
accessible	can be approached or entered
spaghetti	

▶ **Exercise 12** Developing a Spelling List Look carefully at each word below. On a piece of paper, write *correct* if the word is spelled correctly, or change the spelling if it is incorrect. Check each word in a dictionary. Add any words that give you trouble to your personal spelling list.

1. avenue	11. potatoe
2. compleet	12. sincerely
3. encouragment	13. tomatoe
4. expense	14. weapon
5. ninteenth	15. width
6. defeat	16. excape
7. riligion	17. medecine
8. science	18. cafeteria
9. ninty	19. punctuation
10. season	20. Wensday

Internet Tip

On the Internet, you can find lists of words that are frequently misspelled. To access them, type "commonly misspelled words" in the query field of your search engine.

⏱ TIME AND RESOURCE MANAGER

Resources
Print: Academic and Workplace Skills Activity Book, pp. 26–33

In-Depth Coverage	Accelerated Pace
• Work through all key concepts, pp. 666–675. • Assign and review Exercises 12–23.	• Assign pp. 666–675 for independent student review.

Studying Your Spelling Words

It is important to study the words on your spelling list regularly. To make this task more manageable, divide your list into groups of five or ten words. Study each group separately for about a week. As you master more and more words, test yourself on larger groups from your list.

KEY CONCEPT Review your spelling words each week, several times a week. ■

A METHOD FOR STUDYING YOUR SPELLING WORDS

1. *Look* at each word. Notice any unusual features about the spelling of the word. For example, in the word *argument*, the *e* in *argue* is dropped before the ending is added. Concentrate on the part of the word that gives you the most trouble. Then, cover the word and try to picture it in your mind.

2. *Say* the word aloud. Then, sound the word out slowly, syllable by syllable.

3. *Spell* the word by writing it on a sheet of paper. Say each syllable aloud as you write it down.

4. *Compare* the word that you wrote on the paper with the word in your notebook. If you spelled the word correctly, put a small check in front of the word in your notebook. If you misspelled the word, circle the letter or letters on your paper that are incorrect. Then, start over again with the first step.

Exercise 13 Checking Spelling Skills Fill in the missing letter in each word below. Add any words you misspelled to your personal spelling list.

1. element ___?___ ry
2. nurs ___?___ ry
3. courage ___?___ us
4. import ___?___ nce
5. experi ___?___ nce
6. confu ___?___ ion
7. competi ___?___ ion
8. accept ___?___ ble
9. terr ___?___ ble
10. comfort ___?___ ble

Exercise 14 Identifying Commonly Misspelled Words Record in your notebook any words you have misspelled in your work. Check your writing portfolio, corrected tests, essays, and homework to find these words. After you have studied the words, have a partner test you on them.

Studying Your Spelling Words

1. Have students review the spelling of words by practicing and testing themselves regularly.

2. Encourage them to keep track of words that are confusing and to eliminate their confusion by studying those words especially carefully.

Answer Key

Exercise 13

1. elementary
2. nursery
3. courageous
4. importance
5. experience
6. confusion
7. competition
8. acceptable
9. terrible
10. comfortable

Exercise 14

After students have completed this exercise, ask them to write self-tests for themselves to reinforce difficult words. Students should base their tests on their performance with their partners.

More Practice

Academic and Workplace Skills Activity Book
• pp. 27–28

Improving Your Spelling • 667

Applying Spelling Rules

1. Refer students who have difficulty spelling words containing the letters *ie* or *ei* to the bulleted list of rules. Ask them to write these rules in their vocabulary notebook and memorize them.

2. Have students work in pairs, writing sentences that correspond to the list of *ie* and *ei* words in the chart. Have students practice these difficult words in Exercise 15.

Answer Key

> **Exercise 15**

1. brief
2. freight
3. receiver
4. thief
5. beige
6. weigh
7. deceive
8. pierce
9. pier
10. reindeer

29.4

Applying Spelling Rules

Choosing Between *ie* and *ei*

Follow basic rules when you spell a word containing the letters *ie* or *ei*. Exceptions to these rules should be memorized.

- When a word has a long *e* sound, use *ie*.
- When a word has a long *a* sound, use *ei*.
- When a word has a long *e* sound preceded by the letter *c*, use *ei*.

COMMON *ie* AND *ei* WORDS

Long *e* Sound: Use *ie*	Long *a* Sound: Use *ei*	Long *e* Sound preceded by *c*: Use *ei*
brief	eight	ceiling
chief	freight	deceive
niece	reign	perceive
piece	sleigh	receipt
relieve	vein	receive
shield	weight	
yield		

EXCEPTIONS: either, neither, seize

> **KEY CONCEPT** Remember the rule: *i* before *e* except after *c* and when sounded like *ay* as in *neighbor* and *weigh*. ■

Try to Think of Additional Words If you can add more words to the chart above, it will help you to remember the basic rules. Add any words you find difficult to your spelling list.

> **Exercise 15** Spelling *ie* and *ei* Words Fill in the blanks below with either *ie* or *ei*. Check the spellings in a dictionary. Add difficult words to your personal spelling list.

1. br __?__ f
2. fr __?__ ght
3. rec __?__ ver
4. th __?__ f
5. b __?__ ge
6. w __?__ gh
7. dec __?__ ve
8. p __?__ rce
9. p __?__ r
10. r __?__ ndeer

> **More Practice**
>
> Academic and Workplace Skills Activity Book
> • p. 29

668 • Vocabulary and Spelling

STANDARDIZED TEST PREPARATION WORKSHOP

Spelling Many standardized tests require students to recognize correct spelling in a passage. Ask students which is the correct spelling of the underlined word.

The neighbor <u>briefed</u> the family on the block party they missed while they were on vacation.

A No change

B breifed

C breefed

D breafed

The correct answer is **A**, because *briefed* is spelled correctly. The *i* is before the *e*, which conforms to the long *e* sound.

Adding Prefixes and Suffixes

A prefix is one or more syllables added at the beginning of a word to form a new word. A suffix is one or more syllables added to the end of a word.

KEY CONCEPT Adding a *prefix* to a word does not affect the spelling of the original word. Adding a *suffix* often involves a spelling change in the word. ∎

Prefixes When a prefix is added to a word, the spelling of the root word remains the same.

EXAMPLES:
mis- + spell = misspell
un- + finished = unfinished
re- + act = react
dis- + service = disservice
co- + exist = coexist
im- + movable = immovable
de- + press = depress
in- + accurate = inaccurate

Investigate Long Words The way in which the words in the above list are divided may help you to remember something important to spelling success. Long words (*circumnavigate*) are often made up of small words (*navigate*) and word parts (*circum-*). When you have to spell a long word, try to spell the small words within it.

Exercise 16 Spelling Words With Prefixes Make new words by combining the words and prefixes in parentheses below. Check each word in a dictionary to make sure that it is spelled correctly. Add any difficult words to your spelling list.

1. operate (co-)
2. compression (de-)
3. satisfaction (dis-)
4. polite (im-)
5. offensive (in-)
6. fortune (mis-)
7. elect (re-)
8. natural (un-)
9. author (co-)
10. fault (de-)

▼ Critical Viewing How might focusing on correct spelling, as well as on the content of his report, be likely to improve this student's chances of receiving a good grade? **[Connect]**

Adding Prefixes

1. Prefixes are pieces of words that can be added without altering the spelling of the original word.
2. Ask students to think of other words to which these prefixes can be added.

Critical Viewing

Connect Students may suggest that often the meaning of a word depends on its prefix or suffix. The student who understands the meaning of the words he or she is using will have clarity in his or her report.

Answer Key

▶ **Exercise 16**

1. cooperate
2. decompression
3. dissatisfaction
4. impolite
5. inoffensive
6. misfortune
7. reelect
8. unnatural
9. coauthor
10. default

Adding Suffixes

1. Students may find the rules for adding suffixes confusing. Go over each of the rules, using additional words as examples.

2. Have students memorize the rules for adding suffixes and write a sentence for each rule, using a word they already know.

3. These rules are complicated, but frequent reading and practice will enable students to incorporate these rules into their writing with no trouble.

Answer Key

▶ **Exercise 17**

1. fixed
2. tried
3. movable
4. lately
5. meowing
6. greedily
7. beautify
8. usable
9. tapped
10. mysterious
11. crying
12. joyous
13. hungrily
14. lovable
15. dropped

29.4

Suffixes The following three lists summarize the major kinds of spelling changes that can take place when a suffix is added. Pay close attention to the exceptions to the rules.

Adding Suffixes to Words Ending in -*y*

1. Rule: When a word ends in a consonant plus -*y*, change *y* to *i* when adding a suffix.

   lazy + -ly = lazily   happy + -ness = happiness

   Exception: Most suffixes beginning with -*i.*

   try + -ing = trying   cry + -ing = crying

2. Rule: When a word ends in a vowel plus -*y*, do not change the spelling when adding a suffix.

   annoy + -ance = annoyance   enjoy + -ment = enjoyment

   Exception: A few short words.

   day + -ly = daily   pay + -ed = paid

Adding Suffixes to Words Ending in -*e*

1. Rule: When a word ends in -*e*, drop the *e* when adding a suffix beginning with a vowel.

   move + -able = movable   drive + -ing = driving

   Exceptions: (1) words ending in -*ce* or -*ge* with suffixes beginning with -*a* or -*o*, and (2) words ending in -*ee*.

   trace + -able = traceable   courage + -ous = courageous
   see + -ing = seeing   agree + -able = agreeable

2. Rule: When a word ends in -*e*, make no change when adding a suffix beginning with a consonant.

   peace + -ful = peaceful   brave + -ly = bravely

   Exception: A few special words.

   argue + -ment = argument   true + -ly = truly

Doubling the Final Consonant Before Suffixes

1. Rule: When a word ends in a consonant + vowel + consonant in a stressed syllable, double the final consonant when adding a suffix beginning with a vowel.

   mud´ + -y = mud´ dy   submit´ + -ed = submit´ ted

   Exception: Words ending in *x* or *w*.

   mix + -ing = mixing   row + -ing = rowing

▶ **Exercise 17** Spelling Words With Suffixes Make new words by combining the words and suffixes in parentheses below. Check the spelling of each word in a dictionary. Add any difficult words to your personal spelling list.

1. fix (-ed)	6. greedy (-ly)	11. cry (-ing)
2. try (-ed)	7. beauty (-fy)	12. joy (-ous)
3. move (-able)	8. use (-able)	13. hungry (-ly)
4. late (-ly)	9. tap (-ed)	14. love (-able)
5. meow (-ing)	10. mystery (-ous)	15. drop (-ed)

Understanding the Influence of Other Languages and Cultures

Consider this simple English sentence: "The raccoon ignored the sauerkraut but ate three crayons." It sounds like English, and it *is* English, but three of the words come directly from other languages. *Raccoon* is an Algonquian Indian word, *sauerkraut* is a German word, and *crayon* is a French word. Each of these borrowed words comes with the unique features of the spelling and pronunciation of the original language. That is why English uses a wide variety of letters to spell certain sounds and why some words contain "silent letters"—letters that are not pronounced. Use a print or electronic dictionary to confirm the spelling of any word about which you are unsure.

KEY CONCEPT Because English borrows many words from other languages, different words might use different letters to spell the same sound. ■

EXAMPLES:	stu**ff**	**f**un	**g**entle	**ch**rome	pa**ck**
	tou**gh**	**ph**one	**j**ealous	**c**all	la**k**e
				kite	chi**c**

Use Memory Aids To help you remember the spelling of words that don't follow the English spelling rules, try making up sentences that will serve as memory aids.

EXAMPLES: **G**ee! **H**e's tou**gh** enou**gh**!
 Gee! **H**e's rou**gh** enou**gh**!

Exercise 18 Choosing the Correct Spelling Identify the word in each group below that is spelled correctly. Check your answers in a dictionary, and note the language from which each word originated. Add misspelled words and their languages of origin to your personal spelling list.

1.	catchup	ketchup	kachup
2.	tycoon	tiecoon	tyecune
3.	canuw	kannew	canoe
4.	cindergartin	kindergarten	kindargarden
5.	beautyfull	beutiful	beautiful
6.	photograph	fotograf	photoegraph
7.	taco	tacoh	takoe
8.	skope	scope	scohpe
9.	nayburr	neahbor	neighbor
10.	coyote	kyotee	ciyoty

► More Practice

Academic and
Workplace Skills
Activity Book
• p. 30

Answer Key

► Exercise 18

1. ketchup—Chinese
2. tycoon—Sino-Japanese
3. canoe—Spanish < Caribbean
4. kindergarten—German
5. beautiful—Middle English < Old French < Latin
6. photograph—Greek
7. taco—Spanish
8. scope—Latin < Greek
9. neighbor—Middle English < Old English
10. coyote—Spanish < Nahuatl

Forming Plurals

1. Have students review the chart of forming regular plurals.

2. Have students work in small groups and brainstorm plural words that exhibit these common patterns.

3. Encourage students to write these rules into their vocabulary notebooks.

4. Have a spelling bee of plurals, in which students are tested on the various rules of making words plural.

29.4

Forming Plurals

The word *plural* means "more than one." Most nouns form their plurals according to a general rule. These are regular plural forms. Nouns with irregular plural forms do not follow this rule.

KEY CONCEPT Most nouns have regular plurals. Regular plurals are formed by adding *-s* or *-es* to the singular form of the noun. ■

FORMING REGULAR PLURALS		
Word Ending	**Rule**	**Examples**
-s, -ss, -x, -z, -zz, -sh, -ch	Add *-es*.	bus, buses mass, masses fox, foxes buzz, buzzes crash, crashes punch, punches
-o preceded by a consonant	Add *-es*.	tomato, tomatoes EXCEPTIONS: solo, solos (and other musical terms)
-o preceded by a vowel	Add *-s*.	radio, radios
-y preceded by a consonant	Change *y* to *i* and add *-es*.	party, parties discovery, discoveries
-y preceded by a vowel	Add *-s*.	day, days monkey, monkeys
-ff	Add *-s*.	bluff, bluffs staff, staffs
-fe	Change *f* to *v* and add *-es*.	knife, knives
-f	Add *-s*. OR Change *f* to *v* and add *-es*.	chief, chiefs calf, calves leaf, leaves

Learn More

See Chapter 24 to review the ways in which nouns and pronouns must agree with plural nouns.

Step-by-Step Teaching Guide

Irregular Plurals Irregular plurals are not formed according to the rules on the previous page. If you are unsure of how to form a plural, check a dictionary. Irregular plurals are usually listed right after the pronunciation of the word. (If no plural form is given in the dictionary, the word has a regular plural. Simply add -s or -es to the singular form.)

KEY CONCEPT Use a dictionary to look up the correct spelling of irregular plurals. Memorize them. ■

EXAMPLES OF IRREGULAR PLURALS

Singular	Plural
ox	oxen
child	children
tooth	teeth
man	men
mouse	mice
fish	fish
pants	pants

Plural Forms of Compound Nouns Most one-word compound nouns have regular plural forms. If one part of the compound noun is irregular, the plural form will also be irregular.

EXAMPLES: bedroom, bedrooms (regular)
policewoman, policewomen (irregular)

Most compound nouns written with hyphens or as separate words form the plural by making the modified word plural. The *modified word* is the word being described, or modified, by the other part.

EXAMPLES: lady-in-waiting, ladies-in-waiting
string quartet, string quartets
mile per hour, miles per hour
run batted in, runs batted in

Exercise 19 Forming Plurals Write the plural form for each of the following words. Use the rules in this section or a dictionary. Add any difficult words to your personal spelling list.

1. bush
2. mouse
3. snake
4. fly
5. box
6. hero
7. wife
8. fisherman
9. cowboy
10. cello
11. boy
12. lunch
13. goose
14. rice
15. city
16. torpedo
17. basketball
18. donkey
19. holiday
20. business

More Practice
Academic and Workplace Skills Activity Book
• p. 31

Irregular Plurals

1. Review the chart of irregular plurals.
2. Encourage students to memorize irregular plurals and write them in their vocabulary notebooks.
3. Have students practice plurals by doing Exercise 19 in class and comparing their answers.

Answer Key

Exercise 19

1. bushes
2. mice
3. snakes
4. flies
5. boxes
6. heroes
7. wives
8. fishermen
9. cowboys
10. cellos
11. boys
12. lunches
13. geese
14. rice
15. cities
16. torpedoes
17. basketballs
18. donkeys
19. holidays
20. businesses

Spelling Homophones

1. Have students memorize the homophones on the page.

2. Ask students to write sentences using each of the homophones. A challenge is to use an entire pair or triple in one sentence. An extra challenge is to use more than one pair in a single sentence.

Customize for
ESL Students

Students learning English may find homophones especially difficult to spell or use correctly in sentences. Encourage them to write the definitions for the homophones on a special page in their vocabulary notebook and refer to them regularly. Ask them to write sentences that use the homophones and to say them aloud to get as much meaning from context as possible.

Answer Key

▶ **Exercise 20**

1. peace
2. two
3. tail
4. right
5. They're

▶ **Exercise 21**

After students complete this exercise, have them share their papers with a partner and review the different ways these homophones are used. Or students may write their answers on the board and discuss them with the class.

29.4

Spelling Homophones

▶ **KEY CONCEPT** Homophones are words that sound the same but have different meanings. Homophones may also have different spellings. ■

Study the following list of common homophones to make sure that you use and spell each of them correctly.

1. **their, they're, there**
   their: A possessive pronoun that means "belonging to them"
   they're: A contraction for "they are"
   there: A place word or sentence starter, as in "There are lots of people outside"
2. **tail, tale**
   tail: The flexible part at the rear of an animal
   tale: A story
3. **piece, peace**
   piece: A part or fragment
   peace: The condition of not being at war
4. **write, right**
   write: Put words on paper
   right: Correct
5. **to, too, two**
   to: Begins a prepositional phrase or infinitive
   too: Also
   two: A number

▶ **Exercise 20** Using Correct Homophones Choose the correct word from the homophones in parentheses below. Check your answers in a dictionary. Add any misspelled words to your spelling list.
1. The generals finally agreed to a (piece, peace) treaty.
2. I bought (to, too, two) shirts, one yellow and one blue.
3. The horse's (tail, tale) was braided for the horse show.
4. He made the (right, write) choice and won the prize.
5. (Their, They're) going to the game on Saturday.

▶ **Exercise 21** Writing Sentences With Homophones Write a sentence for each lettered word in each numbered pair below. Check a dictionary to make sure that you are using each word correctly.
1. (a) by (b) buy
2. (a) bear (b) bare
3. (a) stair (b) stare
4. (a) through (b) threw
5. (a) rain b) reign

▶ **More Practice**

Academic and Workplace Skills Activity Book
• pp. 32–33

Proofreading and Using References

Proofreading is a simple way to double-check your spelling and eliminate any spelling errors. If you are unsure about the correct spelling of a word, use a reference such as a dictionary to check it.

▶ **KEY CONCEPT** Use dictionaries, electronic spell-checkers, and glossaries to check for the correct spellings of words. ■

▶ **Exercise 22** Proofreading Sentences Copy and proofread the following sentences, correcting misspelled words. Use a reference to confirm the spelling of words about which you are unsure.
 1. The princess recieved her guests at the gates of the castle.
 2. Michael saw a bare during his trip to the mountins.
 3. Ten sheeps left the fold and ate the farmer's daisys.
 4. My naybor's dog chased the racoon until it climed a tree.
 5. Emily's mother was crying with happyness at the site of her daughter singing in the choir.

▶ **Exercise 23** Proofreading a Paragraph Copy and proofread the following paragraph. Correct any words that are written incorrectly. Use a reference to confirm the spelling of words about which you are unsure.

My mother brought home the knew puppy today! He is part retreiver, part boxer. We chose him at the local animal shelter. The first thing he did when he got to our house was to sniff everywhere. Then, he hungryly eight a bowl of food. After that, we let him outside, where he promptily chased a squirrel and a chipmonk.

Reflecting on Your Spelling and Vocabulary

Think about what you have learned by answering the following questions:

• Which of the techniques in this chapter do you find most effective for studying spelling words?

• Which do you find most helpful for studying vocabulary words?

• What do the techniques have in common? In what ways are they different?

Improving Your Spelling • 675

Proofreading and Using References

1. Encourage students to use all resources at hand to spell words correctly.

2. Acquaint students with dictionaries, spell-checkers, and glossaries and remind them of their own vocabulary notebooks.

3. Ask students to review their own writing as if proofreading it for mistakes.

4. Have students work in pairs, proofreading each other's writing for spelling errors. Have students discuss any mistakes and write corrected words into their vocabulary notebooks.

Answer Key

▶ **Exercise 22**

1. The princess received her guests at the gates of the castle.
2. Michael saw a bear during his trip to the mountains.
3. Ten sheep left the fold and ate the farmer's daisies.
4. My neighbor's dog chased the raccoon until it climbed a tree.
5. Emily's mother was crying with happiness at the sight of her daughter singing in the choir.

▶ **Exercise 23**

My mother brought home the new puppy today! He is part retriever, part boxer. We chose him at the local animal shelter. The first thing he did when he got to our house was to sniff everywhere. Then, he hungrily ate a bowl of food. After that, we let him outside, where he promptly chased a squirrel and a chipmunk.

Step-by-Step Teaching Guide

Using Context to Determine Word Meaning

Teaching Resources: Standardized Test Preparation Workbook, Chapter 29

1. Review with students the strategies for answering vocabulary questions.

2. Remind students that many words can have different meanings, depending on how they are used in a specific passage.

3. Make sure students carefully read the passage to get a sense of the overall meaning. This will prevent them from making careless mistakes.

Standardized Test Preparation Workshop

Using Context to Determine Word Meaning

Standardized tests often contain vocabulary questions. These types of questions require you to find the meaning of a word using the context of a passage. Use the context to help you determine the meanings of idioms, expressions, words with multiple meanings, figurative language, and specialized and technical terms.

The following strategies will help you answer vocabulary questions on standardized tests:

• Read the sentence; carefully focus on the underlined word.

• Determine the overall meaning of the passage.

• Look for clues in the surrounding words.

• Use these clues to guess which answer choice best defines the meaning of the new word.

Test Tip

Before making a final selection, read your choice in place of the underlined word. Evaluate whether it makes sense.

Sample Test Items	Answers and Explanations
Directions: Read the passage. Then, read each question that follows the passage. Decide which is the best answer to each question. The <u>counter</u> indicated a <u>record</u> number of visitors to the Web site.	
1 In this passage, the word <u>counter</u> means— **A** a place for preparing food **B** a person who counts things **C** a computer hardware device **D** software designed to collect specific data electronically	The correct answer for item 1 is *D*. Although both *A* and *B* are correct definitions of the word, the only meaning that applies in the context of the passage is *D*.
2 The word <u>record</u> in this passage means— **F** evidence of **G** greatest **H** keep details **J** a recording	The correct answer for item 2 is *G*. The adjective *record* is used in this sentence to indicate the highest number of visitors to the Web site.

676 • Vocabulary and Spelling

✎ TEST-TAKING TIP

When students are in doubt of a word's meaning, have them replace the word in the passage with each of the choices. Students may be able to make an educated guess based on how the choice sounds in the context of the passage.

Practice 1 Directions: Read the passage. Then, read each question that follows the passage. Decide which is the best answer to each question.

Collecting antiques is a fast-growing <u>craze</u>. Everything from old furniture to tin toys is showing up in antique stores and flea markets and even on the Internet. Sometimes, <u>individual</u> items gain much greater meaning and value when added to other like items. For example, a signed picture of the <u>late</u> President Eisenhower, although valuable on its own, may triple in value when paired with an <u>original</u> letter from the President.

1 In this passage, the word <u>craze</u> means—
  A fad
  B insanity
  C cult
  D whim

2 In this passage, the word <u>individual</u> means—
  F human being
  G unusual
  H exclusive
  J single

3 The word <u>late</u> in this passage means—
  A behind schedule
  B postponed
  C recent
  D deceased

4 In this passage, the word <u>original</u> means—
  F unique
  G not copied
  H sincere
  J creative

Practice 2 Directions: Read the passage. Then, read each question that follows the passage. Decide which is the best answer to each question.

Toward the end of winter, a gardener's <u>fancy</u> turns to spring. Seed <u>catalogs</u> begin to arrive in the mail. Periodically, a warm day will allow the gardener to spend some time pulling weeds and turning the soil in preparation for <u>sowing</u>. If you have a <u>green thumb</u>, all you need is the hope of an early growing season!

1 In this passage, the expression <u>fancy</u> means—
  A decorative
  B to be inclined to
  C imagination
  D ornamental

2 The word <u>catalogs</u> in this passage means—
  F lists
  G classifies
  H sales brochures
  J categories of garden tools

3 The word <u>sowing</u> in this passage means—
  A spreading seed in the ground
  B attaching two pieces of fabric with thread and needle
  C harvesting crops
  D preparing the garden

4 In this passage, the expression <u>green thumb</u> means—
  F a fungal infection of the thumb
  G skill at gardening
  H little experience with gardening
  J a gardening club recognized by its members with green thumbs

Answer Key

▶ **Practice 1**
1. A
2. J
3. D
4. G

▶ **Practice 2**
1. C
2. H
3. A
4. G

In-Depth Lesson Plan

	LESSON FOCUS	PRINT AND MEDIA RESOURCES
DAY 1	**Reading Methods and Tools** Students learn and apply reading skills such as using sections and features of a textbook and using reading strategies (pp. 679–684).	**Teaching Resources** *Academic and Workplace Skills Activity Book,* pp. 34–37
DAY 2	**Reading Nonfiction Critically** Students learn and apply such critical reading skills as identifying author's purpose, distinguishing fact and opinion and reasoning and textual analysis skills (pp. 685–690).	**Teaching Resources** *Academic and Workplace Skills Activity Book,* pp. 38–43
DAY 3	**Reading Literary Writing** Students learn and apply strategies for reading fiction, drama, poetry and folk tales and myths (pp. 691–695).	**Teaching Resources** *Academic and Workplace Skills Activity Book,* pp. 44–50
DAY 4	**Reading from Varied Sources** Students learn skills for reading from such sources as newspapers, magazines, manuals, electronic texts and anthologies (pp. 696–697).	**Teaching Resources** *Academic and Workplace Skills Activity Book,* p. 51

Accelerated Lesson Plan

	LESSON FOCUS	PRINT AND MEDIA RESOURCES
DAY 1	**Reading Methods and Reading Nonfiction Critically** Students learn reading methods and skills for reading nonfiction critically (pp. 679–690).	**Teaching Resources** *Academic and Workplace Skills Activity Book,* pp. 34–43
DAY 2	**Reading Literary Writing and Varied Sources** Students learn skills for reading different genres of fiction and varied sources (pp. 691–697).	**Teaching Resources** *Academic and Workplace Skills Activity Book,* pp. 44–51

Options for Adapting Lesson Plans

HOMEWORK

Have students complete any stage of the lesson for homework.

FEATURES

Extend coverage with the Standardized Test Preparation Workshop (pp. 698–699).

TECHNOLOGY

Students can complete any stage of the lesson on computer. Have them print out their completed work.

INTEGRATED SKILLS COVERAGE

Workplace Skills
ATE p. 697

Viewing and Representing
Critical Viewing SE pp. 678, 687, 691, 697

BLOCK SCHEDULING

Professional Development Support
• *How to Manage Instruction in the Block* This Teaching Resource provides management and activity suggestions.

ASSESSMENT SUPPORT

Standardized Test Preparation Workshop SE p. 698; ATE p. 688

Standardized Test Preparation Workbook, pp. 59–60

Scoring Rubrics on Transparency, Ch. 30

Formal Assessment, Ch. 30

Writing Assessment and Portfolio Management

MEETING INDIVIDUAL NEEDS

Less Advanced Students ATE p. 690; see also Ongoing Assessments ATE pp. 681, 684, 686, 689, 692, 695

Verbal/Linguistic Learners ATE p. 693

WRITING AND GRAMMAR WEB SITE

The Interactive Writing and Grammar Web site provides a wide array of support for students, teachers and parents. Writing support includes:

• Interactive revision checkers
• Scoring rubrics with complete models

www.phschool.com

Lesson Objectives

1. To learn how to use sections and features of textbooks.
2. To use reading strategies.
3. To interpret graphic organizers.
4. To comprehend nonfiction.
5. To distinguish fact from opinion.
6. To identify the author's purpose.
7. To apply forms of reasoning.
8. To analyze the text.
9. To apply reading strategies to fiction, drama, poetry, and tales from the oral tradition.
10. To learn how to read various sources.

Critical Viewing

Draw Conclusions Students may suggest that she is reading for pleasure because she is not taking notes or even sitting up straight at a desk. She looks relaxed and absorbed.

Chapter 30 Reading Skills

Good readers use different reading skills for different kinds of reading. You probably use different skills when you read a comic book or magazine than when you read a textbook or a novel. No matter what you read, however, it is important to be able to focus on the most important information, understand the ideas being presented, and determine whether the information makes good sense. These skills are especially important when you are reading textbooks and research materials for school.

In this chapter, you will explore new ways to develop your reading skills. The topics discussed in the following pages will teach you how to locate information in your textbooks more easily, how to organize the information you read, and how to apply reading strategies to understand both nonfiction and fiction materials more successfully.

▲ **Critical Viewing**
Point out details from the picture that help you determine whether this girl is reading a textbook or a book for pleasure. **[Draw Conclusions]**

Reading Methods and Tools

In order to better understand the materials you read, become an active reader. Don't just follow the author's words. Build your own meaning by determining the organization of the text, asking questions as you read, and identifying experiences of your own that fit with the ideas in the text.

Using Sections in Textbooks

Most textbooks have special sections in the front and back of the book and at the beginning and end of each chapter to help you find and understand the information each chapter contains. Pick up one of your textbooks, and locate each of the sections discussed below.

> **KEY CONCEPT** Use the special sections of your textbook to become familiar with its contents. ■

Table of Contents The table of contents is at the front of your textbook. It lists the units and chapters of the book in the order in which they appear, and the pages on which each begins.

Chapter Introduction and Summaries A chapter introduction describes main ideas you will find in the chapter. The chapter summary, at the end, reviews the main points covered. These parts help you focus on information and remember it.

Glossary The glossary is usually located at the back of the textbook, just before the index. It lists and defines, in alphabetical order, special subject-related terms.

Appendix The appendices at the back of a textbook contain additional information. The appendix often includes charts, maps, formulas, timelines, essays, and biographical or historical information.

Index Found at the back of a textbook, the index lists alphabetically all the subjects covered in the book and tells the specific pages on which each subject is discussed. The index provides more details than the table of contents. Index topics beginning with *a* or *the* are listed alphabetically by the first main word.

GLOSSARY

fraction: petroleum part with its own boiling point
freezing: change of a liquid into a solid
freezing point: temperature at which a substance changes from liquid to solid
frequency (FREE-kwuhn-see): number of waves that pass a certain point in a given amount of time
friction: force that acts in the opposite direction of motion
fulcrum: fixed pivot point of a lever
fundamental tone: note produced at the lowest frequency at which a standing wave occurs
fuse: thin strip of metal used for safety because when the current flowing through it becomes too high, it melts and breaks the flow of electricity

galvanometer: device that uses an electromagnet to detect small amounts of current
gamma (GAM-uh) **ray:** high-frequency electromagnetic wave released during gamma decay; strongest type of nuclear radiation
gas: phase in which matter has no definite shape or volume
Geiger counter: device that can be used to detect radioactivity because it produces an electric current in the presence of a radioactive substance
generator: device that uses electromagnets to convert mechanical energy to electrical energy
gram: one thousandth of a kilogram
gravitational potential energy: potential energy that is dependent on height above the Earth's surface
gravity: force of attraction that depends on the mass of two objects and the distance between them; responsible for accelerating an object toward the Earth
group: column of elements in the periodic table; family

fraction: petroleum part with its own boiling point
freezing: change of a liquid into a solid
freezing point: temperature at which a substance changes from liquid to solid
frequency (FREE-kwuhn-see): number of waves that pass a certain point in a given amount of time
friction: force that acts in the opposite direction of motion
fulcrum: fixed pivot point of a lever
fundamental tone: note produced at the lowest frequency at which a standing wave occurs

holography: ... uses lasers to produce three-dimensional photographs
homogeneous (hoh-moh-JEE-nee-uhs) **mixture:** mixture that appears the same throughout
hot-water system: heating system in which hot water is pumped through pipes to a convector that heats a room by means of convection currents
hydraulic device: machine that takes advantage of the fact that pressure is transmitted equally in all directions in a liquid; obtains a large force on a large piston by applying a small force with a small piston
hydrocarbon: organic compound that contains only hydrogen and carbon
hypothesis (high-PAHTH-uh-sihs): proposed solution to a scientific problem

illuminated object: object that can be seen because it is lit up
incandescent light: light produced from heat
inclined plane: flat slanted surface that multiplies force
index of refraction: comparison of the speed of light in air with the speed of light in another material

---

⏱ TIME AND RESOURCE MANAGER

Resources
Print: Academic and Workplace Skills Activity Book, pp. 34–37

In-Depth Coverage	Accelerated Pace
• Cover pp. 679–684 in class. • Assign and review Exercises 1–5.	• Assign pp. 679–684 for independent student review.

PREPARE and ENGAGE

Interest GRABBER Display the following passages about bears on an overhead projector. Ask students to read them, then tell how they read them differently, and why.

> Isabel met an enormous bear,
> Isabel, Isabel, didn't care;
>
> The bear was hungry, the bear was ravenous,
> The bear's big mouth was cruel and cavernous.
>
> The bear said, Isabel, glad to meet you,
> How do, Isabel, now I'll eat you!
>
> Isabel, Isabel, didn't worry,
> Isabel didn't scream or scurry.
>
> She washed her hands and she straightened her hair up,
> Then Isabel quietly ate the bear up.
>
> Grizzly bears in the extreme north can survive on the icy, treeless sedgelands of the tundra, but populations are greater in woodlands and forests, especially where there are plenty of river valleys and open, grassy areas.

Activate Prior Knowledge

Ask students why they use the table of contents, glossary, and index of a textbook.

TEACH

> **Step-by-Step Teaching Guide**

Using Sections in Textbooks

1. Go over the list of textbook sections. Using this textbook as an example, ask students to locate and point out the various sections. Remind students that not all textbooks have every section listed here. This is simply a general indication of what students can expect to find in textbooks.

2. A glossary is a minidictionary. It includes important terms in a textbook. Students can add to their understanding of a glossary word by using a dictionary.

Using Features of Textbooks

1. Writers of textbooks want students to understand the material. It is easier for students to understand a paragraph if they know beforehand what it is about and why they are reading it. The title of this page is in large type and a different color. The key concept stands out. The headings underneath are in large type also. All these features announce what follows and why.

2. In this textbook, exercises appear at the end of each chapter, at the end of each section, and throughout the sections.

3. Emphasize the usefulness of reading captions. Ask students to open a history or science textbook to an illustration. Captions often give information not mentioned in the text.

Answer Key

> **Exercise 1**

Answers will vary.

> **Exercise 2**

Answers will vary.

30.1

Using Features of Textbooks

Within each chapter of a textbook are a number of special features that will help you to read and study the material the chapter contains.

> **KEY CONCEPT** Use the special features of your textbook to aid your reading and studying. ■

Chapter Titles, Headings, and Subheadings These are printed in large, heavy type and help you focus on what the material is about. They also divide the material into sections, so you can learn it more easily.

Questions and Exercises These are located at the end of the chapter to help you retain the information you have read. You might want to preview the questions and exercises before reading the chapter to help you focus on the main ideas.

Pictures and Captions A picture can make a confusing idea clearer. Often, next to a picture there is a printed caption that describes the picture and explains its significance.

> **Exercise 1** Examining the Sections in a Textbook Look at one of your textbooks, and answer the following questions.

- Read the table of contents. How many units and chapters does the textbook contain?

- Does your textbook have a glossary? If so, write the definitions of three words you didn't already know.

- If there is an appendix, tell what types of materials it contains.

- Using the index, find a subject that is discussed on at least four different pages in the book. Locate the subject on each of those pages.

> **Exercise 2** Examining the Features of a Textbook Look at one of your textbooks, and answer the following questions.
> 1. How many headings and subheadings does the first chapter contain? Describe how the publisher has used size and color to make these headings stand out.
> 2. Which of these features—introduction, summary, exercises, questions—does each chapter contain? What information can be learned from each?
> 3. Find three pictures in the textbook that have captions. Describe how the captions explain the pictures. What information in the text does each picture help to explain?

> **More Practice**

Academic and Workplace Skills Activity Book
• pp. 35–36

Using Reading Strategies

You can use special reading strategies to improve your reading of textbooks. Three helpful reading strategies are varying your reading style, learning *Question-Answer Relationships* (QARs), and using the SQ4R method.

▶ **KEY CONCEPT** Use a combination of reading strategies to help you better understand the material you read. ■

Vary Your Reading Style Three types of reading styles are *skimming, scanning,* and *close reading.* You use each style for a different purpose. Before you start to read, consider your purpose, and use the reading style that best fits that purpose.

Skimming a text means looking it over quickly to get a general idea of its contents. When you skim, look for highlighted or bold type, headings, topic sentences, and photo captions.

Scanning involves looking over material to find a specific word or idea and ignoring other information. You scan, for example, when you use a telephone book.

Close Reading is reading the material carefully to understand and remember information, to link ideas, and to draw conclusions about what you read.

Use Question-Answer Relationships (QARs) You can better understand your reading if you ask questions about it. Get into the habit of asking and answering these four types of questions as you read:

? **RIGHT THERE**
The answer is right there in the text, usually in one or two sentences. To answer this question, scan the text to locate specific information.

? **THINK AND SEARCH**
The answer is in the text, but you need to think about the question's answer and then search the text for the evidence to support it.

? **AUTHOR AND YOU**
The answer is not only in the text. Answer this question by thinking about what the author has said, what you already know, and how these fit together.

? **ON YOUR OWN**
The answer is, for the most part, not in the text. To answer this question, you need to draw from your own experiences. You can, however, revise or expand your answer based on your reading.

🖥 Research Tip

Try using these same skills when you conduct research using library reference sources. *Skim* to discover the kinds of information available. *Scan* to locate specific pieces of information. Finally, *read closely* to obtain the facts and ideas you need for your report.

Step-by-Step Teaching Guide

Using Reading Strategies

1. Differentiate among the three reading styles. For a research report on whales, a student would read closely. To find the section about blue whales, a student would skim. To find the size of blue whales, a student would scan the text for numbers.

2. Use "Turkeys" by Bailey White (*Timeless Voices, Timeless Themes,* Copper, pages 602–605) to practice QARs. Right there: What kind of rare bird did Bailey's mother have? A red cockaded woodpecker. Think and search: Why did the ornithologists put the turkey eggs in bed with Bailey? Her body was warm and would help hatch the eggs. Author and you: Was the ornithologists' idea a good one? Explain. Yes, because the eggs did hatch and the baby turkeys were healthy. On your own: Would you like to wake up and find your bed full of just-born turkeys? Why or why not? Yes, they are cute and soft. No, I'd be scared.

continued

☑ ONGOING ASSESSMENT: Monitor and Reinforce

If students have trouble varying their reading strategies according to their purpose, try the following option.

Propose questions for students to answer. Ask them what kind of source they would use to find each answer and how they would have to read the source (skim, scan, or read closely). Have students explain their answer. Continue until students begin to understand the reason for changing reading style.

3. The SQ4R method is useful with a book students are reading for study or research. Students need to use the first two steps to determine whether a book will be useful to them. The next four steps will help them get what they need out of the book.

Answer Key

▶ **Exercise 3**

Answers will vary.

▶ **Exercise 4**

Answers will vary.

30.1

Use the SQ4R Method Once you have examined your textbook's special sections and features, you can use this knowledge to help you read it more effectively. A good reading plan to follow is called SQ4R, which stands for *Survey, Question, Read, Record, Recite,* and *Review.* Use this method to help you focus on your reading and to assist you in recalling information.

SQ4R METHOD

Survey → Look over the material you are going to read for these features: chapter titles, headings, subheadings, introduction, summary, and questions or exercises.

Question → Ask questions about what information might be covered under each heading. Ask the questions *who, what, when, where,* and *why* about it.

Read → Search for the answers to the questions you thought of in the previous step.

Record → Take notes to remember information better. List the main ideas and major details.

Recite → Aloud or silently, recall the questions and their related answers.

Review → Review the material on a regular basis, using some or all of the steps above.

▶ **Exercise 3** Creating Your Own QAR Questions, and Using Reading Styles to Answer Them Using the description of *Question-Answer Relationships* on the previous page, create and answer questions of the four general types for your next reading assignment. Use the various reading styles to answer your questions. *Scan* the text to answer a Right-There question. *Skim* the text to answer a Think-and-Search Question, and *closely read* the text to answer an Author-and-You question.

▶ **Exercise 4** Using the SQ4R Method Use the SQ4R method to study a chapter or section of a textbook that has been assigned to you. Then, write a brief account of how the method helped you learn and remember the information.

682 • Reading Skills

Using Graphic Organizers

A graphic organizer is a diagram that shows how ideas fit together in the materials you read. You can use a graphic organizer to arrange reading information in an organized way to help you better understand the ideas and to prepare for writing assignments on the material.

KEY CONCEPT Use graphic organizers to help you understand relationships among ideas in a text. ■

Following is a description of three different types of organizers you can use to help you understand what you are reading. Before you make a graphic organizer, think about how the parts of your subject are related. Then, you can choose a format that best fits your needs.

Timeline A timeline shows the order of related events and the amount of time between each. It is a good way to organize historical information, arrange events in the plot of a story, or present data from science experiments.

TIMELINE

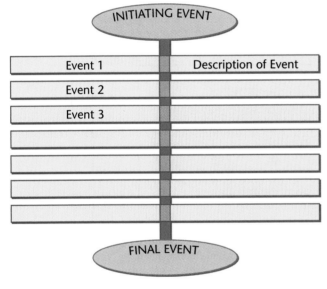

Using Graphic Organizers

1. A timeline is useful when students need to remember many events that happen at specific times, such as the events in Harriet Tubman's life.

2. A modified timeline can help students with science topics too. A timeline labeled Winter, Spring, Summer, Fall could chart an animal's annual cycle, for example.

continued

⊙ Technology Tip

Some computer applications will create graphic organizers for you. Simply enter your data, select a type of chart or graph, and press Enter or Return. You will then have an opportunity to edit the results.

▶ More Practice

Academic and Workplace Skills Activity Book
• p. 37

3. Have the class make a sample K-W-L chart for "Mummy No. 1770" (*Timeless Voices, Timeless Themes,* Copper, pages 47–50). (Possible chart: K: Mummies were made in Egypt; Mummies were dead people wrapped up. W: How did Egyptians make mummies? What is special about this mummy? L: This mummy didn't have legs; It was a girl; She was younger than 20; She had been sick.)

4. Use two story characters all students know to practice making a Venn diagram.

Answer Key

▶ **Exercise 5**

Answers will vary.

30.1

K-W-L Chart Use this graphic organizer as a guide for reading and as a tool for doing research. Begin your K-W-L chart by writing the topic you want to explore at the top of the organizer. Before you read, record all the facts you know about the topic in the *What I Know* column. Write, in the form of questions, the information you want to know about the topic in the *What I Want to Know* column. Use these questions to focus your reading. If you develop new questions during your reading, also write them in this column. After you have finished reading, write your answers to these questions in the last column, *What I Learned.*

KWL CHART		
K	W	L
What I **K**now	What I **W**ant to Know	What I **L**earned
(Fill this in before you read)	(Fill this in before and as you read)	(Fill this in after you read)

Venn Diagram Use this graphic organizer if you want to show how two subjects are compared or contrasted in a textbook, or to prepare an essay comparing or contrasting two subjects. To make a Venn diagram, draw two overlapping ovals. In the overlapping section of the ovals, write the characteristics that the two subjects share. In the other sections of the ovals, write their differences.

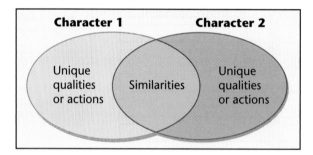

▶ **Exercise 5** **Using Graphic Organizers** Read a chapter from one of your textbooks or from a work of fiction. Then, use a timeline, a K-W-L chart, or a Venn diagram to organize information from the chapter. Explain why you chose that particular chart format and why it is best suited for presenting the chapter material.

☑ ONGOING ASSESSMENT: Monitor and Reinforce

If students are having trouble using graphic organizers, try the following options.

Option 1 Have students create a timeline of a recent trip or vacation. Then have them present their work to the class. You may wish to have your students draw their timelines on the chalkboard.	**Option 2** Suggest two familiar subjects to your students, such as snowboarding and skiing. Have them compare and contrast the two by creating a Venn diagram.

Reading Nonfiction Critically

Section 30.2

Step-by-Step Teaching Guide

Reading Nonfiction Critically

1. Remind students of the different kinds of nonfiction they have read: history, science, biography and autobiography.

2. Emphasize that works of nonfiction are not automatically trustworthy sources of information. Every writer interprets his or her subject, and since different writers see things from different points of view, they can produce books that say entirely different (and contradictory) things about the same topic.

Do good readers believe everything they read? Probably not. They think about the material and judge its value. They consider the author's purpose in writing. They ask themselves whether they can rely on what the author says. They analyze in a critical way the kind of information they are receiving.

Comprehending Nonfiction

The first step in reading a text critically is to get a general understanding of the material. This involves finding and analyzing the key ideas and details. It also involves figuring out the author's purpose and determining how the material relates to the topic you are studying.

> **KEY CONCEPT** Use your reading strategies to analyze and judge what you read. ■

Use these strategies to better comprehend nonfiction:

Find Main Ideas and Major Details Determine the main points the writer wants to get across, and locate the major details that explain and support the main ideas.

Interpret What You Read Use your analysis of the main ideas and major details to help you paraphrase—state in your own words—the information in the text. Restating the information will help you remember how ideas relate to one another.

Identify the Author's Purpose in Writing Once you have a general idea of the material, the next step is to identify the author's purpose. You can do this by examining the words the writer uses and the details the writer includes (or does not include) in the text. As you continue to read, look for additional clues to support this purpose.

Reflect on What You Have Read After you have finished reading, take time to review what the author has written. Answer the following questions as a starting point: How does the material relate to what I am studying? How does it fit with other information I have read? In what ways does the information relate to my life?

> **Exercise 6** **Comprehending Nonfiction** As you read a chapter from one of your textbooks, use the strategies mentioned above. Answer the following questions: What main points and major details did I find? What was the author's purpose? What details did I use to identify it? What is the importance and value of the information I read?

🔍 Learn More

It will be helpful to use these reading skills when you revise your own writing. See the revision strategies in Chapter 2.

More Practice

Academic and Workplace Skills Activity Book
• pp. 38–39

Answer Key

> **Exercise 6**

Answers will vary.

Reading Nonfiction Critically • **685**

⏱ TIME AND RESOURCE MANAGER

Resources
Print: Academic and Workplace Skills Activity Book, pp. 38–43

In-Depth Coverage	Accelerated Pace
• Cover pp. 685–690 in class. • Assign and review Exercises 6–11.	• Assign pp. 685–690 for independent student review.

Distinguishing Fact From Opinion

1. A fact is something known; an opinion is something believed.

2. Not all facts are true. *Whales are mammals* is a fact, and it is true. *Whales are fish* is also a fact, but it is false.

3. Students may have trouble distinguishing between supported and unsupported opinions. *Vanilla is the best flavor; I always ask for a vanilla ice cream cone* is an unsupported opinion. *Vanilla is the best flavor; ice cream stores report that they sell three times as much vanilla as any other flavor* is a supported opinion.

Answer Key

> **Exercise 7**

1. fact
2. opinion, unsupported
3. opinion, supported
4. opinion, supported
5. opinion, unsupported

30.2

Distinguishing Fact From Opinion

Part of being a critical reader is learning to tell the difference between statements that express facts and those that contain opinions.

Fact Statements A statement of fact is one that can be proved true (or found to be false) in one of the following four ways: by measurement, by observation, by consulting a reliable source, or by experiment.

FACT STATEMENT: Joe's brother is five feet ten inches tall.

FACT STATEMENT: It is raining now.

FACT STATEMENT: Plants need water and sunlight to survive.

You could test the first statement by measuring Joe's brother's height. You could test the second statement by looking out the window. You could test the third statement by doing an experiment, consulting a textbook, or talking to an expert.

Opinion Statements A statement of opinion, unlike a statement of fact, cannot be completely proved. An opinion may simply express a person's feeling or attitude. Before you trust an opinion statement, you should feel confident that the writer has supported it with evidence, such as related facts or a reliable authority.

OPINION STATEMENT: Basketball is an exciting sport.

OPINION STATEMENT WITH SUPPORT: Basketball is an exciting sport; turnovers are frequent, and points are scored nearly every minute of play.

The first example is purely opinion, unsupported by any facts. The second opinion is more reliable than the first one because it is based on facts.

> **Exercise 7** Evaluating Fact and Opinion Statements
Identify each statement below as *fact* or *opinion*. If the statement expresses an opinion, tell whether it is supported or unsupported by facts. Consult a reference book if necessary.
1. Mount Everest is the tallest mountain on Earth's surface.
2. I have heard that Mount Everest is not as difficult to climb as K2, which is located in the same range.
3. According to this biography, the teddy bear was named for Theodore Roosevelt.
4. Ty Cobb was a great baseball player; his lifetime batting average is the highest of all time.
5. Dogs make better pets than cats do.

🔎 Learn More

For more about doing research, see Chapter 11.

> **More Practice**

Academic and Workplace Skills Activity Book
• pp. 40–41

☑ ONGOING ASSESSMENT: Monitor and Reinforce

If students have trouble separating statements of fact from statements of opinion, try the following option.

Give students a series of statements of opinion. Have them discuss each one, deciding whether it is supported by reliable evidence. Ask students to give their reasons for finding each statement a supported or an unsupported opinion.

Identifying the Author's Purpose

One important critical reading skill involves examining an author's purpose—why he or she is writing. As you read, remember to look for clues to help you identify the author's purpose. When you think you know the author's purpose, confirm your choice by linking it to details in the text.

KEY CONCEPT Learn to identify the author's purpose by using clues found in the text. ■

The list below describes several common purposes, along with clues to recognize each purpose. Use the clues to help you identify the author's purpose in books or articles you read.

1. **To Inform**—presents a series of factual statements.
2. **To Instruct**—includes a step-by-step explanation of an idea or process.
3. **To Offer an Opinion**—presents a topic from a certain point of view or with a certain intention in mind.
4. **To Sell**—uses persuasive techniques designed to sell a product.
5. **To Entertain**—narrates an event in a humorous manner, sometimes to lighten a serious topic.

Exercise 8 Determining the Author's Purpose Read the following sentences, and determine the author's purpose. Explain your answers.

1. This guide, in four easy steps, tells you how to hook up and operate your stereo system.
2. For the most refreshment possible, try an ice-cold *Lemon Zest Cola.*
3. Mark Twain was born in Hannibal, Missouri, in 1835.
4. I am going to tell you why we should all be using public transportation instead of driving cars.
5. If the dinosaurs could make a comeback, would they enjoy breathing the air or drinking the water on modern Earth?

▼ Critical Viewing Describe how a writer might write about this photograph for each of the five purposes. **[Relate]**

Reading Nonfiction Critically • **687**

Step-by-Step Teaching Guide

Identifying the Author's Purpose

1. Give students the following titles and ask what is the author's purpose for writing each one.
   - How to Hit a Home Run (instruct)
   - The Best Baseball Bloopers (entertain)
   - The History of America's Favorite Sport (inform)
   - Hank Aaron: The Best Hitter Ever (persuade)
   - Buy Magic Bat and Improve Your Score (sell)
2. Some works have more than one purpose. A biography of film director George Lucas, for instance, can both tell about his work (inform) and evaluate it (offer an opinion).

Answer Key

Exercise 8

1. To instruct; explains step-by-step process
2. To sell; suggests a particular brand
3. To inform; states a fact
4. To offer an opinion; sets out to persuade
5. To entertain; wonders about dinosaurs in a humorous way

Critical Viewing

Relate Answers will vary. Students may suggest that three children or students are playing basketball. [to inform]

Applying Forms of Reasoning

Use Aesop's "The Lion and the Bulls" (*Timeless Voices, Timeless Themes,* Copper, page 303) to demonstrate conclusions and generalizations. A conclusion is right there in the moral. It is the main idea, the idea Aesop wanted readers to learn. A valid generalization might be that lions like to eat other animals. An invalid generalization might be that bulls are not as smart as lions.

Answer Key

> **Exercise 9**

1. generalization, unsupported
2. conclusion, unsupported
3. conclusion, unsupported
4. generalization, supported
5. generalization, unsupported

30.2

Applying Forms of Reasoning

Once you have learned how to examine and evaluate reading material, you are ready to start drawing your own conclusions about the work's *central idea*—the overall message of the work.

▶ **KEY CONCEPT** Examine the details of the text you read to help you draw conclusions about the work's *central idea.* ■

Draw Conclusions Often, an author does not state a central idea directly. As you read, you must look for clues to the central idea in the way information is organized and presented. Then, draw your own conclusions based on the clues.

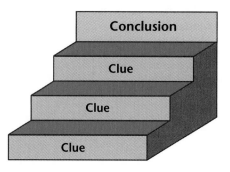

Make Generalizations Another way to draw conclusions is to make generalizations. A **generalization** is a general statement based on a number of facts or examples. A ***valid generalization*** is an accurate conclusion supported by many examples. A ***hasty generalization*** may be inaccurate because it is based on too few examples. Ask yourself:

- What facts or cases are presented to make the generalization?
- Will the generalization hold true for all or most cases? Are there exceptions to the statement?
- Are enough examples given to make the generalization valid?

▶ **Exercise 9** Evaluating Conclusions and Generalizations
Identify each sentence below as a *conclusion* or a *generalization.* Then, explain whether it is supported by evidence or not.
1. All PG-rated movies are boring.
2. Ann attends one of the best ballet schools in the country, so she must be a good dancer.
3. Matt failed his last math test; he knows nothing about math.
4. Children have often been known to mistake medicine for candy, so all medicine bottles should have childproof caps.
5. I got lost in the park. Nobody can get around that park.

688 • Reading Skills

▶ **More Practice**

Academic and Workplace Skills Activity Book
• pp. 41–42

✎ STANDARDIZED TEST PREPARATION WORKSHOP

Standardized tests often ask students to identify particular kinds of sentences. Ask students which of the statements below is a generalization.

A I spent last summer at a camp in Maine.

B Maine is always beautiful in the summer.

C Everyone had a great time at the camp.

D I want to go back there every summer.

C is the only sentence that makes a broad statement about a large number of examples. **B** is an opinion.

Analyzing the Text

When you analyze the text of your reading material, you study the language the writer uses and the way the material is put together—its structure. This analysis can help you better understand the author's purpose and the key information presented in the material.

> **KEY CONCEPT** Learn to identify different uses of language and how the text is structured. ■

Examine the Author's Words Authors can sometimes present information in a direct way, or they can "load" their words to create certain feelings in readers about the information being presented. *Word choice* and *tone* are two ways that authors use language to influence readers' thinking.

Word Choice can affect meaning. The words an author uses can affect how a reader feels about a subject. Some words are neutral and do not influence a reader's feelings. Other words may create either positive or negative feelings in a reader.

NEUTRAL WORDS: The convertible was long with a large engine.
POSITIVE WORDS: The convertible was sleek and supercharged.
NEGATIVE WORDS: The convertible was slick and overpowered.

Tone Sometimes an author's attitude about a subject comes across both in the words used and by the way they are put together in sentences. Like word choice, tone can be neutral, positive, or negative.

NEUTRAL TONE:	The heat and humidity in our community in the summer often keep visitors away.
NEGATIVE TONE:	If you hate heat and humidity, you will be like other visitors and avoid our community in the summer.

> **Exercise 10** **Analyzing Word Choices** For each set of words below, tell which has a neutral meaning, which is positive, and which is negative. Use a dictionary if you need help.
> 1. gobble, dine, eat
> 2. stingy, economical, thrifty
> 3. talk, babble, communicate
> 4. gawk, observe, see
> 5. handwriting, scribbling, calligraphy
> 6. house, palace, shack
> 7. mature, old, haggard
> 8. hard, impossible, challenging
> 9. brisk, freezing, cold
> 10. well-dressed, elegant, showy

> 🗣 **Speaking and Listening Tip**
>
> Get together with two or three of your classmates, and practice neutral, positive, and negative tones orally. For each word in Exercise 10, write a sentence. Then take turns reading the sentences in a way that conveys the tone of the word used. Pay attention to how word choice affects tone.

Step-by-Step Teaching Guide

Analyzing the Text

When reading nonfiction, students should be alert for language that imposes the writer's opinions on the facts. A history book might say that millions of people died, were killed, or were slaughtered during the Vietnam War. Each affects how readers react to the information. Sometimes writers purposely insert their feelings; other times they do so without being aware of it. In either case, it is up to readers to pay attention.

Answer Key

> **Exercise 10**

1. negative, positive, neutral
2. negative, neutral, positive
3. neutral, negative, positive
4. negative, positive, neutral
5. neutral, negative, positive
6. neutral, positive, negative
7. positive, neutral, negative
8. neutral, negative, positive
9. positive, negative, neutral
10. neutral, positive, negative

☑ **ONGOING ASSESSMENT: Monitor and Reinforce**

If students have trouble analyzing word choice, try the following option.

Have students find reviews of movies they have seen and look for examples of positive, negative, and neutral language in the reviews. Have them describe the effect of the different types of language. Challenge them to paraphrase positive and negative sentences into neutral language and then describe the change in the effect of the review.

Identify Text Structure

An author's choice of text structure depends on what he or she wants to communicate. Chronological order to narrate an Iditarod race preserves the suspense of which sled dog team won. Cause and effect would show why one team won and another lost. Order of importance would give a good idea of what factors are most important in preparing for, participating in, and winning the race.

Customize for
Less Advanced Students

Let students practice the text structures with an easy topic—what they have done today. Have them write three paragraphs, each using a different structure.

Answer Key

> **Exercise 11**

Answers will vary.

30.2

Identify Text Structure The structure of the text refers to how ideas are arranged and how they relate to one another. Authors arrange their writing so they can communicate their ideas in a clear and effective way.

> **KEY CONCEPT** Learn how authors arrange ideas in a text so you can locate and understand information more easily. ■

Chronological Order An author uses chronological order when he or she wants to show events or details in the order in which they occur. Word clues identifying chronological order are shown in the illustration below.

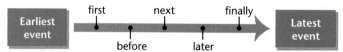

Cause and Effect A cause is an event that makes another event happen. An effect is the event that happens because of a cause. A cause-and-effect structure shows a series of events. Also, note that most effects can also become causes for subsequent events. Some word clues identifying cause and effect are listed in the following illustration.

Order of Importance When an author uses this text structure, he or she arranges events or details from the least to the most significant, or from the most significant to the least. The illustration below contains some of the word clues you can use to identify order of importance.

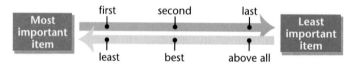

> **Exercise 11** Analyzing Text Structure Go back to the cause-and-effect professional and student models in Chapter 9, and identify a cause and effect in the essays. Show the details that support your answer. For chronological order, turn to Chapter 10, and list in order the events of the essay.

Reading Literary Writing

Section 30.3

When you read literary works—short stories, novels, poems, or plays—you need to use some special strategies to understand what is happening, who the characters are, what the words mean, and what ideas the writer wants to get across to you. You may need to use different strategies for different types of literary works.

▶ **KEY CONCEPT** Practice a variety of reading strategies that fit the type of literary work you are reading and help you to understand it better. ■

Strategies for Reading Fiction

Fiction is filled with made-up characters and events. Two familiar kinds of fiction are short stories and novels. As you read fiction, you explore a new world. The author's words and your imagination create a map of this world. The strategies that follow can help you find your way:

Identify With a Character or a Situation Imagine that you are the character you're reading about in a story. Put yourself in that character's place. Imagine that you are saying and doing the same things. If you've been in a similar situation or had similar friends or family members, you may find it easier to identify with the character.

Predict As you read, make predictions about what will happen next. Base your predictions on your experience or on information in the story. As you read, new information may lead you to predict new and different outcomes.

Envision the Action and Setting As you read, create mental pictures of the action, setting, and characters. Look for the following kinds of words to help you create these pictures:

- **Action words**—interesting or unusual verbs and nouns
- **Adverbs**—words that tell how an action is performed
- **Sensory words**—descriptive adjectives that tell how things look, feel, taste, smell, and sound

▶ **Exercise 12** **Reading Short Stories** Read a few pages of a short story, and then begin to list experiences or qualities you share with the main character. Find at least three similarities. Make a prediction about what might happen to the character. You can check your prediction when you finish the story. Find at least two action words, two adverbs, and two sensory words. Use them to describe the action taking place.

▲ **Critical Viewing**
What kinds of places make good settings for reading a novel or short story? Why would you choose them? **[Evaluate]**

▶ **More Practice**

Academic and Workplace Skills Activity Book
- pp. 44–45

Reading Literary Writings • 691

Strategies for Reading Fiction

1. Have students share information about fictional characters with whom they identified, such as Laura Ingalls Wilder or Tom Sawyer. Ask how comparing characters to themselves added to their enjoyment of the story.

2. Predicting outcomes can keep readers interested and alert. Even if all the predictions are wrong, they keep readers focused on what is happening and why. Wrong predictions simply mean that the author's surprise ending really was surprising. They do not necessarily mean that the predictions were faulty.

Answer Key

▶ **Exercise 12**

Answers will vary.

Critical Viewing

Evaluate Students may suggest quiet, well-lit places, such as one's room or a park, because the tranquility allows for better interaction with the narrative.

⏱ TIME AND RESOURCE MANAGER

Resources
Print: Academic and Workplace Skills Activity Book, pp. 44–50

In-Depth Coverage	Accelerated Pace
• Cover pp. 691–695 in class. • Assign and review Exercises 12–15.	• Assign pp. 691–695 for independent student review.

Strategies for Reading Drama

1. Stories include description—what people and places look like, what characters think and feel. Plays rely on dialogue and have fewer clues to help readers.

2. Have students look at "The Phantom Tollbooth" (*Timeless Voices, Timeless Themes,* Copper, pages 630ff). Point out the case, the sets, and the lengthy text in italics. All these help readers visualize the characters, setting, movements, and emotions.

Answer Key

▶ **Exercise 13**

Answers will vary.

30.3

Strategies for Reading Drama

When you read a play, you focus mainly on the words spoken by the characters, and on the characters themselves. A written play also contains stage directions to tell actors how to move or to speak their lines. Stage directions also describe sets, costumes, and any special lighting or sound effects. To imagine how the play would be performed on stage, use the following strategies:

Preview the Characters Read the list of characters at the beginning of the play. This will help you to know the different characters and how they relate to one another.

Envision the Setting and the Action Form a picture in your mind of what is happening and where. If the play does not take place in the present, consider what you already know about the time in history during which it does take place.

Predict After you have read the first act or scene, try to predict what will happen in the next act or scene. Look for hints in what the characters say or in the action. Using an organizer like the one below, write the reasons for your predictions. Afterward, write the reasons for the actual events.

Question As you read, ask yourself questions like these:
- Why did the character do or say that?
- What does the character mean by that?
- What caused this to happen?

Summarize Dramas are usually divided into parts called acts. Acts are divided into scenes. At the end of a scene or an act, stop and think about what has happened to that point.

▶ **Exercise 13** Reading Drama Read the first few scenes of a drama. List three characters, and explain how they relate to one another. Describe three things you learned about the setting from stage directions. Based on dialogue, make a prediction about what might happen later in the play. After you finish the play, check how accurate your prediction was.

▶ **Internet Tip**

Try looking up famous characters from literature on the Internet. You may find descriptions that help you get involved in the story.

▶ **More Practice**

Academic and Workplace Skills Activity Book
- pp. 46–49

☑ **ONGOING ASSESSMENT: Monitor and Reinforce**

If students have trouble with reading comprehension, or do not enjoy what they read, try the following option.

For their next reading assignment, allow students to read anything they want, including comic books or reading that is above or below their grade level. Have students try several of the reading strategies described on these pages, and meet with them individually to discuss the experience. Ask questions based on the strategies, such as, "When were you able to predict the ending?" By applying the strategies to literature of their own choice, students should begin to improve their reading skills.

Strategies for Reading Poetry

When you are reading poetry, you need to focus on how the words sound, what the words mean, and what emotions the poet causes you to feel. In a poem, even everyday words take on new and special meaning. When you read a poem, you should give every word the attention it deserves. Here are some strategies to use:

Read Lines According to Punctuation Even though poems are divided into lines, thoughts and images may continue from one line to the next. Read poems without pausing unnecessarily. Follow these suggestions:

- Don't stop at the ends of lines where there is no punctuation.
- Pause slightly when you come to a comma and a bit longer for semicolons or dashes.
- Make the longest stops for end marks.

Read aloud these lines from "February Twilight" by Sara Teasdale. Pause at the comma and period, and continue to read where there is no punctuation:

EXAMPLE: I stood beside a hill
                    Smooth with new-laid snow,
                 A single star looked out
                    From the cold evening glow.

Identify the Speaker The poet is not always the speaker in the poem. The speaker is the voice that "says" the words. He or she can be a character in an imaginary situation. Look for clues to who the speaker is. What clues do you have about the speaker in the lines of poetry above?

ANALYZING THE SPEAKER

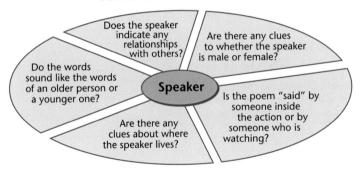

Speaking and Listening Tip

Reading a poem aloud will enable you to hear the sounds and feel the rhythm of the words. Hearing yourself or someone else read a poem will give you a deeper understanding and appreciation of the work.

Strategies for Reading Poetry

1. There is no reason for students to be intimidated by poetry. The basic rule is to read it the same way they read fiction, by pausing at punctuation, not at the end of a line.

2. Some students think poetry is "too hard," or they think they are not smart enough to understand it. Sara Teasdale's "February Twilight" is a good example of a serious poem that every student should "get." Like all poems, it does not have one correct meaning that students must figure out. Whatever it means to any individual reader is valid.

3. Ask students how the poem makes them feel. Does it remind them of a time they stood in the snow? Of a time they looked up at a star? Even students who live in Hawaii and have never seen snow could respond. Maybe the poem reminds them of a time they stood on the beach. Or a time they were alone anywhere and it felt good.

continued

Customize for
Verbal/Linguistic Learners

Suggest that students each choose a poem they like and practice reading it aloud. When they are ready, they can present a poetry reading to the class.

4. Read aloud the following phrases from poems and ask students to label them simile, metaphor, or personification.

- Let the rain sing you a lullaby (personification)

- Ankylosaurus was built like a tank (simile)

- The willow's music is like a soprano (simile)

- Fame is a bee (metaphor)

- Some words are lazy, . . . some words are quick (personification)

Answer Key

> **Exercise 14**

Answers will vary.

Use Your Senses As you read a poem, try to experience the sights, smells, sounds, tastes, and feelings the words express.

Paraphrase the Lines If a line or passage is difficult to understand, try putting it in your own words. Read this example from T. S. Eliot's poem "The Naming of Cats."

EXAMPLE: The Naming of Cats is a difficult matter,
             It isn't just one of your holiday games;

PARAPHRASE: Finding the right name for a cat is not an easy task.

Understand Figurative Language Language that is used to make you see and feel things in a new way is called *figurative language*. Listed below are three types of figurative language:

- **Simile**—uses "like" or "as" to compare things that are usually not alike: *We travel as happily as birds.*

- **Metaphor**—compares unlike things by describing one item as if it were another, not using "like" or "as": *Life is a journey.*

- **Personification**—gives human qualities to nonhuman objects: *The leaves danced across the road.*

> **Exercise 14** Reading Poetry According to Punctuation
Copy a short poem onto your paper. Put an arrow at the end of any line that has no punctuation, a + after each comma, and an X after each end mark. Then, read the poem aloud, using your symbols to decide when to pause, when to stop, and when to read without stopping. After you have read the poem aloud, identify the speaker in the poem, if possible. Give two or three images from the poem, and name the senses to which they appeal. Paraphrase one line of the poem.

Strategies for Reading Folk Tales, Myths, and Fables

Folk tales are stories about ordinary people. They have been shared and passed along by people of a particular country or culture and often point out certain cultural values. Often, folk tales will give fictional explanations for natural occurrences. **Myths** are old stories of gods, goddesses, and heroes. Like folk tales, myths frequently explain natural occurrences. In addition, they often teach a moral lesson. **Fables** usually feature animals that speak like people. They offer lessons about how to live one's life.

> **More Practice**
Academic and Workplace Skills Activity Book
• p. 50

Step-by-Step Teaching Guide

Reading Folk Literature

For Exercise 15, suggest that students ask the school librarian to help them find a work from their culture. After the exercise, encourage students to tell the story to the class.

Understand the Oral Tradition What these stories all share is a tradition—namely, the oral tradition. The **oral tradition** is the passing along of stories from one generation to the next by retelling them aloud. Eventually, these stories were written down so people could read them.

Understand the Cultural Background Because folk literature developed from stories told among people who shared a way of life, it reflects the values and ideas of their culture. Understanding these cultural characteristics will help you understand the story. While you read, look for details that tell you about the culture.

Recognize the Storyteller's Purpose You will understand why characters behave the way they do if you know the reason a fable, myth, or folk tale was told. The chart below shows the general purposes behind several types of folk literature.

Purpose	Explain	Teach	Entertain
Type of Folk Literature	Myths Folk Tales	Myths Folk Tales Fables	Folk Tales Fables

Predict As you read, make predictions about what will happen in the story. Notice that in many folk tales, events occur in threes. After the first event, ask yourself what the second or third event might be. In addition, good deeds are usually rewarded, and foolish or selfish actions bring bad fortune. Predict how a good deed may be rewarded and how a selfish act might be punished.

Exercise 15 Reading Folk Literature Read a myth, folk tale, or fable from your literature book or a book you find in the library. Make a chart like the one above to use while you are reading.
1. Above the chart, identify the type of folk literature and the country or culture from which it comes.
2. In the first column, list several characteristics about the culture that are reflected in the story.
3. In the second column, tell the purpose of the piece, and point out morals it contains, or lessons on how to live one's life.
4. In the third column, list several predictions about events to come in the story or about its ending. Later, circle each prediction that turned out to be correct.

Learn More

To learn more about ways of responding to literature, turn to Chapter 12.

Answer Key

Exercise 15

Answers will vary.

ONGOING ASSESSMENT: Prerequisite Skills

If students are having trouble with the strategies for reading literary writing, try the following option.

Have students rewrite one of the pieces of literature that they have studied in class. If it is a poem, have them write it out as a paragraph. If it is a work of prose, have them isolate two characters from the piece, and then write a dialogue. If it is a play, have them rewrite one of the acts or episodes into prose. Then have the students form groups and discuss the formal difference between the original work and their rewrites.

Reading From Varied Sources

1. Bring in daily newspapers from a single week and one or two newsmagazines that cover the same period. Have students compare how they cover the same events.

2. Emphasize the need to read instructions from beginning to end before beginning to install a new computer game or put together a toy. Ask how many students have realized halfway through a project that they have made crucial mistakes simply because they failed to read the directions carefully. In the long run, it is always faster to spend a little extra time reading than a lot of extra time doing a project over.

3. Warn students of the dangers of reading or researching on the Internet. Because anyone can post anything on the Internet, sources may well not be reliable. Students should use caution.

Section 30.4

Reading From Varied Sources

Many different kinds of reading materials are available for you to choose for different purposes. For example, you may read articles and ads in a newspaper or magazine to find current information or to learn about styles and products. You might focus on Internet Web pages for specialized information or up-to-the-minute sports scores. You might read a textbook to study for school, a pamphlet to find data for a research paper, or a manual to get "how-to" details. What you read depends on why you are reading.

Reading Newspapers

Reading daily and weekly newspapers is one of the best ways to find out what is happening in your community, in the state, in the country, or in the world. Suppose that you are looking for local news. If you live in a small community, is there a local newspaper? If you live in or near a large city, are there parts of the big-city or regional daily newspaper that deal with local news items? Make a quick inventory of the newspaper you get regularly at home or that comes to the school or public library. Find its table of contents or index. Note how the news is laid out in sections for local, state, national, or international news. Are there special sections for news, editorials, style, sports, and features such as comics, puzzles, and advice columns? If you have several newspapers from which to choose, evaluate which paper you think best covers the information you want and is the best organized. Decide which paper you should read on a regular basis.

Reading Magazines

Reading magazines is a good way to find information about a specific interest, such as a hobby, sports, fashions, or celebrities. Some magazines deal with news and current events and provide more analysis than newspapers. Other magazines aim at a specialized audience, such as teenagers, cooks, runners, or model train hobbyists. Unlike newspapers, magazines usually offer an opinion or a point of view on a topic they present. Try to recognize where a magazine article reports facts and where it presents opinions.

Reading Manuals

If you want to learn how to do something or how to use a product you have bought, you should read a manual carefully. Look first for the table of contents, main headings, and diagrams. Follow the steps, one-by-one, without rushing ahead.

More Practice

Academic and Workplace Skills Activity Book
• p. 51

696 • Reading Skills

⏲ TIME AND RESOURCE MANAGER

Resources
Print: Academic and Workplace Skills Activity Book, p. 51

In-Depth Coverage	Accelerated Pace
• Cover pp. 696–697 in class.	• Assign pp. 696–697 for independent student review.

Reading Electronic Texts

Internet Web pages and electronic texts on disk or CD-ROM provide detailed, specific information on a wide variety of subjects. When you read a Web page, think about who posted the page and whether the information can be trusted as factual or should be considered biased, based upon your opinion of the author. You need to make your own evaluation of how reliable the information is before you use it for a paper or report. You might want to use a search engine to find several pages on a subject, and compare the information you find. Some electronic texts are provided by retailers—companies that want to sell you something. Think of these texts as ads rather than as factual information. Try to recognize which parts seem true and which are sales pitches.

Reading Anthologies

An anthology is a collection of literature. Some anthologies contain a specific kind of literature, such as poems or short stories. Some are organized around one theme; others, around several different themes. Most present works of a variety of writers. Some focus on a specific period of time, such as early American literature or modern short stories. You might choose an anthology if you find a specific kind of literature that interests you. Anthologies are also good references for reports or good ways to get introduced to an interesting or unusual writer or topic.

▲ **Critical Viewing** While doing research on the Internet, what kinds of publications might these students find? **[Relate]**

Integrating Workplace Skills

On the job, people have to read every kind of text mentioned here, and other kinds as well. Correspondence, memos, and reports make up daily office reading for many people. They need to apply the reading skills taught in this chapter to all these different texts.

Critical Viewing

Relate Students may suggest that in addition to scholarly publications, they will find publications posted by other students.

Reflecting on Your Reading Skills

After a week of practicing your reading skills, write a paragraph about your progress. Use the following questions to get you started:

- Which sections of my textbooks do I use on a regular basis?
- How does varying my reading style help me to find information and to study?
- Which reading strategies do I find most useful?
- How can I become a more careful and reflective reader?
- What different types of materials do I most often read? Why do I read each type?

Making Inferences and Predictions

Teaching Resources: Standardized Test Preparation Worbook, Chapter 30

1. Make sure students understand that making inferences involves drawing conclusions about what they read. Students will use information directly stated by a writer, as well as information implied through details and descriptions, to make these inferences.

2. Review with students the Test Tip. Explain that it is always a good idea to eliminate any choices to make choosing the correct answer easier.

Standardized Test Preparation Workshop

Make Inferences and Predictions

Standardized tests usually include reading questions that measure your ability to make inferences, or to draw logical conclusions about what you have read. You can make inferences about characters and stories, or you can make them about the author's purpose or point of view. Some questions require you to make a prediction or anticipate what may happen in the future, based on the clues in the reading material. These questions are typically multiple choice. In addition, some tests will ask you to read a passage, then answer, in writing, a specific question about that passage. The following sample test items will help you prepare for answering these types of questions on standardized tests.

Test Tip

Even when you are unsure of an answer, you can usually rule out at least one or two obviously incorrect choices. Rule out choices that directly contradict the information in the passage. Then, make your selection from the remaining choices.

Sample Test Items	Answers and Explanations
Read each passage. Then, answer the questions that follow the passage. from "The Outcasts of Poker Flat," Bret Harte Two or three men, conversing earnestly together, ceased as he [Mr. Oakhurst] approached, and exchanged significant glances. There was a Sabbath lull in the air which, in a settlement unused to Sabbath influences, looked ominous.	

1 When the men see Mr. Oakhurst, they—
 	
  A are glad to see their friend
  B are afraid he will hurt them
  C are curious because he is a stranger
  D stop talking so he will not hear them
	The answer for item 1 is *D*. By using the information provided in the passage, you conclude that the men are conversing about Mr. Oakhurst, and do not want him to hear what they are saying.

Answer the following question. Base your answer on "The Outcasts of Poker Flat." What is Poker Flat usually like? Support your answer with details from the story.	Your answer should consist of a paragraph that includes a topic sentence and details from the passage that support it. The following is part of a possible response: *The town is a place that is usually full of activity, much of it related to gambling and the saloon. By referring to the Sabbath, a holy day, Harte gives the impression that Poker Flat is not a "clean-living" town.*

698 • Reading Skills

✎ TEST-TAKING TIP

Encourage students to mark up the passages as they read, underlining or circling key details, or taking notes about the passage in the margin. They can then use this information to help them answer the questions.

▶ **Practice 1** **Directions:** Read the passage. Then, answer the questions that follow the passage.

From "Everyday Use," Alice Walker

I will wait for her in the yard that Maggie and I made so clean and wavy yesterday afternoon. A yard like this is more comfortable than most people know. It is not just a yard. It is like an extended living room. When the hard clay is swept clean as a floor and the fine sand around the edges lined with tiny, irregular grooves, anyone can come and sit and look up into the elm tree and wait for the breezes that never come inside the house.

Maggie will be nervous until after her sister goes: she will stand hopelessly in corners, homely and ashamed of the burn scars down her arms and legs, eyeing her sister with a mixture of envy and awe. She thinks her sister has held life always in the palm of one hand, that "no" is a word the world never learned to say to her.

1 The author writes in first person to—
  A share the character's personal thoughts and feelings
  B use a traditional story form
  C keep the reader guessing
  D create suspense

2 Maggie and her sister are—
  F close friends and confidantes
  G strangers who are about to meet for the first time
  H sisters who spend little time together, and have little in common
  J vicious enemies

3 Maggie's home is—
  A a wealthy plantation
  B a run-down, ill-kept shack
  C a clean, small, rural home
  D a small suburban ranch house

4 The narrator is probably—
  F Maggie's mother
  G Maggie's best friend
  H a stranger to Maggie and her sister
  J Maggie's daughter

5 Why will Maggie be nervous until after her sister goes?
  A She wants to make a good impression on her sister.
  B She is afraid her sister will make fun of her scars.
  C She hopes her sister will move home.
  D She is intimidated by—yet wishes she were more like—her sister.

6 How does the narrator feel about the impending visit?
  F She is tired from the work, and wishing the visit were over already.
  G She is well prepared and ready for the company.
  H She is afraid her visitor will be disappointed.
  J She is so excited she is unable to concentrate.

▶ **Practice 2** **Directions:** Read the following question. Base your answer on "Everyday Use."

READ, THINK, EXPLAIN Describe Maggie's self-image and her relationship with her family. Use details from the story to explain your answer.

Answer Key

▶ **Practice 1**

1. A
2. H
3. C
4. G
5. D
6. G

▶ **Practice 2**

Students' responses will vary. Be sure they use details from the passage to support their ideas.

Time and Resource Manager

In-Depth Lesson Plan

	LESSON FOCUS	PRINT AND MEDIA RESOURCES
DAY 1	**Basic Study Skills** Students learn and apply such basic study skills as setting up a study area and schedule, keeping an assignment book and taking notes (pp. 700–703).	**Teaching Resources** *Academic and Workplace Skills Activity Book,* pp. 52–53
DAY 2	**Reference Skills** Students learn and apply such reference skills as using the library, encyclopedias and periodical indexes (pp. 704–709).	**Teaching Resources** *Academic and Workplace Skills Activity Book,* pp. 54–56
DAY 3	**Reference Skills** Students learn and apply such reference skills as using dictionaries, other reference sources and the Internet (pp. 710–714).	**Teaching Resources** *Academic and Workplace Skills Activity Book,* pp. 57–58
DAY 4	**Test-Taking Skills** Students learn and apply test-taking skills (pp. 715–719).	**Teaching Resources** *Academic and Workplace Skills Activity Book,* pp. 59–60

Accelerated Lesson Plan

	LESSON FOCUS	PRINT AND MEDIA RESOURCES
DAY 1	**Basic Study Skills** Students learn and apply basic study skills (pp. 700–703).	**Teaching Resources** *Academic and Workplace Skills Activity Book,* pp. 52–53
DAY 2	**Reference Skills** Students learn and apply reference skills for using a library, reference sources and the Internet (pp. 704–714).	**Teaching Resources** *Academic and Workplace Skills Activity Book,* pp. 54–58
DAY 3	**Test-Taking Skills** Students learn and apply test-taking skills (pp. 715–719).	**Teaching Resources** *Academic and Workplace Skills Activity Book,* pp. 59–60

Options for Adapting Lesson Plans

HOMEWORK

Have students complete any stage of the lesson for homework.

FEATURES

Extend coverage with the Standardized Test Preparation Workshop (pp. 720–721).

TECHNOLOGY

Students can complete any stage of the lesson on computer. Have them print out their completed work.

INTEGRATED SKILLS COVERAGE

Language
Language Highlight ATE p. 712

Vocabulary
ATE p. 710

Technology
ATE pp. 708, 710

Viewing and Representing
Critical Viewing SE pp. 700, 703, 707, 709, 714, 717

ASSESSMENT SUPPORT

Standardized Test Preparation Workshop SE p. 720; ATE p. 718

Standardized Test Preparation Workbook, pp. 61–62

Scoring Rubrics on Transparency, Ch. 31

Formal Assessment, Ch. 31

Writing Assessment and Portfolio Management

MEETING INDIVIDUAL NEEDS

Less Advanced Students ATE pp. 703, 709, 714, 716; See also Ongoing Assessments ATE pp. 703, 712, 717

ESL Students ATE pp. 708, 717

BLOCK SCHEDULING

Professional Development Support
• *How to Manage Instruction in the Block* This Teaching Resource provides management and activity suggestions.

MEDIA AND TECHNOLOGY

For the Teacher
• *Resource Pro* CD-ROM

WRITING AND GRAMMAR WEB SITE

The Interactive Writing and Grammar Web site provides a wide array of support for students, teachers and parents. Writing support includes:

• Interactive revision checkers
• Scoring rubrics with complete models

www.phschool.com

Lesson Objectives

1. To form a study plan, including setting up a study area, creating a schedule, and using an assignment book.

2. To use an outline and practice writing summaries.

3. To learn how to use the library catalog to find books.

4. To learn and apply the uses of reference materials.

5. To practice using and judging the reliability of Web sites.

6. To learn how to budget time for test preparation.

7. To know the different kinds of objective questions and strategies for answering them.

8. To learn how to budget time during a test.

Critical Viewing

Infer Students may suggest that because the boy is studying in a comfortable, quiet, and familiar place, he will be able to concentrate on his work more effectively.

Chapter 31 Study, Reference, and Test-Taking Skills

This chapter will help you to improve your skills in studying, researching, and taking tests. If you know how to study and where to look for information, your school experience will be more rewarding. These skills will also come in handy throughout your life. In this chapter, you will learn how to make the most out of your study time, as well as how to research information using printed and electronic reference sources. You will even find useful ideas to help you improve your test scores.

▲ **Critical Viewing** In what ways does this boy benefit from having a special place to study? **[Infer]**

700 • Study, Reference, and Test-Taking Skills

⏱ **TIME AND RESOURCE MANAGER**	
Resources **Print:** Academic and Workplace Skills Activity Book, pp. 52–53	
In-Depth Coverage	**Accelerated Pace**
• Work through all key concepts, pp. 701–703. • Assign and review Exercises 1–4.	• Assign pp. 701–703 for independent student review.

PREPARE and ENGAGE

Section 31.1 *Basic Study Skills*

Study skills—the patterns or habits that you set up to help you study—allow you to get the most out of the time you spend studying. You should have a specific study area, a scheduled study time, an assignment book, and an organized notebook in which you can take useful notes.

Setting Up a Study Area and Study Schedule

You should have a place where you can study and plan for study time. Use these suggestions to improve your study area:

- Your study area should be in the same place every day.
- It should be comfortable and free of interruptions.
- It should have a desk or table, a chair, and good lighting.
- It should have all of the supplies you may need: pens and pencils, paper, erasers, tape, stapler, paper clips, scissors, ruler, felt-tip markers, index cards, and a dictionary.

▶ **KEY CONCEPT** Make a study schedule that allows time for daily assignments and long-term projects. ■

Use the sample study schedule below as a model. Each day, allow some time for the review of difficult subjects, extra study for upcoming tests, and work on long-term projects.

SAMPLE STUDY SCHEDULE	
Time	Activity
3:30–4:00	after-school activity
4:00–4:30	after-school activity
4:30–5:00	homework
5:00–5:30	homework
5:30–6:00	dinner
6:00–6:30	homework
6:30–7:00	homework
7:00–7:30	television
7:30–8:00	television
8:00–8:30	pleasure reading

▶ **Exercise 1** Rating Your Study Area List the features and supplies that are available in your study area, then compare them with the ones listed above. Write down the improvements you could make to your study area.

▶ **More Practice**

Academic and Workplace Skills Activity Book
• p. 52

Study, Reference, and Test-Taking Skills • **701**

Step-by-Step Teaching Guide continued

8. Ask students to recall the last two or three days and how they spent their study time at home. Review the text suggestions. Have students compare their study schedule with the text and make suggestions about what changes they think might help them.

PREPARE and ENGAGE

🖊️ **Interest GRABBER** Ask students to use their imaginations to make a list of what their favorite sports team or music group needs to practice every day. Discuss that in order to learn or improve at anything, we need time to practice, tools or resources, and the appropriate space.

Activate Prior Knowledge

Ask students to describe their most successful day of studying—where they studied, what they used, and how they used their time.

TEACH

Step-by-Step Teaching Guide

Setting Up a Study Area and Study Schedule

1. Not all students have a study area at home that belongs solely to them. Nevertheless, there are ways they can make their studying more effective.

2. A student who studies at the kitchen table after dinner can keep all study tools—pens, tape, dictionary, paper clips, and so on—in a shopping bag and not waste time every night searching for what he or she needs.

3. A student who works in the living room can turn his or her table and chair to face the wall so he or she isn't distracted by what others are doing.

4. If a student is working on a long-term project, she can hang up a large sign: CAROLE'S SCHOOL PROJECT. HANDS OFF!!! She could get a carton from the supermarket to place over her work to keep it safe from hands and paws.

5. Review the text suggestions for a study area.

6. Have students share their own tricks in adapting to their home environments to carve out some privacy and cozy study areas.

7. The basic idea with a study schedule is to get students thinking in terms of time management and planning.

continued

Keeping an Assignment Book

1. Though it is a small item, not all students will be able to afford an assignment book or be organized enough to keep track of one.

2. Ask students to share adaptations—how can they make their own assignment book using just their loose-leaf or bound notebook. The key here is a system for recording and keeping track of assignments.

3. There is no "right" method for keeping an assignment book as long as the assignments are successfully kept track of. Encourage students to explore what works best for them, without allowing them to overly indulge in their own idiosyncrasies.

4. You could help students in keeping track of assignments by always having them listed in the same place on the board.

5. Encourage students to set up a buddy system for keeping track of assignments, especially after absences.

Answer Key

Exercises 1–3

Students can do these exercises in small groups, sharing tips and ideas.

31.1

Exercise 2 Making a Study Schedule Using the model on page 701, make a study schedule of your own. Follow the schedule for two weeks. Notice where you need to spend more time or less time, and make adjustments accordingly. At the end of two weeks, evaluate your schedule, and make any final changes. Keep a copy of your schedule in your notebook.

Keeping an Assignment Book

Keep an assignment book to record tasks you must complete every day for each class. Use your assignment book to keep track of the dates of tests and due dates of long-term projects, as well. Write down each assignment as you receive it. This will help you plan what to work on in your scheduled time. Keeping an assignment book will help you to complete each assignment on time and to be prepared for class discussions and tests.

KEY CONCEPT Use an assignment book to record homework assignments and due dates. ■

Date	Subject	Assignment	Due	Completed
11/19	English	Read pages 126-136	11/20	✔
11/19	Math	Study for test on decimals	11/20	
11/20	Science	Report on fruit flies	11/30	
		—Research	(11/23)	
		—Drafting	(11/25)	
		—Revising	(11/27)	
		—Final draft	(11/30)	

Exercise 3 Organizing an Assignment Book Organize an assignment book page like the one shown in the model. Use this format for one week's assignments. Notice whether you have left enough space to write your assignments and whether you have written your assignments down in enough detail. At the end of a week, discuss with a partner any additional information you might add to an assignment book page.

More Practice

Academic and Workplace Skills Activity Book
• p. 52

Taking Notes

The ability to take notes is important to achieving success in school. To take good notes, listen and read carefully. Record only main ideas and significant details. Use your notes as a framework for studying.

> **KEY CONCEPT** Use a modified outline to take notes while listening or reading. ■

Make a Modified Outline A modified outline breaks down information so that you can remember it. It also helps you organize ideas and information for a composition.

Crazy Horse ⟩———————— heading
1. Chief of Oglala Sioux
2. One of the greatest Native Americans ⟩— details
3. Led Battle of Little Big Horn

> **KEY CONCEPT** Write summaries of chapters or lectures to review what you have learned. ■

> **Exercise 4** **Taking Notes in Outline Form** Choose a section in your science or social studies textbook, and take notes on the important information. Use the modified outline form.

◀ **Critical Viewing** How would you write an outline detailing the various features of this bear? **[Analyze]**

Basic Study Skills • 703

Technology Tip

Most word-processing programs have an outline feature. When preparing an outline on a computer, choose Outline from the appropriate menu on the toolbar. If you are unsure about how to proceed, select "Creating outlines" from the Help index.

Step-by-Step Teaching Guide

Taking Notes

1. Ask students to remember times they have forgotten material they thought they knew and other situations when they were able to recall it thanks to a written note of some form.

2. The reason we all need to take notes is that our memories are not perfect. When we hear or read something, it can seem so clear that it would be impossible to forget it, yet a few minutes or paragraphs later, it's gone. That's why we take notes and write down the important facts.

3. Review the modified outline and discuss how it could help students remember and organize important information.

4. A summary is useful for capturing the important points of a chapter or lecture.

Customize for
Less Advanced Students

Students can have problems organizing information in order to take notes or summarize. Help them recognize main idea and supporting details. Use an essay that features strong topic sentences with the main idea and several supporting details. Show students how capturing the main ideas and maybe one detail per paragraph can be put into an outline or summary.

Critical Viewing

Analyze Students may suggest that their outline's heading should be *Bear*. Then under the 3 headings they will list and number the various details, such as *large*, *brown*, *hairy*, and *wet*.

Answer Key

> **Exercise 4**

Suggest that groups of four choose the same section. They can make individual outlines, then compare them.

☑ **ONGOING ASSESSMENT: Monitor and Reinforce**

If some students are having difficulty mastering note-taking skills, use one of the following options.

Option 1 Work with students in creating outlines that list the main idea and supporting details for each paragraph.	**Option 2** Have students work in small groups to share ideas on how to take notes from class materials.

Activate Prior Knowledge

Ask students to make a list of all the places they can think of where they could find out information about a subject.

TEACH

Using the Library

1. Discuss how to find books in a library. Establish that libraries use different systems to make it easier to locate books. Tell students that before computers, all libraries had card catalogs. Card catalogs are organized by *author, title,* and *subject.* Libraries also use a numbering system, which students will learn about later.

2. Review the entry on the card, making sure that students understand each entry. Tell them that they will learn about the call numbering system shortly.

3. All catalog systems are based on alphabetical order. For a quick practice, write the following author names on the board and ask students to place them in the correct alphabetical order.

   Bradbury, Ray

   Asimov, Isaac

   Chekhov, Anton

   Carroll, Lewis

   Alvarez, Julia

   Brooks, Gwendolyn

   (Alvarez, Asimov, Bradbury, Brooks, Carroll, Chekhov)

Reference Skills

As technology becomes more sophisticated, information is easier to find. Many references that used to be available only in print can now be accessed with a computer. You can get information on CD-ROMs or on-line.

Using the Library

Libraries contain many different kinds of resources. The key to finding the information you need is to understand how the books and other materials are organized.

Use the Library Catalog When you are looking for a book, start with the *library catalog.*

> **KEY CONCEPT** Use the library catalog to find valuable information about the books in a library. ■

The library catalog will be in one of these three forms:

Card Catalog This index system lists books on cards, with each book having a separate *author card* and *title card.* If the book is nonfiction, it also has at least one *subject card.* Cards are filed alphabetically in small drawers, with author cards alphabetized by last names and title cards alphabetized by the first words of the titles, excluding *A, An,* and *The.*

CARD CATALOG (AUTHOR CARD)	
737.4 **Hendin, David**	call number / author
He **Collecting Coins**	part of call number; title
New York:	city of publication,
Signet, 1978	publisher, / publication date
170 p; illus; 25 cm	number of pages / size of book
Coins	subject illustrated

Printed Catalog This catalog lists books in printed booklets, with each book listed alphabetically by author, by title, and—if nonfiction—by subject. Often, there are separate booklets for author, title, and subject listings.

Research Tip

Use the subject catalog in your library when you need to locate information on a specific topic but don't have the name of a particular book or author.

⏰ **TIME AND RESOURCE MANAGER**	
Resources **Print:** Academic and Workplace Skills Activity Book, pp. 54–58	
In-Depth Coverage	**Accelerated Pace**
• Work through all key concepts, pp. 704–714. • Assign and review Exercises 5–13.	• Assign pp. 704–714 for independent student review.

Electronic Catalog This catalog lists books on a CD-ROM or in an on-line database that you can access from special computer terminals in the library. Usually, you can find a book's catalog entry by typing in the title, key words in the title, the author's name, or, for nonfiction, the appropriate subject.

ELECTRONIC CATALOG

Author:	Hendin, David.
Title:	Collecting Coins.
Published:	New York: Signet, 1978.
Description:	170p.; ill.; 25 cm.
Subject:	Coins.
Call No.:	737.4 He
Status:	On shelf.

> **Exercise 5** Working With Catalog Entries Answer the following questions, using either of the two catalog listings shown.
> 1. How can you tell that this is an author card?
> 2. What is the title of the book?
> 3. When was the book published?
> 4. How many pages does the book have?
> 5. What is the subject of this book?

Finding the Book You Want Libraries organize books so that people can find them. Most books are classified as either *fiction* (novels and stories) or *nonfiction* (factual information).

> **KEY CONCEPT** Fiction books are arranged in alphabetical order, using the author's last name. If an author has written several books, they are arranged alphabetically according to the first words of the titles. ∎

Fiction Books If you are looking for the novel *Charlotte's Web*, you can locate it without the card catalog if you know the author's name (E. B. White) and where the fiction section is located.

First, go to the fiction section. Find the books by authors whose names begin with *W*, and find E. B. White. Then. find *Charlotte's Web*. (If you do not know the author of a book, you can locate the book under its title in the card, printed, or electronic catalog.)

> **More Practice**
> Academic and Workplace Skills Activity Book
> • pp. 53–54

Electronic Catalog

1. Many libraries have replaced individual cards with electronic catalogs. If your library has one, take students there and have them practice looking up books. Use a peer support system to have students who are familiar with the catalog's use show classmates how to use it.

2. If your library does not have an electronic catalog, review the example entry. Explain that electronic catalog systems will have slightly different ways of operating. Usually there are on-screen directions, but if not, instruct students to ask a librarian for help.

Answer Key

> **Exercise 5**

1. The author is listed first.
2. <u>Collecting Coins</u>
3. 1978
4. 170 pages
5. coins

Fiction and Nonfiction Books

1. Fiction books are arranged alphabetically according to the author's last name. Books by the same author are then arranged alphabetically by title.

2. It is not always clear from the title if a book is fiction or nonfiction. If students are not sure, they should consult the catalog under the author or title entry.

3. Write the following titles on the board and ask students to classify them as fiction or nonfiction.

   Charlotte's Web

   Dairy Farming in Charlotte, Vermont

   Charlotte's Ghost

   The first and third sound like fiction, and the second sounds as if it deals with factual information.

4. Review the Dewey Decimal System. Some students may be unfamiliar with the terms for each category. Tell them that *philosophy* is the study of basic beliefs and ideas about life; the *social sciences* are the study of such things as history, economics (business), society (sociology), other cultures (anthropology), and psychology (how our minds and feelings work); *pure sciences* are the study of living things (biology), matter (physics), chemistry, and geology (Earth); *technology* is the study of how things work.

5. Write the following numbers on the board and ask students to supply the category of the Dewey Decimal System.

   268 (religion)

   655 (technology)

   923 (history)

   481 (languages)

   742 (the arts)

31.2

> **KEY CONCEPT** To find a nonfiction book, look it up in the catalog, and make a note of its *call number*. ∎

Nonfiction Books The *call number* is a combination of a number and one or more letters. It is found on the upper left corner of a catalog card and on the spine of the book.

Libraries usually display a range of call numbers for each stack of shelves. Most libraries use the **Dewey Decimal System** to classify nonfiction books.

This illustration shows the number ranges of the main content areas, or classes, of the Dewey Decimal System.

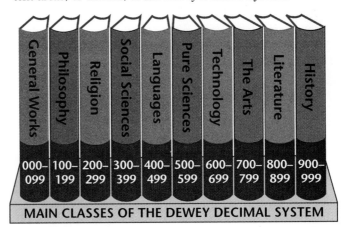

MAIN CLASSES OF THE DEWEY DECIMAL SYSTEM

Biographies These stories about the lives of real people are listed under 921 in the Dewey Decimal System. However, they are often shelved in a special Biography section that is alphabetized by the last name of the person about whom a book is written.

Reference Books Dictionaries, atlases, encyclopedias, and so on may be shelved in a special section. If a book has *R* or *REF* before its call number, go to the library's reference section, and then use the call number to locate the book.

> **Exercise 6** **Finding Fiction** Arrange the following listings according to the way you would find these books on a library shelf.
> 1. *Julie of the Wolves* by Jean Craighead George
> 2. *The Lion, the Witch, and the Wardrobe* by C. S. Lewis
> 3. *Alice's Adventures in Wonderland* by Lewis Carroll
> 4. *The Last Battle* by C. S. Lewis
> 5. *Across Five Aprils* by Irene Hunt

706 • Study, Reference, and Test-Taking Skills

🔦 Challenge

With one or two partners, choose a single topic, and then see in how many Dewey Decimal classes you can find information related to the topic. Using *China*, for example, you would find Chinese *philosophy, religion* in China, Chinese *language,* Chinese *literature,* and so on.

> **More Practice**
>
> Academic and Workplace Skills Activity Book
> • p. 55

> **Exercise 7** Working With the Dewey Decimal System

Write the correct call numbers of the group (the range) to which each title below would belong.
1. *A History of Ancient Greece*
2. *The New Columbia Encyclopedia*
3. *Making Masks*
4. *The Plays of Shakespeare*
5. *Snakes, Lizards, and Other Reptiles*

Using Encyclopedias

With the exception of dictionaries, encyclopedias are the most frequently used reference books because they contain concisely presented information on almost any subject.

> **KEY CONCEPT** Use an encyclopedia for three purposes:
> 1. to get background information on a subject
> 2. to learn basic facts about a subject
> 3. to find out where else to go for information. ■

Alphabetical Listings Each encyclopedia is made up of volumes, which are arranged in alphabetical order. Inside each volume, the articles are also in alphabetical order.

Index Most encyclopedias will have an *index*, which is usually in a separate volume. The index shows the volume and page on which you can find the article you need.

Use these tips when using an encyclopedia:

• Look up the subject under its most common name.

• If there is no article for your subject, you may find "*See* ___?___ " instead.

• At the end of an article, you may sometimes find "*See also* ___?___."

• Some articles list additional readings for further study.

• You can find more sources of information in the index.

> **Exercise 8** Finding Information in Encyclopedias Look up and read the article about your state in an encyclopedia. Follow up on any *See also* directions. Then, check the index. Write a short paragraph that describes the information you found in addition to what was written in the main article.

▲ Critical Viewing
What suggests that this student is still trying to locate information on his subject? **[Deduce]**

Reference Skills • 707

Step-by-Step Teaching Guide

Using Encyclopedias

1. Ask students to describe their experience in using an encyclopedia.

2. Review the uses of an encyclopedia and their alphabetical structure.

3. Ask students to generate a list of subjects they are interested in. If it is possible, have them use an encyclopedia in the library to look up one or two of the subjects.

4. Write the following topics on the board and ask students to place them in alphabetical order:

   dogs

   Australia

   Arkansas

   dinosaurs

   dandelions

   (Arkansas, Australia, dandelions, dinosaurs, dogs)

Answer Key

> **Exercise 6** (page 706)

3, 1, 5, 4, 2

> **Exercise 7**

1. 900–999
2. 000–099
3. 700–799
4. 800–899
5. 500–599

> **Exercise 8**

If your school library has several different encyclopedias—one volume, multivolume, children's—have some students use each one. Then they can compare the information they found.

Critical Viewing

Deduce Students may say he is reading a book without taking notes.

Customize for
ESL Students

You may want to remind students of
Spanish that not so long ago the
letters "ch" were considered as a
different consonant, and so, words
like *chocolate* would be found under
"ch" and not "c." Today, this is no
longer the case. Ask students if they
can think of other entries that
wouldn't be found in an English
language dictionary.

Integrating Technology

If you have access, have students use
an electronic encyclopedia and print
out articles on topics of interest.

Periodicals and Periodical Indexes

When you need current information on a subject, you will
usually find it in a **periodical**—a newspaper, magazine, or other
printed matter that is published at regular intervals.

Using Periodical Indexes The most frequently used periodical index is the *Readers' Guide to Periodical Literature.* In
its many volumes, you will find information telling where and
when articles on a particular subject were published. Each
volume covers a certain time span, and the entries within it
are in alphabetical order by subject. You will find some indexes that focus on a particular subject. On-line indexes provide
the full text of an article. Check with a librarian if you need
help using a periodical index or finding a particular periodical.

Using Dictionaries

A **dictionary** is a collection of words and their meanings,
along with other information about the words. A dictionary also
tells how words are pronounced, how they are used in a sentence, and their *etymology*—how they came into the language.

> **KEY CONCEPT** Dictionaries contain a wealth of useful
> information. ■

Types of Dictionaries Some dictionaries are for scholars.
Others are for general readers. Still others are for people
studying a special area of knowledge. *Unabridged* dictionaries
have a greater number of words, including more detailed information, than *abridged* dictionaries.

Learn More

To learn more about
how dictionaries can
help expand your
vocabulary, see
Chapter 29.

THREE TYPES OF DICTIONARIES

Unabridged	Exhaustive study of the English language containing over 250,000 words.
Abridged	Compact edition containing from 55,000 to 160,000 listings.
Specialized	Limited to words of a particular type or field, such as foreign languages or mathematics.

Finding a Word Dictionaries can be large, cumbersome books, but they are arranged to help you find a word quickly. In printed dictionaries, all the items are listed in strict **alphabetical order.** To speed your search, use these features:

Thumb Index Some dictionaries have a thumb index—indentations along the side of the book printed with letters. Words that begin with those letters are listed in that section of the book.

Guide Words At the top of each page are *guide words.* The guide word on the left tells you the first word on the page. The guide word on the right tells you the last word on the page.

If you use an *electronic dictionary,* you type a word and the computer searches the dictionary database.

> **Exercise 9** Finding Words in a Dictionary Find the following words in a dictionary. Then, list the guide words that appear at the top of each page.

Word	Guide Words	
1. leaf	?	?
2. evening	?	?
3. roadrunner	?	?
4. Arizona	?	?
5. snack	?	?

> **More Practice**

Academic and Workplace Skills Activity Book
• pp. 56–57

◀ Critical Viewing
Name three kinds of information about a particular word that this student might be looking up in the dictionary. **[Speculate]**

Using Dictionaries

1. Review the different types of dictionaries with students. Ask students what kind of dictionary they would most likely use. Elicit that an abridged dictionary, one that is designed for use by students, is best suited to their uses.

2. If you have a dictionary with a thumb index, show it to students. Most abridged dictionaries do not have a thumb index.

Customize for
Less Advanced Students

Give students additional practice in using the alphabetical organization of a dictionary. For words that start with the same letter, instruct them to look first at the second letter, then the third and the fourth, until they find the word they are looking for. For an example, work with them to alphabetize the following words: *paid, pail, paint, pair.*

Answer Key

> **Exercise 9**

Answers will vary.

Critical Viewing

Speculate Students may say the word's pronunciation, its origin, and its definition.

Understanding Dictionary Entries

1. Point out the guide words on a dictionary page. The word on the left is the first word on the page and the word on the right, the last.

2. Ask students what they have used a dictionary for. Students' responses will probably highlight definitions and spelling. Tell them that there is a lot more information about each entry word as you examine the sample entry.

3. Direct interested students to Chapter 29 to see how to use dictionaries to expand their vocabularies.

4. Have students practice using guide words by looking up words and recording the guide words on the page.

Integrating Technology

Have students use the electronic dictionary on your word processor. See that they know how to use the toolbar to find the dictionary and then to type the entry word into the appropriate field and hit *Enter*.

Integrating Vocabulary Skills

Dictionaries are a treasure of information about words. Challenge students to look up, study, and memorize two new words a day and use each word in a sentence in a special vocabulary notebook.

31.2

Understanding Dictionary Entries

The words listed in a dictionary are called *entry words*. An entry word with all of the information about that word is called a *main entry*.

MAIN ENTRY IN A DICTIONARY

① ② ③ ④ ④ ⑤
pret•ty (prit´ē) *adj.* **-ti•er, -ti•est** [ME. *prati* < OE. *prættig*, crafty < *prætt*, a craft, trick] **1.** Pleasing or attractive in a dainty, delicate, or graceful way rather than through striking beauty, elegance, grandeur, or stateliness **2.** *a)* fine; good; nice: often used ironically [a *pretty* fix] *b)* adroit; skillful [a *pretty* move] **3.** [Archaic] elegant **4.** [Archaic or Scot.] brave; bold; gallant **5.** [Colloq.] considerable; quite large [a *pretty* price] —**adv.** **1.** fairly; somewhat [*pretty* sure]: sometimes, by hyperbole, quite or very [*pretty* angry] **2.** [Colloq.] prettily [to talk *pretty*] —**n.,** *pl.* **-ties** a pretty person or thing —**vt. -tied, -ty•ing** to make pretty (usually with *up*) —**SYN.** BEAUTIFUL —☆**sitting pretty** [Slang] in a favorable position —**pret´ti•ly** *adv.* —**pret´ti•ness** *n.* —**pret´ty•ish** *adj.*

⑥ ⑦ ③ ⑥ ⑦ ⑧ ⑦ ⑧ ⑧

---

1. **Entry Words** This may be a single word, a compound word (two or more words acting as a single word), an abbreviation, a prefix or suffix, or the name of a person or place. Dots, spaces, or slashes in an entry word indicate the syllables. Note that words of one syllable are never divided.

2. **Pronunciations** Appearing immediately after the entry word, the pronunciation uses symbols to show how to say the word and which syllable to stress. The syllable that gets the most emphasis has a *primary stress*, usually shown by a heavy mark after the syllable (´). Words of more than one syllable may also have a *secondary stress*, usually shown by a shorter, lighter mark (´).

3. **Parts-of-Speech Labels** Labels that tell whether the word functions as a noun, a verb, or some other part of speech are given as abbreviations, usually immediately following the pronunciation.

 **Learn More**

To learn more about parts of speech, see Chapters 14–18.

4. **Plurals and Inflected Forms** After the part-of-speech label, the dictionary may also show the plural forms of nouns, as well as inflected forms—past tense and participle forms of verbs—if there is anything irregular about their spelling.

5. **Etymology** The word's etymology, or origin, usually appears in brackets, parentheses, or slashes near the start or end of the entry. Abbreviations used for languages are explained in the dictionary's key to abbreviations.

6. **Definition** A definition is the meaning of a word. Definitions are numbered if there are several meanings, and often will include an example illustrating that meaning.

7. **Usage Labels** These labels show how the word is generally used. Words labeled *Archaic (Arch.)*, *Obsolete (Obs.)*, *Poetic*, or *Rare* are not widely used today. Those labeled *Informal (Inf.)*, *Colloquial (Colloq.)*, or *Slang* are not considered part of formal English. Those labeled *Brit.* are used mainly in Great Britain, not the United States.

8. **Idioms and Derived Words** The end of an entry may list and define idioms or expressions that contain the entry word. It may also list derived words (words formed from the entry word) along with a part-of-speech label.

Field labels show whether a word is used in a special way by people in a certain occupation or activity, such as *History (Hist.)* or *Mathematics (Math.)*. Not all entries have field labels.

> **Exercise 10** Working With Main Entries Use a dictionary to answer the following questions.
>
> 1. In what order would these entry words appear?
>   *toast—sadness—field—Arkansas—northwest*
> 2. Which of these entry words would appear on a page with the guide words *nose* and *note*?
>   *north—not—Norway—notch—notify*
> 3. What two guide words appear on the page with *raspberry*?
> 4. What is the origin of the word *paper*?
> 5. Give the definition of the verb *clasp* and the noun *clasp*.
> 6. Give two field labels and definitions for the word *pocket*.
> 7. What is the origin of the word *kindergarten*?
> 8. Which word is not spelled correctly?
>   *spaghetti—mispell—athletic—scissors*
> 9. Which word is spelled correctly?
>   *aniversary—permanant—cematery—calendar*
> 10. Write one idiom using the word *chip*.

Reference Skills • 711

Step-by-Step Teaching Guide (continued)

5. Review each of the items contained in a dictionary entry. This information is always found in unabridged dictionaries but not always contained in abridged dictionaries.

6. Review how the entry word item shows spelling and syllables and possible hyphens in compound words.

7. The pronunciation cue can be confusing. Review the symbols and abbreviations with students. Write the following sentences on the board.

   I read the newspaper every day.

   I read a good book last week.

   Write the pronunciation for both words (rēd, rĕd) on the board and interpret them.

8. Write the following abbreviations on the board and see that students understand their meaning.

   n. noun

   v. verb

   adj. adjective

   adv. adverb

   prep. preposition

9. Tell students that many words in English come from Latin (*L.*), the language of ancient Rome. Other words come from Greek (*Gr.*) and Old English (*OE.*), the language spoken in England 1,500 years ago.

Answer Key

> **Exercise 10**

1. Arkansas, field, northwest, sadness, toast
2. not, notch
3. Answers will vary, depending on the dictionary.
4. from Greek *papyros*, meaning "papyrus"
5. to fasten, to hold in the hand; a device that holds things together
6. Possible responses: baseball: a hollow in a baseball mitt; bowling: space between pins
7. from German for "children's garden"
8. mispell
9. calendar
10. Possible responses: chip off the old block, chip on one's shoulder

711

Almanacs

1. Ask students if they have ever used an almanac to find information. Review that an almanac is organized by topics. An alphabetical index is the best way to look up information.

2. An almanac contains statistics that never change, such as the lengths of rivers, the heights of mountains, and past yearly information.

3. Ask students to speculate on what events or human achievements that have happened this year might be included in next year's almanac.

Atlases and Electronic Map Collections

1. Ask students who have used an atlas to describe the kinds of information they have found there. Elicit that an atlas contains different types of maps, charts, and graphs about geography.

2. Have students use an atlas to find examples of the eight items in the chart.

3. Review the Dolley Madison entry from a biographical reference book. Discuss how biographical reference books are useful for short identifying information about famous people. For more extensive information, students should consult an encyclopedia or a full biography in the library.

4. Students may be puzzled by the word *nee* that follows *Dolley* in the entry. Tell them that it is a French word meaning "born." It is commonly used in English to state a woman's maiden name.

Language Highlight

Atlas Tell students that the word *atlas* comes from Greek. Atlas was a Titan in Greek mythology who was condemned to carry the world on his shoulders. This was the Greeks' explanation of why the sky does not fall.

31.2

Using Other Reference Works

In addition to encyclopedias and dictionaries, there are many other reference tools in school and public libraries. Three important resources are *almanacs*, *atlases*, and *biographical reference books*.

Almanacs An almanac is a book of facts and statistics about subjects of interest to many people, such as government, history, geography, weather, science, technology, industry, sports, and entertainment. It is made up mostly of lists, tables, and charts. Most almanacs are updated every year. With an *electronic almanac*, you can find information by typing in a subject or key word.

KEY CONCEPT Use an almanac to get a brief answer to a question involving facts or statistics. ■

EXAMPLES: What is the distance between Mercury and the sun? (3 million miles)
Who won the 100-meter dash for women in the 1960 Olympics? (Wilma Rudolph, USA)

Facts and statistics are grouped under subject headings. You must look in the index under an appropriate subject heading. For example, if you wanted to know the population of a particular city, you could look it up under either *Cities* or *Population*.

Atlases and Electronic Map Collections Atlases contain maps and geographical information based on them, such as cities, bodies of water, mountains, and landmarks. In *printed atlases*, use an index to locate information. In *electronic atlases*, type the name of a place, and the computer will search the database to find the appropriate map.

KEY CONCEPT Use an atlas for information on the geography of a region. ■

Biographical References These books provide brief life histories of famous or important people.

KEY CONCEPT Use biographical reference books to learn important facts about a person's life. ■

Useful Information Biographical reference books are useful for facts such as the correct pronunciation of a person's name; dates of birth and death; main dates and events of a person's life; and a person's main accomplishments.

712 • Study, Reference, and Test-Taking Skills

Technology Tip

You can use atlases to plan the route for a trip, get local directions, or learn about the rise and fall of empires and changes in countries' borders throughout world history.

✓ ONGOING ASSESSMENT: Monitor and Reinforce

If some students are reluctant to participate fully in learning about reference materials, use one of the following options.

Option 1 Set up a contest for finding information. Divide the class into teams and come up with a series of questions that utilize several reference sources: geographical information, biographical identity, recent political or sports events, and word questions.

Option 2 Set up an extra-credit assignment for individual students and ask them to research information about a topic of their choosing using at least three different reference sources.

Answer Key

Exercise 11

1. sugar, tobacco, rice, coffee, fruit—almanac
2. Answers may vary according to atlas used.
3. 1506—biographical reference book
4. 51–30 B.C.—biographical reference book
5. E. M. Péligot—biographical reference book
6. Answers may vary according to almanac used.
7. minerals, oil, silk—almanac
8. 58 (born 1942)—biographical reference book
9. live oak—almanac
10. more than 200—almanac

Step-by-Step Teaching Guide

Thesauruses

1. Ask students what reference work they would use to find a synonym for a word. Although some dictionary entries list synonyms, a thesaurus contains only synonyms, and lots of them.
2. Ask students to find synonyms for the following words: *friend, nice, cold.*
3. If an electronic thesaurus is available, show students how to access it using the toolbar.

Answer Key

Exercise 12

Answers may vary. Reference works listed.

1. electronic database
2. atlas
3. thesaurus
4. almanac
5. almanac
6. almanac
7. electronic database
8. thesaurus
9. atlas
10. electronic database

Exercise 11 Using Almanacs, Atlases, and Biographical Reference Books For each item below, find the information requested. Indicate the type of reference book you used.
1. chief crops of Cuba
2. rainfall in Brazil
3. year Columbus died
4. length of Cleopatra's rule
5. who discovered uranium
6. number of hijacked planes in a particular year
7. China's natural resources
8. Paul McCartney's age
9. state tree of Georgia
10. baseball players in the Hall of Fame

Printed and Electronic Thesauruses A thesaurus is a specialized reference that lists *synonyms*, or words with similar meanings. It may also list *antonyms*, or words with opposite meanings. *Printed* thesauruses usually arrange words alphabetically, although some are arranged according to subject. In *electronic* thesauruses, you type in or highlight a word, and the computer searches a database to provide one or more synonyms.

Electronic Databases Available on CD-ROM and the Internet, electronic databases let you access large collections of data on particular topics. These databases have search features that allow you to access related information in a variety of ways.

Exercise 12 Using Reference Works Use printed or electronic reference works to answer the following questions. Indicate the type of reference you used.
1. What are three kinds of poisonous snakes, and what is their habitat?
2. What are the latitude and longitude of Anchorage, Alaska?
3. What are five synonyms for the word *good*?
4. Who won the Academy Award for Best Supporting Actor in 1967?
5. What is the average temperature in Morocco in the month of February?
6. What teams won the last four soccer World Cups?
7. Who was the twenty-fourth president of the United States?
8. What word is the opposite of *mercenary*?
9. What countries border the African country of Botswana?
10. What languages are spoken in Switzerland?

More Practice
Academic and Workplace Skills Activity Book
• p. 58

Using the Internet

1. The World Wide Web offers virtually unlimited research possibilities but creates the problems both of reliability and student access to inappropriate information. Ask a knowledgeable student volunteer or tell the class to describe the simple process by which web sites are created. The message is simple: just because it's on the Web doesn't mean it's true.

2. See that all students know how to connect to the web and use search engines such as *Excite* or *Yahoo* to search for information.

3. For practice ask students to go to www.weather.com and find out the weather forecast for the next five days in your area.

Customizing for
Less Advanced Students

Although the Internet can be a big distraction for many students, it can also be a valuable vehicle for reaching and motivating otherwise disinterested students. Customizing lessons and assignments to integrate using the Internet can provide a valuable motivational link.

Critical Viewing

Relate Students may suggest links having to do with astronomy.

Answer Key

> Exercise 13

Answers will vary.

31.2

Using the Internet

The *Internet* is a worldwide network of computers connected over phone and cable lines. The World Wide Web is the part of the Internet that offers text, graphics, sound, and video over the Internet. When you go *on-line*, you have access to an almost unlimited number of Web sites, where an amazing amount of information can be found. Each Web site has its own address, or URL (Universal Resource Locator). If you don't have the address, you can type a key word or words into a *search engine*, which finds related Web sites for you.

> **KEY CONCEPT** Use the Internet for all kinds of information, but judge Web sites for reliability. ■

Here are some guidelines for finding reliable information on the Internet:

- If you know a reliable Web site and its address (URL), simply type the address into your Web browser. Often, television programs, commercials, magazines, newspapers, and radio stations provide Web site addresses where you can find more information about a show, product, company, and so on.

- Consult Internet coverage in library journals (like *Booklist* and *Library Journal*) to learn addresses of Web sites that provide useful and reliable information.

- If you don't know particular Web sites, you can do a general search for a key term on a search engine.

- Remember to bookmark, or save as a favorite, the interesting and reliable sites you find while searching the Web.

> **Exercise 13** **Using the Internet** On a library, school, or home computer, use the Internet to answer the following questions.
> 1. Find the postal ZIP Code for your town or city.
> 2. Find the top-five popular songs for the current year.
> 3. Choose a current-events topic. Do a search on it, and list four Web sites that have information on the subject.
> 4. Find the five children's movies that have made the most money at the box office to date.
> 5. Choose a science topic related to the outdoors. Do a search, and list two Web sites that have information on the subject.

▼ **Critical Viewing** These students have found a Web page on the solar system. What kinds of links to other Web sites do you think they will be able to access from this page? **[Relate]**

> **More Practice**
>
> Academic and Workplace Skills Activity Book
> • p. 59

Section 31.3 *Test-Taking Skills*

This section provides strategies that will help you to improve the way in which you prepare for and take a test, so you can feel more confident and perform more effectively.

Preparing for a Test Doing well on a test depends a lot on how much preparation you have done.

▶ **KEY CONCEPT** Follow these strategies to prepare for a test:

- Review your notes right after you take them, a few days later, and again before the test.
- Test yourself, or ask someone to quiz you.
- Use memory tricks (rhymes, sentences, related words).
- Do not wait until the last minute to begin! ■

Taking a Test In addition to test preparation, you can use strategies to help you relax and concentrate during the test.

▶ **KEY CONCEPT** Budget your time as you preview the test, answer the questions, and proofread your answers. ■

PREVIEW THE TEST

1. Put your name on your paper.
2. Skim the test to see the different kinds of questions.
3. Decide how much time you will spend on each section.
4. Allow time for difficult or high-point questions.

ANSWER THE QUESTIONS

1. Answer easy questions first.
2. If you can, use scratch paper to jot down your ideas.
3. Read each question at least twice before you answer.
4. Give one answer unless the instructions say otherwise.
5. Answer all questions unless you are told not to guess.
6. Do not change your first answer without a good reason.

PROOFREAD YOUR ANSWERS

1. Check that you have followed directions.
2. Reread test questions and answers.
3. Make sure that you have answered all of the questions.

🖥 Internet Tip

If you are interested in learning more about preparing for and taking tests, find one or more Internet sites on the subject. Type "test-taking strategies" in the query field of your search engine.

⏱ TIME AND RESOURCE MANAGER

Resources
Print: Academic and Workplace Skills Activity Book, pp. 59–60

In-Depth Coverage	Accelerated Pace
• Work through all key concepts, pp. 715–719. • Assign and review Exercises 14–15.	• Assign pp. 715–719 for independent student review.

PREPARE and ENGAGE

Interest GRABBER Have the class role-play the following situation: Announce that a test will take place in three days on a current subject. Ask students first to describe their feelings on hearing the word *test* and what their plan would be to prepare for the test and for taking the test itself.

Activate Prior Knowledge

Ask students to recall a test they did well on and try to account for their success. Engage them in the following questions: How did they prepare? How did they feel before and during the test? What strategies did they use during the test? Immediately after the test, how did they feel? What ideas do they have about how they could repeat that success?

Step-by-Step Teaching Guide

Preparing for a Test

1. Test taking is an ordeal for many people. The key to success is good preparation and a good attitude.

2. Engage students in a discussion about strategies for preparing and taking tests. Planning study time is important.

3. Discuss test-taking strategies. First, listen carefully to the test assignment and ask good questions to find out what work needs to be studied for the test. The point here is to budget study time appropriately, giving the most important material the most time. Second, develop study strategies—memory devices like little sayings (*Thirty days hath September . . .*) Also ask students to share their strategies for the actual test—previewing questions, evaluating point distribution, not spending too much time on low-point difficult questions.

4. Discuss the problem of anxiety. Fear about a test, or a negative, defeatist attitude prevents students from using any of the strategies they know. Ask students to share ideas on building confidence. At the same time, talk about the motivational value of a little bit of healthy fear and the dangers of overconfidence.

Answering Objective Questions

1. Ask students why they give wrong answers to questions they know. Many times it is because they did not read the question and answer choices carefully enough. Students want to work efficiently on tests, but rushing can lead to mistakes.

2. Another cause of errors can be reading too much into a question. Encourage students to try to read questions in the context in which the material was presented in class and in their textbooks.

3. About guessing: Students need to know if they are penalized for wrong answers, as is the case on some standardized tests. If there is no penalty, then they must answer every question even if they take a wild guess. Discuss how performance on multiple-choice questions can be improved by using smart guessing. Even if they are not sure of the answer, if they can eliminate two of the four possible answers, they have a 50 percent chance of guessing the right answer. For example, if a math test asks for the area of a circle, students can eliminate any choice(s) that is not in square units.

Customizing for *Less Advanced Students*

Poor test performance often results from students having little idea how to prepare and lacking in resources such as class and text notes to prepare from. To instill some success in these students, set up a workshop situation where you teach a simple model lesson and work with them on the preparation of class and text notes. Follow up with a workshop on time management and studying and another workshop on test-taking strategies. Walk them through the test, showing how they are prepared to answer each question. You could repeat the process, the second time allowing them to take the test on their own. A successful showing will both build confidence and a skill base to work from in the future.

31.3

Answering Objective Questions

KEY CONCEPT Know the different kinds of objective questions and the strategies for answering them. ■

Multiple-Choice Questions This kind of question asks you to choose from several possible responses.

EXAMPLE: The opposite of *fierce* is ___?___ .
  a. angry   b. gentle   c. ready   d. funny

In the preceding example, the answer is *b*. Follow these strategies to answer multiple-choice questions:

• Try answering the question before looking at the choices. If your answer is one of the choices, select that choice.

• Eliminate the obviously incorrect answers, crossing them out if you are allowed to write on the test paper.

• Read all the choices before answering. There are often two *possible* answers, but only one *best* answer.

Matching Questions Matching questions require that you match items in one group with items in another.

EXAMPLE:
  ___?___ 1. menace   a. plentiful
  ___?___ 2. colossal   b. threat
  ___?___ 3. abundant   c. huge

In the preceding example, the answers are 1. *b*, 2. *c*, and 3. *a*. Follow these strategies to answer matching questions:

• Count each group to see whether items will be left over. Check the directions to see whether items can be used more than once.

• Read all the items before you start matching.

• Match the items you know first, crossing them out if you are allowed to write on the test paper.

• Match remaining items about which you are less certain.

Fill-in Questions A fill-in question asks you to supply an answer in your own words. The answer may complete a statement or may simply answer a question.

EXAMPLE: An ___?___ is a word's opposite.

In the preceding example, the answer is *antonym*.

• Read the question or incomplete statement carefully.

• If you are answering a question, change it into a statement by inserting your answer and seeing whether it makes sense.

Technology Tip

If you are taking a test on CD-ROM, be careful not to answer too quickly. Some electronic tests will not allow you to go back and change your answer if you change your mind.

True/False Questions True/false questions require you to identify whether a statement is accurate.

EXAMPLE: __?__ All citizens vote on Election Day.
__?__ High-school students always take three math courses.
__?__ Some schools have a foreign language requirement.

In the preceding example, the answers are *F, F,* and *T.* Follow these strategies to answer true/false questions:

- If a statement seems true, be sure that the entire statement is true.
- Pay special attention to the word *not,* which often changes the entire meaning of a statement.
- Pay special attention to the words *all, always, never, no, none,* and *only.* They often make a statement false.

▶ **Exercise 14** Answering Objective Questions Answer the following questions.

Multiple Choice

1. The word *wealthy* means __?__ .
   a. happy   b. rich   c. worldly   d. successful
2. The opposite of *return* is __?__ .
   a. pay   b. keep   c. remain   d. resound

Matching

3. __?__ heathen   a. hungry
4. __?__ dispute   b. famous
5. __?__ renowned   c. argument
6. __?__ ravenous   d. uncivilized

Fill-in

7. __?__ is the opposite of *generous.*
8. __?__ is the opposite of *rude.*

True/False

9. __?__ All cats have long tails.
10. __?__ Most birds have feathers, lay eggs, and can fly.

▶ Critical Viewing What suggestions would you make to help this student improve her test performance? **[Apply]**

▶ **More Practice**
Academic and Workplace Skills Activity Book
• p. 60

Test-Taking Skills • 717

Step-by-Step Teaching Guide

Answering True/False Questions

1. For true/false questions, the odds of guessing right are 50 percent, so unless there is a penalty for wrong answers, students should always choose an answer.

2. Stress that things are rarely always or never true. A safe guess for any *all, always, none, never* questions is always "false."

Customize for
ESL Students

Students can work individually or with classmates who share the same home language. Have them think of strategies they use to prepare for an English test. Encourage them to share their strategies with the class.

Answer Key

▶ **Exercise 14**

1. b
2. b
3. d
4. c
5. b
6. a
7. Possible answer: Selfish
8. Possible answer: Polite
9. false
10. true

Critical Viewing

Apply Students' responses will vary.

☑ **ONGOING ASSESSMENT: Monitor and Reinforce**

If some students are having difficulty mastering test-taking skills, use one of the following options.

Option 1 Let small groups of students share strategies for test preparation and taking.	**Option 2** To help master test-taking anxiety, use a workshop setting to have students first take open-book tests, then closed-book tests.

Answering Analogies

1. Review the types of analogies. Be sure that students know the difference between synonyms and antonyms.

2. Write the following analogies on the board for extra practice.

   UP : DOWN :: EAST :

   a. north   b. south   <u>c. west</u>
   HILL : MOUNTAIN :: PONY :

   <u>a. horse</u>   b. cow   c. calf

Answer Key

> **Exercise 15**

1. b
2. b
3. c
4. c
5. b

31.3

Analogies An analogy asks you to find pairs of words that express a similar relationship.

EXAMPLE: ELM : TREE :: WHALE :
            a. mammal   b. horse   c. fish

In the preceding example, the answer is *a*. The relationship between the pairs of words is *kind*. An elm is a *kind* of tree, and a whale is a *kind* of mammal.

▶ **Exercise 15** Answering Analogies Fill in each blank below, choosing the word that best expresses the relationship in the given pair.

1. WAGES : EARNINGS :: FEE : ___?___
   a. debt   b. cost   c. coins

2. MUSICIANS : BAND :: FLOWERS : ___?___
   a. aroma   b. bouquet   c. vase

3. TEACHER : INSTRUCTS :: MECHANIC : ___?___
   a. engines   b. cars   c. repairs

4. INVADE : RETREAT :: INTRIGUE : ___?___
   a. trick   b. interest   c. bore

5. LOYAL : FAITHFUL :: CONSTANT : ___?___
   a. happy   b. consistent   c. changing

COMMON ANALOGY RELATIONSHIPS	
Relationship	**Example**
synonyms (same meaning)	enrage : anger
antonyms (opposite meaning)	love : hate
an item and its function	ruler : measurement
a part to a whole	page : book

▶ **More Practice**

Academic and Workplace Skills Activity Book
• p. 60

✏ STANDARDIZED TEST PREPARATION WORKSHOP

Analogies Standardized test questions may require students to complete analogies. Write the following analogy on the board and ask students to choose the correct answer.

FISH : SEA :: DEER :

A forest   **C** bears
B city   **D** grass

A is the correct answer. Fish live in the sea; deer live in a forest.

Answering Short-Answer and Essay Questions

Some test questions require you to supply an answer, rather than simply select a correct answer. Identify these questions when you preview the test. Allow time to write complete, accurate answers.

KEY CONCEPT Allow time and space to answer short-answer and essay questions. ■

Identify Key Words Whether you are responding to a short-answer question or an essay prompt, identify the key words in the test item. Look for words like *discuss, explain, identify,* and any numbers or restrictions. If the question asks for three causes, make sure you supply three.

Check Your Space On some tests, you will be given a certain number of lines on which to write your answer. Make sure that you understand whether you are limited to that space or whether you can ask for more paper. If you are limited to a certain amount of space, use it for the most significant and relevant information.

Stick to the Point Do not put down everything you know about a topic. If the question asks you to identify three steps Jefferson took to limit government power, you will not get extra credit for including information about Jefferson's childhood. In fact, including unrelated information may cause you to lose points.

Answering Short-Answer and Essay Questions

1. Answering short-answer and essay questions requires some different skills from true/false and multiple-choice questions, since there are no sample answers to prompt students' memory. Yet many of the strategies used for those questions apply here. The key is to stay calm and use common sense, read the question carefully, and understand what is being asked.

2. Discuss what strategies students would use in answering short-answer and essay questions. Elicit that a simple outline can be very useful in writing essay questions. It enables students to plan their answer and allot their time.

3. Ideally, students will be fully prepared for a test. But when they are not, talk about the strategy of emphasizing what they do know in longer essay questions. Since essays are usually graded on content, getting them half or two-thirds right is better than a weak answer that misses most of the main points.

4. Encourage students to share their answers to Reflecting on Your Study, Reference, and Test-Taking Skills.

Reflecting on Your Study, Reference, and Test-Taking Skills

Think about what you have learned about the way to study, use reference tools, and take tests. Ask yourself these questions:

- What strategies do I already use for test preparation, and how can I become better prepared?

- Which types of test questions do I find easiest to answer? Which are most difficult?

- Which reference tools do I use most frequently? With which ones should I become more familiar?

Use your answers to identify ways in which you can improve your study, reference, and test-taking skills.

Constructing Meaning from Informational Texts

Teaching Resources: Standardized Test Preparation Workbook, Chapter 31

1. Emphasize to students that their key to success in most standardized essay tests is for them to address the question being asked. Students should read the questions carefully, and confine their answers to the topic area indicated.

2. Remind students that the evidence required to construct meaning of the informational text is within the text itself. Emphasize to the students that they can save time by jotting down the main idea in a passage and key words and dates.

Standardized Test Preparation Workshop

Constructing Meaning From Informational Texts

Standardized tests usually include reading questions. These questions test your ability to construct meaning from the information provided in the passage. The following types of questions will test your ability to read informational texts:

- Identify the main idea, stated or implied, of the passage.
- Identify the best summary—a concise restating of the key points of the passage.
- Distinguish between facts and nonfacts—opinions and untrue, or unprovable, statements.

The following sample test item will give you practice answering these types of questions.

Test Tip

As you read the passage, remember to look for the main idea and the key points.

Sample Test Item	Answer and Explanation
Directions: Read the passage. Then, read the question that follows the passage. Decide which is the best answer to the question. Sidney Lanier was a talented musician as well as a gifted poet. Lanier was born in Macon, Georgia, in 1842. Lanier believed that poetry should have the natural rhythm and fluidity of music.	
1 Which of the following is an OPINION of the writer expressed in the passage? **A** Sidney Lanier was a talented musician as well as a gifted poet. **B** Lanier believed that poetry should have the natural rhythm and fluidity of music. **C** Lanier was born in Macon, Georgia. **D** Lanier was born in 1842.	The correct answer is *A*. The writer of the passage states that Lanier was "talented" and "gifted." The statement is a supportable opinion, but not necessarily a fact. Choice *B* does reflect an opinion, but not the opinion of the writer.

720 • Study, Reference, and Test-Taking Skills

✏ TEST-TAKING TIP

Remind students that it is important to pay attention to words that can clue them in on the tone of the statements within a given passage itself. Awareness of positive, negative and neutral words and phrases will help them to distinguish between fact and opinion.

Answer Key

▶ **Practice 1**
1. C
2. J

▶ **Practice 2**
1. C
2. G

▶ **Practice 1** **Directions:** Read the passage. Then, read each question that follows the passage. Decide which is the best answer to each question.

World War I began in 1914 and was one of the bloodiest and most tragic conflicts ever to occur. Although President Wilson wanted the United States to remain neutral, that proved impossible. In 1915, a German submarine sank the *Lusitania*, the pride of the British merchant fleet. After the sinking, most Americans favored the British and their allies. It soon became impossible for the United States to remain neutral.

1 What is the main idea of this passage?

A President Wilson wanted the United States to remain neutral.

B In 1915, a German submarine sank the *Lusitania*.

C It was impossible for the United States to remain neutral.

D World War I was one of the bloodiest and most tragic conflicts ever to occur.

2 Which of the following is an OPINION expressed in the passage?

F World War I began in 1914.

G In 1915, a German submarine sank the *Lusitania*.

H After the sinking of the *Lusitania*, most Americans favored the British and their allies.

J World War I . . . was one of the bloodiest and most tragic conflicts ever to occur.

▶ **Practice 2** **Directions:** Read the passage. Then, read each question that follows the passage. Decide which is the best answer to each question.

When Christopher Columbus reached North America in 1492, several hundred Native American tribes already populated the continent. Although the history of these earliest Americans is shrouded in mystery, we do know that the Native Americans usually greeted the early European settlers as friends. The settlers were pleased to be greeted by the knowledgeable natives. Native Americans instructed the newcomers in New World agriculture and woodcraft and introduced them to maize, beans, and squash.

1 Which of the following is an OPINION expressed in the passage?

A When Christopher Columbus reached North America in 1492, several hundred Native American tribes already populated the continent.

B Native Americans instructed the newcomers in New World agriculture and woodcraft.

C The settlers were pleased to be greeted by the knowledgeable natives.

D The history of these earliest Americans is shrouded in mystery.

2 Which of the following is the best summary of this passage?

F Native Americans introduced the settlers to maize, beans, and squash.

G Native Americans who lived in North America before Christopher Columbus arrived were friendly and helpful to early European settlers.

H The settlers were pleased to be greeted by the knowledgeable natives.

J Christopher Columbus made friends with Native Americans in 1492.

Standardized Test Preparation Workshop • 721

Citing Sources and Preparing Manuscript

The presentation of your written work is important. Your work should be neat, clean, and easy to read. Follow your teacher's directions for placing your name and class, along with the title and date of your work, on the paper.

For handwritten work:

- Use cursive handwriting or manuscript printing, according to the style your teacher prefers. The penmanship reference below shows the accepted formation of letters in cursive writing.
- Write or print neatly.
- Write on one side of lined 8 1/2" x 11" paper with a clean edge. (Do not use pages torn from a spiral notebook.)
- Indent the first line of each paragraph.

- Leave a margin, as indicated by the guidelines on the lined paper. Write in a size appropriate for the lines provided. Do not write so large that the letters from one line bump into the ones above and below. Do not write so small that the writing is difficult to read.
- Write in blue or black ink.
- Number the pages in the upper right corner.
- You should not cross out words on your final draft. Recopy instead. If your paper is long, your teacher may allow you to make one or two small changes by neatly crossing out the text to be deleted and using a caret [^] to indicate replacement text. Alternatively, you might make one or two corrections neatly with correction fluid. If you find yourself making more than three corrections, consider recopying the work.

PENMANSHIP REFERENCE

For word-processed or typed documents:

- Choose a standard, easy-to-read font.
- Type or print on one side of unlined 8 $\frac{1}{2}$" x 11" paper.
- Set the margins for the side, top, and bottom of your paper at approximately one inch. Most word-processing programs have a default setting that is appropriate.
- Double-space the document.
- Indent the first line of each paragraph.
- Number the pages in the upper right corner. Many word-processing programs have a header feature that will do this for you automatically.

- If you discover one or two errors after you have typed or printed, use correction fluid if your teacher allows such corrections. If you have more than three errors in an electronic file, consider making the corrections to the file and reprinting the document. If you have typed a long document, your teacher may allow you to make a few corrections by hand. If you have several errors, however, consider retyping the document.

For research papers:

Follow your teacher's directions for formatting formal research papers. Most papers will have the following features:

- Title page
- Table of Contents or Outline
- Works-Cited List

Table of Contents

.... 6
.... 10
.... 12

.... 15

Cited

Sybil Luddington:
Female Paul Revere

Megan Mahoney
Language Arts
3rd Period
March 26, 20- -

Incorporating Ideas From Research

Below are three common methods of incorporating the ideas of other writers into your work. Choose the most appropriate style by analyzing your needs in each case. In all cases, you must credit your source.

- **Direct Quotation:** Use quotation marks to indicate the exact words.
- **Paraphrase:** To share ideas without a direct quotation, state the ideas in your own words. While you haven't copied word-for-word, you still need to credit your source.
- **Summary:** To provide information about a large body of work—such as a speech, an editorial, or a chapter of a book—identify the writer's main idea.

Avoiding Plagiarism

Whether you are presenting a formal research paper or an opinion paper on a current event, you must be careful to give credit for any ideas or opinions that are not your own. Presenting someone else's ideas, research, or opinion as your own—even if you have rephrased it in different words—is *plagiarism*, the equivalent of academic stealing, or fraud.

You can avoid plagiarism by synthesizing what you learn: Read from several sources and let the ideas of experts help you draw your own conclusions and form your own opinions. Ultimately, however, note your own reactions to the ideas presented.

When you choose to use someone else's ideas or work to support your view, credit the source of the material. Give bibliographic information to cite your sources of the following information:

- Statistics
- Direct quotations
- Indirectly quoted statements of opinions
- Conclusions presented by an expert
- Facts available in only one or two sources

Crediting Sources

When you credit a source, you acknowledge where you found your information and you give your readers the details necessary for locating the source themselves. Within the body of the paper, you provide a short citation, a footnote number linked to a footnote, or an endnote number linked to an endnote reference. These brief references show the page numbers on which you found the information. To make your paper more formal, prepare a reference list at the end of the paper to provide full bibliographic information on your sources. These are two common types of reference lists:

- A **bibliography** provides a listing of all the resources you consulted during your research.
- A **works-cited list** indicates the works you have referenced in your paper.

Choosing a Format for Documentation

The type of information you provide and the format in which you provide it depend on what your teacher prefers. These are the most commonly used styles:

- **Modern Language Association (MLA) Style** This is the style used for most papers at the middle-school and high-school level and for most language arts papers.
- **American Psychological Association (APA) Style** This is used for most papers in the social sciences and for most college-level papers.
- ***Chicago Manual of Style* (CMS) Style** This is preferred by some teachers.

On the following pages, you'll find sample citation formats for the most commonly cited materials. Each format calls for standard bibliographic information. The difference is in the order of the material presented in each entry and the punctuation required.

MLA Style for Listing Sources

Book with one author	Pyles, Thomas. *The Origins and Development of the English Language.* 2nd ed. New York: Harcourt Brace Jovanovich, Inc., 1971.
Book with two or three authors	McCrum, Robert, William Cran, and Robert MacNeil. *The Story of English.* New York: Penguin Books, 1987.
Book with an editor	Truth, Sojourner. *Narrative of Sojourner Truth.* Ed. Margaret Washington. New York: Vintage Books, 1993.
Book with more than three authors or editors	Donald, Robert B., et al. *Writing Clear Essays.* Upper Saddle River, NJ: Prentice-Hall, Inc., 1996.
A single work from an anthology	Hawthorne, Nathaniel. "Young Goodman Brown." *Literature: An Introduction to Reading and Writing.* Ed. Edgar V. Roberts and Henry E. Jacobs. Upper Saddle River, NJ: Prentice-Hall, Inc., 1998. 376–385. [Indicate pages for the entire selection.]
Introduction in a published edition	Washington, Margaret. Introduction. *Narrative of Sojourner Truth.* By Sojourner Truth. New York: Vintage Books, 1993, pp. v–xi.
Signed article in a weekly magazine	Wallace, Charles. "A Vodacious Deal." *Time* 14 Feb. 2000: 63.
Signed article in a monthly magazine	Gustaitis, Joseph. "The Sticky History of Chewing Gum." *American History* Oct. 1998: 30–38.
Unsigned editorial or story	"Selective Silence." Editorial. *Wall Street Journal* 11 Feb. 2000: A14. [If the editorial or story is signed, begin with the author's name.]
Signed pamphlet	[Treat the pamphlet as though it were a book.]
Pamphlet with no author, publisher, or date	*Are You at Risk of Heart Attack?* n.p. n.d. [n.p. n.d. indicates that there is no known publisher or date]
Filmstrips, slide programs, and videotape	*The Diary of Anne Frank.* Dir. George Stevens. Perf. Millie Perkins, Shelley Winters, Joseph Schildkraut, Lou Jacobi, and Richard Beymer. Twentieth Century Fox, 1959.
Radio or television program transcript	"The First Immortal Generation." *Ockham's Razor.* Host Robyn Williams. Guest Damien Broderick. National Public Radio. 23 May 1999. Transcript.
Internet	*National Association of Chewing Gum Manufacturers.* 19 Dec. 1999 <http://www.nacgm.org/consumer/funfacts.html> [Indicate the date you accessed the information. Content and addresses at Web sites change frequently.]
Newspaper	Thurow, Roger. "South Africans Who Fought for Sanctions Now Scrap for Investors." *Wall Street Journal* 11 Feb. 2000: A1+. [For a multipage article, write only the first page number on which it appears, followed by a plus sign.]
Personal interview	Smith, Jane. Personal interview. 10 Feb. 2000.
CD (with multiple publishers)	Simms, James, ed. *Romeo and Juliet.* By William Shakespeare. CD-ROM. Oxford: Attica Cybernetics Ltd.; London: BBC Education; London: HarperCollins Publishers, 1995.
Article from an encyclopedia	Askeland, Donald R. (1991). "Welding." *World Book Encyclopedia.* 1991 ed.

APA Style for Listing Sources

The list of citations for APA is referred to as a Reference List and not a bibliography.

Book with one author	Pyles, T. (1971). *The Origins and Development of the English Language* (2nd ed.). New York: Harcourt Brace Jovanovich, Inc.
Book with two or three authors	McCrum, R., Cran, W., & MacNeil, R. (1987). *The Story of English.* New York: Penguin Books.
Book with an editor	Truth, S. (1993). *Narrative of Sojourner Truth* (M. Washington, Ed.). New York: Vintage Books.
Book with more than three authors or editors	Donald, R. B., Morrow, B. R., Wargetz, L. G., & Werner, K. (1996). *Writing Clear Essays.* Upper Saddle River, New Jersey: Prentice-Hall, Inc. [With six or more authors, abbreviate second and following authors as "et al."]
A single work from an anthology	Hawthorne, N. (1998) Young Goodman Brown. In E. V. Roberts, & H. E. Jacobs (Eds.), *Literature: An Introduction to Reading and Writing* (pp. 376–385). Upper Saddle River, New Jersey: Prentice-Hall, Inc.
Introduction to a work included in a published edition	[No style is offered under this heading.]
Signed article in a weekly magazine	Wallace, C. (2000, February 14). A vodacious deal. *Time, 155,* 63. [The volume number appears in italics before the page number.]
Signed article in a monthly magazine	Gustaitis, J. (1998, October). The sticky history of chewing gum. *American History, 33,* 30–38.
Unsigned editorial or story	Selective Silence. (2000, February 11). *Wall Street Journal,* p. A14.
Signed pamphlet	Pearson Education. (2000). *LifeCare* (2nd ed.) [Pamphlet]. Smith, John: Author.
Pamphlet with no author, publisher, or date	[No style is offered under this heading.]
Filmstrips, slide programs, and videotape	Stevens, G. (Producer & Director). (1959). *The Diary of Anne Frank.* [Videotape]. (Available from Twentieth Century Fox) [If the producer and the director are two different people, list the producer first and then the director, with an ampersand (&) between them.]
Radio or television program transcript	Broderick, D. (1999, May 23). The First Immortal Generation. (R. Williams, Radio Host). *Ockham's Razor.* New York: National Public Radio.
Internet	National Association of Chewing Gum Manufacturers. Available: http://www.nacgm.org/consumer/funfacts.html [References to Websites should begin with the author's last name, if available. Indicate the site name and the available path or URL address.]
Newspaper	Thurow, R. (2000, February 11). South Africans who fought for sanctions now scrap for investors. *Wall Street Journal,* pp. A1, A4.
Personal interview	[APA states that, since interviews (and other personal communications) do not provide "recoverable data," they should only be cited in text.]
CD (with multiple publishers)	[No style is offered under this heading.]
Article from an encyclopedia	Askeland, D. R. (1991). Welding. In *World Book Encyclopedia.* (Vol. 21 pp. 190–191). Chicago: World Book, Inc.

CMS Style for Listing Sources

The following chart shows the CMS author-date method of documentation.

Book with one author	Pyles, Thomas. *The Origins and Development of the English Language,* 2nd ed. New York: Harcourt Brace Jovanovich, Inc., 1971.
Book with two or three authors	McCrum, Robert, William Cran, and Robert MacNeil. *The Story of English.* New York: Penguin Books, 1987.
Book with an editor	Truth, Sojourner. *Narrative of Sojourner Truth.* Edited by Margaret Washington. New York: Vintage Books, 1993.
Book with more than three authors or editors	Donald, Robert B., et al. *Writing Clear Essays.* Upper Saddle River, New Jersey: Prentice-Hall, Inc., 1996.
A single work from an anthology	Hawthorne, Nathaniel. "Young Goodman Brown." In *Literature: An Introduction to Reading and Writing.* Ed. Edgar V. Roberts and Henry E. Jacobs. 376–385. Upper Saddle River, New Jersey: Prentice-Hall, Inc., 1998.
Introduction to a work included in a published edition	Washington, Margaret. Introduction to *Narrative of Sojourner Truth,* by Sojourner Truth. New York: Vintage Books, 1993. [According to CMS style, you should avoid this type of entry unless the introduction is of special importance to the work.]
Signed article in a weekly magazine	Wallace, Charles. "A Vodacious Deal." *Time,* 14 February 2000, 63.
Signed article in a monthly magazine	Gustaitis, Joseph. "The Sticky History of Chewing Gum." *American History,* October 1998, 30–38.
Unsigned editorial or story	*Wall Street Journal,* 11 February 2000. [CMS states that items from newspapers are seldom listed in a bibliography. Instead, the name of the paper and the relevant dates are listed.]
Signed pamphlet	[No style is offered under this heading.]
Pamphlet with no author, publisher, or date	[No style is offered under this heading.]
Filmstrips, slide programs, and videotape	Stevens, George. (director). *The Diary of Anne Frank.* 170 min. Beverly Hills, California: Twentieth Century Fox, 1994.
Radio or television program transcript	[No style is offered under this heading.]
Internet	[No style is offered under this heading.]
Newspaper	*Wall Street Journal,* 11 February 2000. [CMS states that items from newspapers are seldom listed in a bibliography. Instead, the name of the paper and the relevant dates are listed.]
Personal interview	[CMS states that, since personal conversations are not available to the public, there is no reason to place them in the bibliography. However, the following format should be followed if they are listed.] Jane Smith. Conversation with author. Wooster, Ohio, 10 February 2000.
CD (with multiple publishers)	Shakespeare, William. *Romeo and Juliet.* Oxford: Attica Cybernetics Ltd.; London: BBC Education; London: HarperCollins Publishers, 1995. CD-ROM.
Article from an encyclopedia	[According to CMS style, encyclopedias are not listed in bibliographies.]

Sample Works-Cited List (MLA)

Carwardine, Mark, Erich Hoyt, R. Ewan Fordyce, and Peter Gill. *The Nature Company Guides: Whales, Dolphins, and Porpoises.* New York: Time-Life Books, 1998.

Ellis, Richard. *Men and Whales.* New York: Knopf, 1991.

Whales in Danger. "Discovering Whales." 18 Oct. 1999. <http://whales.magna.com.au/DISCOVER>

Sample Internal Citations (MLA)

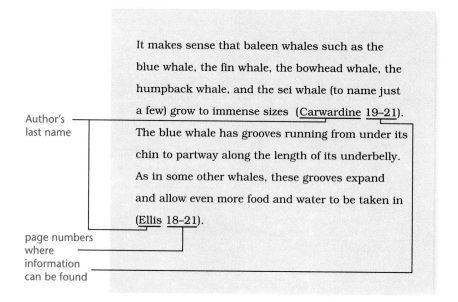

Author's last name

It makes sense that baleen whales such as the blue whale, the fin whale, the bowhead whale, the humpback whale, and the sei whale (to name just a few) grow to immense sizes (Carwardine 19–21). The blue whale has grooves running from under its chin to partway along the length of its underbelly. As in some other whales, these grooves expand and allow even more food and water to be taken in (Ellis 18–21).

page numbers where information can be found

Internet Research Handbook

Introduction to the Internet

The Internet is a series of networks that are interconnected all over the world. The Internet allows users to have almost unlimited access to information stored on the networks. Dr. Berners-Lee, a physicist, created the Internet in the 1980's by writing a small computer program that allowed pages to be linked together using key words. The Internet was mostly text-based until 1992, when a computer program called the NCSA Mosaic (National Center for Supercomputing Applications at the University of Illinois) was created. This program was the first Web browser. The development of Web browsers greatly eased the ability of the user to navigate through all the pages stored on the Web. Very soon, the appearance of the Web was altered as well. More appealing visuals were added, and sound was also implemented. This change made the Web more user-friendly and more appealing to the general public.

Using the Internet for Research

Key Word Search

Before you begin a search, you should identify your specific topic. To make searching easier, narrow your subject to a key word or a group of key words. These are your search terms, and they should be as specific as possible. For example, if you are looking for the latest concert dates for your favorite musical group, you might use the band's name as a key word. However, if you were to enter the name of the group in the query box of the search engine, you might be presented with thousands of links to information about the group that is unrelated to your needs. You might locate such information as band member biographies, the group's history, fan reviews of concerts, and hundreds of sites with related names containing information that is irrelevant to your search. Because you used such a broad key word, you might need to navigate through all that information before you find a link or subheading for concert dates. In contrast, if you were to type in "Duplex Arena and [band name]" you would have a better chance of locating pages that contain this information.

How to Narrow Your Search

If you have a large group of key words and still don't know which ones to use, write out a list of all the words you are considering. Once you have completed the list, scrutinize it. Then, delete the words that are least important to your search, and highlight those that are most important.

These **key search connectors** can help you fine-tune your search:

AND: narrows a search by retrieving documents that include both terms. For example: *baseball AND playoffs*

OR: broadens a search by retrieving documents including any of the terms. For example: *playoffs OR championships*

NOT: narrows a search by excluding documents containing certain words. For example: *baseball NOT history of*

Tips for an Effective Search

1. Keep in mind that search engines can be case-sensitive. If your first attempt at searching fails, check your search terms for misspellings and try again.

2. If you are entering a group of key words, present them in order, from the most important to the least important key word.

3. Avoid opening the link to every single page in your results list. Search engines present pages in descending order of relevancy. The most useful pages will be located at the top of the list. However, read the description of each link before you open the page.

4. When you use some search engines, you can find helpful tips for specializing your search. Take the opportunity to learn more about effective searching.

Other Ways to Search

Using On-line Reference Sites *How* you search should be tailored to *what* you are hoping to find. If you are looking for data and facts, use reference sites before you jump onto a simple search engine. For example, you can find reference sites to provide definitions of words, statistics about almost any subject, biographies, maps, and concise information on many topics. Some useful on-line reference sites:

    On-line libraries
    On-line periodicals
    Almanacs
    Encyclopedias

You can find these sources using subject searches.

Conducting Subject Searches As you prepare to go on-line, consider your subject and the best way to find information to suit your needs. If you are looking for general information on a topic and you want your search results to be extensive, consider the subject search indexes on most search engines. These indexes, in the form of category and subject lists, often appear on the first page of a search engine. When you click on a specific highlighted word, you will be presented with a new screen containing subcategories of the topic you chose. In the screen shots below, the category *Sports & Recreation* provided a second index for users to focus a search even further.

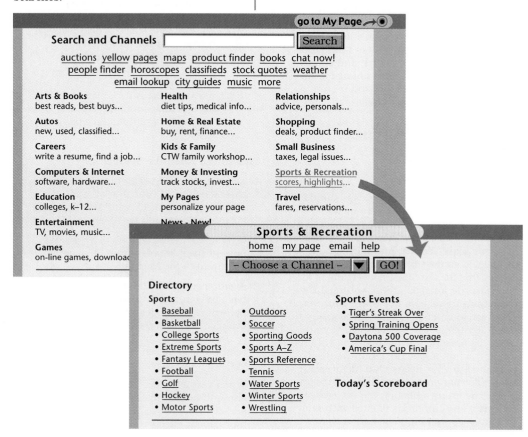

Evaluating the Reliability of Internet Resources

Just as you would evaluate the quality, bias, and validity of any other research material you locate, check the source of information you find on-line. Compare these two sites containing information on the poet and writer Langston Hughes:

Site A is a personal Web site constructed by a college student. It contains no bibliographic information or links to sites that he used. Included on the site are several poems by Langston Hughes and a student essay about the poet's use of symbolism. It has not been updated in more than six months.

Site B is a Web site constructed and maintained by the English Department of a major university. Information on Hughes is presented in a scholarly format, with a bibliography and credits for the writer. The site includes links to other sites and indicates new features that are added weekly.

For your own research, consider the information you find on Site B to be more reliable and accurate than that on Site A. Because it is maintained by experts in their field who are held accountable for their work, the university site will be a better research tool than the student-generated one.

Tips for Evaluating Internet Sources

1. Consider who constructed and who now maintains the Web page. Determine whether this author is a reputable source. Often, the URL endings indicate a source.

   - Sites ending in *.edu* are maintained by educational institutions.
   - Sites ending in *.gov* are maintained by government agencies (federal, state, or local).
   - Sites ending in *.org* are normally maintained by nonprofit organizations and agencies.
   - Sites with a *.com* ending are commercially or personally maintained.

2. Skim the official and trademarked Web pages first. It is safe to assume that the information you draw from Web pages of reputable institutions, on-line encyclopedias, on-line versions of major daily newspapers, or government-owned sites produce information as reliable as the material you would find in print. In contrast, unbranded sites or those generated by individuals tend to borrow information from other sources without providing documentation. As information travels from one source to another, the information has likely been muddled, misinterpreted, edited, or revised.

3. You can still find valuable information in the less "official" sites. Check for the writer's credentials and then consider these factors:

   - Don't let official-looking graphics or presentations fool you.
   - Make sure the information is updated enough to suit your needs. Many Web pages will indicate how recently they have been updated.
   - If the information is borrowed, see whether you can trace it back to its original source.

Respecting Copyrighted Material

Because the Internet is a relatively new and quickly growing medium, issues of copyright and ownership arise almost daily. As laws begin to govern the use and reuse of material posted on-line, they may change the way that people can access or reprint material.

Text, photographs, music, and fine art printed on-line may not be reproduced without acknowledged permission of the copyright owner.

Glossary of Internet Terms

attached file: a file containing information, such as a text document or GIF image, that is attached to an e-mail message; reports, pictures, spreadsheets, and so on transmitted to others by attaching these to messages as files

bandwidth: the amount of information, mainly compressed in bits per second (bps), that can be sent through a connection within a specific amount of time; depending on how fast your modem is, 15,000 bits (roughly one page of text) can be transferred per second

bit: a binary digit of computerized data, represented by a single digit that is either a 1 or a 0; a group of bits constitutes a byte

bookmark: a feature of your Web browser that allows you to place a "bookmark" on a Web page to which you wish to return at a later time

browser: software designed to present material accessed on the Web

bulletin-board system: a computer system that members access in order to join on-line discussion groups or to post announcements

case-sensitivity: the quality of a search engine that causes it to respond to upper- or lowercase letters in different ways

chat room: informal on-line gathering sites where people share conversations, experiences, or information on a specific topic; many chat rooms do not require users to provide their identity, so the reliability or safety of these sites is uncertain

cookie: a digitized piece of information that is sent to a Web browser by a Web server, intended to be saved on a computer; cookies gather information about the user, such as user preferences, or recent on-line purchases; a Web browser can be set to either accept or reject cookies

cyberspace: a term referring to the electronic environment connecting all computer network information with the people who use it

database: a large collection of data that have been formatted to fit a certain user-defined standard

digerati: a slang term to describe Internet experts; an offshoot of the term *literati*

download: to copy files from the Internet onto your computer

e-mail: electronic mail, or the exchange of messages via the Internet; because it is speedier than traditional mail and offers easier global access, e-mail has grown in popularity; e-mail messages can be sent to a single person or in bulk to a group of people

error message: a displayed communication or printout that reports a problem with a program or Web page

FTP site (file transfer protocol): a password-protected server on the Internet that allows the transfer of information from one computer to another

GIF (Graphic Interchange Format): a form of graphics used on the Web

graphics: information displayed as pictures or images instead of text

hits: items retrieved by a key word search; the number tracking the volume of visits to a Web site

home page: the main Web page for an individual or an organization, containing links to subpages within

HTML (HyperText Markup Language): the coding text that is the foundation for creating Web pages

interactivity: a quality of some Web pages that encourages the frequent exchange of information between user and computer

Internet: a worldwide computer network that supports services such as the World Wide Web, e-mail, and file transfer

JPEG (Joint Photo Experts Group, the developers)**:** a file format for graphics especially suited to photographs

K: a measurement of file size or memory; short for "Kilobyte," 1,000 bytes of information (see *bit*)

key word: search term entered into the query box of a search engine to direct the results of the search

link: an icon or word on a Web page that, when clicked, transfers the user to another Web page or to a different document within the same page

login: the procedure by which users gain access to a server or a secure Web site; usually the user must enter a specific user name and password

modem: a device that transfers data to a computer through a phone line. A computer's modem connects to a server, which then sends information in the form of digital signals. The modem converts these signals into waves, for the purpose of information reception. The speed of a modem affects how quickly a computer can receive and download information

newbie: jargon used to describe Internet novices

newsgroup: an on-line discussion group, where users can post and respond to messages; the most prevalent collection of newsgroups is found on USENET

query box: the blank box in a search engine where your search terms are input

relevance ranking: the act of displaying the results of a search in the order of their relevance to the search terms

search engines: tools that help you navigate databases to locate information; search engines respond to a key word search by providing the user with a directory of multiple Web pages about the key word or containing the key word

server: a principal computer that provides services, such as storing files and providing access to the Internet, to another computer

signature: a preprogrammed section of text that is automatically added to an e-mail message

surfing: the process of reading Web pages and of moving from one Web site to another

URL (Uniform Resource Locator)**:** a Web page's address; a URL can look like this:

http://www.phwg.phschool.com or
http://www.senate.gov/~appropriations/ labor/testimony

usenet: a worldwide system of discussion groups, or newsgroups

vanity pages: Web sites placed on-line by people to tell about themselves or their interests; vanity pages do not have any commercial or informational value

virus: a set of instructions, hidden in a computer system or transferred via e-mail or electronic files, that can cause problems with a computer's ability to perform normally

Web page: a set of information, including graphics, text, sound, and video, presented in a browser window; a Web page can be found by its URL once it is posted on the World Wide Web

Web site: a collection of Web pages that are linked together for posting on the World Wide Web

W3: a group of Internet experts, including networking professionals, academics, scientists, and corporate interests, who maintain and develop technologies and standards for the Internet

WWW (World Wide Web)**:** a term referring to the multitude of information systems found on the Internet; this includes FTP, Gopher, telnet, and http sites

zip: the minimizing of files through compression; this function makes for easier transmittal over networks; a receiver can then open the file by "unzipping" it

Commonly Overused Words

When you write, use the most precise word for your meaning, not the word that comes to mind first. Consult this thesaurus to find alternatives for some commonly overused words. Consult a full-length thesaurus to find alternatives to words that do not appear here. Keep in mind that the choices offered in a thesaurus do not all mean exactly the same thing. Review all the options, and choose the one that best expresses your meaning.

about approximately, nearly, almost, approaching, close to

absolutely unconditionally, perfectly, completely, ideally, purely

activity action, movement, operation, labor, exertion, enterprise, project, pursuit, endeavor, job, assignment, pastime, scheme, task

add attach, affix, join, unite, append, increase, amplify

affect adjust, influence, transform, moderate, incline, motivate, prompt

amazing overwhelming, astonishing, startling, unexpected, stunning, dazzling, remarkable

awesome impressive, stupendous, fabulous, astonishing, outstanding

bad defective, inadequate, poor, unsatisfactory, disagreeable, offensive, repulsive, corrupt, wicked, naughty, harmful, injurious, unfavorable

basic essential, necessary, indispensable, vital, fundamental, elementary

beautiful attractive, appealing, alluring, exqui-

site, gorgeous, handsome, stunning

begin commence, found, initiate, introduce, launch, originate

better preferable, superior, worthier

big enormous, extensive, huge, immense, massive

boring commonplace, monotonous, tedious, tiresome

bring accompany, cause, convey, create, conduct, deliver, produce

cause origin, stimulus, inspiration, motive

certain unquestionable, incontrovertible, unmistakable, indubitable, assured, confident

change alter, transform, vary, replace, diversify

choose select, elect, nominate, prefer, identify

decent respectable, adequate, fair, suitable

definitely unquestionably, clearly, precisely, positively, inescapably

easy effortless, natural, comfortable, undemanding, pleasant, relaxed

effective powerful, successful

emphasize underscore, feature, accentuate

end limit, boundary, finish, conclusion, finale, resolution

energy vitality, vigor, force, dynamism

enjoy savor, relish, revel, benefit

entire complete, inclusive, unbroken, integral

excellent superior, remarkable, splendid, unsurpassed, superb, magnificent

exciting thrilling, stirring, rousing, dramatic

far distant, remote

fast swift, quick, fleet, hasty, instant, accelerated

fill occupy, suffuse, pervade, saturate, inflate, stock

finish complete, conclude, cease, achieve, exhaust, deplete, consume

funny comical, ludicrous, amusing, droll, entertaining, bizarre, unusual, uncommon

get obtain, receive, acquire, procure, achieve

give bestow, donate, supply, deliver, distribute, impart

go proceed, progress, advance, move

good satisfactory, serviceable, functional, competent, virtuous, striking

great tremendous, superior, remarkable, eminent, proficient, expert

happy pleased, joyous, elated, jubilant, cheerful, delighted

hard arduous, formidable, complex, complicated, rigorous, harsh

help assist, aid, support, sustain, serve

hurt injure, harm, damage, wound, impair

important significant, substantial, weighty, meaningful, critical, vital, notable

interesting absorbing, appealing, entertaining, fascinating, thought-provoking

job task, work, business, undertaking, occupation, vocation, chore, duty, assignment

keep retain, control, possess

kind type, variety, sort, form

know comprehend, understand, realize, perceive, discern

like (adj) similar, equivalent, parallel

like (verb) enjoy, relish, appreciate

main primary, foremost, dominant

make build, construct, produce, assemble, fashion, manufacture

mean plan, intend, suggest, propose, indicate

more supplementary, additional, replenishment

new recent, modern, current, novel

next subsequently, thereafter, successively

nice pleasant, satisfying, gracious, charming

old aged, mature, experienced, used, worn, former, previous

open unobstructed, accessible

part section, portion, segment, detail, element, component

perfect flawless, faultless, ideal, consummate

plan scheme, design, system, plot

pleasant agreeable, gratifying, refreshing, welcome

prove demonstrate, confirm, validate, verify, corroborate

quick brisk, prompt, responsive, rapid, nimble, hasty

really truly, genuinely, extremely, undeniably

regular standard, routine, customary, habitual

see regard, behold, witness, gaze, realize, notice

small diminutive, miniature, minor, insignificant, slight, trivial

sometimes occasionally, intermittently, sporadically, periodically

take grasp, capture, choose, select, tolerate, endure

terrific extraordinary, magnificent, marvelous

think conceive, imagine, ponder, reflect, contemplate

try attempt, endeavor, venture, test

use employ, operate, utilize

very unusually, extremely, deeply, exceedingly, profoundly

want desire, crave, yearn, long

Commonly Misspelled Words

The list on these pages presents words that cause problems for many people. Some of these words are spelled according to set rules, but others follow no specific rules. As you review this list, check to see how many of the words give you trouble in your own writing. Then, read the instruction in the "Vocabulary and Spelling" chapter in the book for strategies and suggestions for improving your own spelling habits.

abbreviate	athletic	catastrophe	curious
absence	attendance	category	cylinder
absolutely	auxiliary	ceiling	deceive
abundance	awkward	cemetery	decision
accelerate	bandage	census	deductible
accidentally	banquet	certain	defendant
accumulate	bargain	changeable	deficient
accurate	barrel	characteristic	definitely
ache	battery	chauffeur	delinquent
achievement	beautiful	chief	dependent
acquaintance	beggar	clothes	descendant
adequate	beginning	coincidence	description
admittance	behavior	colonel	desert
advertisement	believe	column	desirable
aerial	benefit	commercial	dessert
affect	bicycle	commission	deteriorate
aggravate	biscuit	commitment	dining
aggressive	bookkeeper	committee	disappointed
agreeable	bought	competitor	disastrous
aisle	boulevard	concede	discipline
all right	brief	condemn	dissatisfied
allowance	brilliant	congratulate	distinguish
aluminum	bruise	connoisseur	effect
amateur	bulletin	conscience	eighth
analysis	buoyant	conscientious	eligible
analyze	bureau	conscious	embarrass
ancient	bury	contemporary	enthusiastic
anecdote	buses	continuous	entrepreneur
anniversary	business	controversy	envelope
anonymous	cafeteria	convenience	environment
answer	calendar	coolly	equipped
anticipate	campaign	cooperate	equivalent
anxiety	canceled	cordially	especially
apologize	candidate	correspondence	exaggerate
appall	capacity	counterfeit	exceed
appearance	capital	courageous	excellent
appreciate	capitol	courteous	exercise
appropriate	captain	courtesy	exhibition
architecture	career	criticism	existence
argument	carriage	criticize	experience
associate	cashier	curiosity	explanation

extension
extraordinary
familiar
fascinating
February
fiery
financial
fluorescent
foreign
forfeit
fourth
fragile
gauge
generally
genius
genuine
government
grammar
grievance
guarantee
guard
guidance
handkerchief
harass
height
humorous
hygiene
ignorant
illegible
immediately
immigrant
independence
independent
indispensable
individual
inflammable
intelligence
interfere
irrelevant
irritable
jewelry
judgment
knowledge
laboratory
lawyer
legible
legislature
leisure
liable

library
license
lieutenant
lightning
likable
liquefy
literature
loneliness
magnificent
maintenance
marriage
mathematics
maximum
meanness
mediocre
mileage
millionaire
minimum
minuscule
miscellaneous
mischievous
misspell
mortgage
naturally
necessary
negotiate
neighbor
neutral
nickel
niece
ninety
noticeable
nuclear
nuisance
obstacle
occasion
occasionally
occur
occurred
occurrence
omitted
opinion
opportunity
optimistic
outrageous
pamphlet
parallel
paralyze
parentheses

particularly
patience
permanent
permissible
perseverance
persistent
personally
perspiration
persuade
phenomenal
phenomenon
physician
pleasant
pneumonia
possess
possession
possibility
prairie
precede
preferable
prejudice
preparation
prerogative
previous
primitive
privilege
probably
procedure
proceed
prominent
pronunciation
psychology
publicly
pursue
questionnaire
realize
really
recede
receipt
receive
recognize
recommend
reference
referred
rehearse
relevant
reminiscence
renowned
repetition

restaurant
rhythm
ridiculous
sandwich
satellite
schedule
scissors
secretary
siege
solely
sponsor
subtle
subtlety
superintendent
supersede
surveillance
susceptible
tariff
temperamental
theater
threshold
truly
unmanageable
unwieldy
usage
usually
valuable
various
vegetable
voluntary
weight
weird
whale
wield
yield

Abbreviations Guide

Abbreviations, shortened versions of words or phrases, can be valuable tools in writing if you know when and how to use them. They can be very helpful in informal writing situations, such as taking notes or writing lists. However, only a few abbreviations can be used in formal writing. They are: *Mr., Mrs., Miss, Ms., Dr., A.M., P.M., A.D., B.C., M.A, B.A., Ph.D.,* and *M.D.*

The following pages provide the conventional abbreviations for a variety of words.

Abbreviations of Common Titles

Ambassador	Amb.	Lieutenant	Lt.
Attorney	Atty.	Major	Maj.
Brigadier-General	Brig. Gen.	President	Pres.
Brother	Br.	Professor	Prof.
Captain	Capt.	Representative	Rep.
Colonel	Col.	Reverend	Rev.
Commander	Cmdr.	Secretary	Sec.
Commissioner	Com.	Senator	Sen.
Corporal	Cpl.	Sergeant	Sgt.
Doctor	Dr.	Sister	Sr.
Father	Fr.	Superintendent	Supt.
Governor	Gov.	Treasurer	Treas.
Honorable	Hon.	Vice Admiral	Vice Adm.

Abbreviations of Academic Degrees

Bachelor of Arts	B.A. (or A.B.)	Esquire (lawyer)	Esq.
Bachelor of Science	B.S. (or S.B.)	Master of Arts	M.A. (or A.M.)
Doctor of Dental Surgery	D.D.S.	Master of Business Administration	M.B.A.
Doctor of Divinity	D.D.		
Doctor of Education	Ed.D.	Master of Fine Arts	M.F.A.
Doctor of Laws	LL.D.	Master of Science	M.S. (or S.M.)
Doctor of Medicine	M.D.	Registered Nurse	R.N.
Doctor of Philosophy	Ph.D.		

Abbreviations of States

State	Traditional	Postal Service	State	Traditional	Postal Service
Alabama	Ala.	AL	Montana	Mont.	MT
Alaska	Alaska	AK	Nebraska	Nebr.	NE
Arizona	Ariz.	AZ	Nevada	Nev.	NV
Arkansas	Ark.	AR	New Hampshire	N.H.	NH
California	Calif.	CA	New Jersey	N.J.	NJ
Colorado	Colo.	CO	New Mexico	N.M.	NM
Connecticut	Conn.	CT	New York	N.Y.	NY
Delaware	Del.	DE	North Carolina	N.C.	NC
Florida	Fla.	FL	North Dakota	N.Dak.	ND
Georgia	Ga.	GA	Ohio	O.	OH
Hawaii	Hawaii	HI	Oklahoma	Okla.	OK
Idaho	Ida.	ID	Oregon	Ore.	OR
Illinois	Ill.	IL	Pennsylvania	Pa.	PA
Indiana	Ind.	IN	Rhode Island	R.I.	RI
Iowa	Iowa	IA	South Carolina	S.C.	SC
Kansas	Kans.	KS	South Dakota	S.Dak.	SD
Kentucky	Ky.	KY	Tennessee	Tenn.	TN
Louisiana	La.	LA	Texas	Tex.	TX
Maine	Me.	ME	Utah	Utah	UT
Maryland	Md.	MD	Vermont	Vt.	VT
Massachusetts	Mass.	MA	Virginia	Va.	VA
Michigan	Mich.	MI	Washington	Wash.	WA
Minnesota	Minn.	MN	West Virginia	W. Va	WV
Mississippi	Miss.	MS	Wisconsin	Wis.	WI
Missouri	Mo.	MO	Wyoming	Wyo.	WY

Common Geographical Abbreviations

Apartment	Apt.	National	Natl.
Avenue	Ave.	Park, Peak	Pk.
Block	Blk.	Peninsula	Pen.
Boulevard	Blvd.	Point	Pt.
Building	Bldg.	Province	Prov.
County	Co.	Road	Rd.
District	Dist.	Route	Rte.
Drive	Dr.	Square	Sq.
Fort	Ft.	Street	St.
Island	Is.	Territory	Terr.
Mountain	Mt.		

Abbreviations of Traditional Measurements

inch(es)	in.	ounce(s)	oz.
foot, feet	ft.	pound(s)	lb.
yard(s)	yd.	pint(s)	pt.
mile(s)	mi.	quart(s)	qt.
teaspoon(s)	tsp.	gallon(s)	gal.
tablespoon(s)	tbsp.	Fahrenheit	F.

Abbreviations of Metric Measurements

millimeter(s)	mm	liter(s)	L
centimeter(s)	cm	kiloliter(s)	kL
meter(s)	m	milligram(s)	mg
kilometer(s)	km	centigram(s)	cg
milliliter(s)	mL	gram(s)	g
centiliter(s)	cL	Celsius	C

Other Commonly Used Abbreviations

about (used with dates)	c., ca., circ.	manager	mgr.
and others	et al.	manufacturing	mfg.
anonymous	anon.	market	mkt.
approximately	approx.	measure	meas.
associate, association	assoc., assn.	merchandise	mdse.
auxiliary	aux., auxil.	miles per hour	mph
bibliography	bibliog.	miscellaneous	misc.
boxes	bx(s).	money order	M.O.
bucket	bkt.	note well; take notice	N.B.
bulletin	bull.	number	no.
bushel	bu.	package	pkg.
capital letter	cap.	page	p., pg.
cash on delivery	C.O.D.	pages	pp.
department	dept.	pair(s)	pr(s).
discount	disc.	parenthesis	paren.
dozen(s)	doz.	Patent Office	pat. off.
each	ea.	piece(s)	pc(s).
edition, editor	ed.	poetical, poetry	poet.
equivalent	equiv.	private	pvt.
established	est.	proprietor	prop.
fiction	fict.	pseudonym	pseud.
for example	e.g.	published, publisher	pub.
free of charge	grat., gratis	received	recd.
General Post Office	G.P.O.	reference, referee	ref.
government	gov., govt.	revolutions per minute	rpm
graduate, graduated	grad.	rhetorical, rhetoric	rhet.
Greek, Grecian	Gr.	right	R.
headquarters	hdqrs.	scene	sc.
height	ht.	special, specific	spec.
hospital	hosp.	spelling, species	sp.
illustrated	ill., illus.	that is	i.e.
including, inclusive	incl.	treasury, treasurer	treas.
introduction, introductory	intro.	volume	vol.
italics	ital.	weekly	wkly
karat, carat	k., kt.	weight	wt.
left	L.		

Proofreading
Symbols Reference

Proofreading symbols make it easier to show where changes are needed in a paper. When proofreading your own or a classmate's work, use these standard proofreading symbols.

insert	I proofred. *a*
delete	Ip proofread.
close up space	I proof read.
delete and close up space	I proofreade.
begin new paragraph	¶ I proofread.
spell out	I proofread (10) papers. (sp)
lowercase	I Proofread. (lc)
capitalize	i proofread. (cap)
transpose letters	I proofraed. (tr)
transpose words	I only proofread her paper. (tr)
period	I will proofread⊙
comma	I will proofread and she will help.
colon	We will proofread for the following errors⋮
semicolon	I will proofread she will help.
single quotation marks	She said, "I enjoyed the story The Invalid." ˅ ˅
double quotation marks	She said, I enjoyed the story. ˅ ˅
apostrophe	Did you borrow Sylvias book? ˅
question mark	Did you borrow Sylvia's book ?/
exclamation point	You're kidding !/
hyphen	online /=/
parentheses	William Shakespeare 1564–1616 ( )

Student Publications

To share your writing with a wider audience, consider submitting it to a local, state, or national publication for student writing. Following are several magazines and Web sites that accept and publish student work.

Periodicals

Creative Kids P.O. Box 8813, Waco, TX 76714

Merlyn's Pen: The National Magazine of Student Writing
P.O. Box 1058, East Greenwich, RI 02818

Skipping Stones P.O. Box 3939, Eugene, OR 97403

The McGuffey Writer McGuffey Foundation School, 5128 Westgate Drive, Oxford, OH 45056

Writing! General Learning Corporation, 900 Skokie Boulevard, Northbrook, IL 60062

On-line Publications

Kid Pub http://kidpub.org/kidpub

MidLink Magazine http://longwood.cs.ucf.edu/~MidLink/

Wild Guess Magazine http://members.tripod.com/~WildGuess/

Contests

Annual Poetry Contest National Federation of State Poetry Societies, 3520 State Route 56, Mechanicsburg, OH 43044

National Written & Illustrated By . . . Awards Contest for Students Landmark Editions, Inc., 1402 Kansas Avenue, Kansas City, MO 64127

Paul A. Witty Outstanding Literature Award International Reading Association, Special Interest Group for Reading for Gifted and Creative Students, c/o Texas Christian University, P.O. Box 32925, Fort Worth, TX 76129

***Seventeen* Magazine Fiction Contest** *Seventeen* Magazine, 850 Third Avenue, New York, NY 10022

The Young Playwrights Festival National Playwriting Competition
321 East 44th Street, Suite 906, New York, NY 10036

Glossary

A

accent: the emphasis on a syllable, usually in poetry

action verb: a word that tells what action someone or something is performing (*See* linking verb.)

active voice: the voice of a verb whose subject performs an action (*See* passive voice.)

adjective: a word that modifies a noun or pronoun by telling *what kind* or *which one*

adjective clause: a subordinate clause that modifies a noun or pronoun

adjective phrase: a prepositional phrase that modifies a noun or pronoun

adverb: a word that modifies a verb, an adjective, or another adverb

adverb clause: a subordinate clause that modifies a verb, an adjective, an adverb, or a verbal by telling *where, when, in what way, to what extent, under what condition,* or *why*

adverb phrase: a prepositional phrase that modifies a verb, an adjective, or an adverb

allegory: a literary work with two or more levels of meaning—a literal level and one or more symbolic levels

alliteration: the repetition of initial consonant sounds in accented syllables

allusion: an indirect reference to a well-known person, place, event, literary work, or work of art

annotated bibliography: a research writing product that provides a list of materials on a given topic, along with publication information, summaries, or evaluations

apostrophe: a punctuation mark used to form possessive nouns and contractions

appositive: a noun or pronoun placed after another noun or pronoun to identify, rename, or explain the preceding word

appositive phrase: a noun or pronoun with its modifiers, placed next to a noun or pronoun to identify, rename, or explain the preceding word

article: one of three commonly used adjectives: *a, an,* and *the*

assonance: the repetition of vowel sounds in stressed syllables containing dissimilar consonant sounds

audience: the reader(s) a writer intends to reach

autobiographical writing: narrative writing that tells a true story about an important period, experience, or relationship in the writer's life

B

ballad: a song that tells a story (often dealing with adventure or romance) or a poem imitating such a song

bias: the attitudes or beliefs that affect a writer's ability to present a subject objectively

bibliography: a list of the sources of a research paper, including full bibliographic references for each source the writer consulted while conducting research (*See* works-cited list.)

biography: narrative writing that tells the story of an important period, experience, or relationship in a person's life, as reported by another

blueprinting: a prewriting technique in which a writer sketches a map of a home, school, neighborhood, or other meaningful place in order to spark memories or associations for further development

body paragraph: a paragraph in an essay that develops, explains, or supports the key ideas of the writing

brainstorming: a prewriting technique in which a group jots down as many ideas as possible about a given topic

C

case: the form of a noun or pronoun that indicates how it functions in a sentence

cause-and-effect writing: expository writing that examines the relationship between events, explaining how one event or situation causes another

character: a person (though not necessarily a human being) who takes part in the action of a literary work

characterization: the act of creating and developing a character through narration, description, and dialogue

citation: in formal research papers, the acknowledgment of ideas found in outside sources

classical invention: a prewriting technique in which writers gather details about a topic by analyzing the category and subcategories to which the topic belongs

clause: a group of words that has a subject and a verb

climax: the high point of interest or suspense in a literary work

coherence: a quality of written work in which all the parts flow logically from one idea to the next

colon: a punctuation mark used before an extended quotation, explanation, example, or series and after the salutation in a formal letter

comma: a punctuation mark used to separate words or groups of words

comparison-and-contrast writing: expository writing that describes the similarities and differences between two or more subjects in order to achieve a specific purpose

complement: a word or group of words that completes the meaning of a verb

compound sentence: a sentence that contains two or more independent clauses with no subordinate clauses

conclusion: the final paragraph(s) of a work of writing in which the writer may restate a main idea, summarize the points of the writing, or provide a closing remark to end the work effectively (See introduction, body paragraph, topical paragraph, functional paragraph.)

conflict: a struggle between opposing forces

conjugation: a list of the singular and plural forms of a verb in a particular tense

conjunction: a word used to connect other words or groups of words

connotation: the emotional associations that a word calls to mind (See denotation.)

consonance: the repetition of final consonant sounds in stressed syllables containing dissimilar vowel sounds

contraction: a shortened form of a word or phrase that includes an apostrophe to indicate the position of the missing letter(s)

coordinating conjunctions: words such as *and, but, nor,* and *yet* that connect similar words or groups of words

correlative conjunctions: word pairs such as *neither . . . nor, both . . . and,* and *whether . . . or* used to connect similar words or groups of words

couplet: a pair of rhyming lines written in the same meter

cubing: a prewriting technique in which a writer analyzes a subject from six specified angles: description; association; application; analysis; comparison and contrast; and evaluation

D

declarative sentence: a statement punctuated with a period

demonstrative pronouns: words such as *this, that, these,* and *those* used to single out specific people, places, or things

denotation: the objective meaning of a word; its definition independent of other associations the word calls to mind (See connotation.)

depth-charging: a drafting technique in which a writer elaborates on a sentence by developing a key word or idea

description: language or writing that uses sensory details to capture a subject

dialect: the form of a language spoken by people in a particular region or group

dialogue: a direct conversation between characters or people

diary: a personal record of daily events, usually written in prose

diction: a writer's word choice

direct object: a noun or a pronoun that receives the action of a transitive verb

direct quotation: a drafting technique in which writers indicate the exact words of another by enclosing them in quotation marks

documentary: nonfiction film that analyzes news events or another focused subject by combining interviews, film footage, narration, and other audio/visual components

documented essay: research writing that includes a limited number of research sources, providing full documentation parenthetically within the text

drafting: a stage of the writing process that follows prewriting and precedes revising in which a writer gets ideas on paper in a rough format

drama: a story written to be performed by actors and actresses

E

elaboration: a drafting technique in which a writer extends his or her ideas through the use of facts, examples, descriptions, details, or quotations

epic: a long narrative poem about the adventures of a god or a hero

essay: a short nonfiction work about a particular subject

etymology: the history of a word, showing where it came from and how it has evolved into its present spelling and meaning

exclamation mark: a punctuation mark used to indicate strong emotion

exclamatory sentence: a statement that conveys strong emotion and ends with an exclamation mark

exposition: writing to inform, addressing analytic purposes such as problem and solution, comparison and contrast, how-to, and cause and effect

extensive writing: writing products generated for others and from others, meant to be shared with an audience and often done for school assignments (See reflexive writing.)

F

fact: a statement that can be proved true (See opinion.)

fiction: prose writing about imaginary characters and events

figurative language: writing or speech not meant to be interpreted literally

firsthand biography: narrative writing that tells the story of an important period, experience, or relationship in a person's life, reported by a writer who knows the subject personally

five W's: a prewriting technique in which writers gather details about a topic by generating answers to the following questions: Who? What? Where? When? and Why?

fragment: an incomplete idea punctuated as a complete sentence

freewriting: a prewriting technique in which a writer quickly jots down as many ideas on a topic as possible

functional paragraph: a paragraph that performs a specific role in composition, such as to arouse or sustain interest, to indicate dialogue, to make a transition (See topical paragraph.)

G

generalization: a statement that presents a rule or idea based on particular facts

gerund: a noun formed from the present participle of a verb (ending in -ing)

gerund phrase: a group of words containing a gerund and its modifiers or complements that function as a noun

grammar: the study of the forms of words and the way they are arranged in phrases, clauses, and sentences

H

helping verb: a verb added to another verb to make a single verb phrase that indicates the time at which an action takes place or whether it actually happens, could happen, or should happen

hexagonal writing: a prewriting technique in

which a writer analyzes a subject from six angles: literal level, personal allusions, theme, literary devices, literary allusions, and evaluation

homophones: pairs of words that sound the same as each other yet have different meanings and different spellings, such as *hear/here*

how-to writing: expository writing that explains a process by providing step-by-step directions

humanities: forms of artistic expression including, but not limited to, fine art, photography, theater, film, music, and dance

hyperbole: a deliberate exaggeration or overstatement

hyphen: a punctuation mark used to combine numbers and word parts, to join certain compound words, and to show that a word has been broken between syllables at the end of a line

I

I-Search report: a research paper in which the writer addresses the research experience in addition to presenting the information gathered

image: a word or phrase that appeals to one or more of the senses—sight, hearing, touch, taste, or smell

imagery: the descriptive language used to recreate sensory experiences, set a tone, suggest emotions, and guide readers' reactions

imperative sentence: a statement that gives an order or a direction and ends with either a period or an exclamation mark

indefinite pronoun: a word such as *anyone*, *each*, or *many* that refers to a person, place, or thing, without specifying which one

independent clause: a group of words that contains both a subject and a verb and that can stand by itself as a complete sentence

indirect quotation: reporting only the general meaning of what a person said or thought; quotation marks are not needed

infinitive: the form of a verb that comes after the word *to* and acts as a noun, adjective, or adverb

infinitive phrase: a phrase introduced by an infinitive that may be used as a noun, an adjective, or an adverb

interjection: a word or phrase that expresses feeling or emotion and functions independently of a sentence

interrogative pronoun: a word such as *which* and *who* that introduces a question

interrogative sentence: a question that is punctuated with a question mark

interview: an information-gathering technique in which one or more people pose questions to one or more other people who provide opinions or facts on a topic

intransitive verb: an action verb that does not take a direct object (*See* transitive verb.)

introduction: the opening paragraphs of a work of writing in which the writer may capture the readers' attention and present a thesis statement to be developed in the writing (*See* body paragraph, topical paragraph, functional paragraph, conclusion.)

invisible writing: a prewriting technique in which a writer freewrites without looking at the product until the exercise is complete; this can be accomplished at a word processor with the monitor turned off or with carbon paper and an empty ballpoint pen

irony: the general name given to literary techniques that involve surprising, interesting, or amusing contradictions

itemizing: a prewriting technique in which a writer creates a second, more focused, set of ideas based on an original listing activity. (*See* listing.)

J

jargon: the specialized words and phrases unique to a specific field

journal: a notebook or other organized writing system in which daily events and personal impressions are recorded

K

key word: the word or phrase that directs an Internet or database search

L

layering: a drafting technique in which a writer elaborates on a statement by identifying and then expanding upon a central idea or word

lead: the opening sentences of a work of writing meant to grab the reader's interest, accomplished through a variety of methods, including providing an intriguing quotation, a surprising or provocative question or fact, an anecdote, or a description

learning log: a record-keeping system in which a student notes information about new ideas

legend: a widely told story about the past that may or may not be based in fact

legibility: the neatness and readability of words

linking verb: a word that expresses its subject's state of being or condition (*See* action verb.)

listing: a prewriting technique in which a writer prepares a list of ideas related to a specific topic. (*See* itemizing.)

looping: a prewriting activity in which a writer generates follow-up freewriting based on the identification of a key word or central idea in an original freewriting exercise

lyric poem: a poem expressing the observations and feelings of a single speaker

M

main clause: a group of words that has a subject and a verb and can stand alone as a complete sentence

memoir: autobiographical writing that provides an account of a writer's relationship with a person, event, or place

metaphor: a figure of speech in which one thing is spoken of as though it were something else

meter: the rhythmic pattern of a poem

monologue: a speech or performance given entirely by one person or by one character

mood: the feeling created in the reader by a literary work or passage

multimedia presentation: a technique for sharing information with an audience by enhancing narration and explanation with media, including video images, slides, audiotape recordings, music, and fine art

N

narration: writing that tells a story

narrative poem: a poem that tells a story in verse

nominative case: the form of a noun or pronoun used as the subject of a verb, as a predicate nominative, or as the pronoun in a nominative absolute (*See* objective case, possessive case.)

noun: a word that names a person, place, or thing

noun clause: a subordinate clause that acts as a noun

novel: an extended work of fiction that often has a complicated plot, many major and minor characters, a unifying theme, and several settings

O

objective case: the form of a noun or pronoun used as the object of any verb, verbal, or preposition, or as the subject of an infinitive (*See* nominative case, possessive case.)

observation: a prewriting technique involving close visual study of an object; a writing product that reports such a study

ode: a long formal lyric poem with a serious theme

onomatopoeia: words such as *buzz* and *plop* that suggest the sounds they name

open-book test: a form of assessment in which students are permitted to use books and class notes to respond to test questions

opinion: beliefs that can be supported but not proved to be true (*See* fact.)

oral tradition: the body of songs, stories, and poems preserved by being passed from generation to generation by word of mouth

outline: a prewriting or study technique that allows writers or readers to organize the presentation and order of information

oxymoron: a figure of speech that fuses two contradictory or opposing ideas, such as "freezing fire" or "happy grief"

P

parable: a short, simple story from which a moral or religious lesson can be drawn

paradox: a statement that seems to be contradictory but that actually presents a truth

paragraph: a group of sentences that share a common topic or purpose and that focus on a single main idea or thought

parallelism: the placement of equal ideas in words, phrases, or clauses of similar types

paraphrase: restating an author's idea in different words, often to share information by making the meaning clear to readers

parentheses: punctuation marks used to set off asides and explanations when the material is not essential

participial phrase: a group of words made up of a participle and its modifiers and complements that acts as an adjective

participle: a form of a verb that can act as an adjective

passive voice: the voice of a verb whose subject receives an action (*See* active voice.)

peer review: a revising technique in which writers meet with other writers to share focused feedback on a draft

pentad: a prewriting technique in which a writer analyzes a subject from five specified points: actors, acts, scenes, agencies, and purposes

period: a punctuation mark used to end a declarative sentence, an indirect question, and most abbreviations

personal pronoun: a word such as *I, me, you, we, us, he, him, she, her, they,* and *them* that refers to the person speaking; the person spoken to; or the person, place, or thing spoken about

personification a figure of speech in which a nonhuman subject is given human characteristics

persuasion: writing or speaking that attempts to convince others to accept a position on an issue of concern to the writer

phrase: a group of words without a subject and verb that functions as one part of speech

plot: the sequence of events in narrative writing

plural: the form of a word that indicates more than one item is being mentioned

poetry: a category of writing in which the final product may make deliberate use of rhythm, rhyme, and figurative language in order to express deeper feelings than those conveyed in ordinary speech (*See* prose, drama.)

point of view: the perspective, or vantage point, from which a story is told

portfolio: an organized collection of writing projects, including writing ideas, works in progress, final drafts, and the writer's reflections on the work

possessive case: the form of a noun or pronoun used to show ownership (*See* objective case, nominative case.)

prefix: one or more syllables added to the beginning of a word root (*See* root, suffix.)

preposition: a word that relates a noun or pronoun that appears with it to another word in the sentence to indicate relations of time, place, causality, responsibility, and motivation

prepositional phrase: a group of words that includes a preposition and a noun or pronoun

presenting: a stage of the writing process in which a writer shares a final draft with an audience through speaking, listening, or representing activities

prewriting: a stage of the writing process in which writers explore, choose, and narrow a topic and then gather necessary details for drafting

problem-and-solution writing: expository writing that examines a problem and provides a realistic solution

Glossary • 749

pronoun: a word that stands for a noun or for another word that takes the place of a noun

prose: a category of written language in which the end product is developed through sentences and paragraphs (*See* poetry, drama.)

publishing: a stage of the writing process in which a writer shares the written version of a final draft with an audience

punctuation: the set of symbols used to convey specific directions to the reader

purpose: the specific goal or reason a writer chooses for a writing task

Q

question mark: a punctuation mark used to end an interrogative sentence or an incomplete question

quicklist: a prewriting technique in which a writer creates an impromptu, unresearched list of ideas related to a specific topic

quotation mark: a punctuation mark used to indicate the beginning and end of a person's exact speech or thoughts

R

ratiocination: a systematic approach to the revision process that involves color-coding elements of writing for evaluation

reflective essay: autobiographical writing in which a writer shares a personal experience and then provides insight about the event

reflexive pronoun: a word that ends in -*self* or -*selves* and names the person or thing receiving an action when that person or thing is the same as the one performing the action

reflexive writing: writing generated for oneself and from oneself, not necessarily meant to be shared, in which the writer makes all decisions regarding form and purpose (*See* extensive writing.)

refrain: a regularly repeated line or group of lines in a poem or song

relative pronoun: a pronoun such as *that, which, who, whom,* or *whose* that begins a

subordinate clause and connects it to another idea in the sentence

reporter's formula: a prewriting technique in which writers gather details about a topic by generating answers to the following questions: *Who? What? Where? When?* and *Why?*

research: a prewriting technique in which writers gather information from outside sources such as library reference materials, interviews, and the Internet

research writing: expository writing that presents and interprets information gathered through an extensive study of a subject

response to literature writing: persuasive, expository, or narrative writing that presents a writer's analysis of or reactions to a published work

revising: a stage of the writing process in which a writer reworks a rough draft to improve both form and content

rhyme: the repetition of sounds at the ends of words

rhyme scheme: the regular pattern of rhyming words in a poem or stanza

rhythm: the form or pattern of words or music in which accents or beats come at certain fixed intervals

root: the base of a word (*See* prefix, suffix.)

rubric: an assessment tool, generally organized in a grid, to indicate the range of success or failure according to specific criteria

run-on sentence: two or more complete sentences punctuated incorrectly as one

S

salutation: the greeting in a formal letter

satire: writing that ridicules or holds up to contempt the faults of individuals or of groups

SEE method: an elaboration technique in which a writer presents a statement, an extension, and an elaboration to develop an idea

semicolon: a punctuation mark used to join independent clauses that are not already joined by a conjunction

sentence: a group of words with a subject and a predicate that expresses a complete thought

setting: the time and place of the action of a piece of narrative writing

short story: a brief fictional narrative told in prose

simile: a figure of speech in which *like* or *as* is used to make a comparison between two basically unrelated ideas

sonnet: a fourteen-line lyric poem with a single theme

speaker: the imaginary voice assumed by the writer of a poem

stanza: a group of lines in a poem, seen as a unit

statistics: facts presented in numerical form, such as ratios, percentages, or summaries

subject: the word or group of words in a sentence that tells whom or what the sentence is about

subordinate clause: a group of words containing both a subject and a verb that cannot stand by itself as a complete sentence

subordinating conjunction: a word used to join two complete ideas by making one of the ideas dependent on the other

suffix: one or more syllables added to the end of a word root (*See* prefix, root.)

summary: a brief statement of the main ideas and supporting details presented in a piece of writing

symbol: something that is itself and also stands for something else

T

theme: the central idea, concern, or purpose in a piece of narrative writing, poetry, or drama

thesis statement: a statement of an essay's main idea; all information in the essay supports or elaborates this idea

tone: a writer's attitude toward the readers and toward the subject

topic sentence: a sentence that states the main idea of a paragraph

topic web: a prewriting technique in which a writer generates a graphic organizer to identify categories and subcategories of a topic

topical paragraph: a paragraph that develops, explains, and supports the topic sentence related to an essay's thesis statement

transition: words, phrases, or sentences that smooth writing by indicating the relationship among ideas

transitive verb: an action verb that takes a direct object (*See* intransitive verb.)

U

unity: a quality of written work in which all the parts fit together in a complete, self-contained whole

V

verb: a word or group of words that expresses an action, a condition, or the fact that something exists while indicating the time of the action, condition, or fact

verbal: a word derived from the verb but used as a noun, adjective, or adverb (*See* gerund, infinitive, participle.)

vignette: a brief narrative characterized by precise detail

voice: the distinctive qualities of a writer's style, including diction, attitude, sentence style, and ideas

W

works-cited list: a list of the sources of a research paper, including full bibliographic references for each source named in the body of the paper (*See* bibliography.)

Index

Note: **Bold numbers** show pages on which basic definitions or rules appear.

A

a, an, the, **332**
Abbreviations, 738–741
-able, 664
Accent, **744**
accept, except, 466
Action, **82**, 691, 692
Action Verbs, **87**, **315**–316, 318–319, **744**
Active Voice, **744**
-acy, 664
Addresses, Punctuating, 570–571
Adjective Clauses, **744**
Adjective Phrases, 417–419, **744**
Adjectives, 328–339, 342–349
  adverbs modifying, **340**–341
  articles used as, **332**–333
  color-coding, 60
  commas with, 113
  comparative form of, 162
  conjunctions, connecting, 364, 366
  defined, **330**, **744**
  degrees of comparison for, **538**–541, 543, 544–545
  demonstrative, **338**
  distinguishing, **342**–343
  irregular forms for, **540**–541
  possessive, **336**–337
  predicate, **407**–408
  pronouns used as, **336**–337
  proper, **334**–335
  test items for, 348–349
  underlining, 111
  See also Modifiers; Using Modifiers
Adventure Stories, 73
Adverb Clauses, **211**, **744**
Adverb Phrases, **211**, **420**, **744**
Adverbs, 328–329, **340**–349
  color-coding, 60
  conjunctions connecting, 364, 366
  defined, **340**, **744**
  degrees of comparison for, 541–545

distinguishing, **342**–343, **354**–355
  in fiction, 691
  here and *there* used as, 396
  irregular forms for, **540**–541
  starting sentences with, 451
  test items for, 348–349
  usage of, **340**–341
  See also Modifiers; Using Modifiers
Advertisements, 144–145
advice, advise, 466
affect, effect, 466
Agreement, 518–535
  pronoun-antecedent, 164, **528**–531, 533
  subject-verb, 162, **520**–527, 532–535
ain't, 85
Allegories, **744**
Alliteration, **744**
Allusions, **744**
Almanacs, 646, 712, 730
American Psychological Association (APA) Style, 724, 726
Analogies, 310–311, 718
Analysis, Text, 689
and, 162, 261, **364**, 368, **522**, **528**
and, both, 366
Annotated Bibliographies, **744**
Antecedents
  compound, **528**
  possessive adjectives and, 336
  pronouns and, **300**, 301, **528**–533
  See also Pronoun-Antecedent Agreement
Anthologies, 189, 697
anti-, 663
Antonyms, 310–311
APA Style. *See* American Psychological Association (APA) Style
Apostrophes, 510, **589**–594, **744**
Appendixes, Textbook, 679
Appositive Phrases, 421–422, **744**
Appositives, **421**, **744**
Arguments, Logical, 131

See also Persuasion
Art, Fine
  basic elements of, **644**
  capitalizing titles of, **610**
  citing titles of, 582–583
  explained, 10
  visual, 195
  See also Humanities; Responding to Fine Art and Literature; Spotlight on the Humanities
Art Museums, 644
Articles, Definite and Indefinite, 60, **332**–333, **744**
Articles, Published, 583, 682
Assessment, 27
  See also Rubric for Self-Assessment; Writing for Assessment
Assignment Book, 702
Assonance, **744**
at, 466
Atlases, 712
Attached Files, Electronic, **732**
Audiences
  for autobiographical writing, 55
  background and interest of, 229
  categorizing, 181
  for comparison-and-contrast essays, 157
  creating profile for, 18
  defined, **744**
  familiarity to topic of, 253
  for how-to essays, 204
  identifying, 17–18
  persuading, 130
  providing descriptions to, 104
  for short stories, 81
Audiotapes, 165
Audiovisual Tools, 11
Authors
  letters to, 247, 264
  strategies of professional, 9, 23, 49, 73, 99, 125, 151, 175, 199, 223, 247
Autobiographical Writing, 48–71
  defined, **49**, **744**
  drafting, 56-57
  editing and proofreading, 62
  prewriting, 52-55
  publishing and presenting, 63

writing prompts, 274
See also Topic Bank Ideas
Chronological Order, 106, 206, 230, 690
Circling
  direct statements, 85
  fragments, 137
  short sentences, 234
  supporting evidence, 135
  vague modifiers, 25
  verb tenses, 186
  See also Coding; Color-Coding; Highlighting; Underlining
Citations, **745**
  conventions for writing, 582–583
  internal, 236, 728
  in research reports, 236
Citing Sources, Guide for, 722–728
Clarity, in Writing, 132
Classical Invention, 745
Classifications, Organizing, 277
Clauses, 414–415, 424–435
  adjective, **744**
  adverb, 211, **744**
  defined, **261**, **424**, **745**
  fragments of, 456–**457**
  main, 428, **748**
  noun, **748**
  revising and editing, 434–435
  See also Independent Clauses; Subordinate Clauses
Climax, 82, 745
Clues
  context, 656–657
  leaving, 51
  varying sentences with, 210
Cluster Maps, 17, 234
CMS. *See* Chicago Manual of Style (CMS)
Coding
  ands, nors, ors, 162
  for organization, 108
  See also Circling; Color-Coding; Highlighting
Coherence, 745
  checking for, 136
  in compositions, 39
  in paragraphs, 38
Collaborative Writing, 7
  See also Cooperative Writing Opportunities; Peer Review

Colon Marks, **575**–576, **745**
Color-Coding
  comma splices, 110
  commas, 113
  details, 160, 258
  main ideas, 23
  revision clues, 23
  sentences, 24, 60
  technical terms, 235
  verbs, 87
  See also Circling; Coding; Highlighting; Underlining
Color, in Paintings, 644
Comma Splices, 110, 281
Commands, **394**
Commas, **564**–572
  with adjectives, 113
  color-coding clues for, 113
  in compound sentences, 261
  before conjunctions, 375
  correcting run-ons with, **460**
  defined, **745**
  marking, 110
  separating series with, 213
Common Expressions, Punctuating, 569
Common Nouns, **297**–299
Commonly Misspelled Words, 736–737
Communication. *See* Listening; Media and Technology Skills; Reading; Representing; Viewing; Writing
Comparative Degree, **538**–545
Comparison-and-Contrast Essays, 150–173
  defined, **151**, **273**, **745**
  organizing, 277
  drafting, 157–159
  editing and proofeading, 164
  model from literature, 152–153
  prewriting, 154–157
  publishing and presenting, 165
  revising, 160–163
  rubric for self-assessment, 165
  test prompts for, 172–173
  types of, **151**
Comparisons
  adjectives used in, **538**–541
  adverbs used in, **541**–545
  double, 540

of literary works, 151, 247
  product, 151
Complements, **745**
  subject, **404**–409
  types of, 398, 400
  See also Direct Objects; Indirect Objects
Complete Predicates, **386**–389
Complete Sentences, 137, 281, 412–413
Complete Subjects, 386–389
Complex Sentences, 428–430
Compositions, **32**
  paragraphs in, 37–41
  parts of, **39**
  See also Paragraphs
Compound Antecedents, **528**
Compound Nouns, **296**, 673
Compound Objects, 441–442
Compound Predicates, **390**–393, **405**, **407**
Compound Sentences, **745**
  elements of, **261**
  forming, **427**, 429, **443**
Compound Subjects, **390**–393, 441–442, 522–523
Compound Verbs, 441–442
Computers
  electronic portfolios in, 5
  "help" forms in, 219
  making graphics on, 645
  taking tests on, 287
  See also Word-Processing Programs
Concluding Words, Punctuating, **578**
Conclusions, 745
  clarity in, 132
  for compositions, 39
  forming, 688
  in well-organized drafts, **256**
Concrete Poems, **119**
Conflict, **82**, **745**
  in cartoons, 95
  internal and external, **80**
  mapping, 56, 80
Conjugations, Verb, 494, **745**
Conjunctions, 362–369, 373–375
  combining sentences with, 446
  compound subjects and, 522
  correlative, **366**–367, **745**

770 • Index

Acknowledgments

Staff Credits

The people who made up the *Prentice Hall Writing and Grammar: Communication in Action* team—representing design services, editorial, editorial services, electronic publishing technology, manufacturing and inventory planning, marketing, marketing services, market research, on-line services and multimedia development, product planning, production services, project office, and publishing processes—are listed below. Bold type denotes the core team members.

Ellen Backstrom, Betsy Bostwick, Evonne Burgess, **Louise B. Capuano, Sarah Carroll, Megan Chill,** Katherine Clarke, Rhett Conklin, Martha Conway, Harold Crudup, **Harold Delmonte,** Laura Dershewitz, Donna DiCuffa, Amy Fleming, Libby Forsyth, Ellen Goldblatt, Elaine Goldman, Jonathan Goldson, **Rebecca Graziano,** Rick Hickox, Kristan Hoskins, Jim Jeglikowski, Carol Lavis, **George Lychock,** Gregory Lynch, William McAllister, **Frances Medico,** Perrin Moriarty, Loretta Moser, Margaret Plotkin, Maureen Raymond, Shannon Rider, **Steve Sacco,** Gerry Schrenk, **Melissa Shustyk,** Annette Simmons, Robin Sullivan, **Elizabeth Torjussen, Doug Utigard**

Additional Credits

Ernie Albanese, Diane Alimena, Susan Andariese, Michele Angelucci, Penny Baker, Susan Barnes, Louise Casella, Lorena Cerisano, Cynthia Clampitt, Elizabeth Crawford, Ken Dougherty, Vince Esterly, Kathy Gavilanes, Beth Geschwind, Michael Goodman, Diana Hahn, Jennifer Harper, Evan Holstrom, Alex Ivchenko, Leanne Korszoloski, Sue Langan, Rebecca Lauth, Dave Liston, Maria Keogh, Christine Mann, Vicki Menanteaux, Gail Meyer, Artur Mkrtchyan, LaShonda Morris, Karyl Murray, Omni-Photo Communications, Kim Ortell, Patty Rodriguez, Brenda Sanabria, Carolyn Sapontzis, Ken Silver, Slip Jig Image Research Services, Sunnyside, NY, Ron Spezial, Barbara Stufflebeem, Gene Vaughan, Karen Vignola, Linda Westerhoff

Grateful acknowledgment is made to the following for permission to reprint copyrighted material:

The Boy Scouts of America
"Twist and Shout" by K. Wayne Wincey from *Boy's Life Magazine*, August 1999. Copyright © 1999 by The Boy Scouts of America.

Doubleday, a division of Bantam Doubleday Dell Publishing Group, Inc.
"Child on Top of a Greenhouse," copyright © 1946 by Editorial Publications, Inc., from *The Collected Poems of Theodore Roethke* by Theodore Roethke. Used by permission of Dell Books, a division of Bantam Doubleday Dell Publishing Group, Inc.

Harcourt, Inc.
Excerpt from *My Sister Eileen* by Ruth McKenney. Copyright © 1938, 1966 by Ruth McKenney.

Henry Holt and Company, LLC
"A Great American Symbol" by Richard Durbin from *Elements of Writing*. Copyright © 1998 by Holt, Rinehart and Winston.

William Morrow and Company
Excerpt from *The Tom Sawyer Fires* by Laurence Yep. Copyright © 1984 Laurence Yep.

National Geographic Society
Excerpt from *Sharks* by Susan McGrath from *National Geographic World*, February 1994. Copyright © 1994 by The National Geographic Society. Reprinted by permission. "Gentle Giants in Trouble: Manatees" by Ross Bankson from *National Geographic World*, Number 199, March 1992. Copyright © 1992 by The National Geographic Society. Reprinted by permission.

Reader's Digest Limited
"More Than a Pinch of Salt" from *Did You Know?* Copyright © 1990 by The Reader's Digest Association Limited. Used by permission.

Scribner Laidlaw
"The Snow in Chelm" from *Zlateh the Goat and Other Stories* by Isaac Bashevis Singer. Translated from the Yiddish by the Author and Elizabeth Shub. Text copyright © 1966 by Isaac Bashevis Singer.

The World Publishing Company
"How This Book Came to Be Written" by May Lamberton Becker from *The Last of the Mohicans: A Narrative of 1757* by James Fenimore Cooper. Copyright © 1957 by The World Publishing Company. Used by permission.

Note: Every effort has been made to locate the copyright owner of material reprinted in this book. Omissions brought to our attention will be corrected in subsequent editions.

Photo Credits

Cover: Stamp Designs © United States Postal Service, All Rights Reserved; Luis Castenada/The Image Bank; **vi–vii:** Corel Professional Photos CD-ROM™; **ix:** CORBIS/Annie Griffiths Belt; **x:** *Flight of the Thielens,* Thomas Hart Benton, © T. H. Benton and R. P. Benton Testamentary Trusts/Licensed by VAGA, New York, NY; **xi:** Robert Holmes/CORBIS; **xii:** AP/Wide World Photos; **xiii:** Carl Purcell/Photo Researchers, Inc.; **xiv:** *Blowing Bubbles,* John Kane, The Phillips Collection; **xv:** Photofest; **xvi:** © James Watt/Animals Animals; **xvii:** The Granger Collection, New York; **xviii:** © 1999 VCG/FPG International Corp.; **xix:** (top) Courtesy National Archives, photo no. 306-NT-111998; (bottom) Italian Government Tourist Board; **xx–xxiii:** Corel Professional Photos CD-ROM™; **xxiv:** © The Stock Market/Jose L. Pelaez; **xxv:** (top) Lynn Saville; (bottom) Corel Professional Photos CD-ROM™ **1:** *Am Kaffeetisch (At the Coffee Table),* Carl Schmitz-Pleis, © Christie's Images, Ltd. 1999; **2:** Myrleen Ferguson Cate/PhotoEdit; **4:** © Tom Till Photography; **6:** © The Stock Market/Tom & DeeAnn McCarthy; **7:** © The Stock Market/LWA-Dann Tardiff; **9:** (top) D. DeMello © Wildlife Conservation Society; (middle) Pearson Education; (bottom) Pearson Education; **10:** Archaeological Museum, Istanbul, Turkey, © Photograph by Erich Lessing, Art Resource, NY; **14:** Will Hart; **15:** Tony Freeman/PhotoEdit; **28:** © Walt Disney Productions/Photofest; **32:** Dave G. Houser/CORBIS; **35:** GK and Vikki Hart/The Image Bank; **37:** S. Gazin/The Image Works; **43:** David Young-Wolff/PhotoEdit; **44:** Art Resource, NY; **48:** © The Stock Market/Rob Lewine; **50:** David Young-Wolff/PhotoEdit; **51:** The Purcell Team/CORBIS; **53:**

Great Catch, Moses Ros/Omni-Photo Communications, Inc.; **55:** CORBIS/Annie Griffiths Belt; **64:** © The Stock Market/Paul Barton; **65:** Craig Aurness/CORBIS; **66:** Kathy Ferguson/PhotoEdit; **68:** (top) *Self-portrait with Bandaged Ear,* Vincent van Gogh, Giraudon/Art Resource, NY; (bottom) © Frank Capri/Saga/Archive Photos; **72:** *St. George and the Dragon,* Paolo Uccello, Art Resource, NY; **74:** Earl & Nazima Kowall/CORBIS; **75:** © The Stock Market/Rob Matheson; **76:** *Green Violinist,* Marc Chagall, Photo by Francis G. Mayer/CORBIS © 2001 Artists Rights Society (ARS), New York/ADAGP, Paris; **77:** *Winter Night in Vitebsk,* Marc Chagall/SuperStock © 2001 Artists Rights Society (ARS), New York/ADAGP, Paris; **79:** *Noah's Ark,* Aaron Douglas, Fisk University Fine Art Galleries, Nashville, Tennessee; **82:** *Flight of the Thielens,* Thomas Hart Benton, © T. H. Benton and R. P. Benton Testamentary Trusts/Licensed by VAGA, New York, NY; **85:** David Young-Wolff/PhotoEdit; **91:** Paul Ekman, Ph.D., Professor of Psychology; **92:** Russell L. Ciochon, University of Iowa; **93:** Will Hart; **94:** *Andromeda rescued from the monster by Perseus riding Pegasus,* Parisian copy, c. 1410–15, Works of Christine de Pisan (c. 1364–1430), British Library, London/The Bridgeman Art Library, London/New York; **98:** *Bok Choy and Apples,* Pamela Chin Lee/Omni-Photo Communications, Inc.; **100:** © The Stock Market/Bill Stormont; **103:** *Farberware Coffeepot,* No. VI, Jeanette Pasin Sloan, National Museum of American Art, Washington, D.C./Art Resource, NY; **104:** Robert Holmes/CORBIS; **106:** Corel Professional Photos CD-ROM™; **109:** George Lepp/CORBIS; **112:** Mary Kate Denny/PhotoEdit; **115:** Alan Oddie/PhotoEdit; **116:** Robert Brenner/PhotoEdit; **117:**

Sid Greenberg/Photo Researchers, Inc.; **120:** (top) Canyon de Chelly, Ansel Adams; (bottom) *Among the Sierra Nevada Mountains, California, 1868,* Albert Bierstadt, National Museum of American Art, Washington, DC/Art Resource, NY; **124:** Michael Newman/PhotoEdit; **126:** AP/Wide World Photos; **129:** *Silence, Voices, Money, Danger,* Martin Wong, courtesy of the artist; **141:** Tom Prettyman/PhotoEdit; **142:** © The Stock Market/Paul Barton; **143:** David Young-Wolff/PhotoEdit; **144:** Artwork copyright 2000 by Phil Yeh (www.ideaship.com); **146:** Scala/Art Resource, NY; **150:** © 1999 Steven M. Jones/FPG International Corp.; **152:** Carl Purcell/Photo Researchers, Inc.; **153:** Dave G. Houser/CORBIS; **155:** *Black Mesa,* 1982, Woody Gwyn, Courtesy of the artist; **156:** © 1999 Richard Embery/FPG International Corp.; **161:** (left) Rick Doyle/CORBIS; (right) AP/Wide World Photos/Matt York; **166:** (left) Robert Clay/Monkmeyer; (right) CORBIS/Lowell Georgia; **167:** Brendan Barraclough/courtesy of Megan Chill; **168:** Randy Verougstraete; **170:** (top) The Metropolitan Museum of Art, The Elisha Whittelsey Collection, The Elisha Whittelsey Fund, 1972. (1972.655.1), Photograph © 1977 The Metropolitan Museum of Art; (bottom) Photofest; **174:** © Telegraph Colour Library/FPG International Corp.; **176:** © The Stock Market/Kennan Ward; **177:** (top left) CORBIS/Robert Garvey; (top right) CORBIS/Ralph A. Clevenger; (bottom left) CORBIS/Joe McDonald; (bottom center) Myrleen Ferguson/ PhotoEdit; (bottom right) CORBIS /Stuart Westmorland; **190:** (left) Tony Freeman/ PhotoEdit; (right) Jeremy Walker/Tony Stone Images; **191:** image © copyright

1998 PhotoDisc, Inc.; **192:** Spencer Grant/PhotoEdit; **194:** The Kobal Collection; **195:** Joel Librizzi; **198:** Pat Olear/PhotoEdit; **200:** Wolfgang Kaehler/CORBIS; **203:** *Practice Session,* Phoebe Beaseley, from the collection of Mr. and Mrs. E. C. Hanes, Winston-Salem, NC; **204:** (left) Michael Newman/PhotoEdit; (right) Gary Cralle/The Image Bank; **209:** David Young-Wolff/ PhotoEdit; **211:** Jonathan Nourok/ PhotoEdit; **215:** David Young-Wolff/ PhotoEdit; **217:** Pearson Education/PH College; **218:** (top & bottom) Photofest; **222:** © The Stock Market/Tom Stewart; **224:** © James Watt/Animals Animals; **227:** Moses Ros/Omni-Photo Communications, Inc.; **228:** Tony Arruza/CORBIS; **230:** David A. Northcott/CORBIS; **232:** David A. Northcott/CORBIS; **235:** Corel Professional Photos CD-ROM™; **238:** Louis A. Goldman/Photo Researchers, Inc.; **239:** Museo Archeologico Nazionale, Naples, Italy/The Bridgeman Art Library, London/ New York; **240:** Roger Wood/ CORBIS; **241:** PhotoEdit; **242:** Photofest; **246:** © The Stock Market/Shotgun; **248–249:** Photofest; **251:** *Children's Round,* Hans Thoma, Corel Professional Photos CD-ROM™; **253:** Myrleen Ferguson/PhotoEdit; **255:** Photo Researchers, Inc.; **256:** Layne Kennedy/CORBIS; **258:** © National Gallery Collection; By kind permission of the Trustees of the National Gallery, London/ CORBIS; **262:** Bob Krist/CORBIS;

265: National Museums of Scotland; **267:** David Young-Wolff/PhotoEdit; **268:** (top) Photofest; (bottom) The Granger Collection, New York; **272:** © 1999 VCG/FPG International Corp.; **273:** Andy Whale/Tony Stone Images; **275:** © 1999 Telegraph Colour Library/FPG International Corp.; **277:** David Young-Wolff/PhotoEdit; **279:** Esbin/Anderson/Omni-Photo Communications, Inc.; **283:** Jeff Vanuga/CORBIS; **284:** Aaron Horowitz/CORBIS; **285:** Mary Kate Denny/PhotoEdit/ PictureQuest; **286:** (top) UPI/CORBIS-BETTMANN; (bottom) Ashmolean Museum, Oxford, UK/The Bridgeman Art Library; **291:** Sandy Novak/Omni-Photo Communications, Inc.; **292–295:** Corel Professional Photos CD-ROM™; **297:** Courtesy National Archives, photo no. 306-NT-111998; **303:** Corel Professional Photos CD-ROM™; **312:** Silver Burdett Ginn; **314 & 317:** Corel Professional Photos CD-ROM™; **318:** Courtesy of the Library of Congress; **321:** Italian Government Tourist Board; **328:** Corel Professional Photos CD-ROM™; **331:** Pearson Education Corporate Digital Archive; **332–343:** Corel Professional Photos CD-ROM™; **350:** Courtesy of the Library of Congress; **354–384:** Corel Professional Photos CD-ROM™; **387:** Courtesy of the Library of Congress; **391–436:** Corel Professional Photos CD-ROM™; **439–445:** NASA; **448–**

478: Corel Professional Photos CD-ROM™; **480:** CORBIS; **485:** Corel Professional Photos CD-ROM™; **486:** Courtesy of the Library of Congress; **490:** U.S. Forestry Service; **491–492:** Corel Professional Photos CD-ROM™; **495:** Courtesy of the Library of Congress; **499:** Corel Professional Photos CD-ROM™; **506:** PH College; **509:** Corel Professional Photos CD-ROM™; **510–580:** Corel Professional Photos CD-ROM™; **583:** Joel Greenberg/ Omni-Photo Communications, Inc. **587–604:** Corel Professional Photos CD-ROM™; **608:** Courtesy of the Library of Congress; **611:** Corel Professional Photos CD-ROM™; **631:** *Concept,* Charlie Hill, SuperStock; **632:** Jonathan Nourok/PhotoEdit; **635:** Denis Poroy/AP/Wide World Photos; **641:** Corel Professional Photos CD-ROM™; **644:** *Parkville, Main Street (Missouri),* 1933, Gale Stockwell, National Museum of American Art, Washington, DC/ Art Resource, NY; **650:** Frank Siteman/PhotoEdit; **654:** SuperStock; **659:** © The Stock Market/Jose L. Pelaez; **663:** David Young-Wolff/PhotoEdit; **669 & 678:** Peter Cade/Tony Stone Images; **687:** Lynn Saville; **691:** David Young-Wolff/PhotoEdit; **697:** Tony Stone Images; **700:** Michael Newman/PhotoEdit; **703:** Corel Professional Photos CD-ROM™; **707:** Mary Kate Denny/ PhotoEdit; **709:** CORBIS; **714:** © The Stock Market/Charles Gupton; **717:** Tony Freeman/ PhotoEdit